Photography
A Cultural History

FOURTH EDITION

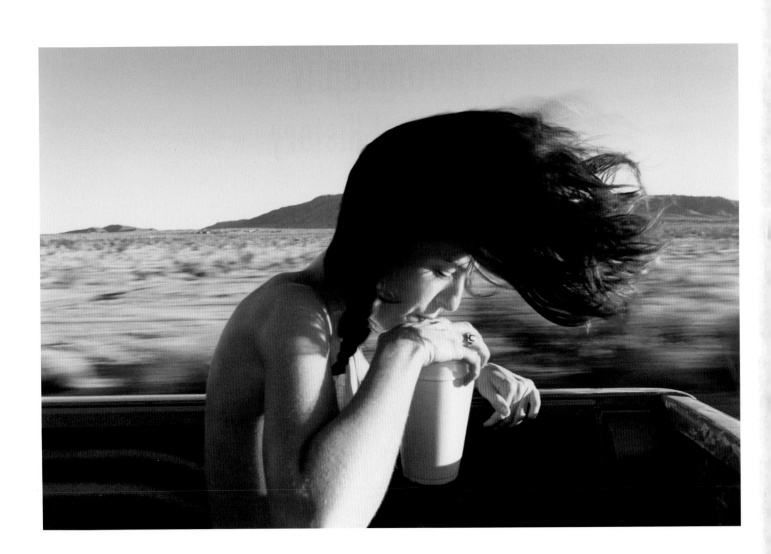

Photography
A Cultural History

FOURTH EDITION

Mary Warner Marien

PEARSON

Boston   Columbus   Indianapolis   New York   San Francisco   Upper Saddle River   Amsterdam
Cape Town   Dubai   London   Madrid   Milan   Munich   Paris   Montreal   Toronto   Delhi
Mexico City   Sao Paulo   Sydney   Hong Kong   Seoul   Singapore   Taipei   Tokyo

For Pearson Education, Inc.:
Editor-in-Chief: Sarah Touborg
Senior Sponsoring Editor: Helen Ronan
Editorial Assistant: Victoria Engros
Senior Managing Editor: Melissa Feimer
Project Liaison: Joe Scordato
Senior Operations Specialist: Diane Peirano
Director of Marketing: Brandy Dawson
Executive Marketing Manager: Kate Stewart
Marketing Assistant: Paige Patunas

Library of Congress Cataloging-in-Publication Data

Marien, Mary Warner.
 Photography : a cultural history / Mary Warner Marien. -- Fourth edition.
   pages cm
 Includes bibliographical references and index.
 ISBN-13 978-0-205-98894-5
 ISBN-10 0-205-98894-6
 1. Photography--History. I. Title.
 TR15.M273 2015
 770--dc23
                              2013030572

10 9 8 7 6

PEARSON

(paperbound) ISBN-10: 0-205-98894-6
ISBN-13: 978-0-205-98894-5

This book was designed and produced by
Laurence King Publishing Ltd, London
www.laurenceking.com

For Laurence King Publishing:
Commissioning Editor: Kara Hattersley-Smith
Project Editor: John Parton
Designer: Grita Rose-Innes
Picture Researcher: Peter Kent

Printed in China

Front cover: Paul S. Taylor, *Dorothea Lange in Texas on the Plains*, c. 1935.
© The Dorothea Lange Collection, Oakland Museum of California, City of Oakland.
Gift of Paul S. Taylor.

Back cover: Doug Rickard, *#39.177833, Baltimore, MD (2008)*, 2011.
Courtesy Doug Rickard

Frontispiece: Ryan McGinley, *Dakota (Hair)*, 2004. Courtesy Ryan McGinley.

CONTENTS

Preface

Despite the impressive increase in college photography courses, autodidacts such as myself make up the bulk of photohistorians. Like many others, I became a photographic historian in my parents' living-room, while looking at copies of *Life* magazine. We photohistorians revel in our passionate preferences. If I had thought I could get away with it, I would have filled this book with my favorite pictures, such as those that French photographer Robert Doisneau made of Paris in the 1950s and 1960s. I have not yet found a tactic to show Doisneau's work in my survey, but have reproduced the portrait that is pinned above my desk: a broadly grinning Doisneau pointing directly at me, prompting me to expect the unexpected (Fig. 1).

In writing this book, I have tried to survey photography's history in such a way that readers can gauge the medium's manifold developments, and appreciate the historical and cultural contexts in which photographers lived and worked. Some readers may long for a comprehensive taxonomy of photography, a unified field with movements and ideas carefully delineated like kingdoms, phyla, orders, and species. Indeed, this sort of categorization is a practical, if sometimes blunt, instrument with which to create order and highlight dominant ideas and visual approaches. Yet it is crucial to remember that people living in a particular era do not synchronize their thoughts. They interpret, refine, resist, oppose, or ignore the prevalent attitudes of their time. Years of teaching have brought home to me the dangers of homogenizing subtly distinctive viewpoints or creating periods so watertight that they leave no residue in the next chapter.

My students have taught me that, contrary to conventional wisdom, they do not dislike history, but are instead hungry for it. Consequently, I have tried to sketch the political and economic events that shaped the circumstances in which photography was practiced, while paying special attention to the particular ideas generated by and about photography in each period. Each Part concludes with a "Philosophy and Practice" section, centered on how beliefs shaped photographic practice. In addition, the Focus boxes in this book discuss particular ideas and historical moments.

Photography generates its own special excitement, in part because it quickly reacts to encompass fresh material and new analytic tools, underscoring its vital, interdisciplinary character. Although photography was a Western discovery, students are rightly curious about its many manifestations in the wider world. To serve that interest, I have incorporated both recent research into non-Western photographers and Western visions of the non-Western world as they were directed toward science, anthropology, journalism, and art.

I am mindful that, despite the existence of several lengthy histories and many monographs, comprehensive surveys of photography in Asia (which makes up about 60 per cent of the world's population) have yet to be created, though scholars in China and India are pursing this goal. As the numbers of photographers and historians from these countries increase, so too does the opportunity for wide-ranging historical recall. Although photography became a business in its first decade, the photographic archives of business and industry have scarcely been mined, and the history of advertising photography, which has shaped the modern experience internationally, remains mostly unwritten.

Influential photographers have often led long lives, traversing eras during which many changes took place. For example, Alfred Stieglitz (1864–1946) was born one year before the American Civil War ended, and he died one year after World War II finished. Having taught an introductory course, I realized that newcomers to the field appreciate an overview of individual careers such as that of Stieglitz, even if this occasionally requires disrupting the chronological order of the presentation. Hence I have included a number of Portrait boxes that concentrate on certain influential photographers.

1
GERARD MONICO, *Robert Doisneau*, 1986.

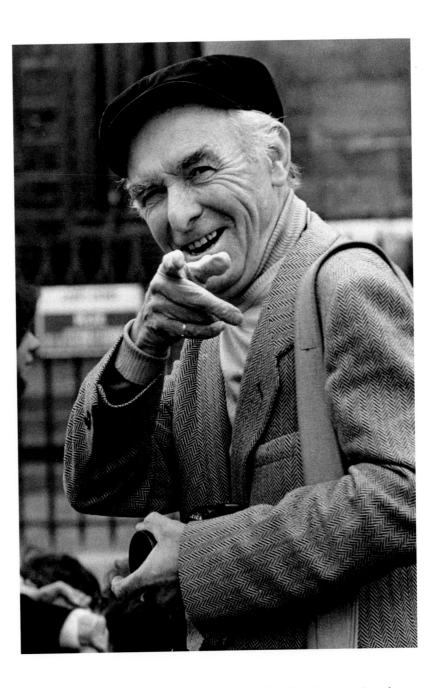

I have discovered in the classroom that today's students, accustomed to encountering art and documentary expression in non-traditional media, are puzzled by the lengthy struggle waged through the nineteenth and twentieth centuries to have photography accepted as an art form. I have narrated that contest, not simply as a large-scale attempt to achieve parity with painting, but as it relates to wider social issues, such as the ascent of a professional, moneyed middle class and the rise of consumer culture.

At present, globalization and digital media encourage the convergence and blurring of photographic genres: photojournalists show their work in art galleries; photographers create new websites to foster social change; practitioners from developing countries depict indigenous motifs using digital tools. The computer, invented—as its name suggests—to facilitate computations, spun a technology and a communications network

that are actively investigated and refined by photographers from many fields. Along with my student colleagues, I am intrigued by emerging visual technologies, and I have concluded this survey with a review of the digital tools as well as some of emerging trends that are shaping the new millennium.

NEW TO THIS EDITION

The fourth edition has been revised to include new material and to expand topics that have received recent scholarly and public attention. For example, prompted by the 2011 exhibition at the Reina Sofía Museum in Madrid, Spain, a Focus box has been created on European worker photography, a long-neglected area of study. The discussion on Conceptualism has been enlarged to show its importance to both Postmodern thought and contemporary photography. In that regard, a new Portrait box has been added on the Conceptual artist, Ed Ruscha. Throughout the new edition, material on the history of photography in China, ranging from the nineteenth century to the present, has been added. In addition to many new pictures, a spirited redesign visually integrates the chapters.

Of course, the twilight of analog photography and the vigorous ongoing rise of digital photography—along with editing software, dependable computer uplinks, and websites—have had an immeasurable impact both on photographic history, contemporary practice, and everyday life. Access to and identification of historic photographs has greatly increased, and many photographers now maintain elaborate websites on which one can view their past work and present ventures. As seen in the last chapter of this book, the ease and frequency with which people worldwide use digital cameras and camera phones to make and upload images is just beginning to impact the medium. In briefest words, there have never been so many photographers!

ACKNOWLEDGMENTS

Many people generously offered information and assistance with this edition, including Anne McCauley, Alan Griffiths (and his brain-child, the website, Luminous Lint), Larry Schaaf, and James Zeng Huang. Special thanks to David Melbye and his students for their observations and questions. I should also like to extend my gratitude to the members of the photographic history listserv, whose exchanges have been helpful and stimulating. As always, I have relied on the keen eye and good judgment of my spouse and live-in editor Michael Marien. I also wish to thank the following reviewers who made useful comments for the development of the fourth edition:

Rihab Kassatly Bagnole, Savannah College of Art & Design; Terri Weissman, Univesity of Illinois, Urbana-Champaign; Joanne Lukitsh, Massachusetts College of Art and Design; Margaret Denny, Columbia College Chicago; Morna O'Neill, Wake Forest University.

I am fortunate to have had the bright and able assistance of the staff at Laurence King Publishing Ltd. Kara Hattersley-Smith has good judgment, patience, and wisdom. John Parton's editorial comments and advice have been as nimble as his turns on the snowboard. Picture editor Peter Kent's enthusiasm for images is matched by his resourcefulness and soothing sense of humor, and Simon Walsh has smoothed this complicated book's path to the printers with continued expertise.

My thanks to Grita Rose-Innes of Rose-Innes Associates who was responsible for the wonderful redesign of the fourth edition, and to Kirsty Seymour-Ure and Angela Koo for their painstaking copy-editing and proofreading throughout.

DEDICATION

My greatest debt continues to be to a legion of people I have never met, whose ongoing research and writing on photography's history informs and shapes my thinking. Without their insights, I could not have conceived this book, nor offered revised editions. I humbly dedicate this book to the international community of photographers, scholars, and critics, whose efforts enrich our field.

Mary Warner Marien
Emeritus Professor
Syracuse University
Syracuse, New York
April 2013

Introduction

LIGHT WRITING: FROM THE DAGUERREOTYPE TO DIGITAL

The basic meaning of the word "photography" is light writing. The medium received that designation in 1839, soon after photography was announced to the world. Despite its many rapid technical changes, from the DAGUERREOTYPE to DIGITAL, the photograph is still an image rooted in the agency of light. When a nineteenth-century photographer placed a leaf on light-sensitized paper and exposed the paper to sunlight, the result was a photograph. Today, digital cameras make electronic records of light, from which one can make prints, or emails, or archives.

The concept of light writing is a starting point for understanding photography. At the same time, it is important to appreciate that photography has never been one thing. In 1839, there were three types of photography. The daguerreotype, an image produced on a silver-coated copper plate, was named for its inventor, Louis-Jacques-Mandé Daguerre. In addition, two forms of photography on paper were invented by William Henry Fox Talbot. One employed a camera and the other, called photogenic drawing, was a contact print made by placing an object on light-sensitive paper. While the daguerreotype was a one-of-a-kind image, photographs on paper and photogenic drawings had the potential to be made into NEGATIVES, from which additional copies could be produced. Throughout its history, photography rapidly changed its technological means, though each type was a variant of light writing.

Even before photography was presented to the world, the medium was grasped through the imagination and prior experience of those who read or heard about it. In other words, photography was a set of assumptions in advance of experience. Soon manifold uses for photography appeared. Within a decade of its presentation to the world, photography was enmeshed in modernity while it helped to shape the modern condition in which knowledge is increasingly visualized. By 1852,

photographic practice had extended to so many applications that one observer concluded "photography is at the same time a science, an art, and an industry."[1]

Photography has always been cross-disciplinary. Photographers who used the medium for artistic expression, record-keeping, journalism, scientific documentation, family history, or other diverse photographic endeavors reached beyond their immediate fields for inspiration and information. Indeed, photographers are omnivores. When asked if there were any influences she wanted to mention, American photographer Helen Levitt (1913–2009) replied, "Everything I ever saw influenced me." It comes as no surprise that photographers have been at the forefront of digital invention.

Cross-disciplinary awareness and interest do not equate with harmony. By 1850 photography was immersed in societal debates and deeply at odds with itself. It was conjectured to be variously an art, a danger to art, a science, a revolutionary means of education, a mindless machine for rendering, and a threat to social order. Because photography appeared to be a relatively cheap way to disseminate information, it seemed to augur either a modern, bloodless, egalitarian revolution, or a social degeneration in which viewers would glut themselves with pleasing but trivial images of reality.

Some of these old battles are still being waged. The camera's objectivity continues to be both beloved and berated by photographers and the general public. The easy manipulation of photographs using digital software has enlivened the protracted concern with the character of photographic realism. Vernacular and popular photographs, such as camera-phone and paparazzi pictures, are persistently blamed for lowering the public's judgment.

In 1923, the filmmaker and photographer Paul Strand spoke to students at the Clarence White School of Photography in New York, and reflected on the future of photography. He urged photographers to be lifelong students of the changing technical dimensions of the medium, its history, and its contemporary expression. He lamented that painters had easy reference to their heritage in museums, while photographers did not. Although Strand was right about the need for students to engage actively with photography's past and present, he erred in underrating access to photography's history.

Of course, early photographic collections could not rival the breadth of art held in galleries like the Louvre in Paris. Nevertheless, the reproducibility of photography renders the medium unusually available. Early in its history, photographic images were regularly displayed in shop windows and shown by photographic societies. Prints began to be collected by public institutions in the mid-1850s. Photographic books and journals contained photographs reproduced by printing techniques, and, occasionally, actual photographic prints. In the late nineteenth century, when technology allowed photographs to be printed directly in books and magazines, the age of mass media began to take shape. Today, the instant and broad access to photography made possible by the Internet is unprecedented. Students of photography now have ever-increasing opportunities to view historic and contemporary images in digital form.

The basic relationship of the photograph and the viewer rests on a few elements: informed observation, research, and contemplation. Photographic historian Estelle Jussim wisely counseled that students of photography's past and present must "expect complexity." The richness and reward of photographic study comes from exploring the comprehensiveness of the medium.

UNDERSTANDING PHOTOGRAPHS

Because it is an everyday activity, looking at photographs seems less complicated than looking at paintings. In fact, we encounter so many photographs in one day that to attend to each would be both time consuming and exasperating. Looking at a painting usually involves going to a space especially reserved for that activity. By contrast, looking at photographs is mostly unavoidable in life. Newspapers, magazines, television programs, billboards, Internet sites, and camera-phones thrust photographs at us. The stream of images is so intense that contemporary observers have honed skills that allow them to assess and reject swiftly much in the daily rush of images. Where a person in the 1840s might dwell lengthily on a single, carefully stored daguerreotype, someone these days might hurriedly review and delete numerous images from an email or camera-phone, in expectation of many more equally valuable ones to follow soon.

Understanding photographs is different from looking at them. Understanding a photograph requires time and willingness to set aside the rapid-fire judgments applied to images in the stream of daily life. Thought, research, and an occasional revision of initial impressions are necessary, and these take more time than a brief look.

Even when the subject of a photograph is apparent, it is useful to recall that photographs have many and sometimes overlapping storylines. One of those storylines involves technique, but we do not need to be able to make a particular type of photograph to recognize how a photographer has employed a technique. Most people who looked at daguerreotypes in the 1840s were not able to create them. Nevertheless, they could appreciate the effects of the polished surface and the intimacy of holding the small picture in their hand, moving it forward and back for a better view.

The subject of a photograph has many facets. Subject includes, but reaches beyond, who or what is pictured in a photograph. For instance, to Western eyes—especially in the nineteenth century—a photograph of a Greek temple was associated with ancient Greek government and the arts, as well as their influence on Western political and cultural history. Of course, associations are not permanent, but circumscribed by time, place, and audiences. Moreover, the subject of a photograph is inflected by elements of composition: the angle from which the picture was taken, the visual information given in the foreground and background, the amount of detail used to render all or parts of the picture, and the deliberate manipulation of light, shade, texture, and color. Though it is often unfeasible to know how the image was treated in the darkroom or with photo-editing software, it is still necessary to remember that the photographer may make the picture after taking the picture. All of these components must be appreciated as choices made by the photographer, sometimes in an instant.

Style—that is, the characteristic methods and ideas employed in a movement—exists in photography, just as it does in the other arts. But style and period in photography are not always synchronized with the other arts. The technique called COLLAGE, the arrangement of various materials, usually on a flat surface, so as to create a new composition, was employed before and after the technique was made prominent in pre-World War I modern art. The first photographic collages may have been crafted by mid-nineteenth-century women for family albums. In the 1920s, the widespread, international use of photo-collage techniques across art, advertising, and newspaper photography drew less on prewar examples than on ideas prominent in photographic criticism.

Realism, the depiction of the external world as it appears to the eye, has long been a powerful pulse in Western art, ranging from Roman portraits to Dutch paintings of household scenes. But the distinctive realism of photography does not often fit neatly into various historic moments of fine-art realism. The camera seemed to have the unique ability to soak up large quantities of visual detail. Therefore, its images were judged to be far less subjective than those made by other methods. Because photography was thought not to have an inherent style of its own, it quickly became synonymous with the making and collecting of objective images. Yet it is important to remember that the absence of style—stylessness—is a style in its own right. When it appears, it points to the expectations of the photographer and of the image's anticipated audiences. Although the pursuit of photographic evidence in science and law is nearly as old as the medium, the underlying concepts of evidence and documentary expression have been frequently challenged. These contests of meaning—and all such disputes—are as much part of photography's history as are its technical accomplishments.

The reception of photographic images is shaped by the fact that photography has been, for the most part, a medium based on multiples. The sense that there is one original that exists in only in one place, like the *Mona Lisa* in the Louvre in Paris, usually does not apply to photography. Prints made by the photographer are sometimes valued more than prints made by an assistant or after the photographer's death. Even in the era of digital printing, some photographic prints are technically and aesthetically preferable to others. To understand photography is to understand that the photographer was probably thinking about multiple images when the picture was taken. Sequencing photographs, whether for an exhibition, a book, a newspaper article, or a website, is an ongoing aspect of photography. Thinking in series may be done for a short period, or over a lifetime. Also, a photographer may consider making multiple, but slightly different prints from one original, by varying depth of shadow or color in the darkroom or through photo-editing software.

Marketing also plays a role in multiple images. For example, the nineteenth-century San Francisco photographer Carleton Watkins used a special camera to make negatives from which he created mammoth prints (approximately 18 × 22 inches) of the American West. These large prints were mostly bought by prosperous collectors as showpieces. Yet Watkins also made smaller, more affordable photographs for tourist albums. The same image was understood differently in separate contexts. Today, when mass-media images of the American West are well known to casual viewers through magazines, films, television, and websites, Watkins's Western images do not carry the same associations that they had in an era when most Americans had never seen the mountains and vistas of the West.

Time, place, and circumstance involve knowing whose time, what place, and what was happening in and outside the picture. A photograph may show what an important event looked like to an observer standing near the camera, but it cannot indicate the historical background. To understand why a photograph of an event looks the way it does, it is necessary to look beyond the frame and to ask how the picture relates to what happened. For instance, in war photography from late in World War II to the present day, portraits of individual soldiers have been more popular with the public than images of generals and battles. To appreciate that situation, one has to look at public perception of modern warfare, and at how prior pictures in all media, especially in mass media, have shaped pictures of soldiers. Yet however widespread a photographic approach may seem,

it is likely that images also possess a particular local resonance that cannot be generalized.

The practice of photography has been formed by expectations originating in the settings for which the photographs were initially created, and by the circumstances of subsequent observation. Photo editors help shape photojournalism through suggestions given to the photographer before the pictures are taken, and through selection from the array of resulting images. When these same images are shown in a gallery, the maker and curators work together, creating a different effect with placement, lighting, and sequencing.

It is important to keep in mind that photographic genres have been very porous. Art photography has influenced newspaper imagery and vice versa. Aspects of experimental art photography—for instance, the odd and abrupt angles of Russian photography after the Revolution or collages created in the years between World War I and World War II—were adapted for advertising and documentary work. Scientific photographs of phenomena not seen by the human eye have been displayed for their aesthetic qualities, not their factual content. In current and historic photographic practice, photographers have blended visual and literary sources to create photofictions. Especially in recent years, ordinary snapshots have influenced art and photojournalism. In addition, when photographs are presented in installations that make use of large projections, they sometimes come close to contemporary video and film in their visual investigations of perception and time.

Just as photographic genres absorb ideas and images from each other, so too are photographers' intentions an amalgam of visual and topical possibilities. Aesthetic experimentation and self-expression are not limited to art photography, but encompass all genres, including amateur and casual photography, as evidenced on the flourishing Internet-based camera-phone galleries. A photographer's influences are not restricted to the visual arts. Although painting has regularly inflected photographic practice, literature, film, and mass media have also played significant roles in the field. Pinning down an image-maker's influences is as slippery a business as analyzing how any individual comes to do and make things. Autobiographies, biographies, and artists' statements are valuable, but a life, like an image, always seems to evade exhaustive description.

Polymath and critic John Berger summed up the photographic condition when he observed that "the relationship between what we see and what we know is never settled."[2] The meaning of photographs shifts over time and in the appreciation of different audiences. Understanding photographs can be pleasurable, challenging, perplexing, edifying, painful, disappointing, or uplifting. What it can never be is complete.

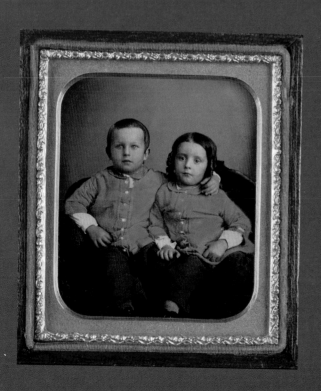

Photography was invented twice: once during a period of largely concealed and scattered technological development, from the end of the eighteenth century to 1839, and then again in the decades after its disclosure, when it would be ceaselessly reinvented by the social uses to which it was put and the cultural dialogue surrounding it.

The invention of photography—or photographies, since several different image-making methods were created—did not depend directly on the impetus of a particular visual tradition, or even on a demonstrable social need. Instead, the climate of congenial attitudes toward material progress, research, and innovation encouraged its conception. Around 1800, Western European countries began to define government's role as fostering economic development through the expansion of industry and commerce. Social progress was understood to flow from the intellectual freedom of individuals seeking to solve scientific problems that would lead to practical applications. Those with the most to gain from this attitude toward change were the educated classes, as well as entrepreneurs, manufacturers, and enlightened landlords—people making up a growing middle class whose status was based on their achievements and earnings.[1] The petite bourgeoisie, or lower middle class, also benefited from the outlook that linked achievement to ability.

The primary elements of the photographic process began to come together and were experimented with in an era when practical, commercially feasible applications of scientific experiments were encouraged by national policy and cultural values. Independent entrepreneurs and business people started to believe that their investments in research might be rewarded. Much of the history of early experiments in photography shows cultural attitudes prompting resourceful individuals to resolve practical problems and technical puzzles. Not every inventor sought financial gain and acclaim, but each of the originators whose stories we know believed in tinkering with devices and testing formulas. In 1839, when the medium was disclosed, the industrializing world eagerly began to explore how it might be applied to portraiture, record-keeping, political persuasion, academic investigation, and travel accounts. Ten years later, photographic subjects and applications began a swift proliferation that constituted a second invention, based partially on the inclinations of individual photographers, but also on the needs of society. The market for portraits expanded, historical events began to be photographed, science and social science took up the medium, and artists and artistically inclined photographers used the camera for personal expression and aesthetic exploration.

LOUIS-JACQUES-MANDÉ DAGUERRE, *View of the Boulevard du Temple,* c. 1839.
Daguerreotype. Bayerisches Nationalmuseum, Munich, Germany.

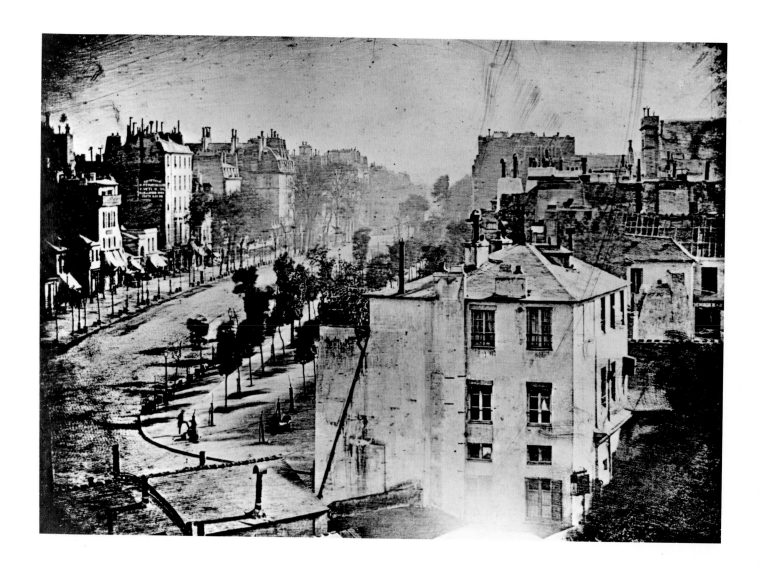

CHAPTER ONE

The Origins of Photography (to 1839)

Since ancient times, devices have been used to aid the eye and hand in reproducing the appearance of optical reality. Indeed, the legend of the Corinthian Maid who preserved the look of her departing lover by tracing his cast-shadow outline on a wall points to the antiquity of the desire for lifelike replicas. Ultimately, photography was invented by individuals working independently from each other, in a relatively short period during the early years of the Industrial Revolution. Their inventions sparked other discoveries, and created a broad social discourse about the meaning of the new medium.

Photography was presented to the world on August 19, 1839, at a joint meeting of the Academy of Science and the Academy of Fine Arts in Paris. Claiming a sore throat, Louis-Jacques-Mandé Daguerre (1787–1851), the specified inventor, did not make the initial presentation. He left the demonstration and technical discussion to François Arago (1786–1853), a scientist and member of the Chamber of Deputies, the lower house of the French parliament. For his accomplishment, Daguerre was awarded a lifelong pension from the French government. The only requirement placed upon him was that he fully reveal his method, which he did in his booklet *Historique et description du procédé du Daguerréotype et du Diorama* (*History and Description of the Process of the Daguerreotype and the Diorama*) (1839). The text was quickly translated into many languages and published around the world.

Tradition still casts Daguerre as the originator of photography, a consensus initiated by François Arago almost two centuries ago. Yet the history of the development of photography is a more complicated tale, involving partial successes, missed opportunities, good fortune, and false starts. The oft-repeated story of the presentation of photography in 1839 says little about the precursors of the medium, the specific course of invention, or the social environment in which the medium was conceived, nor about others who contributed to Daguerre's work or who formulated different photographic processes.

The basic ingredients of photography—a light-tight box, lenses, and light-sensitive substances—had been known for hundreds of years before they were combined. If the invention of photography had depended solely on the availability of materials, it could have taken place during the late Renaissance. Indeed, all but the light-sensitive material was present in a technique for astronomical observation that used some European cathedrals like cameras. Beginning in the sixteenth century, the dark interiors of churches such as Santa Maria del Fiore in Florence, Italy, and Saint-Sulpice in Paris, France, were punctured with a small hole in the roof, which worked like a lens to focus an image of the sun on the floor below. There the sun's movements were measured and used to establish the modern calendar. Ironically, these gauges verified Galileo's proof of Copernicus's theory that the sun, not the earth, is the center of our universe, an idea repudiated by the Roman Catholic Church.[1] With the cathedral serving as a camera, a light-sensitive material might have been found in silver. Silversmithing was an advanced art in the Renaissance, and the perception that silver darkens when exposed to light was an ancient commonplace. If someone ever tried placing a polished silver plate on the floor of a cathedral, however, to see whether it would register the sun's image, no record of that experiment has survived.

Before the end of the eighteenth century, imagining the photographic process seems to have been difficult. Unlike other transformational technologies, such as air travel and automobiles, photography was not foreseen in the centuries before it was invented. Looking back on what was widely perceived as the medium's abrupt appearance, American essayist and medical doctor Oliver Wendell Holmes (1809–1894) remarked that "in all the prophecies of dreaming enthusiasts, in all the random guesses of the future conquests over matter, we do not remember any prediction of such an inconceivable wonder. … No Century of Inventions includes this among its possibilities."[2] In utopian and speculative fiction written prior to 1800, only the 1760 novel *Giphantie*, by French writer Charles-François Tiphaigne de la Roche (1723–1774), anticipated something like the detailed transcription of the observable world that would occur with photography. In *Giphantie*, a narrator visits the hollow of the earth's center, where a group of spirits creates highly illusionistic paintings. A canvas is smeared with a mysterious viscous material and placed before a desired scene. Like a mirror, it records every color and detail. After an hour's drying time in a dark place, the picture becomes permanent. Arguably, *Giphantie* anticipated the use of light-sensitive chemicals, but the story did not involve a light-tight box or lenses—or a human operator.

Although it seems that the invention of photography should be related to the start of the Industrial Revolution, its connection to the technical, social, and political changes that accompanied the initial mechanization of production during the late eighteenth and early nineteenth centuries in Europe is not easy to establish. The desire for reliable visual reproductions has been linked to the needs of expanding commerce and industry, and the wish of the emerging middle class for realistic portraits. But around 1800, when the first documentable experiments attempted to record the visible world by means of light-sensitive materials, these trends were not clearly discernible to contemporaries.

BEFORE PHOTOGRAPHY

Describing the late eighteenth century, historian Eric Hobsbawm persuasively depicted a world that was largely rural, in which there was no urban, mass culture pressing for realistic, multiple images.[3] Even in Britain, where industrialism was most advanced, the stream of reports, novels, and documents describing the Industrial Revolution did not begin to appear until the 1830s and 1840s. In the early nineteenth century,

the visual arts were dominated by Neoclassical idealism and Romantic expression. Naturalistic depiction of reality was occasionally pursued, for example, in the style of German landscape painting known as Biedermeier, or British watercolors such as those of John Sell Cotman (1782–1842), although this trend did not yet seem influential. While the British artist John Constable (1776–1837) struggled to render his observations of the changing light effects of sun and clouds in the rural landscape, his successful contemporary Joseph Mallord William Turner (1775–1851) produced fantastical medleys of color unfettered by mere depiction. Similarly, during the 1820s, French artist Eugène Delacroix (1798–1863) was fascinated with expressionistic color and theatrical lighting effects, and was less interested in realism. By the mid-1830s, when many painters became more concerned with the appearance of mundane reality, as in the work of the Barbizon School of artists such as Théodore Rousseau (1812–1867), photography had been invented by several people.

TECHNOLOGICAL AND ARTISTIC FOREBEARS

Because our culture places great value on imaginative art, it is sometimes forgotten that one of the most common uses for visual depictions in the centuries before photography was to copy the observable world and to communicate visual information in an uninflected manner. Routine commissions for landscapes and portraits did not generally call for the artist's personal interpretation or stylistic flair. Similarly, engravers and etchers, who produced multiple images from drawings cut into a wooden or metal plate, were expected faithfully to copy historic monuments, machines and devices, animals and botanical specimens, and even works of art.

Contraptions to help artists produce images had existed for centuries. French printmaker Abraham Bosse (1602–1676), who wrote and lectured on perspective, showed how artists could achieve greater fidelity by employing a screen with equally

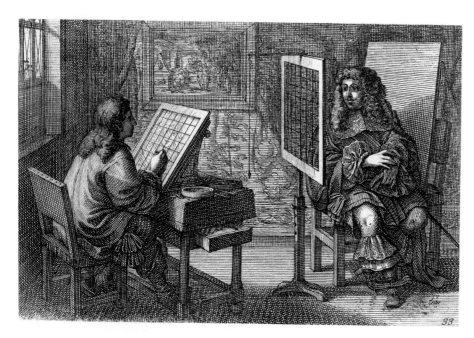

1.2
ABRAHAM BOSSE, *Engraving Depicting Artist at Work*, c. 1737.

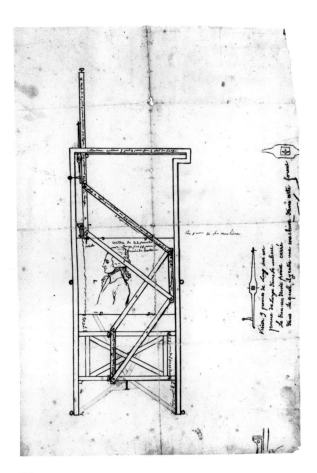

1.3
ARTIST UNKNOWN, *Gilles-Louis Chrétien's Physionotrace*, c. 1786.
Drawing. Bibliothèque Nationale de France, Paris.

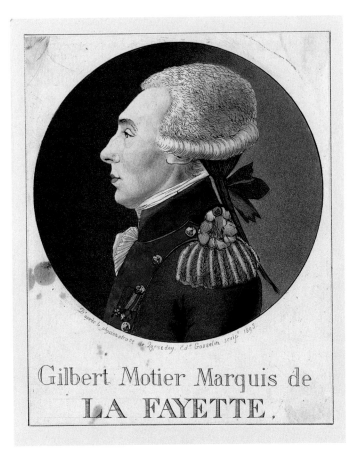

1.4
ARTIST UNKNOWN, *Gilbert Motier, Marquis de La Fayette*, 1895; (below image)
D'après le physionotrace de Quenedey. Aquatint, colored, after physionotrace
drawing. Marquis de Lafayette Print Collection. David Bishop Skillman Library.
Lafayette College Library, Easton, Pennsylvania.

spaced squares (Fig. 1.2).[4] This simple device was particularly
useful in foreshortening—that is, contracting the image of
an object or human figure so as to create the appearance of
perspective. A variant of the technique, employing graph paper,
is used today.

The PANTOGRAPH, familiar since the seventeenth century,
and still available as a drafting tool and as a child's toy, helped
artists copy, enlarge, or reduce drawings. French engraver
Gilles-Louis Chrétien (1754–1811) adapted the pantograph to
engraving in 1786, calling his invention the PHYSIONOTRACE
(Fig. 1.3). The physionotrace mechanized a technique for making
profiles (Fig. 1.4) that can be traced back to the time of Louis
XIV (1638–1715; r. 1643–1715). Not only did the physionotrace
permit users to make multiple copies, but it also allowed color
to be applied.[5] SILHOUETTES, or shadow portraits, were part
entertainment and part artistic venture. Silhouette-makers
primarily served the bourgeoisie, but they also sold profile
portraits on the streets and at parties. Some dextrously cut dark
paper while observing a subject standing in profile; others used
a candle to project the outline of a subject's head on to a sheet of
paper (Figs. 1.15, 1.5).

The public acceptance of the silhouette, usually a single
image, and the physionotrace, which produced multiple,

engraved images, accompanied the growth of the middle classes
in eighteenth-century Europe, and their taste for likenesses
rendered without the idealization and ornament flaunted in
aristocratic portraits. A seemingly neutral descriptive approach
to portraits in all media began to distinguish middle-class
likenesses from those created for the upper classes. In addition
to being quicker to produce than a painting, and certainly less
expensive, the silhouette and the physionotrace responded

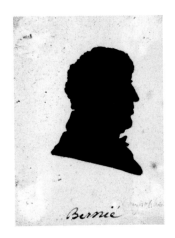

1.5
ARTIST UNKNOWN, *Bernie*. Silhouette
portrait, 1790s. Ink on paper mounted
on 5⅓ × 4⅛ in. (13.5 × 10.6 cm) paper.
Hans P. Kraus, Jr. Collection, New York.

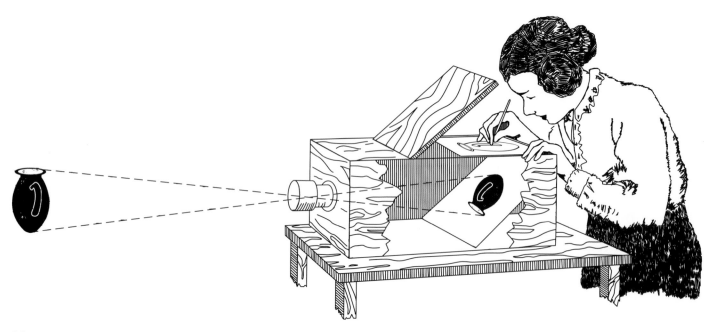

1.6
CAMERA OBSCURA

A simple tool for making drawings, the camera obscura projected an upside-down image onto a mirror, which reflected the image upward onto a pane of translucent glass. The user put a piece of thin paper over the glass, and traced the image.

to the middle-class view of itself as a distinct social group. Such portraits exemplified a sense of individualism and accomplishment among professionals and business people, expressed not simply through the ownership of portraits but also through a preference for likenesses that accentuated such personal features as the shape of the nose and the slant of the forehead. Treatises on physiognomy, the study of physical features as a means to deduce human character, appealed to a middle class seeking new ways, beyond pedigree, to understand temperament and personal achievement. As they evolved, mechanical aids to drawing became more exact, emphasizing outlines and contours rather than shading, or atmospheric effects, or personal interpretation. A similar idea of a neutral representation found favor in the sciences—especially biology, botany, and geology, which sought methods to convey visual data objectively.

The drawing aid with the most direct effect on photography was the CAMERA OBSCURA, literally, a "dark room." Actually, the camera obscura was originally a darkened, room-size chamber, in which a tiny opening in one wall acted like a lens, focusing an upside-down image of the scene outside on to the opposite wall. Over time, the room-size chamber was made smaller and portable (Fig. 1.6). It was equipped with lenses, and constructed with an internal mirror so that the upside-down image was righted and could be traced on a piece of paper placed on a translucent glass plate installed in the top of the device. Like other machines to aid drawing, the camera obscura did not encourage imagination or personal style, and usually produced stiff, formal images (Fig. 1.7). It could help artists to trace the outlines of shapes, but it obviously could not copy the religious, historical, or mythological scenes that were central to art production until the nineteenth century.

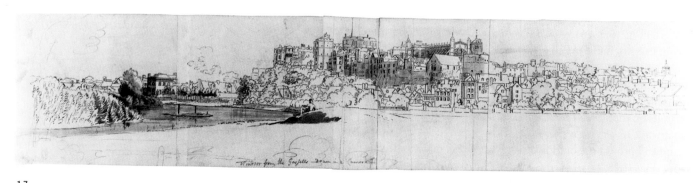

1.7
THOMAS SANDBY, *Windsor from the Goswells,* **1770. Camera obscura drawing. The Royal Collection. © 2002 Her Majesty Queen Elizabeth II.**

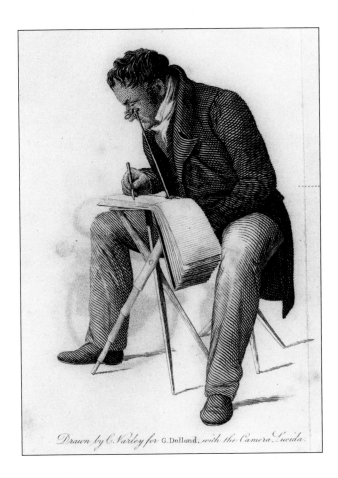

Drawn by C. Varley for G. Dolland, with the Camera Lucida.

An even more transportable and lightweight aid to drawing was patented in 1806 by British scientist William Hyde Wollaston (1766–1828). Simple, if somewhat awkward to use, the CAMERA LUCIDA, or light room, consisted of a rod to which was affixed a glass prism having two silvered sides that reflected the scene at which it was aimed. A person wishing to draw a scene would attach the camera lucida to a drawing table and adjust the prism so as to reflect an image directly into the eye. Looking down, the user then moved the prism slightly to create the illusion of the scene existing on the drawing paper. The would-be artist could then trace the outlines of the scene directly on to the drawing paper, while looking up occasionally to check the actual scene. The camera lucida was useful to travelers who wanted to record topographic or architectural views (Figs. 1.8, 1.9).

There were, in sum, two general categories of drawing aid. The first, such as the camera lucida, helped artists produce a single image. The second, such as the physionotrace, yielded multiple copies. The development of these devices in the years prior to photography indicates different needs, not a concerted

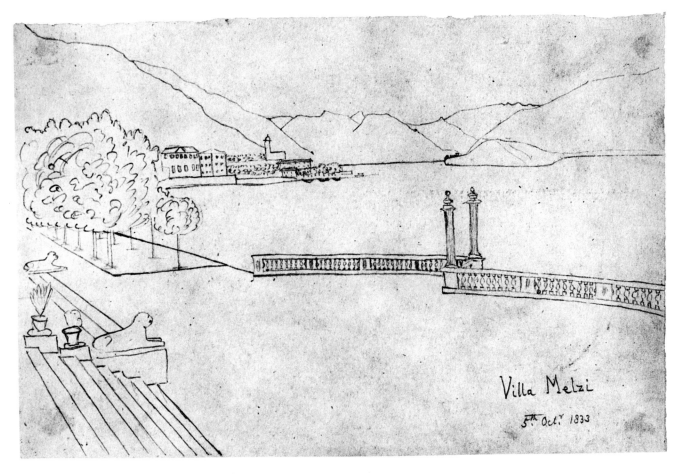

Villa Melzi

5th Oct.ʸ 1833

focus

The First Photograph

When a small photograph came up for auction in 2008,
Dr. Larry J. Schaaf, an expert on early British photography,
challenged its attribution. He observed that the image's
dark red color and darkened highlights indicated that the
photograph had not been fixed—that is, its light sensitivity
had not been completely deactivated. In addition, the
photograph originated in an album originally owned by a
collector who attended meetings of the Lunar Society. Equally
intriguing is what looked like part of the letter "W" inscribed in
ink in the upper right-hand corner. Could this be an example
of the photographs made by Wedgwood and Davy, or by
James Watt? Unfixed images become pale in the light, yet we
know that some of Wedgwood and Davy's pictures were still
visible in 1885. Keeping unfixed images in the dark would
retard fading, but for more than two hundred years? If so, the
early photographs in this album would be the oldest existing
photographs known. The auctioned image is now in private
hands. While not the newly attributed image, this photograph
is from the same album.

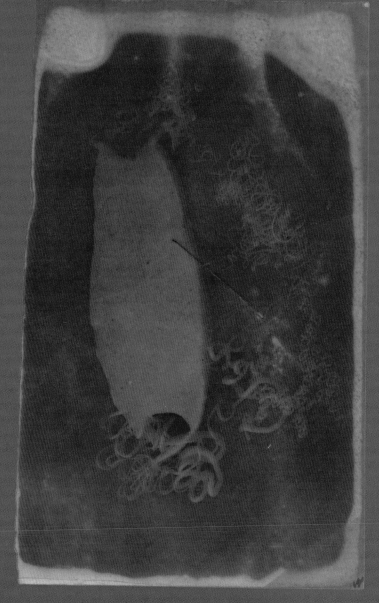

1.10
SHARK EGG CASE, 1840–45. Metropolitan Museum of Art, New York.

social demand. For example, landscape artists used drawing devices to make a visual record as part of the preparation for a painting. Travelers employed these tools to render mementos of a scene. In either case, the user did not ordinarily intend to make multiple copies of the image, like copy-artists, engravers, and printers. Similarly, when photography was invented by a number of individuals, some created systems that produced unique single images, and others fashioned techniques that could make multiple copies.

THE INVENTION OF "PHOTOGRAPHIES"

The history of the first photographs has been made to fit into the conventional notion that invention is regular and progressive, with each experiment building in an orderly, successful way on the achievements of the past. However, none of photography's pioneers reported making headway in that fashion.

ANTOINE FLORENCE AND THE QUESTION OF SIMULTANEOUS INVENTION

French artist and cartographer Antoine Hércules Romuald Florence (1804–1879) traveled through the interior of Brazil with German naturalist Baron Georg von Lansdorff (1774–1852) to record the area's peoples and natural settings. After the 1824–29 expedition he settled in Campinas, a city located in the province of São Paulo, where he painted views and portraits. In 1830, while trying to publish a book on animal sounds, he became frustrated by the lack of nearby printing shops and invented his own printing technique, which he called *poligraphie*, meaning "multiple writing." Soon after, Florence conceived photography after noticing that certain fabrics faded when exposed to light. According to Boris Kossoy, Florence was successful because he was removed from centers of scientific learning, and had to think unconventionally.[6] With the aid of the local druggist, Florence experimented with the camera obscura to see if he could make its images permanent. Unsuccessful, he investigated the printmaking potential of glass plates that were covered with a dark mixture of gum arabic and soot. Like an engraver, he scratched designs into the plates, and then placed them on paper that had been made light sensitive through a treatment with silver chloride, which darkens in the presence of light. The paper's light sensitivity could be halted by the application of an ammonia solution, which stopped the darkening action.

Florence's diaries show precise drawings of small cameras and of printing frames that used sunlight to print an image. In 1832, he began using the term *photographie* for his process, deriving it from the Greek words for light and writing.[7] He used his photographic technique to produce diplomas, tags, and labels, but appears not to have fared well in reproducing camera images. When Daguerre's photography was announced in 1839, Florence realized that his humble efforts could not compete, and he directed his energies toward other aspects of the printing business.[8] Writing to newspapers in São Paulo and Rio de Janeiro, he modestly declared that he would not "dispute anyone's discovery … because two people can have the same idea."[9]

The notion of simultaneous invention—that two or more people can develop the same concept at about the same time—was mentioned by Florence and by another of photography's pioneers, William Henry Fox Talbot (1800–1877), whose experiments are discussed later in the chapter.[10] Simultaneous invention makes it difficult to construct a linear chronology of photography and suggests, moreover, that there may have been other successful yet unknown attempts to invent photography. If Florence, living in a remote area, could originate a way to reproduce labels using a light-sensitive silver compound, others elsewhere in the world may have had similar partial success. It is probable that, while the work of individuals such as Florence was to become better known, the precise history of photography's invention will never be fully ascertained.

THE PROBLEM OF PERMANENCE: WEDGWOOD AND DAVY

Many histories of photography trace the development of European photography through the research of Thomas Wedgwood (1771–1805) and Humphry Davy (1778–1829), both of whom—unlike Florence—were in touch with up-to-date scientific inquiry. Wedgwood, son of Josiah Wedgwood (1730–1795), the British amateur scientist and pottery manufacturer who helped popularize Neoclassicism with his designs, attended meetings of the Lunar Society, a distinguished group that included physician-scientist Erasmus Darwin (1731–1802), inventor James Watt (1736–1819), and the political theorist and scientist Joseph Priestley (1733–1804). The group kept abreast of scientific discoveries in Europe and America, and deliberately sought practical applications for new findings. Thomas Wedgwood's special interest was the new, or French, chemistry developed by Antoine-Laurent Lavoisier (1743–1794), who mandated repeated testing of hypotheses in the laboratory, a practice he helped to establish as the standard for the field. The new chemists were animated by the sense that they were discovering the world afresh.

An enthusiasm for science, especially the new chemistry, prompted Wedgwood and his friend Davy, then a humble apothecary's apprentice, to experiment with light-sensitive materials. They sought to fix the image of an object's shadow cast on paper or leather that had been made light sensitive by immersion in a silver nitrate solution, and they also attempted to capture images formed in a camera obscura. In addition, they tried to copy paintings on glass by letting light pass through the glass on to light-sensitive paper. Unknown to them, silver nitrate was not sufficiently light sensitive to hold the image projected inside the camera obscura. The more direct approach, shadow images of objects and paintings on glass, did leave a photographic imprint, although it was not permanent since the silver nitrate continued to react to light until the surface darkened. In his 1802 report on their work, Davy announced that "nothing but a method of preventing the unshaded part of the delineation from being coloured by exposure to the day is wanting, to render the process as useful as it is elegant."[11] Wedgwood was prevented by illness from taking part in further joint experiments, and Davy moved on in other scientific directions, eventually becoming president of the Royal Society.

Although Wedgwood and Davy's experiments in fixing a light-induced image were less successful than the later efforts of Florence, their efforts were known in scientific circles. James Watt, whose perfected steam engine helped power the Industrial Revolution, corresponded with Wedgwood and may have attempted to make some photographs. Publication of the Wedgwood and Davy experiments in the influential *Journal of the Royal Institution of Great Britain* (1802) furthered their reputation. By contrast, Florence's contribution was not recognized until 1970. Even so, their work did not become a stepping stone for subsequent successful attempts to stabilize an image through photochemical reactions.

THE "SUN WRITING" OF NIÉPCE

Another precursor of photography was the "sun writing" developed in France by Joseph Nicéphore Niépce (1765–1833). Born to a family of people who had worked for French royalty, Niépce received a fine education, and he came of age with high expectations. The French Revolution, which began in 1789, altered his prospects and, from the seclusion of a country estate, he sought ways of making a living. With his brother Claude, he spent years perfecting an internal combustion engine intended to power riverboats. Dubbed the *pyréolophore*, this engine was intended to rival the new onboard steam engine by burning vegetable oil or other similar substances; it received a French patent in 1807. Like many would-be entrepreneurs who saw the development of new machines and processes as the source of prosperity, Niépce turned his attention to the potential of the lithographic process.

LITHOGRAPHY, a technique for reproducing images, uses drawings on a flat surface, usually a smooth stone (ancient Greek: *lithos*), rather than a metal or wood recessed surface, as in engraving and etching. It was perfected in 1798 by the German actor and writer Alois Senefelder (1771–1834). For communicating information the lithograph had several advantages. It could yield quite a large number of prints, and it could render tones and shadows more subtly than etching and engraving, which gained their effects of light and dark from the closeness of individual lines scratched into the surface of the plate. Lithography appealed to painters, who could work directly on the lithographic stone without having laboriously to cut lines into the surface. But it also intrigued early nineteenth-century entrepreneurs, who saw in lithography a process that could surpass existing methods for illustration. In the early 1800s, lithography aroused the kind of get-rich-quick excitement generated by small computer and software companies in the late twentieth century.

Lacking the ability to draw on the lithographic stone, Niépce began to experiment with ways to produce an image through the action of light upon photosensitive materials. His early efforts, begun in 1816, involved the use of paper made light sensitive by the application of a silver chloride solution. After exposing the photosensitive paper in a camera obscura, he experienced some of the very same problems as Wedgwood and Davy. The image was too indistinct, and the action of the light could not be thoroughly stopped. Moreover, the tones of the image were reversed: dark became light, and light became dark, creating what was later known as a NEGATIVE. Niépce tried, without success, to use the negative as it is used today—that is, printing it to create a positive image, in which the tones are re-reversed and thereby corrected. He also failed to alter the reversed dark and light areas through chemical means.

Undaunted, Niépce continued to try out various light-sensitive materials. He does not seem to have known about the experiments of Wedgwood and Davy; nor, like them, did he encounter many past investigations of such materials. An obscure 1727 paper on the effects of light on silver nitrate by German scientist Johann Heinrich Schulze (1687–1744) might have been difficult to locate, but experiments with light-sensitive materials conducted by Swedish chemist Carl Wilhelm Scheele (1742–1786), published in 1777, and the work of Swiss librarian and botanist Jean Senebier (1742–1809), published in 1782, would have been available to a researcher living in an academic and intellectual capital such as early nineteenth-century Paris. The discovery by British scientist John Herschel (1792–1871), published in 1819, that hyposulphite of soda dissolves silver chloride, thereby stopping its reaction to light, also seems to have been unknown to Niépce, although he did receive advice about photosensitive materials from French chemist Louis-Nicolas Vauquelin (1763–1829). Niépce's approach to photography was thus largely independent of the research of others.[12]

Beginning in 1822, Niépce shifted his interests to copying engravings by means of the action of light. To do so, he saturated an engraving with oil to make it more transparent. He then placed it on a pewter plate that had been coated with bitumen of Judea, a substance known to harden when exposed to light. After light exposure, the areas beneath the engraving's dark lines remained soft, while those beneath the light parts of the engraving hardened. The plate was rinsed with lavender oil, washing away the soft areas. What remained became an engraving plate, after Niépce etched the now blank areas with acid. He then printed it (Fig. 1.11).

Finding this procedure more encouraging than his experiment with silver chloride, Niépce put a similarly prepared plate in a camera obscura and exposed it in a window at his estate, Le Gras, near Chalon-sur-Saône. After about eight hours, he removed the plate, washed it with a mixture of oil of lavender and petroleum oil, and rinsed away those soluble areas of the plate where the bitumen of Judea had received less light. The resulting plate contained a poor but visible negative of the scene outside the window where the camera obscura had been placed. The image itself was reversed laterally—that is, left to right. Niépce then took the plate and exposed it to iodine fumes. The iodine did not fully reverse the tones, but it created greater contrasts.[13] In effect, Niépce made what is now called a DIRECT POSITIVE image, one that, as the name implies, produces a

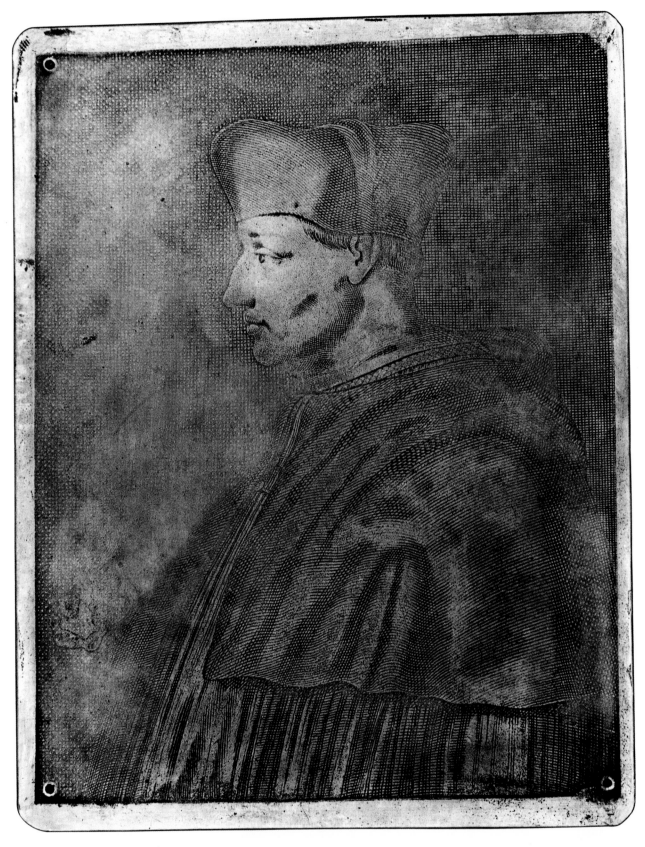

1.11
JOSEPH NICÉPHORE NIÉPCE, *Cardinal d'Amboise,* **1826. Heliograph on pewter plate (reproduction of an engraving). Musée Nicéphore Niépce, Chalon-sur-Saône, France.**

A seventeenth-century image of Cardinal d'Amboise was one of the most popular and commercially successful engravings in France. Niépce copied the image on to a pewter plate by photographic means as an experiment to show that the process would make it possible to print multiple copies, although he never seems to have done so.

photograph without a separate negative. Because there was no negative from which to print copies, the image could not be reproduced. Though not completely stable, Niépce's *View from the Window at Gras* (c. 1826) is considered to be the world's first permanent photograph (Fig. 1.12).

In 1827, Niépce brought examples of his process—called heliography, from the Greek words for sun and writing—to London, where he was visiting his brother Claude, who still hoped to get financial backing for the combustion engine to power riverboats. Claude's ill-health and the increasing financial strains on the family prompted Niépce to seek funding for his photographic process. He managed to get the attention and support of Francis Bauer (1758–1840), a fellow of the Royal Society, for whom he prepared a short "Notice sur l'héliographie" ("Notice on Heliography") (December 8, 1827), describing the process in general terms. His failure to generate interest in the process may have been due to Niépce's cautious concealment of his exact technique. Before returning to France in February 1828, Niépce left many heliographs of engravings and the *View from the Window at Gras* with Francis Bauer.

THE COLLABORATION OF NIÉPCE AND DAGUERRE

While traveling through Paris on his journey to Britain, Niépce met with Daguerre, at that time known as a painter, designer of stage sets, and co-proprietor of the Diorama, a distinctive kind of theater that presented realistic special effects to thrill audiences (Fig. 1.13). To plan his stage illusions, especially the impression of deeply recessed theatrical space, Daguerre employed the camera obscura. He also made some ineffectual attempts to capture photochemically the images that were produced by the camera obscura.

Daguerre and Niépce were introduced to one another by Charles Chevalier (1804–1859), a Parisian maker of optical instruments and devices such as the camera obscura, with whom both men did business. After his disappointing trip to England, coupled with the death of his brother Claude in February 1828, Niépce redoubled his efforts to find a photochemical method to obtain permanent camera obscura images. He moved from using pewter plates to highly polished silver plates and copper plates covered with silver. He continued to use bitumen of Judea, which yielded better picture quality when employed on a silver backing.

Niépce had decided to work with Daguerre to improve the photographic process, even though, as the photographic historians Alison and Helmut Gernsheim concluded, Daguerre could not produce a successful photograph to show Niépce. In a contract signed by both on December 14, 1829, Daguerre promised to give Niépce an improved camera obscura, and

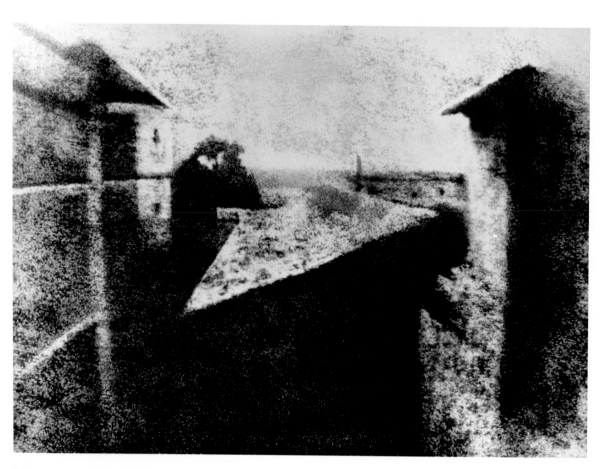

1.12
JOSEPH NICÉPHORE NIÉPCE, *View from the Window at Le Gras*, c. 1826. Heliograph. Gernsheim Collection. Harry Ransom Humanities Research Center, University of Texas at Austin.

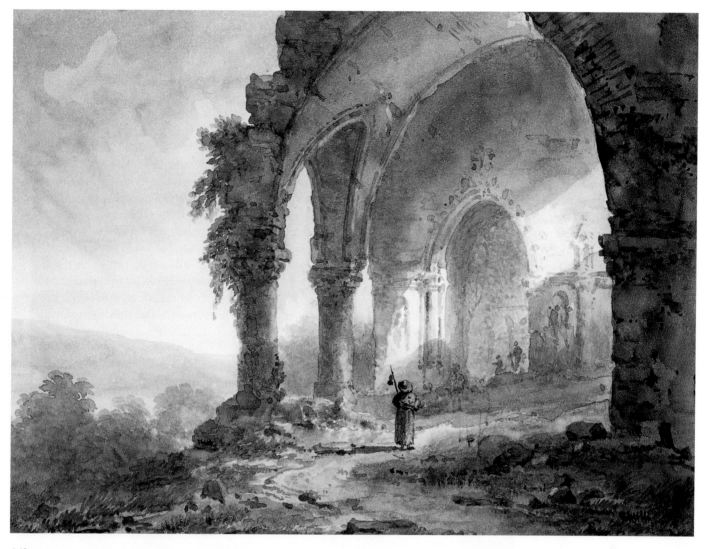

1.13
LOUIS-JACQUES-MANDÉ DAGUERRE, *Landscape with Gothic Ruins and Figures,* 1821. Brown ink and wash drawing. George Eastman House, Rochester, New York.

Daguerre's watercolor of the mists and shadows in a ruined Gothic church gives a sense of the dramatic style of the Diorama's entertainment. Through carefully planned shifting lighting, transparent paintings on thin fabric, and sound effects, audiences were given the impression of being in a ruin, on an alpine hill, or near a waterfall.

Niépce agreed to show Daguerre the means by which he was able to capture camera obscura images, which he did at his estate. Daguerre later admitted that the camera obscura he gave to Niépce was ineffective in producing clearer images. When Niépce died suddenly in 1833, Daguerre took up his research.

DAGUERRE AND THE LATENT IMAGE

Daguerre's personal circumstances were very different from Niépce's. Born into a petite-bourgeois family, he lacked much formal education. Nevertheless, his outgoing personality and drive to succeed contrasted with Niépce's docile yet mistrustful attitude toward others. Daguerre was poised to take advantage of social forces in the 1830s. In France, the hold of upper-class landowning interests remained strong, but was challenged by the growing power of middle-class commercial and industrial development. Business people, bureaucrats, and managers

were part of an emerging elite based not on birth but on intelligence and hard work. Daguerre's humble beginnings and rise to prominence as a co-owner of the Diorama in Paris and, subsequently, in London made him something of a class hero.

By 1835, Daguerre's experiments with Niépce's materials—silver plates, silver-plated copper plates, and iodine—led to his concentrating on the creation of a LATENT IMAGE—that is, an image that had been registered on the silver surface of a plate, but which was not yet visible. Like Niépce, who treated *View from the Window* with iodine fumes, Daguerre realized that treatments after exposure could effectively bring out the image. Where Niépce started with a visible image, and intensified the tones using iodine fumes to give the picture greater contrast, Daguerre found that there was a latent image on the exposed silver plate, which could be treated with mercury fumes, further developing the picture and making it visible. Soon after, in 1837, he discovered that a solution of common table salt dissolved in hot water would stop the light-sensitive material from continuing to react (Fig. 1.14).

In the end, Daguerre's photographic process was so simple that he, like Niépce before him, began to worry about someone stealing it, and robbing him of both his place in history and his long-sought financial reward. To make a DAGUERREOTYPE, a copper sheet plated with silver was given a high polish. The plate, as it was called, was placed with the silver side down over a closed box containing iodine. The iodine fumes fused with the silver to create silver iodide, which is light sensitive. The plate was then fitted into a camera obscura adapted for it and exposed to light. Exposure times varied, but the earliest daguerreotypes took about four to five minutes (Fig. 1.1), according to one of the reports sent to the French Chamber of Deputies. The plate, with its latent image, was then put in a special box and exposed to mercury fumes, which blended with the silver to produce a visible image. The still light-reactive image was thoroughly washed with a sodium chloride (table salt) solution, which stopped the response to light, and then carefully rinsed with plain water.

With his success, Daguerre renegotiated the contract he had made with Niépce, which was held by Niépce's son Isidore (1805–1868). In 1837, Daguerre demanded and received the right to call himself the inventor of the process, and to have the process bear his name. Isidore Niépce secured his father's legacy by getting Daguerre to agree that accounts of both photographic processes would be published together. Additionally, Daguerre and Isidore Niépce arranged to market the processes by subscription—that is, by selling shares to the public. However, an initial attempt in 1838 to convince the public to buy shares in the new business failed. Paradoxically, Daguerre's reputation for creating optical illusions at the Diorama seems to have made the public suspicious of his methods. For a second attempt in late 1838, Daguerre prepared a broadsheet describing his research and that of Niépce. He subtly promoted his own process, while paying sentimental, faintly belittling attention to Niépce's early efforts. The broadsheet boasted that the daguerreotype

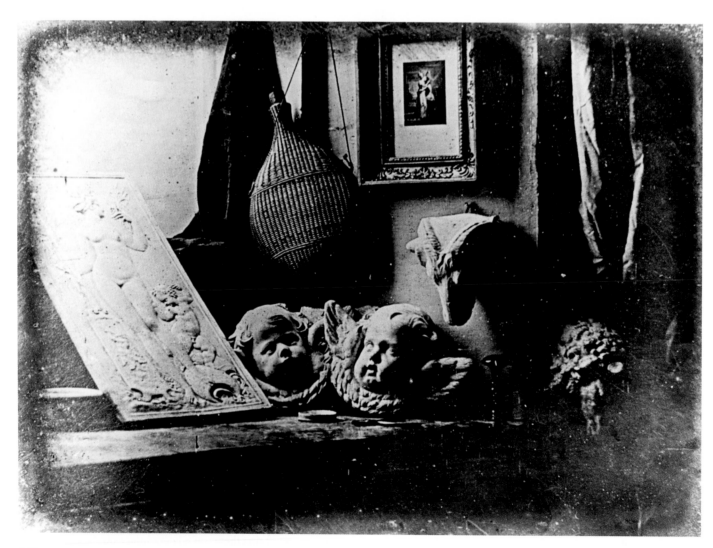

1.14
LOUIS-JACQUES-MANDÉ DAGUERRE, *Still Life (Interior of a Cabinet of Curiosities)*, **1837. Daguerreotype.**
Société Française de Photographie, Paris.

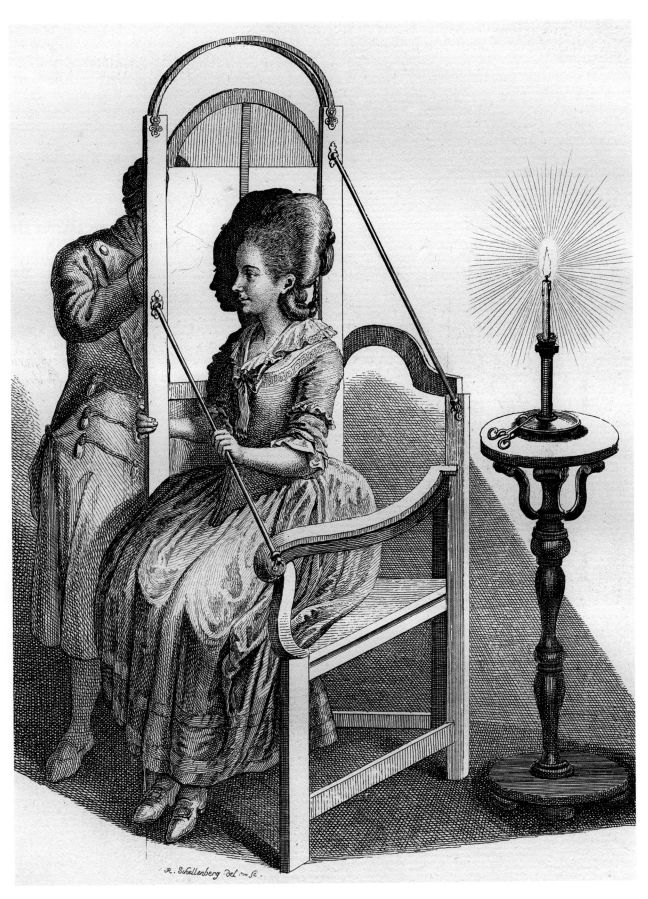

1.15
JOHANN KASPAR LAVATER, *Silhouette Machine*, c. 1780. Engraving from Lavater's *Essays on Physiognomy*. Gernsheim Collection.
Harry Ransom Humanities Research Center, University of Texas at Austin.

required only three to thirty minutes' outdoor exposure to light, and speculated on future uses. Daguerre considered that the daguerreotype would be used by the "leisured class," making renderings of country houses, and providing the means to "form collections of all kinds." "The little work it entails," he concluded, "will greatly please ladies."[14]

At about the same time, Daguerre attempted to persuade prominent scientists and artists to endorse his photographic process. When the astronomer and politician François Arago saw the daguerreotype, he soon set about securing French government assistance for the process. Government support for science and invention was an important feature of French intellectual life.[15] With the sponsorship of a member of the French Academy of Science, and the approval of the Academy, a French citizen could approach the relevant government department for funds. Arago, a liberal and progressive member of the Chamber of Deputies, had already sponsored bills for the development of the railroad and the telegraph. While he may have seen in Daguerre's process a counterpart to his own attempts to measure the intensity of light, he also recognized that the ingredients of the daguerreotype process were sufficiently simple and easily available for the procedure to be quickly copied. Since copyright would not readily secure rights to the process, Arago cleverly suggested that the government provide Daguerre and Isidore Niépce with pensions, and that the new process be magnanimously given to the world by France.

On January 7, 1839, Arago made a statement to the French Academy of Science describing the process in general terms, and emphasizing the originality of Daguerre's invention. The day before, H. Gaucheraud, a journalist writing for the *Gazette de France*, previewed the new process, suggesting that the fine detail of the daguerreotype would not substantially challenge drawing and painting, because the appearance of the daguerreotype was much closer to the look of engravings and of mezzotints, a printing process able to produce a greater range of tones than etchings and engravings.[16]

RESPONSES TO THE ANNOUNCEMENT OF THE DAGUERREOTYPE

News of Daguerre's invention was quickly broadcast, and caught the attention of those who recalled related experiments and those who were working on similar photographic processes. Francis Bauer, to whom Niépce had given some heliographs, quickly organized a British exhibit of these works, in an effort to publicize his deceased acquaintance's earlier accomplishments. In a March 1839 paper on photography, John Herschel recalled that a book by Elizabeth Fulhame, *View to a New Art of Dying* [sic] *and Painting* (1794), proposed capturing and retaining images on cloth through the interaction of light and certain metals.[17] The historian of photography Pierre G. Harmant has

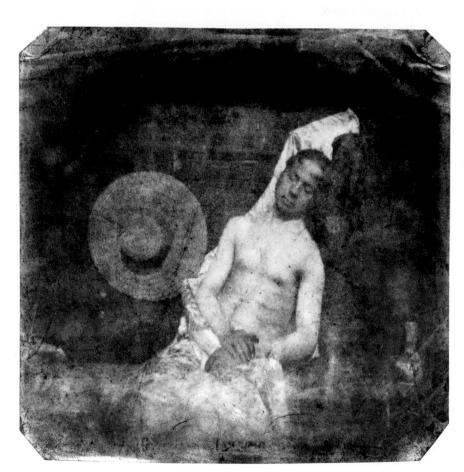

1.16
HIPPOLYTE BAYARD, *Self-Portrait as a Drowned Man*, **1840. Direct paper positive. Société Française de Photographie, Paris.**

Playing on the Romantic notion of the misunderstood artist who commits suicide, Bayard penned a note on the back of this photograph, suggesting that he ended his life in penniless despair. Noting the darkness of his hands and face, Bayard added that these indicated decomposition, since no one even came to the morgue to claim his body![19]

revealed that, from 1839 on, twenty-four persons claimed to have invented photography.[18] Among them was Hippolyte Bayard (1801–1887), who attempted to deduce Daguerre's process before the specific information was released to the public.

BAYARD'S DIRECT POSITIVE PROCESS

Bayard, a minor official in the French Ministry of Finance with no scientific training, responded to the 1839 announcement of Daguerre's method by undertaking photographic experiments. He aimed at making a direct positive print, such as that produced by Niépce and Daguerre, but one that he and others considered to be a simpler and more elegant process than theirs. Bayard completely darkened light-sensitive paper that had been soaked in sodium chloride by exposing it to light. He then took the blackened paper and soaked it again, this time in a solution of potassium iodide. When this paper was placed in a camera obscura and exposed, the light bleached the paper according to its intensity. Like the daguerreotype, Bayard's unnamed process produced a single, unique print that could not be used as a negative to make multiple copies.

Hoping to share Daguerre's success, Bayard showed his images to Arago, who was disconcerted by the prospect of another inventor. Doubtless aware of such famous challenges to discovery as the struggle between British scientist Joseph Priestley and French scientist A.-L. Lavoisier for the discovery of oxygen, Arago secured some small funds to enable Bayard to continue his experiments, but asked him not to announce his findings. Although Bayard exhibited about thirty of his direct positive prints on July 14, 1839, lack of official recognition prevented him from achieving Daguerre's celebrity. Using his direct positive process, Bayard created a comic yet critical response to his nation's neglect of his work. In an image he titled *Self-Portrait as a Drowned Man*, Bayard photographed himself feigning death by suicide (Fig. 1.16). Although Bayard's melodramatic pretense did not earn him the honor he desired, he did not drown himself, but went on to make further photographs, some of which, like his *Self-Portrait*, teased the viewer into thinking about what could be represented in photography, and what could not (see p. 30; Fig. 2.12).

HERSCHEL'S "PHOTOGRAPHIC SPECIMENS"

In Britain, meanwhile, John Herschel, like many scientists, became intrigued with the recent announcement of the daguerreotype, even though the precise formula and materials had not been divulged. Two decades before, in 1819, Herschel had explored the properties of a chemical called hyposulphite of soda, discovering that it would dissolve silver salts. Hypo (now the term for sodium thiosulfate), used today in the development process of black-and-white photography, got its nickname from Herschel's nineteenth-century work. Another of Herschel's early photographic experiments was his 1831 exploration of the light reactions of platinum salts.

A few weeks after Daguerre's announcement, Herschel began to try his luck with photography. In his notebook for January 29, 1839, he wrote: "Expts [experiments] tried within

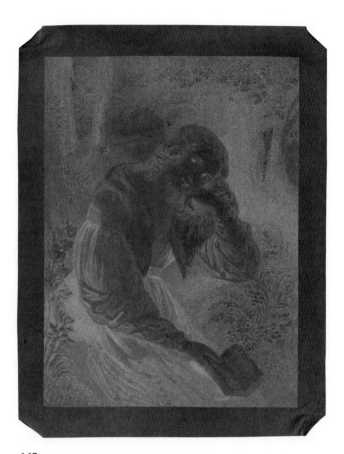

1.17
JOHN HERSCHEL. *Untitled*, 1842. Cyanotype. Harry Ransom Humanities Research Center, University of Texas at Austin.

the last few days since hearing of Daguerre's secret & that Fox Talbot has also got something of same kind."[20] On the very next day, with no understanding of Daguerre's process, but a wealth of knowledge about light-sensitive chemicals and lenses, Herschel succeeded in fixing a camera image and conceived making prints from a negative image. On February 7, 1839, he showed some of his images at the Royal Society in London. Writing to his friend and colleague Talbot a few days later, he referred to his "photographic specimens." Herschel was not the only one of Talbot's correspondents to use the term. Charles Wheatstone, the scientist and inventor of the stereoscope, wrote to Talbot on February 2, 1839, referring to Talbot's "photographic experiments."[21] The word "photographic" quickly evolved into "photography," the general term for the medium. (The term *photographie* employed by Florence may have been used earlier, but his work was unknown in Europe.)

Herschel's photographic investigations continued into the 1840s. He experimented with the possibilities of color photography using vegetable dyes; he also used iron salts to create a process he dubbed CYANOTYPE, which produced an image in which the dominant tones were deep Prussian blue and white (Fig. 1.17). Herschel was one of the first to voice the democratic potential of photography; of the cyanotype he wrote that every person might be a printer and a publisher.[22] While it never became a major form of photography, the simplicity and low cost of the cyanotype made it a commercial success in the

focus

The Stranger

A mythical inventor of photography arrived late on the scene during the 1850s. Accounts of photography's history, published in journals aimed at a general audience, recounted the appearance of "the Stranger," a bedraggled man who enters the Paris shop of optical instrument-maker Charles Chevalier in January 1826. The Stranger wants to purchase a camera obscura, but his poverty prevents him from buying the best instrument. The Stranger recounts his attempts to fix the images in a camera obscura, and shows Chevalier some photographs. As he is about to depart the shop, the Stranger leaves a vial of a secret brown liquid with Chevalier, telling him that it is the substance that produces photographs. The Stranger does not leave instructions for its use, and when he does not return to the shop, Chevalier asks Daguerre to try the brown liquid. Daguerre has no success, but his attempts use up the mysterious substance.

As the story of the Stranger moved from source to source, it grew in complexity. The Stranger became poorer, and his physical needs became more urgent. Conjectures were added. Why did the Stranger not return to Chevalier's shop? Did he end his days in a charity hospital, shivering with cold and hunger? Did he plunge himself into the Seine, discouraged that Daguerre, not he, had got credit for photography? For a person of genius, the later stories concluded, life's disappointments are sharper than for the rest of us.

Like Hippolyte Bayard's self-portrait of himself as a drowned man (see Fig. 1.16), the story of the Stranger was infused with notions of doomed Romantic genius. Indeed, it has been speculated that Bayard's disheartening experience in gaining acceptance for his photographic process may be the origin of the story (Fig. 1.18).

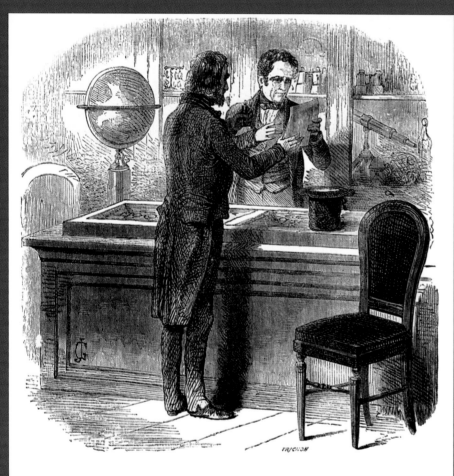

L'inconnu montrant une épreuve photographique à M. Charles Chevalier. Dessin de M. Gustave Janet.

1.18
ARTIST UNKNOWN, "*The Stranger*," from Francis Wey, *Comment le soleil est devenu peintre: histoire du daguerréotype et de la photographie*. Musée des Familles, June 1853. Wood engraving. Widener Library, Harvard University, Cambridge, Massachusetts.

1840s, and a favorite at the end of the nineteenth century for amateurs and scientists working in the field. Until the advent of digital image processing, it was widely used to produce blueprints for architects and builders.

TALBOT'S PHOTOGENIC DRAWING

"Change rules supreme in the affairs of men," reflected Herschel's friend and scientific colleague Talbot, upon hearing about the daguerreotype. Talbot had conceived fixing light-induced images as early as 1833, and had also had some modest success the following year, well before Daguerre achieved provable results. Musing intently, Talbot reflected on the quirk of fate by which

after having devoted much labour and attention to the perfecting of this invention, and having now brought it, as I think, to a point in which it deserved the notice of the scientific world,—that exactly at the moment that I was then engaged in drawing up an account of it, to be presented to the Royal Society, the same invention should be announced in France.[23]

As historian Gail Buckland observed, "Talbot was staggered."[24] He had no way of knowing whether his method was the same as that developed by Daguerre, but he sensed the prospect of losing his claim to be the first to capture a camera image.

Talbot, a multitalented British scientist, classical scholar, and linguist, was educated at Cambridge University and lived at the family estate of Lacock Abbey. He dated his photographic efforts to 1833, when he got disappointing results using a camera lucida as an aid to drawing scenes near Lake Como in Italy. "After various fruitless attempts I laid aside the instrument and came to the conclusion that its use required a previous knowledge of drawing which unfortunately I did not possess," he recalled. "I then thought of trying again a method which I had tried many years before," he continued:

This method was, to take a camera obscura and to throw the image of the objects on a piece of paper in its focus—fairy pictures, creations of a movement, and destined as rapidly to fade away. It was during these thoughts that the idea occurred to me—how charming it would be if it were possible to cause these natural images to imprint themselves durably, and remain fixed upon the paper.[25]

By 1834 Talbot had experimented with two methods of fixing a photochemically induced image. The least known was similar to that concocted by Florence. While staying in Geneva, Switzerland, Talbot prepared glass plates by darkening them with candle smoke, varnishing the surface so that the soot would stay in place. He then drew or wrote on the plates with a tool that cut through the black coating, and placed them over paper that had been made light sensitive. When exposed to light, the lines of drawing or writing were transferred to the paper. He suggested that the technique could be used by friends to share letters and images.[26]

In addition, Talbot formulated a method of sensitizing paper similar to the procedure of Wedgwood and Davy, although he later claimed not to have read their published results from 1802. Aware of the light sensitivity of silver compounds, Talbot discovered that the strength of a solution of ordinary table salt (sodium chloride) in water was key to making images and then stopping the action of light. He first soaked paper in a weak solution, and allowed it to dry. He then applied a solution of silver nitrate, which reacted with the sodium chloride to form light-sensitive silver chloride. He did not put the sensitized paper in a camera obscura, but placed an object to be copied—such as a leaf, lace, or fern frond—directly on the paper, sometimes flattened it down with a piece of glass to make greater contact with the paper, and then exposed the sandwiched object to light. When the object was removed, a pale rendering of its shape remained on the paper (Fig. 1.19). Depending on the strength of the sunlight to which it was exposed, from ten minutes to thirty minutes were necessary to make a print. The area surrounding the image darkened due to exposure to light.

After the object was removed from the paper, Talbot had to prevent the light area from darkening in response to further exposure. He tried various chemicals to inhibit the continuing action of light upon the paper, among them potassium iodide, and a strong solution of table salt. Because of the use of table salt, both in sensitizing the paper and in fixing its image, the process would eventually be called a SALT PRINT. Talbot referred to his work as PHOTOGENIC DRAWING (that is, light-caused drawing) or "sciagraphy" (shadow writing). Prints such as these are still made today, and they are often called shadowgraphs or PHOTOGRAMS.

Although a reminder in his notebook for May 1834 reads "Patent Photogenic Drawing," Talbot did not do so.[27] Since each sheet of paper used in his technique had to be processed separately, the results were uneven and labor-intensive. Perhaps Talbot was waiting until he could perfect the reliability and consistency of photogenic drawing. He continued to experiment

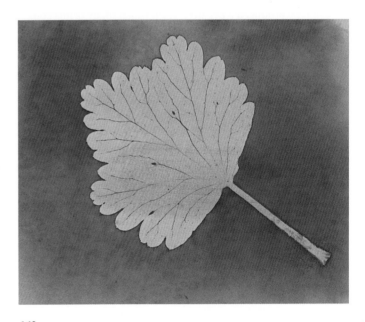

1.19
WILLIAM HENRY FOX TALBOT, *Leaf*, c. 1840. Metropolitan Museum of Art, New York.

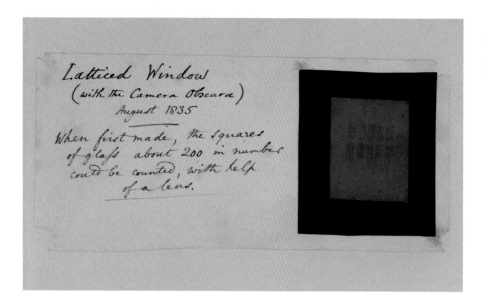

1.20
WILLIAM HENRY FOX TALBOT, *Latticed Window
Taken with the Camera Obscura,* August 1835.
Photogenic drawing negative, mounted on blackened
paper. National Media Museum, Bradford, England.

and, in 1835, he managed to make a picture after exposing sensitized paper in a small camera (Fig. 1.20). In February of that year, Talbot noted that his photogenic drawings might be used to yield what he called a second drawing. In other words, he conceived the photogenic drawing not simply as an end in itself, but also as a NEGATIVE from which POSITIVE prints might be made, although he did not actually use the term or print from one of his early photogenic drawings.

In 1841, after improving the capability of photogenic drawings to make multiple copies, Talbot would patent a photographic process he called the CALOTYPE. The name derived from *kalos*, the Greek word for "beauty." Like the daguerreotype, it made use of the latent image, the invisible picture on the negative that had to be further developed after exposure in the camera. Unlike the daguerreotype, with its single, unique picture, the calotype produced a negative, from which many prints could be made. Thus the calotype would become the basis for modern photographic reproduction. But in the mid-1830s, before the announcement of the daguerreotype, Talbot was losing interest in his photographic experiments. He returned to his study of mathematics and optics for more than three years, until Daguerre's announcement spurred him to demonstrate not only that his own method was original, but also that it had generated photographs before 1839.

THE POLITICS OF INVENTION

Talbot read about Daguerre's image-making process within days of the January 7, 1839, announcement, and quickly moved to make his own work known. He wrote to Arago, claiming prior invention, and prepared a paper titled "Some Account of the Art of Photogenic Drawing, or, the Process by which Natural Objects May be Made to Delineate Themselves without the Aid of the Artist's Pencil," which he read at the Royal Society on January 31, 1839. The first exhibit of his photogenic drawings took place as

part of the regular Friday evening lecture of the Royal Institution on January 25, 1839. The scientist Michael Faraday (1791–1867) spoke about Daguerre's invention, and then urged the audience to examine a display of Talbot's work. The *Literary Gazette* (Saturday, February 2, 1839) recorded that the purpose of the exhibition was to establish Talbot's claim to original invention, should he be challenged by Daguerre. The journal went on to exclaim that "No human hand has hitherto traced such lines as these drawings displayed; and what man may hereafter do, now that Dame Nature has become his drawing mistress, it is impossible to predict."[28]

While photography itself had not been predicted, many of the nineteenth-century uses of photography were soon foreseen after its disclosure in 1839. Arago, for instance, thought that it could aid archeological research and restoration, and also be employed as a kind of objective retina (*rétine physique*) that would assist scientists in studying the properties of light.[29] He thought it might be used to record the art painted and incised on the walls of ancient Egyptian buildings—a task begun in the nineteenth century, yet still far from complete at the beginning of the twenty-first century.

In his arguments for making the daguerreotype a French gift to the world, Arago also anticipated the mistrust and wrangling that would follow the near simultaneous announcements of two competing photographic processes. Talbot, for example, was very wary of showing the French his process. Writing to Herschel in February 1839, he suggested "that it might be best not to disclose at present the washing out process, the retransfer & c. until brought to a state more worthy of publication, inasmuch as the Parisians would hardly be able to discover it immediately if it is not part of Daguerre's process, & I wish to show them that we could do something here which they could not imitate as yet."[30]

In France, Arago hastened to establish Daguerre as the exclusive inventor of photography. He saw to it that Talbot and Herschel, along with other well-known scientists, were boldly invited to Paris to see the daguerreotype and, presumably, to witness its exceptional rendering ability. Talbot refused, but asked Herschel, who was already planning a visit there, to view Daguerre's work. "I shall be glad to hear from you, what you think of them," he wrote. "Whatever their merit, which no doubt is very great, I think that in one respect our English method must have the advantage." "To obtain a second copy of the same view," Talbot continued, "Daguerre must return to the same locality & set up his instrument a second time; for he cannot copy from his metallic plate, being opaque."[31]

When Herschel saw Daguerre's pictures, he reported back to Talbot that "it is hardly saying too much to call them miraculous." The daguerreotypes, he wrote, "surpass anything I could have conceived as within the bounds of reasonable expectation ... Every gradation of light & shade is given with a softness & fidelity which sets all painting at an immeasurable distance." Herschel also added that the exposure time needed for Daguerre's process was very short.[32] In effect, Talbot's respected colleague and friend was compelled to acknowledge the visual superiority of the daguerreotype, a difference in quality so great that it seemed to trivialize Talbot's objection that the daguerreotype could not make multiple copies.

When Daguerre's Diorama burned to the ground in March 1839, Arago strengthened his efforts to award him a pension and to claim the invention of photography for France. He wrote to the minister of the interior hinting that various nations had made Daguerre tempting offers, which the inventor refused. Arago also arranged a display of daguerreotypes for the Chamber of Deputies, and showed the process to the Chamber of Peers. In addition, he orchestrated the major themes of various formal reports presented to these two chambers. In the Chamber of Deputies, Arago stressed the potential scientific importance of Daguerre's invention to the science of photometry (measuring the properties of light) and astronomy. His friend and scientific colleague Joseph Louis Gay-Lussac (1778–1850) reiterated the notion in the Chamber of Peers. Both attempted to raise national pride and rouse a rivalry with Britain by pressing the need to make photography a French cultural achievement. Arago and Gay-Lussac stirred memories of the contest between British

and French linguists to translate the Rosetta Stone, which led to the modern understanding of Egyptian hieroglyphics, and they alluded to the dispute between France and England as to the origin of the Gothic style in architecture. At a time when memories of the Napoleonic Wars between the two countries were still fresh, clear claim to the invention of photography would be read as evidence of national superiority.

In this effort to make Daguerre the sole inventor, reports on his process made to the Chamber of Deputies, Chamber of Peers, and the French Academy of Science distanced his achievement from that of Niépce. Arago insisted that the daguerreotype was "entièrement neuf" (entirely new), and that Daguerre's work of genius was threatened by the efforts of would-be geniuses.[33] From January to August 1839, when the process had its first public demonstration, Daguerre's reputation as an original intellect steadily grew. During that period, no details of his process were revealed, enveloping the daguerreotype and its inventor in irresistible mystery. Indeed, although he was required to produce a booklet describing the daguerreotype process in detail, Daguerre never revealed exactly how he developed it, but allowed tales of fortuitous accidents and miraculous visual events to fill in the blanks. In the end, he and Isidore Niépce secured government pensions, with Daguerre receiving the larger of the two.

The excitement following the first public demonstration of Daguerre's process, at the joint meeting of the Academy of Science and the Academy of Fine Arts in Paris on August 19, 1839, was captured by Marc-Antoine Gaudin (1804–1880), a maker of optical instruments:

We all felt an extraordinary emotion and unknown sensations which made us madly gay ... Everyone wanted to copy the view offered by his window, and very happy was he who at first attempt obtained a silhouette of roofs against the sky: he was in ecstasies over the stove-pipes; he did not cease to count the tiles on the roofs and the bricks of the chimneys; he was astonished to see the cement between each brick; in a word, the poorest picture caused him unutterable joy, inasmuch as the process was then new and appeared deservedly marvellous.[34]

RETAKE

Compared to the steam engine, another prominent creation that altered nineteenth-century life, the first invention of photography was swift. The rudimentary steam engine was patented at the end of the seventeenth century, but not perfected until the dawn of the Industrial Revolution. Despite the centuries-long history of the camera obscura and other mechanical means to aid drawing, such as the silhouette machine and the physionotrace, the photograph seems to have been conceived and invented during a fifty-year period culminating in its presentation to the world in 1839.

Not one, but several approaches to photography were made available: the daguerreotype, with its sharp and detailed picture; the calotype, which displayed more muted tones; and the photogenic drawing, a contact print often recording bits of nature, such as leaves. While the daguerreotype was a unique image—that is, it could not be easily copied—the calotype and the photogenic drawing could create a negative from which copies were made. In photography's second invention, during the fifteen years following 1839, the social, artistic, and scientific potentials of its first invention were investigated and debated.

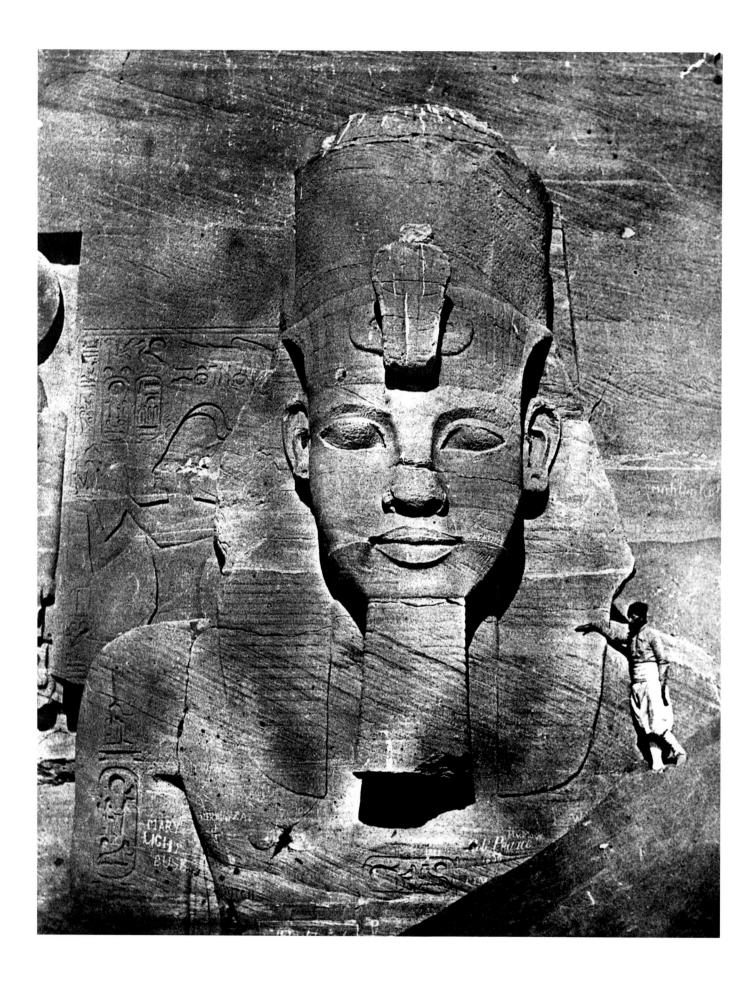

CHAPTER TWO

The Second Invention of Photography (1839-1854)

THE SECOND INVENTION

During the months following Daguerre and Arago's first presentation in 1839, photography and its potential were energetically discussed in Europe, Russia, and the United States, as well as in some parts of Asia and Latin America (Fig. 2.2). But the basic outlines of photography's uses and social meanings—its second invention—took more than fifteen years to emerge. Especially in the early years of its second invention, photography was flexible and experimental, neither a sharply delimited art form nor only the province of science and technology. One tendency occurred across the medium's many applications. Photographers began to assemble series of photographs, ranging from before-and-after pictures of events to microscopic studies and travel pictures. Celebrity photography, whether of political or cultural figures, quickly emerged as photographers tested new applications for their work. The public quickly came to consider that viewing a photograph of a public figure or a public event was an entitlement. The spread of photography included not only the reproduction of art objects, but the creation of an infant art poised between formal consideration of light and shade and the impact of subject matter.

One of the earliest indications of photography's transition from an invention to an active agent in the social world was the patenting of both the CALOTYPE and the DAGUERREOTYPE processes. In the summer of 1839, Daguerre was quietly working

2.1 MAXIME DU CAMP, *Head of a Pharaoh at the Egyptian Temples of Abu Simbel,* 1852.

with an agent in Britain to patent his process there, and to assign the manufacture of his camera and supplies to a French firm run by Alphonse Giroux (active 1840s). Daguerre received the patent, restricting the making of daguerreotypes in Britain to those who paid to do so. Similarly, Talbot patented the calotype process in 1841, although he charged only commercial photographers to use it. In part, the patenting of the daguerreotype and the calotype was motivated by nationalistic competition, but it also indicated the transformation of photography from an invention into a commodity with commercial promise.

Daguerre's instruction manual arrived in the United States in September 1839, but news of the invention had come months earlier. In April 1839, when few people had seen a photograph, the *New Yorker* was sufficiently confident in the medium's future to extol both Daguerre's contrivance and Talbot's PHOTOGENIC DRAWING. The article humorously proposed that photography would conquer the other arts: "The Dagueroscope [*sic*] and the Photogenic revolution are to keep you all down, ye painters, engravers, and, alas!, the harmless race, the sketchers."[1] On a more serious note, the article discussed photography as a modern innovation, situating it among the "phantasmagoria of inventions [that] passes rapidly before us."[2] Another commentator, who had never seen a daguerreotype, nonetheless praised it as "more like some marvel of a fairy tale or delusion of necromancy than a practical reality."[3]

In the 1840s, as photography began to proliferate as a craft, a fledgling industry, a means of record-keeping, and an aspiring art form, it also became a topic in newspapers, magazines, and other areas of public debate, where it was regularly called an "art-science." The term recognized that photographic images were not only generated by a mix of science and art, but also applied

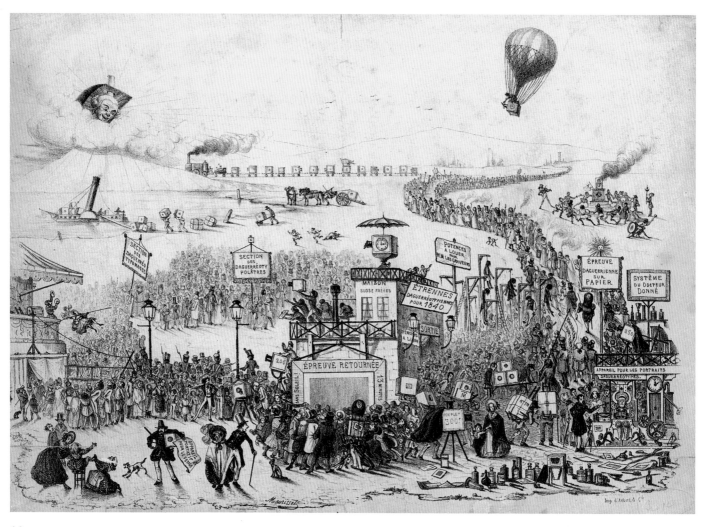

2.2
THÉODORE MAURISSET, *La Daguerréotypomanie*, 1840. Lithograph on card. Private Collection.

in both activities. The ambiguous character of photography in its early years was fostered by the equally uncertain definitions of art and science. Art could mean a skill or a craft, as well as specific media such as painting, sculpture, and engraving. Science referred to areas of knowledge such as biology and geology, and also to techniques for making experiments and observations, such as objective scrutiny and recording.[4] To many observers, photography seemed a science wedded to a craft, fundamentally dependent on the photographer's knowledge of chemistry and willingness to experiment.

Images that appear primarily aesthetic might result from scientific inquiry. For example, the Austrian scientist Anton Georg Martin (1812–1882) studied photography soon after it was announced, and used it to picture an ordinary farmyard in winter (Fig. 2.3). Martin's aim, indicated by a note on the back of the image, was to experiment with exposure time, light, and equipment.[5] Those who took up the new medium found themselves refitting traditional visual arts subjects, such as landscape, to photography's capabilities. The blending of custom

and camerawork is evident in French photographer Alexandre Clausel's (1802–1884) *Landscape near Troyes*, in which a transitory moment is anchored within a carefully chosen point of view whose symmetry and balance derive from the rules of artistic composition (Fig. 2.4).

Writing in the *Athenaeum*, an anonymous author expressed the absence of a distinct category for photography. Describing a meeting of the Calotype Club in London, which was founded in 1847, the writer noted that the members had "associated together for the purpose of pursuing their experiments in this art-science (we scarcely know the word fittest completely to designate it)."[6] The "art-science" label survived into the 1850s. In an early issue of *La Lumière*, France's first photographic magazine, Francis Wey (1812–1882) announced that the journal would be "neutral ground" for photography, which inherently embraced both science and art.[7] There is little evidence that this categorization was unsettling; instead, the term "art-science" seemed productively vague, expressing an interplay between the humanities and the sciences, and the broad interests of people

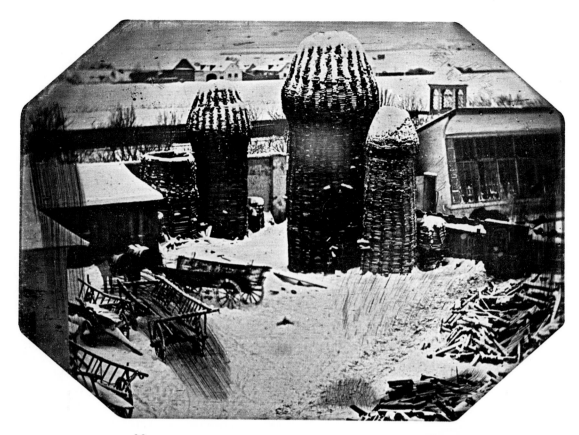

2.3
ANTON GEORG MARTIN, *Vienna: Winter Landscape,* 1841. Daguerreotype.
Museum für Kunst und Gewerbe, Hamburg, Germany.

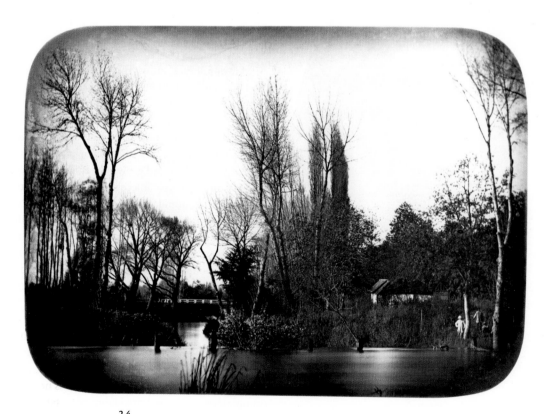

2.4
ALEXANDRE CLAUSEL, *Landscape near Troyes, France,* c. 1855. Daguerreotype.
George Eastman House, Rochester, New York.

who took up the new medium. Images such as those produced by William Henry Fox Talbot's friend, the botanist and scientific illustrator Anna Atkins, could be simultaneously aesthetically pleasing and scientific, without any perceived contradiction (see Fig. 2.16).

Although the daguerreotype was primarily adopted when exact renderings in portraiture and in science were desired, and the calotype was used when softer effects and multiple copies were wanted, no rigid conventions governed their use. Thus, despite the daguerreotype's superior detail and sharp focus, the calotype's ability to make multiple copies, and to be retouched on the negative, made it valuable to scientists as well. Similarly, the daguerreotype could occasionally be made to approximate landscape painting, as Alexandre Clausel convincingly did through his well-balanced composition and attentive use of many middle-gray tones that evoke the look of multiple thin layers of paint.

Reactions to early photography ranged from the exuberant to the cautious. American poet and short-story writer Edgar Allan Poe (1809–1849), the subject of a haunting 1849 portrait (Fig. 2.5), wrote three articles on photography for popular magazines in 1840. Describing the daguerreotype's "most miraculous beauty," Poe opined that "all language must fall short of conveying any just idea of the truth ... but the closest scrutiny of the photogenic drawing discloses only a more absolute truth, a more perfect identity of aspect with the thing represented." He urged readers to imagine a "positively perfect mirror" that "is infinitely more accurate in its representation than any painting by human hands."[8]

Despite the *New Yorker* magazine's playful 1839 foreboding that photography would stifle art, few painters saw early photography as a threat. Still, when John Jabez Edwin Mayall (1810–1901), a British-American photographer working in London, proposed that the daguerreotype was capable of illustrating history, an editorial response in an 1847 issue of the *Athenaeum* corrected him: "At best, he [Mayall] can only hope to get a mere naturalist's rendering. Ideality is unattainable,—and imagination supplanted by the presence of fact."[9] Nevertheless, Mayall went on to document history—or at least a photographic version of it. His mammoth plate daguerreotype, one of fourteen made of the Crystal Palace at Hyde Park, London, depicted the interior of Joseph Paxton's (1801–1865) remarkable large metal and glass structure that housed the Great Exhibition of the Works of Industry of All Nations in 1851 (Fig. 2.6).

Because the photograph was commonly conceived as nature delineating nature, some found it lacking in imagination. The *New Yorker*'s anonymous commentator was convinced that "Nature is only become handmaid to Art, not her mistress ... Painters need not despair; their labours will be as much in request as ever, but in a higher field: the finer qualities of taste and invention will be called into action more powerfully: and the mechanical process will be only abridged and rendered more perfect."[10]

Many of photography's modern applications emerged in the 1840s and early 1850s, together with an equally enduring dialogue about visual representation and multiple imaging. The medium's expansion was inextricably associated with world-shaping forces. Industrial capitalism created a middle class of professionals, such as scientists, who began to use photography in their work. The rapid growth of cities facilitated the exchange of ideas among people interested in the medium of photography, and the shift of populations from the countryside to the cities accentuated the desire for observable personal identity, fueling the market for photographic portraits. Whereas in small towns and villages people were usually known to their neighbors, in the burgeoning cities strangers gawked at strangers, trying to size them up in an instant. In this milieu of unstable social identity, photography offered sitters a chance to fix an outward appearance for all time.

As the medium's capacities grew during its first dozen years, photography also provided a way to enact a public personality through which sitters might be known and remembered. While urban populations increased, rural peoples, traditional occupations, and unpolluted landscapes emerged as sentimental and nostalgic subjects in the visual arts, and, ultimately, in photography. Meanwhile, the expansion of Western powers

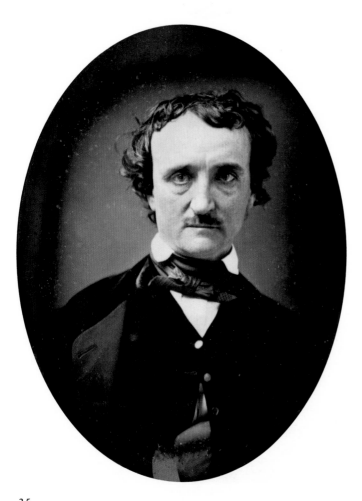

2.5
PHOTOGRAPHER UNKNOWN, *Edgar Allan Poe*, 1849. Daguerreotype.
The J. Paul Getty Museum, Los Angeles, California.

focus

Iron, Glass, and Photography

The Great Exhibition, dubbed the "Crystal Palace Exhibition" by the press, opened in London in May 1851. This early world's fair brimmed with excitement for technological progress and material prosperity. Nearly eight hundred examples from six countries were exhibited. The Crystal Palace, visited by about six million people, boasted Britain's lead in industrial production and promoted the idea that modern mass manufacturing and engineering could be applied in the cause of economic and social betterment. For example, a model, modular house for the working class was on display.[11] Observers noted the resemblance of Joseph Paxton's building to a glass house, the space used by photographers, and associated both structures with social advancement (Fig. 2.6).

Included in the Crystal Palace displays were cameras, other photographic equipment, and photographs. Commercial portraits and landscape photographs were shown with photographic equipment, while art photography was displayed in the Fine Arts Court. Roughly the same number of daguerreotypes and calotypes were shown.[12] The connections between technological progress, social advancement, modern architecture, and the new medium of photography also occurred in France, where Hector Horeau (1801–1872), an architect, Egyptologist, and publisher of prints based on early photographs, was an avid proponent of glass and iron building construction. His philosophy for public works emphasized education and communication for the working class, an idea also expressed by proponents of photography. Ironically, Horeau had successfully competed in the contest to design the Crystal Palace, only to be replaced a month later by Paxton.

2.6
J. J. MAYALL, *The Crystal Palace at Hyde Park*, London, 1851. Daguerreotype. The J. Paul Getty Museum, Los Angeles, California.

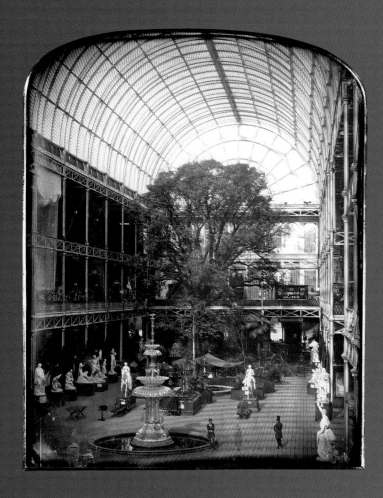

into Asia, Africa, and Latin America provided fresh vistas to be photographed, and a persuasive visual means to rationalize foreign adventurism.

TALBOT AND *THE PENCIL OF NATURE*

While Daguerre took little part in the development of photography after 1839, Talbot continued his efforts. His 1839 account of photogenic drawing conceived the photographic image as a kind of "natural magic"[13] with potential for science and art. He went on to explore both these aspects.

In 1835 Talbot produced what may be the world's first photomicrograph—that is, a photograph of a magnified small object. Talbot believed that photography would "be especially useful for naturalists since one can copy the most difficult things, for instance crystallizations and minute parts of plants, with a great deal of ease,"[14] but he was also interested in its art applications. He considered *The Open Door* (Fig. 2.7), in which he emulated seventeenth-century Dutch painting of scenes from

everyday life, an example "of the early beginnings of a new art."[15] Larry Schaaf has observed that the photograph draws on the doorway as a traditional symbol of the passage between life and light, and death and darkness.[16]

The Open Door was included as plate 5 in Talbot's book *The Pencil of Nature*, which he published in six sections, between 1844 and 1846. One of the first books illustrated with actual photographs rather than engraved versions, *The Pencil of Nature* contained twenty-four calotype images. Since the calotype process created a negative, from which positive prints could be made, actual calotypes were tipped in (pasted at the corners to the page). Each image was accompanied by an explanatory text. *The Pencil of Nature* demonstrated the breadth of Talbot's investigation into the applications of photography. Some images, such as *Articles of China*, showed photography's record-keeping ability (Fig. 2.8), while others demonstrated how photography could variously depict biological specimens, architecture, and sculpture, and reproduce sketches and engravings. Talbot even

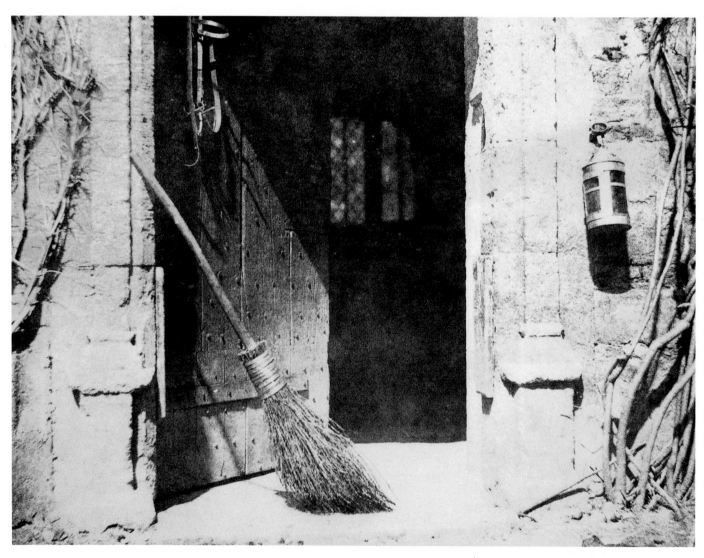

2.7
WILLIAM HENRY FOX TALBOT, *The Open Door*, 1844, plate 5 from *The Pencil of Nature*, 1844–46. Salt print from a calotype negative.

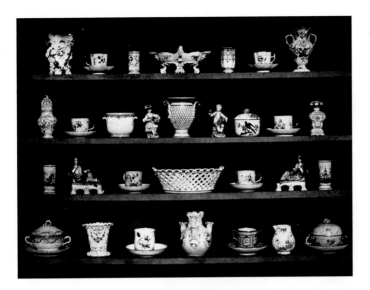

2.8
WILLIAM HENRY FOX TALBOT, *Articles of China*, plate 3 from *The Pencil of Nature*, 1844–46. Calotype. Fox Talbot Collection. National Media Museum, Bradford, England.

suggested that in the future photographs might be taken in the dark, making possible secret surveillance.

Throughout the 1840s, Talbot mingled art, science, and what would eventually be called documentary photography in such works as the series of haystack studies produced on his property. Early on, he understood photography's ability to present a sequence of images, the meaning of which proceeded not just from one example, but from all of them and from their arrangement. As the French Impressionist painter Claude

Monet (1840–1926) would do later in the nineteenth century, Talbot studied the effects of light, and he also delighted in the configuration of geometric shapes found in the natural and built environments. *The Haystack* is a virtuoso piece, taken when the light best revealed the prickly surface of the stack and as shadows defined its sturdy geometry (Fig. 2.9). The image's negative (Fig. 2.10) further reveals its compositional values. Talbot thought to accentuate the leaning ladder and its upright shadow.

Talbot also pursued commercial experiments with photography. Exploiting the calotype's ability to furnish multiple prints, he founded a photographic studio and printing establishment in Reading, a town about forty miles west of London (Fig. 2.11). The business was part of the mid-century industrialization of photography; here Talbot produced *The Pencil of Nature* as well as other views for sale.

BAYARD: THE DOUBTING CAMERA
After Hippolyte Bayard produced his *Self-Portrait as a Drowned Man* (see Fig. 1.16), he continued to test the limits of photographic representation, sometimes exploring ways in which it could be misleading or unsettling (Fig. 2.12). Some contemporary viewers recognized Bayard's unusual approach; Francis Wey wrote that Bayard's images united "the impression of reality with the fantasy of dreams."[17] Ultimately, Bayard took up both daguerreotype and calotype photography, in which he enjoyed professional success. In some photographs he lingered on the textural richness and attractive shapes of such ordinary objects as leaves, tools, stone, and straw. But a teasing sense continued to inform his work: what the eye sees, and what the photograph records, may not be trustworthy.

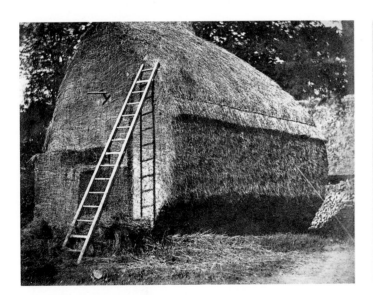

2.9
WILLIAM HENRY FOX TALBOT, *The Haystack*, from *The Pencil of Nature*. Department of Special Collections, Glasgow University Library, Glasgow, Scotland.

Published in Talbot's *The Pencil of Nature*, the plate *The Haystack* became especially popular with the public, perhaps because the new medium of photography was used to pay homage to an agricultural practice that endured into the modern era.

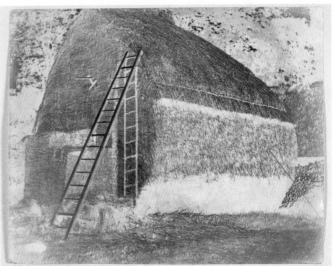

2.10
WILLIAM HENRY FOX TALBOT, negative of *The Haystack* from *The Pencil of Nature*. National Media Museum, Bradford, England.

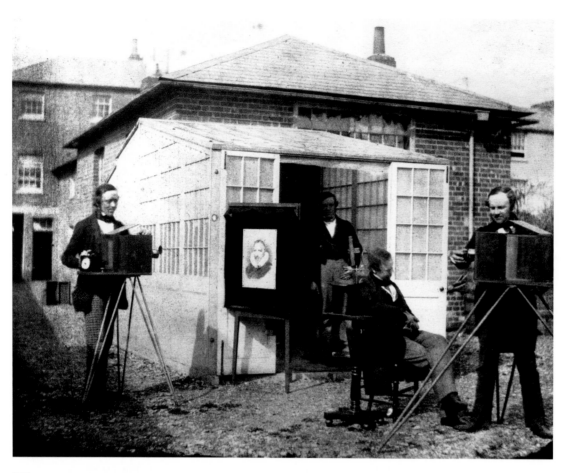

2.11
PHOTOGRAPHER UNKNOWN, *Untitled* (Panorama showing Talbot's Reading establishment), c. 1845. Calotype.
National Media Museum, Bradford, England.

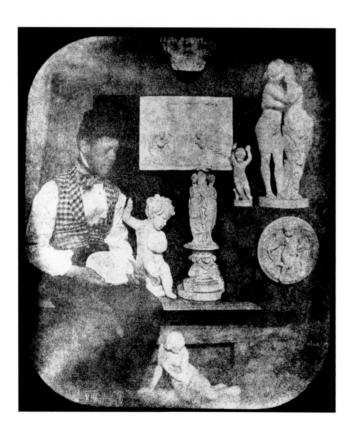

2.12
HIPPOLYTE BAYARD, *Self-Portrait with Plaster Casts*, 1850. National Gallery
of Canada/Musée des Beaux-Arts du Canada, Ottawa.

PHOTOGRAPHY AND THE SCIENCES

Though few early photographers were as multifaceted in
their interests as Talbot, as early as May of 1839 scientists had
attempted to employ Talbot's photogenic drawings in their work.

THE MICROSCOPE AND THE TELESCOPE

After witnessing Daguerre's Paris presentation of his invention
and studying directly with Daguerre, the Viennese physicist and
mathematician Andreas Ritter von Ettingshausen (1796–1878)
created startlingly detailed microscopic images (Fig. 2.13).
Ettingshausen was a member of an informal circle of artists,
mathematicians, and scientists who explored photography,
but, like many of its early users and advocates, he did not
pursue the new invention throughout his scientific career.
The scientist Léon Foucault (1819–1868), who would later do
distinguished research into the speed of light, became involved
with photography while still a medical student. He helped to
produce eighty-six microscopic daguerreotypes, which were

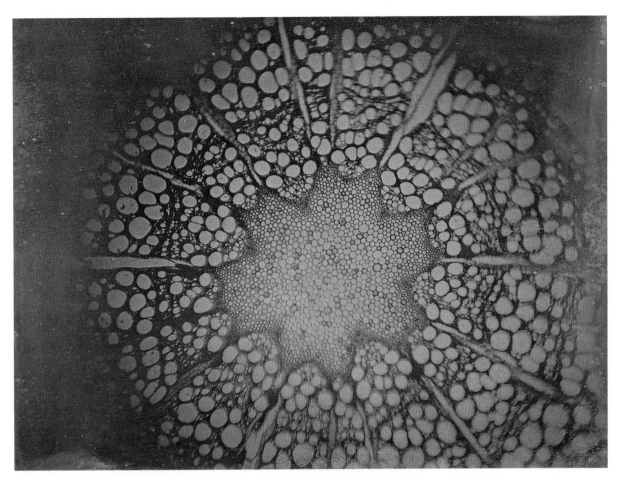

2.13
ANDREAS RITTER VON ETTINGSHAUSEN, *Section of Clematis*, March 4, 1840. Daguerreotype. Ezra Mack, New York.

then engraved for the textbook *Cours de Microscopie* (*Course in Microscopy*) (1845), written by his mentor, the physicist Alfred Donné (1801–1878) (Fig. 2.14). Because the daguerrean process was a tricky, time-consuming way to make duplicates, during its early years the usual course for reproducing daguerreotypes in both scientific and artistic illustrations was to hand-copy the image on to an engraving plate.

Beginning in the early 1840s, several daguerreotype experiments reduced printed matter to a size so small that it had to be read with a microscope. This microform technique promised to condense rare books and manuscripts to an easily transportable and storable size. Celestial photographs were also tried, although the dim light of distant stars, with the obvious exception of the sun, made clear and detailed photographs difficult. Daguerre himself made a faint image of the moon to prove the potential benefits of the medium to his sponsor, the astronomer and politician François Arago. In 1845, with Arago's encouragement, Foucault and another French scientist, Hippolyte Fizeau, had some success in photographing the

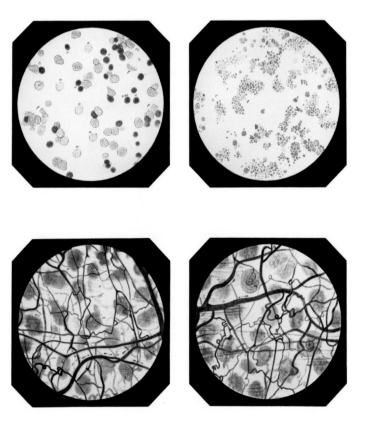

2.14
LÉON FOUCAULT, Microscopic studies, plates 21, 22, 23, 24, from Alfred Donné's *Cours de Microscopie*, 1845. Engravings from daguerreotypes. The J. Paul Getty Museum, Los Angeles, California.

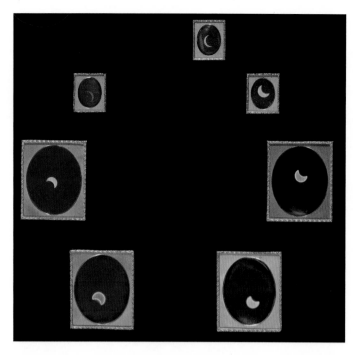

2.15
WILHELM AND FRIEDRICH LANGENHEIM, *Seven Daguerreotypes Showing Eclipse of the Sun*, May 26, 1854. Daguerreotypes. Metropolitan Museum of Art, New York.

An eighth image, now lost, probably showed the total eclipse

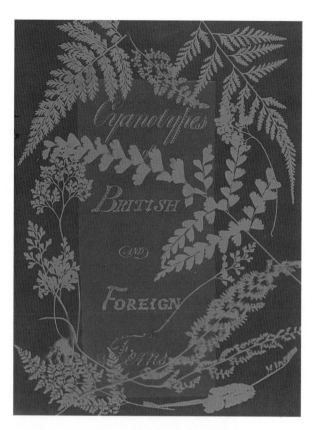

2.16
ANNA ATKINS, Cover of *Cyanotypes of British and Foreign Ferns*, 1854. Cyanotype. The National Media Museum, Bradford, England.

sun with sunspots. The result was published as a lithograph in Arago's *Astronomie populaire* (*Popular Astronomy*) (1858). In America, John William Draper (1811–1882) made a series of early daguerreotypes of the moon, as did George Phillips Bond (1825–1865) and John Adams Whipple (1822–1891) (Fig. 2.42) in the 1850s. Philadelphia photographers and dealers in photographic equipment Wilhelm Langenheim (1807–1874) and his brother Friedrich (1809–1879) recorded the solar eclipse of 1854 (Fig. 2.15). Seven images remain.

BIOLOGY

In the nineteenth century, many men and women of the upper classes were active amateur scientists. They collected and classified biological specimens and attempted to preserve them for further study. Those who could draw or work in watercolor also rendered copies of their finds. For more than a decade, scientific illustrator Anna Atkins (1799–1871) created impeccable CYANOTYPE impressions of algae species and other specimens. A member of the Botanical Society of London and an accomplished book illustrator, Atkins used the technique developed by John Herschel to combine scientific exactitude with aesthetic sensitivity to form and presentation (Fig. 2.16). Because her prints were originals and bore a one-to-one relationship to their subjects, they were thought to constitute persuasive documentation. Similar work was done by Thereza Llewelyn (1834–1926), whose photogenic rendering

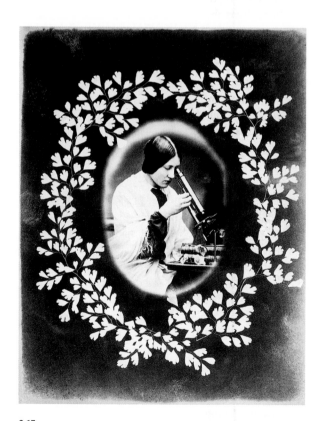

2.17
JOHN DILLWYN LLEWELYN, *Thereza*, c. 1853. Salted paper print. Metropolitan Museum of Art, New York.

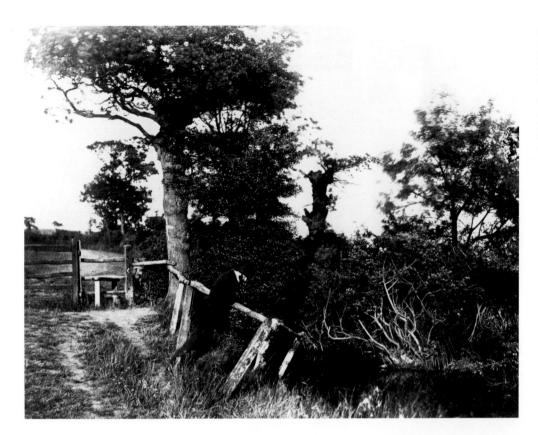

2.18
GEORGE SHADBOLT, *Watching the Newts*, c. mid-1850s. Salted paper print. George Eastman House, Rochester, New York.

Observing newts, aquatic salamanders so small that the camera does not register them, was one of many hobbies pursued by people of means. The image is less about science than social class.

of a maidenhair fern surrounds her portrait by her father, John Dillwyn Llewelyn (1810–1882) (Fig. 2.17). He had been introduced to photography by his wife, Emma Thomasina Talbot (William Henry Fox Talbot's first cousin), and was typical of the amateur photographers who experimented with the technical and chemical aspects of photography, while making a variety of landscape images and family pictures. Like many amateurs, he benefited from meetings with others, and from exchanges, often by mail, of information and photographs from men and women with similar interests. Another British amateur, active in both scientific and artistic photography, was George Shadbolt (1819–1901). The country paths and venerable trees in his *Watching the Newts* (Fig. 2.18) are characteristic of British amateur subject matter, which generally ignored industrial and urban views in favor of ancient buildings and traditional agricultural pursuits.

ANTHROPOLOGY AND MEDICINE

From the first, practitioners of anthropology and medicine saw in photography a good opportunity to generate historical and research archives. The notion was still in force at the end of the century when Robert Sommer, a German professor of psychiatry, proclaimed that photography should "replace the written record (or at least supplement it)," because the medium "is uncontaminated by the interpretive problems inherent in language."[18]

Hugh Welch Diamond (1809–1886), a British medical doctor and active amateur, photographed still lifes and took pictures of antiquarian interest. He also made photographs of mental patients (Fig. 2.19). He professed that mentally ill patients

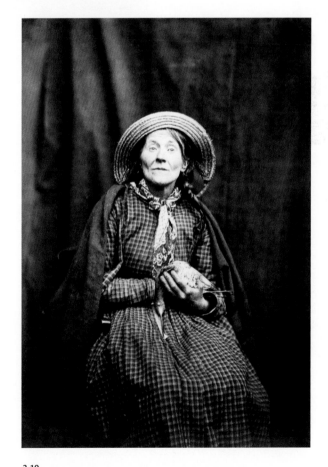

2.19
HUGH WELCH DIAMOND, *Seated Woman with Bird*, c. 1855. Albumen print. The J. Paul Getty Museum, Los Angeles, California.

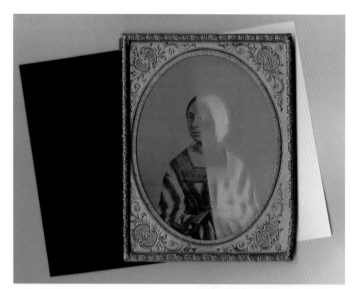

could look at photographs of themselves and understand their afflictions better. For Diamond, the photograph was a transparent medium that allowed the therapist and the patient to interpret the language of nature accurately. "The picture speaks for itself," he asserted.[19] Diamond maintained that "the Photographer secures with unerring accuracy the external phenomena of each passion, as the really certain indication of internal derangement, and exhibits to the eye the well known sympathy which exists between the diseased brain and the organs and features of the body."[20] Addressing the Royal Society in 1856, he stressed that photography's scientific objectivity would give it historical

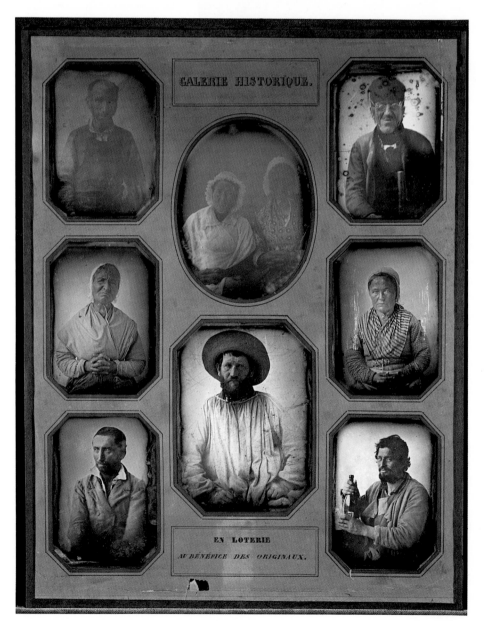

importance. "Photography," he concluded, "gives permanence to these remarkable cases … and makes them observable not only now but for ever."[22] Because these photographs were understood to be both effective therapeutic and educational instruments, patients were obliged to pose for them.

Dr. Diamond was one of the first photographers to experiment with the COLLODION PROCESS, or wet-plate process, a new negative–positive process published by Frederick Scott Archer (1813–1857) in 1851. Although still time-consuming, the wet-plate process used glass, rather than paper, to support the light-sensitive material. It boasted a greater sensitivity and shorter exposure time than previous processes, including the albumen glass-plate NEGATIVES devised in the late 1840s by Claude-Félix-Abel Niépce de Saint-Victor (1805–1870), a relative of Joseph Nicéphore Niépce. The wet-plate process furnished multiple images that were free from the imprint of texture rendered by the paper negatives. The AMBROTYPE, a popular adaptation of the glass negative, was patented in 1854 by James Ambrose Cutting. The ambrotype was a glass negative backed by a dark substance, such as black varnish, cloth, or paper (Fig. 2.20). The ambro may have been so-named because Cutting's middle name, Ambrose, derives from the Greek word for immortality, a desirable quality in photographs. The ambro was a one-of-a-kind image, like the daguerreotype; unlike the daguerreotype, it was appealingly inexpensive.

Most photographs of mental patients were intended for scientific study, but in rare instances some were used to raise money for an asylum. A French example, mounted individual daguerreotypes in a poster-like format, publicized a lottery to benefit patients (Fig. 2.21). Photography was also used during its first decade to describe, compare, and rank "racial" types. The notion of race was renewed in the late eighteenth and early nineteenth centuries, when it was used to describe innate qualities of nations and ethnicities, sometimes with the aim of arousing nationalistic feeling. With the rapid colonization of the non-Western world, human diversity was increasingly discussed and classified.

The French photographer E. Thiésson (active 1840s) produced annotated images of the residents of Sofala, a town in Mozambique (Fig. 2.22), and of the Botocudo people in Brazil. Thiésson omitted names and personal details in an attempt to accentuate the scientific objectivity of his photographs. He developed a specific visual vocabulary, posing his subjects from the side and from the front, and sometimes using a plain background. The appearance of neutrality and the distance of subjects from the camera were conventions that developed slowly and unevenly during photography's first decades, as ethnographers concocted a standard, "styleless" style to connote truth. In fact, many early images of non-Westerners employed the customs of middle-class portraiture, as in a subtle daguerreotype by the Philadelphia photographers Wilhelm and Friedrich Langenheim (Fig. 2.23). With its simple background, three-quarter profile, and the sitter's contemplative pose, the image wavers between anthropological record and formal portraiture.

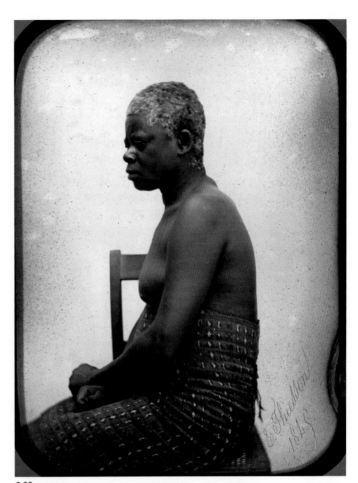

2.22
E. THIÉSSON, *Native Woman of Sofala,* 1845. Daguerreotype. Gift of Eastman Kodak Co. George Eastman House, Rochester, New York.

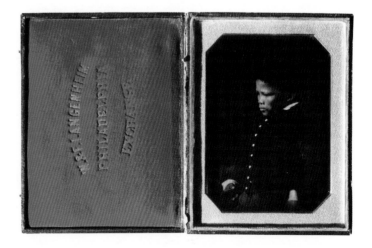

2.23
WILHELM AND FRIEDRICH LANGENHEIM, *African Youth,* 1848. Daguerreotype. Peabody Museum, Harvard University, Cambridge, Massachusetts.

focus

Photography, Race, and Slavery

The Langenheim daguerreotype (see Fig. 2.23) was probably in the collection of the Swiss-born naturalist Louis Agassiz (1807–1873), who came to the United States in 1846. The founder of Harvard University's museum of comparative zoology, Agassiz was an avid proponent of photographic data and perhaps the best-known scientist in mid-nineteenth-century America.[23] His ethnological interests led him to authorize a southern colleague to commission front, back, and side views of slaves from a North Carolina plantation in 1850. Agassiz hoped to provide visual evidence for his theory that the races were created separately at different times and in different parts of the world, an idea that slavery's proponents felt would scientifically justify racial inequality. Agassiz's colleague hired J. T. Zealy (1812–1893), who ran photographic studios in Columbia, South Carolina, and Petersburg, Virginia, to make a series of fifteen daguerreotypes.

In two images of a slave named Jack, the key assumption of middle-class portraiture—that personal character was expressed through physical appearance—vies with the desire to record objectively a generic physical type (Figs. 2.24, 2.25). Zealy's subjects were identified not by their African names but by their slave names and the names of the plantations on which they served. In the first picture, Jack is romantically lit, emphasizing facial features that make him appear noble, pensive, and unassenting. His eyes are fixed beyond the camera. But in the second, side view, his personality traits are diminished, and the romantic side light of the first image is used to intensify anatomical features that would substantiate Agassiz's thesis. Although the photographs were meant to compare and contrast physical types, no images of comparably posed white men and women accompanied these daguerreotypes.

The main purpose of Zealy's slave photographs was to convince viewers of the truth of a racial theory. But they also raise questions about the authorship of images. Although Agassiz commissioned them as part of his fieldwork, he was not there when the images were made. A colleague communicated to the photographer what the aim of the photographs was to be and labeled the final prints, yet Zealy actually made the exposures. Obviously, the subjects of these photographs had no say in their representation.

Today, Zealy's name is appended to the images, because in contemporary law and ethics photographers are understood to be the originators of their work. But in nineteenth-century terms, Zealy was, in this instance, an operator—that is, a person who exposed and/or developed photography.

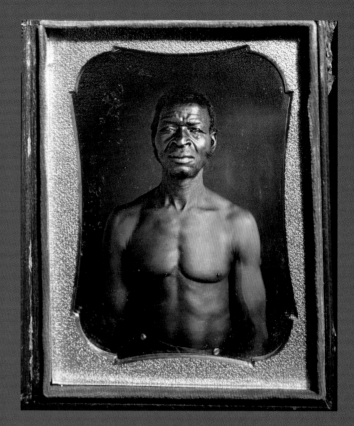

2.24
J. T. ZEALY, *Jack*, 1850s. Daguerreotype. Peabody Museum of Art, Archaeology and Ethnology, Harvard University, Cambridge, Massachusetts.

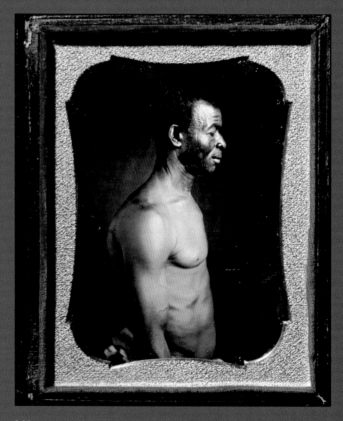

2.25
J. T. ZEALY, *Jack (from the side)*, 1850s. Daguerreotype. Peabody Museum of Art, Archaeology and Ethnology, Harvard University, Cambridge, Massachusetts.

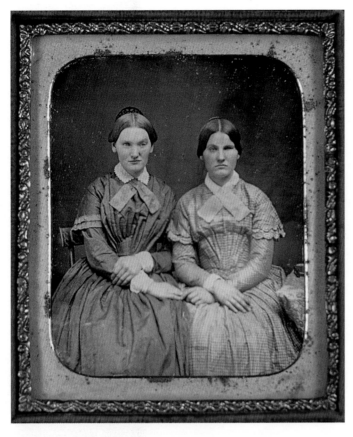

2.26
PHOTOGRAPHER UNKNOWN, *Untitled* (Deformity about the left eye in two sisters), c. 1847. Daguerreotype. Burns Archive, New York.

Early medical photographs showed patients in street clothes, posed as if for a formal portrait. This image shows two sisters with a deformity about the left eye, which in one sister has a more exposed eyeball and in the other is almost closed.

Some medical evidence was collected in early photographs, yet highly detailed, sometimes hand-colored engravings continued to be used because they revealed fine points of anatomical structures more clearly than photographs.[24] Patients were photographed according to the conventions of portraiture, rather than to show only wounds and diseases. They seldom posed in clinical settings, but were pictured in surroundings such as those used for middle-class portraits, and their faces were usually identifiable (Fig. 2.26). Modern protocols for photographing illness—concealing personal identity and emphasizing symptoms—did not become prevalent until the later nineteenth century. The patients in early medical photographs resembled the portraits that doctors took of themselves.[25] As the medical profession grew in numbers and prestige throughout the second half of the nineteenth century, however, largely owing to the increasing use of antiseptics and anesthesia, so too did the rhetoric of therapy and medical education. This in turn fostered more revealing medical imaging that focused on wounds, marks, or dysfunctions. The explicitness of photographs picturing American Civil War casualties (see Fig. 4.17) far exceeded the decorum afforded patients a decade earlier.

PERFORMING HISTORY? THE DR. MORTON CONTROVERSY

Where art conventions influenced early photographic practice, a contradictory blend of old ideas and new expectations was created. A series of daguerreotypes taken in Boston, Massachusetts, by the firm of Southworth and Hawes combined notions associated with older media, such as printmaking and painting, with emergent ideas about the purpose of photography. As a result, it was not immediately clear whether these photographs showed the actual surgery in which ether was first used to relieve pain during an operation, or whether the event was re-enacted for the camera (Fig. 2.27).

Dr. William T. G. Morton, the discoverer of ether and the man who first used it in surgery, could not be identified in the pictures, nor could the original patient. The suggestion that these images were re-enactments did not invalidate them, however. The *tableau vivant*, or living picture, was a popular entertainment in which people donned costumes to recreate historic scenes or famous works of art. Moreover, the visual arts traditionally sanctioned artists who were not present at historical events to depict those events, even to embellish such scenes. If the surgery scene employed artistic license, this would not make it a falsification calculated to deceive viewers. The views may simply have been made to commemorate the historical event, or as devices with which to petition Congress for an award to Dr. Morton.

Certain viewers interpreted the presence of medical instruments in cases as evidence of an authentic operating room. Others also argued that, if the daguerreotypes were re-enactments, they would have emulated the original surgery more closely, in which the patient probably sat in an operating chair. Skeptics also observed that participants appeared to be posing for the camera in a manner not possible during actual surgery. Some scholars observed that Dr. John Collins Warren, shown with his hands on the patient's draped leg, may have asked Southworth and Hawes to pose the scene so as to emulate Rembrandt's famous painting *The Anatomy Lesson of Dr. Tulp*.[26]

By modern hygiene standards, the surgeon and his colleagues, mostly in street clothes, and the patient, still in his stockings, seem prepared not for surgery but for photography. Moreover, the statue visible in the upper right-hand corner appears outlandish in an operating room. But medical historians pointed out that, if the image recorded the preoperation application of anesthesia in an anteroom, then the poses, garb, setting, and even that statue, would be plausible.

Eventually, another photograph was found that convincingly showed the subsequent post-operative scene, thus clearing up the mystery. Real surgery, though not the first use of anesthesia, had taken place before the camera of Southworth and Hawes. While the first surgery under ether was not photographed, in the public memory these later images came to stand for that momentous event. In effect, these daguerreotypes were at once commemorative, documentary, scientific, symbolic, and aesthetic. This rich multiplicity, a result of the mixing of science and art in early photography, did not persist long. The tensions

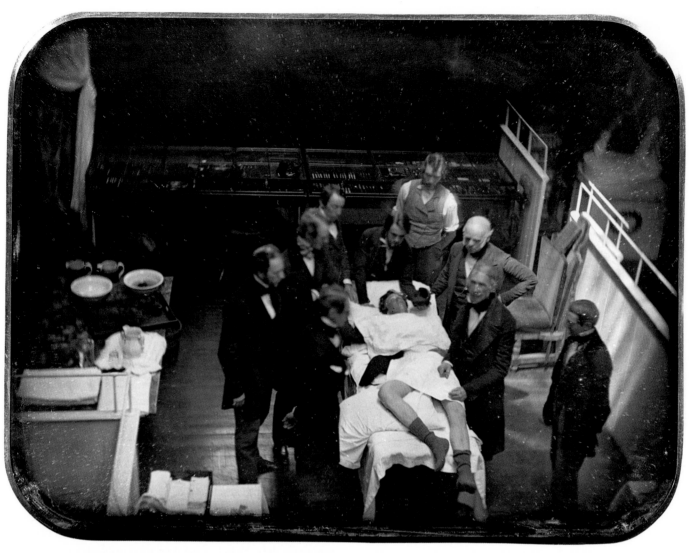

2.27
ALBERT SANDS SOUTHWORTH AND JOSIAH JOHNSON HAWES, *Early Operation Using Ether for Anesthesia*, 1847.
Daguerreotype. The J. Paul Getty Museum, Los Angeles, California.

between realism and symbolism were taken up again in the twentieth century in such art movements as Surrealism and Conceptual Art, as well as in advertising (see Chapter Eight).

RECORDING EVENTS WITH THE CAMERA

Although both the calotype and the daguerreotype processes were too slow to record rapid action, early attempts were made to photograph public events on the spot. For example, Hermann Biow (1804–1850), a portrait photographer living in the German city of Hamburg, is credited with photographing the ruins of the great fire that devastated the city between May 5 and May 8, 1842 (Fig. 2.28). George N. Barnard (1819–1902), an American who would become famous for his American Civil War photographs

(see Fig. 4.14), used the daguerrean process to record a lakeside granary fire in Oswego, New York (Fig. 2.29).

In Hamburg and Oswego, the photographers happened to be nearby when these dramatic scenes occurred, and could have had no preconceived plan to make, sell, or publish these daguerreotypes. By contrast, when historic happenings were anticipated, photographers could arrange to be present. In France, a remarkable pair of "before and after" daguerreotypes were made with the explicit intention of rushing them to publication as wood engravings. During the Revolution of 1848, middle-class demands for greater political influence and the right to vote flared up into street conflicts that led to the abdication of King Louis-Philippe and the establishment of a provisional government, which declared a republic. A daguerreotypist named Eugène Thibault (active 1840–70) was

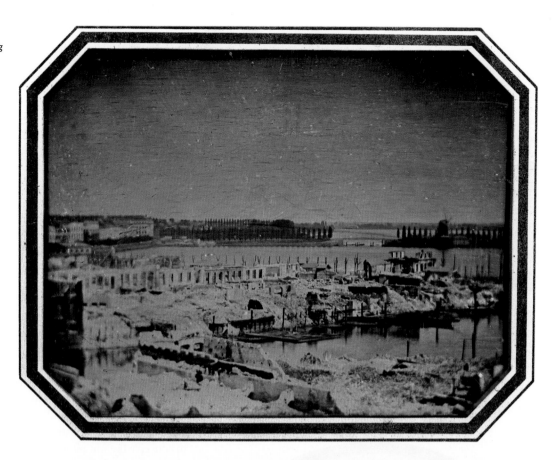

2.28
HERMANN BIOW, *Ruins of Hamburg Fire*, 1842. Daguerreotype. Museum für Hamburgische Geschichte, Hamburg, Germany.

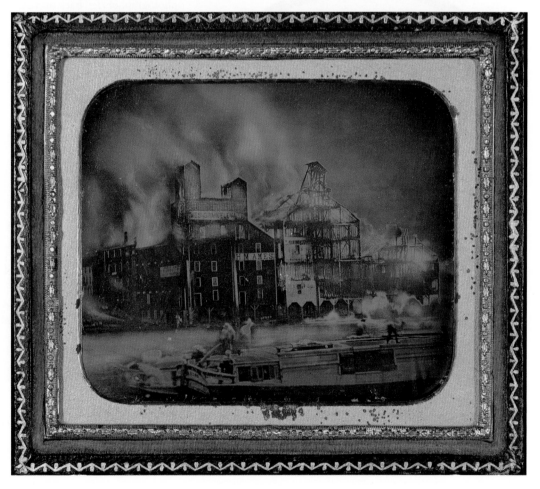

2.29
GEORGE N. BARNARD, *Burning of Oswego Mills*, July 5, 1853. Daguerreotype. George Eastman House, Rochester, New York.

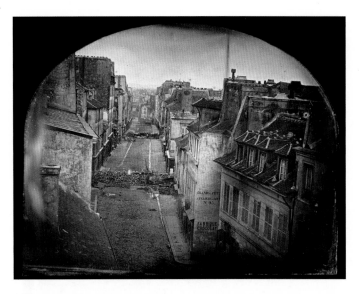

2.30
EUGÈNE THIBAULT, *The Revolution of 1848: Before the Attack*, 1848.
Daguerreotype. Count Geofroy de Beaufort Collection.

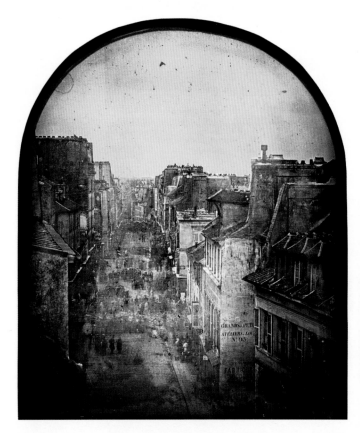

2.31
EUGÈNE THIBAULT, *The Revolution of 1848: After the Attack*, 1848.
Daguerreotype. Count Geofroy de Beaufort Collection.

commissioned by the weekly Paris journal *L'Illustration* to photograph the barricades prior to and after a skirmish between the revolutionaries and French troops. The resulting images were published on July 1, 1848 (Figs. 2.30, 2.31).

While painters and printmakers could enhance their images with sharply rendered scenes of gallantry and heroism, photographers were hard pressed to express the full historical significance or emotional impact of events. The London photographer W. E. Kilburn (1818–1891) took daguerreotypes of a meeting of the Chartists, a coalition of working-class people and social activists seeking political and economic reforms, on April 10, 1848. But his static views fail to convey the exhilaration of the assembly and the speeches made in defiance of the government (Fig. 2.32).

WAR AND PHOTOGRAPHY

IMAGING WAR

Early photographers faced both philosophical and technical difficulties when they attempted to document the facts, causes, and experience of conflict. Both the daguerreotype and the calotype required lengthy preparation of materials prior to exposure in the camera and a cumbersome development process; neither was able to register the rapid action of battle. In having to conceive the war photograph without scenes of active conflict, photographers fell back on visual conventions established in other media, and on the public's expectations of what war pictures should look like. War photographers had to cope with the lack of an established market or viewing space for their work, and the fact that, unlike painters and engravers, they were

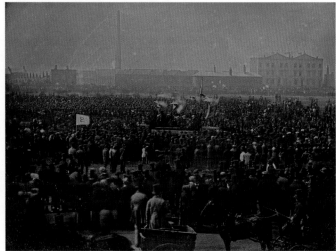

2.32
W. E. KILBURN, *The Great Chartist Meeting on Kennington Common*, April 10, 1848.
Daguerreotype. Royal Archives. © 2002 Her Majesty Queen Elizabeth II.

Photographs of historical events sometimes failed to find a visually striking event or symbol with which to represent the occasion. Kilburn's image does not show the importance of the scene to viewers.

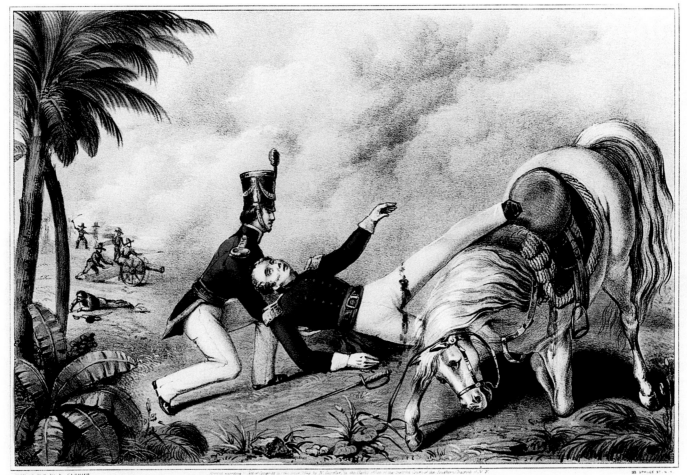

DEATH OF MAJOR RINGGOLD.
OF THE FLYING ARTILLERY.
AT THE BATTLE OF PALO-ALTO, (TEXAS) MAY 8ᵗʰ 1846.

2.33
ARTIST UNKNOWN, *Death of Major Ringgold of the Flying Artillery, at the Battle of Palo-Alto (Texas)*, May 8, 1846. Lithograph. Amon Carter Museum, Fort Worth, Texas.

restricted to what happened in front of the lens. Artists in other media could devise patriotic symbols and emotionally affecting scenes, but the war photographer was faced with transforming the real into the symbolic, and with finding or staging heart-rending incidents. These and other perplexities surfaced in the first photographed wars.

The Mexican–American War (1846–48) coincided with the rise of American newspapers. Daily papers in cities benefited not only from new high-speed presses but also from news carried across the nation by couriers and sometimes by telegraph. Public interest in the war accelerated the appearance of wood-engraving illustrations in newspapers, and increased the popularity of lithographs. But these images were not based on photographs, nor was there a call to make them more authentic by copying camerawork. In the long term, however, the war brought about a change in journalism that affected photography. For the first time war correspondents dispatched from major American papers could send back reports that were rushed into print. Speedier

reporting by war correspondents eroded the domination of the Washington, D.C. newspapers, and the military as major sources of war information. The Mexican–American War also fostered an appetite for up-to-date news. Within a decade, communications systems were specifically developed to transport both images and text describing distant hostilities. In Britain, for example, topical images of the Crimean War (1853–56) would be displayed for viewing and sale (see pp. 98–102).

During and after the Mexican–American War, patriotic themes and sensational melodramas dominated the images produced for the press and the market. A popular hand-colored lithograph theatrically portraying the death of Major Samuel Ringgold, the first officer to fall in the Mexican–American War, could not have been matched by the camera without overt staging (Fig. 2.33). Early war photographs, however, were not always innocent of manipulation. The amputation scene in an intriguing Mexican daguerreotype was probably restaged for the camera. It shows a sergeant who has just been operated on,

focus

The Mexican–American War

In 1836, led by American residents, the Mexican province of Texas declared itself an independent republic. The separation was the result of long-running quarrels between the two nations about land rights and financial reparations due to Americans for property lost during civil unrest in Mexico in the 1830s. Peace negotiations were hampered by the American residents' campaign to have Texas annexed by the U.S. (Texas eventually achieved statehood on December 29, 1845). Relations between Mexico and the U.S. were further troubled by the escalating American desire to fulfill its "manifest destiny" by acquiring more North American soil, including the Mexican territories of California and New Mexico. The prospect of Texas's entry into the Union as a state in which slavery was legal also intensified the national debate about the future of slavery. After skirmishes with Mexican troops in 1846, the U.S. declared war. The war ended in 1848 with the treaty of Guadalupe Hidalgo, in which Mexico ceded extensive territories, including most of what became Arizona, California, Colorado, Nevada, and New Mexico.

The fifty or so anonymous photographs remaining from the conflict—often referred to as the first photographed war—show the faltering beginnings of a war photography largely cut off from battle scenes and troop movements. Some general tendencies are apparent: as happened in many subsequent conflicts, for example, photographs of soldiers were made either before they left for the war or in military encampments. Disruptions in trade and transportation caused shortages of photographic materials near the front, yet scarce supplies did not keep photographers from boasting about their ability to make images. Photographers also made images of war heroes, along with a few landscapes and town views. One of the best-preserved examples is the daguerreotype of Brigadier General John Ellis Wool, accompanied by his staff, on a street in the Mexican town of Saltillo (Fig. 2.34). Because of the daguerreotype's long exposure time, the group had to pause to have a photograph taken. Nevertheless, some blurring occurred on the left side of the image.

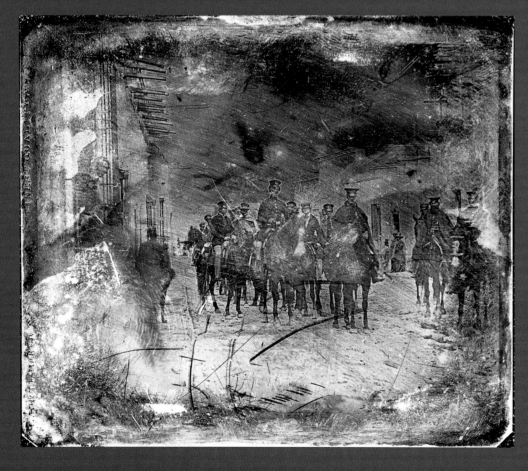

2.34
PHOTOGRAPHER UNKNOWN, *General Wool and Staff, Calle Real, Saltillo, Mexico,* c. 1847. Daguerreotype. Amon Carter Museum, Fort Worth, Texas.

presumably by Dr. Pedro Van der Linden, inspector general of Mexico's Military Medical Corps[27] (Fig. 2.35). Van der Linden, on the far right, is holding an amputated lower leg. Other participants point to the patient's stump, and someone has added a sign noting the place and date. It seems unlikely that this image was made immediately after the operation; more probably it was re-enacted later. Historian Gina Rodriguez Hernández believes that the group was arranged for the camera because the participants appear too clean for battlefront surgery.[28] Van der Linden recounted being interrupted by North American soldiers while performing an amputation. Thrusting out his bloody hands, he pleaded for humanitarian respect, and, as his story goes, the Americans not only retreated but became his protectors and received his medical services.

A daguerreotypist accompanying the United States troops may have made the picture to commemorate the brief eruption of peace during combat.[29] Posed like a history painting, the image evokes the same sort of contradictions surrounding the Southworth and Hawes daguerreotypes of the first uses of surgical anesthesia.

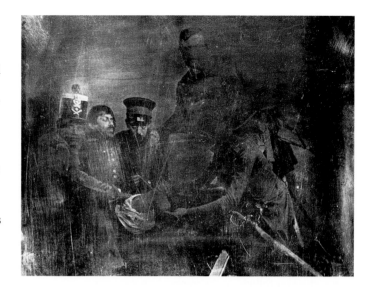

BRITISH CONFLICTS IN ASIA

John McCosh (1805–1885; occasionally spelt MacCosh) is the earliest war photographer whose name is known. He took photographs not of troops but of fellow officers in India, where he served as a surgeon with the East India Company during the Second Sikh War (1848–49), a conflict between the Sikh minority and the British. McCosh made calotype photographs as a hobby in the mid-1840s. In addition to military colleagues, he also photographed local people in Burma, in photographs that tended not to exaggerate their physical characteristics. During the Second Burma War (1852–53), between the Burmese and the British, McCosh produced large photographs, such as his view within the city of Prome (Fig. 2.36).

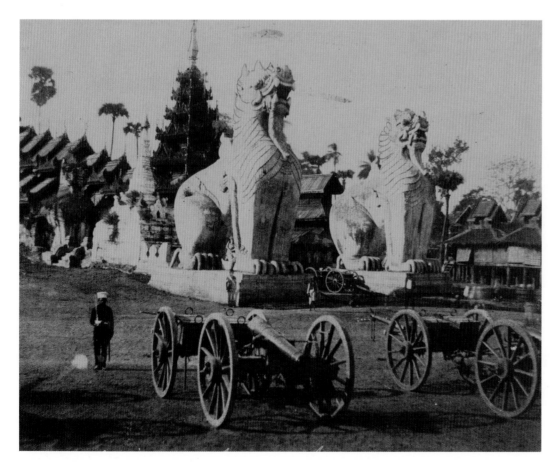

2.35 (above)
PHOTOGRAPHER UNKNOWN, *Amputation,* **Mexican–American War, Cerro Gordo, 1847. Daguerreotype. National Institute of Anthropology and History, Mexico City, Mexico.**

A damaged daguerreotype made in Mexico pays homage to a brief pause in the conflict to allow a doctor to perform a grisly amputation. Proof of the battlefield surgery is evidenced by the patient raising his bloody stump, and by the surgeon's presentation to the camera of the severed limb.

2.36
JOHN MCCOSH, *Artillery in Front of Stone Dragons,* **Prome, Burma, 1852. Calotype. National Army Museum, Chelsea, London.**

Images such as John McCosh's 1852 photograph of British artillery in front of the Stone Dragons in the Burmese city of Prome confidently juxtapose non-Western culture with symbols of imperialist might.

EXPEDITIONARY AND TRAVEL PHOTOGRAPHY

The global expansion of European and American power spurred the growth of photographic practice. Despite its unwieldy equipment and technical limitations, photography was seen as an important tool for information gathering. John Herschel had unsuccessfully suggested that photographic equipment be included in an 1839 British expedition to the Antarctic; then, in 1842, American photographer Edward Anthony (1811–1888) accompanied a government survey of the northeast boundary of the United States and Canada.[30] None of Anthony's daguerreotypes survives, however. Despite modest success, the era's enthusiasm for exploration found a strong symbol in the camera. In 1846 the journal *Art Union* called it "an indispensable accompaniment to all exploring expeditions," which would "greatly … abbreviate the toils and diminish the dangers of those who may follow" in the tracks of the explorer.[31]

EGYPT AND THE HOLY LAND

As early as 1839, François Arago had urged the use of the new medium of photography in copying the hieroglyphic inscriptions on ancient Egyptian buildings. He envisioned a continuation of the extensive French documentation of ancient Egypt begun under Napoleon. Yet while Egypt was one of the first sites to attract daguerrean photographers, they did not fulfill Arago's hope for a systematic visual survey of Egyptian antiquities. Instead, they composed views that responded to the European taste for picturesque ruins. The picturesque, meaning literally "like a picture," was a broad aesthetic category in nineteenth-century thought. In general, it meant that a natural scene was composed in such a way that it stirred fine feelings or thoughts in the viewer, just as a painting or a sketch might do. By selecting topics and designing scenes reminiscent of prints and paintings, photographers validated their efforts and won public acceptance.

Early photographers took advantage of the fact that several regions of the Middle East contained both ancient monuments and biblical sites. The Swiss-born Canadian Pierre-Gustave Joly de Lotbinière (1798–1865) set out for Greece and Egypt as soon as he could obtain reliable daguerreotype equipment. Although the nearly one hundred daguerreotypes he made from 1839 to 1840 no longer exist, we know his work from reproductions.

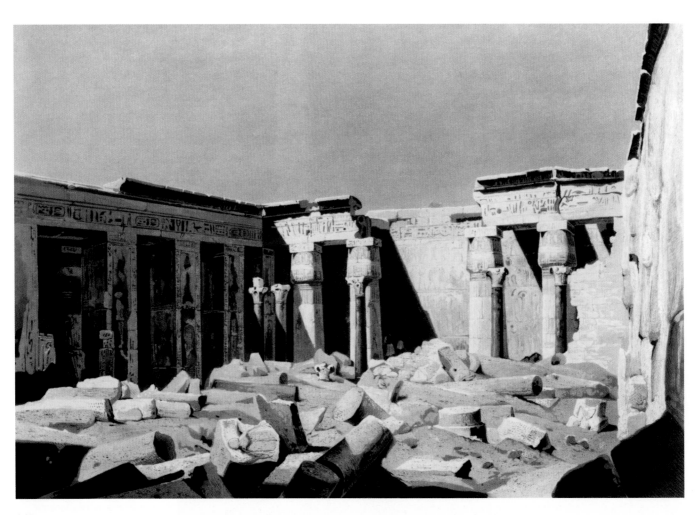

2.37
HECTOR HOREAU, *Medinet Habu,* **plate 18 from** *Panorama d'Égypte et de Nubie,* **1841. Aquatint from daguerreotype by Joly de Lotbinière.**
Resource Collections of the Getty Center for the History of Art and the Humanities, Los Angeles, California.

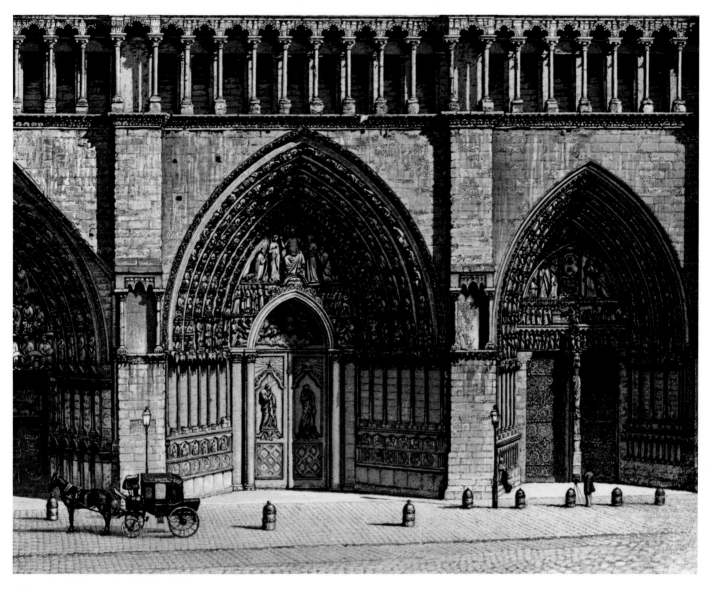

2.38
N. M. P. LEREBOURS, *Portail de Notre Dame de Paris* (detail), plate 43 from *Excursions Daguerriennes*, 1840–44. Engraving after a daguerreotype.
George Eastman House, Rochester, New York.

Some of his daguerreotypes became the basis for the AQUATINTS issued by the architect and egyptologist Hector Horeau in *Panorama d'Égypte et de Nubie* (*Panorama of Egypt and Nubia*) (1841) (Fig. 2.37). Similarly, French publisher Noël Marie Paymal Lerebours (1807–1873) relied on daguerreotypes when he assembled a multivolume work titled *Excursions Daguerriennes, representant les vues et les monuments les plus remarquables du globe* (*Daguerrian Excursions, Showing the World's most Remarkable Views and Monuments*) (1840–44). Lerebours, who bought daguerreotypes and commissioned others for his publications, calculated that prospective buyers would not appreciate a straightforward transcription of daguerreotype views, so he adjusted harsh shadows and other elements to make his scenes more appealing to contemporary taste (Fig. 2.38).

The addition of a photographic camera near the portal on the right added a modern touch.

Lerebours's *Excursions Daguerriennes* credits him as publisher for conceptualizing, organizing, and printing the photographs by many anonymous photographers who contributed daguerreotypes. In the era of early photography, conceptualization was routinely prized over the actual taking and making of a photograph. In the portrait studio, for instance, the photographer might pose a client and arrange the lighting, while an assistant actually exposed and developed the image. For a long time Scottish photographer David Octavius Hill was bestowed more distinction for the art direction of his pictures than his partner, Robert Adamson, was given for the execution of them (see p. 69).

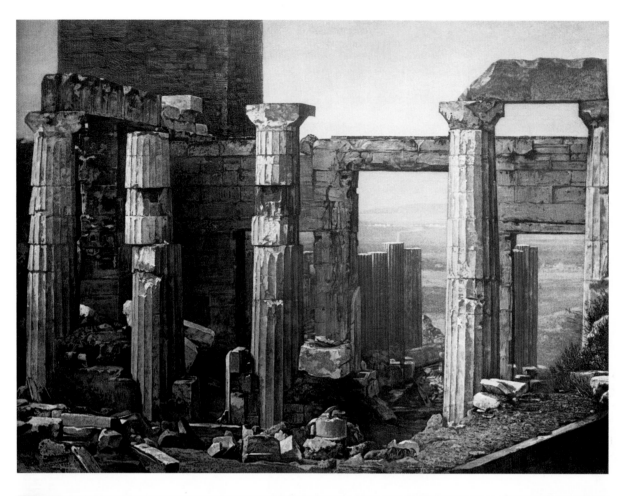

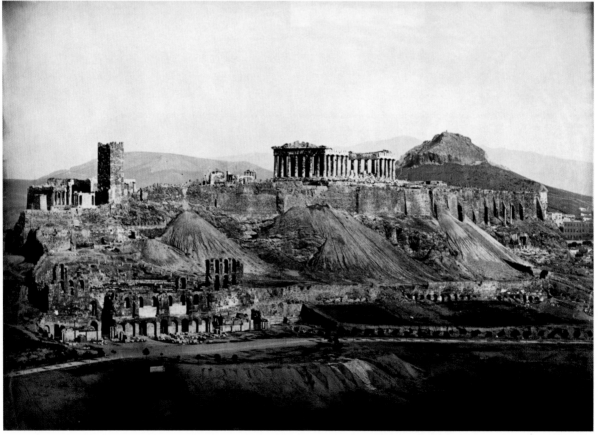

Among more than a hundred travel subjects included in *Excursions Daguerriennes* is a view of the Propylaea, or gateway to the Athenian Acropolis, taken by Lotbinière (Fig. 2.39). Greek photographers, too, photographed ancient remains, but daguerreotypes taken by Greeks of their homeland in the early 1840s do not survive.[32] A remarkable daguerreotype of a general view of the Acropolis from the hill of Philopappus was taken later by Greek painter Philippos Margaritis (1810–1892)[33] (Fig. 2.40).

The Holy Land was another destination for many early photographers, and the site for one of the first planned attempts to use photography as a form of persuasion. When working on a new edition of *Evidence of the Truth of the Christian Religion*, Alexander Keith (1791–1880) (see Fig. 2.67) asked his son the medical doctor George Skene Keith (1819–1910), of Edinburgh, to make daguerreotypes that would show the veracity of the Bible. An earlier edition contained drawings probably not done on the site,[34] but for the new edition, published in 1844, George Keith took about thirty daguerreotypes, eighteen of which were made into engravings for the book, in order to "convince the unprejudiced inquirer or the rational and sincere believer, that it is impossible that his faith be false."[35] Keith's images were accompanied by biblical quotations. Not all Western photographers focused exclusively on places and buildings important to Christian belief. The artist Joseph-Philibert Girault de Prangey (1804–1892) traveled for three years throughout Egypt, Greece, Lebanon, Palestine, and Turkey, making more

than eight hundred daguerreotypes of ancient buildings. An admirer and student of Islamic architecture, Girault de Prangey photographed such famous buildings as the Dome of the Rock (Fig. 2.41).

Different methods of producing light-sensitive paper for photographs were also employed by travelers. French writer, amateur Egyptologist, and student of Arabic literature Maxime Du Camp (1822–1894) adapted the process for an extended trip with writer Gustave Flaubert (1821–1880) to Egypt, Nubia, and the Holy Land. Du Camp was commissioned by the French Ministry of Public Education to photograph Egypt's monuments. Flaubert, then largely unknown, held a commission from the Department of Agriculture to study crop production and trade. These commissions functioned like passports, allowing travelers to circumvent questions and delays.

After many struggles with the medium, Du Camp managed to make more than two hundred paper negatives, 125 of which were printed, mounted on paper, and bound with an introduction. The photographs were printed by Louis Désiré Blanquart-Evrard (1802–1872), who perfected the calotype and also increased its yield. Blanquart-Evrard coated the light-sensitive paper with whey and albumen, derived from milk and eggs respectively. The coating allowed the so-called ALBUMEN PAPER to be prepared ahead of time, which quickly led to the commercialization of its production. With another entrepreneur, Blanquart-Evrard also operated a photographic printing factory, a further sign of photography's impending transition from a handicraft to an industrial process.

Unlike volumes that depended on engravings or aquatints based on daguerreotypes, Du Camp's *Égypte, Nubie, Palestine et Syrie* (*Egypt, Nubia, Palestine, and Syria*) (1852) contained actual photographs, one of the first travel books to do so. Breaking with the newly established style of adjusting shadows and adding human figures to daguerreotype-based travel pictures,

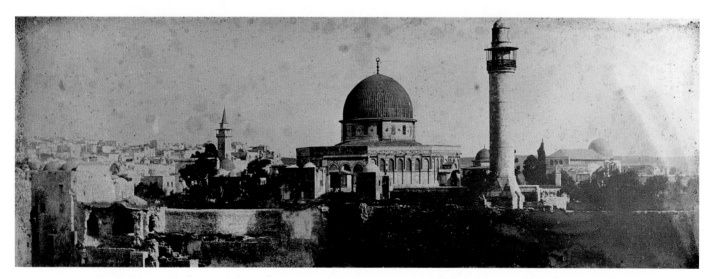

2.41
J. - P. GIRAULT DE PRANGEY, *The Dome of the Rock and the Wailing Wall* (laterally reversed view), c. 1850. Daguerreotype. Bibliothèque Nationale de France, Paris.

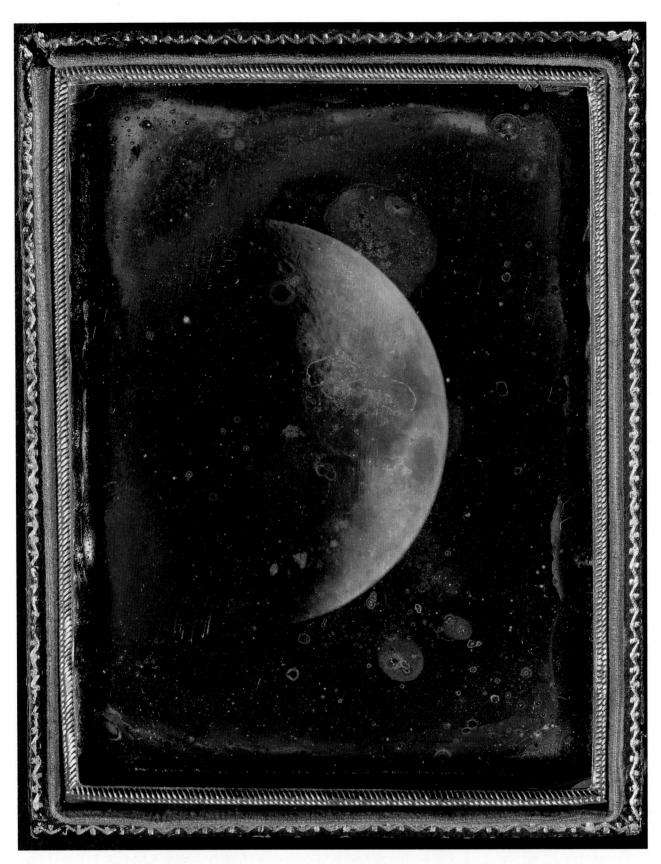

2.42
GEORGE PHILLIPS BOND AND JOHN ADAMS WHIPPLE, *Moon,* **c. 1851. Daguerreotype. Harvard College Observatory, Cambridge, Massachusetts.**

The *Great Refractor* telescope was thought to be the largest in the world at the time that astronomer Bond and daguerreotype portraitist Whipple amazed their colleagues with views that clearly captured the lined and cratered surface of the moon. The technical achievement of their moon photographs was recognized at the Crystal Palace Exhibition in London in 1851 (see p. 27).

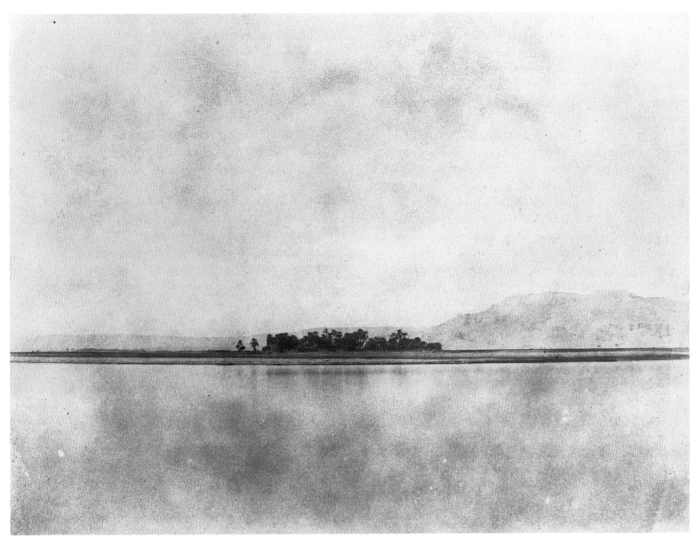

2.43
JOHN BEASLEY GREENE, *The Banks of the Nile at Thebes*, 1854. Salted paper print from a waxed paper negative. George Eastman House, Rochester, New York.

Du Camp chose more neutral views of ancient Egyptian art and architecture (Fig. 2.1). Having defined his goal as an accurate account of ancient Egyptian monuments, he made precise measurements of buildings as well as photographing them. He also recorded contemporary Arab culture, only to have most of these pictures rejected by his publisher, who thought they had no commercial value. Toward the end of his journey, Du Camp traded his photographic equipment for yards of embroidered fabric and never resumed his photographic work.

Not every photographer in Egypt was as scrupulously committed to scientific detachment and neutral description as Du Camp. John Beasley Greene (1832–1856), born in France of an American family, actively pursued the study of both photography and ancient cultures, becoming one of the earliest archeologists to use the new medium in his work. Most of his images parallel those of Du Camp in depicting ancient Egyptian architecture, sculpture, and inscriptions with legibility and precision, yet a few works seem more like evocative watercolors than systematic records (Fig. 2.43). More than ninety of Greene's Egyptian images were published by Blanquart-Evrard in *Le Nil:*

Paysage, explorations photographiques (*The Nile: Landscape and Photographic Explorations*) (1854).

The idea of the photographic series—that is, of creating and arranging images in meaningful sequences—was increasingly adopted in historical, archeological, travel, scientific, medical, and even art photography. During the medium's earliest years, compilations of dissimilar and unrelated images, such as those found in Lerebours's *Excursions Daguerriennes* and Talbot's *The Pencil of Nature*, were prevalent. But as photography proliferated, arrangements of related images were published more frequently. Photographic series expanded the notion of photography from that of an image-making process to something akin to writing. Nineteenth-century albums and books containing interrelated pictures underscored the photographer's skill in building up what the twentieth century would know as the photographic essay. Slowly, commentators began to concede that some photography—series, aesthetic endeavors, and scientific improvements—involved intellectual exertion, a claim that would serve to distance professional and serious amateur photographers from itinerant and part-time practitioners.

THE HISTORIC MONUMENTS COMMISSION

In its historical and civic interest, as well as its convenient stillness and large masses, architecture was suited to photography. Moreover, as historian Janet Buerger observed, in the medium's early period cityscapes were more popular in photography than in any previous art medium. The growth of urban areas during the mid-nineteenth century doubtless helped make the city an object of increased interest. Photographers often chose to picture the enduring monuments from the past with which the public customarily identified cities. For example, Frederick von Martens (1809–1875), a French photographer of German descent who made photographs for Lerebours, invented a rotating camera. His panoramic view of Paris sweeps down the Seine River to the Cathedral of Notre-Dame, which was enclosed in scaffolding for repairs (Fig. 2.44).

A grand series of architectural photographs was undertaken by the Historic Monuments Commission of the French Ministry of the Interior. Formed prior to the disclosure of photography to the world, the commission was charged with listing, surveying, and making recommendations for the historically correct restoration of French medieval and Gothic architecture. This task seemed urgent for several reasons. The aftermath of the French Revolution, the expansion of urban populations, and the industrial disruption of the countryside all nurtured a sense that the future would be markedly different from the past. In turn, this recognition of rapidly passing time heightened public appreciation of history and historical landmarks, many of which had been very seriously neglected or damaged. Moreover, French medieval and Gothic buildings were cherished symbols of cultural achievement, intensified by France's political and economic rivalry with Britain.

This politically charged atmosphere helped to revitalize the Historic Monuments Commission, which by 1850 was considering whether to use photography in its architectural inventory. It might have been expected that the commission would choose the daguerreotype, a French invention that rendered a more detailed image than did the British calotype. Yet the commission rejected the daguerreotype's cold metallic tinge in favor of the softer forms produced by the calotype. Further, a leading member of the commission complained that people of taste had not fully accepted the daguerreotype, because its mass of details was more distracting than artful. By contrast, the calotype's less sharply defined shapes and details and its evocative shadows more eloquently expressed nostalgia for the medieval past. The large size of the calotype was also an attractive feature, as was its ability to produce negatives from which multiple copies could be made.[36]

The photographic enterprise, which came to be known collectively as the Missions Héliographiques, employed several French photographers, the first of whom was Hippolyte Bayard, then vice-president of the recently founded professional association the Société Héliographique. Like many early photographic organizations, it did not specialize in any one kind of photographic practice. It encouraged artistic, scientific, and technical discussions, and published a journal. Within this group, and others similar to it in Europe and America, scientists created what would be called artistic photographs, and artists freely experimented with the chemistry of photography.

Five members of the Société Héliographique (Edouard Baldus, Hippolyte Bayard, Gustave Le Gray, Henri Le Secq, O. Mestral) were chosen by the Historic Monuments Commission. Edouard Baldus (1813–1889) brought a remarkable inventiveness to the task. Typically, Missions Héliographiques photographers were assigned areas of France and particular monuments. Among Baldus's destinations was the Church of Saint-Trophîme in Arles, a city in the south of France. In the adjacent medieval cloister, the self-styled "painter-photographer" Baldus cleverly devised an image-making process that went beyond the scope of his camera's vision. He created a large print of the cloister of Saint-Trophîme by joining many negatives, and by retouching them where necessary (Fig. 2.45). In this effort, Baldus defined the photograph not as the pure product of a single camera

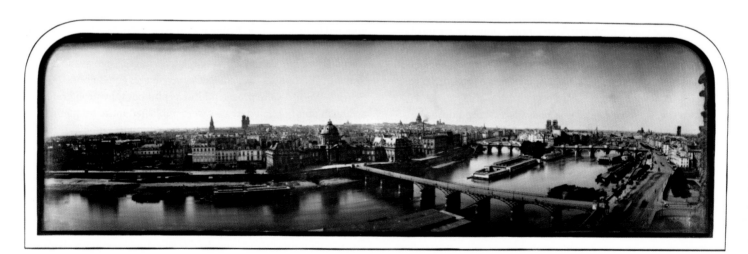

2.44
FREDERICK VON MARTENS, *Panorama of Paris*, c. 1846. Daguerreotype. George Eastman House, Rochester, New York.

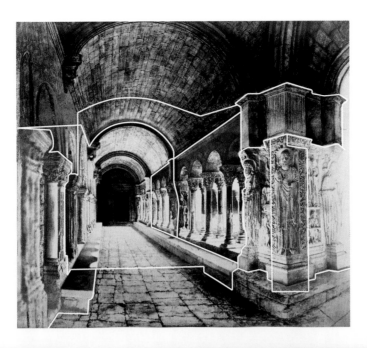

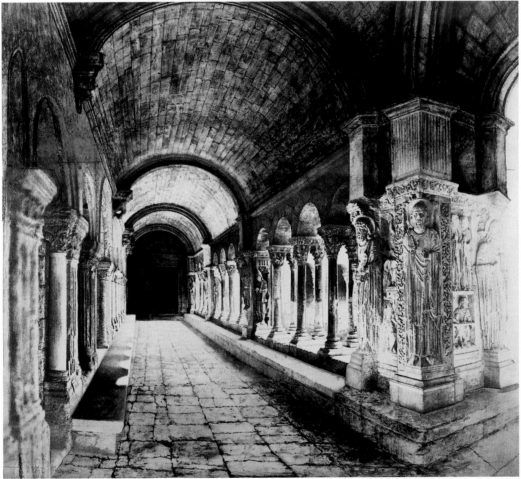

2.45 (above and below)
EDOUARD BALDUS, *Cloister of Saint-Trophîme, Arles,* **1851. Partly hand-painted paper print. Musée National des Monuments Français, Paris.**

Rather than accept the modest range of his lens, which could not encompass the full scope of the cloister, Baldus made ten sharply focused negatives and subtly connected them (see the white lines in the thumbnail, above). He retouched the joins, and accentuated tones across the negative's surface. The image of the vault directly above where Baldus would have stood is not a camera image at all, but a hand-painted negative, carefully affixed to the rest.[37]

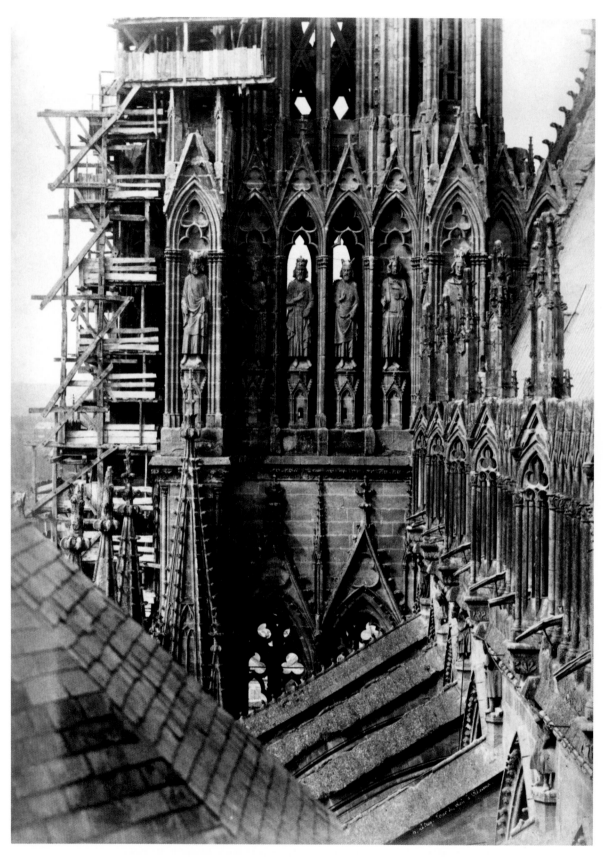

2.46
HENRI LE SECQ, *Tower of Kings, Reims Cathedral,* **1851. Salted paper print. The J. Paul Getty Museum, Los Angeles, California.**

The photographic journal *La Lumière* praised this image by Le Secq as having been reported stone by stone.[38] Le Secq recorded the tower from an angle few visitors would have seen, and thereby showed details that could not be viewed from the ground. The scaffolding on the left side of the picture indicates that restoration has already begun; it was carried out between 1845 and 1864.

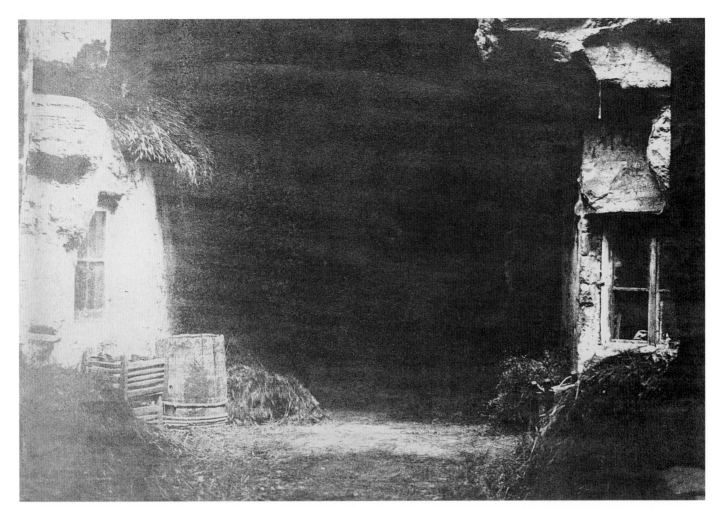

2.47
HENRI LE SECQ, *Farmyard Scene, near St. Leu-d'Esserent,* c. 1852. Cyanotype print from paper negative. Museum Purchase. George Eastman House, Rochester, New York.

exposure, but as a flexible basis for picture-making. Throughout its subsequent history, photographers would juggle two notions, either aligning themselves with the idea of the inherently unique value of the unretouched negative and print, or maintaining that camerawork is, and should be, multifold, embracing not only the pure print but also all manipulations of the images.

Henri Le Secq (1818–1882), another of the Missions Héliographiques photographers, was also a painter and antiquarian. His undertakings for the Historic Monuments Commission often produced finely detailed registers of architecture and sculpture, as in the *Tour des Rois* (*Tower of Kings*) from the south tower of Reims Cathedral (Fig. 2.46). In his other work, Le Secq orchestrated images in which deep shadows mute detail and create such sharp contrasts that the photographs even approach abstraction (Fig. 2.47); he also made ingenious still-life photographs.

The subject matter of the Historic Monuments Commission was also taken up by other photographers without official appointments to the commission, notably Charles Nègre

(1820–1880). Nègre, a painter, progressed from daguerreotype to paper photography in the late 1840s. He made architectural photographs and a unique series of street photographs, including images of organ grinders, rag pickers, and chimney sweeps (Fig. 2.48).

A skilled photographic technician and chemist who worked for the Historic Monuments Commission, Gustave Le Gray (1820–1882), advanced the idea that profuse photographic detail did not have artistic merit. With critics such as Francis Wey and photographers such as Hill and Adamson, Le Gray advocated a theory of sacrifices—that is, of giving up particulars, and composing the picture surface either with sharply defined tonal areas, or through softness.[39] As early as 1853, the English painter and photographer William Newton (1785–1869) similarly advocated the development of an art photography that consciously worked against the glut of details produced by "chemical Photography." Newton proposed rendering a subject a little out of focus.[40] Le Gray's support of the new medium and his excitement about its possibilities are expressed in his treatises;

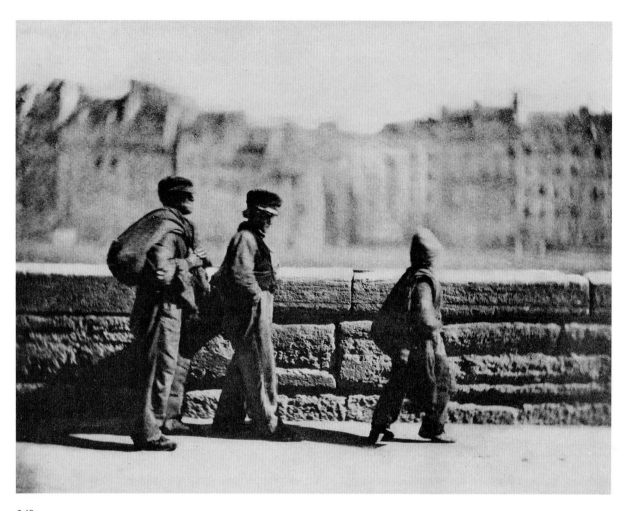

2.48
CHARLES NÈGRE, *Chimney Sweeps Walking*, 1851. Salted paper print. Museum of Modern Art, New York

where some critics considered that photography would lower public appreciation for art, he argued that it would advance taste by allowing the public to study the fullness of nature.[41]

In the *Forest of Fontainebleau* (Fig. 2.49), Le Gray pictured a spot thirty-five miles south of Paris that was a favorite of the Barbizon School[42] painters, such as Jean-Baptiste-Camille Corot (1796–1875) and Jean-François Millet (1814–1875), who sought new artistic subjects in the commonplace landscape near the village of Barbizon. Photographers and painters interacted and exchanged ideas about the depiction of nature. In wild fields and forests the scenery was unrestricted by the conventions that governed formal gardens.

Le Gray filled the frame of his Barbizon views with impressions of filtered woodland light and, in the mono-chromatic palette available to him, rendered the rich varieties of green, from verdant lichen patches to silvery leaves. Where some photographers preferred to make portraits of venerable trees (see Fig. 3.16), Le Gray tried to convey the feeling of being in the forest. His approach to photography combined science and art. He experimented with techniques to render delicate gradations of tone, and he invented his own dry WAXED-PAPER PROCESS, which kept the paper sensitive for two weeks and allowed the

photographer to develop it up to a week after exposure. Le Gray's famous seascapes reveal the extent of his resistance to the idea that photography was merely an automatic recording of scenes before the lens. He manipulated the photograph in a number of ways. He sometimes photographed dramatic cloud formations separately from sea views, merging the resulting two negatives, and printing the sky and the sea separately. To complete the picture, he carefully retouched the horizon line where the two negatives met. *The Great Wave, Sète* merged one negative of the sea and one of the sky, combining them in the printing process to create a dramatic image with blazing light in the center of the picture (Fig. 2.50). Le Gray's concern with the overall aesthetic harmony of the print also led him to retouch clouds, subtract figures, and accentuate horizontal or vertical elements, and to vignette scenes—that is, to darken the edges of the print to emphasize the center. The technique of printing more than one negative to create a single picture, as Baldus had done in *Cloister of Saint-Trophîme, Arles* (see Fig. 2.45), became known as COMBINATION PRINTING. Like the out-of-focus photograph and the photograph to which paint has been added, combination printing challenged the notion of photography as an unadulterated transcription of optical reality.

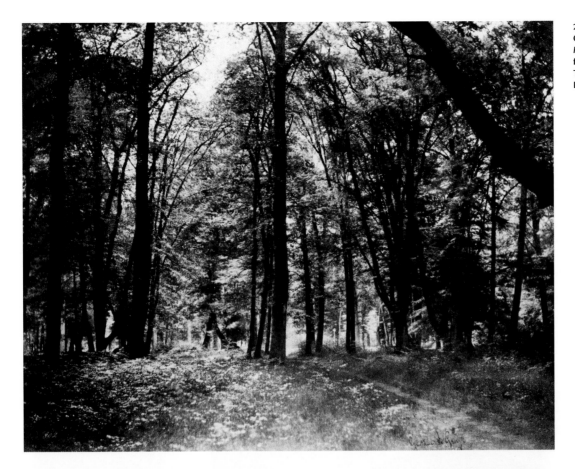

2.49
GUSTAVE LE GRAY, *Forest of Fontainebleau*, c. 1851. Salt print from a wax paper negative. The J. Paul Getty Museum, Los Angeles, California.

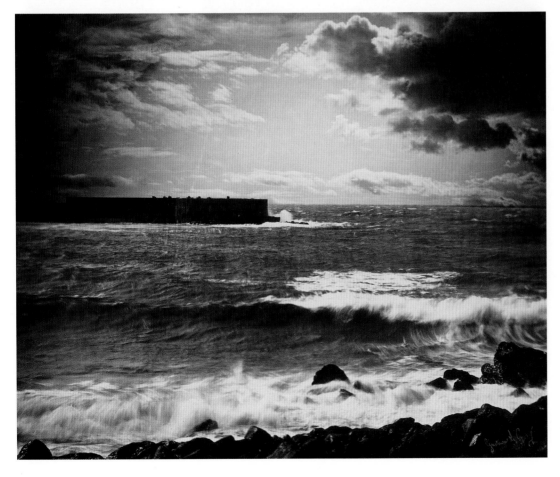

2.50 GUSTAVE LE GRAY, *The Great Wave, Sète*, 1857. Albumen silver print from two glass negatives. Metropolitan Museum of Art, New York.

PORTRAITURE AND THE CAMERA

A wide range of photographic practice developed rapidly in the medium's early years. Yet neither landscape, nor still life, nor the variety of scientific practice acquired quite the aura of magic that the portrait photograph did. At first, Daguerre thought that portraits were impracticable, and the otherwise imaginative François Arago likewise declared that there was little hope that the technique could be used for portraiture. In the earliest daguerreotypes (Fig. 2.51), sitters tended to move during the long exposure time required, blurring the images. They sometimes held themselves in a rigid posture and widened their eyes slightly in an effort to prevent blinking. It was some time, too, before the modern smile became an omnipresent convention. The chemistry making possible shorter exposure times improved swiftly, and devices to hold heads still were soon invented, bringing on a rush of daguerrean portraits (Fig. 2.52). The detailed, silver-surfaced daguerreotype was resolutely preferred to the more atmospheric calotype prints. American scientist, inventor, and artist Samuel F. B. Morse (1791–1872)

was in Paris when Daguerre's invention was first announced. In March 1839, in exchange for an invitation to see how the telegraph worked, Daguerre showed Morse his photographic process. Morse's interest in camera images, however, had predated that of Daguerre. About thirty years earlier, he had unsuccessfully attempted to fix images obtained in a camera obscura.

Once instructions for making the daguerreotype became available, Morse was among the first to make images. Although occasionally frustrated by the unpredictable medium, he is reputed to have produced an extraordinary image of members of the Yale University class of 1810, as they gathered in August 1840 for their thirtieth reunion (Fig. 2.53). The frame surrounding the collection of portraits measures only 3¼ by 4¼ inches, and each image is only ½-inch square. It is not known if the images were somehow reduced in size from larger portraits, or whether the ingenious maker used a special camera to make diminutive originals, which were then rephotographed.[43]

The earliest daguerreotype portraits are often rigidly frontal. The sitter sat beneath a skylight, while reflectors directed more

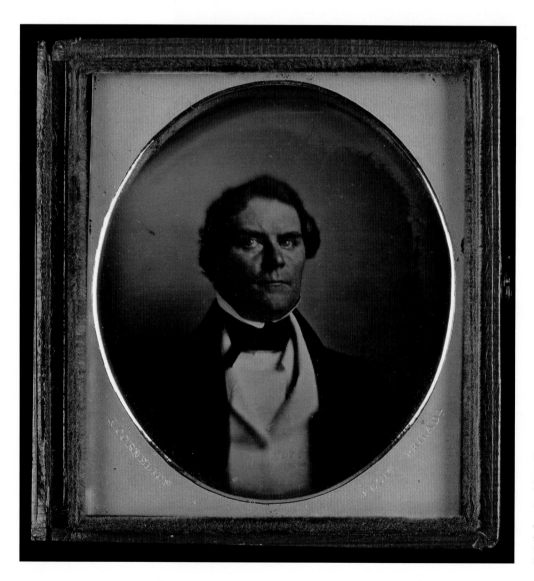

2.51
ROBERT CORNELIUS, *Portrait of Samuel Bispham,* **c. May 1840. Daguerreotype. Wm. B. Becker Collection, American Museum of Photography.**

Cornelius displayed himself as well as the sitter, adding the words, "R. Cornelius Fecit Philada" (R. Cornelius made this in Philadelphia).

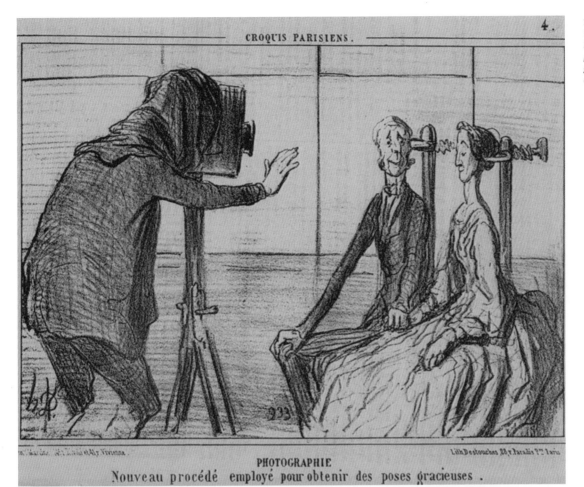

2.52
HONORÉ DAUMIER,
Nouveau procédé employé pour obtenir des poses gracieuses, c. 1856. Lithograph on paper. Private Collection.

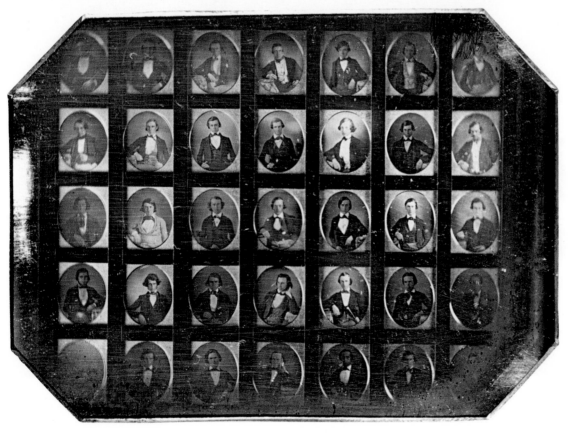

2.53
S. F. B. MORSE (?), *Graduates of Yale, Class of 1810*, 1840. Daguerreotype.

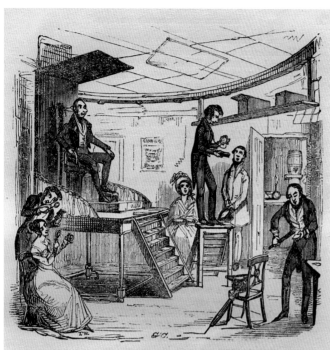

2.54
GEORGE CRUIKSHANK, *Photographic Phenomena*, 1842. Paper print. Private Collection.

light on selected features (Fig. 2.54). Given the discomfort involved, the *Daguerrean Journal* suggested that resolute indifference was "the best expression for a Daguerreotype."[44] Subsequently, viewers would pore over daguerreotypes with magnifying lenses, marveling at the details of representation, especially the outlines of family resemblance and the contrast between youth and age.

In London, in March 1841, Richard Beard (1802–1885) opened a daguerreotype studio, the first licensed public source for daguerreotypes in Britain. It was quickly followed by the studio of another licensee, the London firm of French entrepreneur Jean-François-Antoine Claudet (1797–1867). In 1851, Claudet enlarged his London offices, establishing what he called the "Temple to Photography," a studio decorated with painted portrait medallions of artists, scientists, and photographic pioneers. A tireless innovator, Claudet invented a so-called "safe light" to be used in the darkroom. Claudet's attempt to claim for photography the status of both a science and an art would be variously repeated throughout the nineteenth century.

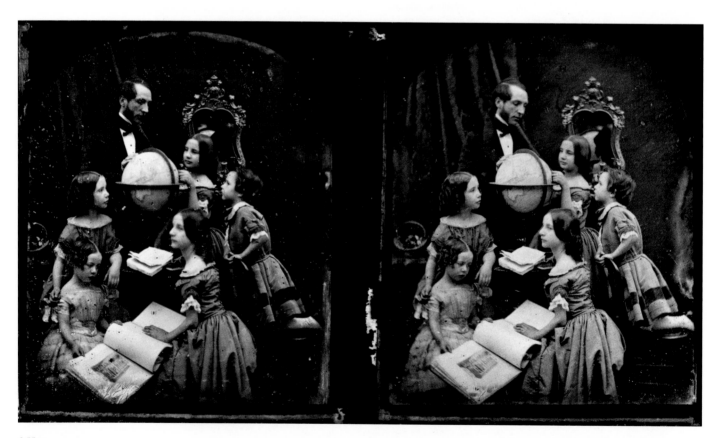

2.55
J.-F.-A. CLAUDET, *The Geography Lesson*, 1851. Stereoscopic daguerreotype. Gernsheim Collection. Harry Ransom Humanities Research Center, University of Texas at Austin.

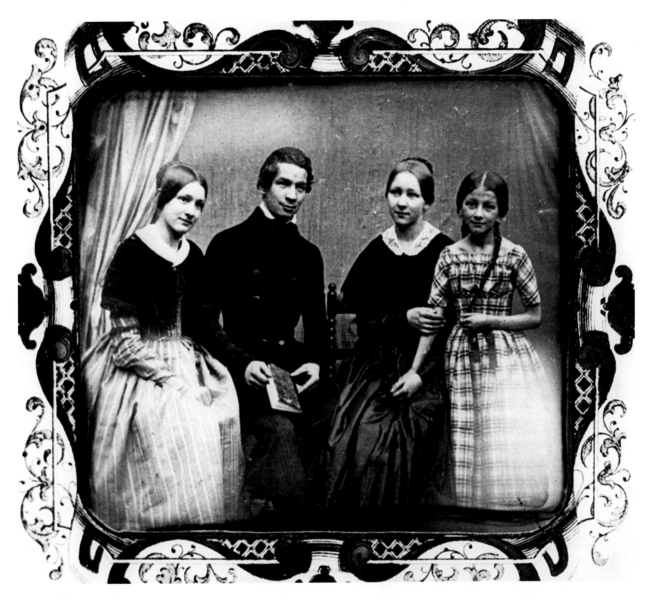

2.56
GUSTAV OEHME, *Group Portrait in Oehme's Studio*, Berlin, April 11, 1847. Daguerreotype. Robert Lebeck Collection. Rheinisches Bildarchiv, Cologne, Germany.

By the late 1840s, sitters preferred to appear casual and affectionate. Smiles began to replace the stern faces of the early 1840s.

Claudet's portrait work quickly diversified: he added back–drops and studio props, and he grouped his sitters in aesthetically pleasing arrangements. His 1851 daguerreotype *The Geography Lesson* shows a man standing before a globe, and children with books, the central one of which shows a print of a Classical building (Fig. 2.55). The image is a daguerreotype using the STEREOGRAPHY technique—that is, produced by two cameras spaced to imitate human binocular vision. In a special viewer, the two stereographic images appeared to be a single three-dimensional scene. Though obviously posed, Claudet's picture is not far-fetched. Books such as Lerebours's *Daguerrian Excursions* were used to teach geography to a generation of children.

In Berlin, Gustav Oehme (1817–1881), an optician who studied with Daguerre, set up a photography studio. He seems to have arranged the family in his 1847 group portrait to maximize the appearance of casual good-naturedness (Fig. 2.56). The necessity for clients to hold a pose is nevertheless evident on the right, where the girl is steadied by the woman next to her. Photographers and sitters abandoned rigid appearances as soon as technical improvements permitted; clients learned to appear joyful, studious, or reflective, and smiles and signs of congeniality swept through photographic practice. In the literature of the time, the idea of enacting an emotion for the camera was not felt to conflict with the notion that photographs rendered truth to experience. The photographic studio emerged as a new social space in which sitters could compose and record an image of how they desired to appear for acquaintances, strangers, and posterity.

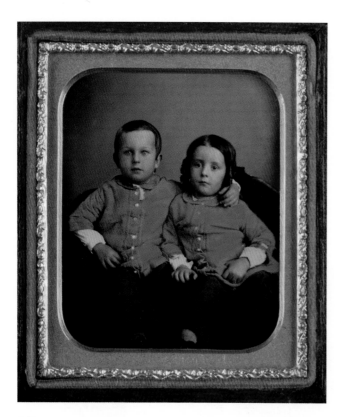

2.57
UNKNOWN PHOTOGRAPHER (U.S.), *Brother and Sister*, c. 1850.
Daguerreotype. Wm. B. Becker Collection, American Museum of Photography.

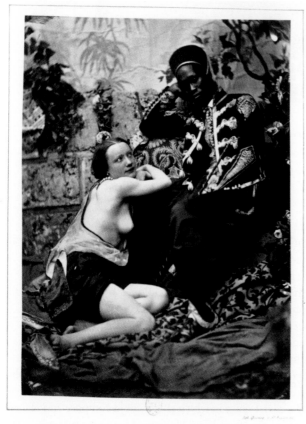

2.58
J. A. MOULIN, *Étude: Séduction*, c. 1852. Paper print.
Bibliothèque Nationale de France, Paris.

COLORING THE IMAGE

When the Russian daguerreotypist Aleksei Grekov (1779/80–1850s) titled his 1840 booklet *A Painter without a Brush and Paint, Photographing any Images, Portraits, Landscapes, etc., in their True and Faithful Colour in a Few Minutes*, he was referring to the gray scale of the daguerreotype, not to hues on the color spectrum.[45] However, daguerreotypes were sometimes hand-tinted, to avoid the gray tones that customers identified with illness and death.[46] French critic Francis Wey denounced the unrelenting gray of the daguerreotype portrait as "fried fish pasted on to metal plaques."[47] Some photographers attempted to invent a daguerreotype process that would be automatically colored by chemical reactions to light rays.

Expertly applied color added warmth to complexions and detail to attire (Fig. 2.57). Color was applied by an artist painting directly on to the daguerreotype, probably with a thin camel-hair brush. In this image, the colorist tinted selected parts of the image only, leaving the boy's trousers and the girl's chair untouched. In other parts of the world, daguerreotypes and other kinds of photographs were more extensively and thickly painted.

Soft pastel colors were often added to warm the skin tones in erotic daguerreotypes, the market for which expanded when stereographic daguerreotypes began to be produced. The creation of so-called *académies*, photographs of nude and semi-nude women, professedly made for the use of artists, provided some daguerreotypists and calotypists with additional income, as did frankly erotic photographs (Fig. 2.58). Pictured singly or in groups, the nude female figure substantially outnumbered male nudes (Fig. 2.59). The capability of the paper photograph to make multiple prints allowed the output of nude photographs to increase rapidly; as historian Elizabeth Anne McCauley has shown, despite some attempts at censorship, soft-core pornographic photographs were one of the first mass-market products.[48]

As materials became more widely available and reliable, photographic practice grew. An 1848 American article declared that "in our great cities, a daguerreotypist is to be found in almost every square; and there is scarcely a county in any state that has not one or more of these industrious individuals busy at work catching 'the shadow' ere the 'substance fade.'"[49] The idea of securing the shadow, or image, before the sitter deceased was not always possible; it sometimes meant commissioning images of dead people. The custom of creating a deathbed image, by making a death mask or a painting, was democratized through photography and became a routine practice among the mid-nineteenth-century middle classes. Because of the high mortality rate, infants and children were the frequent subjects of such photographs, which were not, as today, considered ghoulish (Fig. 2.60). The post-mortem photograph became widespread in America and throughout Europe. Later, when most people had photographs of their family and friends, the practice declined.

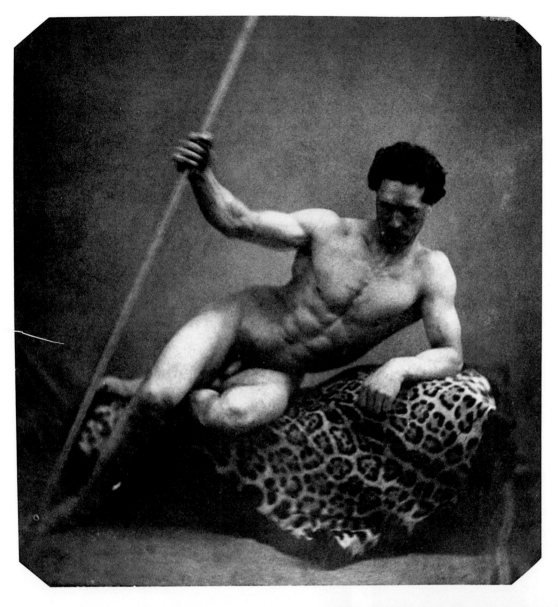

The painter Eugène Delacroix commissioned several photographic studies for his work, such as this male nude. Delacroix maintained that photography was too unimaginative to be a genuine art.

2.60
PHOTOGRAPHER UNKNOWN, *Father and Mother Holding a Dead Child*, c. 1850–60s. Daguerreotype. Strong Museum, Rochester, New York.

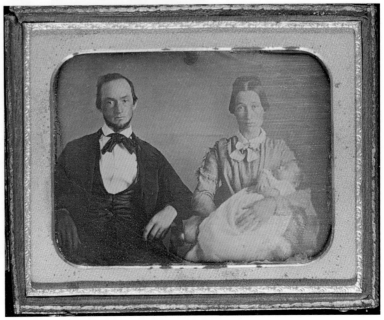

THE PHOTOGRAPHY STUDIO

A European observer remarked that "American daguerreotypists go to enormous expense for their rooms, which are most elegantly furnished … Everything is … united to distract the mind of the visitor from his cares and give to his countenance an expression of calm contentment."[50] In the biggest American cities, daguerrean studios began to rival part-time and itinerant photographers. Salon owners might employ fashion and hair stylists, while less-expensive venues too began to provide visual symbols of personal achievement and economic success for their portraits. Plain backgrounds were replaced by painted backdrops, such as garden scenes, and studio props such as columns, chairs, tables, rugs, books, sculptures, and flowers were added to reflect the sitter's interests, attitudes, or aspirations. The historian Alan Trachtenberg observed that "sitters were encouraged to will themselves into the desired self-expression," thereby creating "a role and a mask."[51]

The shift from relatively unaffected pictures to images in which sitters used the new medium to enact an appearance gave photographers more leeway in which to design photographic representations. As one example, the powerful portrait of American abolitionist John Brown by Augustus Washington (1820/1821–1875) depends on the orchestration of Brown's hands (Fig. 2.61). One is raised in the position of vow-making or challenge, while the other grasps a flag thought to be that of the Subterranean Pass Way, Brown's unrealized scheme for an organization similar to the Underground Railroad, which assisted runaway slaves. Washington, the son of a former slave and an Asian woman, learned to make daguerreotypes in order to pay his way through Dartmouth College. He was an active abolitionist who eventually emigrated to Liberia, the African country acquired by the American Colonization Society, which promoted the repatriation of freed slaves. Washington prospered in Africa, running several photographic studios, farming sugarcane, and serving in the Liberian Congress.

Like Washington, other African-American photographers catered to both white and black customers. At least fifty black daguerreotypists are known to have practiced in the United States during photography's first decade.[52] J. P. (James Presley) Ball (1825–1904), also an active abolitionist, began his career in Cincinnati, Ohio, and soon built the city's largest and most successful photographic practice in a studio he called the "Great Daguerrian Gallery of the West" (Fig. 2.62). During his long life, he attracted a wide clientele, including celebrities such as Frederick Douglass and Charles Dickens. He worked in a variety of photographic processes and established studios in Montana, Washington, and perhaps also Hawaii, where he died.

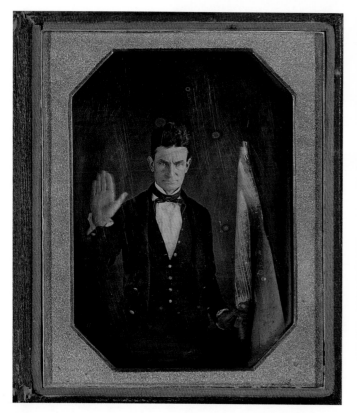

2.61
AUGUSTUS WASHINGTON, *John Brown*, c. 1846–47.
Quarter-plate daguerreotype. National Portrait Gallery,
Smithsonian Institution, Washington, D.C.

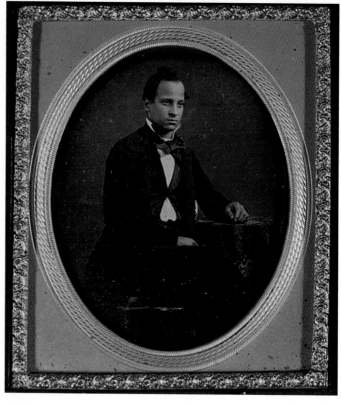

2.62
JAMES PRESLEY BALL, *Alexander S. Thomas*, late 1850s–early 1860s.
Daguerreotype. Cincinnati Art Museum.

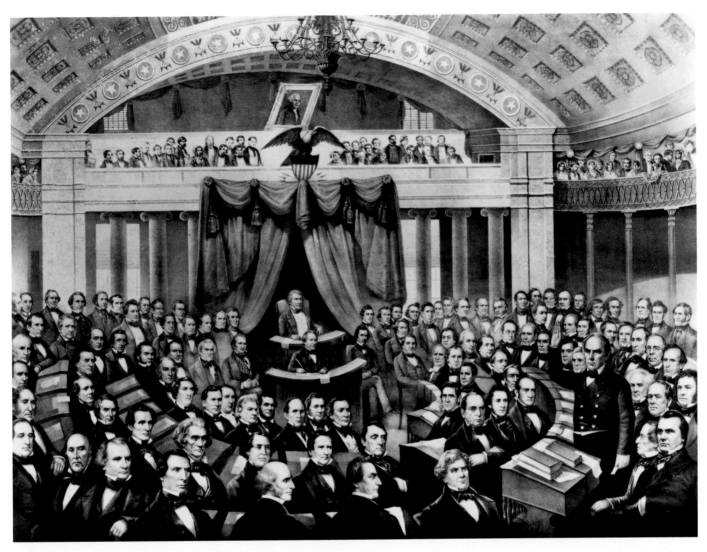

2.63
PHOTOGRAPHER UNKNOWN, *Daniel Webster Addressing the U.S. Senate in the Great Debate on the Compromise Measures of 1850, 1850.*
Lithograph made from daguerreotypes by Eliphalet M. Brown. Library of Congress, Washington, D.C.

The heads of the senators listening to Daniel Webster were copied from daguerreotypes made by Eliphalet Brown, who later accompanied
Commodore Matthew C. Perry to Japan (see p. 122).

CELEBRITY PHOTOGRAPHY

Numerous photographic studios attracted customers
by exhibiting images of celebrities. Studios offered free
daguerreotypes to celebrities from all walks of life in exchange
for the right to exhibit their likenesses, and to reproduce them,
mostly as engravings or lithographs. In the mid-1840s, John
Plumbe (1809–1857), an American photographer who was born
in Wales, devised a plan to mass-produce celebrity photographs
by offering subscribers a daily portrait of the rich and famous.[53]
Though this scheme failed, early photographers encouraged the
public taste for celebrity likenesses. Realistic images of political
figures helped to shift the public's perception of politics away
from events and toward personalities. Lithographs based on
photographs also featured well-known public people, as in a
print showing Daniel Webster's 1850 address to the United States
Senate (Fig. 2.63). This was part of the fiery debate that led to
the Compromise of 1850, which allowed slavery to continue in
the states where it existed, but not in the newly acquired state
of California. To create the lithograph, engraved versions of
daguerreotype portraits were affixed to hand-drawn bodies, with
the disturbing result that the senators' out-of-scale heads look
like an arrangement of fruit.

THE FIRM OF SOUTHWORTH AND HAWES

The Boston photographic establishment run by Albert Sands
Southworth (1811–1894) and Josiah Johnson Hawes (1808–
1901) exhibited large daguerreotypes of political and cultural
celebrities, along with scenes of Boston's economic prosperity

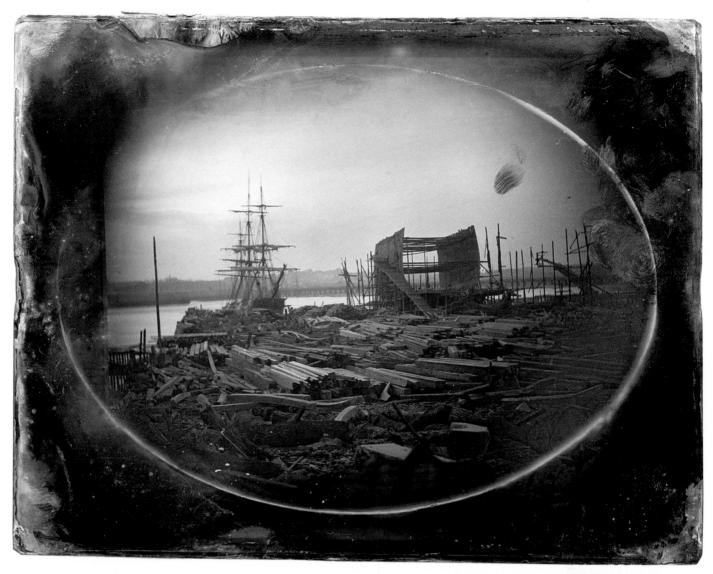

2.64
ALBERT SANDS SOUTHWORTH AND JOSIAH JOHNSON HAWES, *McKay's Shipyard, East Boston*, c. 1855. Daguerreotype.
Museum of Fine Arts, Boston, Massachusetts.

and historical heritage (Figs. 2.64, 2.65). Southworth and Hawes specialized in large—that is, whole-plate—daguerreotypes (usually 6½ inches wide by 8½ inches high) that cost about $15. At a time when commonplace daguerreotypes sold for about $2, and some were even advertised for as little as 25 cents,[54] Southworth and Hawes boasted that they did no cheap work.

The notion of the daguerreotypist as an artist was forcefully advanced by Albert Sands Southworth, in his self-portrait and in his writing (Fig. 2.66). He maintained that "the artist, even in photography, must go beyond discovery and the knowledge of facts. He must create and invent truths, and produce new developments of facts." Playing on the mid-nineteenth-century interest in character study, Southworth described the role of the photographer as catching "the whole character of the sitter … at

first sight." He affirmed that "Nature is not all to be represented as it is, but as it ought to be, and might possibly have been."[55]

THE CALOTYPE PORTRAIT: HILL AND ADAMSON
The absence of specialization in early photography produced remarkable hybrids. The work of David Octavius Hill (1802–1870) and Robert Adamson (1821–1848) in Scotland encompassed landscape, portraiture, and ethnographic recording. Hill was originally a landscape painter and lithographer, who decided to create a painting commemorating the so-called Great Disruption of 1843, when 470 Scottish ministers split with the established Church of Scotland to form the Free Church. Daunted by the thought of sketching the multitude present at the event, he asked Edinburgh engineer-

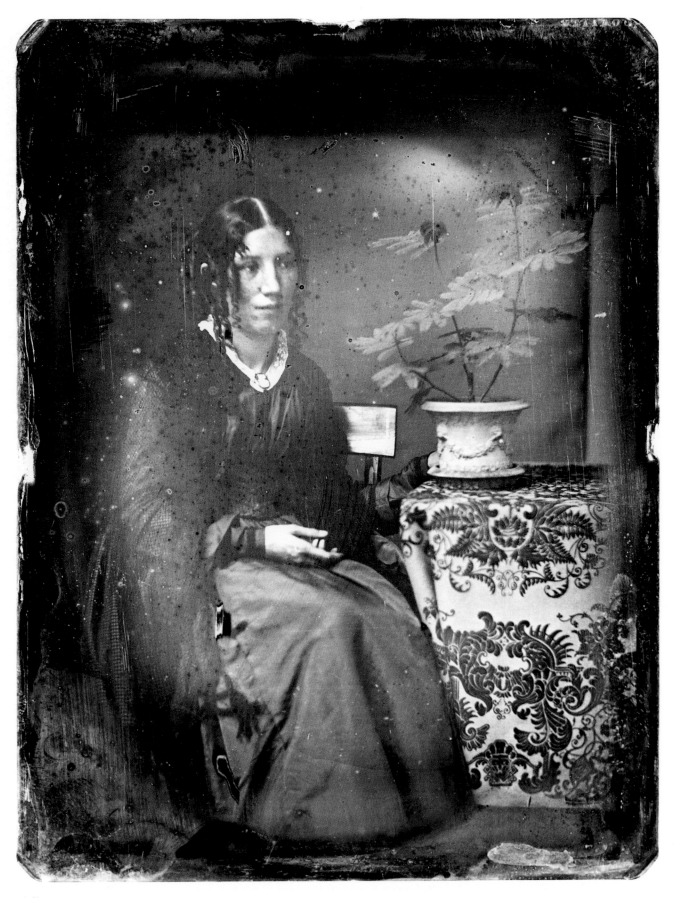

2.65
ALBERT SANDS SOUTHWORTH AND JOSIAH JOHNSON HAWES, *Harriet Beecher Stowe*, c. 1850. Quarter-plate daguerreotype.
Metropolitan Museum of Art, New York.

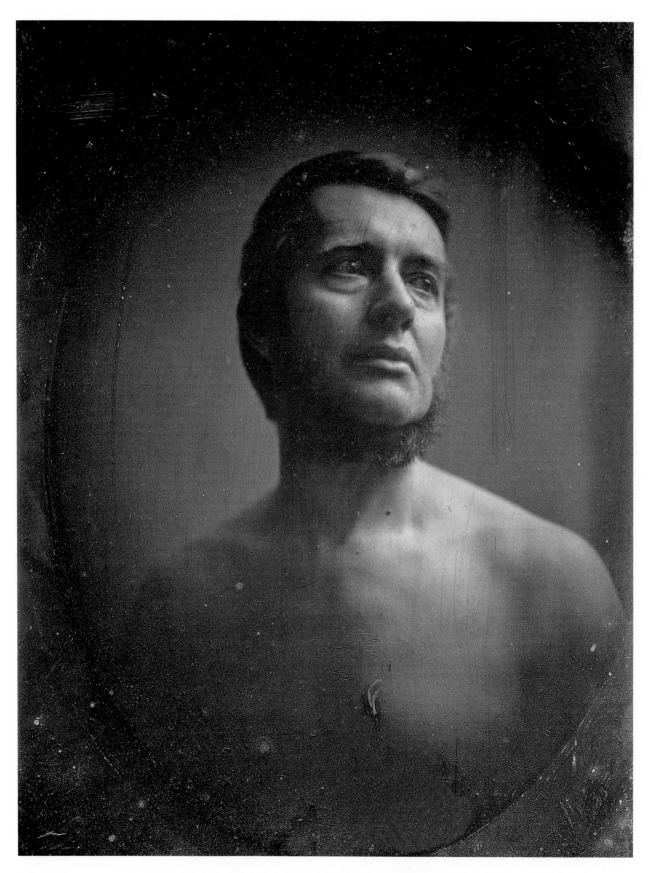

2.66
ALBERT SANDS SOUTHWORTH, *Self-Portrait,* **c. 1848. Daguerreotype. Metropolitan Museum of Art, New York.**

Southworth contrived a dramatically lit picture, with a delicate, rich progression of gray tones. Back-lighted, as were many of his clients, Southworth showed himself in the guise of a thoughtful, long-suffering, Romantic painter.

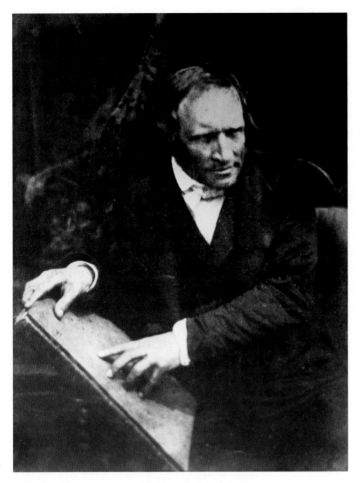

2.67
DAVID OCTAVIUS HILL AND ROBERT ADAMSON, *Dr. Alexander Keith*, c. 1843.
Paper print. Scottish National Portrait Gallery, Edinburgh.

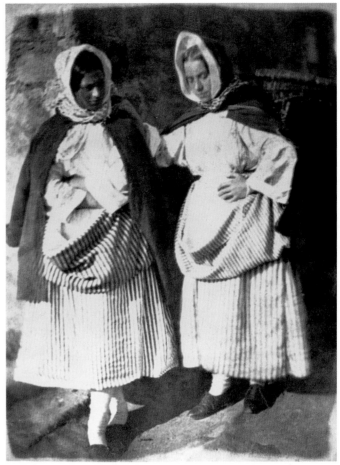

2.68
DAVID OCTAVIUS HILL AND ROBERT ADAMSON, *Mrs. Elizabeth Hall and Unknown Woman (Newhaven Fishwives)*, c. 1845. Salted paper print. Scottish National Portrait Gallery, Edinburgh.

turned-photographer Robert Adamson to photograph the participants. Adamson grew up in St. Andrews, a hub of early photographic practice and writing. He learned photography from his brother John Adamson (1809–1870) and from Dr. David Brewster (1781–1868), a friend of William Henry Fox Talbot and an enthusiastic supporter of the new medium.[56] Trading on the traditional understanding of the commemorative painting, Hill included portraits of persons who were not present at the original event in the work, finished twenty years later, titled *The Signing of the Deed of Demission*.[57] Like the print of Daniel Webster speaking to the Senate (see Fig. 2.63), the painting relinquished perspective and enlarged the proportions of the heads so that the faces would show clearly. But with the calotypes generated during their brief collaboration, Hill and Adamson were more visually inventive.

They turned the calotype's formal qualities to their advantage. Rather than imitating the itemizing detail of the daguerreotype, Hill and Adamson composed within the softer forms resulting from the calotype's paper negative. Adapting artistic principles of light and shade (CHIAROSCURO), they orchestrated the surface with large areas of shadow, which suppressed fine detail.

They posed sitters artfully, and used sunlight and reflected light to create unnaturalistic and theatrical effects (Fig. 2.67). Viewers compared Hill and Adamson's style to the light-and-shadow effects in Rembrandt's works, a resemblance that Talbot had also remarked on in relation to his early work.[58] Hill was especially pleased with what others, particularly proponents of the daguerreotype, found inferior in the calotype process. He admitted that "The rough surface, and unequal texture throughout of the paper is the main cause of the Calotype failing in details, before the process of Daguerreotypy [*sic*]." Of calotypes, he wrote that "they look like the imperfect work of a man—and not the much diminished perfect work of God."[59]

The exposure time for Hill and Adamson's calotypes could be as long as two minutes. They photographed outdoors, usually in direct sunlight, often using monuments in Edinburgh's Greyfriars Kirkyard (churchyard) as a backdrop. They encouraged sitters to enrich their portraits with expressive props, such as books or drawing implements. In addition to their portrait work, Hill and Adamson made some of the earliest anthropological photographs in the nearby fishing village of Newhaven (Fig. 2.68), whose waning traditional way of life contrasted with

focus

The First Police Pictures?

An exceptional early series of 220 photographic portraits of itinerant people was made by the Swiss photographer and lithographer Carl Durheim (1810–1890) between 1852 and 1853. During a large-scale Swiss government operation, stateless, itinerant people were held in open confinement in the city of Bern, and forced to adopt a more settled life. They had generally been poor tradespeople who moved from town to town, subsisting as tinkers and grinders, or by making simple products such as baskets (Fig. 2.69).

The images were to be transformed from paper photographs into lithographs and given to the police to identify any of the itinerants who strayed from Bern. Thinking that it would make identification easier, the photographer tried to show as much of the person's body as possible. Although police pictures did not become routine until the 1880s, occasional portraits of criminals were made in the late 1850s and 1860s. The slow development was due to the absence of an accepted standard format with which to standardize them and of an adequate circulation network.

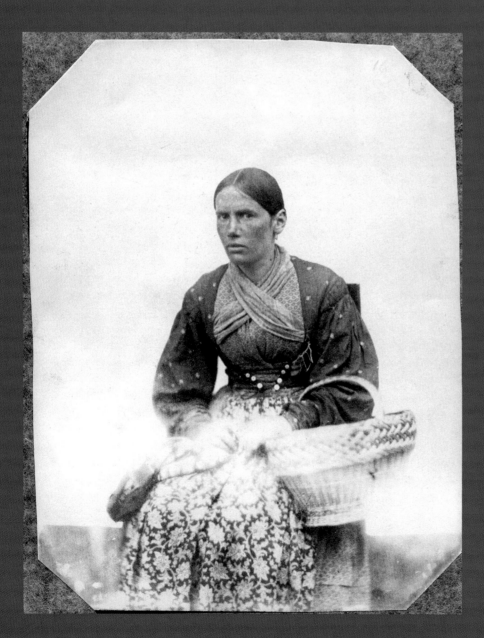

2.69
CARL DURHEIM, *Katharina Josephine Wächter*, 1852–53. Salted paper print. Swiss Federal Archive, Bern.

that of industrializing Edinburgh. These and other prints by Hill and Adamson appealed to the yearning for simpler, preindustrial times. They were sold singly or in albums, through booksellers and galleries, thus extending the market for photographs.

When the images were shown at the Royal Scottish Academy, Adamson was listed as executing the photographs, while Hill gave artistic direction. This information was perhaps intended to convince painters that photographs might be shown in their gallery. But it also indicates the split between conceptualization and implementation in early photography. For about a century after Hill's death in 1870, their collaborative work was largely credited to Hill's imagination as a painter, rather than to Adamson's technical virtuosity.[60]

THE REALITY EFFECT

Unlike painting and engraving, photography left relatively few visible traces of its manufacture. Compared with brushstrokes and a network of lines, the daguerreotype seemed like a smooth mirror that did not betray how it was made. As a result, the photograph was seen as an automatic recording device that required no interpretation. Increasingly the photograph was believed to be what the average person would have seen standing in the same spot at the same time as the photographer. Stereoscopic daguerreotypes, such as *The Geography Lesson* (see Fig. 2.55), added the illusion of three-dimensionality. The fact that photographers such as Baldus (see p. 51) manipulated and retouched negatives did not significantly affect the public's belief in photographic truth. Neither did the increasing use of calculated poses and studio props in portrait photography.

Belief in the medium's objective reflection of reality was reinforced by photographers' efforts to intensify the appearance of truth. For example, while ornate backgrounds and symbolic objects continued to be used, some photographers returned to the plain backgrounds of the earliest daguerreotypes, and had the sitter look directly into the camera. This technique made the photograph seem unaffected. By using bust shots, facial features were enlarged, sometimes to life size, giving the impression of a personal encounter, as if the viewer personally knew the sitter well enough to enter his or her private space.

With the increased "reality effect" came a lasting dilemma, detectable in many early photographs: the tension between visual intensity taken as truth and the larger, societal significance of a subject. This problem is evident in what may be the first daguerreotypes of Native Americans. During the 1840s, St. Louis photographer Thomas M. Easterly photographed the Sauk and the Fox, who were resettled by the U.S. government to the Nemaha Reservation in what is now the state of Kansas. His image of the chief Keokuk (Fig. 2.70) uses impressive detail, a simple backdrop, and restrained hand-coloring to connote immediacy and truthfulness. Yet this image was far from historically comprehensive. At the time it was made, Keokuk had been appointed by United States Indian Affairs officials to replace a more rebellious leader. He and other Sauk and Fox companions were in St. Louis to give an entertainment performance of so-called war dances at a circus. Like the photograph of the

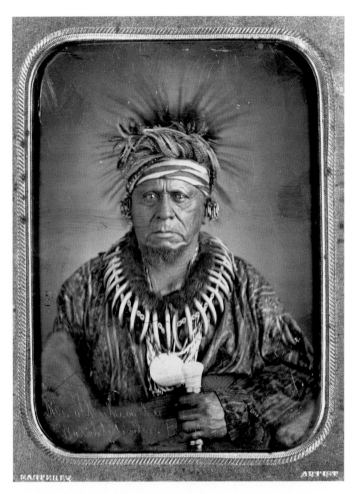

2.70
THOMAS EASTERLY, *Keokuk, or the Watchful Fox*, **1847. Hand-colored quarter-plate daguerreotype. Missouri Historical Society, St. Louis, Missouri.**

Easterly's portrait of Keokuk, or the Watchful Fox, a chief of the Sauk and Fox, concentrated on the sitter's worn face and distinctive clothing. He relied on a plain, neutral background to accentuate the sitter's pensive look, while he highlighted the exotic elements of Native American apparel.

1848 Chartist meeting (see Fig. 2.32), Keokuk's portrait does not lie, but nor does it tell the full story. In public discussions and literature, the capacity of the photograph to seem whole and complete, while omitting relevant truths, was rarely addressed directly. Nevertheless, the conflicts in society's understanding of photography and the problems of truth-telling found some expression in mid-nineteenth-century literature.

PHOTOGRAPHY AND FICTION

In overwrought language and outlandish plots, popular fiction played on the visual veracity of photography, suggesting that the medium could reach beneath the surface to penetrate the minds of sitters. It could thwart villains and make straight the path of true love. This good magic was complemented by stories of bad photographic magic, in which Svengali-like daguerreotypists

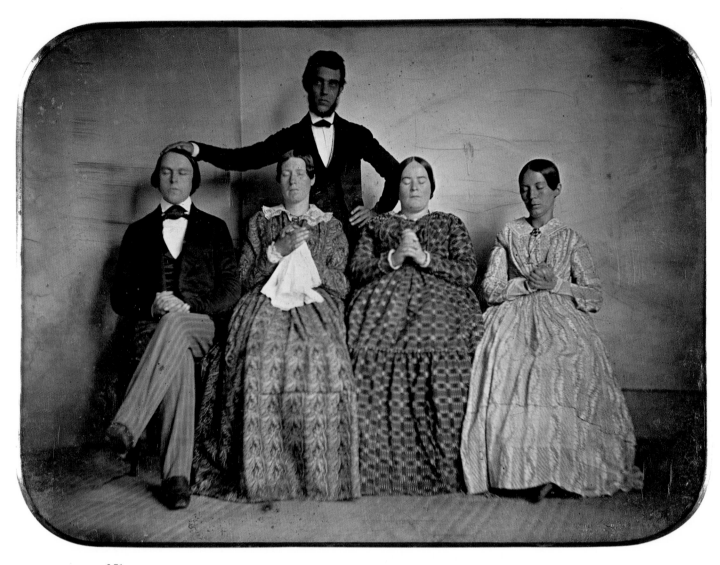

2.71
JOHN ADAMS WHIPPLE, *Hypnotism*, c. 1845. Daguerreotype, no. 113. Metropolitan Museum of Art, New York.

Hypnotism and photography were both associated with magic and mystery in the public mind. John Adams Whipple was the Boston scientist who, with George Phillips Bond, successfully made daguerreotype views of the moon in about 1851 (see Fig. 2.42).

spied on newlyweds and lured innocents from their families. In such stories, the mysterious and compelling powers of hypnotism and mesmerism (a variety of hypnotism thought to be induced by magnetic fields, in vogue during photography's early years) were merged with photography. Some sitters reported that they felt drawn to the camera's eye, or unnerved by the experience of being photographed, as if they were being scrutinized, or compelled to act like a marionette. In a daguerreotype of a hypnotism session, most of the participants appear unaware of the camera's presence, as though they are in what was termed a "magnetic sleep" (Fig. 2.71).

The best-known story about photography's double life as a recorder of reality and a mysterious generator of insights into character is Nathaniel Hawthorne's *The House of the Seven Gables*. By 1851, when Hawthorne published the novel, public perception of photography's relationship to truth had

emerged as a pivotal metaphor for knowledge and ignorance. The story's central character, Mr. Holgrave, is a daguerreotypist. His portraits have special powers, extending human sight into insight, and revealing what ordinary vision cannot bring into focus: the moral character of individuals.

The nineteenth-century trust in character reading of facial features and human gestures, which predated the invention of photography, soon transferred to photography. In *The House of the Seven Gables*, that faith was enhanced by the association of magic with daguerrean realism. Belief in the extraordinary powers of photography was manifest in sitters' requests to photographers, such as the one that photographers use tokens of the dead, for example a scarf or hat, to summon forth the image of the departed one for a photograph.[61] Fiction gave voice to the way in which growing public confidence in photographic representation was mixed with wariness about its power.

RETAKE

In the first years after photography's presentation to the world, photographers were cooperative and experimental. As a result, the medium was not sharply defined as either art or science, but frequently termed an art-science. Similarly, artists who took up photography in its early years enjoyed a hyphenated identity as painter-photographers.

But as more and more people tried the new medium, the diversity of photographic imagery grew and photography became a profession. During its second invention, photography evolved from a hobby and a handicraft to a local, national, and even international industry. Scotland's David Octavius Hill and Robert Adamson earned a living with their diverse images. Booksellers and publishers found markets for multiple copies of photographs. In England, William Henry Fox Talbot produced copies of his book *The Pencil of Nature* at the photographic processing establishment he founded. Noël Marie Paymal Lerebours's *Excursions Daguerriennes* recognized and whetted the public's appetite for images of faraway places. With another entrepreneur, Louis Désiré Blanquart-Evrard founded a photographic printing firm, where he mass-produced images and albums by photographers such as John Beasley Greene, Maxime Du Camp, and Henri Le Secq. In addition, photographers devised ways to expand their enterprises by offering photographs or photographically based images of political figures and entertainment celebrities.

Photographers began to specialize in a particular practice, such as portrait-making or landscapes. By the mid-1850s, the medium that initially seemed a wondrous phenomenon was rapidly becoming a routine part of Western life. At the same time, many of the profound changes arising in the first fifteen years of photography were less visible than the profusion of images generated by the new medium. Faith in photography as an impartial image-maker began to alter the human relationship to memory. No prior medium fully presaged the common photograph's ability to externalize remembrance, or to produce images conceived of as genuinely akin to actual experience. The sense of a personal encounter, of being there, connected individual experience with national and scientific events. What twentieth-century French philosopher Michel Foucault (1926–1984) called "compulsive visibility" began to play a much larger part in human affairs.[62] Societal, scientific, and even personal progress started to be understood as dependent on increased visibility of data in all fields of government and in intellectual inquiry.

As the notion that something might be photographed hardened into the expectation that it ought to be photographed, the public began to perceive a natural claim to see images of all sorts. This perception gave impetus to the making and marketing of a great array of pictures, from individual portraits to scientific images and the first efforts of photojournalism. The assumption that one would own a single photograph of oneself eventually yielded to the notion that one desired to own, or at least to see, many photographic images, including those of strangers and distant events. During photography's first fifteen years, the stage was set for the intense commercialization and dissemination of photography, which in turn sharpened the question of photography as a fine art, while deepening its acceptance as a chronicler.

philosophy and practice

A Threat to Art?

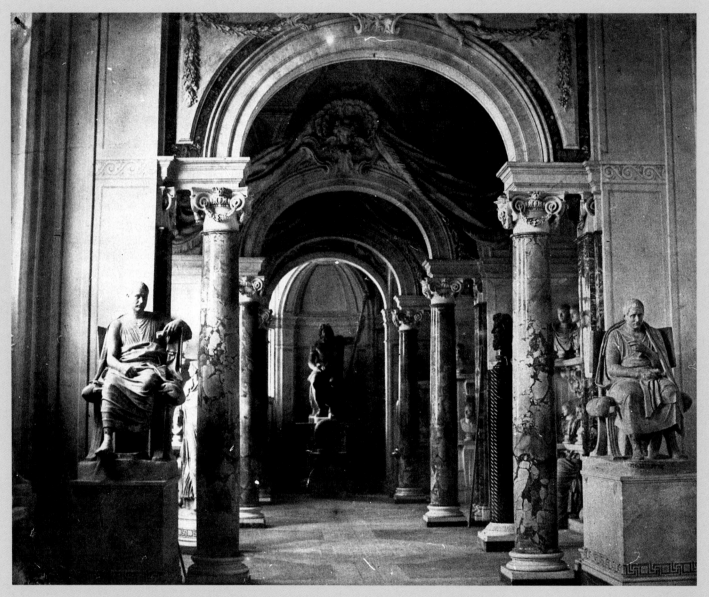

2.72
GIACOMO CANEVA, *Vatican Museum, view of interior*, 1847–52. Salted paper print. Biblioteca Panizzi, Reggio Emilia.

Two successful but different methods of making photographs were presented to the world in 1839. Although the daguerreotype and the calotype had different technical specifications, they were similarly portrayed as methods by which pictures could be made independently of the physical talent and mental effort of the camera operator. Talbot, Daguerre, and Niépce shied away from explaining photography as an invention that makes images through human agency. Each insisted that photography originated in nature and was disclosed by nature. Talbot wrote that photography depicts its images "by optical and chemical means alone"; the image is "impressed by Nature's hand." Daguerre put it this way: "the daguerreotype is not an instrument which serves to draw nature; but a chemical and physical process which gives her the power to reproduce herself." Niépce defined his accomplishment as "spontaneous reproduction, by the action of light." The initial legal agreement, drawn up by Niépce and Daguerre, spoke of Niépce's attempts "to fix the images which nature offers, without the assistance of a draughtsman."[63] Of course, photography's inventors observed the medium's verisimilitude and its reliable visual reproduction, but they stressed its apparent spontaneity: "auto-graphy," that is, nature's automatic writing.

Through these concepts, the medium was integrated with Western notions of empiricism, especially its core belief that knowledge should be based on disinterested observation, not personal opinion. The shared cultural imagining of photography—that is, the idea of photography—emphasized photography as a natural and neutral vision. The camera image was thought to be like the picture on the retina of the human eye, confirming an eighteenth-century proposition that the retinal image is completely independent of the subject's thoughts and feelings. Photography's neutral vision was conceived not only as a boon to science, but also as a socially symbolic anticipation of a future in which the world could be better known by more people—a means to democratize knowledge.

Photography is arguably the most historically aware visual medium. The writing of its history began with the disclosure of the medium to the world in 1839, and persisted as a preoccupation throughout nineteenth-century photographic literature. Isidore Niépce, son of Joseph Nicéphore Niépce, attempted to assert his father's place in history with a slim 1841 volume called *Historique de la découverte improprement nommé daguerréotype* (*History of the Discovery Improperly Called Daguerreotype*). In the same year, Robert Hunt (1807–1887), a geologist and staunch advocate of photography from the first, published *A Popular Treatise on the Art of Photography*, which served to introduce the public to both photographic history and techniques.

Photography's association with the broad technological changes taking place in the industrializing world was firmly fixed within the medium's first decade. Both its proponents and its critics likened photography to such major modern inventions as the steam engine and the telegraph. Writing in 1840 about Italian Renaissance art, British critic Francis Palgrave (1788–1861) produced a vituperative aside on modern inventions, including photography: "Steam-engine and furnace, the steel plate, the roller, the press, the Daguerreotype, the Voltaic battery, and the lens, are the antagonist principles of art."[64] By contrast, an unnamed commentator for an 1843 issue of the *Edinburgh Review* effused that photography "is indeed as great a step in the fine arts, as the steam-engine was in the mechanical arts … and … it will take the highest rank among the inventions of the present age." Yet this writer urged his readers to make a clear distinction between the linear, cumulative development of science and technology, and what constitutes genuine advancement in art. Progress in art, the reviewer declared, was not endlessly incremental: "It would be hazardous to assert that Apelles and Zeuxis were surpassed by Reynolds and Lawrence, and still more so that Praxiteles and Phidias must have yielded the palm to Canova and Chantrey."[65]

As belief in the objectivity of photography took hold, the medium was belittled as a potential art form. Influential British critic John Ruskin (1819–1900) contradicted himself on the matter of the daguerreotype. After calling it a blessing in 1845, less than a year later he found it a matter of serious concern. Acknowledging the daguerreotype as "the most marvellous invention of the century," Ruskin worried about its effects on viewers' perceptions of art: "As regards art, I wish it had never been discovered, it will make the eye too fastidious to accept mere handling."[66]

Photography, for Ruskin, was so wedded to minute appearances that it could not express the personality and soul of the artist. His was a new twist on an old theme: after an October 1839 exhibition of daguerreotypes at the Academy of Arts in St. Petersburg, Russia, one reviewer reported that "the daguerreotype is a useless means of making portraits," because "mathematical verisimilitude and lifeless precision do not do justice to a portrait, for which one needs expression and life; these can only be conveyed by the animating strength of talent and thought of an individual—no machine can do this."[67] Similarly, Eugène Delacroix, who sometimes used photographs as aids for his work, called the camera a machine that makes pictures untrue to human perception. Where the mind filters and emphasizes, the machine does not. It cannot engage the world as the mind can, and its intractable verisimilitude prevented the dialogue of soul to soul that Delacroix deemed the central activity of art.[68]

Criticism of photography's mechanical simplicity merged easily with passionate contemporary reproach of the damaging social effects inherent in mass culture. In France, Flaubert recoiled from what he called "a whorish century," filled with "fake materials, fake luxury, fake pride." Literary critic C.-A. Sainte-Beuve (1804–1869) decried the advent of industrial literature, which he thought was served up to satisfy base emotions, rather than edify.[69] In this intellectual atmosphere, photographic verisimilitude became a bludgeon in the hands of photography's critics. French critic Étienne-Jean Delécluze (1781–1863) saw photography as a science imposing its mode of dogged imitation on art.[70] Advocates of photography responded by suggesting that photography could improve public taste, particularly through art reproduction, which was attempted early in the 1840s[71] (Fig. 2.72).

Controversy about the meaning and social impact of photographic realism was just beginning. The debate that was born with the medium continues in different forms, of course, in the early twenty-first century.

PART TWO

The Expanding Domain (1854-1880)

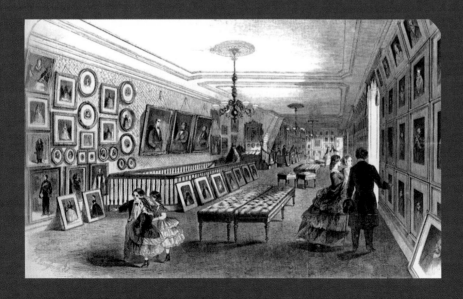

In an 1857 journal article, Lady Elizabeth Eastlake (1809–1893) marveled at the growth of photography since its disclosure to the world in 1839. "Since then," she wrote, "photography has become a household word and a household want; it is used alike by art and science, by love, business, and justice; it is found in the most sumptuous salon, and in the dingiest attic."[1] Photographic images were displayed in shop windows, and newspapers used photographic sources for their illustrations. At the same time, with the continued spread of photography, the development of new applications, and the intense commercialization of the medium in the late 1850s, amazement at its ability to capture appearances declined. As photography became more commonplace, the medium's societal and artistic impact was more frequently debated.

The rapid commercialization of photography sprang from the interaction of social needs and technical inventions. The convenience of the COLLODION, or wet-plate, process, and the resulting availability of low-priced prints stimulated the market for portraits of family, friends, and public figures. As the telegraph, railroad, steamship, and clipper speeded up communications, commerce, and travel, the desire for portraits and views kept pace. For instance, in the months leading up to the outbreak of the American Civil War in 1861, the market for inexpensive portraits of people in the news grew at an unparalleled rate.[2] Also, war and topical photography began to increase the public's demand for recent images of important events. Photographs from the Crimean War, from the so-called Indian Mutiny, and from the American Civil War were shown in galleries. Views of biblical and exotic places were also wanted. In Britain, the views of Egypt by British photographer Francis Frith (1822–1898) were anticipated keenly.

At the same time, the growing market for low-priced photographs intensified the contrast between the so-called "cheap johns" who churned these out and those who hoped to elevate photography to the status of a fine art. By the mid-1850s, members of the Photographic Society in England worried that members who made their living as photographers would degrade the society, and some attempted to pass a rule that would exclude from the society's exhibitions any photograph that had hung in a shop window.[3] Ultimately, "High Art photography" was brought into being by photographers and critics concerned to link the new medium to the betterment of individuals. It put photography in the service of public morality by trying to make the medium ennoble and instruct its viewers in proper conduct. The perceived divide between popular and art photography, begun in the middle of the nineteenth century, lasted almost one hundred years.

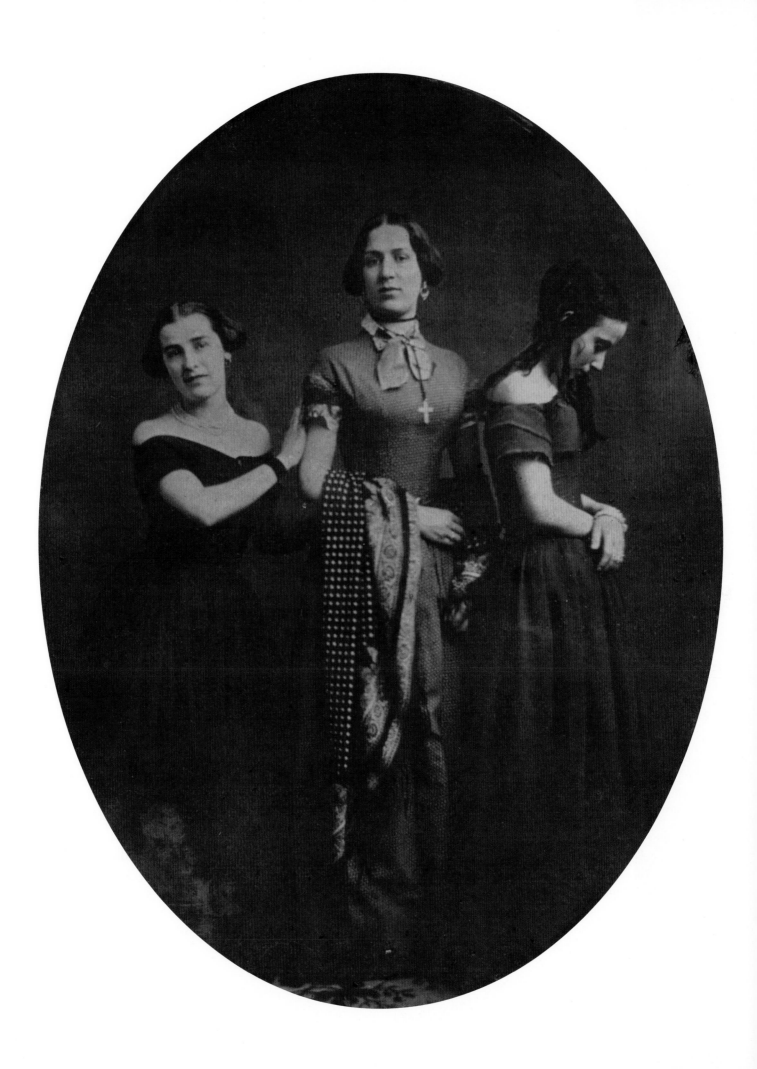

CHAPTER THREE

Popular Photography and the Aims of Art

The idea of photographic imaging as acutely accurate representation permeated many aspects of life and invigorated lively discussion in the art world. An 1860 issue of the *Art Journal* contended that "the photograph cannot deceive; in nothing can it extenuate; there is no power in this marvellous machine either to add or to take from: we know what we see must be *true*."[1] To many artists and critics, photographic truth seemed somehow allied with moral truth. Writing in 1859, Francis Frith argued that

We can scarcely avoid moralizing in connection with this subject; since truth is a divine quality, at the very foundation of everything that is lovely in earth and heaven; and it is, we argue, quite impossible that this quality can so obviously and largely pervade a popular art, without exercising the happiest and most important influence, both upon the tastes and the morals of the people.

At the same time, Frith wrote, photography was "too truthful. It insists upon giving us 'the truth, the whole truth, and nothing but the truth.' Now, we want, in Art, the first and the last of these conditions, but we can dispense very well with the middle term."[2]

The debate over how to make room for imaginative camerawork while maintaining respect for the utilitarian uses of photography became a war of words. A British portrait photographer, C. Jabez Hughes (1819–1884), suggested that photography ought to be divided into three classes. The first, mechanical photography, was literal or exact depiction. In the second category, art photography, the maker, not content with

things as they appear, "determines to infuse his mind into them by arranging, modifying, or otherwise disposing them, so they may appear in a more appropriate or beautiful manner." The last category included "certain pictures which aim at higher purposes than the majority of art-photographs, and whose aim is not merely to amuse, but to instruct, purify, and ennoble."[3] The many tensions between depiction and imagination, objective description and moral uplift, education and amusement permeate photographic practice and criticism.

PHOTOGRAPHIC SOCIETIES, PUBLICATIONS, AND EXCHANGE CLUBS

The expansion of photographic practice in the mid-nineteenth century promoted the growth of photographic associations. Photographers with divergent interests formed societies in order to promote the medium to the general public, hold exhibitions, trade technical information, and publish newsletters or journals. As cheap photographs became increasingly available, the photographic societies viewed themselves as bulwarks against inferior products and assaults on public taste.

Some groups, such as the Photographic Exchange Club in Britain, modeled themselves on organizations in the graphic arts, and traded images. Also in Britain, the Photographic Society of London, founded in 1853, was quickly followed by city-based photographic societies. The status of the Photographic Society was enhanced when Queen Victoria and Prince Albert became patrons. The society published the *Journal of the Photographic Society*, which later became the *Photographic Journal*. Other societies and journals helped to disseminate

3.1
GABRIEL HARRISON, *Past, Present, Future,* **1854. George Eastman House, Rochester, New York.**

technical information and news of exhibits. The French Société Heliographique, which began in 1851, published the influential journal *La Lumière*. The group was succeeded by the French Photographic Society in 1855. The Photographic Society in Vienna, Austria, founded in 1861, was the first in the German-speaking world. Photographic clubs and publications sprang up throughout Europe, North and South America, and in colonial India and Asia.

In addition, private publishers set up such journals as the *Photographic Art Journal*, which was founded by Henry Hunt Snelling in 1851, and *Anthony's Photographic Journal*, published by E. and H. T. Anthony & Co. from 1870. The rise of the periodical press in the mid-nineteenth century, especially newspapers and journals that began to use photographically derived engravings, opened new markets. Two American weekly papers with readerships that promptly soared into the millions were *Frank Leslie's Illustrated Newspaper*, started in 1855, and *Harper's Weekly*, begun two years later. Each was dedicated to bringing the public visual accounts of current events.[4]

The increase in photographic organizations and publications helped to create commentators and critics who specialized in reviewing exhibitions and new work, not just for their members and readers, but also for large-circulation magazines and newspapers.

THE STEREOGRAPH

Chief among the low-priced photographs that burgeoned in the later nineteenth century was the STEREOGRAPH. Stereographic photographs helped turn photography into an industry, by stoking the viewer's desire to see more of the world. The principle of the stereograph was known before the invention of photography, and applied to daguerreotypes (see Fig. 2.55). Stereographs became immensely popular from the mid-1850s to the early twentieth century, with improvements in the technology of paper photography, and with the development of special cameras that used two lenses. During the 1840s, stereographic daguerreotypes had been made by joining images produced by two separate cameras, but the new stereographic camera produced two simultaneous images, photographed as if one were seen with the left eye and the other with the right (Fig. 3.2). Placed in a special viewer, the images recombined to give the illusion of receding space. Given their ease of production, photographers and publishers quickly sought ways of mass-producing and distributing stereographs. One of the largest nineteenth-century photographic supply houses and publishers of photographs, E. and H. T. Anthony & Co. in New York, was said to have stereographs of fifty thousand different subjects, including views of Broadway traffic.[5] Producers of stereographs manufactured millions of images, and set up the distribution networks with which to market them (Fig. 3.3).

To twenty-first-century viewers, stereographs may seem airless, static, and artificial. But to nineteenth-century viewers, the stereograph was a quite unprecedented leap forward in realistic representation, which opened up great expectations. In a swooning 1859 essay on "The Stereoscope and the Stereograph," Oliver Wendell Holmes (see p. 3), the well-known Boston-area physician, photographer, and writer on photography, noted

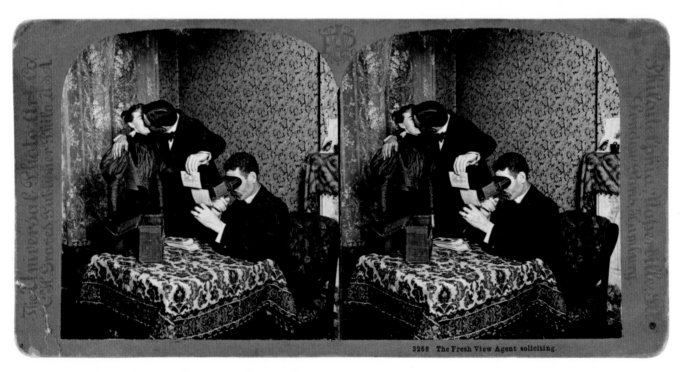

3.2
PHOTOGRAPHER UNKNOWN, *The Fresh View Agent Soliciting*, from *Stereoscopes in Use*, c. 1860s. Stereograph. George Eastman House, Rochester, New York.

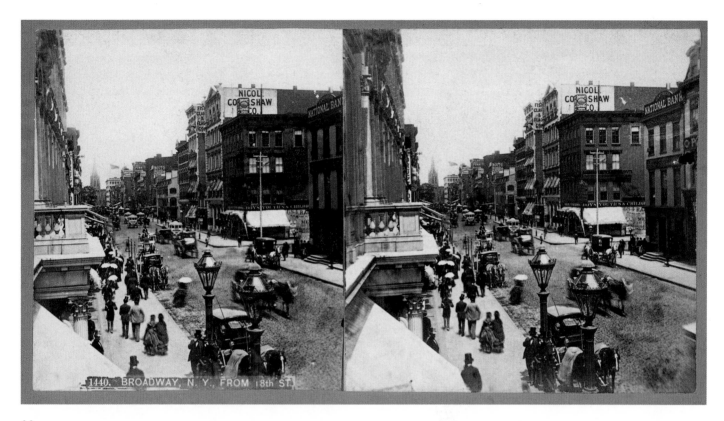

3.3
PHOTOGRAPHER UNKNOWN, *Looking up Broadway from the Corner of Broome Street*, 1868. Stereograph. Albumen silver print, 1868–71.
Library of Congress, Washington, D.C.

that when looking at the image, "the mind feels its way into the very depths of the picture," awestruck at its inexhaustible detail.[6] Holmes had a knack for describing the physical feelings experienced when using the viewing instrument: "The shutting out of surrounding objects, and the concentration of the whole attention … produce a dreamlike exaltation of the faculties, a kind of clairvoyance, in which we seem to leave the body behind us and sail away into one strange scene after another, like disembodied spirits."[7] Holmes thought the stereograph surpassed painting in its intense illusionism and in its potential to broadcast knowledge to a wide audience. It would become "the card of introduction to make all mankind acquaintances," and it would simulate the feeling of being present at natural wonders such as the Alps and human marvels such as the pyramids. For Holmes, the stereograph was a watershed moment in the progress of human history:

Form is henceforth divorced from matter. … Give us a few negatives of things worth seeing. … There is only one Coliseum or Pantheon; but how many millions of potential negatives have they shed— representatives of billions of pictures. … Every conceivable object of Nature and Art will soon scale off its surface for us. … The time will come when a man who wishes to see any object, natural or artificial will go to the Imperial, National, or City Stereographic Library and call for its skin or form. … We do now distinctly propose the creation of a comprehensive and systematic stereographic library, where all men

can find the special forms they particularly desire to see as artists, or as scholars, or as mechanics, or in any other capacity.[8]

The growth of science and its organizing systems, particularly in such areas of public interest as geology, geography, biology, and ethnography, helped to stimulate the stereograph market, as did colonial expansion and global commerce. Behind the eagerness for stereographs was the ideal of democratic access to information. "What an educational revolution is here, my countrymen," wrote a critic in an 1858 issue of the British journal the *Athenaeum*. "Why our Tommys and Harrys will know the world's surface as well as a circumnavigator. … What a stock of knowledge our Tommys and Harrys will begin life with! Perhaps in ten years or so the question will be seriously discussed … whether it will be any use to travel now that you can send out your artist to bring home Egypt in his carpetbag to amuse the drawing room with."[9] Stereography thus concocted a pleasing combination of education and entertainment that presaged what the late twentieth century would call "infotainment." In the words of a French commentator, photography increasingly seemed capable of "enlightening the masses so as to elevate and amend them."[10]

Stereographs were produced and marketed through a global network of publishers and dealers. The public's desire to collect "stereos," as they were called, created a boom-and-bust economy in the images as photographers and publishers attempted to entice the public with new subjects to view. Sometimes a photographer or publisher created a best-selling stereo or set of stereo cards; at other times the images moldered in warehouses while the company that issued them went bankrupt. The vogue highlighted the issue of images as property. When stereographs were pirated from one publishing house and published by another, civil penalties were seldom applied and copyright laws proved inadequate.

Demand led more photographers to carry stereo cameras along with their regular equipment. Moreover, ambitious photographers started to conceive the image with reference to the stereograph's ability to render depth. In landscape photography, for example, the photographers picked or even composed scenes in which an object such as a fallen tree or wedge patterns of dark and light would lead the eye from the foreground to the middle ground, and then on to distant hills (see Fig. 4.56).

Portraits were seldom done in the stereo format, because the illusion of deep pictorial space would have been distracting. But almost every other subject was conceivable as a stereograph.

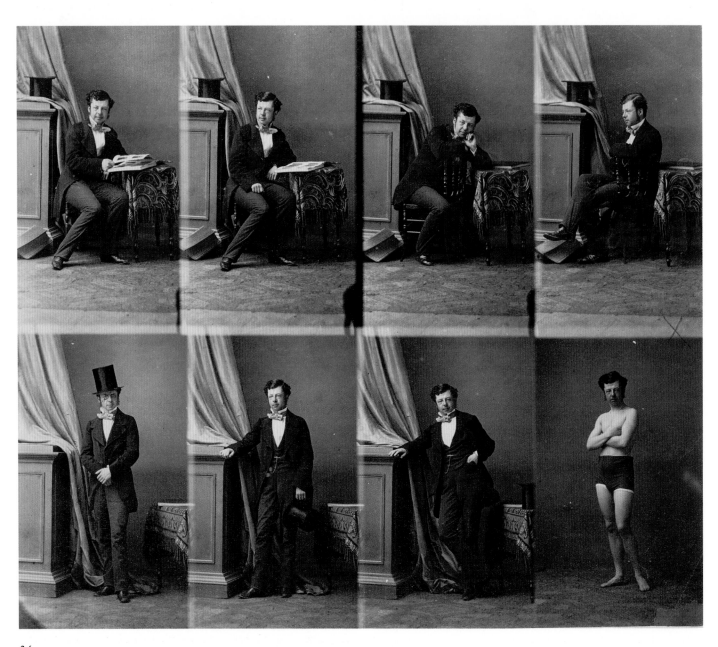

3.4
ANDRÉ ADOLPHE EUGÈNE DISDÉRI, *Prince Lobkowitz*, 1858. Metropolitan Museum of Art, New York.

The market swelled with sets of stereographs devoted to such themes as travel, religion, urban vistas, and architecture. Romance and courtship were depicted by photographers who contrived stories and used actors to perform scenes. Pornographic stereos were available for beholding in small, discreet viewing devices. When photographers from the North and the South went forth to photograph the American Civil War (1861–65), they often brought along a stereographic camera. Because these cameras were lighter and more portable than the standard view camera, photographers sometimes used them to make images that they did not intend to issue as stereographs.

THE *CARTE-DE-VISITE*

Whereas the appeal of the stereograph is easy to understand, the success of the *CARTE-DE-VISITE*, or "card photograph" as it was called in the United States, is less obviously apparent. Perfected and patented in 1854 by French photographer André Adolphe Eugène Disdéri (1819–1889), the *carte-de-visite* was a small portrait photograph originally intended to be pasted to the back of a regular visiting card (4 by 2½ inches) (Fig. 3.4). Like the stereographic camera, the standard *carte-de-visite* camera had more than one lens. But whereas the stereo camera took two pictures at the same time, the *carte-de-visite* camera was constructed so that up to eight different images of the sitter could be exposed on one photographic plate.

The cheapness of the *carte-de-visite* portrait, resulting from its efficient means of production, partly explains its rapid acceptance. Many *cartes-de-visite* were full-length portraits, or bust-length shots, rather than close-up studies of the face. The distance from the camera, especially in the full-length portraits, eliminated the need for and expense of careful lighting and time-consuming retouching. The success of the *carte-de-visite* also derived from the liberal use of fancy furniture and painted backdrops calculated to make the sitter appear rich. Like the later daguerreotypes, *cartes-de-visite* encouraged sitters to construct an image of self-satisfaction and financial prosperity. Some photographers even stocked lavish clothing, which they rented to sitters for the photographic moment.

The vogue for *carte-de-visite* photographs was, like that for stereographs, propelled by a collecting urge. People amassed *cartes* of famous people much as they accumulated stereos of notable natural wonders, placing them in plush albums. Such renowned figures as France's Emperor Napoleon III, President Abraham Lincoln in the United States, and members of Britain's royal family recognized the public's craving to possess their likenesses, and willingly posed for photographers. In Mexico, Emperor Maximilian shifted the *carte* from the famous to the infamous, when he ordered that prostitutes be registered and *cartes* made of them so as to protect soldiers. But, as scholar John Mraz concluded, the women often used the photographs as an opportunity to construct a visual identity at odds with the emperor's intent.[11]

Eventually, speculation in *carte* subjects ran high, and overproduction was common, resulting in an even more precarious market than that for the stereograph. The vogue lasted about ten years, having saturated the market with millions of images.[12]

ART AND PHOTOGRAPHY

ART REPRODUCTION

On the face of it, the photographic reproduction of artworks seems a simple project. Suggested early in photography's history by François Arago and William Henry Fox Talbot (see pp. 19–21), the reproduction of works of art began as an effort to combine the cataloging capability of photography with the interests of education. In 1852, Roger Fenton was employed to photograph prints, drawings, and sculpture at the British Museum in London, a position he took up again at the end of the Crimean War.[13] The art dealers P. & D. Colnaghi negotiated with the museum to sell the museum's photographs.[14] Similarly, Charles Thurston Thompson, the photographer at the South Kensington Museum who trained British Royal Engineers in the medium (see p. 129), photographed items from the museum's collections.

As early as 1851, Francis Wey suggested that the Musée du Louvre in Paris create a gallery of photographs of paintings by French artists not represented in French museums.[15] In Paris, the Print Room of the Bibliothèque Nationale and the Bibliothèque des Arts Décoratifs collected photographs of architecture and art during the second half of the nineteenth century. At the same time, museums were collecting, however haphazardly and sporadically, works by leading photographers who specialized in picturesque views or architectural photography.

Photographers soon formed firms largely devoted to art reproduction. In 1866, Alsatian photographer Adolphe Braun (1812–1877) began an art reproduction business that quickly became international both in the scope of its reproductions and in its sales. Fratelli Alinari Fotografi Editori, a company that still sells art reproductions, was founded in Florence, Italy, in 1852. *Photographic Art Treasures* (1856), a collection of picturesque views, art reproductions, and morally edifying photographs, appeared in Britain. Throughout the 1860s and 1870s, publishers in Italy, Germany, and France produced *cartes-de-visite* that illustrated art objects. Lantern slides, sometimes called "magic lantern slides," were made of art objects and architecture. The magic lantern was a device for projecting images on to a screen; early lanterns used oil lamps. In the 1870s, when courses on the history of art were slowly introduced into America, Great Britain, Germany, and France, the market for slides increased.[16]

In the later nineteenth century, the rationale for making photographs of art objects available to the public was more democratically phrased than Arago or Talbot had considered, and came to the fore in a more commercial culture than either of them envisaged. American photographer Marcus Aurelius Root (1808–1888) emphasized that images of culture, as well as nature, could benefit "the lowliest of the community." Photographs could bring to "the masses … abundant and infinitely various stores of knowledge and entertainment," invented in 1839 by British engravers and renewed by several experimenters, including French image-makers A. Cuvelier (1812–1871) and L. Granguillaume (active 1850s), in 1853. It employed a glass plate covered with a dark coating, like opaque black varnish, something akin to Talbot's earliest experiments (see p. 19). The artist scratched an image into the coating with a sharp stylus, making what amounted to a hand-drawn negative. The plate was placed on sensitized paper, and exposed to light; many prints could be made from one plate (Fig. 3.5). Because the *cliché verre* seemed neither sufficiently handmade nor wholly photographic, however, it found only limited success.

The notion that photography could replicate art more accurately than other reproductive media arose because of the belief that photography itself was not an art—that is, not a medium open to imagination or subjective response. This belief in photography's objectivity prompted a variety of responses from those who defined art as an expression of human imagination. The American painter Rembrandt Peale (1778–1860) succinctly summed up the complaint when he wrote, "We do not see with the eyes only, but with the soul."[20]

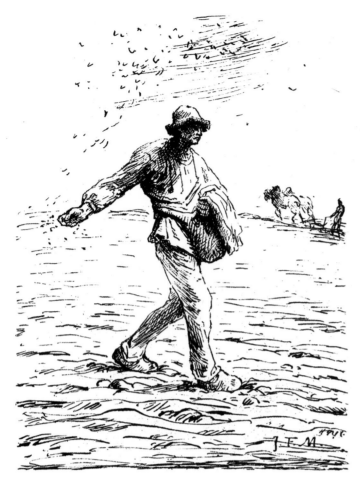

3.5
JEAN-FRANÇOIS MILLET, *The Sower*, 1862. *Cliché verre*. Victoria and Albert Museum, London.

and "no small measure of artistic training."[17] Art education was linked with the process of cultivating taste and temperament in the poor; in an era that stressed self-improvement, art reproduction was touted as a social equalizer. "With a pile of pictures by their sides, which cost almost nothing, they can make the European tour of celebrated places, and not leave the warm precincts of their own firesides," wrote one observer.[18] Reviewing an exhibit of art reproductions, the *Athenaeum* pronounced that "The old selfish aristocratic days of hoarding are gone for ever. Rare Titians, kept in cases to be gloated over at a miserly moment, will be seized and photographed … Great and true Art is republican, and is for all men, needing no education to appreciate it—no more than we need education when we fall in love."[19]

PHOTOGRAPHY AS A FINE ART

The emphasis on photographic imagery as rendering what actually took place before the camera helped to suppress the use of a partially photographic technique called the CLICHÉ VERRE,

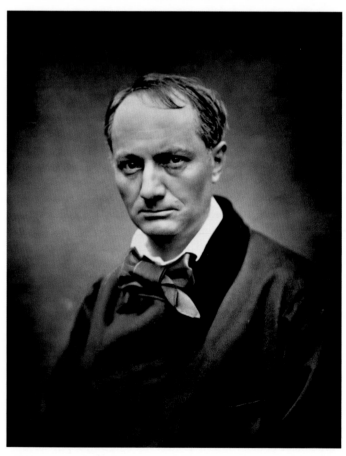

3.6
ÉTIENNE CARJAT, *Charles Baudelaire*, c. 1862. Woodburytype. Metropolitan Museum of Art, New York.

Although he was friendly with such photographers as Carjat and Nadar, Baudelaire did not believe that photography could be an art. Carjat set up his portrait of Baudelaire against a plain background, and carefully modulated the lighting of the face to bring out the poet's strength of concentration.

French poet and critic Charles Baudelaire (1821–1867) (Fig. 3.6) accepted photography as a means of record-keeping, yet lamented what he saw as its broad social consequences. He contended that photography's supporters were unwittingly constricting the range of human imagination. Baudelaire wrote that "each day art further diminishes its self-respect by bowing down before external reality; each day the painter becomes more and more given to painting not what he dreams but what he sees."[21] He thought that those who considered that "Photography and Art are the same thing"[22] thinly rationalized soul-deadening matter-of-fact pictures. Similarly, the French painter Eugène Delacroix insisted on a crucial differentiation between the insights that follow on the interaction of eye and mind and what occurs in the process of photography. Although Delacroix commissioned photographic studies of models to be used in his paintings (see Fig. 2.59), he insisted that the camera was a machine that yielded pictures untrue to the complexities of human perception. For him the central activity of art—soul speaking to soul—was foreclosed by photography.[23] While many painters in Europe and America collected, commissioned, and used photographs, they insisted that the camera was merely a recording instrument. The influence of the photograph on art was seldom discussed positively, even by painters such as Jean-Léon Gérôme (1824–1904), whose highly detailed views of the Middle East resemble contemporary photographs in glossy appearance, fine detail, and subject matter.[24]

Both Baudelaire and Delacroix sat for photographers and socialized in their circles. French photographer Étienne Carjat (1828–1906) was typical of the emergent artist-photographer who led a bohemian life. Trained as a painter and working as a caricaturist and writer, Carjat moved in the world of Paris culture, where he met writers, musicians, artists, and their patrons (see Fig. 3.6). Comparable portrait work was done by another French caricaturist turned photographer, Nadar (real name Gaspard-Félix Tournachon). Nadar drew political cartoons and caricatures of prominent figures, and conceived his Panthéon Nadar as a lithograph that would show a thousand portraits of contemporary celebrities. He managed to complete only one section of the grandiose work, in 1854 (Fig. 3.7). Nadar learned photography late in 1853, at about the same time as his

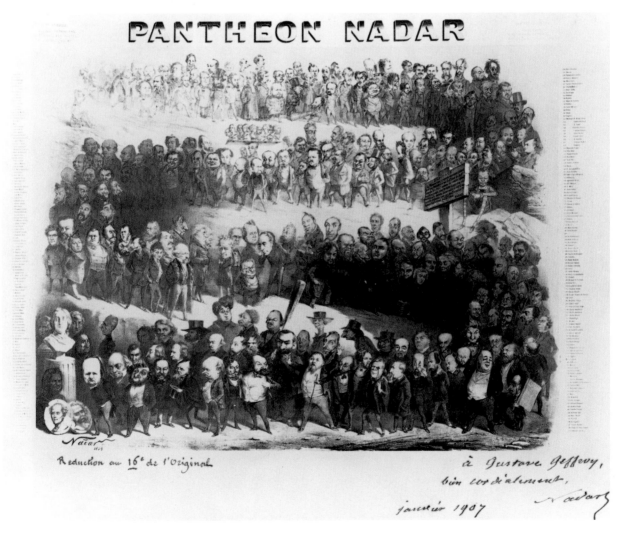

3.7
NADAR, *Panthéon Nadar*, 1854. Lithographic print. George Eastman House, Rochester, New York.

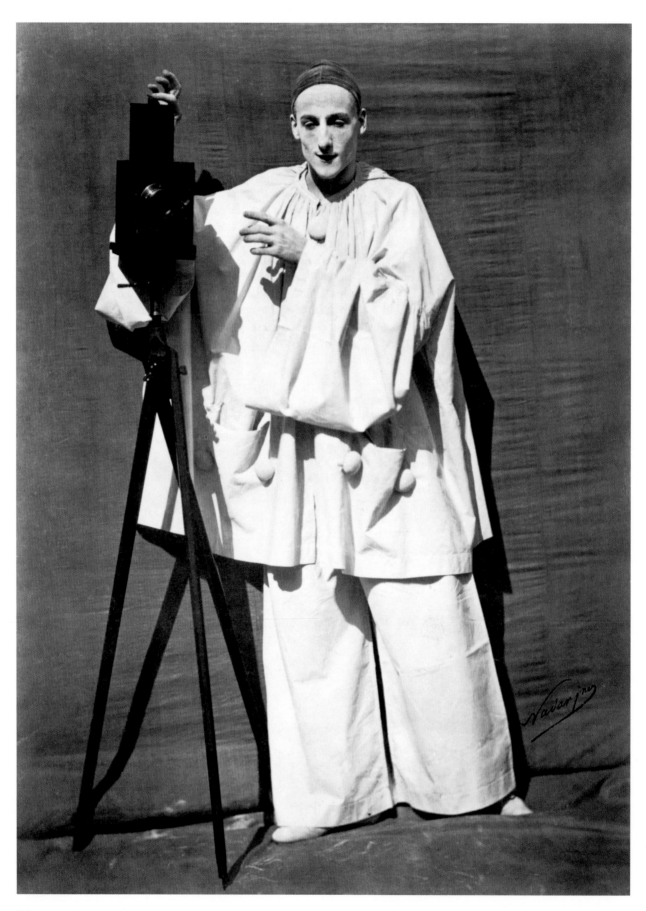

3.8
NADAR AND ADRIEN TOURNACHON, *Pierrot the Photographer*, 1854–55. Paper print. Musée Carnavalet, Paris.

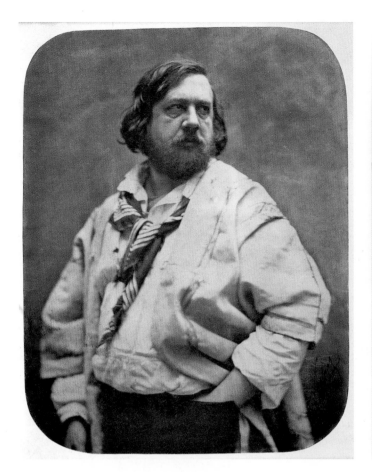

3.9
NADAR, *Théophile Gautier*, 1854–55. Albumen salted paper print, mounted on Bristol board. Musée d'Orsay, Paris.

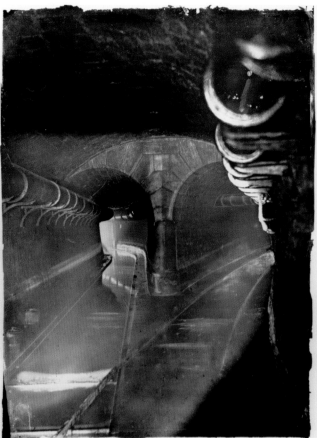

3.10
NADAR, *The Sewers of Paris*, 1864–65. Modern print from a glass negative. Caisse Nationale des Monuments Historiques et des Sites, Paris.

Nadar used a carbon arc lamp to create an eerie, ghostly apparition of subterranean Paris, etched into immortality by Victor Hugo's book *Les Misérables*.

brother Adrien Tournachon, who would go on to aid Duchenne de Boulogne (see p. 150). In a short-lived partnership, the brothers produced a series of photographs of the mime artist Jean-Charles Deburau, posed as Pierrot (Fig. 3.8).[25]

Nadar initially capitalized on the upper-class taste for images of creative people. His quick perception and judgment, learned as a caricaturist, helped him to specialize in making heroic portraits of contemporary cultural figures, especially bohemian artists and writers. Nadar not only sold large, high-priced images, but also marketed his public persona. With photographer Gustave Le Gray (see Figs. 2.49, 2.50), he maintained that he was not a simple operator of photographic equipment but an artist, sensitive to the nuances of personal character as well as rules of composition. "What can't be learned," he wrote, "it's the sense of light, it's the artistic appreciation of the effects produced by different and combined qualities of light."[26]

Nadar's photographic studio became a fashionable intellectual salon.[27] Like David Octavius Hill (see p. 64) and Mathew Brady (see p. 104), he conceptualized photographs, and he posed his sitters, but the image was produced and developed by a staff that grew in numbers with his success. Nadar's portrait of Théophile Gautier (1811–1872), boisterous proponent of art for art's sake and author of the influential novel about Parisian bohemian life *Mademoiselle de Maupin* (1835), visually summarizes the writer's antagonism toward the middle-class values of orderliness and civility (Fig. 3.9).

In addition to photography, Nadar was a fervent advocate of balloon transportation and aerial reconnaissance. He produced the first photographs of Paris from the basket of his balloon *Le Géant* (*The Giant*), and he administered the airmail service during the siege of Paris.[28] Nadar also experimented with artificial light, making the first photographs of the Paris sewers using a carbon arc lamp powered by Bunsen batteries (Fig. 3.10). His interest in science and technology complemented his reputation as a multitalented originator. Coupled with the artistic and literary circles in which he moved, this helped considerably to elevate the status of the photographer generally.

HIGH ART PHOTOGRAPHY

Other efforts to elevate the public perception of photography included emulating the conventional subjects of painting. The popularity of photographic still lifes, beginning with Daguerre,

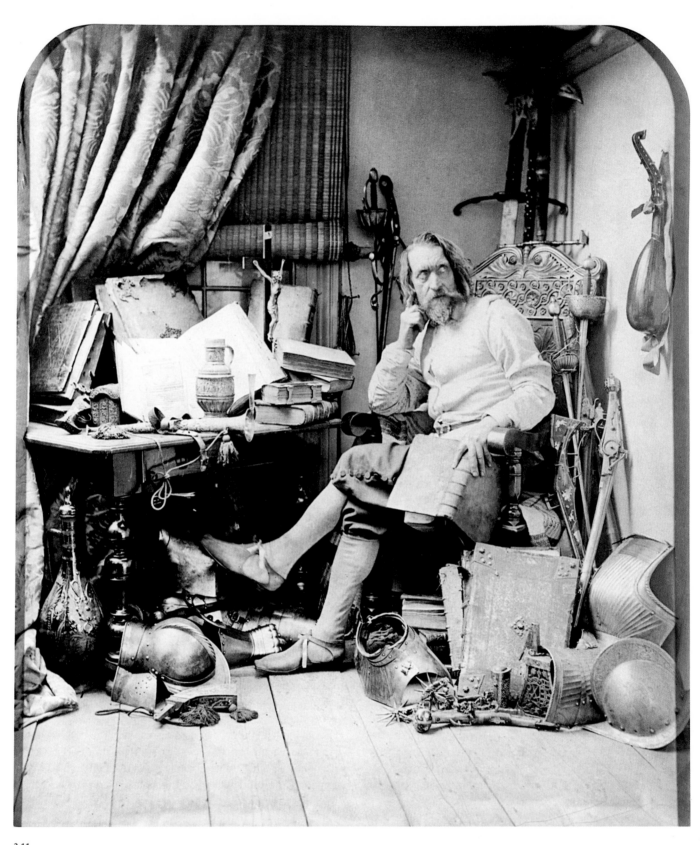

3.11
WILLIAM LAKE PRICE, *Don Quixote in his Study*, **early 1850s. Albumen print from a wet collodion negative.**
Victoria and Albert Museum, London.

indicates the success of this course, while Gabriel Harrison (1818–1902), who had strong interest in the theater, posed actors in dramatic scenes that were appreciated in his time as an exploration of the poetic in photography (Fig. 3.1). A different approach, which occurred mostly in Britain, also borrowed from the painterly tradition. It took up the notion of High Art photography outlined by photographer C. Jabez Hughes, "to instruct, purify, and ennoble." In this photography, emphasis was placed not simply on artistic scenes but on edifying subject matter, such as incidents from the Bible or literary sources, including Shakespeare, Alfred, Lord Tennyson, and Walter Scott. *Tableaux vivants*, literally "living pictures," were popular subjects for early photographers. The *tableau* required that the actors hold their poses for about twenty seconds, a time well suited to photography.[29] Photography was also influenced by sentimental or moralizing paintings and engravings, as in the stereographs of British photographer James Elliott (1835–1903).

William Lake Price (1810–1896), a British painter who adopted photography, made portraits of famous people, scenes from everyday life, still-life studies, and *tableaux vivants* from literature. His image of Don Quixote, hero of the romance of the same name by Miguel de Cervantes (1547–1616), drew upon the tradition of inspirational or uplifting painting (Fig. 3.11). It also engaged the interest in historically accurate representation that was flourishing in painting at the time. Lake Price combined his knowledge of art principles and the techniques of photography in his 1858 publication *A Manual of Photographic Manipulation*.

The most famous High Art photograph was constructed by Oscar Rejlander (1813–1875), who worked with Charles Darwin to create studies of human expression (see p. 151). Like many mid-century photographers, Rejlander began as a painter. While studying art in Rome, he made a living by copying Old Master paintings. There he became acquainted with Raphael's famous fresco *The School of Athens*, whose composition and theme of opposing points of view became the basis for a large photographic work, *The Two Ways of Life*, exhibited in 1857 (Fig. 3.12). In the center of the Raphael fresco, Plato points toward the heavens, the realm of the ideal, and Aristotle seems to point to the earth, source of material knowledge. In Rejlander's *The Two Ways of Life*, a sage introduces two youths to life: the one on the right embraces the moral life of honest industry; on the left, a callow rake is about to venture into a life of dissipation and debauchery. The women who posed were from Madame Warton's (sometimes Wharton) Troupe, a popular theatrical group who performed *tableaux vivants* derived from paintings and, especially, Classical sculpture.[30]

The large print, about 31 inches wide, was made from more than thirty individual negatives in a technique termed COMBINATION PRINTING, which required a great deal of handwork. Rejlander argued that the labor involved, combined with the image's inspiration from a Renaissance source and the morally uplifting theme, distanced the work from ordinary photography and aligned it with painting.[31] Despite its fame, however, Rejlander made few more moralizing pictures. Like many photographers, his main means of support was portraiture.

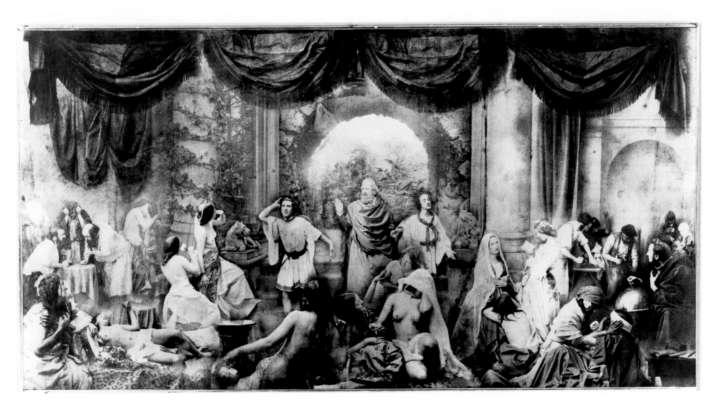

3.12
OSCAR REJLANDER, *The Two Ways of Life*, 1857. Albumen print. George Eastman House, Rochester, New York.

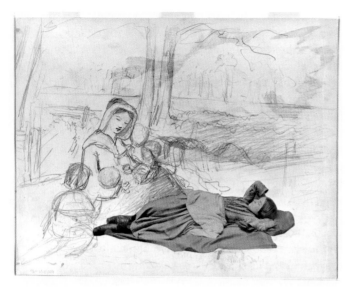

Henry Peach Robinson (1830–1901), another painter-photographer, learned from Rejlander how to combine negatives. A hand-drawn sketch with a photograph inserted shows how Robinson planned his work (Fig. 3.13). The subject of his 1858 combination-print photograph *Fading Away* (Fig. 3.14) disturbed the public with its scene of a dying young girl being attended by her family. Although the space between the girl and the wall beyond the window is unnaturally compressed, the illusion of the image having been taken in one camera shot, not built up from individual pictures, is stronger in *Fading Away* than in Rejlander's *The Two Ways of Life*. Robinson depicted another dying heroine in a combination print titled *The Lady of Shalott* (1861), illustrating a scene in a famous poem by Tennyson. His book *Pictorial Effect in Photography* (1869) was a standard work throughout the nineteenth century.

WOMEN BEHIND THE CAMERA

WOMEN AS AMATEURS

On rare occasions, a woman such as Harriet C. Tytler (1828–1907), who was married to a British officer in India, learned photography, traveled extensively, and produced a body of work alone, or as a joint effort with a spouse. Harriet Tytler

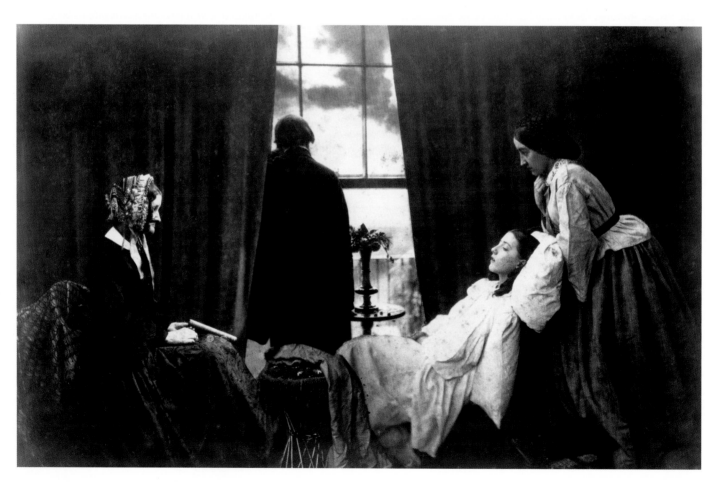

focus

Lewis Carroll's Photographs of Children

Charles L. Dodgson (1832–1898) was an ordained clergyman and lectured in mathematics at Oxford University in Britain, but he is better known as the author of *Alice's Adventures in Wonderland* and *Through the Looking-Glass*, written under the pen name Lewis Carroll. He also created about three thousand negatives during twenty-five years of photographing.[32] His landscape and architectural photographs are unremarkable, and his portraits of adults are mostly conventional, but the photographs he made of the female children of his friends and colleagues have been the subject of much debate. Carroll photographed Alice Liddell, the Alice of his stories, alone and with her sisters. His contrived image of her as a beggar child in artfully ripped clothing and bare feet is perplexing. It is difficult to reconstruct the Victorian attitude toward children of the upper middle class, and Carroll may have been more than a little enthralled with Alice (Fig. 3.15). Certainly, Alice cannot

be mistaken for a pauper: her costume, her grooming, and especially her pose suggest a child playing a role. But is it a sexually charged image?

In recent criticism, Carroll has been accused of instilling private erotic innuendo into his photographs of young girls.[33] The nude and semi-dressed photographs, most of which were destroyed by Carroll before his death, or ordered by him in instructions to his executors to be scrapped, were made with the knowledge of the girls' parents. Amidst the tumultuous changes in the Victorian period, the child became a potent symbol of purity and simplicity. The era insisted on childhood as a time of innocence, and Carroll's pictures pivot on the girls' ignorance of the teasing sexuality of their poses.

3.15
LEWIS CARROLL, *Alice Liddell as "The Beggar Maid,"* **c. 1859.
Hand-colored albumen print.**

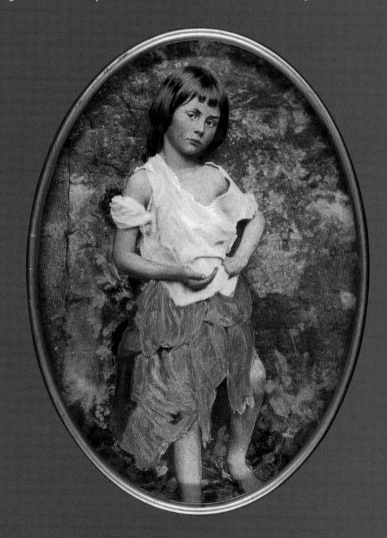

and Robert Christopher Tytler (1818–1872) made about three hundred photographs, some of them as large, two- and three-part panoramas, and exhibited them in India and in the India Office Records in London, where they remain today.[34] But many more women participated in formally arranged and informal exchange clubs for photographers who made non-commercial images. Called "amateurs" for their love of the pursuit, they were not amateurs in the modern sense of being unskilled or beginners. Most amateur photographers were people of means and accomplishment. Their work ranged from scientific pursuits to architectural and landscape views. John Dillwyn Llewelyn

(see p. 33) shared his interests in botany, landscape, and still-life photography through exchanges with other amateurs. *The Sunbeam: Photographs from Nature* (1859), an album of photographs and poems edited by Philip Henry Delamotte (1820–1889), distilled a mood of quiet meditation in nature that attracted many amateurs.

A few privileged women such as Lady Augusta Mostyn (1830–1912) and her sister, Lady Caroline Nevill (1829–1887), were accomplished photographers who participated in the Photographic Exchange Club in Britain (Fig. 3.16). In 1901, Lady Augusta established the Mostyn Art Gallery to show

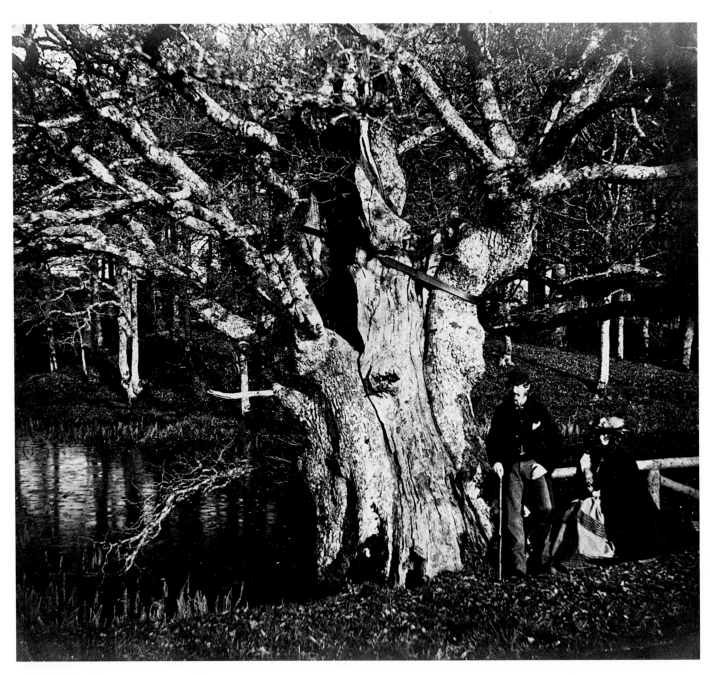

3.16
LADY AUGUSTA MOSTYN, *Oak Tree in Eridge Park*, **Sussex, 1856. Albumenized print of collodion negative. George Eastman House, Rochester, New York.**

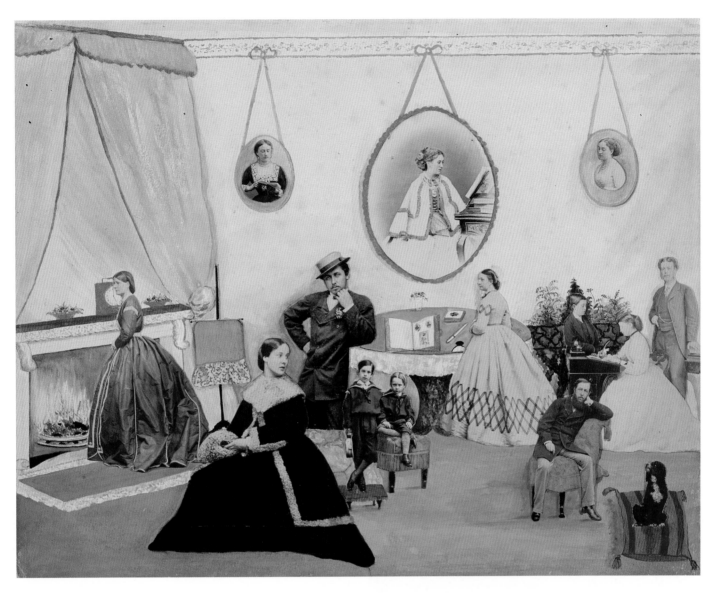

3.17
LADY FILMER, Untitled leaf from the Filmer Album, c. 1865. Photo and watercolor. Paul F. Walter Collection, New York.

the work of the Gwyneed Ladies Art Society, thereby creating the first gallery built specifically to show women's artwork. The photographic work of upper-class women in the nineteenth century is not widely known because outside of the exchange clubs their photographs were not exhibited, and many remain in private family collections. One such elusive figure is Lady Filmer (1838–1903), an intimate of Queen Victoria's court, who made portraits, and who cut up photographs and inventively arranged them on sheets of paper upon which she painted watercolors (Fig. 3.17).

Perhaps the most intriguing amateur photographer in the Victorian era was Lady Clementina Hawarden (1822–1865), who took up photography in the late 1850s and in the seven years before her death in 1865 produced about eight hundred images. Elected to the Photographic Society of London in 1863, she won silver medals for her work in that year and in 1864. Although she made some landscape images, her most intriguing pictures were made of her daughters, mainly in the family's London townhouse, where an upper floor was devoted to her photographic pursuits.[35]

Expert in lighting and composing a scene that seems tantalizingly part of a story, Hawarden often photographed the young women in costumes that probably came from the family's collection. She frequently used a mirror, which not only added depth to the scene, but also employed a favorite Victorian symbol for the tension between reality and appearance and the

portrait

Julia Margaret Cameron

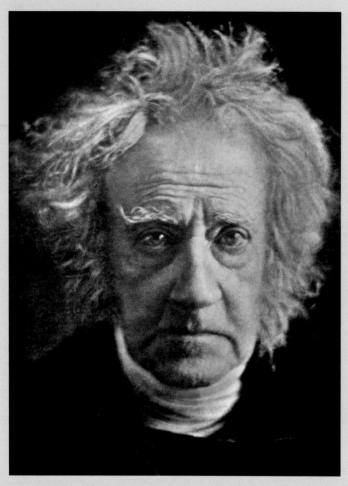

3.18
JULIA MARGARET CAMERON, *Herschel,* **1867. Albumen print.**
Victoria and Albert Museum, London.

The Victorian period's most enduringly famous photographer, Julia Margaret Cameron (1815–1879), did not take up photography seriously until she was given a camera in 1863, at the age of forty-eight. Born Julia Margaret Prattle, in India, she was schooled in France, married when she was twenty-three years old, and took up photography only when her children were grown and her domestic duties reduced.

Cameron eagerly experimented with the medium, and during the next decade produced images in order "to ennoble photography and to secure for it the character and uses of High Art by combining the real and ideal and sacrificing nothing of Truth by all possible devotion to Poetry and beauty."[36]

Cameron took portraits of friends, and friends of friends, as well as of Victorian cultural figures such as Charles Darwin and Alfred, Lord Tennyson. Her likeness of scientist and photography pioneer John Herschel, with whom she had been acquainted since 1836, illustrates her distinctive approach to male portraiture (Fig. 3.18). Herschel's hair, recently washed and, at her request, left uncombed, becomes an outward manifestation of his active mind. In her autobiographical writing, "Annals of my Glass House," Cameron recalled photographing Herschel and another Victorian sage, Thomas Carlyle (1795–1881). "When I have had such men before my camera," she wrote, "my whole soul has endeavoured to do its duty towards them in recording faithfully the greatness of the inner as well as the features of the outer man."[37]

In Cameron's work, friends, family, and servants were changed into characters from the Bible, Greek myth, and Renaissance painting, as well as figures in British lore and literature. By careful draping and delicate lighting, Cameron transformed her parlormaid Mary Hillier into the Virgin Mary. Like many women photographers, she posed more women than men. Because women generally did not have the identity and authority in the cultural and intellectual world enjoyed by men such as Darwin, Herschel, and Tennyson, they were more easily transformed into literary personages. Most of the time, she chose a crucial psychological moment in a story that would be well known to her audience (Fig. 3.19). She illustrated an edition of Tennyson's *"Idylls of the King" and Other Poems,* published in two volumes in 1874–75. Cameron appreciated the languidly beautiful women in medieval costume who appeared in paintings by artists of the Pre-Raphaelite Brotherhood, and made several images especially similar to the work of Dante Gabriel Rossetti (1828–1882).

Cameron explained that the slightly blurred focus that became her characteristic style resulted from her early attempts at photography, when she was using a lens with such a short focal length that only a small region of the sitter's face would be sharp. However accidentally Cameron may have come upon her technique, and no matter how much she was criticized as being technically inexpert for continuing to use it, the style suited her subject matter. A detailed picture of the Virgin Mary would look too much like someone acting out the role, but a cloudy version appears like an imagined vision or a remembered dream. Unlike many women photographers, Cameron publicly displayed her photographs and attempted to sell them, using the well-established print dealers P. & D. Colnaghi in London. Even though her religious and cultural subjects would have been considered appropriate for a pious woman, her attempts to ease family financial difficulties with the sale of prints was frowned on, and provoked criticism of her style as ignorant or slovenly.[38]

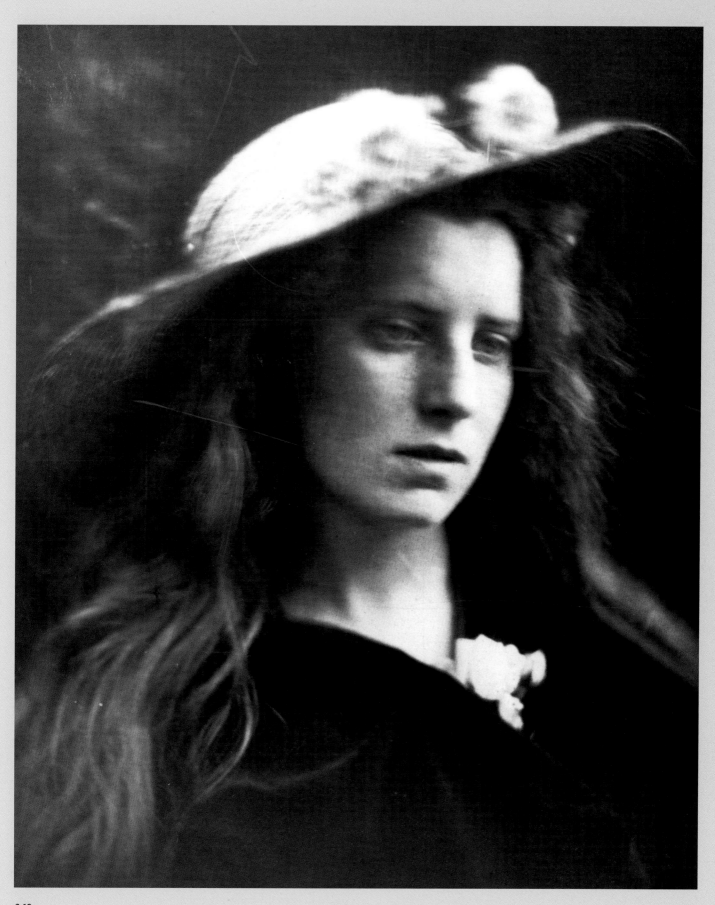

3.19
JULIA MARGARET CAMERON, *Ophelia, Study no. 2*, 1867. Albumen print. George Eastman House, Rochester, New York.

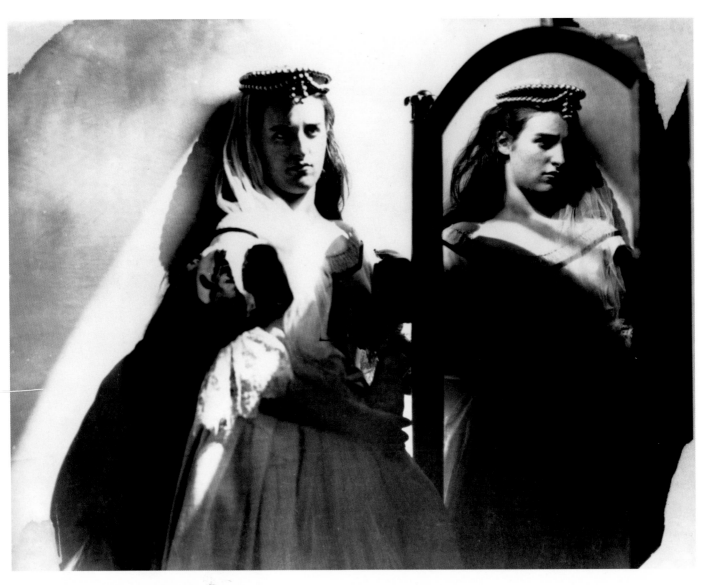

3.20
LADY HAWARDEN, *Girl in Fancy Dress***, c. 1860. Collodion print. Victoria and Albert Museum, London.**

line between art and life (Fig. 3.20). Though the photographs resemble *tableaux vivants*, they are mostly untitled, giving no direct clues to their meaning. They remained largely unknown in a family collection, until they were given to the Victoria and Albert Museum in London in 1939.

WOMEN AS PROFESSIONALS

Few women had the resources to set up full-time commercial photographic studios, but women were present in all phases of photographic production. Some, such as Marie Lydie Cabanis Bonfils (1837–1918), wife of the photographer Félix Bonfils (1831–1885), were actively engaged in the studio (see p. 144 and Fig. 5.6).

As ALBUMEN PAPER, which used egg white to give the final photograph a sheen, became more popular, women were employed by the thousands to break and separate eggs. Women had sometimes been employed to add color to the cold silver tinge of the daguerreotype. When paper photographs supplanted the daguerreotype, women continued as colorists. As the *carte-de-visite* and stereograph industries boomed, women found employment as laboratory assistants, print cutters, and print mounters.[39] Except for some work with noxious chemicals, C. Jabez Hughes concluded that "in photography there is room for a larger amount of female labour, that it is a field exactly suited to even the conventional notions of women's capacity, and further, that it is a field unsurrounded with traditional rules, with apprenticeships, with vested rights, and it is one in which there is no sexual hostility to their employment."[40]

Professional training in photography could be more easily obtained than training in painting or sculpture. Women might be excluded or discouraged from art academies, but they could study with photographers who advertised for students, or learn through the many technical manuals. Women could not travel abroad as freely as did John Thomson and Francis Frith, for example, but they did produce landscape work based on local scenery, as well as routine studio portraiture. Tellingly, women did not seem to secure copyright, or to publish their work to the extent that men did, possibly because these activities involved being in the world of business and commerce to a greater degree than was deemed suitable.[41]

RETAKE

By the middle decades of the nineteenth century, photography's development was so rapid and broad that it created a new milieu for both art and popular photography. The medium was caught up in the conflicts associated with democratic movements and the growth of the middle class. It became an active force in the beginnings of mass culture, along with popular fiction and newspapers, inexpensive lithographs, and engravings. In many ways, the praise and censure for art photography expressed a barely concealed concern for the future of society.

As photography lost its novelty, it gained both adherents and detractors, and they often focused on the relationship of photography to art and culture. One the one hand, the medium was the most exact way of creating art reproductions that could be viewed by more people than could travel to see the originals. Stereographs could enhance learning by transmitting the appearance of cultures, geography, and events that most people would never see for themselves. *Cartes-de-visite* made it possible for many more people to own likenesses of themselves and others. On the other hand, critics were quick to point out that the passion for optical exactitude suppressed the public's appreciation for nuance and opportunities for quiet rumination on images. The transcription of visual appearances, however adeptly rendered, did not seem capable of conveying higher sentiments and moral example. In reaction, High Art photography strove to instruct viewers in moral values and refined sympathies by utilizing themes and ideas from other media, such as poetry and painting.

4.1
CARLETON E. WATKINS, *Cape Horn, near Celilo*, 1867. Albumen silver print
from glass negative. Metropolitan Museum of Art, New York.

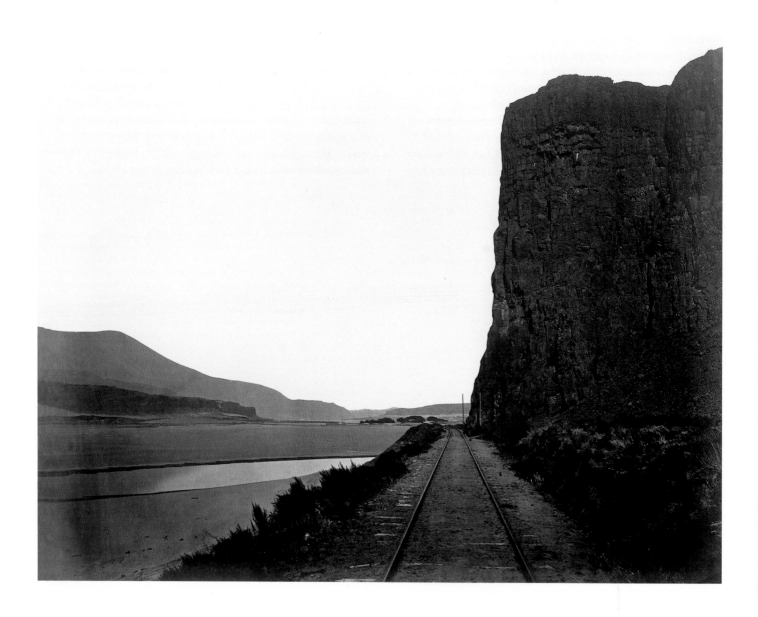

CHAPTER FOUR

Imaging of the Social World

Military, commercial, and propagandistic uses of photography were exploited during war and colonial expansion. In addition, land surveys around the world employed photographers who not only made descriptive topographical images but also created pictures that explored the history and aesthetic appeal of the terrain. While the camera and the gun were routinely allied, it was not clear from the start how to circulate, sell, and archive images of conflict. Would audiences want to see combat photographs made weeks and months before they reached an exhibition hall? Should a photographer censor the violence of the battlefield? Would consumers buy photographs of a war after it was resolved? These questions could not be answered beforehand, because there were no precendents to follow. War was a risky business, even for its photographers.

WAR AND PHOTOGRAPHY

Writing in the *Atlantic Monthly* for July 1859, Oliver Wendell Holmes forecast that "the next European war will send us stereographs of battles."[1] His prediction was darkly realized when the next major war, the American Civil War, erupted in the United States. On the eve of the conflict, there was widespread naïveté about the conduct of war and its effects on camerawork. John Draper, who created early daguerreotypes of the moon, later became editor of the *American Journal of Photography*, where he mused that "there will be little danger … for the photographer [who] must be beyond the smell of gunpowder or his chemicals will not work."[2]

Photographs and photographers' accounts from previous conflicts, such as the Mexican–American War and the Second Burma War (see p. 43) had not been widely distributed. Hence, the possibility that war photographs might be different from heroic war paintings and engravings was not much discussed before photographs of mid-nineteenth-century wars began to

be circulated through exhibitions and newspaper engravings. Commentators mostly failed to take into account the technical inadequacy of photography to register the swift action of battle, which supplied one of the major visual art themes, or the likelihood that such disruptions as low light or a strong breeze could halt picture-taking at crucial moments. Few mentioned that photographic equipment was still cumbersome, or that plates had to be processed soon after exposure, forcing the photographer to hurry to a makeshift darkroom.

Despite high hopes for photography, sketch artists—often amateurs attached to military units in semi-official positions, or entrepreneurial individuals who sold their works to journals for reproduction as engravings—continued to produce the majority of war images that the public saw. Photographers recorded what they could: fortifications and landscapes, as well as troops and military leaders, before and after battle. What it lacked in spontaneity, photography began to make up for in quantity, both in the number of views taken and in their extensive circulation.

During the nineteenth century, European countries were involved in many so-called "small wars," a term used by Major Charles Callwell to describe the conflicts associated with the expansion of colonial European powers in Asia, North Africa, India, and the Middle East.[3] Callwell saw these conflicts as inevitably "a heritage of extended Empire."[4] Britain was involved in about thirty such wars during the nineteenth century, almost two dozen of which were fought in India, between the Indian Mutiny of 1857 and 1900. The presence of photographers at these colonial struggles strengthened the public perception of a link between photography's expansion and territorial conquest.

In February 1856, as peace negotiations after the Crimean War (1853–56) were being conducted, retired statesman and photographer Eugène Durieu (1800–1874) (see Fig. 2.59) reported to the French Photographic Society that photography would conquer unknown territories as the victorious armies of France conquered land.[5] Indeed, photography became a formalized element in military organization: in 1856, a photographic section was formed as part of the Telegraphic School run for the Royal Engineers in Chatham, England; and in 1861, the French minister of war ordered that one officer in every brigade be trained in photography.[6] By 1870, the camera was commonly used for many tasks, such as copying maps, teaching recruits, and recording experiments with weaponry.

THE CRIMEAN WAR

The conflict in the Crimea, a peninsula at the northern end of the Black Sea, sprang from a tangle of issues relating to European influence in the Ottoman Empire, and pitted Russia against Britain, France, Turkey, and Sardinia. The war required joint action and cooperation from the allies to plan strategy and to furnish supplies. Newspaper reports by William Howard Russell (1820–1907), published by *The Times* of London late in 1854, revealed how mismanagement and disunity among Britain's allies produced severe hardships, food scarcities, and lack of medical care among the troops. In a dispatch written on November 25, 1854, Russell described torrential rains that flooded tents and chilled soldiers, who lacked warm, waterproof clothing. The "wretched beggar who wanders the streets of London in the rain," wrote Russell, "leads the life of a prince compared with the British soldiers who are fighting out here for their country." "These are hard truths," he warned, "but the people of England must hear them."[7] Political cartoons denounced the situation of the soldiers.

Early in the conflict the War Department ordered two ultimately unsuccessful photographic forays in an attempt to counteract the negative newspaper accounts of the war. The next British efforts to photograph in the Crimea were undertaken separately by Roger Fenton (1819–1869) and James Robertson (1813–1888).

Roger Fenton

A well-known British amateur photographer, Roger Fenton (see p. 81) helped to found the Photographic Society in 1853. An artist by inclination and a lawyer by training, he studied painting in France and learned the waxed-paper photographic process invented by Gustave Le Gray (see p. 54). In the fall of 1852, Fenton was off again, this time to Russia, where he photographed historic architecture, as well as the construction of a bridge across the Dnieper River at Kiev, a structure commissioned by Czar Nicholas I (1796–1855; r. 1825–1855) from Fenton's friend and promoter of photography, the British engineer Charles Vignoles (1793–1875).

By the mid-1850s, governments and publishers were speculating about the potential of war photographs. In Manchester, England, the firm of print publishers Thomas Agnew & Sons commissioned Fenton to make images in the Crimea, to which Agnew would retain the reproduction rights. Fenton eventually exhibited his Crimean War photographs in London, and in 1856 Agnew published 160 of Fenton's more than 300 photographs, which could be purchased singly or in handsome volumes. At this time peace negotiations were well under way, and the project proved to be less financially rewarding than the publisher had hoped. Along with some Crimean photographs by James Robertson, Fenton's unsold photographs and negatives of the war were auctioned at a discount in 1856.

Although his letters from the front clearly show that he was frustrated by the war's mismanagement, and, like many others there, suffered from cholera, Fenton's photographs were less explicit (Fig. 4.2). Most did not make direct reference to the war's calamities: he did not depict fallen soldiers, the wreckage of battle, or the results of supply shortages that caused soldiers to loot civilian homes. Like war artists in the past, he made heroic

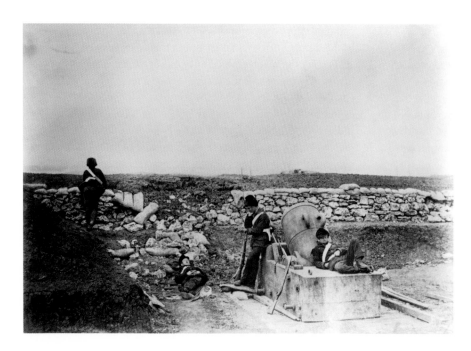

4.2
ROGER FENTON, *A Quiet Day at the Mortar Battery*, 1855. Salted paper print. The J. Paul Getty Museum, Los Angeles, California.

focus

The Valley of Death

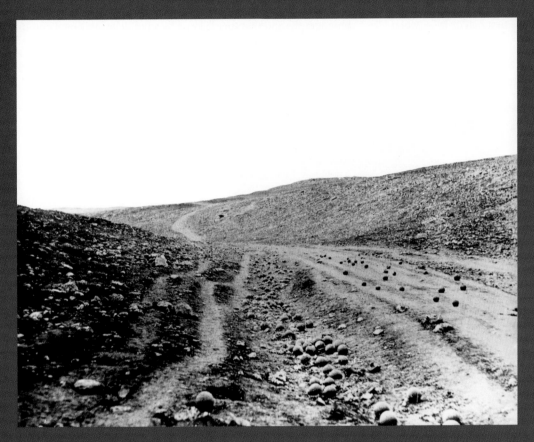

Theirs not to make reply,
Theirs not to reason why
Theirs but to do and die.
Into the valley of Death
*   Rode the six hundred.*

Alfred, Lord Tennyson,
"The Charge of the Light Brigade"

4.3
ROGER FENTON, *The Valley of the Shadow of Death*, 1855. Paper print. Victoria and Albert Museum, London.

Even before it became immortalized in a famous poem and a famous photograph (Fig. 4.3), the area in the Crimea where so many British troops met their deaths was called "the valley of death."[8] The desolate lowland lived up to its biblical name when, on October 25, 1854, Russian artillery in a strong position fired on a British cavalry brigade whose attack orders had been confused through the chain of command. The Light Brigade incurred heavy losses. Tennyson incorporated the line "Someone had blundered" from newspaper accounts of the incident. When Fenton's photograph was exhibited in 1855, the editor of the *Photographic Journal* in London wrote that the show was the "most remarkable and in certain respects the most interesting exhibition of photographs ever opened." The writer singled out *The Valley of the Shadow of Death* "with its terrible suggestions, not merely those awakened in the memory, but actually brought materially before the eyes, by photographic reproduction of

the cannon-balls lying strewd like moraines of a melted glacier through the bottom of the valley."[9]

Fenton did not arrive in the Crimea until months after the event and after Tennyson wrote the first draft of his poem. He was aware of the national sentiments surrounding the valley when he left Britain. In fact, Fenton made two photographs on the site, the second of which became famous. In the first, there are hardly any cannon balls in the road; but in the second and better-known photograph, cannon balls have been strewn on and near the road, perhaps by Fenton and his staff, to create the impression that the battle had recently taken place.[10] The renown of his photograph of the site grew in subsequent years, propelled by the Tennyson poem, the Christian symbolism of death and eternal life, and the complex sentiments felt by the British about the war. The charge of the Light Brigade, not a pivotal battle, became an emblem of devotion to duty during senseless conflicts.

images of military leaders, and his photographs of the soldiers showed them in no danger, often enjoying the same social activities they might at home.

Fenton's tact may have derived from the instructions to the first, failed, government-sponsored photographic party, which was to bring back visual evidence that newspaper accounts of the war exaggerated the disease and starvation endured by the troops. Moreover, Fenton's acquaintance with Queen Victoria (1819–1901; r. 1837–1901) during the first half of 1854, when he created a flattering likeness of the monarch, photographed the royal children (Fig. 4.4), and instructed the royal couple in the rudiments of photography, may have tempered his images.[11] Further, the worst privations occurred during the winter of 1854, when lack of supplies was exacerbated by severe cold and rampant cholera. Fenton visited the Crimea in 1855, when the previous winter's situation had to some extent been alleviated. Aware that the print-publishing firm would be marketing the photographs and that there would be a public exhibition, Fenton

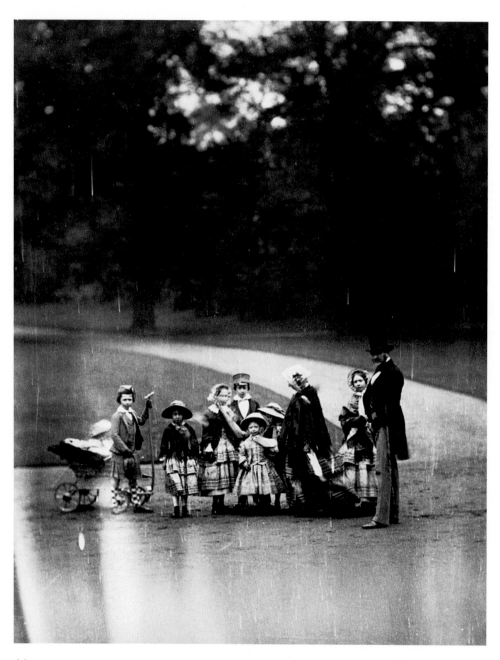

4.4
ROGER FENTON, *The Royal Family in Buckingham Palace Garden,* **May 22, 1854. Paper print. The Royal Archives.**
© 2002 Her Majesty Queen Elizabeth II.

Queen Victoria was aware of the power of photography to form her public image. Her more formal portraits are counterbalanced by casual views and family scenes. She also amassed a collection of 100,000 photographs, which she put into ten albums.

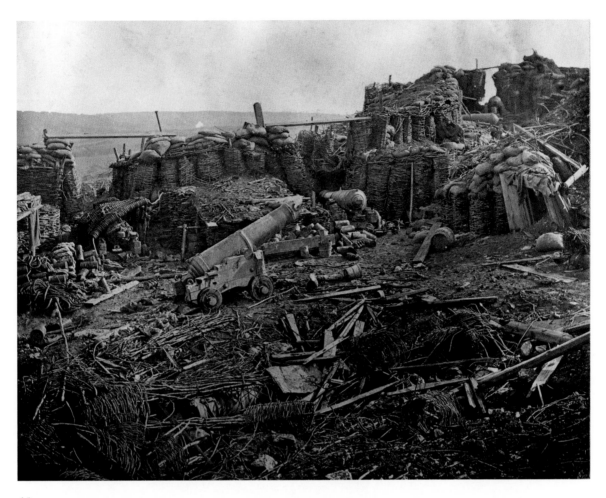

4.5
JAMES ROBERTSON, *Interior of the Redan, June 1855*. Salted paper print. Gernsheim Collection. Harry Ransom Humanities Research Center, University of Texas at Austin.

may have assumed that few people would want to see or to buy images of suffering and carnage. Interestingly, the public and press did not raise issues of content—Fenton's photographs were praised by critics for their factual quality and their superiority to words.

James Robertson and other Crimean Photographers

James Robertson was a British citizen working as chief engraver of the Imperial Mint in Constantinople, and an accomplished amateur landscape photographer, who made views in the Middle East. Early in the war he traveled to the area, taking some images about which little is known, before returning to the war zone in 1855. Robertson's trip may have been sponsored by print publishers looking for someone to carry on when Fenton left, or he may have set off on his own initiative. He made approximately sixty images, including the ruins of a redan, or fortification, at Sebastopol, which had been secured only after numerous bombardments (Fig. 4.5). Robertson's photographs were published by Thomas Agnew, who auctioned the unsold photographs and negatives along with Fenton's surplus images.

Fenton and Robertson are the best-known photographers of the Crimean War, because their work was published in

engraved interpretations in newspapers and issued in multiple photographic prints. But there were other photographers on the scene, including Karl Baptist von Szatmari (1812–1887), an amateur painter and photographer from Bucharest, Romania. He used his social connections to visit the opposing armies of Turkey and Russia early in the conflict that led to the Crimean War. Although all but one of his photographs have perished, the range of subjects, known from a show of his work at the Paris Exposition of 1855, included group portraits and troop movements. Legend has it that the young Russian novelist Leo Tolstoi, who was in an artillery unit at Sebastopol, made a number of photographs. Readers commented on the vivid visual accounts offered in his *Sebastopol Sketches*, published serially in 1855–56. The French painter and war historian Colonel Jean-Charles Langlois (1789–1870) arrived late in the war, sent by Napoleon III to bring back images of the conflict. Accompanied by the architect and photographer Léon-Eugène Méhédin (1828–1905), he made photographs that were developed in Paris by panoramic photographer Frederic von Martens (see p. 50). Langlois joined fourteen of these prints to create a 360-degree view, and later used some of the Crimean photographs that displayed deep recessive landscape views as sources for his

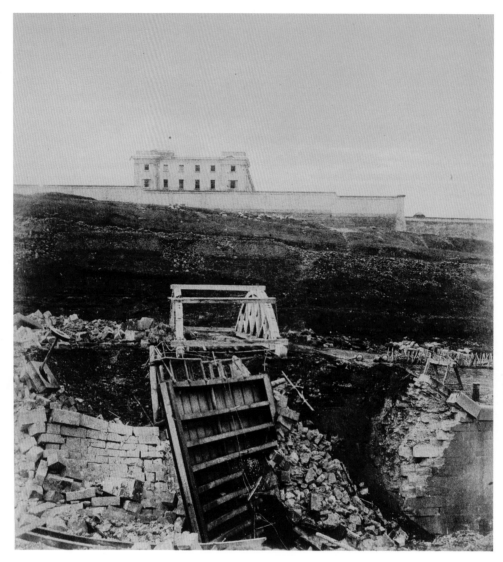

4.6
JEAN-CHARLES LANGLOIS, LÉON-EUGÈNE MÉHÉDIN, FREDERICK VON MARTENS, *Ruins at Sebastopol*, 1855.
Musée d'Orsay, Paris.

illusionistic panoramic painting of the fighting in the city of Sebastopol (Fig. 4.6).

THE AMERICAN CIVIL WAR

For decades, economic and political tensions in the United States between the industrialized northern states and the largely agricultural southern states had been patched over by fragile concessions. One such agreement, the Compromise of 1850, admitted California to the Union as a free—that is, non-slave—state but allowed slavery to continue in the states where it existed, and mandated the return of fugitive slaves from free states. Abolitionist feeling in the North was roused by the provision that runaway slaves had to be returned to the South, and the immediate cause of the war, the secession from the Union by the state of South Carolina, was partly motivated by the dispute over fugitive slaves.

Fighting between North and South began with the shelling of Fort Sumter in South Carolina on April 12, 1861, and ended with the Southern surrender at Appomattox, Virginia, on April 9, 1865. During the hostility, war correspondents, artists, and photographers furnished the public with news and images. Unlike in the Mexican–American War (see p. 41–43), Americans understood from the beginning that this conflict would be photographed extensively, and that photographs, and the engravings taken from them, would create a comprehensive visual chronicle—the first of its kind in American history.[12] The first pictures from the conflict were taken by Southern photographers such as George S. Cook (1819–1902) the day after Fort Sumter fell. Born in Connecticut, Cook settled in the South in his twenties, but maintained his contacts with Northern photographers, publishers, and suppliers, such as E. and H. T. Anthony & Co.[13]

When the division between North and South deepened, Cook centered his work on Confederate subjects. In February 1861, Cook made a portrait of Major Robert Anderson, who commanded the Federal troops at Fort Sumter, in the mouth of

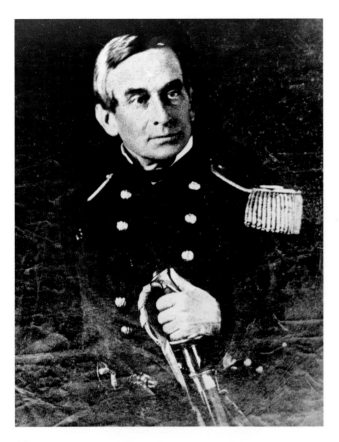

4.7
GEORGE S. COOK, *Portrait of Major Robert Anderson*, 1860–65.
Wet-plate collodion. Valentine Museum, Richmond, Virginia.

Charleston Harbor (Fig. 4.7). In the succeeding months, as the quarrel between the North and the newly declared Southern Confederacy focused on the continued presence of Federal troops in the fort, wood engravings of Cook's photograph were reproduced in the Northern press, and *cartes-de-visite* made from the photograph were sold by the thousand. When Fort Sumter fell to Southern forces, Cook made many photographs, including the lowering of the American flag. After the war, Cook amassed ten thousand Civil War photographs, largely by other photographers, which were later acquired by the Valentine Museum in Richmond, Virginia.

The Effect of the War on Photography
While only one photographer, Andrew J. Russell (1830–1902), was actually paid by the United States government, many quasi-official photographers from the North and South saw the conflict as an opportunity to expand their markets. Photographic portraits of such politicians as Abraham Lincoln were popular, as were images of military leaders. Families of soldiers going off to war desired pictures of their young men, who, in turn, wanted photographic keepsakes of their families. Photographers such as the three Bergstresser brothers from Pennsylvania set up makeshift studios at military camps to provide photographs to soldiers (Fig. 4.8). An article in the *New York Tribune* for August 20, 1862, reported that the Bergstresser brothers had

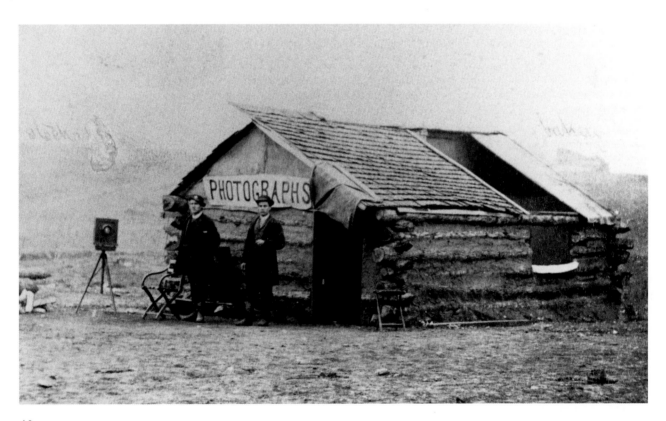

4.8
BERGSTRESSER BROTHERS, *Bergstresser's Photographic Studio, 3d Div., 5th Corp, Army of the Potomac*, c. 1862–64. Albumen silver print.
U.S. Army Military History Institute, Carlisle Barracks, Carlisle, Pennsylvania.

portrait

Mathew Brady

Mathew Brady is best remembered for the battlefield photographs that his firm took during the American Civil War. But, as historian Mary Panzer noted, Brady's wartime photographs were dominated by representations of individuals and groups of soldiers.[14] Brady's emphasis on specific people reveals a philosophy that history is shaped by great persons, not abstract historical forces or political controversies.

Brady's interest in portraiture began early in his professional life. Like many enterprising photographers of limited means, the young Brady undertook a number of different tasks that might offer a steady photographic practice. He began his career in New York City during the early 1840s, making cases for painted miniatures and jewelry, as well as daguerreotypes. By 1844, he had opened a daguerreotype studio and was winning awards for his images. He produced a series of portraits of criminals, which were made into wood engravings and published in the American edition of Marmaduke Sampson's *Rationale of Crime*.

By the late 1840s, celebrity photography had become Brady's stock in trade. He produced unflinching portraits, including that of John C. Calhoun, the powerful South Carolina politician who opposed northern abolition movements (Fig. 4.9). This and other daguerreotypes of prominent Americans were transformed by Francis D'Avignon (b. 1813) into lithographs (Fig. 4.10) and published in Brady's *The Gallery of Illustrious Americans* (1850). Produced during the debate that led to the Compromise of 1850, *The Gallery* struck a delicate balance by including images of opposing politicians.

Throughout the 1850s, Brady created portraits of distinguished American figures in law, government, business, society, and the arts, and exhibited them in his photographic studios (Fig. 4.12). Brady's images were sometimes used for personal publicity, being reproduced as inexpensive popular prints. His status rose with the fame of his sitters, whose reputations were strengthened in turn because their images bore his name and were displayed in his gallery. Before the outbreak of the Civil War in 1861, Brady had amassed more than ten thousand photographs of celebrities, mostly Americans. Even United States presidents were not immune from the potential of photography.

Mathew Brady's famous photograph of Abraham Lincoln (1809–1865) was taken on the day in 1860 when he gave an address in New York at the Cooper Union (Fig. 4.11). Brady sold prints of the photograph, and it was reproduced in newspapers and magazines. Most people had never seen Lincoln, but rumors of his physical ugliness were rife during the presidential

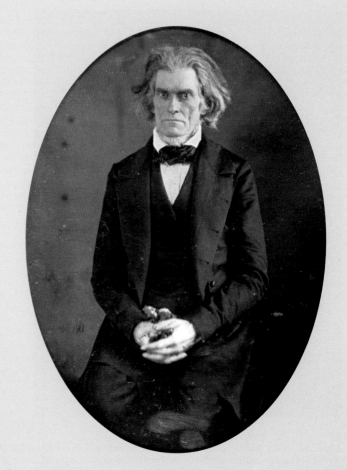

4.9
PHOTOGRAPHER UNKNOWN, *John C. Calhoun*, c. 1848–49. Daguerreotype. The Beinecke Rare Book and Manuscript Library, Yale University, New Haven, Connecticut.

campaign. The Democrat opposition sang a song at rallies that ended "We beg and pray you—Don't, for God's sake, show his picture."[15] Brady distracted attention from Lincoln's gangliness by directing light to his face. He posed the future president in a statesmanlike attitude and took care that he curled his fingers (especially of his right hand), so that they would not appear too long and large. Lincoln credited Brady for part of his success, remarking that "Brady and the Cooper Institute made me President."[16] By 1864, Brady and his firm had created more than thirty photographs of Lincoln, who himself sat for dozens of photographers, one of which was later used for the "Lincoln head" penny, and another of which was the source for Lincoln's image on the $5 bill.

Perhaps because of poor eyesight, Brady did not take most of the photographs that bore his name. Like David Octavius Hill (see p. 69) in Scotland, Brady conceptualized images, arranged the sitters, and oversaw the production of pictures. In his Civil War work, Brady stressed his conceptual and administrative capacity by frequently appearing in photographs with military leaders.

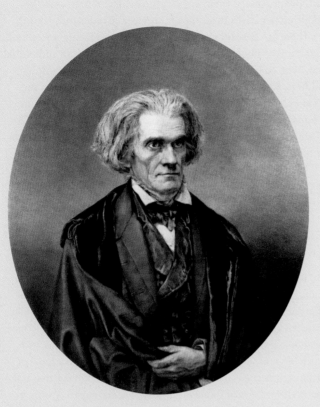

4.10
FRANCIS D'AVIGNON, *John C. Calhoun*, c. 1861. Lithograph.
National Portrait Gallery, Smithsonian Institution, Washington, D.C.

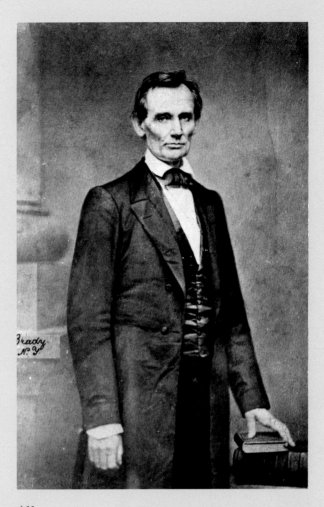

4.11
MATHEW BRADY, *Abraham Lincoln*, 1860. Salted paper print
(*carte-de-visite*). Library of Congress, Washington, D.C.

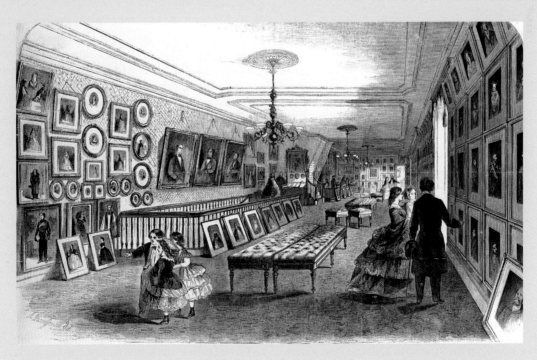

4.12
ALBERT BERGHAUS, *M. B. Brady's New Photographic Gallery, Corner of Broadway and Tenth Street, New York*, from *Frank Leslie's Illustrated Newspaper*, 1861. Wood engraving. Library of Congress, Washington, D.C.

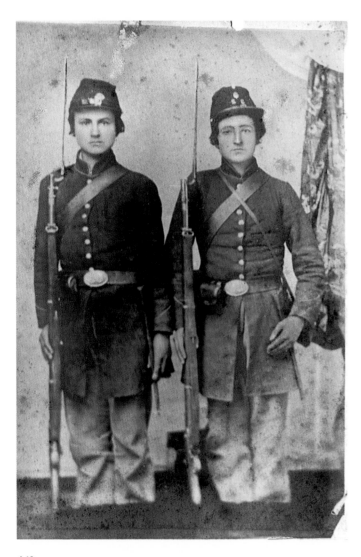

4.13
PHOTOGRAPHER UNKNOWN, *John and Nicholas Marien of Terre Haute, Indiana*, c. 1862–64. Tintype (original lost). Courtesy of the author.

scarce not simply because of the ravages of war, but also because of the severe shortages of photographic materials brought on by economic turmoil and military blockades. Photographers initially processed their work in the field, and then sent the resulting negatives to studios in towns and cities for printing.

There are few differences among the subject categories found in Civil War photographs. Whether of battlefields or individuals, they tend to be stiff and formal. Casual camaraderie among soldiers, such as that pictured in Roger Fenton's work in the Crimea, was seldom recorded. Although African-American troops were photographed and occasional images were made of abused slaves, the Civil War did not engender a far-reaching photographic record of slavery and its aftermath.

The restraints and omissions in subject matter, as well as the carefully balanced compositions, probably owe to the sense prevalent during the war that photography was a type of history writing, dedicated to recording the events, not investigating their tangled causes. The *New York Times* for July 21, 1862, observed:

Mr. Brady deserves honorable recognition as having been the first to make Photography the Clio of war [in Greek myth, Clio is the muse of history] … His artists have accompanied the army on nearly all its marches, planting their sun batteries by the side of our Generals' more deathful ones, and "taking" towns and cities, forts and redans, with much less noise and vastly more expedition. The result is a series of pictures christened "Incidents of War," and nearly as interesting as the war itself; for they constitute the history of it, and appeal directly to the great throbbing hearts of the North.[18]

Throughout the war, it was customary for major photographers to copyright their images, even though they were frequently published by other firms or individuals. For example, George N. Barnard, who worked for Mathew Brady, copyrighted his work, and later published *Photographic Views with Sherman's Campaigns* (1866), in which he recorded the well-organized destruction of the city of Atlanta, as well as of the infrastructure of the South, especially its railroads (Fig. 4.14). Indeed, Northern troops often lined up along the tracks, and on a signal simultaneously picked up one side of the railroad ties and tipped them over. The rails were then burned at high heat so that they twisted themselves into ruin.[19]

Recognition of photographers who worked for other image-makers also became more common during the Civil War. Timothy O'Sullivan (1840–1882), who left Brady's studio in 1862 or 1863 to work with Alexander Gardner (1831–1882), was given credit for his work in Gardner's publications. He made hundreds of war photographs, including *The Harvest of Death*, his most famous image, taken on the Gettysburg battlefield (Fig. 4.15). It was included, along with the work of several other photographers, in Gardner's *Photographic Sketch Book of the Civil War*, published in two volumes in 1865–66. In the last years of the war, photographs of battles and leading military officers were less sought after. The initial enthusiasm for the vast photographic record that could be made of the war was replaced by a sense of what could not be photographed.

"followed the army for more than a year and taken, the Lord only knows how many thousand portraits. In one day, since they came here [to Fredericksburg] they took in one of their galleries, 160 odd pictures at $1.00 each (on which the net profit was probably ninety-five cents)."[17] The recently invented TINTYPE photographs, developed on thin sheets of iron, were particularly popular, cheap, and lightweight (Fig. 4.13). Their name derives from the colloquial term for iron sheets, that is, "tin." Photographs from the front lines were published in many formats, including the popular *carte-de-visite*. E. and H. T. Anthony & Co. issued more than a thousand pictures per day, sent in by semi-professional photographers and celebrities such as Mathew Brady (1823–1896).

The war was extensively reported by newspaper reporters and magazine journalists. Of the more than 1,400 photographers who made images of troops, military installations, and battle sites, most were from the North. Southern photographs are more

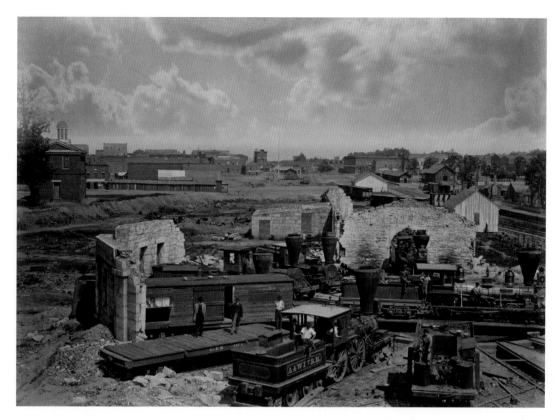

4.14
GEORGE N. BARNARD, *City of Atlanta No. 1*, 1866. Albumen print. Library of Congress, Washington, D.C.

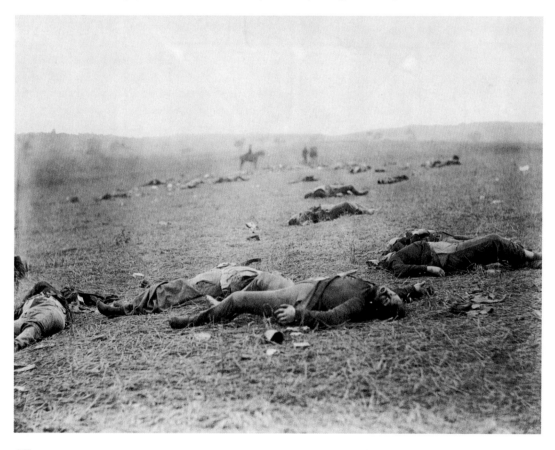

4.15
ALEXANDER GARDNER, *The Harvest of Death, Gettysburg, Pennsylvania*, July 1863, from Gardner's *Photographic Sketch Book of the Civil War*. Stereoscope. Negative by Timothy O'Sullivan. Library of Congress, Washington, D.C.

portrait

Alexander Gardner

When Alexander Gardner emigrated from Scotland to the United States in 1856, he was already an accomplished photographer. His association with Mathew Brady, whom he may have met in London when both attended the Crystal Palace Exhibition in 1851 (see p. 27), proved to be beneficial to both photographers. Beginning in 1856, Gardner, an adept accountant and organizer, brought order and a modicum of financial stability to Brady's Washington gallery. With Brady, Gardner foresaw the potential market for photography brought about by the impending Civil War.

Brady's corps of photographers gained access to battlefields and fortifications through the efforts of one Allan Pinkerton (1819–1884), head of the presidential protective organization that became known as the Secret Service. Pinkerton, a Scot, arranged for Gardner and a contingent of photographers who worked with him to be given access to Union encampments, where the photographers carried on covert activities—for example, photographing groups of soldiers among whom spies were thought to dwell. These photographers also made copies of maps for the Secret Service, and pictures of feasible battlefields and of structures such as bridges, tunnels, and railroad lines for the War Department.

Gardner and his subordinates made many of the photographs associated by the public with Mathew Brady. The battle at Antietam, Maryland, in September 1862 resulted in shocking photographs of the dead (Fig. 4.16), eight of which were engraved and published by *Harper's Weekly* on October 18. On the occasion of their exhibition in New York City, the *New York Times* brooded on their effect: "Mr. Brady has done something to bring home to us the terrible reality and earnestness of war. If he has not brought bodies and laid them in our dooryards and along the streets, he has done something very like it."[20] After seeing the Antietam photographs, Oliver Wendell Holmes, who visited the battlefield soon after the conflict took place, similarly commented:

Let him who wishes to know what war is look at this series of illustrations. These wrecks of manhood thrown together in careless heaps or ranged in ghastly rows for burial were alive but yesterday. … It was so nearly like visiting the battlefield to look over these views, that all the emotions excited by the actual sight of the stained and sordid scene, strewed with rags and wrecks, came back to us, and we buried them in the recesses of our cabinet as we would have buried the mutilated remains of the dead they too vividly represented.[21]

When President Lincoln removed General George McClellan as head of the Union army, Alexander Gardner lost his favored position as "Photographer, Army of the Potomac." He then

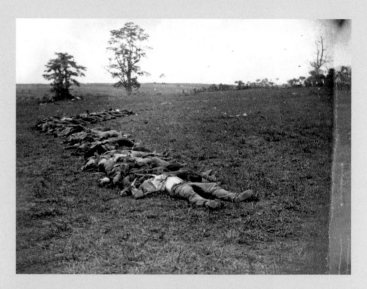

4.16
MATHEW BRADY, *Soldiers on the Battlefield*, 1862. Albumen silver print by Alexander Gardner. Library of Congress, Washington, D.C.

resigned from Brady's staff, but kept good, if competitive relations with his former employer. Both Gardner and Brady made images at the battle of Gettysburg in Pennsylvania, the Civil War's bloodiest engagement. Most of Gardner's views of Gettysburg feature death and destruction. It was on the Gettysburg battlefield that Gardner reconfigured a scene for the camera, so as to intensify its visual and emotional effects. To make *Home of a Rebel Sharpshooter* (Fig. 4.17), he had the corpse moved to a stone wall, and supported the dead man's head on a knapsack so that it faced the camera.[22] The rifle leaning on the wall is a prop that Gardner carried with him. The fact that Gardner did not keep his arrangement of this scene a secret indicates that the public was willing to allow the photographer to construct a scene that was true in a larger sense than fidelity to visual fact. Soon after Gettysburg, Gardner was briefly captured by Confederate troops, but released after they had assured themselves that he was not a spy. Like the ability of Southern photographer George S. Cook to obtain photographic supplies during the conflict, this incident suggests that photographers were regarded as neutral observers of war, not partisans.

Gardner's eye for the sensational is evident in the series of photographs he made of the conspirators who plotted the assassination of Lincoln. He photographed several of them after their arrest and published images of their execution (Fig. 4.18). Although the series from which this image comes seems like an innovative precursor of the photo-essays that would appear in twentieth-century magazines such as *Life*, it was probably made primarily for Secret Service records. Images derived from Gardner's photographs were published in *Harper's Weekly* (July 22, 1865), but the actual photographs did not sell well.

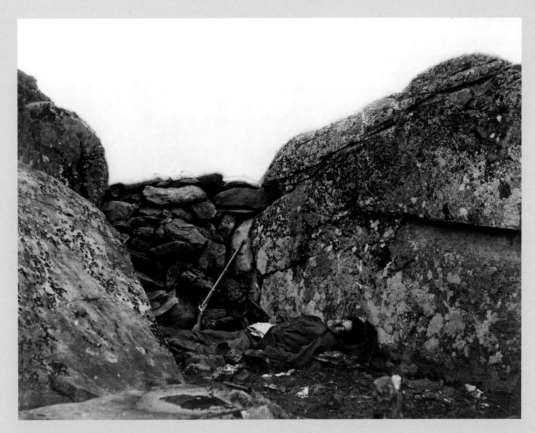

4.17
ALEXANDER GARDNER, *Home of a Rebel Sharpshooter, Gettysburg*, from Alexander Gardner's *Photographic Sketch Book of the Civil War*, plate 41, July 1863. Wet collodion print. Library of Congress, Washington, D.C.

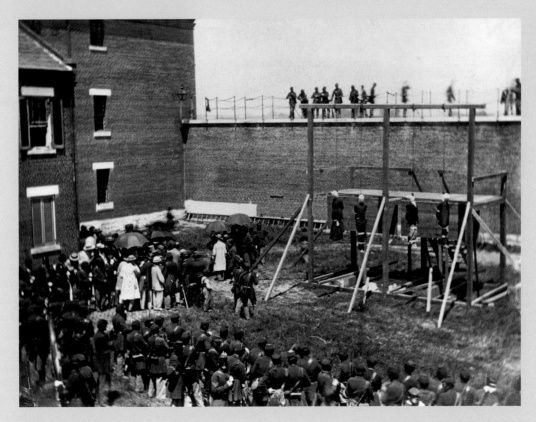

4.18
ALEXANDER GARDNER, *Execution of the Lincoln Conspirators*, 1865. From an original glass negative. George Eastman House, Rochester, New York.

THE CIVIL WAR AND REMEMBRANCE

After the Civil War, *Frank Leslie's Illustrated Newspaper* published images derived from photographs of prisoners in Southern prisoner-of-war camps such as that at Andersonville, Georgia (Fig. 4.19). These photographs initiated one of the most lasting debates about the Civil War. While no one doubted the truth of the soldiers' dire condition, its cause has been disputed. About eighty thousand prisoners were held by both the North and the South, while prisoner-of-war exchanges stalled over such issues as whether black Northern soldiers would be returned by the South. As the war dragged on, the North's blockades became more punitive, denying food and medical supplies to the South. The editors of *Harper's Weekly* wrote of the Confederates: "they do not [starve their prisoners] intentionally, perhaps, but that does not help the matter. … We are surely not obligated to tolerate the torture of Union prisoners because we wage the war so strictly that the rebels' supplies fail."[23] In Northern newspapers, the poor condition of Union captives was contrasted with what was thought to be the decent and

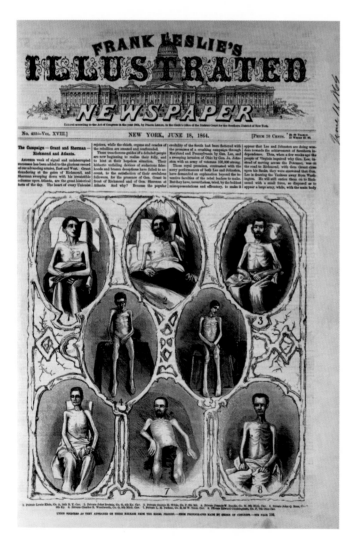

4.19
PHOTOGRAPHER UNKNOWN, *Frank Leslie's Illustrated Newspaper,* June 18, 1864. Woodblock print. Library of Congress, Washington, D.C.

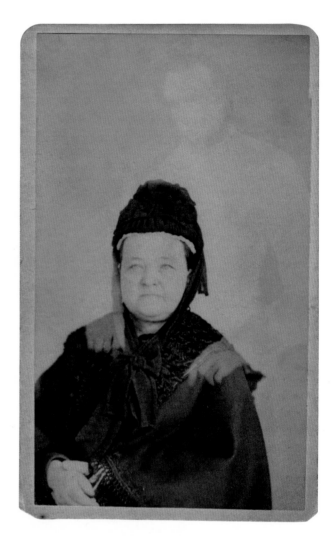

4.20
WILLIAM HOWARD MUMLER, *Mary Todd Lincoln with the Ghost of Abraham Lincoln,* after 1865. Albumen *carte-de-visite.* Wm. B. Becker Collection, American Museum of Photography.

honorable condition of Southern prisoners in Northern detention centers. Little attention was paid to broadcasting the misery endured by Southerners in prisons such as that at Elmira, New York.[24]

After the Civil War, and well into the twentieth century, the photographic books of the war were rumored to have been financial failures. It is true that Brady struggled for a decade to place his Civil War photographs in a public institution; it was not until 1875 that Congress paid him for the title to his prints and negatives. Current research suggests that Gardner's book and Barnard's volume, issued in small numbers, were both moderately profitable.

In 1869, both Brady and Gardner petitioned Congress to purchase, and hence preserve, their negatives. Both proposals were rejected, partly because the government was unsure how to store large numbers of photographs. About ninety thousand of Gardner's glass-plate negatives passed to a portrait photographer in Washington, D.C., who, in turn sold them to a scrap-glass dealer. The dealer recognized the historic importance of the work and tried unsuccessfully to market the images; finally, the glass and the silver in the emulsion were salvaged, destroying the negatives. Other sources, including the collection of E. and H. T. Anthony & Co., who distributed both Brady and Gardner images, were ultimately obtained by the United States Library of Congress.

Photography also figured in another sort of remembrance. The huge death toll of the Civil War, estimated at about 620,000 for Northern and Southern troops, encouraged grieving relatives and friends to try to contact the dead through spiritualists. So-called spirit photographs purported to show ethereal loved ones, or wisps of smoke indicating their presence. Among the best-selling images was a portrait taken by the leading American spiritualist photographer, William Howard Mumler (active 1832–84). It shows Mary Todd Lincoln with the ghost of the slain president standing behind her (Fig. 4.20). The vogue was also popular in Europe, where French spirit photographer Édouard Buguet was accused of creating fraudulent images. Although he clearly admitted to deceiving his customers with simple double exposures, some clients were unconvinced and maintained that his photographs recorded visits from the Other Side. When X-rays were invented (see p. 212), they deepened belief in unseen spiritual activity. For lyrically inclined spiritualists, French photographer Louis Darget (1847–1921) created images of dreams and thoughts.

LATER CONFLICTS

THE WAR OF THE TRIPLE ALLIANCE, SOUTH AMERICA

The day after Christmas, 1864, eighty thousand troops under the direction of Paraguay's leader, Francisco Solano Lopez (1826?–1870), invaded Brazil. In May 1865, Brazil, Uruguay, and Argentina formed a triple alliance to defeat the Lopez government. The conflict arose over disputes about navigation routes and land claims. Tens of thousands of troops from the four countries were mobilized. The war, which thundered on until 1870, was especially devastating for Paraguay; some estimate that 80 per cent of the country's population died during the hostilities.

As in the American Civil War, photographers were sent to the fronts. One of the first Latin American war photographers, Esteban García (active 1860s), from Uruguay, organized their efforts. Little is known about García, but his images were published by Bate & Co., a Montevideo studio financed by investors in the United States. The North Americans were hoping to reproduce what they mistakenly thought was the substantial financial success of Brady's American Civil War photographs.[25] Sold in sets of ten, called *La Guerra Ilustrada* (*The War Illustrated*) (1866), the photographs show the troop formations and battle preparations characteristic of nineteenth-century war photographs (Fig. 4.21). As with American Civil

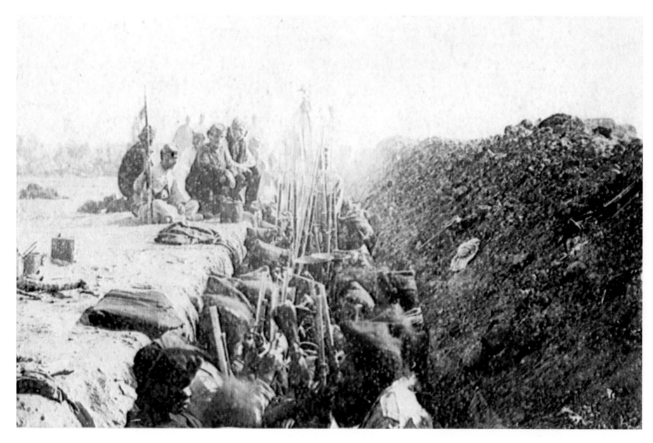

4.21
ESTEBAN GARCÍA, *First Battalion April 24 in the Trenches of Tuyuty,* 1866. Collodion print. Biblioteca Nacional de Uruguay, Montevideo.

War images, the daily personal experiences of the combatants are virtually absent.

THE FRANCO-PRUSSIAN WAR AND THE PARIS COMMUNE

The Franco-Prussian War sprang from the political and economic rivalry between France, under Emperor Napoleon III (1808–1873; r. 1852–70), and Prussia, led by Otto von Bismarck (1815–1898), who orchestrated the confrontation. France declared war on July 10, 1870, only to experience repeated defeats that culminated in the decisive German victory at the battle of Sedan (September 1, 1870), when Napoleon III was captured. A provisional government was declared in Paris, and in the winter of 1870 Prussian troops laid siege to the city. Passenger balloons, with such names as *Daguerre* and *Niépce*, attempted to carry communications from the beleaguered city, whose telegraph lines had been cut. In the lore of war and photography, the extensive use of carrier pigeons has become legendary. Packaged in tiny containers and tied to the tails of homing pigeons, more than a hundred thousand messages of photographically reduced text passed between the city and French officials outside the siege line. Sometimes the images were projected on to a wall so that a group of people could view them. The Prussians used falcons to chase and kill the French pigeons.[26] Despite the Parisians' efforts, the city fell after German bombardment.

Resentment at the royalist leanings of the postwar French government was especially keen in Paris. The move to disarm the National Guard, townsmen who fought the Germans and who supported an idea of a French republic, further angered Parisians. In mid-March, a group of anti-royalists and working-class activists declared themselves the "Paris Commune." Although the Commune lasted less than three months, it became an abiding emblem of a righteous people's revolution, in France and around the world. During so-called Bloody Week (May 21–May 28, 1871), when the French government repossessed the city, around twenty-five thousand Parisians were killed, more than during the Reign of Terror in the French Revolution or the recent German siege[27] (Fig. 4.22).

During and after the Commune, photography was used to record events as well as to promote, explain, and rationalize political positions. For example, the Communards posed for photographs before and after they tore down the Vendôme Column, erected in 1815 by Napoleon Bonaparte (1769–1821; r. 1804–14), whose statue stood on top of it. The decree for the destruction of the column belittled it as "a monument

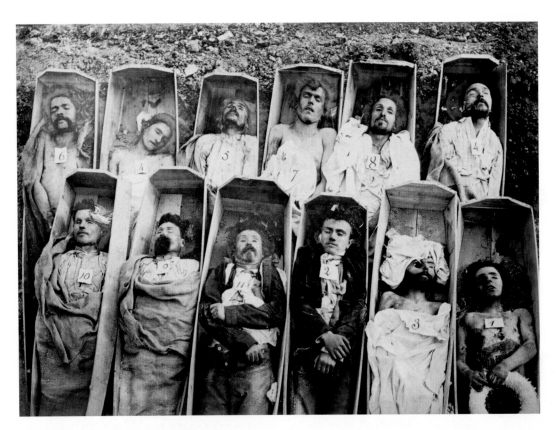

4.22
PHOTOGRAPHER UNKNOWN, *Communards in their Coffins*, May 1871. Albumen print. Gernsheim Collection. Harry Ransom Humanities Research Center, University of Texas at Austin.

An unknown photographer captured the carnage with an image of numbered corpses slumped in their coffins. This photograph of dead Communards could be read by their supporters as a symbol of tragedy and by their enemies as a symbol of triumph.

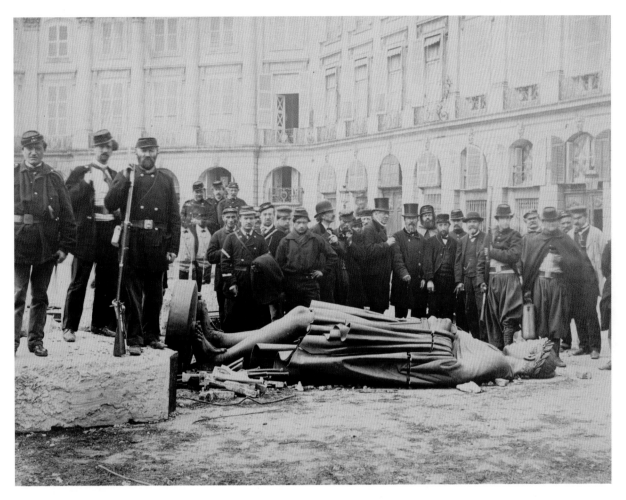

4.23
BRUNO BRAQUEHAIS, *The Fall of the Vendôme Column*, 1871. Bibliothèque Nationale de France, Paris.

of barbarianism, a symbol of brute force and of false glory, a confirmation of military rule contrary to the international rights of man."[28] These photographs were taken by the Paris photographer Bruno Braquehais (1823–1875), who favoured the Communards (Fig. 4.23). Braquehais's work took several forms, including portraits, art reproduction, and a few gauzy bits of pornography. He took 109 views of the Commune, which were sold in a bound album called *Paris during the Commune*. Regardless of their political leanings, many Parisian photographers realized what the domestic and foreign commercial potential of Commune-related images was. Ironically, photographs of the Communards were soon used to identify and arrest them, when the French government retook the city.

The activities of photographers in Paris after the fall of the Commune were the subject of a satirical illustration in the *Illustrated London News* for June 24, 1871[29] (Fig. 4.24). It is difficult to gauge completely the meaning of this print. British criticism of French radicalism had run high since the French Revolution of 1789; here, however, the placement of the photographer, and his disregard for the urgent task of the firefighters and the acute suffering of the woman and child

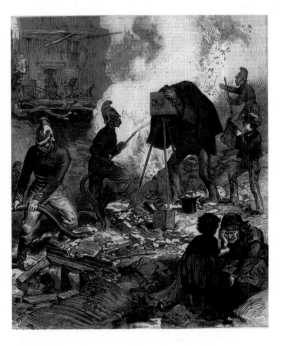

4.24
ARTIST UNKNOWN, *The Ruins of Paris*, from *Illustrated London News*, June 24, 1871. Newspaper illustration.

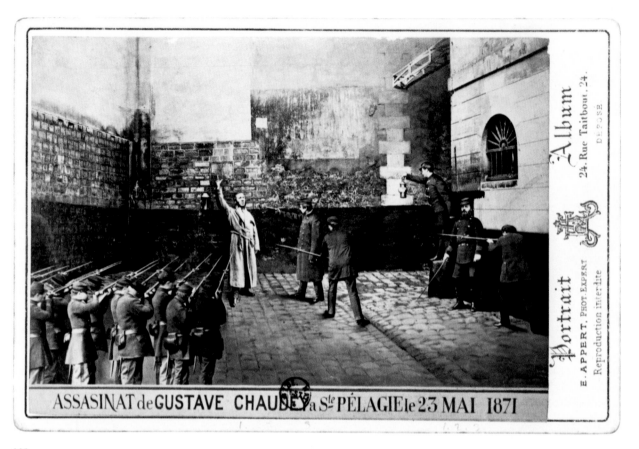

4.25
EUGÈNE APPERT, *Assassination of Gustave Chaudey at Sainte Pélagie, 23 May 1871*, 1871. Composite photograph. Bibliothèque Nationale de France, Paris.

in the right foreground, seem to criticize the neutrality and intrusiveness of photography and the public's hankering for sensational photographs.

After the Commune, the French photographer Eugène Appert (active 1870s), who favored the French government, made dramatic, deliberately contrived photographs of the events. In his *Crimes of the Commune* he included nine fabricated prints of events that visually presented the government's strong opposition to the Communards. After obtaining portraits of the leaders of the Commune, Appert hired actors to enact historic scenes from the point of view of the anti-Commune forces. In the studio, he cut out the individual figures, pasted on them the heads of the Communards, then rephotographed the image. These composite photographs vary considerably in quality (Fig. 4.25).

"SMALL WARS," COLONIAL EXPANSION, AND PHOTOGRAPHY

The Crimean War, the American Civil War, the War of the Triple Alliance, and the Franco-Prussian War were conflicts that, for the most part, engaged national armies against each other. But most conflicts during the nineteenth century pitted troops from the great powers against non-European peoples. Military, commercial, and propagandistic uses of photography were exploited during these small wars and subsequent colonial expansion. The combat-related uses of photography, such as the duplication of maps, description of terrain, and depiction of armaments, became more routine. Photographers increasingly accompanied troops from the major powers, both to record military exploits and to picture foreign countries for audiences back home. In India, China, North Africa, Abyssinia (now Ethiopia), the Middle East, and Asia, photographers were granted the right to photograph troops and the aftermath of battles. They also produced views of foreign lands that stressed the exotic look of the landscape, architecture, and people. In the 1850s and 1860s, dozens of Western photographers without military obligations relocated abroad and set up studios in countries where they hoped to make images for markets back home and for colonial settlers.

The landscape and architectural views produced by photographers attached to military expeditions and those made by commercial photographers are strikingly similar. Both tend to emphasize the unusual aspects of a landscape, an extraordinary temple or public building, or the remoteness of a site. In effect, the photographs, sold singly or in albums, promoted the notion of the photographer as a brave and resourceful explorer, akin to other expatriates, such as military personnel and entrepreneurs, who were living large at the edges of the world.

In the November 1859 edition of the *Photographic News*, an anonymous reviewer noted an exhibition of stereoscopic photographs published by the London firm of Negretti & Zambra. The writer observed that "as … the camera became more common in Egypt and the Holy Land, the more adventurous photographers turned their steps to more distant and less known countries. Even the jealously-guarded countries of China and Japan cannot shut out the camera."[30] Especially in places where intertwined Western political and economic interests expanded, photographers very quickly followed. In Asia, photography was first known primarily in port cities, but from the 1850s photographers began trekking to remote interior regions, photographing the residue of war, the wonders of the natural world, and indigenous art and architecture.

India

It is not clear what brought the German photographer John Christian A. Dannenberg (d. 1905) to northern India, but from the mid-1850s on, he seems to have been both an active commercial photographer and a member of the Bengal Photographic Society. His photographic portrait of Maharaja Jaswant Singh of Bharatpur (1851–1893) (Fig. 4.26) was subsequently overpainted by an anonymous artist, in a distinctly Indian style dating from the early daguerreotypes in India. Indian royals and the well-to-do had photographs made to mark historic events, and as presentation pieces for dignitaries at important meetings and events. Also, they sometimes became dedicated amateur photographers. When the young maharaja succeeded his father in 1862, he and his court were photographed by the firm of Shepherd & Robertson.

After arriving in India in 1863, British photographer Samuel Bourne (1834–1912) made three climbs high in the Himalayan wilds. Despite the physical obstacles and technical problems that beset his treks, Bourne excluded the hardships of the trail from his photographs, restricting difficulties to the long descriptive letters he wrote home to the *British Photographic Journal*. These helped to make him the epitome of the heroic photographer abroad. Bourne wrote that the mountain "scenery was not well adapted for pictures—at least for photography. … The character of the Himalayan scenery in general is not picturesque."[31] Consequently, he carefully selected scenes and camera angles, in order to depict the Himalayas as a compliant and serene landscape, waiting to be recorded by the camera (Fig. 4.27). One photographic historian credits Bourne with initiating "an imperial picturesque"—that is, an adaptation of European notions of pictorial organization and subject matter to the look of an exotic locale.[32]

After his journey to photograph the Crimean War, James Robertson traveled with photographer Félice Beato (c. 1820s– c. 1907) throughout the Middle East. Pictures of India were published under the name of Robertson and Beato, or Robertson Beato et Cie, though it is possible that Robertson never actually visited the subcontinent.[33] Beato, however, was certainly in India making photographs, some of them staged, soon after the Indian Mutiny, which began with the 1857 uprising of Indian-born troops in the employ of the British East India Company, the private corporation that controlled trade in India, against

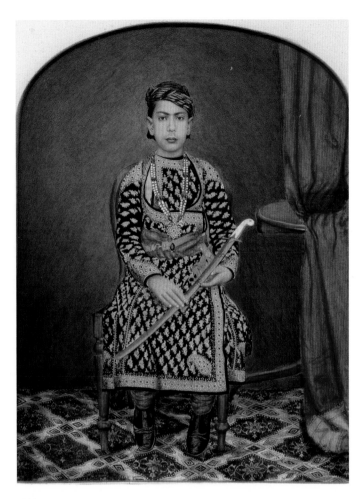

4.26
J. C. A. DANNENBERG AND UNKNOWN ARTIST, *Maharaja Jaswant Singh of Bharatpur (1851–1893)*, **1863. Albumen print and watercolor. The Alkazi Collection of Photography, London.**

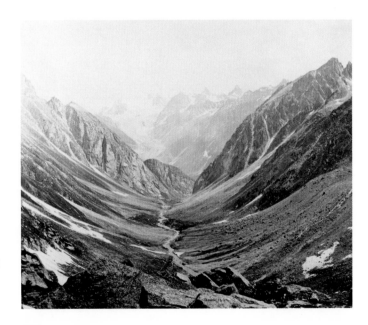

4.27
SAMUEL BOURNE, *Valley and Snowy Peaks Seen from the Hamta Pass, Spiti Side,* **1863–66. Albumen print from wet collodion negative. Victoria and Albert Museum, London.**

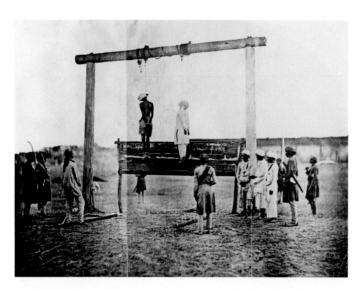

4.28
FÉLICE A. BEATO (attrib.), *The Execution of Mutineers in the Indian Mutiny*, 1857.
Victoria and Albert Museum, London.

During the Indian Mutiny, or First War of Independence, Beato photographed
from the British perspective, which included severe punishments for the rebels.

the regular British Army (Fig. 4.28). Later called by Indians the
First War of Independence, the uprising spurred the British to
reorganize the army and restructure colonial rule. For years, the
British public feasted on newspaper remembrances and novels
based on the Mutiny, which portrayed the British as martyrs and
served to justify further colonial expansion and conflicts such as
the Boer War. In fact, both sides were guilty of appalling savagery.

Beato was not the first Western photographer in India. John
Murray (1809–1898), a medical doctor who had worked for
the East India Company, and who taught medicine in Agra,
was also a photographer (Fig. 4.29). Some of his eight hundred
images of India, including the Taj Mahal, were exhibited
in London in November 1857, and gained large audiences
because of the Mutiny. Murray was skilled in making large-
format images and panoramas that consisted of two or three
connected photographs. The East India Company itself had
employed photographers to document Indian landscape and
antiquities since the mid-1850s.[34] Three brothers—Adolph
(1829–1857), Hermann (1826–1882), and Robert (1833–1885)
Schlagintweit, natural scientists and Alpine explorers—were
commissioned by the company to do biomagnetic measurement
in India and the Himalayas. During their four-year stay, Robert
made photographic renderings for their report of the scientific
mission, and for Hermann's book *Travels in India and High
Asia* (1869–80). One measure of the presence of Western
photographers in India is the formation of three photographic
societies, in Bombay, Madras, and the province of Bengal, from
1854 to 1856. Another indication of photography's capacity
to replicate the British imperial view of India is found in a
monthly publication, the *Indian Amateur's Photographic Album*
(1856–58), and in combinations of text and pictures, such as
the two-volume *The Oriental Races and Tribes: Residents and
Visitors of Bombay* (1863–66), produced by William Johnson
of the Bombay Photographic Society[35] (Fig. 4.30). As in China,
Western photographers employed painters trained in the art of
the miniature to color photographs.[36]

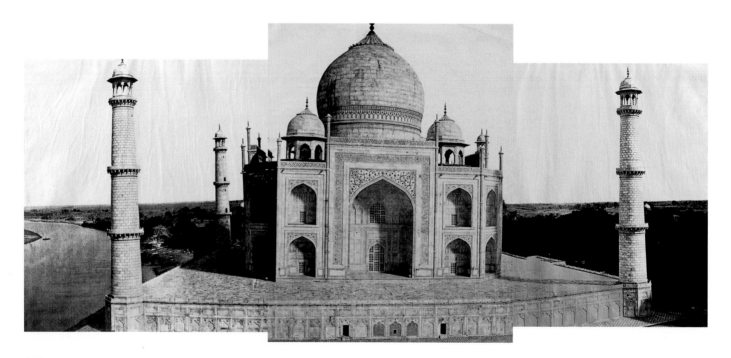

4.29
JOHN MURRAY, *Panorama of the West Face of the Taj Mahal*, c. 1850s–60s. Albumen print from mixed-type paper negatives. Victoria and Albert Museum, London.

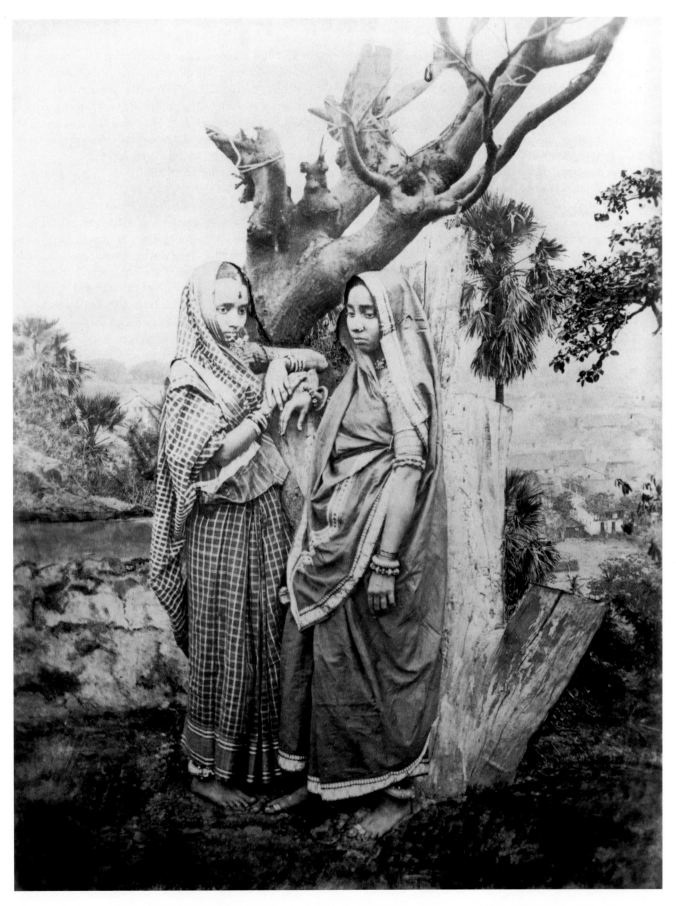

4.30
PHOTOGRAPHER UNKNOWN, *Nagar Brahmin Women*, from *The Oriental Races and Tribes: Residents and Visitors of Bombay*, 1863. Albumen print.

China

Félice Beato was with Anglo-French troops in China in 1860, during the Second Opium War (1856–60), perhaps in a semi-official capacity. At this period, China had endured a decade of civil war and economic instability, amidst Western pressure to open the country to commerce. The opium trade, hugely profitable to the British, French, Dutch, and Americans, flourished despite being outlawed by the Chinese government. After the First Opium War (1839–42), negotiations with European powers and the United States opened some ports to trade, but hostilities reignited in 1856, when Chinese officials searched a British ship. In 1860, the Western allies took the forts at Taku, near Tientsin, a critical step in the advance on the capital city of Peking (now Beijing). Beato's sequential documentation of the China campaign is among the first such conscientious series of images. He methodically photographed the aftermath of the allies' efforts to capture the forts at Taku; the interior of one of the strongholds shows the unburied Chinese dead inside the conquered fort (Fig. 4.31). A few months later an image from this series by Beato was reproduced as a wood engraving for the Christmas Eve edition of the *Illustrated London News*. The bold picturing of carnage predates the grisly photographs taken in the American Civil War (see Figs. 4.16, 4.17).

However vivid the devastation, Beato's photograph by itself did little to explain the condition of China and its relations with the West. After the signing of peace accords between the Chinese government and the Western powers, which Beato tried unsuccessfully to photograph, he managed to photograph Prince Kung, brother of the emperor, who negotiated with representatives of the West. Kung's image, and Beato's views of war and commerce, were sold in both Asia and Britain.[37]

For the London firm of Negretti & Zambra, which manufactured scientific instruments for the world trade, the production of photographic equipment and of photographs was a profitable sideline from the mid-1850s. To increase their stock of foreign views, they hired Swiss photographer Pierre Joseph Rossier (1829–1883/98) to photograph in Asia. His work resulted in a series of stereographic views that showed scenes in the southern city of Canton (now Guangzhou) after it had been captured by the Western allies, as well as images made in Japan. Around the globe, photographs of international ports, wharves, and Western commercial buildings were regularly created. Beato crafted a panorama of the British fleet in Hong Kong harbor (Fig. 4.32). Stereotypical images of indigenous peoples and local scenes also became popular.

The American expatriate photographer Milton M. Miller (active 1850s–70s) set up practice in the thriving city of Hong Kong, which had been deeded to the British in 1842. Miller acquired photographs of Beijing by Beato, which he marketed in addition to his portrait practice. Though active for only a few years, Miller worked in both Hong Kong and Canton, selling photographic prints and producing images of influential Chinese and foreign citizens, as well as occasional city views.

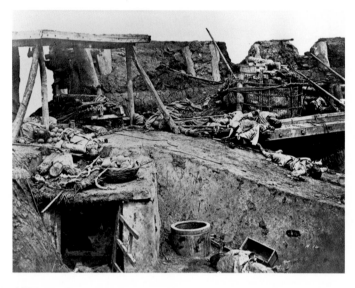

4.31
FÉLICE A. BEATO, *Interior of the Angle of North Fort at Taku on August 21, 1860*, 1860. Albumen print. Victoria and Albert Museum, London.

There is some evidence to suggest that Beato had corpses dragged into this scene and artfully arranged, a staging method he employed in some of his photographs of the Indian Mutiny.

4.32
FELICE A. BEATO, *Panorama of Hong Kong, Showing the Fleet for the North China Expedition*, March 18–27, 1860. Panorama consisting of six albumen silver prints from five wet collodion glass-plate negatives, each mounted on paper and joined by Japanese tape. Victoria and Albert Museum, London.

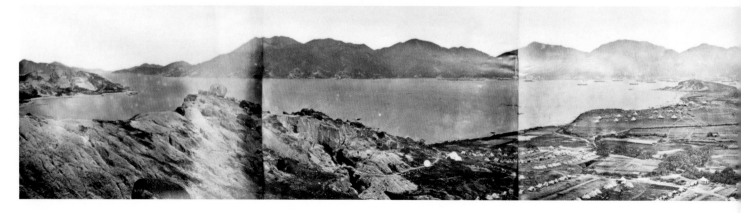

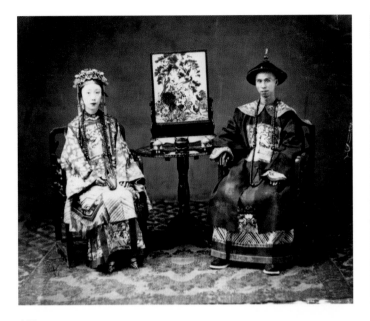

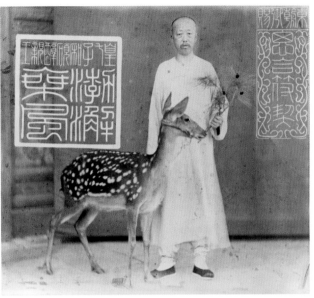

4.33
MILTON M. MILLER, *Cantonese Mandarin and his Wife*, 1861–64. Paper print.
Royal Asiatic Society, London.

4.34
LIANG SHITAI (SEE TAY), *Seventh Prince Feeding Deer*, 1888. Albumen Print.
Library of Congress, Washington, D.C.

The standards for middle-class portraiture, developed in the West, were adapted to the tastes of a new, well-to-do Chinese clientele. Lavish furnishings, placed in an enclosure marked off by a cloth backdrop, formed the setting for people who dressed in fine clothing and displayed artistic treasures. Miller's portraits, mostly of the Chinese upper and middle classes, and persons working for foreign traders, usually show the sitters directly facing the camera (Fig. 4.33). A hint of expression is occasionally evidenced on a sitter's face, but as a rule the camera kept its distance from the sitter.

Recent writing reveals the extent to which the Chinese understood photography as one of the Western technologies they needed to master. The reform effort of the 1860s known as the Self-Strengthening Movement embraced military machinery, the railroad, the telegraph, and to a lesser extent, the camera. Photographer Liang Shitai (also known as See Tay) (active 1870s–80s) created formal and informal photographs of the

emperor's seventh son, Prince Chun Xian, blending Western imaging and Chinese representation. In *Seventh Prince Feeding Deer*, the prince, who dressed like a scholar, feeds a deer, a symbol of longevity (Fig. 4.34). The prince's official seals are stamped on the photograph.[38]

The Scottish photographer John Thomson (1837–1921) observed what he thought to be a Chinese photographic aesthetic, which he satirized through the words of a fictional photographer, A-hung:

"You foreigners," says A-hung, "always wish to be taken off the straight or perpendicular. It is not so with our men of taste; they must look straight at the camera so as to show their friends at a distance that they have two eyes and two ears. They won't have shadows about their faces, because, you see, shadows form no part of the face. It isn't one's nose or any other feature; therefore it should not be there. The camera, you see, is defective … it won't recognize our laws of art."[39]

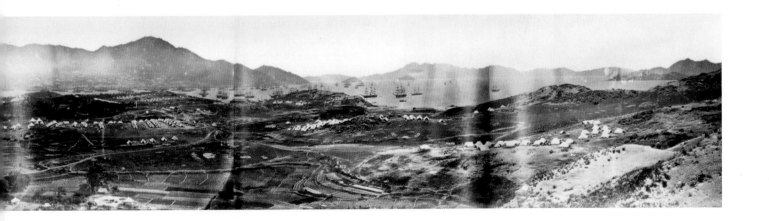

His remarks indicate the rapid growth of photography in China (see Fig. 4.35). Especially in Chinese cities such as Hong Kong, which had established trade with foreigners, artists were employed to copy paintings of Chinese scenes for sale to Western business people and travelers. These images, rendered in a more three-dimensional style than was used in traditional Chinese painting, dwelled on what seemed unusual and exotic to Western eyes. Such elements as rickshaws and sedan chairs, and pictures of workers and tradespeople in typical dress, were also drafted into photographic practice. Chinese costume, particularly the bound feet of women (see Fig. 4.33), and Chinese punishments, such as the *cangue* (Fig. 4.36), were frequent subjects. With the arrival of photography in China in the 1840s, some Chinese copy-painters turned to reproducing photographs in paint. In time, after training in the studios of foreigners or under the tutelage of Western missionaries, they began making photographs. Hong Kong seems to have been a photographic training center for Chinese, who then went on to set up practice in other cities.

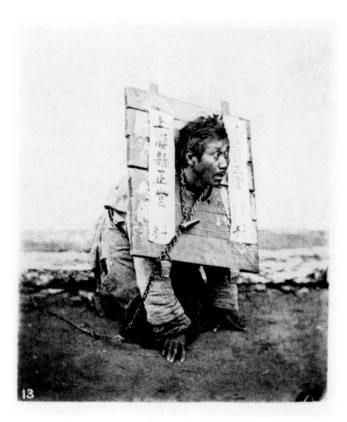

4.36
JOHN THOMSON, The *Cangue*, 1871–72, from *China and its People*, 1874. **Victoria and Albert Museum, London.**

The *cangue* was a Chinese punishment in which a wooden board was worn around the neck like a portable pillory. Photographs of Asian criminal punishments, especially beheadings, became a persistent theme in Western photography, beginning in the mid-nineteenth century.

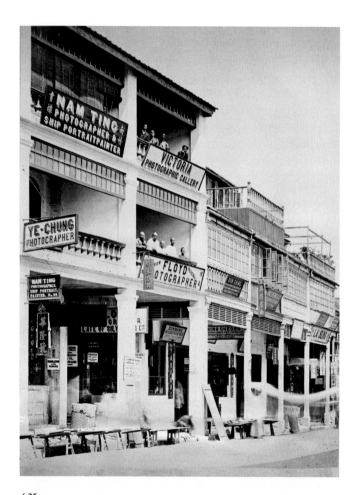

4.35
WILLIAM PRYOR FLOYD, *Photographers' Studios* (Floyd's studio among other studios, Queen's Road, Hong Kong), late 1860s–early 1870s. **Albumen print. Gift of Mrs. W. F. Spinney, 1923. Peabody Essex Museum, Salem, Massachusetts.**

Photography studios flourished in areas where colonial forces traded. Western photographers frequently hired Asian assistants, who soon set up their own rival businesses.

Unlike many Chinese photographers, who used the medium to augment their painting income, the famed Chinese photographer Afong Lai (1840–1900), probably did camerawork full-time. The quality of his work was noted in 1872 by Thomson, who wrote that "there is one Chinaman in Hong Kong, of the name Afong, who has exquisite taste, and produces work that would enable him to make a living even in London."[40] Lai advertised his up-to-date knowledge of photographic processes, as well as the resources of his well-stocked studio. He also published an album of prints taken after the typhoon that hit Hong Kong on September 22, 1874 (Fig. 4.37).

By the time he became acquainted with Lai's work, Thomson had spent several years traveling around Asia making photographs. His work pattern was to settle in an area for a while, make images, then strike out for new territory. He moved to Singapore in 1863, but made long photographic excursions over the next three years to India, Siam (now Thailand), and Cambodia. His first book, *The Antiquities of Cambodia*, was published in 1867. By 1868, he had resettled in Hong Kong. Thomson's images may stand alone aesthetically (Fig. 4.38), but they were integrated with geographic observation, and

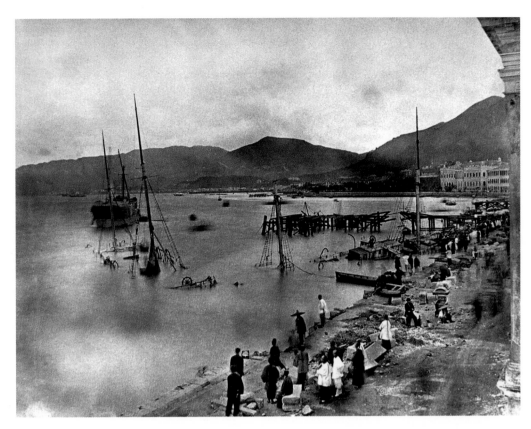

4.37
AFONG LAI, *Wreck of the Steamers "Leonor" and "Albay," Praya and Douglas Wharf Destroyed by Typhoon, 22 September 1874,* from *Hong Kong and Macao: The Typhoon of 22 September 1874.* Albumen silver print. Foreign and Commonwealth Office Library, London.

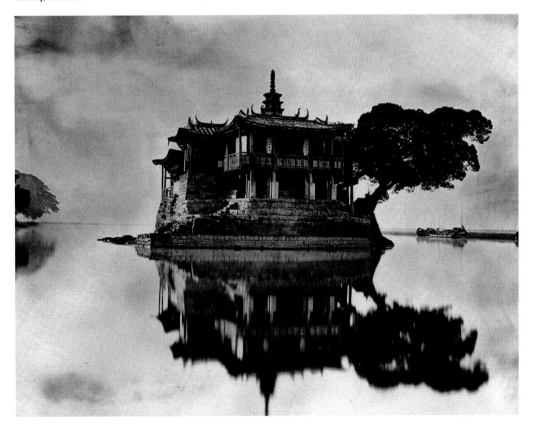

4.38
JOHN THOMSON, *Island Temple Foochow, Fukien Province, China,* 1870–71. Stereograph. The Wellcome Library, London.

with ethnographic research in his texts and lectures. Like other photographers aware of viewers' tastes, he took photographs of Chinese laborers, punishments (see Fig. 4.36), and street people. Thomson published six books of text and photographs on China, including *Illustrations of China and its People* (1873–74), a four-volume work of two hundred photographs produced by the COLLOTYPE process, an advancement that allowed images to be printed along with text.

Japan

The introduction of photography to Japan seems to have come about in the early 1840s, through scientific exchanges between the Japanese and a small Dutch trading outpost. But the rapid growth of commercial photography in Japan began in the 1850s, coinciding with the modernization of the country. Although momentous economic and social changes began to transform the country, it is difficult to discern these alterations through the photographic images produced during the mid-nineteenth century. In 1853 and 1854, Commodore Matthew C. Perry used shows of force to establish political and economic relations between the United States and Japan, and helped start the process of modernization in that largely feudal country. On his second mission, Perry brought along a daguerreotypist, Acting Master's Mate Eliphalet Brown (1816–1886), who made photographs while Perry negotiated with the Japanese for nearly five months. Along with wood engravings and lithographs, one-of-a-kind daguerreotypes illustrated Perry's official trip report to the United States Congress.[41]

Given widespread curiosity about Japan, which had been all but closed to foreigners, it was likely that Western and, in time, Japanese photographers would grasp the commercial potential for making views. From the late 1850s, a steady trickle of Western photographers entered Japan; by the early 1860s, Japanese professionals were serving a clientele of wealthy

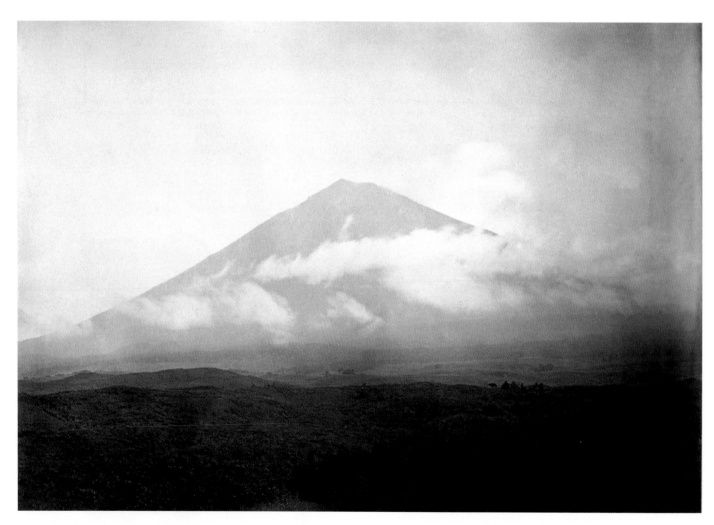

4.39
FÉLICE A. BEATO, *Mount Fuji*, 1868. Paper print. Old Japan Collection, Surrey, England.

Beato often photographed Mt. Fujiyama, the highest and most sacred mountain in Japan, either highlighting its reach through the clouds or the way in which it dominated the surrounding countryside.

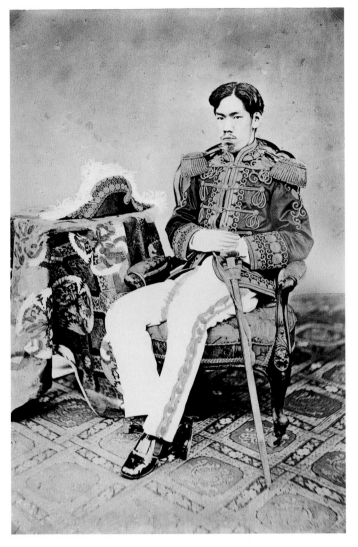

4.40
UCHIDA KYUICHI, *Mutsuhito, the Emperor Meiji*, c. 1872. Albumen print.
Richard Gadd Collection. Monterey Museum of Art, Monterey, California.

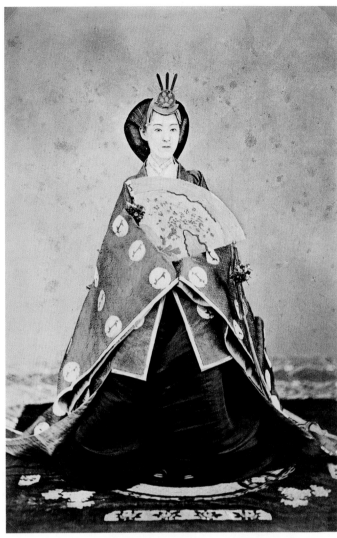

4.41
UCHIDA KYUICHI, *Haru-Ko, the Empress of Japan*, c. 1872. Albumen print.
Richard Gadd Collection. Monterey Museum of Art, Monterey, California.

Japanese patrons, as well as foreigners. When Beato arrived in Japan from China, he probably saw the growing economic opportunity. The *Illustrated London News* for July 13, 1863, indicates that he had set up a studio in Yokohama. Despite the political conflict between pro- and anti-modernization supporters, Beato's views imaged a tranquil country, unchanged for centuries (Fig. 4.39). He also made images of what he called "native types," including hand-tinted, somewhat romantic images of the samurai, the Japanese warrior class, whose privileges were repealed as Japan modernized its armaments and built a centrally controlled military. Travelers were able to purchase photographs in a variety of sizes from Beato and other photographers who catered to travelers. Complete albums of topographical views or occupational types were also available. Beato kept his thumb on the pulse of public opinion. In 1864, when two British officers were murdered by a

feudal lord and his entourage, their assailants were beheaded. Beato recreated the execution in a setting, and sold the images. Japanese samurai captivated the interest of foreign travelers, and many photographers, including Beato, satisfied the market by photographing them. Some even staged scenes of the samurai ritual suicide.

Many of Beato's images were delicately hand-colored by Japanese artists, including Kusakabe Kimbei (1841–1934), who worked as a colorist before setting up his own studio in Yokohama (Fig. 5.7). Contact with Western photographers was presumably one of the main ways in which the Japanese learned photography. In 1872, Uchida Kyuichi (1844–1875) made two photographs of Emperor Mutsuhito (1852–1912; r. 1867–1912) and Empress Haru-Ko, who ruled over Japan as it modernized (Figs. 4.40, 4.41). When offered for sale, these images quickly became popular;[42] they were withdrawn from the market in 1873, however, when the government decided that they represented an inappropriate commercialization of the monarchs. Photographs of the emperor were not officially offered for sale again until 1889.[43]

PHOTOGRAPHY IN THE MIDDLE EAST

During the 1850s and 1860s, the popularity of an extended trip to view ancient sites around the Mediterranean, often called the Grand Tour, stimulated the market for views of Italy, Greece, Palestine, and Egypt. Thomas Cook (1808–1892), founder of the popular Cook's Tours, escorted travelers to Egypt and the Holy Land, where he usually hired photographers to take group pictures. The books, prints, and stereographs produced by British photographer Francis Frith (1822–1898) were extremely popular. They introduced a generation of British viewers to the sights of Egypt and the Holy Land.

Frith's photographs in Egypt encompassed such well-known monuments as the pyramids at Giza, and less familiar works such as the buildings on Philae, an island in the southern reaches of the Nile near Aswan (Fig. 4.42). Frith was also a publisher of photographic books, and arranged his pictures of Egypt in such volumes as *Egypt and Palestine Photographed and Described by Francis Frith* (1858–60). Like the photographs themselves, Frith's books mix the ancient and the modern; awestruck descriptions of ancient architecture are interspersed with amusing accounts of recent travels. Frith also worked on an 1862 edition of the

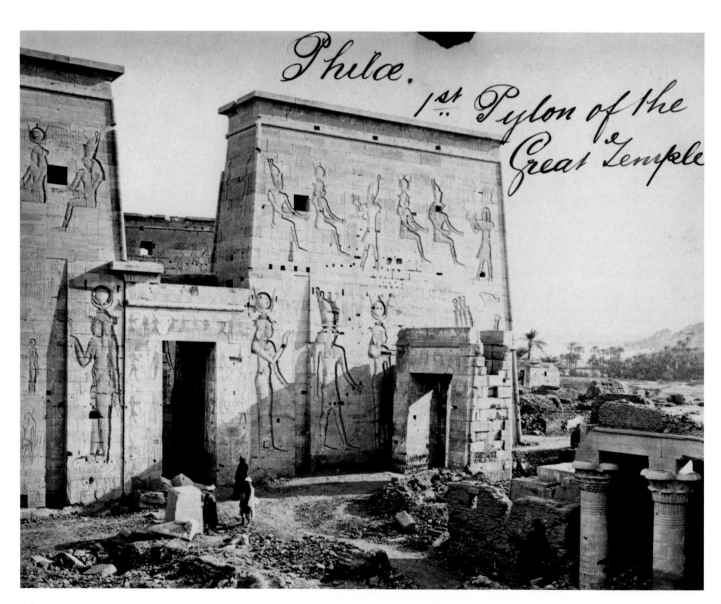

4.42
FRANCIS FRITH, *First Pylon View of the Great Temple,* **1850s. Wet collodion paper print. Victoria and Albert Museum, London.**

Frith's view of the deeply incised relief sculpture on the outer gate of Philae's temple of Isis is characteristic of his approach to Egyptian artifacts. He liked to include some local people, not simply to demonstrate the scale of the sculpture, but also to contrast the present with the past, and to let viewers glimpse contemporary Egypt.

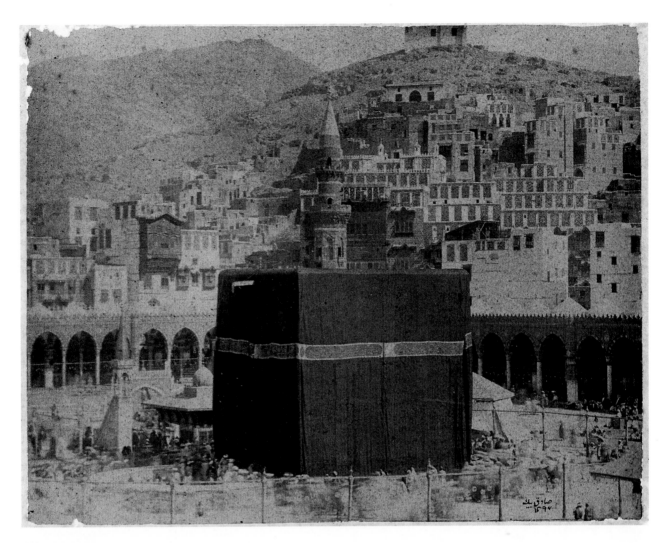

4.43
MUHAMMAD SADIQ, *The Holy City*, c. 1880. Albumen print.

Bible, which contained fifty-five of his Middle East photographs. Spurred, perhaps, by the popularity of his books on Egypt and the Holy Land, Frith and his assistants set out in 1859 to photograph every city and town in England, Scotland, Ireland, and Wales, including historic monuments and natural sites.[44] This encyclopedic urge, which struck many photographers and publishers, resulted in thousands of images that were sold singly on newsstands and similar venues.

While Frith photographed sites in the Middle East, Egyptian colonel and amateur photographer Muhammad Sadiq (sometimes Sadic Bey) (1832–1902) set out on a military mapping mission to explore Arabia. Although the exploration did not officially include photography, Sadiq was able to make the first-known photographs of the holy city of Medina (Madinah), where the Prophet Muhammad was born. In 1880, Sadiq accompanied a cortege of pilgrims from Egypt to Mecca (Makkah), where he produced a panorama of the Sacred Mosque with the draped Kaaba, or sacred structure, in the center (Fig. 4.43).

TOPOGRAPHICAL SURVEYS AND PHOTOGRAPHY

In the second half of the nineteenth century, the United States, Canada, and many European countries carried out numerous surveys of their own land, colonies, and foreign territories. Surveys were organized for a variety of purposes, including providing clean water to European settlers, transcribing the geology of an area, scouting routes for railroads, and recording archeological or architectural sites. Often the surveys were carried out by military engineers, who had already recognized the value of photography for determining artillery range and reproducing maps and sketches.

Because the terrain encountered by the foreign surveyors and the photographers who accompanied them was little known, the surveys' sponsors could not thoroughly predetermine what would be photographed. Nevertheless, photographers observed subtle cultural guidelines when selecting, arranging, and framing their shots. For example, Christians associated photographs of

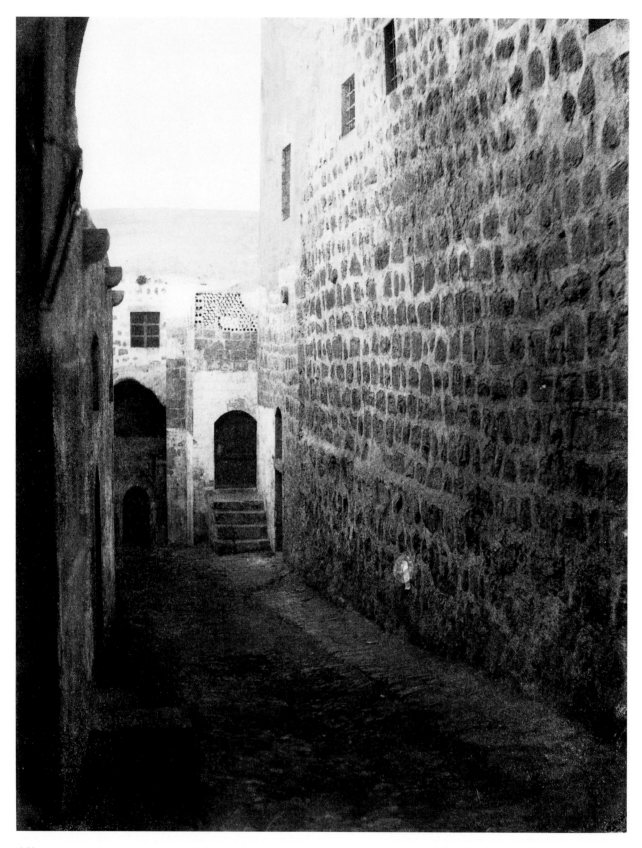

4.44
LOUIS DE CLERCQ, *Eighth Station of the Cross: Jesus Consoles the Daughters of Jerusalem,* **from** *Voyages en Orient: Les Stations de la Voie Douloureuse à Jerusalem (album 4), 1859–60.* **Albumen print. Collection Centre Canadien d'Architecture/Canadian Centre for Architecture, Montreal.**

While photographing castles built by crusaders in Syria and Palestine, French photographer Louis de Clercq (1836–1901) applied his spare, modernistic style to a photograph of the Way of the Cross—that is, the route of Jesus on the way to the Crucifixion.[45] His *Voyages en Orient 1859–1860* contained a separate album of these images.

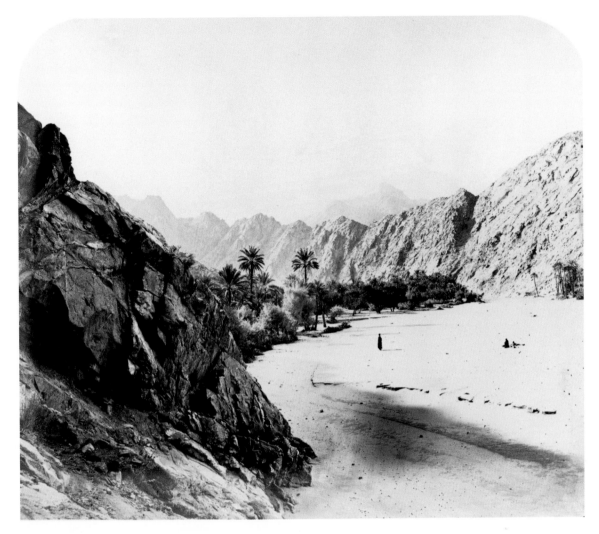

4.45
JAMES MCDONALD, *Distant View of Jerbel Serbal, from the Palm Grove, Wady Feiran*, 1868–69, from *Ordnance Survey of the Peninsula of Sinai*, part III: Photographs, vol. 2. Albumen print. Harry Ransom Humanities Research Center, University of Texas at Austin.

the Middle East with the Bible, regardless of the initial intent or context of the image. Photographers were aware of the intellectual and emotional interaction viewers had with such photographs, and they understood its commercial potential. Consequently, they ignored contemporary conditions in places associated with the Bible, and stressed the very timelessness of the setting (Fig. 4.44).

Sergeant James McDonald, assigned by the British Royal Engineers to survey Jerusalem and later the Sinai, photographed early Christian inscriptions and pilgrimage sites. His images of the Sinai peninsula are composed almost as paintings (Fig. 4.45). As was typical of photographers traveling through the Middle East, McDonald regularly took ethnographic images.

THE ABYSSINIAN CAMPAIGN, OR THE MAGDALA EXPEDITION

It is sometimes difficult to distinguish survey photography from the photography done by major powers during military campaigns. For example, during the Magdala expedition to Ethiopia, launched in 1867 by the British government when Christian missionaries and other Europeans were taken hostage by the emperor, the Royal Engineers furnished Sir Robert Napier's troops with a team of photographers. They reportedly managed to make an astounding fifteen thousand images, despite the hazards of conflict and the difficulties of terrain.[46] As might be expected, the Magdala expeditionary photographers made routine military photographs of leaders and troop formations. But they also created aesthetically attentive landscapes, including a view of the emperor's mountain fortress, together with images of indigenous houses, and pictures of the Ethiopians in typical clothing or with interesting implements.

DÉSIRÉ CHARNAY AND EXPEDITIONARY PHOTOGRAPHY

French photographer Désiré Charnay (1828–1915) received financial support from a branch of the French government for

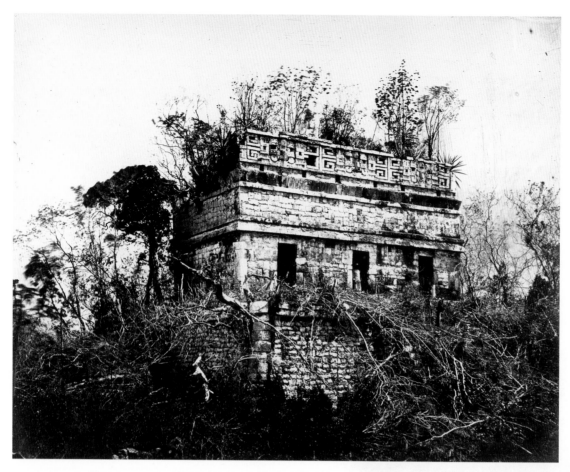

4.46 (above)
CLAUDE-JOSEPH-DÉSIRÉ CHARNAY, *The Prison, Chichen-Itza*, 1857–89. Albumen silver print from glass negative. Metropolitan Museum of Art, New York

4.47 (right)
CLAUDE-JOSEPH-DÉSIRÉ CHARNAY, *"Marou – Malgache – Marou," Three Women*, from *Album of a Mission in Madagascar*, 1863. Musée d'Orsay, Paris.

Charnay used the rapidly accepted conventions for photographing non-Western peoples by comparing the bodies of three residents of Madagascar.

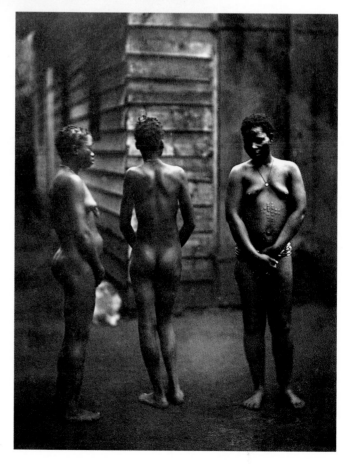

his photographs of pre-Columbian sites in Mexico, and locations associated with Spanish conquistador Hernán Cortés (Fig. 4.46). Soon after returning to France, Charnay joined his country's 1863 expedition to Madagascar to extend French political and trade influence[47] (Fig. 4.47). When Charnay returned to Mexico in 1864, he accompanied French troops who were sent to support Emperor Maximilian (1832–1867; r. 1864–67), who had been put on the throne by Napoleon III. After Maximilian was captured and executed by his rival Benito Juárez (1806–1872) in 1867, Charnay stayed in the United States for three years. He later ventured through South America, Java, and Australia, where his interest in writing about and photographing exotic landscapes, ancient ruins, and ethnographic types continued.

THE 49TH PARALLEL SURVEY
Photography of the shared northwestern border of the United States and Canada, running along the 49th parallel, was begun

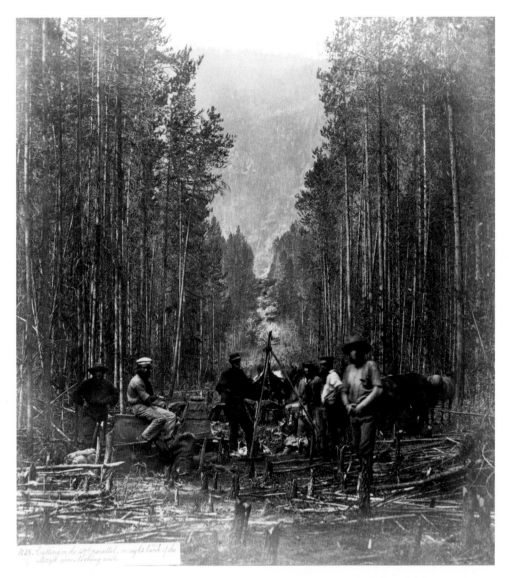

4.48
PHOTOGRAPHER UNKNOWN (ROYAL ENGINEERS), *Cutting on the Forty-Ninth Parallel, on the Right Bank of the Mooyie River Looking West*, 1860–61. Albumen print from wet collodion negative. Victoria and Albert Museum, London.

by an American survey team in 1857, and completed jointly with a British team of Royal Engineers from 1858 to 1861 (Fig. 4.48). Beginning in 1855, some members of the Royal Engineers had been given photographic training. Soon after, Sir John Burgoyne (1782–1871), inspector general of fortifications, originated a program of systematic training in photography under the direction of one Charles Thurston Thompson (1816–1868), official photographer to the South Kensington Museum (now the Victoria and Albert Museum) in London. The photographer engineers were charged "to send home periodical photographs of all works in progress, and to photograph and transmit to the War Department all drawings of all objects, either valuable in a professional point of view, or interesting as illustrative of history, ethnology, natural history, antiquities, etc."[48] As in most surveys, scientists accompanied engineers to the borderlands. They wrote about the fossils, plants, and animals they encountered.

The final map-making and scientific report writing took place in Washington, D.C., though it was never finished because the American Civil War pressed other duties on many of the contributors.[49] The British photographers also joined expeditions in Palestine, the Sinai, China, India, Greece, and Panama.

GOVERNMENT SURVEYS IN THE UNITED STATES

In 1838, the United States Army Corps of Topographical Engineers became a separate branch of the military assigned to explore and map the undeveloped parts of the United States.[50] The corps remained a military unit, capable of fighting, yet its work was directed toward the advancement of civilian enterprise and public works. After the Civil War, surveys of the American West covered vast regions. As the historian William Goetzmann observed, the corps could perform scientific exploration, such as mapping unknown terrain, while also serving political and commercial ends, such as scouting roads and railway passages for private entrepreneurs, which would, in turn, displace native peoples.[51] Similarly, photographs of the American West could be simultaneously scientific, commercial, political, and aesthetically pleasing.

In the expansive lands west of the Mississippi River, surveys mixed dispassionate scientific investigation with research on the commercial potential of natural resources. Attempts to map possible routes for a transcontinental railroad line were spurred by pressure from settlers, from business, and by gold and silver finds, such as the discovery of the Comstock lode in 1859, near Virginia City, Nevada. Government surveys often had an encyclopedic mission, attempting to construct orderly records of Native American life, geology, plants, and animals, as well as investigate commercial potential. For instance, the huge Pacific Railroad Reports included whole volumes on zoology.[52]

Photography and the Transcontinental Railway

After years of speculation and surveying, the United States Congress in 1862 authorized the construction of a trans–continental railroad. Two years after the end of the Civil War, Alexander Gardner was appointed chief photographer to the eastern division of the Union Pacific Railway. Along with images made by photographers under his supervision, his photographs were published in an album titled *Across the Continent on the Kansas Pacific Railway (Route of the 35th Parallel)*, offered for sale in April 1869. The album included scenes of small-town life, settlers' homes, Native Americans, and military installations, as well as Gardner's primary topic, the construction of the railroad. *Westward, the Course of Empire Takes its Way* shows workers and pioneers laying track at the end of the line (Fig. 4.49). The title alludes to a famous mural painted by Emanuel Leutze for the United States Capitol in Washington, D.C., completed in 1862 (Fig. 4.50). Gardner was working for Mathew Brady in

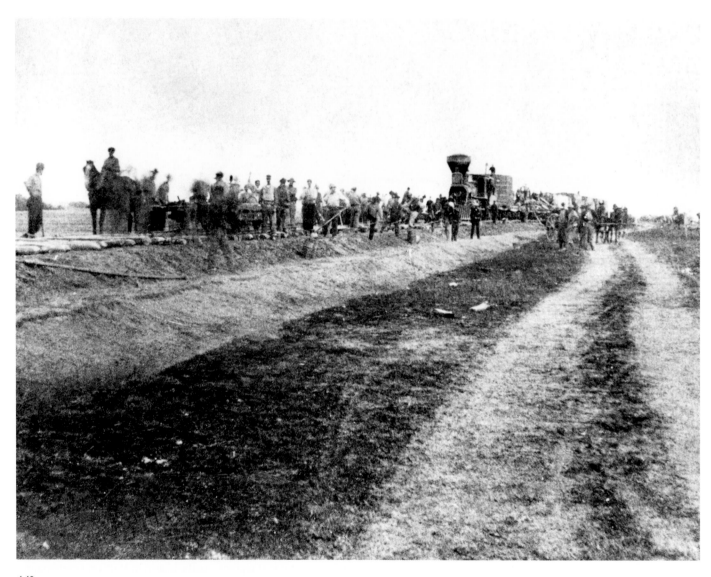

4.49
ALEXANDER GARDNER, *"Westward, the Course of Empire Takes its Way": Laying Track 600 Miles West of St. Louis, outside Hays City, Kansas: End of the Line*, plate 152 from *Across the Continent on the Kansas Pacific Railway*, n.d. Stereograph. Kansas State Historical Society, Kansas, Missouri.

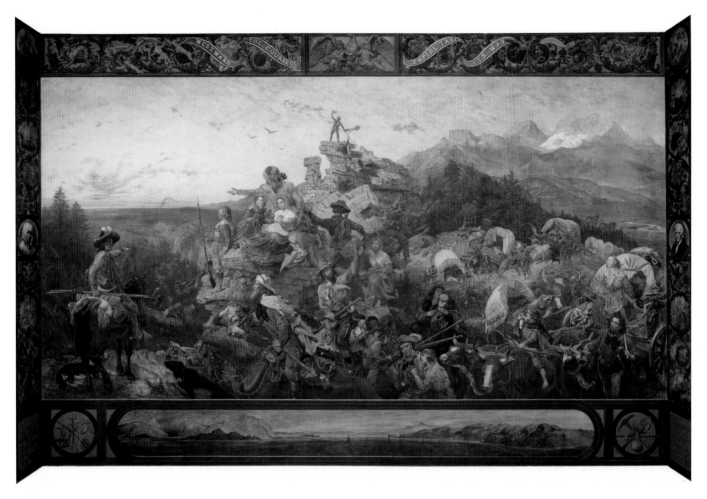

4.50
EMANUEL LEUTZE, *Westward, the Course of Empire Takes its Way (Westward Ho!)*, 1861. Oil on canvas, 33 x 43 in. (84 x 110 cm). National Museum of American Art, Smithsonian Institution, Washington, D.C.

Washington as the painting was being executed, and reports of its progress appeared in newspapers along the East Coast. The mural shows pioneers crossing the continent on horseback and in covered wagons; in applying the title to his static, posed photograph, Gardner may have hoped to associate the railroad with the sense of adventure and accomplishment depicted by Leutze.[53]

Andrew J. Russell (1830–1902), who had been the only officially assigned photographer in the American Civil War, was hired by the Union Pacific Railway to photograph the building of a northern route across the American West that competed with the proposed track of the Kansas Pacific, for which Alexander Gardner photographed. Russell's album *The Great West Illustrated in a Series of Photographic Views Across the Continent; Taken along the Line of the Union Pacific Railroad* was published in 1869 (Fig. 4.51).

Timothy O'Sullivan and Survey Photography

The May 2, 1867, issue of the *New York Times* noted the departure of a "party of young men on an important surveying expedition to a section of the Rocky Mountains and the great basin westward."[54] The journey, sponsored by the U.S. Congress

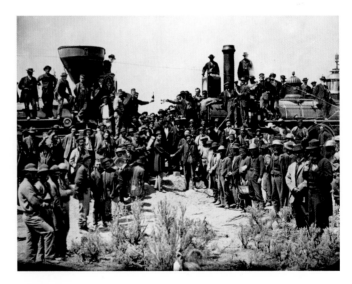

4.51
ANDREW J. RUSSELL, *Meeting of the Rails, Promontory Summit, Utah*, 1869. Albumen print. Union Pacific Historical Museum, Omaha, Nebraska.

Russell's photographs celebrated the engineering feats required to build a railroad across the rugged terrain of the western United States. His images of the meeting of the Union and Central Pacific railroads in Promontory Summit, Utah, on May 10, 1869, are part of the collective visual memory of Americans.

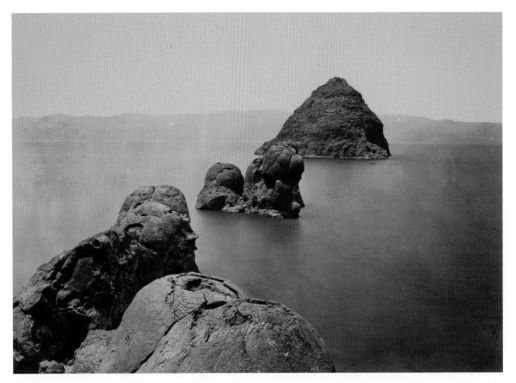

4.52
TIMOTHY O'SULLIVAN, *Pyramid and Tufa Domes, Pyramid Lake, Nevada*, 1878. Albumen print. Library of Congress, Washington, D.C.

O'Sullivan photographed members of the United States Geological Expedition of the 40th parallel clambering on the unusual rock formations in Pyramid Lake. But in this, his best-known image of the area, he showed it undisturbed by human presence. The far shore is only lightly suggested, while the bold diagonal composition suggests the tremendous volcanic forces that pushed up the domes.

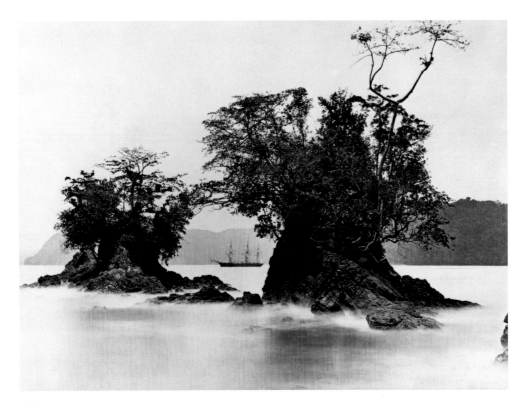

4.53
TIMOTHY O'SULLIVAN, *The Nipsic in Limón Bay, at High Tide*, 1871. Albumen print. George Eastman House, Rochester, New York.

and carried out by the United States Engineers, was directed by scientist Clarence R. King (1842–1901). The surveying party was to follow part of the proposed route of the transcontinental railroad, and included Timothy O'Sullivan as the official photographer.

Like his colleague and friend Alexander Gardner, Timothy O'Sullivan journeyed through the American West after the Civil War. With King's survey, he made views of the strangely shaped lava domes that erupted from Pyramid Lake in Nevada (Fig. 4.52). While the survey wintered in Virginia City, Nevada, in 1868, O'Sullivan ventured several hundred feet underground into the Comstock mine, the most famous deposit of gold and silver in America.

O'Sullivan was scarcely back in Washington, D.C., when he joined another survey. The Darién Survey Expedition of 1870 set out to explore the isthmus of Darién (or Panama), led by Lieutenant-Commander Thomas O. Selfridge under the auspices of the secretary of the navy. The group also included sixty Marines, a show of force for the Panamanian people, who suspected that the proposed canal would endanger their way of life.[55] O'Sullivan found photographing in the jungle difficult because of the humidity, the frequent rain, and the thick vegetation, which allowed little light to penetrate. Nevertheless, he produced more than two hundred stereo images and one hundred glass plates.[56] Some of his pictures adapt the Panamanian landscape to Western tastes (Fig. 4.53), as Bourne had done in India (see Fig. 4.27).

O'Sullivan accompanied two other important American surveys: the 1871 United States Geographical Survey West of the 100th Meridian, commonly called the Wheeler Survey for its leader George Montague Wheeler (1842–1905); and an independent 1873 survey sponsored by Wheeler to photograph Native Americans and the ruins of a cliff-dwelling culture in the Cañon de Chelly, in what is now Arizona (Fig. 4.54). The trip's reputation was tarnished in the press for having allegedly abandoned two white guides, and resulted in the shooting dead of several Native Americans. The photographs taken by O'Sullivan, however, depict none of the ill-feeling or tragedy of the journey, indicating that he, like many nineteenth-century photographers, understood that his documentary work was bound by his assignment and by commercial considerations.

Preservation of the Wilderness: Yellowstone and Yosemite

Westward expansion and development in the United States were driven by political and economic motives, as well as spiritual yearnings for unity, which seemed to compromise the notion of the West as an inviolable wilderness. There were two Wests in American perception: the West of such natural resources as minerals, timber, and arable land; and the West of ancient Native American peoples, vast geological wonders, and trackless wilderness. The Gold Rush era and subsequent closing of the western frontier threatened to do away with a central psychic dynamic in American life—the attitude that, in a pinch, one could head out west beyond the taint of human society and live simply. Settlement and enterprise appeared to endanger the

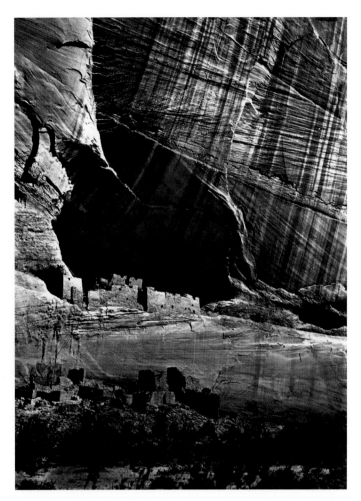

4.54
TIMOTHY O'SULLIVAN, *Ancient Ruins in the Cañon de Chelly*, 1873. Albumen print. Library of Congress, Washington, D.C.

unique American landscape, but the wilderness seemed hostile to robust economic development. The history of photographic imaging of the Yosemite Valley in California and the Yellowstone area of Wyoming demonstrates how closely intertwined were the notions of pure nature and civilized progress.

Carleton E. Watkins (1829–1916) was not the first person to photograph the dramatic scenery of the Yosemite Valley, but he was the best known and most influential. Another San Francisco photographer, Charles Leander Weed (1824–1903), had visited Yosemite in 1859. Watkins's early career brought him near Yosemite, to the vast Mariposa estate, where he was commissioned to photograph the property's mining activities. The photographs were used to entice foreign investors with the estate's gold and mineral potential. In his early commercial photographs, Watkins developed the practice of showing that human enterprise did not disturb the natural order (Fig. 4.1). He was one of the first American artists in any medium to construct a commercial sublime, rendering nature's grandeur with subtle, unobtrusive traces of new economic ventures.

Watkins probably made his initial 1861 trip to Yosemite in the company of one of the Mariposa estate's entrepreneurs.

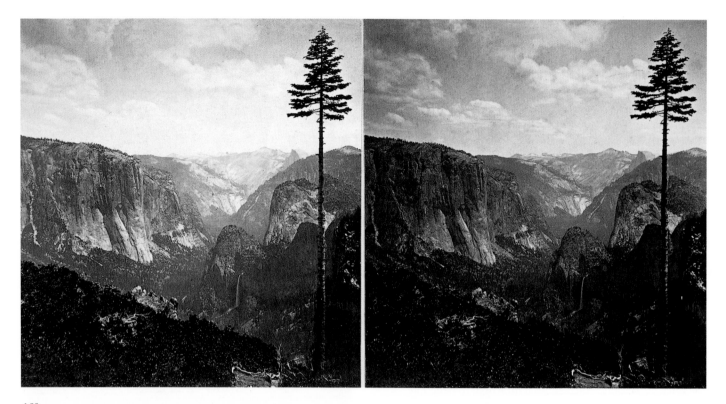

4.55
CARLETON E. WATKINS, *From the "Best General View," Mariposa Trail*, c. 1865–66, from Watkins's, *Pacific Coast* stereo series, no. 1134.
Albumen print. Center for Creative Photography, University of Arizona, Tucson, Arizona.

Watkins's photograph shows the Yosemite Valley as he imagined it might have existed at the time of creation. The dark foreground area and the tall tree on the right help to inflate the three-dimensional effect of the stereograph by creating a sense of deep recessive space.

He returned to Yosemite in 1865 and 1866, under the informal auspices of the California State Geological Survey, whose members studied the geology, biology, and mineral potential of the region, as well as likely sites for roads. The Gold Rush years had quickened American and foreign interest in California. Watkins, alert to opportunity, if not always adept in business matters, began a series of photographs at Yosemite, whose scenic beauty was already attracting both a growing curiosity back east and a few intrepid tourists. Like O'Sullivan at Pyramid Lake, Watkins preferred to show Yosemite as an Eden of unsullied awe. The absence of people accentuated the area as a prime site in which to witness the processes of nature.

Watkins's stereograph *From the "Best General View," Mariposa Trail* (Fig. 4.55) typifies the soaring sublime that he contrived to express in the expansiveness of the valley and the height of its crags. Although more tourists were arriving in Yosemite by the mid-1860s, Watkins still took his photograph from a vantage point that eliminated all traces of the human presence, and dislocated the view from contemporary life. Moreover, the viewer is not situated in a particular spot, but invited to soar above the valley, a feeling that would have been made all the more intense in stereographic viewing. German-American painter Albert Bierstadt (1830–1902) saw Watkins's photographs and magnified the conventions, creating sensational tourist-pleasing images of Yosemite as a primordial, cotton-candy-swathed Alps.

Eadweard Muybridge (1830–1904), who would later become renowned for his photographs of human movement (see pp. 208–9, 211), also gained a national reputation as a photographer of Yosemite. Born in Britain, Muybridge settled in San Francisco. Following the success of Watkins's views of the valley, Muybridge made his first trip to Yosemite in 1867. By 1872, he was producing large-plate prints that competed with those of Watkins.

Muybridge's images of Yosemite frequently fill the sky with dramatic atmospheric effects. Even when he chose a point of view that would dangle the viewer over a precipice (Fig. 4.56), Muybridge did not imitate the hypnotic detail and airless clarity of Watkins's work. Muybridge sometimes printed cloud studies separately in the upper portion of his Yosemite scenes. He also relished moonlight effects, and invented a device that minimized overexposure of the sky, and thereby allowed clouds to appear. In *Spirit of Tutohannula* (1867), he responded to the American association of ancient peoples with wilderness by having an individual enact the ghostly presence of the Native American chief said to have lived on the summit of El Capitán in Yosemite. It was good practice for his staged photographs of the Modoc War (see Fig. 4.59).

William Henry Jackson's (1843–1942) photographs of the Yellowstone area, though not the first, were the images that became enduring visual symbols of this locale. Jackson began his photographic career coloring and retouching portrait photographs. His philosophical outlook on nature was informed by American writers such as Henry David Thoreau (1817–1862) and Ralph Waldo Emerson (1803–1882), who saw nature as infused by a higher spiritual intelligence. Nevertheless, Jackson was a shrewd businessman, and embellished his photographs with descriptive words such as "castle" and "temple" to describe the sites at Yellowstone. Jackson settled briefly in Omaha, Nebraska, where he made studio pictures and locale shots of the Pawnee, Otoe, and Omaha peoples living in the area. In the *Descriptive Catalogue of Photographs of American Indians by W. H. Jackson, Photographer of the Survey of 1877*, he spoke of Native Americans in terms that were becoming increasingly prevalent. He saw them as dwindling vestiges of a primitive time in America, who could only purchase survival by adopting the values of white Americans.

Like several photographers of the West, Jackson worked for a government-sponsored survey. He joined the first official government and scientific survey of the Yellowstone area, directed by Ferdinand Vandeveer Hayden in 1871.[57] Previous explorations to Yellowstone, which would become the country's first official national park, aroused public interest in the area's geological wonders, as did the prospect of a rail service for tourists. Aware of public curiosity about the area, Hayden brought with him the landscape painter Thomas Moran (1837–1926), who had made sketches for a recent article in *Scribner's* magazine on "The Wonders of Yellowstone." He also invited sons and protégés of such powerful Washington politicians and lobbyists as Massachusetts senator Henry L. Dawes, the principal spokesperson in the campaign that resulted in Yellowstone being designated a national park in 1872.[58] Along the way, Jackson made photographs of gold mining. But for his treatment of the

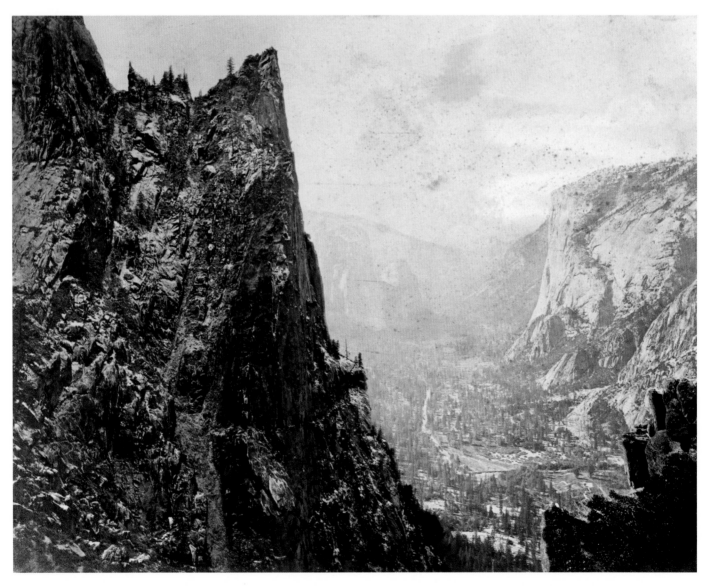

4.56
EADWEARD MUYBRIDGE, *Valley of the Yosemite from Union Point*, c. 1872. Albumen print. The J. Paul Getty Museum, Los Angeles, California.

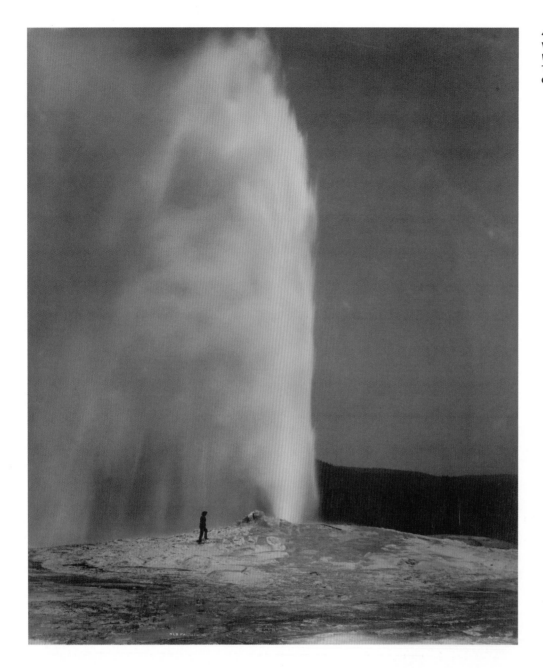

4.57
WILLIAM HENRY JACKSON, *Old Faithful, Wyoming*, 1870. Albumen silver print. The J. Paul Getty Museum, Los Angeles, California.

Yellowstone geysers, such as *Old Faithful, Wyoming* (Fig. 4.57), he turned to retouching, embellishing the steamy emissions.

WAR AND THE PHOTOGRAPHY OF NATIVE AMERICANS

The movement westward brought about regular conflicts with Native Americans, who fought removal from their ancient homelands and consolidation with other, unrelated groups.

The Modoc War

In northern California and Oregon, longstanding tension between the Modoc people and white settlers escalated between 1872 and 1873. Unhappily moved by the United States. government to the Klamath Reservation in Oregon, many Modocs returned to their ancestral homelands along the California–Oregon border. In November 1872, cavalry troops arrived to remove the Modocs from settler-claimed land. Eventually the Modocs hid in caverns and depressions found in the rugged lava beds south of Tule Lake, where the remainder of the campaign against them was fought.

The terrain of the lava beds was so unfamiliar to the U.S. military that the Corps of Engineers was called in to make a reconnaissance.[59] The photographer hired to record the topography and, perhaps, copy maps and sketches was Louis Heller (1839–1928). A German-born photographer who worked in California, Heller was the first to reach the war front. His images of Modoc prisoners were used on the cover of *Frank Leslie's Illustrated Newspaper* for July 12, 1873[60] (Fig. 4.58). At the time, Muybridge was a San Francisco photographer in the employ of Bradley and Rulofson, commercial photographers who sold images of California as well as current events.

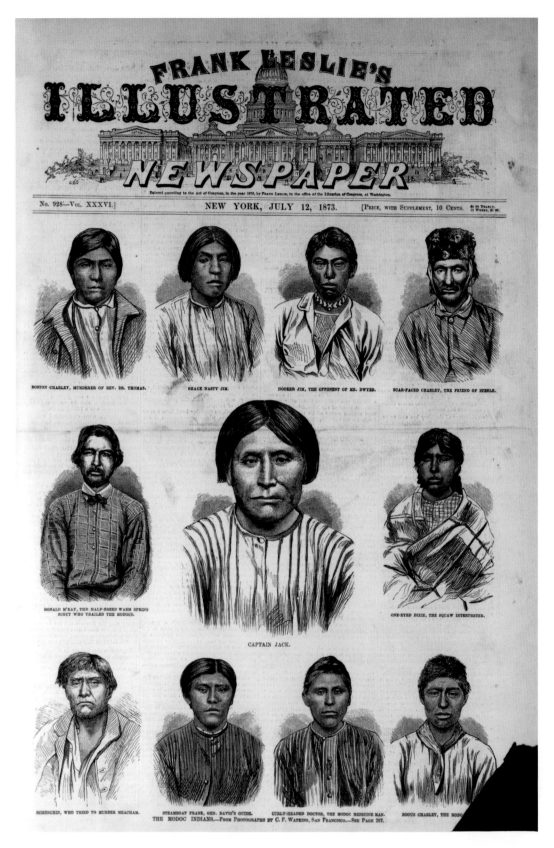

4.58
LOUIS HELLER, *Frank Leslie's Illustrated Newspaper*, July 12, 1873. Woodblock print from a photograph by Louis Heller.
Library of Congress, Washington, D.C.

The cover of the newspaper erroneously credited Heller's photographs of Modoc prisoners to Carleton Watkins. The note, in small print at the bottom of the page, tells readers that the images were derived from photographs, an increasingly common announcement that expressed the authenticity of the images.

His photographs of the troops and the locale were sent to Washington to show the difficult circumstances in which the military had been operating against the Modoc (Fig. 4.59). These pictures were also used to illustrate the June 21 issue of *Harper's Weekly*.

The Fort Laramie Treaty

Although dozens of wars such as the Modoc War were fought between 1850 and 1886, the preparation, conduct, and aftermath of battles and skirmishes were seldom reported by the camera. Photographic portraits of Native American leaders were sometimes made, both in their own settlements and in towns where photographers maintained studios. Newspaper articles on the so-called Indian Wars were generally illustrated by artists' conceptions, rather than photographically derived pictures. From time to time, Native American artists rendered the engagements with paintings on animal hide.

A photograph taken by Alexander Gardner in 1868 of the participants in the peace talks and treaty negotiations at Fort Laramie (Fig. 4.60) shows Civil War general William Tecumseh Sherman (third from the right of the U.S. delegation), commander of the army's Division of the Mississippi, which included the Great Plains. Sherman took his Civil War philosophy of "total war" and applied it to relations with Native Americans, for whom it meant the annihilation of villages and supplies, as well as battle.[61] The treaty negotiated at Fort Laramie in 1868 followed the war for the contested Bozeman Trail, which

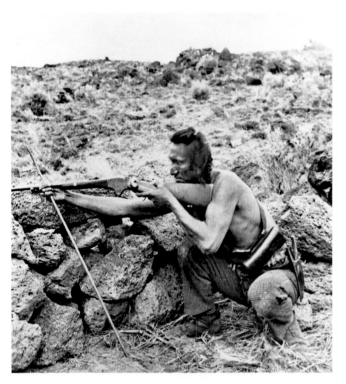

4.59
EADWEARD MUYBRIDGE, *A Modoc Brave on the War Path*, 1872–73. Paper print. National Anthropological Archives, Washington, D.C.

Muybridge posed a Native American scout working for the U.S. Army as an enemy Modoc brave, although he was not a Modoc.

4.60
ALEXANDER GARDNER, *Untitled* (Commissioners, General Sherman among them, seated with Indians), May 10, 1868. Paper print. National Anthropological Archives, Washington, D.C.

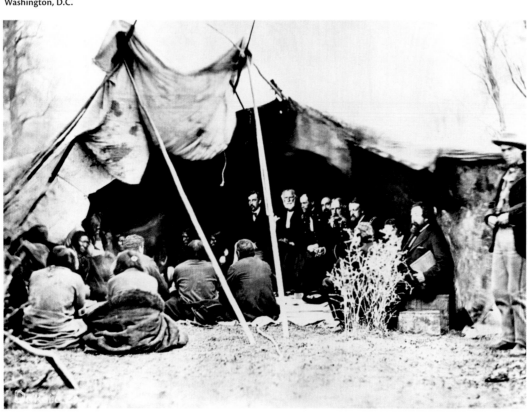

gave white settlers a passage westward. It came after the most decisive Native American victory in all of the western wars.[62] Nevertheless, the May 1868 photograph visually reversed the temporary fortunes of war. It depicted the beaten white men in a physically superior position, even though the treaty they were negotiating was highly favorable to the Native Americans.

Little Big Horn

The provisions of the 1868 Fort Laramie treaty were violated by both sides, each of whom entered the other's territories. Survey parties scouting a route for the Northern Pacific Railroad entered Native American territory, where they clashed with warriors led by Sitting Bull. The discovery of gold in the Black Hills of present-day South Dakota motivated thousands of white miners to invade the legendary home of the Sioux gods.[63] In 1874 Colonel George Armstrong Custer (1839–1876) led a reconnaissance force of more than a thousand heavily armed troops. There were about one hundred wagons in his train, some carrying equipment to be used by the engineers, geologists, and other scientists who accompanied him. A photographer, W. H. Illingsworth (1842–1893), captured the expedition entering the Black Hills (Fig. 4.61). After several smaller battles, U.S. troops under Custer were thoroughly defeated at Little Big Horn in 1876. Custer's Last Stand, as it came to be called, inflamed the American public, whose support for harsher treatment of the Native Americans gathered strength during the last decades of the nineteenth century.

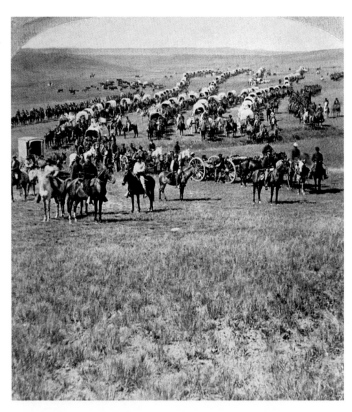

4.61
W. H. ILLINGSWORTH, *Columns of cavalry, artillery, and wagons, commanded by General George A. Custer, crossing the plains of Dakota Territory during the 1874 Black Hills expedition*, 1874. Paper print.

RETAKE

During the middle of the nineteenth century, photography not only accompanied conflicts and imperialist expansion, but also provided visual rationales for domination and the extension of economic power. For example, the Western presence in Asia was underscored by panoramas of Hong Kong. Despite lumber mills, railroads, and mines, views of the American West took on the look of a primordial paradise in the photographs of Timothy O'Sullivan and Carleton Watkins. In addition, indigenous people were portrayed as too weak or too wicked to be allowed to stand in the way of civilization.

The market for photographs grew, but not always in foreseeable ways. Across the globe, the practice of photography directly followed the expansion of Western interests. Expatriates, traveling businessmen, tourists, and viewers in Europe and America provided a ready market for pictures. Photographers and publishers continually speculated about new views and markets, and began traveling abroad, or sending photographers abroad, to seek their fortunes (see Fig. 4.35). In addition, the appetite for

vernacular photography also expanded, ranging from tintypes of American Civil War soldiers to *cartes-de-visite* of presidents. Once Southworth and Hawes invited the public to come to their studio to see a pantheon of public figures. But in the middle years of the nineteenth century, people increasingly wanted to own images themselves and implicitly felt the right to see things photographed. Hence the desire for photographs sparked one of the first mass-marketed media.

Yet this proliferation of photographs proved to be a mixed blessing: seeing many images eventually reduced the impact of each of them, and considerably hindered the emergence of a single image as a symbol of the conflict and a rallying point. As photographs achieved a new degree of topicality, they were also liable to lose value as their immediate newsworthiness faded. Together with mass-produced stereographic photographs and *cartes-de-visite*, war photographs taught viewers a modern skill: how to ignore or forget images when confronted by an excess of them.

ICONO-PHOTOGRAPHIQUE

MÉCANISME DE LA PHYSIONOMIE HUMAINE

Pl. 6.

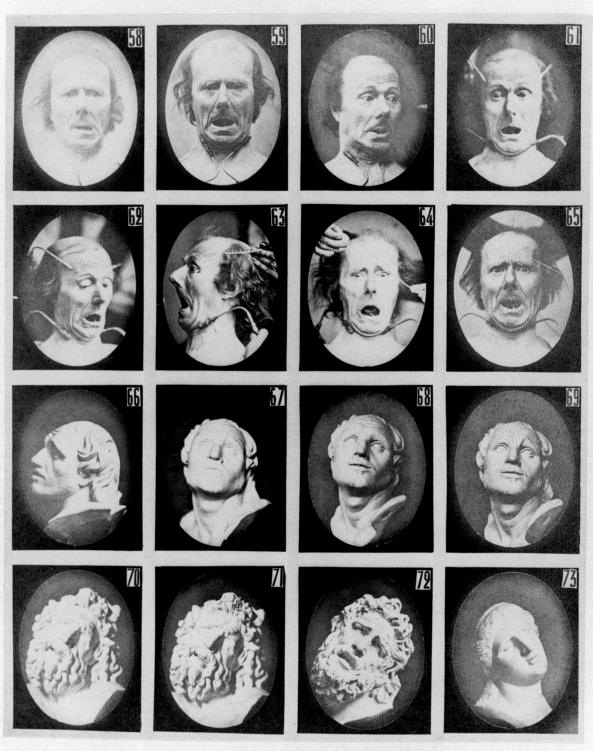

Duchenne (de Boulogne). phot.

CHAPTER FIVE

Science and Social Science

The photographers assigned to military missions frequently carried out ethnographic, topographic, and other kinds of scientific research. Likewise, topographical survey teams were sometimes accompanied by military troops tasked to protect and advance survey work and photography. It was not unknown for photographer-adventurers to enlist the help of armed guards. Thomas Cook, founder of Cook's Tours, arranged military transport and cultivated the protection of rulers to safeguard them and the high-end tourist groups he escorted to Egypt and the Holy Land. Another component of Cook's Tours was the photographer hired to make and sell group pictures to the sightseers.

Although they increasingly used photography as evidence, science and social science were not firmly differentiated until the end of the nineteenth century. In India, the Schlagintweit brothers (see p. 116) combined geological study with landscape photography, and took time to practice some ethnology by making plaster heads of Indian subjects. Their successors, the Western military and civilian amateur photographers stationed in India, spent years amassing statistical data as well as photographs for the multivolumed *The People of India* (1868–75). To record the 1874 transit of Venus (when the planet Venus passes directly between the earth and the sun, causing a small, round dot on the sun) scientists traveled to distant vantage points. With the relentless expansion of Western political and economic interests during the mid-nineteenth century, photographers increasingly sought to highlight cultural,

gender, and physiognomic differences among people. Sexuality and ethnicity merged in images of the exotic; often the normal was implicitly defined with reference to images of people with mental disabilities. As popular and professional science and social science proliferated, they helped to make photography a global activity. Locally powerful people saw the advantages of photography and sometimes took it up as amateurs. Westerners routinely trained assistants, who, having learned the trade, went on to found their own photographic enterprises.

PHOTOGRAPHY AND THE SOCIAL SCIENCES

Photography participated in the production of evidence in many fields. Geology, biology, botany, medicine, astronomy, and chemistry used photography to collect and exhibit evidence. European efforts to establish comprehensive and systematic classifications of human beings were enhanced by the intense discussion of Charles Darwin's writings on evolution and the origins of the human species. Theories about the multiple origins of human beings, akin to those that motivated Louis Agassiz to commission photographic studies of slaves (see p. 36) persisted, despite Darwin's insistence on a single human origin. Some commentators also interpreted his writings to validate a natural hierarchy of development, from the lower to the higher races, based on visible differences in anatomy, and on cultural characteristics.

ETHNOGRAPHIC STUDIES AND DISPLAY

Grand schemes to compare and contrast races and to photograph them were launched throughout the later nineteenth century. For instance, it was proposed that the Calcutta exhibition of 1869 should bring together "tribal" peoples from Asia, Polynesia, and Australasia, for purposes of examination and photography.[1] The scheme failed, but ethnographic studies and exhibitions,

5.1
G. B. DUCHENNE DE BOULOGNE, *"Electrical contraction of the eyelids, the forehead with voluntary lowering of the jaw: terror. ..."* plate 63 from *Mécanisme de la physionomie humaine: ou analyse electro-physiologique de l'expression des passions,* 1876. Paper photograph tipped in book. Victoria and Albert Museum, London.

Duchenne used electrical currents to stimulate facial expressions. He seems to have had few scientific or moral reservations about provoking the appearance of emotions in his subjects.

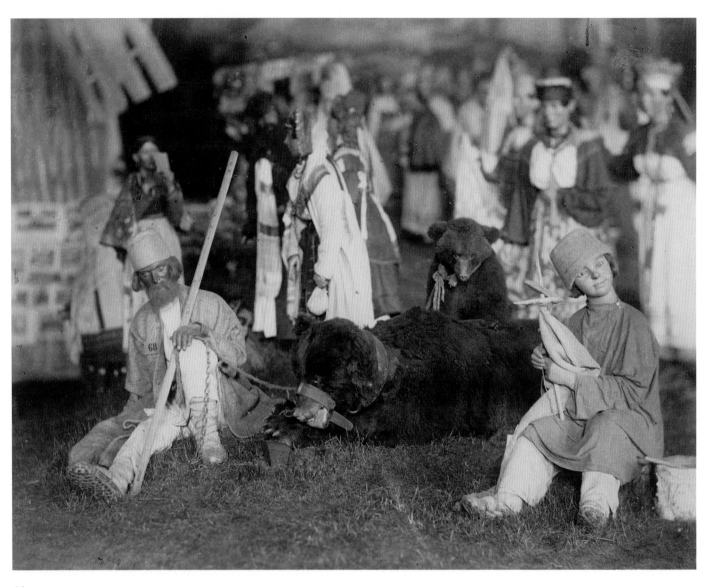

5.2
PHOTOGRAPHER UNKNOWN, *A Bear Trainer*, exhibited in the Western and Slav section of the Moscow Ethnographic Exhibition, 1867. Paper print.
Royal Anthropological Institute, London.

extensively illustrated by photographs, flourished throughout the 1860s and 1870s. With his brother, F. W. Dammann, German photographer Carl Dammann (active 1870s) issued an album of six hundred small images titled *Ethnological Photographic Gallery of the Various Races of Man* in 1875.

In Russia, more systematic fieldwork aimed at describing physical types and local costumes began to use photography. The Russian Geographical Society issued special instructions for photographers who were attempting to create a scientific study of difference. Full-face, profile, and full-length views of people were considered to be the most scientifically useful.[2] The Moscow Ethnographic Exhibition of 1867 displayed dioramas showing about three hundred mannequins in regional costume (Fig. 5.2).

The People of India (1868–75) was an eight-volume series of text and photographs. Begun in response to a casual request for

a souvenir album by the British governor general, Charles John Canning, it developed into a huge project involving civilian and military photographers. The 468 tipped-in prints generally show people identified by tribe and caste, holding a tool or weapon denoting their work and social position (Fig. 5.3).

The lack of standardization in anthropological photography led scientists such as Thomas Henry Huxley (1825–1925) and John Lamprey (active 1870s) to create systems by which humans could be photographed for observation and comparison. Huxley's anthropometric poses were cumbersome, but Lamprey's recommendations in his 1869 journal article "On a Method of Measuring the Human Form" became influential (Fig. 5.4). Both Huxley and Lamprey proposed that the scientific study of race should be based on observations of the nude human body, so that differences in skin color, hair texture, physique, and the like would be recorded. Using a portable silk-thread grid for

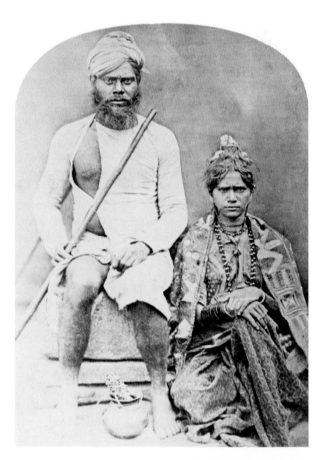

5.3
PHOTOGRAPHER UNKNOWN, *Brinjara and Wife*, plate 161 from *The People of India*, 1868. Paper print. Harry Ransom Humanities Research Center, University of Texas at Austin.

the background of anthropological studies was encouraged. This strategy strengthened the belief that there were basic differences among human races, observable through distinctions in physical appearance.

Orientalism

One of the most persistent of such types of ethnographic photography showed women from the Middle East and Asia in sexually suggestive poses. The term "Orientalism," adopted by cultural critic Edward Said in a 1978 book of the same title, has come to mean the wholesale social labeling of non-Western peoples as passive, rather than active; childlike, rather than mature; feminine, rather than masculine; and timeless—that is, separate from the progress of Western history. More specifically, it describes the phenomenon of titillating sexual interest or intrusive observation of people from non-Western cultures, especially women.[4]

In Western literature, travel accounts, and art before the invention of photography, Middle Eastern women were contradictorily described as closeted in harems, swathed in

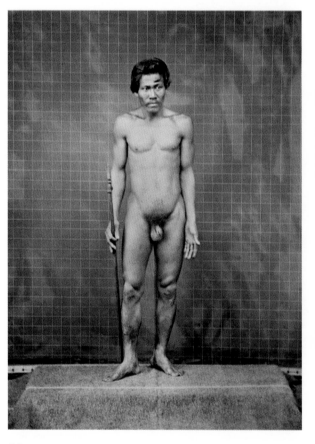 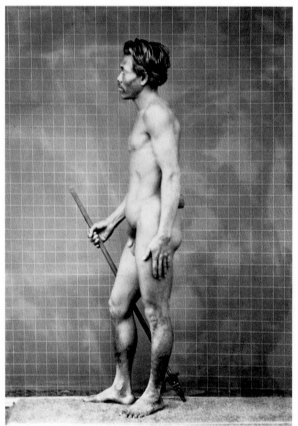

5.4
JOHN LAMPREY, *Front and Profile Views of a Madagascan Male*, c. 1868–69. Carbon prints. Royal Anthropological Institute, London.

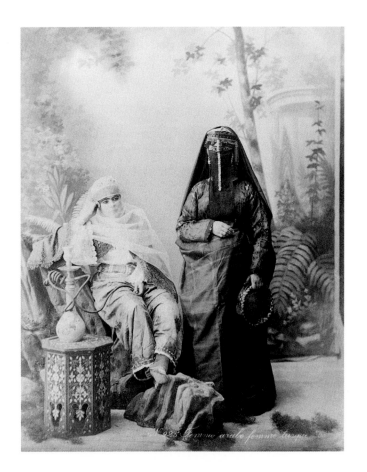

In this studio photograph, a Turkish woman is masked by a semi-transparent veil, reclining in the manner of an odalisque, suggestively holding a *narghileh* (water pipe). The standing woman grasps a tambourine. By the time this image was made, the harem had been a fixture in Western culture for hundreds of years. The image gratifies the fantasy view of the "Orient" as a place where time has stood still.

thick clothing and veils, and sexually aggressive. Images of the odalisque, the drowsily reclining naked or semi-nude female pictured in an intimate or exotic setting, were frequent in Western art. In photography, the mystery and unavailability of Middle Eastern women were enhanced by costume and pose (Fig. 5.5). Not all pictures of Middle Eastern women, however, were made to please foreign fantasies: Marie Lydie Cabanis Bonfils (see p. 94) is reputed to have made the photographs of women who came to the Bonfils family's Beirut studio (Fig. 5.6.[5] In India, legitimate photography of women in purdah—that is, in seclusion—was done by British women, such as a certain Mrs. Carrick, who is said to have run a studio in Calcutta. By 1885, Indian women had taken up photography.[6]

Nude and semi-nude images of Eastern women were marketed in many ways. Sensual pictures, in which the model wore traditional clothing to mark her ethnic identity, were issued in CARTES-DE-VISITE, miniatures, postcards, and ALBUMEN

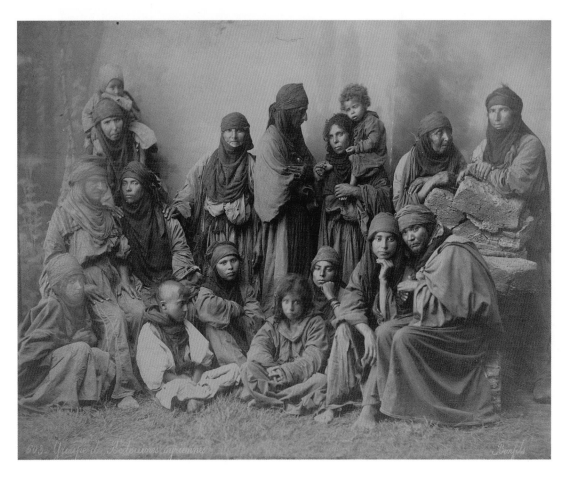

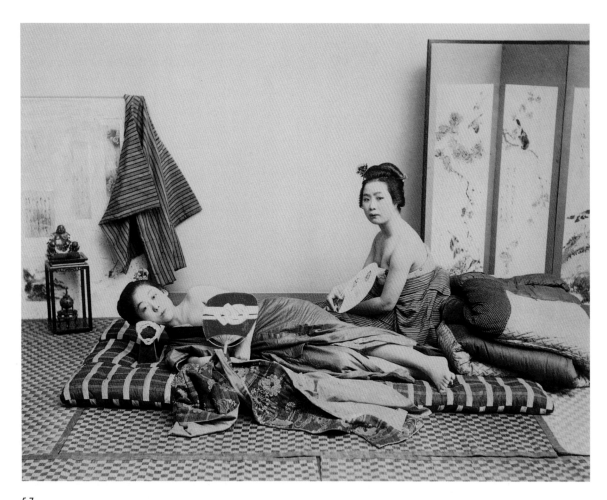

5.7
KUSAKABE KIMBEI, *Geisha Resting*, c. 1885. Hand-colored albumen print. Richard W. Gadd Collection, Monterey Museum of Art, California.

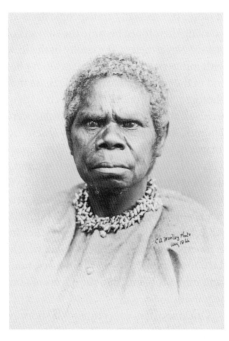

5.8
C. A. WOOLLEY, *Trucanini*, 1866. Paper print.
Royal Anthropological Institution of Great Britain
and Ireland, London.

prints (Fig. 5.7). The *académies*, or figure studies of women ostensibly sold as aids to painters, sometimes featured Middle Eastern women, whose hairstyle and jewelry signaled their identity and class to the viewers.

Explicit photographs of sexual acts, featuring Western and non-Western participants, were marketed in European capitals and sold by mail order catalog.[7] Bruno Braquehais, who photographed the French Commune (see Fig. 4.23), also made images of individuals and couples engaged in sexual activities.[8]

"Dying Cultures"

Anthropological photography took on a moral urgency as the notion spread that indigenous peoples did not have the physical and mental strength to survive the encroachment of Western civilization. At the 1866 Intercolonial Exhibition in Melbourne, Australia, a section was devoted to "The Last of the Tasmanians."[9] The number of aboriginal Tasmanians was indeed severely reduced—in 1847, only forty-six individuals had remained. Professional photographer C. A. Woolley (1834–1922) made a studio study, in the style of Western portraiture, of a Tasmanian woman named Trucanini (Fig. 5.8). The notion of vanishing races was also applied to Native North Americans (see p. 191), though they ultimately fared better than the Tasmanians.

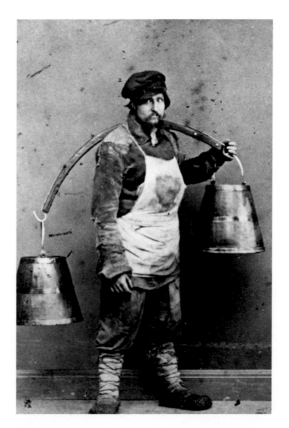

5.9
WILLIAM CARRICK, *Russian Water Carrier*, c. 1860–78.
Carte-de-visite.

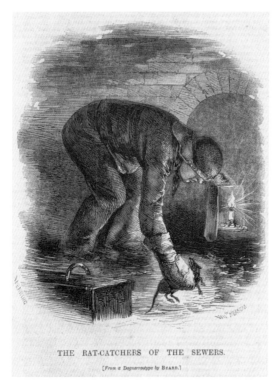

THE RAT-CATCHERS OF THE SEWERS.

[*From a Daguerreotype by* BEARD.]

5.10
ARCHIBALD HENNING, *The Rat-Catchers of the Sewers.*
Engraving from a daguerreotype by Richard Beard, illustration
from *London Labour and the London Poor* by Henry Mayhew,
1851. Private collection.

In 1879, responding to the belief that the traditional life of Native Americans was endangered by development, the United States established the Bureau of Ethnology.[10] John K. Hillers (1843–1925) was appointed staff photographer under John Wesley Powell (1834–1902), the agency's first director. Hillers had met Powell while working as a boatman for Powell's survey of the Colorado River in 1871. The expedition's photographer, E. O. Beaman (1837–1876), had taught Hillers how to use the camera, and when Beaman left the group, Hillers took over from him, making about three thousand images of the Grand Canyon and of Native Americans. For the Bureau of Ethnology, he produced more than twenty thousand negatives.[11] After the massacre at Wounded Knee in 1890, when the Indian Wars all but ceased, photographers took up the "grand endeavor" to capture the likeness of Native Americans before they disappeared altogether.

POPULARIZING ETHNIC AND ECONOMIC TYPES

The idea of creating assemblages of thematically related photographs of people was not restricted to scientific pursuits. Studios around the world offered exotic images of people deemed typical of an ethnic group. In Rio de Janeiro, a portraitist advertised "a large collection of black tipos [characters] and their customs, very appropriate for those who are leaving for Europe."[12] The Scottish-born photographer William Carrick (1827–1878) worked in Saint Petersburg, Russia, photographing "Rasnoshchiki," the street sellers of that city[13] (Fig. 5.9). He also made photographic expeditions to rural areas in Russia, gathering images of workers, farmers, boatmen, and the landscape.

In the later nineteenth century, factories and industrial sites were photographed with increasing frequency, and studio shots of laborers, especially craftspeople dressed in work clothes and carrying their tools, became the subjects of many *cartes-de-visite*.[14] Nevertheless, the reality of the urban poverty associated with industrial capitalism was seldom photographed before the end of the nineteenth century. Despite the historical interests of photography's proponents, subjects with no evident scientific, archival, artistic, or commercial value were neglected. Child laborers, for instance, are largely absent from early photography. Images of working men and women, except when stiffly posed with tools or clothed in quaint ethnic and regional costume, are also uncommon. Scenes of ordinary activities such as preparing food are exceedingly rare, unless these activities are performed in an exotic culture. The absence of unpleasant and ordinary subjects is highlighted by their presence in other media, such as newspaper and book illustration, which showed child labor, the poor, factory abuses, workhouses, ramshackle homes, urban sanitation problems, and the effects of famine and overcrowded neighborhoods.

One important exception to the norm was created by Henry Mayhew (1812–1887), a newspaper reporter and editor. When Mayhew published the first three volumes of *London Labour and the London Poor* in 1851, they contained engravings based on photographs that Mayhew commissioned Richard Beard

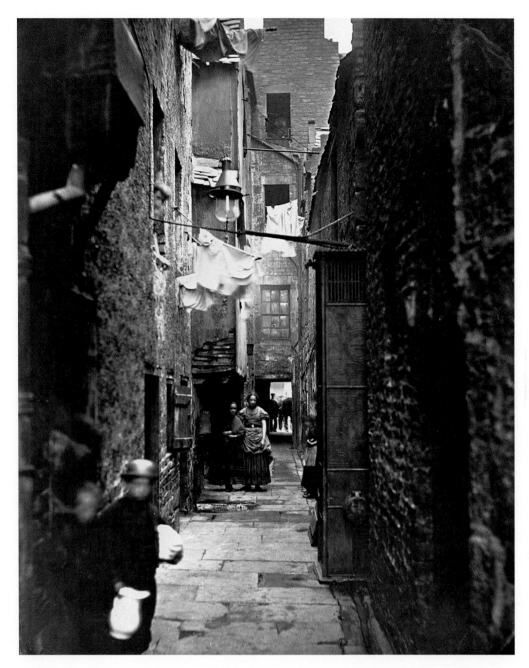

5.11
THOMAS ANNAN, *Close No. 37, High Street*, 1868, from *The Old Closes and Streets of Glasgow, from Photographs Taken for the City of Glasgow Improvement Trust*, 1900. Photogravure. Gernsheim Collection. Harry Ransom Humanities Research Center, University of Texas at Austin.

(see p. 58) to take (Fig. 5.10). The book, which blends pictures, anecdotes, statistical inquiry, and interviews, did not fully escape the biases of its times. It was a financially successful publication, perhaps because public opinion was turning toward the acceptance of minimal government-sponsored welfare programs as a necessary component of modern life. Photographs of strikes, even during the European depression of the 1870s and its labor unrest, are also rare. The poor could not afford photographs, and newspaper images tended to reflect the point of view of private industry. Moreover, reformers in the mid-nineteenth century were generally not stirred to photograph societal problems or

remedial programs, because for them the camera was largely associated with the evils of industrialization.

As European cities implemented modernization schemes, the people displaced by renovation were seldom photographed, although the buildings were. An unusual picture was made by Thomas Annan (1829–1887), a photographer in Glasgow, Scotland, who was asked by the Glasgow City Improvement Trust in 1866 to record the vast slums that had grown up around mills and factories before the buildings were torn down and rebuilt (Fig. 5.11). Charles Marville (1816–1879), a French artist and photographer, was commissioned by the city of Paris to record

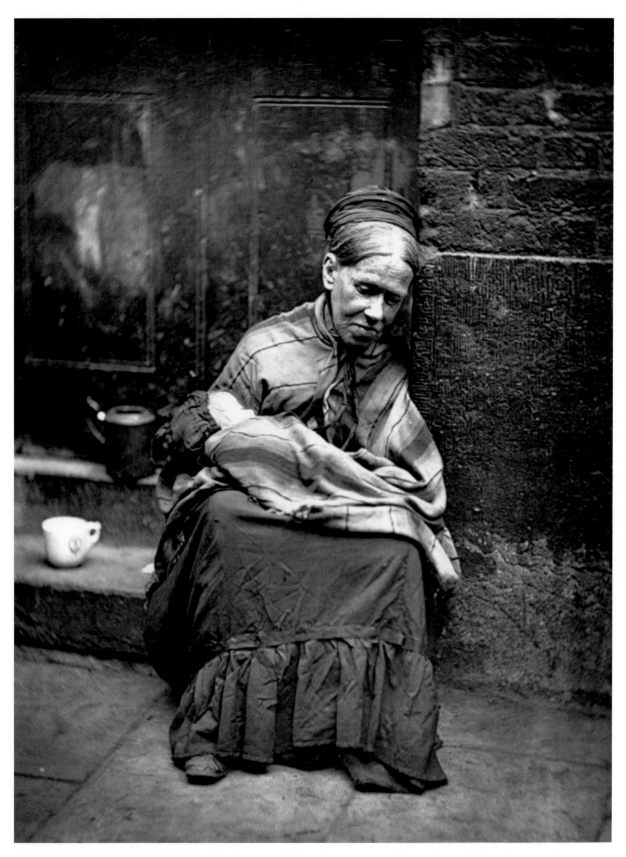

5.12
JOHN THOMSON, *The Crawlers*, 1877–78. Woodburytype. Victoria and Albert Museum, London.

Street-dwellers such as the woman pictured here were termed "crawlers," because they would occasionally have enough cash to buy tea leaves, then "crawl" to a pub for hot water. The image of the crawler shows greater emphasis on the individual, in contrast with Thomson's often static presentation of street types.

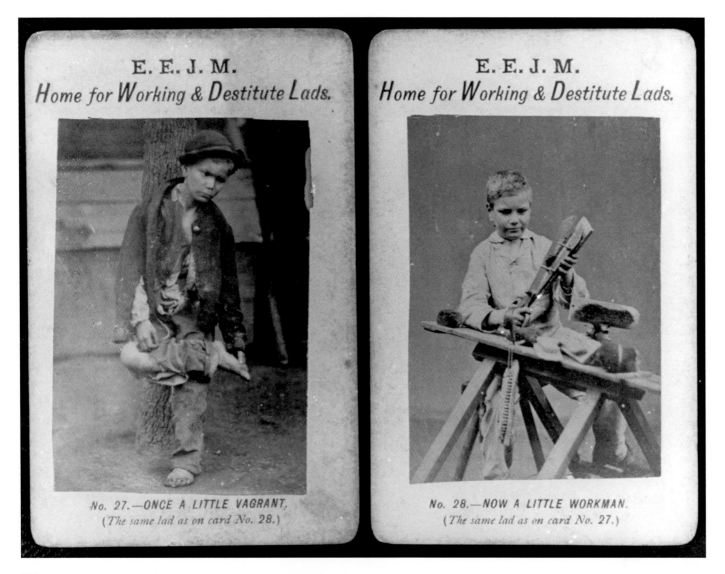

5.13
PHOTOGRAPHER UNKNOWN, *Before and After Photographs of Young Boys*, c. 1875. Albumen prints. Barnardo Photographic Archive, Ilford, England.

old Paris, before the implementation of Baron Haussmann's (1809–1891) improvements (Fig. 5.14), and the new Paris of buildings like the Paris Opera House.

When John Thomson (see p. 119) returned from Asia to Britain, he became a portrait photographer, whose studio was equipped with the usual painted backdrops and fancy posing chairs. He also undertook a photographic survey of London's poor with writer and social activist Adolphe Smith Headingly, who wrote under the name of Adolphe Smith. *Street Life in London* was issued in twelve monthly installments, beginning in February 1877, and was published as a bound book one year later. Thomson and Smith acknowledged Mayhew's efforts on behalf of the poor, presenting their own work as an updated version. Their preface stresses the function of photography to document objectively, without omission or exaggeration. One remarkable picture shows an impoverished homeless widow who made her living minding the children of poor working women (Fig. 5.12).

In the last third of the nineteenth century, photographs were used slightly more often in private social reform efforts. Thomas Barnardo (1845–1905), who administered homes and training programs for poor and homeless children, made before-and-after images to advertise his work and to raise funds (Fig. 5.13). In most of the images, Barnardo exaggerated the children's poverty, dressing them in torn clothes and posing them in pitiful positions. The images could be purchased singly or in packets.

PHOTOGRAPHIC STUDIES OF HUMAN EXPRESSION

The notion that inner human character could be interpreted through facial expressions persisted throughout nineteenth-century portraiture in all visual media. In fact, as photographs became more generally available, they seemed to encourage the reading of inner character. Gallery displays of photographs taken of public figures supported the public's speculation, as did growing personal collections of photographs. Writing in the July 1863 issue of the *Atlantic Monthly*, Oliver Wendell

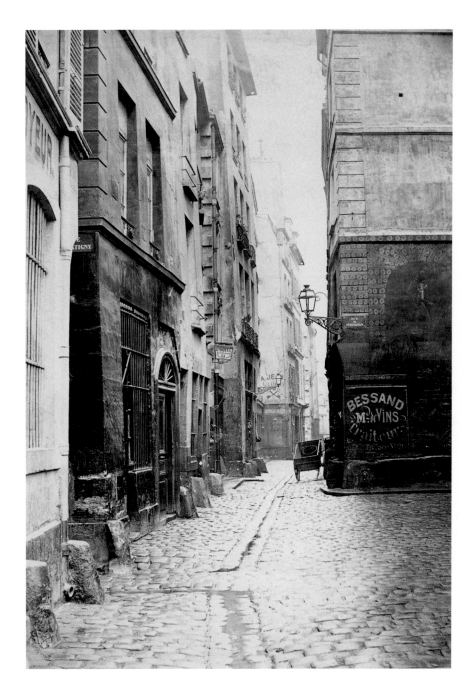

Holmes envisaged a new human possibility called "photographic intimacy," a friendship established by the exchange of photographs, between two people who have never met. The relationship starts after the exchange of letters and views of scenery. It culminates in an exchange of photographic self-portraits carefully staged among personal objects, and the sharing of photographic pictures of loved ones. In time, Holmes wrote, photography would make the "outer and … inner life a reality … but for his voice, which you have never heard, you know … [the photographic correspondent] better than hundreds who call him by name, as they meet him year after year."[15] The conviction that a clear correspondence existed between inner moods and outward appearances also informed scientific experiments on human gestures and facial expressions, such as

the photographs of mental patients taken by Dr. Hugh Welch Diamond in the 1850s (see p. 33).

Duchenne de Boulogne

Outwardly, the explorations undertaken by the French doctor Guillaume Benjamin Duchenne de Boulogne (1806–1875) resemble Diamond's work. Duchenne was a physician at the Paris hospital La Salpêtrière, which treated people suffering from epilepsy, neurological problems, and insanity. Duchenne's *Mécanisme de la physionomie humaine* (*The Mechanism of Human Physiognomy*), published in 1862, was accompanied by an atlas of eighty-four photographs taken between 1852 and 1856 of human subjects whose facial muscles were stimulated by an electric current (Fig. 5.1). With the technical advice of photographer Adrien Tournachon (1825–1903), brother of the famous Parisian photographer Nadar (see pp. 83–85), Duchenne attempted to arouse through electrical stimulation the individual facial muscles that he considered to be involved in human expression. Most of his photographs were of people with mental retardation; forty-five of the eighty-four images are of one old mentally retarded man.

To aid the camera's recording, swift and subtle muscular reactions were ignored in favor of more dramatic and visible ones. Duchenne took his subjects' emotional responses to be typical of all humans; the individual's personality and distinctive range of reactions did not interest him. Unlike Diamond's efforts, Duchenne's work was very specifically related to art as well as science. His *Mécanisme* contained plates in which works of art were compared with his photographic experiments, so as to show how art did not always show physiologically true depictions of human emotional responses. Photographic historian Nancy Roth found that, to his contemporaries, Duchenne's representations seemed too naturalistic for art: one critic wrote that "he's … to be reproached for stripping art of its every ideal, reducing it to an anatomical realism every bit in keeping with the tenets of a certain modern school of art."[16] The nineteenth-century clash between two approaches to painting, represented by the realism of Gustave Courbet (1819–1877) and the idealism of Jean-Auguste-Dominique Ingres (1780–1867), was specifically referenced by the commentator in relation to Duchenne's physiological photography.

Darwin

After he published *The Origin of Species* (1859) and *The Descent of Man* (1871), the British scientist Charles Darwin (1809–1882) completed a study that he had begun in 1838. *The Expression of the Emotions in Man and Animals* (1872) argued that the physical signs of emotional states were inherently the same in all humans, regardless of culture, and that animals had emotions that they expressed in ways similar to people. The volume underscored Darwin's hypothesis that humans were not a separately created species, but resulted from the processes of natural selection and evolution.

About nine thousand copies of the book sold in the first four months of publication, both because Darwin was a well-known, controversial author, and because the subject of emotional expression was popular at the time.[17] Darwin's introduction acknowledged his debt to the insights and photographs of emotion made by Duchenne de Boulogne. In fact, Duchenne lent Darwin photographs, which he published as part of his study. With some of Duchenne's images, Darwin asked the engraver who worked on the photographs to temper the wrinkles and to remove the instrument that directed an electrical stimulus to the subject's face. Along with illustrations provided by artists, Darwin also included photographs commissioned from the London photographer Oscar Rejlander (see Fig. 3.12), who personally acted out some of the emotional states before the camera. Believing that babies exhibited the purest, least acculturated signs of emotion, Darwin used photographs of babies made by Rejlander (Fig. 5.15) and the German photographer Adolph Diedrich Kindermann (1823–1892). In all, five photographers provided images to Darwin.

Darwin investigated the means by which photographs might be inexpensively included in the text. This had proved difficult because the presses that printed text ran too fast to reproduce photographs and type at the same time, and because

5.15 OSCAR REJLANDER, *Rejlander with Baby*, 1872. Darwin Collection, Cambridge University Library, England.

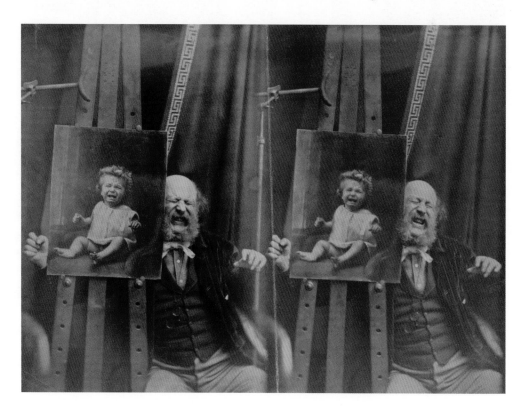

most photographs needed to be printed on special paper, not newsprint. But a technique known as HELIOTYPE, invented by the photographer Ernest Edwards (1837–1903), who made a portrait of Darwin in 1868, used printing-press plates to reproduce photographs, and thus keep down the price of the book. The resulting images are not sharp and detailed, but they do convey facial gestures adequately.

Charcot

Like his teacher Duchenne de Boulogne, the French physician and neurologist Jean-Martin Charcot (1825–1893) worked at La Salpêtrière, where he drew upon photographs to document his case studies, and was interested in the expression of emotion in art. In one sense, Charcot carried Duchenne's work to an extreme, making weekly public presentations of his patients, many of them female, to an audience of scientists and socialites.[18]

Charcot's particular concern with hysteria attracted his most famous admirer, Sigmund Freud (1856–1939).

From 1877 to 1880, Charcot published *L'Iconographie photographique de La Salpêtrière* (*Photographic Iconography of the Salpêtrière Hospital*), a three-volume work that contained photographs of hysterics (Fig. 5.16). Collaborating with the clinician Désiré Magliore Bourneville (1840–1909), and assisted by Paul Régnard (1858–1927), an intern at La Salpêtrière, Charcot sought to photograph the physical expression of mental states. He chose subjects who were known throughout France to be able to respond well to hypnotic suggestion.[19] Like those of Hugh Welch Diamond, Duchenne, and Darwin, Charcot's work and his photographs emphasized facial expression as an infallible indicator of psychological states. And like them, Charcot regarded himself as a neutral observer. Of his visual recording, he stated: "I stand here merely as a photographer, I write down what I see."[20]

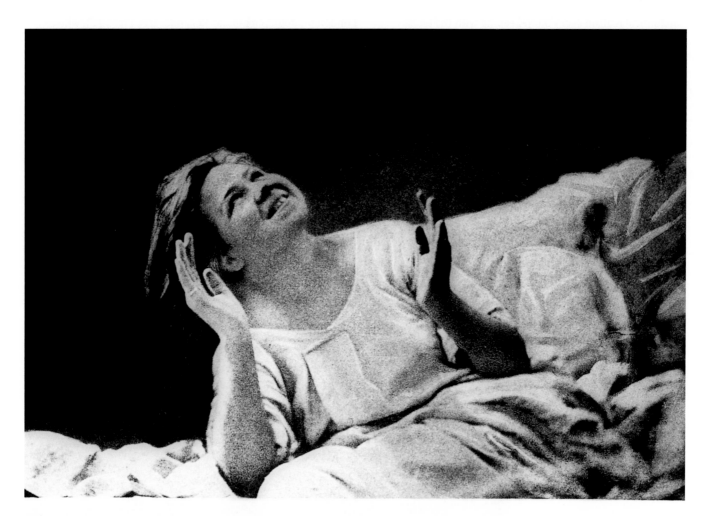

5.16
PHOTOGRAPHER UNKNOWN, *Attitudes Passionelles*, plate 21 from Charcot's *L'Iconographie photographique de La Salpêtrière*, 1876. **Paper print. Bibliothèque Interuniversitaire de Médecine, Université René Descartes, Paris.**

Charcot not only photographed sitters acting out various symptoms of mental illness but also invited the public to his sanatorium on Tuesdays to see the performances. His subjects' exaggerated expressions and physical positions resemble poses assumed by actors in the theater, largely because they were called upon to act out their symptoms for the camera, not experience them afresh.

PHOTOGRAPHY IN MEDICINE AND SCIENCE

Because the American Civil War was fought near towns and cities, there was acute public awareness of battle injuries and the needs of soldiers. The Sanitary Commission was a charitable organization of private citizens who came together to do whatever the U.S. government did not do for soldiers during the war. The commission, modeled on the British equivalent that was active during the Crimean War, worked with the government to provide food and medical supplies, ambulance service, rehabilitation, and aid to dependent families. To raise money, the Sanitary Commission held fairs, which included the sale of photographs of landscapes and famous individuals. Disabled soldiers were the subject of postwar photographs.

Throughout the war, Clara Barton (1821–1912), the first woman clerk in the United States Patent Office, organized relief efforts for wounded soldiers. She managed to secure permission to be on the front lines, where she ministered to Northern and Southern soldiers. Like many of Brady's sitters, she was a popular figure in American civic life, and gave many public lectures (Fig. 5.17).

The number of amputations suffered by Civil War soldiers shocked both doctors and the general public. In the May 1863 issue of the *Atlantic Monthly*, Oliver Wendell Holmes described how photographs of able-bodied people walking on city streets might be observed in order to devise effective and comfortable artificial limbs.[21] Medical practitioners and hospitals, meanwhile, commissioned photographs of soldiers with wounds (Fig. 5.18). During the war, the surgeon general founded the Army Medical Museum in Washington, D.C., one of whose purposes was to collect photographs of war injuries.[22] More than a thousand pictures were collected in compendiums of photographs

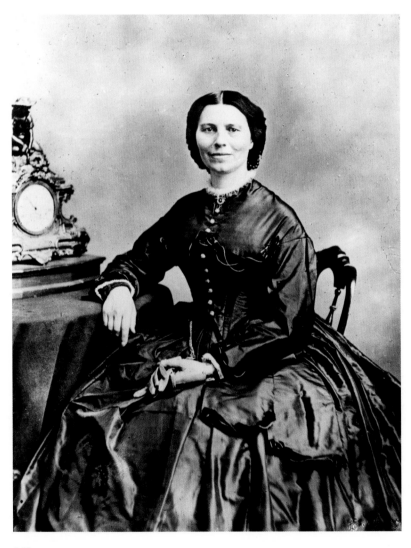

5.17
MATHEW BRADY, *Clara Barton*, c. 1866. Albumen silver print. Library of Congress, Washington, D.C.

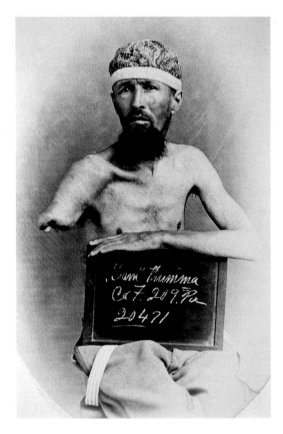

5.18
PHOTOGRAPHER UNKNOWN, *Untitled* (Corporal Samuel Thummam, wounded at the battle of Petersberg), 1865. Burns Archive, New York.

Photographs of wounded American Civil War veterans were made and circulated to teaching hospitals for study in an effort to improve battlefield care, recovery, and the quality of prosthetics.

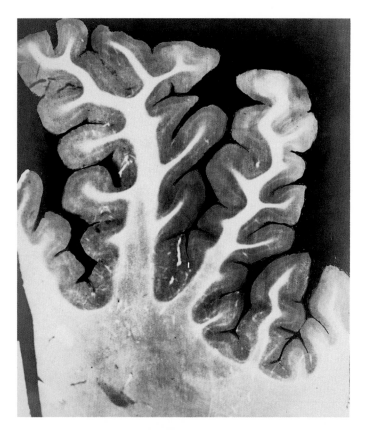

5.19
JULES-BERNARD LUYS, *Four-Diameter Cross-Section of Segments of Cerebellum*, plate 68 from *L'Iconographie photographique des centres nerveux*, c. 1873. Albumen silver print. Bibliothèque de l'Institut de France, Paris.

and engravings based on photographs, including the eight-volume *Photographs of Surgical Cases and Specimens* (1866). Though thwarted by shortages of paper and printing supplies, Confederate doctors were also able to publish a journal largely devoted to battlefield medicine. The *Confederate States Medical and Surgical Journal*, issued from January 1864 to February 1865, printed a few photographically derived woodcuts of injured soldiers.[23]

PHOTOMICROGRAPHY AND ASTRONOMICAL PHOTOGRAPHS

From the very beginning, objects and organisms made visible by microscopes and telescopes were subjects of photography (see Figs. 2.13, 2.14, 2.15, 2.42). Indeed, photomicrography became a photographic specialty beginning in the 1850s.[24] For the French physician and anatomist Dr. Jules-Bernard Luys (1828–1897), photomicrography provided an important aid to scientific objectivity. In his work *L'Iconographie photographique des centres nerveux* (*Photographic Iconography of the Nerve Centers*) (1873), which was issued with an atlas of photographs and lithographs of neurological subjects, Luys wrote that photography substituted "the action of light for … personality, in order to obtain an image both impersonal and accurate"[25] (Fig. 5.19).

From the late 1850s on, proposals to miniaturize and store information in photographs became more frequent. The *American Journal of Photography* for 1858 recommended storing public documents on photographic negatives. With its usual exuberance, *Photographic News* opined that "the whole archives of a nation might be packed away in a snuff-box." Businesses were founded to produce microscopic photographs, either as a means of record-keeping or for novelties, such as penholders fitted with a lens that magnified tiny calendars.[26]

Despite much enthusiasm for its potential, telescopic photography did not proceed as rapidly as photomicrography. Astronomical photography was beset with technical problems resulting from low light, the movement of the earth, and the limitations of photosensitive materials, while the sun's brightness created its own difficulties. Nevertheless, many astronomers, such as John Herschel, saw the potential to create systematic recording of the sun and its features. Others, in the spirit of François Arago's original conjectures (see p. 16), considered that photochemical reactions might be used to measure light rays.

Photographers continued to have difficulty creating clear images of the moon. Throughout the 1870s, American astronomer and photography advocate Lewis M. Rutherfurd (sometimes spelt Rutherford) (1816–1892) circulated his 1865 photograph of the moon (Fig. 5.20). Working together,

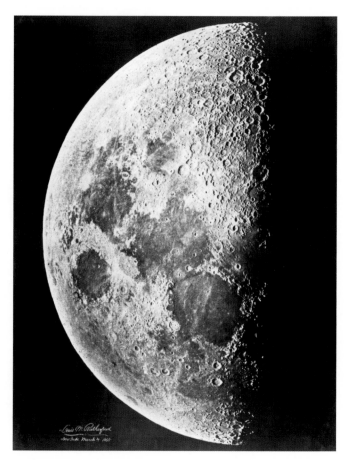

5.20
LEWIS RUTHERFURD, *Moon*, March 4, 1865. Albumen silver print. George Eastman House, Rochester, New York.

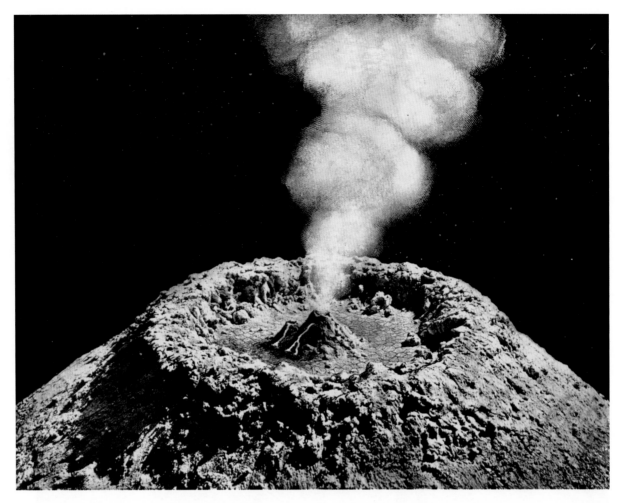

5.21
JAMES NASMYTH AND JAMES CARPENTER, *Moon, Crater of Vesuvius*, 1864. From *The Moon, Considered as a Planet, a World, and a Satellite*, 1874. Woodburytype. National Media Museum, Bradford, England.

engineer James Nasmyth (1808–1890) and astronomer James Carpenter (1840–1899) created a unique series of astronomical pictures. Among the images in their 1874 publication *The Moon, Considered as a Planet, a World, and a Satellite*, were WOODBURYTYPE PRINTS of photographs of plaster models of the moon, constructed in accordance with Nasmyth's drawings based on telescope observations. Far from fakery, in their minds, the model was conceived as an instructional tool that provided clear, close-up details not technically possible in actual moon photographs. Nasmyth and Carpenter even created events, such as a volcanic eruption on the moon's surface (Fig. 5.21), and drew parallels between such natural phenomena as the creases on the surface of the moon, a human hand, and an apple[27] (Fig. 5.22).

The largest international effort in astronomical photography during the period took place in December 1874, when scientists from Germany, Britain, and France entered into a friendly competition to record the passing, or transit, of the planet Venus across the face of the sun.[28] The French team included the scientist and photographer Pierre-César Jules Janssen (1824–1907), who developed a revolver camera, in effect

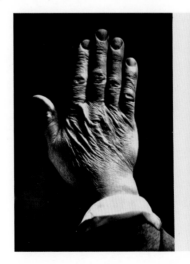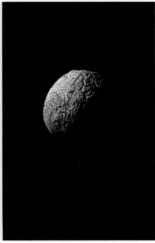

5.22
JAMES NASMYTH AND JAMES CARPENTER, *Back of Hand, Wrinkled Apple*, 1864, from *The Moon, Considered as a Planet, a World, and a Satellite*, 1874. Woodburytype. National Media Museum, Bradford, England.

The search for universal laws in nature led Nasmyth and Carpenter to compare the wrinkling of the human hand to that of an apple, and, eventually, the processes that created the furrowed surface of the moon.

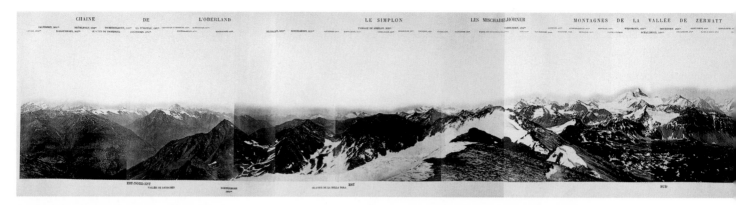

5.24
AIMÉ CIVIALE, *Circular Panorama Taken from Bella Tolla (3030 metres)*, 1866. Collotype, printed by Jean-Dominique Gustave Aroca, 1882 or earlier. Bibliothèque Centrale du Musée National d'Histoire Naturelle, Paris.

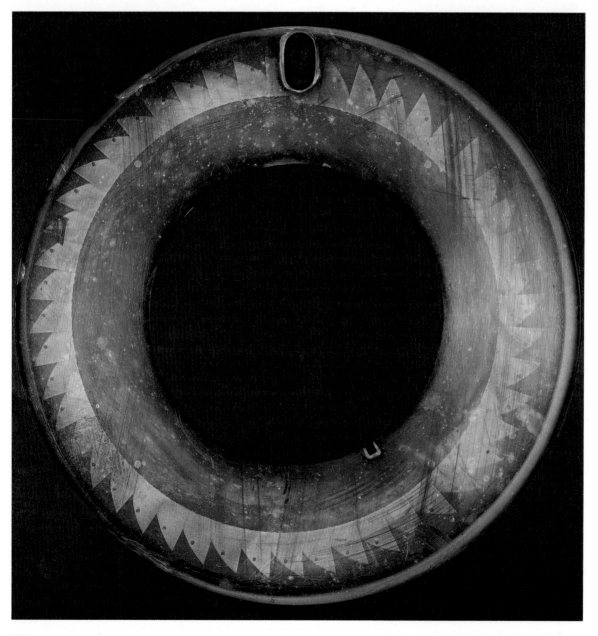

5.23
PIERRE-CÉSAR JULES JANSSEN, *Transit of Venus*, 1874. Daguerreotype, partly colored, full plate. Société Française de Photographie, Paris.

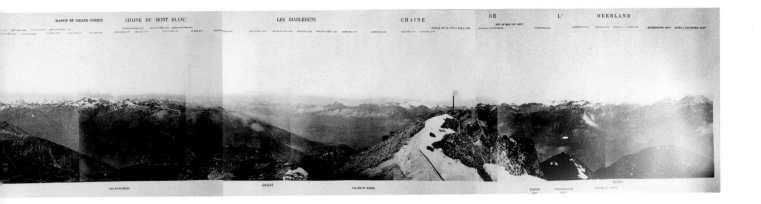

a gun fitted with a lens, to make sequential exposures on a DAGUERREOTYPE plate (Fig. 5.23). Though outmoded for portrait and landscape photography, the daguerreotype was chosen by the French team, in part because its metal plates were not subject to breakage, as were glass plates.

In the second half of the nineteenth century, the public experience of photographs depicting human society and the natural world increased. With that expansion came an intensification of the visual effects of images. The three-dimensionality of STEREOGRAPHS is perhaps the most prominent example, but there are others. Photographers created panoramic views, some of which mimicked the span of human vision, others of which attempted to reproduce a circular, 360-degree view. Throughout the nineteenth century, painted and photographed panoramas were used for popular entertainment and education. Whereas painted panoramas were rendered on long canvas scrolls, photographic panoramas were constructed from connected sequences of camera images.

From 1859 to 1866, French geologist Aimé Civiale (1821–1893) made a striking series of twenty-eight large photographic panoramas in the Italian, French, Austrian, and Swiss Alps (Fig. 5.24). Civiale did not conceive his photographs to show how a human might perceive the scene, nor to render the beauty of the Alps. He wanted the panoramas to illustrate the tremendous geological uplift that originally formed the European mountain systems. Civiale developed a scientific aesthetic for his purposes, in which the large patterns of the mountains' geological development were emphasized and the myriad surface details were decreased. His work was shown in the exhibitions of the French Photographic Society for a decade, from 1859 to 1869.[29]

RETAKE

Photography made possible a new age of discovery comparable to that of the explorers who charted the globe from the fifteenth to the seventeenth centuries. From the mid-nineteenth century onward, great and small explorations were routinely photographed, as were medical achievements. Topographical survey teams made pictures of the terrain, mineral deposits, and potential transportation routes, as well as the lives and customs of indigenous peoples along the way. Scientists developed special instruments to record astronomical events, and planned lengthy expeditions, like those to view the transit of Venus in 1874. Prompted by the thin premise that the psychological and moral qualities of human beings are unerringly written in their physical appearances, amateur and professional scientists sought to use the camera to create a visual dictionary of the inner life. Like the earlier age of discovery, the photographically driven exploration of the mid-nineteenth century increased human knowledge while extending Western influence around the globe. But where earlier explorers could paint and draw their discoveries, later ones could fix their finds with the camera's glass eye and disseminate their views as never before. While more and more people were able to make virtual visits to the world's various cultures and natural wonders, they were able to do so often through a configuration of ignorant and prejudicial ideas. Photographs of non-Western people exaggerated their physical and cultural difference from Westerners. The falsehoods of science and social science, aided by the camera, were as undeniable as their advances.

philosophy and practice

"Superseded by Reality"

During the mid-nineteenth century, photography was defined by its makers and users as a complex and contradictory medium. At issue was the central notion of realism. For some, such as Oliver Wendell Holmes, realistic photographic images and the development of a commercial network of publishers promised a more democratic diffusion of knowledge in an era when acquired skills and mechanical invention were effectively eroding the authority of traditional power structures. For governments and the military, as well as topographical surveys, photography became a routine adjunct to operations. In science, specialty photography developed hand-in-hand with geology, biology, astronomy, chemistry, and other empirical pursuits. Photography not only recorded findings, but also made it easier to arrange these findings into taxonomies—that is, broad classifications and categories.

Writing in 1864, Robert Cecil (1830–1903), later, as the Marquess of Salisbury, British prime minister (1885–92, 1895–1902), summed up the general feeling. "It is to science … that photography, the child of science, renders, and will unceasingly render, the most valuable aid. … Photography is never imaginative, and is never in any danger of arranging its records by the light of a pre-conceived theory."[30]

The growing acceptance of photography as a reliable representation of the world increased the credibility of photographic evidence. Cecil considered that "the noblest function of photography [is] to remove from the paths of science in some degree the impediments of space and time, and to bring the intellects of civilized lands to bear upon the phenomena of the vast portion of the earth whose civilization has either not begun, or is passing away."[31] Individual photographs thus became building blocks in systems that have since proved to be more fanciful than empirical. For example, notions of racial difference were supported by photographs that emphasized some bodily distinctions, while neglecting similarities.

In law and police work, photographic evidence of personal identity, clothing, locales, signatures, and the like were increasingly used. In the 1880s these applications developed into internationally accepted systems to organize visual data. Photographic affidavits (photographs used in legal briefs as sworn evidence) proved to be a potent challenge to hearsay evidence in the courtroom.[32] In addition, schemes to prevent crime by creating national identity cards containing a photographic likeness were proposed in Britain in the late 1860s. As one notable advocate of photography put it in 1869,

the expanding domain of photography made earlier forms of evidence "superseded by reality."[33]

Because it was accepted as proof, photography confirmed whatever was photographed. This sense of authenticity was applied broadly, not only in war, science, and law, but also in everyday portraiture and views of foreign lands. It teased into being a craving for pictures of political, social, and cultural celebrities. As photography emerged as evidence, events and personalities began to be fashioned with an eye for public circulation.

At the same time, the absence of photographs effectively denied the significance of a subject or theme that was not regularly depicted. New bridges and railroads were photographed; non-picturesque agricultural and industrial workers actually toiling in fields and factories were generally not pictured. The American Civil War military installations and battles were thoroughly photographed; the dismal record of slavery was not. Foreign wars and landscapes were programmatically photographed, as were foreign natural disasters, such as the Hong Kong typhoon (see Fig. 4.37), when they affected Western commerce. But devastating events and calamities outside the Western sphere mostly were not photographed, even though public faith deepened in photography's ability to confirm events.[34]

Writing from southern India during the Madras famine, a certain Dr. Cornish lamented: "I often regret that I have not a photographer temporarily attached to my office while moving amongst the famine-stricken people. … Words at best can but feebly represent the actual facts, but if members of Government could see the living skeletons."[35] Moving as they are, images of human suffering, such as those taken to raise relief funds by British photographer Willoughby Wallace Hooper (1837–1912) during the Madras famine in India in the late 1870s, were not routinely or methodically produced.

Generally speaking, it was easier for photographers to conjecture the opening of the Suez Canal (1869) as an aesthetically challenging and commercially lucrative subject for photography,[36] than for cameraworkers to imagine how to photograph the intangible ways in which life was swiftly changing in the developing world. Locomotives could be photographed; the speed of life could not. In effect, photography developed unevenly, omitting or neglecting the social and psychological responses to modernization that became the stuff of fiction and of art movements, such as Impressionism.

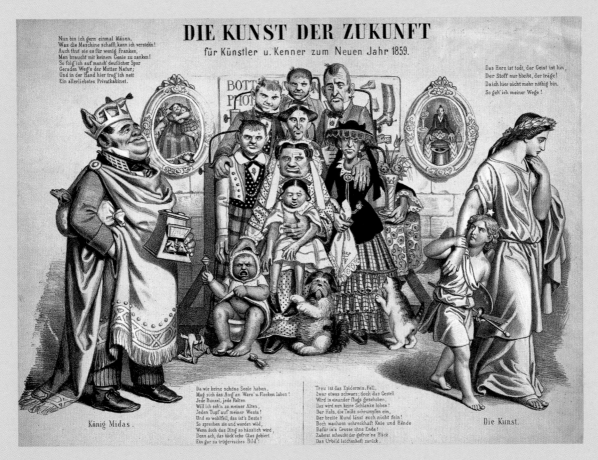

5.25
ARTIST UNKNOWN, *Die Kunst der Zukunft* (*The Art of the Future*), 1859. Lithograph. Museum Ludwig Köln/Agfa Foto-Historama, Germany.

In the face of the societal acceptance of photography as evidence, those who pursued the possibilities of photography as art began to think of ways to counteract the look of photographic testimony. As early as 1853, the British painter and photographer William Newton advocated the development of an art photography that consciously worked against the glut of details produced by "chemical Photography." Like Julia Margaret Cameron (see p. 92), he proposed rendering a subject a little out of focus.[37] For artists and cultural commentators, the association of photography with scientific and industrial progress was not a blessing. British artist and critic John Ruskin came to consider it a detriment to art and to society. He wrote that photography could not be an art because art "expresses the personality, the activity, and living perception of a good and great human soul."[38] "Almost the whole system and hope of modern life," Ruskin wrote, "are founded on the notion that you may substitute mechanism for skill, photography for picture, cast-iron for sculpture."[39] The camera and the machine both tamped down human imagination, replacing creativity, observation, and insight with mediocre readymade goods. In 1859, French critic Henri de la Blanchère (1821–1880) succinctly phrased the complaint: "The less machine, the more the art."[40]

High Art photography, with its emphasis on moral values and literary topics, was no match for the tide of photographic evidence that defined the wider social understanding of the medium. Julia Margaret Cameron's spiritually infused photographs were popular in her circle, but they did not influence ordinary portraiture. Oddly enough, critics raised few questions about the exactness of photographic realism outside the arts, even when scenes in such photographs as *Home of a Rebel Sharpshooter* (see Fig. 4.17) were openly admitted to be arranged for the camera. Although the difference between an object seen and an object photographed was not much discussed, photographic realism was sometimes the brunt of humor, especially in portraiture, where realism seemed ugly, though truthful (Fig. 5.25). Yet the idea that there could be varieties of photographic realism, ranging from the sublimity of Samuel Bourne's Himalayan photograph (see Fig. 4.27) to the theatrical performance of mental states in the photographs produced for Charcot (see Fig. 5.16) and to the grittiness of John Thomson's views of street life in London (see Fig. 5.12), did not become part of a social dialogue.

As photography emerged as scientific and social evidence, it was also increasingly labeled counterfeit in art. The link between art and science in the popular phrase "the art-science of photography" weakened. In the last decade of the nineteenth century and the early years of the twentieth century, art and science would be painstakingly disconnected.

PART THREE
Photography and Modernity (1880-1918)

Chapter Six
The Great Divide

Chapter Seven
Modern Life

Philosophy and Practice
The Real Thing

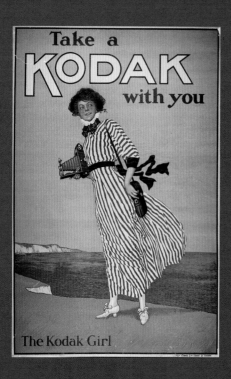

Take a
KODAK
with you

The Kodak Girl

The decades before World War I were symbolized not by photography but by electricity, which was lighting cities, running street cars, and powering large factories. As a machine, the camera was aligned with the First Industrial Revolution. Electricity powered the Second Industrial Revolution, which also included: the telephone; the radio; the combine, which reaped and threshed grain; automatic looms in the textile industry; the adding machine; the widespread use of typewriters; and the electric light bulb, together with power plants and the network delivering electrical power. Many late nineteenth-century writers saw electricity as a metaphor for rapid and powerful change; the camera gave way to the dynamo as a symbol of modernity. The perceived need for speed prompted Mark Twain to promote "mental telegraphy." Mind reading seemed the next step, because, as Twain put it, "telephones, telegraphs, and words are too slow for this age."[1] No wonder that tireless boy-inventor Tom Swift improved his camera, in Victor Appleton's 1914 *Tom Swift and his Photo Telephone*, by hitching it to the telephone and electricity.

While the camera-phone was only an imaginary device, photography was linked to the expansion of industrialization in other ways. Increasingly, the production of multiple photographs resembled that of the late nineteenth-century factory, which was coupled to national and international markets. Postcards and stereographs were mass produced for new audiences. Photography was subjected to the division of labor, not just in the small factories that made stereographs and postcards, but in the experience of the amateur snapshooter. When the Kodak camera hit the market in 1888, it separated the act of taking photographs from the process of making photographs. Instead of processing photographs in the home darkroom, users sent the camera and film to Kodak, which developed and printed the images. The Kodak advertising slogan, "You push the button—We do the rest," was part of the division of labor seen in the industrial realm. Perhaps the greatest correlation between photography and the second industrialization was found in the production of illustrated newspapers and magazines. Half-tone printing allowed images and text to be printed together on high-speed presses, which, in turn, fostered the production of inexpensive daily illustrated newspapers, some of whose income came from photographically illustrated advertisements. These highly competitive publications also promoted themselves by publishing topical and celebrity photographs.

The perceived vulgarity of mass culture and the excitement of modern art com–bined to encourage photographers interested in art and personal expression to create a separate aesthetic, supported by publications, galleries, and exclusive societies. Optical realism, which was photography's major asset in mass media, was targeted in the European art movements that influenced art photography. At the same time, the photography of movement and the X-ray undermined the certainty of human perception. By the end of the era, the extensive death and brutality of World War I brought into question both the social responsibility of science and the aspirations of art.

6.1
SUZANNE PORCHER, *Among the Irises, Public Gardens of Tours, France.* 1924.
Autochrome. Wm. B. Becker Collection/PhotographyMuseum.com.

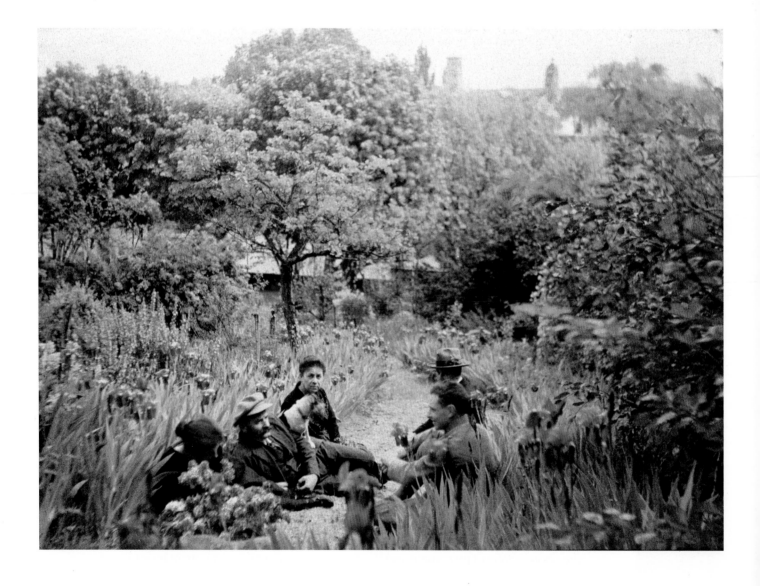

CHAPTER SIX

The Great Divide

By 1880, photography had been quietly absorbed into the texture of everyday life. In the late 1880s, there were more than sixty photographic journals and 161 photographic societies around the world.[1] By the turn of the century, manufacturers of STEREOGRAPHS, such as Underwood and Underwood, were producing twenty-five thousand images a day.[2] The increase in amateur photography prompted newspaper editors to run camera columns that served the people sometimes jokingly called "fotophiends." An 1884 article in the *New York Times* tried to be humorous by comparing "the camera epidemic" to the rampant cholera epidemic in Europe: "The camera epidemic threatens the gravest danger even to those who have never come into actual contact with a camera," the newspaper reported: "In watering places where the disease rages persons who venture from one place to another are sure to be stopped by the cry: 'Hullo there! don't walk in front of my camera.'"[3] The large photographic firms and news agencies in the developed countries continued to expand sophisticated networks for the accumulation and dissemination of images worldwide. In other words, the period witnessed an explosion of vernacular photography.

At the same time, art photographers were compelled to engage modern life. Some believed that art photography should take its lead from contemporary scientific findings. Others rejected science as hazardous to the timeless values of art and to the need for self-expression through art forms. Many felt that mass-media photography was not only vulgar and sensational, but also a symbol of the cheapening of modern life. Just as the fine arts had inspired some Victorians to devise High Art photography, turn-of-the-century photographers contrived PICTORIALISM—that is, a kind of photography that rejected industrialization for evocative, often hand-painted photographic images.

MASS MEDIA AND MASS MARKETS

During the vast expansion and societal absorption of photography, there was no particular moment or event to mark the point at which the medium fundamentally altered the experience of modern life. Instead, the transformation was expressed in multiple, interrelated technological developments during the 1880s, which occurred in response to the immense demand for photographs and the voracious information systems in Western society. Experiments in photomechanical processes led to the development of the HALF-TONE PROCESS, which allowed publications to reproduce photographic images directly, rather than through engravings. During the 1890s, it became cheaper, easier, and faster to use half-tones than to hire artists to make sketches, or to translate photographs into engravings. Spurred by advertising and illustrated periodicals, millions of half-tone images were produced. Along with the stereograph and the postcard, the half-tone invested modern life with visual information to an unprecedented degree.

The speed with which photographs could be reproduced with text, combined with the fast pace of urban life, altered newspapers, which had previously consisted mostly of columns of text with occasional line drawings, engravings, and advertisements. Specialized press photographers, agencies, and networks emerged, and pages were redesigned to include more photographs in place of descriptive text. Rather than wait for news to happen, news photographers were sent around the world to places where incidents were likely to occur. Political figures were regularly photographed, and the pictures were rushed to press by land or sea, since, unlike text, they could not yet be cheaply wired to newspapers over telephone lines. Interestingly, a specific date was not appended to many news photographs, perhaps because of the time-lag between taking a picture and publishing it. For example, illustrations derived from photographs of the great flood of May 31, 1889, in Johnstown, Pennsylvania, where more than two thousand people lost their lives, were published in New York's *Daily Graphic* on June 6. The delay was longer for international pictures. Photographs from the World War I battles near the Somme in France (June 24 to November 13, 1916) ran in *Leslie's* on January 25, 1917.

In the 1880s and 1890s, such periodicals as the *Berliner Illustrirte* [sic] *Zeitung* (*Illustrated Berlin Newspaper*), the *Illustrated London News*, and the *Illustrated American* presented political news together with entertainment listings, social happenings, and society reporting. Non-news, human interest

articles, and reports on the doings of celebrities increased and were accompanied by photographs. For news and feature stories, editors sought unusual, candid, or dramatic pictures. American audiences could be counted on to buy papers with scenes of natural and human-induced disasters, such as earthquakes and fires.[4] Although press photography created full-time work for photographers, their output was considered to be the property of the paper. The images were routinely cropped, retouched, and sequenced without the photographer's prior knowledge or permission.

The popularity of illustrated newspapers spawned new daily and weekly newspapers, as well as magazines, all of which engaged in intense rivalry for original pictures (Fig. 6.2).

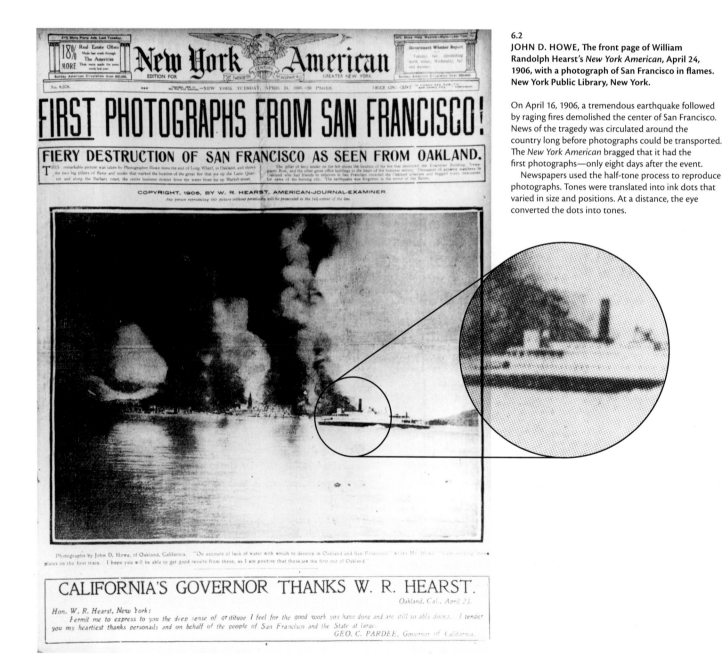

6.2
JOHN D. HOWE, The front page of William Randolph Hearst's *New York American*, April 24, 1906, with a photograph of San Francisco in flames. New York Public Library, New York.

On April 16, 1906, a tremendous earthquake followed by raging fires demolished the center of San Francisco. News of the tragedy was circulated around the country long before photographs could be transported. The *New York American* bragged that it had the first photographs—only eight days after the event.

Newspapers used the half-tone process to reproduce photographs. Tones were translated into ink dots that varied in size and positions. At a distance, the eye converted the dots into tones.

The competition for pictures to sell to the press spurred photographers to invade the privacy of public figures, such as German statesman Otto von Bismarck, who was clandestinely photographed on his deathbed by photographers who climbed in a window.[5] In 1899, the *Penny Pictorial Magazine* started a feature called "Taken Unawares," which contained snapshots of famous people. At the same time, public figures and celebrities often orchestrated events for the cameras that followed them. Theodore Roosevelt (1858–1919) welcomed the picture and print press on his election campaigns. Photographers Wade Mountford, Jr. (active early twentieth century), and William Warnecke (1881–1939) were with New York City mayor William Jay Gaynor moments after a 1910 assassination attempt, and made pictures showing his startled alarm (Fig. 6.3).

Advertisers began using photographs to sell an ever-increasing number of products. Along with the growth of department stores, catalog shopping, and national advertising campaigns, photography's own association with modernity gave products cachet and fostered a culture of display. In the cities, window shopping became a Sunday afternoon activity. The multifaceted increase in merchandising gave photographers opportunities to enlarge their practices. Because women were increasingly the modern family's designated shopper, they were thought to have an instinct for what products and promotions would succeed in the market. Consequently, women were often sought for jobs as copywriters and photographers. In Chicago, portrait photographer Beatrice Tonnesen (1871–1958) turned to advertising photography and eventually developed a national practice. With her sister Clara Tonnesen Kirkpatrick (1861–1944), who acted as the firm's business manager, she sometimes used the working name the Tonnesen Sisters. In an era accustomed to the use of drawings in advertising, the Tonnesens' photographs of live models gave them a competitive advantage (Fig. 6.4).

It was not only that photographs could be produced quickly and cheaply, but that people increasingly thought and planned in terms of multiple photographs. In 1893, when Abdulhamid II (1842–1918; r. 1876–1909), ruler of the Ottoman Empire, learned that his dominion was being perceived as "the sick man of Europe," he sent elaborate photographic albums to Britain, France, Germany, and the United States, hoping to change perceptions. Rather than images featuring timeless peasant life, the albums contained photographs of girls' schools, fashionable Western-style shops, a modern military, and factories located in the empire. Whereas the Ottoman Empire album comprised actual photographs, the half-tone process enabled localities to produce "booster books," illustrated descriptions of cities emphasizing only those aspects that would encourage commerce.

The invention of DRY PLATES made photography faster and easier. In contrast to the cumbersome wet-plate process, mass-manufactured dry plates did not need to be prepared and processed close to the time of exposure. Writing in 1894, photographer James Lawrence Breese (1854–1934) concisely summed up the impact of the new process: "the photographic artist has … a wider range at the present time than ever

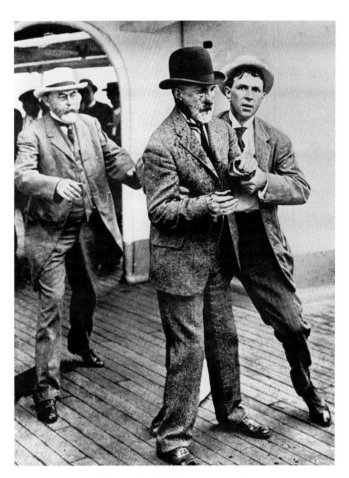

6.3
WILLIAM WARNECKE, *The Shooting of Mayor Gaynor*, 1910.

Warnecke was given a standard assignment from the *Evening World*, to photograph New York City mayor William Gaynor, who was leaving for a European vacation. As Warnecke loaded his last plate holders for his last shot, a would-be assassin stepped forward and shot Gaynor. The mayor recovered, but died three years later from the bullet's lingering effects.

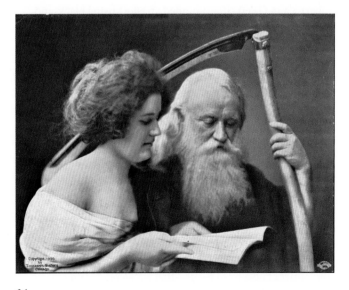

6.4
Advertising agencies used actors to play parts in images. The Tonnesen Sisters frequently employed character actors, like the man with the long white beard. He enacts Father Time for a calendar illustration. Courtesy of the author.

before, for the modern dry plate, so rapid in its action, permits photography from the rigging of a ship in motion, as well as on the busiest thoroughfare of the metropolis."[6] In 1839, exposures could take several minutes; by the end of the nineteenth century, exposure time was reduced to 1/5,000 of a second.

In addition, early photographic chemicals were not sensitive to the full range of colors in the natural world. They rendered some shades of red and blue as dark black. But by 1900, the responsiveness of black-and-white film to the range of colors was perfected and applied to the dry plate, making it better able to reproduce tonal variation in monochromatic prints.

Yielding faster exposure times throughout the 1880s, dry plates worked well with new, smaller, and more portable cameras, called hand cameras. In part, the short exposure time of the dry plate led to the design of camera shutters, which could open and close more quickly than the hand could remove and replace a lens cap. The dry plate allowed photographers to record movement, and permitted them greater mobility and anonymity. Because the image registered so quickly, the photographer did not need a tripod. In addition, an elaborate process for making color photographs called AUTOCHROME was developed in 1904 by the brothers Louis Lumière (1864–1948) and Auguste Lumière (1862–1954), inventors of the motion-picture projector in 1895. It involved depositing tiny potato-starch granules, dyed red-orange, green, and blue, on a glass plate, which was then coated with the light-sensitive emulsion used for black-and-white photographs. The grains served as color filters and the resulting image was a unique direct-positive photograph (Fig. 6.1). Basically, the autochrome was a slide, requiring light to be passed through it so viewers could look at the image. It remained the most advanced method for making color photographs until Kodachrome was introduced in 1935.

Subject to fading, expensive to create, and not capable of being duplicated, the autochrome enjoyed a vogue with amateur photographers. Despite its drawbacks, French banker-financier Albert Kahn (1860–1940) funded an effort using black-and-white photography and the autochrome process to create a visual record of everyday life around the globe. Initiated in 1912 and ending during the Great Depression, Kahn's archive amassed film and photographs from about fifty countries. The *Archives de la Planète* (*Archives of the Planet*) contains four thousand black-and-white photographs, approximately one hundred hours of film, and seventy-two thousand autochromes, the largest of its kind in the world. Kahn believed that when his collection was viewed by people it would motivate them to embrace human differences and, thereby, contribute to world peace.

"YOU PRESS THE BUTTON—WE DO THE REST"
In 1888, the Eastman Dry Plate Company in Rochester, New York, began manufacturing the Kodak camera, the first of many cameras intended for casual use by middle-class consumers. The camera had a fixed focus—that is, the photographer did not focus the lens, nor look through a viewfinder. The No. 1 Kodak, introduced in 1888, used what the company founder, George Eastman (1854–1932), called American film, a roll of

paper coated with light-sensitive material. The camera came loaded with film containing a hundred exposures. When all the pictures had been taken, the entire camera was sent back to the company in Rochester, where the prints were developed and the camera was reloaded. In other words, Kodak invented a customer-friendly photo-finishing business, as well as an uncomplicated camera. Indeed, the Kodak camera was one of the first standardized consumer items mass-produced in the United States.[7] The company slogan, "You press the button—We do the rest," enticed people to carry a camera and make spontaneous shots in a way that had not been done before. The resulting snapshots—the word was probably coined by John Herschel in the mid-nineteenth century—were 2½-inch diameter circular pictures (Fig. 6.6).

The No. 2 Kodak, which came on the market in 1889, yielded 3½-inch images. In 1900, the company launched the inexpensive Brownie camera, which it marketed initially to children. Increasingly, cameras were available in department stores, rather than shops specializing in professional photographic needs.

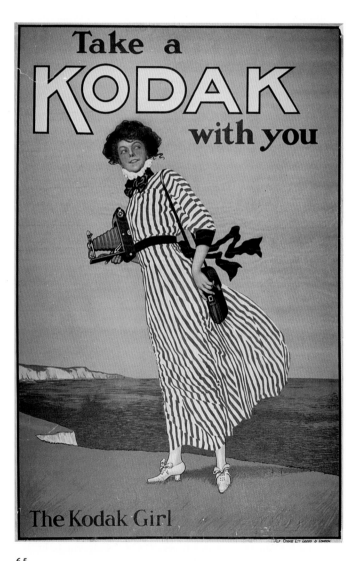

6.5
ARTIST UNKNOWN, *Untitled* (Advertisement for Kodak cameras), c. 1910. Poster. George Eastman House, Rochester, New York.

Though snapshots were mostly personal pictures, they did have a significant public impact. Snapshots not only reduced the number of professional portrait photographers; they also deepened the association between informality and photographic truth. Increasingly press photographs emulated the casual look of the snapshot, and the few artists remaining at newspapers made their drawings look more sketchy, as if done quickly on the spot.

Small cameras were not merely intended for casual shooters. Manufacturers slimmed down cameras and experimented with roll film to create compact, lightweight hand-held devices such as Hawkeye, P.D.Q. (Photography Done Quickly), and, of course, Kodak, to be used by professionals and amateurs alike. The Kodak camera even made its way into Bram Stoker's 1897 novel *Dracula*, where it was used by the protagonist Jonathan Harker. About the same time, the camera was miniaturized. Tiny cameras fitted into walking-stick handles, pistols, and jewelry were marketed as detective or secret cameras, capable of taking pictures covertly. The SINGLE-LENS REFLEX CAMERA, such as the Graflex, was rigged with an internal mirror that allowed photographers to examine the scene before the lens. It became the standard news photographer's camera.

THE POSTCARD CRAZE

The private world exposed by the detective camera contrasted with the public world broadcast by the postcard, which rivaled stereography in popularity and sheer range of subject matter. Picture postcards evolved after changes in nineteenth-century postal regulations in Europe and the United States authorized a simple, undecorated card with a message to be mailed. At the turn of the century, when printing methods such as the half-tone process facilitated reproduction of pictures and text, photographic postcards began to appear in large numbers. Like *CARTE-DE-VISITE* and stereograph images, they were both collected and sent to others (Fig. 6.7). Before long-distance telephoning became common, when radio and the movies were infant technologies, people wrote often to each other. Notes jotted on postcards were casual hellos, like emailed friendship cards.

Photographic postcards depicted tourist spots as well as ethnic types and news events. Erotic images, such as those

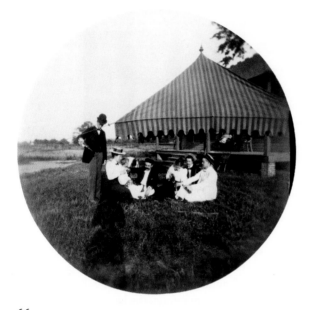

6.6
PHOTOGRAPHER UNKNOWN, *Untitled*, c.1888. Early Kodak print. George Eastman House, Rochester, New York.

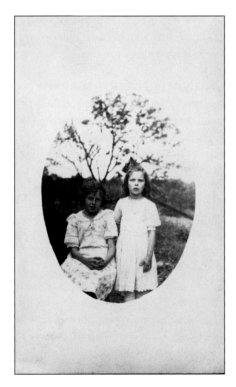

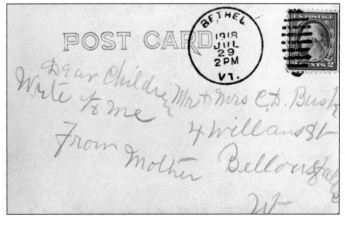

6.7
PHOTOGRAPHER UNKNOWN, *Untitled* (front and back of postcard), 1918. Courtesy of the author.

The front of this postcard shows Ida Root (Sarazen) and Anne Northrup (Warner). Before telephones became common in rural areas, postcards were often sent over short distances to convey friendship and affection. This card was dispatched by a woman in Bethel, Vermont, to her daughter and niece visiting at a nearby farm in Bellows Falls. The message on the back reads, "Dear Children, Write to me, From Mother."

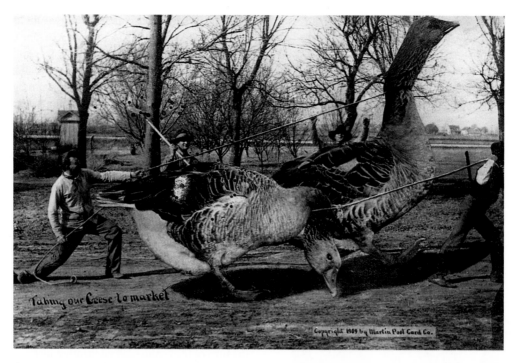

6.8
WILLIAM H. MARTIN, *Taking our Geese to Market*, 1909. Silver print postcard. Franklin County Historical Society, Kansas.

displaying partially clad women from colonial Africa, were produced in great numbers. Veiled Islamic women, long a subject for ethnographic and erotic photography, were also pictured on postcards.[8] At the end of the nineteenth century, photographer William Henry Jackson (see p. 134) joined with two other entrepreneurs to form the Detroit Publishing Company. Postcards, sometimes in boxed sets, comprised most of the seven million images issued by the company in an average year. Panoramas, slides, and hand-colored prints—mostly of American farms, factories, cities, natural wonders, and that ubiquitous favorite the cowboy—were marketed worldwide to schools, libraries, and governments, as well as to individuals.[9]

At the height of the craze, Kodak manufactured the Folding Camera 3A, especially for producing picture postcards. The United States Post Office reported that from June 1907 to June 1908 more than 667 million postcards, many of them picture postcards, were sent.[10] The postcard rage originated a type of popular image that would not have seemed humorous in photography's first decade, when trifling with the appearance of reality was considered misplaced. Photographic exaggerations showed grasshoppers the size of turkeys, apples as large as mansions, and geese twice as tall as men (Fig. 6.8). The postcard vogue faded after World War I (1914–18), in part because of new postal regulations that discouraged it.

THE CHALLENGE FOR ART PHOTOGRAPHY

On the occasion of photography's fiftieth anniversary in 1889, American artist J. Wells Champney (1843–1903) wrote an article surveying the familiar list of its social and technological accomplishments in the fields of science, anthropology, criminology, and military applications. He ended with what would become a frequent refrain: the lack of parallel progress in art photography. "As an aid to science, as a recorder, as a duplicator, photography has helped advance civilization," Champney remarked. Yet "it has failed to occupy the place it may yet hold as a means for expressing original thought of a fine order."[11] At the turn of the twentieth century, more people came to believe that a modern art must evolve at a pace and with an inventiveness similar to those of science and technology.

NATURALISTIC PHOTOGRAPHY
Perhaps Champney overlooked the writings of British photographer Peter Henry Emerson (1856–1936), who a few years earlier had taken up eagerly the perceived challenge of science to art and art photography. Emerson acquired his first camera during his medical training at Cambridge University. By 1885, with the assurance of a private income, he chose to practice photography rather than medicine. He insisted that, in the modern world, science was the only authentic basis for art and photography. Just as the French novelist Émile Zola (1840–1902) had adopted the scientific method and outlook of the doctor Claude Bernard (1813–1878), so Emerson seized on the ideas of German scientist Hermann von Helmholtz (1821–1894), whose studies of the human eye's range of focus he took as instructive for photography. Both Zola and Emerson attempted to align art with the cutting edge of science, and to make it part of the modern world. In 1880, Zola famously proclaimed that "metaphysical man is dead; with physiological

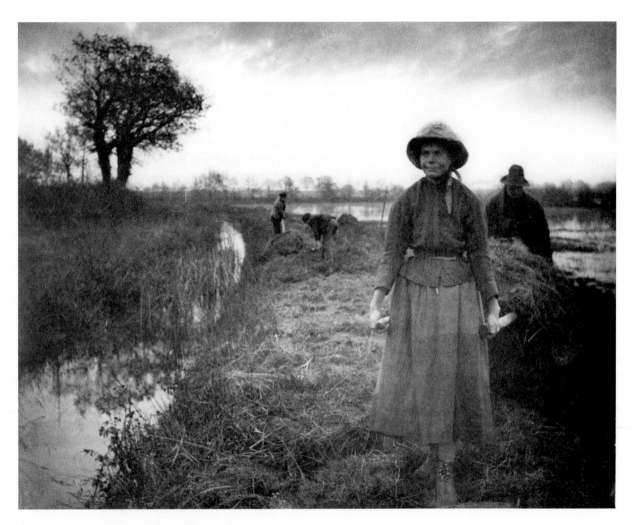

6.9
PETER HENRY EMERSON, *Poling the Marsh-Hay*, plate 17 from his book *Life and Landscape on the Norfolk Broads*, 1886.
Victoria and Albert Museum (Library), London.

man our position changes."[12] Speaking to the Camera Club of London in March 1886, Emerson likewise declared that "the days of metaphysics are over."[13]

In his most important theoretical work, *Naturalistic Photography* (1889), Emerson expounded his theory of photography. He rejected the idea of art as primarily a vehicle for personal and emotional expression. While maintaining that the artist was a person of special character and ability, he derided works of the imagination as untrue.[14] His own notion of naturalism was based on contemporary science, not art theory, notably on Helmholtz's idea that "perfect artistic painting is only reached when we have succeeded in imitating the action of light upon the eye."[15] At a time when technical improvements enabled photographers to make sharper pictures, Emerson denied that the camera could make art by merely transcribing physical reality. Instead, he argued that the artist should translate exactly how the eye sees, concluding that the photographer should focus on the main subject of a scene, allowing the periphery and the distance to become indistinct. Called differential or selective focus, this approach varied from William Newton's

earlier idea of making the entire image slightly out of focus (see p. 159).

Much of Emerson's photography was done on the Norfolk Broads, a marshy area in eastern England where industrialization had not penetrated to the degree that it had in other parts of the country. There Emerson found rural life and traditional occupations; he ignored the beginnings of tourism, which was bringing people to the shallow, navigable waters of the Broads. His first major work, *Life and Landscape on the Norfolk Broads* (1886), was a folio of forty mounted PLATINUM PRINTS (called platinotypes in the period) with accompanying text by Emerson and his friend and traveling companion the artist Thomas Frederick Goodall (1857–1944). Emerson's pictures emphasized the unchanged relationship of people to the land (Fig. 6.9).

Emerson was known as an eccentric art celebrity, whose ideas and work were controversial, like those of American painter James McNeill Whistler (1834–1903). When he rejected his own theory in a black-bordered pamphlet titled *The Death of Naturalistic Photography* (1890), the public was skeptical. Yet Emerson maintained that his early theory was based on a belief that TONES in a photograph could be manipulated to a greater degree than chemists now proved possible. Many people today find Emerson's rationale insufficient. Having promoted art photography as a cutting-edge application of recent science, he seems to have abruptly cast it off because he saw it as limiting the individuality of the artist.

PICTORIALISM

Although Emerson wrote that he thought much amateur and art photography pretentious, many practitioners ignored his insults, and based their ideas of art photography on his photographs, with their subdued middle-gray tones, soft focus, and peaceful, agrarian subjects. Amateurs of art photography creatively misunderstood Emerson's writings to authorize moving away from faithful depiction toward more evocative and expressive photographs. The resulting international photographic movement known as Pictorialism gathered strength in the mid-1880s, peaked in the 1900s, and persisted into the 1920s.

Pictorialists adopted Emerson's disgust with industrialization and mass-produced goods, as well as his belief in photography as a fully fledged modern art form. They embraced his choice of subjects, but jettisoned allegiance to recent science. In Pictorialist hands, Emerson's selective or differential focus became a dislike of the distracting details associated with vulgar commercial photography. Pictorialist photographers favored scenes infused with fog and shadows. In contrast to their simple subjects, they strove for tonal complexity, choosing techniques such as platinum printing, which yielded abundant soft, middle-gray tones. They favored procedures that allowed for handworking of both NEGATIVES and prints. Their results were in obvious visual opposition to the sharp black-and-white contrasts of the commercial print. Pictorialist photographs were frequently printed on textured paper, unlike the glossy surface of commercial photographs, so that they resembled watercolors, evoking the earlier Victorian photographs of David Octavius Hill and Julia Margaret Cameron, which they admired and exhibited.

Pictorialists valued their symbolic control over the growing photography industry, and they cultivated a sense of superiority over the snapshooters, who did not even develop their own film. One Pictorialist asserted that "the photographer is not helpless before the mechanical means at his disposal. He can master them as he may choose, and he can make the lens see with his eyes, can make the plate receive his impressions."[16] Pictorialist writing encouraged a self-image of cultural heroism, striking back at the worst of the modern world. In his influential 1901 book *Photography as a Fine Art*, critic Charles H. Caffin (1854–1918) described the "men and women who are seeking to lift photography to the level of one of the Fine Arts" as "advanced photographers," and Alfred Stieglitz (1864–1946), who would later emerge as the foremost art photographer, as an "artist, prophet, pathfinder."[17]

As Emerson's justification of selective focus—that is, to match the way the eyes see—faded from currency, the writings

of Henry Peach Robinson, which Emerson strongly disliked, were devoured by a new generation. Robinson, best known for his COMBINATION PRINTS (see p. 88), was probably even more responsible for popularizing the word "pictorial" than Emerson. His book *Pictorial Effect in Photography*, first published in 1868, was still read at the turn of the century. A few photographers made elaborate *tableaux vivants* of Old Master paintings, extending Robinson's own practice. Serious amateurs, as they were called, sometimes blended contemporary styles and themes in their work. Jane Reece (c. 1869–1961), a commercial portraitist in Dayton, Ohio, combined turn-of-the-century

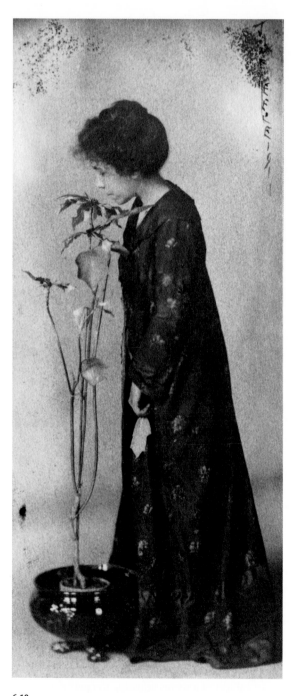

6.10
JANE REECE, *The Poinsettia Girl (Self-Portrait)*, 1907. Sepia-toned gelatin silver print. Dayton Art Institute, Dayton, Ohio.

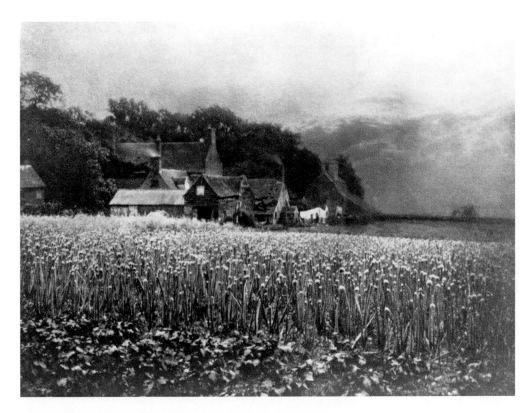

6.11
GEORGE DAVISON, *The Onion Field*,
1889, from *Camera Work*, January 1907.
Photogravure. Library of Congress,
Washington, D.C.

The blur in Davison's image was produced
using a pinhole camera, which softened
edges and imparted a dreamy haze not
necessarily present at the time of exposure.
Printed as a gravure, a technique favored by
Pictorialists because it suppressed detail, the
image seems to have flowed into the fabric
of the paper on which it is printed.

interest in Japanese prints, with their flattened space, and the principle that one should beautify the experience of everyday life, an idea promoted by the Arts and Crafts movement and the followers of Art Nouveau (Fig. 6.10).

To Emerson's annoyance, another British photographer, George Davison (1854–1930), expanded upon his theories and promoted an imprecise notion of impressionistic photography. Whereas Impressionism, the French art movement of the 1870s–80s, aimed at capturing a momentary visual imprint of a scene, impressionistic photography attempted to render a personal response to a subject. Soon the words "poetic," "art," "naturalistic," and "impressionistic" all came to signal Pictorialist photography, exemplified by Davison's *The Onion Field* (Fig. 6.11). Unlike Emerson's work, where the main subject was in focus, the entire surface of *The Onion Field* is indistinct. Davison thus shifted the foundations of art photography from science to art. Paradoxically, the anti-industrial, hand-crafted "fuzzygraph," as Pictorial photographs were sometimes mockingly called, helped foster a new segment of photographic manufacturing. Commercial producers rushed to make soft-focus lenses and textured photographic papers for amateur use.

Emerson's renunciation of naturalistic photography did not stop him making pictures or criticizing the growing popularity of the GUM-BICHROMATE PROCESS, which made it possible to add pigment and texture to a print. French photographer Robert Demachy (1859–1936) promoted the technique in influential articles and worked extensively in it himself (Fig. 6.12). Another proponent of so-called gum printing was German photographer Heinrich Kühn (1866–1944), whose painterly photographs using the technique vexed viewers at the first amateur photographic

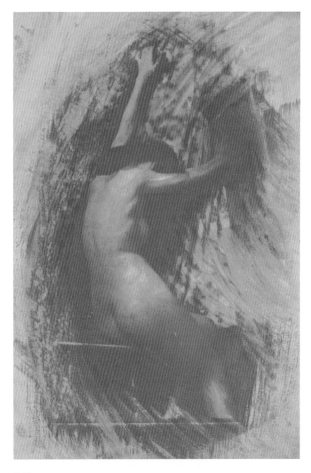

6.12
ROBERT DEMACHY, *Struggle*, from *Camera Work*, January 1904.
Photogravure. Metropolitan Museum of Art, New York.

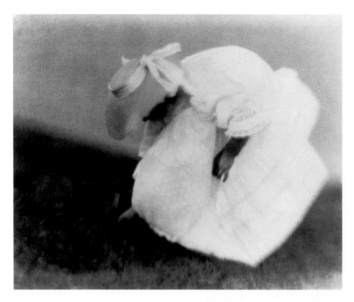

6.13
HEINRICH KÜHN, *On the Hillside*, 1910. Gum-bichromate print. Metropolitan Museum of Art, New York.

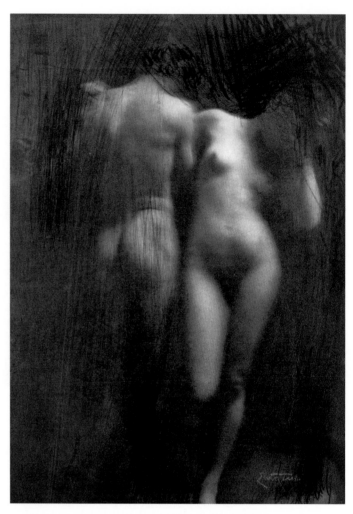

6.14
FRANK EUGENE, *Adam and Eve*, 1910, from *Camera Work*, April 1910. Photogravure. Library of Congress, Washington, D.C.

exhibition held in Berlin in 1896 (Fig. 6.13). Like Emerson, Kühn was a scientist and a doctor, but his training did not lead him to a scientifically based theory of art. He also disliked the new snapshot photography, claiming that humans do not see the way that "quick shots" look. However spontaneous his photographs may appear, Kühn planned them by selecting a location and sketching possible scenes, including poses for his subjects, whose apparel he frequently selected. With photographers Hans Watzek (1848–1903) and Hugo Henneberg (1863–1918), Kühn exhibited under the name Das Kleeblatt (The Trifolium, or Cloverleaf, referring both to the three-lobed leaf and to the three-part window of Gothic architecture). Kühn moved easily between groups of European photographers and painters. American-born Frank Eugene (1865–1936) was equally international. He sometimes combined photography and printmaking (Fig. 6.14), and favored dreamy views of leisured women enjoying nature, a popular theme in Pictorialist photography. In 1906, he moved to Germany, where he made both paintings and photographs.

Like Art Nouveau artists in Europe and America, the Pictorialists raised aesthetic experience to a paramount life goal. From their point of view, what was needed was aesthetic reform of the whole society, and they hoped to start the process by banishing the harsh and unsightly realm of industry from their work. Pictorialism created international networks of artists and amateurs. The movement was strong in Russia, where Sergei Lobovikov (1870–1942) adopted it to render traditional peasant life, not as ethnographic data, but as an expression of nostalgia for nature and simpler times (Fig. 6.15). Like other Pictorialists, Lobovikov worked with gum bichromate and made platinum prints; he also favored the BROMOIL PROCESS, which allowed him to apply color to the print with a brush. In Japan, the Pictorialist look dominated portraits, street scenes, landscapes, and ethnographic photography until the mid-1930s, when it finally gave way to the pressures of Modernism and abstraction.

MOVEMENTS AND MAGAZINES

The first photographic associations brought together people with diverse interests and occupations. Their publications covered subjects from art exhibits and travel to technical instructions and new commercial products. In the 1890s, however, Pictorialist photographers felt constrained by the uncritical commercialism of the older photographic organizations and the mediocrity of the images their members produced. They worried haughtily that snapshot photography was impairing the aesthetic sensibility of the public. Believing their medium to be equal to the other arts, and a source of spiritual and aesthetic fulfillment, they wanted to associate with like-minded people and to arrange their own exhibits.

Among the first associations formed solely to advance art photography was the Wiener Kamera Klub (Vienna Camera Club), which celebrated its founding in 1891 with a show of six hundred art photographs. Its members included Watzek, Henneberg, and Kühn. Artists in other media acknowledged the aesthetic aspiration of Pictorialist photographers by sitting on juries for photographic exhibitions, and by showing art

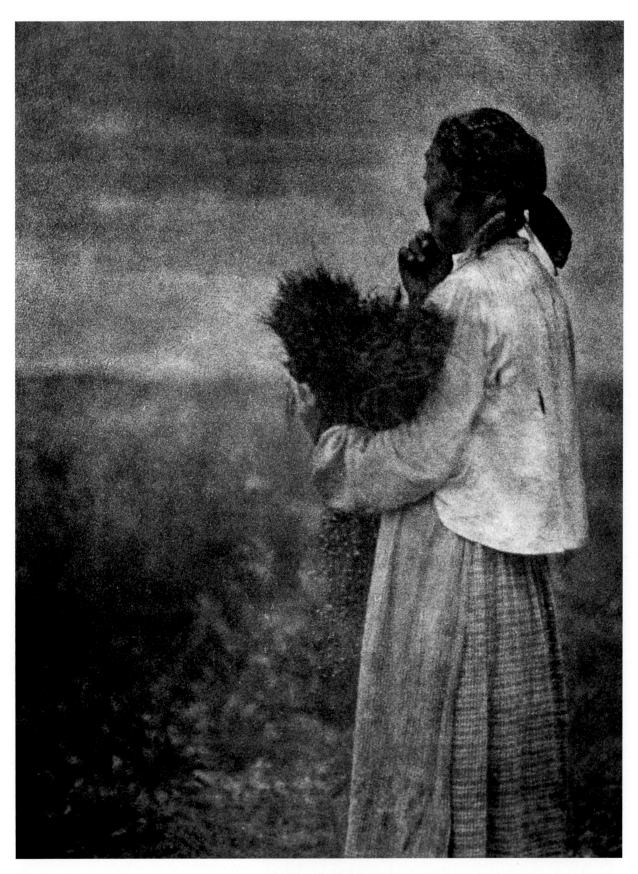

6.15
SERGEI LOBOVIKOV, *The Widow's Pillow*, c. 1900. Bromoil and varnish. Mikhail Golosovskii Collection, Krasnogorsk, Russia.

Despite the blurry image, the woman's raised hand makes clear that she has endured a life of manual labor. She clutches a bundle of straw gleaned, perhaps, from the field before her. As indicated by an intent gaze at the horizon, her thoughts seem to be on times long gone and faraway places.

photographs at their own shows. For example, Watzek's gum bichromate photographs were presented at an 1898 exhibit sponsored by the Munich Secession, an association of artists formed in 1892 with interests akin to those of the Pictorialists. A similar group, the Vienna Secession, showed Henneberg's gum prints in 1902 (Fig. 6.16).

Art photography organizations were typically international in membership: Watzek, Henneberg, and Kühn, for example, were also members of the Photo-Club de Paris, which broke from the more conservative Société Française de Photographie in 1894. Two of the Photo-Club's founders, Robert Demachy and Charles Émile Joachim Constant Puyo (1857–1933), had

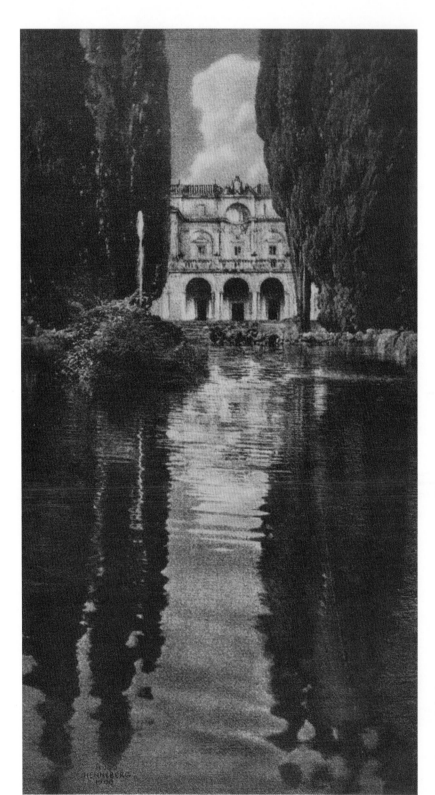

6.16 (left)
HUGO HENNEBERG, *Villa Falconieri,* **from** *Camera Work,* **1906. Photogravure. Museum of Modern Art, New York/Scala, Florence.**

As it had for generations of painters, the Italian landscape and its ancient villas attracted Pictorialist photographers. Henneberg's image shows the Pictorialist concern with light, water, clouds, and reflections.

6.17 (opposite top)
CHARLES É. J. PUYO, *Puyo, Robert Demachy, and Paul de Singly with Model,* **1909. Platinum print. Metropolitan Museum of Art, New York.**

6.18 (opposite bottom)
JAMES CRAIG ANNAN, *Miss Janet Burnet,* **1893. Vintage tissue photogravure from** *Camera Work* **by Alfred Stieglitz, 1907.**

Annan's photograph of Janet Burnet shows how Pictorialists blended artistic themes and ideas. He sometimes printed the photograph with the subject looking left and sometimes to the right. He may have been influenced by *Whistler's Arrangement in Gray and Black* (*Whistler's Mother*). In the background, the sitter's name is rendered as it might be in a print by German artist Albrecht Dürer (1471–1528).[18]

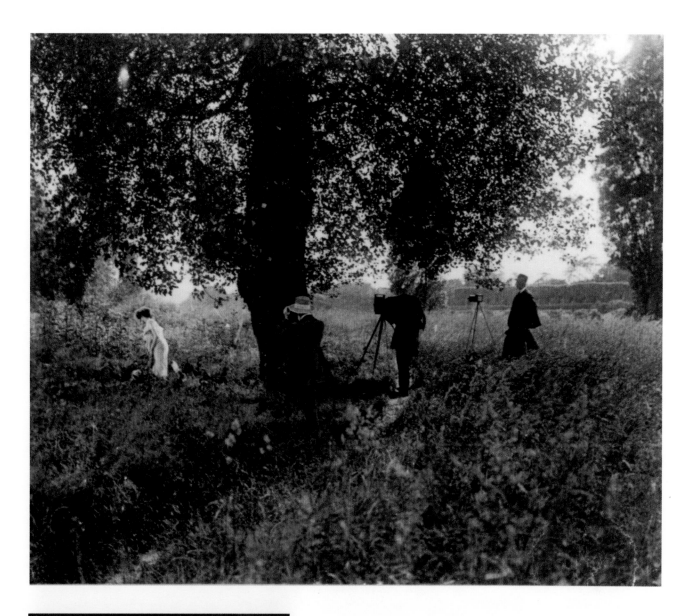

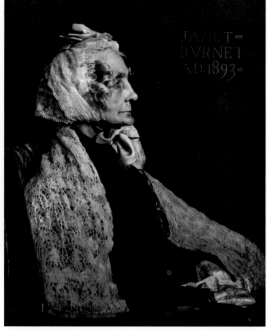

an international audience for their writings about the gum-bichromate process (Fig. 6.17).

Watzek, Henneberg, and Kühn were also elected to the British association called the Linked Ring—formed in 1892 in opposition to the Photographic Society of Great Britain—whose fifteen founders included Henry Peach Robinson and George Davison. The "Links" thought of themselves as members of a spiritual and aesthetic fellowship. Their Photographic Salons were held yearly, exhibiting work they approved, such as that of James Craig Annan (1864–1946), son of photographer Thomas Annan, who had photographed the Glasgow slums before they were demolished (see Fig. 5.11). James Craig Annan admired the work of Hill and Adamson; as a youngster he met Hill, and in the 1890s he began making prints from Hill and Adamson negatives. Having learned the GRAVURE process in Vienna from its inventor, Karl Klič (1841–1926), Annan began working with his father on fine printing (Fig. 6.18). The gravure process allowed photographers to translate their photographs into printer's ink by means of a copper plate that was etched by chemicals, then inked, and printed on a hand-turned printing press.

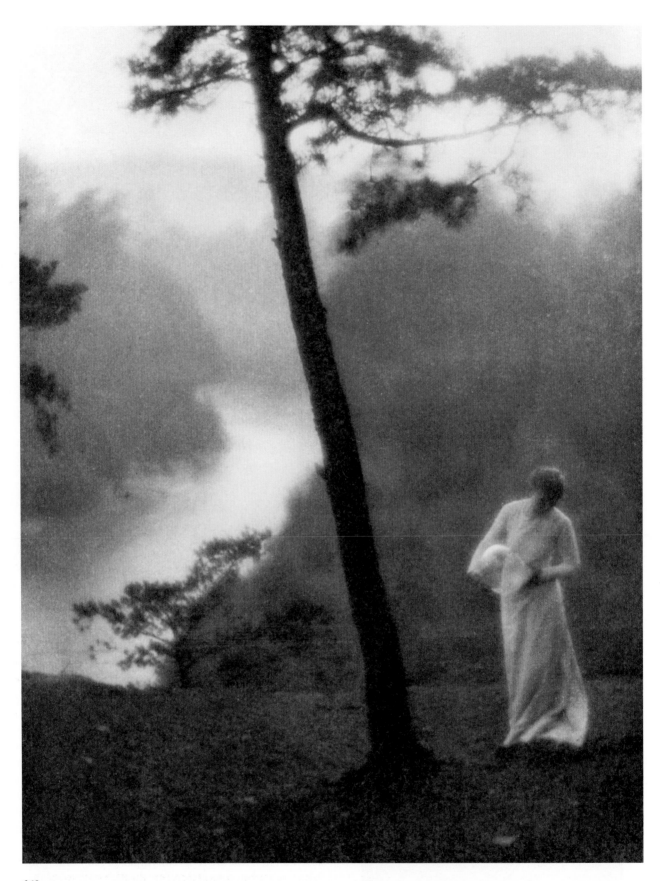

6.19
CLARENCE H. WHITE, *Morning*, **1908. Photogravure print. George Eastman House, Rochester, New York.**

The purity of morning and the idea of a fresh beginning are indicated by bright light filtering through fog. The glass globe that the model carries appears in several of White's images.

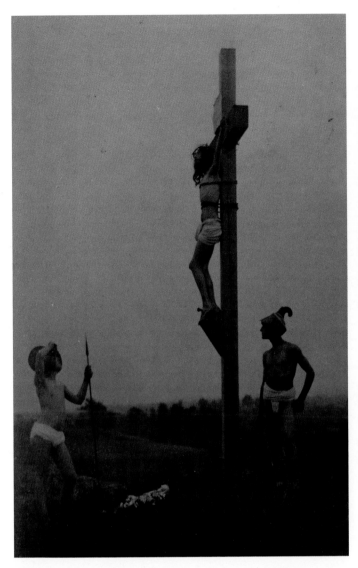

6.20
F. HOLLAND DAY, *Untitled* (Crucifix with Roman soldiers), 1896. Platinum print. Library of Congress, Washington, D.C.

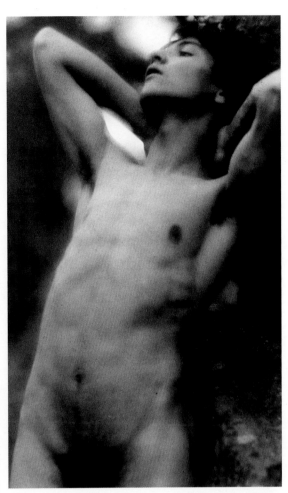

6.21
F. HOLLAND DAY, *Nude Youth with Laurel Wreath Standing against Rocks*, c. 1907. Platinum print. Library of Congress, Washington, D.C.

Day's sensuous images of the male nude blend a fondness for Classical sculpture with eroticism. Somewhat obscured by his Pictorialist technique, Day's nudes were not censored for their explicitness but applauded for their refinement.

American photographer Clarence H. White (1871–1925) was also elected to the Linked Ring. White's photographs centered on familiar Pictorialist themes, rendered with delicate atmospheric effects (Fig. 6.19). Through his teaching at Columbia University in New York City, White became influential in American photography. Eventually, he went on to found a photography school in his own name in 1914. His students included such luminaries as Dorothea Lange, Margaret Bourke-White, and Paul Outerbridge.

White was hired at Columbia by the painter and theorist Arthur Wesley Dow (1857–1922), whose understanding of *notan*, a Japanese concept of graphic patterning that interpreted the relationship of positive and negative spaces, was widely experimented with by the Pictorialists. In 2002, when Dow's large photographic work came to light, its flat, geometric patterning suggested that the Pictorialists may have learned directly from his art, as well as his theory.

Yet another American, F. Holland Day (1864–1933), was also elected to the Linked Ring. Day explored the possibility of using the camera to depict religious scenes in his *Sacred Art* series (Fig. 6.20). These photographs provoked ardent discussions about what constituted a proper photographic subject. A man of independent means, Day was the co-founder of the Boston publishing firm Copland and Day, which published the American editions of such controversial volumes as Oscar Wilde's *Salomé* and Aubrey Beardsley's *The Yellow Book*. His interest in the erotic human form was expressed in a number of nude and semi-nude photographs (Fig. 6.21).

Another Linked Ring member, British photographer Frederick H. Evans (1853–1943), rejected the special lenses and negative manipulations used by many Pictorialists, in favor of what he called "pure photography."[19] He called for plain prints from plain negatives. Writing about his work, mostly platinum prints, Evans explained that he found architecture best suited

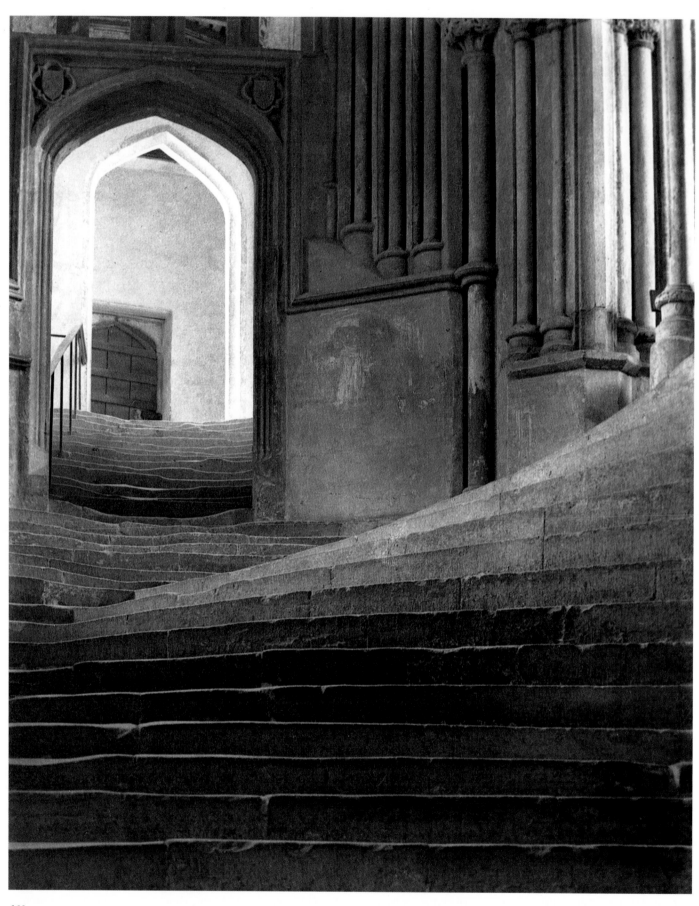

6.22
FREDERICK H. EVANS, *Steps to Chapter House: A Sea of Steps*, Wells Cathedral, 1903. Platinum print. Museum of Modern Art, New York.

to art photography. His goal was to record an emotional and aesthetic response to space, light, and shadow, especially in the interiors of historic English churches, cathedrals (Fig. 6.22), and French chateaux.

THE PHOTO-SECESSION

Writing in *American Amateur Photographer* in 1904, critic Sadakichi Hartmann (1867–1944) used an exhibition at the Carnegie Institute in Pittsburgh, Pennsylvania, as a spring-board for his thoughts on contemporary photography. Not attempting to disguise his distaste, he called the organizers "pictorial extremists, who lay more stress on 'individual expression' than on any other quality." Some works, he scolded, "overstep all legitimate boundaries and deliberately mix up photography with the technical devices of painting and the graphic arts." He wondered whether the Pictorialist photographers were doing an "injustice to a beautiful method of graphic expression"—that is, photography. "Why then," he asked, "should not a photographic print look like a photographic print?" He called instead for "straightforward depiction" or "straight photography."[20]

One of the organizers of the 1904 Pittsburgh show was the American photographer Alfred Stieglitz, who was well positioned to lead an art movement. Through his work as an editor of *American Amateur Photographer* and *Camera Notes*, the journal of the Camera Club of New York, Stieglitz knew the work of the major Pictorialist photographers in Europe and America. He wanted *Camera Notes* to be international in scope, and to make American photography the equal of European painting, much revered in the United States. By the time Camera Club members objected to his aesthetic agenda, Stieglitz had already built up a following of art photographers ready to form their own association. Adopting the word "secession" from the art movements in Vienna and Berlin that were "seceding" from conventional academic work, and in the spirit of the Linked Ring, in February 1902 Stieglitz launched the Photo-Secession. Three weeks later, the Photo-Secession sponsored a large exhibition of "American Pictorial Photography" with the works of thirty-two photographers, among them Frank Eugene, F. Holland Day, Gertrude Käsebier, Clarence H. White, and Stieglitz himself. In December, the Photo-Secession issued a statement of purpose:

The object of the Photo-Secession is:
To advance photography as applied to pictorial expression;
To draw together those Americans practicing or otherwise interested in the art, and
To hold from time to time, at varying places, exhibitions not necessarily limited to the productions of the Photo-Secession or to American work.[21]

In effect, Stieglitz emphasized American artistic expression while accepting modern, mostly European, art movements. He became a major organizer of the new art photography, but this role was not unprecedented. Influential shows had been organized in Berlin by his mentor Hermann Wilhelm Vogel (1834–1898),

by the Amateur Photography Club in Vienna, by the Society for the Advancement of Amateur Photography in Hamburg, and, of course, at the annual salon sponsored by the Linked Ring.[22] In the United States, too, Clarence White proved an able advocate for photography with the shows he sponsored at the Camera Club of Newark, Ohio. Before the founding of the Photo-Secession, F. Holland Day proposed an "American Association of Pictorial Photographers," to be based in Boston. In 1900, he organized an exhibition of about three hundred images, called the "New School of American Photography," which was sponsored by the Royal Photographic Society and shown in London, and the next year by the Photo-Club de Paris in the French capital. Though Day's photographs were shown by the Photo-Secession, he never formally joined the group, perhaps because of his rivalry with Stieglitz.

One advantage Stieglitz possessed was his periodical *Camera Work*, published from 1903 to 1917. Modeled on fine-art publications, this was printed in decorative typography on deluxe paper; abundant samples of the new photography were mostly reproduced in gravure. Other journals advocating art photography included such lavishly illustrated German magazines as *Photographische Rundschau* (*Photographic Review*) and *Die Kunst in der Photographie* (*Art in Photography*). Stieglitz enlarged the scope of *Camera Work* to encompass the other arts and art theory. In July 1912, for example, he published selections from *Concerning the Spiritual in Art* by Russian painter Wassily Kandinsky (1866–1944).

The covers for *Camera Work* were designed by Edward Steichen (1879–1973), a painter-photographer who was also a founding member of the Photo-Secession. Outside *Camera Work*, Stieglitz continued to promote photography in popular magazines and journals. In a 1903 pamphlet, he manifested the outlook that made him notoriously difficult to work with. In scarcely veiled self-praise, he announced that progress is not achieved by the masses, but by the "fanatical enthusiasm of the revolutionist, whose extreme teaching has saved the mass from utter inertia." Photo-Secessionists, he announced, possess a feeling of "rebellion against the insincere attitude of the unbeliever, of the Philistine."[23]

Stieglitz also ran the Little Galleries of the Photo-Secession, which opened in November 1905 at 291 Fifth Avenue, New York, in Steichen's former studio. Steichen organized the first exhibition at 291, as the gallery became known, followed by a show of French photography selected by Demachy. Prints by Hill and Adamson (see Figs. 2.67, 2.68), greatly admired by Pictorialist photographers, were also shown, and reproduced in *Camera Work*. Working with Steichen, Stieglitz showed artwork in other media: drawings by Auguste Rodin (1840–1917), Henri Matisse (1869–1954), and Picasso (1881–1973); watercolors by Paul Cézanne (1839–1906) and Picasso; sculpture by Constantin Brancusi (1876–1957) and Elie Nadelman (1882–1946); LITHOGRAPHS by Henri de Toulouse-Lautrec (1864–1901); artwork by Americans such as Marsden Hartley (1877–1943), John Marin (1870–1953), and Georgia O'Keeffe (1887–1986); and children's art and Japanese prints.

portrait

Alfred Stieglitz

Born in Hoboken, New Jersey, Stieglitz took up photography while he was an engineering student in Berlin, studying photochemistry with Hermann Vogel. Soon his photographs were winning awards, and he was writing essays on the aesthetics and technical obstacles of the field. His early work includes the familiar tranquil scenes and all-over blurriness of Pictorialism, but his depiction of light and textures is clearer than Pictorialist photography. For instance, *Sun's Rays—Paula, Berlin* (1889) delineates the bands of light that pass through the shutter slats outside the room (Fig. 6.23). The technical virtuosity required to create a photograph in this lighting would be understood by photographers, but the personal symbols Stieglitz included would be grasped only by his immediate circle. On the wall behind his companion, Paula, are photographs of and by Stieglitz himself. One of them shows the letter-writer in bed, suggesting the couple's intimate relationship. The Valentine hearts and the caged bird also speak to the private subject-within-a-subject, a favorite visual strategy that Stieglitz would use throughout his life.

When he returned to the United States from Europe in 1890, Stieglitz worked for five years at the Photochrome Engraving Company in New York, and continued to make photographs. His marriage to Emmeline Obermeyer, a woman of financial means, and an allowance from his father, permitted him to leave the business and pursue photography full-time. His street photographs in New York City and during extended European trips centered on such everyday scenes as horse-drawn streetcars, rain-slicked avenues, and street children. Foreshadowing the 1904 critique of Sadakichi Hartmann (see p. 179), Stieglitz's images in the 1890s became more straightforward, with an increasing emphasis on form rather than atmosphere. His interests in contemporary art moved toward urban realism, like that of American painter Robert Henri (1865–1929), whom Stieglitz nonetheless accused of making "colored photographs."[24] Stieglitz also responded to the geometric experiments of such European painters as Pablo Picasso.

While sailing on a trip to Europe aboard the *Kaiser Wilhelm II*, Stieglitz experienced what he recalled as a pivotal moment in his understanding of art. Looking into the steerage section of the ship, he saw there not the disheartened immigrants returning to Europe, but a combination of abstract forms that evoked a profound response:

A round straw hat, the funnel leaning left, the stairway leaning right, the white draw-bridge with its railings made of circular chains—white suspenders crossing on the back of a man in the steerage below, round shapes of iron machinery, a mast cutting into the sky, making a triangular shape ... I saw a picture of shapes and underlying that the feeling I had about life.[25]

Decades later, he contended that *The Steerage* (Fig. 6.24) would best represent him, if all his other images were destroyed. Recent research suggests that he created an aura around this image to prove his early connection of abstraction and symbolism, as well as his knack for transforming the ordinary into pictures, as in his *Equivalents* (see p. 184).[26] The instantaneous visual recognition of a personal, not public, symbol informed much of Stieglitz's photography. His numerous photographs of his second wife, painter Georgia O'Keeffe, show how he, like Picasso, used daily life as a basis for art.

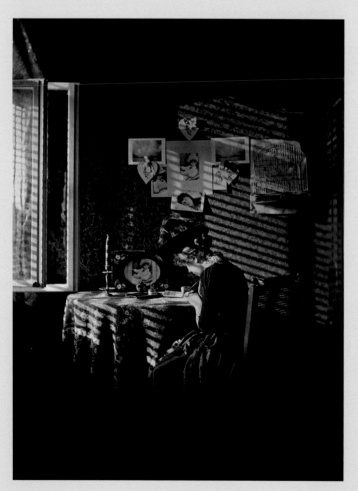

6.23
ALFRED STIEGLITZ, *Sun's Rays—Paula, Berlin*, 1889. Chloride print. Alfred Stieglitz Collection. Art Institute of Chicago, Chicago, Illinois.

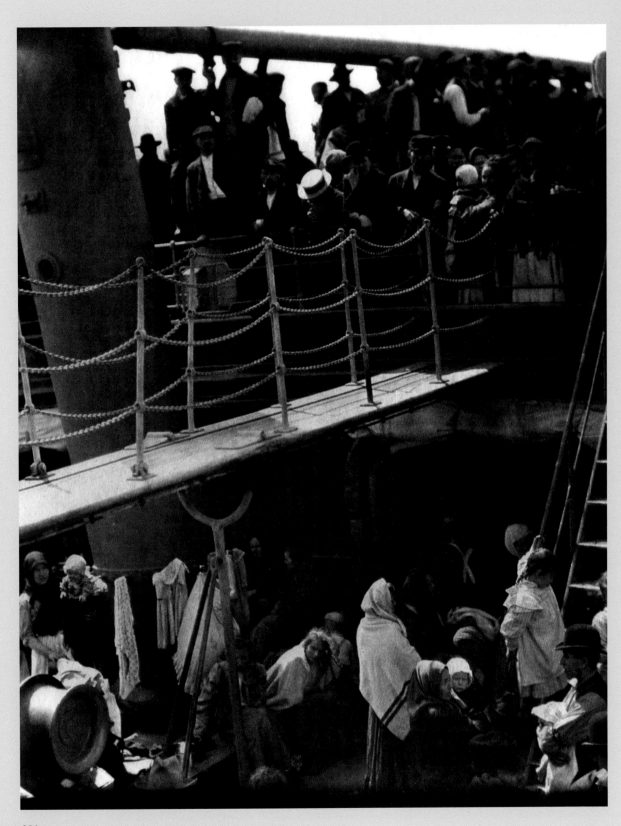

6.24
ALFRED STIEGLITZ, *The Steerage*, 1907, from *Camera Work*, no. 34. Photogravure.
Museum of Modern Art, New York.

portrait

Edward Steichen

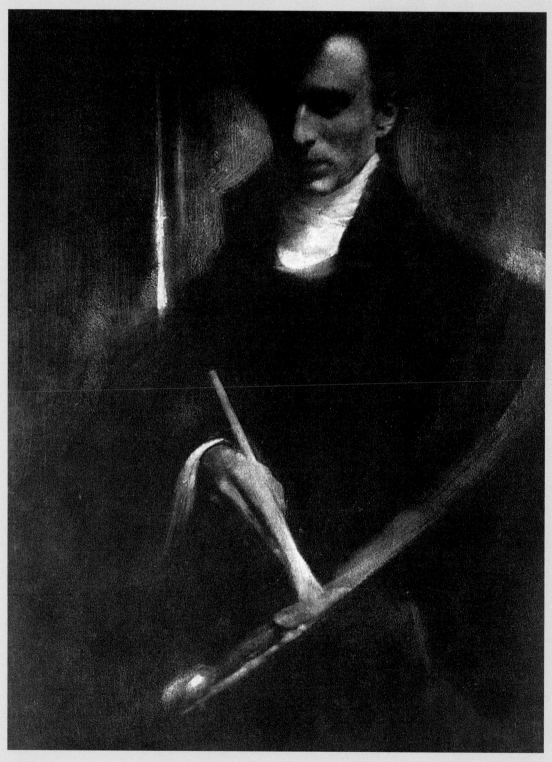

6.25
EDWARD J. STEICHEN, *Self-Portrait*, 1902. Photogravure. Library of Congress, Washington, D.C.

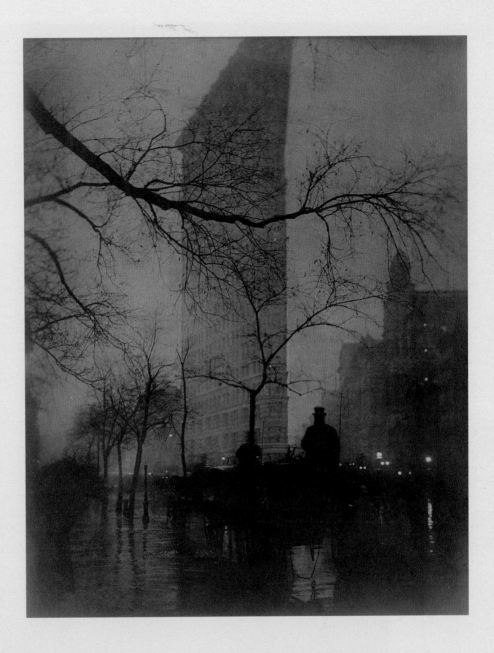

Were it not a gumprint, the self-portrait of Edward Steichen might be mistaken for that of an emotionally intense Romantic artist, with his head, hands, and palette brightly highlighted, and his face partially sunk in shade (Fig. 6.25). Early in his career, Steichen took up painting and photography, both of which he pursued until World War I. After two years studying art in Paris, he returned to the United States in 1902 and opened a portrait studio at 291 Fifth Avenue, which later became the Little Galleries of the Photo-Secession. A close friend of Stieglitz, Steichen collaborated with him on *Camera Work* and on exhibitions. Elected to the Linked Ring in 1901, and a founding member of the Photo-Secession in 1902, Steichen worked on the exhibits that brought modern European art to 291. His Pictorialist work resembles that of Alvin Langdon Coburn (1882–1966) (see Figs. 6.41, 6.42) in its emphasis on design and powerful graphic contrasts (Fig. 6.26). With Stieglitz and other Pictorialist photographers, Steichen

also experimented with the color photography process known as autochrome (see p. 166 and Fig. 6.1).

Unlike Stieglitz, Steichen had no family money. He supplemented his income as an art photographer by doing portrait, advertising, and other commercial work. Born in Luxembourg, he felt he had to show his allegiance by enlisting in the United States Army, where he set up a department of aerial photography. In 1923, he began a career as the chief photographer for Condé Nast publications. During World War II (1939–45), he returned to military service, directing United States naval combat photography. He also organized two patriotic photographic exhibitions at New York's Museum of Modern Art, "Road to Victory" (1942) and "Power in the Pacific" (1945), which helped him become director of the influential Department of Photography at the museum. In 1955, he organized "The Family of Man" (see Chapter Ten).

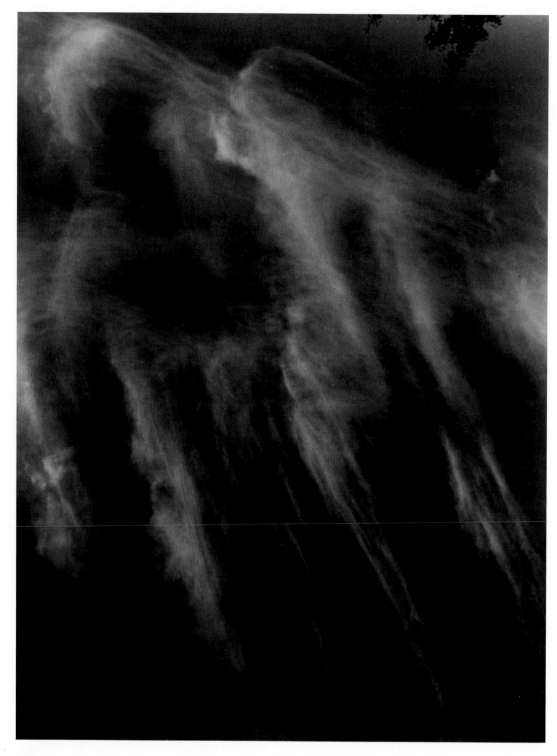

6.27
ALFRED STIEGLITZ, *Equivalent,* **1930. Gelatin silver print. The J. Paul Getty Museum, Los Angeles, California.**

The 291 gallery regularly showed modern art, including the first American exhibition of Picasso in 1911. Stieglitz praised Picasso's "antiphotographic" work, meaning that it had renounced the simple vanishing-point perspective imposed by the camera. He advocated that art photography should be similarly anti-photographic, not necessarily through abstraction, but by reaching beyond subject matter for personal and spiritual expression. Stieglitz's own work was shown only once in a one-person exhibition at 291, during the so-called Armory Show in 1913, when about 1,300 pieces of modern European art were exhibited in New York, including *Nude Descending a Staircase # 2* by Marcel Duchamp (1887–1968) (see Fig. 7.15).

During the 1920s, Stieglitz continued his photographic experimentation, creating hundreds of what he eventually

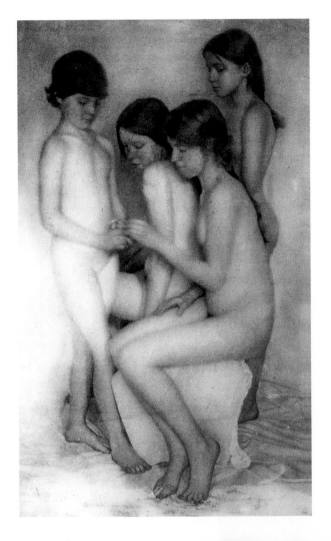

titled *Equivalents* (Fig. 6.27). These cloud studies, originally called "songs of the sky," show how he never relinquished the assumption of Pictorialist photography that the ordinary world abounded with evocative symbols of emotion.

THE NUDE AND PICTORIALISM

Pictorialism's emphasis on nature and the natural gave rise to studies of the male and female nude, created by White, Steichen, Demachy, Puyo, and Anne Brigman (1869–1950), among others. Since boys customarily swam nude, the beach was a likely place to photograph them. Alice Boughton (1865–1943), a member of the Photo-Secession, published an image that subtly compared the bodies of pubescent and pre-pubescent girls in a 1909 issue of *Camera Work* (Fig. 6.28). Those interested in creating more explicit and sexually arousing images took advantage of the acceptance of the Pictorialist nude, imitating its soft-focus, painterly surface, or Classical references. Wilhelm von Gloeden (1856–1931) mixed the exoticism of earlier nineteenth-century sexual photographs with Pictorialist themes. In Sicily he photographed Italian lads, reclining on animal skins and Persian rugs, and surrounded by planters bearing Classical motifs (Fig. 6.29). Von Gloeden's less explicit photographs were popular with educated American and European viewers, who sought them out for their evocation of Classical times. His nude photographs were sold as postcards, though they were seldom put in the mail.

WOMEN IN THE PICTORIALIST MOVEMENT

The longstanding association of women with both nature and domesticity made feminine subjects a favorite in Pictorialist

6.28 (above)
ALICE BOUGHTON, *Nude*, from *Camera Work*, April 1909. Library of Congress, Washington, D.C.

6.29 (right)
BARON WILHELM VON GLOEDEN, *Nude Sicilian Youths*, c. 1885. Gelatin silver print. The J. Paul Getty Museum, Los Angeles, California.

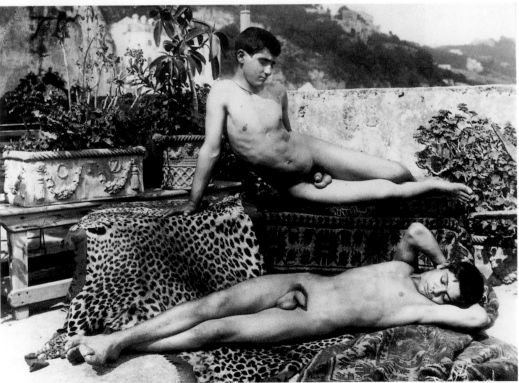

practice. Women, too, worked with these themes; in particular, Californian photographer Anne Brigman portrayed women as spirits or souls of trees, rocks, water, and even photography (Fig. 6.30). Portraiture was thought to be done better by women, who were considered to possess a more intuitive grasp of the sitter's personality and a wider range of emotional response than men. With the increased acceptance of women's aptitude, their work was shown in large exhibits and magazines.

Frances Benjamin Johnston (1864–1952) ran a successful business, branching out from flattering Pictorialist portraits of prominent people in Washington, D.C. She photographed architecture and industrial sites, and documented the activities of the Hampton Institute in Virginia, where young African

Americans received training in the trades. Johnston's Hampton photographs were among those also included in the "American Negro" exhibit, which African American W. E. B. Du Bois helped organize for the international Exposition Universelle in 1900. Johnston promoted photography as a means of employment and recreation for women, writing upbeat essays in such magazines as *Ladies' Home Journal*. In 1900, she was asked to be one of the delegates to the International Congress of Photography, held in Paris in conjunction with the Exposition Universelle. She arranged a show of about 150 images by amateur and professional women for the Congress's July 1900 meeting. The show traveled to Moscow, and then back to Paris, but never found a venue in the United States. Johnston created a self-

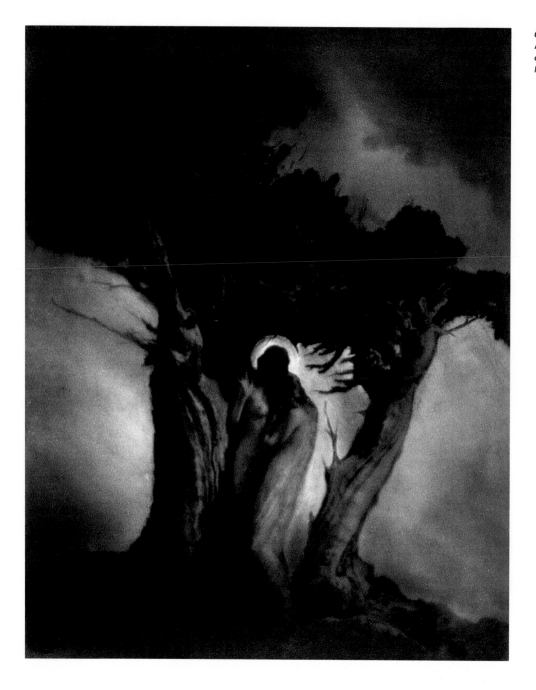

6.30
ANNE BRIGMAN, *The Heart of the Storm*, c. 1910. Platinum print. The J. Paul Getty Museum, Los Angeles, California.

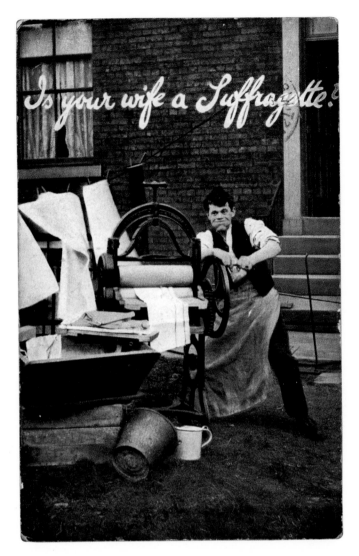

6.31
PHOTOGRAPHER UNKNOWN, *Untitled* (*Is your wife a Suffragette?*), postmarked 1908. Postcard.

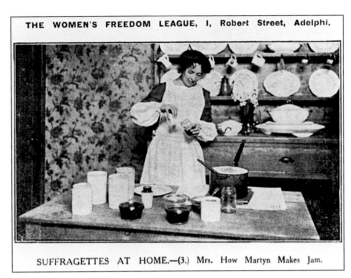

6.32
PHOTOGRAPHER UNKNOWN, *"Mrs. How Martyn Makes Jam,"* from *Suffragettes at Home*, n.d. Postcard. Museum of London.

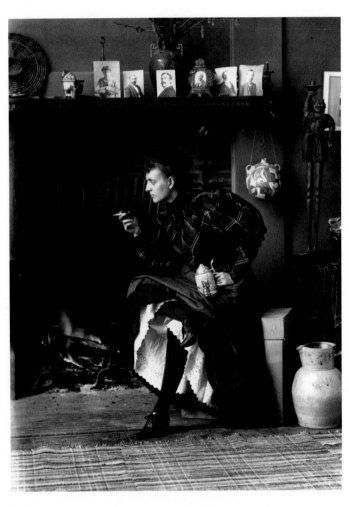

6.33
FRANCES BENJAMIN JOHNSTON, *Self-Portrait (as New Woman)*, c. 1896. Gelatin silver print. Library of Congress, Washington, D.C.

The New Woman was the subject of serious essays, novels, and poems as well as parodies. Johnston's self-portrait seems like a gentle joke, for despite the "masculine" crossed legs and the cigarette, she is surrounded by souvenirs from her travels and portraits, probably from her successful Washington, D.C. studio.

portrait as a caricature of the New Woman, a figure in revolt against contemporary standards of feminine behavior (Fig. 6.33). More subtly, women photographers frequently photographed themselves holding a camera, creating a sign of their art and their self-determination.

In its depiction of women, Pictorialist photography expressed a deep-seated conservatism at the historical moment when more women were working outside the home in schools, factories, and offices, and when there were focused international efforts to gain women the right to vote. In Britain, anti-suffragist imagery ridiculed women activists as mannish brutes who neglected their domestic duties and showed men as reduced to doing housework (Fig. 6.31). To counter such propaganda, suffragists portrayed themselves as tender mothers and caring homemakers who wanted to influence government policy on children (Fig. 6.32).

The acceptance of women practicing photography, especially as amateurs, was expressed in the advertising image of the Kodak Girl, introduced in 1901, and continued, with fashionable updates, for decades[27] (Fig. 6.5). Pictorialism's soft focus and

portrait

Gertrude Käsebier

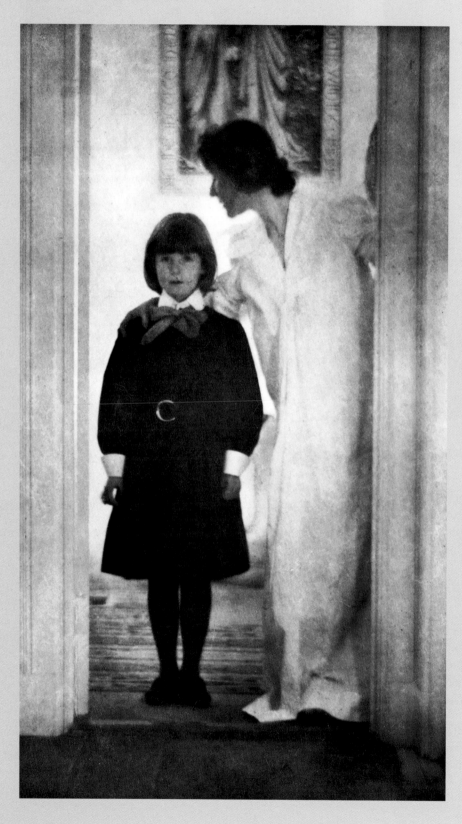

6.34
GERTRUDE KÄSEBIER, *Blessed Art Thou among Women*,
1899. Platinum print on Japanese tissue. Museum of
Modern Art, New York.

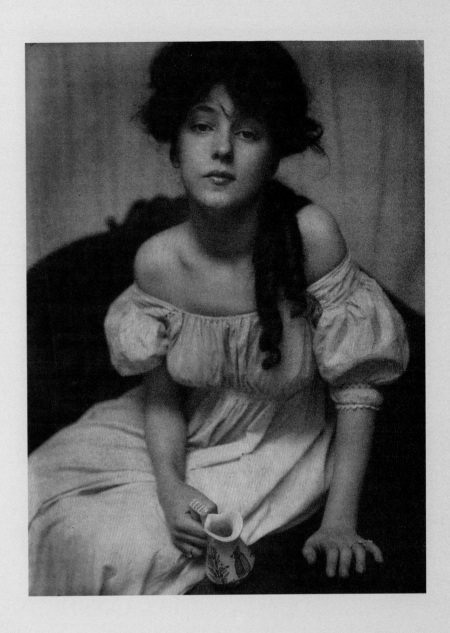

6.35
GERTRUDE KÄSEBIER, *Portrait—Miss N. (Evelyn Nesbitt)*, 1902.
Platinum print. Musée D'Orsay, Paris.

Gertrude Käsebier (1852–1934) was probably the most successful American portrait photographer in the first decade of the twentieth century. Like Julia Margaret Cameron, Käsebier came to photography later in life, first as a hobbyist, then as an art photographer, and finally as a sought-after portraitist. Her photographs of women sometimes relied on implicit storytelling in the manner of Lady Hawarden. *Blessed Art Thou among Women* (1899) shows a mother about to send her child into the world (Fig. 6.34). The mother-and-child theme, prominent in Käsebier's photography, was often depicted with the mother helping the child negotiate the passage into life, rather than holding the child close. The photograph, with its religious overtones, is a portrait study of Agnes Rand Lee and her daughter Peggy. A print of the Annunciation (when the Angel Gabriel appears to the Virgin Mary) hangs on the wall behind the figures. Agnes Lee is dressed in loose, flowing robes, as advocated by British artist and reformer William Morris

(1834–1896). Soon after the photograph was made, Peggy Lee died. Agnes then posed as the sorrowful mother in Käsebier's 1904 photograph *The Heritage of Motherhood*.

Käsebier's photographs were honored abroad, and she was elected to the Linked Ring in 1900. *Blessed Art Thou among Women* was included in the first exhibition of the Photo-Secession, and her work was showcased in the first issue of *Camera Work* (January 1903).

Käsebier's sensuous *Portrait—Miss N.* redresses the saccharine charms of motherhood so much associated with her work. It depicts Evelyn Nesbitt, the sixteen-year-old model, actress, and mistress of prominent architect Stanford White (Fig. 6.35).[28] Nesbitt figured in a sensational early twentieth-century scandal and murder fictionalized by E. L. Doctorow in the novel *Ragtime* (1975): she married railroad heir Harry K. Thaw, who, spurred by jealousy over her previous relationship with Stanford White, shot him dead in 1906.

association with women, the major purchasers of home products, were particularly persistent in portraiture and advertising[29] (Fig. 6.36).

ANTHROPOLOGICAL PICTORIALISM

Together with Pictorialism, the international Arts and Crafts movement, with its emphasis on hand-crafted art objects and on home life, provoked an interest in Native American peoples. Idealized as living close to nature, they were also known to be under threat from the incursion of Western civilization into their lands.[30] To meet amateurs' interest in Native American life, George Eastman sponsored the photographic expedition of Frederick Monsen (1865–1929). Monsen's *With a Kodak in the Land of the Navajo* (1909) was both a photographic booklet and an advertising device. Edward S. Curtis (1868–1952) made numerous photographs of Native American life using gravure or platinum printing techniques, lending the pictures a soft, faded quality (Fig. 6.37). Curtis also asked his subjects to enact

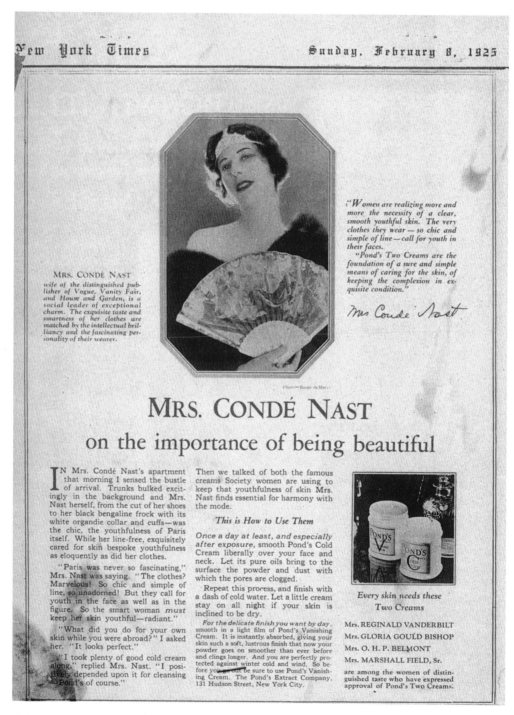

6.36
Advertisement for Pond's Cold Cream, from *New York Times*, February 8, 1925. Duke University, Durham, North Carolina.

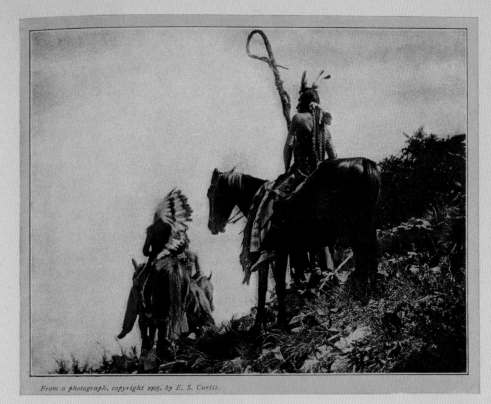

From a photograph, copyright 1905, by E. S. Curtis.

Crow warriors on the edge of a precipice in the Black Canyon.

VANISHING INDIAN TYPES
THE TRIBES OF THE NORTHWEST PLAINS

By E. S. Curtis

ILLUSTRATIONS FROM PHOTOGRAPHS BY THE AUTHOR

THE Northwest Plains Indian is, to the average person, the typical American Indian, the Indian of our school-day books—powerful of physique, statuesque, gorgeous in dress, with the bravery of the firm believer in predestination. The constant, fearless hunting and slaughtering of the buffalo trained him to the greatest physical endurance, and gave an inbred desire for bloodshed. Thousands of peace-loving, agricultural-living Indians might climb down from their cliff-perched homes, till their miniature farms, attend their flocks, and at night-time climb back up the winding stairs to their home in the clouds, and attract no attention. But if a fierce band of Sioux rushed down on a hapless emigrant train the world soon learned of it.

The culture of all primitive peoples is necessarily determined by their environment. This, of course, means that all plains tribes —though speaking a score of languages— were, in life and manner, broadly alike. They were buffalo-hunting Indians, and only in rare cases did they give any attention to agriculture. Buffalo meat was their food, and the by-products their clothing, tools, and implements.

The plains tribes in earlier times were certainly true nomads. For a time, in the

VOL. XXXIX.—68

657

6.37
EDWARD S. CURTIS, Photograph and article "Vanishing Indian Types," from *Scribner's* magazine, June 6, 1906. Library of Congress, Washington, D.C.

ritual dances and battles. He carried Native American costumes, which his customers associated with preindustrial life, using them occasionally to dress his subjects in what his viewers saw as authentic garb. Curtis produced a twenty-volume work, *The North American Indian* (1907–30), which contained more than 1,500 photogravures as well as text. Like Stieglitz's *Camera Work*, the books were produced in limited editions on fine paper. Curtis was also skilled in motion-picture making. His film *In the Land of the Head Hunters* (1914) was based on a Pacific

Northwest coast legend, and enacted by the Kwakiutl people of the area.

NON-PICTORIALIST VISIONS

As the invention of dry plates, roll film, and hand cameras encouraged a greater number of hobbyists, it also allowed them to go their own way. Pictorialism did not appeal to everyone. As amateur photographer Charles L. Mitchell (active 1890s) put it bluntly in 1900: "There are too many 'impressions' and too few

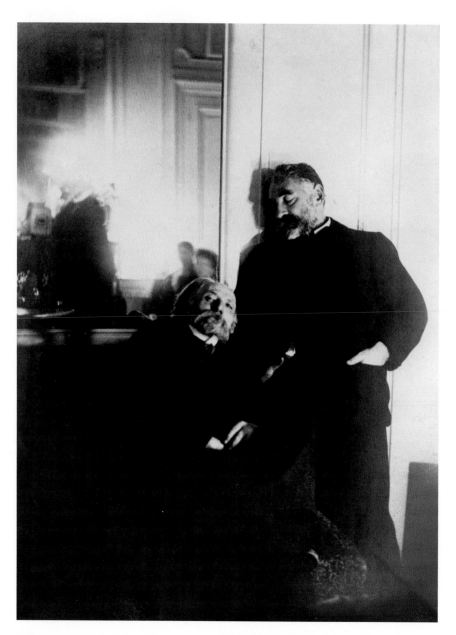

6.38
EDGAR DEGAS, *Berthe Morisot's Salon: Auguste Renoir and Stéphane Mallarmé,* **c. 1890. Albumen print. Museum of Modern Art, New York.**

Degas's portrait of painter Auguste Renoir (1841–1919) and poet Stéphane Mallarmé (1842–1898) reveals Degas in the mirror, operating his camera, while Mallarmé's wife and daughter watch. Degas's face is obscured by the intense light of an oil lamp.

6.39
AUGUST STRINDBERG, *Celestograph XII*, 1893–94. Royal Library, Stockholm.

clearly conceived, thoroughly expressed realities; too few real pictures, and too much 'trash.'"[31] Non-Pictorialist efforts can be seen in the work of amateurs whose fame in other endeavors preserved their photographic work. For example, the novelist Émile Zola took up photography in the late 1880s, producing unexceptional family portraits and trip mementos. Occasionally, though, he created a bold experiment with composition. French painter Edgar Degas, whose paintings of the ballet inspired some Pictorialist photographers, also found a visual challenge outside of Pictorialist photography. Degas seems to have enjoyed resolving particular formal and aesthetic photographic problems. "Daylight gives me no problem," he commented, "What I want is difficult—the atmosphere of lamps or moonlight"[32] (Fig. 6.38).

Norwegian painter Edvard Munch (1863–1944) used photography throughout his life, not only as a sketching instrument for his paintings, but also to create a series of what he called *Fatal Destiny Photographs*, in which melancholic sitters, including the painter, appear transparent, with the background visible through them. Munch's photographs resemble some of the experiments of Swedish playwright August Strindberg (1849–1912), who took up autobiographical photography, and hoped to make psychological photographs of sitters by intuiting their innermost thoughts. He developed a "Wunderkamera"—a large camera able to take life-size photographs of faces and thereby increase the sense of psychological presence. He also wrote a defense of spirit photography, as photographs purporting to depict the presence of the dead were called.[33] Strindberg experimented with what he called "celestographs," photographic plates lengthily exposed to starry skies (Fig. 6.39). The results resemble abstract paintings. Irish critic, playwright, and social activist George Bernard Shaw (1856–1950) took more than ten thousand pictures. His self-portraits, pictures of friends, and landscapes typify the varied output of amateurs. Shaw also wrote extensively about photography, defending it as an art and advocating that photographers stick to the inherent qualities of the camera, which he considered to be sharp focus and no handworking of the negative and the print. Of George Davison (see Fig. 6.11), Shaw wrote: "if I saw the edges of a house blur as they blur in Mr. Davison's pictures, I should conclude that I was going to faint, and probably do it too."[34]

A whimsical child in an eccentric, privileged French family, Jacques Henri Lartigue (1894–1986) took his first photograph at the age of six. His photography seems to have been guided more by his interest in stopping action than in making art images. He photographed early racing cars, flying machines, and fashionable people parading the boulevards. Although they seem worldly and sophisticated, many of his photographs were taken while he was a child or young adult. While his photographs were mostly taken with a stereographic camera, better able to stop time, they were not meant to be three-dimensional or commercial (Fig. 6.40).

PICTORIALISM: A CONSERVATIVE AVANT-GARDE

By 1909, the Photo-Secession was open to assault by its own revolutionary rhetoric. A vast 1909 international show in Dresden, Germany, arranged by Stieglitz with Steichen's help, was criticized for "doing nothing new,"[35] and some considered the art photography in *Camera Work* to be repetitive. When

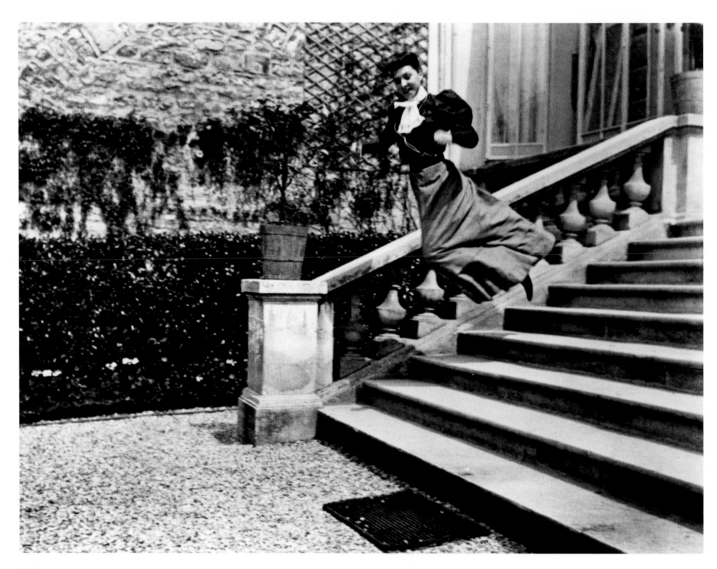

6.40
J. H. LARTIGUE, *My Cousin Bichonnade*, 1905. Association des Amis de J. H. Lartigue, Ministry of Culture, Paris.

Lartigue wittily pictured the life of his fashionable French family. Caught jumping from the middle of the staircase, cousin Bichonnade seems to fly forward, defying gravity.

asked to prepare a large exhibit for the Albright Art Gallery (now the Albright-Knox Art Gallery) in Buffalo, New York, Stieglitz staged what photohistorian Robert Doty called "a finale."[36] The 1910 exhibition of about six hundred photographs was organized as a retrospective of Pictorialism, with contributors asked to provide old and new work. The show is often cited as marking the historical moment when photography was accepted as an art form worthy of museums. It was also the point at which the creative possibilities of the Pictorialist style were thoroughly explored, though the "fuzzygraph" vocabulary continued for another decade in commerce and advertising, and was popular into the 1930s in many countries, including Spain, Poland, Czechoslovakia, Japan, and South Africa.

Was Pictorialism an avant-garde movement? Certainly it introduced a visual fashion dominant for thirty years, and mixed painting and photography in a way that anticipated the hybridization of art media in the late twentieth and early twenty-first centuries. At the same time, its sentimental subject matter and its rendition of otherworldly women harked back to the nineteenth-century view of women as angels trapped in a domestic environment. Through Stieglitz and 291, art photography did engage with the European avant-garde, such as the FAUVES and CUBISTS. Nevertheless, until the Armory Show in 1913, it was the rebellious spirit of the European avant-garde, rather than their visual strategies, that influenced American art photography. The Pictorialists largely ignored the raw emotionality and anxiety that marked Expressionism, the mainly German art movement much discussed in the 1890s. When Stieglitz and his colleagues took the city as a subject, they did so when atmospheric effects, such as fog, rain, and snow, softened the bleakness.[37]

Like other late nineteenth-century avant-gardists, the Pictorialists and Photo-Secessionists advocated self-expression as soul preserving in the world of mass production and mass taste. At the same time, their magazines practiced promotional techniques akin to those of the newly formed field of advertising. Also they established a network of institutions, publications, and selection strategies to validate their work, while laying claim to unsullied virtue.[38]

As historian Ulrich Keller pointed out, art photography was not primarily concerned with art theory so much as with "spiritual exclusiveness," being "away from 'the Philistine' and 'the masses.'"[39] Stieglitz disparaged those who let money taint their art, though of course he was in a financial position that enabled him to take the moral high ground. In 1899, he wrote that "nearly all the greatest work is being, and has always been done by those who are following photography for the love of it, and not merely for financial reasons."[40] In an age of raging labor disputes, Stieglitz praised working for love, not money. After the horrors of World War I, the ideology of Pictorialism was in full retreat. Nevertheless, Pictorial-style photographs continued to be made, especially in advertising and amateur work, despite the challenges of Russian CONSTRUCTIVISM, which stressed design as a way for artists to participate in changing society for the better, and European DADAISM, which questioned the

plausibility of beauty and purity after the horrors of trench warfare (see Chapter Eight).

Advocates of art photography have viewed Pictorialism as avant-garde on account of its tendency to stress abstract patterns, which emerged as a key visual characteristic of art photography in the 1920s. The work of such photographers as Alvin Langdon Coburn used the visual conventions of Pictorialism, including flattened space and diminished detail, to create abstract patterns on the surface of the photographic print. Coburn corresponded with American painter Arthur Wesley Dow about *notan* (see p. 177) and the Japanese use of perspective (Fig. 6.41). Despite the surface values of Coburn's prints, neither Emerson's differential focus nor Davison's notion of personal impressions is prominent in his work. Instead, drawn to spiritualism and religious symbolism, Coburn sought out patterns in nature as clues to a great spiritual immanence. It is ironic that Coburn, who spurned modernity later in his life and became a druid, also made the first completely abstract photograph.

Through the influence of the poet Ezra Pound (1885–1972), Coburn briefly took up Vorticism, a short-lived English art movement named by Pound in 1913, and promoted by the painter Wyndham Lewis (1882–1957). The movement's magazine, *Blast*, explained that Vorticism would integrate the dynamic movement of FUTURISM with the static geometric analysis of Cubism. The movement hoped to blast away the remnants of the past. Coburn experimented with abstraction, building a Vortescope, a combination of mirrors that produced an image like that of a kaleidoscope, and photographing the result (Fig. 6.42). Coburn's interest in total abstraction lasted only about a month; he never embraced the notion that radical changes in the visual arts could promote change on the social front, an assumption that would guide experimental photography in the 1920s (see Chapter Eight).

In the last issue of *Camera Work* (June 1917), Stieglitz featured work by Paul Strand (1890–1976). Strand was younger than Stieglitz and Steichen, and a student of Lewis Hine at the New York Ethical Culture School in 1907, where he learned photography in an intellectual atmosphere of moral concern for humankind. Ironically, Hine introduced Strand to Stieglitz's 291 gallery, where European paintings and experimental art photography influenced the younger photographer, who did not follow in his mentor's footsteps.

Strand frequented the Little Galleries of the Photo-Secession, where he became acquainted with abstract art, as well as with Pictorialism. Like critic Sadakichi Hartmann, Strand rejected the soft-focused "fuzzygraph" in favor of what he called "absolute unqualified objectivity" and "straight photographic means."[41] The 1913 Armory Show of contemporary European art, especially abstraction, also impressed him. In 1917, when *Camera Work* devoted its last issue to Strand's photography, Stieglitz wrote that Strand's work was "brutally direct," and "devoid of trickery and any 'ism.'" "These photographs," Stieglitz concluded, "are the direct expression of today."[42] Stieglitz included two areas of Strand's work: close-up,

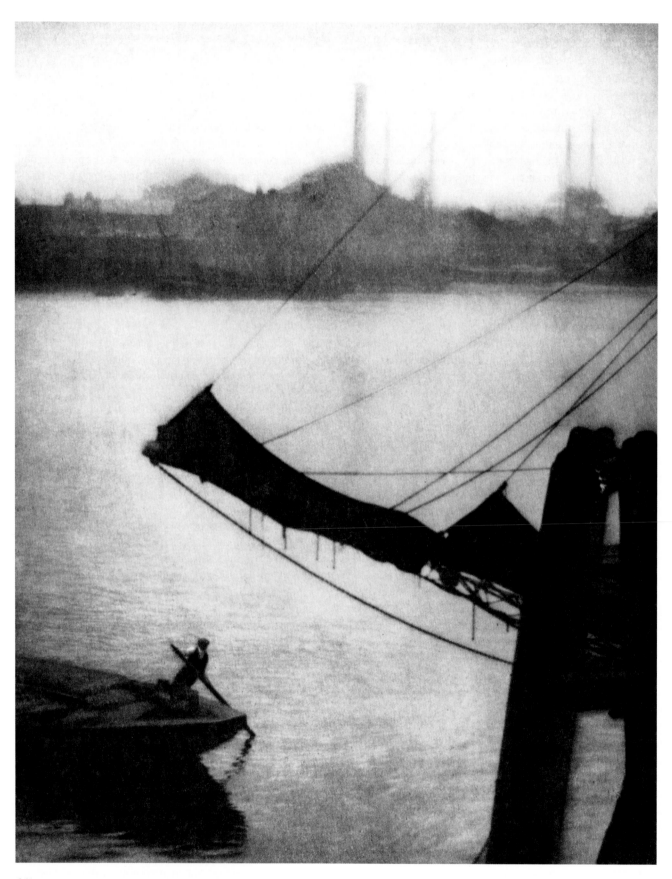

6.41
ALVIN LANGDON COBURN, *Wapping,* plate 10 from his book *London,* 1909. Victoria and Albert Museum, London.

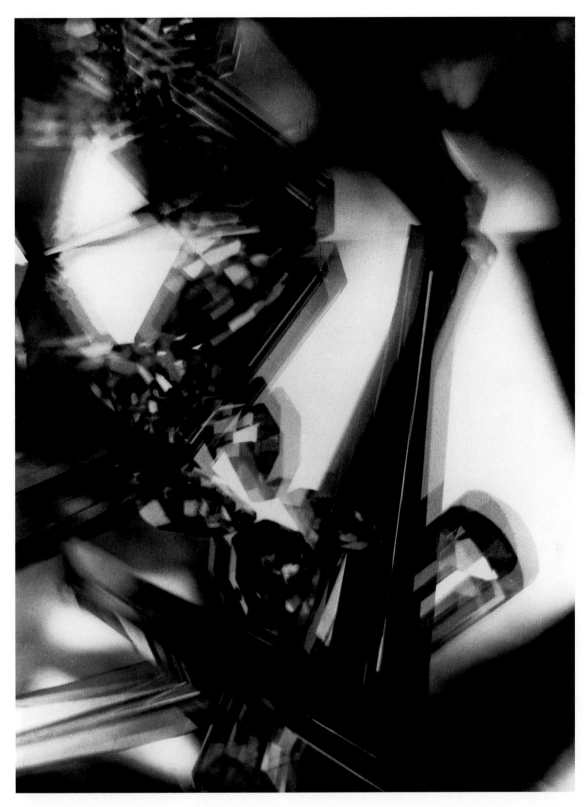

6.42
ALVIN LANGDON COBURN, *Vortograph*, **1917. Coburn Collection. George Eastman House, Rochester, New York.**

Coburn created abstract photographs called Vortographs that resemble the work of British painter Wyndham Lewis, the primary Vorticist painter. Both borrow heavily from Cubism and Futurism. In some of his Vortographs, like this one, Coburn used multiple exposure to increase the abstract effect.

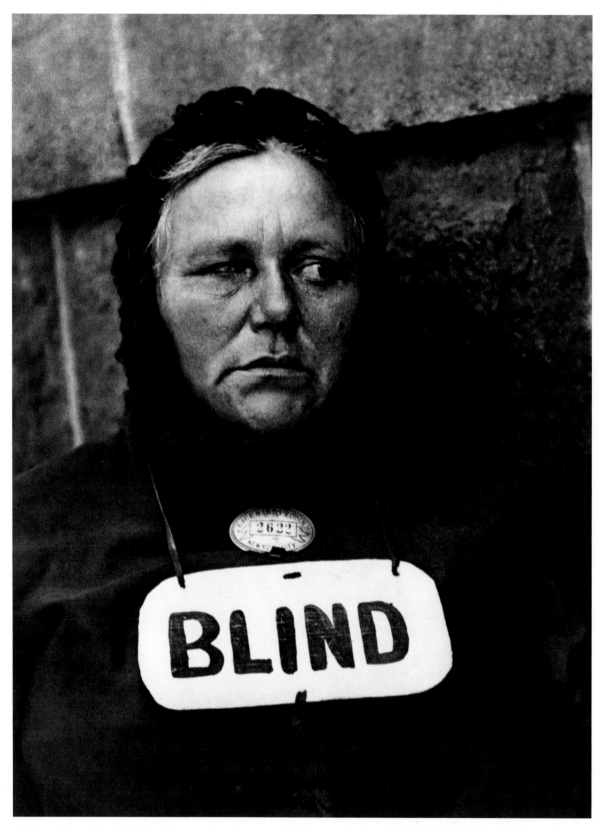

6.43
PAUL STRAND, *Photograph—New York* **(Woman with sign that reads "Blind"), from** *Camera Work***, June 1917. Photogravure.**
Library of Congress, Washington, D.C.

Strand took his street photographs with a trick camera that led people to believe he was shooting in another direction. His portraits of the poor were not part of a social reform program, but intended to be matter-of-fact examples of life. His audience would not have known about the trick camera, but they would have understood the picture's ironic slant, namely, the contrast between the camera's clear eye and the woman's blindness.

unsentimental portraits of street people, and near abstractions made by focusing on repeated patterns of light and dark found in the experience of everyday life (Figs. 6.43, 6.44).

In an essay accompanying his photographs, Strand stated his dislike of Pictorialism. He called gum-printing, oil-printing, and handworking of the negative and the print "the expression of an impotent desire to paint." Yet Strand understood the Pictorialist goal to make photography responsive to the photographer's perception and intuition, which he called the "organization of objectivity."[43] Strand credited Stieglitz for creating, through *Camera Work*, a true American art. "America has really been expressed in terms of America without the outside influence of Paris art schools or their dilute offspring here," Strand wrote, comparing the work of White, Steichen, Käsebier, and Eugene to the unique experimentation manifested by the builders of skyscrapers.[44] He was wrong, of course, about the absence of European influence on American photography, including his own, but right to sense that Pictorialism had had its day.

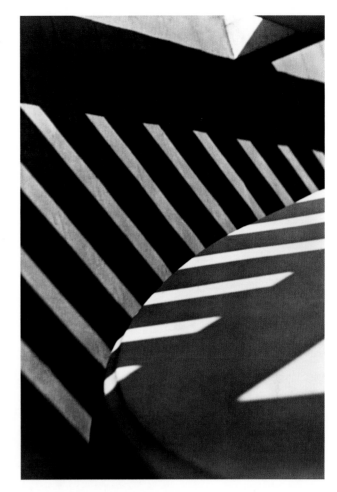

6.44
PAUL STRAND, *Abstractions, Porch Shadows, Connecticut*, 1916. Gelatin silver print by Richard Benson. Museum of Modern Art, New York.

Strand obscured his subject matter—shadows cast by a porch railing and posts—in a pleasingly balanced abstraction of complementary geometric shapes and tones of light and dark.

RETAKE

The expansion of vernacular photography, which began in the mid-nineteenth century with stereographs and *cartes-de-visite*, continued to extend the medium to new users through the marketing of inexpensive cameras, the growth of illustrated newspapers, and the popularity of postcards. At the same time, it promoted the growth of the photographic industry. Overall, the technological developments in photography relocated some control and definition of the image from the individual photographer to large manufacturers and the press. This tendency paralleled the development of other major networks and industries, such as the power companies that produced and delivered electricity, and also the large corporations that manufactured and distributed name brands.

In the years before World War I, a great divide separated the photography of everyday life from art photography. Snapshots, stereographs, postcards, newspaper illustrations, and advertise–ments made photography omnipresent; art photography was based in aesthetic values and personal insights translated into images

seen mostly in little magazines and a few galleries, such as 291, run by Alfred Stieglitz, the founder of the Photo-Secession. The blurry appearance of Pictorialism established a niche in upscale product marketing, but art photography remained rooted in private experience. For art photographers, taking pictures meant making pictures—that is, developing and retouching them in the darkroom. They often worked with processes like gum-printing that involved handwork, or sought out expensive platinum-printing paper, whose multiple gray tones exceeded those available in the black-and-white process used by the casual weekend photographers.

Underlying the split between vernacular and art photography was the assumption that mass culture depreciated what in the prewar years was called highbrow culture. The notion that mass-culture media could be employed not simply as propaganda, but also as a fruitful form of expression, was mostly beyond the grasp of the pre-World War I chic and well-heeled. After the war, High Art and mass culture would meet and meld in the heat of a Modernist vogue (see Chapter Eight).

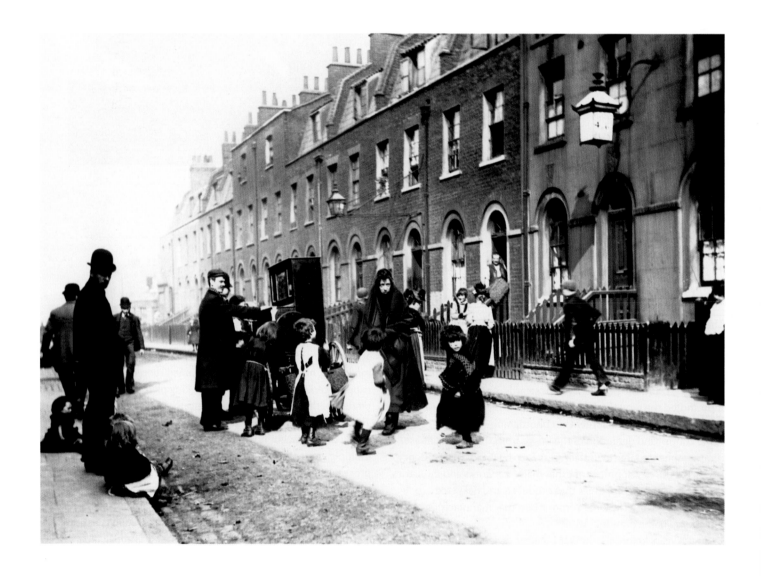

CHAPTER SEVEN

Modern Life

In the last decades of the nineteenth century, photography was no longer associated with new and sudden social shifts. Instead, the modern world was denoted by a quickening of technological and scientific progress, the increased consequence of urban life, and patterns of life and labor that involved mass manufacturing. The notion of change infiltrated modern life, and encouraged social reform movements in which photographs played a major role. Photographs became part of statistical reports and emotional pleas for urban improvement. They helped to produce visual archives, not only of substandard living conditions, but also of criminals. Photography was not simply used to verify what could be seen, but also to prove what the eye could not see. In Europe and the United States, photographs recorded physical movements too swift and subtle for the human eye. When they first saw X-rays, some people found them indecent. World War I, which ended the era, was the first industrialized war. Professional, amateur, and soldier photographers used their cameras to record the boredom and the horror of the trenches.

THE MODERN CITY

Pictorial photographers occasionally photographed the urban environment, modifying it with a mantle of color or cloud. Photographers independent of Pictorialism also rendered the city and its inhabitants. Often employing a concealed camera, French-born British photographer Paul Martin (1864–1944) recorded street life and seaside entertainment in a casual style associated with the snapshot (Fig. 7.1). E. Alice Austen (1866–1952) of Staten Island, New York, photographed the social life of her genteel friends, but also ventured into Manhattan to photograph immigrant life (Fig. 7.3). Neither photographer's work was ever aimed at bringing about social improvements.

New York City, especially after the opening of Ellis Island in 1892, was the port through which most of the immigrants

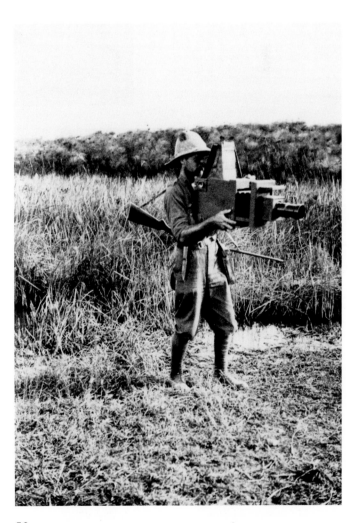

7.2
ARTHUR RADCLYFFE DUGMORE, *The Author and his Camera,* from *Camera Adventures in the African Wilds,* **1910. Royal Geographical Society, London.**

Arthur Radclyffe Dugmore's *Camera Adventures in the African Wilds* appeared in 1910. Opposing big-game hunting in Africa, he claimed that hunting with the camera was more exciting than hunting with the gun.[1]

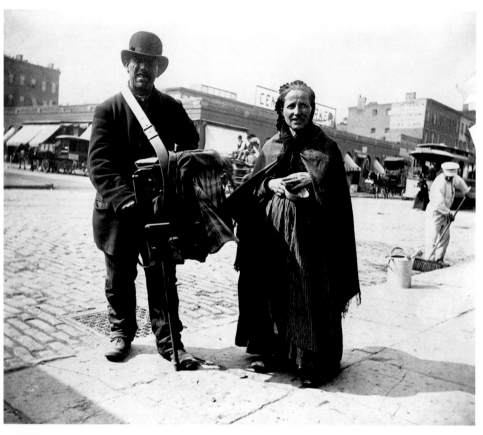

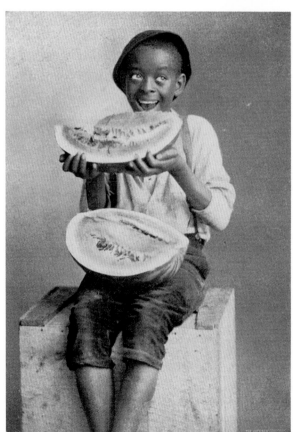

7.4
SIGMUND KRAUSZ, *Oh golly, but I'se Happy!* **Illustration from**
Street Types of Great American Cities, **1896. Private collection.**

entering the United States passed. In 1900, more than 35 per cent of the population in big cities such as New York and Chicago was foreign-born. Immigrant neighborhoods became the subject of much public curiosity and concern. Photographers in expanding American cities provided the public with an array of images of the poor. Firms such as Underwood and Underwood issued boxed sets of stereographs depicting immigrants and urban life. Some pictures, for example the lantern slides and book illustrations for the book *Street Types of Great American Cities* (1896), produced by Chicago photographer Sigmund Krausz (1857–after 1927), reinforced ethnic stereotypes and clichés about urban workers and the poor (Fig. 7.4). Like the so-called miscellanies of the period, *Street Types of Great American Cities* also paired popular poetry and prose with photographs.

By contrast, the rural poor were not major photographic subjects, apart from in the idyllic scenes produced by Pictorialist photographers.

SOCIAL REFORM PHOTOGRAPHY

From the beginning, British suffragists used photography to record the lives of poor women and children, arguing that giving women the vote would draw more attention to the issue of poverty. After a slow start, reform organizations and settlement houses—privately run charities that did social work among the poor—began using photography to promote their work.[2] As social work moved from a voluntary occupation to full-time professional employment, photographs were increasingly used in conjunction with other data. As the public became more familiar

7.5
JACOB RIIS, *Bandits' Roost*, New York, 1888. Gelatin silver print from the original
negative. Museum of the City of New York, New York.

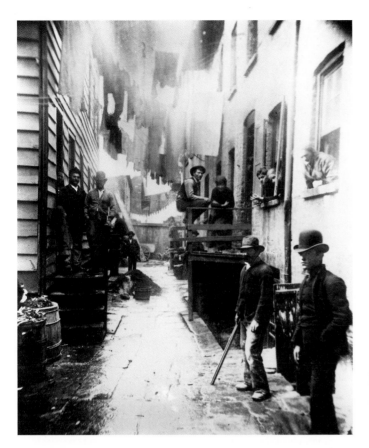

many modes of reform photography. Among them were the
photographs of living conditions taken by the *Berlin Wohnungs-
Enquete* (*Berlin Housing Inquiry*) from 1903 to 1920. This report,
which concluded that the city had the world's largest number
of tenement and other deficient dwellings, pictured not only
the crowed attics and cellars where poverty forced thousands of
Berliners to live, but also carefully recorded sanitary conditions,
square footage of the residences, and the number of occupants
(Fig. 7.6). Also often overlooked are the photographs made by
American novelist and avid amateur photographer Jack London
(1876–1916) for *The People of the Abyss* (1903), his account of the
slums of London's East End. London used photographs, mostly
his own, to depict the effects of industrialization on the poor,
and to conclude that criminal mismanagement of society was to
blame for poverty.

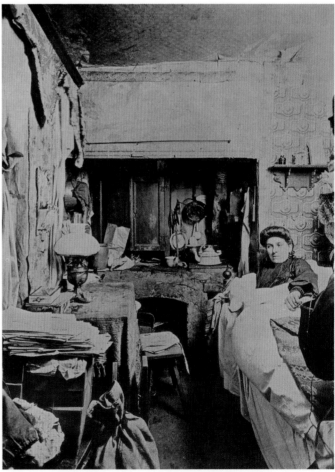

7.6
PHOTOGRAPHER UNKNOWN, Dwelling interior from the Berlin Housing
Enquiry, 1905.

An extensive housing survey reported on the health and general welfare of
the crowded Berlin slums, and used photographs to underscore the statistical
evidence.

with photographs of the poor, there were two unexpected
consequences: repeated images of people in squalid conditions
bolstered stereotypes of the poor as inferior; and what is now
called "compassion fatigue" set in, as happened toward the end
of the American Civil War when, as photographic coverage
increased, public response declined.

Photographs of the poor were still novel and engaging when
Jacob Riis (1849–1914) produced his book *How the Other Half
Lives* (1890), which contained fifteen half-tone images, and
forty-three drawings based on photographs. Riis, a Danish
immigrant who became a journalist in New York City, lectured
on the condition of the slums, and projected stereopticon
lantern slides to illustrate his points. Like many reformers, Riis
believed that individuals were formed by their environment.
For him the crowded, unsanitary tenements—that is, shoddy
apartment houses—were the cause of crime and moral decay. By
contemporary standards, Riis was conservative in his suggestions
for reform: he did not call for government intervention, but
hoped that the wealthy would consider tenement construction
as a work of charity and that private investors would take less
profit when building tenements, in order to provide adequate
lodgings (Fig. 7.5).

Like many social observers, Riis implicitly divided the poor
into two categories: deserving and undeserving. Women and
small children often fitted the first category, with unemployed
and criminally inclined males in the second. Oddly enough, Riis's
photographs have come to stand for late nineteenth- and early
twentieth-century social reform. Nevertheless, the era embraced

portrait

Jacob Riis

Jacob Riis emigrated from Denmark to the United States in 1870, but endured hardships there while looking for work during the depression years of the 1870s. Riis acquired a job as a police reporter in the Lower East Side of Manhattan, and began writing about the slums, using photography to illustrate his points. Initially he used photographs by others, but eventually took his own. He presented his work in several formats. Lantern-slide lectures were given to mostly middle-class audiences in New York, who had little direct experience of the slums, where they were afraid to venture. Riis dramatized his shows with pauses for hymn singing and sometimes showed an image of Jesus as the concluding slide. He also published his photographs in newspapers and magazines. "Flashes from the Slums: Pictures Taken in Dark Places by the Lightning Process," an 1888 illustrated newspaper article in the *Sun*, described a foray made by Riis and a group of photographers to research and photograph the life of the "other half."[3] His party toured at night, using the now standard magnesium flash powder to illuminate the darkness and to surprise subjects. The harsh look of the sudden burst of intense white light and the shock registered on the faces of those photographed came to stand for candid and objective photography (Fig. 7.7). Riis's photographs acquired credibility in part because their compositions resembled the spontaneous look of the newly introduced snapshot. Nevertheless, several of his photographs were posed, such as his images of street children, which show them obviously feigning sleep.

Riis's photographs have been the subject of debate, both because of the photographer's intrusion on the lives of the poor, and because of the interpretations to which they have been subject since Riis's death. The first Jacob Riis exhibit at the Museum of the City of New York in 1947 presented prints that were cropped and enlarged to increase their impact. In grand, artful exhibition prints, the technical defects and spontaneous character of Riis's photographs were suppressed. The show exemplified changes in Riis's reputation following his death in 1914. With the popularity of documentary photography in the 1920s and 1930s, Riis, who photographed only for a short period and downplayed his efforts, was cast as a major recorder of the American experience and a forerunner of the documentary approach. Questions persist about his lack of sympathy with his subjects, and about the transformation of his untidy photography by the museums from its original context in social reform into American art.[4]

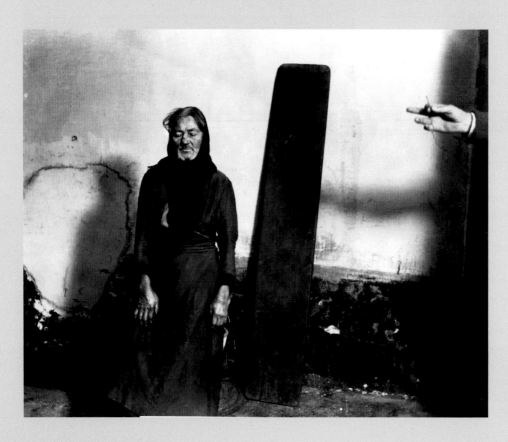

7.7
JACOB RIIS, *Police Station Lodgers* (Eldridge Street Station, an old lodger, and the plank on which she slept), c. 1898. Museum of the City of New York, New York.

portrait

Lewis Hine

Like Jacob Riis, Lewis Hine (1874–1940), did not have a back–ground in art photography. Although he visited Alfred Stieglitz at 291, and introduced Paul Strand to him, Hine jokingly called the members of the Photo-Secession the "Seceshes."[5] Hine taught a number of subjects at New York's Ethical Culture School, a progressive institution. He learned photography at the school's request, and went on to work exclusively in the medium. Beginning in 1904, as part of the school's curriculum, Hine made photographs of immigrants arriving at Ellis Island and living in the poor neighborhoods, so that the students might "have the same regard for contemporary immigrants as they have for the Pilgrims who landed at Plymouth Rock"[6] (Fig. 7.8).

While working at the Ethical Culture School, Hine began freelancing for the National Child Labor Committee (N.C.L.C.), a private agency founded by Dr. Felix Adler, who also established the Ethical Culture Society. The N.C.L.C. attempted to reform child labor by urging legislation to control industrial hiring practices. Hine traveled around the United States between 1907 and 1918, taking about five thousand photographs of child labor. He often assumed a false identity to photograph children at work in factories, mines, canneries, and mills (Fig. 7.9). Working for

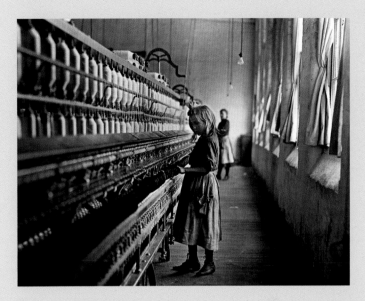

7.9
LEWIS W. HINE, *Child in Carolina Cotton Mill*, 1908. Gelatin silver print on masonite. Museum of Modern Art, New York.

the N.C.L.C. and other social welfare organizations, Hine created what he called the "photo story," a narrative composed of pictures and words to be published in journals and magazines. Hine's layouts were often non-linear, linked more by ideas than a flow of narrative images. In 1937, he criticized the photographs in the new *Life* magazine for "the fetish of having a unified thread."[7]

Hine frequently insisted on receiving a credit line for his images, at a time when photographic reproductions generally did not carry them. He also took advantage of the possibilities for illustration offered by the half-tone process and the recently created illustrated magazine. He worked extensively on *The Pittsburgh Survey* (1909–14), a multivolume study of working-class life in a city whose mix of immigrants and comfortable professionals, as well as its bitter history of labor conflict, seemed to many to epitomize the industrial metropolis. Hine's images and words aligned with the objective orientation of economic reports and the emergent profession of social work, in contrast to the personal approach favored by Riis. Hine went on to photograph the work of the Red Cross in Europe after World War I, and to publish *Men at Work: Photographic Study of Men and Machines* (1932), which showed the construction of the Empire State Building.

After his years with the N.C.L.C., Hine's attitude toward social photography shifted away from showing abuse to picturing the dignity of the working class. His later photographs, especially what he called "work portraits," put laborers in the center of the picture, celebrating their skill and perseverance. Although he addressed the workers as his audience, most of his photographs appeared in journals read by professional and volunteer social reformers.

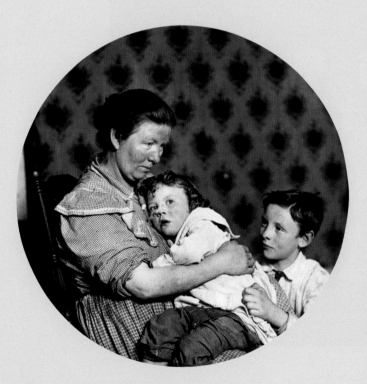

7.8
LEWIS W. HINE, *A Madonna of the Tenements*, c. 1911. Gelatin silver print on glass. George Eastman House, Rochester, New York.

Speaking to the National Conference of Charities and Corrections in 1909, social photographer Lewis Hine suggested that workers be encouraged to photograph their own situations. The idea of worker photography later briefly took hold in Europe, between world wars (see p. 289). The turn of the twentieth century was an active time for the formation of labor unions in industrialized nations, but there was no systematic network to distribute photographs recording labor grievances, or offering union interpretations of the many labor actions and strikes that took place. As historian Larry Peterson observed: "workers' organizations adopted photography more slowly and haltingly than corporations." He contended that even such militant new unions as the International Workers of the World (I.W.W.) failed to adopt the mass-media publicity techniques associated with corporations.[8] Instead, labor groups promoted craft skills and art historical knowledge because they were thought to stimulate the mind and the feelings. During the 1913 textile strike in Paterson, New Jersey, for instance, workers used posters that looked like rough woodcuts, and staged a pageant of their complaints just a few blocks from the Armory Show (see p. 184). There was no

extensive photographic protest showing workers trying to keep pace with speeded-up assembly lines, or learning to perform repetitive actions more quickly. More often than not, it was newspaper photographs of labor confrontations, not photographs taken by the unions, that galvanized worker opinions.

Industry, by contrast, used photography to present a positive vision of the company to the workers. The Pullman Company, makers of railroad sleeper cars, was the site in 1894 of a violent labor strike. *The Story of the Pullman Car* (1917) contained thirty-four photographs describing the work of the company, and the company newspaper, the *Pullman Car Works Standard* (1916–19), presented the company as "Pullman's Big Family" to the public and employees.[9] Companies used their financial resources and ready access to the factory floor to make photographs that served their interests; images of admirable working conditions and engineering feats were encouraged in the press (Fig. 7.10). The paternalistic attitude toward workers that developed in some factories was exemplified in the Ford Motor Company's booklet *Helpful Hints and Advice to Employes* [sic] (1915), which contained photographs showing proper

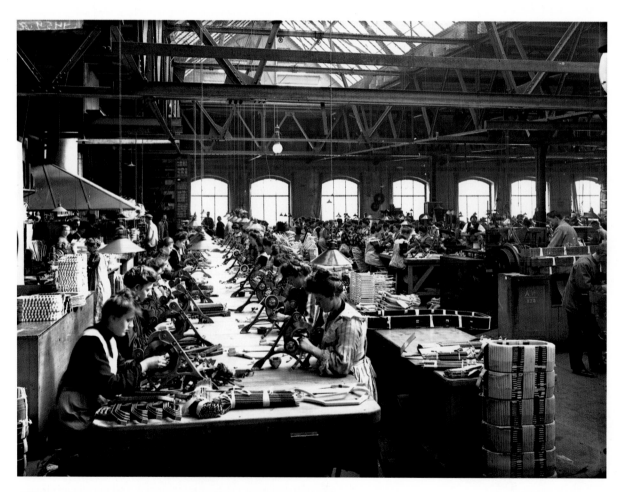

7.10
PHOTOGRAPHER UNKNOWN, *Female Employees at AEG,* **1906. Deutsches Technikmuseum, Berlin.**

The AEG company in Germany hired women to assemble electrical appliances. Although women's employment in factories is associated with wartime labor shortages, in 1907 women comprised nearly 36 per cent of the working population in Germany.[10]

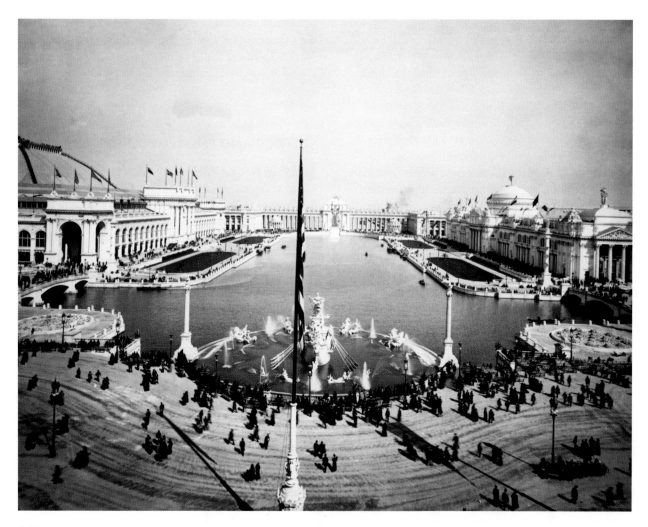

7.11
CHARLES DUDLEY ARNOLD, *Basin and the Court of Honor*, 1893. Platinum print. Chicago Historical Society, Chicago, Illinois.

living conditions for a Ford worker. The company's Sociological Department took photographs of ideal kitchens and bathrooms as examples to workers,[11] and hired about one hundred inspectors to check employees' homes. More benignly, the General Electric Company began publishing a magazine called *Work News*, which emphasized the notion of community through photographs of workers and company sports teams.[12]

THE IDEAL CITY

The ideal city at the turn of the century was presented at a world's fair held in Chicago during 1893, called the World's Columbian Exposition, which was attended by twenty-eight million people. Dubbed "the White City," for its classically derived, all-white BEAUX-ARTS architecture, the exposition expressed the notion that American economic success could renew cities and make them the centers of civilization. Charles Dudley Arnold (1844–1927), director of the Photographic Division of the exposition, made every effort to control photographs of the fair. All newspapers and periodicals had to use photographs issued by him and his office, or approved by them.[13] His view of the

exposition is best expressed in the official images he made on mammoth plates and printed on platinum paper (Fig. 7.11). As photographic historian Peter Bacon Hales noted, Arnold's view resonates with the painting of American artist Thomas Cole (1801–1848), in whose work *The Consummation of Empire* (part of *The Course of Empire* series) Classical architecture is celebrated as a symbol of American advancement.[14] Night-time photographs of the White City were calculated to demonstrate the union of culture and progress, symbolized by electricity, as the fair's buildings were traced by thousands of incandescent lights. In the photographs overseen by Arnold, the presence of people was minimized, thereby magnifying a vision of order.

The White City featured a Midway or "Midway Plaisance," with the first Ferris wheel, constructed as an engineering feat meant to rival the Eiffel Tower in Paris, which was built for the 1889 Exposition Universelle. From atop the Ferris wheel, visitors could look down at living ethnological exhibitions placed along the Midway in a conscious effort to merge information and entertainment. Strollers could enter the most talked-about area, a street in Cairo, modeled not after an actual street, but after a similar stretch at the 1899 Paris Exposition. Native villages with ethnic types, including Native Americans, dotted the Midway area, where the daily life of residents was periodically punctuated with ceremonial rituals, some of which had long passed from practice. Anthropologist Franz Boas (see p. 229) recruited Kwakiutl people from British Columbia, whom he asked to execute ritual dances in front of a white sheet, so that their various moves were easier to see and to photograph. Frederic Ward Putnam (1839–1915), the anthropologist in charge of the ethnological exhibits, helped to prepare one of the six hundred souvenir photographic booklets. Titled *Portrait Types of the Midway Plaisance* (1894), it linked information with entertainment, announcing that "Truly there was much of instruction as well as joy on the Merry Midway."[15]

African Americans were discouraged from participating in the exposition. They protested their lack of visibility in letters to newspapers and visits to public officials when they were represented on the Midway by people from Dahomey (now Benin), in West Africa. Abolitionist Frederick Douglass spoke from the Haitian pavilion, asking the crowd to live up to the ideals of the Constitution. Suffragist and civil rights worker Ida B. Wells (1862–1931) handed out pamphlets that documented the increase in lynching. She noted that lynching victims were often photographed, and the images sold as individual prints or postcards. Soon afterward she published the book, *The Red Record: Tabulated Statistics and Alleged Causes of Lynching in the United States* (1895), which contained drawings and photographs of lynchings.

SCIENCE AND PHOTOGRAPHY

THE PHOTOGRAPHY OF MOVEMENT

In 1878, French physiologist Étienne-Jules Marey (1830–1904) was reading the science journal *La Nature* when he came across images derived from photographs taken by Eadweard Muybridge, who had previously photographed at Yosemite in California (see Fig. 4.56). Muybridge's photographs resolved an age-old question for equine experts and painters: do all four legs of the horse leave the ground when the horse moves quickly (Fig. 7.12)? To make the photographs, Muybridge lined a raceway with 15-foot-wide sheeting, upon which lines were drawn at 21-inch intervals. As a horse rushed past, its hooves tripped cotton threads, which in turn tripped shutters on twelve cameras set up opposite the sheeting. Marey, who had been studying human and animal locomotion for a decade,

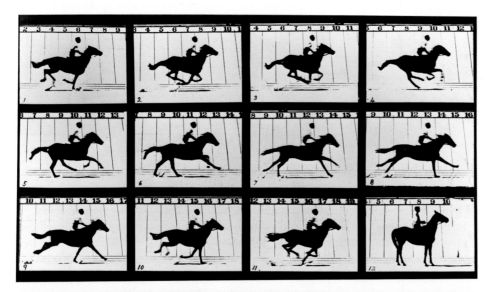

7.12
EADWEARD MUYBRIDGE, *Untitled*
(Sequence photographs of a galloping horse),
from *La Nature*, December 1878. Gravures.

The third photograph in the top row clearly shows all four hooves of the galloping horse in the air, rather than extended or touching the ground, as most painters had rendered them. Muybridge's work had begun in the 1870s at the instigation of former California governor Leland Stanford, who owned race horses.

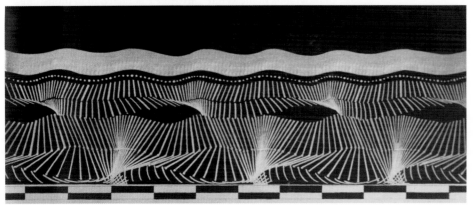

7.13
ÉTIENNE-JULES MAREY, *Joinville Soldier Walking,*
1883. Collège de France, Paris.

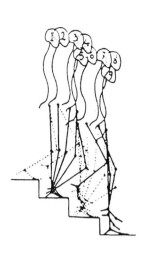

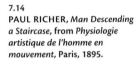

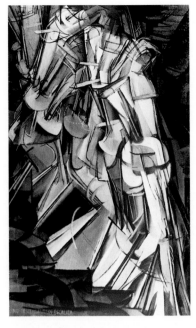

7.14
PAUL RICHER, *Man Descending a Staircase,* **from** *Physiologie artistique de l'homme en mouvement,* **Paris, 1895.**

7.15
MARCEL DUCHAMP, *Nude Descending a Staircase # 2,* **1912. Oil on canvas, 58 × 35 in. (147.3 × 88.9 cm). Louise and Walter Arensberg Collection. Philadelphia Museum of Art, Pennsylvania.**

The photographer Albert Londe (1858–1917), who worked with Charcot (see p. 152) at La Salpêtrière during the 1880s, extended his medical photography into the creating of X-ray photographs (see p. 212) and the study of movement. A line drawing by Paul Richer (1849–1933), based on one of Londe's stop-action photographs, may have provided the visual vocabulary for *Nude Descending a Staircase # 2* (1912), the influential painting by Marcel Duchamp (1887–1968). In addition, the dotted lines in the center of the canvas probably derive from Marey's geometric drawings[16] (Figs. 7.14, 7.15). Perhaps the greatest effect in the art world of late nineteenth-century photographs of movement was on the Italian FUTURISTS, who came to prominence in 1909 (see p. 210).

As his fame and influence grew, Muybridge became a science celebrity, traveling and giving lectures. He visited France, where he met Marey, and he was invited by the University of Pennsylvania in Philadelphia to carry on his experiments there in a specially built outdoor studio. One of Muybridge's supporters at the university was the American realist painter Thomas Eakins (1844–1916). An accomplished amateur photographer, Eakins used Muybridge's photographs in both his teaching and his art to show how humans and animals actually moved. His 1879 painting *A May Morning in the Park* referred to Muybridge's studies of the horse's gait. By blending scientific accuracy with artistic color and composition, Eakins made his point that modern art had to take the findings of science into account. He helped to bring Muybridge to the University of Pennsylvania, and worked with the photographer in 1884 (Fig. 7.16). Though he later lost interest in perfecting photographs of human movement, Eakins used outdoor photographs of the nude male for his paintings, both as figure studies and to learn how sunlight illuminates the body. Recent research indicates that he sometimes projected photographs on to his canvases and traced the outlines of forms, a practice occasionally used to create

was motivated by the Muybridge images to experiment with photography. In the early 1880s, he invented a gun-camera like that used by Pierre-César Jules Janssen (see pp. 157–59), with which he made exposures rapid enough to record the bodily movements of a bird in flight. Marey's work was greatly aided by the speed of DRY-PLATE technology, which made possible the fast exposure time necessary to make instantaneous photographs.

Another of Marey's inventions used a simple but elegant addition to the camera that let him record the flow of human and animal movement on a single photographic plate. A rotating disk with small slots cut into it at regular intervals was spun in front of an open camera lens. A person walking in front of this apparatus would be in a different position each time the open slot on the disk allowed an image to register. The result showed human movement in time and space. Marey called his work chronophotography—that is, time photography.

Marey's images are visually puzzling and attractive, yet he was primarily interested not in their aesthetic merit, but in the way in which they isolated the imperceptible phases of movement (Fig. 7.13). He continued to improve his photographic devices so that he could eliminate any overlapping of moving figures. He created a camera in which light-sensitive material moved with each exposure. When continuous photographic film, like that used today, was invented, Marey employed it to produce a short film in July 1889, showing how the human hand works. He published his results in articles and books, notably in *The Flight of Birds* (1890), which influenced early attempts to build airplanes.

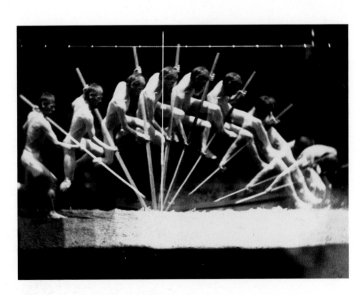

7.16
THOMAS EAKINS, *Motion Study: George Reynolds nude, pole-vaulting,* **1885. Gelatin silver print. Philadelphia Museum of Art.**

focus

Photography and Futurism

The Italian Futurists were a pre-World War I group of artists thrilled by the prospect of a future filled with motion, activity, and change. They were intrigued by the visual language of stop-action photographs. Giacomo Balla (1871–1958) interpreted photographs of sequential movements in a humorous painting, *Dynamism of a Dog on a Leash* (1912). Balla and his celebrated painting were photographed in the photodynamic style developed by Anton (or Antonio) Bragaglia (1890–1960). A photographer and filmmaker associated with the Futurists, Bragaglia accentuated the blur of motion that most action photographers regarded as a fault in their images and tried to remove.

Bragaglia's photodynamic images appeared in a 1913 book, *Fotodinamismo futurista* (Fig. 7.17). In words that approximate the goals of Victorian High Art photography, Bragaglia thought his multiple exposures would help revolutionize photography, by "purifying[,] ennobling and truly elevating it to art."[17] Unlike other practitioners, who tried to elevate photography by making pictures carry a moral lesson or by copying Old Masters, Bragaglia believed that the photographic artist should render the world's invisible vital energy. He proceeded to dissolve the clear resolution and distinctly segmented pictures of motion studies. He adapted Marey's strictly scientific images to his metaphysical aims, believing that both art and science should seek to reveal the spiritual. The photodynamic photograph, with its obscure and blurry areas, allowed him to record reality "unrealistically."

7.17
ANTON GIULIO BRAGAGLIA, *The Futurist Painter Giacomo Balla*, 1912, from *Fotodinamismo futurista*, Rome, 1913.

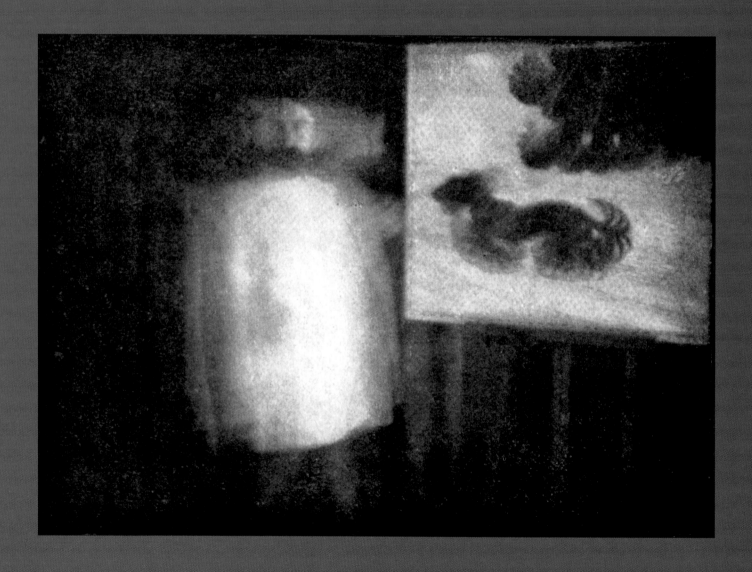

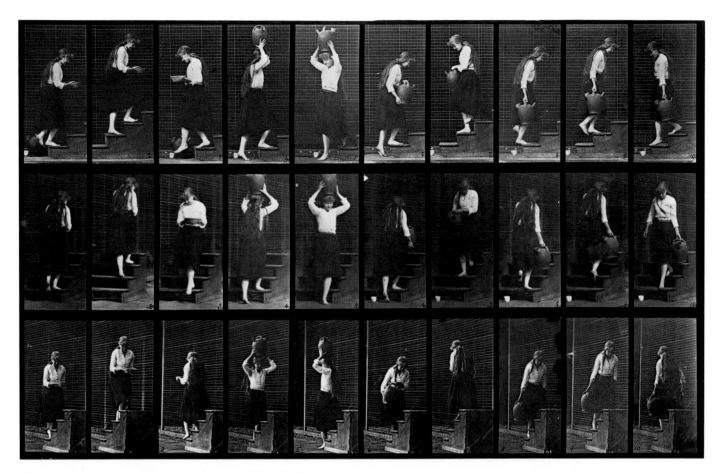

7.18
EADWEARD MUYBRIDGE, *Ascending and Descending Stairs*, from *Animal Locomotion*, plate 504, 1870s. Library of Congress, Washington, D.C.

charcoal and painted portraits from photographic sources. In his own way, Eakins attempted to refresh the Classical nude. "Nature," he said, "is just as varied and just as beautiful in our day as she was in the time of [the ancient Greek sculptor] Phidias."[18]

Muybridge's time in Philadelphia proved highly productive. He refined his techniques, creating 100,000 images of movement. He photographed female and male nudes, some in casual poses such as turning to embrace a child or laying bricks, which, if not strictly scientific, may have been influenced by Eakins's location of beauty in everyday modern life. After setting up a studio in the zoological gardens, Muybridge recorded the movements of such animals as elks, camels, and elephants. His eleven-volume work *Animal Locomotion* (1887) offered 781 large plates (19⅛ inches by 24⅜ inches). The studies attracted a varied audience, including prominent scientists such as Louis Agassiz, inventors such as Thomas Edison (1847–1931), and artists including Auguste Rodin.

Muybridge's notes indicate that he always made twelve lateral and twenty-four foreshortened (that is, from the front, or from the back) views of his subjects. But few of his final prints contain thirty-six images (Fig. 7.18).[19] As scholar Marta Braun

discovered, Muybridge often fabricated his final composite pictures, assembling images that play upon the willingness of the eye and mind to see photographs arranged from left to right as having been taken in that order. About 40 per cent of Muybridge's photographs of movement are composed of images that were not taken successively, as he had claimed.[20] Muybridge's stop-action pictures contrast with the unaltered scientific investigations of Marey. Possibly his artistic sensibilities intervened when he encountered a technical difficulty, or perhaps his willingness to give the appearance of truth began with his misleading photographs from the Modoc War (see pp. 136–38).

Directly or indirectly, chronophotographs influenced art. Most immediately, such artists as the French painter Jean-Louis-Ernest Meissonier (1815–1891) and Thomas Eakins, both of whom carried out their own motion studies, made their paintings of horses accord with what the photographs showed, rather than with what the eye perceived. At the same time, each painter recognized how the human brain confirms the truth of optical realism, and adapted science to art. These modifications were seen by some critics as a capitulation to the machine. As stop-action photographs became known outside of scientific circles, they fueled the discussion about the role of human perception in modern art.

PHOTOGRAPHY AND THE INVENTION OF MOVING PICTURES

Although devices creating the illusion of moving pictures existed before the development of photography, in the late nineteenth century there was a burgeoning of parlor-game machines and what were called "philosophical toys," which whirled images around a horizontal cylinder. Viewed through tiny slits in the cylinder, the sequence of pictures showing running horses and the like created the impression of movement. Limited by the size of the cylinder, devices such as the zoëtrope, the praxinoscope, and the phenakistoscope operated on the same general principle of tricking the eye into seeing motion. Muybridge experimented with a contrivance he called the zoöpraxiscope, which added the magic lantern's ability to project an image to the zoëtrope's simulation of movement. Muybridge used his own photographs of movement, heavily outlined or painted over, to form SILHOUETTES. The device, first demonstrated in 1879, was again limited by the size of the turning disks.

About the same time that he was developing the phonograph to record and project sound, Thomas Edison took a hint from the success of Muybridge's zoöpraxiscope and began work on making pictures move. His kinetoscope, introduced in 1894, made images move in a boxlike structure with a viewer. Commonly called a "peep show," after the popular street entertainment begun in the eighteenth century, the kinetoscope used flexible film about 50 feet in length. The film was illuminated behind a magnifying lens, and it sped by the viewer at forty-eight frames per second, generating a show that lasted only thirteen seconds. In Europe, several inventors added public projection to the private peep show. In France, the Lumière brothers introduced their film projector to the Parisian public late in 1895.

Although attempts to make pictures move predated the invention of photography, the concurrent invention of motion pictures by different inventors in the late 1880s and the 1890s seems to have been sparked by stop-action experiments, such as those of Marey and Muybridge. Photographic skills expedited the leap from still to moving pictures: for example, Edison viewed Marey's photographs of movement placed on a moving film strip, and the Lumière brothers manufactured photographic supplies in Lyon, before creating their Cinématograph.

The effect of motion pictures on photography within professional, artistic, amateur, and hobbyist circles is a little-known aspect of photographic history. Some photographers became filmmakers, but the wider impact of moving pictures on still photography has yet to be written. Where the first photographs immediately explored artistic, travel, and documentary uses, the first films tended to demonstrate movement itself: the arrival of a train, acrobats prancing and tumbling, workers leaving a factory. Photography's varieties were well established by the 1890s, and none seems to have been superseded by the emergence of film.

THE X-RAY

The 1895 discovery of the X-ray by Wilhelm Conrad Röntgen (1845–1923), a Dutch-German physicist working in Germany, had profound effects outside science and medicine. Röntgen, who had a practical knowledge of photography, was experimenting with electricity and a cathode ray tube, which beamed an image on a screen, when he chanced to observe a force he would later call the "X" or unknown ray. It emanated from the cathode tube and caused a piece of cardboard coated with a fluorescent material to glow in the dark. He soon learned that the rays could pass through the human body, blackening a photographic plate except where they were absorbed by the calcium in bones (Fig. 7.19). His X-ray photographs looked like shadowgraphs, such as those made by William Henry Fox Talbot and others decades earlier (see p. 19). The public defined the X-ray as a kind of photography, even though it was not created by light waves.

X-ray apparatus, like early photographic gear, could be easily constructed. Moreover, like the initial response to the DAGUERREOTYPE and CALOTYPE, the reception of the X-ray was essentially confident. Earlier scientific uses of photography had not provoked the immense fascination that the X-ray did. An inquisitive public could gawk at X-rays at amusement parks and department stores—also new phenomena on the urban scene. Department store customers stood in line to look

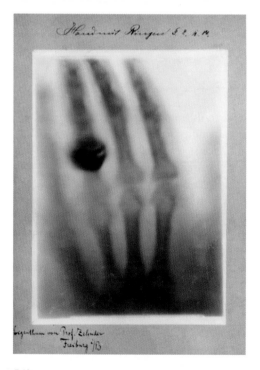

7.19
WILHELM RÖNTGEN, *Frau Röntgen's Hand,* 1895. X-ray. **Deutsches Röntgen Museum, Remscheid, Germany.**

Röntgen's X-ray of his wife's hand accompanied his initial scientific paper reporting on the phenomenon. He exposed the left hand of his wife, Bertha, to the X-ray for fifteen minutes to create one of the first images of its kind. The large bulge is her ring.

focus

Worker Efficiency: The Gilbreths' Time and Motion Studies

Studies of human movement were not confined to the realm of science. The American engineer Frederick Winslow Taylor (1856–1915) studied the steps laborers use to perform tasks. In 1898 he was hired to reorganize the machine shops at Bethlehem Steel in Pennsylvania. To make the shop operate in a linear, rational way, akin to the machine itself, Taylor renovated the shop floor. His most influential change came from his observation of the most efficient workers and the motions they employed to accomplish a task. After breaking down these actions into the smallest units, Taylor ordered the workers to imitate exactly the motions used by the efficient workers to accomplish tasks. His name became synonymous with what he called scientific management. An idea that had been suggested as early as the 1851 Crystal Palace exhibition's celebration of mass production, what became known as "Taylorism" spread through the world, boosting productivity and giving management increased control.

Followers of Taylorism used photography to isolate the individual actions used by workers to perform mechanical acts. As electrification of factories and the use of the assembly line and conveyor belts speeded up production in the early twentieth century, Frank Gilbreth (1868–1924) and Lillian Moller Gilbreth (1878–1972) claimed to demonstrate to industrial laborers the most efficient way to get the job done with a minimum of fatigue. In their essay "The Effect of Motion Study upon the Workers," they contended that the orderly performance of tasks would make the workers happier and more prosperous.[21] To make what was called a chronocyclegraph, or time-cycle image, Frank Gilbreth attached small light bulbs to a worker's hands, and photographed the lights as they traced the worker's actions (Fig. 7.20). The Gilbreths then made models of the light tracings in wire. These wire replicas of the most efficient and speedy actions were used to train workers, who ran their hands over the wires to learn the best pattern for their hands to take.[22]

The Gilbreths also filmed "micro-motion" studies of workers' actions. Their work was influenced by the photographs of Muybridge and Marey. The Gilbreths' time-and-motion studies were seen as modern, scientific management of business, and their work, like Taylor's, was imitated around the world. Labor unions soon protested against intrusive cameras and a philosophy of business that reduced humans to a set of standardized, repetitive actions.

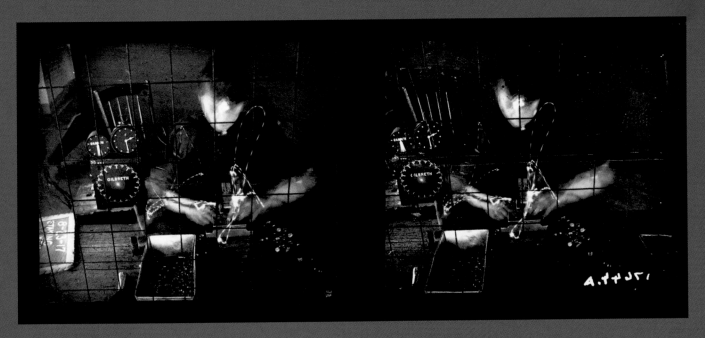

7.20
FRANK B. GILBRETH, *Chronocyclegraph of Woman Staking Buttons*, 1917. Gelatin silver print. National Museum of American History, Smithsonian Institution, Washington, D.C.

through their own hands at the living bone. Since X-rays did not cause physical pain, people assumed they were safe. Even when Edison created the fluoroscope in 1896, eliminating the use of the photographic plate, people still associated the X-ray with photography. Indeed, before the professionalization of radiology, photographers thought of the X-ray as a branch of their practice; "radiophotographers" were not required to have long medical training. After only a year's preparation, Elizabeth Fleischmann (c. 1865–1905) became the first person to open an X-ray laboratory in California, and pioneered the use of multiple views of a patient's body.[23]

In the public imagination, the X-ray photograph was sometimes associated with the occult. If the X-ray, a powerful but unseen element, could reveal hidden existence, perhaps it could do other things, such as reviving the dead.[24] Perhaps X-ray glasses would allow ordinary people to see through buildings. The technique was, after all, popularly referred to as "The New Sight." Maybe there were other imperceptible rays that could make ghosts visible and humans invisible, reveal human thoughts, or locate a fourth dimension. The idea of a fourth dimension, simplified from mathematics and philosophy, extended the promise of a break with traditional thinking.[25] Some saw the X-ray photograph as proof that spirit photographs—that is, images purporting to record invisible emanations coming from ghosts—were authentic. What seems today like pseudo-science was taken seriously in certain academic circles. In 1909, at the Sorbonne in Paris, a committee was established to study transcendental photography of invisible beings and forces.[26]

To some viewers, seeing beneath clothing via the X-ray had the erotic shiver of the forbidden. A London store even offered X-ray-proof undergarments. Literature's most famous X-ray photograph may be that in Thomas Mann's famous 1924 novel *The Magic Mountain*, in which the main character, Hans, finds an X-ray of his beloved sexually arousing, but identifies a fluoroscope of his own hand with death. One of the most enduring science-fiction novels, H. G. Wells's *The Invisible Man* (1897), is based on the idea that a man's exposure to "roentgen rays" can make his body invisible.

A few doctors and dentists purchased X-ray machines as soon as they were manufactured. Public acceptance grew gradually, along with medical use during armed conflict, beginning with X-ray-equipped field hospitals set up by the Italians in their 1896 attempt to colonize Abyssinia, and culminating in the routine use of the X-ray during World War I. Soon X-ray photographs were taken from many angles, to pinpoint the location of bullets and shrapnel. As research trickled in about the dangers of X-rays, in an era when the average medical exposure was about one hour long, the public had to adjust to the idea that they could be injured by a substance that could not be seen or tracked, and which took months or years for its effects to develop. California X-ray pioneer Elizabeth Fleischmann died from cancer induced by the new technology.

As historian Bettyann Holtzmann Kevles points out, X-rays were "the first invisible substances generated by scientists to

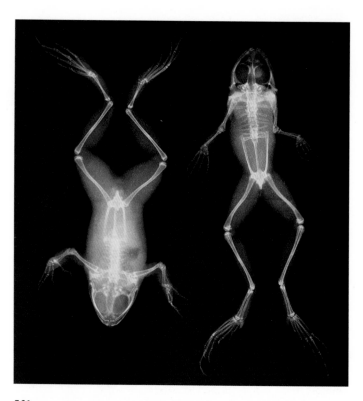

7.21
EDUARD VALENTA & JOSEF MARIA EDER, *Frogs*, 1896, from the portfolio *Versuche über photographie mittlest der Röntgenschen Strahlen*. X-ray. George Eastman House, Rochester, New York.

profoundly affect human perception."[27] Several scholars have suggested that the multiple perspectives and monochromatic CUBIST palette of Picasso and Georges Braque (1882–1963) may relate to X-ray photographs. The Italian Futurists embraced the X-ray. One of the movement's founders, Umberto Boccioni (1882–1916), believed that the X-ray would help to wipe away outworn attitudes. "Who can still believe in the opacity of bodies," he wrote. Futurist art, he maintained, was like the X-ray—they both "sharpened and multiplied sensitiveness."[28] A 1913 watercolor by Francis Picabia (1879–1953), a Paris-born artist who worked in France and the United States, was titled *New York Seen Through the Body*. (In France, the phrase *à travers le corps*—literally, "through the body"—was used by practitioners to advertise X-ray examinations.) Picabia's painting let viewers see through buildings to the structure behind them.

Experiments with X-ray technology by Viennese chemists Eduard Valenta (1857–1937) and Josef Maria Eder (1855–1944) (who would write one of the histories of photography) led them to issue a portfolio of X-ray photographs that expressed aesthetic delight in the revealing images (Fig. 7.21).

PHOTOGRAPHY, SOCIAL SCIENCE, AND EXPLORATION

While art photography was influenced by science and technology, travel, exploration, survey, and social-scientific photography continued patterns set in the mid-nineteenth century. The encyclopedic urge to collect images was newly invigorated by the growing sense that traditional life around the world was disappearing so rapidly that it must be recorded. In the *British Journal of Photography* (1889), Cosmo Burton suggested that a responsible photographic society should "keep a library of great albums containing a record as complete as it can be made, and in *permanent photographs only* of the present state of the world."[29] Similarly, British anthropologist and colonial administrator Everard im Thurn (1852–1932) wrote that "primitive phases of life are fast fading from the world in this age of restless travel and exploration, and it should be recognised as almost the duty of educated travellers in the less known parts of the world to put on permanent record, before it is too late, such of these phases as they may observe."[30] Roland Bonaparte (1858–1924), a relative of Napoleon I, commissioned thousands of photographs from around the world, and photographer John Thomson wrote in 1885, "no expedition, indeed, now-a-days, can be considered complete without photography to place on record the geographical and ethnological features of the journey."[31]

Official expeditions set out to clarify national and regional borders, as well as to research roadways, railroads, and resources. As in the mid-nineteenth century, the camera and the gun were accepted equipment for the journey (Fig. 7.2). Likewise, the classification of human types through physical differences continued apace, aspiring to become ever more comprehensive. In short, while photographic realism was hotly debated in art circles, the medium's objectivity was increasingly central to social science.

PHOTOGRAPHING AFRICA

In Africa, the Western imagination constructed an alternative to the industrializing world, while simultaneously exploiting its natural wealth. Notions of Africa as the "dark continent," historically cut off from the European Enlightenment and racially inferior, were rekindled in the late nineteenth century. Social Darwinists misinterpreted Darwin's theories to mean that people and societies that had not developed in the manner of Western culture were inherently inferior. Africa, and in particular sub-Saharan Africa, was seen as a prime example of timeless backwardness.

Renowned missionary Dr. David Livingstone (1813–1873), famously assumed lost during one of his attempts to bring Christianity to Africa, took along his brother Charles (1821–1873) as a photographer on an earlier Zambezi expedition (1858–64). Livingstone the missionary also commanded an official British exploration, seeking mineral wealth and agricultural potential. He favored visual aids to his work, referring to the magic lantern he brought with him to show Bible stories as the "oxyhydrogen light of civilization."[32] Charles Livingstone was replaced by John Kirk (1832–1922), who made the first camera images of an official British expedition in Africa.[33] In some of Kirk's photographs, the dense African foliage indicated fertile land, potentially suitable

for Western agriculture. At the same time, the jungle also symbolized to Europeans the triumph of nature over civilization.

While writing for the *New York Herald* in 1871, Henry Morton Stanley (1841–1904) found the ailing missionary, and uttered the now well-known greeting, "Dr. Livingstone, I presume?" There were no photographers on the scene, and Livingstone's death in 1873 in a remote area of Africa precluded photographs being made of him. But public curiosity was served when Stanley was photographed in a London studio, supposedly dressed in the very clothes he wore when he met Livingstone (Fig. 7.22).

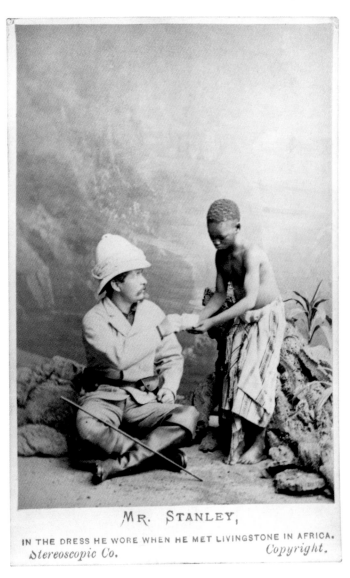

7.22
PHOTOGRAPHER UNKNOWN, *Henry Morton Stanley and Kululu* (detail), c. 1872. Albumen *carte-de-visite*. London Stereoscopic Company, National Portrait Gallery, London.

The setting of this *carte-de-visite* was a painted backdrop in a London studio. Stanley is being served tea by Kululu (Ndugu M'hali) (1864–1877), who was given to him by a slave-trader. From the age of eight, Kululu was Stanley's personal servant. He died crossing the Congo River during Stanley's 1874–77 expedition.[34]

By 1880, companies that commissioned and published photographs were established in coastal areas of colonial Africa.[35] Interest in Africa grew after the 1885 Berlin Conference, which authorized European nations with coastal bases to expand their interests into the African interior so long as they did not impinge on other colonial territories. Beginning in the 1880s, large photographically illustrated books depicting people, land, and riches were published.[36] Trophy animals hunted during safaris were also frequently photographed. Typically, photographs showed Africans as primitive, and European culture and enterprise as progressive. At the turn of the nineteenth century, when the postcard fad flourished, images of Africans were often reproduced in this format (Fig. 7.23). It has been argued that Picasso adapted poses of Africans on postcards made by François-Edmond Fortier (1862–1928), who published more than eight thousand postcards of Africa, for his work during 1906–07, including *Les Demoiselles d'Avignon* (1907).[37]

The spirit of African expansion was expressed in *The Queen's Empire* (1897), a British book celebrating Queen Victoria's Diamond Jubilee. It contained three hundred photographic images, including customs, education, and Western engineering feats. The text boasted that "in every part of the Empire we shall find some trace of the work which Britain is doing throughout the world—the work of civilizing, of governing, of protecting life and property, and of extending the benefits of trade and commerce."[38] Armed conflict in Africa was photographed, but was subject to censorship, as in the Boer War (1899–1902). Soldiers and armaments were regularly photographed, yet, as historian Jorge Lewinski remarked, "there are no pictures of barbed wire, of the results of the scorched-earth policy, of Boer women and children in prison camps where the mortality rate was nearly 50 per cent and where some 20,000 died."[39] Instead, photographers produced symbolic and sentimental pictures. Underwood and Underwood issued individual views and boxed

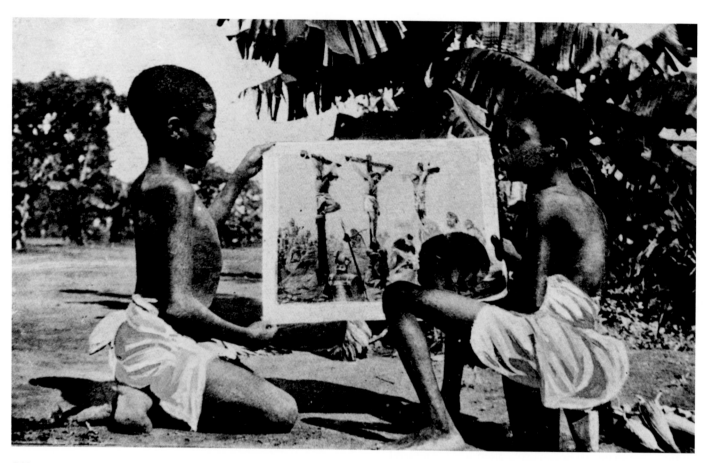

7.23
PHOTOGRAPHER UNKNOWN, *The Sons of the Cannibals Contemplating the Passion of the Redeemer,* c. 1910. Postcard. Archivio Provinciale dei Padri Cappuccini, Milan, Italy.

Schools were often set up by missionaries in Africa. The exaggerated shadow of the child's head on the print of the Crucifixion was probably added to show symbolically that Christianity was appropriate for Africans.

focus

The *National Geographic*

The National Geographic Society in the United States began in 1888 as a relatively small group of professional geographers and sponsors. When Alexander Graham Bell (1847–1922), the inventor of the telephone, took over the society's leadership, he stressed dissemination of knowledge. Gilbert H. Grosvenor (1875–1966) was employed to build circulation of the society's publication, which he did by studying the content and marketing of widely read magazines, such as *Harper's*. The *National Geographic*'s friendly tone and especially its uncomplicated pictures made it a success. While the society's 1915 policy statement underscored "absolute accuracy," it also envisaged an "abundance of beautiful, instructive, and artistic illustrations." Moreover, *National Geographic* promised that "nothing of a partisan or controversial character is printed."[40] The possible conflicts between these goals, such as the clash between accuracy and aesthetics, were not engaged. In his 1909 book *Scenes from Every Land*, Grosvenor reprinted upbeat, pleasant images from the magazine, offering armchair adventure, while avoiding the worst stereotypes of native people. Still, *National Geographic* often pictured people in the less developed world as primitive, implicitly suggesting that non-industrial societies remain static without Western intervention. Despite early twentieth-century prudery, the magazine did show nudity, especially female nudity (Fig. 7.24). In the United States, a longstanding joke had it that American teenagers got their first look at naked bodies in *National Geographic*. Its policy of accuracy, and its announced educational goal, allowed, even invited, readers to look. In effect, *National Geographic* carried forward the high-minded dual pursuit of information and entertainment beloved by fans of the stereographic photograph.

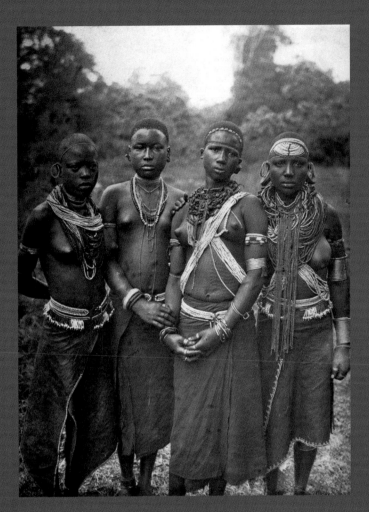

7.24
UNDERWOOD AND UNDERWOOD, *Girls in a Village of East Equatorial Africa*, 1909. Photo and copyright by Underwood and Underwood, New York.

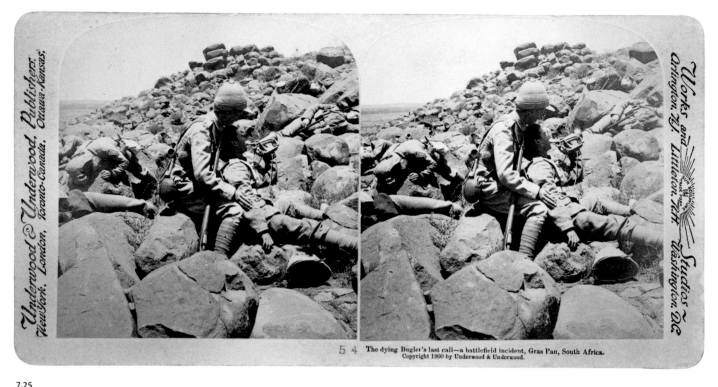

7.25
UNDERWOOD AND UNDERWOOD, *The Dying Bugler's Last Call—A Battlefield Incident, Gras Pan, South Africa*, 1900. Stereograph, gelatin silver print.
Gernsheim Collection. Harry Ransom Humanities Research Center, University of Texas at Austin.

sets from the Boer War for an international market, including a staged stereographic photograph of a patriotic dying soldier making a last bugle call (Fig. 7.25).

PHOTOGRAPHING THE PACIFIC PARADISE: SAMOA

In Western art and literature, the Pacific islands were long mythologized as a paradise, where labor was almost unknown and physical wants, including sexual ones, were easily gratified. At the same time, the inhabitants were seen as exotic primitives, unable or unwilling to live according to Western standards. Great curiosity about the Pacific area was sustained in the eighteenth and nineteenth centuries by the teasing contradictions between the Western Puritan work ethic and a life of reputedly unearned ease and abundance. In particular, images of nude or sparsely clad Pacific island women were taken to indicate a sexual and moral slackness, owing to the lack of struggle with nature.

Commercial photographers were aware of these powerful preconceptions and were quick to respond. In the late 1890s, as the Samoan Islands became trade and naval bases for the United States and Germany, they attracted widespread interest. John Davis (active mid-1870s; d. 1893), the first commercial photographer in Apia (then German Samoa, now the capital of Western Samoa), told a visitor that "hundreds of native girls and youths presented themselves at his studio in hopes that they would make photographs of commercial value for book illustrations and for selling to tourists." Yet he chose "only two, or three at the most, who possessed the thick lips and sensual

features which coincided with the stock European idea of the South Sea type."[41]

Photography supported social stereotypes, even for people who had been there and bought photographs as souvenirs. Historian Alison Devine Nordström suggested that, because the commercial photographs used for postcards, stereographs, and half-tones were stereotypical, once dealers and distributors collected enough images to satisfy customers, they did not require new ones.[42] These images reinforced the notion that Samoa, like most of the Pacific islands, was a timeless, uneventful place. Postcards of Samoa frequently featured Samoans in scanty native clothing, as well as beaches, palm trees, and waterfalls (Fig. 7.26). The Western presence, in the form of commercial and governmental buildings, was also pictured. Anthropological photographs often featured body tattoos, long associated in visual representations with the Pacific islands.[43]

CRIMINAL LIKENESSES

During the 1880s, photographs of criminals became routine in police work. In the past, the camera had been used occasionally to record the appearance of suspects and criminals. In the 1850s, the Swiss government used it to register indigents and stateless persons, and Alexander Gardner made portraits of President Lincoln's assassins and of their execution (see Fig. 4.18). But in the late nineteenth century, the photography of criminals became as standardized as anthropological photography, largely because of the work of Paris police official Alphonse Bertillon

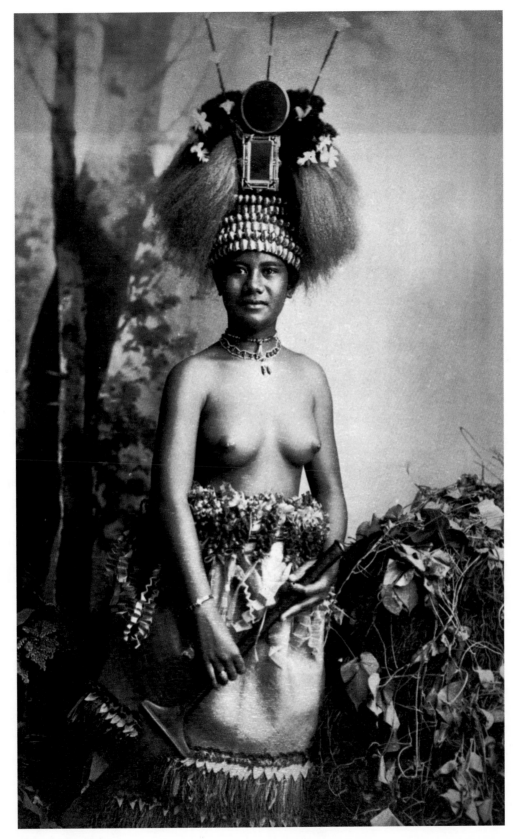

7.26
JOHN DAVIS, *Samoa Princess Fa'ane, Apia,* **c. 1893. Albumen print on board. Phillips Library Collection. Peabody Essex Museum, Salem, Massachusetts.**

Bare-breasted Samoan women were often pictured wearing an elaborate traditional headdress and carrying a large club. Western photographers favored the exotic look of the *taupou,* or village maiden, a position of honor in Samoan society. Thus anthropological imagery mixed with tourist visions of the Pacific.

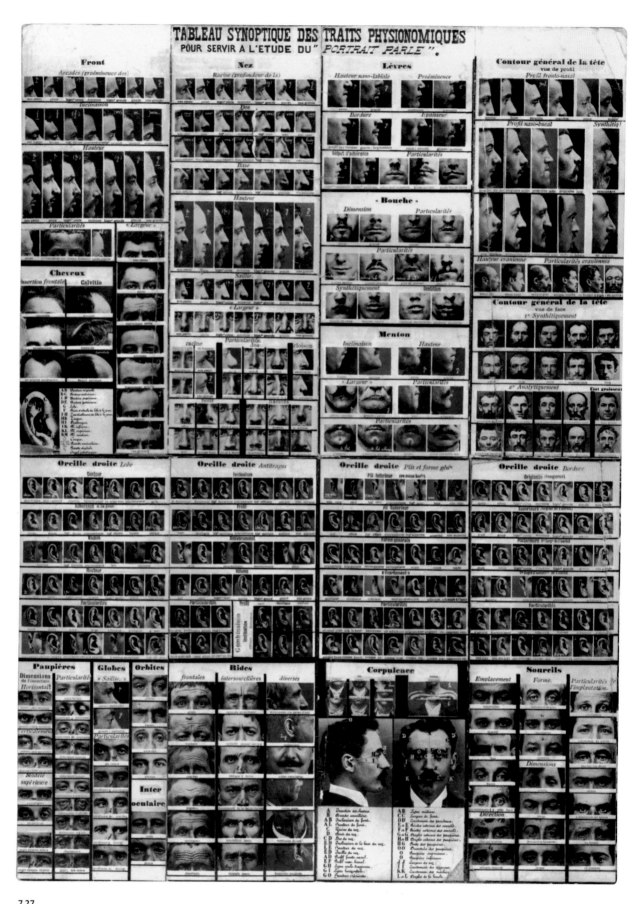

7.27
PHOTOGRAPHER UNKNOWN, *Synoptic Table of Facial Expressions for the Purposes of Systematic Identification, according to Alphonse Bertillon's system,*
n.d. Musée de la Préfecture de Police, Paris.

(1853–1914). Son of Louis-Adolphe Bertillon, a well-known anthropometrician who used statistics to describe humankind, Alphonse Bertillon developed a verbal and visual system to describe criminals (Fig. 7.27). His main interest was to identify recidivists—that is, repeat offenders. Called "speaking likenesses," Bertillon's invention was what is known today as the mugshot.

As historian Allan Sekula pointed out, Bertillon's system resembled the efficiency systems developed by Frederick Winslow Taylor and Frank and Lillian Gilbreth (see p. 213). Breaking down physical appearance into small, standardized units allowed unskilled clerks to file and retrieve criminal photographs.[44] The creation of large information archives, such as those used in police work, strengthened government control of the populace and, with anthropological photography, came close to fulfilling the abiding nineteenth-century dream of a vast, encyclopedic collection of images.

Bertillon's publications, such as *L'Identité des récidivistes et la loi de régulation* (*The Identity of Recidivists and Legal Regulation*) (1883) and *Identification anthropométrique* (*Anthropometric Identification*) (1893), influenced criminology and police procedures around the world. They fitted into an existing trend that saw criminality as evidence of degeneration—that is, of faulty innate tendencies in the individual brought out by the pressures of modern society.

French statistician Gabriel Tarde published *La Criminalité comparée* (*Comparative Criminality*) (1886), and British science writer Havelock Ellis followed with his own tract *The Criminal* (1890), which contained photographs of American, Russian, and Australian criminals, purporting to show the stigmata, or physical signs, of their moral defects. Ellis's friend the American

medical doctor Eugene S. Talbot proclaimed that "criminals form a variety of the human family quite distinct from law-abiding men," and liberally illustrated the 1901 edition of his book *Degeneracy: Its Causes, Signs, and Results* with photographs of criminals and others whom he considered deviant.[45] New York City police inspector Thomas Byrnes glamorized detective work in his 1886 *Professional Criminals of America*, which was also illustrated with photographs. Perhaps the most influential crime tract, Italian Cesare Lombroso's *L'Uomo delinquente* (*The Criminal Man*) (1876), was expanded in the 1890s with added illustrations. Unlike Bertillon, Lombroso thought criminality inherent, the expression of a biological element persisting from primitive times. In the late nineteenth century, fingerprinting, developed under British colonial rule in India and promoted by British scientist Francis Galton (1822–1911), was gradually introduced alongside the mugshot.[46]

Even small, local police departments commissioned mugshots of criminals. In Marysville, California, a small town north of Sacramento, portrait photographer Clara Sheldon Smith (1862–1939) fulfilled a contract with the city from 1900 to 1908, contributing about five hundred photographs to the local rogues' gallery (Fig. 7.28). Because prisoners were often brought to her studio unannounced, she sometimes photographed them using the backdrops and lighting set up for her regular customers.[47]

Another systematizing approach to human description and photography was used by Francis Galton, best known for his studies of heredity and for founding the science of eugenics, which he defined as "science which deals with all influences that improve the inborn qualities of a race."[48] In Galton's words, an improved humankind (presumably British) "should be better

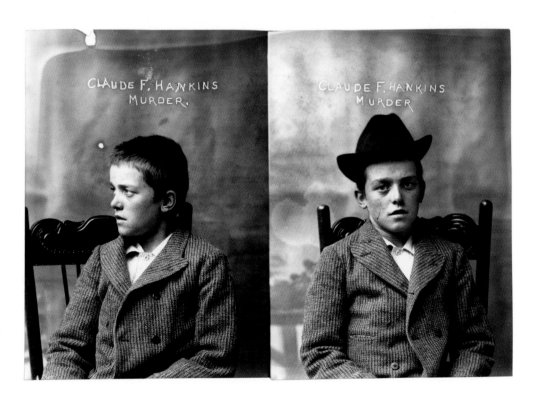

7.28
CLARA SHELDON SMITH, *Claude F. Hankins: Murder*, 1904. Arne Svenson Collection.

On July 1904, fourteen-year-old Claude F. Hankins shot and killed an older man whom he claimed tried to commit "a crime against nature" with him. He was sentenced to sixteen years in San Quentin State Prison. He received early parole in 1914.

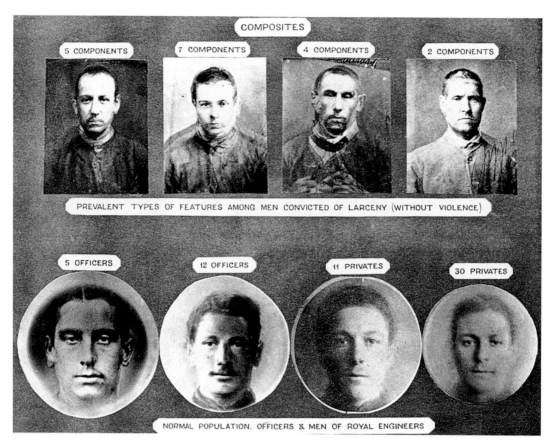

7.29
FRANCIS GALTON, *Untitled,* **from** *Inquiries into Human Faculty and its Development,* **1883.**

On a single photographic plate, Galton combined images of the mental and physical types, exposing one negative after another until all had been registered. He computed the exposure time by dividing the exposure time for one plate by the number of photographs he planned to register. Galton used composite photography to obtain what he called "representative faces" and "pictorial statistics" that condense large statistical tables.

fitted to fulfill our vast imperial opportunities."[49] Eugenics suggested a natural social order based on human ability that would surpass social class and wealth; Galton believed that photographs would show human superiority, just as they showed mountains and cathedrals. Photography was touted by reformers such as Galton as superior to painting, which was based on subjectivity, not objective description. Eugenics and photography attracted people in science, industry, academia, and government who had gained success through intellectual achievement rather than birthright. Galton used the mugshot format to photograph prisoners as well as patients, and recommended that the public create family albums with full-face and profile portraits arranged chronologically.[50]

Where Bertillon hoped to use photography to find unique individuals within a vast photographic archive, Galton sought to show general hereditary laws. For his 1883 *Inquiries into Human Faculty,* he invented a form of composite photography to make his points. Relying on the belief in photography's truthfulness, he called such images "real generalization,"[51] of criminals, tuberculosis patients, Jews, and families (Fig. 7.29). Composite images never ceased to interest viewers. They were powerfully invigorated in the late twentieth century by the ease with which images could be melded by computers.

WAR AND REVOLUTION

Because photographs could be quickly reproduced and generously displayed in the press, the quantity of up-to-the-minute war information and imagery consumed by the public escalated. The effect, as historian Susan D. Moeller argued, was that the Spanish–American War became the first "living-room" war.[52]

THE SPANISH–AMERICAN WAR
The conflict between Spain, which ruled Cuba, and the United States simmered for several years before American troops were sent into Cuba. Egged on by many inflammatory articles and shocking photographs of atrocities published in newspapers owned by the Hearst and Pulitzer syndicates, Americans empathized with the Cuban guerrilla forces fighting for independence. American newspapers further inflamed the

situation by blaming the Spanish for the sinking of the U.S. battleship *Maine*, on February 15, 1898, in the harbor of Havana, Cuba. "Remember the *Maine*" became a popular slogan, and large photographic firms marketed stereographs of the incident. Of all their pictures, Keystone View Company sold more of the wreckage of the *Maine* than any other.[53] The Spanish–American War (April 25–August 12, 1898) was probably the first war filmed by the motion-picture camera. Some early filmmakers even simulated battle scenes on the roofs of New York City buildings, using toy boats floating in bathtubs, and cigar smoke as fake fumes.

On April 25, 1898, the American Congress voted for war, setting off a stream of volunteers to serve in the military. Among them was the then assistant secretary of the navy, Theodore Roosevelt, who formed the First Volunteer Cavalry, known as the Rough Riders. The war's lack of planning, shortages of supplies, and general mismanagement recall the Crimean conflict. Roosevelt's famous cavalry charge up San Juan hill, sung in the press as a valiant and heroic act, was in fact a rash strategy born of desperation. There were no photographs of the actual charge, and the celebrated paintings of the incident by Frederick Remington (1861–1909), who was in Cuba to make illustrations for William Randolph Hearst's *New York Journal*, were created after Remington had returned to the United States. Nevertheless, the favorable publicity generated by the charge ushered Roosevelt into the governorship of New York (1898–1901). In office, Roosevelt acquired a permanent retinue of reporters and photojournalists.

Despite the public interest in the war, few photographers were assigned to it. Frances Benjamin Johnston, who was running a successful portrait studio in Washington, D.C. (see p. 186), worked as a correspondent for the Bain News Service, one of the earliest in the United States. When Admiral George Dewey was returning from the American victory in the Philippine Islands, a Spanish possession ceded to the United States at the end of the conflict, she got the first interview with him, titled the "Hero of Manila Bay." Johnston was also hired in 1899 by the Hampton Institute in Virginia, to portray its work. Founded as a training school for ex-slaves, Hampton continued to educate African Americans. Some of the photographs Johnston took were displayed at the Paris Exposition Universelle of 1900 in the "American Negro" exhibit organized by leading figures such as W. E. B. Du Bois. With Jessie Tarbox Beals (1870–1942), the first American woman to hold a full-time position as a staff photographer on an American newspaper, Johnston was among the earliest women photojournalists.

James Henry Hare (1856–1946) gained a reputation for war photography (Fig. 7.30). Journalists about to sail to cover the Mexican Revolution (1911–14) asked, "Where is Jimmy Hare? This cannot be a war. Jimmy Hare is not here."[54] His fame

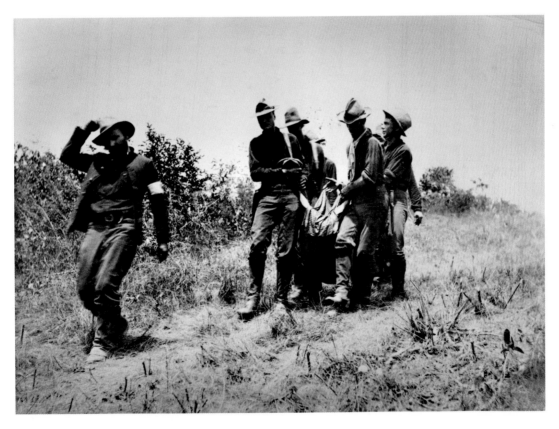

7.30
JAMES "JIMMY" HARE, *Carrying out the Wounded During the Fighting at San Juan*, c. 1914. Gernsheim Collection. Harry Ransom Humanities Research Center, University of Texas at Austin.

bespeaks the hot competition among magazines and newspapers that sparked the expansion of photojournalism in the early twentieth century. Hare became part of a team of writers from *Collier's*, which covered both sides of the war between Russia and Japan (1904–05), and his Spanish-American War photography significantly increased the magazine's circulation. He also photographed the San Francisco earthquake of April 1906, the First Balkan War (1912–13), and World War I. The magazine boasted that "wherever there is an army in the field, and clash of arms and bullets and the tragedies of war … there, too, is a man from *Collier's*."[55]

WORLD WAR I

During the Spanish–American War, while news stories could be cabled to newspapers competing for the most topical articles, photographs still had to be transported by sea and land. Nevertheless, the potential existed for civilians to see war in greater detail than ever before. By World War I, it was clear to

military officials that both photographs and news stories should be broadly managed to keep clandestine operations secret, and to keep up spirits at home. The assassination of Archduke Franz Ferdinand (1863–1914), heir to the Austro-Hungarian monarchy, in the Bosnian city of Sarajevo on June 28, 1914, became the trigger for conflict between Germany, Austria-Hungary, and Italy (the Triple Alliance), and Belgium and the Triple Entente, which consisted of France, Russia, and Britain. The United States did not enter the engagement until April 1917. Trench warfare, which characterized the conflict on the Western, or European, Front, caused unprecedented loss of life (see Fig. 7.33). Ten to thirteen million people died in hostilities sustained by the mass production of armaments.[56] On average, troops endured a death and injury rate of 58 per cent.

During the Spanish–American War, newspapers led public opinion in the United States, but during World War I, governments took the lead. Home-front morale proved less of a problem than expected, because the press practiced

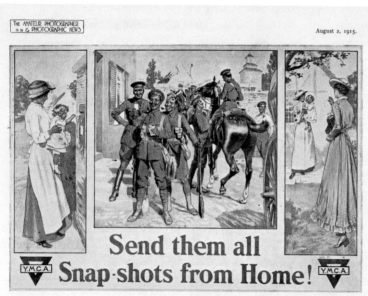

7.31
ARTIST UNKNOWN, *Send them all Snap-shots from Home!* from *Amateur Photographer*, August 2, 1915. Birmingham Central Library, Birmingham, England.

Part of the British volunteer effort on the home front was the coordinated effort to send soldiers abroad pictures of their loved ones at home. In a poster made for the Y.M.C.A., which sponsored the drive, the woman on the right can be seen taking a photograph of a young child. In the center, a soldier brags about the image he has just received.

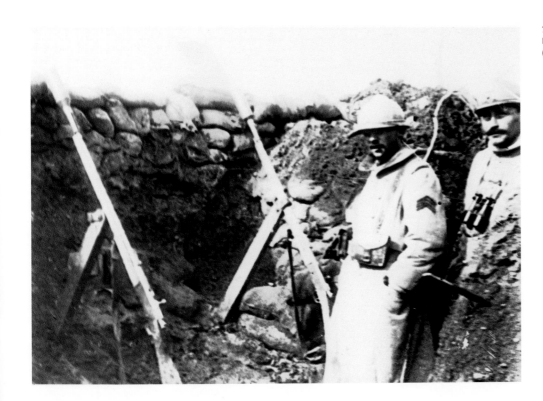

self-censorship. During the war, photographs were shown in galleries, including the Grafton Galleries in London, which in December 1916 exhibited work done for the Canadian War Records Office. The prints, enlarged to 3 by 3 feet and up to 6 by 10 feet, resembled traditional heroic painting in both size and subject matter.[57] Although the press did not seek to undermine official pronouncements, or to offer the soldier's view of battle, it did critique the photographs of the enemy. In Germany, a regular column in the *Deutsche Photographen Zeitung* (*German Photographic Newspaper*) reported on "the photographic lies our enemies tell."[58] Britain prohibited making photographs of corpses or scenes of conflict. After 1916, soldiers were buried where they were killed, rather than transported home.[59] Horrific tales from battles such as Gallipoli and Verdun were generally not backed up with photographs that the public could see, creating a profound difference between the experience of soldiers and public awareness, especially in Britain, which did not undergo trench warfare on its own soil.[60]

Photographers were eventually banned from the Western Front, causing newspapers and illustrated serials to rely on artists, and on photographs already in stock. Another problem troubled photographers and editors alike. The *War Illustrated*, a serial, announced in November 1914 that "from the pictorial point of view modern warfare lacks much which the battlefields of the past provided. Soldiers today are fighting enemies on the continent whom they never see … For this reason the great mass of photographs which reach us do not show actual hostilities."[61] Others complained that the war, conducted on flat plains, under cover of cloud and darkness, offered uninspired photographs. Occasionally, events such as soldiers "going over the top" of

the trenches were staged for the camera, the presence of which would draw fire during a real charge.[62]

Press photography was not the only kind made during the war. In Britain, the Snapshots from Home League encouraged citizens to send comforting pictures to soldiers (Fig. 7.31). German, Italian, British, Russian, and American nurses, ambulance drivers, and soldiers brought small cameras to the war (Fig. 7.32), creating an unauthorized archive that is still making itself known to researchers. Newspapers printed photographs found on battlefields, in hopes of identifying the soldiers who might have possessed them. Personal photographs recorded shocking material not considered appropriate for general circulation. The military, meanwhile, experimented with official photographers, whose numbers were limited, but who were given privileged access to troops and events. Britain, Australia, Canada, New Zealand, France, the United States, and Germany all employed official photographers, often military personnel, whose role was to record, rather than issue photographs to the press. International photographic distributors, such as Underwood and Underwood and Keystone View, sent photographers to the war. Aerial photography for military reconnaissance was perfected; in 1918 Edward Steichen became chief of the newly formed Photographic Service for the United States military.

As in previous wars, gruesome images of the enemy dead were published, but pictures of one's own casualties were mostly limited to the injured receiving speedy humane treatment. A German directive urged photographers to record the "fairness of the German troops and the destructive cruelty of the enemy."[63] Yet as the war went on, greater recognition

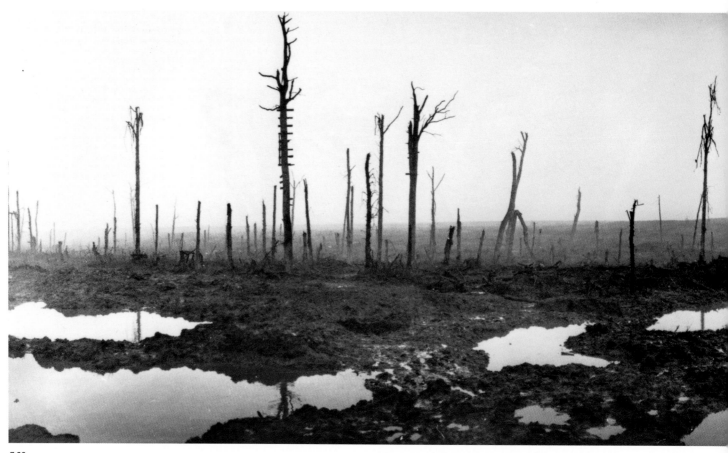

7.33
WILLIAM RIDER-RIDER, *Untitled* (Devastation on the battlefield of Passchendaele taken with a panoramic camera), 1917. Imperial War Museum, London.

of its terrible cost began to show up in photographs. Official Canadian photographer William Rider-Rider (1889–1979) took photographs of the dismal, muddy trenches at Passchendaele, where the Germans used mustard gas (Fig. 7.33). After the war, as the public learned more of its horrors, images of the trenches came to epitomize the conflict.

THE RUSSIAN REVOLUTION

The uprising of workers and intellectuals against the Russian monarchy was facilitated by the government's distraction during World War I. The various confrontations between March and November 1917 were not programmatically photographed, and, until recently, most photographs of the Revolution seemed to derive from motion-picture film of such events as the storming of the Winter Palace. In the post-Cold War period, images are beginning to emerge from Russian archives, promising more information about the use of photographic propaganda by all the factions. One series of images of the Russian Revolution was made by the Bulla photographic agency (Fig. 7.34). Founded by Karl Bulla (1854–1929), the agency sent photographs to such publications as Germany's illustrated newspapers. Bulla, who also made photographs of the Russian elite, emigrated to Estonia after the Revolution, leaving his sons to carry on the business. Viktor Bulla (1883–1944) became one of the first to film the news with a motion-picture camera.

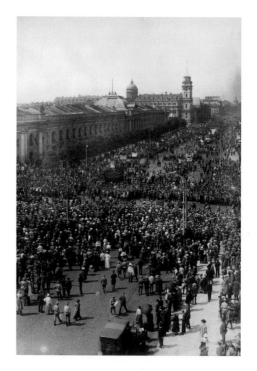

7.34
PHOTOGRAPHER UNKNOWN, *Demonstration by Revolutionary Democrats, Petrograd*, June 18, 1917. Silver bromide print. Saltykov-Shchedrin State Public Library, St. Petersburg, Russia.

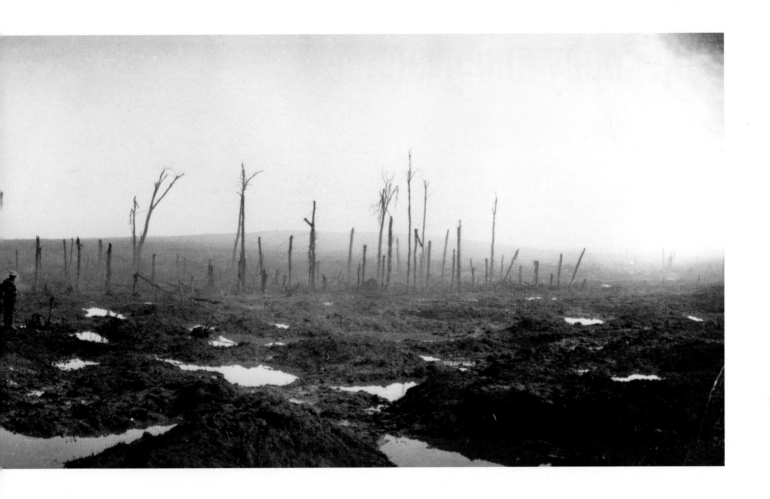

RETAKE

At the turn of the twentieth century, a split emerged between those who maintained that photography was a channel for intuitive insight and self-expression, and those who set up systems relying on the medium's objectivity. This divide was implicit in photographic practice from the first, but it broadened as that practice expanded. The wide separation echoed the conflict between positivism—the outlook adopted by science and social science, which asserted that knowledge was derived from the observation of facts—and metaphysics, which suggested that there were important meanings beyond those perceptible in human intellectual systems. While art photography continued to celebrate aesthetic sensitivity, the photographs of motion taken by Muybridge and Marey challenged the veracity of human perception with mechanical vision.

At the same time, the capacity of newspapers and magazines to print photographs, the growth of journals devoted to contemporary events, and increased speed in communications and transportation systems, made it technically possible for the public to see much more of war than in the past. During the American Civil War, topical photographs had to be viewed in a gallery, photographic studio, or bookseller's shop, often weeks after an event. Only engraved interpretations of photographs appeared in journals. But at the turn of the century, with the success of the half-tone processes for printing photographs with text, the public's access to contemporary events greatly increased. Social reform photographers, such as Lewis Hine, were in touch with the proliferation of imagery. Hine recognized the public's increased ability to contemplate multiple pictures, and presented his images in narrative sequences or photostories.

Photographers seeking to represent reality were quickly caught up in contradictions. At the 1904 World's Fair in St. Louis, which presented about two thousand indigenous peoples in the largest anthropological exhibition ever staged to date, visitors were invited to travel from Africa to Asia, visiting simulated environments and buying photographs and postcards of places that were staged especially for the fair. The effect was far more sophisticated than the painted scrim and gently tinkling cowbells of Daguerre's Diorama. At the same time, turn-of-the-century audiences were more media savvy than those in the mid-nineteenth century. They accepted the photographs and the environments as simulations, a category between the real and the false that was neither actual nor deceptive.

philosophy and practice

The Real Thing

In his 1893 short story "The Real Thing," Henry James tells of a handsome and prominent husband and wife who have lost their fortune. Once they were such social celebrities that photographers made their likenesses to sell in shops. Now financially desperate, the couple visit an artist who makes illustrations of contemporary life for magazines. They hope to earn money by posing as "the real thing; a gentleman, you know, or a lady."[64] The artist agrees, but is quickly frustrated in his attempt to create the illusion of wealth and elegance around them. He resorts to employing a lower-class man and woman who can more convincingly act out an affluent attitude. The formerly well-to-do couple briefly become servants in his home, then disappear into the city.

The contrast between appearance and reality was a central issue in the late nineteenth and early twentieth centuries. In both the visual arts and literature, it appeared in the repeated concern with masks and identity. In Oscar Wilde's *The Picture of Dorian Gray* (1884), the main character does not age or betray the effects of his debauched behavior, but a portrait of him evidences

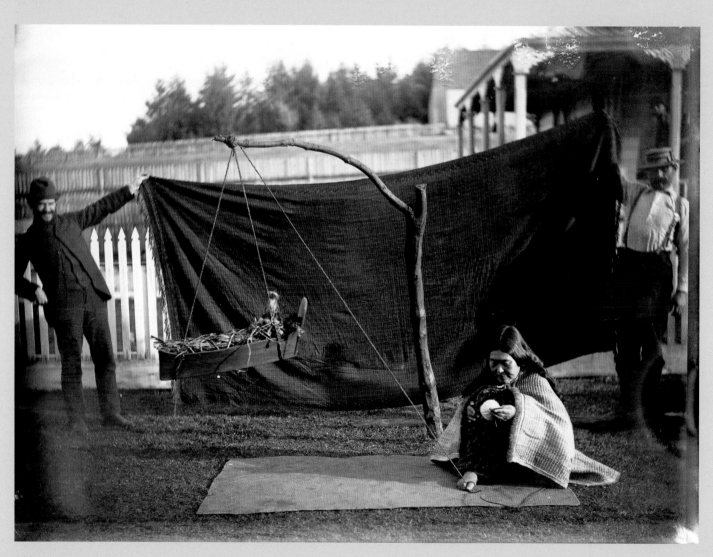

7.35
FRANZ BOAS AND GEORGE HUNT, *Untitled* (Anthropologist Franz Boas, left, and photographer George Hunt hold up a backdrop for a photograph of a Kwakiutl woman in the process of cedar-bark weaving), n.d. American Museum of Natural History, New York.

The poses assumed by Boas's subjects were often those that he hoped to recreate in New York's Museum of Natural History, whose president had sponsored his expedition.

physical and spiritual decay. The developing relationship between acceptable public appearance and the avid consumption of mass-produced commodities is portrayed in Theodore Dreiser's *Sister Carrie* (1900), a novel whose eponymous heroine is an actor who defines herself in fantasies of material goods, especially as arrayed in a department store.

In the late nineteenth century, photography, the supposed truth-telling medium, was increasingly used in the fabrication of biased social evidence. A much reprinted story in legal journals during the late 1880s told of a lawyer who meets a photographer. The attorney accuses the photography profession of making him lose a case. The photographer replies, "you should get some photographs taken on your side also."[65] In effect, the photograph simultaneously confirmed and denied truth, while emphasizing the appearance of accuracy. The same phenomenon was apparent in the early twenty-first century, when comedian Stephen Colbert famously coined the term "truthiness."

During a 1909 address to the National Child Labor Committee, Lewis Hine spoke directly to the question of photographic truth. He held that the photograph itself was a symbol of reality, not reality. He warned that an "unbounded faith in the integrity of photographs is often rudely shaken," because "while photographs may not lie, liars may photograph."[66]

The problem of appearances took many forms, sometimes highlighting the limits of ordinary human sense perception. Some photographers, such as Alfred Stieglitz, were influenced by the French philosopher Henri Bergson (1859–1941), extracts from whose *Creative Evolution and Laughter* appeared in Stieglitz's journal *Camera Work*. Bergson's concern with the limits of intelligence and the need for intuition to perceive beyond appearances was deliciously vague and readily popularized. It blended with notions of the occult and the fourth dimension, and fostered the belief that the spirit photograph and the X-ray revealed a world not previously perceptible. To art photographers, intuitive insight meant rejecting the appearance of optical reality, and investigating a world of symbols and clues to hidden meanings. In that sense the haze of Pictorialism did not mask reality, but suggested its promise.

In contrast to the static, compartmentalized domain of the archive, Bergson's world was in constant flux. It resembled the experience of the modern, dynamic city, where anonymous people flowed along the streets, an endless current—like the electricity increasingly lighting the metropolis and energizing the factories. While Bergson himself saw camera images as stubbornly mundane, others found just the opposite in scientific photographs of movement, which they argued hinted at a spiritual world.

For artists and scientists, reality proved to be tricky. While studying the indigenous peoples of the northwest coast of Canada and the northeast coast of Siberia, anthropologist Franz Boas (1858–1942) eliminated traces of the contemporary world, photographing people performing traditional tasks in front of backdrops (Fig. 7.35). Performances before the camera were as old as photography itself, but the practice that would eventually be called documentary photography maintained the myth of objective and unaltered observation.

The conundrum was summed up by a commentator for a popular magazine in 1894: "Wherein [photography] presents facts, it is a science. Wherein it presents ideas, it is an art."[67] Science was not without ideas, but it derived its legitimacy from impersonal observation and record-keeping. Art, on the other hand, originated in the personal and intuitive experience, and yielded another, even greater sort of truth. Scientific observation rested on a separation between the observed and the observer that did not acknowledge that photographers tinkered with what was observed, as, for example, Muybridge did when he reordered sequences of photographs, or as Hine did when he deliberately eliminated from his picture "non-essential and conflicting interests."[68] Bergson rejected this sort of editing, in favor of a fluid interchange between the observer and the observed.

At the end of World War I (1918), fiercely explicit photographs of the sufferings of the troops began to circulate. The ultimate shocking collection was *War against War!* (1924), gathered by the German pacifist Ernst Friedrich (1894–1967) and published in German, English, French, and Dutch. The experience of the war led some intellectuals and artists to believe that Western civilization itself had lost its authenticity—that is, a claim to a superior cultural and scientific achievement. This perception followed on the declaration of Sigmund Freud (1856–1939) that human nature harbored an unconscious psychic realm that influenced behavior, but which could not be fully known. Alienation, arising from the experience of war and the psychological fragmentation of self, finally did away with Pictorialism's grander assumptions about making life an art, and brought into question the very concept of representation in the post-World War I era.

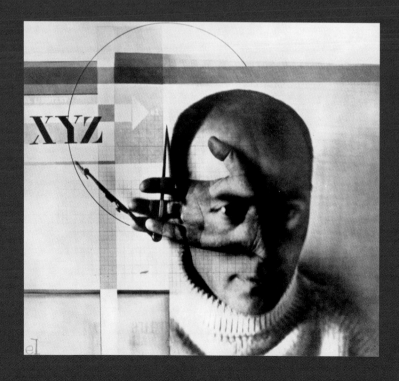

In the 1920s, the industrialization of photography reached a new level, with the expansion of newspapers, general- and special-interest magazines, and professional periodicals, all of which employed photomechanical means of reproducing images. In addition, the automatic photo machine, better known as the photo-booth, was patented in 1928 and first set up in New York City's theater district, where it became immensely popular.

By 1920, there were about ten million registered automobiles in the United States, and automobile production was on the brink of becoming one of the nation's leading industries. In 1900, the United States had one million telephones; by 1920 there were 7.5 million.[1] Widespread electrification made possible radio stations and home radio receivers. Especially in European art movements, photographic realism was associated with the forces that culminated in World War I. The psychological devastation in the wake of the war seemed to clear a path of experimental and non-linear art. Clear subject matter and tidy compositions were critiqued and challenged by abstract images in which flat planes, strange shapes, and irrational shadows perplexed simple understanding. Indeed, experimental art broke out of the sedate gallery and into small but widely circulated avant-garde publications. Advertising for upscale consumer items employed what was called the new vision, to glamorize products.

The sustained world economic and industrial growth of the 1920s ended abruptly in 1929. In the United States, the stock market crash on October 24, 1929, wiped out more than 60 per cent of the value of securities, and set off a chain reaction of bank failures, factory shut-downs, and mortgage foreclosures. Unemployment grew, while foreign trade declined. By the election of 1932, one worker in four was unemployed, at a time when families depended primarily on a single breadwinner, and when relief programs were minimal. Franklin D. Roosevelt (1882–1945) came to the American presidency with a broad series of recovery plans collectively known as the New Deal. Roosevelt was keenly aware of maintaining public faith in his good health; he banned photographs showing him in his wheelchair or wearing the heavy leg braces that he needed as a result of having had polio. The press largely complied. When he fell flat approaching the speaker's platform at the 1936 Democratic Convention, no written reports noted it and no photographs of it appeared in the press.[2]

In the United States, the Depression challenged the notion of America as a land of limitless opportunity for those willing to roll up their sleeves and work. As hard times were gradually perceived as an enduring, not a temporary, experience, many photographers relaxed the stiff graphics of Modernist photography and adapted them to interpretations of how people now lived. The clear close-ups of troubled faces, angled pictures of ragged breadlines, and angry contrasts between poverty and wealth were frequently called documentary photographs.

The outbreak of World War II in Europe and the entry of the United States into the conflict were well recorded by the camera. The work of war photographers was carefully censored, lest they betray troop movements and other kinds of secret information. In response, image-makers took to recording the daily life and war experience of soldiers and civilians.

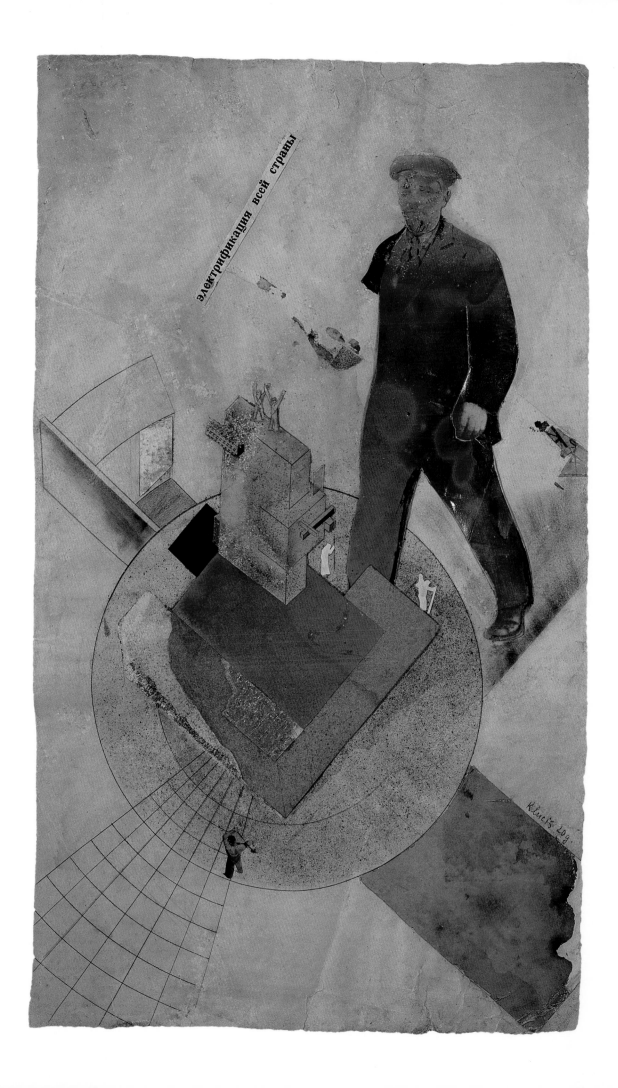

CHAPTER EIGHT

Art and the Age of Mass Media

It is not hard to understand how the DADA movement in Europe drew on artists' reactions to the killing fields of World War I. More puzzling is the postwar zest that propelled extensive experimentation. In a 1921 article, English artist and writer Percy Wyndham Lewis declared that "we are at the beginning of a new epoch, fresh to it, the first babes of a new and certainly better day."[1] The huge gush of experimental photography after the war was propelled by that buoyant, sometimes militant perception that the war's devastation shattered Victorian conventions of artistic conduct and generated a new, modern covenant with the social world. In the post-revolutionary Soviet Union, some artists began to think of themselves as social engineers, reshaping optical experience. In Germany, and in the territories once under its control, the dogma of a new vision propelled multidisciplinary art exploration intended to shake up vestiges of the past while shaping the future. In this heady atmosphere, creators working in film and photography underscored the notion that their media were not only similar to each other but also like the proliferating illustrated newspapers and magazines read by the public. They each spawned a rapidly changing, sometimes confusing, but always exciting jumble of successive images oscillating at the speed of modern life.

PHOTOJOURNALISM

As mass-market illustrated journals proliferated, the word "photojournalism" entered common usage. The inescapable presence of photomechanical illustration influenced many of the artistic movements that took root in Europe. Where the previous generation of artists and photographers had condemned mass-media newspapers as damaging peoples' spirits and impairing their intellects, the next generation saw both their visual excitement and communications potential. Berlin, Germany, with its edgy modern art and culture, became known throughout Europe and Russia for its visual arts experiments. The popular weekly periodical *Berliner Illustrirte* [sic] *Zeitung* (*Illustrated Berlin Newspaper*) (Fig. 8.2), started in 1890, but having been redesigned to carry many photographs, had a circulation of more than two million during the 1920s.[2] *BIZ*, as it was popularly called, pioneered the photo-essay, which was rapidly copied both at home and abroad. Politically aligned

8.1
GUSTAV KLUTSIS, *Electrification of the Entire Country,* **1920. Vintage gelatin silver print. Merrill C. Berman Collection, New York, copy photo by Jim Frank.**

Klutsis used photomontage to advocate the continued modernization of the Soviet Union, symbolized by electricity and the figure of Lenin striding into, and towering over, the future. Designed as a poster, this propaganda image is combined with abstract shapes that resemble Lissitzky's work (see Fig. 8.6).

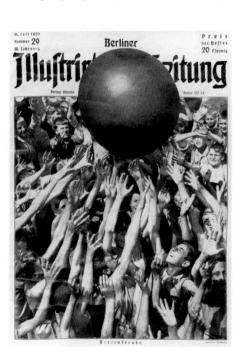

8.2
MARTIN MUNKACSI,
Cover of *Berliner Illustrirte Zeitung,*
July 21, 1929.
Bildarchiv Preussicher Kulturbestitz, Berlin.

illustrated magazines soon appeared, such as the German left-wing *Arbeiter Illustrierte Zeitung* (*Workers' Illustrated Newspaper*; *AIZ*), which was established in 1921 by Willi Münzenberg (1889–1940) specifically to foster liberal and humanitarian causes and to critique capitalism.³ On the political right, the Nazi Party founded the *Illustrierter Beobachter* (*Illustrated Observer*), which became one of its official papers. In France, *Vu* (*Seen*) was launched in 1928 with the aim of communicating liberal ideas to the working class. Many of these new illustrated publications favorably compared themselves to the cinema, with its constantly changing images.

The hardships of postwar Germany and central Europe forced many art photographers to turn to photojournalism for a living, among them Hungarian-born Martin Munkacsi (1896–1963),⁴ who photographed for *BIZ* and other magazines owned by the Berlin firm of Ullstein Verlag, then the world's largest publishing house. A decade later influential mass-circulation picture magazines were still being set up. In the United States, *Life* magazine, founded in 1936, took its cue from European models, both in terms of their style and their use of expert photographers (see Fig. 9.9). Britain's *Picture Post* began in 1938, under the direction of Stefan Lorant (1901–1997), who had previously

made the *Münchner Illustrierte Presse* (*Munich Illustrated Press*) an outstanding picture newspaper.

Between the two world wars, the average person in the industrialized nations saw more photographs than his or her late nineteenth-century counterpart, although these images were not original prints but photomechanical reproductions in newspapers and magazines. Photographic historians Colin Osman and Sandra S. Phillips concluded that "taking 1927 as the departure point of the new thinking in picture journalism, the progress made by 1937 was far greater than in the whole of the previous history of press photography."⁵ While mass-manufactured images, in the form of *cartes-de-visite* and stereographs, had been common in the home in the late nineteenth century, these were chosen by viewers, arranged in personal albums or collections, and could be looked at repeatedly. Newspaper and magazine images, by contrast, were selected by photoeditors or advertising designers, circulated for a short time, then superseded by more images. Photographers had many more outlets for photographs, representing a wide range of political positions. Moreover, the glut of images was producing an increasingly visually sophisticated audience that rapidly came to see printed images as transitory and expendable.

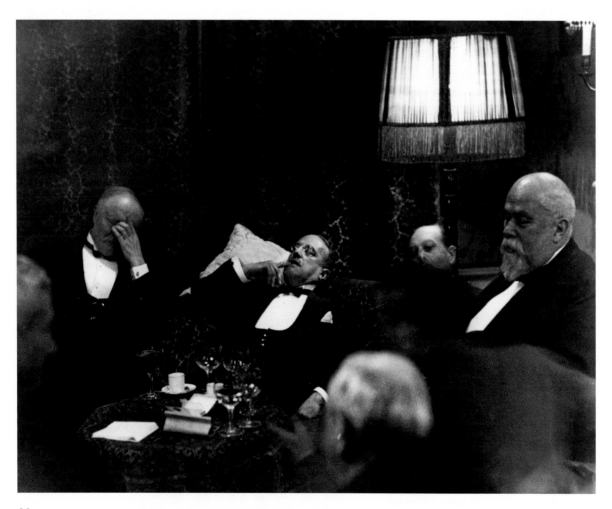

8.3
ERICH SALOMON, *Hague Conference*, January 3–20, 1930. Gelatin silver print. Bildarchiv Preussischer Kulturbesitz, Berlin.

Technological improvements boosted the range of pictures that could be taken. The Leica camera, developed before World War I as a device to test movie film, was introduced to a wider audience in 1924. The Leica and its rival, the Contax camera, used 35mm roll film, whose sensitivity, that is, "fastness," was continually being improved. Also in 1925, magnesium flash power was replaced by the safer flashbulb developed in Germany. Preferring the greater detail rendered by larger negatives, some photographers continued to use big cameras, but there was a universal tendency to mimic the spontaneous look made fashionable by the small-camera users. The public delighted in "candid photography," a phrase first used to describe the work of German photojournalist Erich Salomon (1886–1944), whose social connections gave him access to the corridors of power, where he made photographs that seemed beyond artifice (Fig. 8.3). Salomon's work, published in the *Berliner Illustrirte Zeitung*, implied the importance of the public's right to see behind the scenes of important political events.

The interwar period witnessed the rapid development of journals largely devoted to pictures, especially the TABLOID newspaper, a compact journal featuring eye-catching pictures and far less text than the earlier broadsheet newspapers. Tabloids featured sensational crime and violence pictures, candid celebrity shots, and spectacular disaster photographs— just the thing to pick up while traveling to work on the streetcar, or while downing a quick meal in the factory lunch room. Tabloids told their stories quickly, through large pictures and brief captions.

In London, a women's magazine called the *Daily Mirror* was transformed in 1904 into a picture-driven daily newspaper. In the United States, the *New York Illustrated Daily News*, which became the *New York Daily News*, appeared in June 1919. The original masthead of the *New York Daily News* featured a camera with wings, symbolizing the speed with which photographers pursued their stories. By 1930, its circulation had grown to more than 1.5 million. Typical of the audacious spirit of the *Daily News* was the quest by photographer Tom Howard (c. 1893–1961) for a picture of murderer Ruth Snyder at the moment of her electrocution. The picture ran with the one-word headline: "DEAD!" (Fig. 8.4). Then, as now, there was highbrow opposition to the prevalence of pictures in tabloids. As journalism historian Michael L. Carlebach observed, "abundant use of pictorial material" was understood "as conclusive proof both of declining literary standards and a nefarious plan to exploit hopelessly naive and illiterate people."[6]

Newspapers aimed at middle-class audiences were also lavishly illustrated. ROTOGRAVURE, a printing process that allowed photographs and text to be imaginatively intermingled, was pioneered in *Vu* magazine, and also employed in special lavishly illustrated inserts included with Sunday newspapers. Fashion and high society were all the rage in the section called "the roto," as noted in Irving Berlin's popular song "Easter Parade" (1933), in which a lad boasts to his lady that "On the Avenue/Fifth Avenue/The photographers will snap us/And you'll find that you're/in the rotogravure."

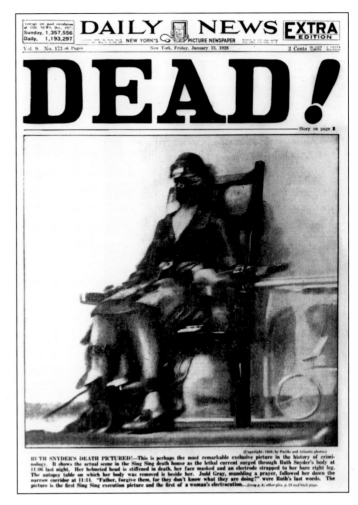

8.4
TOM HOWARD, *Dead!* (Execution of Ruth Snyder), front cover of *Daily News*, January 13, 1928. Daily News, New York.

The *Daily News* encouraged photographers to get images by whatever means possible. The blurry photograph of murderer Ruth Snyder at the moment of her electrocution was taken by their photographer Tom Howard, who strapped a hidden camera to his ankle and raised his leg at the appropriate moment.

Newspapers responded to competition from radio by adding more pictures, in particular, dramatic pictures. Although experiments with wire and radio transmission of photographs began before World War I, in the early 1920s publication still depended on the mails or special couriers to deliver photographs. Consequently, newspapers and magazines turned to "evergreen" features—that is, non-time-linked single-topic photo-series and essays about a person, place, or event. Such features were so popular that they continued even after technology allowed instant transmission of news photographs. Photographs achieved some of radio's immediacy when more reliable, though expensive image-transmission systems became available in the late 1920s. The founding of the Associated Press Wirephoto division in January 1935 marked the start of cheaper transmitting systems and networks, which remained technologically similar until replaced by electronic systems in the 1980s. The you-are-there feeling of radio and photography was jointly captured in May 1937, when the fashionable transatlantic airship the

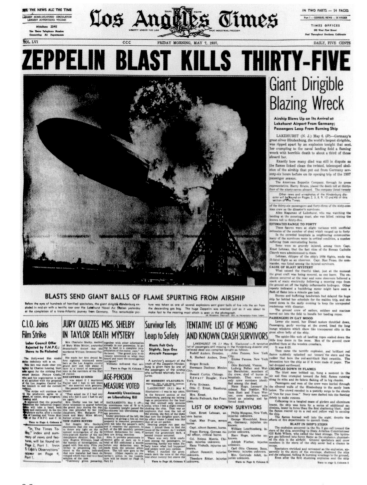

8.5
PHOTOGRAPHER UNKNOWN, *"Zeppelin Blast Kills Thirty-Five,"* from
Los Angeles Times, Friday, May 7, 1937. Newsprint.

Hindenburg crashed and burst into flames in Lakehurst, New Jersey (Fig. 8.5).

During the 1920s, motion pictures evolved from an arcade amusement to a widespread public entertainment. From 1935 on, stylish newsreels, such as *The March of Time*, preceded the featured film. The emergence of a technologically driven popular culture in which a literate, largely urban mass audience could see the same photographs, go to the same films, and hear the same records, affected the way photographers conceived their images. No longer was a photograph from a faraway place thrilling in itself. Kurt Schwitters (1887–1948), a successful advertising designer and avant-garde artist, remarked that "modern man hears and sees such an enormous amount of impressions, that already he is accustomed to unconsciously turn off."[7]

In his 1925 article on "The Magazine as a Sign of the Times," German editor and radio personality Edlef Köppen linked the hectic activity of modern life to the character of the illustrated magazines. "The mark of our age is haste, hurry, nervousness," he wrote. "People have no time, indeed they flee the calm of contemplation." The public, Köppen scolded, wanted the pleasure, variety, and brevity of short acts in a theatrical review.[8] The speed of modern life found its expression in the compression

of meaning in modern media. In his book on the motion pictures, Vachel Lindsay wrote that "American civilization grows more hieroglyphic everyday. The cartoons … the advertisements in the back of the magazines and on the bill-boards and in the street-cars, the acres of photographs in the Sunday newspapers make us into a hieroglyphic civilization … ."[9]

The social significance of mass media was quickly perceived by artists. Hungarian-born painter and sculptor László Moholy-Nagy (1895–1946) asserted the unique qualities of sound recording, film, and photography, which he thought were the best media for representing the modern experience. Similarly, in 1921, Vienna-born German artist Raoul Hausmann (1886–1971) asked, "Why don't we paint works today like those of Botticelli, Michelangelo, Leonardo, or Titian? Because our spirits have utterly changed. And not simply because we have the telephone, the airplane, the electric piano, and the escalator. Rather, because above all these experiences have transformed our entire psycho-physiology."[10]

Hausmann was among the first artist-critics to argue that there may be a threshold in human biological capacity at which the proliferation of mediated experiences provided by photography, film, radio, and sound recording alters the individual's perception of the world. That claim is still contested, especially in relation to television and the Internet. Nevertheless, the readiness with which people in the 1920s both desired and accepted reproductions of events not directly experienced was remarkable. It was in Germany and Russia, countries in which the legacy of war was particularly far-reaching, that the dream of a utopia achieved through technological means found its most animated vision. "The mechanization of our planet," as German architect Hannes Meyer (1889–1954) called it in 1926, offered "palpable proof of the victory of human consciousness over amorphous nature." For him, the speed of planes and automobiles broke the bounds of place and tradition. The speed of life made us live faster, and therefore longer. It made us see that things could change: "We learn Esperanto," Meyer wrote; "we become citizens of the world."[11]

REVOLUTIONARY ART: THE SOVIET PHOTOGRAPH

In Russia, the Revolution of 1917 (see p. 226), which placed revolutionary socialists in power, had a deep impact on artists, particularly the avant-garde. Even before the overthrow of the czar, abstraction had already become a symbol for a future untainted by the past. After the Revolution, artists experimenting with Cubism and Futurism responded to the Communist Party's buoyant utopianism, expressed in *The ABC of Communism* (1919), which proclaimed that "within a few decades there will be quite a new world, with new people and new customs."[12] El Lissitzky (1890–1941), an architect who worked in many media, including photography, was one of the most politically committed artists. He renounced self-expression in art, along with easel painting, which he associated with a corrupt past and stagnant aesthetics. With others, Lissitzky insisted that the artist's role was now linked to industry and to reshaping everyday life. In avant-garde circles, the terms "production art" and "production artist" began being used, to indicate that the artist would employ technology in order to mold a new society. Photography was favored precisely because it was the product of a machine that could be mass produced by other machines.

Lissitzky's *The Constructor* (1924) (Fig. 8.6) shows the artist in his new role as builder or engineer. It features the austere geometric overlays frequently used by Russian avant-garde image-makers, who favored non-realistic, intersecting planes that flattened Renaissance perspective and thereby condemned the older art of morally bankrupt elites. In Lissitzky's image, the artist's hand fingers a compass, which seems to have drawn a perfect circle around his head. The circle forms a halo, as in a Russian religious painting.[13] The "sainted" new Soviet artist worked with geometric shapes and signs, as well as printers' type, which emerged as primary elements in Soviet poster design and magazine illustrations. Lissitzky also designed trade exhibitions, demonstrating Soviet industrial progress. In these installations, he transformed the shape of the room by having images and text bulge out from the wall or droop from the ceiling.

Many Soviet artists were also writers and theorists addressing national and international audiences. Latvian-born Gustav Klutsis (1895–1944) realized that it was imperative "to construct iconic representations for a new mass audience."[14] He used photomontage (see pp. 239–47), assembling images and text from a variety of mass-media sources, such as newspapers and magazines. The result overturned the expectations of everyday experience and of realistic painting with arresting

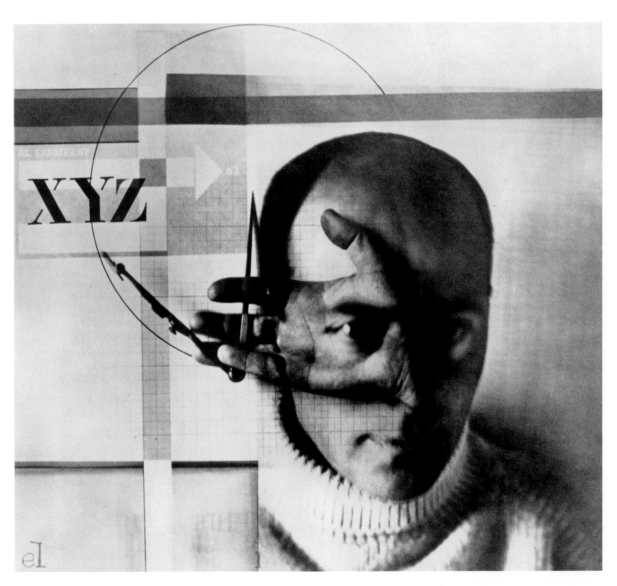

8.6
EL LISSITZKY, *The Constructor*, 1924. Photomontage. Getty Research Institute, Los Angeles, California.

Borrowing from two Russian art movements, Suprematism and Constructivism, both of which favored abstract geometric shapes in unshaded colors, Lissitzky superimposed an image of himself on a piece of graph paper, and layered on top a picture of his hand, uniting hand and eye in a symbol of ideal labor. Superimposing one image on another recalled the experiments of Cubism.

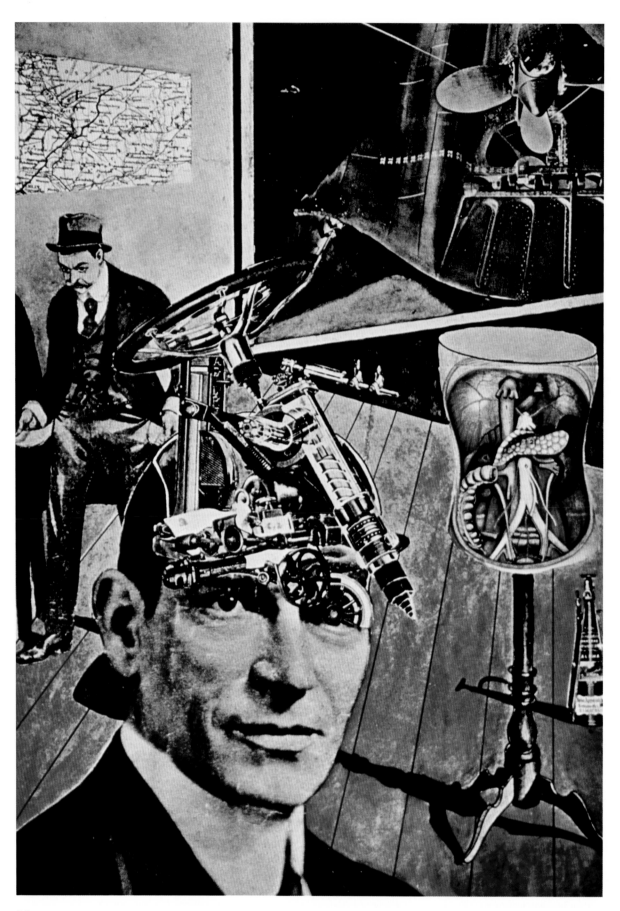

8.7
RAOUL HAUSMANN, *Tatlin at Home*, 1920. Collage (destroyed). Statens Konstmuseet, Moderna Museet, Stockholm.

image collisions. Klutsis, however, insisted that his images should be understood by the illiterate as well as the educated. In *Electrification of the Entire Country* (1920) (Fig. 8.1), a giant-size Soviet leader, Vladimir Lenin (1870–1924), strides forward confidently into the future as workers on the Modernist building's roof-top cheer him on.

The prospect of a revolutionary art was eagerly taken up by Aleksandr Rodchenko (1891–1956), a Russian painter and sculptor who had absorbed the geometric abstractions of CUBISM and who valued the process of collage, pioneered by the Cubists in the decade before World War I. As his political activity increased in the new arts organizations initiated by the Soviet government in its early years, Rodchenko investigated the role art might play in society. He resolved to make art less theoretical and more practical. With other artists, he went to factories to learn design needs first hand, and he conceived posters, fabrics, and furniture. Rodchenko wholeheartedly accepted photography because he felt it freed artists from inherited aesthetic ideas, especially perspective and the other techniques used to render the world as it is, rather than as it might be. He promoted the notion that new concepts could not be expressed in old media, and was a leading proponent

of *faktura*, the idea prominent in Soviet art theory that an artist should discover a medium's distinctive capabilities by experimenting with its inherent qualities.

Looking at the work of photographers who traveled to foreign countries, Rodchenko scoffed, "They photograph with museum eyes, the eyes of art history."[15] Rodchenko's hope for new media such as film and photography was enhanced by looking at German art and fashion magazines, such as *Die Dame* (*Woman*), *Junge Welt* (*Young World*), and *Moderne Illustrierte Zeitschrift* (*Modern Illustrated Journal*), which featured experimental German photography. In turn, Rodchenko's work appeared in the Russian magazine *LEF* (*Left Front of the Arts*), a left-wing arts magazine founded by poet Vladimir Maiakovskii (1893–1930). In 1923, Rodchenko gathered images from the picture press, and also commissioned a series of photographs from another photographer. He joined these images to make PHOTOMONTAGE illustrations for Maiakovskii's poem "Pro Ito" ("About This") (Fig. 8.8). These images are visually arresting, but it is hard to see how uninitiated viewers could have interpreted their symbolic meanings.

The post-revolutionary Russian avant-garde advocated making images in such a way as to obstruct habits of seeing.

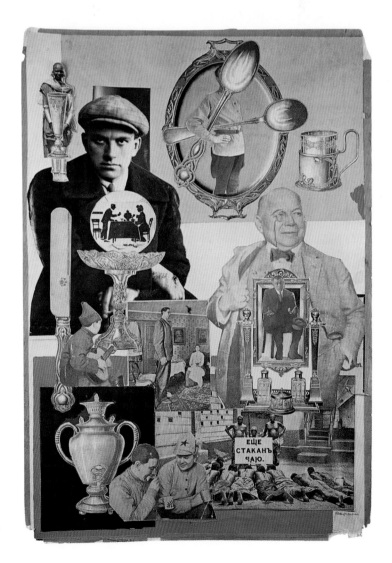

8.8
ALEKSANDR RODCHENKO, *Untitled*, **1923, to accompany Maiakovskii's poem "Pro Ito" ("About This"). Photomontage. Rodchenko Archives, Moscow.**

Rodchenko's photomontages for Maiakovskii's poem use the class of incongruous objects to evoke the poet's seething anxiety about the absence of his lover.

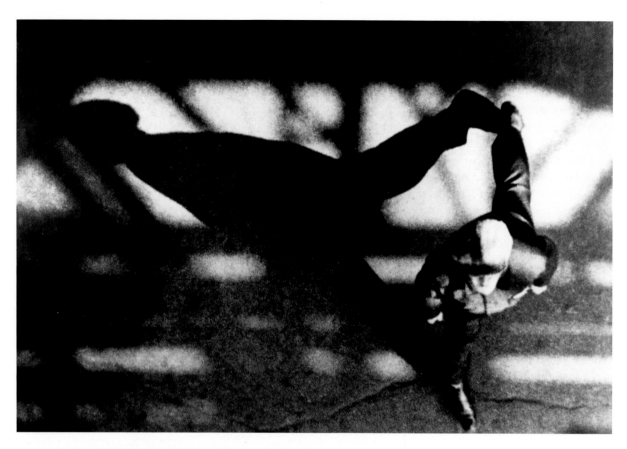

8.9
ALEKSANDR RODCHENKO, *Untitled* (Walking figure), 1928. Gelatin silver print. Rodchenko Archives, Moscow.

Odd camera angles, unrecognizable close-ups, multiple exposures, and confused perspective all served to "make strange" the expected appearance of the world.[16] In the mid-1920s, Rodchenko learned to make his own photographs and moved from photomontage to straight photography (Fig. 8.9). Nevertheless, he continued to disparage "belly button" camerawork—that is, the conventional, balanced picture taken with a camera held near the waistline while the photographer peered into the viewing screen.

In the years immediately after the Revolution, the Soviet government courted experimental artists in its search for innovative methods of mass communication. But by the early 1930s, the romance turned sour. Official policy shifted from avant-garde art—seen as intellectual, bourgeois, and thus part of the capitalist system—and instead promoted Socialist Realism, that is, a conventionally realistic style used as a vehicle for rousing propaganda messages that could be universally understood by the workers.

As the avant-garde was losing official sanction, Rodchenko began the huge official task of photographing the construction of the White Sea Canal, or Stalin Canal (1931–33). Using a less startlingly inventive approach than in his earlier work, he produced about three thousand photographs, some of which were published in a special 1933 edition of *USSR in Construction*, a magazine intended to show Soviet progress, especially to audiences abroad. Tellingly, Rodchenko did not focus on the

use of forced labor, or the deaths of thousands of workers at the site—subjects forbidden by the propaganda controls enforced in the Soviet Union under Stalin's leadership in the 1930s.

DADA AND AFTER

During World War I, a group of writers, artists, and poets met at the Cabaret Voltaire in Zurich, Switzerland, a cultural outpost in a politically neutral country. The group strongly objected to the war and to the bankrupt materialism of the age. They envisioned a new art that expressed their despair, but that would also sweep away tiresome conventions and intellectual barriers. The Romanian-born artist Tristan Tzara (1896–1963), who wrote the *Dada Manifesto* of 1918, saw the task to be done as "a great negative work of destruction."[17] The origins of the name "Dada" seem to owe to a moment when two enthusiasts thrust a paper knife into a French–German dictionary, and it pointed to the word "dada," or hobby horse. The nonsensical-sounding word may have been chosen because it has different meanings in several European languages, such as "yes, yes" in Romanian and "there, there" in German. Through the visual arts and performances, Dada accentuated the disruptiveness of chance collisions of images and sounds.

Christian Schad (1894–1982), a German artist associated with the Zurich Dada group, was influenced by the French artist and

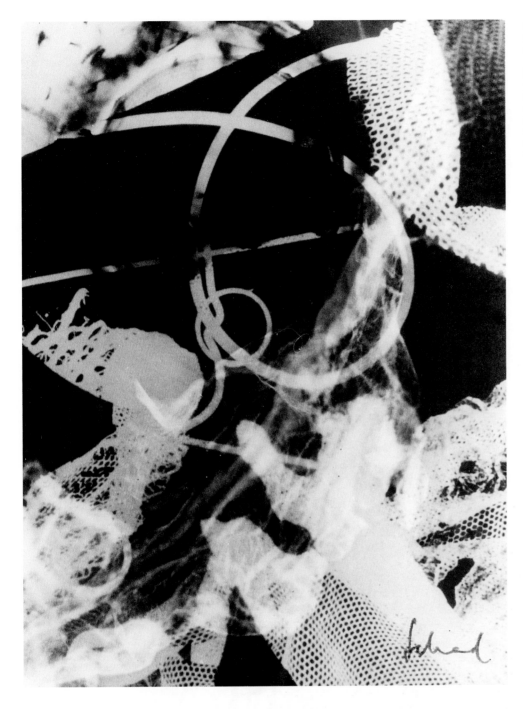

8.10
CHRISTIAN SCHAD, *Schadograph 24b*,
c. 1920. Gelatin silver print.

Schad placed pieces of randomly collected
paper and objects atop photographically
sensitive paper, pressing them down with a
sheet of clear glass. As the assemblage was
exposed to light on a windowsill, Schad
observed its development and occasionally
moved objects around as they were appearing
on the paper.

poet Jean (or Hans) Arp (1887–1966), who emphasized the need
to be unconstrained by traditional notions of composition, and
who made low-relief sculptural collages of found objects. Schad,
too, created small collages of newspaper clippings and odd bits of
paper, and used a similar method to make abstract photographs
(Fig. 8.10). Several of Schad's abstract photographs were acquired
by Tzara, who dubbed them "schadographs." This sounds like
"shadowgraph," a process used by such early photographers
as Talbot (see p. 19). Tzara may have been aware of this, but
was perhaps also alluding to the meaning of the German word
schaden, which means "damaged," evoking the Dada sense of
things falling apart.

Another group of Dada artists met in Berlin as Germany was
disintegrating toward the end of the war. More political than the
Zurich Dadaists, they wanted to make social statements. In the
words of one their leaders, Richard Hülsenbeck (1892–1974),
"the highest art will be that which in its conscious content
presents the thousandfold problems of the day, the art which has
been visibly shattered by the explosions of last week, which is
forever trying to collect its limbs after yesterday's crash."[18] Berlin
Dadaists adopted photomontage as a key medium. Often the
initial *Klebebild* or "paste picture" was photographed, producing
a more finished look, and preparing the image for reproduction
in one of the many avant-garde magazines.

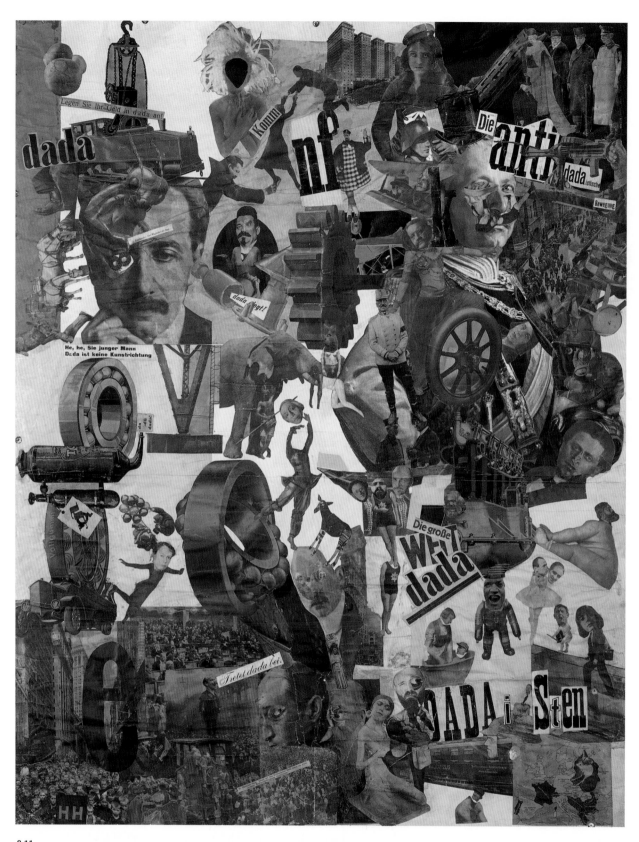

8.11
HANNAH HÖCH, *Schnitt mit dem Küchenmesser Dada durch die letzte weimarer Bierbauchkulturepoche Deutschlands (Cut with the Kitchen Knife Dada through the last Weimar Beer Belly Cultural Epoch of Germany),* **1919. Photomontage. Nationalgalerie Staatliche Museen, Preussischer Kulturbesitz, Berlin.**

In the center a popular dancer of the time pirouettes beneath the head of the artist Käthe Kollwitz. The head has been speared by a man in front of an elephant. The dancer's right foot rests on a giant ball-bearing. Beneath that is a young revolutionary sailor who is saying "Tretet Dada bei" ("Join Dada"). The word "Dada" is also scattered throughout the work.

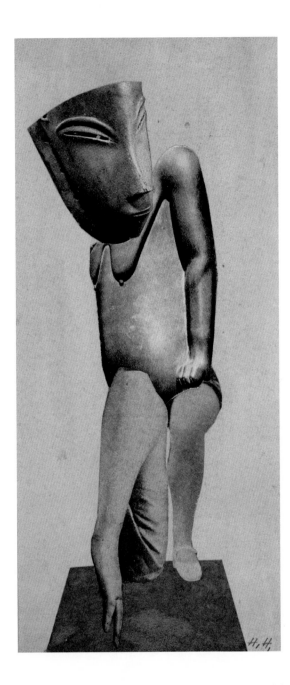

8.12
HANNAH HÖCH, *Denkmal I: Aus einem ethnographischen Museum* (*Monument 1: From an Ethnographic Museum*), 1924. Collage, photomontage. Berlinische Galerie, Landesmuseum für Moderne Kunst, Photographie und Architektur, Berlin.

change. Nevertheless, some parts of *Cut with the Kitchen Knife* can be decoded (they are described in the caption).

Like American photographer Frances Benjamin Johnston, Höch engaged the theme of the New Woman.[20] She juxtaposed images of smartly dressed contemporary women with women in traditional social roles and with such symbols of modernity as automobiles, machinery, and electric light bulbs. While she criticized contemporary politics and society's hypocrisy toward women as both workers and sexual objects, the jazzy exuberance of her compositions reveals optimism for avant-garde art and the joy of artmaking. During the 1930s, Höch collaged pictures of objects in German ethnographic collections with symbols of Modernism, so as to contrast Western materialism and non-Western traditional practices. Her photomontage series *From an Ethnographic Museum* produced unsettling effects by juxtaposing snippets of male and female body parts and non-Western sculpture (Fig. 8.12).

Höch's lover for seven years, Raoul Hausmann, was one of the few communists to insist on women's equality in any new society. More subtle than his copious political writing, Hausmann's photomontage images included his contribution to the 1920 Dada Fair, *Tatlin at Home* (Fig. 8.7). This photomontage was more an exercise in freewheeling mental associations and concern for artistic form than a penetrating portrait or social critique. For example, Hausmann explained that he added machinery, including an automobile steering wheel, to the main figure's head because he was interested in portraying a man who had machines for brains. The man with his pockets turned inside out was included because Hausmann fancied that Tatlin could not be rich. Like many photomontagists, Hausmann painted parts of the picture, such as the background.[21]

Another Berlin Dadaist, George Grosz (1893–1959), one of the most politically active artists to emerge from the Berlin Dada group, was also a pioneer of photomontage. Grosz's photomontages have a plainly discernible message, expressed in an apparently spontaneous accumulation of images and texts (see Fig. 8.13).

MOHOLY-NAGY AND THE BAUHAUS

László Moholy-Nagy arrived in Berlin just before the 1920 Dada Fair. He soon met Höch, Hausmann, and other members of the Berlin Dada group. Like them, Moholy-Nagy favored the use of industrial materials and concepts, and he adopted the Soviet artists' notion of *faktura*, which he understood to mean that a new vision could be created only when photography was practiced for its own inherent qualities, not as an imitation of painting. While the Dadaists were politically active, many joining the Communist Party, Moholy-Nagy concentrated instead on technology and its relation to art. He insisted that "the first and foremost issue" for photography was to determine "a more or less exact photographic language," independent of the past.[22]

The origins of the photomontage have long been debated, but it seems that Hannah Höch (1889–1978) and Hausmann were two of the earliest Dadaists to make such images. Höch's large photomontage *Schnitt mit dem Küchenmesser Dada durch die letzte weimarer Bierbauchkulturepoche Deutschlands* (*Cut with the Kitchen Knife Dada through the last Weimar Beer Belly Cultural Epoch of Germany*) (1919) made its appearance at the First International Dada Fair in Berlin (1920) (Fig. 8.11). As art historian Maud Lavin observed, the diversity of mass-media sources in Höch's picture testifies to the vast proliferation of newspapers and journals in the years following World War I, and the growing perception that mass-media images were forming a common visual culture.[19] Even though the individual images in early photomontage were generally easy to read, their combination yielded pictures whose meaning was difficult to decipher. In effect, photomontage itself was the message of

focus

Photomontage or Photocollage

Narrowly speaking, photocollage began with the cut-and-paste work of album-makers such as Lady Filmer and the combination printing of photographers such as Oscar Rejlander. But the anti-establishment photographic experiments that originated in both Soviet and German experimental photography had different social roots and dissimilar social aims from these Victorian forebears.

Photomontage originated in Germany, but was adopted in Russia soon after World War I, through artists' visits and through magazines. The avant-garde Dada movement, initiated by artists who took refuge in Switzerland during the war, spread to Berlin, and from there to Moscow. Experimental artists cut pictures from magazines and newspapers and pasted them together in composite images whose jumbled scale and perspective challenged conventional expectations (Fig. 8.13). These collages (from the French word for "glue") were sometimes photographed so that the unique first image could be printed in multiple versions. Soviet experimental artists called such images not photocollages but photomontages. The word "montage" has various sources. In silent film, for example, it specified the

rapid succession of images that indicated a change of place or the transition of ideas. The Berlin Dadaist Hausmann wrote that the group agreed on the term "photomontage" because of "our aversion at playing the artist and, thinking of ourselves as engineers (hence our preference for working-men's overalls) we meant to construct, to assemble [*montieren*] our works."[23] Experimental artists used the word "photomontage" almost exclusively after World War I. Although a photomontage may resemble a Cubist painting, on to which such materials as tickets and menus have been pasted, experimental artists in Germany and Russia aimed to use such materials in a different way. The jumbled appearance of photomontage was more than formal inventiveness; it was a token of the quick changes and disruptions of modern life that seemed, in the period immediately after World War I and the Russian Revolution, to promise progressive social change.

8.13
GEORGE GROSZ AND JOHN HEARTFIELD, *Leben und Treiben in Universal City um 12 Uhr 5 Mittages (Life and Activity in the Universal City at Five Past Twelve),* 1919. Akademie der Künste, Berlin.

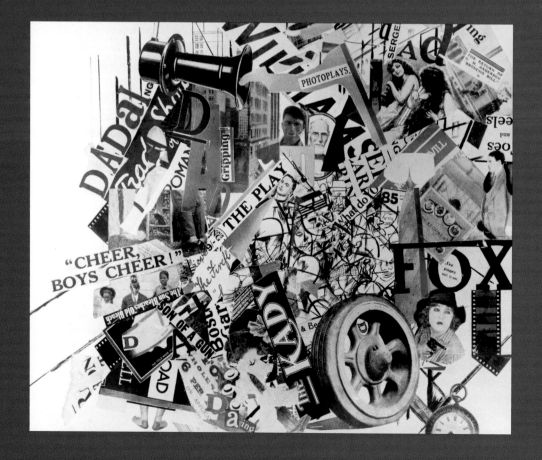

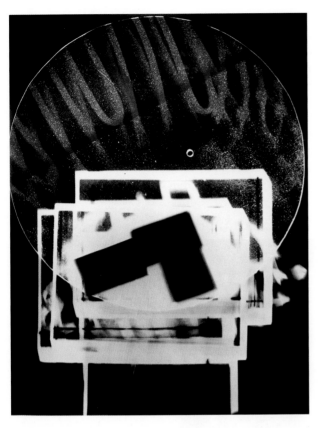

8.14
LÁSZLÓ MOHOLY-NAGY AND LUCIA MOHOLY, *Photogram*, 1924.
Gelatin silver print. Museum Ludwig, Cologne, Germany.

His social concern was expressed in his theory that mass production, especially the wide circulation of images, made it possible for an artist to change perceptions of the world, thereby creating a desire for social revolution.

Moholy-Nagy claimed that photography's chief characteristic was light, and that artists should experiment with patterns of light and shade. "This century belongs to light," he argued, and "photography is the first means of giving tangible shape to light, though in a transposed and … almost abstract form."[24] "Today," he wrote, "everything is concentrated, more powerfully than ever before, on the visual." Moholy-Nagy looked to science to research the physiological and psychological basis for visual presentations, which would be as effective as written language. He announced that "the illiteracy of the future will be ignorance of photography."[25]

Like Rodchenko, Moholy-Nagy proposed that photographers should radically change the angle of camera vision. He advocated such devices as distorting mirrors that would alter normal views, and he anticipated the invention of new sorts of cameras that would allow the operator to play with perspective. He also envisaged photographers adapting microscopes, telescopes, and X-ray equipment to their repertoire of image-making. Among his proposals was the making of cameraless photographs, which he called PHOTOGRAMS (Fig. 8.14).

In 1923, Moholy-Nagy was invited to join the faculty of the Bauhaus, the German art school established by architect Walter Gropius (1883–1969), whose goal was to integrate the arts with industry. Moholy-Nagy already had an international reputation for his abstract paintings and sculptures, some of which used industrial materials and processes, such as porcelain enamel on steel; he was an energetic member of a faculty that would later include artists Wassily Kandinsky (1866–1944) and Paul Klee (1879–1940). The Bauhaus curriculum did not include classes in photography until soon before it was closed by the Nazis in 1933, but Moholy-Nagy's ideas were influential. In addition, his 1925 book *Malerei, Photographie, Film* (*Painting, Photography, Film*), published by the Bauhaus, became an international reference for the new photography.

The upbeat mood of experimental photography was captured in the title of an article by Bauhaus artist Johannes Molzahn (1892–1965), "Stop Reading! Look!" ("Nicht mehr lesen! Sehen!"). Molzahn was convinced that formal education should adapt to the increasingly visually portrayed world rendered in mass-media newspapers and magazines. He offered "Stop Reading! Look!" as the guiding motto for teaching and learning.[26] Also at the Bauhaus was Austrian-born designer and photographer Herbert Bayer (1900–1985), whose design for the first cover of the institution's publication, *Bauhaus*, was a photomontage (Fig. 8.15). Bayer's post-Bauhaus career included

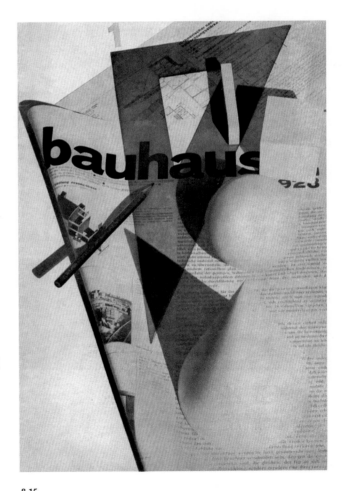

8.15
HERBERT BAYER, Cover of *Bauhaus* 1, 1928. From a photomontage.
Bauhaus-Archiv, Berlin.

the design of an infamous Nazi brochure, which demonstrated the extent to which photomontage was not a technique intrinsically wedded to progressive politics, but a style whose aesthetic features could serve any political persuasion (see Fig. 8.47).

Born in East Prussia, a section of Germany that became part of Poland after World War I, photographer Germaine Krull (1897–1985) typified the international contacts and movements of artists after the war. She studied photography in Munich, absorbed the techniques promoted by Moholy-Nagy, and grasped the swift interplay of images advocated by Russian filmmaker and writer Sergei Eisenstein (1898–1948). She and her companion (later husband), Dutch activist and filmmaker Joris Ivens (1898–1989), lived in Paris. Like the French painter Fernand Léger (1881–1955), she celebrated industrialization as a marvelous marriage of the human body and the machine. Her 1928 collection of images, *Métal*, was advertised as "the dance of the metal nudes."[27] The portfolio's cover showed a disconcerting view of the elevator wheels that lifted people to the top of the Eiffel Tower in Paris (Fig. 8.16). Krull's sixty-four unbound prints of French and Dutch industrial sites in *Métal* were uncaptioned, and sequenced so as to jump from soothing conventional views

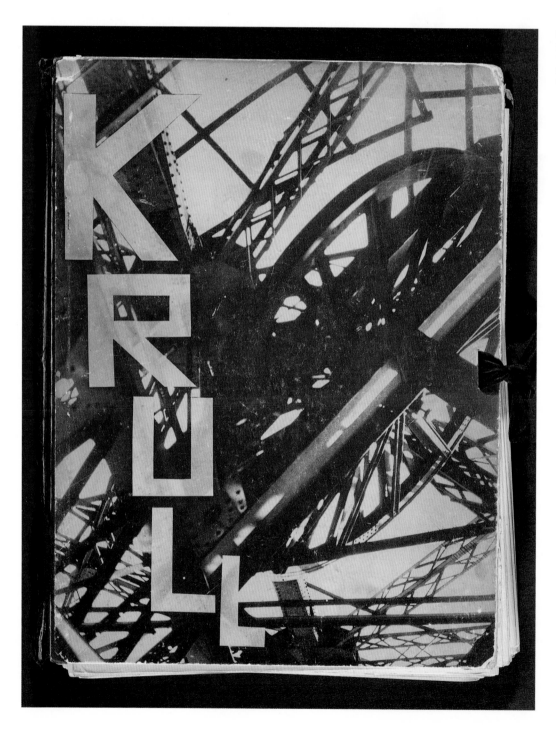

8.16
GERMAINE KRULL, Cover of *Métal*, 1928. Collotype. Museum Folkwang Fotografische Sammlung, Essen, Germany.

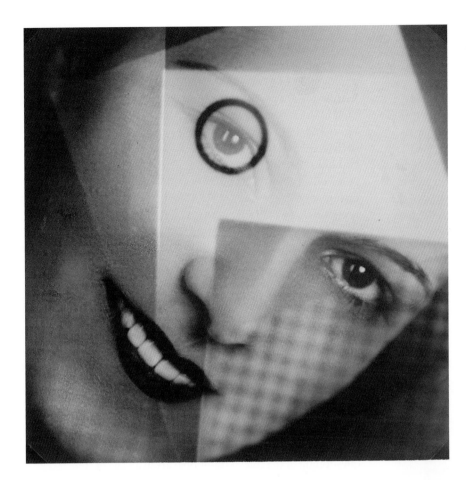

8.17
JAROSLAV RÖSSLER, *Untitled*, 1931. Museum of Decorative Arts, Prague, Czech Republic.

Endlessly experimental, Rössler extended his art to advertising and to commercial work.

to slippery superimpositions. Because of her dizzying dynamic angles and other techniques, many of the actual locations were unrecognizable, and had to be taken as symbols of modern life rather than depictions.

PARIS—BERLIN—PRAGUE

Although the experimental art and thought of Russia and Germany quickly reverberated throughout Europe and North America, they did not extinguish the international influence of French Cubism. For example, Germaine Krull seems to have intermingled these strands. Despite its closeness to Berlin, artists in the newly minted, post-World War I republic of Czechoslovakia also embraced French and German concepts. Jaroslav Rössler (1902–1990), a Czech artist and photographer whose work included portraiture and advertising, explored Cubist angles and layers in his photomontages (Fig. 8.17). The abstract photographs produced by Jaromír Funke (1896–1945) do not simply respond to a panoply of influences; more precisely they exemplify a ready openness to the modern spirit of experimentation. To create *Abstract Photo*, Funke gathered an assortment of materials at hand in the darkroom, such as glass negatives and mat board. He arranged them to create a puzzling space of shade and shape (Fig. 8.18). Interestingly, both Rössler and Funke slightly blurred their images, not as a tribute to Pictorialism, but to detach the images from the experience of ordinary reality.

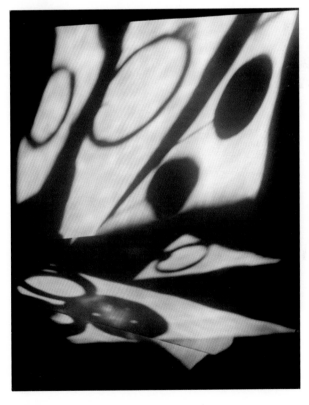

8.18
JAROMÍR FUNKE, *Abstract Photo*, 1928–29. Moravian Gallery in Brno, Czech Republic.

DADA AND PARIS

In Paris, Dadaists turned away from the Berlin group's political activism in order to take up a wider cultural criticism. It was in Paris that Marcel Duchamp drew a mustache on a photographic reproduction of the *Mona Lisa* by Leonardo da Vinci (1452–1519), and relabeled it with a title that sounded lewd when read aloud in French (Fig. 8.19). Before he came to Paris and met with the Dadaists, German painter Max Ernst (1891–1976) was already making psychologically disorienting photographic collages and creating disquieting effects on canvas and paper using such techniques as frottage (rubbing a surface so that the texture of an object beneath it shows through). Eerie enigmas pervaded his work (Fig. 8.20). Ernst had little respect for the Berlin Dada's political orientation: "German intellectuals can't even shit or piss without ideology," he snarled.[28]

André Breton (1896–1966), one of the leaders of Paris Dada, praised Ernst and lauded his photography, relating it to the Dada practice of automatic writing. This entailed writing or speaking a haphazard sequence of words to evade the censorship of the rational mind: "Automatic writing," Breton wrote, "is a true photography of thought."[29] Breton's curiosity about psychic states led him toward psychology, especially the theories of Sigmund Freud, which suggested that human behavior is motivated by forces and desires hidden deep within the human psyche, which individuals and society are generally reluctant to acknowledge. Around 1924, Breton rejected the anarchism of Dada, which relied on an ability (difficult to sustain indefinitely) to shock, disturb, or outrage viewers. He sought a more constructive program that would still be based on the power of the unconscious and irrational mind. This led to the founding of the Surrealist movement, of which Breton became one of the major theorists.

DADA AND THE MACHINE AGE IN NEW YORK

In the United States, meanwhile, Dada had had a further manifestation, spurred by contact between exiled European artists and their American counterparts. Man Ray (1890–1976), the American artist born Emmanuel Radnitzky, maintained that there was no such thing as New York Dada,[30] and indeed conditions there were markedly different from those in Europe. Involved in World War I in only the final stages, the United States also did not endure years of conflict on its own soil, and was therefore spared the disillusioned anguish that led to the questioning of the role of traditional art in an age of trench warfare. Moreover, Americans did not identify non-objective, or abstract, art with political revolt and social change to the degree that many European experimenters did. New Yorkers responded to the visually provocative 1913 Armory Show, the first large-scale exhibition of modern art from Europe and the United States, as a display of art, not as progressive social propaganda. Through the influence of Duchamp and Picabia, both of whom arrived in New York from Europe during 1915 for extended stays, a spirited group of artists came together around the notion that the machine and industrial society formed the fountainhead of a new cultural expression. Duchamp found workspace in the New York home of Walter and Louise Arensberg, wealthy collectors whose residence emerged as the gathering-place for artists including Man Ray, Morton Schamberg (1881–1918), and Charles Sheeler (1883–1965).

The first and only issue of the magazine *New York Dada* appeared in 1921 with a photograph of Duchamp disguised as his female *alter ego* Rrose Sélavy, which had been affixed to a recycled perfume bottle (see Fig. 8.37). The issue also carried an experimental photograph by Alfred Stieglitz, whose circle of friends overlapped with those in the Arensberg salon. Stieglitz permitted Picabia and others to use his 291 gallery on Fifth Avenue as the title of a magazine inspired mostly by European Dada experimentation. Despite its liveliness, the New York Dada movement had little enduring impact on photography in the United States.[31]

Schamberg and Sheeler were painters who initially took up photography to make a living, and gradually gained attention

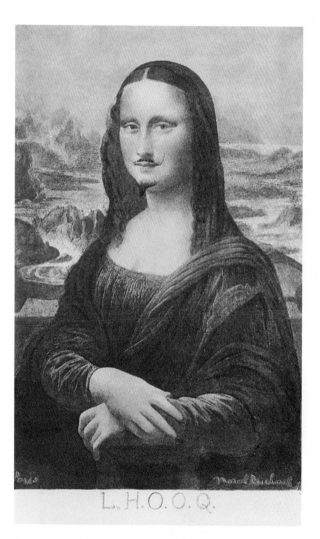

8.19
MARCEL DUCHAMP, *L.H.O.O.Q.*, 1919. Color reproduction of *Mona Lisa* altered with a pencil. Private collection.

Duchamp's comical addition to a postcard of Leonardo da Vinci's *Mona Lisa,* and his bawdy retitling of the image, expressed his attitude toward unthinking acceptance of tradition.

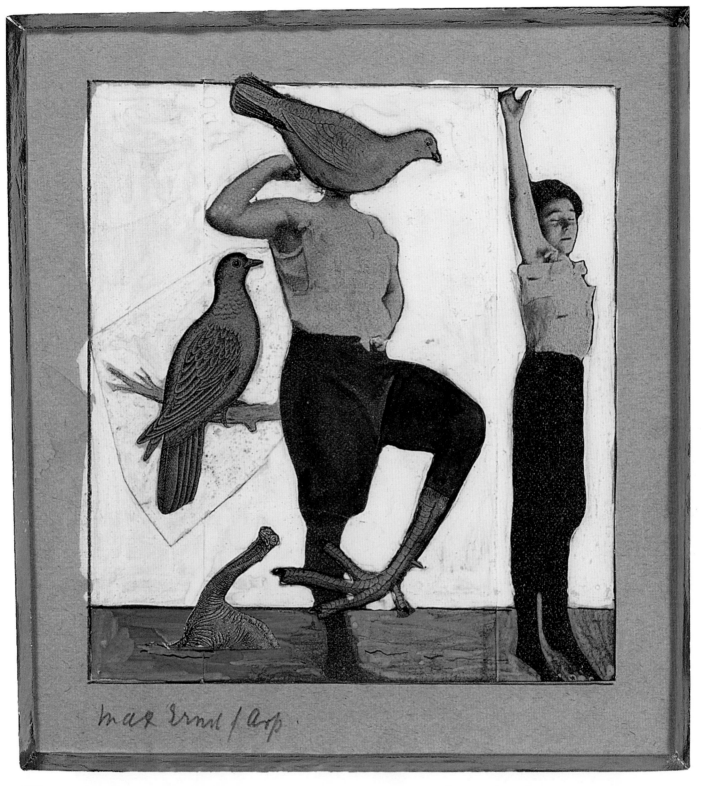

8.20
MAX ERNST AND HANS ARP, *Physiomythological Diluvian Picture*, 1920. Collage with fragments of a photograph, gouache, pencil, pen and ink on paper laid on card. Sprengel Museum, Hanover, Germany.

Combining the optical realism of a photograph (the woman's head) with media suggestive either of flatness or perspective allowed Ernst and Arp to create an image full of puzzling contradictions.

for their camerawork. In both his painting and photography, Schamberg moved toward the sharp, flat delineation of geometric forms that was later to influence the group of American abstract realists known as the Precisionists (Fig. 8.21). Sheeler, a founder of Precisionism who specialized in art and architectural photography, made several photographs of Duchamp's *Nude Descending a Staircase* (1912; Fig. 7.15). The term PRECISIONISM has been used to describe paintings depicting specifically American building types, such as skyscrapers and barns, in a near-abstract manner that stresses geometric form. Although

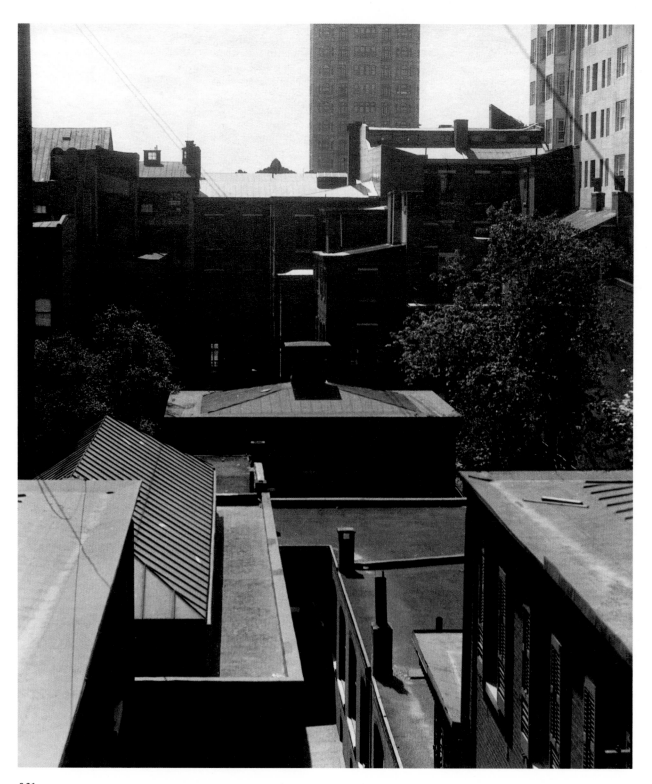

8.21
MORTON SCHAMBERG, *Untitled* **(Cityscape), 1917. Vintage gelatin silver print. The Nelson-Atkins Museum of Art, Gift of Hallmark Cards, Inc., Kansas, Missouri.**

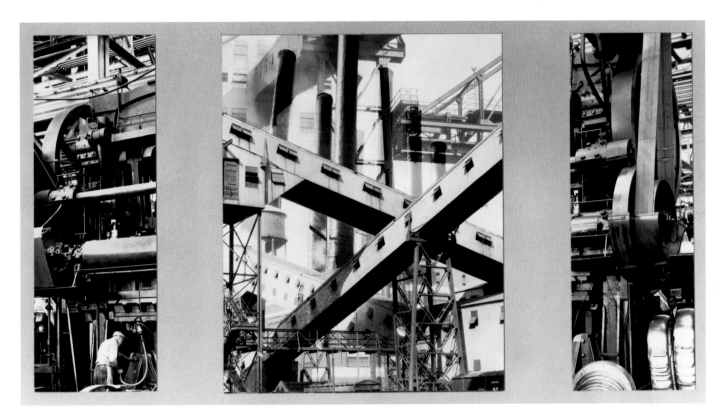

8.22
CHARLES SHEELER, *Industry*, 1932. Gelatin silver prints (triptych). Art Institute of Chicago, Chicago, Illinois.

Sheeler did much the same thing in his photographs, they are not routinely called Precisionist. With Paul Strand, Sheeler worked on the 1920 experimental film *Manhatta*, which celebrated the city as a wellspring of progressive modern life, from its newly erected skyscrapers to its smoke-belching chimneys. Geometrically lean and striking shots of the city were interspersed with high-spirited quotations from American poet Walt Whitman (1819–1892). Reflecting on the experience, Strand remarked that "both of us were well along the road of abstract organization of reality."[32]

Sheeler supported his art by working in advertising, producing promotional pictures for spark plugs, tires, and typewriters. In 1927 he received a commission to photograph the Ford Motor Company's plant near Detroit on the Rouge River.[33] Sheeler put few workers in his shots, for fear that viewers would concentrate on them rather than the plant's machinery; and he overlooked contemporary labor issues by attending to the massive mechanical elements that took raw materials and converted them into automobiles. His large three-part mural *Industry*, now generally known only through its much smaller study, centers on the criss-crossed conveyors that carried coal and coke (Fig. 8.22). On either side of the central panel, Sheeler placed photographs of gigantic stamping presses. The buildings at the Rouge River plant thrilled Sheeler, as much as the French Gothic cathedrals whose dynamic architecture he later photographed. For him, industrial architecture marked a stupendous movement in human progress. "Our factories are

our substitute for religious expression," he proclaimed.[34] Many of Sheeler's canvases take up the same subjects as his photographs, profiting from the simplification of tones and generalization of forms that he learned through the use of the camera.

SURREALIST PHOTOGRAPHY

The Surrealist movement was born in Paris in the mid-1920s. Unlike Dada, which always remained individualistic, Surrealism was a self-proclaimed movement. André Breton's *Surrealist Manifesto*, published on October 15, 1924, announced the primacy of the irrational and the belief in a truth beyond realism. Surrealism was deeply indebted to Freud's theory of the unconscious and the methods he proposed for revealing a person's unconscious desires, notably dream analysis and free-association sequences of words and ideas. Rather than emphasizing social change on the state level, the Surrealists advocated the transformation of human perception and experience through greater contact with the inner world of imagination.

Photography was central to Surrealist practice. In theory, at least, making photographs could be the visual equivalent of free association and other methods of side-stepping the monitoring rational mind. Some Surrealists pointed their cameras haphazardly, recording whatever happened to be in front of the lens. Other efforts were more purposeful, such as

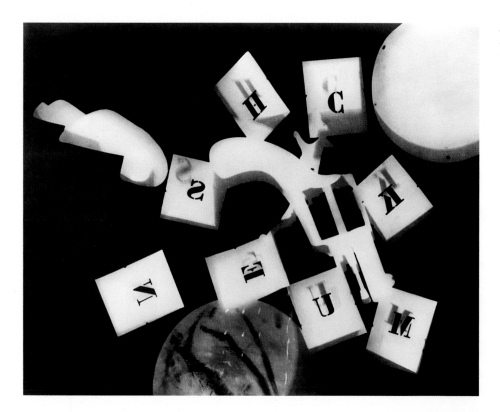

8.23
MAN RAY, *Abstract Composition*, 1921–28.
Rayograph. Victoria and Albert Museum, London.

Man Ray's experiments with the photogram, or RAYOGRAPH
(Fig. 8.23). His untitled rayographs, featuring unlikely
conjunctions of mundane, recognizable objects, such as a
knife and a comb, were published as *Les Champs délicieux* (*The
Delicious Fields*) (1922). Tzara contributed a preface cleverly
titled "Photography Inside Out" ("La photographie à l'envers"),
referring both to the reversal of tones in the rayographs, and to
the idea that photographic practice might be turned on its head.

Brassaï (1899–1984), born Gyula Halász in Brasso,
Transylvania, the town from which he adapted his name, was
working as a correspondent for both Hungarian and German
newspapers when he met the Paris Surrealists. His 1933 series
Involuntary Sculpture shows Surrealist influence (Fig. 8.24) in its
emphasis on chance discoveries.

Most Surrealist photography alludes to psychological
intimations and innuendoes, a scenario in which something has
just happened or is about to happen, as in Man Ray's untitled
image for the Surrealist publication *Minotaure* (Fig. 8.25).
Like several early twentieth-century art groups, the Surrealists
believed that "primitive" art and myth bypassed conscious,
rational thought to reach into the fertile unconscious. In
response to the French government's 1931 international Paris
Exposition Coloniale, several Surrealists joined forces to curate
a section of the anti-imperialist exhibition "La Verité sur les
Colonies" ("The Truth about the Colonies"), which emphasized
the originality and spiritual integrity of art created by indigenous
peoples living in Africa and Indochina.

Forbidden sensuality and sexuality were frequent Surrealist
topics. Hans Bellmer (1902–1975), born in the German-
dominated area of Poland called Silesia, encountered the

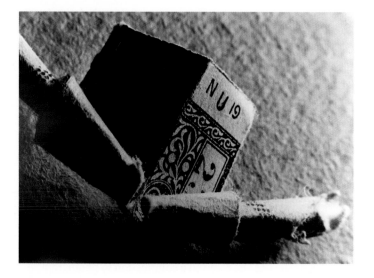

8.24
BRASSAÏ (GYULA HALÁSZ), *Sculpture involontaire* (*Involuntary Sculpture*), 1933.
Courtesy Edwynn Houk Gallery, New York.

Berlin Dadaists while studying engineering. Following the
well-trodden path to Paris in 1924, he came in touch with the
Surrealists. After a number of eerie personal incidents, including
attending a performance of Jacques Offenbach's (1819–1880)
opera *The Tales of Hoffmann*, about a beloved automated doll
that is demolished, he was inspired to create his own dolls and
photograph them (Fig. 8.26).

Belgian-born Raoul Ubac (1910–1985) was as technically
experimental as his sometime collaborator Man Ray. Both
made solarized prints, a technique Man Ray originally

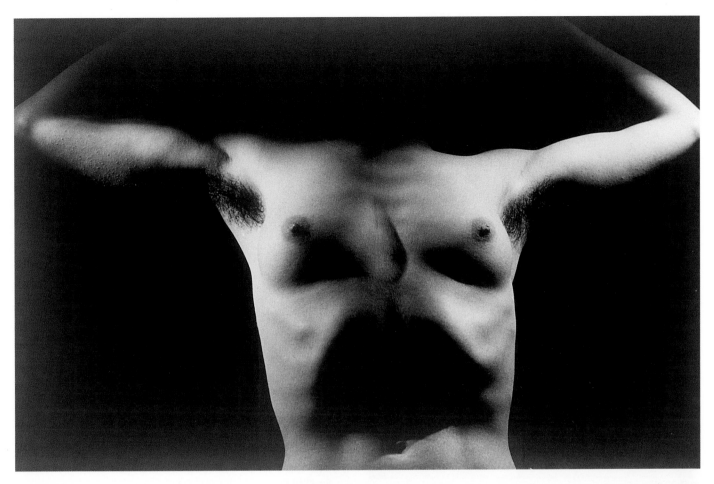

8.25 (above)
MAN RAY, *Untitled*, **from** *Minotaure*, **1933–35. Silver print.**
Michael Senft Collection, East Hampton, New York.

For the Surrealist publication *Minotaure*, Man Ray used ominous shadows to suggest that a woman's upper torso was transforming itself into the head of a bull. In Greek mythology, the Minotaur was a creature half-man, half-bull, to whom the Athenians periodically sent young men and women for sacrifice on the island of Crete.

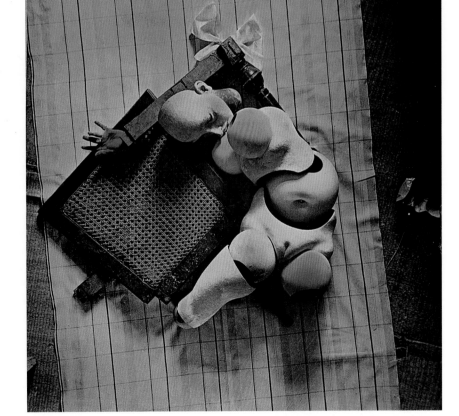

8.26
HANS BELLMER, *Doll* (*La Poupée*), **1935. Gelatin silver print with applied color. George Eastman House, Rochester, New York.**

In these photographs, Bellmer mismatched and twisted mannequins body parts. His grotesque figures have been scrutinized for insights into his personal Oedipal conflicts, and read as a sophisticated retaliatory response to the fair-haired stereotypes of the normal—that is, Aryan—body, celebrated in Nazi propaganda pictures.[35]

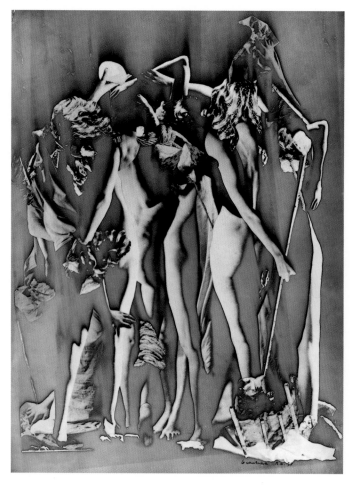

8.27
RAOUL UBAC, *La Conciliabule*, 1938. Brûlage print. Galerie Adrien Maeght, Paris.

The prints Ubac produced using *brûlage* depict slippery-looking dissolving forms that signal the transitory quality of human identity. The technique gives the whole print a shimmering, dreamlike quality.

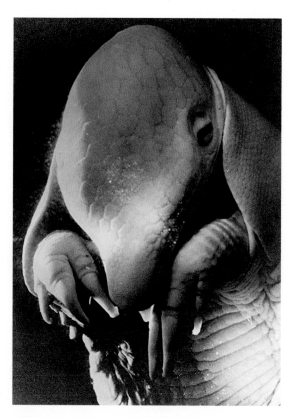

8.28
DORA MAAR, *Père Ubu*, 1936. Gelatin silver print. Metropolitan Museum of Art, New York.

Maar found an element of something extraordinary—and disturbing—in this close-up shot of an armadillo.

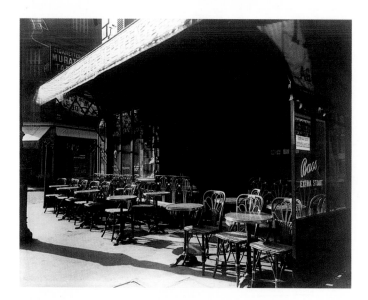

8.29
EUGÈNE ATGET, *Café, Avenue de la Grande-Armée*, 1924–25. Silver print from glass negative. Metropolitan Museum of Art, New York.

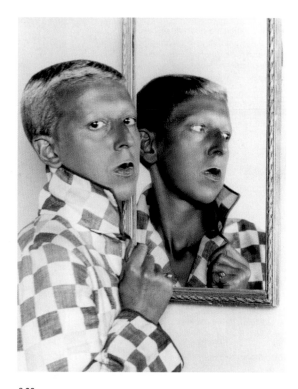

8.30
CLAUDE CAHUN, *Self-Portrait*, 1928. Gelatin silver print. Musée des Beaux-Arts, Nantes, France.

investigated with Berenice Abbott and Lee Miller, who were his studio assistants at different times (see pp. 286, 288, 304). SOLARIZATION involves briefly exposing a print or negative to light during the development process. The result is a reversal of tones, especially along the edges of objects. Sometimes called edge reversal, solarization is unpredictable, which made it a favorite technique of the Surrealists. Ubac also developed a technique called *brûlage*, or burning, in which film emulsion was melted to produce swirling shapes (Fig. 8.27).

Attracted to the bohemian life of Paris in the 1920s, Berenice Abbott worked for Man Ray from 1924 to 1926. While in Paris, she also studied with Eugène Atget (1857–1927), a photographer who roamed Paris and its environs, producing about ten thousand prints in the early twentieth century (Fig. 8.29). Using a box camera and glass negatives, Atget resisted the then fashionable Pictorialist photographic style, and compiled clear objective images, which he called "documents." The Paris Surrealists found Atget's "documents" unsettling and evocative, and briefly put the reluctant Atget forward as an instinctive voice for their philosophy. By contrast, Abbott admired his methodical approach. After his death, she acquired Atget's images, which in time became part of the collection at New York's Museum of Modern Art.

Male Surrealist painters and photographers often used female forms as symbols of the primitive, the mysterious, and the erotic. As recent feminist critics have pointed out, they also pictured women's bodies caged, distorted, or dismembered, as if they were primal forces to be trapped, observed, or punished. The women artists in Surrealist circles did not generally adopt this iconography. Painter Dora Maar (1909–1997), often unjustly remembered only as a lover of Picasso and as a subject in his paintings, was also a member of Man Ray's circle and an experimental photographer with a knack for contriving unsettling images (Fig. 8.28). Claude Cahun (1894–1954), an activist writer and photographer involved with Surrealism in Paris during the 1930s, made self-portraits exploring shifting subjective moments and female gender identity (Fig. 8.30). Born Lucy Renée Mathilde Schwob, Cahun adopted the first name of Claude, which in French can be either a male or a female name.

The Surrealist sensibility persisted well beyond its historical high point in the 1920s and 1930s, although shorn of its early radicalism and intense psychologizing. Brassaï's recognition that the extraordinary always prowls close to the ordinary informs his book of photographs *Paris de nuit* (*Paris by Night*) (1933), which teems with people who exist at the twilight of respectable society. To many photographic artists, such outsiders as vagrants and prostitutes represented freedom and nonconformity.[36] Brassaï's *Paris by Night* carried no message of social reform or personal redemption, but showed such people of the night as "Bijou" ("Jewel"), who relished the extremes of life (Fig. 8.31).

For André Kertész (1894–1985), a Hungarian-born photographer and mentor to his Paris friend Brassaï, Surrealist distortion of the human figure was a short-lived, if much discussed, experiment (Fig. 8.32). Nevertheless, the Surrealist feeling for the magic of coincidence and presence of the

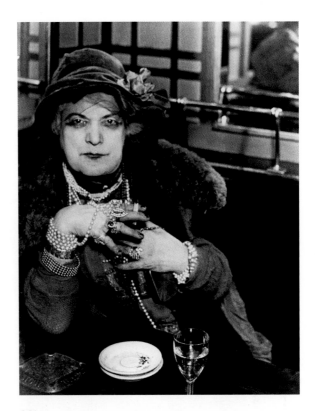

8.31
BRASSAÏ (GYULA HALÁSZ), *"Bijou" of Montmartre*, from *Paris de nuit (Paris by Night)*, c. 1933. Gelatin silver print. David H. McAlpin Fund. Museum of Modern Art, New York.

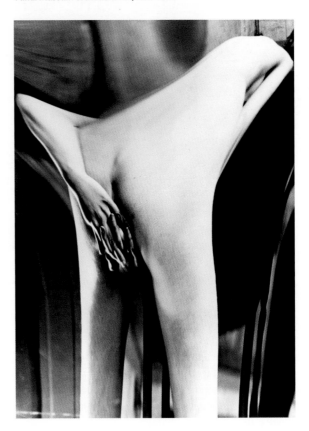

8.32
ANDRÉ KERTÉSZ, *Distortion # 102*, 1933. Gelatin silver print. Gift of Graham Nash. San Francisco Museum of Modern Art, San Francisco, California.

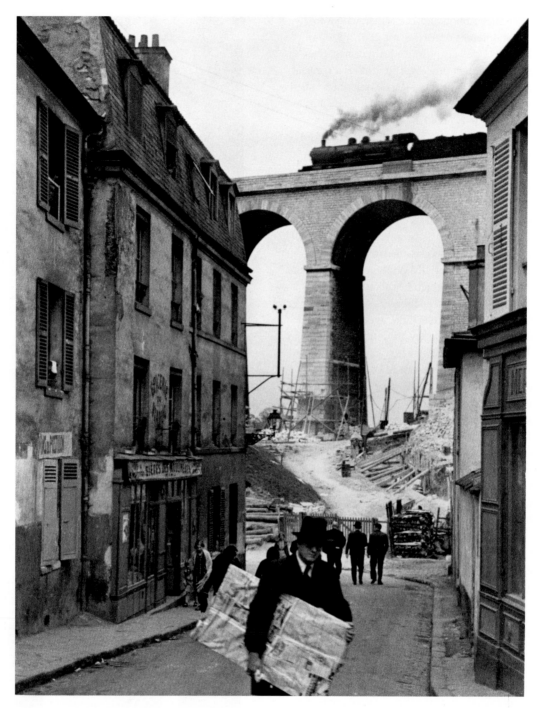

8.33
ANDRÉ KERTÉSZ, *Meudon*, 1928. Gelatin silver print. Museum of Modern Art, New York.

mysterious in everyday life stayed with him throughout his career, as in *Meudon* (Fig. 8.33). Kertész's joy in seizing a fleeting yet resonant visual moment influenced many twentieth-century photographers, including Robert Capa (see pp. 300–01) and Henri Cartier-Bresson (1908–2004).

A painter and student of art history, Cartier-Bresson recalled that he was influenced more by Surrealist theories of the irrational than by Surrealist art practice. He fastened on to

"the role of spontaneous expression … and of intuition and, above all, the attitude of revolt."[37] He is legendary for describing his instantaneous composition of a scene as "the decisive moment," which he defined as "the simultaneous recognition, in a fraction of a second, of the significance of an event as well as of a precise organization of forms which gave that event its proper expression."[38] A famous example is his image of a man momentarily suspended over a rain-drenched area (Fig. 8.34).

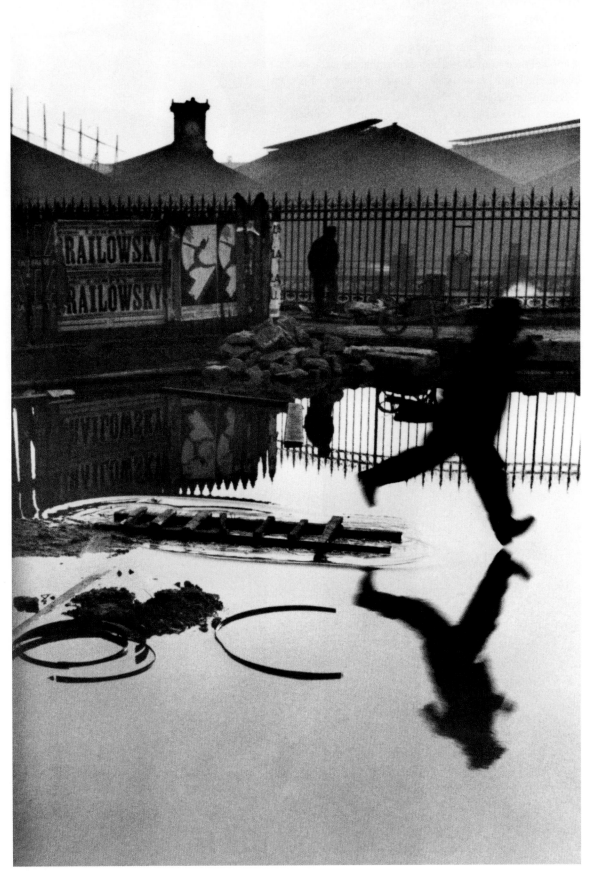

8.34
HENRI CARTIER-BRESSON, *Behind the Gare St. Lazare*, 1932. Gelatin silver print.

EXPERIMENTAL PHOTOGRAPHY AND ADVERTISING

Experimental photographers in Europe and, to a lesser extent, America applied their graphic techniques and theories to commerce. In the United States, with its lingering affection for the serious amateur Pictorialist who created works of art for love, not money, advertising work was widely seen as a betrayal of artistic talent. Nevertheless, such photographers as Canadian-born Margaret Watkins (1884–1969) (Fig. 8.35) and her protégé American Paul Outerbridge (1896–1958) (Fig. 8.36) both contrived images that translated Modernist visions to advertising aimed at men and women who thought of themselves as up to date. The proliferating presence of the slightly eroticized female image in advertising may have been part of the inspiration for Marcel Duchamp's *alter ego*, Rrose Sélavy (Fig. 8.37).[39]

In Europe, advertising carried less of a stigma, and was even considered a meritorious photographic pursuit. Some Soviet artists saw it as a crucial aspect of modern mass media that could be used to change the public's outlook. Especially in the Soviet Union, theorists were careful to distinguish between capitalist advertising, which they saw as misleading the public, and socialist advertising, which they argued was an educational tool. In 1923, Maiakovskii and Rodchenko formed an association that they called Maiakovskii-Rodchenko Advertising-Constructor. Maiakovskii's manifesto "Agitation and Advertising" argued

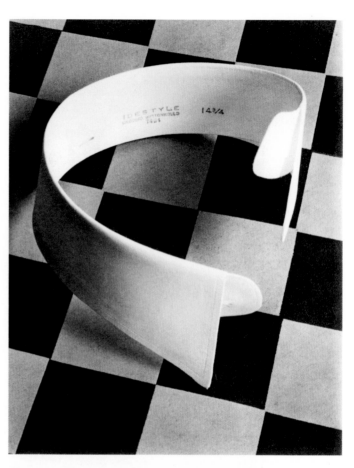

8.36
PAUL OUTERBRIDGE, *Ide Collar*, 1922. Platinum print. Metropolitan Museum of Art, New York.

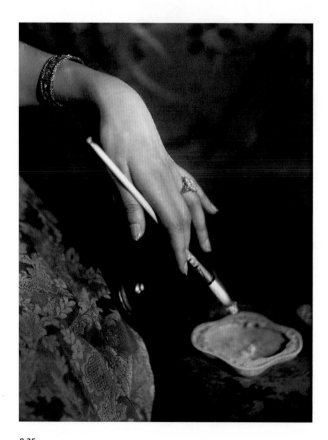

8.35
MARGARET WATKINS, Advertisement for Myer's Gloves, 1920s. Gelatin silver print. J. Mulholland Collection, Glasgow, Scotland.

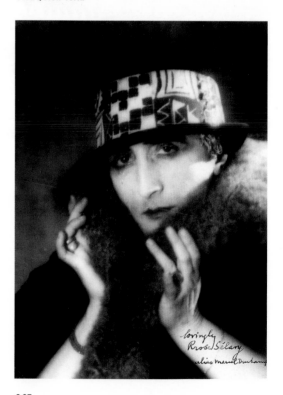

8.37
MAN RAY, *Marcel Duchamp Dressed as Rrose Sélavy*, 1924. Gelatin silver print. Philadelphia Museum of Art, Pennsylvania.

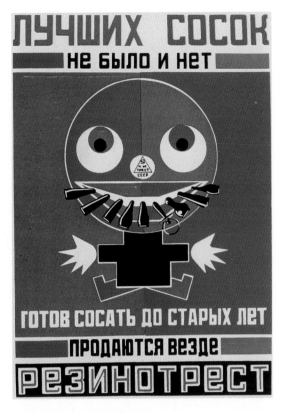

8.38
ALEKSANDR RODCHENKO, Advertisement for baby pacifiers, 1923. Rodchenko Archives, Moscow.

Despite a mouthful of pacifiers, this baby still seems wide-eyed and fretful.

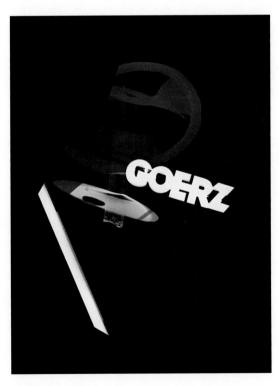

8.39
LÁSZLÓ MOHOLY-NAGY, *Goerz*, 1925. Gelatin silver print. George Eastman House, Rochester, New York.

that he and Rodchenko "had to put into action all the weapons that the enemy also uses, including advertising."[40] Similar aims guided the formation of the Adbusters Media Foundation in the late twentieth century (see p. 490). Maiakovskii-Rodchenko produced bold graphic designs that occasionally integrated photographs. The firm aimed their advertising at a proletarian audience, and promoted a variety of products, including state-manufactured candy, pacifiers, and beer (Fig. 8.38).

In capitalist countries such as Germany, Modernist chic sold upscale products. Moholy-Nagy routinely produced commercial photographs for clients including fashion magazines, publishers, an airline, and an optical company[41] (Fig. 8.39). German photographer August Sander (1876–1964) created an uncharacteristic photomontage for a brand of cologne, and German Krull photographed for automobile companies such as Citroën and Peugeot. French artist and commercial photographer Maurice Tabard (1897–1984) brought a touch of sophistication and class to a glittering advertisement for a Dunhill cigarette lighter (Fig. 8.40). Speculating on the effectiveness of advertising photography in 1930, German writer Willi Warstat concluded that "the public simply believes without reservation that the photographic representation of an object is truer and more real than any artist's graphic representation."[42]

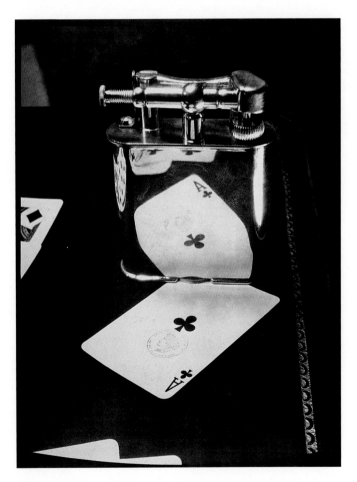

8.40
MAURICE TABARD, *Publicité Dunhill*, 1930. Gelatin silver print. Musée National d'Art Moderne, Centre Beaubourg, Paris.

focus

Film and Photography

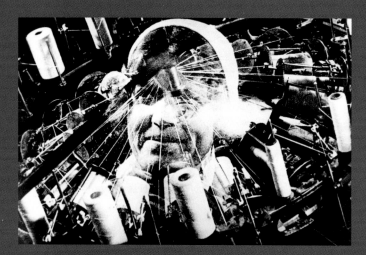

8.41
DZIGA VERTOV, *Man with a Movie Camera,* 1929.

Throughout the 1920s and 1930s, photographers and film–makers embraced many of the same radical social theories about the visual arts, and used similar techniques to break down preconceptions. For example, Rodchenko interacted with pioneering filmmakers such as Sergei Eisenstein, and even had a small role in one of his films.

In the Soviet Union, cinematographer Dziga Vertov (1896–1954) employed unusual camera angles, superimpositions, and rapidly montaged scenes in such films as the exhilarating *Man with a Movie Camera* (1929), in which a cameraman sweeps through a city recording modern life (Fig. 8.41). Vertov famously announced:

I am kino-eye [film-eye]. I am in constant motion. I draw near, then away from objects, I crawl under, I climb onto them. I move apace with the muzzle of a galloping horse, I plunge full speed into a crowd, I outstrip running soldiers, I fall on my back, I ascend with an airplane, I plunge and soar …[43]

Film posters were equally experimental. Vladimir Stenberg (1899–1982) and his brother Georgy (1900–1933) tried to combine the zesty spirit of collage with the need for mass appeal. Because Russia lacked the technology to print large, photo-based posters, the Stenberg brothers meticulously copied photographs by hand.

Much the same could be said for the quick changes of meaning in photomontage, or the surprising angles in Rodchenko's photographs (see Fig. 8.9). Both photographers and filmmakers scorned the laws of gravity, and propelled the viewer on a visual roller-coaster ride. Eisenstein used the new techniques in such patriotic films as *Battleship Potemkin* (1925) and *October*

(also known as *Ten Days that Shook the World*) (1927). *October* re-enacted the Russian Revolution of 1917, with realistic scenes of the storming of the Winter Palace, a crucial moment in the Revolution when the Bolsheviks toppled the czarist regime. The film scenes were later converted into photographs purporting to have been made during the actual assault (see p. 226).

In the years after World War I, before the monopoly of big film studios, artists and photographers were attracted to film as a medium. In his 1922 book *Foto Kino Film* (*Photography Cinema Film*), Czech artist and writer Karel Teige wrote enthusiastically about film's potential. Duchamp, Moholy-Nagy, and Man Ray all made non-commercial films. In fact, Man Ray's *Le Retour à la Raison* (*The Return to Reason*) (1923) applied the rayograph process directly to cinema. Among the Surrealist films with visual parallels in photography was *Un Chien Andalou* (*An Andalusian Dog*) (1926), directed by Salvador Dalí (1904–1989) and Luis Buñuel (1900–1983), which deliberately shocked audiences with such scenes as a woman's eyeball being slit by a straight razor. At the exhibition "Film und Foto" held in Stuttgart, Germany, in 1929, the interplay between cinema and photography was manifest (Fig. 8.42). The show of about one thousand photographic works from Europe, the Soviet Union, and the United States included movie stills, and demonstrated reciprocal uses of camera angles, montages, and superimpositions, which migrated from experimental film and photography to mainstream movies by emulation and the changing employment of cinematographers and writers.

The year 1929 was pivotal in film history. Film speed was standardized at twenty-four frames per second, to accommodate simultaneous sound projection—an indirect indicator of the transformation of filmmaking into big business, and the subsequent influence of the large studios. Experimental film and photography gave way to documentary film and photography, forms thought to appeal to wider audiences. In Depression-era America, the Resettlement Agency (R.A.), which evolved into the Farm Security Administration (F.S.A.) (see p. 278), sponsored both photography and film. In 1935, filmmaker Pare Lorentz (1905–1992) was hired to chronicle the Dust Bowl—that is, the dire consequence of soil erosion in the Great Plains that coincided with the economic depression. Working with influential photographers such as Paul Strand, Lorentz made the poignant film *The Plow that Broke the Plains* (1936), employing visual techniques and emotional subjects that F.S.A. photographers would soon emulate.[44] Similarly, members of Film and Photo Leagues included still photographers and motion-picture makers. The New York branch made a Workers' Newsreel, which they attempted to have shown in theaters.

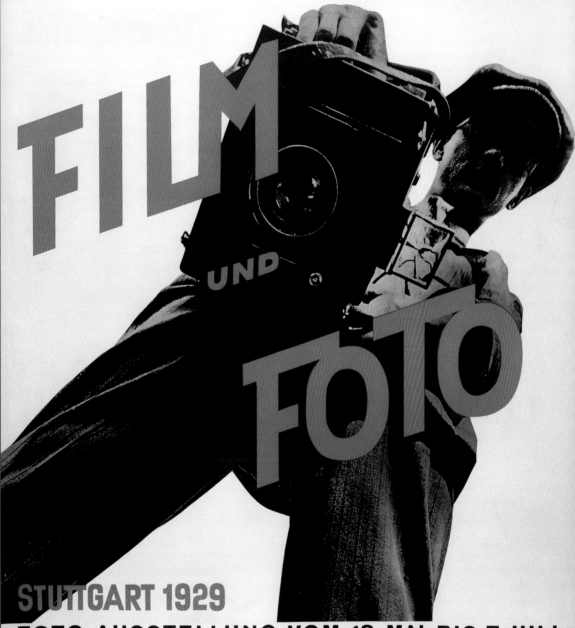

8.42
JAN TSCHICHOLD, "Film und Foto" exhibition, Stuttgart, 1929. Poster. Stadtmuseum, Stuttgart, Germany.

portrait

August Sander

The detached approach to subject matter favored by European New Objectivity (Neue Sachlichkeit) artists and what might be called "the archival tendency" came together in the haunting images produced by German photographer August Sander (1876–1964). While running his own commercial studio, Sander began making portraits of farmers in the rural Westerwald area of Germany, which spurred him to plan a systematic portrait gallery of occupational types, beginning with farmers, continuing through the industrial jobs, the professions, and the arts, and ending with unemployed and disabled people. He planned to have forty-five portfolios, each consisting of twelve related images, which would be collectively called *People of the 20th Century*. Sander was not unique in preparing a survey of the German people. As a post-World War I morale booster, perhaps, books containing a panoply of German portraits came into fashion during the 1920s.[45] Sander's plan extended the encyclopedic urge of nineteenth-century photography into the twentieth century.

During decades of shooting, Sander used a set formula reminiscent of early photography. His usual method was to take sharp full-length or half-length portraits of subjects, posed with props and garments suggesting their work (Fig. 8.43). Most of his images show that he arranged his sitters, carefully focusing so that facial characteristics were distinctive, even unique. The relationship of the figure to the surroundings in his work is novel—a process of distance and isolation that unmasks qualities in the subjects such as their relationship to others. This was a Modernist project, at least as it was understood by whole generations of photographers who came afterward.

Sander's technique—and moments of humor—sometimes undermined the emotionally detached scheme he had in mind. He was not interested in the odd angles and cameraless photographs of the German experimentalist photographers, and he renounced both his youthful infatuation with Pictorialism and the casual spontaneity of the snapshot. Instead, he insisted on three guiding concepts: "See, observe, and think correctly!"[46] Although the immense project was never completed, Sander did publish sixty photographs in *Antlitz der Zeit* (*Face of the Time*) (1929). He also gave a pioneering series of radio lectures in 1931 on the history of photography.

In 1936, after the Nazi Party came to power, remaining copies of *Face of the Time*, along with the printing plates used to produce them, were destroyed by order of the Government Bureau of Fine Arts. Sander's images showed how, in reality, many German people did not have the "Aryan" facial features and physiques promoted by the Nazis as the infallible marks of the German race. Moreover, his series ended with unemployed

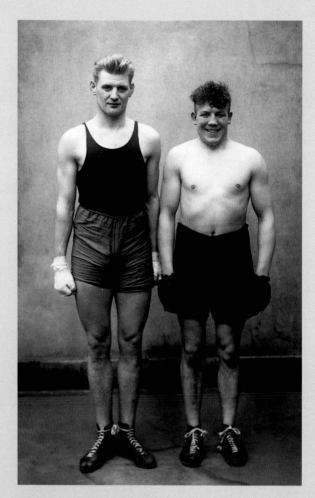

8.43
AUGUST SANDER, *Boxers Paul Roderstein and Hein Heese, Cologne*, 1929. Gelatin silver print. August Sander Archive, Cologne, Germany.

and disabled people—the very types the Nazis first targeted for removal to "purify" the Aryan race. After World War II, Sander added photographs of political prisoners and persecuted Jews to his work *People of the 20th Century*. He continued to work after the war, although wartime bombing was responsible for the destruction of his studio and a postwar fire that destroyed about thirty thousand negatives.

Sander did not live to see the enormous influence his work and ideas would have on late twentieth-century photography. His detachment from the subject, coupled with his urge to create comprehensive series, fed the imaginations of Bernd and Hilla Becher in their ongoing sequences of antiquated technological structures (see Fig. 11.61). Through the Bechers, many prominent German contemporary photographers, such as Andreas Gursky (see p. 395), adopted photographic objectivity as a visual stance in relation to the built environment. Sander's work has been a touchstone of past and present international Conceptual artists, who have investigated the qualities peculiar to photography, such as how far a subject is placed from the camera. Indeed, his images have nourished the notion that physical distance is an effective visual metaphor for psychic remove.

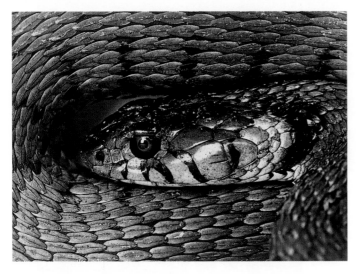

8.44
HANS FINSLER, *Untitled* (Toothpaste and brush), c. 1930. Gelatin silver print. San Francisco Museum of Modern Art, San Francisco, California.

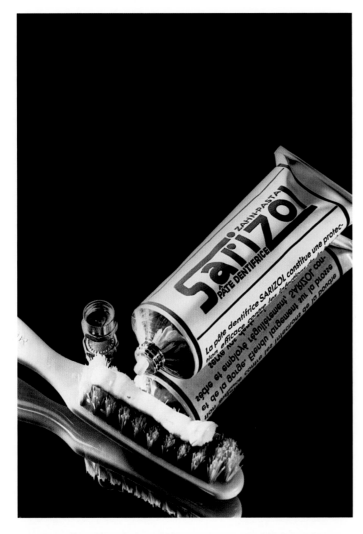

8.45
ALBERT RENGER-PATZSCH, *Snake Head*, 1927. Gelatin silver print. Metropolitan Museum of Art, Gilman Collection, Purchase, Ann Tenenbaum and Thomas H. Lee Gift, 2005.

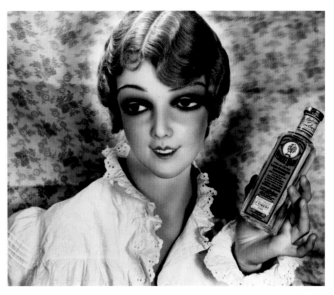

8.46
foto ringl + pit, *Petrole Hahn Advertising*, Berlin, 1931. Bauhaus-Archiv, Berlin.

foto ringl + pit counted on viewers being so accustomed to the pose of a glamorous model that they would only gradually detect not a living woman but a mannequin.

Warstat maintained that advertisers must take advantage of that illusion of truth. Advertising photographs in fact presented goods as more than they were, endorsing them with suggestions of sexual allure and financial success. Through advertising, the product became a commodity favored not because it cleaned teeth or provided transportation, but because it pledged to gratify human desires. Swiss-born photographer Hans Finsler (1891–1972), who taught art history and ran a commercial studio in Germany, was one of the best photographic enchanters (Fig. 8.44).

The techniques of experimental photography, including photomontage, close-ups, and severe angles, were gradually disengaged from utopian aspiration for social change of the sort that followed the Russian Revolution. Nevertheless, the experimental look remained closely associated with dapper newness and swanky modernity. For example, the intense close-up advertisements of German photographer Albert Renger-Patzsch (1897–1966) resembled his art photographs (Fig. 8.45) by zeroing in on the repetitive patterns of rows of commodities, ranging from coffee beans to bathtubs. Former Bauhaus students Ellen Auerbach (1906–2004) and Grete Stern (1904–1999) used their childhood nicknames for their Berlin partnership, foto ringl + pit. They accepted commissions for advertisements and magazine illustrations (Fig. 8.46), as well as fashionable portraits. By 1931, when the New York show called the "Exhibition of Foreign Advertising and Industrial Photography" brought to America the work of European Modernists including Moholy-Nagy, Man Ray, and Bayer, their politics were out of the picture.

EXPERIMENTAL PHOTOGRAPHY AS STYLE

Moholy-Nagy was influential in organizing the international 1929 "Film und Foto" exhibition held in Stuttgart, Germany, to which he contributed ninety-seven photographs, photomontages, and photograms (see Fig. 8.14).[47] At Fifo, as the exhibition was called, viewers could see how far photography had changed from the fuzzy look and rural subjects of turn-of-the-century Pictorialism. Collectively, the Fifo photographs dwelled on the urban-industrial environment, emphasizing form and texture. Borrowing the name of a contemporary German art movement, observers described such work as exemplifying the Neue Sachlichkeit, or New Objectivity. More imprecise terms, such as "New Vision" (neue Optik), "Modernist Photography," or "New Photography," were also used to denote the emphasis placed on industrial subjects, close-ups, odd angles, and repeated visual patterns.

Some critics decried the commercialization of the Modernist style. Karel Teige (1900–1951) angrily observed that "Film und Foto", as well as the 1930 Munich exhibition "Das Lichtbild" ("The Photograph"; literally "the light picture" in German), propagated a visual fashion emptied of its initial social activism. He noted the tendency in such popular books as *Es kommt der neue Fotograf!* (*Here Comes the New Photographer!*) by writer and filmmaker Werner Graeff (1901–1978), and the triple-titled *Foto-Auge = Oeil et photo = Photo-eye*, a 1929 compilation of seventy-six contemporary photographs edited by photographer-critic Franz Roh (1890–1965) and proponent of experimental typography Jan Tschichold (1902–1974). In particular, Teige targeted the book *Die Welt ist Schön* (*The World is Beautiful*), by Renger-Patzsch, claiming that its concentration on formal beauty spawned a modish, socially irresponsible version of art for art's sake.[48]

Originally titled *Die Dinge* (*Things*), the book consisted of one hundred photographs organized in eight sections,

including technology, architecture, and plants. Renger-Patzsch emphasized "thingness" by choosing a view that standardized and regularized the subject (Fig. 8.45). While praising the new photography for tearing the medium "loose from the grip of the petty business machinations of the studios, and from artistic dilettantism," Teige insisted that "photography did not triumph over painting in order to take its place."[49] He appealed for a photography that was grounded in social life, not the art gallery, and invited photographers to recognize that the medium could be successfully practiced by amateurs. Not surprisingly, Teige admired Soviet photography, asserting that it had not lost sight of its ideological mission. "Service," he concluded, "is the future of modern photography and its tasks will be utilitarian: to serve science, ideas, and social progress." In effect, he called for a progressive, socially committed documentary photography.

For similar reasons, Renger-Patzsch's book was also denounced by German critic Walter Benjamin (1892–1940), who called its style "the posture of a photography that can endow any soup-can with cosmic significance but cannot grasp a single one of the human connections in which it exists."[50] Benjamin mocked what he called creative photography, the tendency to look for engaging visual juxtapositions that delighted the eye but ignored the mind. He maintained that taking subjects out of context, as in severe close-ups, turned photography "into a sort of art journalism."[51]

The depoliticizing of experimental photography at Fifo was not an overt, organized effort. In fact, the show seemed progressive in its inclusion of a wide variety of work, ranging beyond art to X-rays, photomicrographs, press photographs, and advertising. Yet the continuous repetition of the style

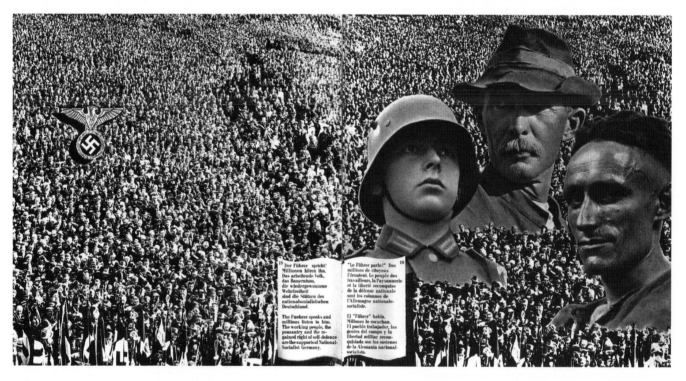

8.47
HERBERT BAYER, Brochure for the exhibition "Deutschland", Berlin, 1936.

in newspapers and advertisements dulled its newness. The art director for Condé Nast publications, M. F. Agha (1896–1978), shrewdly remarked, "Modernistic photography is easily recognized by its subject matter." He continued:

Eggs (any style), twenty shoes standing in a row. A skyscraper, taken from a modernistic angle. Ten tea cups standing in a row. A factory chimney seen through the ironwork of a railroad bridge (modernistic angle). The eye of a fly enlarged 2000 times. The eye of an elephant (same size). The interior of a watch. Three different heads of one lady superimposed. The interior of a garbage can. More eggs …[52]

While the Modernist style descended into triteness, the Soviet government shifted its support away from photographic experimentation (see pp. 236–40), in favor of high-impact, easily understood propaganda images.

During the 1930s in Germany, the rise of the Nazi Party, with its love of nationalistic pictures, and disgust with what it called cultural Bolshevism, cooled photographic experimentation

and sent many photographers seeking asylum abroad. At the same time, the Nazis recognized the power of photography, and organized their first successful propaganda event around photography in October 1933. The exhibition "Die Kamera" ("The Camera") in Berlin took to heart the words of Joseph Goebbels, the Nazi propaganda minister, who declared that "the experience of the individual has become the experience of the people, thanks solely to the camera." Through photography exhibitions such as "The Camera," the Nazis tried to create a glory-strewn chronology of their rise to power.[53] Ironically, they used the graphic impact of new-vision photography in a brochure designed by Bayer (see p. 245–46) to accompany the 1936 Berlin Olympic Games[54] (Fig. 8.47). By the end of the 1930s, the experimental photography developed in the 1920s knew no nationalism or political persuasion. It could be used by Nazis, or against them, as on the cover of *Vu* for April 25, 1934, designed by photographer and innovative designer Alexander Libermann (1912–1999) (Fig. 8.48).

8.48
ALEXANDER LIBERMANN, *"In Germany, toward a mass army,"* **from** *Vu*, **April 25, 1934. Neogravure. Victoria and Albert Museum (Library), London.**

The huge gun barrel that looms over the ranks of Nazi soldiers is not merely an emblem of conflict. It also refers to Germany's continuing investment in and development of long-range guns such as "Big Bertha," which during World War I was capable of hurling shells nearly 10 miles.

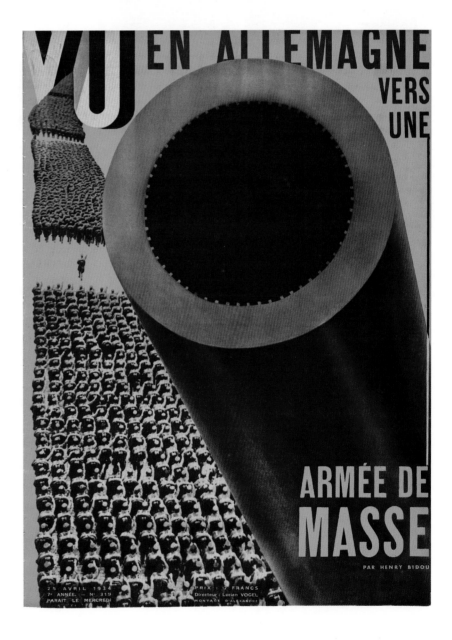

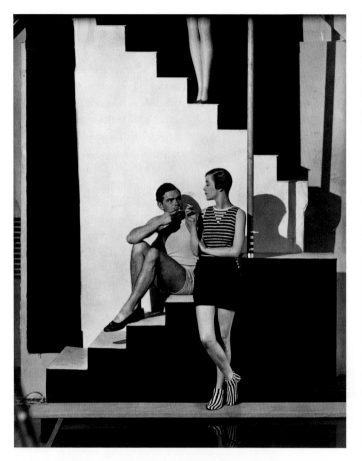

8.49
GEORGE HOYNINGEN-HUENE, *Schiaparelli Beachwear*, 1930, from *Harper's Bazaar*, 1935. Gelatin silver print. Victoria and Albert Museum, London.

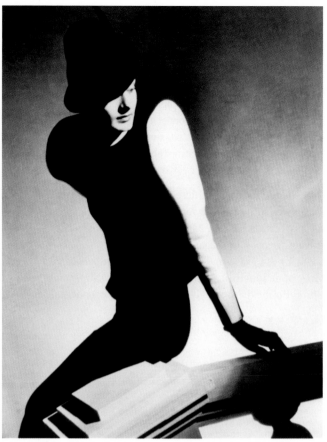

8.50
HORST P. HORST, *Untitled*, 1936. Victoria and Albert Museum, London.

Horst used the slim, overlapping planes of Cubism, as well as the negative–positive look of photograms, in his carefully lit fashion photography. Here he seems to have merged the look of photomontage with the appearance of the rayograph, invented by his friend Man Ray.

Reflecting on the evolution of photomontage, one of its inventors, Raoul Hausmann, noted that "over time the technique of photomontage has undergone considerable simplification, forced upon it" by application in "political or commercial propaganda."[55] Commercial propaganda—that is to say, advertising—brought experimental techniques quickly to the mainstream. Packaging and advertising design were coordinated to conflate the newness of the imagery with claims for a commodity's originality and effectiveness. Where earlier forms of product promotion used extensive text, designers now turned to the terse forms in modern art and photography.

The visual techniques of Surrealism were adapted for commercial purposes, most notably in fashion photography. Russian-born George Hoyningen-Huene (1900–1968) worked in Paris, where he moved in the same circles as Man Ray and Salvador Dalí. He photographed such international celebrities as Marlene Dietrich and Charlie Chaplin, as well as the former British monarch Edward VIII, who took the title Duke of Windsor after his abdication in 1936 to marry the American divorcee Wallis Simpson. Hoyningen-Huene quickly moved

into the world of haute couture, fusing experimental techniques and surreal suggestion in photographs for such magazines as *Vanity Fair* and *Harper's Bazaar* (Fig. 8.49).

Hoyningen-Huene's friend and student Horst P. Horst (1906–1999) also learned from experimental photography and Surrealist art (Fig. 8.50). The most outlandish advertising photographs in the period were made by Lejaren à Hiller (1880–1969), who revived the *tableau vivant* (see pp. 37, 170–71) for a collection of photographs depicting the history of medicine in the 1933 series *Surgery through the Ages*, commissioned by the firm of David and Geck, which made surgical sutures (Fig. 8.51). These photographs were often reprinted and used to decorate doctors' offices.[56]

CALIFORNIA MODERN

In the United States, advanced technological image-making came to be associated with corporate propaganda, as in Sheeler's images for Ford (see Fig. 8.22). Left-wing political movements

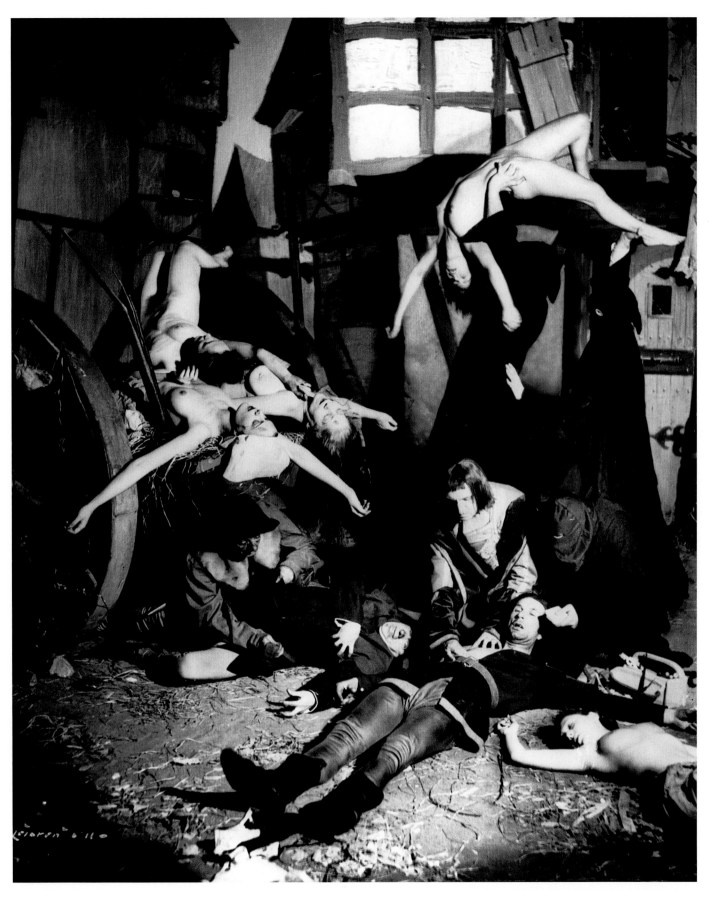

8.51
LEJAREN À HILLER, *Étienne Gourmelen*, c. 1933, from *Surgery through the Ages*, 1933. Gelatin silver print. George Eastman House, Rochester, New York.

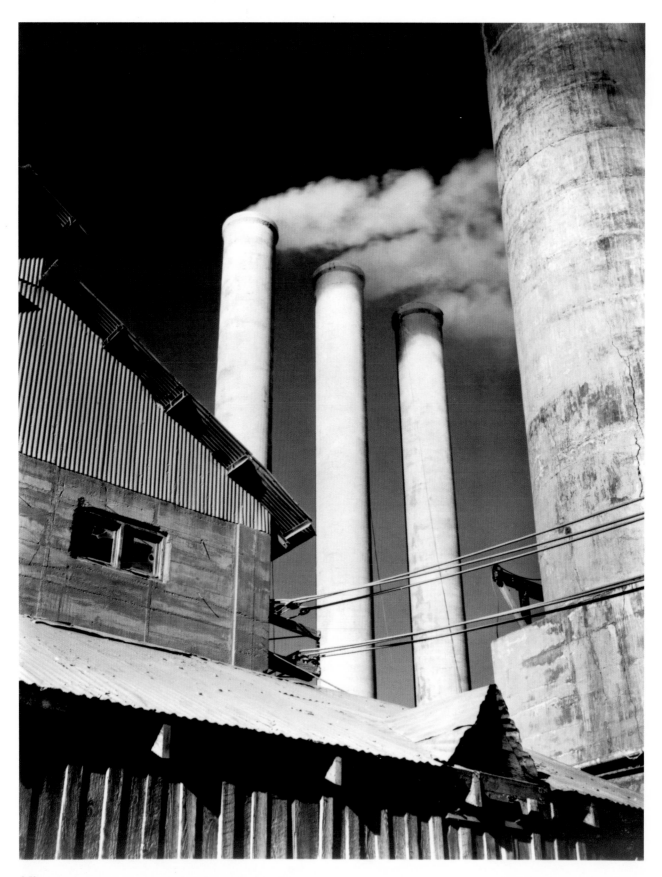

8.52
WILLARD VAN DYKE, *Cement Works, Monolith, California,* **1931. Gelatin silver print. Private collection.**

Van Dyke's angle of vision made the large chimney on the right appear flattened and tipped inward slightly, as if it were applied to the surface of the picture, similar to a Cubist collage.

mostly rejected such visual effects, favoring instead the look of hand-crafted images to communicate their message. Advertising photography had recourse both to the blurry appearance of the Pictorialist "fuzzygraph" and the lean lines and crystalline light derived from European experimental art and photography. Abstraction, which in Europe had been strongly associated with the social utopianism of early Modernism, was valued by American photographers more for its aura of artistic seriousness. Surrealism similarly lost its political content (closely bound with the fight against fascism in 1930s' Europe) when it crossed the Atlantic.

The mists of Pictorialist photography (see pp. 170–199) were still thick in California in the late 1920s, when a loose affiliation of friends dubbed themselves Group f.64, and issued a manifesto: "The members of Group f.64 believe that Photography, as an art-form, must develop along lines defined by the actualities and limitations of the photographic medium, and must always remain independent of ideological conventions of art and aesthetics that are reminiscent of a period and culture antedating the growth of the medium itself."[57] In other words, Group f.64 dismissed Pictorialism, despite the fact that several of its members had practiced it, and urged the exploration of camera vision. Their name referred to the small lens opening on their large-format cameras that produced clear detail in the foreground as well as the background, and indicated that they had more in common with regard to the appearance of the photograph than its subject matter.

It is difficult to say exactly how the general strains of Modernism reached the group. Certainly they traveled, and they were familiar with contemporary magazine design and advertising. In addition, the Oakland Art Gallery in California exhibited Bauhaus abstract art, German posters, and works by the Blue Four (*Die Blaue Vier*), who were Bauhaus painters. The Blue Four included Kandinsky and Klee, formerly associated with the more famous German Expressionists collectively called the Blue Rider (*Der Blaue Reiter*), a name derived from the title of a painting by Kandinsky. In fact, the Blue Four was not a formal organization, but a term chosen specifically to acquaint American audiences with their work, while alluding to the success of the Blue Rider. The first American Blue Four show was held in Oakland, and led to criticism that Group f.64's notions were drawn from the German artistic invasion of America. Opponents discounted the fact that f.64 did not promote social change, as did the Germans. In West Coast parlance, the Modernist work of Moholy-Nagy was called "pure photography," a term f.64 used at the "First Salon of Pure Photography" (1934), and which their enemies derided as the "carcass" of transatlantic ideas.[58]

The group's energetic organizer, Willard Van Dyke (1906–1986), photographed a cement works, usually a dusty business, as if it were a sun-drenched Cubist apparition (Fig. 8.52). As the Depression deepened, Van Dyke responded to the growing sentiment that artists should contribute directly to the nation's economic recovery. He did a stint as camera operator for Pare Lorentz (see p. 260) on the shooting of *The Plow that Broke the*

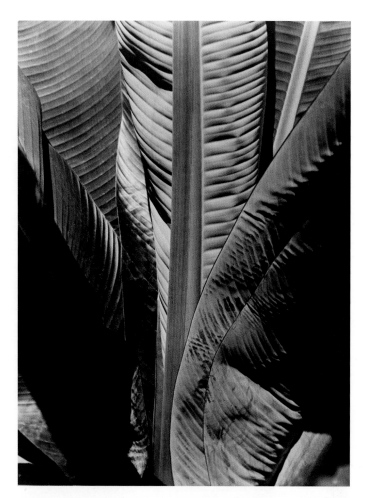

8.53
IMOGEN CUNNINGHAM, *Banana Plant*, c. 1929. Gelatin silver print. Museum purchase, George Eastman House, Rochester, New York.

Plains, which recorded the plight of Midwestern farmers, and went on to make other documentary films.

As a teenager, f.64 photographer Imogen Cunningham (1883–1976) was so impressed with a reproduction of Käsebier's *Blessed Art Thou among Women* (see Fig. 6.34) that she decided then and there to take up the medium. After college, she went to work in the Seattle, Washington, studio of Edward S. Curtis, where she learned the intricacies of PLATINUM PRINTING. Following photographic study in Germany, in 1910 she returned to Seattle to open a portrait studio. When exhibited, her Pictorialist nude interpretation of the Adam and Eve story became the scandal of Seattle. A move to California increased her contact with other photographers, especially Edward Weston (1886–1958). During the 1920s and 1930s, her work shifted toward a starkly geometrical style of straight photography. Her female nude studies and close-ups of plants (Fig. 8.53) and flower portraits began to be compared to the simple, sinuous forms favored by American painter Georgia O'Keeffe (see Fig. 9.21). Some of her plant studies were exhibited at the 1929 "Film und Foto" show in Stuttgart. Cunningham's strength in this period rested on her ability to find visually arresting pictures in small moments of life. Her later work capitalized on her

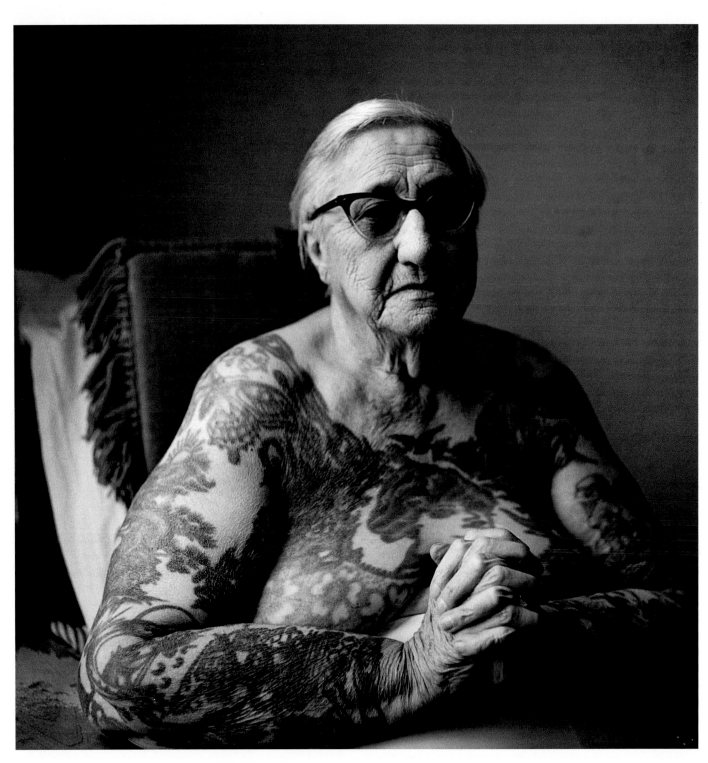

8.54
IMOGEN CUNNINGHAM, *Irene "Bobby" Libarry*, from her book *After Ninety*, 1976. Gelatin silver print.
© The Imogen Cunningham Trust, San Francisco, California.

Cunningham was among the first to photograph older people in a way that respected their individuality.
At first, the image of a woman with many tattoos is startling. But Cunningham kept the image from seeming
voyeuristic by having the woman directly address the camera with an unembarrassed look.

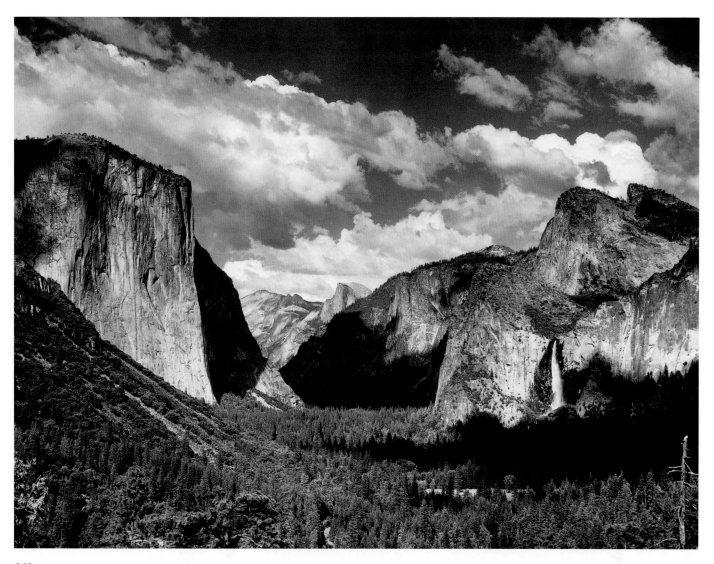

8.55
ANSEL ADAMS, *Valley View, Yosemite National Park, California*, c. 1935. Gelatin silver print. Collection Center for Creative Photography, University of Arizona, Tucson, Arizona.

knowledge of portraiture, as in her informal series picturing older people (Fig. 8.54).

Ansel Adams (1902–1984) and Edward Weston, probably the best-known members of f.64, shared a philosophic regard for natural forms. Adams revealed his belief in the spiritual value of nature to society when he remarked, "I still believe there is a real, social significance in a rock—a more important significance therein than in a line of unemployed."[59] Nevertheless, Adams spoke and showed his prints at the politically involved Photo League in New York. Adams's concentration on dramatic images of natural light effects was fixed well before he became acquainted with f.64. During the 1920s, for example, while working as a guide and custodian in California's Yosemite National Park area, Adams photographed the region (Fig. 8.55).

Meetings with Strand and Stieglitz strengthened Adams's resolve to photograph full-time. At Yosemite, in the midst of the scenery swooningly recorded by Carleton E. Watkins, he worked

out the beginnings of what he would call the "zone system" of photography. His method allowed a photographer to previsualize the finished print by comparing light intensities in the scene to be photographed with a chart showing an ascending scale of tones, ranging from black to white. In other words, the main work of picture-making took place not in the darkroom, but before the film was exposed.

After the United States entered World War II, following the Japanese bombing of Pearl Harbor on December 7, 1941, Adams and Dorothea Lange (1895–1965) expressed their sense of outrage at the forced round-up and confinement of Americans of Japanese descent at the California internment camp called Manzanar Relocation Center in Owens Valley. Though given access to the camp, Adams and Lange were forbidden to photograph guards, guard towers, or barbed wire. Pictures of camp life were also made by Toyo Miyatake (1895–1979), a Modernist Japanese-American photographer interned at

8.56
TOYO MIYATAKE, Three Boys Playing Near a Barbed-Wire Fence, Manzanar Relocation Center, c. 1943.

In recent years, Miyatake's most reproduced photograph has come to stand for the unjust incarceration of Japanese-Americans during World War II. Ironically, the boys were standing outside the fence when Miyatake took this shot.

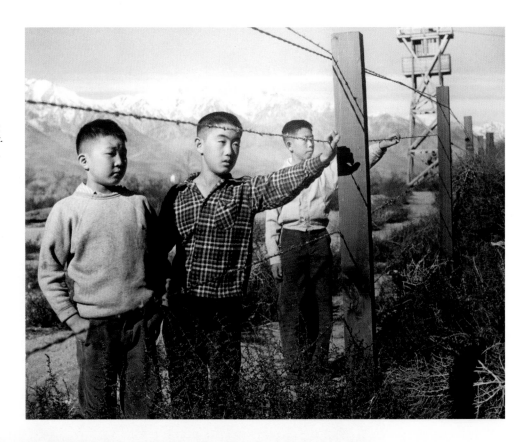

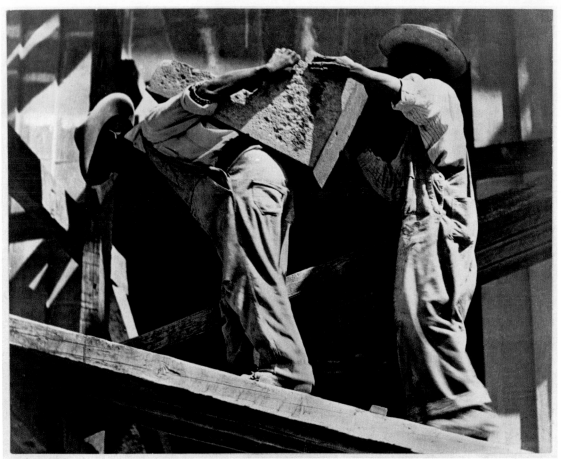

8.57
TINA MODOTTI, *Workers*, Mexico, c. 1926–30. Gelatin silver print. Amon Carter Museum, Fort Worth, Texas.

Manzanar, who eventually gained permission to photograph around the camp (Fig. 8.56).

Though Edward Weston did not originate an elaborate system of tonal equivalents as Adams did, he, too, believed that "the finished print is previsioned on the ground glass while focusing … the shutter's release fixes forever these values and forms."[60] Like Adams, Weston joined the f.64 group when he was already established as a photographer, perhaps to underscore his allegiance to Modernism. His first book of images, *The Art of Edward Weston*, was available at the group's inaugural show at San Francisco's M. H. de Young Memorial Museum in November 1932. A decade before this exhibition, Weston had visited Stieglitz in New York, an event he treasured, even though

the older photographer dropped one after another of Weston's prints on the discard pile. In 1923, Weston left his struggling portrait business and went to live in Mexico with his companion, the photographer Tina Modotti (1896–1942). In Mexico, Modotti came into her own as a photographer, evolving away from Weston's interest in beautiful patterns to a concern for injustice in society (Fig. 8.57). After 1930, she largely gave up photography in favor of political work. Several of her photographs appeared in *Der Arbeiter-Fotograf* (*The Worker-Photographer*)[61] (see p. 289).

In Mexico, Weston made his most notorious image, *Excusado* (the Spanish word for "toilet") (Fig. 8.58). The toilet exemplifies Weston's close-up, sharply detailed approach to

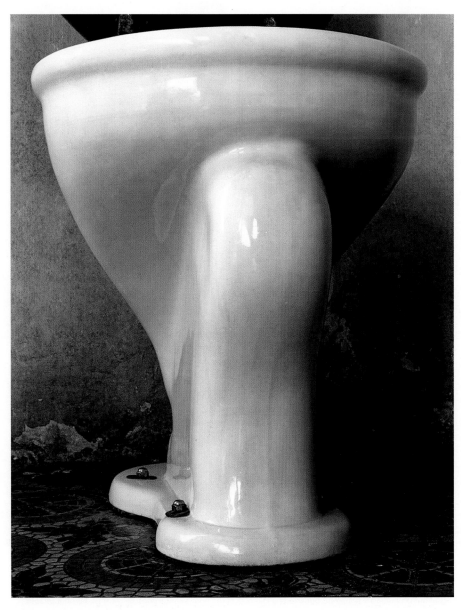

8.58
EDWARD WESTON, *Excusado*, **Mexico, 1925. Gelatin silver print. Center for Creative Photography, University of Arizona, Tucson, Arizona.**

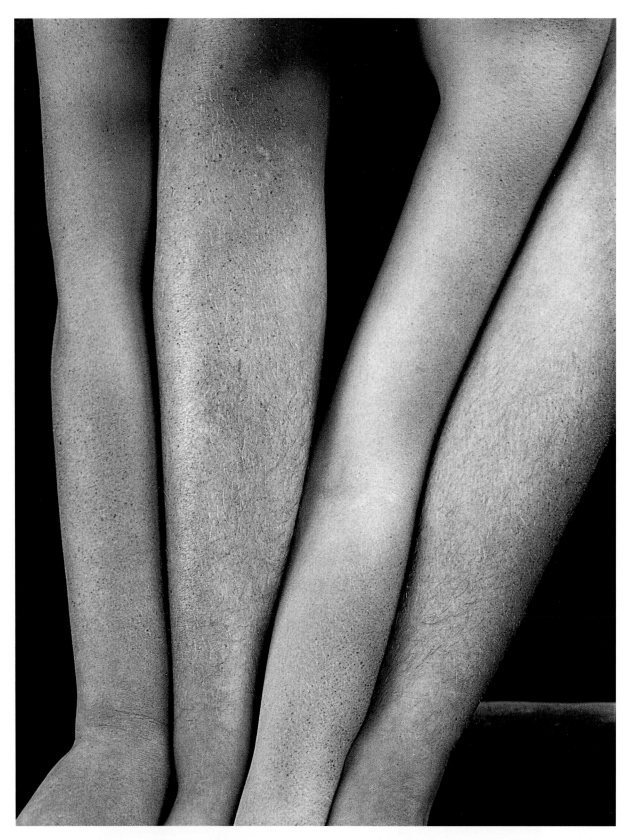

8.59
EDWARD WESTON, *Nude,* **1934. Gelatin silver print. Center for Creative Photography, University of Arizona, Tucson, Arizona.**

Many of Weston's images of human nudes are not erotic, but arresting glimpses of the body's contortions. By contrast, his photographs of subtle, textured shadows originating in nature are often more sensual.

everyday objects such as sea shells and vegetables, especially his celebrated photographs of peppers, which he compared to the sleek sculpture of Romanian Constantin Brancusi (1876–1957), himself an accomplished photographer. By the time of the inaugural f.64 show, Weston had organized the American contribution to the 1929 "Film und Foto" show, enjoyed a major exhibit of his work at the M. H. de Young Memorial Museum in San Francisco, and had two successful shows in New York City.

Though eagerly involved, Weston's active participation in f.64 activities was only a brief phase in his life. Continuing in the style and visual themes he groomed in Mexico, Weston went on to make several series of images involving light, shade, and texture in nature. Oddly enough, his photographs of deeply pleated light and dark patterns of sand dunes, or twisted cypress trees and worn rocks at Point Lobos, California, seem more sensual than his images of the human nude (Fig. 8.59). Where Stieglitz is remembered as the photographer who put modern art and photography on the American cultural radar, Weston is revered as a romantic figure, who sacrificed emotional and economic stability to pursue his creative life.

RETAKE

Newspapers and radio grew in size and influence after World War I. In Europe, many photographers were persuaded that they should follow the example of mass media in order to sway public opinion. As a medium capable of multiple images, photography became more central to art movements. Sometimes, as in the work of Klutsis and Rodchenko in the Soviet Union, and the Nazi Party in Germany, the result was overtly political. By contrast, the photograms and other photographs by László Moholy-Nagy and Lucia Moholy conveyed a sense of newness and Modernist values, without specifically alluding to a particular political philosophy. Photographers and filmmakers explored unexpected angles and collage effects, and closely watched and admired each other's work. Dada art and photography inclined in other directions, smartly ridiculing the pomposities of art or attempting to fathom the nasty bits of the human psyche. Surrealism also targeted the human unconscious, and explored the significance of change and the dream state. Advertising campaigns benefited from experimental photography; products were found floating in shadowy netherworlds or dominating larger-than-life terrains. American photography cultivated close-ups and geometric abstractions. These lively movements were cut short by the Depression of the 1930s, and, of course, by the outbreak of World War II.

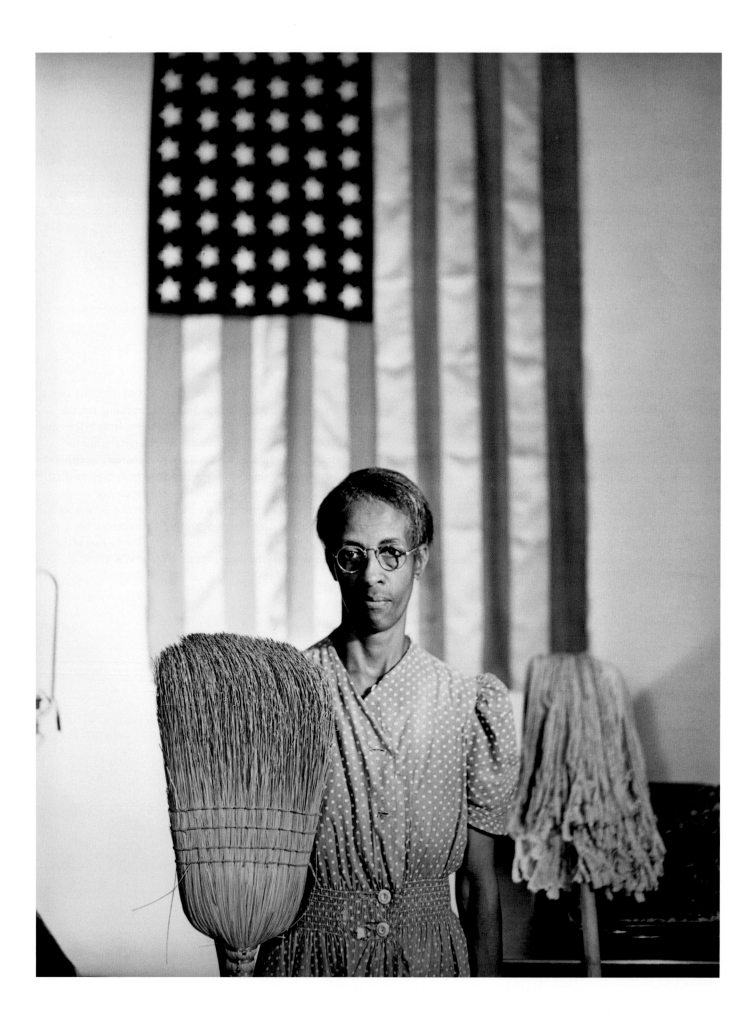

CHAPTER NINE

Documentary Expression and Popular Photography

While many American photographers of the 1930s had been influenced by a Modernist aesthetic, their subject matter during this decade was more profoundly determined by their varied responses to the social and political realities of the Depression. The emergence of documentary photography as a means of addressing those realities had a far-reaching legacy for the medium, reaching into the twenty-first century.

About the same time, the radio took its place as a piece of family furniture, perhaps near the phonograph, which played popular tunes. As the historian William Stott has pointed out, trust in the truth and impartiality of radio broadcasts surpassed belief in newspapers.[1] In the post-World War I era, the radio was as glamorous as today's wide-screen digital televisions. Experimental photographers photographed them, emphasizing the geometrics of radio tubes. In 1930, Walter Ruttmann (1887–1941) sampled street sounds in Berlin. He presented the result, which he called an acoustical film, in a theater where sounds emanated from a deliberately blank screen—in effect, a radio.

Newspaper and magazine photographs were rivaled by the up-to-the-minute news of radio broadcasts, and the proliferation of motion pictures, with which sound had been successfully integrated. Many theaters closed, but those that survived lowered prices and sponsored give-aways to bring in customers. Entertainment and documentary films were often preceded by newsreels, the precursors of post-World War II television news programs. Simply put, during the lean years of the Great Depression, ordinary people began their enduring acquaintance with multimedia.

THE ORIGINS OF DOCUMENTARY

In a broad sense, all non-fictional representation, in books or in images, is documentary. But during the 1930s, when the word "documentary" came into wide usage, its meaning was more limited. Writers, filmmakers, and photographers produced a blend of Modernistic style and realistic subject matter, aimed at educating the public about the experience of hardship or injustice. Earlier photographers such as John Thomson and Jacob Riis had pictured misfortune, but they were not interested in visual innovation, and they tended to present people in categories, such as occupation, class status, or ethnic origin. Documentary photographers in the 1930s strove to present their human subjects as ordinary people who were temporarily down on their luck, hoping that viewers would make the imaginative leap to apply the message to themselves. Earlier social documentary photography, with the exception of Lewis Hine's work, was often more patronizing toward its subjects.

Filmmaking and film theory helped instigate the beginnings of documentary photography. For example, to make his popular *Man with a Movie Camera*, Dziga Vertov left the studio and roamed the streets recording life as it was lived, before editing it into a fast-paced visual roadshow (see p. 260). In the 1920s, documentary film combined derring-do with exotic stories, as in *Grass* (1923), an account of the hazardous yearly migration of the Bakhtiari people of Iran. *Grass* was shot by Merian C. Cooper (1893–1923) and Ernest B. Schoedsach (1893–1979),

9.1
GORDON PARKS, *Ella Watson (American Gothic)*, 1942. Gelatin silver print. Library of Congress, Washington, D.C.

who went on to make *King Kong* (1933), a film whose early island scenes demonstrate the entertaining qualities of early documentary.

American filmmaker Robert Flaherty (1884–1951) spent sixteen months with the indigenous people near Hudson Bay in Canada chronicling their daily lives in the box-office success *Nanook of the North* (1922). Though acting and scripts were discouraged by documentary filmmakers, they were not purists. For example, during the shooting of *Nanook*, Flaherty restaged a walrus kill. Flaherty's public success helped legitimize the documentary mode, and sent the big film studios in search of "another Nanook." The first use of the word "documentary" in its new sense was probably made by influential British filmmaker and theorist John Grierson (1898–1972), in his review of Flaherty's South Sea island film *Moana* (1926).

The documentary current flowed not only through film and photography, but also through social science writing, popular literature, radio programs, and art movements such as the American Ashcan School.[2] Each of these modes reinforced the other, suggesting that the practitioners were neutral observers, boldly recounting facts. Grierson suggested that documentary should be given the power of poetry and prophecy.[3] He maintained that documentary was "an 'anti-aesthetic' movement" that knew how to use aesthetics.[4] However, photographer Ansel Adams rejected the new fusion of art and observation, complaining wryly that "What you've got are not photographers. They're a bunch of sociologists with cameras."[5]

Over time, as questions about the accuracy and completeness of documentary arose, its primary association with social observation and social advocacy weakened. Today the word is popularly used loosely to describe large, visually and thematically related archives or extensive photographic projects, such as the far-ranging photographs of three decades of life in the American South by novelist Eudora Welty (1909–2001) (see p. 286), or the 1,400 portrait photographs of famous individuals by Carl van Vechten (1880–1964) (see Fig. 9.21). Contemporary documentary photography now frequently navigates between visualizing the personal experience of the photographer and a setting of profuse sociological text.

THE FARM SECURITY ADMINISTRATION

Initiated in 1935, the Resettlement Administration (R.A.) was among President Roosevelt's efforts to fight the Depression. It was an umbrella agency, charged with coordinating the various rural relief efforts in government departments, including the Agricultural Adjustment Administration and the Federal Emergency Relief Administration. The agency oversaw loans, flood control, migrant camps, and agricultural education. As its name implies, one of the R.A.'s prominent initiatives was to move distressed farmers into more economically viable service and industrial work. The mission of the R.A., like many of the New Deal agencies, was regularly questioned by conservatives who felt that direct, planned government intervention into the economy and the daily lives of citizens was un-American, or worse, crypto-socialist.

In 1937, the R.A. was subsumed into the Department of Agriculture and renamed the Farm Security Administration (F.S.A.). Roy Stryker (1893–1976), who supervised the photographic activity of the R.A., continued with the F.S.A., directing what was officially known as the "Historical Section—Photographic." His job remained much the same: he was to gather photographic evidence of the agency's good works and transmit these images to the press. Stryker's background as a photo editor consisted solely of his efforts to find illustrations for the textbook *American Economic Life and the Means of its Improvement* (1925), written by his mentor Columbia University professor Rexford Tugwell. When Tugwell moved to Washington to head the R.A., Stryker went with him.

Some scholars argue that the orchestration of public opinion through the mass media practiced by the F.S.A. and other New Deal programs parallels the activities of experimental photographers in the early years of the Soviet Union.[6] Certainly the United States and the Soviet Union both envisioned industrial expansion as crucial to future prosperity. But the R.A./F.S.A. did not financially support revolutionary departures from visual—or political—conventions, as did the Soviet Union. In fact, the United States government feared socialist connotations, and abstained from calling their efforts propaganda, preferring instead the word "publicity."[7]

The R.A./F.S.A. photographers were heir to an understanding of documentary that revolved around emotionally persuasive, stylized depictions of symbolic images. However much they asserted the hard reality of their pictures, they were no more averse to invoking religious imagery than was Lewis Hine. Indeed, the photographs that themselves have become part of American history, such as Arthur Rothstein's *Fleeing a Dust Storm* (see Fig. 9.5) or Dorothea Lange's *Migrant Mother* (see Fig. 9.3), elicited biblical associations of wandering in the desert or the Virgin Mary with the baby Jesus.

Early in his tenure, Stryker envisioned a smooth system in which full-time photographers exhaustively covered the agency's good works around the country, and returned the images to the R.A. for swift nationwide distribution to media outlets. Budget restraints reduced his grandiose vision, yet Stryker still scheduled assignments, drafted shooting scripts, and decided which photographs would be distributed to media outlets ranging from *Time* magazine to the *Junior Scholastic*.[8] By 1940, the agency claimed to be distributing an average of 1,400 images a month.[9] Stryker's pet idea of focusing on life in small towns may have come from conversations he had with sociologist Robert S. Lynd, who with Helen Lynd wrote the influential 1929 book *Middletown: A Study in Modern America*, a classic in-depth study of an average middle-American small city. Stryker once bragged about his ability to shape views of the Depression that avoided tabloid voyeurism and social strife, saying, "You'll find no record of big people or big events … There are pictures that say Depression, but there are no pictures of sit-down strikes, no apple salesmen on street corners, not a single shot of Wall Street, and absolutely no celebrities."[10] Roughly twenty photographers,[11] full- and part-time, shot for the agency until 1942, at which time

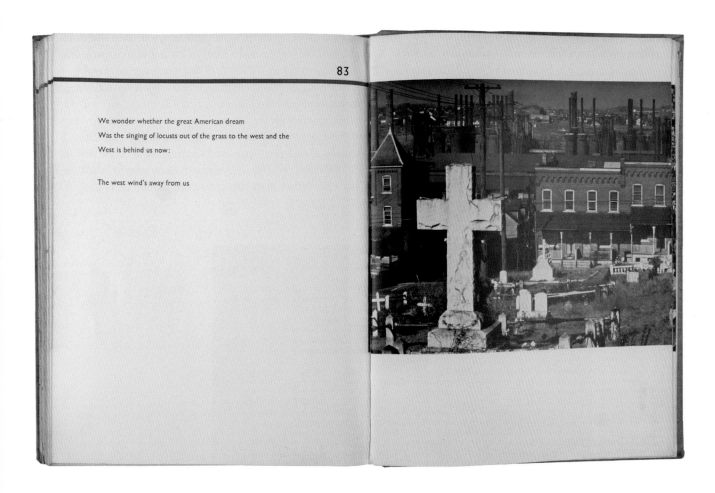

We wonder whether the great American dream
Was the singing of locusts out of the grass to the west and the
West is behind us now:

The west wind's away from us

9.2
WALKER EVANS, *Untitled,* **from** *Land of the Free,* **by Archibald MacLeish, 1937. Library of Congress, Washington, D.C.**

it was subsumed within the Office of War Information. Although some photographs were taken before the R.A. was renamed the F.S.A., and after it was engaged to do war work, the images are collectively known as the Farm Security Administration photographs.

Among Stryker's first hires was Walker Evans (1903–1975), who came to the agency in June 1935 with well-established credentials. Through Berenice Abbott (see p. 288), Evans had had the opportunity to view the photographs of Eugène Atget (see Fig. 8.29), which Abbott had amassed in Paris and brought to New York City. Evans responded to Atget's straightforward recording of historic streets and buildings, as well as worn interiors and architectural detail that bespoke the persistence of the past in the present. Unlike the Surrealist photographers, who found Atget's work full of mystery and the uncanny, Evans located there a reserved and courtly melancholy about the transitions of modern life. He spoke of Atget's "lyrical understanding of the street, trained observation of it, special feeling for patina, eye for revealing detail, over all of which is thrown a poetry."[12] Atget's images heartened Evans's aesthetic inclinations, while the commercial and fashion photographs of Steichen ran counter to his sensibilities. Evans wrote that Steichen's "general note is money, understanding advertising values, special feeling for parvenu elegance, slick technique,

over all of which is thrown a hardness of superficiality that is the hardness and superficiality of America's latter day."[13] In Evans's view, commercialism was not simply Steichen's personal dilemma, but America's national predicament.

Evans believed in finding scenes and objects whose appearance implied a story or acted as a metaphor for an attitude toward life. He felt that his unambiguous, clearly composed images owed a debt to the spare and rhythmic prose style of American author Ernest Hemingway (1899–1961).[14] Evans's image of Bethlehem, Pennsylvania (Fig. 9.2), symbolically guides the viewer from background to foreground through a fatal progression of work, home life, and death. The image shows no people, but uses the locale and flattened perspective to indicate the compass of their restricted lives.

Evans secured a leave of absence from the R.A. to work for *Fortune* magazine on a project with his friend the writer James Agee (1909–1955). Like other publications in the mid-1930s, *Fortune* contrived human-interest photo-essays on how the Depression affected individuals. For their joint venture, Agee and Evans chronicled the lives of three families of impoverished, cotton-growing tenant farmers in Hale County, Alabama. Agee's procrastination, and *Fortune*'s doubts about the project, eventually prompted the company to cancel the assignment. The project was later published as the book *Let Us Now Praise*

Famous Men (1941), with a suite of Evans's uncaptioned photographs preceding Agee's text. Agee explained that his prose and Evans's photographs were to be viewed as "coequal, mutually independent, and fully collaborative."[15] Published in the shadow of the commercially successful *You Have Seen Their Faces* (1937), by Margaret Bourke-White and Erskine Caldwell (see p. 284), the Evans–Agee book was a financial failure. Evans's image of twenty-seven-year-old Allie Mae Burroughs, thinly disguised as "Annie Mae Gudger" in the text, exemplified his approach to picture-making (Fig. 9.7).

Evans's disdain for Stryker's assignment guidelines and deadlines made him the legendary bad boy of F.S.A. photography, and he was dismissed in 1937. It is difficult to imagine that the autocratic Stryker could tolerate Evans's desire to record handmade advertising signs or austere domestic interiors as an anonymous folk art. Evans's images tended to lift poverty and the economic effects of the Depression into a timeless picturesque universe. Spare and serene images comprised the bulk of Evans's pictures in "American Photographs," the title of his 1937 Museum of Modern Art exhibition and of his 1938

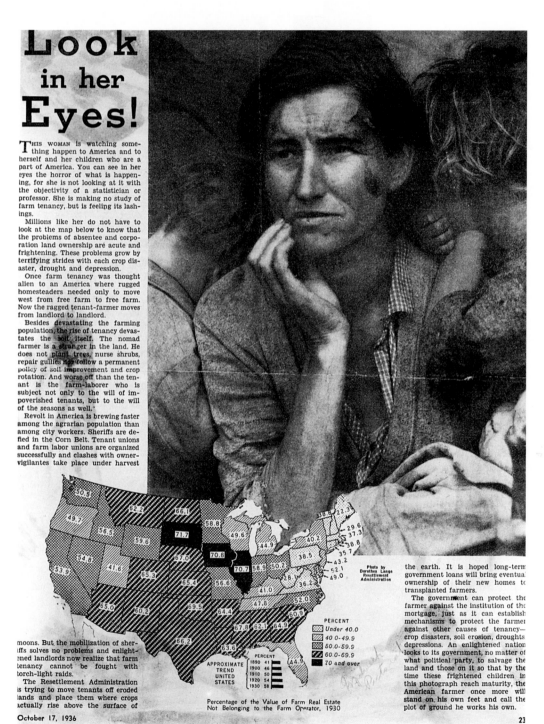

9.3
DOROTHEA LANGE, *Migrant Mother,* **1936, from** *Midweek Pictorial,* **October 17, 1936. F.S.A. Scrapbook, FSA-OWI Written Records. Library of Congress, Washington, D.C.**

Lange's photograph recalls religious images of the Madonna and Child, but also expresses Depression-era values. The children on either side turn away, symbolically ashamed of their wretchedness. The mother's careworn face, her tattered clothes, and the dirty baby near her breast indicate extreme distress, deserving of compassion. Yet her expression hints at a determination to persevere through hard times.

book. This book influenced a generation of younger American photographers, such as Robert Frank (see pp. 342). They admired its dispassionate approach, which for them indicated Evans's caustic alienation from society. His insistence on publishing the images without captions and in no chronological order suggested the sensibilities of an artist who demanded that his work be taken on its own terms.

After the F.S.A., Evans continued his artful documentary in such series as his subway photographs taken with a concealed camera. But his major source of income was ironically as a writer and photographer for *Fortune*, a periodical devoted to big business.

Unlike Evans, Dorothea Lange came to the R.A. in 1935 with a sure sense of social justice and of how photography could reveal inequality. As a statement of her belief, in 1923 she tacked lines by English statesman and writer Francis Bacon (1561–1626) to her darkroom door:

The contemplation of things as they are
without substitution or imposture
without error or confusion
is in itself a nobler thing
than a whole harvest of invention.[16]

The seminar she took in New York City on basic photography, given by Pictorialist Clarence White, did not influence the look or the subject matter of her images. During the early Depression, Lange photographed labor demonstrations and breadlines in San Francisco. Her work with activist-economist Paul Taylor, whom she subsequently married, focused her attention on the plight of migrant farmworkers. For the R.A., she produced the photograph that became the national icon of the Depression. *Migrant Mother* is one of several shots Lange took of a thirty-two-year-old woman and her children, who were stranded in a frozen pea field among the crop they had hoped to pick to earn some money (Fig. 9.3). Undoubtedly the most popular image created during the Depression era, the photograph was repeatedly sent out to newspapers and magazines by the F.S.A.

Though powerful, *Migrant Mother* is not typical of Lange's work. She did not readily repeat the mother-and-child theme. With Taylor supplying the text, Lange published captioned photographs in *An American Exodus: A Record of Human Erosion* (1939; Fig. 9.4), a book whose title refers to the destructive southwestern drought of the mid-1930s, and the migration it caused. In the book, photographs were accompanied by quotations from the sitters, unlike the fictionalized statements

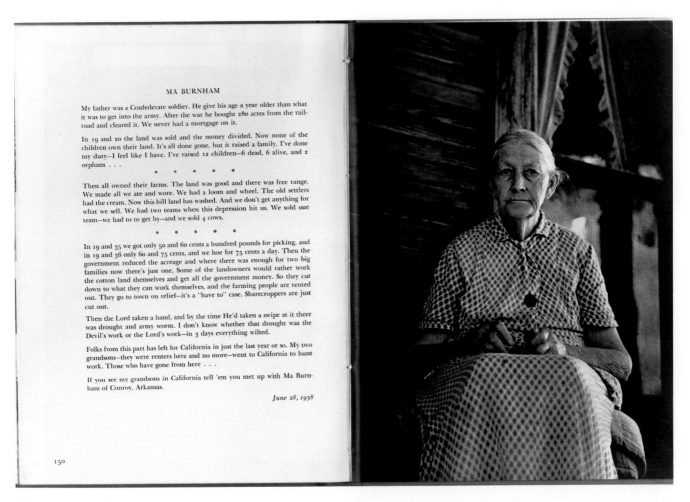

9.4
DOROTHEA LANGE, *Ma Burnham,* **from** *An American Exodus,* **by Dorothea Lange and Paul Schuster Taylor, 1939, pp. 150–51. Library of Congress, Washington, D.C.**

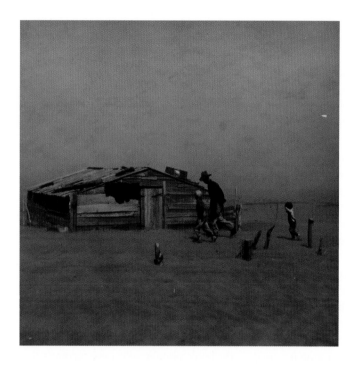

9.5
ARTHUR ROTHSTEIN, *Fleeing a Dust Storm, Cimarron County, Oklahoma*, April 1936. Gelatin silver print. F.S.A. Collection. Library of Congress, Washington, D.C.

created by Margaret Bourke-White and Erskine Caldwell for *You Have Seen Their Faces.*

After her five years with the R.A./F.S.A., Lange continued to make photographs that accorded with her concern for social justice. She and Taylor were adamantly opposed to the 1942 War Relocation Authority (W.R.A.), which forcibly moved Japanese-Americans to internment camps. Like Adams, Lange photographed the internees' life at Manzanar Relocation Center in California. For *Life* magazine, she profiled the daily life of a public defender in Alameda County, California, and chronicled the last days of farming communities in the Berrysea Valley, northeast of San Francisco, on the brink of being flooded by the construction of a new dam.

Another early recruit to the R.A. was Arthur Rothstein (1915–1985), who made a lasting image of the Dust Bowl experience (Fig. 9.5). Rothstein's photography has been

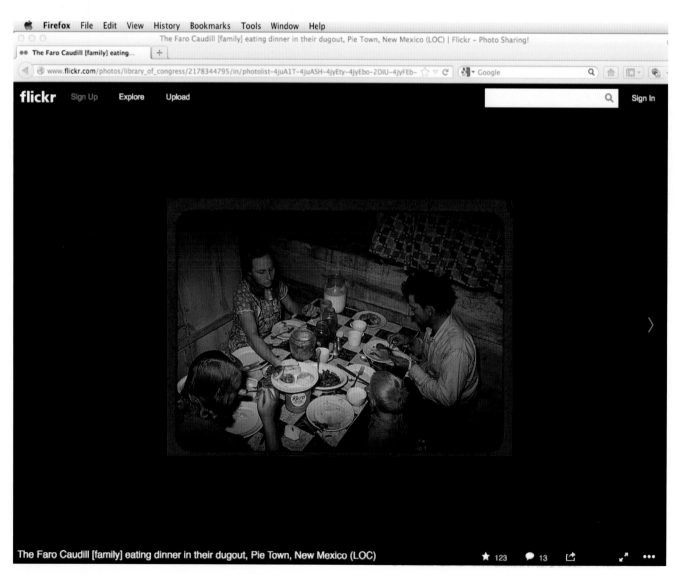

The Faro Caudill [family] eating dinner in their dugout, Pie Town, New Mexico (LOC)

overshadowed by a notorious set of photographs he made in the barren Badlands of South Dakota during the summer of 1936. Having come across the sun-bleached skull of a steer resting on parched soil, he filmed it where he found it, but then moved it, and experimented with close-ups and cast shadows. He was accused of fakery for moving the skull; the agency worried that their funds would be cut back, but did not dismiss Rothstein.[17] In fact, several R.A./F.S.A. photographers could have been charged with altering their images; Lange, for example, had a retoucher airbrush out what she considered a flaw in *Migrant Mother*.[18]

Rothstein was among the F.S.A. photographers to take color pictures using Kodachrome film. Originally developed for motion pictures, the film was adapted for other formats, including the 35mm slide. Known for the longevity of its color sharpness, Kodachrome became a highly successful product for amateur photographers. Along with black-and-white film, Russell Lee (1903–1986) used Kodachrome to photograph in Pie Town, New Mexico (Fig. 9.6), a small rural town selected by Roy Stryker and Lee because they saw it as exemplifying frontier virtues, like self-reliance. Rothstein's work, along with that of other Farm Security Administration photographers, has now been made available on the Internet through the Library of Congress's Photostream.

Photographers came and went at the R.A./F.S.A., some working only a few months. Although about twenty individuals worked for the agency, only a half-dozen or so were employed at any one time.[19] Among the late hires at the F.S.A., when the agency's focus was changing from small town and rural life to urban enterprise and defense activities, were Gordon Parks (1912–2006) and Esther Bubley (1921–1998). Parks came to Washington, D.C., on a prestigious fellowship, which had been held by other African Americans, such as Zora Neale Hurston (1891–1960) and James Baldwin (1924–1987), who wrote about the American South and the black experience. Parks began by photographing the life and work of Ella Watson, who cleaned the agency's office (Fig. 9.1). Parks was eventually hired by *Life* magazine, where he photographed the tumultuous black power movement in the United States. He added filmmaking to his repertoire, and directed the perennial favorite, *Shaft* (1971), about the adventures of a cool black private eye in Harlem.

Esther Bubley was hired in 1942, just as the agency changed its name to the Office of War Information. Her first assignments were in Washington, a city rapidly transforming in response to the United States' entry into World War II. Bubley emphasized women workers, who replaced soldiers. She pictured women at work, driving streetcars and in the new residences for women that were quickly formed in the city and its suburbs (Fig. 9.8). Her images of solitary, pensive women differ greatly from the main visual themes of the F.S.A. In 1943, she rode buses for four weeks, chronicling bus travel, which increased in popularity due to wartime rationing in gasoline and tires. Generally, Bubley's

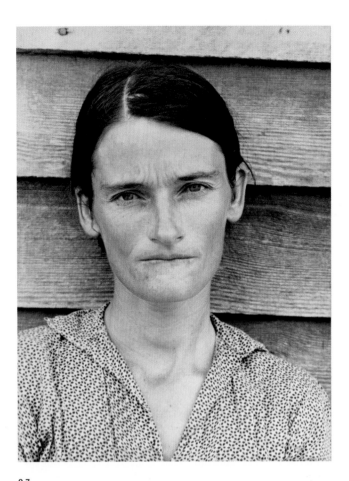

9.7
WALKER EVANS, *Allie Mae Burroughs*, 1936, from *Let Us Now Praise Famous Men*, by Walker Evans and James Agee, 1941. Gelatin silver print. Harry Ransom Humanities Research Center, University of Texas at Austin.

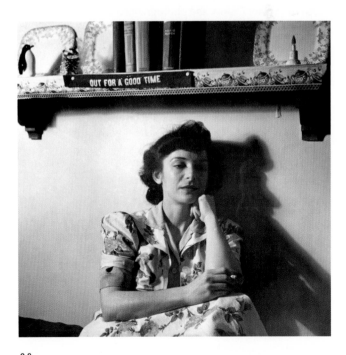

9.8
ESTHER BUBLEY, *Listening to a Murder Mystery on the Radio in a Boarding House Room*, 1943. Gelatin silver print. Library of Congress, Washington, D.C.

9.6 (opposite)
RUSSELL LEE, *The Faro Caudill [family] eating dinner in their dugout, Pie Town, New Mexico*, 1940. Library of Congress, Washington, D.C., screengrab from the Flickr image-sharing website.

portrait

Margaret Bourke-White

By the time she was in her mid-twenties, Margaret Bourke-White (1904–1971) was in the news. Such captions as "This daring camera girl scales skyscrapers for art"[20] show the press's infatuation with a woman who climbed out on to the high steel frame of the Chrysler Building to record its construction, stood on the steel-mill floor amidst flying sparks to photograph a ladle full of molten metal, and shot pictures in remote Canadian logging camps where the temperature went below minus 20 degrees. Bourke-White loved being a celebrity—she even coordinated her camera clothes to match her designer outfits. At the same time, though, she determinedly moved from assignment to assignment, for *Fortune* magazine and then for *Life* magazine, often suggesting her own themes and subjects. Her photograph of the Fort Peck Dam in Montana, then the world's largest earth-filled dam, introduced the American public to the first issue of *Life* magazine on November 23, 1936 (Fig. 9.9). She not only had the cover; she wrote and illustrated the lead article, demonstrating that her ability to find powerful symbols of industrialization easily converted to revealing how people lived in places like the boom town near the dam. Bourke-White is most frequently remembered for her photographs, but she was also the author or co-author of about a dozen books recounting her adventures and imparting her convictions about social inequality.

In the Soviet Union, she photographed the new industrial town of Magnitogorsk, offering a paean of praise to machines and the people who made them work. With Erskine Caldwell (1903–1987), author of steamy southern poverty stories such as *Tobacco Road* (1932) and *God's Little Acre* (1933), she chronicled the impoverished lives of sharecroppers in *You Have Seen Their Faces* (1937), one of the first books to show this kind of imagery in America. The book proved so popular that a less expensive paperback version was issued the same year. Other editions followed. In the book, she and Caldwell contrived dialogue to accompany the images, a deed still debated by those who believe that documentary work must record exactly what people have to say for themselves.

During World War II, Bourke-White photographed German bombs falling on Moscow, was the first woman to fly a combat mission, and sent back raw, painful photographs from the Nazi concentration camp at Buchenwald. Also, she insisted on recording the contributions of the so-called "buffalo soldiers," military units composed of all-black troops. After the war, she photographed Mahatma Gandhi's attempts to gain independence for India, the punishing lives of black gold-miners in South Africa, and guerrilla warfare in Korea. At age forty-nine, her career waned, cut short by Parkinson's disease, which she fought for twenty years with the same courage that she deployed in the course of dangerous assignments.

9.9 (opposite)
MARGARET BOURKE-WHITE, Cover of *Life*, vol. 1, no. 1, November 23, 1936.

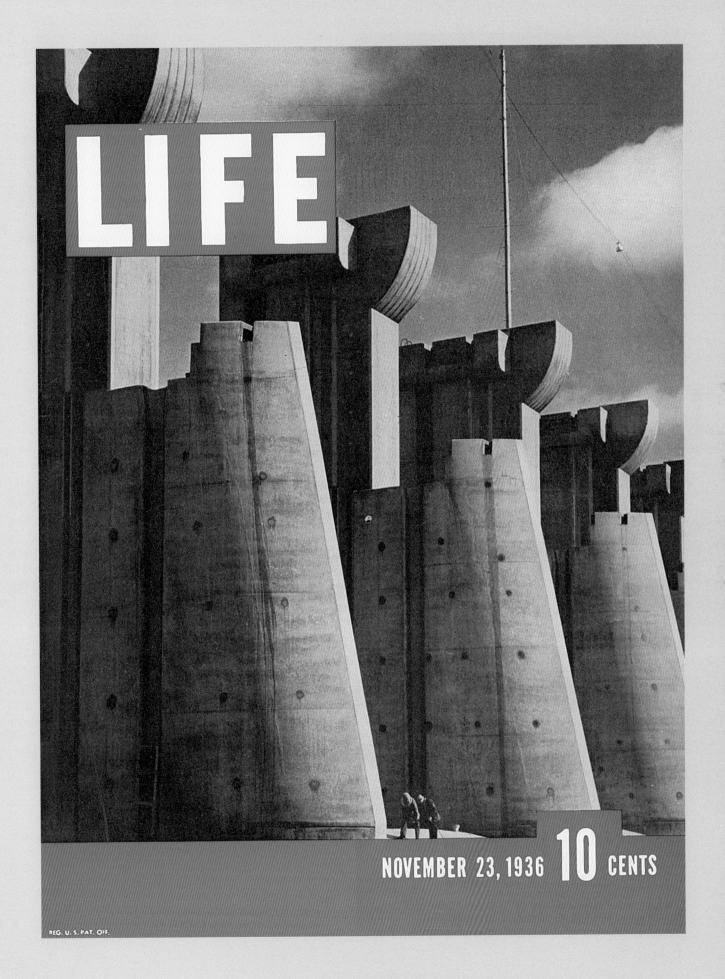

LIFE

NOVEMBER 23, 1936 10 CENTS

REG. U. S. PAT. OFF.

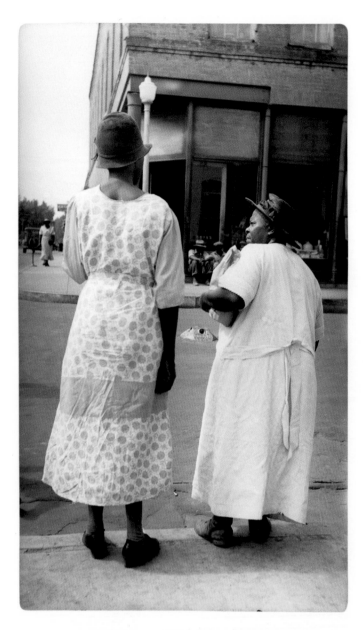

9.10
EUDORA WELTY, *Crossing the Pavement, Utica, Mississippi*, 1930s. Gelatin silver print. Eudora Welty Collection. Mississippi Department of Archives and History, Jackson, Mississippi.

subjects do not suffer the effects of poverty that might be alleviated by a government agency, but are shown coping with the tribulations of war.[21] The bus-trip series and her boarding-house photographs were among the last assignments Bubley did for Stryker. He left the Office of War Information to work in the photographic section of the Standard Oil Company; Bubley eventually joined him there, where she was employed to make another sequence of photographs about a cross-country bus trip.[22]

Stryker sent Jack Delano (1914–1997), another late-comer to the F.S.A., to follow the annual trek from Florida to Maine made by migrant workers who moved northward as crops ripened and required harvesting. Like Bubley, Delano was later employed by the Office of War Information, where he chronicled the industrial build-up before and during World War II (Fig. 9.11), which brought women into factories and spurred African Americans to relocate permanently to jobs in the North, the Midwest, and the West.

OTHER DOCUMENTS

While the R.A./F.S.A. photographs had a lasting effect on America's image of itself, other documentary photography projects were also instigated by government agencies during the Depression era. Berenice Abbott (1898–1991) photographed for the Works Project Administration (W.P.A.), a controversial New Deal program that found public employment for artists, and Eudora Welty, who was hired as a publicity representative for the agency's work in Mississippi, brought her own camera (Fig. 9.10). A bitter look at the Depression and its psychological effects was created by writer and poet Archibald MacLeish (1892–1982), who juxtaposed F.S.A. photographs with his verse in *Land of the Free* (see Fig. 9.2). MacLeish placed images next to pages of text, and in a reference to modern storytelling put a narrow blue line across the top of every text page, alluding to the soundtrack that was placed in a thin line along the edge of motion-picture film. *The Grapes of Wrath* (1939) by John Steinbeck (1902–1968), a stirring account of the lives of poor farmers displaced by the Dust Bowl, was first conceived by Steinbeck as a text with pictures by a *Life* magazine photographer called Horace Bristol (1908–1997).

Richard Wright (1908–1960) was the author of *Native Son*, the best-selling 1940 novel about racism in a northern American city. In the midst of the popularity of *Native Son*, Wright was commissioned to write another text about black life in America, *Twelve Million Black Voices: A Folk History of the Negro in the*

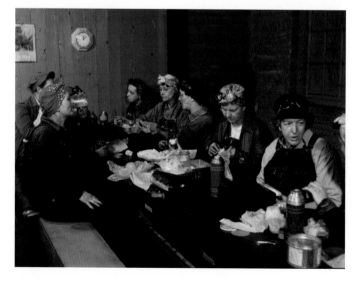

9.11
JACK DELANO, *Women Workers employed as wipers in the roundhouse having lunch in their rest room, C. & N.W. R.R*, 1943. Library of Congress, Washington, D.C.

We answer: "Our problem is being solved. We are crossing the line you dared us to cross, though we pay in the coin of death!"

The seasons of the plantation no longer dictate the lives of many of us; hundreds of thousands of us are moving into the sphere of conscious history.

We are with the new tide. We stand at the crossroads. We watch each new procession. The hot wires carry urgent appeals. Print compels us. Voices are speaking. Men are moving! And we shall be with them. . . .

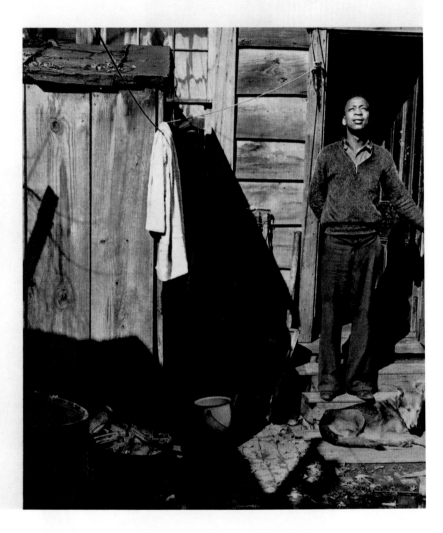

9.12
CARL MYDANS, *Back Yard Alley Dwelling*, from *Twelve Million Black Voices: A Folk History of the Negro in the United States*, by Richard Wright, 1941. Library of Congress, Washington, D.C.

Wright addressed *Twelve Million Black Voices* to whites, using the word "you" from the outset, and he deliberately identified with other African Americans, using "we" and "us" throughout the text.

United States (1941), which was illustrated with photographs from the F.S.A. archive, including those by Carl Mydans (1907–2004) (Fig. 9.12). Listed as photo editor was Edwin Rosskam (1903–1985), a photographer hired as an exhibition designer at the F.S.A., who also worked with Stryker to promote the use of the agency's images in publications.

The winnowing of the archive for images by different photographers, and the recaptioning of the pictures for *Twelve Million Black Voices*, have been questioned by critics. Foreshadowing reactions to "The Family of Man" show (see pp. 311–12), commentators claimed that reprinting works in a different context turned "what was news into history, what

was propaganda into art, or vice versa, altering the relation of the photograph to actuality, confounding hopes for a single, authoritative, stable meaning."[23]

TRANSFORMING THE SOCIAL DOCUMENTARY

Although socially concerned documentary was prominent throughout the 1930s, most photographers were not creating work intended to kindle social change. In fact, like experimental photography, the documentary look became a putatively apolitical visual style. Around the United States, newspapers sent their photographers into the countryside to bring back F.S.A.-like photographs, safely shorn of any social welfare propaganda. The

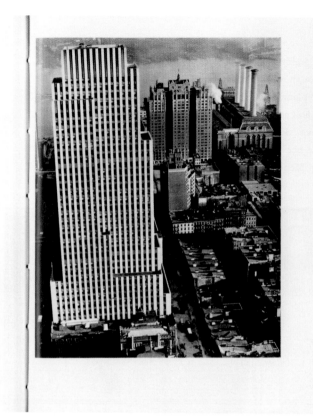

"Daily News" Building, 220 East 42nd Street, Manhattan; November 21, 1935. Completed: February, 1930. Architects: Howells, Hood & Fouilhoux. Owned by News Syndicate Company, Inc.

• Three million circulation Sundays, one and three-quarter million weekdays — more than double that of the next largest American newspaper — this is the DAILY NEWS. Such revenue made possible "The House that Tabloid Built," the DAILY NEWS Building, a 36-story skyscraper, costing $10,000,000.

142

9.13
BERENICE ABBOTT, *Daily News Building,* from her book *Changing New York* (text by Elizabeth McCausland), 1939. Library of Congress, Washington, D.C.

W.P.A. funded American photographer Berenice Abbott to depict the growth of New York City. Her four-year project resulted in the book *Changing New York* (1939) (Fig. 9.13). Abbott typified the New Woman of the 1920s.

Imaging the social world took many forms during the interwar years, including worker photography, photojournalism, and sociologically driven accounts, some of which made photography central to their investigation. A popular theme was a day in the life of an individual or a city. This was taken up in Britain by Mass-Observation, or MO, a group that simultaneously targeted false mass-media images of workers and the middle class, and images promulgated by out-of-touch academic sociologists and self-interested government officials. It published *May the Twelfth*, containing written accounts of a day in the life of more than two hundred observers. On this day—May 12, 1937—King George VI (1894–1952; r. 1936–52) was crowned, ending the crisis that arose when Edward VIII abdicated the throne the previous December. MO's intent in *May the Twelfth* was far from the simplistic "where-were-you-then?" motif. The group hoped to undermine faith in government, by showing that it did not communicate with the people about the impending abdication. At the same time, MO wanted to skewer British psychological reliance on the monarchy, exposing the operation of a modern myth. MO gathered full- and part-time writers, painters, poets, and local people to produce an "anthropology of ourselves."[24] MO was an early instance of what

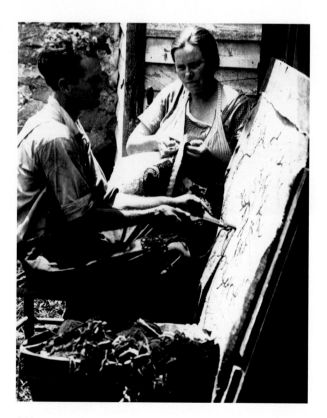

9.14
DORIS ULMANN, *Mr. and Mrs. Anderson, Saluda, North Carolina,* 1933 or 1934. Platinum print.

focus

Worker Photography in Europe

In Europe and the Soviet Union during the 1920s, left-wing groups calling themselves worker-photographers organized to combat what they identified as "bourgeois picture-lies" about working conditions and organized protests.[25] At the same time, they focused on the dignity of work. Their attempt to combat deceptive press images with their own pictures attests to the power of illustrated newspapers and magazines as public display cases for political ideas.

Like the sports and hiking clubs organized in the Soviet Union to motivate and modernize workers, photography groups, exhibitions, and publications were created to raise consciousness through picture-taking, and also to provide a visual record of the emerging new society. The magazine *Sovetskoe foto* (*Soviet Photo*) started in 1926, to foster a new imagery that would replace the obsolete photography of the past. As one contributor to the first issue wrote, "Just as each vanguard comrade should have a watch, so he should also be able to master a photographic camera."[26] Yet, as Erika Wolf pointed out, many of the worker-photographers in the Soviet Union did not have working-class backgrounds, and sought professional assignments in the growing photojournalism sector of Russian life.[27]

Willi Münzenberg, the German publisher who founded *AIZ* (see p. 234), had his periodical carry photo-reports by workers. He also issued *Der Arbeiter-Fotograf* (*The Worker-Photographer*), the journal of the German worker-photography association, which sought to instruct its readers how to make images with a "class eye,"[28] and to break down the customary distinction between producer and consumer of mass-media images (Fig. 9.15). Often anonymously, camera-carrying workers captured protest rallies and strike actions. They photographed workers' families, but were rarely successful in infiltrating factories to make images of hazardous conditions.[29] The worker-photographers brought their class eye to bear on Renger-Patzsch's book *The World is Beautiful* (see p. 264), claiming that the world was ugly and evil, and in need of change.[30] Artists such as George Grosz and Kathe Köllwitz were criticized for making the condition of the workers seem too hopeless.[31]

Worker-photographer groups were also started in the Netherlands, Belgium, France, Czechoslovakia, Hungary, Austria, and Britain.[32] Wherever they appeared, their approach was challenged by groups who embraced left-wing politics but not the conventional imaging approach sometimes taken by the workers. While the German magazine *Der Arbeiter-Fotograf* carried articles critical of photomontage, it also adopted

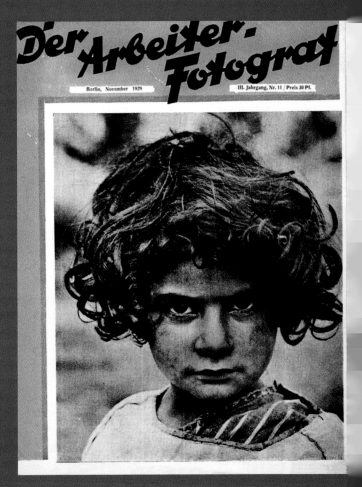

9.15
ERNST THORMANN, Cover of *Der Arbeiter-Fotograf* (*The Worker-Photographer*), November 1929.

the assertive typography and unexpected angles of Modern photography. In Russia, experimental artists and photographers associated with the *Left Front of the Arts* (see p. 239) became active in worker-photography circles. Publications begun as showcases for photography by workers sometimes turned to professional photographers to illustrate sociological reports and news.

These and other observations were part of a groundbreaking 2011 exhibition on worker photography held at the Museo Reina Sofía in Madrid, which brought new prominence to this vital international movement in art and photographic histories.

is now called citizen journalism. Humphrey Spender (1910–2005), a photographer for the *Daily Mirror*, also shot for MO. He traveled to the gritty towns of England's northern industrial areas, building a trove of about nine hundred images, most of which were not published because of the expense involved (Fig. 9.16).

Although he did not work for MO, German-born and -educated Bill Brandt (1904–1983) took up a similarly anthropological form of documentary when he settled in London in 1932, after studying with Man Ray in Paris. Two books of photographs, *The English at Home* (1936) and *A Night in London* (1938), examined British life, particularly its class system and behavior. Brandt's point of view is evident in the interpretive strategies he used in these books. His *Parlormaid and Under-*

Parlormaid Ready to Serve Dinner (1932–35) (Fig. 9.17) is full of astute social observation.

Despite its name, the Workers' Film and Photo League, founded in New York in 1930, was not a working-class organization but a group of filmmakers and photographers committed to depicting urban life, especially in poorer neighborhoods, and to keeping a supply of class-conscious images available for left-wing publications. The filmmakers and photographers soon split into two groups, and the word "worker" was dropped from their titles. Members of the Photo League included W. Eugene Smith (1918–1978), who once served as its president, and Jerome Liebling (1924–2011), whose two years spent with the league anticipated his lifelong career in humanistic documentary work. The Photo League offered

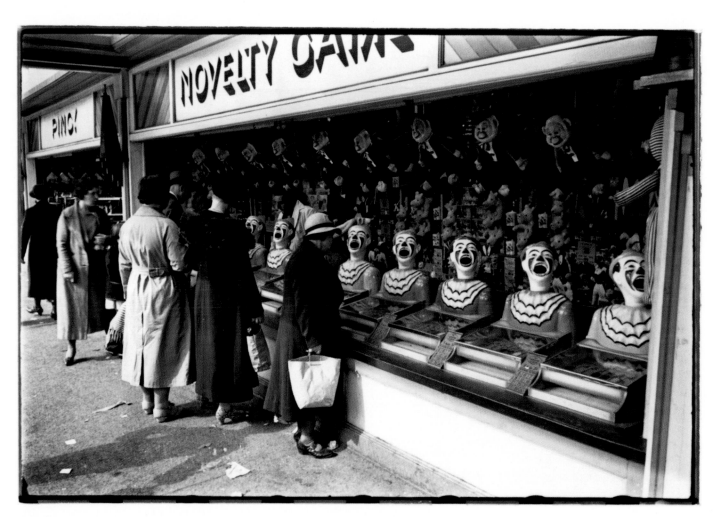

9.16
HUMPHREY SPENDER, *Midway Clowns, Blackpool*, 1937. Gelatin silver print. Bolton Museum and Art Gallery, England.

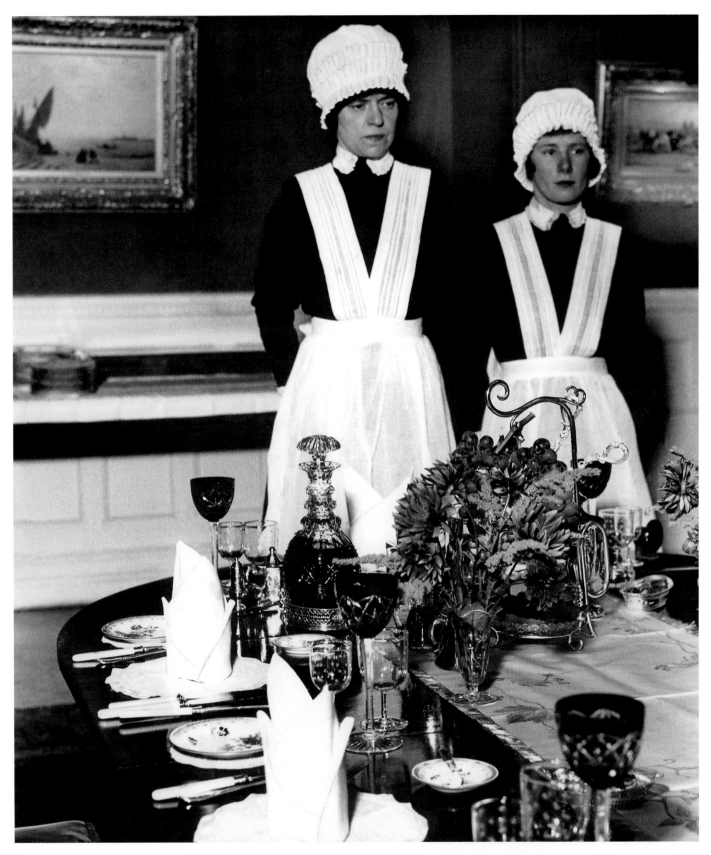

9.17
BILL BRANDT, *Parlormaid and Under-Parlormaid Ready to Serve Dinner*, 1932–35. Gelatin silver print. Bill Brandt Archive, London.

The two servants here are ready to attend at a lavishly set table. Their starched aprons and stiff poses resemble the folded napkins in the foreground. The taller woman's stern expression is set off by the anxious expression of the underling. The scene's implicit drama—the sense that something is about to happen—may owe to Brandt's infatuation with Surrealism.

lectures, classes, and cooperative ventures. While working for *Fortune* magazine, Margaret Bourke-White and Berenice Abbott attended meetings of the New York branch.[33]

Among the league's undertakings were "production groups," like-minded photographers interested in experimentation, or in such themes as contemporary youth and neighborhood life. Under the direction of Aaron Siskind (1903–1991), the so-called Feature Group worked on the Photo League's most widely recognized project, the *Harlem Document*, containing pictures of the area's poor and a text composed by African-American

sociologist Michael Carter[34] (Fig. 9.18). Although Siskind published some of his photographs from the *Harlem Document* in his exhibitions, and some of the pictures appeared in the May, 1940 issue of *Look* magazine, the totality of the images were never published.[35]

While the Photo League was working on its *Harlem Document*, a different, generally more upbeat, Harlem document was being informally created by other image-makers. The work of James Van der Zee (1886–1983), a popular portraitist and street photographer, was steeped in nineteenth- and early

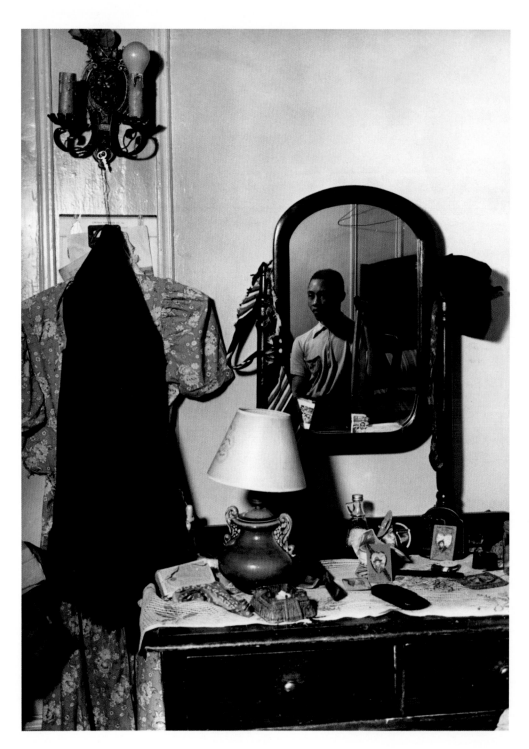

9.18
AARON SISKIND, *Reflection of a Man in a Dresser Mirror*, **from** *Harlem Document*, **c. 1938. Gelatin silver print. George Eastman House, Rochester, New York.**

From 1938 to 1940, the Feature Group was the most publicly visible of the various project-oriented teams at the Photo League. Originally planned as a book, some of the pictures from the *Harlem Document* appeared in *Fortune* magazine, and were exhibited at the 1939 San Francisco World's Fair.

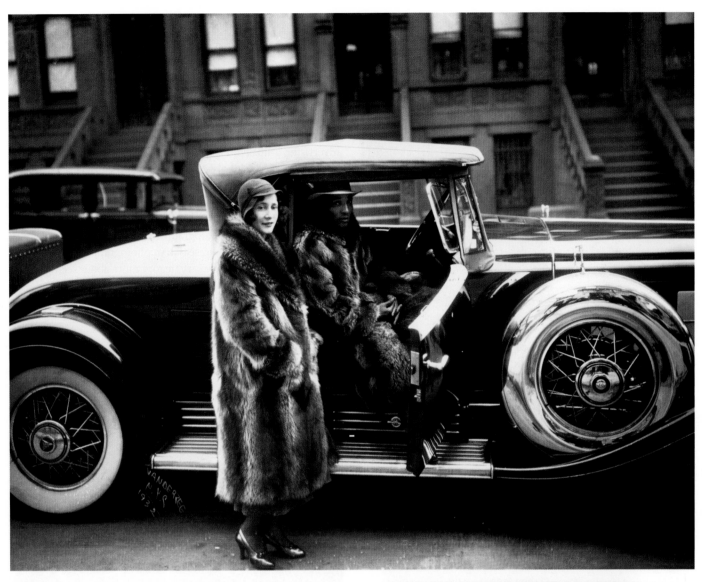

9.19 (above)
JAMES VAN DER ZEE, *Couple in Raccoon Coats*, 1932. Gelatin silver print.

twentieth-century devices, including extensive props and elaborately painted backgrounds. As historian Deborah Willis observed, his photographs of middle-class African-American life often suggest that the postwar mass movement of blacks from the South to take factory jobs in northern cities was a success (Fig. 9.19). Like Van der Zee, Marvin Smith (1910–2003) and Morgan Smith (1910–1993), twin brothers who ran a popular Harlem portrait studio, recorded social affairs and political events, and captured the beginnings of the Civil Rights movement in their pictures of the campaign "Don't Buy Where You Can't Work" (Fig. 9.20). At the same time, Carl van Vechten, the first American critic of modern dance, wrote for the *New York Times* in the era when Isadora Duncan was choreographing

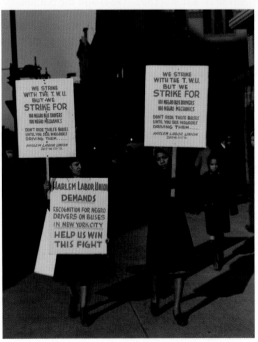

9.20 (right)
MORGAN AND MARVIN SMITH, *Transit Workers Union Strike*, c. 1940.
New York Public Library, Schomburg Center for Research in Black Culture.

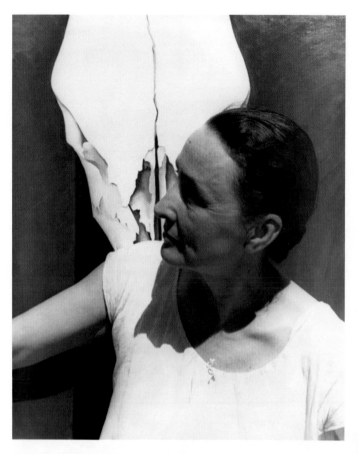

original context and force it into an aesthetic category so that it could function as a museum display. Albin-Guillot had already enlarged the meaning of this type of photography with her choice of title and her selection of pictures.

The artistic and popular appreciation of scientific images owed much to the spread of illustrated magazines and journals aimed at a general audience, as well as the development of textbooks with photographically derived images. Even advertising utilized images drawn from science (Fig. 9.23). Theorists such as Moholy-Nagy encouraged viewers to look at X-rays, which were also included in the Newhall show, not as medical information but as a remedial kind of new vision. At the 1929 "Film und Foto" exhibit, influenced by Moholy-Nagy's ideas, scientific photography was divided into three sections: documentation; research in photographic process; and expansion of the senses, a category more about seeing than about scientific knowledge.[36]

In the late 1930s, Berenice Abbott began experiments with scientific photography. By the early 1940s, she saw the need to invent a visual recording system, called "Projection Photography" or "Supersight," which allowed the user to project and enlarge subjects on a 16- by 20-inch piece of film or paper.[37] When she became photography editor of *Science Illustrated*,

creative rebellion in that field. He promoted black artists and writers, and photographed his large circle of acquaintances, ranging from poet-playwright Langston Hughes (1902–1967) to publisher Alfred A. Knopf (1892–1984) and the painter Georgia O'Keeffe (Fig. 9.21).

POPULAR SCIENCE/POPULAR ART

At the 1937 Museum of Modern Art exhibition of photographic history, the first such comprehensive show in the United States, curator and historian Beaumont Newhall (1908–1993) presented samples of photojournalism, sports photography, film stills, and aerial photography, as well as an array of art photography, organized historically. He also included scientific photography, not simply to record technical advances in that area, but also to display the aesthetic appeal of forms and processes revealed through scientific procedures. From *Micrographie décorative* (*Decorative Micrography*), a 1931 portfolio of views seen through a microscope made by French photographer and scientist Laure Albin-Guillot (1879–1962), Newhall chose a microscopically enlarged view of a diatom (a form of single-celled alga), showing its ornate symmetrical design (Fig. 9.22). Newhall did not, as later critics have suggested, wrench a scientific image from its

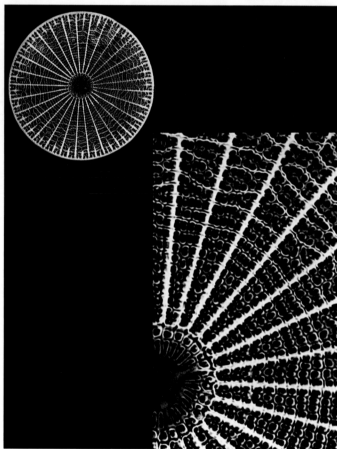

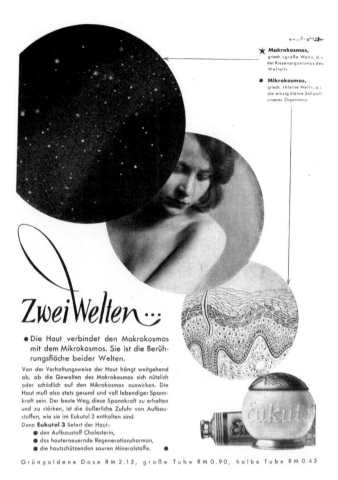

9.23
DESIGNER UNKNOWN, "*Zwei Welten ...*" (*Two Worlds*). Advertisement for Eukutol Skin Cream in *Münchner Illustrierte Presse*, no. 5, January 31, 1932, p. 105. Institut für Zeitungsforschung, Dortmund, Germany.

she carefully selected views that explained scientific principles to lay readers. Her interest in scientific education continued throughout the 1950s, when she worked with a commission of scientists and teachers to improve the illustrations of science textbooks (Fig. 9.24).

After he escaped the Nazi campaign of terror against the Jews, Roman Vishniac (1897–1990) emigrated to the United States in 1940. The Russian-born Vishniac, who was a physician, microbiologist, and Ph.D. art historian as well as a photographer, added photomicrography to his skills, primarily to make a living. He specialized in depicting small living organisms, and wrote and lectured on the hidden beauty revealed by the microscope.

But in the public's mind, it was Harold Edgerton (1903–1990) who was most closely associated with demonstrating the beauty of scientific photography. His early work in the 1930s, taken with the STROBE lighting system he helped to invent, was a fixture in *Life* magazine, and appeared in books marketed to lay readers, such as *Flash! Seeing the Unseen by Ultra High-Speed Photography* (1939), and in short movies such as *Quicker than a Wink* (1940), which won an Oscar. The 1937 Museum of Modern Art display exhibited Edgerton's crowd-pleasing stop-action image of the crown-shaped splash made by a milk drop as it hit the surface

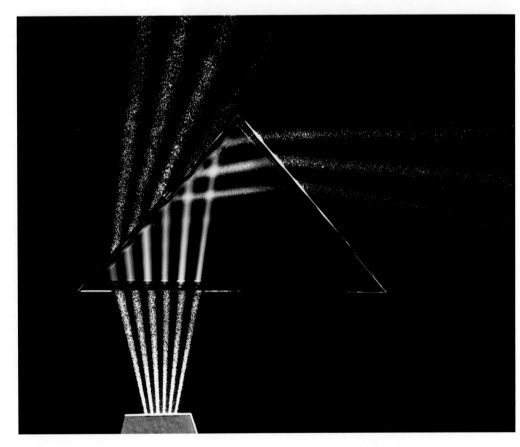

9.24
BERENICE ABBOTT, *Light Rays through a Prism*, Cambridge, c. 1958. Gelatin silver print. New York Public Library, New York.

Abbott invented several devices and techniques for scientific photography. This image, typical of her scientific illustration, clearly shows the properties of light as it passes through a prism. The rays are reflected in the glass, but also bent or refracted on the left and right, as they pass through the prism.

of the liquid (Fig. 9.25). Edgerton perfected strobe lighting throughout the 1930s by synchronizing intense but short bursts of light with turning engine rotors. In 1939, he began working with the military, developing the lighting necessary for night-time aerial photography, a technology that won him the Medal of Freedom in 1946.

During the interwar years, entertainment magazines, such as *Photoplay* (1911–80) and *Modern Screen* (1930–85), increased in number and in circulation. The elegant sophistication of Hollywood film stars was emphasized by George Hurrell (1904–1992). Where Southworth and Hawes (see p. 64) created public personas for their sitters, Hurrell fashioned not only a look but also a glamorous otherworldly habitat for celebrities (Fig. 9.26). As chief photographer at MGM, Hurrell shaped faces with light and shadow, drew in thick, sexy eyelashes, and used his retouching pencil to create flawless skin textures. His shadow inflections are so nuanced and numerous that his works seems, at first glance, to harken back to Pictorialism. A closer look reveals that his celebrity photographs are sharp. When World War II erupted, Hurrell was drafted, and his sensuous pictures were eventually replaced by candid photographs and aggressive photographers who would later be dubbed paparazzi, after a

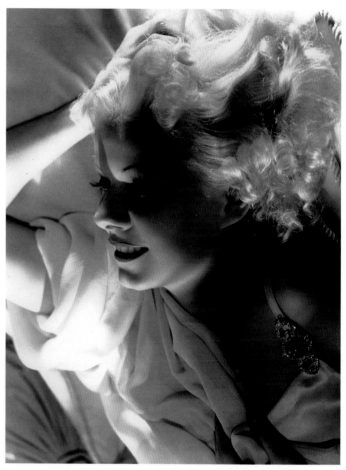

9.26
GEORGE HURRELL, *Jean Harlow,* **1935.**

Such was the appeal of "The Blonde Bombshell," during the Depression, that she frequently made two or three pictures a year.

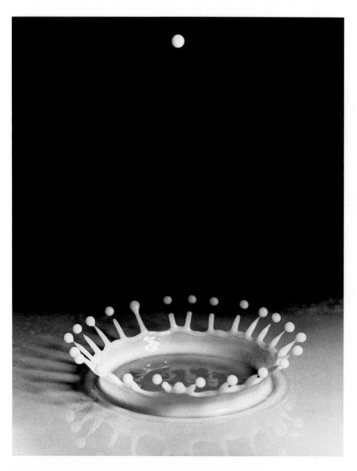

9.25
HAROLD EDGERTON, *Drop of Milk Splashing into a Saucer of Milk,* **1936.**
Stroboscopic photograph. PalmPress, Concord, Massachusetts.

character in Frederico Fellini's 1960 film *La Dolce Vita.* For Fellini the name, which may derive from an Italian dialect word, reminded him of buzzing and pesky mosquitos.

Other kinds of photo-entertainments gave people momentary respite from the Great Depression. All the rage since the late nineteenth century, cross-dressing for the camera flourished during the interwar years. In Europe and North America, men sometimes posed as mannish suffragettes, in a comic effort to belittle the movement. Far more common were cross-dressing theme parties. The photographs that remain suggest that women-dressing-as-men was a more usual theme. Events were mostly recorded with snapshots, although the existence of studio shots shows the extent of the practice's popularity (Fig. 9.27).

The photo-booth also functioned as a distraction from the pressures of daily life. A mechanism for making automatic photographs was introduced at the 1889 Exposition Universelle in Paris, but one of the most popular gadgets was invented by Anatol Josepho (1891–1980) in New York City, just before the Great Depression.

Josepho's early Photomaton employed attendants to help sitters into the photo-booth and to suggest poses. After a wait of

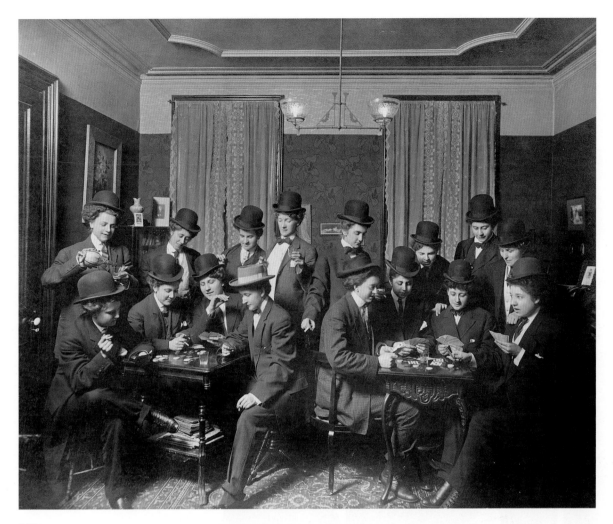

9.27
Photographic studio image of a cross-dressing party, c. 1920. Courtesy of the author.

nearly ten minutes, a strip of eight images appeared and was cut into individual pictures by the attendant. Attendants were not needed and perhaps not wanted for later versions of the photo-booth. Privacy curtains blocked the public's view as the sitter or sitters posed. What happened in the photo-booth stayed in the photo-booth, because the photo-booth process produced a direct positive print—that is, one without a negative. During its heyday, families made photo-booth picture galleries for their photo albums (see Fig. 9.28). Although their popularity has waxed and waned, photo-booths never disappeared. In fact, their humble images have influenced artists from Francis Bacon (1909–1992), who created paintings that resembles photo-booth strips, to Andy Warhol, who owned his own photo-booth and relished the self-portrayal evident in its images (see p. 374). Today, digital versions are found in malls, amusement parks, and theaters.

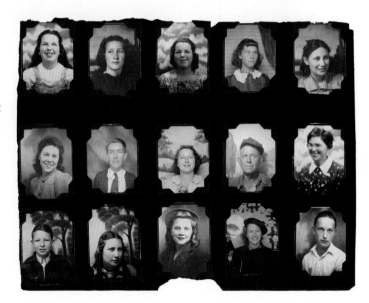

9.28
Photo-booth photograph album, c. 1940. Courtesy of the author.

Scrapbooks and photo albums contained unique displays of friends and family portraits taken in a photo-booth.

WORLD WAR II

While German photographer Alfred Eisenstaedt (1898–1995) was working for the Associated Press, he photographed Joseph

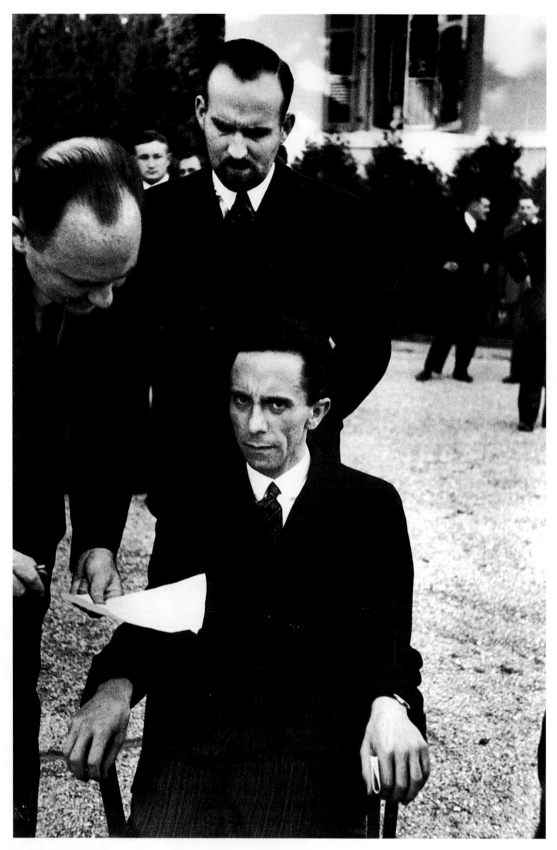

9.29
ALFRED EISENSTAEDT, *Joseph Goebbels*, 1933. Gelatin silver print.

Eisenstaedt's riveting image of the Nazi propaganda minister, Joseph Goebbels, shows him with a menacing expression and claw-like hands. As Eisenstaedt recalled later, "He looked at me with hateful eyes and waited for me to wither. But I didn't wither. If I have a camera in my hand, I don't know fear."

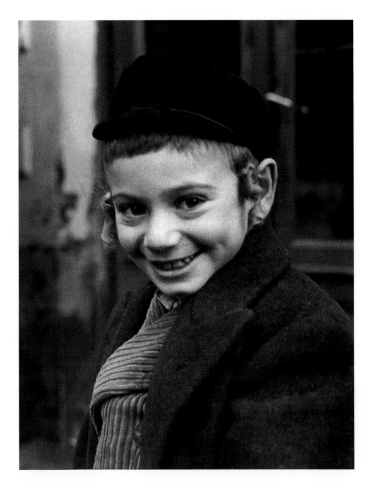

9.30
ROMAN VISHNIAC, *Boy with Earlocks*, 1937. Gelatin silver print.

Goebbels, the Nazi Party's chief propagandist who became the national minister of propaganda, at the 1933 League of Nations Assembly in Geneva, Switzerland (Fig. 9.29). In that year, the Nazis required that all German photographers register with the government, a move that broke the worker-photography movement and sent *AIZ* (the *Workers' Illustrated Newspaper*) into exile in Prague, Czechoslovakia. From the mid-1920s, Hitler's rise to power was orchestrated by the German illustrated press, which was increasingly controlled by Berlin's Ministry of Propaganda. Heroizing portraits of Hitler, montaged over pictures of the vast and carefully staged political gatherings of the Nazi Party, portrayed him as a powerful, popular leader. Two volumes of photographs taken by Hitler's favorite photographer, Heinrich Hoffmann (1885–1957), showed him not only as a political figure, but also as a simple man of the people, reading the newspaper, talking with farmers, and pondering the wonders of nature.[38]

From 1933 on, as the Nazis fomented an atmosphere of race hatred and scapegoating, Jewish people were characterized as lazy and slovenly in print and in press photographs. Boycotts of Jewish shops were encouraged by notices proclaiming, "Jewish business! Anyone shopping here will be photographed."[39] From 1935 to 1938, Roman Vishniac, then living in Berlin, frequently worked with a concealed camera picturing Eastern European

Jewish life. He traveled to Poland, Russia, Hungary, and Romania on behalf of the American Jewish Joint Distribution Committee, making pictures that could assist their money-raising efforts to aid poverty-stricken Jewish communities (Fig. 9.30).

By the time war was imminent, Goebbels determined that there should be no independent media in Germany. Journalists, photographers, writers, film and radio producers, publishers, printers, painters, and poets were conscripted into the Propaganda Division of the army.[40] The twisted logic of Goebbels's schemes was a favorite target of the photomontages created by John Heartfield (anglicized name of Helmut Herzfeld; 1891–1968) for *AIZ*. Heartfield, who had been one of the Berlin Dadaists, turned his talents to satirizing growing Nazi power (Fig. 9.31). A skilled designer of books and posters, he did not make his own photographs, but selected them from mass-media illustrations, or commissioned them from other photographers. His searing PHOTOMONTAGES, which exposed the real effects of Nazi social policies on the ordinary citizen, appeared in *AIZ*. Rumblings of war, official censorship and persecution, and anti-Semitism sent many illustrious photographers in Germany

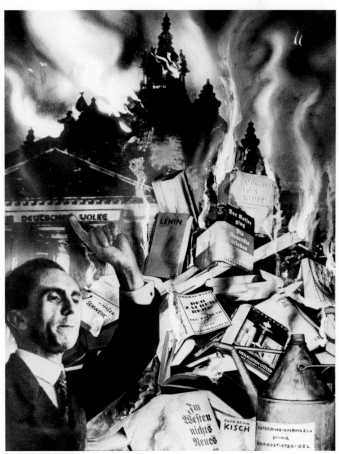

9.31
JOHN HEARTFIELD, *Durch Licht zur Nacht* (*Through Light to Night*), May 19, 1933. Photographic collage. Akademie der Kunst, Berlin.

In his photomontages for *AIZ*, Heartfield criticized Nazi practices. In this image, he shows propaganda minister Joseph Goebbels ordering a book-burning. In the background is the former German parliament building, the Reichstag.

into exile. In 1933, after *AIZ* was banned, Heartfield moved to Prague, and then to Britain in 1938. Moholy-Nagy came to the United States, where he founded a new Bauhaus (1937), soon renamed the Institute of Design, in Chicago. Vishniac also came to America, where insufficient English kept him from practicing medicine, so he went on to do photomicrography. Erich Salomon got as far as the Netherlands, where a Dutch Nazi betrayed him. He and his whole family died in Auschwitz.

WAR AND PHOTOGRAPHY

One of the twentieth century's most famous war photographs, *Death of a Loyalist Soldier* (Fig. 9.32), was taken by Hungarian-born photographer Robert Capa (1913–1954) before World War II formally began. This moment-of-death image purportedly shows an incident during the Spanish Civil War (1936–39), a conflict between a coalition of leftists called loyalists and the fascists, led by Nazi sympathizer General Francisco Franco. The

war inflamed much debate in Europe and America. However, stories that the image was not made by Capa, or that the death was staged, were rumored immediately after World War II, and came to wide public inspection in Phillip Knightley's 1975 book *The First Casualty*.[41] The issue and its evidence have been passionately discussed ever since. In 2008, the existence of three makeshift suitcases belonging to Capa was made public. They contained an extensive cache of Capa's negatives, as well as those by Gerda Taro (1910–1937), his professional and personal partner, and by David Seymour (1911–1956), known as Chim, who also photographed the Spanish Civil War. Historians hoped that the restoration of this find would locate the before and after shots of the long-disputed famous photograph. But in early 2009, when the negatives were scanned, no images were found to have been taken the day the Loyalist photograph was made.

Part of the controversy has to do with Capa's professional and popular reputation. His statement that "if your pictures aren't good enough, you're not close enough" became the dictum for subsequent generations of war and adventure photographers.

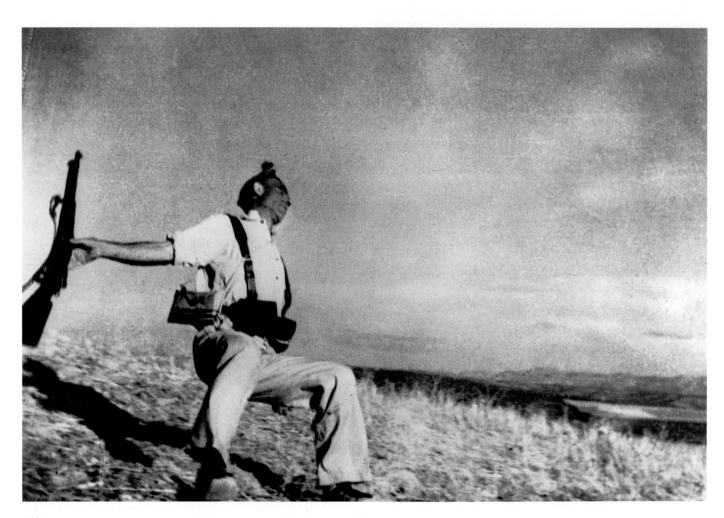

9.32
ROBERT CAPA, *Death of a Loyalist Soldier*, Spain, 1936. Gelatin silver print.

In Capa's image, a lone anti-fascist soldier pitches backwards at the instant bullets seem to rip through him. Published in *Vu* in September 1936 and *Life* in July 1937, it propelled its maker into international celebrity. The circumstances in which he took the picture, however, have been disputed for fifty years.

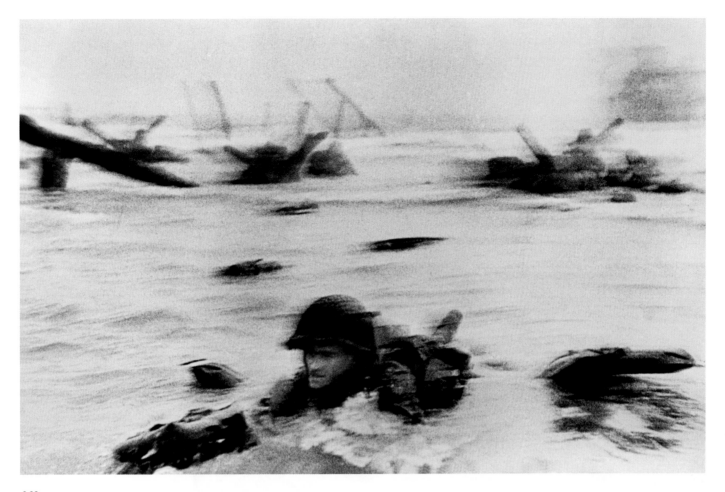

9.33
ROBERT CAPA, *Ed Regan, Veteran of Omaha Beach D-Day Landing,* June 6, 1944. Gelatin silver print.

Capa's images from the Normandy landings have been imitated in many war movies, including Steven Spielberg's *Saving Private Ryan* (1998). This shot of Allied soldiers coming ashore during the invasion that ultimately ended the war in Europe was blemished when a darkroom aide used too much heat and partially melted the film.

Less well known, but still a guideline for photographers, photo-editors, and the public, was his observation on the slight blur in *Death of a Loyalist Soldier*: "if you want to get good action shots, they mustn't be in true focus. If your hand trembles a little, then you get a fine action shot." Ironically, another of Capa's celebrated images was also blurred—but by accident (Fig. 9.33).

When the war broke out in Europe in 1939, correspondents and photographers were sent there, sponsored by publications and photo agencies. As in World War I, war photography was censored. For example, Bourke-White's images were often printed as contact sheets (rows of small, negative-size images on photographic paper) and reviewed by military censors before being sent to *Life* magazine. Some photographs were conveyed by radio transmission, but most, with captions written by the photographer, were physically transported by the military. Photographers often had to form pools, meaning that photographs by any one of them could be used by all of them. The practice reduced the number of photographers in the field and eased the work of censors. The huge improvement in cameras and film since World War I allowed soldiers from all sides to make snapshots and send them back home, although these, too, were supposed to pass through the censors' hands. By using handmade PINHOLE CAMERAS and smuggled film, secret photographs were made by wily American prisoners of war in German camps.

For the Allied troops, motion-picture studios issued millions of free celebrity images, including so-called pin-ups of popular stars such as Rita Hayworth and Betty Grable. The military trained photographers to accompany units, and aerial photography, some done by the naval aviation unit under the command of Captain Edward Steichen, accounted for about 85 per cent of the Allied information on the enemy.[42]

To avoid disclosing information the enemy could use, and because the 1930s' documentary emphasis on individuals and typical days persisted, newspapers and magazines stressed the personal encounter with war far more than in World War I. Stationed in the Pacific, American photographer W. Eugene Smith managed to get so close to the action that he was seriously wounded on the island of Okinawa in 1945. His pictures centered on the physical and emotional experiences of soldiers at the front line (Fig. 9.34). *Life* magazine fought the government to show the American wounded and dead, though not with the explicit horror accorded the enemy dead, especially the Japanese, who were also frequently the subject of racial caricature in print and in cartoons. The United States kept a secret file of ghastly war photographs, called "The Chamber of Horrors," in the Pentagon.[43]

The Museum of Modern Art staged large photographic exhibits to support the war effort. Two such shows, both curated by Steichen, were immensely successful with the public. "Road to Victory" (1942) used many R.A./F.S.A. photographs, updated and recaptioned from Depression themes to such patriotic slogans as "War—they asked for it—now, by the living God, they'll get it."[44] Designed by Herbert Bayer, who emigrated to

the United States in 1938, "Road to Victory" used the exciting shaped-space concepts of European experimental photography INSTALLATIONS. The visual strategies that Bayer had used to promote the Nazi Party were thus turned against them. Steichen's second show, "Power in the Pacific" (1945), utilized images from the United States Navy, whose photographic unit he had himself directed.[45]

Robert Capa's photograph from the Spanish Civil War was not the sole well-publicized photograph to be questioned in this era. The picture by Joe Rosenthal (1911–2006) of the raising of the Stars and Stripes on the Pacific island of Iwo Jima, another American icon, has been long rumored to be questionable[46] (Fig. 9.35). It was, indeed, the second raising of an American flag on the war-torn island, replacing the first which was too small to

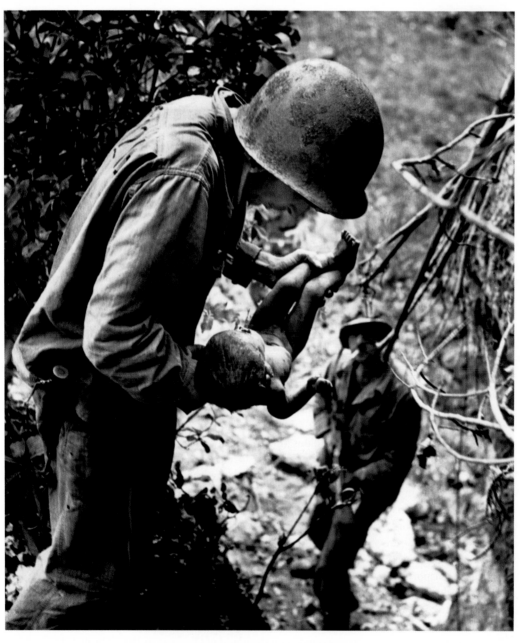

9.34
W. EUGENE SMITH, *U.S. Marines with a Wounded and Dying Infant,* June 1944. Gelatin silver print.

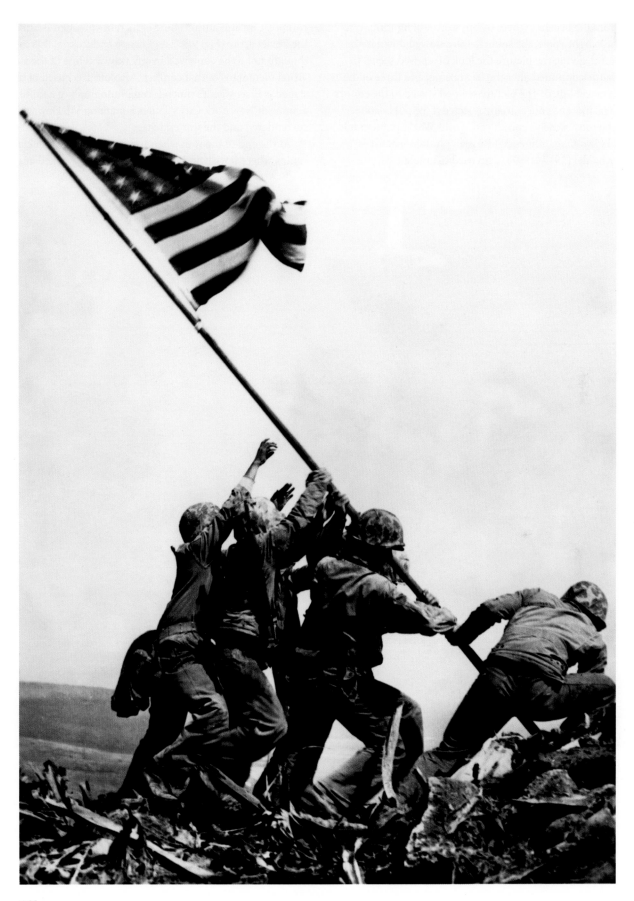

9.35
JOE ROSENTHAL, *Marines Raising the American Flag on Iwo Jima—"Old Glory goes up on Mt. Suribachi,"* February 23, 1945. Gelatin silver print.
Library of Congress, Washington, D.C.

be seen from the beaches where troops were still fighting. While raising the weighty pole, the soldiers were slowed down in the slippery mud, giving the picture the look of a posed scene. In fact, the battle continued after the flag raising, and three of the flag-raisers were killed. The picture seemed staged to the editors at *Life* magazine, and they initially rejected it for publication. Perhaps the most widely reproduced World War II photograph, Rosenthal's *Iwo Jima*, influenced Russian photojournalist Yevgeny Khaldei (1917–1997), who tried to emulate its

composition and attract some of its renown when Berlin fell to the Soviet army (Fig. 9.36). In Europe and Russia, this image, thought not to be contrived in any way, was one of the strongest visual mementos of that conflict. Also often accused of being staged is Eisenstaedt's much loved photograph of a sailor kissing a nurse in New York City's Times Square on V.J. Day, when Japan surrendered and the war ended.

At the end of the war, when troops entered the concentration camps where Jewish and other prisoners had worked and died,

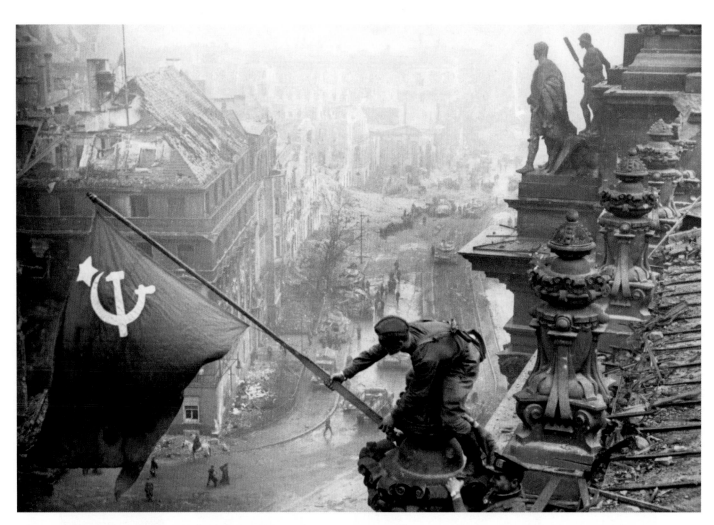

9.36
YEVGENY KHALDEI, *Reichstag*, **Berlin, 1945. Gelatin silver print. Galerie Voller Ernst, Berlin.**

To make his version of Rosenthal's famous photograph (see Fig. 9.35), Khaldei rushed to the blazing Reichstag, the former German parliament building, with a flag that he had his uncle hurriedly make from red tablecloths. With the assistance of three Russian soldiers, he climbed to the roof, positioned the flag, and photographed the city under Russian control.

photographers recorded the grim scenes. At Buchenwald, Bourke-White pictured the charred remains of victims and the shrunken bodies of living skeletons. Lee Miller (1907–1997), the photographer who had developed solarization with Man Ray, was a member of the London War Correspondents Corps, and later an accredited correspondent with the U.S. forces. She, too, defied the prevailing notion that women were too emotionally delicate to face the horrors of extermination camps. Her unsparing photographs at Buchenwald catalog the means of annihilation,

and the lives of those who survived (Fig. 9.37). When she sent her equally shocking photographs of Dachau, she cabled her editor: "I implore you to believe this is true."

Henri Cartier-Bresson was captured by the Germans during the war and imprisoned. He escaped and joined the French Resistance. After the war, he recorded the reaction of French people to those among them who had aided the Nazis. In this image he sought the decisive moment that told the story of the denunciation of a French Gestapo informer (Fig. 9.38).

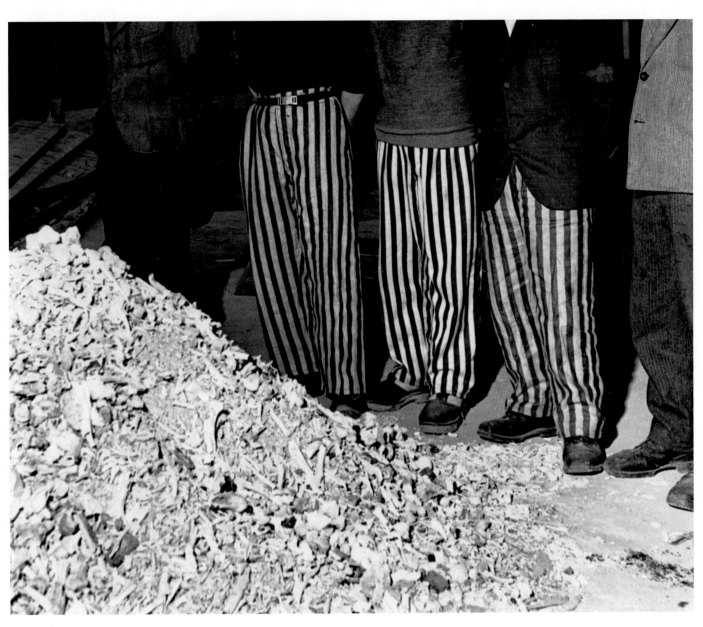

9.37
LEE MILLER, *Buchenwald*, April 1945. Gelatin silver print. Lee Miller Archives, Chiddingly, East Sussex, England.

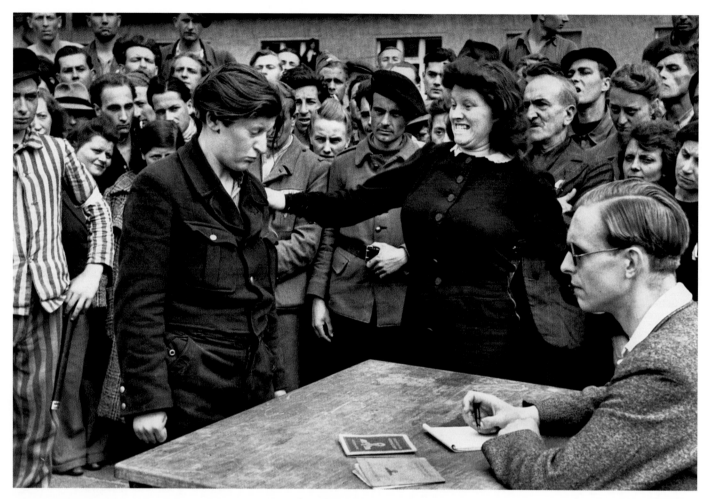

9.38
HENRI CARTIER-BRESSON, *Gestapo Informer, Dessau*, Germany, 1945. Gelatin silver print.

RETAKE

American film and photography entered an age of documentary practice during the Great Depression. Photographs of the conditions of the poor and the efforts to help them became central to photojournalism. The clear-eyed, subject-oriented style favored by the Farm Security Administration became ascendant in newspapers and magazines, as did the photo-essay dedicated to a single theme. Iconic images, such as Dorothea Lange's *Migrant Mother* (see Fig. 9.3), outlived their original circumstances and remain touchstones in American culture. In Europe, worker photography emerged as a philosophy of picture-making as well as a practice. Ordinary people were urged to record the trials and joys of their lives, ranging from strikes and protest rallies to the minutiae of daily life. Photography's capacity for entertainment grew, in magazines devoted to celebrity images and in the ubiquitous photo-booth, where 25 cents got the sitter eight small pictures and a measure of delight. When World War II broke out, the picture magazines and newspapers in the combatant countries were ready to report, protest, and propagandize. The eye-witness documentary style established in photography and film became strongly associated with the Great Depression and the war years. As such it was both the measure of success and the nemesis of subsequent photographic practice.

philosophy and practice

The "Common Man" and the End of Media Utopia

In his much cited 1936 essay "The Work of Art in the Age of Mechanical Reproduction," German critic Walter Benjamin argued that the proliferation of photomechanical means of production marked one of history's watershed moments. For the masses, he forecast that reproducibility would be truly revolutionary. In the end, it would "pry an object from its shell … [and] destroy its aura."[47] Thus removed from "the fabric of tradition," photographically reproduced and widely distributed pictures of once class-bound objects would become strategic elements in fomenting social change among the masses, who could witness at first hand the decline of privilege in their new access to art reproduction. Benjamin's hopes for the mass media were echoed throughout European experimental photography, especially in Germany.

As historian Maud Lavin summed up, "the burning issue for the German avant-garde from 1922 until Hitler's seizure of power in 1933 was not at all a rebellion against art institutions, but rather a serious and prolonged engagement with mass culture."[48] Similarly, American documentary photographers thought their images were self-validating, needing only wide exposure in the press to change the hearts and minds of the people.

Benjamin was wrong about the special aura that unique objects have. Far from destroying the aura, art reproductions served to increase it. Photographs of Leonardo da Vinci's *Mona Lisa* roused people to want to see the original. Oddly, photographic reproducibility sometimes destroyed the aura of the original photograph. For example, the many thousands of people who cut out and saved press pictures of Dorothea Lange's *Migrant Mother* felt that they owned the original, because it was the very one that affected them.

Written from a left-wing perspective, Benjamin's essay is typical of international writing in the 1930s in its concern for what were alternately called "the people," "the masses," "ordinary humanity," and "the common man." Notions of progressive social change aimed at the common man sustained photographs in such divergent styles as those done by the Russian experimental photographers and those published by the F.S.A. The immense brutality and destruction of World War II, and the advent of the atomic bomb, eroded faith in the future of the human race. At the same time, the dissolution of experimental photography into commercially viable styles, and the control of visual media by large corporations and news agencies, dampened belief in the inherently revolutionary nature of camerawork.

One mark of the waning faith in photography, which became widespread after World War II and continues today, is the repeated inquiry into the authenticity of the documentary photographs that emerged as icons of the war, such as Capa's *Death of a Loyalist Soldier* (see Fig. 9.32) and Rosenthal's *Marines Raising the American Flag on Iwo Jima* (see Fig. 9.35) In the postwar phase of the age of mechanical reproduction, iconic images have often been greeted with suspicion. Almost a century earlier, Alexander Gardner could openly describe his staging of *Home of a Rebel Sharpshooter* (see Fig. 4.17). By contrast, war photographers such as Capa and Rosenthal were unable to deflect doubts that anyone can be lucky enough to be at the right place at the right time to make such powerful and well-composed symbols. The war years had seen photography exploited to an unprecedented extent by government and the military on both sides to control public opinion. Prized for its contribution to uniting nations during the war, photography was far less certain of its role in the postwar world.

Through the Lens of Culture (1945–1975)

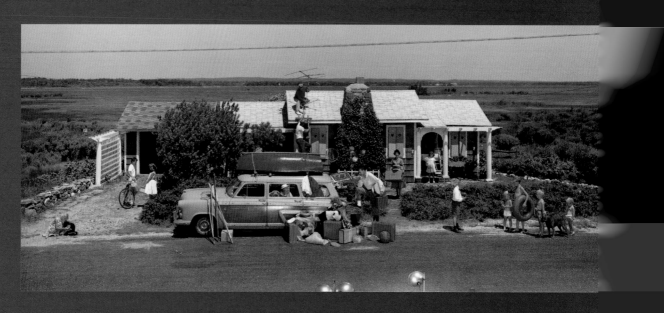

While postwar Europe and Asia staggered under the loss of millions of people, coupled with economic devastation, the United States, which did not suffer physical damage on its mainland, emerged as the world's leading industrial and military power. By 1947, the relief and unity felt by the Allies after their victory in World War II had given way to a world polarized by what the American presidential advisor Bernard Baruch called the Cold War. Beginning in 1945, the Soviet Union established its influence among eastern European nations in the territories previously occupied by Nazi Germany. In addition, the Soviets administered eastern Germany, one of the four zones into which Germany was partitioned at the end of the war.

When the Soviet Union and the eastern European nations in its sphere of influence refused rebuilding funds under the Marshall Plan, initiated by U.S. secretary of state George C. Marshall, suspicion of Soviet long-term expansionist intentions rapidly spread in the West. Fired by the fear that its wartime ally wanted to spread communism throughout the world, and that the human misery of the immediate postwar period would make such a message attractive, the United States redoubled its economic aid to Europe and some Middle Eastern countries.

World War II erased any lingering doubt that global forces affected all nations and regions. The word "globalization" showed up in dictionaries and ordinary parlance during the 1960s.

Like other media of expression, photographic practice was caught up in the cross-currents of postwar upheavals and crises. The "Family of Man" exhibition at the Museum of Modern Art in New York expressed a unity among the world's people that went beyond political differences, and it phrased nuclear war as the greatest threat to global understanding. In the United States, images from the assassinations of John F. Kennedy, Robert F. Kennedy and Martin Luther King quickly became part of the nation's collective visual memory. Filmmakers and photographers not only recorded, but were part of, the 1968 uprising in France and the Warsaw Pact's invasion of Czechoslovakia. The medium aided the beginnings of what would eventually be called identity politics, when photographers chose as topics cultural distinctiveness and idiosyncratic behavior. Similarly, postwar anxieties about spiritual life in an age of material abundance were captured by the lens. In the United States, the Civil Rights movement and reactions to the war in Vietnam were photographed, and the resulting images were shown not only in newspapers and magazines but on television, which quickly became the medium through which average people learned the news. At the same time, photography was adopted by artists who cared less about the medium's historical attempts to join the fine arts and more about its potential to create images whose objectivity accorded with Conceptualism. The distinction between art photographers and artists who use photography continued throughout the twentieth century, as notions of multimedia expressions gained currency.

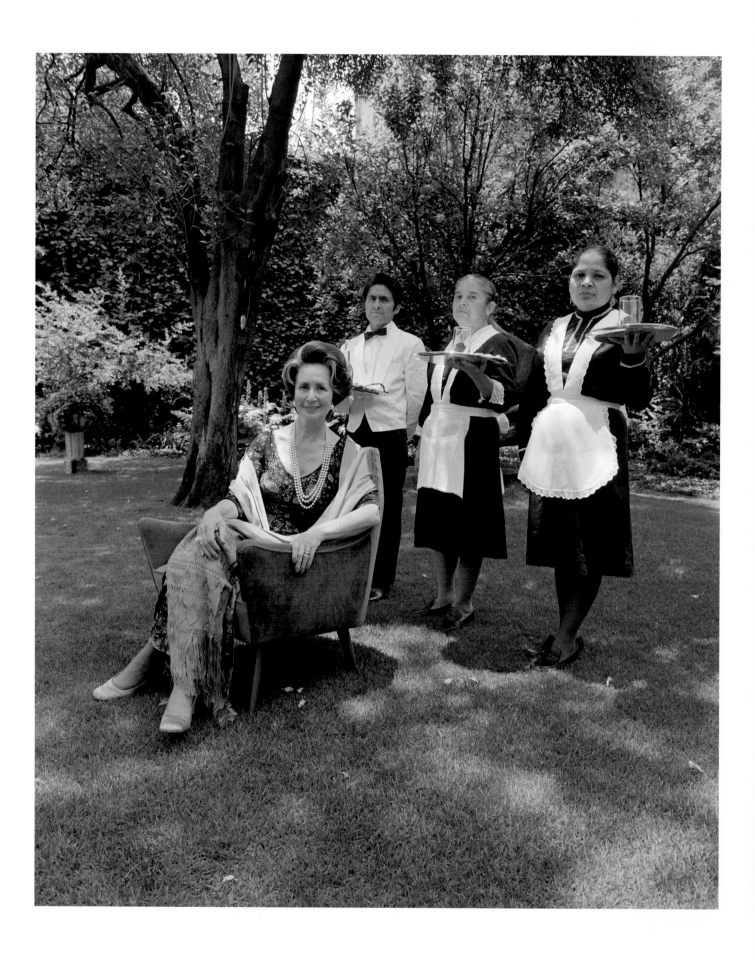

CHAPTER TEN

The Human Family

Hope and melancholy struggled in post-World War II expression. In photography, hope found its manifestation in "The Family of Man" exhibit, which began at the Museum of Modern Art in New York and traveled abroad. The show emphasized the similar experiences and aspirations that humans share. Nevertheless, "The Family of Man" was not a naïve accolade. It placed hope in the context of the threat of nuclear annihilation. Despite the exhibition's call for unity and peace, people around the world came to resent the extensive military, financial, and cultural influence of the United States. Central and South American photographers convened in an effort to create distinctive regional art and documentary photographs. In Africa, South Africans used the medium both to record the evils of racial segregation and to underscore the aspects of social life and cultural expression that survived and even flourished under pressure. In India, photojournalism made extensive contributions to the independence movement. In Japan, representation of contemporary culture took into account the lasting effects of the atomic bombings. Division, opposition, and estrangement quickly dispelled the postwar peace.

THE FAMILY OF MAN

In 1947, John G. Morris, picture editor of the *Ladies' Home Journal*, decided to expand on the magazine's series, "How America Lives." Influenced by the Farm Security Administration project, he decided to craft a more global version, which he called, "People are People the World Over." It would be a series of monthly photo-essays showing common activities in rural

10.1
PEDRO MEYER, *Untitled* (Wealthy woman with two maids and a male servant behind her), 1978, from "Hecho en Latinoamérica" exhibition, 1978. Gelatin silver print.

families around the globe, such as laundering clothes, shopping, and cooking.[1] Henri Cartier-Bresson, whom Morris had met in Europe just before the liberation, contacted him and told him that he would be an ideal first customer for a new cooperative photographic agency that he had founded with three other war-weary photographers, Robert Capa, David "Chim" Seymour, and George Rodger (1908–1995).[2] Thus, Magnum Photos, established in the penthouse restaurant of the Museum of Modern Art in the spring of 1947 by photographers hoping to gain more editorial control over their pictures, began supplying images to the quintessential American women's magazine of the twentieth century.

The World War II experiences of Magnum's founders oriented them toward a photography that would contribute to human betterment. Their aspiration was shared by the organizers of the large 1955 exhibition titled "The Family of Man", mounted at New York's Museum of Modern Art. The show proposed photography as a means through which the alarming tensions and uncertainties of the Cold War era could be seen in a wider context of human values, emphasizing the theme of common humanity against the destructive effects of political polarization and other forms of divisiveness. The exhibit reaffirmed a faith in humanity for an audience shaken by gruesome images in *Life* magazine of Japanese atomic injuries and troubled by the new specter of global nuclear war. It pleased the general public more than any previous photographic exhibition, and the book derived from it became one of the best-selling photographic books of all time.

Edward Steichen, who returned from his wartime duties to head the museum's photography department, selected and organized the images according to universal themes, such as birth, work, and love. To generate the impression of global unity, Steichen homogenized the look of the individual photographs; cropped and shorn of their original titles, the exhibition prints were processed in a commercial lab, where their tonal values were harmonized. The prints were sometimes transformed into poster-size images.

Steichen hoped that "The Family of Man" would illustrate "the essential oneness of mankind throughout the world." Aiming to highlight "human consciousness rather than social consciousness," he discarded images that demonstrated strong political and cultural differences.[3] The unity of humankind was stressed even during the planning stages of the show, when the Museum of Modern Art announced that it would open simultaneously in New York, Europe, Asia, and Latin America—a proposal that was never realized.[4] Steichen's utopian aspiration, in which supposed enemies and outcasts are revealed to share a common humanity and national boundaries are ignored, should be seen against the background of hysterical anti-communism in early 1950s' America and the equally shrill optimism of postwar consumer culture. The United Nations, founded in 1945, and its Universal Declaration of Human Rights, proclaimed in 1948, had offered a vision of the good society rising from the ashes of battle; Steichen's show underlined both the nobility and the fragility of this vision.

To choose from among the 2.5 million photographs submitted, Steichen looked for "swiftness of seeing," the visual summing up of an idea in a single moment that formed the kernel of Modernist photographic practice familiar to audiences from nearly three decades of illustrated magazines and newspapers.[5] In the end, he selected about five hundred images from sixty-eight countries. As Jacob Deschin, camera editor of the *New York Times*, observed, "The Family of Man" was an "editorial achievement rather than an exhibition of photographs."[6] Steichen clustered untitled photographs around concise sayings drawn from cultures around the world. For motherhood, he chose the biblical quotation, "She is a tree of life to them" (Proverbs 3: 18); images of laborers carried a quotation from the ancient Hindu religious poem the *Bhagavad-Gita*: "If I did not work, these worlds would perish... ."

Overall, his installation design owed its dynamic programming of ideas and emotions to the exhibition spaces created by Russian and German artists between the world wars (see pp. 237–47), but critics generally did not acknowledge these European precedents. Indeed, photographer Barbara Morgan (1900–1992) thought that the show was so original that it needed a new term, perhaps "photographic mosaic," "three-dimensional editorializing," or words that related it to rapidly shifting images, such as movies or television.[7]

At "The Family of Man," viewers walked though themed areas (Fig. 10.2). They came across familiar images, such as Lange's *Migrant Mother* (see Fig. 9.3), and met unfamiliar ones as well. At the end of the show, however, the seemingly open-ended themes became more directive. A display of photographs depicted three women, three men, and three children; next to these was placed a stark warning by British philosopher Bertrand Russell (1872–1970) about the capacity of the hydrogen bomb to destroy all human life. Just beyond was a panel showing a dead soldier and a question posed by Sophocles: "Who is the slayer? Who the victim? Speak." Lastly, the viewer passed under an overhead lamp into a darkened area where a 6- by 8-foot back-lighted TRANSPARENCY revealed a red-orange image of the 1954 U.S. hydrogen bomb test explosion on Bikini Atoll in the Pacific Ocean. The glowing picture erupted into the viewers' space, startling them after they had become accustomed to so many black-and-white images. The exhibition plan then directed viewers to a huge photograph of the United Nations General Assembly, and to a final series of images showing children at play.[8]

Although public response to the show was overwhelmingly positive, some photographers objected to Steichen's trans–formation of their work into tonally harmonized, standard-format prints. Further, they charged that the show denigrated the skill involved in making photographs, and lessened the value of the medium just at the moment when it was struggling for acceptance in art museums and galleries. A few critics also felt manipulated by Steichen's agenda, and questioned his underlying ideological message. Phoebe Lou Adams complained:

If Mr. Steichen's well-intentioned spell doesn't work, it can only be because he has been so intent on the physical similarities that unite "The Family of Man" that he has neglected to conjure the intangible beliefs and preferences that divide men into countries and parties and clans. And he has utterly forgotten that a family quarrel can be as fierce as any other kind.[9]

In his zeal to find international common ground from which to work against the widely feared nuclear cataclysm, Steichen had obliterated the specific cultural settings of the images. For example, Farm Security Administration photographs such as *Migrant Mother* were blended with other images of unspecified calamities. Images of workers from the Belgian Congo, Bolivia, Denmark, Germany, and the United States were thematically linked, without regard for the drastically unequal circumstances of labor in those countries. Nathan Farbman's (1907–1988) photograph of an African storyteller in Bechuanaland (now Botswana) became part of a cluster of images on education, twisting its meaning to relate it to Western educational practices. In addition, Steichen ignored most popular forms of photography. He included a few snapshots, but did not show photographs of everyday family life taken by non-professionals with unsophisticated equipment.

CULTURAL RELATIVISM AND CULTURAL RESISTANCE

Steichen's focus on common humanity reflected a larger movement to affirm the basic rights of all peoples. The 1948 Universal Declaration of Human Rights defined those rights as the "common standard of achievement for all peoples and all nations," and listed thirty articles, first among them the idea that "all human beings are born free and equal in dignity and rights." Each of the articles expressed human rights in terms of individual rights. Group, ethnic, racial, and national rights were pointedly absent from the list.[10] As the historian Eric Sandeen

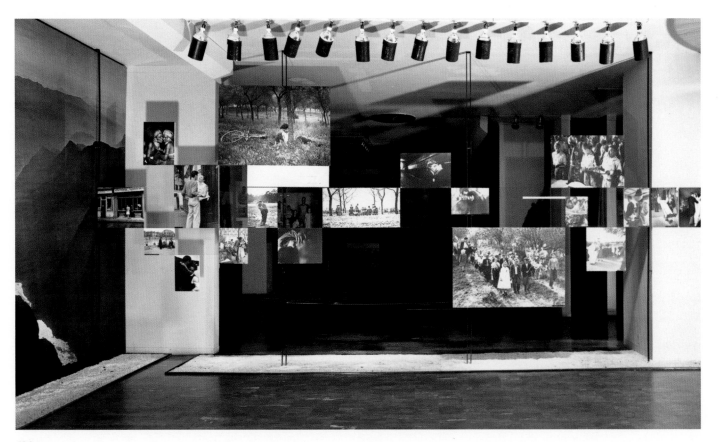

10.2
PHOTOGRAPHER UNKNOWN, *"The Family of Man" Exhibition*, January 24–May 8, 1955. Museum of Modern Art, New York.

"The Family of Man" benefited from earlier experimental European installations, in which the viewer's route was directed. Walking through the show was like leafing through an issue of *Life* magazine. Indeed, Steichen modeled many aspects of the show on picture magazines—from the relative scale of the images, to the use of picture agencies, and the anonymity of the images' authorship.

concisely pointed out, the United Nations, like "The Family of Man," represented a Western view of universal community: "By using the rhetoric of international goals and principles, [the United Nations] bound the members together with one view of what was admirable and what was unacceptable in all human culture."[11] Even as the United Nations announced its Universal Declaration, mainstream cultural outlets from *Life* to *National Geographic* were giving renewed attention to the very different proposals found in the theory of cultural relativism.

Developed by anthropologists in the 1920s and 1930s, the concept of cultural relativism encompassed several interrelated ideas. It asserted that human values are not universally the same, but emerge from dissimilar cultural experiences. In an era when modernization seemed to mean the loss or diminution of diversity, cultural relativism accented the value of tradition. American anthropologist Melville J. Herskovits (1895–1963) clearly articulated one of its core values: "Our civilization may indeed be recognized as in no way inherently superior to another … and this is why the imposition of a foreign body of custom, backed by power is so distressing an experience."[12] His ideas helped fuel an international human rights movement. Around the world, notions of cultural relativism sparked resistance

to outside interference, whether it be military intervention, economic takeover, or the promotion of ideas that might erode cultural identity.

Within the United States and Europe, as well as in other parts of the world, those who disagreed with measuring material wealth as a standard of well-being turned to non-Western and unassimilated indigenous cultures as sources of alternative values. In the United States, photographers again journeyed to Native American groups, not to picture them as vanishing peoples, as had happened in the early twentieth century (see pp. 190–92), but instead to venerate spiritual wisdom and ethical values, which they thought were more in tune with the rhythms of nature than were the artificial demands of modern society. *Through Navajo Eyes* (1972), a report of the 1966 project of Sol Worth (1922–1977) and John Adair (1913–1977) to teach members of the Navajo community to use motion-picture cameras to assert their identity, enlivened many discussions about the potential of the camera to record non-Western experience.

Cold War tension between the United States and the Soviet Union politicized the arts. Both superpowers used artists and exhibitions to promote themselves around the world. Among

focus

Making an Icon of Revolution

In 1960, Cuban photographer Alberto Díaz (1929–2001), more popularly known as Korda, photographed Ernesto "Che" Guevara (1928–1967), who was then serving in Fidel Castro's government. Korda was so impressed by his image of Guevara that he cropped out all extraneous visual information in order to emphasize Guevara's revolutionary zeal (Fig. 10.3). Undoubtedly, Korda's background as a portrait, advertising, and fashion photographer guided him in the process of making what would become a popular symbol of revolution. This image of Guevara, gazing into the future, beneath a beret bearing the revolutionary star, was not published when it was made, but became an international emblem of political resistance after Guevara was killed seven years later in Bolivia. On the evening of the announcement of Guevara's death, a ten-story portrait based on Korda's photograph was hung on the exterior of Havana's Ministry of the Interior building, which faces the plaza where Castro revealed the revolutionary's death to Cubans gathered there. The image was quickly disseminated throughout Latin America, where it became an icon of martyrdom. It was also adopted by American students and antiwar protesters during the Vietnam War era (1964–75). In the 1990s, Korda contested the photo's commercial exploitation in ways he said "dishonored"

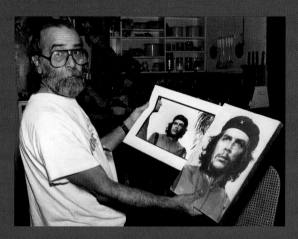

10.3
LIBORIO NOVAL, *Alberto Korda Holding Photos of Che Guevara,* March 5, 1960.

his subject; in 2000 he won a $50,000 settlement from a British advertising agency over the use of the photo in a campaign to market a brand of vodka. He donated the money to buy medicine for children. In 2008, Guevara's family publicly denounced the widespread commercialization of this image as antithetical to Che Guevara's social philosophy.

The news and photography agency UPI (United Press International) inadvertently promoted Guevara's fame when it circulated a photograph of Guevara's corpse posed in a way reminiscent of religious paintings of the dead Christ, and thereby strengthened Guevara's identity as a self-sacrificing fallen martyr in largely Christian Latin America[13] (Fig. 10.4).

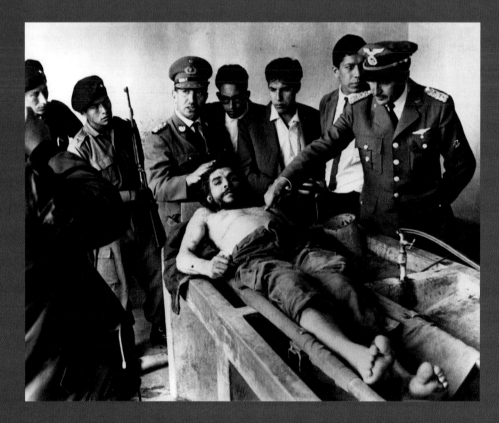

10.4
PHOTOGRAPHER UNKNOWN,
Death Picture of Che Guevara, 1967.

the major cultural programs of the United States Information Agency (U.S.I.A.) was the tour of "The Family of Man," which traveled abroad from 1955 to 1962, appearing in thirty-eight countries to a total audience of nine million people. With additional materials commemorating Hiroshima, the exhibition was mounted in Tokyo and at Ground Zero, the spot in Hiroshima where the atomic bomb exploded. The Soviet authorities even let the exhibit run in Moscow. Publicity framed the show as evidence of the individual freedom that fostered American prosperity, much as the art movement ABSTRACT EXPRESSIONISM, with its gestural handling of paint and absence of realistic subject matter, was cast as an example of American intellectual freedom, in contrast to Soviet Socialist Realism.[14]

The "American Way of Life," as it was called, derived from postwar economic prosperity, manifest in a housing boom, the growth of suburbs and shopping malls, and increased automobile use. It fostered the notion of material abundance as a universal gauge of societal achievement. The propaganda slogan implicitly disparaged "un-American" and "anti-American" societies—such as the Soviet Union, which offered fewer material comforts, but where all citizens were (at least in theory) seen as equal beneficiaries of centralized state-run programs rather than lone competitors in a world governed by free-market capitalism.

Propaganda use of cultural objects during the Cold War set off the rapid politicization of artists and photographers. In Latin America, Africa, and Asia, where American art symbolized American political power and economic clout, photography came to be understood as a means to create and communicate a defiant, or at least oppositional, cultural identity.

CENTRAL AND SOUTH AMERICA

In the postwar period, many people living in Central and South America resented the extensive cultural, political, and economic influence of the United States. They attempted to forge a distinctive Latin American identity in the arts and in photography. These efforts were strengthened by the reaction to U.S. interventions in South America and the Caribbean, beginning with the invasion of Cuba at the Bay of Pigs in 1961, and including U.S. support of Augusto Pinochet (1915–2006), who overthrew the elected Chilean government of Salvador Allende (1908–1973) in 1973, and of the dictatorial regime of Anastasio Somoza (1925–1980) in Nicaragua throughout the 1970s. As Peruvian-born photographer and critic Fernando Castro (b. 1952) recounts, "Latin American photographers busied themselves exposing every trace of U.S. penetration they could find. Those who did not participate in this ideological purge, ridding themselves of any taste for U.S. art, dress, or speech, were branded *alienados*—alienated from their own people and culture."[15]

In the years before World War II, Latin American photographers had responded positively to European experiments in photographic form, such as Surrealism (see Chapter Eight). In the decades after 1945, a wide range of photographic practices persisted, from local photographers using nineteenth-century studio styles to those who were thoroughly conversant with contemporary international styles and techniques. This layering of practices could be found throughout the postcolonial world in the postwar period of modernization and nation-building. As in North America and Europe, photographers increasingly found work creating advertising and other commercial images. Throughout Latin America, photojournalism was carried out by press photographers attached to illustrated newspapers, or by freelancers, who sometimes sold their work through regional photographic agencies. Yet, despite the many professional photographers in Latin America, it was mostly foreign practitioners who were sent in when the area was portrayed in magazines abroad.

During the 1959 Cuban Revolution, local photographers such as Raúl Corrales (1925–2006) documented the progress of the struggle, along with foreign correspondents and photographers. Nevertheless, Cuban images were not purchased by international agencies, and most of the pictures of Cuba seen around the world were taken by foreign photographers. A significant exception was Alberto Díaz (1928–2000), who created a defining image of the revolution (see Fig. 10.3). In the early years of the Fidel Castro (b. 1927) government, photojournalism played an important role in communicating ideas visually to a largely illiterate public. Castro reputedly waved a copy of *Life* magazine in front of one of his associates, saying "I want something like this"; *Revolución*, a picture magazine, was soon founded.[16]

In post-World War II Latin America, photography took many forms, ranging from the work of itinerants to fashionable portraits such as those made by Grete Stern, one of the partners in studio ringl + pit (see pp. 263), who emigrated from Germany to Argentina. Especially before the spread of the Polaroid photograph (see p. 362–63) in the late 1960s, roving rural photographers used old-fashioned paper negatives, created in large wooden cameras constructed from parts of broken, older cameras. These itinerants used painted backdrops showing religious scenes or cityscapes, which they set up in designated spots for photographers near marketplaces and rural fairs. "Los Ambulantes," or the traveling ones, offered inexpensive portrait images (Fig. 10.5).[17]

During the 1970s, Latin American documentarians, photojournalists, and art photographers sought to counteract simplistic or derogatory depiction by foreigners, while still affirming the multicultural character of the region. The First Colloquium of Latin American Photographers, held in Mexico City in 1978, was accompanied by the influential exhibition "Hecho en Latinoamérica" ("Made in Latin America"). The title built ironically on the once common label "Made in America," which identified imported goods from the United States, not the other Americas. In an introduction to the catalog, organizer Raquel Tibol (b. 1923) emphasized the growing desire to view Latin American photography as "an artistic family." "The narrow confinement within our borders was becoming unbearable," she wrote.[18] According to Tibol, Latin American photographers shared several outlooks, including "the rejection of an alienating and unjust society; the denunciation of exploitation,

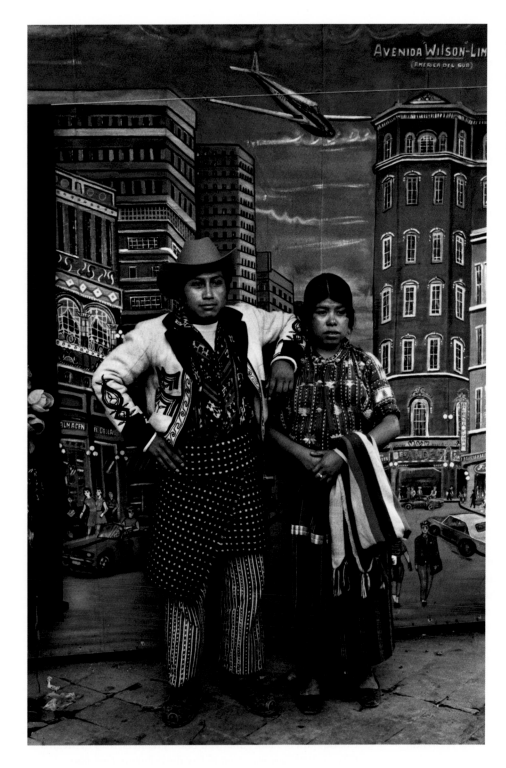

marginalization and colonization; a rupture with conventional
aesthetic models, [and] an impulse toward a reaffirmation."[19]
In other words, she hoped that photographers could unite
a political vanguard with an artistic avant-garde. The socio-
economic contrasts throughout the book underscored the
disparities between rich and poor (Fig. 10.1).

Two more conferences and exhibitions were held in
1981 (Mexico City) and 1984 (Havana, Cuba). These efforts
led to international group shows abroad, and a system of

awards for outstanding work.[20] One result of the heightened
regional identity was the increased activity of Latin American
photographers working in Bolivia, Brazil, Chile, Cuba,
Guatemala, Venezuela, and elsewhere, who chronicled the
daily existence of the indigenous peoples threatened by modern
development and ecological devastation.[21] Pre-Columbian
peoples living traditionally came to symbolize a pure Latin
American experience before colonization, and represented
resistance to external political and cultural interference.

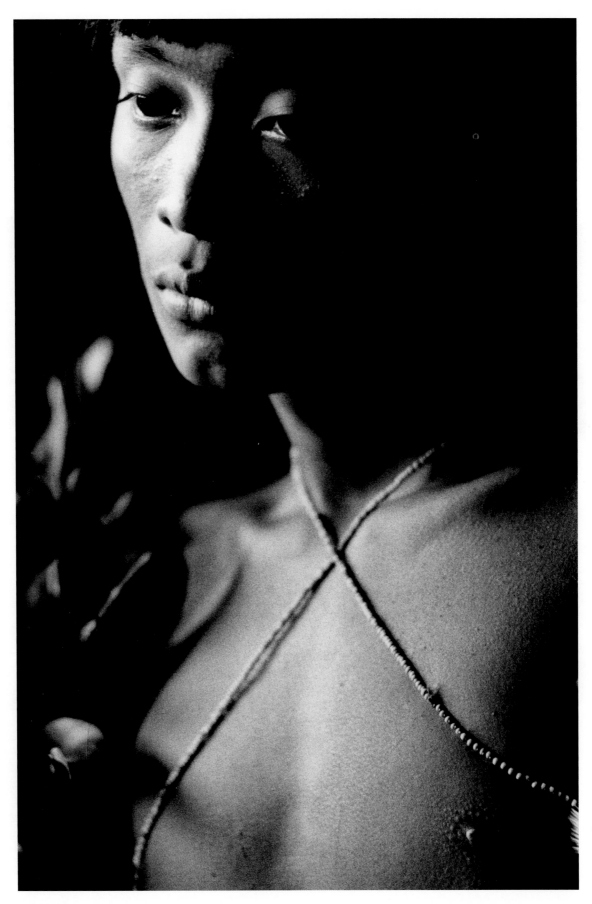

10.6
CLAUDIA ANDUJAR, *Yanomami Youth During a Traditional Reahu Festival*, 1978.

Brazil and Argentina

Claudia Andujar (b. 1931), a Swiss-born photographer who arrived in Brazil in 1955, embraced the outlook proclaimed at the First Colloquium of Latin American Photographers, and she exhibited her work in "Hecho en Latinoamérica." During her treks in the 1970s and 1980s to photograph the Yanomami people of northern Brazil, she witnessed their deaths as a result of epidemics in the wake of a gold rush that brought forty thousand miners to the Amazon basin, and the dislocation of villages when the jungle was leveled to make way for roads. For a time, she gave up photography to set up health clinics among the Yanomami and to lobby the Brazilian government for the creation of a reserve the size of Portugal for them, a feat accomplished in 1992.

Andujar did not adopt the straightforward documentary style of the Farm Security Administration photographers (see pp. 278–86). Rather than rendering her subjects in simple compositions and lighting schemes, she used extreme contrasts

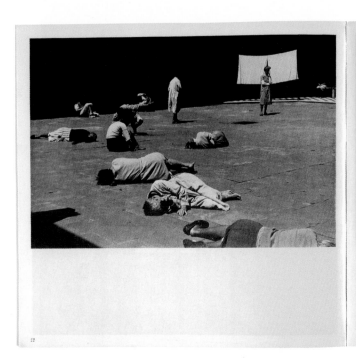

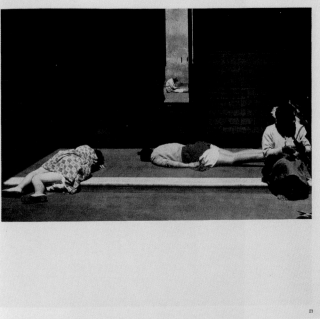

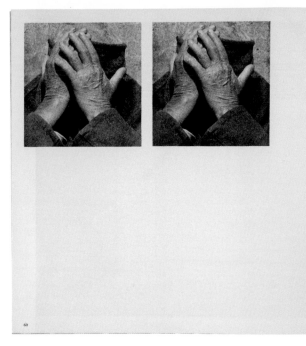

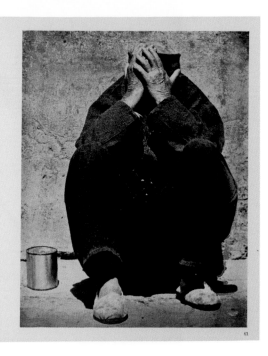

10.7
SARA FACIO AND ALICIA D'AMICO, *Untitled*, from their book *Humanario*, 1976.

of dark and light to add complexity to the image's surface (Fig. 10.6). Unlike the early twentieth-century photographers who showed Native North American people as physically and mentally exhausted, and therefore unable to cope with modern life, Andujar manipulated the graphic contrasts of her work to create sensuous surfaces that suggest vitality. Her book *Yanomami* (1978) conveyed the message that these people were endangered not by their inadequate cultural achievement, but by the moral deficiency of the major culture. She underscored the idea of an impending holocaust by dedicating the book to the people who perished at the Nazi concentration camp at Dachau.

Image-making among indigenous peoples became the hallmark of the photographers interested in portraying Latin American identity, but photographers also looked closer to home for instances of injustice and abuse. Civil unrest, revolutionary activity, and repressive government measures were routinely photographed. Argentinean photographers Sara Facio (b. 1932) and Alicia D'Amico (1933–2001) began collaborating in the late 1960s on a series depicting life in a state-run mental institution, published in 1976 as *Humanario* (Fig. 10.7).

MEXICO

In Mexico, photographers had already avidly turned to local subject matter before the First Colloquium. They recorded the lives of ordinary urban dwellers as well as the persistence of ancient religious practices among rural peoples. In a series of influential photographic essays published in popular Mexican illustrated magazines such as *Hoy* (*Today*) and *Siempre!* (*Always!*), Mexican photojournalist Nacho López (1923–1986) depicted everyday life in Mexico City, sometimes posing his subjects to create a humorous or poignant effect. His photo-essays present the poor as animated, capable actors in their own realm, not as victims awaiting misfortune's next call (Fig. 10.8).[22] López believed that photography found its finest expression in photojournalism, which thrust the image-maker into the midst of life's theater. He came to detest what he and other Latin American photographers called "folkloric" photography, the pursuit of picturesque subjects rather than social contexts.[23] Another Mexican photographer, Héctor García (1923–2012), traveled the country seeking out the survival of ancient, precolonial rituals. He also concentrated on laborers, producing pictures that emphasize their individual imagination (Fig. 10.9).

Foto Hermanos Mayo, or the Brothers of May Day Photography, an anonymous, left-leaning collective originally from Spain, enthusiastically supplied Mexican and foreign illustrated magazines and newspapers with pictures that examined issues from the working-class point of view. The Hermanos Mayo archive of about five million negatives is probably the largest of its kind in Latin America.[24] Although the brothers took many assignments for the Mexican press, they specialized in images that portrayed workers and social change. One of their recurrent themes was the migration of laborers from Mexico to the United States in what was informally called the Bracero Program. Begun in 1942, in response to labor shortages in the United States, the program ended in 1964 in

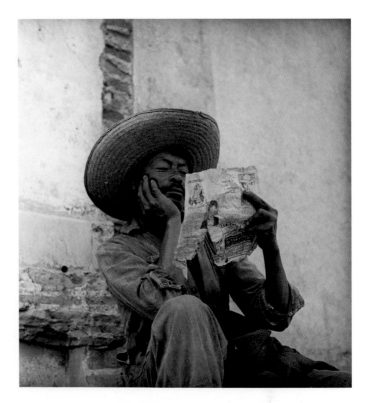

10.8
NACHO LÓPEZ, *Campesino*, 1949. Nacho López Foundation. Fototeca del Instituto Nacional de Antropología e Historia, Mexico City.

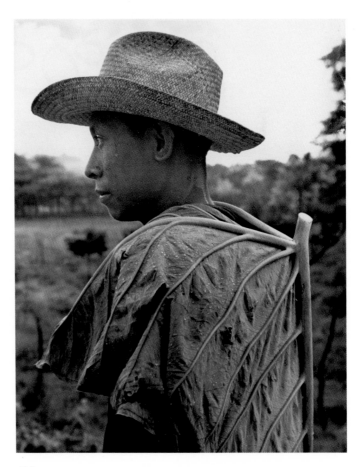

10.9
HÉCTOR GARCÍA, *Campesino Covered with a Leaf*, 1965.

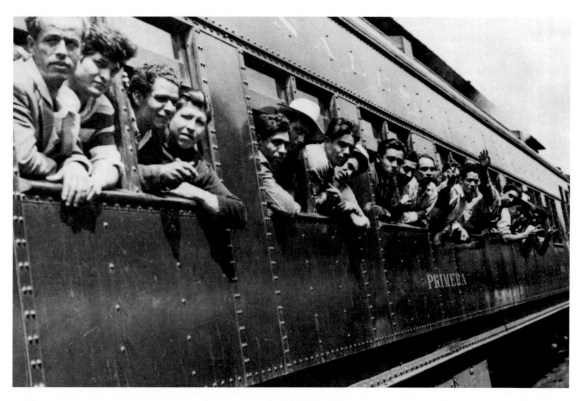

10.10
HERMANOS MAYO, *Buenavista Train Station, Mexico City*, c. 1945. Archivo General de la Nación, Mexico City.

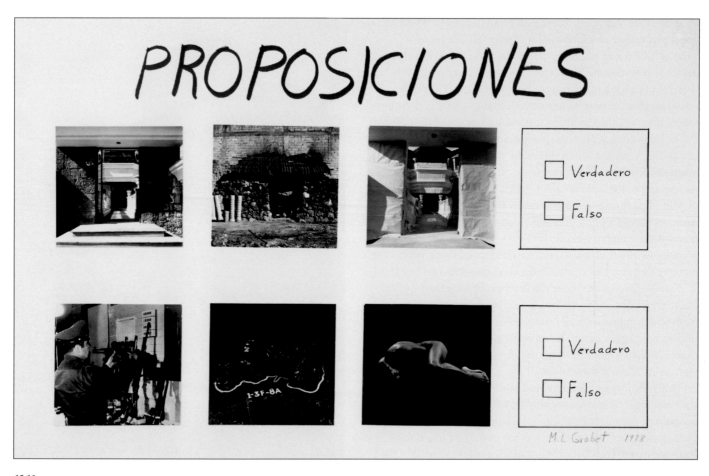

10.11
LOURDES GROBET, *Proposiciones*, 1978. Mixed media.

the midst of controversy about migrant workers' rights and illegal immigration. The Hermanos Mayo photographs typically show a whole narrative, beginning, for instance, with the long lines of laborers hoping to go the United States and ending with expectant faces leaning out of railway cars that will bring them north (Fig. 10.10). In postwar Mexico, photojournalists organized gallery exhibitions of their pictures, and increased the circulation of their images by allowing their work to be published in books, a pattern that was appearing worldwide.

During the 1970s, former painter Lourdes Grobet (b. 1940) used photography as an element in "environments"—that is, multimedia precursors of installation art. She also made a series of bogus referendum ballots, to make her point about the deficiencies of the voting process (Fig. 10.11). Another Mexican photographer, Graciela Iturbide (b. 1942), began her career photographing indigenous and rural people in the 1970s. Her work often focuses on the adaptation of traditional life to the modern world, a prominent motif in Mexican cultural expression (Fig. 10.12). During the 1990s, her work centered on Mexicans living in east Los Angeles, the largest Mexican population outside the country, and along the United States–Mexico border. She does not mourn the loss of cultural identity or romanticize the severe poverty that confines people in traditional cultures. Instead, she shows indigenous Mexican people as constantly in flux, accommodating to change that began half a millennium ago with the Spanish conquest.

AFRICA

Like most photographers living in colonial areas, Africans learned camerawork and business procedures in European-run establishments, or as part of service in colonial military units. Consequently, portrait photography by Africans of Africans adapted many attributes of colonial photography, such as the portrayal of worldly accomplishments, and the display of tokens indicating social class or personal interests. Photography was brought to villages by traveling photographers, who, like those in Latin America, made portraits against the cloth backgrounds they took with them.

Within the constraints of received traditions, photographers such as Mali resident Seydou Keïta (1921–2001) infused the

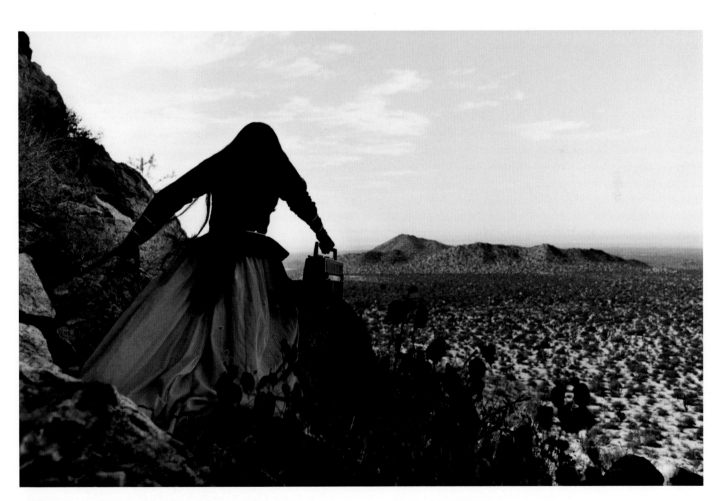

10.12
GRACIELA ITURBIDE, *Woman Angel, Sonara Desert, Mexico, 1979.*

A Seri Indian woman literally balances between modernity, symbolized by the portable radio, and the earth, an emblem of traditional life, which she reaches for with her left hand. Iturbide suggests the abiding spiritual life of her subjects, especially women.

portrait

Manuel Álvarez Bravo

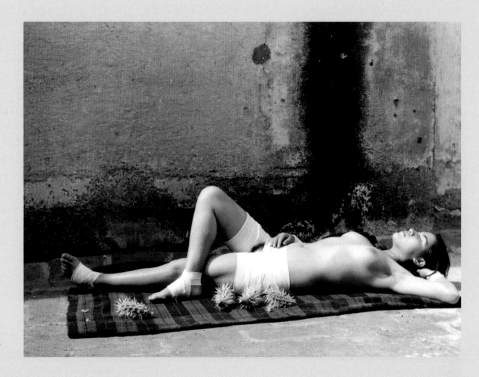

10.13
MANUEL ÁLVAREZ BRAVO, *La Buena Fama Durmiendo*
(*Good Reputation Sleeping*), 1938–39. Gelatin silver print.
Museum of Photographic Arts, San Diego, California.

Nacho López, Héctor García, and Graciela Iturbide all studied with photographer Manuel Álvarez Bravo (1902–2002), the most influential photographer in Mexico during the last half of the twentieth century. Although Álvarez Bravo's uncanny compositions recall the eerie and mysterious visual spectacles favored by Surrealism,[25] he maintained that Surrealism was a minimal influence.[26] More important, he claimed, was his friendship with Tina Modotti during the 1920s, which led him to view the Modernist photographs of her companion, Edward Weston.[27] In addition, he and Henri Cartier-Bresson interacted and mutually influenced each other. Álvarez Bravo also confronted Modernist simplification of forms when he photographed the work of the Mexican muralists José Clemente Orozco (1883–1949), David Alfaro Siqueiros (1896–1974), and Diego Rivera (1886–1957) for the magazine *Mexican Folkways*.[28] "My work is more related to Mexican art and Mexican life than to photographic traditions," he asserted.[29]

Beginning in the 1940s, Álvarez Bravo's photographs were increasingly seen outside Mexico. Three of his images were included under sweeping categories such as "birth" and "death" in Steichen's "The Family of Man" exhibition in 1955. In these non-Mexican contexts, viewers could overlook Álvarez Bravo's many allusions to ancient myth, folklore, and ritual, with their multiple, intertwined inflections on fecundity and death. For example, *La Buena Fama Durmiendo* (*Good Reputation Sleeping*) (1938–39) shows a young woman slumbering in the sun (Fig. 10.13). She rests on a blanket or rug, and her ankles and thighs are wrapped with what look like bandages. Her pubic area is emphasized against the white fabric. The seductive, sexually charged nude intimates Surrealism's concern with eroticism and altered states of consciousness; the image was shown at an exhibition organized by Surrealist leader André Breton.

The photograph is also imbued with particular Mexican themes that owe nothing to Surrealism. Within Mexican folklore, the thorny cactus pieces lying beside the figure are signs of danger. They warn about the perils of sleep, while protecting the sleeper. The bandages, which owe to an incident in which Álvarez Bravo observed dancers binding their feet, suggests an associative link between the sleeping figure and dancers portrayed in the sculptural reliefs of ancient Mexican civilizations. In one interpretation derived from Mexican cultural experience, the image simultaneously alludes to both the Virgin Mary and the ancient earth goddess Coatlicue, both of whom conceived sons without sexual intercourse.[30]

In Álvarez Bravo's work, some of which was specially staged for the camera, the past is alive in the present in a way different from Western history, which firmly situates events in chronological time and keeps the past at bay. It is interesting to note that Álvarez Bravo never offered extensive interpretations of his work, possibly because their poetic nuances might be sapped in prose. Consequently, he did not respond to the charge that his images promote an internal Mexican exoticism of the sort nineteenth-century travelers sought in photographs of colonial subjects.

Western portrait with African qualities. The urbanization of Bamako, a city where the railroad meets the Niger River, is evident in his portraits of government officials, shopkeepers, politicians, and socialites. Unlike anthropological photographs, which stress the primitivism of Africans, the participants and photographer in Keïta's work collaborate to create an image of lively, confident town life (Fig. 10.14). Accordingly, his advertisements promised "The Image You Want."

Though most post-World War II portraiture in Africa, as in Europe, did not employ experimental techniques, a few photographers, such as Kenyan Omar Said Bakor (1932–1993), made composite portraits that sprang from the client's desire to add people to an extant photograph. Unlike European photomontage, however, Bakor's work was not strongly illusionistic. He used the technique in a way that let the process show, as a means of portraying people's inner desires and aspirations, and also perhaps as a visual equivalent to the non-linear nature of African storytelling (Fig. 10.15).

The "Africanization" of portrait photography received fresh impetus in the 1960s, as many countries began to achieve political independence from colonial European powers.

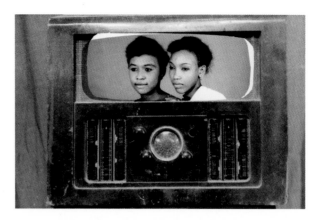

10.15
OMAR SAID BAKOR, *Untitled*, 1975. Photomontage.

African backdrop scenes showed specific African scenes, and sitters increasingly chose to wear traditional African attire.[31] Independence also brought the establishment of official photography agencies, such as AMAP in Mali and A Foto in Angola, tasked with communicating government-approved points of view.[32] Inspired, possibly, by the achievement of independence in other countries, Mozambique photographer Ricardo Rangel (1924–2009) reoriented his own camerawork in the service of social change. During the 1960s, when guerrilla warfare was being waged against Portuguese colonial authority, Rangel shot a series called *Our Nightly Bread*, capturing the night life in the port city of Maputo (Fig. 10.16). Rangel founded a photographic training center, which continues to instruct most students of photography in Mozambique.

By South African custom and law, press photography was reserved for white practitioners. Nevertheless, the medium was enlisted in the fight for social justice during the 1950s. In Johannesburg, the Progressive Photographic Society was formed, and *Drum* magazine, founded in 1951 as an entertainment magazine for urban blacks, was reformulated as a showcase for young writers and photographers who wanted to portray contemporary culture. *Drum* contrived ways to show the work of South African photographers, whether black, white, or of

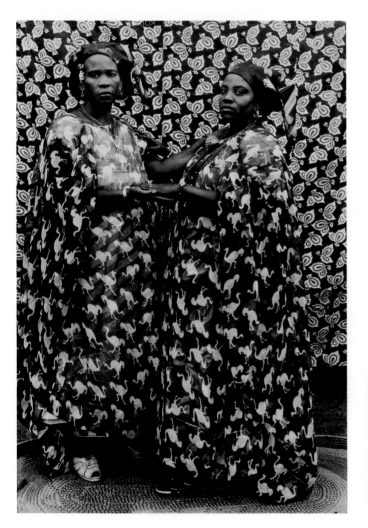

10.14
SEYDOU KEÏTA, *Two Women*, 1959. Private collection.

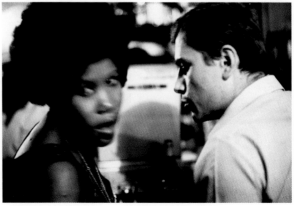

10.16
RICARDO RANGEL, *Untitled*, from *Our Nightly Bread* series, 1960.

Asian extraction, including Cloete Breytenbach (b. 1933), Ernest Cole (1940–1990), Bob Gosani (1934–1972), and Ranjith Kally (b. 1925). They resolutely pictured life under apartheid, the policy of racial separation formalized in 1948 and regulated with increasingly severe laws throughout the 1950s. *Drum* magazine expanded to several other African countries; at its height, its circulation was about 450,000.

Since publications could be banned at any moment, the writers, editors, and photographers at *Drum* were not openly hostile to apartheid. Nevertheless, during the 1950s, the magazine pushed the limits of resistance, publishing Alan Paton's novel *Cry, the Beloved Country*, a best-seller about the conflict between a black minister and a white supremacist farmer. Occasionally *Drum*'s photographers got themselves arrested in order to record the effects of the harsh criminal justice system, or such practices as convict labor.

Peter Magubane (b. 1932), who ultimately became chief photographer at *Drum*, once shrewdly turned the prevalence of black stereotypes to his advantage. In order to make a series of photographs of the 1956 trial of some apartheid protesters

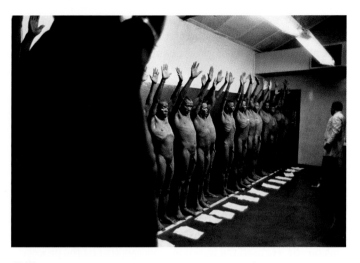

10.17
PETER MAGUBANE, *Untitled* (The Wenela Mine recruiting agency), Johannesburg, South Africa, 1967.

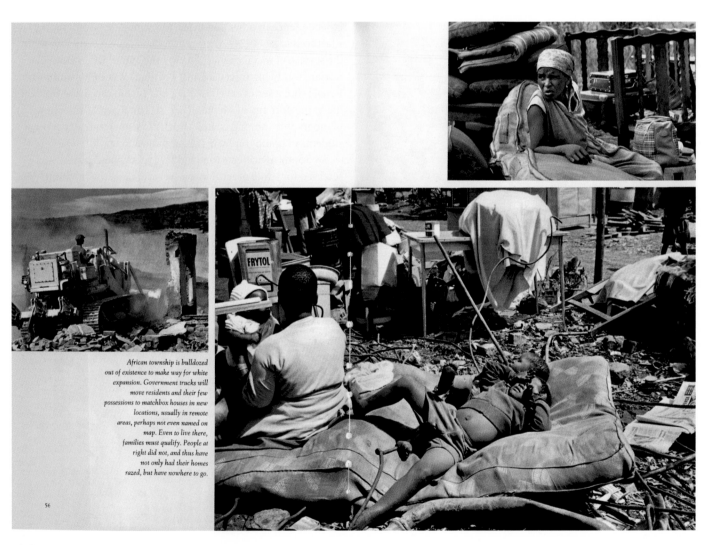

African township is bulldozed out of existence to make way for white expansion. Government trucks will move residents and their few possessions to matchbox houses in new locations, usually in remote areas, perhaps not even named on map. Even to live there, families must qualify. People at right did not, and thus have not only had their homes razed, but have nowhere to go.

56

10.18
ERNEST COLE, *Untitled*, pages from his book *House of Bondage*, 1967. Ridge Press, Random House, New York.

Magubane hid his camera in a loaf of bread and lounged outside the courthouse pretending to eat it, all the while secretly photographing people as they arrived. At considerable risk, Magubane resolved to record abuse of black workers (Fig. 10.17) and anti-apartheid demonstrations, whose activities were distorted in the newspapers that backed government policy. Similarly, when detained by the police, Ernest Cole cleverly played on his captors' biases, claiming that he was doing a report on black juvenile delinquency. Cole's *House of Bondage* (1967) is one of the most comprehensive indictments of South African racial policy produced by a photographer (Fig. 10.18).

Drum photographers also contributed to political resistance by making pictures in such places as jazz clubs, where they showed black social life unfettered by apartheid policy. After 1960, when the ruling government reacted to anti-apartheid activities by declaring a state of emergency, black photographers faced jail or exile. Magubane was held in solitary confinement for a year and a half, and then was banned from taking pictures for five years. Undeterred, during the 1980s, Magubane and other photographers, many of them trained in their craft at *Drum*, used photography to record the oppression and resistance that led to the end of apartheid. Not all anti-apartheid photographs directly pictured incidents of injustice and racial domination. For forty years, David Goldblatt (b. 1930), a white man who left his family's menswear business in 1962 in order to make photographs, shot scenes of ordinary daily activities. His views of shanty towns, billboards, shacks, and public monuments subtly alluded to the condition of racial inequity. In *The Transported: A South African Odyssey* (1989), Goldblatt collected photographs he made during the early morning, two-and-a-half-hour bus ride endured daily by black workers from the segregated "homeland" of Kwandebele to the city of Pretoria, where they labored but were not allowed to live (Fig. 10.19). After the end of apartheid in South Africa, Goldblatt continued his strategy of contrasting visually the environments of the rich and the poor.

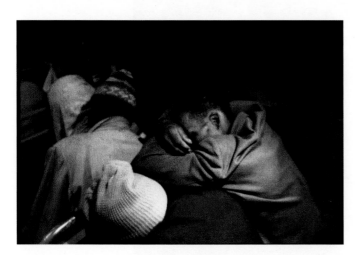

10.19
DAVID GOLDBLATT, *Untitled,* **from his book** *The Transported: A South African Odyssey,* **1989. © David Goldblatt/ South Photographs.**

Shooting in the spotty available light of the interior of a bus, Goldblatt let the forms of human figures suggest themselves out of the gray granular atmosphere.

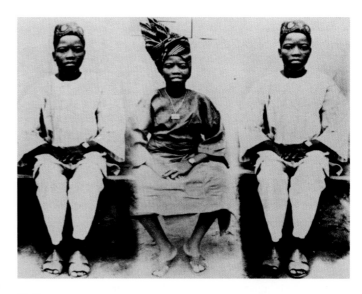

10.20
STEPHEN F. SPRAGUE, *Yoruba Triplets from Yoruba Photography: How the Yoruba See Themselves,* **1978. Photograph by Simple Photo, Courtesy the MIT Press.**

The West began to take notice of Afrocentric photography in the decades after World War II. Stephen F. Sprague's still widely read and cited 1975 study of the use of photography among the Yoruba people of West Africa made the case that they had been integrating photography into their art practice since the 1930s.[33] At the core of Yoruba photography were cultural guidelines about how to render likenesses based on broad rules for human interaction. The notion of *jijora* indicated that an image, including a photograph, should be made at the mid-point between generalization and resemblance; individualizing specificity should be avoided in favor of a modest idealization. At the same time, the concept of *ifarahon*, or visibility, suggested clarity and order. In practical terms, *ifarahon* meant that both the sitter's eyes should be visible, so the sitter had to look directly into the camera. Moreover, the photographer should not employ such poses as the profile view nor introduce dramatic lighting or unusual angles. Sprague described how Yoruba photographs of twins worked against Western realism to confirm the Yoruba belief in the unique spiritual connections of multiple-birth children. He wrote that if one twin were to die, the surviving twin of the same sex was photographed, and the photograph printed twice to show them both. If the twins were of different sexes, the survivor was dressed once as a male and once as a female, to create a double portrait. He documented an unusual case in which two male triplets died, and the surviving female portrayed the two deceased brothers (Fig. 10.20).

Sprague's work is an example of the shift in anthropological and cultural studies toward a consideration of indigenous and postcolonial uses of the medium.

ASIA
India
Photographic practice in India took off quickly within months of the medium's official disclosure to the world in 1839, and grew rapidly among colonial and Indian practitioners

(see pp. 115–17). In the years immediately preceding and following World War II, India constituted a large market for photographic supplies, manufactured by international companies such as Kodak and the German company Agfa. Illustrated publications such as the *Illustrated Weekly of India* provided outlets for Indian-made images. The pre-World War II period saw the start of specialty magazines for photographers, such as *Indian Photography and Cinematography*, launched by S. Lakshiminarasu in 1937, and the Kodak-sponsored *Kodak Indian Magazine* (later *Tropical Photography*), founded in 1940. Camera clubs consisting largely of Indian members were well established in the bigger cities and towns. However, as historian G. Thomas reported, "no deliberate attempt was being made by Indians to establish an Indian idiom in photographic communications."[34] The British Royal Photographic Society's programs and its operations were widely admired. As in nineteenth-century Britain, various groups in India exchanged photographs by mail in what was called the "Postal Portfolio" movement.

Although Margaret Bourke-White photographed in postwar India, publishing a book called *Halfway to Freedom: A Report on the New India* (1949), and Henri Cartier-Bresson worked there several times, the pictures they produced were mostly not for the Indian market. After India achieved independence from Britain in 1947, a new proposal for photography "of Indians, by Indians, for Indians" was eagerly heard, and a national society, the Federation of Indian Photography, was established in 1953.[35] The call for Indian photography followed on the success of the independence movement's wide distribution among the populace of photographic postcard images picturing organizer Mahatma Gandhi (1869–1948). Beginning in the 1930s, the postcards were used as a rallying device that could bypass British-controlled media. After independence, cameras made exclusively for the Indian market were manufactured by New India Industries, in conjunction with Agfa, and Kodak changed its name from Kodak Limited to the Indian Photographic Company. By 1965, film was also being manufactured by Indians for Indians.

Homai Vyarawalla (1913–2012), a self-taught photojournalist who covered World War II for the *Illustrated Weekly of India*, recorded the jubilant crowds celebrating independence and followed the political life of the new country during the 1950s. She worked for the *Times of India*, and as a contributor to *Time* and *Life* magazines. Another photojournalist to emerge during the independence movement was Sunil Janah (1918–2012). His pictures of the 1943–44 famine, the independence struggle, and Gandhi's assassination in 1948 gave him an international

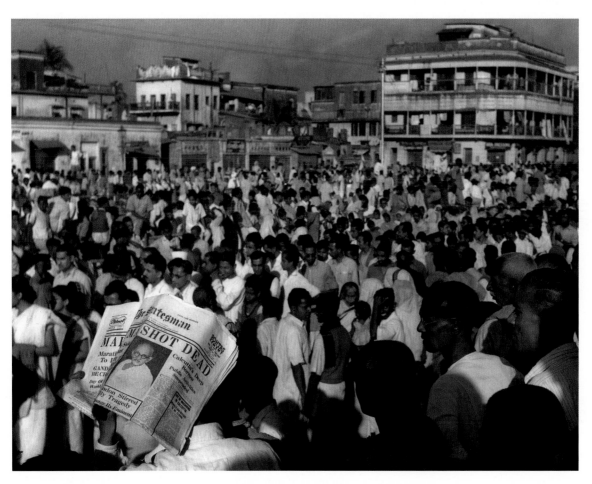

10.21
SUNIL JANAH, *Untitled* (People pouring into the streets of Calcutta after the news of Gandhi's assassination), 1948.

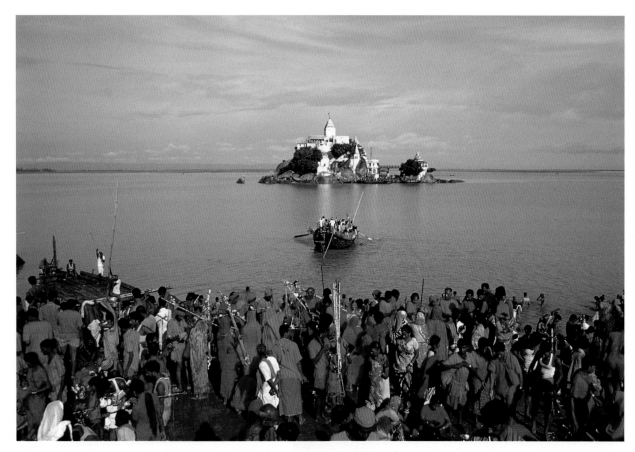

10.22
RAGHUBIR SINGH, *Shiva Temple*, Jahngira, 1983.

reputation (Fig. 10.21). When Margaret Bourke-White began her work in India, she sought him out for advice and contacts. Janah's Calcutta studio became a meeting place for artists and intellectuals, including the filmmaker Satyajit Ray (1921–1992).

India's best-known photographer at home and abroad was Ray's friend Raghubir Singh (1942–1999). Singh credited his interest in photography to his teenage viewing of Cartier-Bresson's 1949 book *Beautiful Jaipur*. Unlike many non-Western photographers, for whom the new reliable color film was too expensive, Singh started his career in color photojournalism, supplying images for international publications such as *National Geographic* and the *New York Times*. During the 1970s, he began creating photographic books on Indian regions, including Kerala in the south, Kashmir in the north, the Ganges River (Fig. 10.22), and cities such as Bombay (Mumbai) and Calcutta (Kolkata). His books were sold internationally and marketed to tourists in India.

Postcolonial Indian photography took another turn in the industrial city of Nagda and the village of Bhatisuda in the central subcontinent. In this area photographic practices developed out of custom and religion, and disregarded Western notions of realism.[36] Like the Yoruba people of Africa, the residents of Nagda and Bhatisuda created an aesthetic form and meaning for their works that ignored the usual studio conventions. Before the advent of widespread color photography,

they freely requested that the photographic image be painted over with color. In addition, photographs of family members were then montaged, sometimes bringing together relatives who could not attend a baptism, wedding, or funeral, in order to create an image of the whole extended family. A distinctive genre of montaged photographs emerged as memorials of the

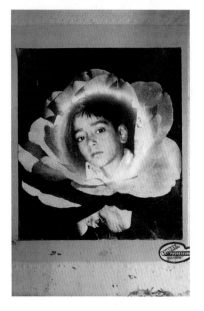

10.23
PHOTOGRAPHER UNKNOWN,
Untitled (Manakal's son), c. 1965.
Photomontage. Bombay Photo
Studio, India.

A dead child is remembered in a photomontage placing his image inside one of a rose, linking scent with memory.

dead (Fig. 10.23). It has been suggested that the development of a moderately independent representational system such as that at Nagda and Bhatisuda may have sprung from classic Indian narratives, notably the story-within-a-story structure of the *Mahabharata*.[37] What might be called non-Western photographic folk practice exists side by side in rural and urban settings with Western-derived photojournalism.

Japan

Taking its cue from Western examples, Pictorialism dominated Japanese still life, landscape, and portrait photography into the 1930s. It was followed by other Western-inspired styles, such as Modernism, whose sharp angles and severe close-ups affected art

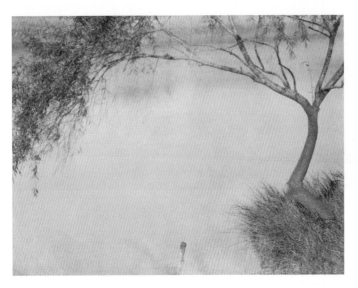

10.24
SHINZO FUKUHARA, *Light With its Harmony 8: Pond*, c. 1910. Shiseido Corporation, Japan.

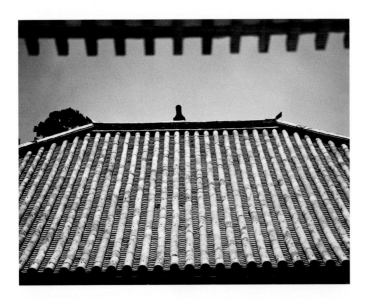

10.25
ROSO FUKUHARA, *Sangaatsudo*, c. 1915. Gelatin silver print. Shiseido Corporation, Japan.

photography, advertising, and portraiture. Likewise, Surrealism and European experimental photography were investigated in Japan, and their disjointed and collaged effects were adapted to create visually exciting commercial art. As in other countries, the pre-World War II period saw the flourishing of illustrated publications and specialty magazines for photographers, and the manufacture of Japanese cameras for the home market. While international styles flourished in prewar Japan, some photographers, such as Shinzo Fukuhara (1883–1948) and his brother Roso Fukuhara (1892–1946), sought to counteract both the fuzzy look of art photography and the deep perspective offered by the camera (Figs. 10.24, 10.25).

Shinzo and Roso Fukuhara were the sons of Arinobu Fukuhara, founder of the cosmetics firm Shiseido. Like their father, who modeled his merchandise on European products, they judiciously borrowed Western visual styles for their photography. Shinzo, who studied pharmacology in the United States, took over the company presidency in 1915, and streamlined the firm's advertising and window displays in the manner of Western Modernist art and photography, but his and his brother's photography was resolutely otherworldly. Much of Shinzo's work was destroyed in a 1923 earthquake.

During World War II, Japanese propaganda and war photographs dwelled on injured or dead enemy bodies and ruined buildings, subjects also pictured by other war-torn countries. Japanese photographers arrived on the scene soon after the atomic bombings of Hiroshima and Nagasaki. At the epicenter in Hiroshima they found a ghastly photograph-like silhouette of a man's shadow scorched into a wall by the heat and light of the bomb. Sent to Nagasaki by the Japanese military, photographer Yosuke Yamahata (1917–1966) spent August 10, 1945, making images of the city's ruins. His 119 pictures are the largest archive of photographs made of an atomic bomb site, gained at the cost of severe radiation exposure that probably contributed to his early death from cancer. Some of his pictures were published in Japanese newspapers immediately after the country surrendered, but the army of occupation under American General Douglas MacArthur soon banned all atomic-related information and pictures for seven years.[38] When Edward Steichen traveled to Japan to gather images for "The Family of Man" exhibition, he met Yamahata and was moved by his book *Atomized Nagasaki* (1952). For the anti-nuclear war section of the show, Steichen used a Yamahata photograph of a small injured boy clutching a rice ball (Fig. 10.26).

PHOTOGRAPHING THE ATOMIC BOMB

Photographs from the atomic bombings of Hiroshima and Nagasaki did not run in U.S. newspapers on the days these cities were bombed (August 7 and August 9, 1945, respectively, United States time). The pictures that were released on August 11, 1945, were taken from the air by George R. Caron, a tailgunner aboard the *Enola Gay*, the airplane that delivered the bomb to

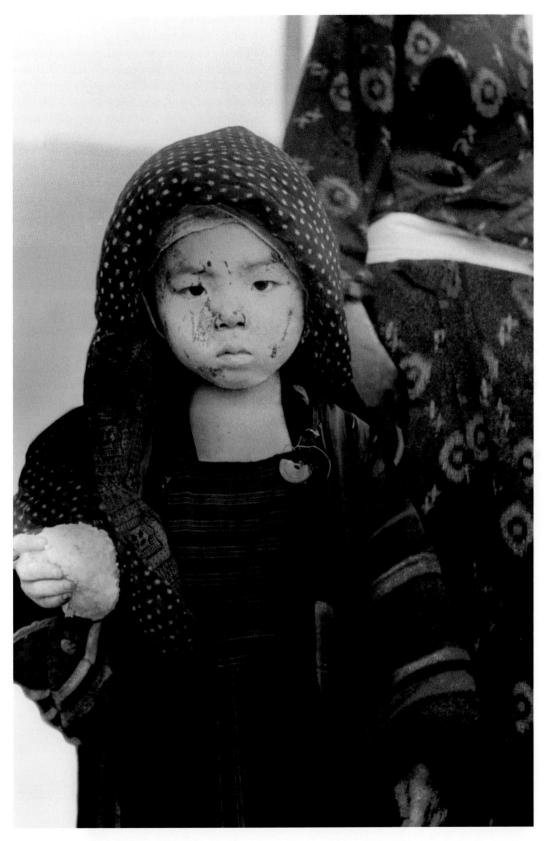

10.26
YOSUKE YAMAHATA, *A Boy with a Rice Ball*, from his book *Atomized Nagasaki*, **1952. Gelatin silver print.**

The cover image from Yamahata's 1952 book, *Atomized Nagasaki*, shows a dazed child, clothed in a headdress thought to protect the wearer from radiation, and looking directly into the camera. Unlike the other photographs hung near it in "The Family of Man" show, which were labeled only with their country of origin, Yamahata's image was specifically labeled "Nagasaki."

Hiroshima. They were published widely in subsequent weeks, appearing, for example, in the August 20, 1945, issue of *Life*. Though they gave many people their first look at the tall, dome-topped cloud rising 20,000 feet over the city, the Hiroshima images scarcely approximated the mushroom-shape cloud that emerged as the emblem of the atomic age. A photograph of the Nagasaki explosion that accompanied it in the same issue of *Life* came closer.

The distinctive shape assumed by the soaring column of dirt and debris that follows an atomic explosion was first compared to a mushroom in military descriptions of the tests preceding the Japanese bombings. In fact, the resemblance began to enter the language vocabulary before the 1946 atomic test on Bikini Atoll that produced a distinctive mushroom shape. The public repeatedly viewed the Bikini blast in photographs as well as through newsreels and television (Fig. 10.27). In a bizarre twist, the Pacific island later gave the famous bathing suit its name.

Aerial views of the destruction at Hiroshima and Nagasaki appeared in the United States within weeks of the bombings, but close-up images of the damage to people and property shot by the Japanese were confiscated by the United States War Department before they could be disseminated. Bits of movie footage, cut from film made by the Japanese shortly after the

Hiroshima explosion, were included in an August 1946 newsreel about the Bikini Atoll tests. The *New York Times* reported that one of the images showed victims who appeared "as though they had been seared by an acetylene torch."[39] In that same month, the *New Yorker* published writer John Hersey's vivid chronicle of what he saw in Hiroshima. Pictures made by Japanese photographers were not widely seen by the American public until a 1952 issue of *Life*. When the magazine ran pictures of the first hydrogen bomb explosion in 1954, it also published an editorial tinged with fear and relieved with deathbed humor, reflecting increased public apprehension about the specter of nuclear warfare.[40] The initial public feelings of awe and patriotism following Hiroshima and Nagasaki eroded throughout the 1950s, allowing the anxiety about the atomic bomb gradually to spread. Nevertheless, atomic energy remained a strong, yet contradictory, prospect for the future. To some, harnessing the atom foretold a utopian tomorrow, in which nuclear power freed humans from work and nuclear medicine cured diseases. To others, experiments with the atom launched a growing pessimism about the dark side of human nature.

Defeat in World War II raised questions about postwar national identity for Japanese artists working in such media

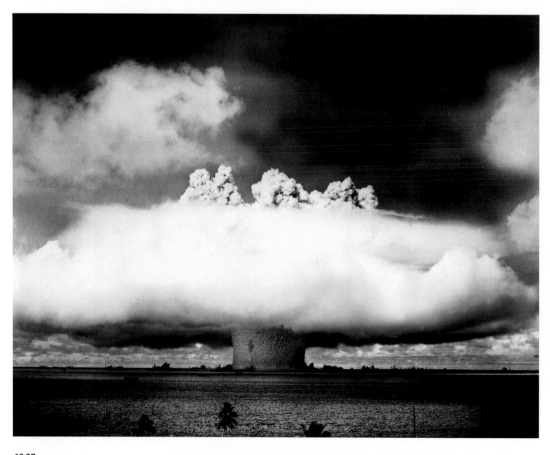

10.27
PHOTOGRAPHER UNKNOWN, *Atomic Cloud During Baker Day Blast at Bikini*, 1946. Gelatin silver print. National Archives, Washington, D.C.

as dance and film, as well as photography. As Mark Holborn observed, "it is impossible to look at postwar Japanese photography without recognizing the effect of the almost inconceivable events of 1945 on the collective imagination of the nation."[41] The war experience reverberates through Japanese postwar artwork, in themes linking death, devastation, and defeat. After the atomic bombings, the anatomy of the human body, not a major subject in traditional Japanese art, was thrust forward as a contradictory symbol of ruin and endurance. The countervailing desire for normalcy also coursed through postwar Japanese photography. Because Japan's museums did not take a major interest in exhibiting and collecting photography, books became the primary way to circulate photographs. Consequently, Japanese photographers conceived their images in series. Their photographs were viewed consecutively on book pages, and reproduced in the deep, dull black and blank white created by printer's ink. The grayscale delicacies of fine photographic prints, best appreciated in a portfolio or in a gallery, became secondary.[42]

After a prohibition by the U.S. authorities on atomic-bomb-related images was lifted in the early 1950s, several photographers began to shape meanings from the experience of Hiroshima and Nagasaki. Indeed, the havoc wrought by the bomb on human beings and on civic life became a central symbol for life and death in the iconography of postwar Japan. Ken Domon (1909–1990), a photographer with wide-ranging interests including the photography of Japanese art, published *Hiroshima* (1958), an unsparing look at the survivors of the blast. For the Japanese, this book became the best-known account of the bombing. Wanting to underscore the perseverance of Hiroshima's people, Domon issued *Living Hiroshima* twenty years after his first study (Fig. 10.28).

In 1950, Domon co-founded the Shudan Photo Group, which renounced prewar Pictorialist prettiness as well as modes of extreme self-expression. The group exhibited in Japan with Western photographers they admired, including Margaret Bourke-White, W. Eugene Smith, Henri Cartier-Bresson, and Bill Brandt.[43] Their philosophy was soon superseded by that of another group, Junin-no-Me (The Eyes of Ten), which favored stylized interpretations of physical existence. After viewing the work of Junin-no-Me, Domon remarked that the period of objective documentary was over and a period of subjective documentary had begun.[44]

In the early 1960s, industrial pollution introduced poisonous mercury into the waters near the fishing village of Minamata, causing profound birth defects. Along with other professional and amateur photographers, doctors, and filmmakers, Shisei Kuwabara (b. 1936) photographed the tragic results in images whose grainy dark surfaces parallel the visual language used by photographers to chronicle the physical effects of atomic devastation (Fig. 10.29). Influenced by these pictures and Kuwabara's book on Minamata, American photographer W. Eugene Smith and his wife, Aileen Mioko Smith, similarly recorded the calamity, producing a large series of photographs that trace the introduction of mercury waste into the water, its

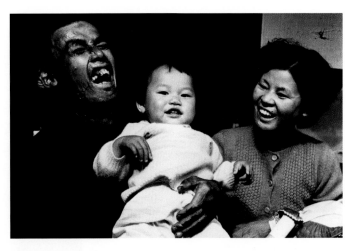

10.28
KEN DOMON, *Hiroshima: The Marriage of A-Bomb Victims*, 1957. Gelatin silver print. Ken Domon Museum of Photography, Yamagata, Japan.

The longing to return to normalcy after exposure to atomic radiation was frequently expressed in pictures of domestic life and the happiness born of daily existence.

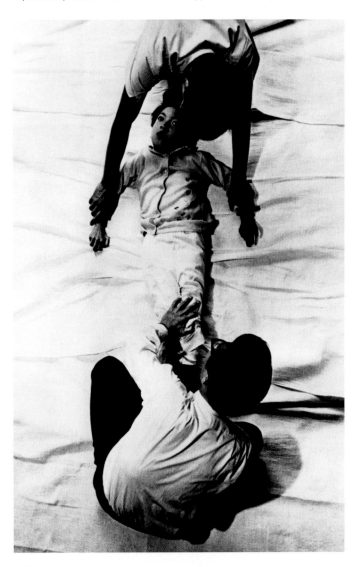

10.29
SHISEI KUWABARA, *Untitled* (People affected by "Minamata Disease"), from his book *Minamata Disease*, 1972.

portrait

Shomei Tomatsu

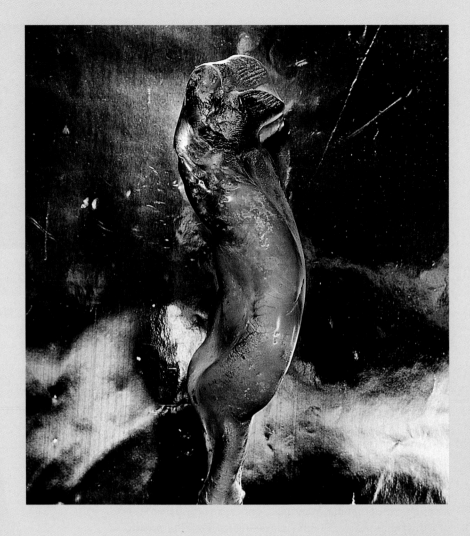

10.30
SHOMEI TOMATSU, *A Bottle Melted and Deformed by Atomic Bomb Heat, Radiation and Fire*, Nagasaki, 1961.

Introducing his photographs about the effects of the atomic bomb blast at Nagasaki, Shomei Tomatsu (1930–2013) wrote: "Nagasaki has two times. There is 11:02, August 9, 1945. And there is all the time since then."[45] The pivotal influence of the explosion on postwar Japanese experience was summarized in the introductory photograph of Tomatsu's book *Nagasaki: 11:02* (1966), which shows a scorched wristwatch stopped at the time of the detonation. The text accompanying Tomatsu's pictures begins with impersonal scientific data on the heat and energy of the blast, as well as the symptoms of radiation exposure, but the photographs are far from objective. For instance, when Tomatsu photographed a beer bottle melted in the infernal heat, he lighted it in such a way that it suggests a skinned animal carcass (Fig. 10.30). In another image, a man's head appears out of black shadows into a spotlight where dark and light abstract shapes reveal themselves to be skeins of scar tissue moving up his neck. The man's face is dramatically lighted to indicate the skull beneath the skin. With Ken Domon, Tomatsu also worked on an extensive project, the Hiroshima–Nagasaki Document (1961).

Tomatsu's work was at the forefront of the trend in postwar Japan toward subjective documentary, in which the presence and the worldview of the photographer fuse with the subject matter.

He forcefully argued that merely reporting a scene does not help to illuminate situations.[46] In many of his photographs, the subject is off-center, or lies at the edge of the work, or is masked with dark shadows. In a hospital just for atomic bomb victims, the face of an obviously ill man addresses the viewer from the extreme upper left of the picture; the disfigured face of a child injured in the womb by radiation is all but lost in a welter of tree leaves that discreetly obscure the face while offering the comforts of nature. Tomatsu was also concerned to show the period of recovery. In his work, immutable human scars and bomb-induced changes in the landscape are balanced by photographs that show the restoration of work and family life in Nagasaki.

The devastation of the atomic bombings caused Tomatsu to think that Japan had to begin afresh, not by trying to revive the past, as some—such as the writer and actor Yukio Mishima (1925–1970)—urged. Consequently, Tomatsu's work examined the emergence of postwar Japanese identity. His willingness to make images of contemporary, often urban life helped sever the allegiance of many photographers to the notion of a purely Japanese aesthetic based on older visual arts traditions. The pensive, personal character of his images, with their deliberate shaping of a subject through exaggerated contrasts of black and white, was a major force in Japanese photography.

effects on a generation of children, and the attempts of citizens to seek justice through the court system. Their most famous photograph, showing a victim of the poisoning, Tomoko Uemura, being gently bathed in a position reminiscent of Michelangelo's *Pieta* was withdrawn from circulation in 1997, on the twentieth anniversary of her death.

Some photographers shunned subjectivity and sought other means to chronicle postwar Japan. Eikoh Hosoe (b. 1933), who was a child during World War II, fused ancient Japanese myth and contemporary experimental dance in his series of thirty-five prints called *Kamaitachi* (1969), which visually narrates the lot of villagers fatally enchanted and wounded by a dancer taking the part of an evil wind, representing the nuclear blast. Throughout the book, the lowering sky threatens the ever-darkening earth, and fear of the vicious wind becomes panic about the atomic explosion. The narrative ends with a picture of total darkness. Presented as a book and an exhibition in 1969, *Kamaitachi* (Fig. 10.31) expresses both a dangerous innocence and the persistent anxiety the Japanese felt about continued American influence.

The war between Japan and the Allied forces lasted three years and eight months; the postwar occupation of Japan, largely administered by Americans, was about twice as long (August 1945 to August 1952), and the United States maintained large military bases in the country after the official end of occupation. During the 1960s, anti-American student demonstrations sparked by indignation at the Vietnam War heightened national interest in elements of traditional Japanese culture and religion thought to have been erased by Americanization. Where *Kamaitachi* spoke to a Japanese audience about these concerns in a mythic structure, Hosoe's most famous book, *Barakei* (*Killed by Roses*) (1963; 2nd, revised edition 1971), established the photographer's international reputation.

In *Barakei*, Hosoe collaborated with Yukio Mishima, whose themes revolved around Japan's humiliation by occupying forces. Their presence compelled the emperor to renounce his divinity and to align himself with modernization and rapid reconstruction. No doubt Hosoe and Mishima were among the millions of Japanese who reeled when what became known as

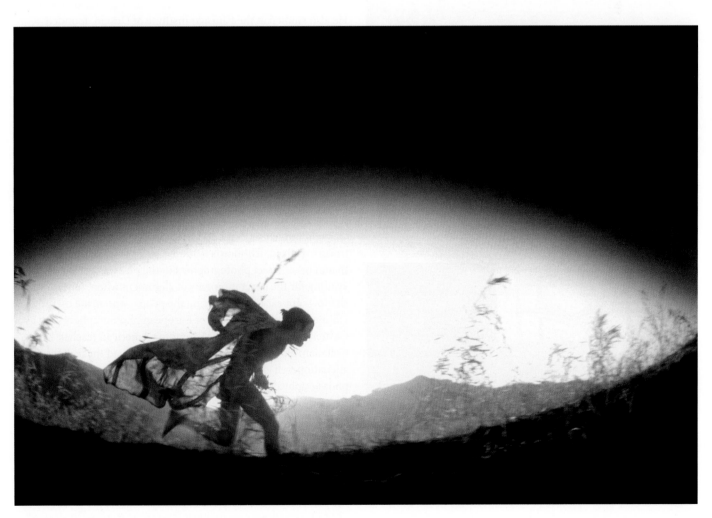

10.31
EIKOH HOSOE, *Kamaitachi 31,* **1968, from his book** *Kamaitachi,* **1969.**

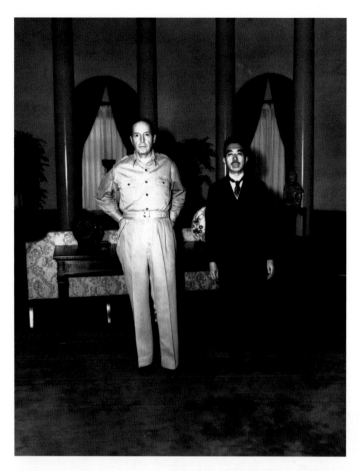

10.32
PHOTOGRAPHER UNKNOWN, *Untitled* ("The Photograph"—the first meeting of General MacArthur and Emperor Hirohito, September 27, 1945), 1945. National Archives, Washington, D.C.

The seemingly simple news photograph upset Japanese viewers, who thought that General MacArthur insulted the emperor by dressing too casually. The picture reputedly marked the moment when the Japanese recognized that they had been defeated and that the Americans were in charge. Yet the picture also showed that the Americans would support some form of continuing monarchy.[48]

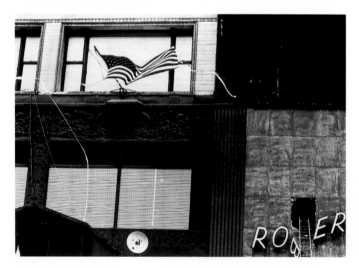

10.33
YASUHIRO ISHIMOTO, *Chicago*, 1962. Gelatin silver print.

"The Photograph" appeared in the press (Fig. 10.32). Depicting the first meeting of the Emperor Hirohito (1901–1989; r. 1926–89) and General Douglas MacArthur (1880–1964), designated supreme commander for the Allied powers in Japan, "The Photograph" showed an informally posed and somewhat casually dressed MacArthur standing beside the self-conscious, formally outfitted emperor.

Hosoe and Mishima both attempted to blend experimental art with ancestral Japanese art forms, and to infuse the postwar Westernizing present with the strength of ancient Asian tradition. Hosoe's portraits of Mishima in *Killed by Roses* dwell on Mishima's fascination with samurai swords and physical pain, an uncanny anticipation of the writer's famous act of ritual suicide. Rehearsed and performed like a theater piece, Mishima's hara-kiri was enacted on November 25, 1970, after he and a band of his supporters took over a military office and demanded to address soldiers about the loss of traditional Japanese values, and the erosion of the emperor's power in modern, democratic Japan.

Despite growing anti-American sentiment, the Modernist photograph was not neglected in Japan. It found a staunch advocate in the work of American-born Yasuhiro Ishimoto (1921–2012), who learned photography in the Colorado relocation camp where he was interned during World War II. He also studied at the Chicago Institute of Design, founded by László Moholy-Nagy as the New Bauhaus in 1937. Under Moholy-Nagy, who brought Aaron Siskind and Harry Callahan (see p. 345) to the school's faculty, the Institute of Design acquired an international reputation for its dedication to experimental techniques and formal innovation in graphic design and photographic practice. Ishimoto traveled to postwar Japan, where he applied the lessons of Moholy-Nagy's new vision photography (see pp. 243–46). Although he continued to spend time in the United States, Ishimoto became a Japanese citizen in 1969. Responding to a comment by photographer Minor White, Ishimoto stated: "I studied at the New Bauhaus in Chicago, so I agree that my work can be said to contain American and German influences, but I do not agree that I have any Japanese traits."[48] Indeed, Ishimoto's work in Chicago strongly resembles that of other street photographers in the postwar period. Waiting for the exact moments of alignment when, for example, shadows appear to be following the people who make them, Ishimoto's work recalls that of European photographers such as Cartier-Bresson and that of Ishimoto's American teacher, Harry Callahan. Never sentimental, Ishimoto grasped the feelings of alienation, self-delusion, and futility expressed in American photography during the 1950s (Fig. 10.33). Misunderstanding Ishimoto's disheartened perception of human relationships, Edward Steichen put two of his photographs in the exhibition "The Family of Man."

Ishimoto's international reputation was sealed when he published the result of his six-year-long study of Katsura Rikyu, the so-called Detached Palace in Kyoto, Japan. In these images, the palace from the early 1600s resembles the spare geometry of Modern architecture. Published in 1971, *Katsura: Tradition and Creation in Japanese Architecture* was a collaboration with

Modernist architect Kenzo Tange (1913–2005), as well as Bauhaus artists Walter Gropius, who wrote an introductory essay, and Herbert Bayer, who designed the book.

Despite the recovery of the Japanese postwar economy and the efforts of several prominent Japanese photographers to recuperate postwar culture, Daido Moriyama (b. 1938) lingered on the notion of social decline, beginning with defeat in World War II and the subsequent "Americanization" of the nation.[49] His most famous image is a gravelly picture of a dirty, exhausted, snarling stray dog (Fig. 10.34). Like his mentors, Shomei Tomatsu and Eikoh Hosoe, Moriyama exploits photography's graphic properties to express fierce emotion. His images are, as

photographer Leo Rubinfien observed, "the visual equivalent of nausea, vertigo or horror."[50] Their tilted, slightly out-of-focus quality shows Moriyama's acknowledged debt to the idiosyncratic work of American photographer William Klein (see Fig. 11.12).

Where Tomatsu's expressionistic images ultimately rely on the factual credibility of what was before the lens, Moriyama's work is radically personal: "My photographs have always been … private letters that I write and send to myself," he explained.[51] He once renounced all hope by rejecting photography in a 1972 collection called "Sashin yo sayonara" (Farewell to Photography or Photography, Good Riddance!), in which pictures were "blurred, too dark, too light, or otherwise hard to read."[52]

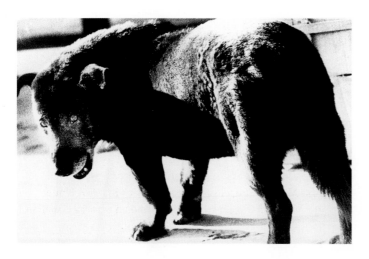

10.34
DAIDO MORIYAMA, *Stray Dog, Misawa Aimori,* **1971. Gelatin silver print. Gift of Van Deren Coke. San Francisco Museum of Modern Art, San Francisco, California.**

Moriyama's stray dog, an unwanted and dangerous animal, is an outcast and a loner and blends the photographer's sense of himself as an angry outsider with the perception that his country is irretrievably conquered. The figure appears elsewhere in Japanese postwar photography and film as a frightening symbol for social isolation, as in Akira Kurosawa's 1949 film *Stray Dog.*

RETAKE

"The Family of Man" was one of the last influential expressions of the documentary social realism that had characterized American photography during the 1930s' Depression era. Had it occurred in the pre-World War II era, it might have avoided criticism. But around the world in the 1950s, photographers were focusing on the cultural values that differentiate, not unite, societies and groups of people. Consequently, photographs of individuals outside the mainstream— such as indigenous people, urban workers, people with mental challenges, and victims of discrimination—became more numerous. Photojournalism in non-Western countries increasingly emphasized national and regional history, struggles, and events. Indeed, the

particular struggles, histories, and contexts that Edward Steichen removed from the images fast became major subjects. For example, Japanese photographers focused on the effects of the war, and especially the lasting physical and psychic consequences of the atomic bomb blasts. A major theme in photography outside the United States was resentment against the perceived Americanization of world cultures. When "The Family of Man" reached Paris, French critic Roland Barthes (1915–1980) identified its "ambiguous myth of the human 'community,'" which suppressed "the determining weight of History."[53] Barthes equated the exhibition's theme of universal oneness with American imperial aspirations.

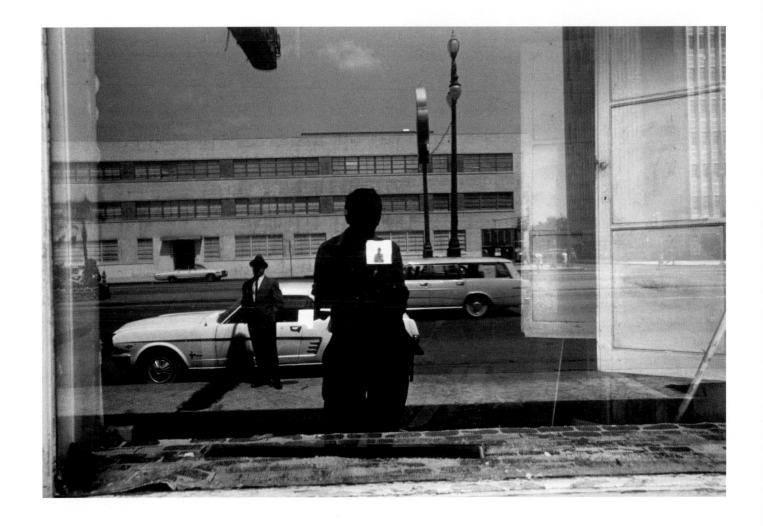

CHAPTER ELEVEN

The Cold War Era

In a 1946 speech, former British prime minister Winston Churchill (1874–1965) described an "iron curtain" dividing Europe; this seemed to come true in 1948, when the city of Berlin was cut off from the West by Soviet occupation forces, and supplies had to be airlifted to the city. Later, the Berlin Wall, built in August 1961, effectively isolated East Germany and the eastern European nations from the West.

The ravaged condition of the European nations, and the surprisingly deep economic downturn of the postwar British economy, helped make the United States a superpower. America's exclusive possession of atomic weapons confirmed that position. In addition, the United States was the only postwar nation sufficiently prosperous to consider direct military and economic confrontation with communist countries. Fear of communism increased with the 1949 victory of Mao Zedong (1893–1976) in China, and mixed with nuclear fear when the Soviets exploded their first atomic bomb in 1949.

The threat of nuclear warfare hung over the war in Korea (1950–53), which was the outcome of festering economic and political discontent in North Korea about the Allies' postwar decision to divide the country in two along the 38th parallel. Soviet- and Chinese-supported North Korean troopers battled South Korean and United Nations forces, composed of fifteen nations, including the United States. In contrast to their patriotic photographic coverage of World War II (see Fig. 9.35), newspapers and magazines heightened public fear of nuclear warfare and stirred doubt about the war's goals, using anti-heroic images of ordinary soldiers enduring danger far from home. Battle-toughened photographers such as Larry Burrows (1926–1971), Carl Mydans (1907–2004), and David Douglas Duncan (b. 1916) sent back close-up photographs of ordinary soldiers suffering cold, privation, and the death of friends. Duncan's photo-essay for *Life*'s 1950 Christmas issue undermined cozy assumptions about what a Christmas essay should contain. Entitled "There Was a Christmas," it showed an image of a young Marine more as victim than victor, his youthful freckles replaced by frostbite and mud (Fig. 11.2). Reflecting on his Korean images, Duncan concluded that "war is in the eyes."

The Korean War ended in 1953, but international tensions continued to rise. In 1955, the Soviet Union and the eastern European nations of Poland, Czechoslovakia, Hungary, Romania, Bulgaria, Albania, and East Germany signed the Warsaw Pact, a mutual defense agreement. In November 1956, a Hungarian revolt against Soviet occupation was suppressed.

In October 1957, the Soviets gained the world stage with the launch of the space satellite Sputnik 1, proving the superiority of its long-range rockets. In the United States, anti-communist hysteria led to fear that "reds" were infiltrating the nation's institutions. Federal employees were asked to sign loyalty oaths. Senator Joseph McCarthy still zealously headed the powerful House Committee on Un-American Activities (H.U.A.C.), which had subpoenaed prominent entertainers as suspected communists in 1947 and 1951.

The livelihood of many within the arts community was seriously threatened by these investigations. In 1954, McCarthy set out to locate communists in the U.S. Army, a campaign that led to his downfall. After more than a decade of highly visible political photography during the New Deal and World War II, artists and photographers left the fray, having been harassed by the government or discouraged by the slowness of social change. Recalling the 1950s, photographer Lisette Model (see p. 349) exclaimed, "It was terrible. You didn't know what to photograph."[1] Disgusted with politics and angered by the shallow materialism of what economist John Kenneth Galbraith famously called "the affluent society" in his 1958 book of the same name, many artists, writers, and photographers turned to the inner world of private contemplation.

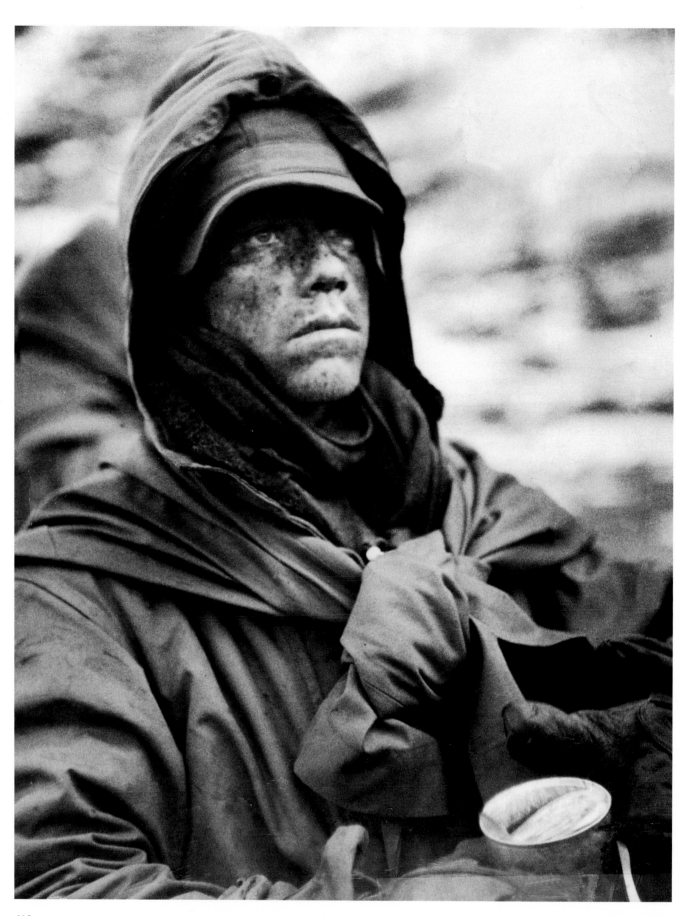

11.2
DAVID DOUGLAS DUNCAN, *Untitled,* cover of *Life* magazine, December 25, 1950.

ANNIHILATION, ALIENATION, ABSTRACTION: AMERICA

As writer Tom Englehardt observed, "from 1945 to 1975 victory culture ended in America."[2] The "heroic war ethos" of 1945 gave way to fear, insecurity, and societal disillusionment. America's inability to end the nightmarish spiral of the arms race slowly undermined the logic of mutually assured atomic destruction and confidence in the nation's place in the world. The national mood was captured in a best-selling book by the sociologist David Riesman. First published in 1950, *The Lonely Crowd* leapt to prominence in a paperback edition of 1953 that sold 1.4 million copies.[3] It warned of a major shift in the American character, a turning away from guidance by an inner compass, toward seeking direction from others. Riesman substantiated readers' worries about the American postwar future. Artist and photographer Ben Shahn (1898–1969), who had made images for the Farm Security Administration (F.S.A.), summed up the parallel changes in photographic practice: "during the thirties art had been swept by mass ideas, so during the forties there took place a mass movement toward abstraction. Not only was the social dream rejected, but any dream at all."[4]

Perhaps the best example of the shift from social documentary to abstraction is provided by Aaron Siskind's work. An active member of the Photo League, and promoter of its famous *Harlem Document* (see Fig. 9.18), Siskind began experimenting in the 1940s with abstract qualities in nature and the built environment. He photographed sites where humans had left their marks, framing and cropping them into abstractions. At the same time, he eliminated any hint of narrative content, and worked against the camera's construction of deep perspective, flattening the photographic image as if it were an ABSTRACT EXPRESSIONIST canvas by an American painter such as Franz Kline (1910–1962), Mark Rothko (1903–1970), or Willem de Kooning (1904–1997), whom he knew and whose artwork he photographed. One of his images was hung at the Ninth Street Show (1951) in New York City, an exhibit that was instrumental in bringing Abstract Expressionism to a wider audience.

As Siskind put it, "the so-called documentary picture left me wanting something." However much close-ups of peeling paint might look like an abstract painting (Fig. 11.3), Siskind insisted that this sort of work was not "a compromise with reality. The objects are rendered sharp, fully textured, and undistorted (my documentary training!)." Siskind described the instant of finding his subjects in the world of visual experience as "emotional," "psychological," and "utterly personal." He concluded that "the inner drama is the meaning of the exterior event." Like many artists in the 1950s, he sought to begin anew in primal experience or, as he put it, to unlearn socially educated responses so as "to see the world clean and fresh and alive, as primitive things are clean and fresh and alive."[5]

While Siskind turned to exploring the inner world, other artists and writers looked to indigenous peoples for lessons on living outside the tainted modern world. John Collier, Sr., who served from 1934 to 1945 as President Franklin Roosevelt's commissioner of Indian affairs, helped arrange the landmark exhibit "Indian Art of the United States" at the Museum of Modern Art in New York (1941). The tone for postwar appreciation of Native Americans was set at that exhibit, when its organizer René d'Harnoncourt dismissed the notion of primitivism as a backward stage of early civilization, and underscored the moral weight of Indian culture.[6] John Collier, Jr. (1913–1992), the commissioner's son, made extensive and generally unromanticized photographs among the Navajo people and among Peru's indigenous peoples. Similarly, Laura Gilpin (1891–1979), who spent the greater part of her career photographing among Native Americans in the Southwest, ardently studied Navajo history and life for her 1968 book *The Enduring Navajo*.

Detached from their origins in Europe between the world wars, Surrealism and abstraction became international visual languages, not only in advertising but also for a younger generation of artists. To escape persecution in Nazi Germany,

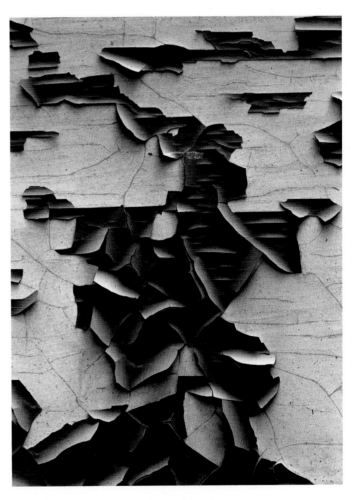

11.3
AARON SISKIND, *Jerome, Arizona*, 1949. Gelatin silver print. Aaron Siskind Foundation. Nelson-Atkins Museum Collection.

By coming in close to what appears to be peeling paint, Siskind isolated a composition with a central, if abstract figure, balanced by an array of shapes in the upper and lower parts of the picture. The photograph may owe to Siskind's close relationship with Abstract Expressionist painters, who employed thick slashes of paint on their canvases.

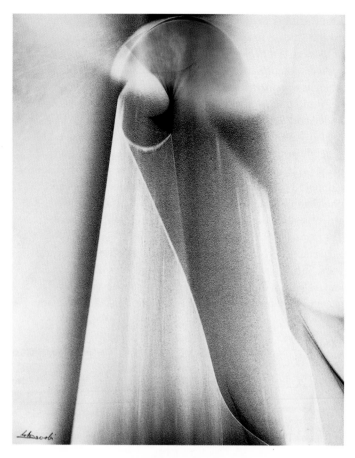

11.4
LOTTE JACOBI, *Photogenic*, c. 1950. Vintage gelatin silver print. Lotte Jacobi Archives, Dimond Library, University of New Hampshire, Durham, New Hampshire. The Nelson-Atkins Museum of Art, Gift of Hallmark Cards, Inc., Kansas, Missouri.

Lotte Jacobi (1896–1990) had to leave 90 per cent of her work behind. After arriving in the United States in 1935, Jacobi set about combining a career in portrait photography with the production of abstractions she called "photogenics." These resulted from drawing with a light source, such as a pen light, on photographically sensitive paper (Fig. 11.4). Working in Arizona for more than fifty years, Italian-born Frederick Sommer (1905–1999) blended Surrealism and abstraction in psychologically disturbing images. He photographed still lifes made from the desiccated corpses of desert animals, fusing formal beauty with frightening decay. Like his friend the Surrealist Max Ernst, Sommer experimented with de-forming the photograph's realism. He superimposed images, created CLICHÉS VERRES, and constructed negatives from oil paint sandwiched between sheets of cellophane. Even his straight photographs look like altered images (Fig. 11.5). Like Siskind, with whom he photographed in 1949, Sommer favored blocking out the horizon line and focusing on surface texture and flatness.[7] Just as Abstract Expressionists such as Jackson Pollock (1912–1956) brought to center stage the physical process of making art, so Sommer emphasized technique at the expense of realistic description.

As happened in Europe, American Surrealist photography gradually lost its sense of outrage and estrangement, becoming more a means of psychic inquiry and fanciful imaginings. Even

though American Jerry Uelsmann (b. 1934) claims that his seamless separate realities draw on what he calls "the darker side of myself,"[8] there are no horrific scenes in his work. A student of Minor White (1908–1976), Uelsmann creates illusionistic images that seem to capture a parallel world, where elements recombine in unexpected but not repugnant ways (Fig. 11.7). In one print he showed himself in the bathtub as Oscar Rejlander and as Henry Peach Robinson, a reference to the nineteenth-century combination-printmakers and their efforts to insert visual information into a photograph that the camera was incapable of recording.

Surrealism and abstraction were among a number of strategies for contesting the notions that photography must record the external world, or that it was obliged to support the humanitarian task of social betterment. Minor White, a photographer who sought spiritual insights in poetry, psychological theory, myth, and religion, did not so much reject the material realm as reconfigure it. White thought of photography as a process wherein the visual world was rediscovered as a font of spiritual illumination for those willing to look. Widely seen as a mystic, White nonetheless stressed that the poet-photographer must move beyond self-discovery to communication. Writing to a person seeking his advice, White counseled: "Your photographs are still mirrors of yourself. In other words your images are raw, the emotions naked. These are private images not public ones. They are 'expressive' meaning a direct mirror of yourself rather than 'creative' meaning so converted as to affect others as mirrors of themselves."[9]

White much admired Stieglitz's photographs, especially the series known as *Equivalents* (see Fig. 6.27), in which he used cloud shots to intimate inner states. Like Stieglitz, White insisted that photographs could be much more than literal transcriptions of optical reality, and he preferred to work in series of images

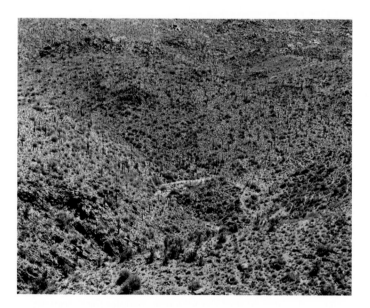

11.5
FREDERICK SOMMER, *Arizona Landscape*, 1943. Gelatin silver print. Center for Creative Photography, Tucson, Arizona.

arranged to form complex poetic meanings. He began making "sequences" soon after returning from service in World War II, and this "cinema of stills" became his basic unit.[10] Wanting a more interactive interpretation of his work, White often spoke of "reading" photographs, not merely glimpsing them. In the 1940s, he was already numbering his sequences, some of which were personal explorations of homoerotic desire that were never publicly exhibited during his lifetime. The order of individual photographs within a sequence was not fixed, but changed from time to time. Certain themes recur in his work, such as the fleeting performances of natural phenomena. Ordinary doors and windows open on to unanticipated glimpses of fantastic yet momentary illumination (Fig. 11.6).

At the end of the nineteenth century, White might have been a Pictorialist, locating spirituality in suggestive haziness. Instead, he looked to the intensely detailed views and vigilant printing methods of Ansel Adams and Edward Weston, and to their use of the straight photograph to convey metaphysical meaning. In the postwar period, when social reform efforts were too often misconstrued as communist ventures, White became a spiritual activist. His teaching at institutions on the East and West coasts, and curatorial position at George Eastman House in Rochester, New York, allowed him to encourage personal insight and spirituality among photographers, and to promote the use of photography as metaphor or symbol. In 1952, White became editor of *Aperture*, a magazine devoted to art photography,

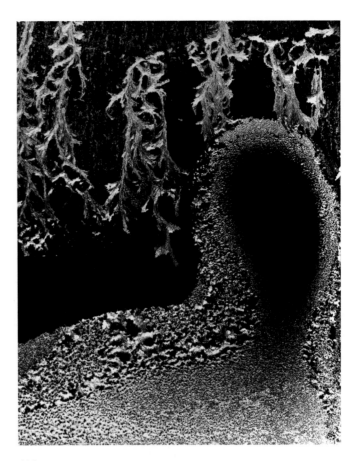

11.6
MINOR WHITE, *Empty Head,* **from sequence 14 of** *Sound of One Hand Clapping,* **1962. Gelatin silver print. Minor White Archive. Princeton Art Museum, Princeton, New Jersey.**

11.7
JERRY UELSMANN, *Untitled*
(Landscape with a floating tree), 1969.
Victoria and Albert Museum, London.

Uelsmann's precise combination-printing techniques allow him to invent alternative worlds in which nature operates in ways contrary to its habits on earth.

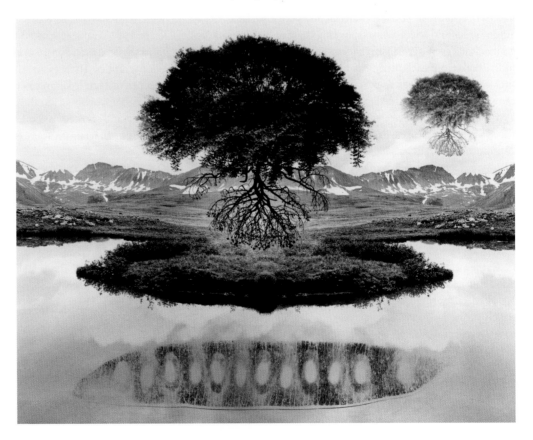

which he founded along with others, including Dorothea Lange and Ansel Adams. Although his work was criticized by Postmodernists in the late twentieth century as "mystical trivia,"[11] White's influence on photography endures in the meditative fine printing of his students, such as Paul Caponigro (b. 1932) and Jerry Uelsmann, as well as the independence of Eugene Richards (see p. 419).

THE AMERICANS

Minor White's spiritualism was not the only personal approach to photography to have a lasting impact on the medium. The photographs of Swiss-born photographer Robert Frank (b. 1924) induced many young photographers to cruise the streets and highways of America looking for pictures. A commercial and fashion photographer when he came to the United States, Frank also made his own work, which came to Steichen's attention while he was selecting images for "The Family of Man" exhibition.

Encouraged by his friend and mentor Walker Evans, Frank began the first of several road trips around the United States, where he made pictures that would unravel the certitude of documentary photography as practiced by the F.S.A. photographers and the picture press. Where Depression-era documentarians witnessed a troubled yet resilient America, summed up in such images as Lange's *Migrant Mother* (see Fig. 9.3), Frank saw a soul-damaged population, fluctuating through violence, ignorance, and despair. In the collection of these images called *The Americans* (French edition, 1958; American edition, 1959), first published in France because no American publishing house would issue it, Frank transformed tokens of American postwar material prosperity, such as automobiles and television sets, casting them as conduits of an insidious commercialism that was profoundly alienating individuals from each other and from the wider society. In this way, he can be seen as part of a wider artistic resistance movement, which included the Beat poets and novelists, engaged in the struggle to find alternatives to the power of consensus-based art forms. Despite Frank's recurrent images of motion and communication, such as highways or telephones, the people in *The Americans* seem stuck in one place: the loneliness of their own psyches. As Peter C. Mazio observed, "The only mobile person in Robert Frank's *The Americans* is the artist himself."[12] In his book, American flags sometimes fly in the faces of observers, obscuring their vision, and people seldom find eye contact with each other (Fig. 11.8).

Rather than the clear, balanced compositions of photojournalism and the documentary tradition, Frank's prints are often gritty, tilted, and blurred. Shot with a 35mm camera, which allowed him to take pictures quickly and secretly, they have an unpremeditated look that—like the action paintings of Jackson Pollock—combines great intensity with a free, risky handling. *The Americans* does not progress through a legible visual narrative, but consists of fragmented "indecisive" moments experienced by the photographer. For some viewers, Frank's concentration on ragtag Americans and his apathetic

attitude toward the craft of photography were tantamount to "un-American" behavior of the kind notoriously persecuted by McCarthy's committee.

With the wider circulation of a 1960s American edition, and subsequent republications that kept the book in print, Frank's photographs gained a wide intellectual presence as a protest against numbing mass culture, materialism, and social conformity. The preface to the United States printing was written by Beat generation writer Jack Kerouac (1922–1969), whose jittery romantic novel of the American highways *On the Road* was published in 1957 and featured Frank as one of its characters. Kerouac's hipster language, reeled off in streams of association, like a poem by Allen Ginsberg (1926–1997), located the authenticity of the pictures in their apparently impromptu nature, reminiscent of Beat-generation poetry and jazz improvisation.

Kerouac also drew Frank—and photography—into the sphere of American existentialism and Beat generation hauteur, with its emphasis on cool, self-absorbed rebelliousness in the face of narrow social conformity. In effect, Kerouac suggested that Frank's photographs could be savored like serious avant-garde literature, which assailed the deeply rooted American tradition of rural innocence and integrity, and prophesied the coming of shabby morality and self-delusion to the American heartland. Like Walker Evans, whose *American Photographs* (1938) pictured automobiles, graveyards, and luncheonettes as signposts of American feeling, Frank became a photographer-hero, both for his vision and for his lifestyle, which reflected personal discoveries. Evans had, in fact, helped to obtain for Frank the Guggenheim Fellowship that allowed him to make the trips on which *The Americans* was based.

In 1962, Frank remarked that "photography is a solitary journey. That is the only course open to the creative photographer. There is no compromise: only a few photographers accept this fact."[13] Taking a cue from the New York Abstract Expressionist painters and Beat generation poets, among whom he lived and worked in the 1940s and 1950s, Frank believed that anti-authoritarianism was a basic form of political resistance.

ON THE STREETS

Street photography is as old as the medium itself; one of Daguerre's early images shows a Paris boulevard (see Fig. 1.1). But in the postwar period, street photography was increasingly practiced by art photographers who discovered in the shifting crowds on America's city streets countless images that expressed the photographer's inner feelings or evinced the seedy

11.8 (opposite)
ROBERT FRANK, *Drug Store*, Detroit, 1955, plate 147 from his book *The Americans*, 1959. Gelatin silver print. Courtesy Pace McGill Gallery, New York. © The artist.

The Americans captures the sense of unfulfilled lives and spiritually vacant environments of the post-World War II period. Whether by accident or design, contemporary issues sometimes intrude on Frank's work, as in this view of a lunch counter where white men are served by African-American women, who would not be welcome to eat at the counter they serve.

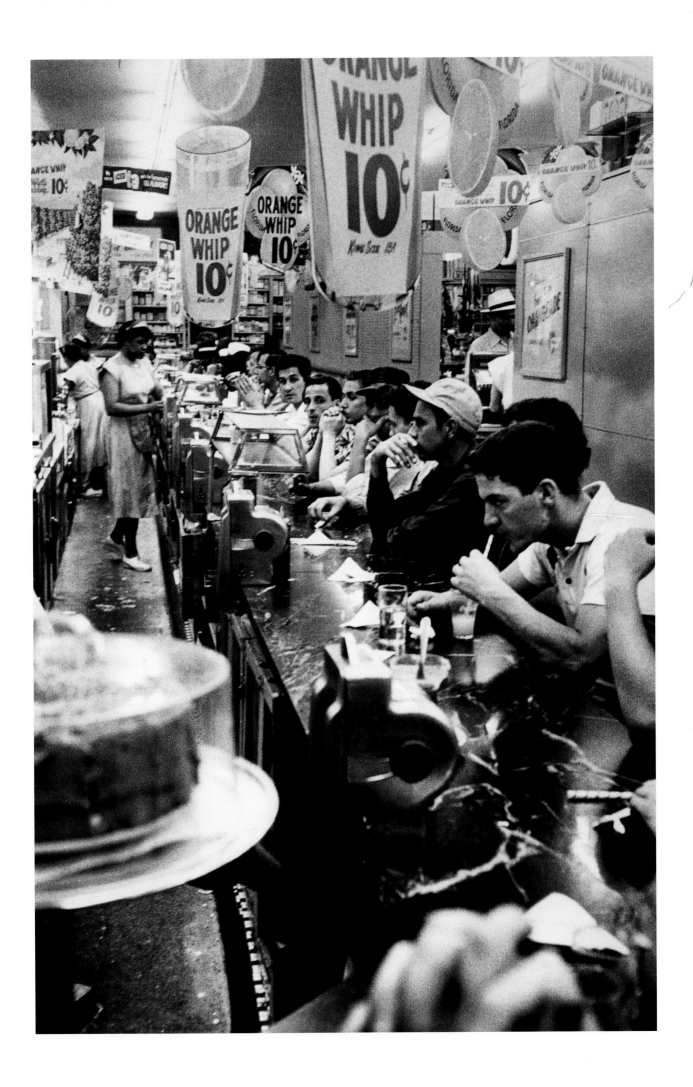

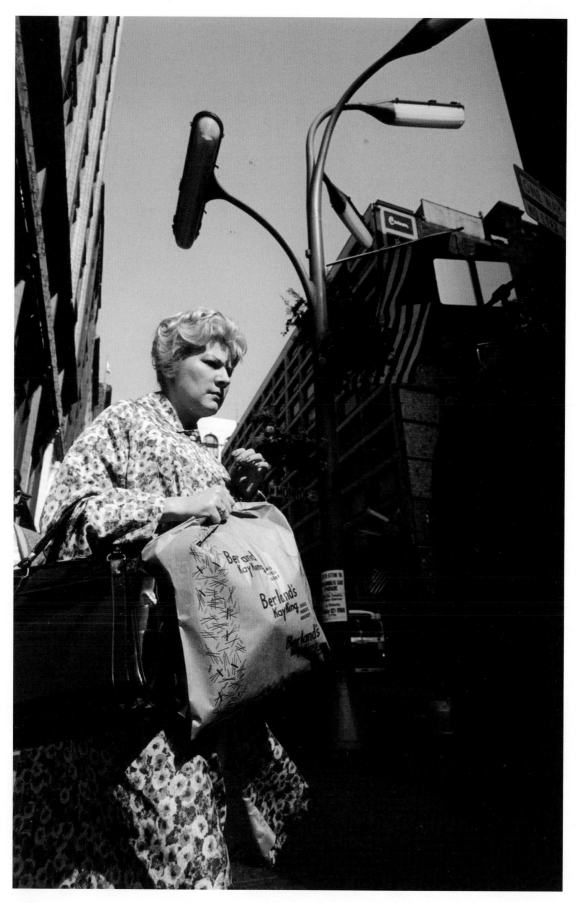

11.9
HARRY CALLAHAN, *Chicago,* **1961. Gelatin silver print.**

materialism of postwar American culture. Harry Callahan (1912–1999), Siskind's colleague at the Chicago Institute of Design, found fresh material on the streets through what he called "seeing photographically."[14] Callahan's brooding street photographs are crammed with stark contrasts of black and white, allowing few middle gray tones (Fig. 11.9). While he viewed the city as tense and inhospitable, he could shift outlooks to savor lyrical flashes of beauty in humble tufts of grass, elegant lines drawn by utility wires against the sky, or the graceful features of his wife's form (Fig. 11.10).

Although Callahan's influence was felt throughout American photography, street photographers were generally more enchanted with what became known as the "snapshot aesthetic," an apparently uncomposed everyday subject, illuminated

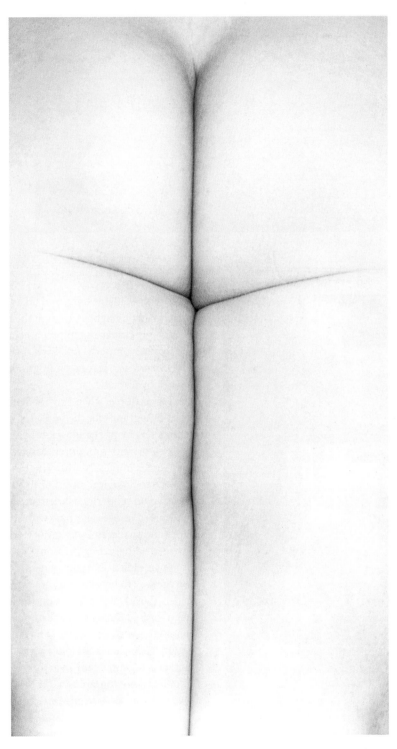

11.10
HARRY CALLAHAN, *Eleanor*, 1947. Gelatin silver print.

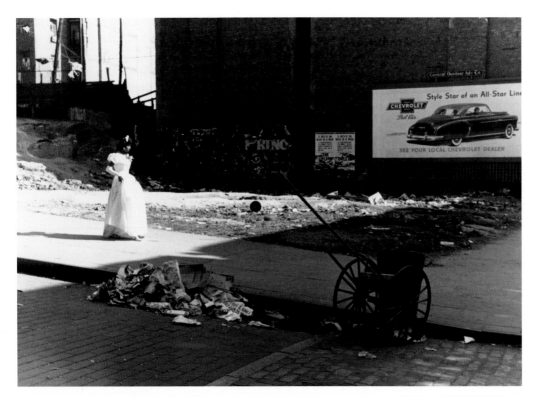

11.11
ROY DECARAVA, *Graduation*, 1949,
from his book *The Sweet Flypaper of Life*,
1955. George Eastman House, Rochester,
New York.

Some of DeCarava's photographs are so
thick with shadow that forms are barely
visible. In this image, however, the girl's
pleasure on the way to a graduation
is highlighted in a wedge of light that
pierces the desolation of the empty lot.
The billboard does double duty, as a
caption for the girl's achievement, and as
an ironic contrast with its surroundings.

11.12 (below)
WILLIAM KLEIN, *Swing and Boy and Girl, New York*, 1954. © William Klein.
Gelatin silver print. Howard Greenberg Gallery, New York.

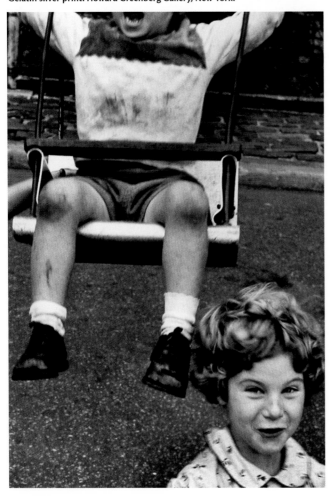

only with available light, and taken in a way that mimics
instantaneous sight. Although the trend toward making these
seemingly casual and unprepared, sometimes blurry, and often
deliberately imperfect pictures owes to the influence of Frank's
The Americans, several photographers had earlier explored the
snapshot aesthetic.

For example, when Roy DeCarava (1919–2009) worked on
the photographs for the book *The Sweet Flypaper of Life* (1955),
with a text by poet and writer Langston Hughes, he balanced
posed portraits with unrehearsed scenes on Harlem's streets and
in people's homes. Neither Hughes nor DeCarava attempted to
make a sociological report or to advocate reform measures. Each
insisted on rendering Harlem artistically.[15] Thickly shadowed
or blurred images alternate with studies of sharply delineated
light and shade. In DeCarava's work, the snapshot aesthetic
merged with Cartier-Bresson's "decisive moment." The mixture
is apparent in a shot showing an elegantly dressed young woman
on the way to her graduation (Fig. 11.11).

In 1963, DeCarava was one of several photographers
who formed Kamoinge, a forum for African-American
photographers. The name, which derives from the Kikuyu
language in Kenya, signifies a group that supports members
and acts together. Still an active center, Kamoinge published
members' photographs in *The Sweet Breath of Life: A Poetic
Narrative of the African-American Family* (2004). The book
adopted an inclusive notion of family current in early twenty-
first-century social thinking (see p. 462).

The former painter William Klein (b. 1928), who spent most
of his career abroad, had begun to snatch cheerless images along

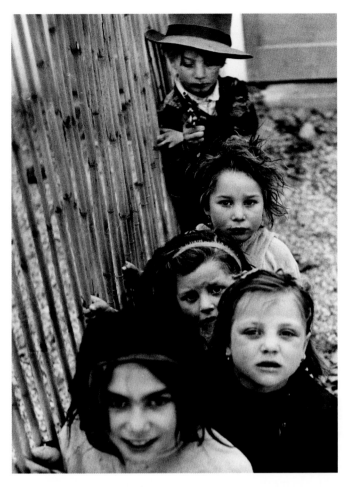

New York City's streets before Frank published *The Americans*. Klein conceived his early work in book form, where he would have greater control over the printing and arrangement of his images, as in his self-published *Life is Good and Good for You in New York: William Klein Trance Witness Revels* (1956). Less well known than Frank, Klein was even more experimental in his camerawork. He distorted the image, overexposing with a flash, or deliberately using wide-angle lenses for close-ups, in order to blur or stretch shapes (Fig. 11.12). Self-taught, Klein bypassed prescribed methods of taking pictures and looked to the tabloids. "My aesthetics was the *New York Daily News*," he wrote. "I saw the book I wanted to do as a tabloid gone berserk, gross, grainy, over-inked, with a brutal layout, bull-horn headlines."[16] Self-taught like Klein, Italian Mario Giacomelli (1925–2000) also dismissed the medium's conventions, willfully warping faces and smudging detail, to heighten the psychic punch of his images. (Fig 11.13)

The impertinent tabloid photographs Klein enjoyed may have been made by Weegee—the nickname of Arthur Fellig (1899–1968)—who sold his specialty, raw crime-scene photography to many New York newspapers. His well-deserved moniker derived either from the squeegee he used in one of his first jobs as a darkroom assistant, or from the ouija board, a device used at séances to contact the dead. With a short-wave radio in his car and home, Weegee monitored police broadcasts and arrived so quickly on the scene that he seemed able to anticipate the crime. Weegee's New York is a place of barely submerged brutality, fear, and confusion (Fig. 11.14). Weegee became an art-world

11.13
MARIO GIACOMELLI, *Roma*, 1957.

11.14
WEEGEE (ARTHUR FELLIG), *Their First Murder*, October 9, 1941. Gelatin silver print.

Weegee photographed murder and mayhem for tabloid newspapers. His signature style often included an array of human reactions, from shock and grief, to excitement about the chance of getting one's picture in the newspaper. He liked to include bystanders, who—in their ability to ignore death and human suffering, and become ghoulish voyeurs—acted as surrogates for newspaper readers.

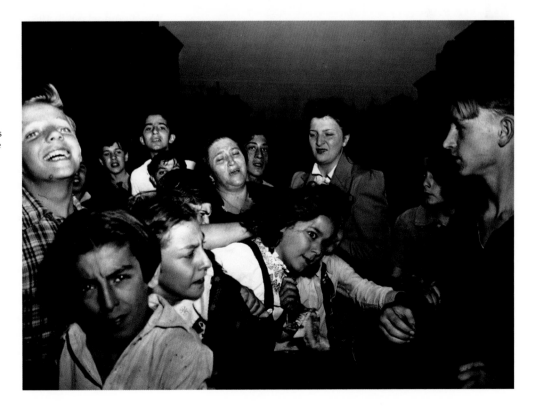

celebrity, who exhibited and lectured at the Museum of Modern Art in New York. His sensational images of crime and violent death, rendered in the harsh light of the exploding flash, were not unique, however. The ubiquitous tabloid newspapers established a stylish visual vocabulary and cast of urban characters (corpse, cop, and criminal) that encouraged *films noirs* such as *Murder, My Sweet* and *Double Indemnity*, both released in 1944, and *The Naked City*, adapted from Weegee's 1945 collection of photographs with the same title.[17]

THE SOCIAL LANDSCAPE

The appearance of a new photographic trend, indifferent to social reform but acutely focused on the qualities of camera vision, was recognized in 1966, at the Brandeis University exhibition "Twelve Photographers of the American Social Landscape." The show gave the style its name, and was quickly followed by another compendium at George Eastman House, Rochester, New York (now the International Museum of Photography at George Eastman House, IMP/GEH), where curator Nathan

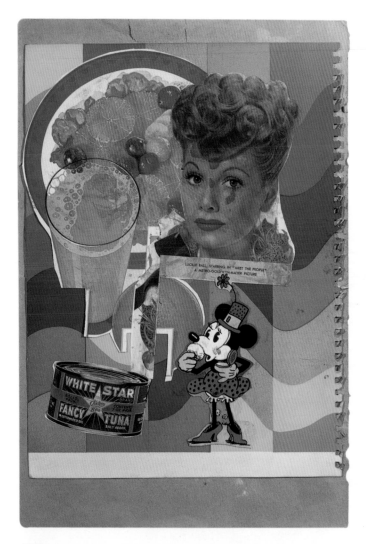

11.15
EDUARDO PAOLOZZI, *Meet the People,* **1948. Collage mounted on card. Tate, London.**

Lyons opened "Toward a Social Landscape" (1966). Soon after, the Museum of Modern Art mounted its exhibition "New Documents" (1967). In these presentations, Lee Friedlander (b. 1934) emerged as a major figure. Friedlander was impressed by Frank's *The Americans*, and made his own road trip around the United States, shooting cemetery stones and memorial statues for an elegiac project called *The American Monument* (1976). Friedlander admired Weegee's hardheaded urban dramas and André Kertész's grasp of visual coincidence. He balked at supplying viewers with clear visual clues with which to decipher his work. Whether picturing the jumble of signs and traffic on the street, or layers of reflections in the glass of storefronts, Friedlander obscurely hinted at a story, only to fall back on an exercise in camera vision. He saw photography as a picture-making system with rules as peculiar to itself as painting. Just as the painter's brush leaves marks on the canvas, so the camera leaves marks of its rectangular framing device, the kind of lens used, and the chemistry of the film and processing. In *New Orleans* (1968), Friedlander toyed with the photographic tradition of deep perspective (Fig. 11.1). He frequently includes his reflection or shadow in his work, not to indicate that the image is a personal metaphor for a state of mind or emotion, but to demonstrate that it is a picture made with the camera whose outlines often show in the print.

More blunt than Friedlander, Garry Winogrand (1928–1984) was also among the new social landscape image-makers. Like Friedlander, he did a stint as a photojournalist for the picture press. One of his images, an uncomplicated view of a couple frisking in the water at a bathing beach, was included in "The Family of Man." It did not give an inkling of the psychologically complex and tense series of street photographs that he would begin in the 1960s. With funding from a Guggenheim grant, Winogrand set out in 1964 to tour America, as Walker Evans and Robert Frank had done before him. But Winogrand had a particular agenda: he wanted to photograph the United States in the wake of the 1963 assassination of President John F. Kennedy.

Winogrand is often quoted as saying "I photograph to find out what the world looks like photographed."[18] Where Friedlander's work resembles fortuitously found collages, Winogrand's pictures home in on human gestures and body stances that indicate interpersonal tension and inner turmoil. Sometimes his caustic view of human nature is echoed in abrupt cropping of the image, or in shots where the camera has been tilted.

Winogrand asserted that the photograph was not simply a window on the world but a new fact. His fear that the subject matter of the street might overwhelm his investigation of photography's unique picture-making qualities was well founded.[19] In his image of a man with multiple amputations (Fig. 11.16), the chance arrangement of figures, oddly reminiscent of a *tableau vivant*, is not so compelling as to blunt the tense human implications of the scene.

Comparing the work of Friedlander and Winogrand to European street photographers such as Kertész, one can see that the American work tips the balance between form and narrative toward form, and tilts the scales between individual expression

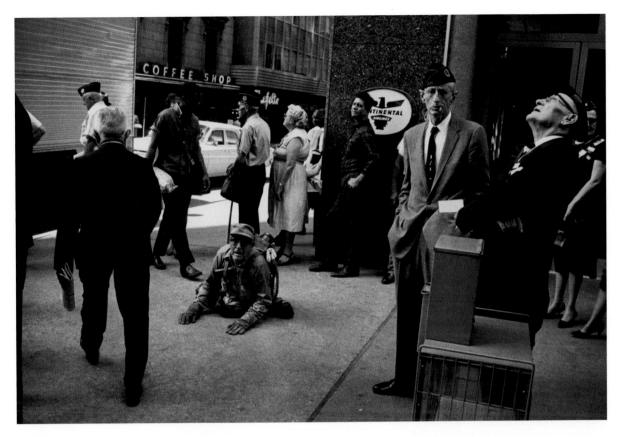

11.16
GARRY WINOGRAND, *American Legion Convention, Dallas, Texas*, 1964. Gelatin silver print. Museum of Modern Art, New York.

11.17
LISETTE MODEL, *Albert-Alberta, Hubert's Forty-Second Street Flea Circus, New York*, c. 1945. Gelatin silver print. Bruce Silverstein Gallery, New York.

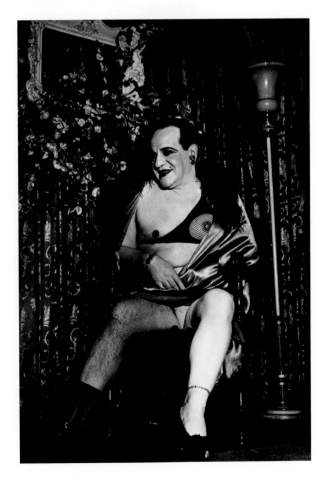

and neutrality toward neutral vision, or disinterested irony. What remains personal in much social landscape photography is the selection of the picture, especially because Friedlander and Winogrand both exposed many rolls of film and picked the picture from contact sheets.

The influence of the social landscape photographers was felt throughout the 1960s, but it did not completely obliterate the work of street photographers with a greater interest in content and personal point of view. For example, when Austrian-born photographer Lisette Model (1901–1983) emigrated to the United States in 1938, she had already polished her observation of human foibles and vanities. In France, where she had lived since 1926, Model's lens recorded the self-delusions of the rich and fashionable as they lounged in the fancy resort area of Nice. In New York, she showed her work at the Photo League, and continued to be fascinated by those who are infatuated by glamour, including people on the margins of society (Fig. 11.17). Because she was not able to make a living from her art and freelance fashion work, Model turned to teaching in 1949, eventually becoming one of New York City's leading photo-educators.

Among her students was Diane Arbus (1923–1971), who took private lessons from Model, and also studied with her at the New School for Social Research. Arbus responded to what she saw as Model's hard-boiled audacity and courage to confront extremes in human situations. In addition, Arbus sharpened her nerve when she accompanied famed New York tabloid ace Weegee on his assignments to photograph murders. Included with Friedlander and Winogrand in the 1967 "New Documents" exhibition at the Museum of Modern Art, Arbus's work was more personal, transforming the social world into a visual terrain to be mined for metaphors resonating with her inner feelings.

Arbus turned normalcy on its head, making the ordinary bizarre and naturalizing the unusual. In her photographs of people, many of them made while she roamed the streets of New York, clothes and cosmetics are futile efforts to camouflage psychic emptiness or damage. When Arbus photographed children, she revealed them as little versions of bad-tempered, mean-spirited adults (Fig. 11.18). On the other hand, her photographs of people at the margins of society, such as female impersonators, show them to be more virtuous for having unmasked their subjective inclinations. For Arbus, marginal people were symbols of her own psychological fragility and trauma.

During the postwar period in American photography, Arbus was not alone in undermining sentimental ideas of the innocence of childhood. Ralph Eugene Meatyard (1925–1972) coaxed children to wear weird masks that did not so much conceal their innocence as reveal their strangeness (Fig. 11.19). Teenage life became a regular subject in the work of many street photographers, including Bruce Davidson (b. 1933). He spent two years chronicling the lives of a Brooklyn gang called the Jokers, and two years photographing the homes of families living on New York City's East 100th Street (Fig. 11.21). Even if his lengthy concentration on one theme contrasted with the more itinerant efforts of Robert Frank, Davidson was nonetheless inspired by Frank's *The Americans*: "in it I saw an America that diminished the dream and replaced it with piercing truth. It was hard for me to endure those bitter, beautiful photographs, for I had still within me the dream of hope and sympathy that I had found in the widow, the dwarf, and the gang."[20]

Davidson's resilient empathy reveals itself in his New York City photographs, which fix on the strong community and family relationships that persist in the face of deprivation. His approach

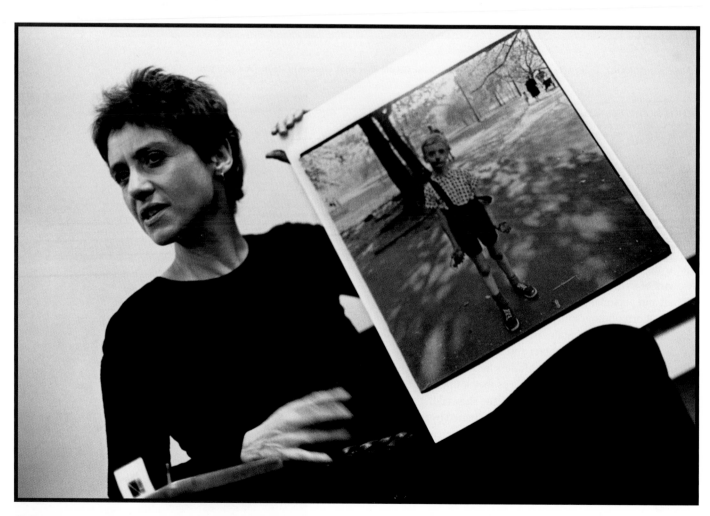

11.18
STEPHEN FRANK, *Untitled* (Diane Arbus with her photo of a boy holding a toy grenade in Central Park, New York), 1970.

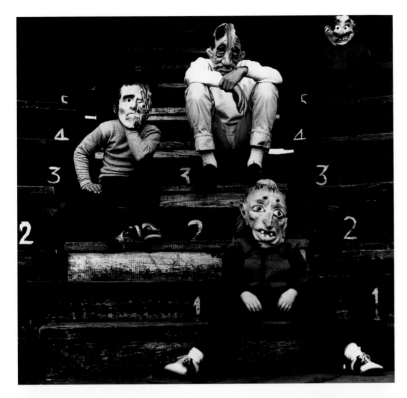

11.19
RALPH EUGENE MEATYARD, *Romance (N) from Ambrose Bierce,
No. 3*, 1962. Gelatin silver print. George Eastman House, Rochester,
New York.

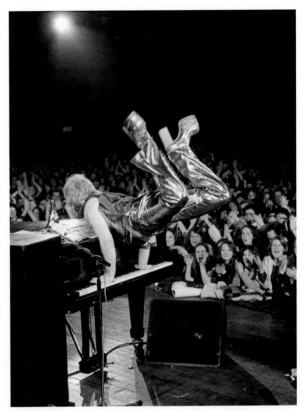

11.20
BARRIE WENTZELL, *Elton John, Sundown Theatre, Edmonton, London*,
1973.

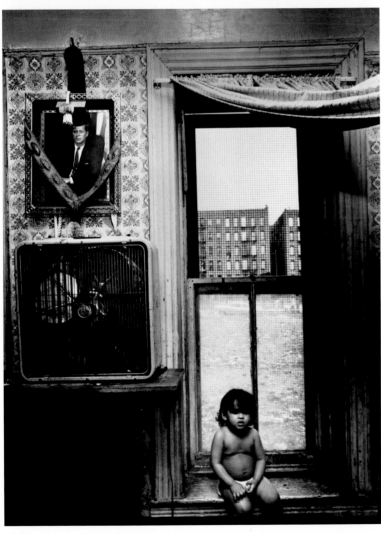

11.21
BRUCE DAVIDSON, *Untitled*, from his book *East 100th Street*, New York,
1966–68.

Davidson was one of the few photographers adept at blending the dark
outlook of postwar photography with the attentive humanism of the
Depression era. Using a large-format view camera and a flash, he spent two
years photographing life on East 100th Street in New York City, where he
balanced scenes of hardship with those of hope and endurance.

stands in sharp contrast to that of other photographers who prowled American streets to expose living symbols of alienation and despair. As historian Jonathan Green observed, "the icons of the sixties have few redeeming features: the dwarf, the freak, the prostitute, the disenfranchised, the outlaw motorcyclists, the drug addict, the insane, the retarded, the prisoner, the napalmed child, the brutal cop, the assassin's assassin."[21] Danny Lyon (b. 1942), who assisted Robert Frank with filmmaking, chronicled motorcycle gangs in his own work, and in 1968 he published *The Bikeriders*, a photographic chronicle of his years as a member of the Outlaws, a Midwestern motorcycle club. Lyon presented these young people as rebels whose choice to live outside middle-class social values paid off in strong bonds of companionship (Fig. 11.22). A major omission on Green's list of icons was the rock-and-roll musician, who appealed not only to teenagers but also to artists. For example, Conceptual artist Dan Graham began his engagement with rock music in the 1960s, writing about the Kinks and using ideas he found in music for his art. Increasingly rock was chronicled by photographers, who often specialized in depicting the field. The connection of youth culture with rock and roll was captured by such photographers as Jim Marshall (1936–2010), Elaine Mayes (b. 1936), and Barrie Wentzell (b. 1942) (Fig. 11.20), who documented the musicians' public and private moments, first for special interest publications such as *Melody Maker* in the U.K., and eventually for general interest newspapers and magazines that saw rock and roll as the music of the counterculture.

Perhaps the most disturbing images of teenagers were rendered by Larry Clark (b. 1943), who gained fresh notoriety for his 1995 film *Kids*, which features explicit scenes of underage drug use and sex. His 1971 book *Tulsa* covered similar territory: it is a first-hand account of the time he spent among drug-users, some of whom were his friends (Fig. 11.24). While postwar photographers, such as Lyon, spent extensive time among their subjects, Clark personally sampled the drug culture he imaged. His candid photographs provoked negative reactions, in part, as critic Joseph Marshall observed, because "Clark implied what [Robert] Frank didn't say … that getting high, despite its social costs and its dangers, is an appropriate response to the banal meaninglessness of American life."[22] Compared to this abrasive nihilism, Helen Levitt's (1913–2009) sometimes whimsical, always compassionate, street photographs of children

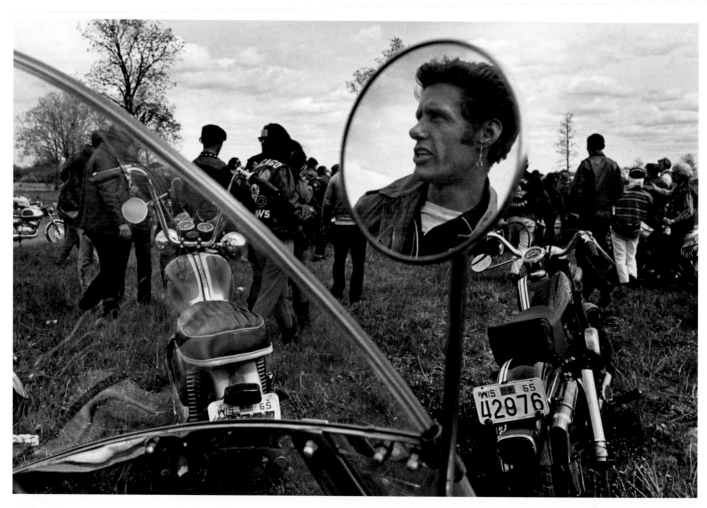

11.22
DANNY LYON, *Cal, Eikhorn, Wisconsin,* 1966. Gelatin silver print.

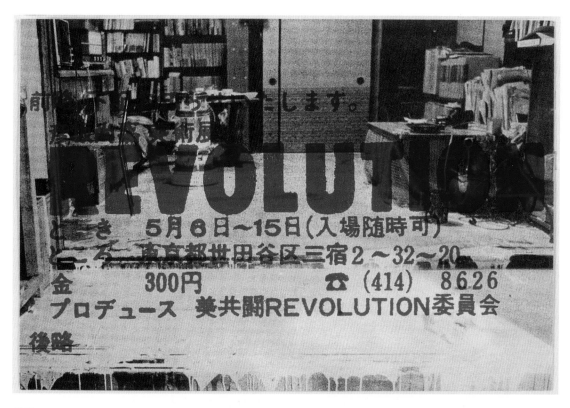

11.23
NAOYOSHI HIKOSAKA, *Revolution*, 1971. Offset printed postcard and silk screen. Getty Research Institute, Research Library.

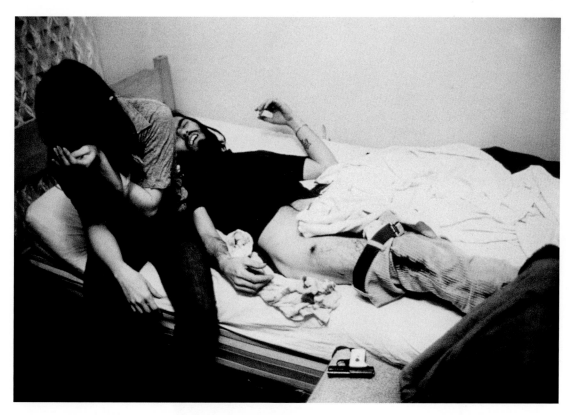

11.24
LARRY CLARK, *Accidental Gunshot Wound*, 1971. Gelatin silver print.

Clark's photographs of the deteriorating lives lived by drug dealers and users in Tulsa, Oklahoma, assailed the bright humanism of Depression-era documentary photography. In this image, in which a man lies in pain from an accidental gunshot wound, the viewer's sympathies are pulled in different directions.

(Fig. 11.25) are exceptional in their amiable and bemused observations, an attitude more familiar in the work of European photographers.

Many postwar photographers worked in extensive series based on life experiences, be they road trips or observations gained through insight and meditation. The scope of these series, dramatized by the photographer's unique perspective on how to order the images, propelled the photographic book into prominence. The rhythm, connections, and contradictions of form and subject generated by sequenced images had a lasting impact on contemporary photographic practice. In the work of Duane Michals (b. 1932), the photographic sequence blended with two other postwar trends, the deliberate staging of scenes to

be photographed, and the addition of text, not as an explanatory caption but as an integral part of the work. A successful advertising photographer, Michals developed a signature blend of photography and the film frame during the late 1960s. His book *Sequences* (1970) contains arrangements of images that narrate appearances of spirits and passages between life and death. Like many postwar photographers, Michals favored a palette of dense black, hazy grays, and form-dissolving light (Fig. 11.26).

SUBURBIA
Postwar prosperity fueled the migration of Americans from the cities to the suburbs, where the prospect of green space and domestic comforts was underwritten by the larger hope of

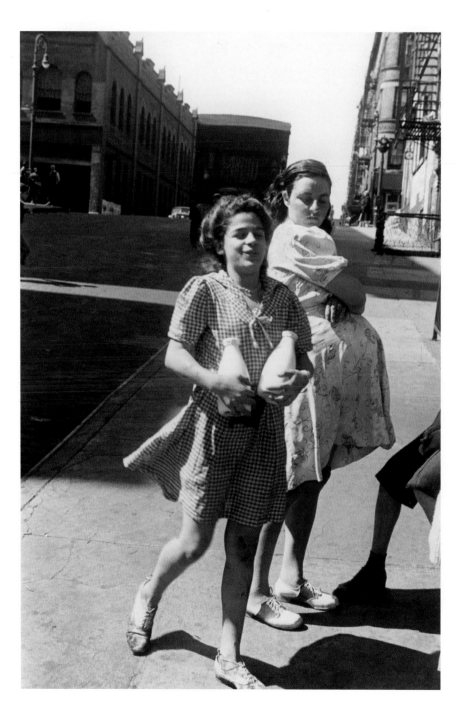

11.25
HELEN LEVITT, *New York,* **c. 1940. Gelatin silver print.**

11.26 (opposite)
DUANE MICHALS, *The Bogeyman,* **1973. Gelatin silver print.**

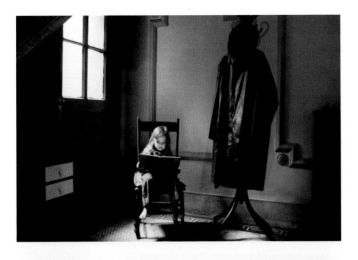
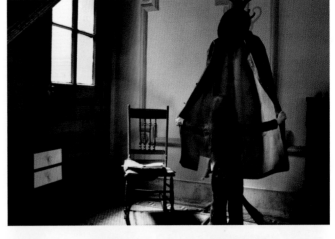
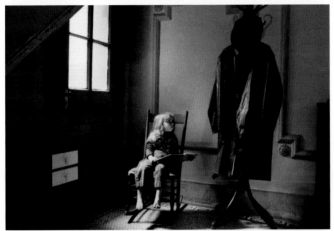
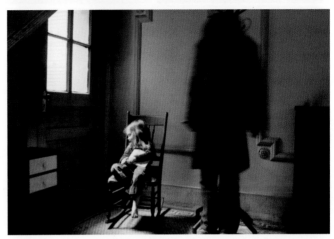
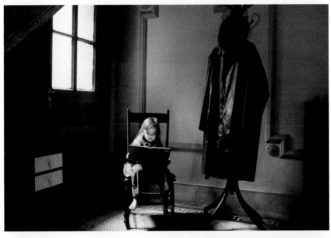
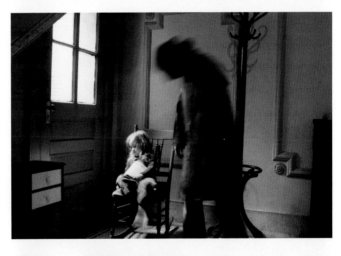
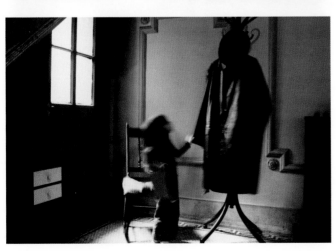
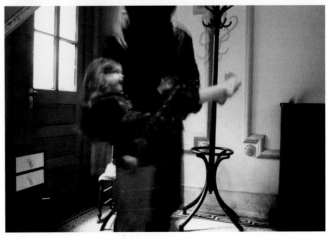

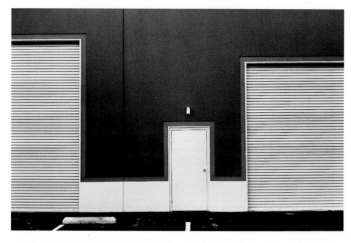

11.27
LEWIS BALTZ, *Southwest Wall, Ware, Malcom & Garner*, from *The New Industrial Parks Near Irvine, California*, 1974. Collection Centre Canadien d'Architecture/ Canadian Center for Architecture, Montreal, Canada.

rising to a higher social class. As historian David Halberstam wrote, many in the freshly minted middle class "were children of people who never owned a home and who had rented cold-water flats in the years before the war."[23] In the American West, long a symbol-laden landscape in art and photography, the spectacular banality of regularized suburban houses suddenly springing up in formerly open expanses caught the critical eye of photographers such as Lewis Baltz (b. 1945) (Fig. 11.27) and Robert Adams (b. 1937), who preferred the distanced view and a seemingly neutral style, the visual analog of their prosaic subjects (Fig. 11.28).

This approach to landscape photography was reported in an influential 1975 exhibition, "New Topographics: Photographs of a Man-Altered Landscape," at Eastman House in Rochester.

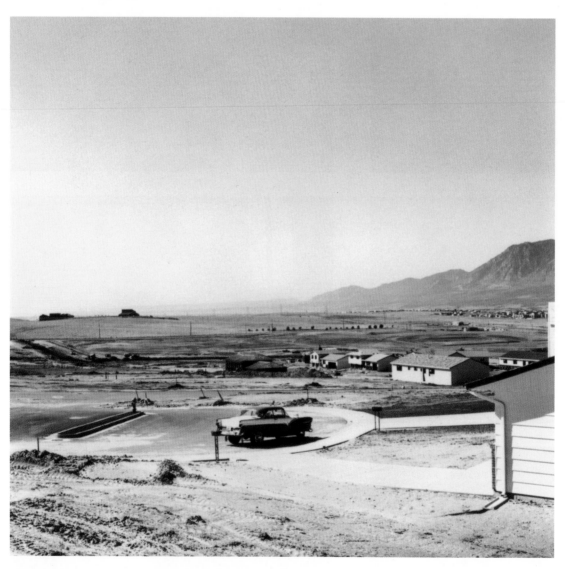

11.28
ROBERT ADAMS, *Newly Occupied Tract Houses*, Colorado Springs, Colorado, 1968.

Many American suburbs were built in the decade following World War II. Their rapid appearance in isolated clumps surrounded by open landscape attracted photographers, who implicitly contrasted the open and vacant suburban terrain with the congested urban environment.

The dispassionate images in this show rebutted the sometimes lush, sometimes sublime attitude toward the land expressed in a photographic tradition derived from nineteenth-century images of the American West, and invoked the dispassionate approach of Walker Evans. Among the photographers were Robert Adams, Lewis Baltz, Bernd and Hilla Becher, and wunderkind Stephen Shore (b. 1947), who began making photographs at the age of six, sold some of his pictures to the Museum of Modern Art when he was twelve, and photographed the goings-on in Andy Warhol's studio when he was just seventeen. As defined in the exhibition, the New Topographics was a form of documentary deliberately divorced from social advocacy. In addition, the neutral vision that framed the New Topographics linked photography with the international art movement called Conceptualism (see p. 376), and helped accelerate the acceptance of camerawork in academia and the art world.[24]

In a series of photographs published in the book *Suburbia* (1972, 1999), Bill Owens (b. 1938), a photographer for a small newspaper in Livermore, near the Bay Area of California, portrayed not only the look of the suburbs but also the dreams, longings, and discontents of the residents. Owens admired the visual sociology of the F.S.A. photographs, and his work is replete with small, telling details.[25] Ungroomed nature is threatening: one photograph shows a teenager straddling the branches of a small tree, shaking off all the leaves to be raked by a second lad below. In another picture, a couple sit in a garage crammed with motorcycles and other vehicles. In the quotation accompanying the photograph they mellowly remark, "We enjoy having these things." When Owens moved inside suburban homes, he found the focus of the modern living-room to be the television set, mostly left on and disgorging advertisements, football, old movies, space launches, and occasional glimpses of a grimly determined President Richard Nixon (1913–1994). Owens captured not only the tackiness of furnishing and omnipresent polyester clothing but also the dissent and dislocation of suburbanites, whom he does not patronize or stereotype. An African-American woman notes that her children are growing up without an anchor in black culture; a Chinese-American family cannot find Asian groceries nearby. Teenagers grumble that there is nothing to do in the suburbs. The impact of the national mood is caught in women's complaints about staying home and taking care of children (Fig. 11.29).

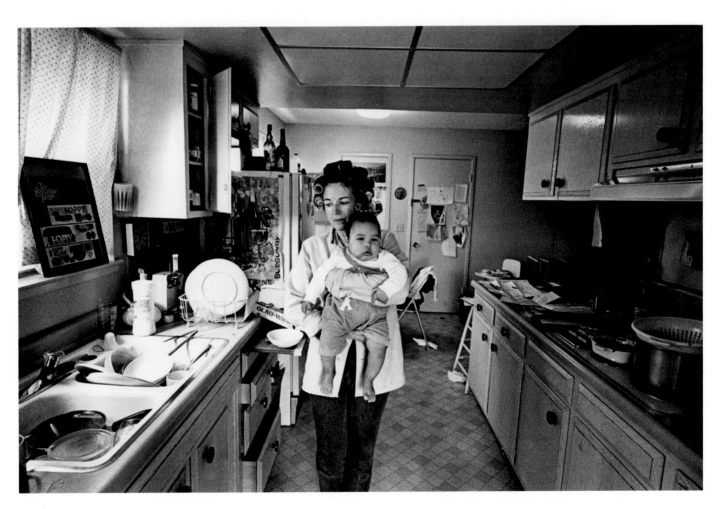

11.29
BILL OWENS, *Untitled*, from his book *Suburbia*, 1972, 1999.

TECHNOLOGY AND MEDIA IN POSTWAR AMERICA

COLOR PHOTOGRAPHY AND THE POLAROID PROCESS

The concluding segment of Steichen's "The Family of Man" exhibition disrupted the long chain of black-and-white photographs with a large color TRANSPARENCY of a hydrogen bomb explosion. Before the war, the Farm Security Administration photographers sometimes used color film, and in the decade after the conflict, magazines such as *National Geographic* used color transparencies. Magazine advertising occasionally appeared in color, and fashion photographers leapt at the chance to use color to depict clothing and to glamorize settings. Horst P. Horst, Paul Outerbridge, Richard Avedon (1923–2004) (Fig. 11.30), and Avedon's student Japanese-born photographer Hiro (b. 1930) (Fig. 11.31) electrified the pages of large-format fashion magazines with strong color accents. Soon color slipped the bonds of description and was used by image-makers such as photographer and art director Bert Stern (1929–2013) to contrive seductive advertisements in which bright color saturates

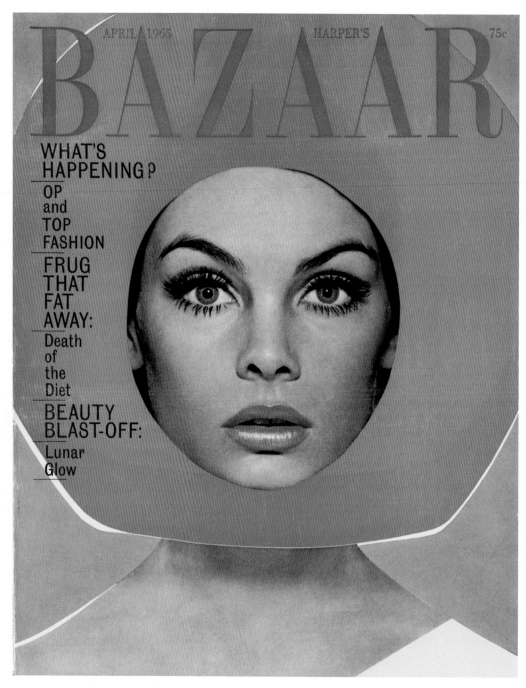

11.30
RICHARD AVEDON, Cover of *Harper's Bazaar*, April 1965.

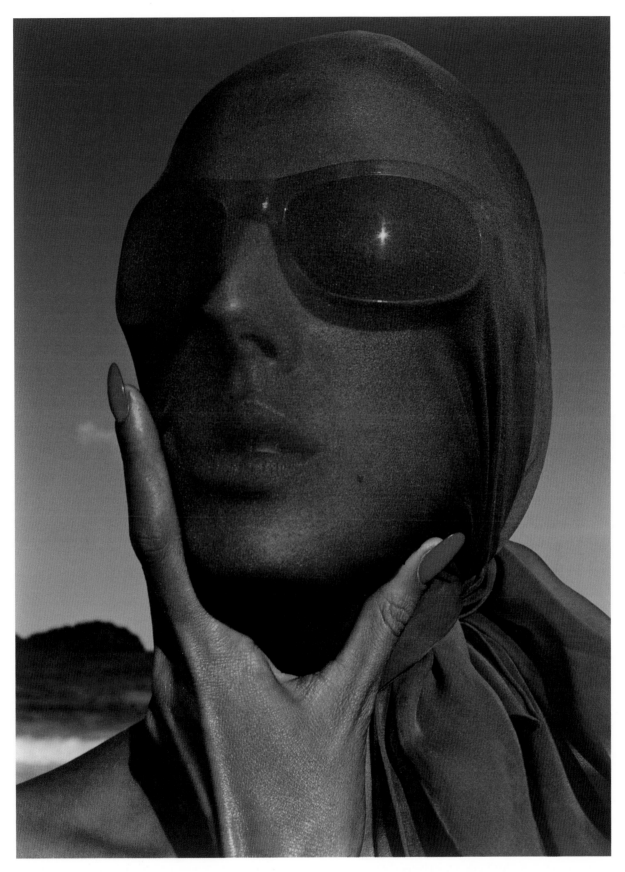

11.31
HIRO, *Tilly Tizzani with a Blue Scarf*, Antigua, 1963, from cover of *Harper's Bazaar*, May 1963. Victoria and Albert Museum, London.

Post-World War II magazine advertising quickly embraced color reproduction. In his fashion photography, Hiro tended to isolate figures and accentuate deeply saturated colors, all of which served to remove models from the real world.

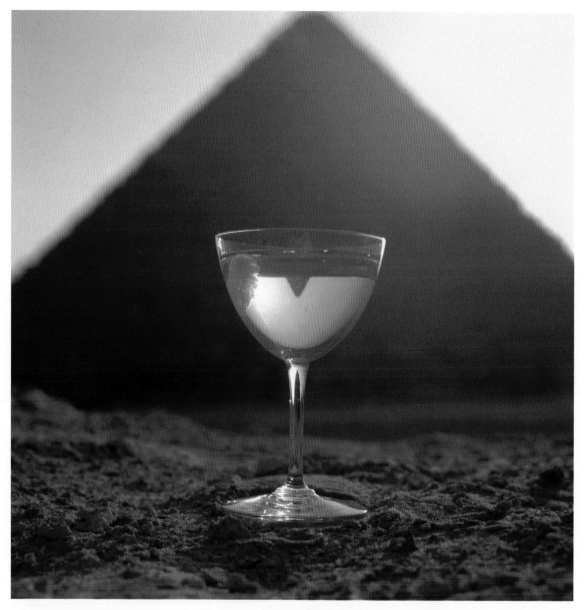

11.32
BERT STERN, *Martini and Pyramid*, **1955. Dye-transfer print.**

Necessity was the mother of Stern's inventive treatment of a cocktail made with Russian vodka. During the Cold War, Russian products seemed un-American. Stern's solution was to make the vodka seem un-Russian, by photographing chic, exotic settings.

the whole environment (Fig. 11.32). Later, Stern became famous for having made numerous photographs of Marilyn Monroe six weeks before she died. During the 1970s, Deborah Turbeville (b. 1937) created her own distinctive cool-toned colors and dusky atmosphere for fashion shoots, and contrived scenarios for the models to perform (Fig. 11.33).

Natural light and hues seemed particularly suited to color work. Radiant pops of chromatic light were rendered in transparencies by Minor White, who even planned programs of dual-screen projection for his work. Eliot Porter (1901–1990), who used color transparencies and the cumbersome but more permanent DYE-TRANSFER system, collected his nature views in the book *In Wildness is the Preservation of the World* (1962)

(Fig. 11.34), and in large-size or "exhibition format" prints, both of which were sponsored by the Sierra Club. The Sierra Club fostered wilderness photography, owing to the active participation of photographers such as Ansel Adams, Eliot Porter, and Minor White. The club's landmark exhibition of photographs and text, "This is the American Earth," opened in San Francisco in 1955, traveled around the United States and Europe, and eventually became a book, edited by Adams and Nancy Newhall.

Despite color's intermittent successes, in the 1950s and early 1960s most magazines continued to run black-and-white images, which were less expensive and less time consuming to produce. In 1955, the year of "The Family of Man," color film that

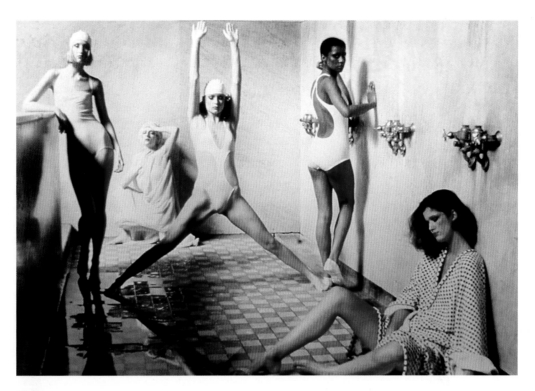

11.33
DEBORAH TURBEVILLE, *The Bath House*, 1975.

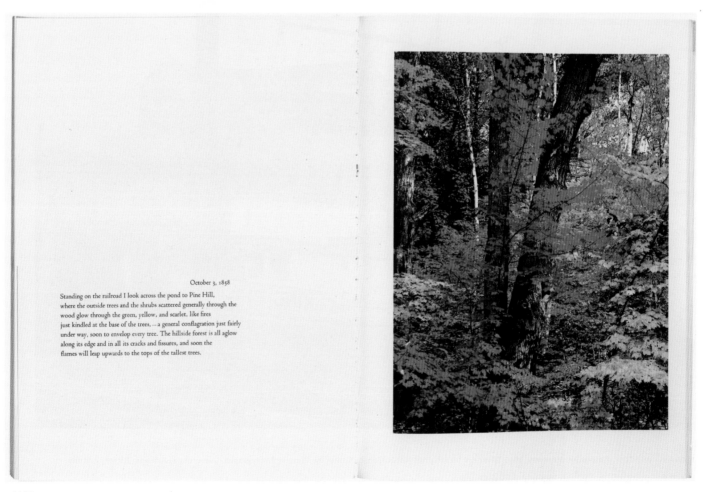

October 3, 1858

Standing on the railroad I look across the pond to Pine Hill,
where the outside trees and the shrubs scattered generally through the
wood glow through the green, yellow, and scarlet, like fires
just kindled at the base of the trees, —a general conflagration just fairly
under way, soon to envelop every tree. The hillside forest is all aglow
along its edge and in all its cracks and fissures, and soon the
flames will leap upwards to the tops of the tallest trees.

11.34
ELIOT PORTER, *October 3, 1858*, from Henry David Thoreau's book *In Wildness Is the Preservation of the World*.

a photographer could process had been available for less than a decade. To promote the use of color film, the Kodak company then attempted to persuade leading photographers such as Ansel Adams, Paul Strand, Charles Sheeler, and Edward Weston to try it by commissioning images from them. When the firm wrote to photographer Weston, asking if he would make an 8- by 10-inch Kodachrome print, Weston reluctantly agreed, saying that he loved the landscape around Point Lobos in California so much that he would have abhorred seeing "it murdered in color by an 'outsider.'"[26] Weston accepted an offer from Kodak to revisit some of his favorite spots, where he rendered images that showed a visible tension between the descriptive powers of color and the expressive qualities of line (Fig. 11.35). Weston's anxiety about color film was grounded in what he perceived as its greater realism—that is, its more comprehensive resemblance to the world of experience.

Walker Evans remained resistant to the process throughout the 1960s. He railed against "screeching hues," and the "bebop of electric blues, furious reds, and poison greens," and asserted that "there are four simple words which must be whispered: color photography is vulgar."[27] Like other art photographers, Evans thought that color was too embedded in commercial culture to be used by serious artists.

Despite these reservations, Evans did experiment with color. During his postwar years as a photographer with *Fortune* magazine, he issued portfolios of photographs that he hand tinted so as to control the selection and strength of the color. In the early 1970s, Evans began to try Polaroid film and cameras.

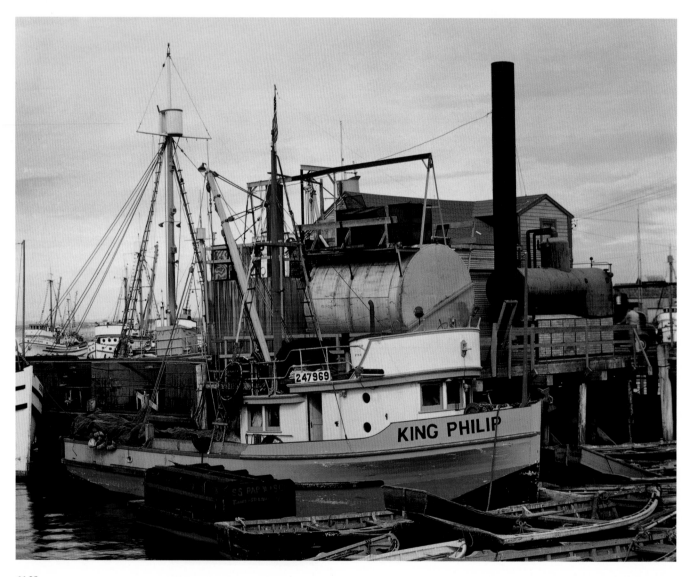

11.35
EDWARD WESTON, *Waterfront, Monterey*, 1946. Silver dye bleach print (Cibachrome). Center for Creative Photography, University of Arizona, Tucson, Arizona.

The black-and-white linear elements of this image, like the masts and lines, set off the color of the boat and the water. Nevertheless, Weston was skeptical about color photography, holding that, "as a creative medium, black and white photography has, at the start, an advantage over color in that it is already a step removed from a factual rendition of the scene."[28]

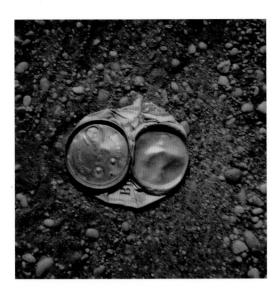

11.36
WALKER EVANS, *Untitled* (Crushed beer can), 1973–74.
Polaroid print. Metropolitan Museum of Art, New York.

his youth and which he carried out in his work for the Farm Security Administration. He praised the Polaroid quick payback process, saying that it encouraged sudden inspiration. As he had in his earlier work, Evans conceived Polaroid images in series. Importantly, he challenged the tenacious complaint that color needlessly prettified photographs. In such prints as the one depicting a crushed beer can (Fig. 11.36), Evans integrated color and form; despite the small (3⅛ by 3⅛ inch) format of the print, the scene has a puzzling monumentality.

In spite of the efforts of Kodak and Polaroid to convince artists to work with the new techniques, the biases against color photography expressed by Weston and Evans permeated the world of serious art photography. Notwithstanding the occasional museum exhibition of color work, art photography persisted mostly as a black-and-white medium. This attitude put it at odds with commercial photography and photojournalism, both of which adapted more quickly to the possibilities of color to promote products or to interest readers. The art photographers' preference for black-and-white sharply contrasted with the adoption of color film by amateurs, who happily moved from black-and-white snapshots to color pictures. The proliferation of color in commercial photography transformed the experience of the average person. The reality effect—the sense of authenticity and honesty—passed from black-and-white film to color. Millions of people gazed up at the Kodak-sponsored 18- by 60-foot color transparencies called *Colorama* hung on the east balcony of the Grand Central Terminal in New York City[29] (Fig. 11.37). Ansel Adams, who occasionally worked on the Kodak projects, nevertheless calculated that these displays were "aesthetically inconsequential but technically remarkable."

Invented in 1947 by Edwin H. Land (1909–1991), the Polaroid process originally generated monochromatic prints. By the 1970s, the method had improved to yield so-called instantaneous color prints—that is, pictures developed on the spot. Evans worked with the Polaroid SX-70 system, a fully automatic method that timed the film's development inside the camera and expelled a final print for which the photographer made no contribution to the color scheme. Using the somewhat subdued colors of Polaroid's SX-70 system, Evans returned to making pictures of American signs and lettering, themes he began in

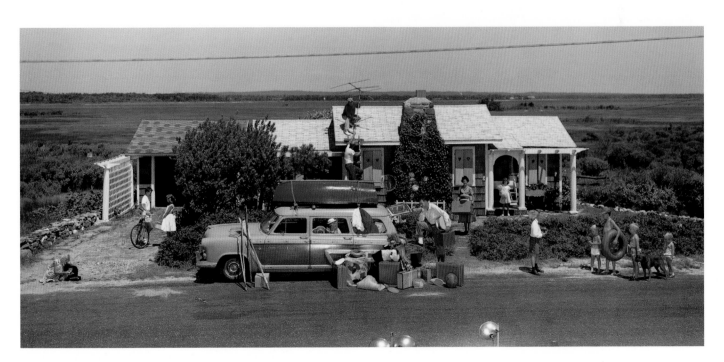

11.37
RALPH AMDURSKY, *Colorama* (Blue "Woody" stationwagon in front of summer cottage), n.d. Kodak print. Eastman Kodak, Rochester, New York.

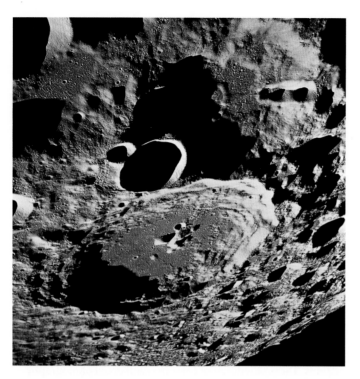

11.38
APOLLO II, *Untitled* (The far side of the moon), *Apollo II* mission, July 1969.

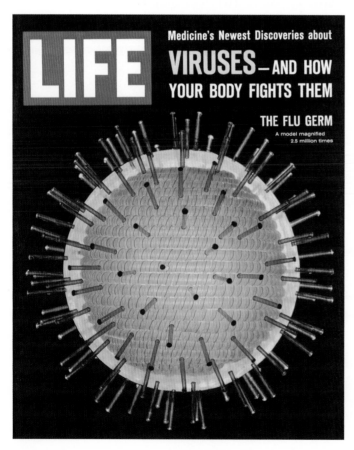

11.39
PHOTOGRAPHER UNKNOWN, Cover of *Life* magazine, February 18, 1966.

The public came to expect that photography would keep up with other kinds of technological advances. In 1969, *Apollo 11*'s pictures of the far side of the moon needed to be as accomplished as the mission was successful (Fig. 11.38). As space exploration continued, audiences took it for granted that the picture magazines would render views of the earth from space in color. Similarly, advances in science were accompanied by parallel accomplishments in scientific imaging. Pictures of a human fetus's development in the womb, patterns observed by particle physicists, and the hypnotic beauty of small viruses were issued in color for audiences to enjoy as scientific and aesthetic wonders (Fig. 11.39).

Color motion pictures, costly to produce before World War II, became less expensive and more common after the 1950s period of *film noir*, with its deeply shadowed, highly stylized ambience. Television, too, began the transformation from black and white to color. In 1955, the children's television show *Howdy Doody* switched from black-and-white to color broadcasting. The show's popularity helped sell color television sets, which began being marketed in the mid-1950s. By the mid-1960s, color television sets became more affordable and so their sales increased.

TELEVISION, PHOTOJOURNALISM, AND NATIONAL EVENTS

Despite increased sales of television sets by the mid-1960s, national television news did not surpass newspapers and picture magazines as the public's major source of current events information until the early 1970s. By that time, television news programs progressed from fifteen-minute readings of the news, accompanied by a few still photographs, to nightly half-hour broadcasts, with reports from news bureaus around the world, supplemented by film, videotape, and occasional live coverage. In effect, television seized the market for instantaneous images, the previous domain of newspapers, and, to some extent, news magazines. Images of the disastrous mercury poisonings at Minamata, Japan, were presented in magazines, newspapers, and films, and on television. The public's shift from print media to television was signaled by the demise of *Life* magazine's weekly publication in 1972, owing to declining advertising revenues, as clients switched to purchasing television commercials. Increasingly, photographers such as Diane Arbus, Robert Frank, Lee Friedlander, and Bill Owens photographed television sets glowing unattended in bars and living-rooms.

Public events, such as the assassination of President John F. Kennedy (1917–1963) and its aftermath, entered the public memory through a blend of photography, radio, film, and television broadcasts. Pictures obtained from the space exploration, which began in the late 1950s, were all photographs, until astronauts sent back a live television broadcast from the moon in 1969. Arresting in themselves, photographs of the earth from space graphically demonstrated the interdependence of earth's natural systems (Fig. 11.40).[30]

Americans also learned about the post-World War II Civil Rights movement, which started in the late 1950s to protest

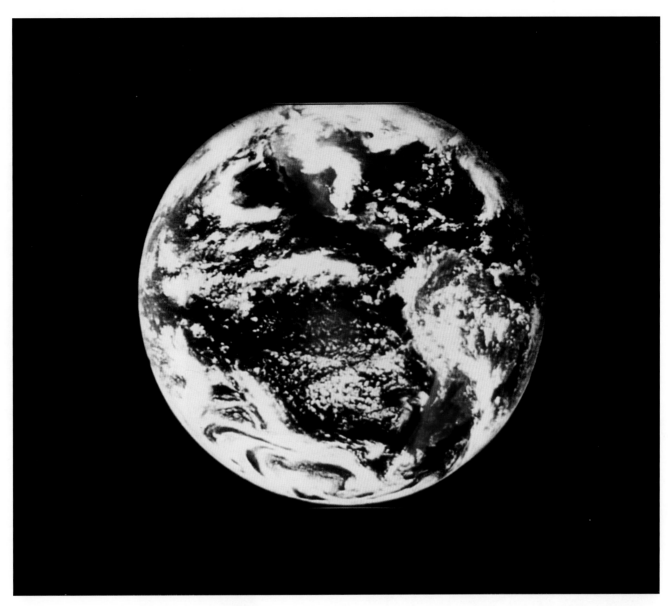

11.40
ATS SATELLITE, *Earth, as Viewed from ATS Satellite,* **November 1967.**

racial segregation in the South and to secure voting rights for African Americans, from a mix of photography and other media. A disturbing image of the disfigured body of Emmett Till, a Chicago teenager killed in 1955 while visiting kin in Mississippi, began circulating in *Jet* magazine, and national photo-based magazines such as *Look* carried the story. The photograph and story of Emmett Till sparked protests, and were memorialized in the literature and art of the 1960s. Historian David Halberstam characterized the lynching of Emmett Till in Mississippi during the summer of 1955 as the first powerful media event of the Civil Rights movement. Photographs taken by David Jackson (1922–1966) were published in the African-American press, but not in mainstream media. They showed Till in an open coffin,

on to which his mother had taped pictures of him as a vibrant youngster. The contrast between his youthful image and his abused corpse galvanized African Americans across the United States, and the photographs remain indelible symbols of racial strife. Because the criminal investigation of the Till case went on for more than fifty years, the image of Emmett Till continues to resonate. For example, photographer Demetrius Oliver (b. 1975) chillingly recalled the image in a self-portrait in which he covered his face with chocolate frosting, to give it the appearance of disintegrating.

In the early 1960s, photographers such as Bruce Davidson and Danny Lyon traveled through the South, picturing events and confrontations. In fact, Lyon joined the Student Nonviolent

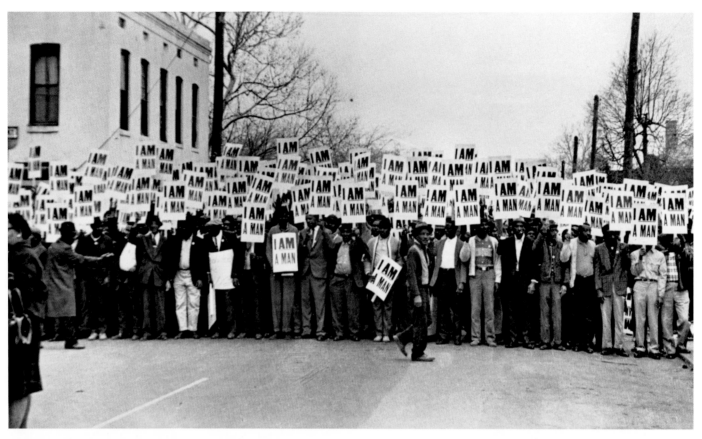

11.41
ERNEST WITHERS, *Workers Assembling for a Solidarity March, Memphis, Tennessee,* **1968.**

Withers took his picture from a spot in which the individual identities of the marchers were somewhat obscured, in effect, replacing faces with the repeating signs declaring, "I am a man." This strike by Memphis sanitation workers brought Civil Rights leader Martin Luther King (1929–1968) to the city, where he was assassinated.

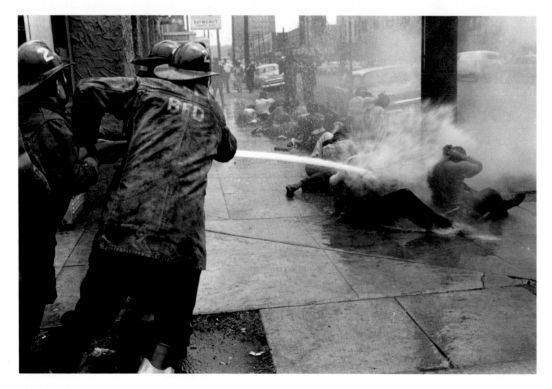

11.42
CHARLES MOORE, *Birmingham,* **1963.**

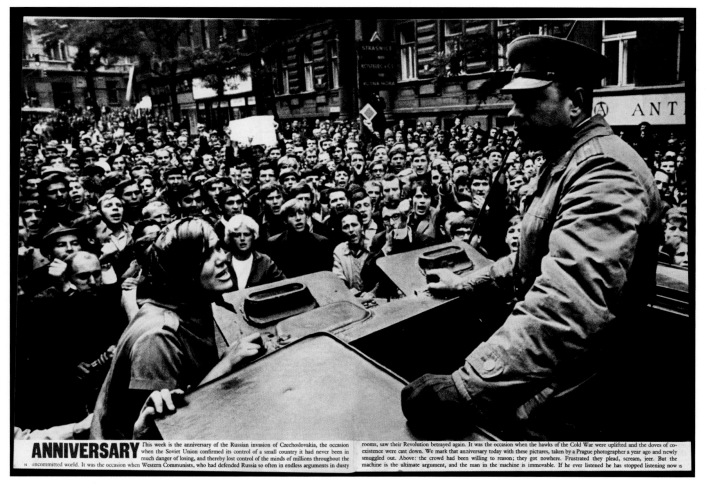

ANNIVERSARY This week is the anniversary of the Russian invasion of Czechoslovakia, the occasion when the Soviet Union confirmed its control of a small country it had never been in much danger of losing, and thereby lost control of the minds of millions throughout the uncommitted world. It was the occasion when Western Communists, who had defended Russia so often in endless arguments in dusty rooms, saw their Revolution betrayed again. It was the occasion when the hawks of the Cold War were uplifted and the doves of co-existence were cast down. We mark that anniversary today with these pictures, taken by a Prague photographer a year ago and newly smuggled out. Above: the crowd had been willing to reason; they got nowhere. Frustrated they plead, scream, jeer. But the machine is the ultimate argument, and the man in the machine is immovable. If he ever listened he has stopped listening now

11.43
JOSEF KOUDELKA, *Soviet Invasion of Czechoslovakia*, 1968. Image from *The Sunday Times Magazine*, anniversary issue, 1969.

Coordinating Committee (S.N.C.C.), where he helped to produce posters and other organizational materials. Civil Rights organizers knew how to use the media to gain publicity, and how to craft events with visual appeal for the nightly television news shots. Ernest Withers (1922–2007), the first African-American police officer hired in Memphis, Tennessee, also worked as a photographer, and expressed his support with a memorable image of the famous march on Memphis by sanitation workers (Fig. 11.41). Photographer Charles Moore (1931–2010) caught members of the Birmingham, Alabama, Fire Department as they turned high-pressure hoses on protesters (Fig. 11.42).

From 1955 to 1975, television and photography combined to disseminate images of war and conflict. When the forces of the Warsaw Pact invaded Czechoslovakia during the month of August 1968 in an attempt to put down democratic reforms, Josef Koudelka (b. 1938) photographed civilian resistance as tanks rumbled through Prague's main streets and squares. His negatives were smuggled out of the country, picked up by the Magnum photo agency, and published worldwide on the one-

year anniversary of the invasion, with a by-line reading "P. P."— that is, Prague Photographer (Fig. 11.43).

While *Life* magazine's photographs never approached the patriotic fervor expressed in Joe Rosenthal's images of the flag-raising on Iwo Jima during World War II (see Fig. 9.35), they did repeatedly communicate the average person's experience of the war, an approach pioneered by W. Eugene Smith. That theme was prominent in the June 27, 1969, issue of *Life*, which displayed "The Faces of the American Dead in Vietnam," in what resembled a high-school yearbook of the perished.[31] Feature stories concentrated on the experience of individual soldiers, as Smith had done in World War II.

For example, the April 16, 1965, edition of *Life* published twenty-two black-and-white pictures by British photographer Larry Burrows, who chronicled the war experiences of a twenty-one-year-old soldier. Burrows, who later died in a helicopter crash, mounted a camera on the airborne machine gun the soldier used during battle so as to record the gunner's facial expressions. But it was the pungency of his color work that

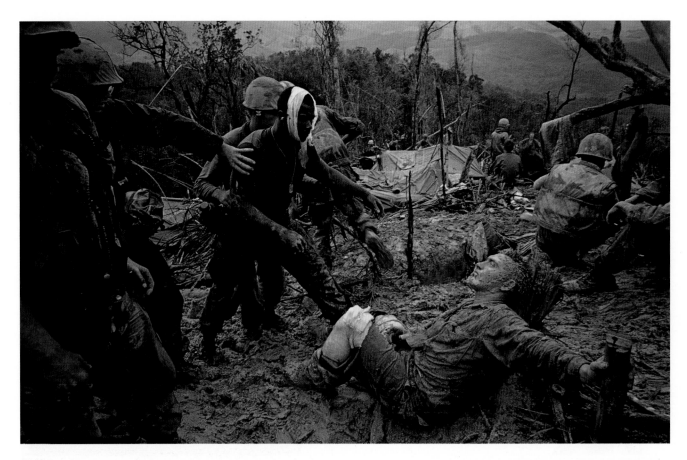

11.44
LARRY BURROWS, *At a First-Aid Center During Operation Prairie*, 1966.
Dye-transfer print. Spencer Museum of Art, University of Kansas, Missouri.

transformed the battlefield's ankle-deep mud into an emblem
for America's futile involvement in Vietnam (Fig. 11.44). David
Douglas Duncan, who saw the ordinary soldier in Korea as a
reluctant aggressor (see Fig. 11.2), was soured by the wanton
violence of Vietnam. The pictures he shot there were gathered
in his book *War without Heroes* (1970). Philip Jones Griffiths
(1936–2008), who would later write and illustrate *Vietnam, Inc.*,
a scalding indictment of the war as big business, photographed
the conflict for three years, mostly as it was experienced by
the Vietnamese peasants (Fig. 11.45). The image of a South
Vietnamese general executing a handcuffed Vietcong suspect
was captured by photographer Eddie Adams (1933–2004)
(Fig. 11.46). During one of his more than twenty-five trips to
Vietnam after the war, Griffiths photographed a widow holding
a copy of the newspaper photograph of her husband, the man
who was killed in Adams's famous photograph.

Some lasting images of the war experience were created only
in photography. For example, when President Richard Nixon
ordered the bombing of enemy camps in Cambodia, student
protests arose around the country. Photography student John
Paul Filo (b. 1948) caught the outcry of a young woman as she
knelt beside the body of a Kent State University student shot
dead by a member of the Ohio National Guard during a student
protest (Fig. 11.47). Vietnamese photographer Huynh Cong

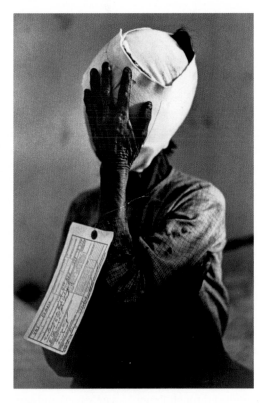

11.45
PHILIP JONES GRIFFITHS, *Napalm Victim*, Vietnam, 1967.
Gelatin silver print.

11.46
EDDIE ADAMS, *General Loan Executing a Vietcong Suspect,* February 1, 1968. Gelatin silver print.

This image, recording the execution of a suspected Communist sympathizer, roused national anger in the United States against the summary street justice administered by a Vietnamese general.

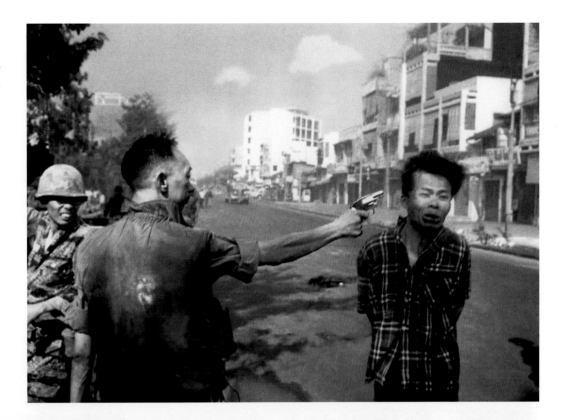

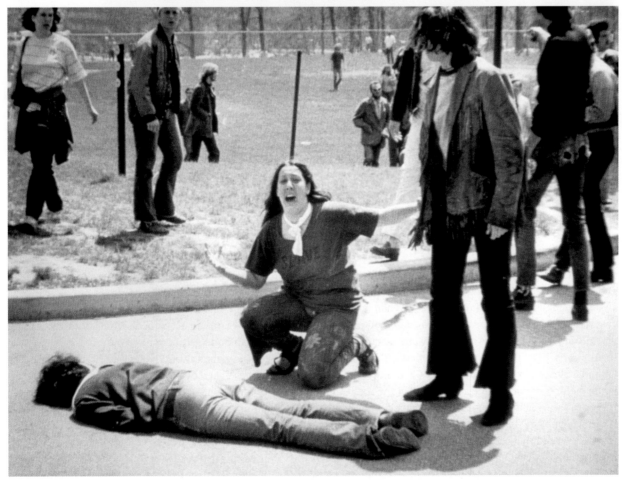

11.47
JOHN PAUL FILO, *Untitled* (Kent State: girl screaming over dead body), May 4, 1970.

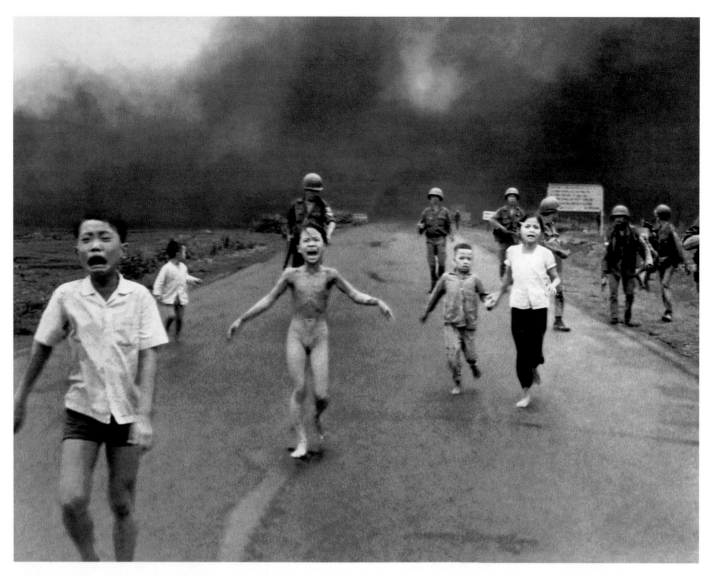

11.48
HUYNH CONG (NICK) UT, *Children Fleeing a Napalm Strike,* June 8, 1972.

(Nick) Ut (b. 1951) provided the lasting document of terrified and injured children running from an accidental napalm attack on a building where non-combatants had taken cover (Fig. 11.48). Motion-picture and video equipment were absent when Ron Haeberle (b. 1941), an army photographer, recorded the massacre of civilians in the Vietnamese village of My Lai by a United States Army company. Haeberle submitted the black-and-white pictures he took to the army, but kept the color film, which he began showing in the United States when he was demobilized. An image published in the Cleveland (Ohio) *Plain Dealer* soon traveled around the world. Working together, staff from the Museum of Modern Art, New York, and members of the Art Workers' Coalition used the image to create a gripping antiwar poster, which the museum later refused to sanction. With the question and answer, "Q: And babies? A: And babies," derived

from a television interview with a soldier who had witnessed the massacre, the poster became a rallying point against the war (Fig. 11.49). Yet it was Eddie Adams's still image (see Fig. 11.46) that became an acclaimed symbol of the war's injustice and its cold-blooded attitude toward the loss of life.

More than twenty-five years after the war ended in 1975, images taken by North Vietnamese civilian and military photographers were published through the efforts of the British photographer Tim Page (b. 1944), who had photographed the war in the south. Page discovered that North Vietnamese photographers such as Vo Anh Khanh (b. 1939) (Fig. 11.50) used mostly inexpensive black-and-white film and relied on the jungle night to create an outdoor darkroom. They seldom photographed the dead, but set out to inspire their embattled viewers with scenes of endurance and patriotism.

11.49
RON HAEBERLE AND PETER BRANT,
"Q. And Babies? A. And Babies," 1970. Offset
lithograph, printed in color. Museum of
Modern Art, New York.

The photograph taken by Haeberle, then a
U.S. Army photographer, showing the result of
deliberate killing of civilians, became the most
famous anti-Vietnam poster in the United States
and around the world.

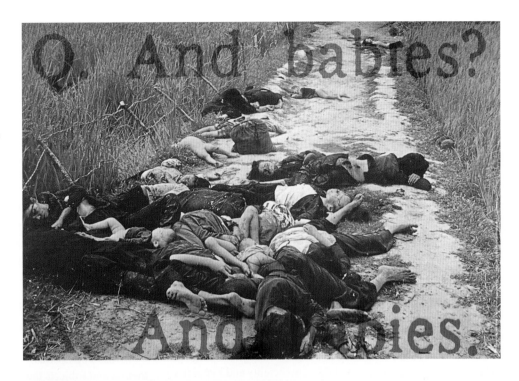

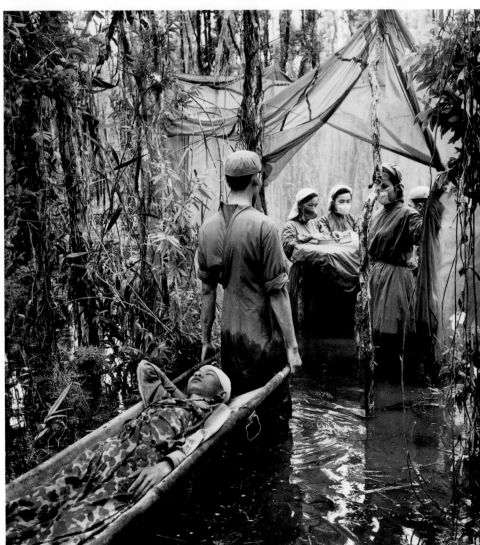

11.50
VO ANH KHANH, *U Minh Forest, Ca Mau,*
September 15, 1970.

During what they called "The American War,"
civilian and military photographers from North
Vietnam rode bicycles to the front to capture
scenes of suffering and courage. Vo's image of a
mosquito-netted operating room located in a
swamp to avoid detection is all the more startling
because its subjects seem so unruffled in their
improbable setting. The victim was a guerrilla
wounded by American bombing.

PHOTOGRAPHY IN ART

During the postwar decades, while photography gained a greater presence in international art movements, photojournalism emerged as a new source for artists interested in topical issues. Sculptor Duane Hanson (1925–1996) modeled his *Vietnam Scene* on published war photographs, and George Segal (1924–2000) created sculptures based on Civil Rights movement images, as well as on the shooting of students at Kent State University during the Vietnam War protests.

The wider use of photography also owed to the fact that artists in many media increasingly employed the camera to record their work. Meanwhile, the growth of mass media, especially in service of advertising, roused artists and critics to attend more closely to the effects of photography. The European avant-garde movement called the Situationist International, which emerged in the late 1950s, based its critique of consumer culture on what French critic Guy Debord (1931–1994) called in a 1967 book of the same title "the society of the spectacle." Inspired by Dadaist debunking, the Situationists attempted to subvert the profusion of mass media by appropriating its images and re-presenting them in ways that demonstrated the superficiality and hypocrisy of advertising and newspaper illustrations. At times, they freely rearranged appropriated images; in other instances, they let captions interpret the image (Fig. 11.51). The Situationists' examination of the mass media's impact on everyday life prefigured the critiques of consumer culture and gender stereotyping in the late 1970s and 1980s (see pp. 450–52). Their ideas helped to propel the 1968 uprisings and strikes in France.

The Situationist movement was generally secretive, its members largely anonymous, and much of its work was intentionally ephemeral; consequently, it was not a primary influence on later movements such as Pop art. Begun in Britain during the 1950s, Pop art derived from the word "popular," as in "popular culture." The seminal Independent Group (I.G.) included artist Richard Hamilton (1922–2011), whose 1956 COLLAGE *Just What is it that Makes Today's Homes So Different, So Appealing?* combined advertising images for products such as television sets and vacuum cleaners (Fig. 11.52). Shown in the 1956 London exhibition "This is Tomorrow", Hamilton's collage is a bittersweet parody that simultaneously critiques and celebrates the prospect of long-denied consumer items, symbolized by American products and attitudes toward conspicuous consumption.

British Pop art was anti-academic, rejecting the traditional themes and subjects taught in art school. Members of the I.G. took inspiration from Moholy-Nagy's 1947 book *Vision in Motion*, and from his belief in the vigor of advertising, and the

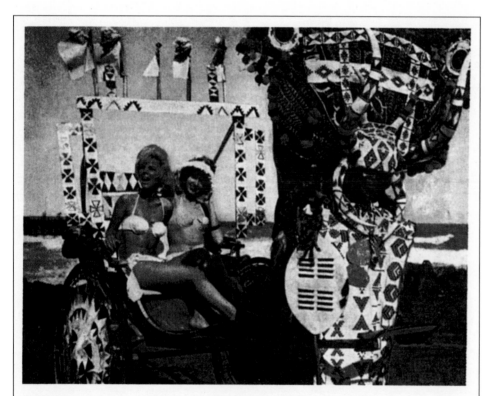

Des rôles réservés au nègre dans le spectacle. — I. Bon nègre, en République Sud-Africaine, 1963.

« Le président Johnson inaugurera mercredi la foire internationale de New-York... un spectacle de 1 milliard de dollars... D'autre part le Congrès pour l'égalité raciale... a fait part de son intention

11.51
PHOTOGRAPHER UNKNOWN, *Roles Reserved for the Negro in the Spectacle*, 1963, from *The World of Which We Speak*, 1970. Situationist International.

Situationists took photographs intended for one purpose, changing their captions to reveal other meanings. In this case, what appears to be a newspaper or travel industry shot has been recaptioned to highlight the condition of black South Africans.

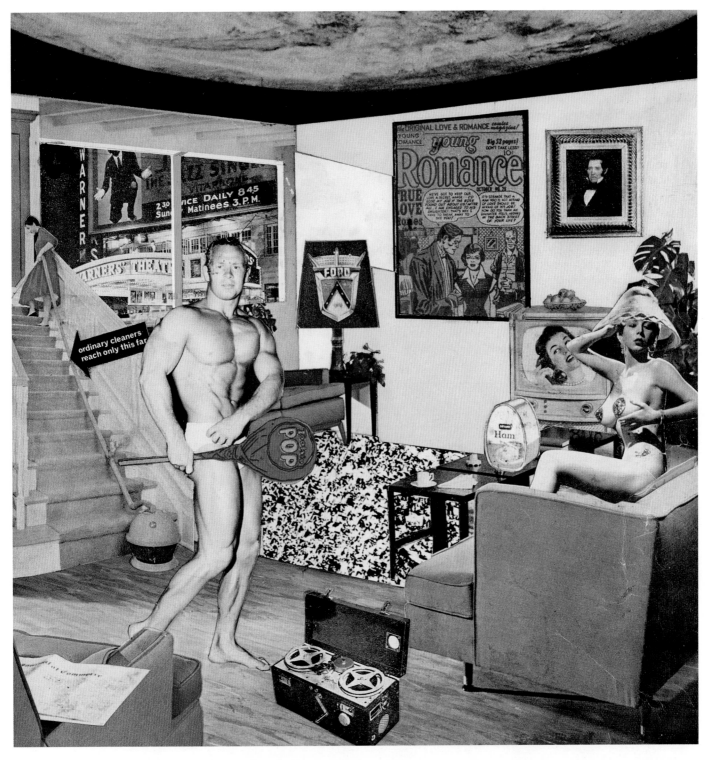

11.52
RICHARD HAMILTON, *Just What is it that Makes Today's Homes So Different, So Appealing?*, 1956. Collage on paper. Kunsthalle, Tübingen, Germany.

need to express the modern world through collage and the reuse of scientific photographs such as X-rays.[32] But they reversed Moholy-Nagy's complaints about the throwaway design of American goods, finding them entirely appropriate for an art that they insisted must be of its time. Hamilton analyzed the admirable elements of popular art as "transient, expendable,

inexpensive, witty, sexy, gimmicky, glamorous, and 'big business.'"[33] Hamilton's collage has been canonized in the history of art, surpassing works by other members of the I.G., for whom photography played a major role, including Nigel Henderson (1917–1985) and Eduardo Paolozzi (1924–2005) (Fig. 11.15), who assembled collages that incorporated mass-media images of movie stars, household products, and hot cars. As famous as Hamilton's collage is, his most iconic work was the design of the Beatles's so-called "White Album" of 1968.

In the United States during the 1960s, Pop artists were nonchalant about "the society of the spectacle," accepting mass-produced commodities and images as the inescapable norm of modern life. Artists Larry Rivers (1923–2002) and Andy Warhol (1928–1987) appropriated sensational tabloid images, such as car crashes, enlarging their scale and deepening their tonality to accentuate the omnipresence of photographic reproduction. Warhol was a dedicated fan of film stars, beginning a collection of their publicity photographs when he was a child. He carried a camera with him to social events, and snapped flattering pictures of people that he felt were always on camera, always performing a public identity. To that end, he bought a photo-booth and cajoled his house guests to photograph themselves. He also concentrated on the paparazzi, or celebrity photographers, who stalked their prey, embodying the public's delirious curiosity about such figures, as in the character of Paparazzo in Federico Fellini's 1961 film *La Dolce Vita*. During the late 1960s, Ron Galella (b. 1931),

whom Warhol called his favorite photographer, epitomized the paparazzi. He pursued celebrities such as actress Elizabeth Taylor, singer Elvis Presley, and First Lady Jacqueline Kennedy, who found their tabloid images recycled into Warhol's art. Warhol exploited the thrill of illicit looking at the same time that he critiqued it in his repetitive images of the famous. Likewise, celebrity photographs were central to *Interview*, the tell-all magazine he founded in 1969.

Warhol urged portrait clients to visit public photo-booths, commonly called Photomats for their brand-name. Before the Photomat lens they could self-dramatize for images that Warhol later turned mostly into SILKSCREEN prints. Some of his most famous work was based on publicity shots of such luminaries as Elvis Presley and Marilyn Monroe (Fig. 11.53). The repetition of the portrait image in such works registered the fan's longing for more glimpses of the celebrity, and anticipated the extraordinary public appetite for photographs of Diana, Princess of Wales (1961–1997), in the 1980s and 1990s.

During the 1960s, fashion photographer David Bailey (b. 1938) created images of such cultural celebrities as the

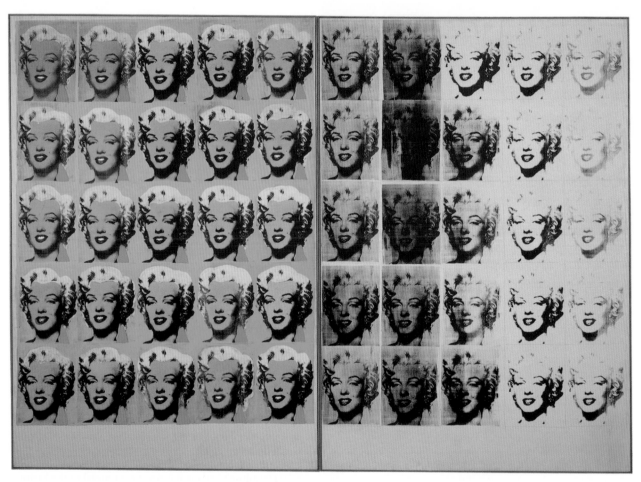

11.53
ANDY WARHOL, *Marilyn Diptych*, 1962. Acrylic on canvas. Tate, London.

Warhol used the silkscreen technique to create repeating rows and columns of Marilyn Monroe's portrait. He altered each of the pictures, letting the colors bleed into each other, smudge, and overlap in an echo of the cheap color printing methods of celebrity magazines. The exaggerated result was a counterpart to the frantic public appetite for celebrity likenesses.

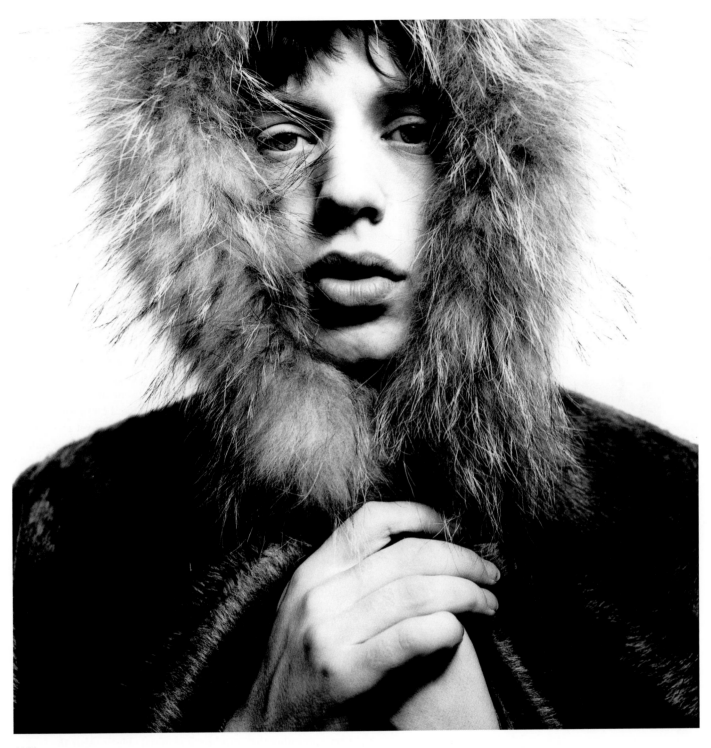

11.54
DAVID BAILEY, *Mick Jagger,* 1964.

Beatles, and with Andy Warhol helped shape the notion of the Swinging Sixties (Fig. 11.54). Bailey was a star in his own right, and his carefree lifestyle became the basis for the internationally popular movie *Blow-Up* (1966), which scrutinized the limits of a photographer's societal observations. Bailey's meteoric rise at *Vogue* magazine was partly due to his insistence on bringing fresh faces, such as models Jean Shrimpton and Penelope Tree, to fashion shoots. His emerging fame also owed to his large black-and-white portraits of hip celebrities, especially those whose humble class backgrounds matched his own, such as Warhol and the actor Michael Caine. Warhol's friend the artist Robert Rauschenberg (1925–2008) had been creating PHOTOGRAMS,

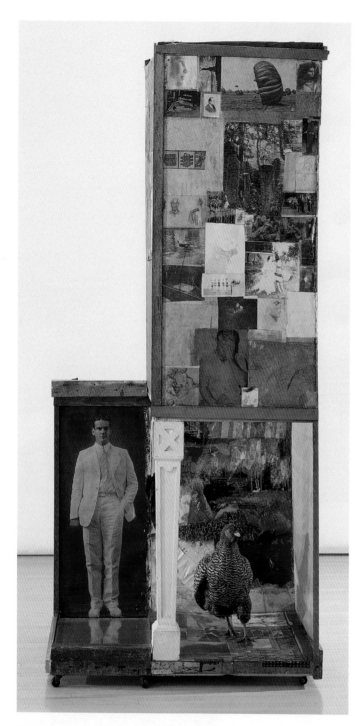

11.55
ROBERT RAUSCHENBERG, *Untitled Combine (Man with White Shoes)*, 1955.
Panza Collection. Museum of Contemporary Art, Los Angeles, California.

Based on a mysterious image of a man in a white suit, Rauschenberg's combination of collaged photographs and a chicken does not so much tell a story as argue that art can be made from the detritus of life.

or cameraless photographs, on blueprint paper since the 1950s. In his "combines," Rauschenberg incorporated mundane objects found along the street, such as pieces of cardboard, bits of signs, magazine photographs, and old postcards, as well as paint (Fig. 11.55). More than Warhol, Rauschenberg wanted to puncture the pretensions of "high art" in traditional media, especially the work of the Abstract Expressionists, by making art that was not conceived as a mirror of life, but actually contained bits of life itself. Like Warhol, he also adapted the silkscreen process, blending images from newspapers and magazines.

At about the same time, some painters adopted a style known as Photorealism to respond to the look of color photographs, in particular their generalization of color and illusion of depth. To render these qualities, they projected photographic slides on to a canvas, then precisely copied details, using an airbrush, which sprays a thin stream of diluted paint that leaves no trace of handwork. Like street photographers, the Photorealists chose mostly urban scenes, and concentrated on highly polished surfaces such as glass and chrome (Fig. 11.56). American Chuck Close (b. 1940) employed the Photorealist vocabulary in portraiture (Fig. 11.57). His eerily airless large-scale, close-up portraits anticipate the approach of late twentieth-century photographers such as Thomas Ruff (see Fig. 12.43), whose big pictures show abundant physical details of sitters, yet are silent about the subjects' personal characters. The photographic source of Photorealism became a favorite theme in the work of Audrey Flack (b. 1931), who arranged snapshots like elements of a still life, and who mimicked the way the camera can exaggerate highlights. The garish colors of her work may also derive from photographic sources, particularly the deeply saturated shades employed in advertising (Fig. 11.58).

PHOTOGRAPHY AND CONCEPTUAL ART

During the 1960s and the 1970s, photography was used by artists who found no irony in making lasting images of ephemeral projects, such as installations, performance art, and the Happenings of the late 1950s and early 1960s, in which impromptu public events or situations were presented to onlookers. Photography was also employed internationally by Conceptual artists not just because they were drifting away from traditional media, but also because its record-keeping function favored their focus on making and communicating ideas or concepts rather than producing material objects. Also, the ordinary, utilitarian snapshot provided artists with an alternative, one that was largely removed from the art market. Indeed, the anti-aesthetic of the snapshot intrigued artists who were looking for alternatives.

Celebrated for his earthworks, such as *Spiral Jetty*, which became familiar mostly through photographic reproduction, Robert Smithson (1938–1973) was one of the many postwar artists who may have come to photography to record their work but who soon began to investigate the medium on its own terms. He dwelled on photography's relationship to time, through what he called "mirror displacements," produced while traveling in the

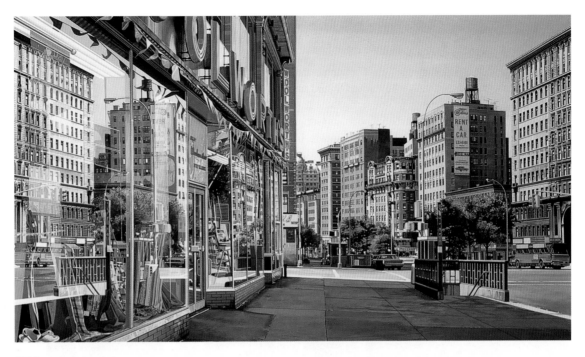

11.56
RICHARD ESTES, *Woolworth's*, 1974. Oil on canvas, 38 × 55 in. (96.5 × 139.7 cm). San Antonio Museum of Art, San Antonio, Texas.

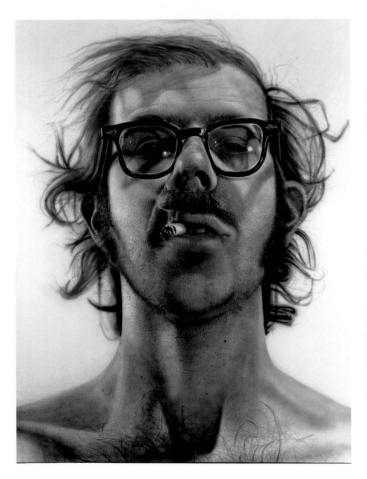

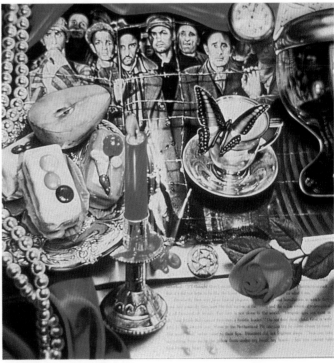

11.58
AUDREY FLACK, *World War II (Vanitas), Incorporating Part of Margaret Bourke-White's Photograph "Buchenwald, April 1945,"* 1976–77. Oil over acrylic on canvas, 8 × 8 ft (2.43 × 2.43 m).

In this work, Flack gathered such objects as a Star of David, and copied part of a photograph by Margaret Bourke-White, showing Jewish survivors of Nazi concentration camps to create a tribute to those lost during World War II.

11.57
CHUCK CLOSE, *Self-Portrait*, 1968. Acrylic on canvas, 8 ft 11½ in. × 6 ft 11½ in. (2.73 × 2.12 m). Walker Art Center Collection, Minneapolis, Minnesota.

Yucatán area of Mexico (Fig. 11.59). In his writings, Smithson imagined an "Infinite Camera," a voracious yet indifferent perpetual machine that would gobble up the visual stream and produce unlimited reproductions.[34] His thoughts parallel those of other artists, such as Warhol, who exalted the impersonal camera, including the inexpensive Kodak Instamatic.

Similarly, the British pair of artists known as Gilbert and George (Gilbert Proesch, b. 1943; George Passmore, b. 1942) moved from performances, in which they presented themselves as living sculpture, to making "photo-pieces." Unlike Smithson, who continued to work in sculpture and earthworks, Gilbert and George turned primarily to the large photoworks. In their living sculpture, which dates from the late 1960s, they collapsed the distinction between art and life. In like fashion, their personal

lives and interests became the subjects of their photo-pieces.[35] An anti-art attitude informed Hikosaka Naoyoshi (b. 1946), one of the founding members of the Japanese Bikyōtō group, which came together during the student protests of the 1960s. The group's concern with political action and rejection of conventional art-making was expressed in Hikosaka's 1971 postcard invitation to *Floor Event*, which invited people to come to his apartment literally to watch paint dry (Fig. 11.23). The card is also an early example of mail art, an international effort that continues today to confound establishment galleries by sending art, often in the form of postcards, through the postal system.

Photography's boundless potential for mimicking appearances prompted American Douglas Huebler (1924–1997)

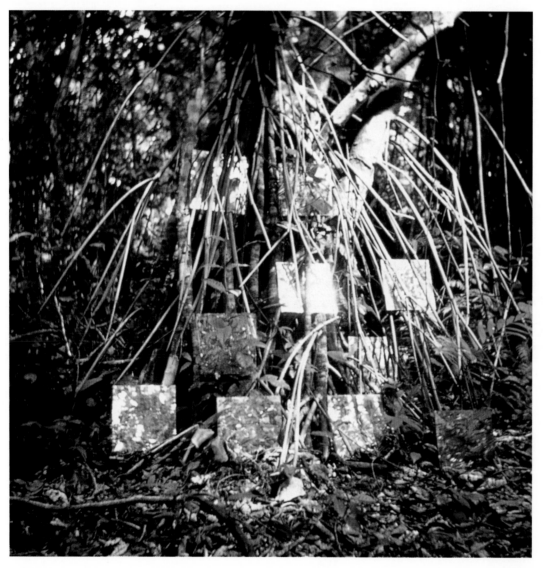

11.59
ROBERT SMITHSON, *Seventh Mirror Displacement,* **1969. Guggenheim Museum, New York.**

Arranging a dozen mirrors in the ordinary landscape, rather than near the often photographed monuments of ancient Mexican cultures, Smithson brought the sky down to earth. He used a small, inexpensive Instamatic camera to record his construction. After the picture was taken, he packed up the mirrors, leaving the landscape as he found it. The brief insertion of mirrors then existed only as a photographic record.

portrait

Ed Ruscha

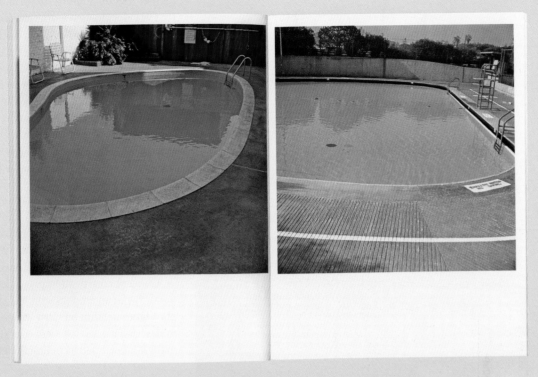

11.60
ED RUSCHA, From *Nine Swimming Pools and a Broken Glass*, 1968.

Ruscha not only made neutral photographs of ordinary subjects such as gas stations, parking lots, and swimming pools; he also gathered them in books without any explanatory text. *Nine Swimming Pools* is just that—nine photographs of swimming pools.

American West Coast artist Ed Ruscha (b. 1937) saw the camera as an essentially bland, inexpensive recording tool with which to record dispassionately a banal human environment. His work not only typifies the first generation of Conceptual artist-photographers, but also marks the beginning of the now well-established trend of artists from other media taking up photography. Rejecting the fine-arts tradition of photography as well as photojournalism, Ruscha remarked in 1972 that "Photography's just a playground for me. I'm not a photographer, at all." [36]

Ruscha's early interests in cartooning, typography, and the graphic arts indicate his attention to vernacular and often urban imagery as well as the relationship between words and pictures. While making his first paintings and working as a commercial artist, Ruscha became preoccupied with the way that photography could capture the essence of Pop art's emphasis on advertising and mass-media imagery (see Fig. 11.52). He was also attracted to contemporary collages of detritus, like those of Robert Rauschenberg (see Fig. 11.55), which mixed objects and images, some of them photo-based.

Ruscha's first book of photographs, *Twentysix Gasoline Stations*, published in 1963, was a selection of twenty-six photographs of gas stations along Route 66. The highway was the renowned "Mother Road" used by people leaving the Dust Bowl in the 1930s, photographed by Robert Frank (see p. 342) for his book *The Americans*, and celebrated in the popular 1960–64 television show *Route 66*. But Ruscha was careful to remove any historical or symbolic hints in his pictures. Indeed, he chose the most austere images for *Twentysix Gasoline Stations*, and for his later photo-based books. He pointed out that "I want absolutely neutral material. My pictures are not that interesting, nor the subject matter. They are simply a collection of 'facts', my book is more like a collection of readymades." [37] In his photobooks, Ruscha often left pages blank. In *Nine Swimming Pools and a Broken Glass*, the ten photo pages are accompanied by fifty-four blank pages that negate the optical pleasure of turning the pages to find new pictures while also reminding the viewer of the book's thingness.

Ruscha's way of working echoes the procedures at the center of Conceptual art and photography. Projects were planned in advance—an important difference from the decisive moment of Henri Cartier-Bresson (see p. 256), which could not be foreseen. The idea or plan became the main motivator of Conceptual work, and what Ruscha called a "factory polish" made the image seem mass-produced, rather than deeply felt. Indeed, in some Conceptual theories, the work need not be made at all.

painter Mel Bochner (b. 1940) and British artist Victor Burgin (b. 1941) formulated work that probed photography's ability to create an aura of authenticity. Bochner's *Misunderstandings (A Theory of Photography)* consisted of an index-card-size negative of a photograph of his arm. Because it is a direct product of the camera, the negative is putatively closer to the original scene, more truthful than the positive. In London, Burgin also alluded to photography's relationship to reality when he created what he called a *Photopath* (1967). Photographing sections of a gallery floor, Burgin then printed images the exact size and tonality of the wood and stapled them to the boards, creating a system in which "images are perfectly congruent with the objects."[39] One of the most famous photographs to emerge in the postwar era—an image that found its way on to public kiosks and studio walls— also toyed with the notion of photographic truth. Idiosyncratic French artist Yves Klein (1928–1962) produced a picture showing himself springing off a wall into space (Fig. 11.62).

Conceptual art's attempts to dematerialize the art object not only put an emphasis on less expensive materials, such as photographic film, but also stressed language, which was used to describe works that were conceived, but never intended to be made. Conceptualists maintained that words, like photographs,

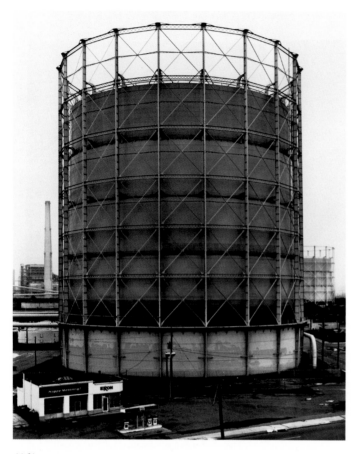

11.61
BERND AND HILLA BECHER, *Gas Tower (Telescoping Type), off Pulaski Bridge, Jersey City, New Jersey, U.S.A.,* **1981.**

to propose his *Variable Piece # 70 (In Progress)*, in which he set out to do the impossible: photograph everyone living on the planet. Huebler was adroit at mining the vein of ridicule that ran through Conceptual art. In his 1969 *Location Place* series, he mocked Alfred Stieglitz's *Equivalents* (see p. 184) when he photographed clouds on a New York to Los Angeles flight, reporting that "the camera was pointed more or less straight out the airplane window (with no 'interesting' view intended)."[38] Deconstructive humor also informed the work of Ed Ruscha.

By contrast, German photographers Bernd (1931–2007) and Hilla Becher (b. 1934) soberly began elevating the photograph's ability to archive the appearance of specifically so-called "dead-tech" objects, namely, antiquated industrial constructions such as blast furnaces and gas towers (Fig. 11.61). Because of their dispassionate style, these images were included in the 1975 show "New Topographics." Yet the rich gray tonalities of their work, along with the public nostalgia aroused by the disappearance of mechanical technologies, prompted audiences to respond with a sentimentality that was alien to Conceptual philosophy.

The photographic interests of Conceptual artists bypassed the fine arts tradition of Alfred Stieglitz, the spiritualism of Minor White, and even the formalism of Lee Friedlander and Garry Winogrand. Instead Conceptualists plunged into an examination of publicly accepted notions of photographic truth. American

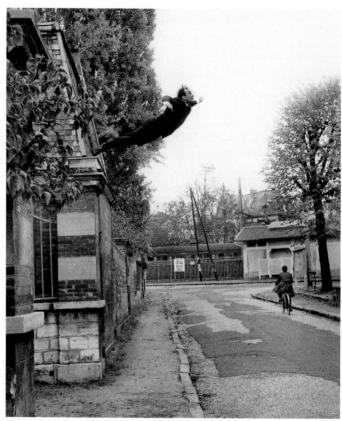

11.62
HARRY SHUNK, *Yves Klein Leaping into the Void, near Paris,* October 23, 1960. **Gelatin silver print.**

Though not primarily a photographer, Klein had himself photographed leaping from a tall stone wall in an image of the artist as risk-taker. He altered the original image to remove the circle of assistants holding a trampoline.

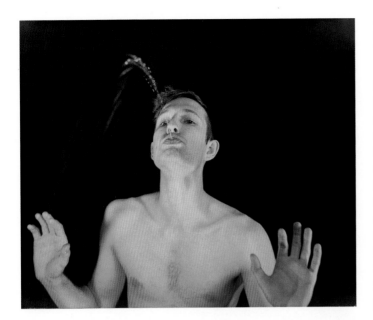

11.63
BRUCE NAUMAN, *Self-Portrait as a Fountain*, from the series *Photograph Suite*, 1966. Chromogenic color print. Whitney Museum of American Art, New York.

function in a web of social meanings. The interaction between image and caption, ever-present in magazines, advertising—and textbooks—had been shunned in art photography, which expected the image to carry the full burden of meaning. But the captioned photograph became a wellspring for Conceptual artists. Bruce Nauman (b. 1941) made a photograph called *Self-Portrait as a Fountain* (1966), in which he spurted water from his mouth (Fig. 11.63). The photographic work of Belgian artist Marcel Broodthaers (1924–1976) often turned on the contradiction between image and words. He amusingly wrote that "the idea of inventing something insincere finally crossed my mind and I set to work straightway."[40] His *La Soupe de Daguerre* (*Daguerre's Soup*) (1976) is a collage of photographs, including photographs of other media, all referring to food (Fig. 11.64).

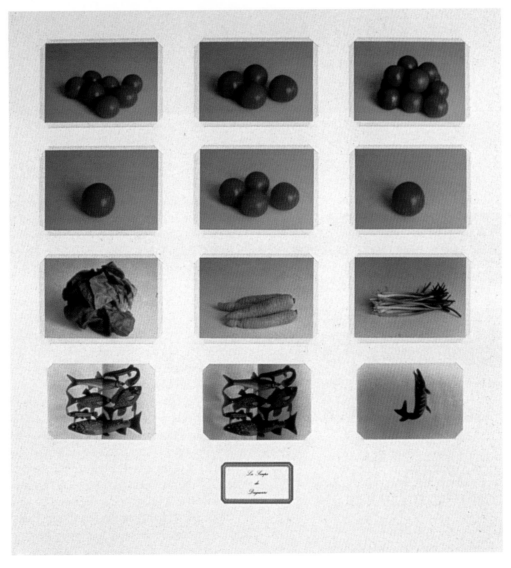

11.64
MARCEL BROODTHAERS, *La Soupe de Daguerre*, 1974. Twelve color coupler prints on paper.

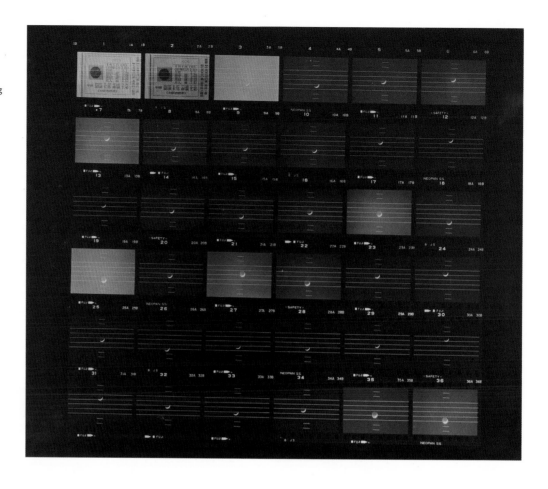

11.65
HITOSHI NOMURA, "Moon" Score, 1977–80. National Museum of Modern Art, Tokyo.

Nomura bluntly stated that "My artmaking begins precisely with a desire not to talk about it."[41] His work gently parodies scientific records. For the *"Moon" Score* series, he shot a full roll of film (thirty-six exposures) each night for more than a decade.

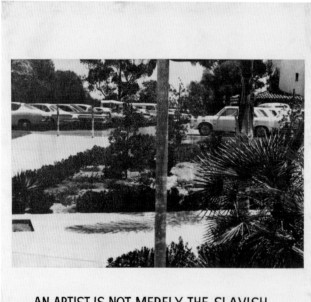

AN ARTIST IS NOT MERELY THE SLAVISH ANNOUNCER OF A SERIES OF FACTS. WHICH IN THIS CASE THE CAMERA HAS HAD TO ACCEPT AND MECHANICALLY RECORD.

Not all Conceptual artists used photography to critique the medium and its myths. Dutch painter Jan Dibbets (b. 1941) turned from monochrome painting to abstract photography to explore time and manipulate the elements of perspective. As its title implied, Dibbets's series of photographs *The Shortest Day of 1970 Photographed in my House every Six Minutes* recorded the passage of daylight before the camera. Similarly, Japanese photographer Nobuo Yamanaka (1948–1982) used the camera to suggest the flow of human sight. In the early 1970s, he helped organize installations that relied on slides projected on to the surface of a river or through suspended sheets of transparent material. He also constructed a large, walk-in camera obscura, not for purposes of tracing a drawing, but to experience a fugitive image hovering on a wall.[42]

Likewise, Hitoshi Nomura (b. 1945) combined an interest in human sight with an inquiry into what he called "after-images," meditations on duration and phenomena, such as decay and evaporation, which must be seen over time. His work is reminiscent of time-lapse photography, like that of Étienne-Jules Marey. Nomura employed the look of scientific photography to tease out an awareness of duration and perception (Fig. 11.65).

The biggest change in the relationship between photography and art was the developing interest of artists in the medium.

11.66
JOHN BALDESSARI, *Untitled*, 1967. Acrylic and photoemulsion on canvas.

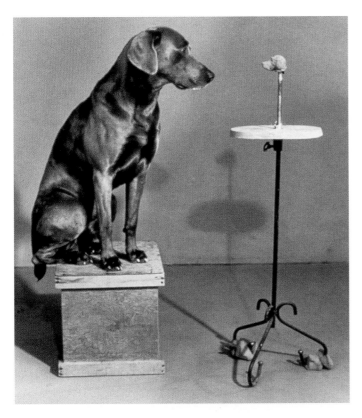

11.67
WILLIAM WEGMAN, *Man Ray Portfolio—Man Ray Contemplating the Bust of Man Ray*, 1978. Silver gelatin print. Collection of the artist.

While recording their work, exploring the possibilities of dematerializing art, or critiquing mass media, artists who had little or no training in photography discovered fresh visual possibilities in it. As they adopted the camera, they did not take up the burden of prejudices and received ideas that weighed down photographic practice throughout the nineteenth and early twentieth centuries. The appeal of what seemed to be an underutilized, non-traditional medium set American artist John Baldessari (b. 1931) on a one-way street away from painting. He burned his easel works and turned to reproducible media, such as photography and video (Fig. 11.66). For most artists, the discovery of photography was not so drastic, but was quietly revolutionary. In the postwar decades, photography gradually emerged as another medium, like paint, wood, or stone, in which artists routinely worked, and it augured the ascent of the late twentieth-century multi- or post-media artist, who works in whatever medium or mediums seem appropriate.

As a young artist and video-maker William Wegman (b. 1943) embraced Conceptual ideas, but he became popular with the general public for his humorous portraits of his dog Man Ray, named for the Surrealist artist. Costumed and posed for black-and-white, as well as color Polaroid photographs and videotape, the dog patiently modeled for Wegman, whose pictures were meant to underscore the theoretical point that representation is the product of a photographer's interpretation and creation, not an objective view of the world. Moderately successful in the art world, the images were a hit on calendars sold around the world to people with little or no knowledge of Conceptual art (Fig. 11.67).

THE CZAR'S PANTHEON

When John Szarkowski (1925–2007), the former director of the Photography Department at New York's Museum of Modern Art, died in 2007, newspapers and blogs were quick to recall his nickname, "the czar." In 1962, he was picked by Edward Steichen to manage what quickly became the most prominent museum department collecting and exhibiting contemporary photography. Although he remained in his post until 1991, the era of his greatest influence extended through the 1960s and 1970s, when he not only organized ground-breaking exhibitions, but also set out a critique of photographic practice that influenced a generation of photographers, artists, and historians.

Szarkowski's central theme, particularly as expressed in the influential *The Photographer's Eye* (1966), was exactly the reverse of the nineteenth-century notion that photography should emulate the other arts, especially painting. Szarkowski insisted that photography needed to abandon its "allegiance to traditional pictorial standards" and be inventive in terms of inherent qualities with which "photography was born whole."[43] In other words, he articulated the excitement about the medium that postwar artists such as John Baldessari had discovered.

Szarkowski repeatedly asserted that the images by little-known photographers, or commercial photographers operating in areas such as photojournalism, could as successfully explore the medium's potential as the work of art photographers.[44] To prove his point, he built a 1973 exhibition called "From the Picture Press" from the archives of the tabloid newspaper the *New York Daily News*. In the show's catalog he wrote that "as images, the photographs are shockingly direct, and at the same time mysterious, elliptical, and fragmentary, reproducing the texture and flavor of experience without its meaning."[45]

Improvising on a seasoned theme in art history, expressed specifically in the work of architectural historian George Kubler, Szarkowski proposed that the history of an art form should be traced through apparent changes in its formal characteristics such as line, not through changes in its subject matter.[46] Simply put, as media evolve, they elaborate and explore their formal potential. In his popular book *Looking at Photographs* (1973), Szarkowski envisioned a kind of historical check-valve in which formal innovations could only go forward. "The chief arbiter of the game is Tradition," he wrote, "which records in a haphazard fashion the results of all previous games, in order to make sure that no play that won before will be allowed to win again."[47] In other words, progress in photography centered on novelty—not new subjects, but fresh formal approaches.

Szarkowski listed five interdependent characteristics unique to photography. The first, "the thing itself," declared that the photograph was a picture, not the equivalent of reality. The second feature, "the detail," referred to photography's "compelling clarity," and also to the fact that photography can only "isolate a fragment" of reality. He emphasized the importance of "the frame," or the "central act of choosing and eliminating," and he noted the "vantage point," which allows photographers to present the subject from unexpected points of view. On a more philosophical note, Szarkowski insisted that "all photographs are time exposures, of shorter or longer duration."[48] Each of the five characteristics of photography was illustrated by the work of historic and contemporary photographers. Whether distance shots or close-ups, virtually all the images in *The Photographer's Eye* are sharply focused and readily accessible.

Among the trends Szarkowski held up as definitive examples of photography's progressive investigation of its inherent characteristics were "the decisive moment" developed by Henri Cartier-Bresson, the "straight photograph" exemplified by Paul Strand and Walker Evans, and the humanistic Depression-era documentary as embodied in the work of Dorothea Lange and Arthur Rothstein. The next in line in the chronological discovery of formal properties were the efforts of contemporary American photographers such as Robert Frank, Lee Friedlander, Garry Winogrand, Harry Callahan, and Danny Lyon.

Szarkowski also extended his standards to color photography, praising the work of William Eggleston (b. 1939) as no less than the "discovery of color photography."[49] Beginning in 1965, Eggleston began to experiment with color film, and centered on vernacular color found on a tricycle, a backyard barbeque, or a cracked ceiling (Fig. 11.68). He made many pictures of many ordinary objects and scenes, a practice he later called "democratic." In the 1976 catalog of Eggleston's work, Szarkowski noted that the photographer was true to the landscape of the Memphis, Tennessee, area where he worked, and also faithful to "photography as a system of visual editing." Recognizing, perhaps, that Eggleston had begun to intensify his colors during the early 1970s by using the saturated pigments of the dye-transfer printing method, Szarkowski observed that photography's goal "is not to make something factually impeccable, but seamlessly persuasive." The photographer's work is to discover "new patterns of facts that will serve as metaphors

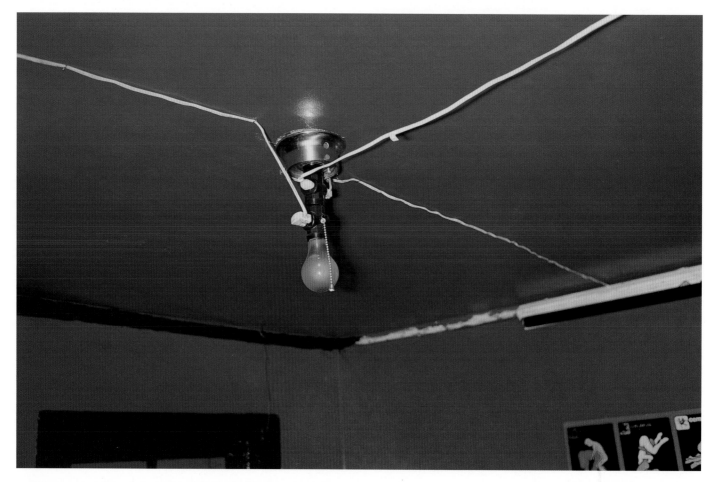

11.68
WILLIAM EGGLESTON, *Greenwood, Mississippi*, 1970. The J. Paul Getty Museum, Los Angeles, California.

William Eggleston's photographs resemble Photorealist paintings, in that they often dwell on qualities of light, and reflections on different surface textures, such as metal and concrete.

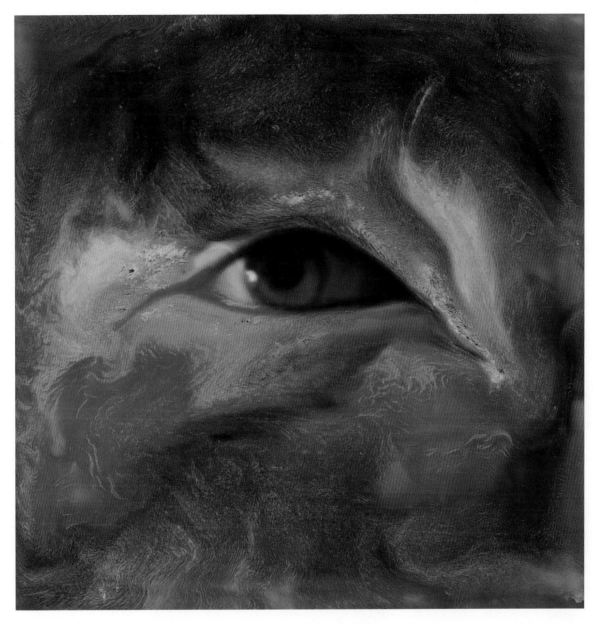

11.69
LUCAS SAMARAS, *Untitled*, **1973. Polaroid. The Nelson-Atkins Museum of Art, Gift of Hallmark Cards, Inc., Kansas, Missouri.**

for their intentions." Color, in Szarkowski's view, challenged the photographer's ability to resist its simple prettiness and devious nullification of form.[50] He argued that in Eggleston's photographs color and subject matter were faultlessly blended into a formally exciting private view of the world.

By 1978, when Szarkowski mounted the extensive exhibition "Mirrors and Windows: American Photography since 1960," it was evident to him that a lot more had been taking place in photographic practice than he had envisioned twelve years earlier in *The Photographer's Eye*. He tried to organize the "Mirrors and Windows" exhibition along a continuum, ranging from the idea of the mirror, or artist's concern with self, typified by the introspective photography and writing of Minor White, and the notion of window, typified by Robert Frank's book

The Americans, with its emphasis on the appearance of the world. But the variety of photographs he selected quickly eluded that terminology and became more of a postwar survey. He included work done mostly in the 1960s through the mid-1970s, including images by Eggleston and Eliot Porter, as well as by such artists as Sol LeWitt (1938–2007) and Robert Smithson. Along with the photographers such as Friedlander and Winogrand, who exemplified the quest for what Szarkowski called photography's inherent characteristics, there were new imaging technologies, including John Mott-Smith's (b. 1930) 1966 series of pictures arising from computer analysis, and the Polaroid pictures of Lucas Samaras (b. 1936), in which the photographer manipulated the soft, freshly exposed chemical emulsion with his fingers or mechanical aids (Fig. 11.69).

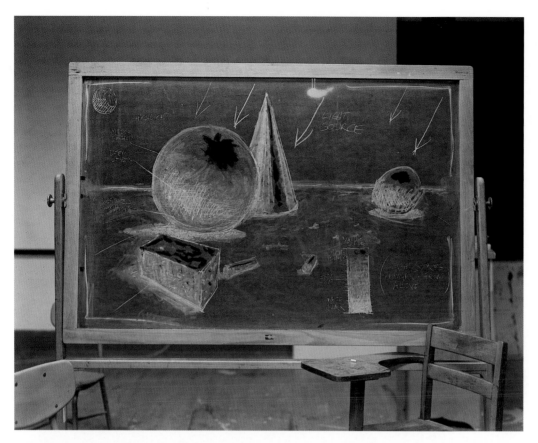

11.70
ROBERT CUMMING, *Academic Shading Exercise*, 1974. Positive contact print.

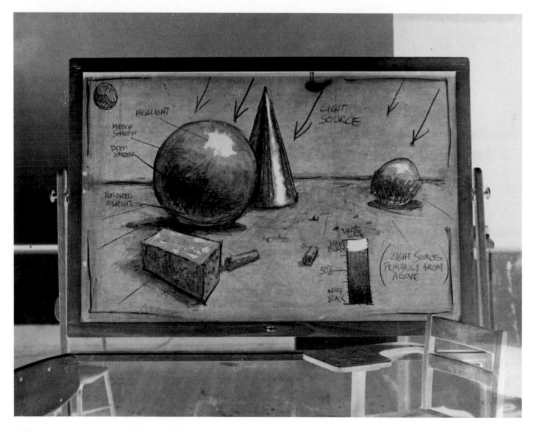

11.71
ROBERT CUMMING, *Academic Shading Exercise*, 1974. Paper negative print.

"Mirrors and Windows" recognized the growing significance of appropriated mass-media images in the work of such artists as Rauschenberg and Warhol. The scoffing humor of Conceptual artist Robert Cumming (b. 1943) was evident in two prints, one a positive and the other a negative, showing blackboard exercises for students learning how to shade shapes such as rectangles and cones to create the illusion of depth. Of course, the negative print reversed the black-and-white values, turning the lesson inside out (Figs. 11.70, 11.71). Cumming was one of the earliest American photographers to construct scenes of this kind solely to be photographed. His work anticipated the fabricated-to-be-photographed style of the 1980s. "Mirrors and Windows" also contained the work of Robert Heinecken (1931–2006), who transformed advertising and pornographic images, and experimented with collage, photograms, printing processes, and even the shape of the work (Fig. 11.72). He thought of himself as a documentarian of manufactured experiences.

Szarkowski also chose images by Ray K. Metzker (b. 1931), and praised his "photomosaic," in which a dimly perceptible human figure appears in forty-nine different poses within a

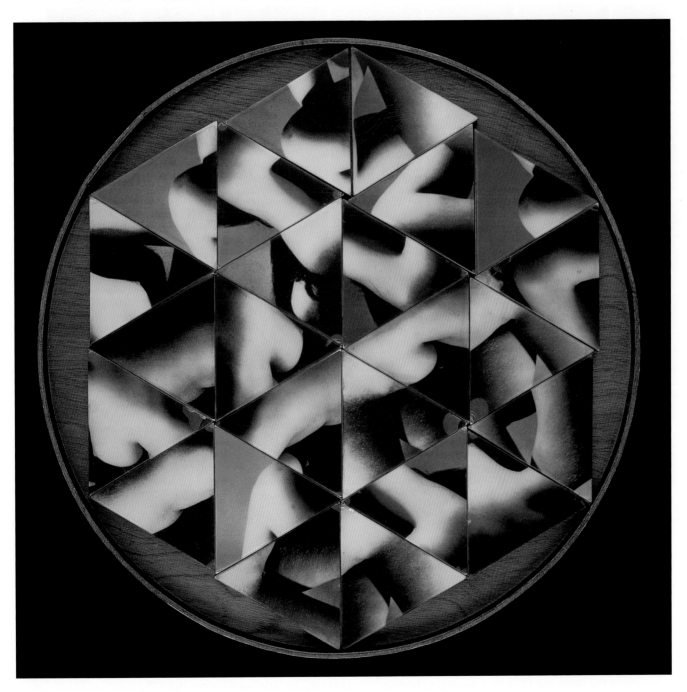

11.72
ROBERT HEINECKEN, *Refractive Hexagon,* **1965. Twenty-four movable photographic pieces on wood. Gelatin silver prints. Center for Creative Photography, University of Arizona, Tucson, Arizona.**

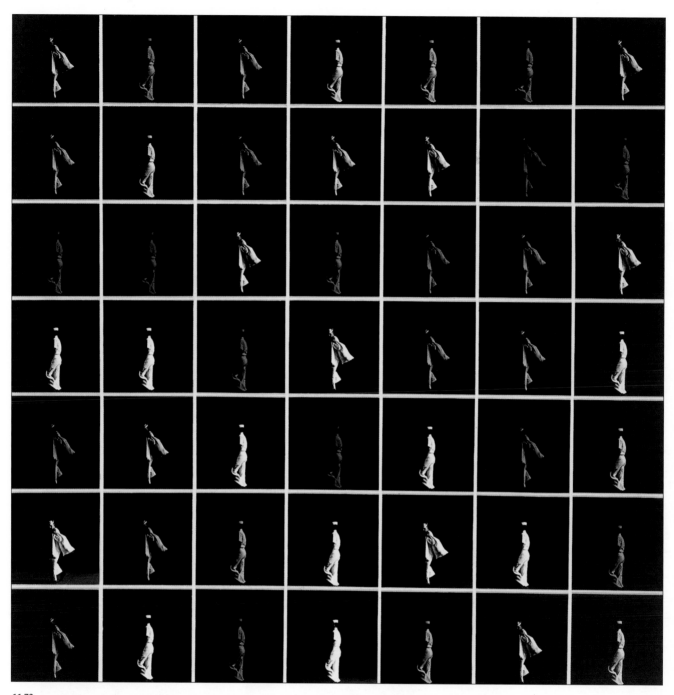

11.73
RAY K. METZKER, *Composites: Philadelphia*, 1964. Gelatin silver print. Purchase. Contemporary Exhibition Fund, Alfred Stieglitz Restricted Fund, Alice Newton Osborn Fund. Philadelphia Museum of Art, Philadelphia, Pennsylvania.

large grid, a successful attempt to find beauty in scientifically derived systems. Metzker's figure is reduced to the significance of a slim squiggle of paint (Fig. 11.73). Likewise, body parts in the Heinecken photomosaic have all but lost their identity. From a standard viewing distance on the gallery wall, both the Heinecken work and the Metzker image rely on the visual rhythm of overall abstract patterns rather than subject matter.

Increasingly in the 1960s and 1970s, artists working in other media, as well as photographers not committed to notions of the medium's uniqueness and purity, began to exploit mass-

media images. Szarkowski included an array of these kinds of pictures in "Mirrors and Windows," but he does not seem to have understood the extent or direction of this change in American art. He mainly argued that in the quarter-century before "Mirrors and Windows," photography had moved from "public to private concerns."[51] Recalling the serious, broadly based social concern of Farm Security Administration and Depression-era American photography, Szarkowski stated that "The Family of Man" exhibition marked the end of the period in which photographers willingly submerged their personal interests to a larger goal. For him, the two major tendencies of new photography could be found in the realistic yet personal pictures of such photographers as Robert Frank and the romantic and spiritual approach typified by Minor White. As he wrote, "neither pretended to offer a comprehensive or authoritative view of the world, or a program for its improvement."[52]

Szarkowski's emphasis on the unique formal properties of photography helped to promote the institutional life of photography in museums and universities. Founded in 1937, the Department of Photography at the Museum of Modern Art, New York, became the major arbiter of trends in the United States during the postwar period.

In 1947, George Eastman House in Rochester, New York, named for the Kodak Corporation's founder, began collecting and archiving historic film and photography under the guiding hand of historian Beaumont Newhall. Especially in the 1960s, departments of photography were established at numerous American colleges and universities to teach what was regarded then as an independent medium with its own distinctive history and methods.

The Society for Photographic Education, an organization of photographers, writers, historians, and curators that came together in 1963, was originally formed on similar assumptions. In other words, just as many image-makers were starting to explore the persuasiveness of mass-media photography, which made the world seem "already seen," the leading photographic institutions were grounding the medium's existence as an academic and museum subject in the notion of its uniqueness.

RETAKE

The climate of cultural alienation that followed World War II found expression in the photography of mavericks like Robert Frank, Diane Arbus, and William Klein. Street photography flourished as image-makers prowled the big cities and small towns detecting loneliness and despair in an age of growing material abundance. The television set, photographed by many photographers in the period, brought people indoors to a darkened room, where they silently listened and did not look at each other. Along with suburban tract homes in which sidewalks had been eliminated, television came to symbolize what sociologist David Riesman characterized as American's postwar condition: the lonely crowd. Photographers captured the Civil Rights movement and the persistent conflict in Vietnam, which unsettled the nation. While their images continued to be shown in newspapers and magazines, television emerged as a major outlet for photographic work. In addition, during the postwar period, photography made a big move into both museums and universities. Propelled by photographers and artists who made photographs, the medium's range was newly viewed as extending beyond reportage and realism to the range of theory and expression accorded other art media. In the work of artists such as Robert Smithson, Chuck Close, Andy Warhol, and Robert Rauschenberg, the emergence of a multimedium or transmedium, embracing several art media, began to appear.

philosophy and practice

Purity and Diversity

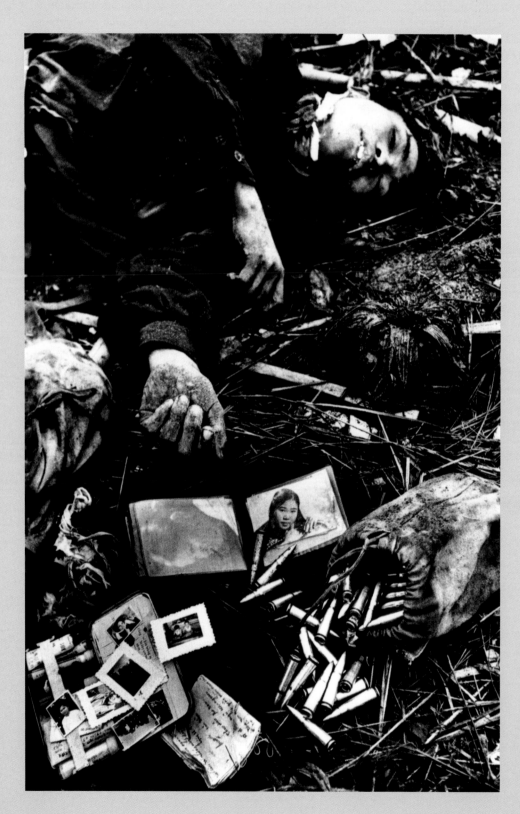

11.74
DON MCCULLIN, *Corpse of North Vietnamese Soldier*, 1968. Copy-negative print.

McCullin juxtaposed the grisly corpse of a fallen North Vietnamese soldier with his personal effects, including photographs and letters, scattered on the ground by plundering American soldiers who did not find them valuable. McCullin admitted this was the only time in his career that he composed a picture, by gathering the objects strewn about and moving them close to the corpse.

In his influential books and exhibitions at New York's Museum of Modern Art, John Szarkowski both recorded and helped shape the dimensions of photographic practice. He underscored photography's shift away from imaging the public realm and social conditions. He sensed that picture magazines were failing in the 1960s—even before *Life* magazine suspended publication in 1972. Indeed, he contended that photo-essays strained beyond their capacity to inform. How could W. Eugene Smith define the ancient culture of a Spanish village in a mere seventeen images? In particular, Szarkowski pointed to "photography's failure to explain large public issues" such as the Vietnam War. He claimed that neither the images of British war photographer Don McCullin (Fig. 11.74) nor those of Larry Burrows (see Fig. 11.44) could even "begin to serve either as explication or symbol for that enormity." Instead, he proposed that the shock of the war was best communicated by the psychologically expressive photographs of Diane Arbus.[53]

For Szarkowski, photography's shrinking authority was due in part to the success of television and to air travel, which made the world seem less exotic. But the basic conundrum was what he perceived to be the inherent limitations of photography. "Most issues of importance," Szarkowski concluded, "cannot be photographed." The world-renowned photograph showing the moment when Jack Ruby shot President John F. Kennedy's alleged assassin, Lee Harvey Oswald, showed a man in pain, but did not—and could not—explain the political and emotional significance of the event[54] (Fig. 11.75).

Szarkowski seems to have ignored the extent to which the emergence of screen culture—that is, the collective environment of projected images found on television, movies, videos, slides, and nascent computer screens—was rapidly altering audience expectations and assumptions. Increasingly, photographers,

artists, and viewers tended to experience the screen as one medium—a heterogeneous blend of projected pictures. The era's media guru, Marshall McLuhan (1911–1980), understood the potency of the media melange, which prompted him to revive a faith in the direct educational powers of media similar to that found in the 1858 issue of the *Athenaeum*, which envisioned young lower-class British lads imaginatively rambling around Egypt by way of the stereograph (see pp. 78–81). Of course, McLuhan got it wrong when he argued that the medium was the message, meaning that the subject of a work was inextricably linked to its means of broadcast, and that the means was more important than the subject. The so-called "cool," disjointed style of television was easily adapted into what McLuhan had thought to be the "hot," or linear character of photography. Indeed, Robert Frank's *The Americans* had the loose, jumpy quality McLuhan felt typified television.

Yet unlike Szarkowski, McLuhan sensed the emergence of global culture and a fusion of the arts, instigated by the widespread use of electronic media. Overinfatuated with media, he was nonetheless attuned to the heightened attractiveness of pluralist approaches and multimedia techniques in the arts, especially those emerging in the late 1960s and early 1970s. Artists were actively looking into what was then called intermedia, combinations of older media such as photography and paint with sound, theater, dance, and newer media such as film and video. By contrast, Szarkowski promoted photography as a unique and pure picture-making process. The conflict of the absolute and the diverse played out in photographic practice and theory throughout the last decades of the twentieth century. In the end, it seems that pure photography was simply one element in a varied and globalizing enterprise.

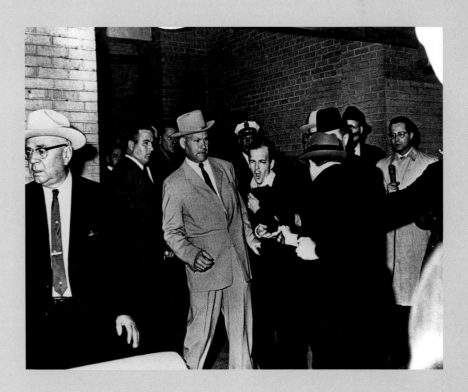

11.75
BOB JACKSON, *Lee Harvey Oswald Shot*, 1963.
Gelatin silver print.

PART SIX

Convergences (1975 to the Present)

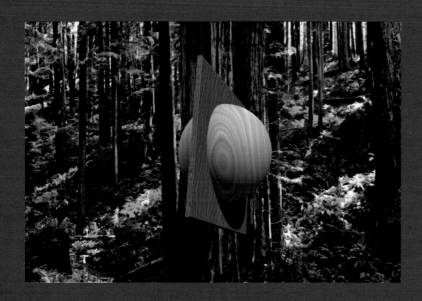

The worldwide convergence of political accords, economic networks, and cultural creations has been escalating for about five hundred years. Nevertheless, people living in the last decades of the twentieth century experienced a globalization that outpaced the past. Advances in communications expedited commercial and cultural exchanges to the speed of computers, aided by the concomitant storage capacity of "the cloud." The integration of financial markets and trade agreements, such as happened in the European Union, stimulated the production and sale of consumer goods, and made globalization a key marketing term. Thus the financial crisis that began in 2008 had a global reach. Record numbers of skilled workers and manual laborers migrated around the world in search of employment. This unprecedented international mobility of people, money, and materials was a key function of globalization, which also encouraged a transnational perspective on such issues as global warming.

The decline of the picture magazine after World War II, and the associated rise of television news, shrank the number of outlets available for documentary and photojournalistic images. Newspaper and magazine photo editors increasingly prescribed the exact subject and style they wanted from photographs, thereby cramping the individual initiative of photojournalists. To a greater degree than in the past, editors rather than photographers chose which, if any, of the images submitted would be published. Yet as newspapers and magazines called for fewer photographs, the possibilities to publish images on the Web greatly multiplied.

Culturally, globalization saw some national and ethnic cultural practices being amalgamated into internationally appreciated forms. World music, a blending of Caribbean, African, and other local musical styles with rock and roll, was heard all over the planet. Conceptual art continued to become a globally available but locally defined set of parameters (see p. 376). Conceptualism's emphasis on art as idea continues to be expressed in photography, film, and video, and has proved adaptable to specific circumstances. As Cuban photography curator Cristina Vives Gutiérrez observed, Conceptualism is an attitude about the function of art, not a clearly identifiable visual style. Its manifestations can be remarkably diverse.[1]

The outlines of digital photographic practice change rapidly, and predictions for the digital future abound. History teaches that it often takes decades for a society to relinquish and revise symbols and ideas. Indeed, societies find it difficult and painful to reach consensus about visual symbols, as shown by the prolonged debate about the plans for new buildings and memorials on the New York City site of the September 11 attacks.

The gradual amalgamation of art photography and photojournalism begun in the twentieth century continues in the twenty-first, aided by the ongoing spread of electronic means of communication. Screen culture, once a term in art theory, has been realized in the daily experience of most people. In this fresh setting, photography has become immaterial—that is, decreasingly printed for everyday use. News-based websites thrive, expanding access to the shots taken by a photographer on assignment and by a citizen who happens to be carrying a camera-phone or digital camera. Around the world, camera-phone images are beamed from person to person. One thing is certain: the proliferation of digital cameras and easy uplinks to the Internet have created more photographers than ever before.

12.1
MARTIN PARR, *Tupperware Party*, **1985, from his book** *The Cost of Living*, **1989.**

While listening to a Tupperware demonstrator, the women in the audience display contrasting expressions of polite boredom. Unlike many other photographers of his generation, Parr admires these visual anecdotes and seeks them out.

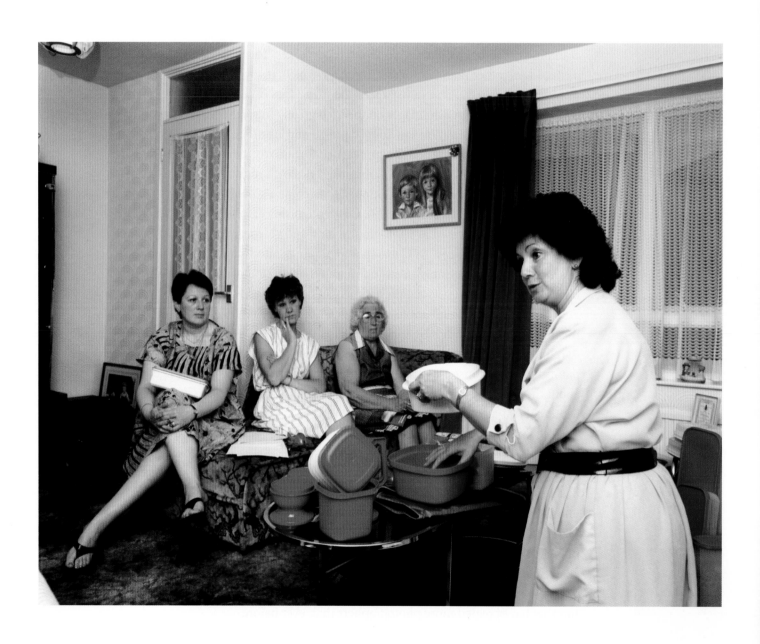

CHAPTER TWELVE

Globalism, Technology, and Social Change

The promises and threats associated with globalization were frequently voiced together in the late twentieth century. Vast global systems seemed to endanger the significance of individual human lives, yet paradoxically provide the means for small cultural groups to maintain their identity. As happened in the era after World War II, cultural and personal identity within a dominant group was a major theme explored by photographers. Similarly, social and personal memories couched in photographs found new existences in artistic expression. As the crises brought on by global warming received more public attention, and the progress in scientific research—like DNA imaging—became better known, photographs by artists took up scientific subject matter. Of course, the most pervasive scientifically based change for photography was the explosion of digital devices for creating and disseminating images. Photographers were among the earliest users of computer-generated images, and they helped to shape their social, as well as artistic, applications. Knowing the means of making and distributing digital images allowed photographers to become cautious critics of potential misuses.

PHOTOGRAPHY AND THE GLOBAL EXPERIENCE

The architectural manifestations of globalization and their impact on people were rendered by German photographer Andreas Gursky (b. 1955) in huge photographs of large contemporary public buildings, such as the Hong Kong Stock Exchange and the German Bundestag or parliament building (Fig. 12.30). Gursky, who studied with Bernd and Hilla Becher, makes images that are simultaneously glamorous and ominous. He favors architectural subjects such as big hotels, office buildings, and stock exchanges that cater to global capitalism. His large photographs, sometimes 10 feet wide, approach the size of historical paintings, and shine with intense color, like that used in William Eggleston's work, which influenced Gursky.

Despite their loud colors, these large prints have a neutral quality, owing to the physical distance of the camera from the subject, and to their high finish, like commercial work, which sometimes makes them look like large pieces of colored plastic. Gursky's images are frequently computer-modified and printed with the aid of computer software, making use of the vast array of new tools for picture-making available to photographers in the digital age. During the last years of the twentieth century, it was often remarked that large photographs like Gursky's put color photography on the physical scale of nineteenth-century history paintings. In that sense, Gursky may be described as an artist who paints with pixels. Nevertheless, he rejects that label and maintains that the heart of his work is photography not post-production editing tools.

Globalization has not meant the total homogenization of cultural values and expression. Despite the proliferation of American popular culture, economic globalization is not yet synonymous with cultural identity. Corporate logos and consumer goods reach into every corner of the world, yet some aspects of cultural experience remain local, regional, and national. Indigenous ways of life have been cruelly disrupted, even destroyed, by the invasion of Western media, yet others have found satellite broadcasts and the Internet to be potent countervailing forces. Globalization seems often to have heightened awareness of regional life and locales. In effect, globalization has been accompanied by an ongoing negotiation of cultural difference, and in that sense cultural globalism is different from economic domination. The extinction of many of the world's languages through the historical process of colonization, and the rise of global media outlets that promote English, now either the first or second language of much of the commercial and scientific worlds, have been met with resistance in areas where language signifies cultural attainment to its speakers. Thus Catalans in Spain use television to maintain the vigor of their language, and Inuits in northern Canada keep the Inuktituk language alive through satellite broadcasts to far-flung settlements. The notion that global capitalism can be tailored to specific cultural settings is clearly problematic—but it has remained popular nonetheless. Russians repeatedly voiced a desire for global ties shaped by a distinctly Russian capitalism that would protect the singularity of the indigenous culture. Similarly, social thinkers in India called for a uniquely Indian modernization that would reject certain industrial and technological pathways as inappropriately Western.[1] In the midst of intense commodification of goods and services, Cuban-born American artist Felix Gonzales-Torres (1957–1996) stacked inexpensively printed black-and-white prints on paper in a gallery and allowed visitors to take one (Fig. 12.2). Likewise, he installed wrapped candies on the gallery floor. By allowing them to take a printed sheet or eat a sweet, Gonzalez-Torres not only made the passive visitor a collaborator, but also created a challenge to the valuation of art objects by the market. His use of clouds for the subject of his photograph recalls Alfred Stieglitz's reply to the accusation that he had special access to great subject matter. Referring to his series *Equivalents* (see p. 184–85), Stieglitz famously pointed out that clouds were freely available to all photographers.

Ironically, the compression of time and space made possible by jet travel and instant electronic communication has enabled transient workers to maintain active ties with political, cultural, and religious practices in their home countries or ethnic groups. By contrast, the European immigrants photographed by Lewis Hine (see Fig. 7.8) shortly after their passage through New York's customs station on Ellis Island might have to wait months for a letter from family and friends back home. Whereas, in the past, moving to a new country often meant severing ties, an immigrant traveling to the United States today can (money permitting) phone home from the plane, or send photographs by email or other application from a computer or a smart phone. Free email accounts and access to the Internet through public libraries and other agencies let new immigrants stay in touch with their homelands and read electronic newspapers in their native languages.

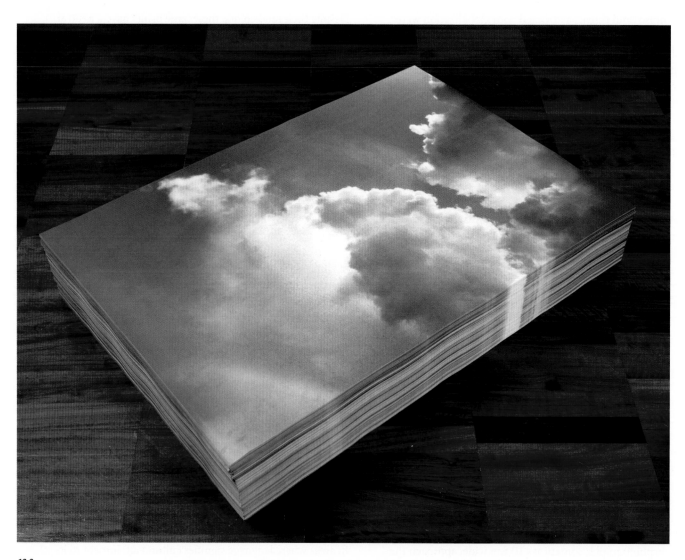

12.2
FELIX GONZALEZ-TORRES, *Untitled (Aparición)*, 1991. Print on paper, endless copies. 8 in. (20.3 cm) at ideal heght x 28.5 x 43 in. (72.4 x 109.2 cm) (original paper size). © The Felix Gonzalez-Torres Foundation. Courtesy of Andrea Rosen Gallery, New York.

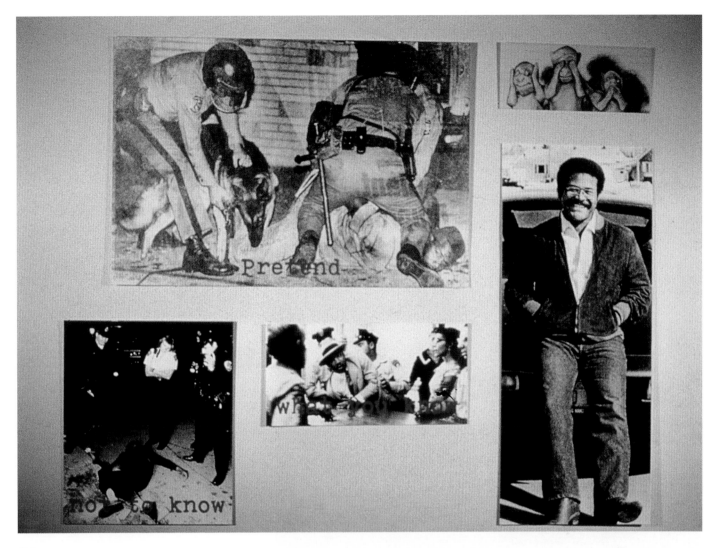

12.3
ADRIAN PIPER, *Pretend No. 3*, 1990. Four black-and-white photographs, one pencil drawing on graph paper, silkscreened texts.

To suggest that the public regularly denied the violence against protesters during the American Civil Rights movement, Piper superimposed red-lettered captions on news photographs, and included a line drawing of the monkeys who, in the popular saying, "see no evil, hear no evil, and speak no evil."

As never before, hybrid cultural identities can be maintained through generations. An Italian-American immigrant during Lewis Hine's time probably did not become fully assimilated into American culture, but the children and grandchildren of immigrants did. In the late twentieth century, however, immigrants and their descendants could choose to hover between the cultural and ethnic identity of their families and the culture of their new country.

Migrations of people from place to place, whether in order to to seek work, escape famine, or flee political tumult and repression, became frequent photographic subjects, both for photojournalists and for those photographers who experienced cultural dislocation first-hand. Writing about her own sense of displacement, the Korean-born image-maker Young Kim (b. 1955) noted, "My work reflects the continuous process of negotiating between two cultures. It is based on my experience of immigration and of locating myself in relation to ever-changing definitions of home in personal, social, and cultural contexts."[2]

Crossing borders was a characteristic of photographic practice itself in the late twentieth century. By the mid-1970s, photography had moved squarely into the art world, and artists active in other media integrated photography into their work, either through the direct use of the medium or by making reference to the ubiquitous presence of camera-generated pictures in the contemporary world. As it had been for sculptor Robert Smithson, photography continued to be an adjunct to late twentieth-century artists working primarily in other media, such as sculptors Kiki Smith (b. 1954) and Damien Hirst (b. 1964). Multimedia artists such as Sophie Calle (b. 1953) regularly depended on the camera to record their performance pieces and installations. Video-maker Matthew Barney (b. 1964) recorded ephemeral work and printed stills from his videos, while Adrian Piper (b. 1948) easily moves among performance, installation,

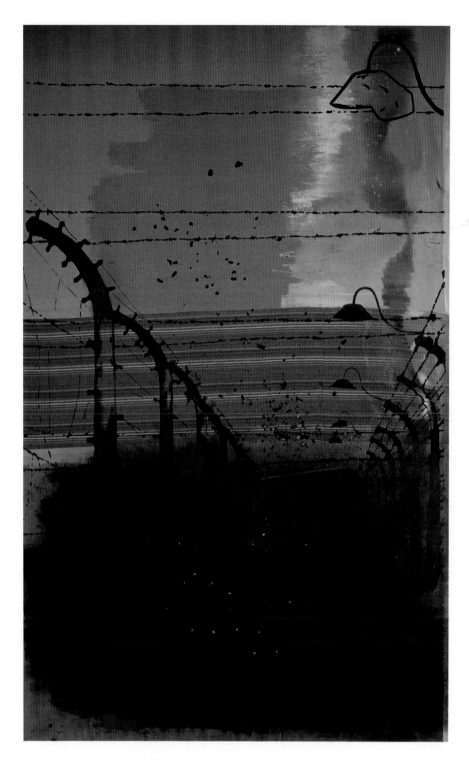

12.4
SIGMAR POLKE, *Lager,* **1982. Acrylic and various pigments
on fabric, 158 × 98 in. (401.4 × 250 cm).**

Polke worked on unprimed canvas so that his pigments would
seep through the fibers like a stain. In this image, the stain
courses through an image of a German concentration camp.

video, and photography (Fig. 12.3). Sigmar Polke (1941–2010)
made reference to the ominous overhead lights and the barbed-
wire enclosure of concentration camps as shown in postwar news
photographs (Fig. 12.4). Likely enough, photographers sensed
this openness, and some, such as Yinka Shonibare (see p. 459),
moved into sculpture and installation work.

Throughout the Western world, artists who came of age after
the skirmishes to confirm photography as an art medium found
the camera to be an exciting picture-making process, whose full
potential had not been explored. German artists Anselm Kiefer
(b. 1945) (Fig. 12.5) and Gerhard Richter (b. 1932) (see p. 444)
employed photography in their image-making, largely without
reference to the celebrated masterworks of photographic history,
or the reigning technical standards of photographic image
production. British artist David Hockney (b. 1937) collaged
sequences of snapshots or Polaroid prints, creating a total picture
that contains myriad alterations of the angle of view and distance
from the subject, in conscious reference to early twentieth-

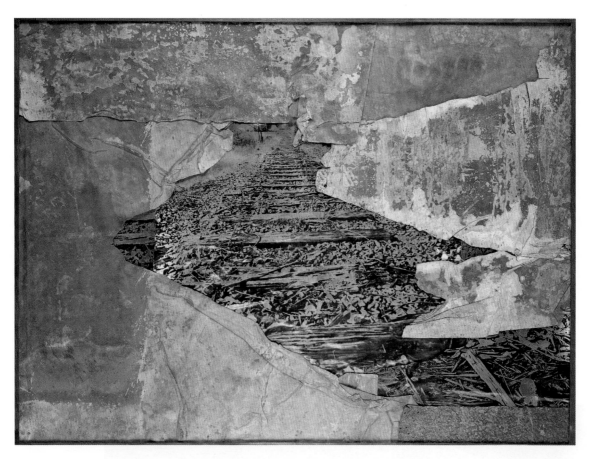

12.5
ANSELM KIEFER, *Siegfried's Difficult Way to Brünhilde*, 1988. Lead and photo in a glazed steel frame.

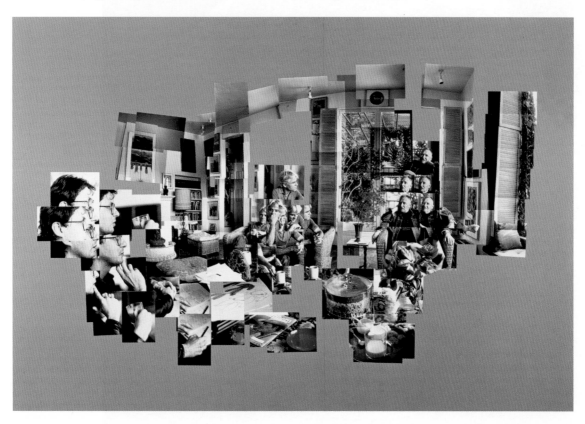

12.6
DAVID HOCKNEY, *Christopher Isherwood Talking to Bob Holman*, Santa Monica, California, March 14, 1983, 1983. Photographic collage.

century Cubist painting and collage (Fig. 12.6). Sliced, crumbled, overprinted, underexposed, blurred, and even cameraless, photography was welcome in the art world.

Once a simple means to record performance art, photography gradually became integral to the initial conception of performance pieces. For French performance artist Orlan (b. 1947), photographs are indispensable traces of the repeated surgical remodeling done on her face to make it resemble famous art-historical versions of feminine beauty. Submitting to the surgeon's knife in cumulative stages, rather than in a single operation, Orlan targets the incessant, intense longing for perfection some feel about their physical appearance. She has used video, photography, and most recently DIGITAL IMAGING to record and investigate the surgical transformation of her face (Fig. 12.7).

The continuing assimilation of photography into the art world was only one of the many camerawork convergences during the period. Photojournalism and documentary work blended with each other, and with art photography. Fashion and celebrity photography adopted techniques from art photography,

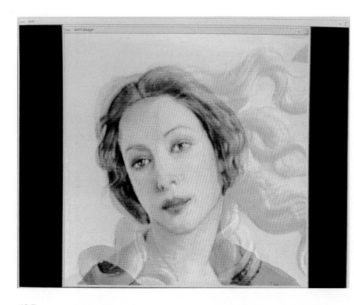

12.7
ORLAN, *Omniprésence Vénus*, 2001. Composite photograph.

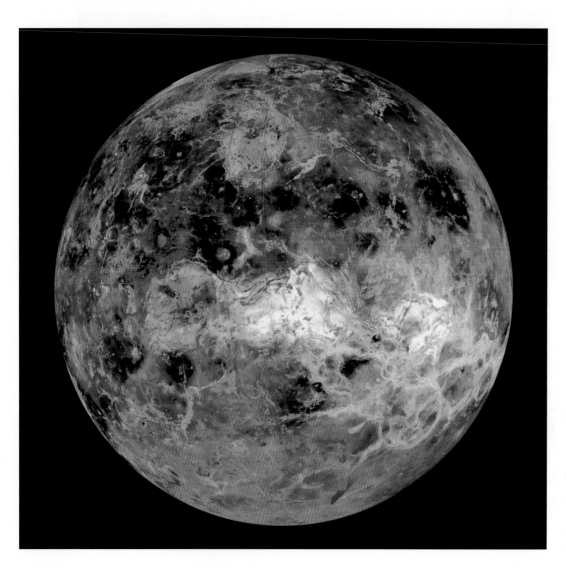

12.8
NASA, *View of Venus*, May 26, 1993.

This image was produced by the Magellan science team at the Jet Propulsion Laboratory in Pasadena. Simulated color was used to enhance small-scale details. The bright area near the center is Ovda Regio, a mountainous area of Venus. The dark areas reveal the results of meteorite collisions.

and art photographers mined the methods of fashion and celebrity images for the sake of social commentary. In addition, advertising photography sometimes took up social issues and the visual language of documentary photography. The effects of these new hybrids are still unfolding, but the preliminary outlines of the changes wrought by these convergences are apparent in a number of new configurations, including the new alignment of photography and science, and, of course, the digital revolution.

PHOTOGRAPHY, NATURE, AND SCIENCE

The relationship between photography, a technologically based medium, and advancements in science has long been a matter of concern. More than a century ago, Peter Henry Emerson asserted that photography had to reject the canons of established art and follow the cutting edge of science for up-to-the-minute instructions on how a photograph should look. Today, the human relationship to nature and to science is examined from a point of view far from Emerson's understanding. Some

contemporary observers, such as Jungian psychologist James Hillman, see science not as an ever-unfolding source of aesthetic options, but as an immense force that demystifies nature and thereby stifles human perception of beauty in nature.[3]

As we learn more about the depletion of the rainforests, global warming, and the extinction of species, and take an expanded custodial attitude toward the planet, the wonder born of innocence and detachment from nature is likely to change (Fig. 12.8). People unable to experience feelings of awe in their regular surroundings tend to seek amplified experiences. In the United States, national parks such as Yosemite that offer extremes of natural magnitude in sheer cliff walls and waterfalls have become overcrowded. Another response is conveyed in Derek Johnston's image of Havisu Falls, near the Grand Canyon in Arizona. In the image, wild nature is bottled and displayed as a specimen contained in a plain gallon jug (Fig. 12.9).

Where nineteenth-century scientific inquiry focused on the visible manifestations of nature, such as geological transformation and biological evolution, in the twentieth and twenty-first centuries attention turned to the invisible yet

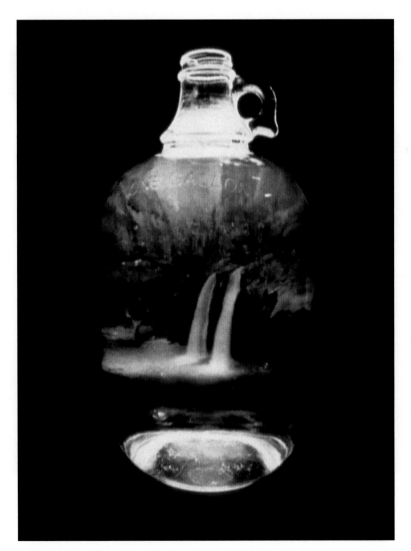

12.9
DEREK JOHNSTON, *Landscape Specimen 004 (Havisu Falls),* 1996. Hand-coated platinum/ palladium print. Museum of Contemporary Photography, Chicago, Illinois.

Johnston pictures Havisu Falls, on the sacred land of the Havisu (Native American people living in Arizona), confined within a manufactured container. The image alludes both to the late twentieth century's notion of nature as an invalid in need of human care, and to the artificial boundaries of the Indian reservation where the waterfall is located.

crucial building-blocks of nature, from subatomic particles to the human genome. For South African-born New York City resident Gary Schneider (b. 1954), science and technology have permanently altered the portrait, shifting it away from external appearances—a traditional source of beauty—to the irreducible kernel of identity lodged in the human chromosome (Fig. 12.10).[4] As historian and curator Ann Thomas observed, Schneider's series of photographs *Genetic Self-Portrait* is simultaneously a depiction of his uniqueness and a portrait of our time, which tries to square cultural conditioning with the strength and scope of biological determinism, implied by the fact that, across the human spectrum, individual differences reside in only 1 per cent of our genetic make-up.[5] Despite its title, Schneider's series extends beyond nuggets of genetic information to personal interpretation. Simply prepared photograms of Schneider's hands and ears accompany chromosome sequences. The medium he uses—the PLATINUM PRINT—was a favorite of the Pictorialists.

High-resolution, often computer-aided microscopic imaging allows the eye to look through the body at its smallest particles. The increasingly common experience of viewing DNA, in both the scientific community and the public realm, marks another

crucial stage in the historical process of seeing inside the body, which began with the X-ray and now includes such techniques as magnetic resonance imaging (MRI), positron emission tomography (PET), and ultrasound scanning. Each of these techniques employs non-photographic means that are translated into computer-enhanced images, which are informally called pictures or photographs. TOMOGRAPHY, an advanced X-ray process, produces thin cross-sections of the body, not just from one point of view, like a photograph, but from 360 degrees. The option to create 2D or 3D images is rapidly increasing. The ongoing Visible Human Project combines photography with the latest imaging devices to draw together an exhaustive archive of cross-sections of the human body to be used for medical research (Fig. 12.11).

The dual response of fascination and revulsion that such investigations into the natural world can inspire has been taken up by American Catherine Chalmers (b. 1957). She poses home-raised insects, such as cockroaches and praying mantises, in front of shiny white backgrounds, as if they were fashion models (Fig. 12.12). In her series of images called *Food Chain*, Chalmers adapted fashion photography to the diminutive realm of rapacious insects, which reduce each other to scattered limbs.

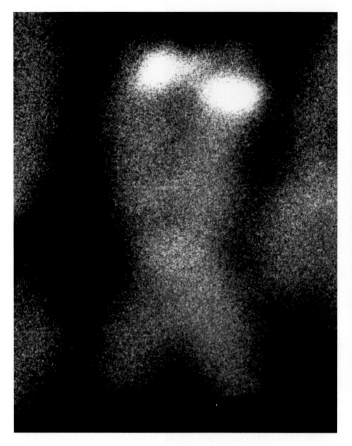
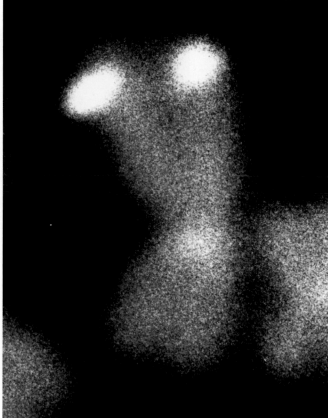

12.10
GARY SCHNEIDER, *Pair of Tumor Suppressor Genes on Chromosome 11*, 1997. Platinum print.

Schneider used sophisticated scientific imaging processes to obtain pictures of his chromosomes, which he then reclaimed as art by printing them using the platinum process.

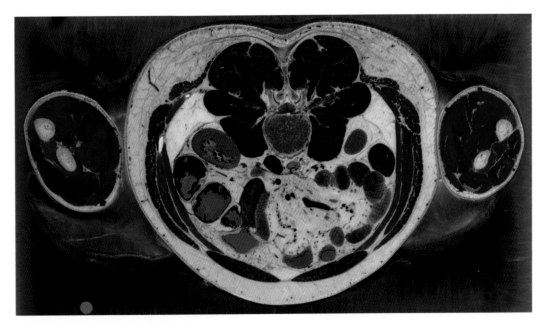

12.11
STANFORD UNIVERSITY, *The Stanford Visible Male*, from the Visible Human Project™, National Library of Medicine, 1990s. Stanford University, California.

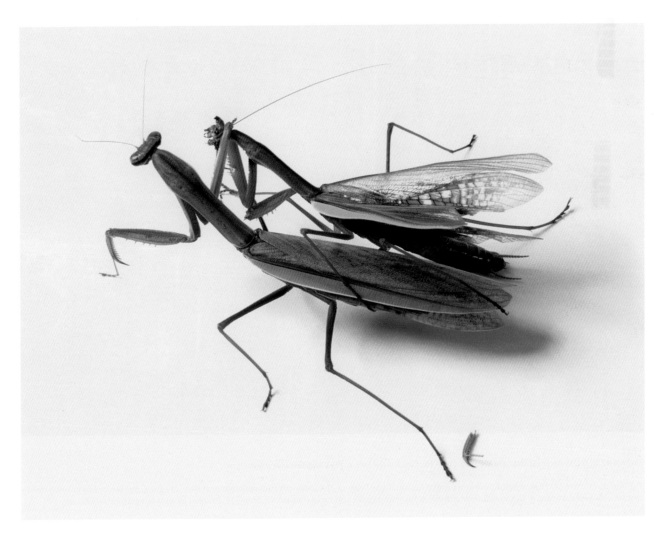

12.12
CATHERINE CHALMERS, *Bug from Food Chain*, 1994–96. Massachusetts Museum of Contemporary Art, North Adams, Massachusetts.

By contrast, Suzanne Bloom (b. 1943) and Ed Hill (b. 1935), pioneers in DIGITAL IMAGING who work under the name MANUAL, see an encouraging watershed moment in humankind's relationship to nature presaged by digital information and imagery. Using image-manipulation software, they made combination-pictures of forests and abstract shapes (Fig. 12.13). Their installation of these photographs, titled *The Constructed Forest,* was subtitled (*This is the End—Let's Go On—El Lissitzky*). It seized the Russian artist's idea that a new society must renounce the old Romantic art of self-expression and embrace industry and machine art, including photography, as the new wave of the future.

For MANUAL, photography is an impotent Romantic art, and the computer a means through which social progress might be made. Nature and culture—the forest and a new, digital art—come together in MANUAL's work, pointing away from the old promise of industrialization toward the positive potential of cyberspace.

No other technological innovation in the history of photography, a medium regularly jolted by inventions and their commercialization, brought on such drastic conjectures about the future as did electronic or digital imaging. Computer-assisted picture-making made a largely unremarked-upon appearance in a 1966 work by American John Mott-Smith (b. 1930), shown in John Szarkowski's 1978 book *Mirrors and Windows.* Extensive discussion about the social consequences of computer-manipulated images sprang not directly from art practice, but from the public's reaction to stunning special effects in such movies as the *Star Wars* series, which began in 1977, and through the rapid spread of computers in the late twentieth century, which supplied the print and broadcast media with enhanced capacity to alter photographs easily and expertly.

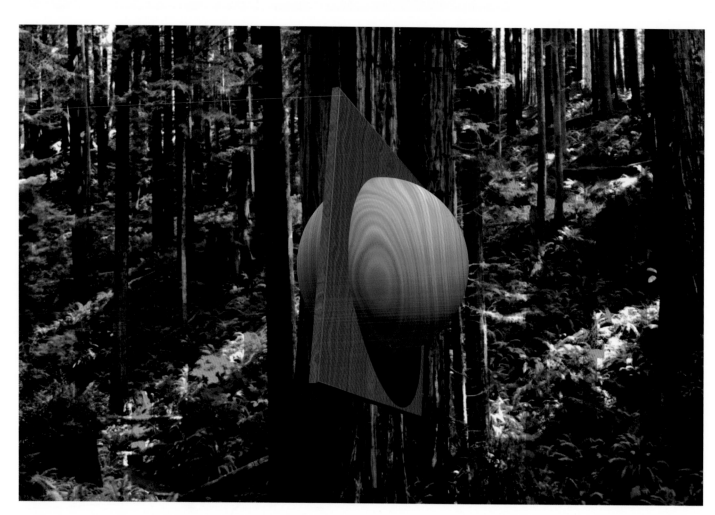

12.13
SUZANNE BLOOM AND ED HILL (MANUAL), From *The Constructed Forest*, 1993. Digital color print.

The duo that formed MANUAL helped pioneer art applications of digital imagery. This image combines conventional views of nature, represented by growing trees, with images that look like wood, but are, in fact, computer inventions. It suggests that the next social transformation will be achieved by embracing digital technology.

When the cover picture of the February 1982 issue of *National Geographic* showed two of the famous pyramids at Giza in Egypt somewhat closer together than they actually are, digital imaging overstepped a previously inconspicuous line between socially accepted fiction, such as *Star Wars*, and unacceptable tampering with the appearance of optical reality. *National Geographic* gave the public the jitters about the capacity for computer-assisted pictures to lie.

POST-PHOTOGRAPHY

THE END

In 1839, when photography was disclosed to the world, painter Paul Delaroche, a supporter of photography, is rumored to have declared, "From today, painting is dead." The attribution is probably apocryphal,[6] and in any event painting is still a very living art. Nevertheless, the remark became part of photographic folklore and has been repeatedly enlisted to insinuate that an ironic, cosmic cadence is at work in the history of the medium. If painting was killed by photography, then photography may be destined to die by means of a new medium. For example, while lauding the success of color photography in a 1985 issue of *Creative Camera*, Susan Butler claimed that "From today black-and-white is dead." Before long, all of photography would be declared vanquished at the hands of an even more robust and welcome reformer.

In the 1990s, the critic Nicholas Mirzoeff looked back and identified traditional camerawork's time of demise, announcing that "photography met its own death some time in the 1980s at the hands of computer imaging."[7] Likewise, William J. Mitchell, an early advocate of digital manipulation at the Massachusetts Institute of Technology in Cambridge, paraphrased Delaroche, announcing in 1992 that "from this moment on, photography is dead—or more precisely, radically and permanently redefined as was painting one hundred and fifty years before."[8]

A more measured yet minority view was expressed by Spanish photographer and critic Joan Fontcuberta (see p. 449), who noted that, because the computer has become "a sophisticated technological prosthesis we cannot do without," it was not surprising that artists would use it as an accessory to their work, like a filter or a telephoto lens.[9] Fontcuberta pointed out that previous technological improvements did not fundamentally alter the medium, and that "the metamorphosis from silver grains to pixels is not itself that significant." After all, he cautioned, "the silver-grained structure of actual photographs has already been replaced in the print media by the photomechanical dot."[10] Moreover, he reasoned, from its inception, all photography has been "altered" in the sense that the camera frames and focuses on a chosen subject, thus eliminating other topics. Manipulation, Fontcuberta argued, "is exempt of moral value." What should be judged is the intent of the manipulation, not the process itself.[11]

Deceitful photographs, perhaps the most prominent concern from the mid-1980s to the early 1990s, did not start with the computer. In the 1870s, photographer Eugène Appert staged scenes with actors and used old-fashioned cut-and-paste methods on the resultant photographs to contrive subtle political propaganda for the forces opposing the French Commune. Comparable attempts to alter recorded history were made on behalf of Joseph Stalin during his dictatorial rule in the U.S.S.R. from 1929 to 1953. Officials such as Leon Trotsky (1879–1940) who fell from favor were physically eliminated and their portraits were airbrushed out of group photographs.[12] Still, the availability of the means to falsify photographs does not mean that photographs will be routinely adulterated.

Anxiety about the effects of digital technology was the latest appearance of photography's oldest ghost, technological determinism, which continued to evoke illusory beliefs that, in its relative simplicity, past photography was more innocent than contemporary modes, and that "straight" photography is the norm of camerawork. During the 1980s and 1990s, concern for the possibly malevolent effects of computer-manipulated photographs overshadowed other powerful ways in which photographs have been and will continue to be deceptive. Omitting images, such as the scenes of forced labor that Aleksandr Rodchenko excluded from his series on the building of the White Sea Canal (see pp. 240), can be as deceitful as reshaping pictures. Moreover, in a medium that thrives in multiples, a potential taken further by computer replication, important subjects can be hidden in plain sight in the midst of a plethora of distracting pictures.

Analyses of photographs of the Gulf War (1990–91) reveal that news magazines such as *Time*, *Newsweek*, and *U.S. News and World Report* ran pictures of military hardware more than any other subject. Virtually no pictures of actual combat were shown, and the few photographs of American casualties that found their way into print followed the iconography established during the Korean War, as in the image by David Turnley (b. 1955) of a grieving, wounded soldier accompanying the body of a dead comrade on an evacuation helicopter. Most television coverage was of military briefings and interviews with politicians and experts.[13] Nevertheless, the public perception persists that Operation Desert Storm was witnessed up close on television screens across the world. Delaying the publication of pictures is yet another form of concealment.

During the Gulf War, *Time* magazine and the Associated Press wire service (AP) both refused to publish or distribute grisly photographs of the charred bodies of Iraqi troops killed along the so-called "highway of death." Eventually *Time* published one of these pictures, in a year-end round-up issue, about nine months after the war. Potentially, computer-assisted and disseminated images may fall into any or all of these modes of misrepresentation. Indeed, computer-assisted photographs have largely followed paths already well trodden by past photographic practice.

The Dystopian Series, created by Aziz and Cucher (American Anthony Aziz, b. 1961, and Venezuelan Sammy Cucher, b. 1958) captured the persistent fear that digital technologies pose a threat that is muffled by enthusiasm for technological advancement.

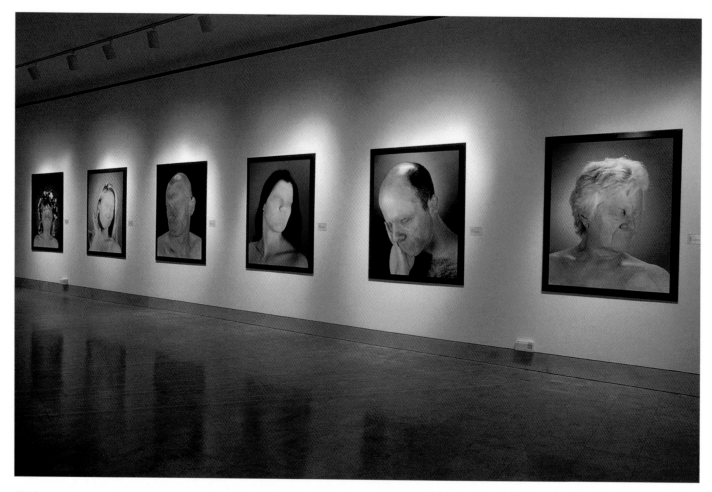

12.14
AZIZ AND CUCHER, *Dystopia,* **1994. Installation at the Jack Shainman Gallery, New York. Digital prints.**

Through digital means, Aziz and Cucher create portraits in which one can see the freckles and wrinkles on the faces of sitters whose senses have been blocked by computer-generated tissue, so as to make the sitters seem cut off from direct experience of the world.

In their large prints, sitters pose thoughtfully, while computer-generated skin closes their eyes, mouths, and ears (Fig. 12.14). These "desensitized" humans, whose minds are cut off from direct perception of the world, stand for the pair's suspicion of blind faith in digital futures, which they perceive as similar to the naïve confidence that people in the second half of the twentieth century had with regard to the promise of nuclear power and the rewards of space travel. Recognizing that cyberspace brings with it the potential "democratization of the artistic impulse,"[14] they still counsel that uncritical attitudes toward the cyberworld will only deepen the individual self-centeredness promoted by an online life, while diminishing the collective experience they deem crucial to society's welfare. Aziz and Cucher accused technophiles of hymning a new romanticism, drawn from the jargon of biogenetics, computer science, and popular psychology, to exalt "a smooth universe of interfaces, amazing speed, multilocality, and superconductivity, populated by friendly cyborgs, artificially intelligent machines and the shallow creations of our transpersonal selves." "No one seems to care," they admonished, "that this idealized world functions on the basis of extreme human isolation, mediated experience, and global consumerism."[15]

FACE VALUE
The Fall 1993 cover of a special issue of *Time* magazine used computer software to create a female image of multi-ethnic America, combining physical attributes of Anglo-Saxons, Asians, Africans, and Hispanics with those of people from southern Europe and from the Middle East[16] (Fig. 12.15). To keep her from looking like the fabricated product she was, designers gave her an engaging semi-smile, and used shadows to imply the slightly asymmetrical face of real humans. The concept of merging portrait photographs has a long history, going back to the late nineteenth-century combination-portraits of English scientist Francis Galton. During the 1980s, American Nancy Burson (b. 1948) achieved notoriety for her eerie computer-generated composite pictures, which blended the facial features of politicians including Stalin, Mussolini, Mao, Hitler, and Khomeni, or film stars such as Bette Davis, Audrey Hepburn, Grace Kelly, Sophia Loren, and Marilyn Monroe. Her blend of

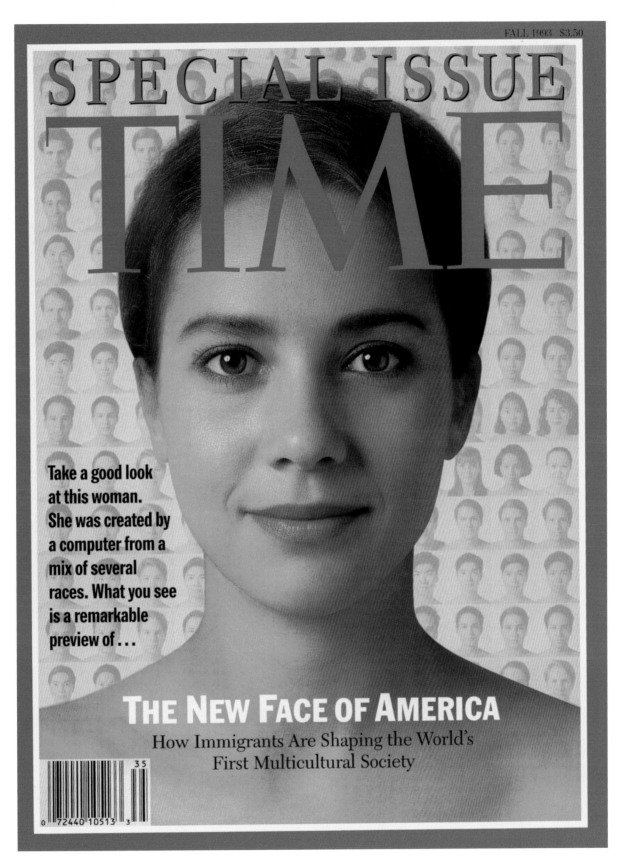

FALL 1993 $3.50

SPECIAL ISSUE
TIME

Take a good look
at this woman.
She was created by
a computer from a
mix of several
races. What you see
is a remarkable
preview of . . .

THE NEW FACE OF AMERICA
How Immigrants Are Shaping the World's
First Multicultural Society

12.15
Time **cover, special issue, Fall 1993.**

Digital combination prints, layering physical aspects of different ethnic groups, proved to be one of the most enticing visual motifs in the last decades of the twentieth century. Fashion photographers such as Hiro did it, photo editors on news magazines called for it, and artists such as Nancy Burson (see Fig. 12.16) explored the overlaid look.

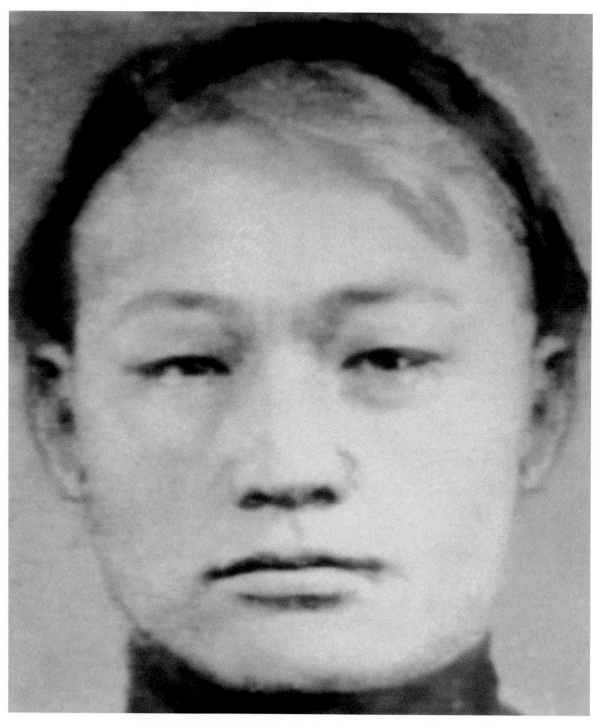

12.16
NANCY BURSON, *Mankind (an Asian, a Caucasian, and a Black blended, weighted according to current population statistics)*, 1983–84. Composite photograph.

Black, Asian, and Caucasian features into an ominous mugshot (Fig. 12.16) struck some critics, such as Allan Sekula (b. 1951), as a pointless use of the computer's skills.

Today, Burson's smudgy black-and-white computer-assisted prints look dated, because more recent digital equipment and software, pioneered in television and advertising production,

offer crisp, ultra-naturalistic, and seamless production values. Contemporary computer imaging in art, journalism, and commerce tends toward sharp realizations, oddly reminiscent of the DAGUERREOTYPE, whose mirror-like surface simultaneously gripped foreground and background visual detail, challenging how the human eye sees. With a little know-how and user-friendly software, the average personal computer user can achieve a professional-looking image. Insofar as image-makers are attracted to changing high-tech systems, they are involved in an incessant and expensive game of catch-up brought about by the vast proliferation of image-enhancing techniques and the rapid obsolescence of software and computers. Today's state-of-the-art gear will soon show up at the recycling center. Even commentators wary of inflated digital enthusiasm were convinced, with Joan Fontcuberta, that "the true computer-photography fusion gives rise to a powerful electronic laboratory, which introduces factors too decisive for us to sustain our conventional views of image making."[17] From the vantage point of 1995, he predicted that the widespread use of digital imaging by amateurs would vanquish the notion of photographic objectivity while permitting a faster and larger dialogue among artists and the public

EVERYTHING OLD IS NEW AGAIN

Describing the work of Mexican artist and photojournalist Pedro Meyer (b. 1935), Joan Fontcuberta observed that his pictures run the gamut from snapshots to digitally altered images that obviously stray far from the appearance of optical reality. In general, that range describes the great extent to which computer-assisted imaging is used in newspapers, books, art, advertising, propaganda, and even pornography. A few photographs are unretouched, while most are adjusted to differing degrees via software programs in what are now called lightrooms, a play on the darkrooms used in the analog film era.

Although it is possible for computers to compile data and create pictures that mimic the appearance of the world without ever using visual bits of information captured from optical reality, at the present time that practice is largely confined to entertainment vehicles, such as animated films and computer games. Most digitally modified pictures are processed so as to make them look more "real," "super-real," even 3D, thereby confounding notions of truth that have freighted the medium from the first. To denote this state of looking real by being enhanced through digital means, Joan Fontcuberta invented the term the "vrai-faux" (true-false) and applied it to Pedro Meyer's particular use of the illusion of three-dimensional, photographic space in his magical, digitally altered photographs (Fig. 12.17).

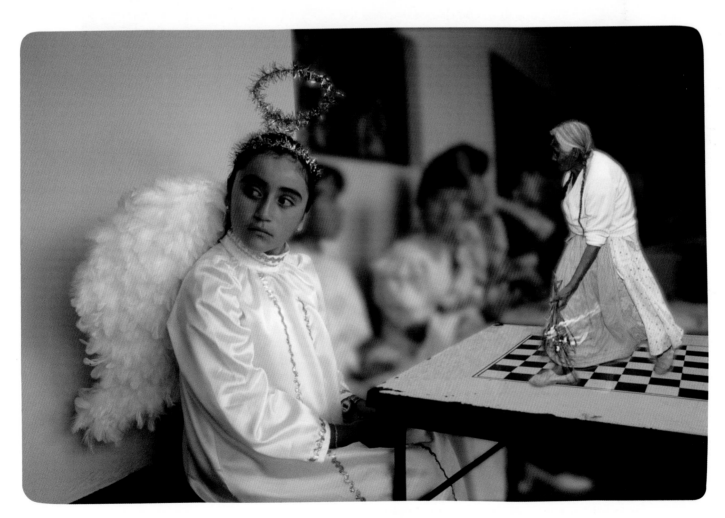

12.17
PEDRO MEYER, *The Temptation of the Angel,* **1991. Digital color print. California Museum of Photography, Riverside, California.**

During the 1990s, Canadian Dyan Marie (b. 1954) began using digital techniques to soften and swirl forms (Fig. 12.18), in the manner of Surrealists such as Salvador Dalí, in whose best-known work, *The Persistence of Memory* (1931), pocket watches melt like warm cheese. The ease with which computer software can appropriate, intermingle, and also dissolve images ensures the perpetuation of Surrealism's taste for the incongruous, what the French poet the Comte de Lautréamont (Isidore Ducasse) (1846–1870) famously called the beautiful "chance encounter of a sewing machine and an umbrella on an operating table" (*Les Chants de Maldoror*, 1868).

Digital processes have also been used by social campaigners and critics such as Hulleah Tsinhnahjinnie (see p. 424), for whom they facilitate copying old photographs and collaging them with bits of appropriated imagery, to create pointed yet humorous indictments of Eurocentric points of view (Fig. 12.19). In his early digital work, Taiwanese artist Chen Chieh-Jen (b. 1960) inserted his own image into disturbing historical images of Chinese history (Fig. 12.20). Like many users of computer-assisted software, Chen painted and drew using a pen attached to a digital touchpad. Some electronic processes rely on a computer mouse to select and merge images, where others depend on traditional manual dexterity. In other words, computer-assisted image production has not completely superseded traditional drafting skills. Perhaps that is one reason why critics lauded Canadian Jeff Wall (b. 1946) for reinventing painting in the 1990s.

Wall continues to work in the system he developed two decades ago. He stages episodes for the camera, and displays the resulting images as large transparencies placed in front of light

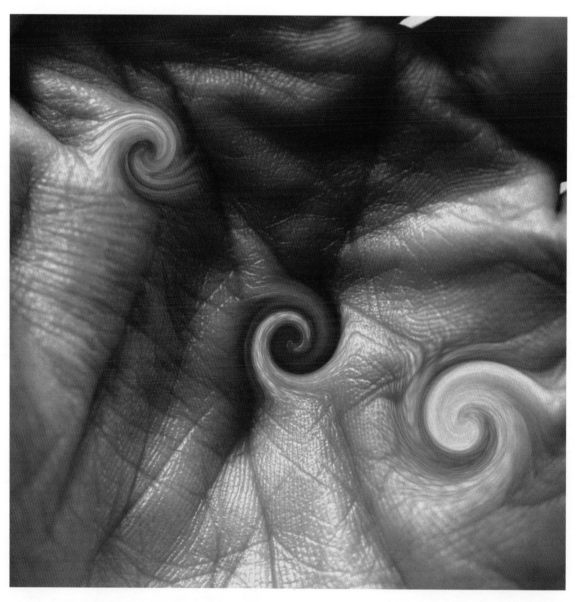

12.18
DYAN MARIE, *Learning to Count THREE: Whirlwind*, **1993. Digital color print.**

Marie's image is an improvisation on the lines of her hand. She uses digital means to deepen crevices into tiny spirals of pliant flesh.

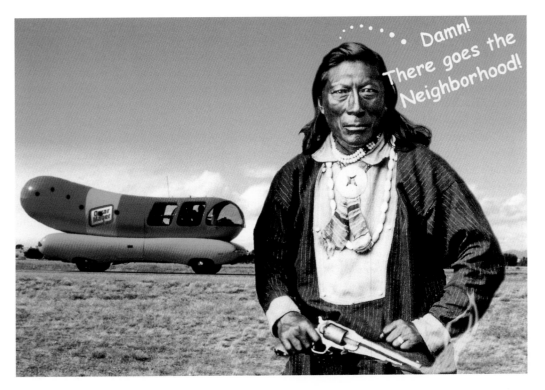

12.19
HULLEAH TSINHNAHJINNIE, *Damn! There Goes the Neighborhood!*, 1998. Digital print.

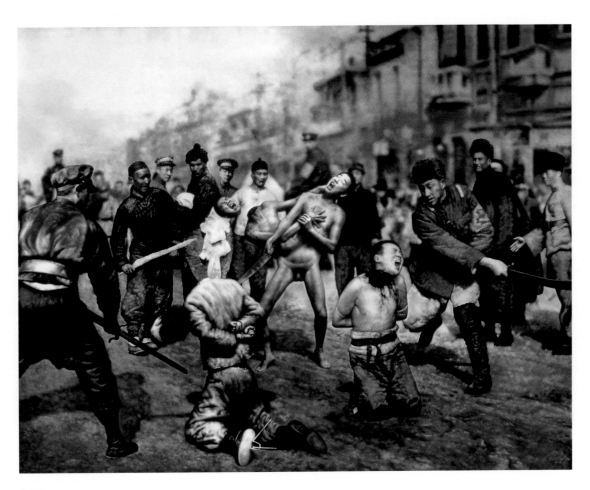

12.20
CHEN CHIEH-JEN, *Self-Destruction*, 1996. Digital print.

boxes, like those used to illuminate advertisements. Sometimes he concocts scenes of contemporary life, making visual reference to famous paintings by Édouard Manet (1832–1883) or Paul Cézanne (1839–1906); in other instances, he draws on literary sources, such as Ralph Ellison's *The Invisible Man* (1952), or recreates scenes from everyday life. Wall's work has been called post-Conceptual, perhaps because his reliance on ideas is coupled with a visual intensity and a complicated narrative that earlier Conceptual artists, such as Douglas Huebler (see p. 378) rejected. Yet his images continue the Conceptual—and Postmodern—concern with knowledge and perception.

Wall's use of software is not usually evident in his final images, except in their large size, whose overall clarity is more readily attained with the assistance of programs. For one of his most discussed works, *Dead Troops Talk (A Vision after an Ambush of a Red Army Patrol, Near Moqor, Afghanistan, Winter 1986)* (Fig. 12.21), is about 7½ feet by 13½ feet, and was created in 1991–92, with actors depicting an incident reminiscent of epic history paintings such as *Napoleon on the Battlefield at Eylau* (1808) by Antoine-Jean Gros (1771–1835). Wall filled a lightbox-illuminated transparency with a harsh winter battlefield, sensational gore, and implausible heroism.

Japanese photographer Yasumasa Morimura (b. 1951) also adapted his analog self-portraits to digital imaging, pursuing notions of gender and ethnic identity. Morimura creates pictures in which he inserts his likeness into famous paintings and photographs, such as the bandaged-ear self-portrait by Dutch artist Vincent van Gogh (1853–1890). In his more recent work, Morimura enacted celebrated photographs of Western movie actresses, including Marilyn Monroe, in her famous pin-up pose published in *Playboy* (Fig. 12.22). Since the computer could have been used to conjure a more convincing imitation, one assumes that he intended to show the artificial breast-bra, polyester wig, lipstick-enlarged lips, and whitish make-up. Especially for a Japanese audience, these accoutrements are reminiscent of Japanese *kabuki*, a traditional form of theater in which men play all the women's roles. In his twenty-first-century work, Morimura has put himself in iconic images from photographic history, such as Yves Klein *Leaping into the Void* (see Fig. 11.62), and the notorious photograph of General MacArthur and Emperor Hirohito (see Fig. 10.32).

Mariko Mori (b. 1967) similarly starred in and produced her own work, employing cutting-edge digital devices. In *Pure Land* (Fig. 12.23), her candy-colored galaxy is inhabited by futuristic

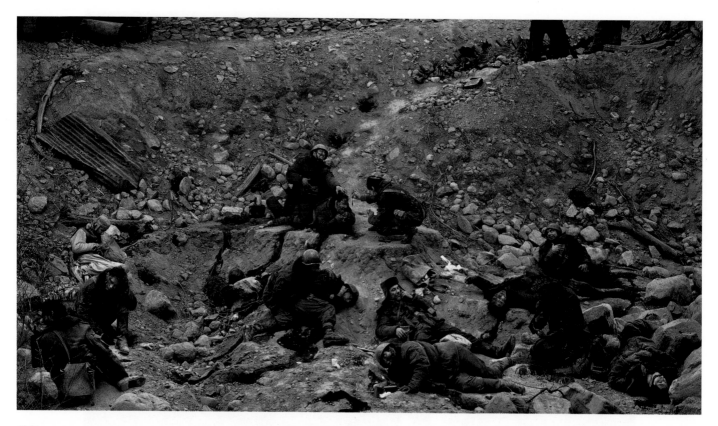

12.21
JEFF WALL, *Dead Troops Talk (A Vision after an Ambush of a Red Army Patrol, near Moqor, Afghanistan, Winter 1986)***,** 1991–92. Cibachrome transparency, fluorescent light, aluminum display case.

By comparison with nineteenth-century history painting, Wall's scene is a domesticated spectacle. Like many artists who came of age in the Postmodern moment, Wall sometimes leaves clues to the image's artificiality, such as the obviously fake blood that stains the clothing of troops.

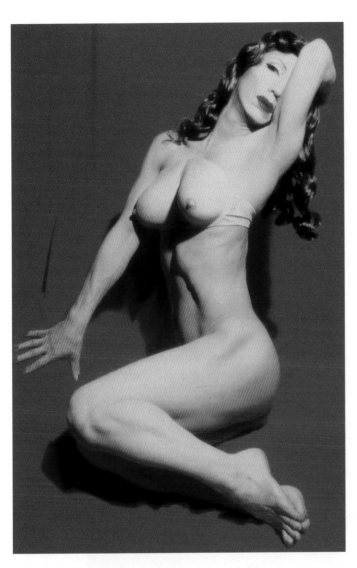

images culled and combined from postwar monster movies, popular toys, and even artificial bubble-gum flavors, such as blueberry. *Pure Land* also recalls the Japanese concept of the "floating world." Once a Buddhist notion for transcendence of the material world, the floating world was appropriated in the seventeenth century to characterize transient pleasures, and eventually applied to the elaborate erotic etiquette of the geisha, whose robes Mori seems to be wearing. Like Morimura, Mori jumbled references to tradition, commerce, fashion, and Japan's infatuation with the West into pictures that play on the persistent bearing of the past on the present. In the early 2000s Mori moved away from her trademark staged digital photography, because she thought it was too judgmental. Instead, she now creates big-budget, high-tech environments that combine light shows, video installations, and some photographs.

Unexpectedly, the time saved by digital means allows some image-makers to make wider use of older, more time-consuming media. For example, Keith Cottingham (b. 1965) electronically

12.23 (below)
MARIKO MORI, *Pure Land*, 1997–98. Glass photo interlayer (1 of 5 panels).

Androgynous space-traveling Smurfs sit like Buddhas and play musical instruments, while hovering with a traditionally garbed Mori over what looks like a post-apocalyptic Japan. The image alludes to atomic-age cinema monsters such as Godzilla and Mothra, who required traditional maidens as sacrifices or as servants. In addition to photographs, Mori has also experimented with three-dimensional photographs and videos.

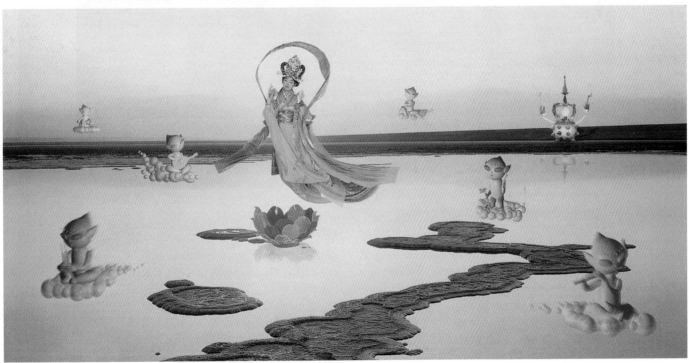

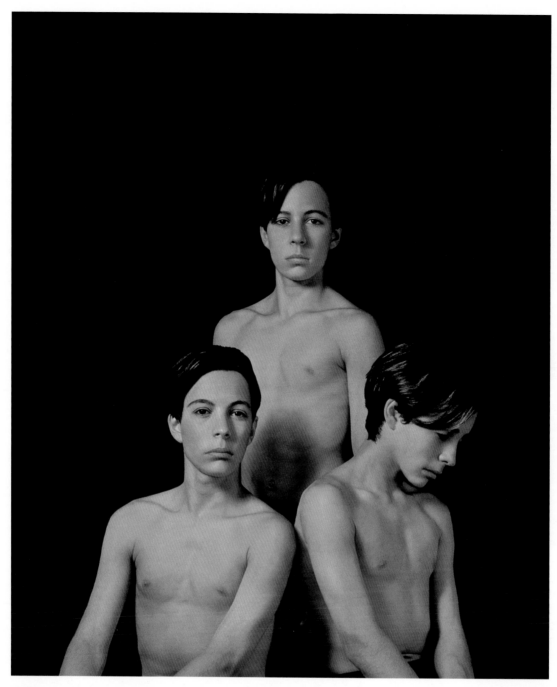

12.24
KEITH COTTINGHAM, *Untitled (Triple)*, **1993. Digitally constructed color photograph.**

Digital triplets pose like the Three Graces of Greek mythology. The too-perfect shadow on the standing figure's abdomen, the breadth of his collarbone, which seems to sweep over his shoulders like the ribbons on a cape, and the highlights in his hair that resemble brushstrokes, remind the viewer that these figures are fabricated.

hybridizes photographs of his soft-clay sculpture and anatomical drawings with appropriated images of race, gender, and age (Fig. 12.24). The resultant image, as in his *Fictitious Portraits* series, recalls the cool light and sensuous skin tones of late Italian Renaissance artist Michelangelo Merisi da Caravaggio (1573–1610). Electronic reproduction permits Cottingham to "use and abuse photography's myth, its privileged claim to the real." Like Andres Serrano's images of bodily fluids (see Fig. 13.19), Cottingham's pictures, are, in his words, "both beautiful and horrific," playing on the psychological longing to substitute the picture for the real thing.[18]

Perhaps in response to a world in which humans increasingly interact with machines, some image-makers have adapted the photograph to electronic environments that reciprocate the

movements of visitors. In *Lover's Leap* by Polish-American artist Miroslaw Rogala (b. 1954), computers track a viewer throughout the installation (Fig. 12.25). *Lover's Leap* is far removed from Edward Steichen's "Family of Man" exhibition, in which the viewer's path through the exhibit was as carefully determined as the images that could be seen there. Describing Rogala's installation, curator Lynne Warren voiced an increasingly familiar declaration: "This is the post-photographic image. The image-maker is no longer the godlike determinant of perspective and viewpoint."[19]

Rogala's work is physically based in a gallery, but long-time critic of American foreign policy, photographer Esther Parada (1938–2005) took advantage of digital montage for almost twenty years, and for a while made work that was entirely Web-based. She orchestrated interactive sites, such as *Transplant: A Tale of Three Continents (Wherein a Victorian love story between a Chicago heiress and an English aristocrat reveals a web of colonial maneuvers connecting the United States, England, and India)* (Fig. 12.26). Viewers were invited to follow their own path among photographs that were plainly or enigmatically labeled.

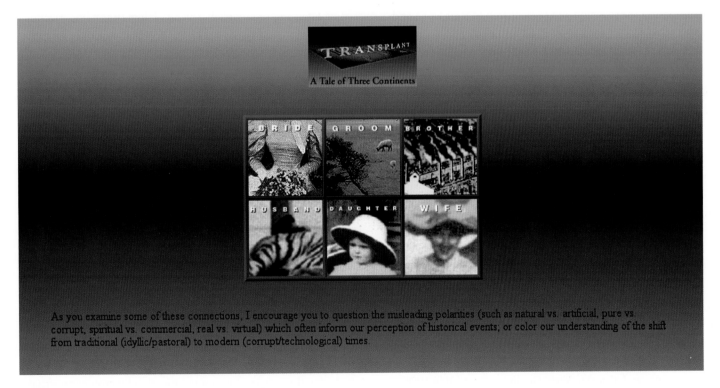

12.26
ESTHER PARADA, *Transplant: A Tale of Three Continents (Wherein a Victorian love story between a Chicago heiress and an English aristocrat reveals a web of colonial maneuvers connecting the United States, England, and India)*, 1996. Website.

A story about a young bride "transported" from her family home and then to India unfolded in an indirect, non-linear way, with clickable asides about such topics as British imperialist conduct in India during the nineteenth century.

While websites may eventually offer more users a global reach into visual information, a strong countervailing trend developed at the beginning of the third millennium. Image-makers, museums, galleries, news organizations, and image archives have responded to the commercial possibilities of the Web by commodifying more and more pictures in extensive pay-per-view or -use operations. For example, *Corbis.com*, an image bank holding more than seventy million pictures, was established by Microsoft founder Bill Gates in 1989. It resembles a nineteenth-century photographic studio from which users could get images in many sizes and qualities, ranging from postcards to archival prints. In image banks, the name of the photographer is often omitted in favor of subject matter. Mark Getty, founder of Getty Images and descendant of the family that founded the Getty petroleum firm, also owns about seventy million photographs. He succinctly summed up the economic potential of images when he remarked that "intellectual property is the oil of the twenty-first century."[20]

THE PREDICAMENTS OF SOCIAL CONCERN

During the 1980s and 1990s, documentary photographers and photojournalists continued to work for newspapers and magazines, but they also published books, and exhibited in museums and galleries, where they were able to exercise greater control over the selection and presentation of their work, and where they did not have to contend with tight deadlines. The presence of documentary and photojournalistic photographs in museums and galleries was not new. From the beginning, reportage images, such as those taken by Roger Fenton of the Crimean War, were presented in art spaces. Images made for the Farm Security Administration also found their way into the art world. Nevertheless, in the past, image-makers, audiences, curators, and scholars had considered art photography, documentary photography, and photojournalism as having their own separate lines of development and different social agendas. But by the late twentieth century these distinct photographic genres were increasingly coming to resemble each other in style and subject. No single term emerged to express this hybridization, but the need for a label to describe the new phenomenon is evident in the attempt of Weston Naef, former curator of photographs at the J. Paul Getty Museum in Los Angeles, California, to characterize the work of Brazilian photographer Sebastião Salgado (see pp. 426–27). Although Naef described him as "an artist, using photojournalism as the vehicle for his art," Salgado has repeatedly maintained that he is not an artist, but a documentarian.[21]

As critic and historian Vicki Goldberg observed in 1988, "some of the most arresting documentary work now leans heavily, even self-consciously, on art and art photography."[22]

Contemplating the origins of what he considers is a shift away from documentary, cultural historian Stuart Hall suggested that no approach can isolate itself from being weakened or co-opted. He speculated that during the last decades of the twentieth century, some artists and photographers lost confidence in the idea that documentary embodied the essential truth of photography.[23] The current blending of documentary work, photojournalism, and art photography, as well as the popularity of constructed and staged photographs (see p. 452), seems to bear out his conjecture.

The merger of art, journalism, and documentary is apparent in the images of Americans Mary Ellen Mark (b. 1941) and Eugene Richards (b. 1944). Both sought employment where their ideas would be least subject to editorial interference. Their work centers on the plight of unfortunate people, yet their images are seldom sentimental. Mark and Richards did not venerate the poor in the manner of the confidently humanistic pictures made by photographers working for the Farm Security Administration. Although Mark's images are frequently seen as having been influenced by Diane Arbus's work, she does not deliberately belittle subjects, nor make symbols for her own psychological expression. Mark's photographic series on homeless children and teenagers in Seattle, Washington, is compassionate yet unflinching (Fig. 12.27).

While photographs showing unfortunate people as victims of political injustice and catastrophic circumstance continued to be made and shown, in the new hybrid of art, documentary, and photojournalism, the romantic humanism of the popular 1955 *The Family of Man* book and exhibit (see pp. 311–12) was overturned. It was replaced by the idea that human nature is a convoluted and unpredictable blend of dignity and imperfection.

To be sure, this chastened estimate of human nature was not simply a photographic phenomenon. The twentieth century's grim record of millions of deaths caused by large and small wars, as well as by many disregarded famines, did not inspire faith in the inherent goodness of humankind. The end of the Cold War, and of the tendency to see the world in terms of sharply competing ideologies, may also have contributed to a diminution of human expectations. From Lewis Hine to the Photo League, social documentary photography was animated by the idea that images could precipitate social change. During the late 1950s and the 1960s, social documentarians began to lose faith in the capacity of pictures to do this.[24] Robert Frank and Diane Arbus used the camera to denote their dissatisfaction with society's shallowness, not the need for social change. Their mood of dark resignation was sustained in the documentary photography of the next generation. For instance, in his book *Interior America* (1978), Chauncey Hare (b. 1934) laid waste to whatever hopefulness Bill Owens had found in suburbia, and cast his camera on the bleak settings that framed the experience of even bleaker Americans.

The work of British photographer Chris Killip (b. 1946) is typical of the ongoing turn away from directly promoting social change towards personal observation and interpretation of particular instances of social life (Fig. 12.28). Killip's book,

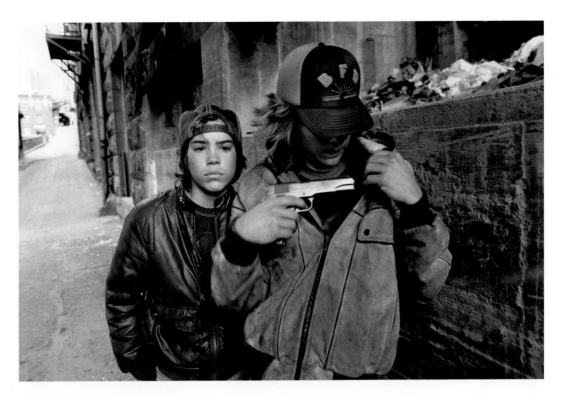

12.27
MARY ELLEN MARK, "Rat" and Mike with a Gun, Seattle, Washington, 1983.

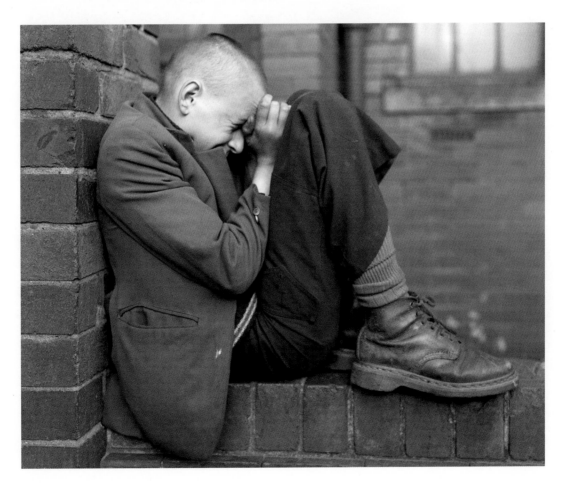

12.28
CHRIS KILLIP, *Youth, Jarrow*, 1976.

In Flagrante (1988), drew its title from the expression *in flagrante delicto*, meaning "caught in the act of committing an offense." While Killip's camera captured the effects of deindustrialization on downtrodden residents in and around the northeastern city of Newcastle upon Tyne, his title focused a critique against the government's efforts to reduce social supports, reduce the power of labor unions, and create free trade. "Britain in 1984," the powerful concept and title of an exhibition at London's The Photographers' Gallery, encouraged photographers to pursue personal documentary projects, especially those that revealed the effects on the poor and working class of Prime Minister Margaret Thatcher's social policies. Among the work shown was that of Paul Graham (b. 1956), who had already jettisoned the documentary tradition of black-and-white photography. With the example of William Eggleston's rambling tour of the American South in mind, Graham set out to show how color could add to the documentary record. His uncompromising 1986 book *Beyond Caring*, an ironically titled look at the frustrations

and failures of Britain's social welfare system, was illustrated by views of people seated on DayGlo orange benches below the abrasive sheen of fluorescent lights installed in the waiting rooms of the Department of Health and Social Security (D.H.S.S.) (Fig. 12.29). For this series of pictures, Graham frequently used signage as chance titles for his pictures, just as many photographers for the Farm Security Administration had done in the late 1930s. Yet unlike them, he took pictures on the sly, and deliberately distanced himself from his subjects, sometimes even placing a physical barrier, such as a table or a bench, between the camera and his subjects. Often the most emotionally affecting person is farthest from the camera. Graham continues to work experimentally. In the images produced during a recent tour of the United States, he intentionally whited out pictures in which people of color appear, as if to indicate that they are invisible. Another British photographer, Martin Parr (b. 1952), achieved an international reputation for his images of self-centered British middle-class suburban life. Unlike Killip's introspective

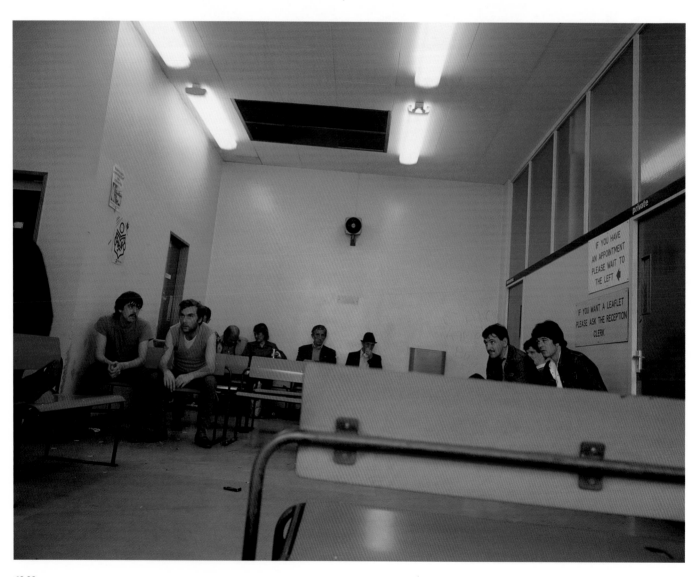

12.29
PAUL GRAHAM, *Waiting Room, Southwark D.H.S.S., South London*, 1984.

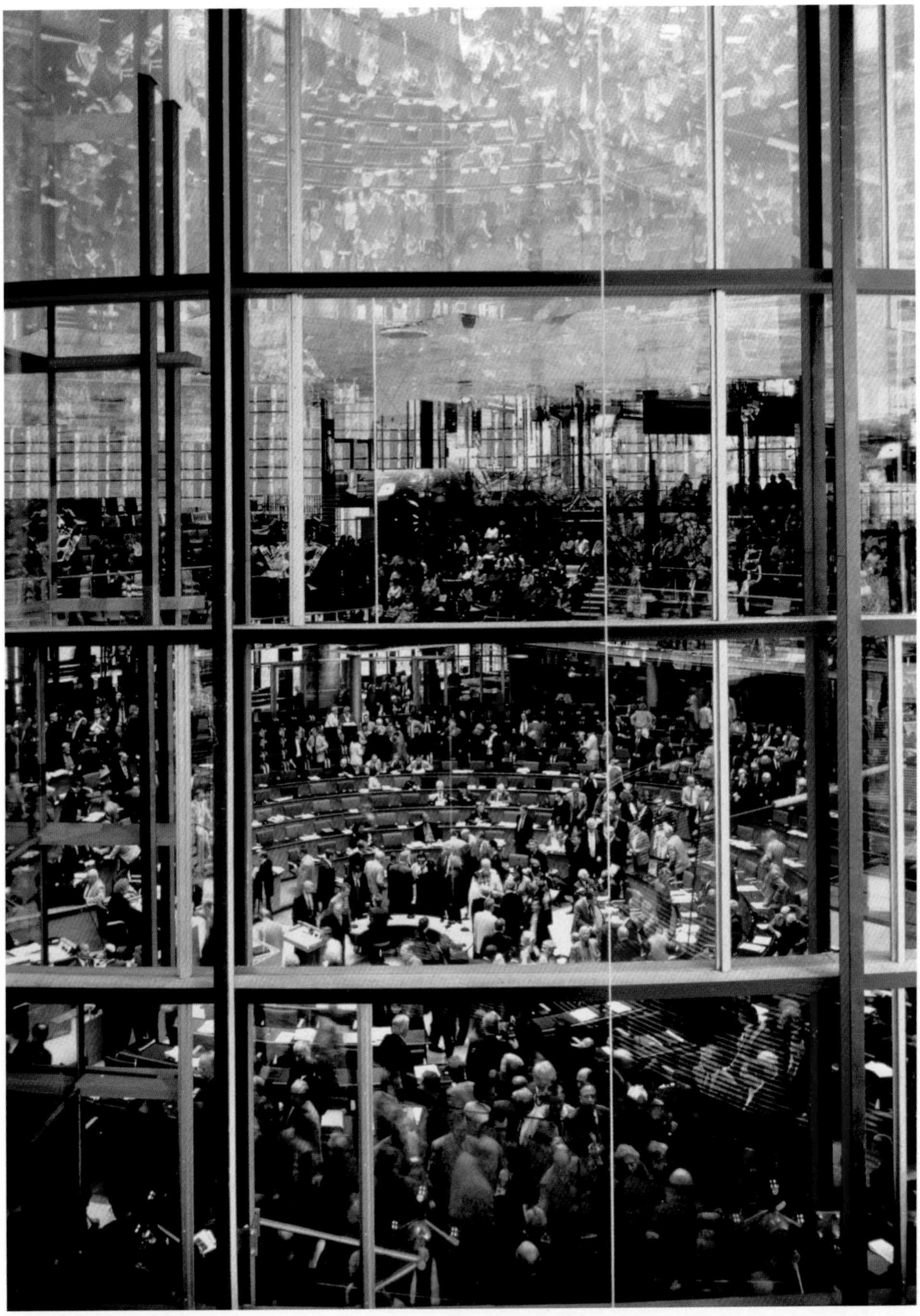

12.30
ANDREAS GURSKY, *Bundestag, Bonn*, 1998.
Mixed media.

views and Graham's subtle symbolism, Parr's *The Cost of Living* (1989) is punctuated with wry, satirical perceptions of human behavior (Fig. 12.1).

Photography's blighted vision of human nature was accompanied by a change in the formal appearance of documentary and photojournalism in the 1980s and 1990s. In a hurried era—with round-the-clock television news, ubiquitous video cameras, and small, concealable digital cameras that could quickly transmit still photographs around the world—the static, balanced, easily discernible images promoted in the past by the Farm Security Administration and picture magazines such as *Life* blurred and shattered. Audiences exposed to television

or Internet images for many hours a day adjusted to rapid, highly condensed picture sequences, such as thirty-second advertisements and rapid-cutting music videos. Largely through exposure to television and film, viewers became accustomed to quick transitions, such as jump-cuts, and shaky hand-held camera motions. Typically, photojournalism and documentary work also picked up on the look of speed and chance.

For example, Eugene Richards's pictures are stylized, and regularly use dim light, surprising angles, and disjointed sequences to remind the viewer of the photographer's presence and interpretive role. Like Mary Ellen Mark, he spends long periods with his subjects, returning time and again to keep

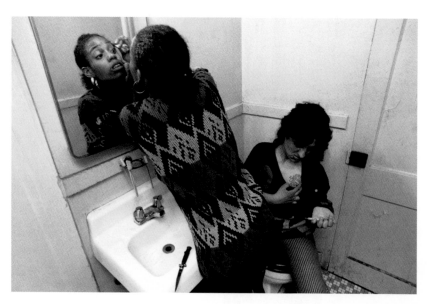

12.31
EUGENE RICHARDS, *Crack Plague in Red Hook*, Brooklyn, 1994. Gelatin silver print.

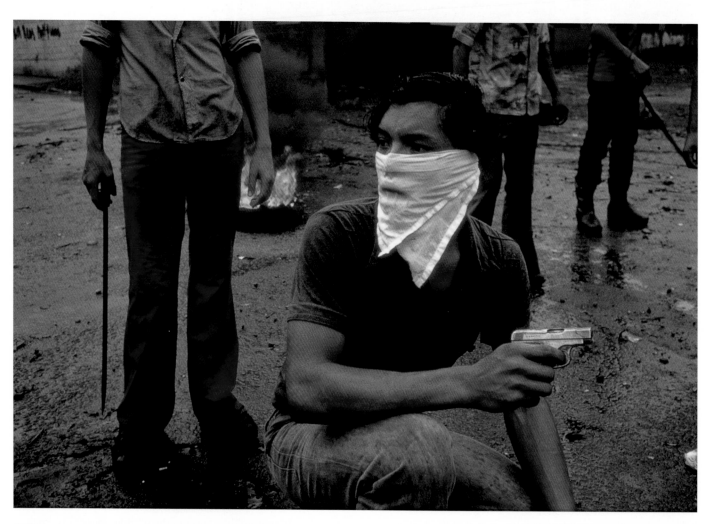

12.32
SUSAN MEISELAS, *Street Fighter in Managua*, from her book *Nicaragua*, 1981.

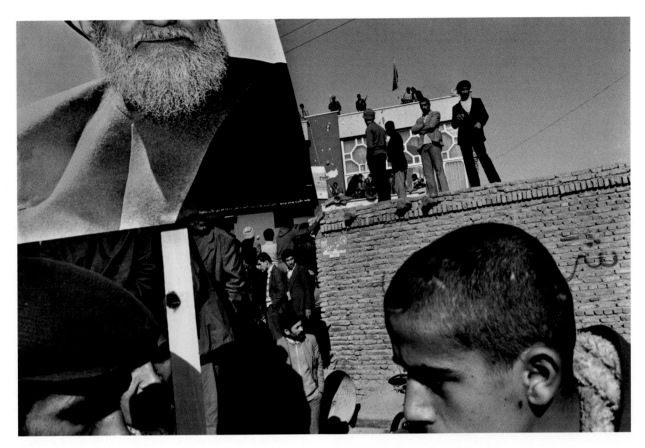

12.33
GILLES PERESS, *Demonstration in Favor of the Ayatollah Shariatmadari, Iran,* **1980. Gelatin silver print. Courtesy the artist.**

Peress disowned the notion of neutral, comprehensive reporting in his book *Telex Iran*, which integrates images with copies of the telegrams sent to and from his photo agency, Magnum. He warned readers that "these photographs, made during a five-week period from December 1979 to January 1980, do not represent a complete picture of Iran, or a final record of that time."[27]

up with their progress, and his photographs are accompanied by text that reads like a personal diary. *Exploding into Life* (1986), Richards's paradoxically titled chronicle of the medical experiences he and his companion Dorothea Lynch endured during her losing battle with breast cancer, is a searingly frank presentation of what was then a largely unphotographed theme, the individual experience of cancer in the milieu of modern medical technology. *Cocaine True, Cocaine Blue* (1994), a controversial collection of pictures and intimate personal stories about drug use, brought viewers into a world of day-to-day self-deception and ruin (Fig. 12.31). Viewing the exhaustion and despair in so much of Richards's work, Cornell Capa, brother of Robert Capa and former director of the International Center of Photography in New York City, commented that "He is too strongly attuned to misery."[25] Others have declared that Richards's intimate pictures encourage voyeurism.[26]

Another characteristic of recent photojournalism and documentary work is an increased reliance on words to contextualize photographs. In the past, large books by socially concerned photographers such as Dorothea Lange relied on extensive text written by someone else. Sociologist Paul Taylor

furnished the data and arguments that accompanied Lange's pictures in *An American Exodus: A Record of Human Erosion* (1939). American Susan Meiselas (b. 1948), who combines history, social science, and photography in her work, emerged as one of the main photographers of the protracted small-scale wars that characterized the last decades of the twentieth century. Her books *Nicaragua* (1981) and the much larger *Kurdistan* (1997) contain not only photographs but also substantial data, orchestrated by Meiselas. In Nicaragua, where she photographed life under the late 1970s regime of dictator Anastasio Somoza, rebels had taken up arms against a brutal right-wing government that was receiving U.S. aid. The hostilities eventually left about fifty thousand dead and one-fifth of the population homeless. Meiselas's images captured the spasmodic flurry of street fighting (Fig. 12.32) and the evidence of atrocities. Akin to Meiselas, French photographer Gilles Peress (b. 1946) prepares extensive historical chronologies to accompany his books and gallery exhibitions. With fragmented foreground close-ups, slanted horizon lines, and visual components that enter the frame at all angles, Peress's images often resemble the work of American street photographers Garry Winogrand or Lee Friedlander (Fig. 12.33). Like them, Peress embraces disunity as a condition

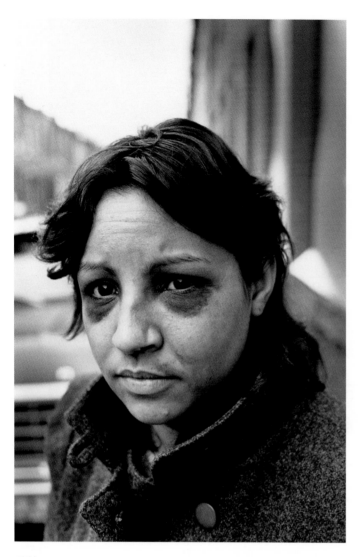

12.34
DONNA FERRATO, Cover photograph of her book *Living with the Enemy*, 1991.

In 1991, the year that *Living with the Enemy* was published, Ferrato started a non-profit organization called the Domestic Abuse Awareness (D.A.A.) to raise funds for women's shelters. She recalled that "I felt it was important to find ways to show as many aspects of the problem as I could."[28]

of the world, and tries to find its visual equivalent for his work, as he did during the genocide in Rwanda and in the Iraq War.

In the late twentieth century, extensive textual descriptions of the sitters' social or personal circumstances were regularly added to documentary photography and concerned photojournalism. Photographs were not expected to stand on their own, presumably communicating to viewers in a universal visual language. In *Living with the Enemy* (1991), for instance, a book recording incidents of domestic violence and their aftermath, American photographer Donna Ferrato (b. 1949) did not linger solely on battered women (Fig. 12.34). In abundant text and many pictures, she related life stories of the battered and the batterers, and she laid bare the circuit of violence, from home, to hospital, to court, to shelters, to prisons, or to therapy sessions. Ferrato's consciousness of domestic violence's large province

earned her commendations by critics who otherwise questioned the effectiveness of documentary work.

THE COLOR OF CONCERN
Concerned photojournalists and documentarians, such as Susan Meiselas and American James Nachtwey (b. 1948), author of the 1989 *Deeds of War* (Fig. 12.35), were sometimes reproved for using sensational high-key colors that so startled the viewer that they hampered contemplation of the image. Black-and-white work continued to be associated with seriousness of purpose, and with a dedication to craft, even though one could argue that color film more accurately equates to the way we see the world. Philip Jones Griffiths (1936–2008), the British war photographer who produced the penetrating indictment *Vietnam, Inc.* (1971), denounced color as "the biggest single hindrance to photojournalism the world has ever seen."[29] Decades of amateur photography, and the broad use of color in advertising, made it seem too facile and too emotionally arousing for somber subjects such as war and human suffering. Moreover, increased use of color film in art photography prompted the association of color with fabrication, fantasy, and self-expression.

Documentarians and photojournalists working in color were accused of adulterating the medium by making the photograph look too much like a painting. Some did indeed mine the history of art and magazine advertising, which they scrutinized for clues to effective color usage. Larry Burrows, for instance (see Fig. 11.44), rummaged through Old Master paintings for ideas, and occasionally did sketches to precast the kind of battle photographs he wanted to make. The increasing custom of photojournalists and documentarians to publish beautifully crafted books and mount art gallery exhibitions added to the unease about blurring the line between personal expression and reporting. Lastly, to photographers who came of age in the first half of the twentieth century, color documentary and color photojournalism repudiated the venerable heritage of socially concerned black-and-white photography, such as the work of Lewis Hine.

The profusion of color photography signaled for many the loss of ethical gravity, and with it the abandonment of the idea that photography could play a role in social change. Even in black-and-white work, raw emotionalism, the equivalent of color's supposed excess, was suspect. Thus, the monochrome images created by Brazilian-born photographer Sebastião Salgado were reproved for what critic and historian Vicki Goldberg called "too much humanism"[30] (see pp. 426–27).

Before the widespread use of digital cameras and photographic computer software, the proliferation of photography using color film in fields such as advertising, commerce, and art highlighted the economic inequities that divided photographers practicing in developing countries from those in the developed world. The color process was more expensive than the black-and-white method, and it required a greater infrastructure, including costly development apparatuses and printers. Black-and-white film could be developed and printed in a simple darkroom. Often newspapers in the

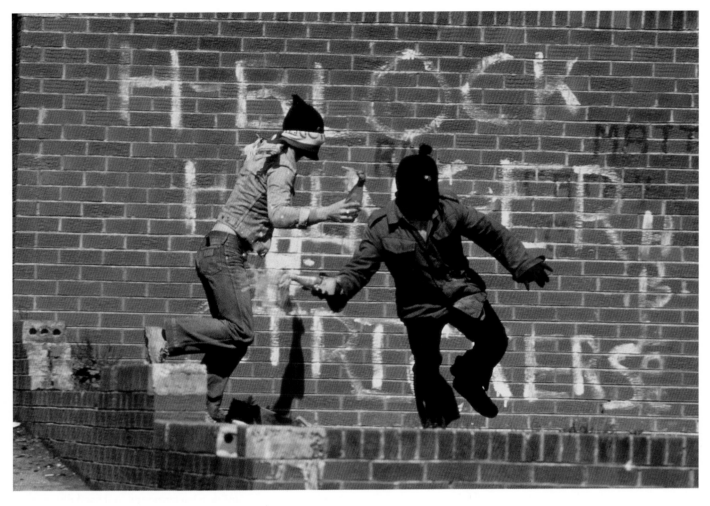

12.35
JAMES NACHTWEY, *Rioters in Belfast, Northern Ireland*, 1981, from his book *Deeds of War*, 1989.

developing world and magazines, especially those aligned with poorly funded opposition causes, did not have the capacity to print color photographs.

During the last decades of the twentieth century, Western photographers were typically college graduates, with specialized education in photography or related subjects that stressed continual innovation and offered exposure to a wide range of historical and contemporary image-making. By contrast, the route followed by the poor throughout photography's history remained self-instruction or informal apprenticeships on newspapers and in photographic studios. For example, Gordon Parks (see p. 283) was inspired to become a photographer when he was working as a railroad porter and happened to pick up a copy of a magazine that contained photographs by Dorothea Lange. He began his career with a pawnshop camera. Raúl Corrales (see p. 315), motivated by Farm Security Administration photographs he saw in newspapers and magazines, bought a plastic camera for a few pesos and began making pictures. Héctor García (see p. 319), who was an orphaned street child and manual worker, learned photography while serving as an office boy at several Mexican publishing

firms. An education like García's does not acquaint learners with many permutations of style, nor does it allow much expensive, technologically based image-making. Until the diffusion of digital cameras, printers, and networked computers, photography produced in and for people in developing regions wanted the means by which to circulate the images to the wider world. Consequently the photography and history of these countries were often ignored outside its immediate domain. The digital revolution has made it possible for more people to make photographs, especially with inexpensive or pirated camera-phones. Yet for many in poorer countries, access to the Internet and to printers remains elusive.

NEUTRAL VISION

During the 1980s and 1990s, the notion of neutral vision was repeatedly examined by cultural critics and by artists, especially those involved with Conceptualism (see pp. 376–83). *The Predicament of Culture* (1987), a much discussed book by American anthropologist James Clifford, investigated

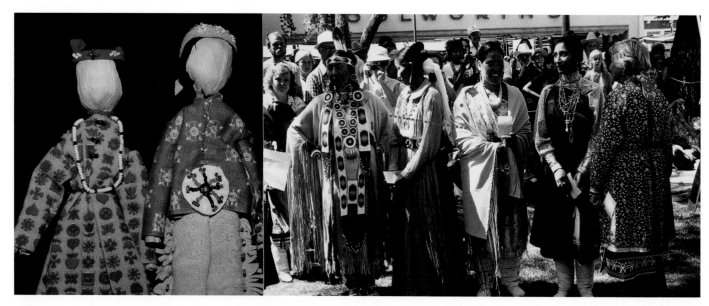

12.36
JOLENE RICKARD, *Untitled*, adapted from the series *Scientifically Unnatural*, 1993.
Ektachrome and silver gelatin print with rubbings.

twentieth-century ethnology and literature, to conclude that photographers had relinquished the idea of objectivity for subjective exploration. British anthropologist Elizabeth Edwards and British critic David Green looked back at earlier, purportedly impartial anthropological photography, such as that initiated by T. H. Huxley (see p. 142), and revealed the means by which these methods were used to demonstrate implicitly the superiority of Western civilization.[31] In a sweeping indictment, photographer-critic Allan Sekula pointed out that Modernist photographic practice is "shielded by a bogus ideology of neutrality."[32]

One reason for the decline of the neutral-record photograph in the social sciences is that non-Western peoples, the former subjects of the record-keeping procedure, have themselves taken up photography as a way of counteracting stereotypes propagated by it. Native American photographer Jolene Rickard (b. 1956) put it clearly: "Working in photography, one is forced to deal with issues of representation or risk promoting visually the ideals other people have placed in your head"[33] (Fig. 12.36). In the United States, the Native American Journalists Association sponsors "shoot out" contests in which Native American photographers vie to present scenes of contemporary everyday life that specifically counterbalance many stereotypes. Globalism and localism operate simultaneously within Native American photographic theory. Theresa Harlan, who taught Native American studies and curated photography exhibits, maintained that in her scholarship she used "the term 'international' in place of 'intertribal' to stress the diversity of indigenous nations within and outside the borders of the United States."[34]

Some photographers, such as Hulleah Tsinhnahjinnie (b. 1954), concentrated on fracturing stereotypes of Native Americans by focusing on intertribal issues, or by investigating the laws that determine who is and who is not considered an Indian. Recently,

Tsinhnahjinnie has begun working with computer-enhanced techniques and has linked up with indigenous people on other continents to share experiences, especially of what it is like to be the subject of tourist cameras (see Fig. 12.19).

Despite the mounting condemnation of neutral vision, it remained a strong component of late twentieth-century imaging. Standardized poses, uniform backgrounds, and fixed distance were used routinely for millions of national identity cards, medical illustrations, passports, drivers' licenses, employee badges, and the like. Mugshots of prisoners looked much as they had in the nineteenth century (see Fig. 7.28). After the defeat of the Khmer Rouge regime in Cambodia in 1979, the public was able to see the conventions of photographic objectivity used to produce more than five thousand standardized images of people who would go on to be killed (see p. 433).

The broad utilitarian use of would-be neutral photographs sparked many political and artistic responses. Internationally, Conceptualism's take on objectivity persisted in the work of such artists as Ed Ruscha, Bernd and Hilla Becher, and a younger generation of photographers, such as Chinese photographer Zhuang Hui (b. 1963), who parodied neutral vision's uniformity by making rigorously unvaried, single-shot panoramas of large

12.37
ZHUANG HUI,
Commemorative Picture of Teachers and Students of Loyang Police School, Hunan Province, May 13, 1997, 1997. Gelatin silver print.

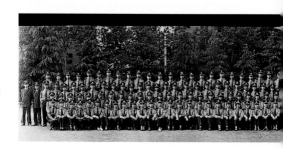

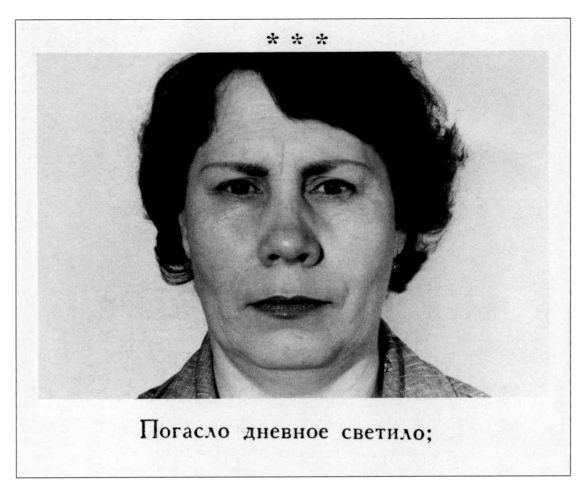

12.38
VLADIMIR KUPREJANOV, *"The lights of the day extinguished,"* **from his series** *In Memory of Pushkin,* **1985.**

groups, such as factory workers or the population of a whole town (Fig. 12.37).

Russian Vladimir Kuprejanov (sometimes Kuprijanov) (1954–2011) energized monotonous ID cards when he photographed sixteen women telephone operators in Moscow, and then placed a line of verse written by Russian poet Aleksandr Pushkin (1799–1837) below the portraits, where one normally would find names and numbers (Fig. 12.38). Kuprejanov orchestrated an oblique political commentary in this sequence, called *In Memory of Pushkin.* The first few pictures in the series show weary, morose middle-aged faces, but the final images present younger, more contented-looking women. At the bottom

of the images, the lines from Pushkin's poem "Farewell to the Sea" metaphorically advance from the present darkness to an inviting view of a distant shore. Created in 1985, the year that Mikhail Gorbachev (b. 1931) assumed the office of general secretary of the U.S.S.R., *In Memory of Pushkin* conveys the Russians' cautious hopes for economic reform and political liberalization. Like Kuprejanov, Ukrainian photographer Boris Mikhailov (b. 1938) found it necessary to tiptoe around the Soviet bureaucratic rules by using literary references as indirect allusions to social and psychological conditions. His series *By the Ground*, begun in 1991 as Soviet control of Ukraine began to diminish, deliberately makes reference to the celebrated Russian

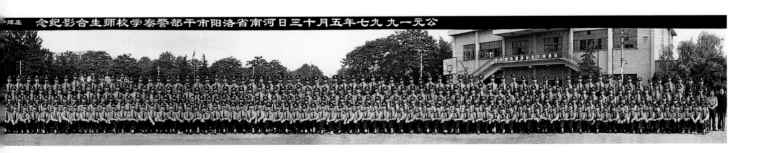

portrait

Sebastião Salgado

Although he was in the right place to make the well-known images showing the 1981 shooting of President Ronald Reagan (1911–2004), Sebastião Salgado (b. 1944) is not a news photographer. An economist who never finished his Ph.D., Salgado has photographed in more than sixty countries, focusing mainly on people who survive day to day: physical laborers, refugees, victims of famines, and groups who migrate because of natural disasters or civil unrest.

Through magazine and newspaper illustration, Salgado's work attracted an appreciative public that was mostly unfamiliar with debates about the efficacy of documentary work. His popularity permitted him to pick his projects and to schedule his own time. Salgado rejects the use of color film, calling it a distraction. He prefers to use available light and highly sensitive black-and-white film, because he finds flash illumination artificial. Salgado pointedly differentiates his image-selection process from the "decisive moment" popularized by Cartier-Bresson (see Fig. 8.34). Where Cartier-Bresson perfected the technique of waiting for the one instant in which compositional elements and the subject of a photograph come together, Salgado attunes himself to the extended rhythms of a particular site.

Salgado's approach can be seen in his best-known series, *An Uncertain Grace*, of 1990, which records the bone-wearying toil of laborers excavating pyramid-size pits in the wilds of northern Brazil in order to extract gold deposits. The series begins with a panoramic establishing shot showing hundreds of tiny, mud-swathed figures straining under loads of earth, and struggling up long ladders to the top of the pit. Salgado, who often packs his pictures with visual references to religious art, makes the workers look like souls trying to climb out of purgatory (Fig. 12.39). The next several pictures move in closer, allowing viewers to see the armed guards who overlook the scene, and to make out individual faces among the throng. Later shots come in closer still, to study the perseverance expressed on sweaty faces, or the grace of a hand holding a heavy burlap bag of earth. The final shot is again a wide expanse of the excavation and its denizens.

Salgado's style harkens back to the Depression era, when press and advocacy photography confidently presented humans as pure of heart, despite their suffering and hardships. Seen primarily in magazine articles, but also through books and exhibitions, Salgado's affecting pictures of human suffering during a famine in northern Africa helped to raise money for the humanitarian aid group Médecins sans Frontières (Doctors without Borders). His photographs of Cambodian children who lost legs to land mines helped to raise funds for a factory to manufacture artificial limbs.

Despite his good works, Salgado has been the subject of two recurring questions—one concerning the implicit politics of his images, the other having to do with the formal qualities of his prints. He has been chastised for neglecting to record local struggles to organize and change conditions. Although Salgado has depicted worker protests, as in his pictures of Brazilian peasants marching for agrarian reform, it is not the dominant theme of his imagery. While showing human suffering at its most wretched, Salgado's images are elegant poems of composition and luminosity. Viewers understand the symbolism of harsh black-and-white pictures used to describe misery in photographs such as those by W. Eugene Smith or Shomei Tomatsu. But Salgado enhances shimmering light so that it transforms burlap sacks of earth into treasure pouches, and warms the gaunt faces of the starving so that they look like tranquil martyrs.

Salgado's books, *Workers, An Archeology* (1993), *Migrations* (2000), and *The Children* (2000), generally disappointed the literati, who label his work "sentimental voyeurism," and who are uneasy in the presence of Salgado's signature mixture of beauty and affliction.[35] While no one openly accused Salgado of building his reputation on the backs of the unfortunate, his approach not only made some viewers uneasy but also seemed to frustrate criticism, for fear of being thought to be insensitive to the plight of the unfortunate. Other observers judged Salgado's radiant prints offensive, because they seemed to suggest that misery is the immutable way of the world, or that a divine presence will ennoble those who suffer.

Salgado's defenders point out that formal beauty has suffused panoramas of suffering throughout Christian art, and that, in an age when news photographs of misery are broadcast around the clock, beauty grips the viewer's attention and is a counterweight to the ubiquitous violence of television and film. In an era that refined remoteness into an art language, Salgado boldly wore his heart on his sleeve. His constant concern for the relief of poverty and disease in Africa helped spur the early twenty-first-century efforts to obtain debt relief for poor countries on that continent. For his recent project, "Genesis" (2004–12), Salgado made the shift from analog to digital, to record the pristine parts of the planet, such as the seas near Patagonia, and the nomadic people of the Siberian Arctic.

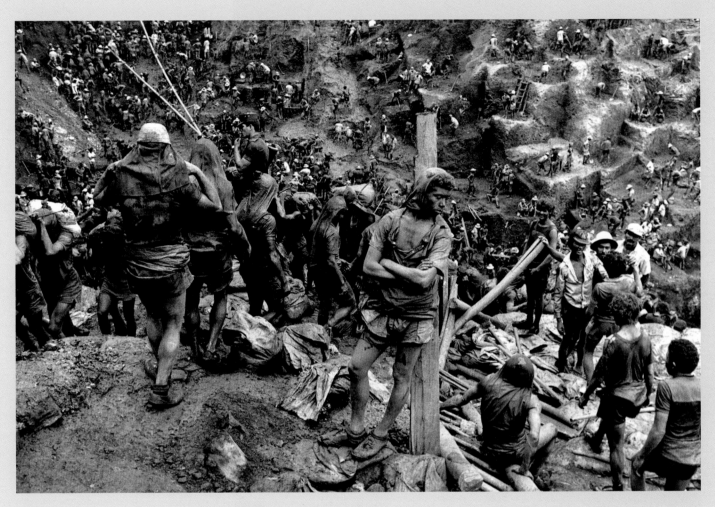

12.39
SEBASTIÃO SALGADO, *Serra Pelada, Brazil*, from his book *An Uncertain Grace*, 1990.

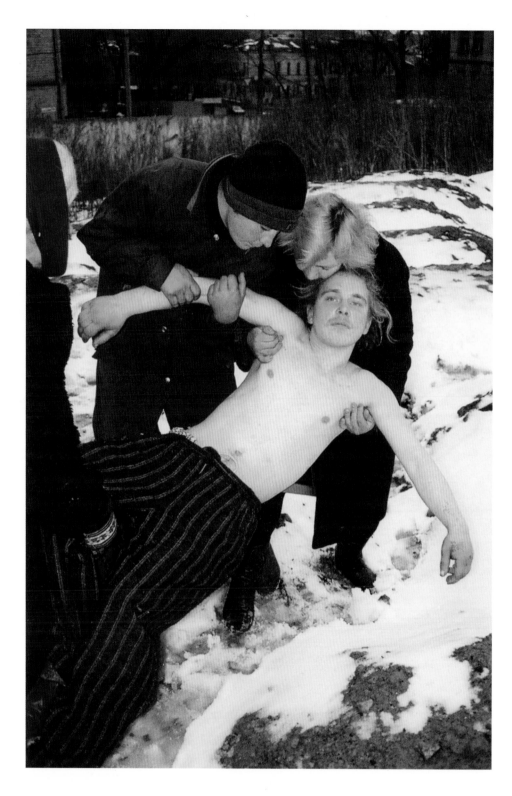

12.40
BORIS MIKHAILOV, *Untitled* **from the** *Case History* **series, 1997–98.**

Mikhailov created more than five hundred photographic "case studies" of homeless people in Kharkov, Ukraine, where he watched the steady post-Soviet decline of social services.

play, *The Lower Depths* (1902) by Maxim Gorky (1868–1936), which poignantly describes the lives of social outcasts. For this series, Mikhailov literally shot his pictures at belly level, to emphasize degradation. In 1997, Mikhailov began the *Case History* series, in which he sarcastically criticized the beginnings of capitalism and its effects by paying hungry, homeless people to pose for him in postures he chose (Fig. 12.40). The pictures remain controversial because of what some perceive as the

camera's cynical, cold-eyed stare at helpless people. One critic cited them as an example of the pornography of power.[36]

In Chile, during the repressive regime of Augusto Pinochet, neutral vision's purportedly non-partisan stance was turned in on itself to create images for the political opposition. Photographer Eugenio Dittborn (b. 1943) mocked the oppressive regime by making an accusatory hybrid of the identity card and the mugshot (Fig. 12.41). Similarly, Korean Conceptual artist

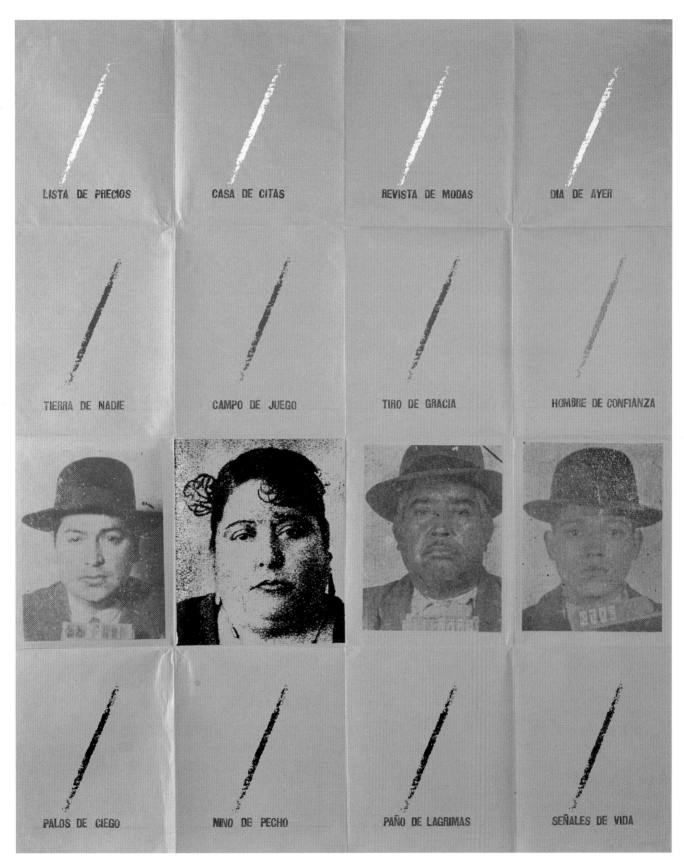

12.41
EUGENIO DITTBORN, *Commonplaces*, 1984. Airmail painting no. 8, rubber stamp and photosilkscreen on wrapping paper.

Park Bul-dong (b. 1956) satirized the appearance and purpose of election campaign posters (Fig. 12.42).

No words inform the large, richly detailed, yet uninformative portraits taken by Thomas Ruff (b. 1958), a German photographer who studied with Bernd and Hilla Becher (Fig. 12.43). Ruff adapted the uniform picture-making techniques used by the Bechers to explore the extent to which viewers contribute interpretations to portrait photographs. In contrast to the dramatically lighted portraits of the past—such as those of Carjat (see Fig. 3.6), where posture, lighting, and facial expressions cued a viewer's response—Ruff's work is resolutely uninflected.

The scientific method, neutral vision's mainspring, figures in the work of American-born Canadian photographer Lynne Cohen (b. 1944). No people appear in the icy interiors of the lecture halls, laboratories, military installations, and corporate headquarters she photographs. Cohen's sterile interiors evoke a claustrophobia that seems to seep through the antiseptic air. Working primarily in black and white, her images share the thin

humor of pictures by Conceptual artists such as Ed Ruscha. As writer and cultural critic David Byrne commented, in Cohen's pictures "coolness is being flipped back on itself to look ridiculous."[37] In the scientific observation room, one of Cohen's repeating subjects, it is never clear what activity is being viewed or why (Fig. 12.44). Cohen focuses on the stale sameness of the observers' world, not on the people, animals, or things they scrutinize.

The public's continuing faith in photographic impartiality is an ongoing motif in the work of French artist Christian Boltanski (b. 1944). He suggests the public importance of his photo-based installations by setting them in civic spaces, such as Grand Central Terminal in New York, or by inventing the look of public places such as hospitals and churches in his museum installations. Boltanski conjures up the darkened interiors of shrines and churches by using miniature lights that glow like candles. He evokes the past by placing old objects, such as letters and clothing, next to portrait photographs. The dim illumination and religious objects of his *Monuments (Les Enfants de Dijon)*

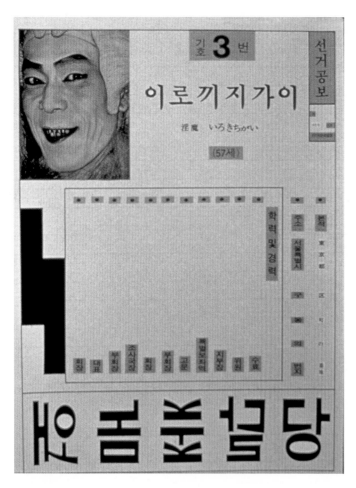

12.42
PARK BUL-DONG, *Nightmare No. 3 (Electoral campaign poster),* 1985. **Collage of photograph and text on paper. Collection of the artist.**

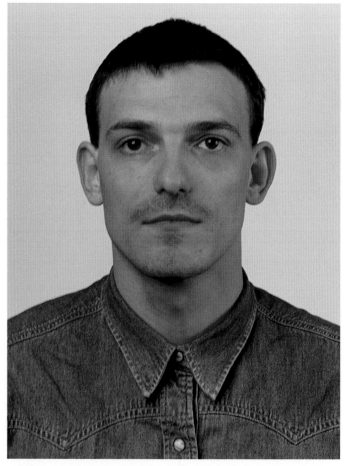

12.43
THOMAS RUFF, *Portrait,* 1987. **Chromogenic color print.**

Ruff's portraits are close-up and impersonal. All the facial details captured by the camera provide physical identity, but offer no clues from which the viewer can ascertain the sitter's mental attitudes or interests. He deliberately attempts to overturn the deeply ingrained notion that one can read personal character from a photograph.

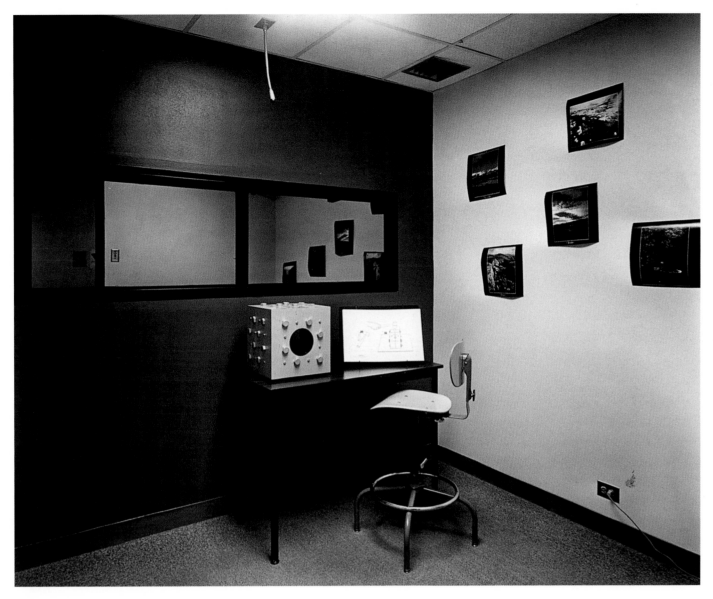

12.44
LYNNE COHEN, *Observation Room,* **n.d. Gelatin silver print.**

Cohen's interior shots are frequently undated, adding to their eerie timelessness and banality. The past presence of never-seen workers, indicated by forgotten briefcases, soiled coffee cups, or, in this case, a sketch mounted on the table, poses questions about the emotional state of people who inhabit these rooms.

(*The Children of Dijon*) hint at a memorial chapel (Fig. 12.45). Black electrical cords, like old cobwebs, power the tiny lights and link the images in an implicit web of meaning.

In France, where Boltanski is considered to be a Conceptual artist who manipulates ideas, his work is understood as a critique of adults' persistent yearning to reclaim the golden days of their youth. Elsewhere, Boltanski's *Monuments* are taken to be poignant mementos filled with emotionally charged references to the Jewish Holocaust. He has resolutely declared neutrality, stating that his art means whatever it means to individual viewers.

The presence of text accompanying pictures that play on the conventions of neutral vision is no guarantee of additional or clearer meaning. American photographer Lorna Simpson (b. 1960) appended words to her neutral photographs, yet the resulting combinations are puzzling (Fig. 12.46). The faces of the African Americans in these life-size or over-life-size photographs are deliberately cropped, and their individuality is disguised by plain backgrounds and simple clothing. Simpson uses standardized observational techniques, such as fixed distance, to disguise the differences among her subjects, which can only be observed by carefully looking beyond the visual structures that suggest sameness. The sitter's arm positions and the folds of her simple gown are not identical in each image. When Simpson began to work in film, she created comparably enigmatic pictures.

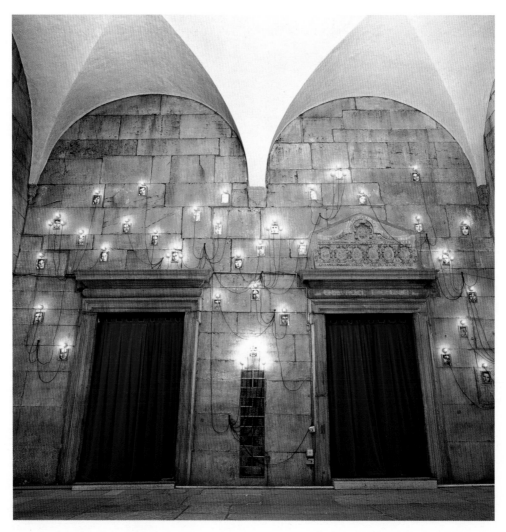

12.45
CHRISTIAN BOLTANSKI, *Monuments (Les Enfants de Dijon) (The Children of Dijon)*, 1985. Installation. Black-and-white and color photographs, metal frames, glass, light bulbs, wire.

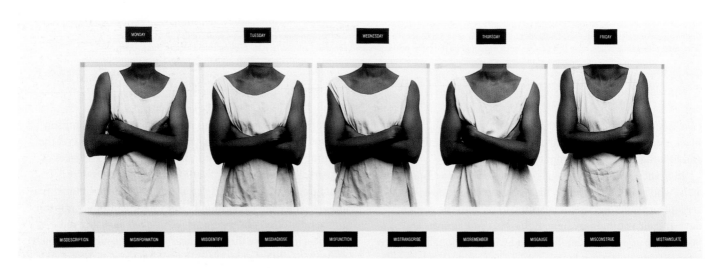

12.46
LORNA SIMPSON, *Five-Day Forecast*, 1988. Five black-and-white prints in one frame and ten engraved plaques.

Although the text and pictures in Simpson's work are clear, their combined meaning is not. The bottom row of words listing mistakes is not aligned with the top row listing the days of the week. Simpson places the burden of interpretation on the viewer, whose habits of linking words with pictures serve as a frustrating lesson in the complexity of meaning.

focus

The Cambodian Genocide Photographic Database

When Cambodian communist leader Pol Pot (c. 1925–1998) assumed leadership in 1975, he directed his troops and supporters, known as the Khmer Rouge, to move urban populations to the countryside to work as farm laborers. Many died by succumbing to starvation, disease, and murder. Ultimately, Pol Pot oversaw the deaths of nearly two million of the country's seven million people. While private possession of a camera was viewed as an emblem of privilege and a tool of political defiance during the Pol Pot era, government-sponsored photographs were produced, among them mugshots of the people who were jailed (Fig. 12.47).

Large-scale rural genocide sites, called the "killing fields," were discovered after Pol Pot's government was defeated by the Vietnamese. Prison records were also uncovered, including those for Phnom Penh's Tuol Sleng prison, known as "S-21," where as many as twenty thousand people were imprisoned, tortured, and murdered. More than five thousand of the Tuol Sleng mugshots have been found. Prisoners in these pictures have official-looking numbers pinned to their clothing, but the function of the images is not clear. The photographs do not identify specific individuals, nor do they reference remaining records of forced confessions. It may prove true that the pictures catalog batches of prisoners.

At Yale University in New Haven, Connecticut, the Cambodian Genocide Project contains a database of more than ten thousand photographic images and thousands of documents related to the Cambodian holocaust. It is available on the Web in the Khmer language as well as English, in hopes that the mostly anonymous victims may be identified. Preserved and restored, the original photographs are part of the collection of the Tuol Sleng Museum of Genocide in Cambodia.[38]

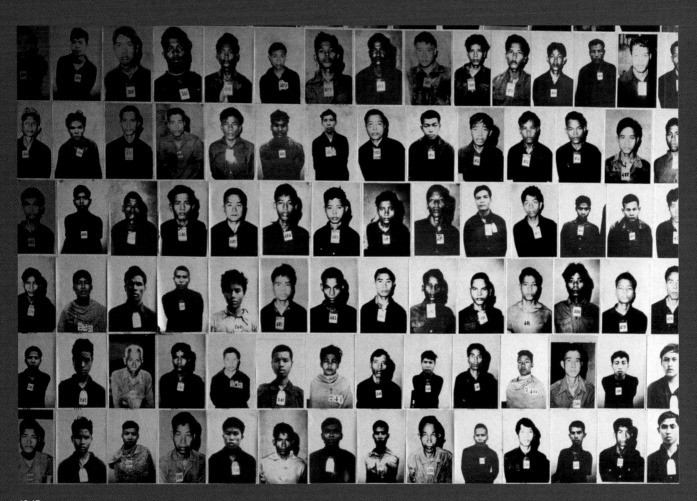

12.47
PHOTOGRAPHER UNKNOWN, *Untitled* (Cambodian prisoners), 1975–79. Gelatin silver prints.

THE LOOK OF POLITICS

During the 1980s in South Africa, photographic agencies and collectives, such as Dynamic Images, The Brotherhood, Vakalisa, The Black Society of Photographers, and Afrapix, were founded to lend support to image-makers such as Peter Magubane and David Goldblatt, who were committed to using photography in the struggle for social change. These collectives furnished images to alternative and underground newspapers, as well as to the world press.

Afrapix, which ceased activity in 1991, included younger members such as Johannesburg-born Santu Mofokeng (b. 1956), who moved from street photography to themed series about everyday life beyond the daily news. As Mofokeng wrote, "I was unhappy with the propaganda images which reduced life in the townships into one of perpetual struggle, because I felt this representation to be incomplete."[39] In the politically charged atmosphere of apartheid in South Africa, when photographers were greeted with suspicion by many factions, the desire to move away from overtly political photography was taken by anti-apartheid partisans as a token of irresponsibility. Still,

Mofokeng persisted in showing aspects of "unvictimized" life in the neighborhoods, as well as moments of camaraderie and enjoyment (Fig. 12.48). Within the context of South African photography, he invented a new social documentary approach.

In a related ongoing project, Mofokeng has been collecting urban family albums made by middle- and working-class African blacks, and presenting the images in slide shows that recall the days before racial policy split South Africa. Like his scenes of everyday life, which were so long excluded from public view, the old family portraits and other scenes had not been accumulated by libraries or museums. Painter-photographer Zwelethu Mthethwa (b. 1960), who lives in Cape Town, is equally concerned to underscore the strength and pride of people who, despite the end of apartheid in 1994, still endure unemployment and live in shanty towns. Since 2000, he has been photographing people in the unique interior settings they have made for themselves (Fig. 12.49). With a host of artists, writers, and photographers, Mofokeng, Mthethwa, and Goldblatt emerged from the isolation that apartheid brought with it and quickly achieved wide recognition in international exhibits.

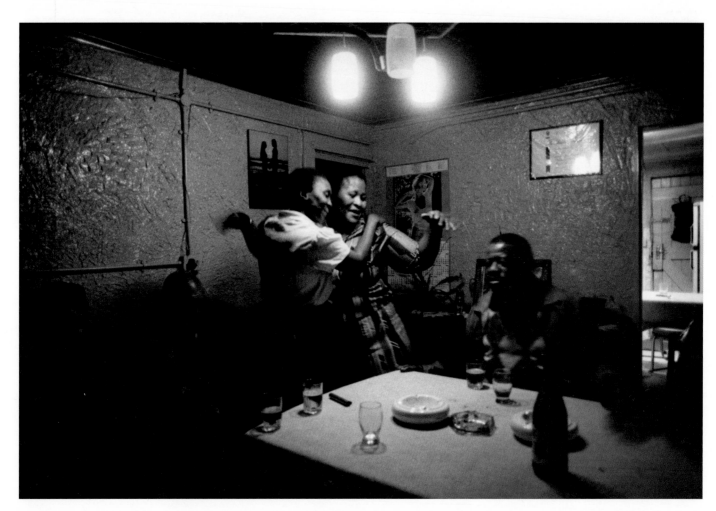

12.48
SANTU MOFOKENG, *Shebeen in White City, Soweto,* c. 1987. Gelatin silver print. © Santu Mofokeng/South Photographs.

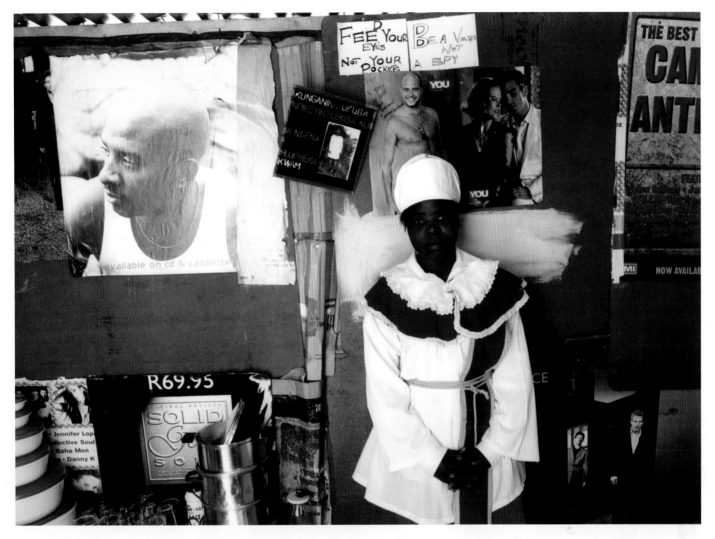

12.49
ZWELETHU MTHETHWA, *Untitled*, 2002. Chromogenic color print.

An emphasis on individual creativity characterizes Mthethwa's extensive study of the private spaces people fashion in their homes. Mthethwa was rigorous in obtaining the approval of the sitters who feature prominently in his images.

RETAKE

Global and local social perceptions vied for attention in the last decades of the twentieth century. For instance, while Andreas Gursky presented huge photographs of large buildings that seemed to overwhelm the identity of the very people who conceived and work in them, the photography of social injustice during and after apartheid in South Africa centered on the experience of strong individuals and their ability to carry on. In the art world, Conceptualism continued to inform photography, in the cool, objective views of the Bechers and the whimsical give-aways of Felix Gonzalez-Torres. The impact of digital technology seemed so abrupt and pervasive that some thought it would obliterate previous understandings of photography, and others were wary of its ability to produce fraudulent images. Digital technology enhanced and encouraged the crossover between scientific imaging and art production, in such work as Gary Schneider's genetic self-portraits. Improbably, digital means were used to create interpretations of history, ranging from Chen Chieh-Jen's insertion of himself in a historic photograph taken during a Japanese assault in Shanghai, to Jeff Wall's fabricated scene of an incident during the Russian occupation of Afghanistan.

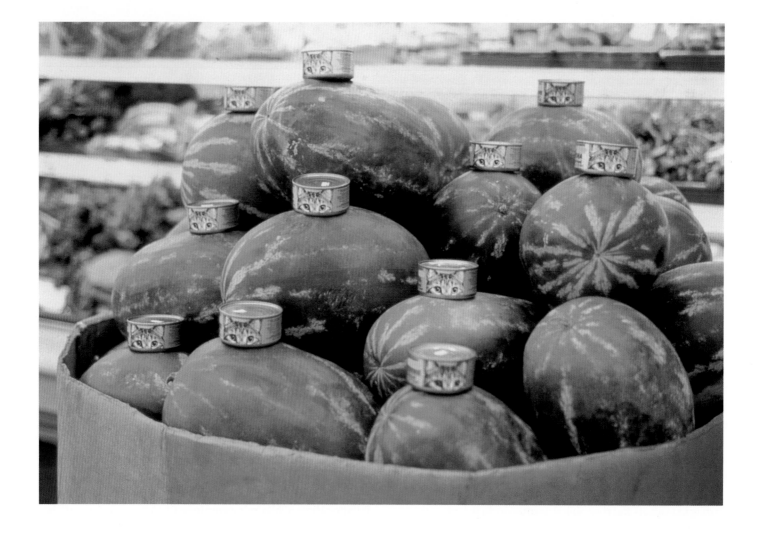

CHAPTER THIRTEEN

The Culture of Critique

Postmodern ideas fostered new thinking about social documentary photography. Assumptions about the causes of poverty and the power of photography to report them were challenged in relation to renowned images from the past, like those by Jacob Riis and the Farm Security Administration. Likely enough, the examination of societal representations dovetailed with ongoing civil rights struggles and with feminist movements. In particular, popular presentations of gender and ethnicity in film and advertising were not only scrutinized, but also incorporated into visual investigations of the power of images. "Thinking photography," as it was dubbed, pervaded such academic fields as textual studies, history, and the visual arts. Though the value of Postmodern theory and criticism are still debated, there is no doubt that they pushed photographic studies out of the darkroom and into the forefront of the humanities.

THE NEW SOCIAL DOCUMENTARY

In the United States, a new social documentary also followed from specific political and social circumstances. A mix of anti-Vietnam War activism and Conceptual art ideas helped shape a new philosophy and practice that differed from the work done by Eugene Richards and Mary Ellen Mark. The ideas and interests of an informal study group that formed during the mid-1970s in California proved important to a generation looking for direction about photographic practice in general, and documentary projects in particular. Members of this group, including Martha Rosler (b. 1943), Allan Sekula (b. 1951), and Fred Lonidier (b. 1942), emerged as intellectual and visual leaders of a new social documentary.

Among the most widely influential writings read by the group, and by others seeking a fresh direction in photography, was a 1936 essay penned by German historian and critic Walter Benjamin, called "The Work of Art in the Age of Mechanical

Reproduction." Benjamin held that mechanical reproduction, principally based in film and photographic techniques, was capable of breaking down what he called the "aura" of the original work of art—that is, our sense of an artwork's uniqueness, based on its having been made at a particular time and occupying a singular physical space. He reasoned that when multiple low-cost reproductions of a work of art such as Leonardo da Vinci's *Mona Lisa* were readily available, many people could own it, and, therefore, would not feel a need to visit the original. In effect, there would be no original, because the actual painting would come to be understood as just another copy. Benjamin held that this ongoing democratization was the forerunner of a sweeping historical change that would break down tradition, making way for revolutionary social and cultural change.

It hardly mattered that Benjamin, writing decades before the glut of mass media, including television, was wrong about the popular effect of mechanical reproduction. In truth, the vast manufacture and marketing of copies, be they of art or music, increased people's desire to see the original in a museum or to hear it played at a concert. What attracted most of his readers was his notion that the original could vanish in a welter of facsimiles. Benjamin's essay confirmed the existence of an image-world that molded people's perception of themselves, forged their desires, and fashioned their political beliefs. Importantly, the essay implied that political action consisted not only of protests, like those during the Vietnam War, but also of an ongoing, vigorous questioning of conventions and stereotypes promulgated by the mass media.

The study group also encountered the thoughts of Benjamin's close friend, the German critic and playwright Bertolt Brecht (1898–1956). Among Brecht's ideas that found favor was his understanding of how to affect an audience with a story. Brecht believed in constructing obviously artificial situations and disrupting the anticipated narrative with the unexpected.

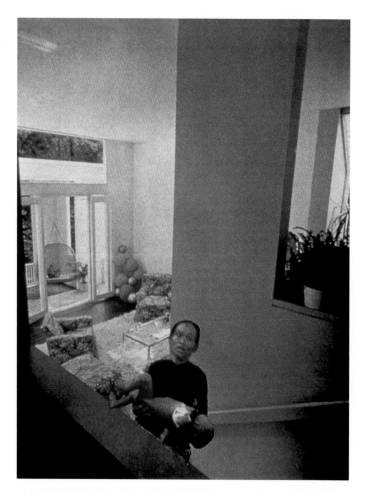

13.2
MARTHA ROSLER, *House Beautiful,* c. 1967–72, from the series
Bringing the War Home. **Collage.**

The study group also looked at contemporary art and film, especially the experimental work of French filmmaker Jean-Luc Godard (b. 1930), from whom they took the idea of recasting older themes and of thwarting the illusion of reality by letting the means of picture-making show. Martha Rosler recalled, "we wanted to be documentarians in a way that documentarians hadn't been. As readers of Brecht, we wanted to use obviously theatrical or dramatized sequences or performance elements together with more traditional documentary strategies, to use text, irony, absurdity, mixed forms of all types."[1]

Even before the study-group sessions, Rosler made political art in the form of three PHOTOMONTAGE series called *Bringing Home the War* (c. 1967–72) that combined mass-media images of the Vietnam conflict with pictures taken from design and architectural magazines (Fig. 13.2). (Almost forty years later, she revived the series in response to the Iraq War.) Similarly, Lonidier integrated his political activities with his black-and-white photography, as in his *Twenty-Nine Arrests: Headquarters of the 12th Naval District, May 2, 1972,* and Sekula was working on what he called a photonovel, titled *This Ain't China* (1974), a fabricated tale about rebellion by food-service workers. Soon, Rosler, Lonidier, and Sekula were at the core of what, by the

mid-1980s, was being called the "new documentary," or the "new social documentary," created by sophisticated, college-educated, politically active intellectuals who wanted to use photography as an important element of social critique.

Historian and critic Abigail Solomon-Godeau observed at the time that "it seems increasingly justified to speak of a new generation of photographers committed to rethinking documentary in a rigorous and serious way."[2] These thinkers did not want to make photographs so much as integrate image-making into political analyses of poverty and injustice. They vigorously studied historical documentary photography, such as that of Jacob Riis, Lewis Hine, and the Farm Security Administration photographers (see Figs. 7.7–7.10), and attempted to find ways in which they could comment on social oppression without generating what they called "victim photographs." Wary of fashioning such images, the new social documentarians surrounded their photographs with copious text that illuminated wider issues of corporate greed and government neglect, and expressed the experiences of manual workers and the poor. With limited success, they struggled to find venues beyond the art world for their work.

Lonidier went on to make investigative series, such as *The Health and Safety Game* (1976), in which he juxtaposed photographs of workers' injuries and appended statements by them.[3] Lonidier wrote that artists who pursue oppositional cultural practice must continually search for non-elitist ways of practicing.[4] Starting with his early photographs, Lonidier worked closely with labor unions hoping to use photography as a teaching tool. The effect of his continuing political agitation was witnessed during his 1999 exhibition in Tijuana, Mexico, which was critical of the North American Free Trade Agreement (NAFTA.) and the establishment of *maquiladoras* (internationally run factories in Mexico, near the United States border, that employ Mexicans at a fraction of American wages). The show was shut down by the concerted efforts of the manufacturers, who put pressure on the Mexican government.

Lonidier's work received less academic attention than the images and ideas circulated by Rosler and Sekula, whose writings were widely read and debated in colleges, universities, and art journals. In particular, Rosler's image-and-text series *The Bowery in Two Inadequate Descriptive Systems* (1974–75) took a familiar Conceptual art technique and used it to condense notions of documentary that held sway throughout the 1980s. Explaining the series, Rosler wrote that it is "a work of refusal. It is not defiant antihumanism. It is meant as an act of criticism."[5] In her *Bowery* series, Rosler demonstrated how both language and images are insufficient to a full description of a poor area of New York City where homeless persons gather to drink alcoholic beverages (Fig. 13.3). She did not set out to provoke concern for the plight of those living in the Bowery; instead, she tried to examine the weakness of words and pictures to encompass social realities while puncturing humanist assumptions about documentary photography's ability to contribute to human progress.[6]

Beginning in the late 1970s, critical essays on the history and theory of photography by Rosler and Sekula—along with Douglas Crimp, Christopher Phillips, Rosalind Krauss, Abigail Solomon-Godeau, and Sally Stein—hit the field of photographic studies like a sharp wind. By 1983, when *New York Times* photography critic Andy Grundberg wrote his essay "Two Camps Battle over the Nature of the Medium," it had become obvious that "lines are drawn between those who think of photography as a relatively new and largely virgin branch of art history, and those who rebel at the very notion of photography being 'estheticized.'" "The split is real," Grundberg commented, "and the rhetoric is fierce."[7]

Among the most forceful new writers was artist-critic Allan Sekula, who combined political theory, social commentary, and photographic criticism in a way reminiscent of the politically engaged European artists and photographers between the world wars. Like Martha Rosler, Sekula insisted that photography was not simply an autonomous picture-making system, but was knit into the broad patterns of global history. He reproached Edward Steichen's "The Family of Man" exhibition for its influential attempts to construct photography as a universal language, and for its covert promotion of the family "as the exclusive arena of all desire and pleasure."[8] With others, including British writers David Green and John Tagg, Sekula examined the history of photography within the development of fact-finding and cataloging systems, such as prison photographs and anthropometric images.[9]

Sekula's essay "On the Invention of Photographic Meaning" (1975) became one of the most read, discussed, and anthologized articles within art and photography circles, and still holds sway today. Its basic premise was that the photograph is not a clear window on reality, but defined by the culture and setting in which it is found. Like Rosler, Sekula bluntly announced that "the ills of photography are the ills of aestheticism."[10]

In his writing and photography, Sekula proved to be less pessimistic than other critics about the ability of photography to document social experience and to effect change. He insisted that he did not want to "ignore or suppress the creative, affective, and expressive aspects of cultural activity, [because] to do so would be to play into the hands of the ongoing technocratic obliteration of human creativity."[11] Sekula praised the photographic collages of John Heartfield for deconstructing Nazi propaganda, and cited Rosler's *The Bowery in Two Inadequate Descriptive Systems* as coming "the closest to having an unrelenting metacritical relation to the documentary genre."[12] He maintained that the window-on-the-world style of concerned documentary and photojournalism had to give way to "a hybridized, pictorially disrespectful narrative approach to the photographic medium."[13] Significantly, Sekula was also one of the few critics to extend his perspective to other than Western settings. While discussing the photography of Ernest Cole, who worked for *Drum* magazine in South Africa (see p. 323–25), Sekula recognized that distinct social situations, such as racial apartheid, called for approaches particular to the circumstances. Moreover, he cautioned critics and photographers that it "would be wise to avoid an overly monolithic conception of realism, [because] not all realisms necessarily play into the hands of the police."[14] Indeed, in Sekula's series, from the early *This Ain't China* (1974), through *Fish Story* (1987–1995; exhibition 2000)—a seven-year-long multi-media investigation of the maritime trades—to *Geography Lesson* (1997), which links changes in the Canadian landscape to the mining industry and wealth-seeking, Sekula remained constant in his efforts to relate the lives of working people to the expansion and changes of global capitalism.

Speculating in 1986, Abigail Solomon-Godeau worried that the political philosophy of the new documentarians would be marginalized within the art and photographic communities. In fact, the opposite occurred. The new

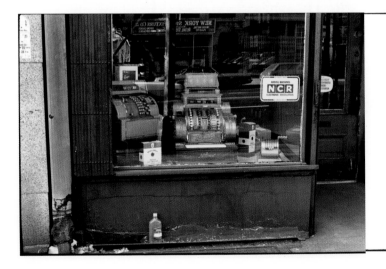

13.3
MARTHA ROSLER, *The Bowery in Two Inadequate Descriptive Systems*, 1974–75. Text and gelatin silver prints.

In this series, Rosler paired photographs and slang words for drunkenness. None of the images shows people, just empty liquor containers. Similarly, the words offer only shorthand stereotypes, not lives as they are lived. The two parallel representational systems do not add up to a conscientious description of the people or the area.

documentarians found ample support within the art world, whose practices and supporters were the subject of their critiques, and at universities, where they gained influential faculty positions. New social documentary joined the panoply of late twentieth-century photographic practice. It did not dislodge the continuing popularity of earlier documentary approaches, such as the alienated vision advanced by Robert Frank (see pp. 342), the personal interaction model used by Eugene Richards, or the universal humanism exhibited at the "Family of Man" show.

In Britain, various activist organizations used photography to communicate with the public at large. Beginning in the mid-1970s, the Hackney Flashers, of which Jo Spence (see p. 463) was a member, produced photographic exhibitions and slide sets on women and inequity in the workplace, which traveled beyond the art gallery to community centers and libraries. Similarly, from the late 1970s to the early 1990s, Lorraine Leeson (b. 1951) and Peter Dunn (b. 1946) collaborated with community groups to conceive visual responses to cutbacks and facility closures in a largely working-class neighborhood. Through such projects as the Bethnal Green Hospital Campaign (Fig. 13.4), the East London Health Project, and the Docklands Community Poster Project, they circumvented government-influenced mainstream

media outlets, distributing eye-catching billboards and street posters as well as postcards. Where American theorists tended to be overwhelmed by what they perceived as the mighty tide of mass-media images crushing all efforts at societal change, social documentarians and activists such as the Hackney Flashers held that political and personal transitions were possible, and could be achieved through photographs that exposed injustice. Similarly, as Nelly Richards reported on the use of the medium under the Pinochet regime in Chile (see p. 428), the opposition to the right-wing dictator believed photography to be a means of exposing the conditions that the military regime sought to hide, including the so-called torture and "disappearances" of protesters. Although Chilean image-makers associated with the opposition, such as Eugenio Dittborn (see p. 428) , acknowledged the sway of mass media, they chose not to accept the nihilistic view that change was unattainable.

THINKING PHOTOGRAPHY
Attempts to conceive a new social documentary were based on a thoughtful rejection of documentary traditions, as well as the incorporation of ideas from outside the area of photographic practice. The 1982 book *Thinking Photography*, edited by artist-critic Victor Burgin, introduced a new audience to the debates

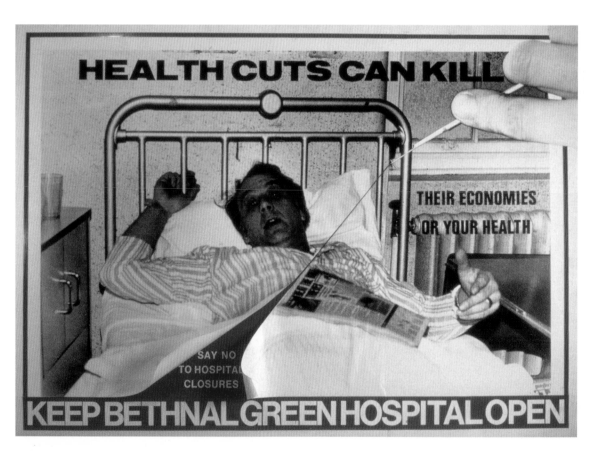

13.4
LORRAINE LEESON AND PETER DUNN, *Health Cuts Can Kill*, one of a series for the Bethnal Green Hospital Campaign, 1978. Street posters.

Leeson and Dunn created posters and billboards to show how closing public health facilities would affect people in the working-class East London neighborhood. The signs told their own story, but also countered proposed plans to turn the neighborhood into a gentrified area.

within the field of photographic studies, through an anthology of Burgin's own writing and that of others, including Benjamin and Sekula.

One of the most influential thinkers in the period was French philosopher Roland Barthes, who coined two terms that were much discussed in photographic criticism. The first, *studium*, designated photographic content that interests the intellect; the second, *punctum*, taken from the Latin word for "to puncture," referred to the sudden arresting effect that a photographic image can have on the viewer. The terms were introduced in Barthes's 1980 book *Camera Lucida*, which, despite its title, referred not to the pre-photographic tool used to make images, but to a philosophical light (*lucida*) thrown on photographic practice. Reviewing family photographs, Barthes found himself reacting only to the *studium*, or factual basis of the images, until he encountered a picture of his mother as a five-year-old child standing with her seven-year-old brother on a little wooden bridge in the family's Winter Garden, or greenhouse. "Something like an essence of the Photograph floated in this particular picture," Barthes wrote. Because the experience was so personal, Barthes refused to illustrate the photograph. "It exists only for me," he observed: "For you, it would be nothing but an indifferent picture, one of the thousand manifestations of the 'ordinary.'"[15]

While contributing *studium* and *punctum* to contemporary critical discourse, *Camera Lucida*'s personal, unsystematic, and mystical essay disappointed some critics, who were hoping that Barthes would (uncharacteristically) use the book as an opportunity to bring together his earlier thoughts on photography. *Camera Lucida* followed other influential writing on photography. In "The Photographic Message" (1961), Barthes wrote that the newspaper photograph has two messages, one brimming with socially inscribed "denoted" and "connoted" meanings, which ride on a second perception that photography is "a message without a code." In other words, he recognized that photography itself is an idea or mental concept, grounded in the notion of neutral vision. Another seminal question, articulated in such books as *S/Z* (1970; English translation 1974) and such essays as "The Rhetoric of the Image" (1964) and "The Death of the Author" (1968), repeatedly queried the notion of originality. Barthes suggested that, for a visual or verbal text to be understood, its meanings must already exist in the social world. Consequently, the text, and, for that matter, perception of the world, cannot be entirely new, but result from a combination of already extant meanings that the reader/viewer brings to the text or image. When images and text exist together, as in photojournalism and advertising, the interplay between the bundles of meaning becomes even more complex, though not original.

Similar ideas were advanced by the French philosopher and historian Michel Foucault, who wrote persuasive books and essays on the furtive nature of power and pondered the originality of authors. Like Barthes, Foucault politicized photography without linking it to any particular social movement or cause.

For photographers and critics, the writings of Barthes and Foucault opened the way to a philosophical and historical reconsideration of photographic practice and discredited pictures of the kind deemed original by virtue of individual expression. Their ideas suggested a new image-making, cognizant of the social reproduction of meaning, especially in mass media. Such ideas were close to those discussed and acted upon by Rosler, Sekula, and Lonidier, who tried to find new ways to integrate political action and camerawork. The photographers who admired both Barthes and Foucault, however, were frequently less politically active than the new social documentarians. They sought new insights and incentives for picture-making, not for directions on how to change society.

One of the most powerful ideas taken from Barthes and other thinkers concerned the futility of originality. Since mass-media photography was replete with messages, new pictures were not needed. In part or in full, existing images could be appropriated and re-exhibited. These "readymades" differed from the everyday objects earlier proposed as art by Marcel Duchamp (see Fig. 8.19), in that they were not things but pictures of things frequently marketed to arouse consumer desire. Some photographers argued that these acts of appropriation were inherently subversive, because the effect of seeing mass-media images framed in a new context would enlighten and politicize beholders. The recognition that images pilfered from magazines and newspapers had visual forebears in Dada photography, as well as in experimental camerawork between the world wars, sparked a renewed interest in what had hitherto been a neglected area of historical scholarship.

Beginning in the late 1970s, American critics such as Rosalind Krauss, Craig Owens, Hal Foster, and Douglas Crimp focused on the demise of the original as a vastly important sign that Modernism, with its enthronement of artistic expression and originality, was also dying. Two widely read essays by Crimp, "Pictures" (1977) and "The Photographic Activity of Postmodernism" (1980), linked photography to French theory and to Benjamin's notions of aura and originality. Crimp was also among the earliest observers to see the fulfillment of contemporary theory in new approaches to photography, such as those employed by Cindy Sherman (b. 1954) (see Fig. 13.6) and Sherrie Levine (b. 1947), whom he included in the 1977 New York exhibition "Pictures," from which the essay was derived. By the late 1970s, photography was rapidly emerging as the vogue art, not simply because of its growing acceptance in the art world, but because of the way it dovetailed in practical terms with contemporary concerns about representation and originality. Simultaneously, the term "Postmodern" became current, to characterize what was increasingly perceived as a new period following Modernism.

THE POSTMODERN ERA

The concept of a Postmodern era was not new in twentieth-century thought, but it was revived when Jean-François Lyotard's dense, short 1979 book *The Postmodern Condition* (English translation, 1984) posited Postmodernism as the next phase of Modernism. Lyotard maintained that Modernism's successor was already at work, disintegrating "metanarratives," or grand, longstanding social rationales about the improvability of the human condition made possible by the progress of knowledge, especially science. As these overarching visions declined, Lyotard argued that they would be replaced not by other unifying ideas but by a welter of competing notions, whose fertile chaos would feed a new freedom from the oppression and authority of scientific knowledge.

Lyotard's analysis was fanciful, underestimating the predominance of science and the prodigious ability of capitalism to adapt to the times. Nevertheless, from his book, philosophers, social commentators, critics, and artists construed a broad theory that explained and justified the present moment as a state of flux, propelled by instantaneous information churned out by mass media, and shaped by global finance and business networks, whose prevalence lessened the importance of the nation state in the world order.

In art circles, Postmodernism came to mean a rejection of themes and subjects that interested Modernist artists, such as abstraction and the subjective expression of unique intellects. Artists in many media reintroduced the human figure, or turned to mass-produced kitsch for image sources. Photographers, too, dwelled on the body, often deriving or appropriating images from commerce, advertising, and film. Some explored the potentials of the blurred image, in which forms were suggested but not clearly delineated.

In his essay for the catalog accompanying the "Pictures" exhibit, Crimp acknowledged how the experience of media created a generation gap between those raised on television, movies, and ubiquitous magazines, and those brought up in the less image-saturated culture of the period prior to World War II. "To an ever greater extent," he wrote, "our experience is governed by pictures, pictures in newspapers and magazines, on television and in the cinema. Next to these pictures, firsthand experience begins to retreat, to seem more and more trivial. While it once seemed that pictures had the function of interpreting reality, it now seems that they have usurped it."[16] Soon after, in response to another exhibit ominously called "Last Exit: Painting," critic Thomas Lawson argued that "the camera, in all its manifestations, is our god, dispensing what we mistakenly take to be truth."[17]

Cultural critic Susan Sontag (1933–2004) built her widely read book *On Photography* (1977) upon the notion of a similar, even more noxious "Image-World," in which photographs injured human memory and drained away the instinct to know the world at first hand. In Sontag's view, this left us as passive viewers at a spectacle of recycled pictures.[18] Sontag did not, however, put forward the consummate Postmodern conviction that, because of its omnipresence, the image-world provided a new source of realism for artists. She maintained that an authentic, valuable, first-hand reality had been plundered and debased. In sum, a chilly, sobering down-draft in the intellectual climate whirled away any remnants of Marshall McLuhan's rapturous 1960s praise for the mass media's educational and peace-making powers (see p. 391).

POSTMODERNIST PHOTOGRAPHY

Among the artists included in Douglas Crimp's "Pictures," and discussed in his "The Photographic Activity of Postmodernism," was Sherrie Levine, who confronted the art world with her rephotographed well-known images made by famous photographers such as Edward Weston, Walker Evans, and Eliot Porter. Called APPROPRIATION, Levine's reuse of images such as Walker Evans's image of Allie Mae Burroughs (see Fig. 9.7), highlighted the ubiquity of the copy and the insignificance of the original. To make her point, she photographed art and photography examples reproduced in books so as to contrast copying a copy with original archival images and printing original negatives. By taking an image, rather than making an image, Levine repressed the notion of her art as original and unique. By the late twentieth century, Levine's appropriations were themselves being appropriated by other artists.

More frequently, appropriationists procured mass-media images. Artist and writer Richard Prince (b. 1949) found his source images in magazines, cutting, cropping, rearranging, and reprinting them to isolate the devices used in advertising to summon up desire (Fig. 13.5). Levine and Prince are typical examples of the powerful convergence of image-making and social analysis that occurred during the last decades of the twentieth century. Social science observation by artists, expressed primarily in art, became known as critical practice.

In "Pictures," Douglas Crimp noted the work of Cindy Sherman, who would become one of the most celebrated image-makers of the 1980s and 1990s. Her series of black-and-white photographs called *Untitled Film Stills* seemed to be derived from 1950s B-movie melodramas, film stills, and the photographs displayed in theater lobbies. The film still exaggerated movie-born gender stereotypes, especially that of the beleaguered, fretful, or frightened heroine. While Sherman found suggestions in film-still poses, she did not make reference to any particular movie. Photographing herself in make-up, wigs, and costumes, she imitated or evoked a culturally prevalent image (Fig. 13.6). Viewers could recognize the source of her images, not because she employed scenes from old movies, but because the poses she assumed condensed the much repeated portrayal of women in films.

As Crimp pointed out, Sherman's self-portraits do not ever reveal Cindy Sherman. Her faux film fragments played up the notion of the Postmodern copy and its opposition to the ideas of invention and genius. Sherman's later work shifted to larger, deeply saturated color pictures, in which she performed appearances based on pin-ups, fairy tales, and Old Master paintings. Eventually, she took herself out of the picture, substituting prostheses or plastic body parts used in medical education, and combining them to form grotesque bodies in the manner of Surrealist photographer Hans Bellmer (see Fig. 8.26).

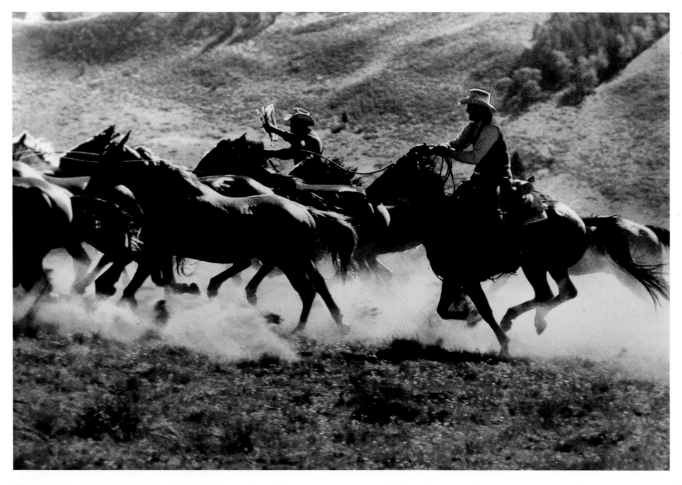

13.5
RICHARD PRINCE, *Untitled* (Cowboys), 1993. Ektacolor print. Barbara Gladstone Gallery, New York.

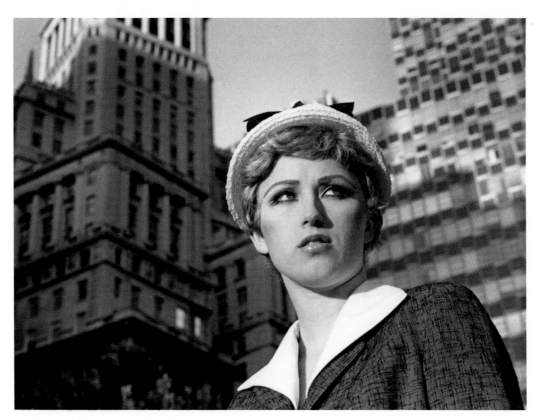

13.6
CINDY SHERMAN, *Untitled Film Still*, 1978.

Sherman costumed and coiffed herself to look like troubled and anxious women from B-movies of the 1950s. She enacted the stereotypical role of the woman in jeopardy, not taken from a specific film, but improvised from an array of them.

Sherman's interest remained constant throughout the last decades of the twentieth century, and she continues to expose not only the shallowness of gender stereotyping but also the titillating pleasure of looking.

ART PHOTOGRAPHY AND PHOTOGRAPHY-BY-ARTISTS

The mid-1970s witnessed the increased use of photography by artists who usually worked in other media, and the retreat from conventional art photography by image-makers such as Cindy Sherman. Noting the development, critic Abigail Solomon-Godeau commented that "although the attempt to draw a distinction between art photography and photography done by artists might initially be taken for a semantic quibble, or worse, as informed by the desire to privilege the photographic work of artists over that of photographers, there remain significant differences in the two forms of practice."[19]

Art photography, of course, had a history going back to the beginnings of the medium. One of Daguerre's first successful photographs rendered a traditional art subject, the still life (see Fig. 1.14). The quintessential art photographer was Alfred Stieglitz, an unashamed elitist who positioned art photography as the spiritual opposite of crass commercial imaging. As Solomon-Godeau pointed out, art photographers continued to treasure subjective and intuitive expression, the intricacies of craft, and the sharp dividing line between fine art and commercial imagery. Briefly put, art photography aspired to the condition of painting, which meant recognition as a fully fledged art, and access to the intertwined realms of gallery and museum.

In contrast, photography-by-artists owed little to the traditional aspirations and values of art photography. It critiqued the notion of personal expression, holding up to public view the way in which the mass media spewed out copies of copies of copies of stereotypes. For those who praised and those who disparaged her work, Cindy Sherman became the exemplar of the photography-by-artists movement. In fact, she was one of the first image-makers who worked exclusively in the medium to be called an artist rather than a photographer.[20] Of course, the renunciation of personal expression was central to the philosophy of Conceptual artists and photographers, such as Edward Ruscha, who dispassionately itemized and compiled ready-made images of ordinary locations and buildings, such as gas stations and motel swimming pools (see Fig. 11.67).

Ideally, photography-by-artists was intended as part of a broad social intervention, aimed at exposing the so-called illusions of individuality and originality that formed the bulwark of the art market. In fact, the boundary between art photography and photography-by-artists broke down almost as soon as it was conceived. By the mid-1980s, photography-by-artists had not shattered or reformed the art market, but had refreshed and recommercialized the notion of the avant-garde artist, whose attacks on mainstream society and consumerism had become an expected and marketable model of artistic behavior. Photography-by-artists was represented in chic galleries and showcased in prominent exhibitions and books. Because of its links to contemporary theories of language,

notions of representation, and gender identity, photography-by-artists received an international academic welcome. It was the recurrent subject of lectures and discussions, not only in art and photography departments but also in literature, philosophy, and sociology classes.

For its part, the art photography exemplified by Stieglitz did not lose its appeal for the public but considerably increased in monetary value, as evidenced by the high auction prices recorded during the late twentieth-century economic boom. During the late 1970s and 1980s, the uncertain distinctions between art photography and photography-by-artists helped break down the compartmentalization of museum departments according to media, a configuration that was already taxed by hard-to-categorize activities such as installation and performance art. Heads of museum painting departments and photography departments vied with each other to collect work by such artists as Cindy Sherman. Sometimes museum photography departments broadened their acquisition goals; at other times new positions were created to embrace what were called "new media."

By the end of the century, the terms "photo-based artist" and "photo-based work" replaced "photography-by-artists," and with that substitution also vanished the association of photography-by-artists with a tough, ongoing social or media criticism. At century's end, photo-based work was normal fare. Surveying the New York gallery scene during the year 2000, critic David Rimanelli observed a "narrowing of that time-honored (if rarely acknowledged) distinction between those spaces devoted to contemporary art (including that which is photographically based) and venues catering to photography." "Given its absolute and tiresome omnipresence," he opined, photography "looks like the academic painting of our time."[21]

BLURRING THE SUBJECT

The Postmodern notion of indeterminate, circular meaning gave the blurred image a new lease on life as a multivalent symbol, alluding to transient and fragmentary moments, fuzzy or disfigured identities, or indistinct and ambiguous knowledge. Interestingly, blur has had many uses in the history of photography, the best-known of which was the Pictorialist image, with its pretensions to High Art. More recently, photographers such as Duane Michals blurred the actions of human figures to add mystery and wonder to a scene. Likewise, Tunisian photographer Kamel Dridi (b. 1951) revealed Muslim religious life in North Africa and Saudi Arabia in photographs published in the leading French newspaper *Le Monde*. He uniquely employed blurred images to evoke, for people brought up in the Muslim faith, early memories of ceremonial movements and gestures (Fig. 13.7).

Since the mid-1960s, German painter Gerhard Richter (b. 1932) has reworked photographic sources, often his own snapshots, creating paintings that maintain photography's deep perspective. While the painting is still wet, he pulls a special squeegee across its surface, blurring the subject almost to the point of unrecognizability. Some of his so-called "photo

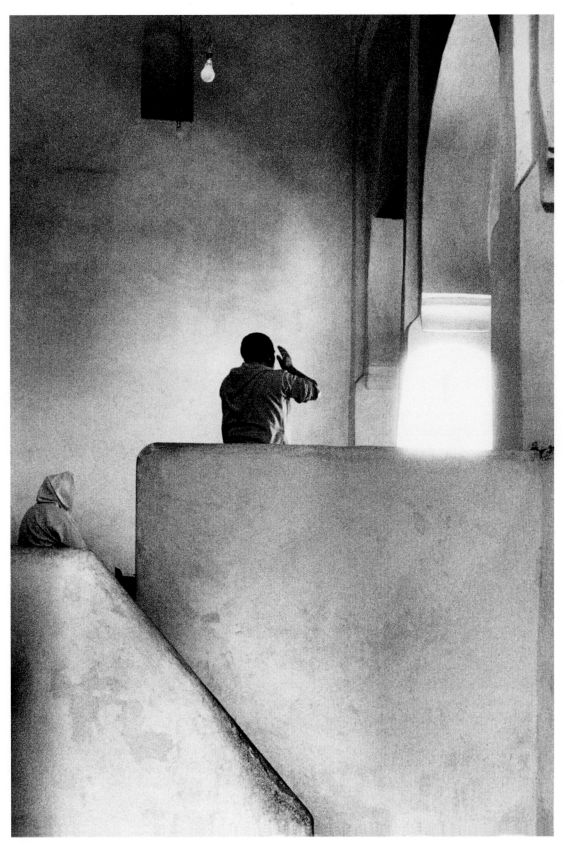

13.7
KAMEL DRIDI, *Mosque, Fes*, 1987. Société Française de la Photographie, Paris.

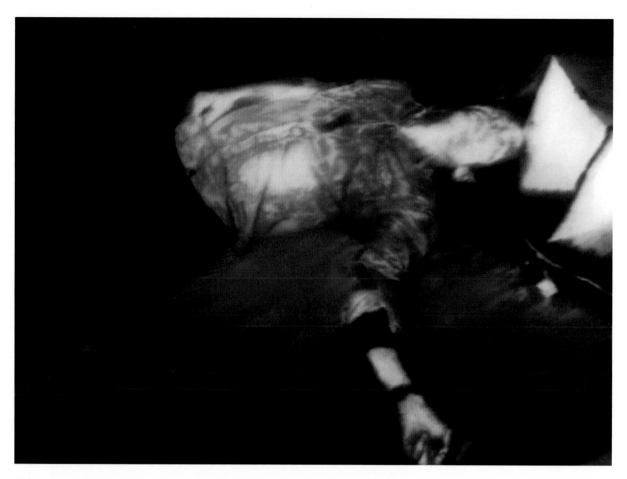

13.8
GERHARD RICHTER, *Shot Down (1)*, 1988, from his series *18 Oktober 1977*. Oil on canvas, 39¼ x 55 in. (99.7 x 139.7 cm).

paintings" glow with suffused Romantic light, but others have a sinister dreaminess to them, as if the subject, hovering between painting and photography, cannot or will not allow itself to be fully grasped (Fig. 13.8). Produced a decade after the events, Richter's paintings refer to a specific incident of the deaths in prison of political activists, only to obscure it like a memory that is ten years old. Through blur, which indicates an eye dimmed with tears and a mind clouded with opinions, he transformed simple archival photographs into symbols for the tangled issue of German historical memory in and of the twentieth century. The smudged surfaces of the canvases erased the sharpness of their newspaper sources, imitating not only hazy recall but also the sense of lost idealism, felt especially by Germans who lived through the tensions and moral compromises of the Cold War.

The work of James Welling (b. 1951) is also deliberately misleading. He has photographed what appear to be black-and-white renditions of abstract paintings, or deeply shadowed abstract photographs in the manner of Aaron Siskind and Frederick Sommer (see Figs. 11.3, 11.5). Welling relies on the viewer's recollection of abstract art, especially as it was seen for years in black-and-white photography, to accept the absence of recognizable subject matter in *August 16a* (Fig. 13.9). In fact, the picture is no more than a shadowy close-up of aluminum foil.

German-born photographer Uta Barth (b. 1958) creates fragmentary, fuzzy pictures that depict light and color punctuated by wisps of identifiable subject matter (Fig. 13.10). In Barth's work, any trace of narrative seems to dissolve, an effect hastened by her off-kilter, seemingly out-of-focus approach. She does focus her work, but on an imaginary plane of space, rather than recognizable objects. She seeks to present the peripheral and marginal—the things that stand on the edge of our attention. To stress her interest in perception, she sometimes hangs her work at eye-level. Her photographs express the impossibility of intelligible experience or certain definition, as well as the desire, however repressed, to seek pleasure in simply looking. Her technique recalls the attitude of Victorian photographer Julia Margaret Cameron, for whom photographic focus had to fit the mood of the subject matter, not necessarily mimic the clarity of ordinary optical experience.

The black-and-white series by New York-based Japanese photographer Hiroshi Sugimoto (b. 1948) shares with Barth a regard for the fragile beauty of uncertainty, expressed in grainy atmospheric effects. Sugimoto often works in series, such as his ongoing work with the wildlife dioramas at the American Museum of Natural History in New York, and including his lush black-and-white images of early twentieth-century movie

13.9
JAMES WELLING, *August 16a*, 1980. Gelatin silver print.

13.10 (below)
UTA BARTH, *Ground #42*, 1994. Color photograph on panel.

The rooms Barth photographs are almost empty, emphasizing their existence as containers for light. She focuses here on the unoccupied foreground space so as to blur the depth of field out of which dimly emerge two reproductions of paintings by Johannes Vermeer, *The Milkmaid* (Rijksmuseum, Amsterdam) on the left and *The Lacemaker* (Louvre, Paris) on the right. Barth's technique recalls Julia Margaret Cameron, for whom the avoidance of focus could suit the mood of her subject matter (see Fig. 3.19).

13.11
HIROSHI SUGIMOTO, *Aegean Sea, Pilion 1*, 1990.

theaters across the United States. For more than two decades, he has traveled the world seeking high vantage points from which to aim his camera at the point where the sky and ocean come together at the horizon (Fig. 13.11). The boundless vistas he portrays are reminiscent of Pictorialism's thronging gray tones. Sugimoto's work manifests the dichotomy between the rapture of visual pleasure and the cold comfort of human systems of measurement.

The PINHOLE CAMERA, favored by Pictorialists such as George Davison (see Fig. 6.11) because its wide angle stretched and fogged photography's typically deep pictorial space, was reinvestigated by late twentieth-century artists such as Barbara Ess (b. 1946) and Nobuo Yamanaka (see p. 382). For Mark McLoughlin (b. 1953?) the pinhole camera was a retreat from the many technological options available in the 1990s. It allowed him to pare down the image-making process and experience what he calls "serendipity over science," and gave him a rationale for image-making into the twenty-first century (see Fig. 13.12).

By contrast, Hungarian artist Zoltán Szegedy-Maszák (b. 1969) turned to pinhole photography in the 1990s to explore imaging with light. For him, pinhole work excited experimental and interactive applications. He folded and crumbled the light-sensitive paper in the pinhole camera in a way that resembles the technique used by Walead Beshty (see p. 516) to create photographic abstractions. What the Kodak Instamatic and other point-and-shoot cameras were to such artists as Andy Warhol and Robert Smithson in the 1960s (see pp. 374–5, 376, 378), the pinhole was to the 1990s and the present era: an alternative to commercial and digital photography.

London-born Adam Fuss (b. 1961) is likewise disposed toward older, elementary forms of photography. He extensively employs cameraless image-making in the form of the PHOTOGRAM or what William Henry Fox Talbot called "photogenic drawing." Using a technique that also fueled experimental photography between the world wars, Fuss sometimes records only the action of light on sensitive film,

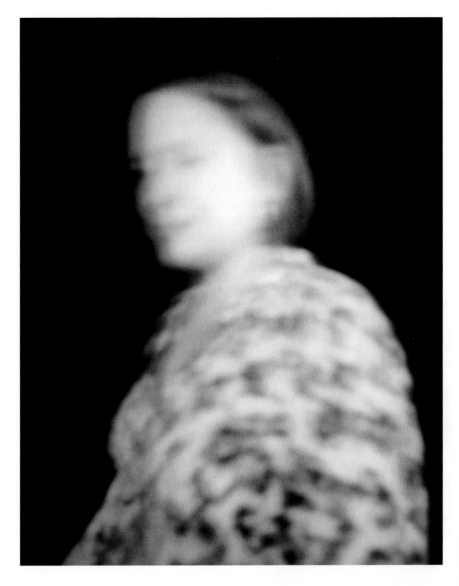

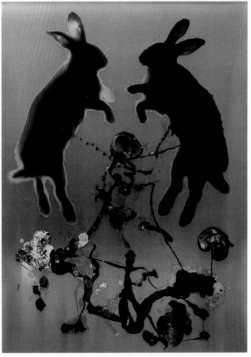

13.13
ADAM FUSS, *Wish*, 1992. Color photogram.

or the concentric circles made by falling droplets of water. For
the enigmatically titled *Wish* (1992), he arranged two rabbits as if
they were heraldic animals on a medieval shield (Fig. 13.13).
Fuss identifies more with painters than photographers, stating
that he is less interested in Postmodern theory than in the
expressive qualities of photographic techniques.

By contrast, Spanish photographer Joan Fontcuberta
was a Postmodernist before the movement began! From his
precocious teenage years, he approached photography as
the art of fabrication—in every sense of the word. His very
first photographs were staged, and he quickly moved into
montage. His use of the photogram is rooted in his axiom that
a photograph best conveys the fact that it is a photograph, an
idea that neatly reinforces Postmodern notions of media and
representation. Even though a photogram is a trace of the objects
set on or near the light-sensitive paper, Fontcuberta toys with
the viewer by not visually disclosing which of the flower images
that impressed themselves on the final photograph were actual

flowers and which were from mass-manufactured wallpaper (Fig. 13.14). In other words, the copy of the real is no more real than a stereotype. Likely enough, Fontcuberta quickly embraced digital imaging and advanced software. For his 2002 series, *Landscapes without Memory*, he uploaded pictures of famous paintings as well as of his body, and asked the sophisticated software to interpret the data and create imagery.

During the last decades of the twentieth century, the DIANA camera and other inexpensive instruments found favor with photographers, who were attracted to its foggy, unevenly lit image and its distortions. Mexican photographer Carlos Somonte (b. 1956) rejected documentary realism. He chose a cheap plastic camera to photograph casual snapshots (Fig. 3.15) as well as images of the poor inhabitants of Mexico's northern and central desert areas. Easy to achieve with a Diana camera, Barbara

Pollack's blurry photographs require considerable planning. Her *The Family of Men* installation (1999), which invoked the design of the 1955 exhibit at the Museum of Modern Art by suspending large-scale pictures at different heights (see Fig. 10.2), showed indistinct color photographs of her husband and son (Fig. 13.16). Pollack's main focus is voyeurism—that is, the desire to look—and what it feels like to be looked at. To that end, she intentionally blurs the image to frustrate the viewer's gaze, and make the viewer more aware of efforts to look.

FEMINISM AND POSTMODERN PHOTOGRAPHY
In an influential article titled "The Discourse of Others: Feminists and Postmodernism," critic Craig Owens pointed out a convergence of "the postmodernism critique of representation," and "the feminist critique of patriarchy."[22] He looked back at

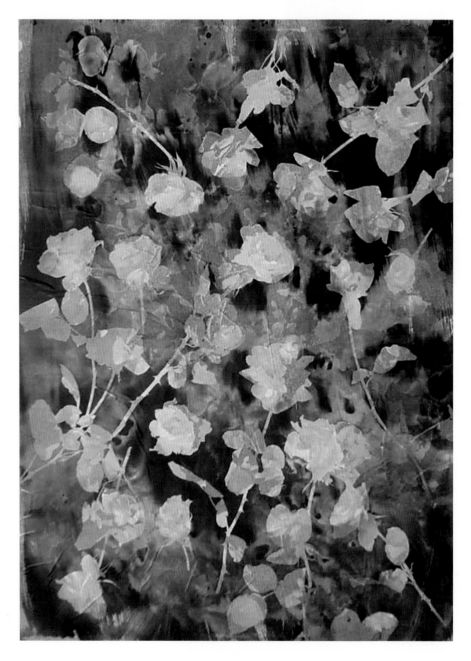

13.14
JOAN FONTCUBERTA, *Ich danke Ihnen für die Rosen*, from his series *Paper Gardens*, 1990. Photogram on foil wrapping paper.

13.16 (opposite)
BARBARA POLLACK, Installation view of *The Family of Men*, Thread-waxing Space, New York, 1999.

Pollack used out-of-date film and old Polaroid cameras to create *The Family of Men*. After exposure, she smeared and smudged the emulsion while it was developing. In contrast to Steichen's 1955 exhibition, "The Family of Man," Pollack's show displays not universal harmony, but interpersonal tension embodied in strained visual distortions.

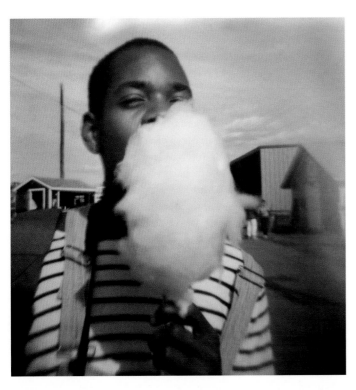

13.15
CARLOS SOMONTE, *Lyle Ashton Harris with cotton candy, Rockport County Fair, Maine, U.S.A., 1986.*

Martha Rosler's series *The Bowery in Two Inadequate Descriptive Systems* (see Fig. 13.3), retroactively casting it as a Postmodern work because of Rosler's attempt to undermine the truth value of visual and verbal texts. Owens also enlisted Cindy Sherman's film stills to point out how the artist assumed roles so as to reveal them as gender stereotypes. Applying the psychoanalytic theory of French thinker Jacques Lacan (1901–1981), Owens was one of the first to fix on the notion that, if gender is not innate but culturally acquired, it can also be culturally rejected and redirected. The initial bridge Owens built between Postmodernism and feminism supported many subsequent accounts, and encouraged comparable investigations of received ideas on race and sexual preference.

The intense focus on gender as a kind of performance, rather than the expression of an inherent feminine or masculine temperament, followed a period in which some feminist photographers and photographic historians had begun to rehabilitate the reputations of nineteenth- and early twentieth-century women photographers such as Julia Margaret Cameron and Frances Benjamin Johnston. After producing the book *The Feminine Eye in Photography* (1973), at a time when the work of many women photographers was largely unknown, Californian

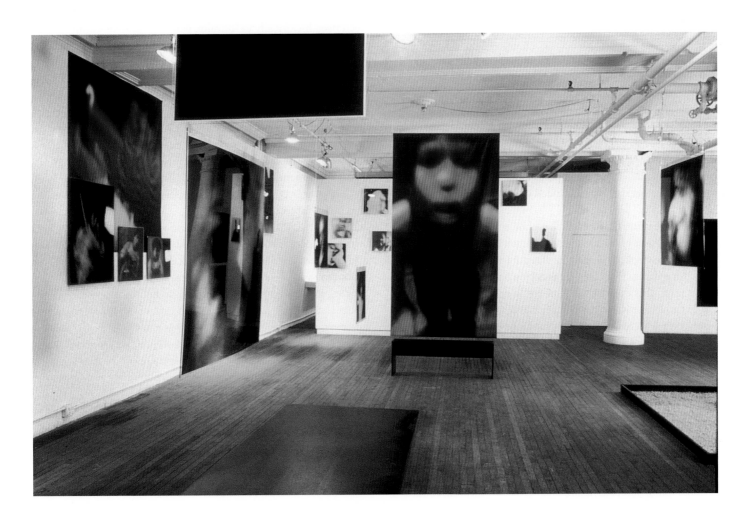

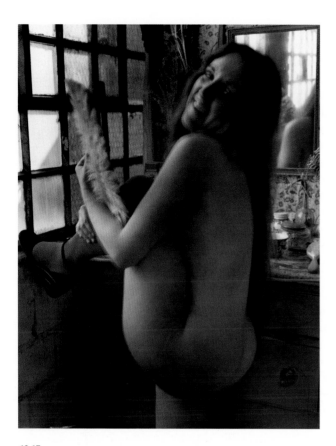

13.17
JUDY DATER, *Maureen with Fan*, 1972, from the book *Women and Other Visions*, 1972.

photographer Judy Dater (b. 1941) created portraits showing women comfortable with their own bodies (Fig. 13.17). Several other studies and exhibitions attempted to show the breadth of women's photographic work. Anne Tucker's *The Woman's Eye* (1973), Val Williams's *Women Photographers: The Other Observers, 1900 to the Present* (1986), and Naomi Rosenblum's *A History of Women Photographers* (1994) helped gather initial data, and gave impetus to the ongoing study of the social factors that have excluded women from histories of photography.

The restoration of women's past photographic pursuits and the presentation of female sexuality began to be berated by critics, who attacked the uncomplicated notion that there was something distinctive about images by women. They believed that it promoted the idea of an inherent feminine essence. For example, British writers Griselda Pollock and Janet Wolff asserted that there is no intrinsic feminine or masculine essence, only complex networks of culturally conditioned markers that construct what superficially appears to be coherent gender identity.[23] They questioned the experimental writings of French theorists Hélène Cixous and Julia Kristeva, both of whom put forward the concept of "writing from the body," or "feminine writing"—that is, the possibility of creative expression that eludes through indirection the dominant male point of view.

The French theorists' ideas were becoming widely persuasive in academic settings, including art schools, where it had already become important to visualize an alternative feminine condition,

one sufficiently protean and anti-authoritarian to evade the pervasive gender stereotype of the nurturing, emotionally ruled woman. Conceptual artists such as the French image-maker Annette Messager (b. 1943) responded to this vein of feminist theory. Messager created her fragmented photo-pieces as an embodiment of Cixous's idea that the feminine was not fixed but was, instead, an aggregate of unstructured perspectives that thwarted summarization. In *Mes Voeux* (*My Vows*), Messager suspended from strings of different lengths several hundred photographs of women's body parts (Fig. 13.24).

Throughout the 1980s and 1990s, essentialist feminists—that is, people who believed that femininity is a real inborn trait—vied with culturalists, who held that gender roles were culturally determined. In photography, this argument ignited competing exhibition rationales and vigorous critical reviews. For instance, the 1987 show "Reclaiming Paradise: American Women Photograph the Land" was conceived to show a basic sameness underlying women's photography from different eras, a resemblance that stood in very opposition to landscape views taken by men. The exhibition hoped to show that women used visual strategies that indicate a caring attitude toward the earth, whereas, by contrast, men frame the land in ways that indicate a desire to possess and own it. Critic and photographer Deborah Bright (b. 1950) was among those who objected to the premise of a woman's landscape photography. She pointed out that aligning women with nature and natural functions had long been used historically to "devalue women and their cultural production." For Bright, the claim that women are "naturally" creative also suggested that men must create "artificially," through cultural and technological means alien to women.[24]

While scholars debated the desired direction of photographic history and practice, American graphic designer Barbara Kruger (b. 1945) culled photographically derived mass-media images for use in an extensive series of confrontational poster-like pictures based on Postmodern assumptions about women in society. Like experimental German photographers between the world wars, she inserted bold, blocky type derived from advertising into her compositions, both as design elements and for their meaning (Fig. 13.18). The art museum was only one location in which Kruger's work appeared; she also sought out public venues and commercial formats, putting her images and slogans on billboards and even department store shopping bags.

Despite the oppositional messages in her images, Barbara Kruger was well incorporated into the art world, the sales gallery, and even advertising, where her work was considered stylish. Indeed, by the mid-1990s, appropriation itself was mocked as a worn-out visual device, as when Amy Adler (b. 1967) photographed her own drawing of Sherrie Levine's appropriation of a photograph by Edward Weston.

CONSTRUCTED REALITIES AND THE DIRECTORIAL MODE

In a period of multiple convergences, one of the most fruitful for photographic practice was the hybridization of Conceptual art's interest in ideas, Postmodernism's investigation into visual

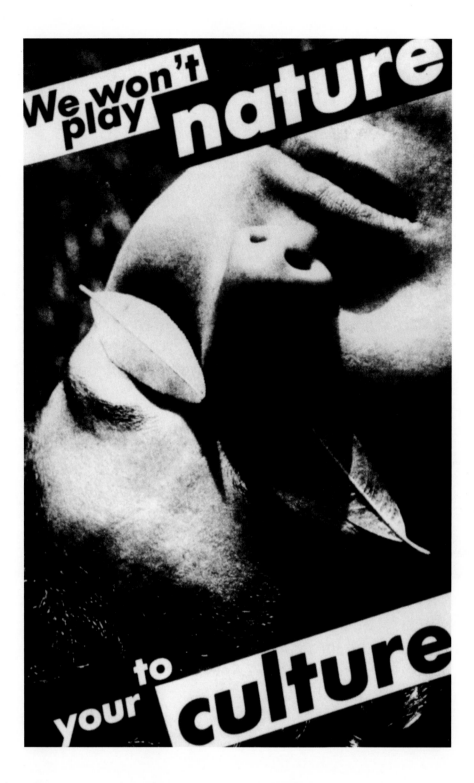

and verbal signs, and the increased presence of installation art beginning in the late 1970s. The mixture was evident in the widespread practice sometimes referred to as the "staged photograph." Interestingly, attempts to create fictions for the camera never acquired an accepted label. Especially in its early years, staging was awkwardly called the "fabricated-to-be-photographed" approach, meaning that a scene was composed mostly, but not always totally, of inanimate objects. Equally ambiguous terms were also tried, such as "the constructed photograph," which did not indicate the collage technique, but referred to any scenes assembled for the camera. As early as 1976, American critic A. D. Coleman outlined an extensive history for what he called the "directorial mode," in which he made the case that contemporary staged photographs had precedents, such as Civil War photographer Alexander Gardner's deliberate moving of a dead Confederate soldier so as to compose a more richly symbolic image (see Fig. 4.17), or the nineteenth-century STEREOGRAPH, in which many narrative scenes were enacted as a matter of course (see pp. 78–81).[25]

focus

Culture Wars

13.19
ANDRES SERRANO, *Piss Christ*, 1987. Cibachrome, silicone, Plexiglas, wood frame, edition of 4.

A fabricated-to-be-photographed image was at the center of a national debate in the United States about public funding for the arts. On May 18, 1989, New York Senator Alphonse D'Amato demonstrated his hostility to public funding of the arts in the United States by ripping up a photograph of a work by the then little-known artist Andres Serrano (b. 1950). The offending image showed a crucifix suspended in an illuminated bubbly, reddish-yellow liquid (Fig. 13.19). The radiant glow around the crucifix made it seem like a work of devout religious fervor. Were it not for the title, *Piss Christ*, viewers could not tell that the liquid was urine.

The piece had been exhibited at a show of fellowship winners held by the Southeastern Center for Contemporary Art in Winston-Salem, North Carolina. The program was sponsored by private foundations, including the Rockefeller Foundation and the Equitable Foundation, as well as the government-funded National Endowment for the Arts.[26] Only the last organization, which channeled public money, was criticized for its support.

Serrano devised and labeled his work to bring about a collision of extremes: intense aesthetic pleasure and strong physical revulsion. Another piece, *Semen and Blood III*, shows these bodily fluids swirling in a dynamic abstraction. But Serrano undercut the enjoyment of shapes and colors with a title that unambiguously declares its unorthodox materials, and put viewers in mind of the connection of sexuality with disease, particularly AIDS. Some observers complained that they were repelled by Serrano's pictures, just as if they were in the physical presence of the substances. Others felt fooled into experiencing visual pleasure from elements repugnant to them.

The dispute ignited by Senator D'Amato raged on, fueled by people of faith who felt that Serrano had desecrated a cherished religious symbol at public expense. Critic Steven C. Dubin observed that the public controversy over *Piss Christ* was prompted by a national sense of uncertainty about the future, which also kindled a longing for traditional values of home and church during the Reagan administration. These feelings found a target in Serrano's picture. In the end, government funding to the arts was placed under the scrutiny of the so-called "Helms amendment," named for its sponsor, North Carolina Senator Jesse Helms. It barred public moneys from underwriting so-called "obscene" work, unless it had "serious literary, artistic, political, or scientific value."[27]

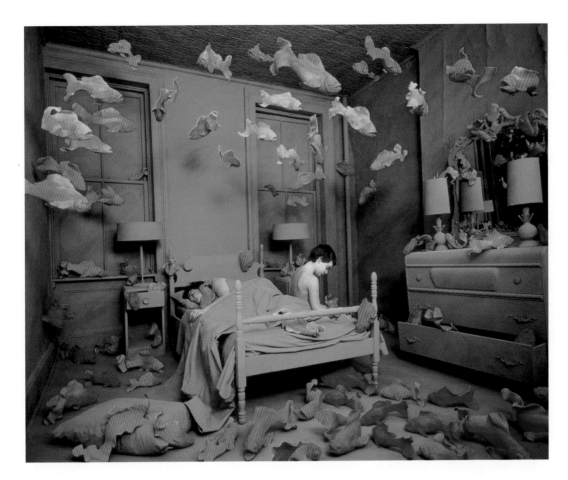

13.20
SANDY SKOGLUND, *Revenge of the Goldfish,* **1981. Silver dye-bleach (Cibachrome) print.**

Skoglund unified the area in her room-size installations by applying the same color paint to the walls, floors, and furnishings. The bright orange goldfish who fly in the air and wriggle on the floorboards make the picture both fanciful and menacing—a balance often achieved in her work.

Of course, the *tableaux vivants* orchestrated by nineteenth-century photographers Oscar Rejlander and Henry Peach Robinson (see Figs. 3.12, 3.14) were assembled to be photographed, but the artists' motives could hardly have been more different from those of late twentieth-century picture-makers. Sometimes Rejlander and Robinson could not make the stubborn paper negatives and imprecise lens clearly capture the image they had mentally conceived. Rejlander and Robinson welcomed the hands-on, directorial aspects of composite photography as a way to negate the criticism that photography was witlessly automatic and therefore not an art.

But when fabricated-to-be-photographed approaches became widespread in the 1980s, former technical difficulties had long been overcome, and the issue of whether a photograph could be art was not raucously contested. Photographers and critics began to adopt the long view, noting that from its beginnings, mundane photographic studio work normally demanded staging, rehearsal, and lighting strategies. In particular, the history of advertising photography is filled with a steady stream of sophisticated fabricating techniques, such as intricate artificial lighting and suggestive, unnatural color, used to enhance the appeal of products. In addition, the omnipresence of movies and television, in which a director orchestrates scenes, may have amplified photographers' desire to direct for the still camera. Though the movement seems to have arisen within photographic practice, it was abetted by the success in the early 1980s of the edgy narrative paintings created by artists such as Eric Fischl (b. 1948) and, more recently, the suburban Surrealism of German painter Neo Rauch (b. 1960).

The lack of an overarching "-ism" for staged photographs may owe to the fact that it was not an art movement driven by a core of beliefs, but an approach that interested image-makers with different artistic perspectives and ideological positions. What the fabricators had in common was not a philosophy but a methodology, and, perhaps, a boredom or anger with the limitations of Modernist idioms. Where Modernist photographers combed the visual field for delightful coincidence, poignant metaphors, or abstract patterns, photographers working in the directorial mode conceived and fabricated subjects, disregarding photography's conventional assignment of finding meaning from the look of the world. In addition, the Postmodern dismantling of photographic truth indirectly encouraged the creation of photographic fictions.

The making of scenes, rather than the taking of scenes, was epitomized in the work of American sculptor-photographer Sandy Skoglund (b. 1946), who created room-size installations to be viewed in their own right as three-dimensional sculptures, as well as photographs. In her work, exaggerated objects, such as cobalt-blue leaves or safety-orange fish, invade spaces occupied by sense-dulled people stranded in monochrome settings (Fig. 13.20). Skoglund's work anticipated the partnership between sculpture and photography that pervaded art in the

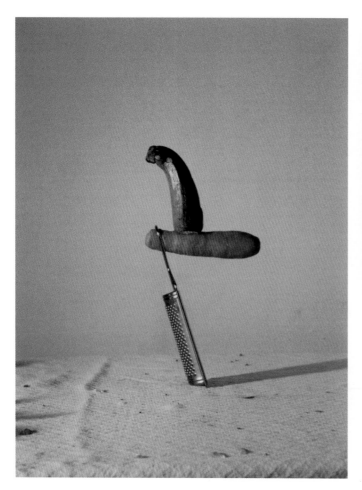

13.21
PETER FISCHLI AND DAVID WEISS, *Untitled*, from the series *Stiller Nachmittag*, 1985. Kunsthaus, Zurich.

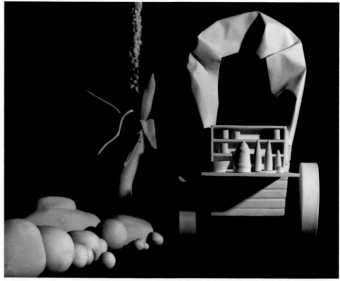

13.22
JAMES CASEBERE, *Chuck Wagon with Yucca*, 1988. Gelatin silver print, edition of 7.

Casebere, who began his career in sculpture, works with both larger-than-life pieces and dollhouse-size objects, all derived from the world of experience but presented in a flat monotone, with the distinguishing edges and textures smoothed away, as in memory or a dream. In this image, the wheels of the chuck wagon are too polished to seem authentic, and the canvas covering lacks roughness.

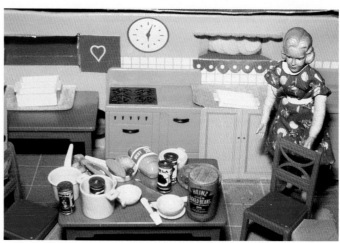

13.23
LAURIE SIMMONS, *Blonde/Red Dress/Kitchen*, 1978.

last decades of the twentieth century, ranging from the tongue-in-cheek balancing acts pictured by Swiss artists Peter Fischli (b. 1952) and David Weiss (1946–2012) (Fig. 13.21) to the cool, cerebral black-and-white world pictured by James Casebere (b. 1953) (Fig. 13.22). Large, richly colored and fabricated-to-be-photographed scenes were also made by German artist Thomas Demand (see Fig. 14.9). By constructing scenes and objects for the camera's eye, the photographer can control every detail of the image.

By contrast, Mexican artist Gabriel Orozco (b. 1962) prizes fleeting perceptions of art, especially the unintentional presence of sculpture in everyday life. Orozco points to the gracefulness of a melting popsicle, chronicles the brief life of a human breath exhaled on to the polished surface of a piano, and fabricates makeshift scenes to be photographed (Fig. 13.1). American Laurie Simmons (b. 1949) works with doll's-house-like settings in which small plastic figures robotically act out routine incidents of domestic life (Fig. 13.23). When Simmons began making images of males, she continued her concern with authenticity and originality by manipulating ventriloquists' dummies. With many other late twentieth-century artists who

use the camera, Skoglund, Fischli and Weiss, Casebere, Demand, Simmons, and Orozco want to be principally known not as photographers but as artists who work with photography, as well as other media.

The success of performance art before a live audience during the late twentieth century influenced the conception of staged photographs. For example, starting in the mid-1980s, Japanese sculptor turned photographer, Tokihiro Satō (b. 1957) initiated what might be called ephemeral sculpture or light performance pieces, not conceived for a live audience but intended solely

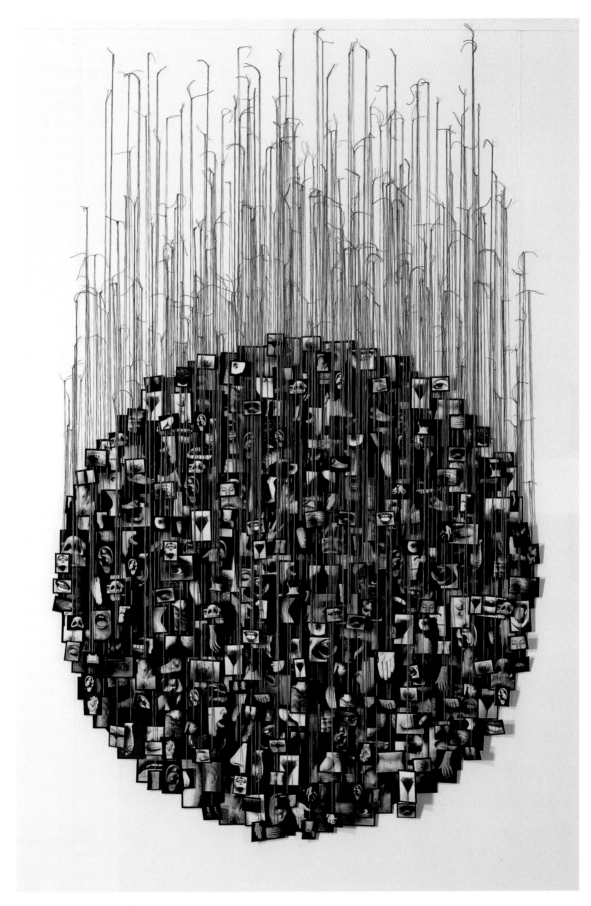

13.24
ANNETTE MESSAGER, *Mes Voeux* (*My Vows*), 1990. Black-and-white photographs and string.

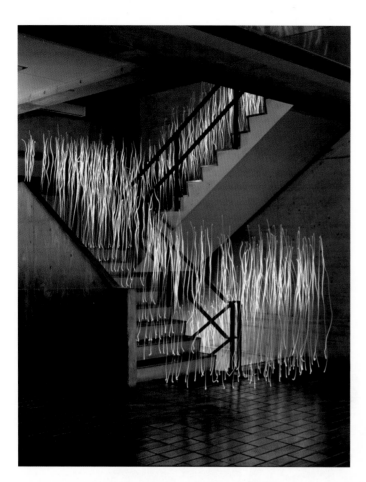

13.25
TOKIHIRO SATO, *Photo-Respiration (Breath-graph no. 22)*, **1988.**

to be viewed as a photograph (Fig. 13.25). In interior settings Sato used projected light, such as a flashlight, and in exterior locations he captured and reflected sunlight with a mirror, all the while moving so quickly that his camera, adjusted for long, slow exposure, could record only twinkles and trails of bright light, not his body. Like Robert Smithson before him, Satō created transient environments that exist only for the camera. Yet where Smithson tried to stop the flow of time, Satō wanted his so-called "breath-graphs" to suggest time's progress; he imagined that his pictures intimated the accumulated streams of human energy that had been expended in the settings he photographed.

The directorial mode was instigated by artists and photographers for whom video constituted an absorbing initial experience of directing, rather than physically making, a work of art. It also benefited from the allure of film and, especially the cultic admiration of film directors such as Alfred Hitchcock, whose exceedingly planned scripts often revolved around the innocence of an ordinary individual who must cope with an extraordinary happening. The disquieting and shadowy scenes of Gregory Crewdson (b. 1962) are produced with big budgets and the assistance of a crew whose jobs are the same as they would be on a film project. Like a film director, Crewdson does extensive post-production additions and alterations, using cutting-edge digital-editing tools. Working in series, he crafts enigmatic

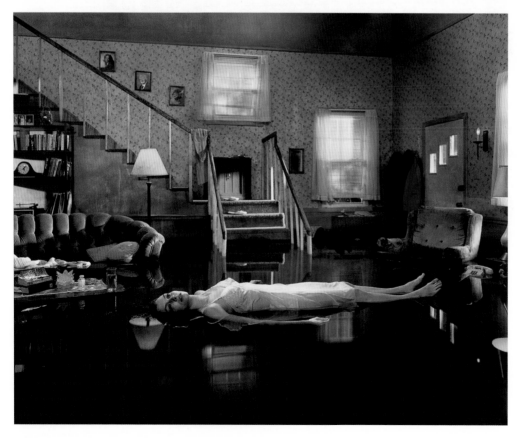

13.26
GREGORY CREWDSON, *Ophelia*, **2001.
Digital C-print.**

Crewdson's melodramatic stagings suggest an undercurrent of abnormal events. His creations were among the most influential on young photographers working in the late twentieth and early twenty-first centuries.

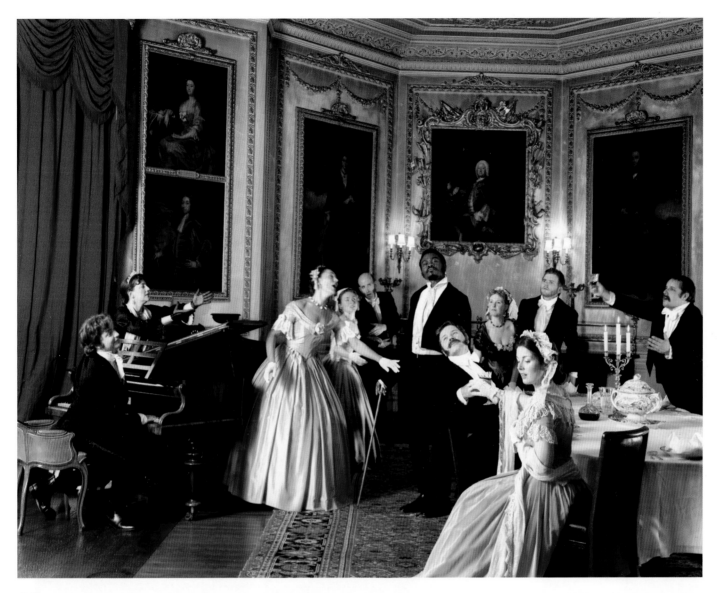

13.27
YINKA SHONIBARE, *Diary of a Victorian Dandy (21:00 hours),* **1998. C-type print.**

scenes that often take place in small towns or suburban tracts. These locales, standard settings for the American dream of the good life, are seen in many films by Steven Spielberg, whom Crewdson admires, but in Crewdson's work suburban life is on the brink of being splintered by nail-biting anxiety. He invokes the uncanny and the edgy supernatural effects that made the television series *The X-Files* popular (1993–2002), and admits to being influenced by David Lynch's 1986 film *Blue Velvet,* which cracked the patina of ordinary hometown life with the revelation of secret sexual behavior. Crewdson wants to explore "the American psyche through the American vernacular landscape, much as [the painter Edward] Hopper did."[28] For example, in Crewdson's *Ophelia* (Fig. 13.26), a scene from the *Twilight* series that he began in 1998, a woman seems to float on water that has mysteriously filled her living room. The subject, drawn from William Shakespeare's play *Hamlet,* is about a sensitive

young woman who becomes mentally unbalanced and drowns herself. Many painters and photographers, such as Henry Peach Robinson and Julia Margaret Cameron (see Fig. 3.19), also took up the subject.

Famous paintings from the canon of Western art also served as sources for fabricated images. The life of Christ, as seen in the history of art, inspired several photographers to stage such scenes as the Last Supper and the Crucifixion. In one of his series the London-born, Nigeria-raised artist Yinka Shonibare (b. 1962), who works in many media, posed himself incongruously in the midst of figures enacting a scene whose setting, gestures, costumes, and colors resemble late eighteenth- and nineteenth-century painting (Fig. 13.27). American photographer Joel-Peter Witkin (b. 1939) also mined art history for ideas, occasionally improvising elaborate tableaux recalling familiar paintings in the Western tradition, and then aging the resultant image by

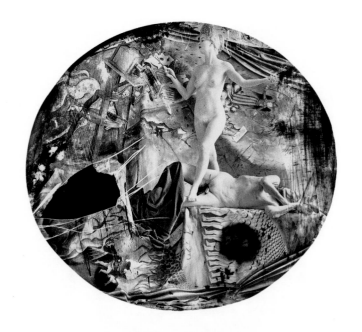

scratching the negative and antiquing the print's tone. The aging appearance adds an unsettling, dreamlike effect to his fantastic visions, which are often charged with an unsettling eroticism (Fig. 13.28).

As image-makers began to "make" and then "take" their pictures, they also increased the size and intensity of their pictures. For example, Satō's *Breath-graph # 22* is 95¼ inches by 77½ inches. This development was showcased in a 1983 exhibit at New York's Museum of Modern Art, called "Big Pictures." Not only did photographs come to emulate the size of large paintings in museums and galleries; they also acquired deeply saturated, tropically hot colors, more obviously associated with paint than with photographic materials. Sandy Skoglund's installations and photographs erupt in the piercing colors of acrylic paint. Similarly, the collages of waste materials gathered together and

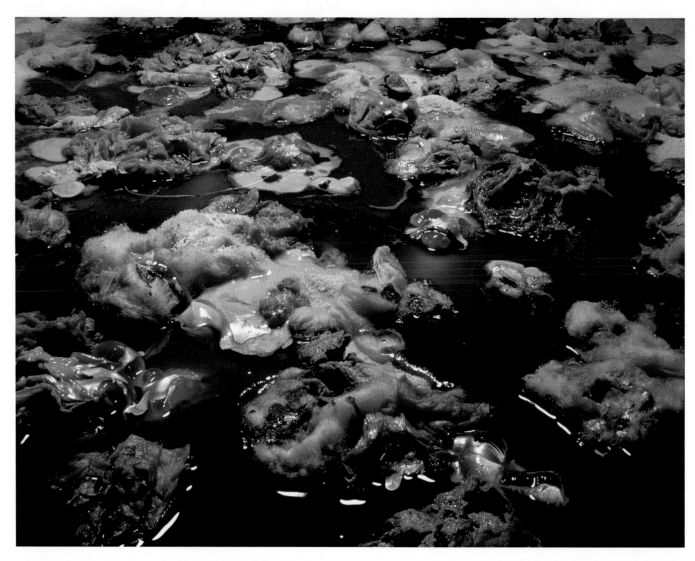

13.29
TIM HEAD, *Toxic Lagoon*, 1987. Cibachrome print.

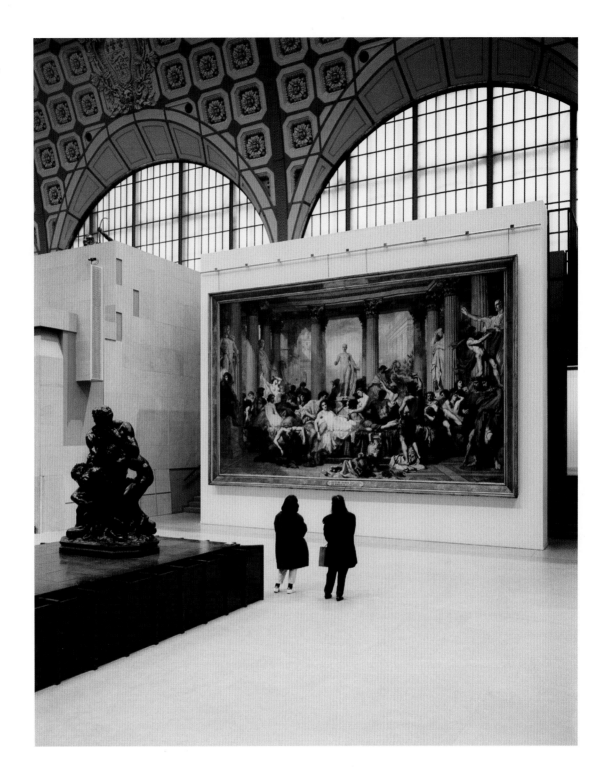

13.30
THOMAS STRUTH,
Musée d'Orsay, Paris, 1989.

photographed by British artist Tim Head (b. 1946) concentrate on the eye-catching density of the color used in packaging consumer goods. During the 1980s, Head began gathering discarded mass-produced materials to serve as the basis for his photographs. At once luridly attractive and repugnant, Head's images of ecological calamities imitate the push–pull of desire and guilt (Fig. 13.29). In the 1990s, the art gallery and the photograph came together in yet another way, in the large photographs of Thomas Struth (b. 1954), who created detailed yet huge studies of people contemplating art in museums (Fig. 13.30). The odd, quasi-religious convention of maintaining silence or talking in hushed tones while visiting an art gallery finds a visual correspondence in the poses and expressions of people attempting to deliberate images considered to be masterworks in Western art. Struth did not use digital means to create his museum series, but achieved his prints employing a large-format camera similar to those used by nineteenth-century photographers.

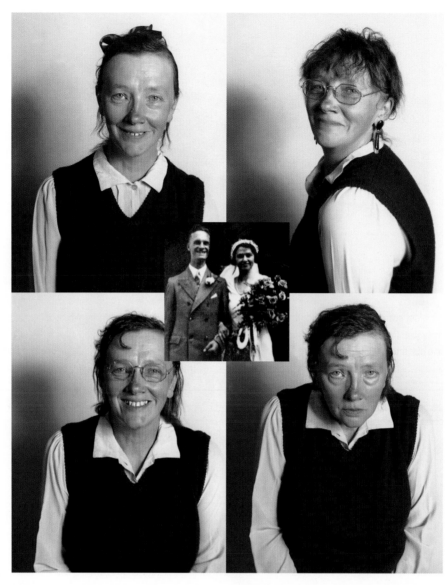

13.31
JO SPENCE, *Transformations,* **from her book** *Putting Myself in the Picture,* **1986.**

FAMILY PICTURES

Although staged photographs did not arise as part of a consistent art movement, several motifs recurred, among them the subject of the family, a topic taken up around the world during the late twentieth century. Focus on domestic life intensified, in part because the concept of the ideal family had been rocked by a high divorce rate, picked over in family therapy, and mangled in the popular media, from *Roseanne* through *The Simpsons.* During the Reagan administration (1981–89) in the United States, and the years that Margaret Thatcher was prime minister of Britain (1979–90), traditional values, in particular the glorified norm of the white, middle-class family, were enlisted as remedies for a tattered social morality thought to reveal itself in the increase of single-parent families, the rising demand for abortion and birth control, and the growth of gay and lesbian activism.

Of course, many early photographers made images of their family members, chiefly because they were near at hand. William Henry Fox Talbot photographed his wife, Constance, who also made her own photographs. From the beginning, amateurs and professionals practiced lighting techniques and rehearsed stances using members of the family. Nevertheless, few nineteenth-century photographers operated like Lady Hawarden and Julia Margaret Cameron, purposefully posing family members in evocative attitudes suggestive of characters in literature and myth. In the postwar period, Edward Steichen's "The Family of Man" exhibition and the best-selling book that accompanied it became conceptual markers to which most photographers had to attend, whether they were inspired by the emphasis on the universal bonds of family life, or distressed by the omission of personal, social, and economic circumstances that differentiate people from each other.

In addition, throughout the twentieth century, families accumulated extensive collections of images, the majority taken with simple cameras and increasingly reliable film. The content of family photographs was dominated by celebratory occasions, such as weddings, birthdays, and vacations. Few families resolutely set out to record the look of everyday life, such as messy kitchens and unmade beds. Fewer still made visual records of emotionally trying times, or used the camera for psychological self-study or therapy. Interestingly, the very themes and subjects omitted in family pictures were explored by a wide variety of photographers, and studied by artists and scholars. British critic and photographer Jo Spence (1934–1992) was one of the first image-makers to use her own baby pictures, family snapshots, and early studio portraits to investigate her socialization into gender and class roles. Out of this experience she and actor Rosy Martin developed what was called "the reconstructive process," a psychological therapy in which new photographic portraits were made in order "to disrupt, replace or rework" an aspect of personality (Fig. 13.31). Artists came to view the casual snapshot, with its innocence of technique and composition, and the cheap camera, with its lack of sophisticated metering or fine lenses,

as exciting means with which to extricate photography from its longstanding infatuation with "artistry." Canadian photographer Jeff Wall dubbed this far-reaching, self-imposed, de-skilling of photographers as "amateurization."[29]

Toward the end of the Cold War in Russia, Soviet photographers "amateurized" their photographs, creasing and spotting the print in experiments with what they called "the aesthetics of defect."[30] Ignoring the fact that the humble and crumpled snapshot could be as riddled with conventions as the refined studio portrait or the news photograph, some photographers looked to it as a means to escape the pervasive influence of Henri Cartier-Bresson's "decisive moment." German writer Ulf Erdmann Ziegler accused the "decisive moment" of being an intellectually and visually reductive technique that diminished photography to a mere anecdote.[31] Family photographs not only refreshed art; they also energized social commentary. In East Germany during the 1980s, Ute Mahler (b. 1949) pictured an array of households that repudiated the official state-sponsored view of the normal family (Fig. 13.32). The Chinese photographer Wang Jinsong (b. 1963) focused on the family as an act of political resistance. His *Standard Family*

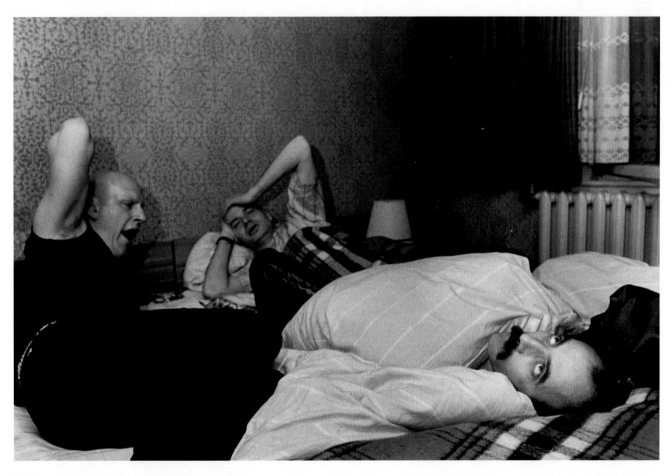

13.32
UTE MAHLER, *Untitled,* **from the series** *Living Together,* **c. 1981.**

Mahler's photographic series *Living Together* focused on the family, an approved subject for East German photography. But she moved beyond the idealized, happy household to show the variety of people who live together, and their idiosyncrasies.

series illustrates the effects of China's policy of one-child families in images of middle-aged and older couples that would be immediately understood by Chinese viewers (Fig. 13.33). Yet, as Wang explained, the image can be appreciated negatively, by those who object to China's rule, and positively, by those who favor population control.[32]

The fall of the Berlin Wall in 1989 and the reunification of the eastern and western halves of Germany the following year marked a change in German photographers' attitude toward the medium's social role. Arguing that the post-1989 period lacked vitality and ideological coherence, they became engrossed by lengthy, non-narrative depictions showing the tedium of daily life. However, the hold of the "decisive moment" was evident, even in the work of image-makers who emphatically tried to escape it. For example, the pictures by Andre Zelck

(b. 1962) of a marginally employed working-class family in the industrialized Ruhr area of Germany vacillate between precise, telling moments, and rambling pictures of miscellaneous scenes (Fig. 13.34).

The notion that home life had eclipsed street life in American art and documentary photography was the theme of a much discussed 1991 exhibition at New York's Museum of Modern Art called "Pleasures and Terrors of Domestic Comfort." Curator Peter Galassi sampled family photographs ranging from the disconcerting staged tableaux of Philip-Lorca di Corcia (b. 1953) (Fig. 13.35) through Tina Barney's representations of affluence (see Fig. 13.44), Sally Mann's controversial images of her immediate family (see Fig. 13.50), and Larry Sultan's views of his parents' daily routine (see Fig. 13.43). In the last decades of the twentieth century, when photographers increasingly created

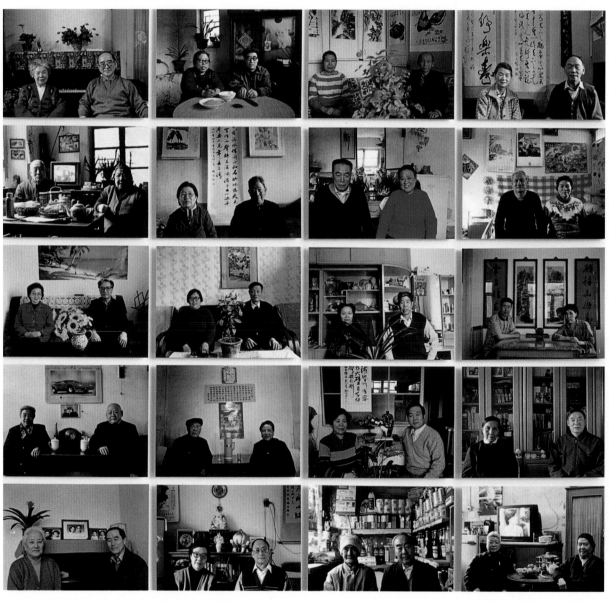

13.33
WANG JINSONG, *Parents,* **1998.**

13.34
ANDRE ZELCK, Untitled, from his series Familienbande (Family Group), 1992–96.

Zelck's family scene seems to show a moment beneath the notice of most snapshot makers. Despite its apparent casualness, the image is composed of interlocking triangular shapes, starting in the lower right-hand corner with the wedge of table that enters the picture. It reveals the difficulties of breaking away from the angular designs of Modernist photography.

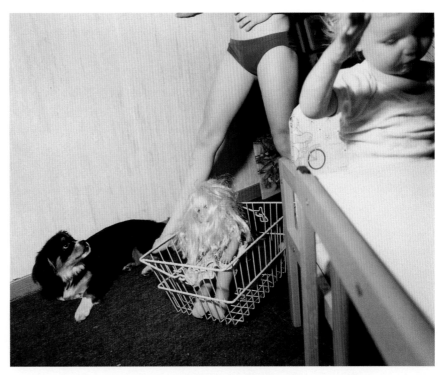

13.35
PHILIP-LORCA DI CORCIA, Brian, 1988, on the cover of the book accompanying the show "Pleasures and Terrors of Domestic Comfort," 1991. Offset, printed in color. Museum of Modern Art, New York.

An edgy foreboding seeps through Philip-Lorca di Corcia's images of ordinary domestic life. In this picture, the boy's thoughts seem far removed from the simple task of making a snack.

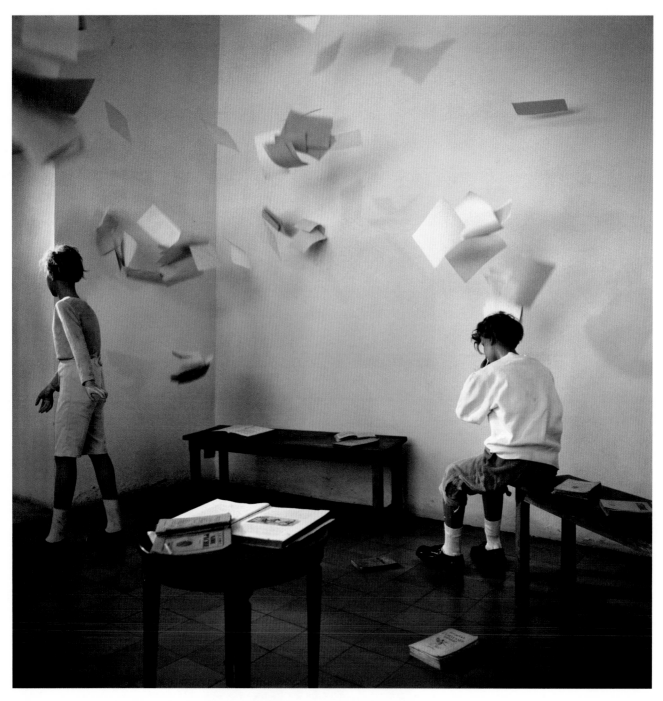

13.36
BERNARD FAUCON, *Les Papiers qui Volent*, 1977–95. Fresson technique, edition of 40.

sets and scenarios, family life and interaction with friends were increasingly pictured. Larry Sultan used his parents' home as the setting for the photographs directed by him, but other photographers, such as French image-maker Bernard Faucon (b. 1950), contrived elaborate backdrops and tableaux for tense, enigmatic domestic dramas (Fig. 13.37).

EXTENDED FAMILY
Photographers of daily life frequently expanded the definition of family from blood relatives to groups with which they associated.

In particular, the ever-expanding domain of youth culture became a fertile terrain for photographic description. German Göran Gnaudschun (b. 1971) assembled his photo-book project *Longe–44 Leningrad* as a chronicle of his life with a folk-punk band called 44 Leningrad. In Gnaudschun's words, *Longe*, or daily life, "does not aspire to relate a story, but the everyday cycle of constantly changing yet always recurring basic feelings."[33]

Similarly, Wolfgang Tillmans (b. 1968), a German living in London, began his career photographing the London club scene and street life for unconventional British fashion magazines

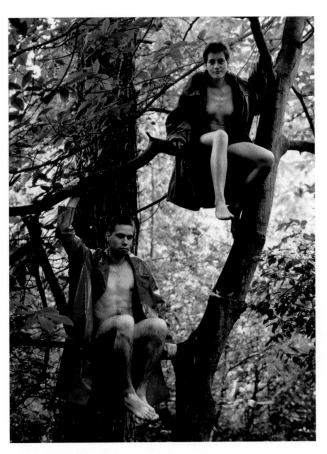

such as *The Face*, but achieved an international reputation for informal photographs of his coterie of friends (Fig. 13.37). Like Charles Baudelaire (see p. 83), Tillmans believes that an artist must render the ever-changing look of the contemporary world and not pursue timeless beauty—a rationale, perhaps, for his continued work in fashion photography. American artist Jack Pierson (b. 1960) created clusters of disjointed, blurry, or overexposed shots of his life and companions (Fig. 13.38). An air of listless "hanging around" is relieved by scenes of sexual longing and melodrama.

Although Tillmans and Pierson bear little resemblance to the politically inspired Postmodern photographers of the late 1970s and 1980s, their outlook on truth as an unrealizable goal for photography is similar. By insisting on portraying the private self, both photographers testify to the modest limits of the medium. At the same time, they further glamorized the mass-media-induced fantasy that it is pleasurable to be incessantly photographed in private life, as well as in public.

During the 1980s, Pierson was a member of an informal network of photographers that has since been called the Boston School. Also in the group were Philip-Lorca di Corcia, Mark Morrisoe (1959–1989), and Nan Goldin (b. 1953), whose work during the last decades of the twentieth century exemplified the trend toward books and exhibitions that mingled private and public views of family and friends. By far the best known and most influential of her efforts was the sound and slide

13.37
WOLFGANG TILLMANS, *Lutz and Alex Sitting in the Trees*, 1992. C-type print.

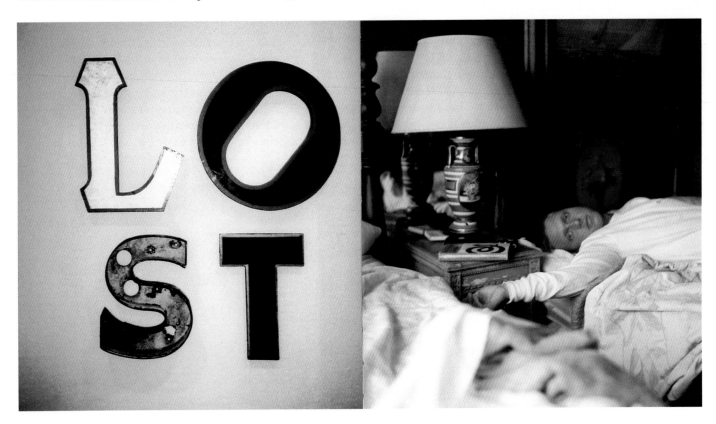

13.38
JACK PIERSON, *Untitled*, from his book *Jack Pierson: The Lonely Life*. Edition Stemmle, Zurich, 1997.

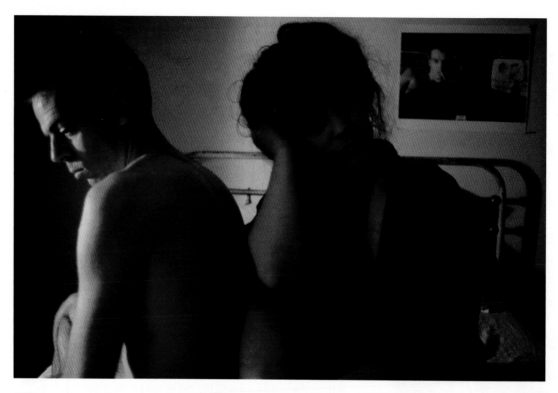

13.39
NAN GOLDIN, *Nan and Brian in Bed, New York City*, 1983, from "The Ballad of Sexual Dependency," 1981–86.

show titled "The Ballad of Sexual Dependency" (1981–86). The show consisted of about seven hundred to eight hundred transparencies (slides) detailing the intimate lives of Goldin and her friends, her "re-created family"[34] (Fig. 13.39). Her 1996 book *I'll Be your Mirror* included personal interviews as well as pictures of friends who were HIV-positive. Goldin has traveled extensively, and her sexually charged work, characterized by a revealing flash and a palette of strong colors, has been internationally influential in validating the use of photography as a diary of daily life. Her approach was widely influential in fashion photography (see p. 487). "Heartbeat," Goldin's 2002 slide

show, with music composed by John Tavener (b. 1944) and sung by Björk (b. 1965), moved away from the portrayal of personal pain evident in "The Ballad of Sexual Dependency" to reveal the domestic routines of couples.

The sexual subjects and shock value of Goldin's images from the 1980s paralleled some of those produced by the Japanese photographer Nobuyoshi Araki (b. 1940), whom Goldin met in the early 1990s. Araki roams the streets of Tokyo collecting photographs with an array of cameras ranging from the latest technological advances to inexpensive devices. Frequently tilted, these views glimpse the friction between traditional and

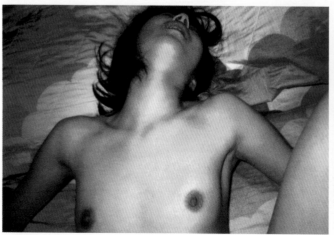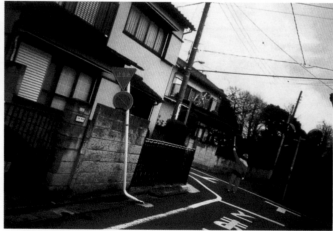

13.40
NOBUYOSHI ARAKI, *Untitled*, from his series *Desire and the Void*, 1996–97.

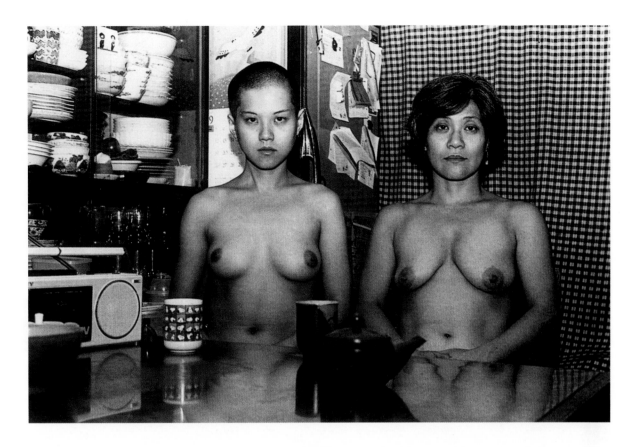

13.41 (above)
YURIE NAGASHIMA, "Self-Portrait," Mother no. 2, 1993. Gelatin silver print.

13.42 (below)
DOUG MUIR, My Brother Gary and his Girlfriend Joanie, Otisco Lake, Amber, New York, 1959. Gelatin silver print of a snapshot.

ultra-modern Japanese life. But Araki's most notorious images show women in sexually submissive or suggestive poses derived from pornography (Fig. 13.40). In both his street scenes and his photographs of women, Araki attempts to show what he believes is an obsessiveness lurking in the Japanese character.[35]

In Japan, Araki's casual, snapshot-like photographs and Nan Goldin's diaries of friends and life experience had an unpredictable impact on young Japanese women photographers.[36] Until the 1980s, when formal training in photography became available through art schools, women in Japan found it difficult to learn the medium. Apprenticeships with master photographers were routinely given to men. A woman who succeeded in learning and practicing the craft was called a "Joryu photographer," meaning one who works in a woman's style.[37] The popularity of the diary-like photographs by Araki and Goldin served to validate women's lives and image-making. Indeed, Yurie Nagashima (b. 1973) became a celebrity for her images of family and friends (Fig. 13.41).

The extent and availability of family photograph collections, some tracing back several generations, spearheaded the late twentieth-century image-makers' reuse of old images, from daguerreotypes to snapshots. Korean photographer Young Kim searched through her family's albums for materials with which to express her anxiety at living between two worlds. Californian Doug Muir (b. 1940) reprinted images he took with an inexpensive, fixed-focus camera during his childhood. His pictures center on gestures and facial expressions that reveal interpersonal relationships that were probably unrecognized by the participants at the time (Fig. 13.42).

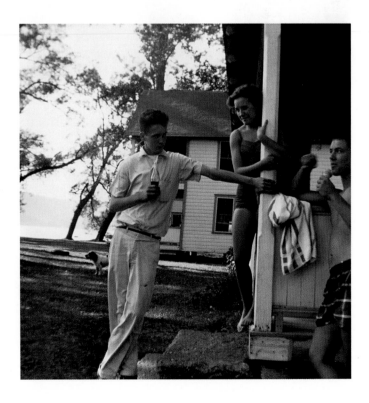

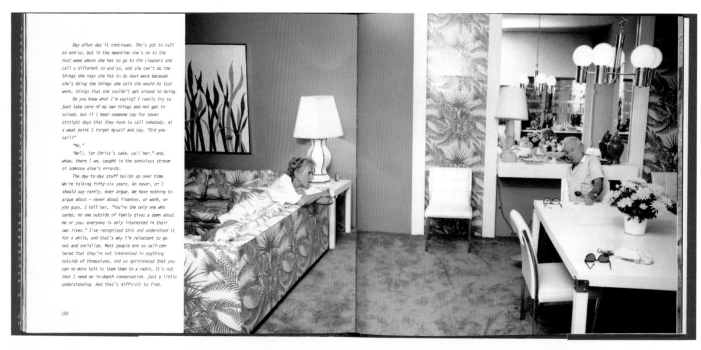

13.43
LARRY SULTAN, *Untitled,* **from his book** *Pictures from Home,* **1992.**

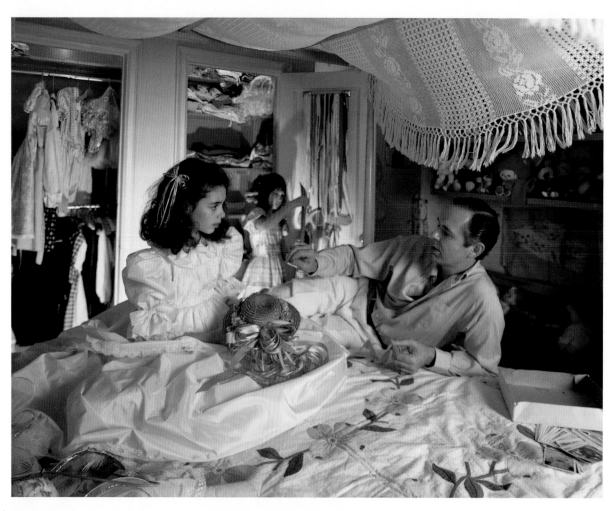

13.44
TINA BARNEY, *Marina's Room,* **1987.**

While Muir does not fundamentally alter the snapshots that form the basis of his work, another Californian, Larry Sultan (b. 1946), plainly demonstrates that his pictures are his interpretations, by bleaching, blurring, and enlarging family snapshots and home movie stills. For "Pictures From Home" (1992), an exhibition and book, Sultan directed his parents in poses for new photographs (Fig. 13.43). Sultan's work went beyond the affections and tensions of his family, to offer a public statement about the acritical exaltation of American family life promoted by the political right wing during the Reagan era.

At first glance, the photographs by Tina Barney (b. 1945) of her relatives offer an inside look at the private lives of the wealthy, who actively work to prevent themselves from being seen candidly. Barney's images feature informal and secluded domestic moments, such as preparations for a party (Fig. 13.44). At the other end of the socio-economic scale, Richard Billingham (b. 1970) photographed people with a seeming indifference to the lens. Employing an inexpensive auto-exposure camera and budget film-processing, Billingham logged his British family's strained existence, much of which turned on his father's alcoholism (Fig. 13.45). The dirt, disorder, and dishevelment pictured in his work have long been associated with truthful photographic documentation, for example in the images made by Jacob Riis (see Figs. 7.5, 7.7). It is intriguing to compare the grime and raw passion in Billingham's pictures with the cleanliness and order transcribed in Barney's work. Despite the apparent artlessness of their images, Barney and Billingham do not break free from the prevailing stereotype that the rich and the poor are the way they are because of their inherent temperaments.

Family pictures also provided an important source for authenticating forgotten social history. During the late twentieth century, museums began to exhibit and create histories for so-called OUTSIDER ART, which drew on non-traditional forms of folk art and shed new light on family photographs. Sociologists such as Pierre Bourdieu scrutinized family picture-making with the belief that its social significance surpassed the stated intentions of the photographer. He and others deduced that family pictures consecrated social identity, within and beyond the family. Interestingly, lower-class families seldom had family-produced photographs of past generations, owing, perhaps, to an unease about the visual signs of their social identity, as well as to practical economics. Groups for whom political powerlessness was accompanied by the lack of public visibility sought out family albums with which to reclaim their ancestors' stories and place in society's collective memory. The big mixed-media works by Radcliffe Bailey (b. 1968), who is based in Atlanta, Georgia, incorporate real TINTYPES and other old photographs handed down in his family. Like Santu Mofokeng (see p. 434), Bailey wants to indicate the existence of a flourishing black middle class, and authenticates his research into late nineteenth-century African-American life by using actual photographs as evidence (Fig. 13.46).

On a large scale, historian and curator Deborah Willis brought together the first comprehensive view of African-American photographers in her *Reflections in Black: A History of Black Photographers, 1940 to the Present* (2000). Willis's earlier work *Picturing Us: African American Identity in Photographs* (1994) gathered reflections penned by black writers, historians, and image-makers on the impact that a special photograph had

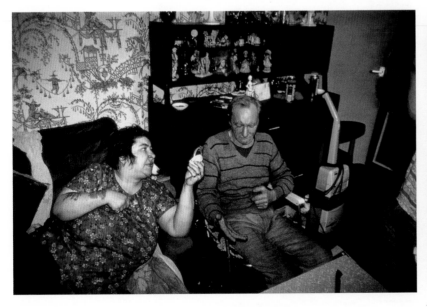

13.45
RICHARD BILLINGHAM, *Untitled*, 1994. Color print on aluminum.

Made while he was an art student, Billingham's candid photographs of his unsettled family life resemble the intrusive images captured with video cameras for reality television, which got its start about the same time.

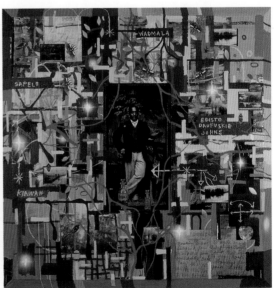

13.46
RADCLIFFE BAILEY, *Untitled*, 1999. Acrylic, photograph, and mixed media on wood. Clarice M. Laubenheimer Collection.

on them. The pictures that American Darrel Ellis (1958–1992) worked with during his short lifetime were taken by his father, who died one month before Ellis was born. Ellis altered the shapes in his father's images, creating fleeting light sculptures by projecting photographs on to irregular plaster surfaces and foam molds. He further distorted the pictures by photographing them from extreme angles that flatten and stretch the pictures' space. For Ellis, these mutations expressed a yearning for memories of his father (Fig. 13.47).

In a similar manner, Albert Chong (b. 1958), a Caribbean photographer of African and Asian descent, uses the medium to create a personal dialogue with his ancestors, and to encourage viewers to acknowledge the mixing of cultures. His self-portraits, called "I-traits," usually involve his moving so quickly in front of the camera that his identity is a blur. Other works incorporate old photographs in assemblages put together as part of a ritual to connect with the past. In *Aunt Winnie*, for instance, Chong constructed a homage to his mother's sister from a studio portrait made in the 1940s (Fig. 13.48). Similarly, Mexican image-maker Adolfo Patiño (1954–2005) accentuated the personal and homemade quality of family photographs by sewing them to handmade bark paper. He worked in series, frequently repeating whole images or miscellaneous snippets, sometimes using a simple family photograph to elicit the feeling of memory and loss (Fig. 13.49).[38]

The rescue and reuse of family photographs further encouraged the growing interest of historians, curators, and artists in past photographic processes. A personal investigation

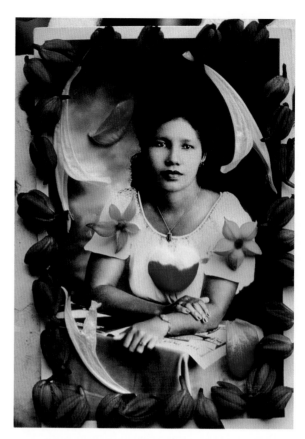

13.48
ALBERT CHONG, *Aunt Winnie,* **1995 (original 1940s). Chromogenic color print.**

13.47
DARREL ELLIS, *Untitled (Grandfather),* **1990.**

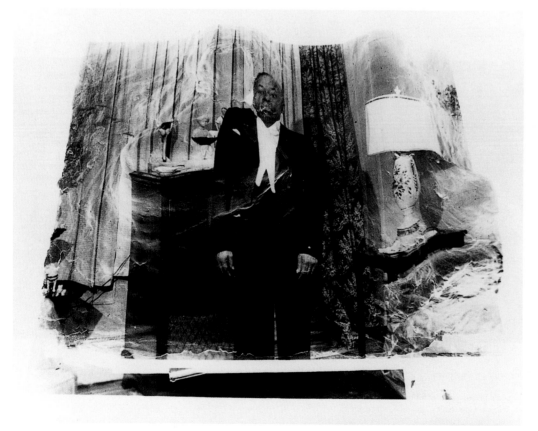

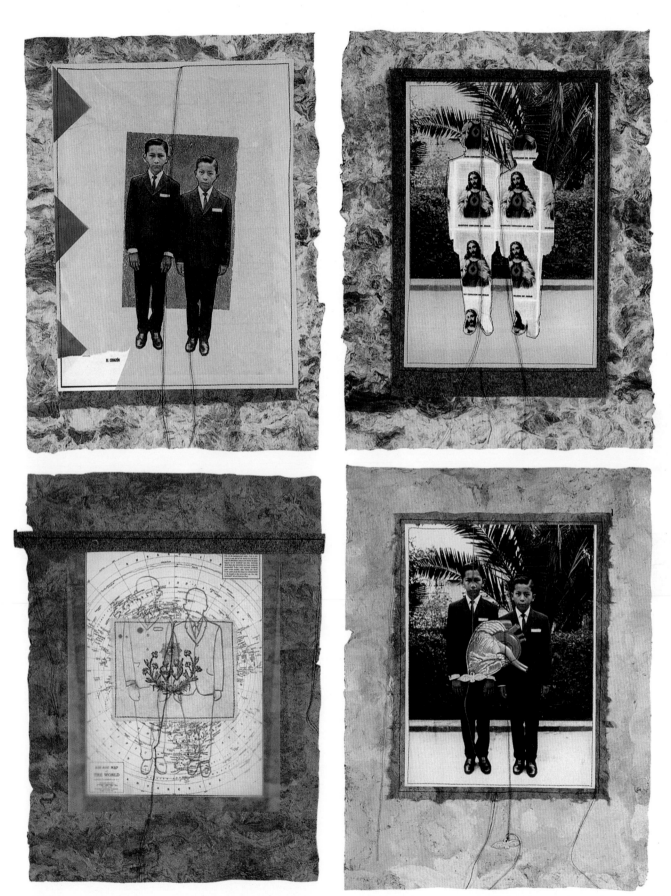

13.49
ADOLFO PATIÑO, *Navegación constante (Constant Navigation)*, 1991–92, from the series *Elementos para una navegación (Elements for Navigation)*, from the larger series *Reliquias de artista (Relics of the Artist)*. Family photographs, Polaroid 669 photographs, negatives, Canon laser copies, Polaroid SX-70 photographs, old postcards, prints on paper sewn with cotton thread on felt, satin, and amate. Enriquez Schneider Family Collection, Mexico.

focus

Looking at Children

During the 1980s and 1990s in the United States, some family photographs provoked boisterous debate about the right of both amateur and professional photographers to show children in poses that revealed genitalia, or to suggest that children possess adult sexual knowledge.[39] Photo-processing laboratories and drugstore photo-developing machine operators were put on notice to report pictures of nude children on the rolls of film brought to them. Laws prohibiting child sexual abuse and the sale of child pornography occasionally punished innocent snapshooters who pictured their naked children romping in a backyard wading pool. In the worst cases, children were temporarily taken away from parents and put in foster care until the legalities were cleared up, and homes were subjected to search and seizure of prints and personal records.

American art photographer Sally Mann (b. 1951) was surprised to find her work at the center of angry criticism from religious and conservative critics, as well as from those who deplored what they felt to be the vulgarization of the American family. Only 20 per cent of the photographs that Mann published in the book *Immediate Family* (1992) showed her children topless

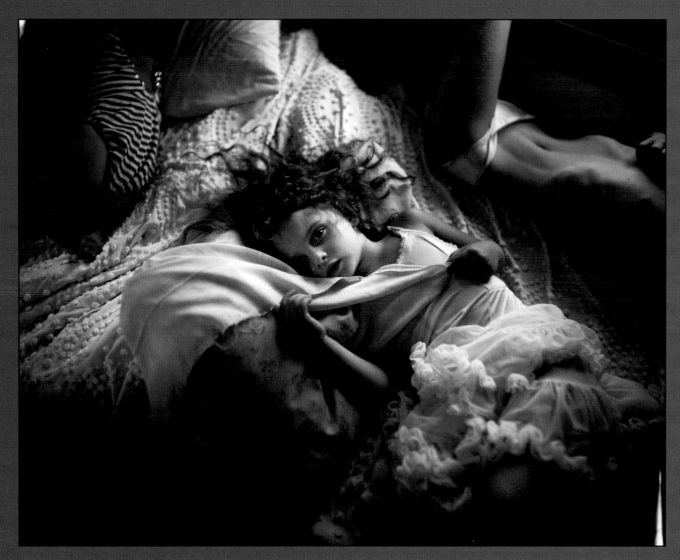

13.50
SALLY MANN, Naptime, 1989, from her book *Immediate Family*, 1992.

or nude, yet for many the volume came to symbolize disturbing changes in American life, including how early it was that children were now becoming acquainted with the demeanor of adult sexual behavior. In addition, some of Mann's pictures, such as *Naptime* (Fig. 13.50), angered viewers who were repulsed by their own identification of erotic innuendo in the image of a young girl with tousled hair and pouting lips who is awaking from sleep.

Unlike the response to Mann's photographs, the explicit prepubescent frontal nudity pictured during the Pictorialist era by photographers such as Alice Boughton (see Fig. 6.28) seems to have gone unremarked. This was perhaps because in the years before the immense use of sexuality in mass-market advertisements, the poses and expressions of children did not so readily suggest sexual awareness or pleasure.

Those who defended Mann's pictures asserted her right to make the images, and maintained that these were truthful portrayals of children's expressions of sexuality. Her advocates were quick to note that male photographers such as Harry Callahan (see Fig. 11.10) were not rebuked for photographing nudity in intimate family pictures. Mann's detractors held that, as an adult, she could comprehend the sexually expressive qualities of the photographs in a way that the children could not. Therefore, they accused her of abdicating her parental responsibility to protect her children from lewd gazes of strangers.

The display of child sexuality became an issue that cut across political divisions, uniting some feminists and some conservative activists in censorship efforts. Within photographic circles, the topic initiated new inquiries into the motivations of nineteenth-century photographers Julia Margaret Cameron and Lewis Carroll (see Fig. 3.15), both of whom showed nude or nearly nude children.[40] Critic Anne Higonnet helped to frame the discussion by contrasting representations of the innocent child, pictured in photographs and paintings as not understanding sexuality, with the knowing child who is sexually precocious. In her study and others, social history and psychological theory directed attention to the photographer, the viewers of such pictures, and the condition of women in the societies that provided a market for such images.

Regardless of circumstance, the fact that a child stood before the lens in a state of undress became the salient point in a number of legal actions. Across the United States, some photographers and arts publications were scorned or punished for presenting images of childhood sexuality. For example, in New York City, the publication *Nueva Luz* (*New Light*), issued by En Foco (In Focus), an organization dedicated to promoting photography by people of color, was criticized by the *New York Post* for publishing photographs by Ricardo T. Barros (b. 1953) that showed his nude wife and children.[41] The newspaper was outraged that the organization received public money with which it supported *Nueva Luz*.

The most notorious incident involving public hostility to sexual images took place in 1989. The threat of losing public funding drove the Corcoran Gallery of Art in Washington, D.C., to cancel an exhibit of photographs by Robert Mapplethorpe (1946–1989), some of which were explicitly homoerotic prints, and a few others of which showed glimpses of children's genitalia. The parents of the children in the Mapplethorpe pictures knew the pictures and gave their permission for the prints to be exhibited. One of those pictures, titled *Rosie*, shows a little girl innocently raising her skirt while adjusting her pose (Fig. 13.51). Eventually the same Mapplethorpe exhibition was exhibited in Cincinnati, Ohio, where it gave rise to a much publicized trial, which, though won by the defendants, raised public ire at the use to which tax dollars were being put. Along with the uproar about Andres Serrano's pictures (see Fig. 13.19), the publicity surrounding the Mapplethorpe show culminated in reduced national and local spending on the arts.

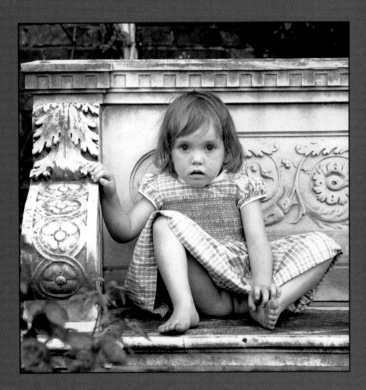

13.51
ROBERT MAPPLETHORPE, *Rosie,* 1976.

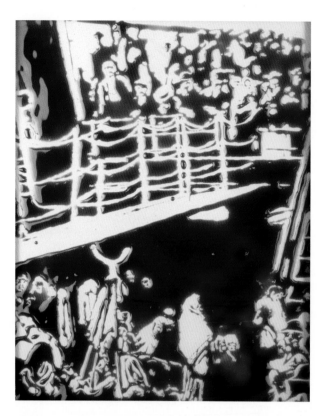

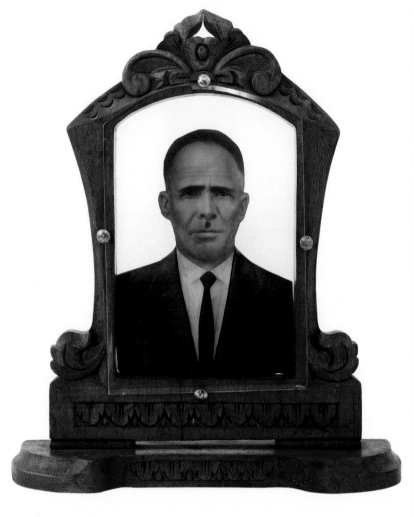

13.52
VIK MUNIZ, *The Steerage (after Alfred Stieglitz)*, 2000. Silver dye bleach print. The Jewish Museum, New York.

13.53 (right)
ARTIST UNKNOWN, *Hombre (Man)*, c. 1950. Hand-painted photograph over wood, plaster, woodframe, glass. Private collection.

of alternatives to silver-based photographic processing led American photographer Bea Nettles (b. 1946) to concoct an enduringly popular 1977 volume called *Breaking the Rules: A Photo Media Cookbook.* Sally Mann (see pp. 474–75) spent the 1990s learning the tricky visual language of the wet-plate COLLODION process, and Cuban-American photographer Abelardo Morell (b. 1948) has revitalized the use of room-size camera obscuras. Brazilian-born Vik Muniz (b. 1961), who is known for his humorous and irreverent use of art media, revived the look of the CLICHÉ VERRE in a series of images based on Rembrandt's etchings. To produce the work, Muniz photographed a composition made of nails, pins, and paperclips, after carefully arranging them to give the illusion of etched lines. Muniz also photographed his gently irreverent version of Alfred Stieglitz's *The Steerage* (see Fig. 6.24), drawn with chocolate syrup (Fig. 13.52). Muniz often draws iconic images such as Leonardo da Vinci's *Mona Lisa* or Stieglitz's *The Steerage* from memory, acknowledging how they have achieved a permanent place in the extended family of cultural recall.

Some nineteenth-century processes now even have their own websites. During the late 1990s, as film-based black-and-white photography was being replaced by digital means, interest in the medium sparked a renewed interest in the darkroom with its sinks, trays, and chemical mixes. Even the tedious and physically hazardous DAGUERREOTYPE method made a return during the late twentieth century. For his 2006 series *A Couple of Ways of Doing Something,* Chuck Close took up the daguerreotype process, asserting that photography never got any better after 1840. One enterprising photographer, Robert Shlaer (b. 1942), employed the technique during a four-year project retracing John C. Frémont's 1848 trip through the American West, deducing from engravings the actual scenes of now lost daguerreotypes made by the expedition's photographer, Solomon Nunes Carvalho (1815–1897).[42] Artists' reuse of ordinary photography supplemented scholarly attention to vernacular photographic practice, such as the heavily overpainted photographs studied by Christopher Phinney in his investigation of camerawork in India, and Mexican *foto-esculturas,* or photo-sculptures. This hybrid between the flat photograph and the sculpture in the round was invented in the 1920s and became popular through the 1950s. It was customary for the sitter to direct the session, or to suggest flattering modifications to the photograph that would be used to make the *foto-escultura.* The practice of photo-sculpture evolved from the public's longing to magnify the vivid sense of personal presence. Not surprisingly, photo-sculptures became meaningful additions to funeral ceremonies (Fig. 13.53).

NATURE AND THE BODY POLITIC

Of the millions of images of nature made by amateur and professional photographers, most operated within the enduring nineteenth-century visual vocabulary of awe and magnificence. Photographs from space followed the tradition of the sublime landscape, accentuating the distance of other galaxies and the breadth of celestial bodies (see Figs. 11.38, 11.40, and Fig. 14.24). As a matter of fact, the hold of the nineteenth-century sublime upon wilderness imagery remained so strong that a few contemporary landscape photographers preferred to operate primarily with cumbersome old equipment, like that used by Carleton Watkins and other nineteenth-century photographers of the American West.

In the late twentieth century, images of nature did not receive as much critical scrutiny as did the concepts of gender and ethnic identity. Occasionally a voice was raised to protest the intrusion of cameras in precincts where endangered species might be disturbed by the presence of the photographer and equipment.[43] A few critics pointed out that photographs and films of animals were not objective, but modeled on an idealized view of Western family life. Some artists, such as Scottish-born sculptor Andy Goldsworthy (b. 1956), created on-site and gallery installations of natural materials, which were either returned to nature or allowed to decay, their only record being a photograph.

Invocations of magic and ritual, which regularly informed installation and performance art in the late twentieth century, were sometimes felt in photographic practice. Adam Fuss's photograms (see Fig. 13.13) sometimes seem like traces of ceremonial acts, and the *Earth Elegies* (1999–2000) of Robert ParkeHarrison (b. 1968) portray him dressed in a priestlike black suit, while he tries to mend a simulated rupture in the earth. Equally sacramental is *Patching the Sky* (1997), in which the formally dressed artist-shaman stands on a makeshift platform attempting to suture a spot in the unmistakably artificial heavens (Fig. 13.54).

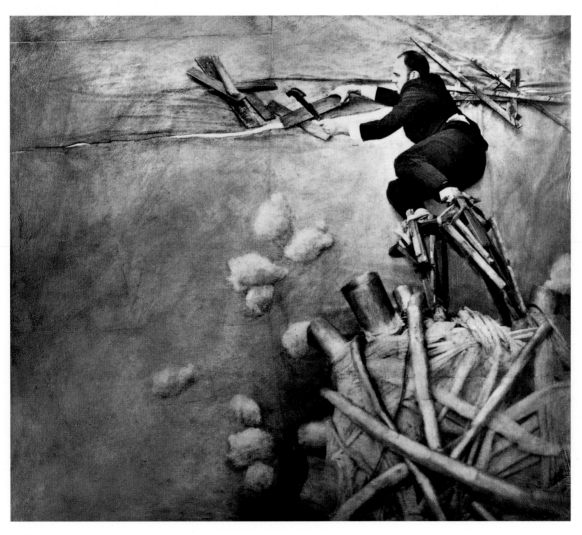

13.54
ROBERT PARKEHARRISON, *Patching the Sky*, 1997. **Photogravure with beeswax.**

Performance art was one of the forces that helped shape photography in the late twentieth century. It is a short step from photographing a performance to make a record of it, to performing for the camera. ParkeHarrison's rituals exist for the moment, and for the record.

More often, nature was a distant presence with which humans could not convincingly connect, but for whose fate they were implicitly responsible. In photography, this feeling of alienation had been foreshadowed by New Topographics photographers, such as Robert Adams (see p. 356), who declared that "Scenic grandeur is today sometimes painful."[44] Where nineteenth-century artists sought spiritual sustenance through sublime and beautiful displays in the natural world, contemporary artists tend to express the loss of transcendence.

American Joel Sternfeld (b. 1944) mastered the distanced landscape photograph, as in his view of dead and dying whales (Fig. 13.55). In his early twenty-first-century work, he has begun to use digital manipulation to reprint these images. The resulting increase in the overall sharpness of these pictures tends to befuddle the eye and increase the sense of detachment. Since the 1970s, American John Pfahl (b. 1939) has been cleverly undermining landscape views with additions that prevent viewers from easily comprehending the spatial relationships before their eyes (Fig. 13.56). Where Pfahl constructs physical impediments to seeing in a landscape view, some photographers exploit obstructions that were already there, especially the automobile. To contrast with postcard and travel-magazine idealization of an uninhabited wilderness, they focus on the inevitable cluster of tourists' automobiles parked near the scenic outlook. Putting the human subject before nature, not being able to discern what is happening in nature, or being at a fixed, dreamlike remove from the landscape has characterized human separation from the natural world.

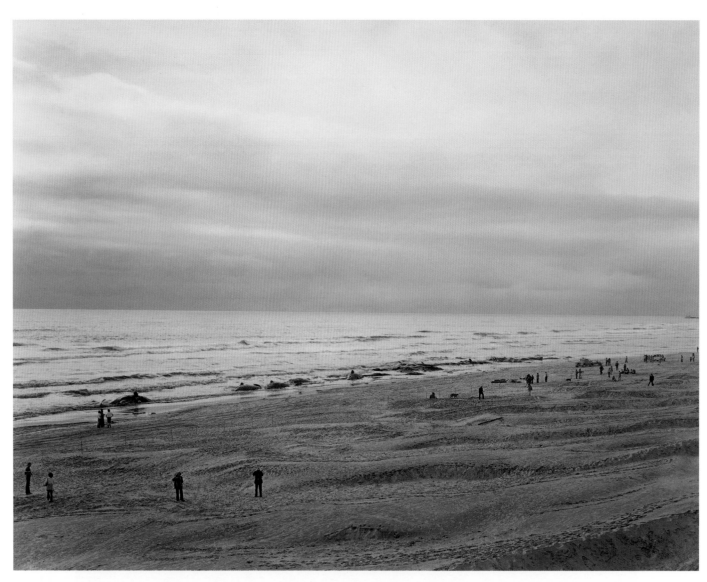

13.55
JOEL STERNFELD, *Approximately 17 of 41 Whales which Beached (and Subsequently Died), Florence, Oregon*, June 18, 1979. Dye-transfer print. The Nelson-Atkins Museum of Art, Gift of Hallmark Cards, Inc., Kansas, Missouri.

Sternfeld uses physical distance to symbolize emotional detachment. The tragic death of the whales takes place in a space remote from the viewer, as if it were impossible to care about their plight.

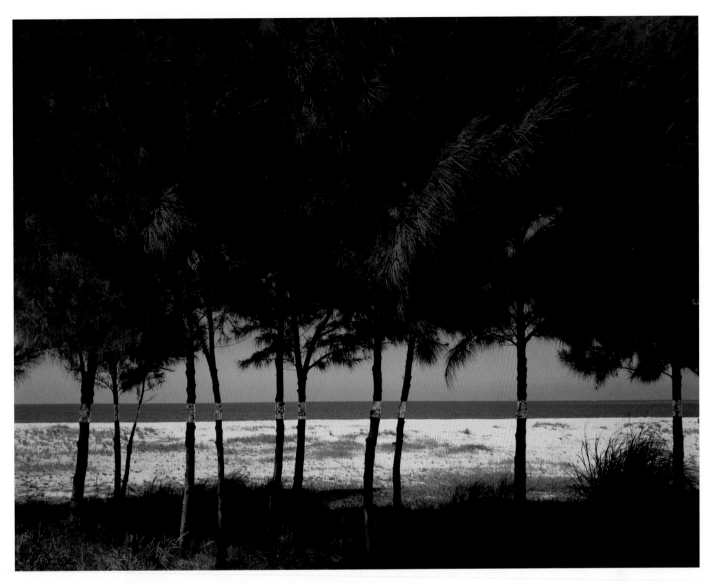

13.56
JOHN PFAHL, *Australian Pines*, 1977.

As Andres Serrano's work showed (see Fig. 13.19), beauty and repugnance can be mingled in the same work. A similar effect sometimes occurs in photographs of nature as a wounded victim. Pictures of strip mines, clear-cut forests, and oil spills flaunt intense coloration and spectral glamour. In the pictures of Bravo 20, a bombing range in northwestern Nevada, by Richard Misrach (b. 1949), the crater and rusting convoy teeter on the edge of abstraction and apocalypse (Fig. 13.57). When the work of Canadian Edward Burtynsky (b. 1955) made its appearance in a 2004 show and book covering his twenty-year career, it revealed a similar tack. Burtynsky exposes the paradoxical relationship between beauty and destruction. He concentrates on landscapes made spectacular through pollution, mining, and industrial decay (Fig. 13.58). Underlying his work is the worldwide reach of industrial development driven by the relatively cheap cost of oil. For example, his 2002 series *Shipbreaking* features the beauty of the Chittagong Delta of Bangladesh, inflected by the rusting orange hulks of oil freighters that have been strewn on the beach, awaiting disassembly for their metal scraps.

Within Postmodern theories of representation, the body was repeatedly theorized as the point at which society's values shape human personality. Cindy Sherman's multiple self-portraits, in which she is always and never herself (see Fig. 13.6), and Annette Messager's fragmented body parts (see Fig. 13.24) epitomized the Postmodern attitude that personality is ever-changing. Similarly, the disjunction between words and pictures in Lorna Simpson's pictures of the human body (see Fig. 12.46) showed the force of societal labeling. History, the body, appropriation, and issues of ethnic identity met in Carrie Mae Weems's (b. 1950) reuse of nineteenth-century daguerreotypes made by J. T. Zealy to support Louis Agassiz's racial theories (see p. 36). By rephotographing, reshaping, and framing the images, as well as

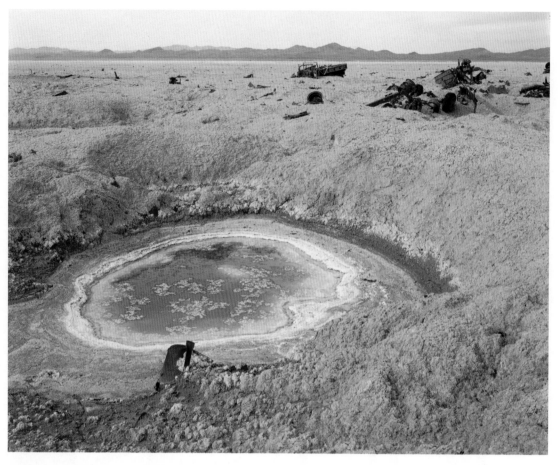

13.57
RICHARD MISRACH, *Bomb Crater and Destroyed Convoy*, 1986. Chromogenic color print.

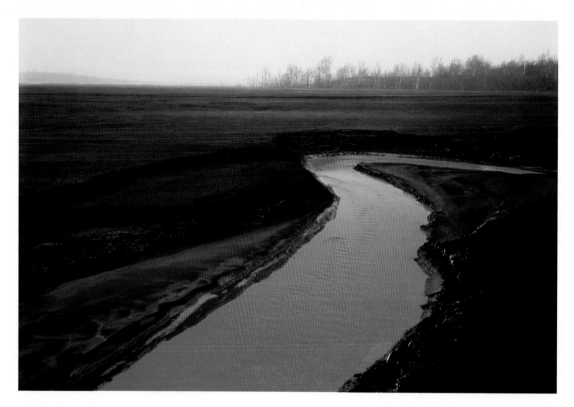

13.58
EDWARD BURTYNSKY, *Nickel Tailings No. 34, Sudbury, Ontario*, 1996.

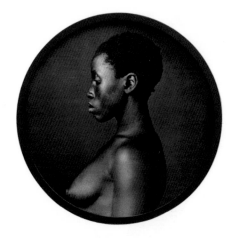
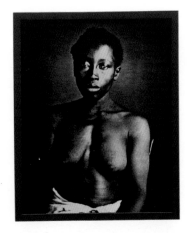
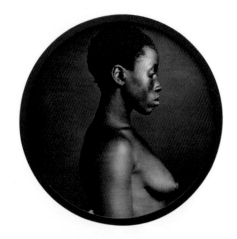

13.59
CARRIE MAE WEEMS, *Diana Portraits*, from the *Sea Island* series, 1992. Ektacolor prints, three panels.

adding a somber blue tone to the circular outer pictures, Weems transformed scientific photographs that made a spectacle of the body into an affecting memorial (Fig. 13.59).

Other sorts of personal identity also focused on the body. Sunil Gupta (b. 1953), an Indian-born Canadian citizen who lives in London, produced the photographic series *Exiles* (1987), depicting gatherings of gay Indian men. His work continues to contrast his daily life with that of ideals (Fig. 13.60). While Gupta appreciates experimental techniques such as photomontage and digital representation, he nonetheless chose

a straightforward view of the plight of those who are seldom represented except in pornographic pictures. In his choice of visual presentation, Gupta, who is gay and HIV positive, is typical of people seeking greater social visibility. As video-maker and writer Marusia Bociurkiw aptly pointed out, "the absence of photographic representations amid a larger culture so heavily saturated by media images can make the act of production seem transgressive."[45] In that spirit, perhaps, the French collaborators Pierre et Gilles (Pierre Commoy, b. 1949, and Gilles Blanchard, b. 1953) have been creating sensuous, color-laden, often

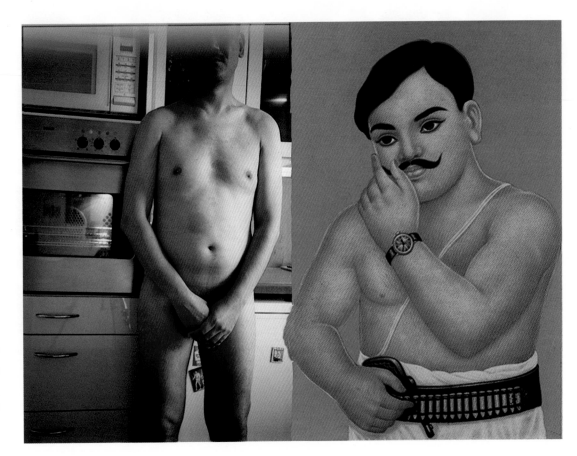

13.60
SUNIL GUPTA,
Untitled from *Trespass II*, 1993

To confront South Asian values and heritage, Gupta compares modes of contemporary life by contrasting his own nude body with a depiction of a robust figure who has a gun tucked into his bullet belt.

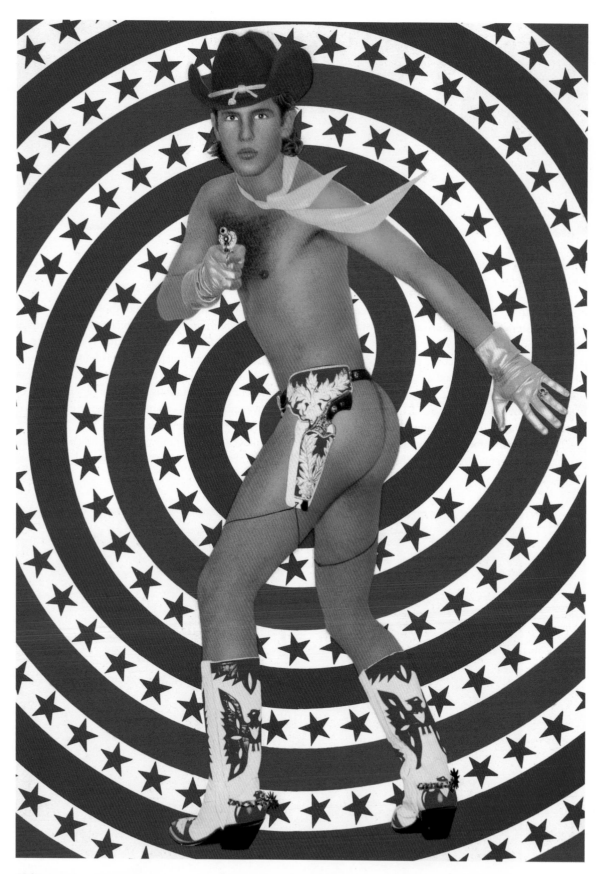

13.61
PIERRE ET GILLES, *Le Cowboy—Victor,* **1978. Painted photograph.**

Adamantly anti-digital, Pierre et Gilles insist on the craft of hand-painting their photographs, which they assert show the beauty inherent in popular culture items such as pulp comics. Their work appears on posters and postcards, as well as in gallery prints.

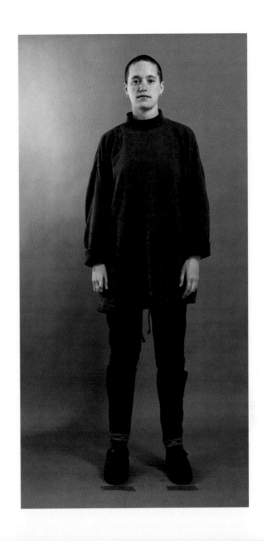

homoerotic photographs since the mid-1970s (Fig. 13.61), and their work is used frequently on album covers.

American photographer Linn Underhill (b. 1936) undermined the conventions for women's portraits by deliberately avoiding the association of the female body with nature. She refused to fragment the body or to deflect the sitter's gaze from the camera, and hence the viewer. Printed life size, and hung nearly ceiling to floor, Underhill's images unsettled viewers who were accustomed to the hint of submission and seduction that characterized formal studio portraits of women (Fig. 13.62). Underhill's women present themselves as uncomplicated everyday people, but Catherine Opie's (b. 1961) sitters in the 1991 series *Being and Having* manifested obviously fake accessories, as if gender clues were something they put on or took off at will (Fig. 13.63). *Chicken* sports a false mustache and even a phony tear. In a later series showing lesbian couples, Opie, like Underhill, reverted to a less experimental format and conventional studio techniques, validating the sitters' frankness with photography's styleless style.

During the period, homoerotic desire was depicted by artists in direct images of sexual arousal, and in pictures that critique received ideas about gays and lesbians. Following the lead of advocates and artists, scholars took renewed interest in the history of homosexuality and its images. The then largely unknown work of French Surrealist photographer Claude Cahun (see Fig. 8.30) was studied and widely exhibited. Indeed, Cahun's

13.63
CATHERINE OPIE, *Chicken*, 1991, from her series *Being and Having*, 1991. Chromogenic print. Patrick Breen Collection.

Opie's images often fuse stereotypes of outward physical appearances, in an attempt to make the viewer struggle to interpret ethnic and gender identity. In this image, the obviously false facial hair and artificial tear do not effectively change the appearance of the person wearing them— a lesson, perhaps, in the futility of gender pretense.

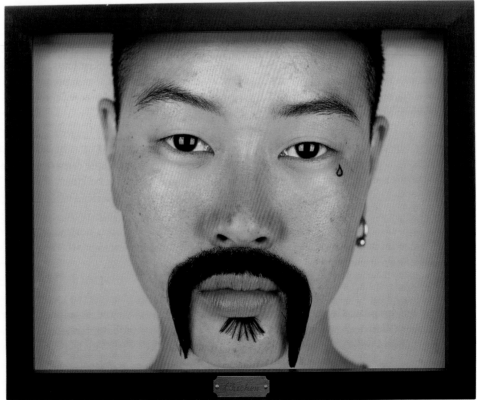

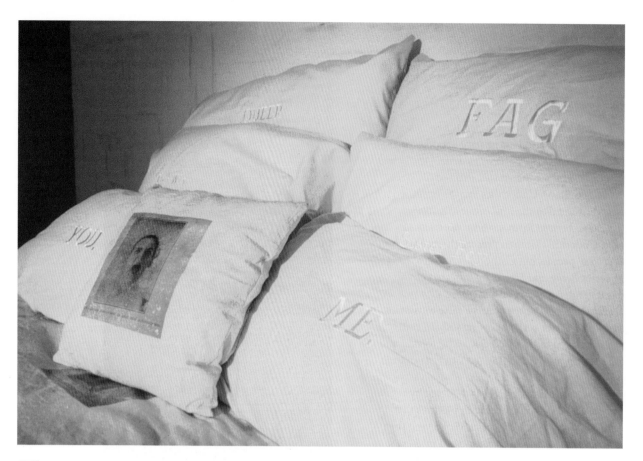

13.64
GARTH AMUNDSON, Detail from the installation *Dr. Kempf's Nightmare*, 1995. Muslin, embroidery, and transfer, queen-sized bed.

Amundson hand-stitched the pictures to muslin sheets that were also embroidered with derogatory labels for homosexuals. Putting the pictures and words on a bed, Amundson not only made reference to erotic desire, but used the display as a ceremonial wedding or acceptance of his homosexuality.

self-portraits were recast as a forebear of Cindy Sherman's investigation of feminine roles.

Because pictures of homosexuals in the mainstream media emphasized stereotypical looks and behaviors, the body became the locus of politically oppositional gay photography. Still, in pictures by Garth Amundson (b. 1963), the body is implicitly rendered. For his 1995 piece *Dr. Kempf's Nightmare*, Amundson recast medical photographs gathered by psychiatrist Edward J. Kempf at the turn of the nineteenth century as part of his attempt to prove homosexuality an illness (Fig. 13.64).

The AIDS crisis of the mid-1980s sparked a variety of artistic responses, the best known of which is probably the Names Project Quilt, with panels sometimes adorned with photographs commemorating individuals who died of the disease. Pictures of emaciated people suffering with AIDS, taken by photographers such as Nicholas Nixon (b. 1947), or those used in advertisements sponsored by the international clothing company Benetton (see p. 488), were subject to debates about what was considered to be an indulgent and counterproductive voyeurism. Activist groups, such as ACT UP, argued for "the visibility of PWAs [People With AIDS] who are vibrant, angry, loving, sexy, beautiful, acting up and fighting back."[46] In response, media-savvy photographers created photographs of healthy-looking AIDS patients, and showed the pictures not only in galleries but also in poster form in the streets. Photography was also the backbone of the safe-sex campaigns around the world, most notably in the internationally traveling exhibition "Visual Aids."

As happened in South Africa under apartheid, people whom society has marginalized have been concerned not only to critique disparaging imagery, but also to originate depictions that had been absent or censored. For instance, when Burmese-American Chan Chao (b. 1966) photographed students and ethnic members of the Burmese resistance, he created large, direct portrait studies, concentrating less on the sitters' military exploits, which were played up in the press, than on their routine daily lives in the encampments along the border between Thailand and Burma (Fig. 13.65). A comparable approach has been taken worldwide by people with disabilities, who attempt to redress photographs that show them as victims. British photographer, writer, and activist David Hevey (b. 1959) has tried to devise what he calls a "post-tragedy form of disability representation." Hevey faults Postmodern theory for not taking into full account the "distribution, audience and production" of images.[47] Like Jo Spence, whom he greatly admired, Hevey

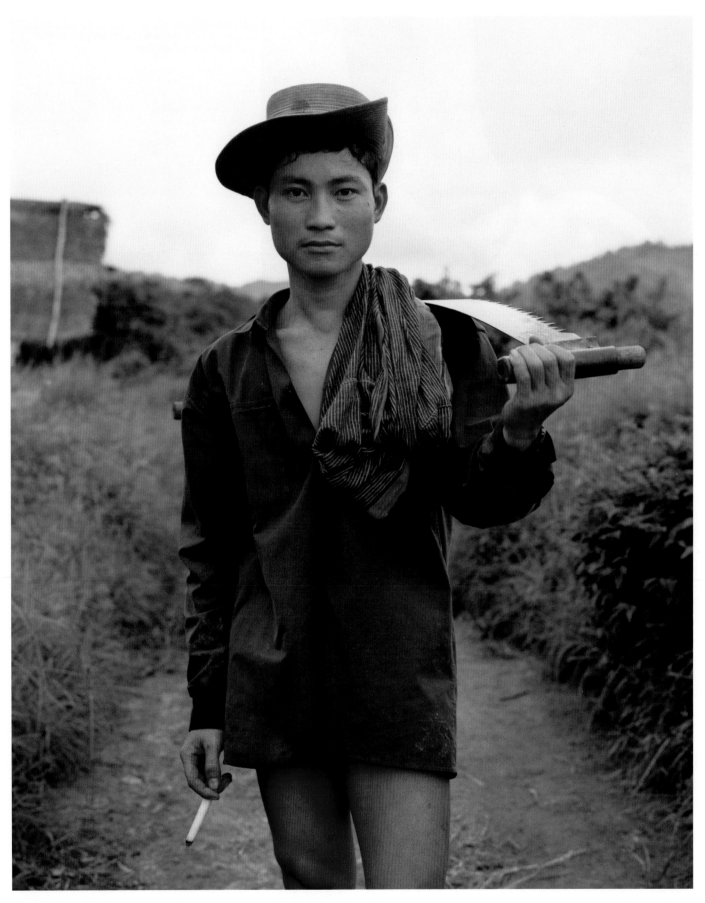

13.65
CHAN CHAO, *Member of KNLA*, from his series *Something Went Wrong*, 1999. C-print.

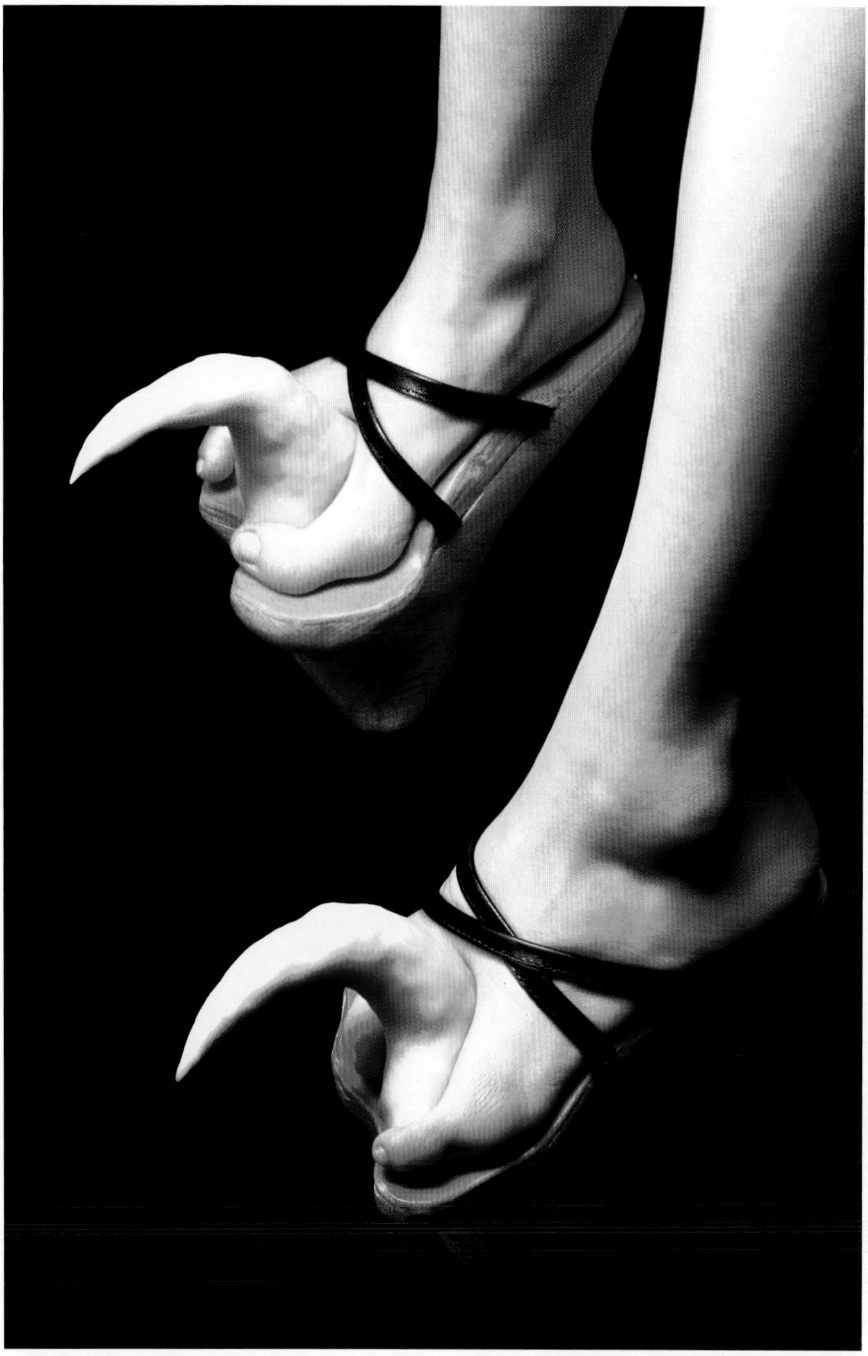

13.66
CHUN-SHAN (SANDIE) YI, *Animal Instinct*, 2005.
Photo: Cheng-Chang Kuo.

distrusts academic nit-picking and bickering, which he believes
obliterates the larger issues of class with psychoanalytic analysis.

Because of its history in representing people with disabilities,
photography continues as a central medium for historical
investigation and creative expression. Like racial and gender
identity, disability emerged in the late twentieth century as
the subject of artistic inquiry. Freed from the medical model
of understanding, disability has been explored from many
viewpoints, ranging from Yinka Shonibare's 2000 video of
fetal ultrasound images called, "effective, defective, creative,"
shown in a science museum, to couture art and photographs of
Taiwan-born Chun-Shan (Sandie) Yi (b. 1981). Working with

photographer Cheng-Chang Kuo, Yi blends prosthetics, fashion
design, and jewelry to surround disability with a fanciful and
alluring improbability that defies simple labeling (Fig. 13.66).

ENTER FASHION

In an era of exceptional hybridization among photographic
genres, none was more surprising than that of fashion
photography, art, and social concern. The merger was somewhat
precedented in the experimental photography of the 1930s, but
the vast growth of goods and media since that time produced a

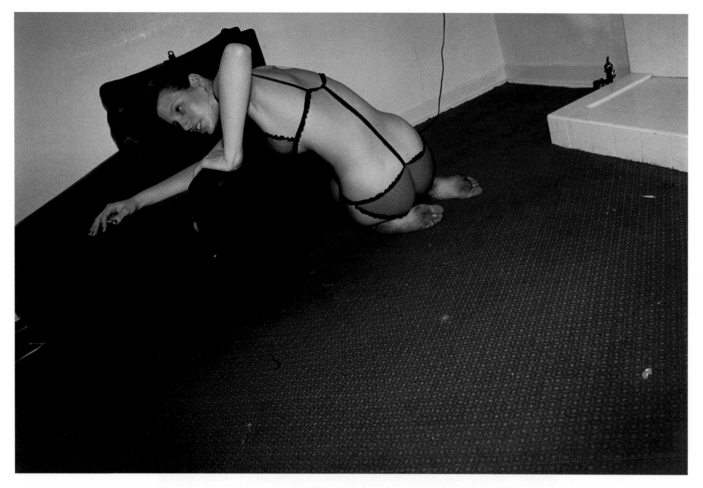

13.67
CORINNE DAY, *Georgina, Brixton,* 1993. C-print.

Late twentieth-century cutting-edge fashion photography favored a gritty realism. In Day's image, a littered room sets the scene for a model with dirty feet who is wearing designer lingerie.

much larger, more dynamic consumer economy in which styles and images changed rapidly and ideas had a short shelf life.

Many art photographers, such as Nobuyoshi Araki, Nan Goldin, Jack Pierson, Cindy Sherman, and Larry Sultan, created fashion advertisements that strongly resembled the implicit narratives of gallery work. In fact, Goldin was able to move some of the lingerie advertisement photographs that she took in the run-down Russian Baths in New York City into her open-ended slide show "The Ballad of Sexual Dependency."

Of course, mainstream fashion magazines continued to feature models whose engaging cuteness or chill beauty reliably sold conventional clothing and cosmetics. But during the last decades of the twentieth century, the urban music and club scene bred an anti-fashion industry and, with it, progressive magazines such as *i-D* and *Dazed and Confused*, which featured clothing and settings that would never have been published in more commercially oriented publications. At the same time, the rapid expansion of the youth market and youth culture, which began accelerating after World War II, fostered the increasing development of clothing, jewelry, and cosmetics just for teenagers and young persons.

Fashion-forward clothing advertisements also abandoned the idealized, pristine locales of high fashion for the grime and disarray of the real world. Likewise, tall, slim, carefully coiffed and rigidly posed models were replaced by everyday people who did their own make-up and had "bad hair days."

Former model Corinne Day (1965–2010) frequently set her fashion shoots in actual lofts and apartments, where dirty coffee cups, old newspapers, littered rugs, and grungy furniture created an ambiance far from the glamorous, squeaky-clean settings of high-fashion photography (Fig. 13.67). Fashion photographers tended to picture evocative interpersonal relationships, putting the product second. For example, in one of Day's pictures, a model's face is blotchy and red from crying because of an off-camera event; in another, a naked young man sprawls across a bed while looking questioningly into the camera's lens. Their anti-establishment approach was dubbed "Slacker photography."

Another British photographer, Nick Knight (b. 1958), frequently conceived his photographs as demimondaine night-time scenes. Like Corinne Day, Knight photographed some internationally known models, but he also favored ordinary people inhabiting favorite hang-outs. His pictures for One in

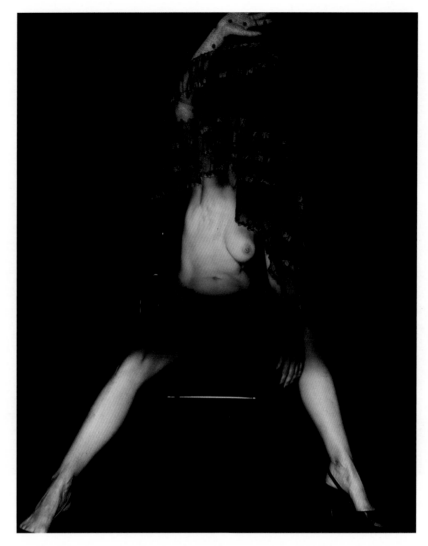

13.68
NICK KNIGHT, *One in Ten*. Photo Nick Knight; styling Katy England. Show Studio and *Dazed and Confused*, 2001.

Ten, an anti-breast-cancer campaign, broke from the topic's sentimentality to show women who had been treated for the disease wearing heavy make-up and posed in sexually alluring postures (Fig. 13.68). The term "heroin chic" arose to describe unkempt settings and models shown with bruises and red-rimmed, unfocused eyes.

Because of its world-weary appearance, the photography of underground or fashion-forward clothing was sometimes labeled Postmodern, though it mostly lacked the theoretical intricacy of art theory. Alternative fashion photography continues to hasten the breakdown of barriers that have separated the medium's genres. It is not unusual or shameful for a documentary photographer, such as Mary Ellen Mark, to do fashion work. The ungainly yet descriptive moniker "fashion-plus-culture" has emerged to describe this continuing trend.

Fashion and social trends met in a different way when Wolfgang Tillmans guest-edited the *Big Issue*, a magazine sold on the streets of the United Kingdom by the homeless. He made the weekly periodical desirable by exhibiting in its pages a mix of photographs from different genres similar to those appearing in upscale galleries (Fig. 13.69). The most notorious combination of fashion and politics was made by the Benetton Group, an international clothing retailer. In the mid-1980s, Benetton began to market multiculturalism by attiring models from different ethnic groups in its clothing. By the 1990s, the United Colors of Benetton ads turned away from displaying the company's products and toward showing people in distress, such as Haitian refugees, prisoners on death row, or persons with AIDS (Fig. 13.70). The fact that these images were widely criticized for reinforcing class, ethnic, and gender stereotypes did not deter the company from expanding its efforts.

During the 1990s, Benetton revived a strategy used by corporations in the 1950s, such as Pepsi-Cola, which hired accomplished photographers such as Esther Bubley (see p. 283) to create "documentary advertising" for a multilingual magazine. Called *Panorama*, Pepsi's bimonthly aimed to lessen the hold of Coca-Cola on the Latin American market by featuring international friendship and understanding.[48] Under the

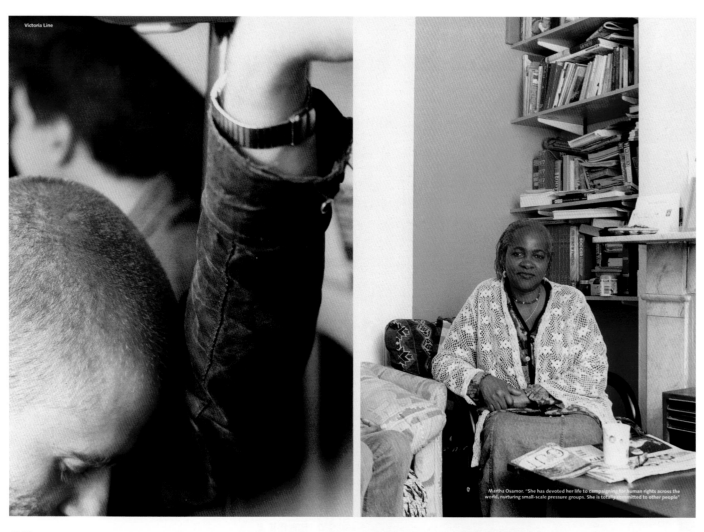

13.69
WOLFGANG TILLMANS, *Victoria Line and Martha Osamor*, from the *Big Issue*, special edition "The View from Here," August 28–September 3, 2000, no. 401.

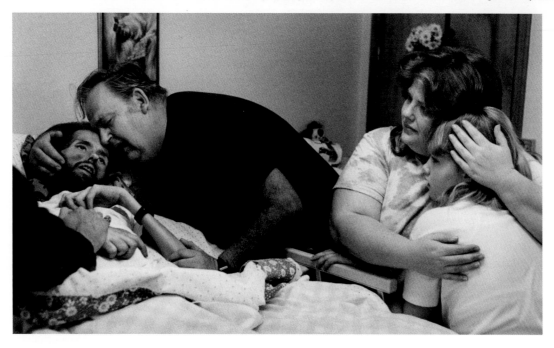

13.70 THERESE FRARE, *Pietà* (AIDS patient), 1992.

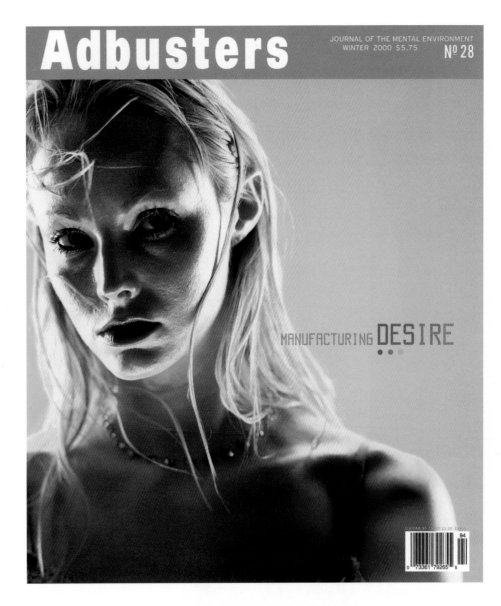

Adbusters

JOURNAL OF THE MENTAL ENVIRONMENT
WINTER 2000 $5.75   Nº 28

MANUFACTURING DESIRE

leadership of designer Tibor Kalman (1949–1999), Benetton created the magazine *Colors*. In the most famous issue, public figures were made to look like people of color, while people of color turned white. The ad campaign and magazine sparked consumer protest, and provoked Benetton dealers in Europe and the United States to sue the company on the grounds that the advertisements had a negative effect on sales. Benetton advertisements prompted the international use of new composite words, such as advertorial (advertising + editorial) and infotainment (information + entertainment). In the early twenty-first century, just as the promise of linking advertising and social concerns was being reconsidered, *Colors* was revamped, turning away from iconoclastic images, while dwelling on less disquieting social movements.

After the Benetton furor, it seemed unlikely that another manufacturer would attempt to join advertising and political action. However, the Adbusters Media Foundation, a countercultural enterprise based in Vancouver, Canada, launched the glossy magazine titled *Adbusters* (vol. 1, no. 1,

Summer 1989), aimed at unraveling marketing strategies and critical of consumerism. Using the high-tech tools of advertising photography, *Adbusters* deconstructed visual clichés, such as the appearance of the cover girl (Fig. 13.71).

THE PASSING OF POSTMODERNISM

In a 1993 interview, photographer-critic Barbara Pollack spoke for many when she announced her frustration with Postmodernism:

It's the nineties. I don't have to discuss Lacan any more. The phrase "postmodernism" presumed that everyone had already shared in the modernist expedition. But I consider myself a prime example of people who are saying, "Hey, before you say that modernism is over, let me share in that adventure." There are myths inherent in modernism that may romanticize the role of the artist or may be sexist but have certainly influenced my life. I am ambivalent about giving up those myths.[49]

The major ideas of Postmodern photography were played out by the mid-1980s. Looking back in 1987, Abigail Solomon-Godeau was convinced that critical practice itself was in a critical condition. Within a decade of Douglas Crimp's 1977 article "Pictures," which allied then little-known photographers such as Cindy Sherman with oppositional writing on the nature of language, power, and representation, Postmodern photography had been incorporated into what Solomon-Godeau called the "emporium of photography." Major Postmodern shows in galleries dedicated to presenting art photography signaled what she aptly called "deconstruction in reverse." Instead of analyzing the art market, with its emphasis on originality and genius, Postmodern photography itself began to be marketed as original and inspired, thereby vitiating its critical stance.

How did the passing of the Postmodern happen? Douglas Crimp, one of the first to announce the arrival of Postmodern photography, was also the critic who noticed its slide into an accepted and marketable commodity. In the wittily titled article "Appropriating Appropriation," written for the 1982 catalog accompanying the show called "Image Scavengers," he observed that Postmodern photography was being diluted by the artists who first fashioned it, such as Richard Prince and Cindy Sherman, while simultaneously being subsumed into the art institutions as just another category of art. In that vein, Solomon-Godeau asserted that the conventions of art history and museum practice easily historicized Postmodern photography as the photography after Modernism, just as Post-Impressionist painting followed Impressionism. Thus categorized, Postmodern photography became what it so desperately attempted not to be, another art-historical style/period. In addition, the roaring art market of the 1980s latched on to Postmodern photography, by then predigested in popular arts magazines and newspapers, and found it a profitable investment.[50]

In an important sense, there were several Postmodern moments in twentieth-century photographic history. The first, starting with the 1977 "Pictures" exhibit in New York,

ended in the mid-1980s, when some of the movement's most persuasive proponents, such as Crimp and Solomon-Godeau, began to question Postmodernist photography's increasingly cozy relationship with the art market. The second period persisted until the mid-1990s, during which time Postmodern theory and photography found a central place in many college art departments, as well as in literary studies, art history, and cultural studies. Future historians may be tempted to date the conclusive demise of Postmodern photographic practice to a particular place and time: New York City, Monday evening, November 8, 2004, when Barbara Kruger's iconic photograph, *Untitled (I Shop Therefore I Am)*, a once heretical and divisive indictment of consumer culture, was sold at auction for $601,600.

Nevertheless, the end of Postmodern photography was less dramatic. By the mid-1990s, Postmodernism was about twenty years old, and of decreasing interest to young artists, for whom the issues it raised about Eurocentrism and colonialism, the construction of social truth, the sources and misuses of gender and ethnicity identity, the conundrums of representing the past and the present, had been absorbed into the majority culture and were part of their education since childhood. As critic Jeff Rian observed, "From the younger perspective, social consciousness is a given."[50] In that sense, Postmodernism was—and is—a highly successful intellectual movement, which reshaped a broad spectrum of high-school and university curricula. Many prior intellectual movements, such as existentialism, cannot make that claim. There is no clear marker for the end of Postmodernism, because many of its most admirable principles are now commonly held.

Postmodernism changed the art and academic worlds in several ways. It shifted emphasis away from traditional art to reproducible media, such as film, photography, video, and computer-based art. Because Postmodernism questioned the tacit assumptions of Western art, it helped to refocus attention on marginal and non-Western art practices.

RETAKE

In art, documentary, and advocacy photography, the human body emerged as nature's chief representative. Issues of gender and ethnicity, which could have been pictured in a wide social context, tended to feature individuals, not milieus. Artists such as Lorna Simpson and Cindy Sherman created images with echoes of cultural stereotypes. Infused with Postmodern ideas, social documentary photographers questioned the act of representation. Martha Rosler's *The Bowery in Two Inadequate Descriptive Systems* exemplified the critique of realism as well as the suspicion of

aesthetic appearances. Feminist and Postmodernist photographers portrayed matters of psychological identity. At the cultural moment that marriage and the nuclear family were declining, photographers showed tensions among kids and couples, and turned to the extended family of friends and lovers. During the same period, what would be called the digital revolution was gaining strength. It appeared both in art and in photojournalism, where it sometimes set off shivers about a dystopian future.

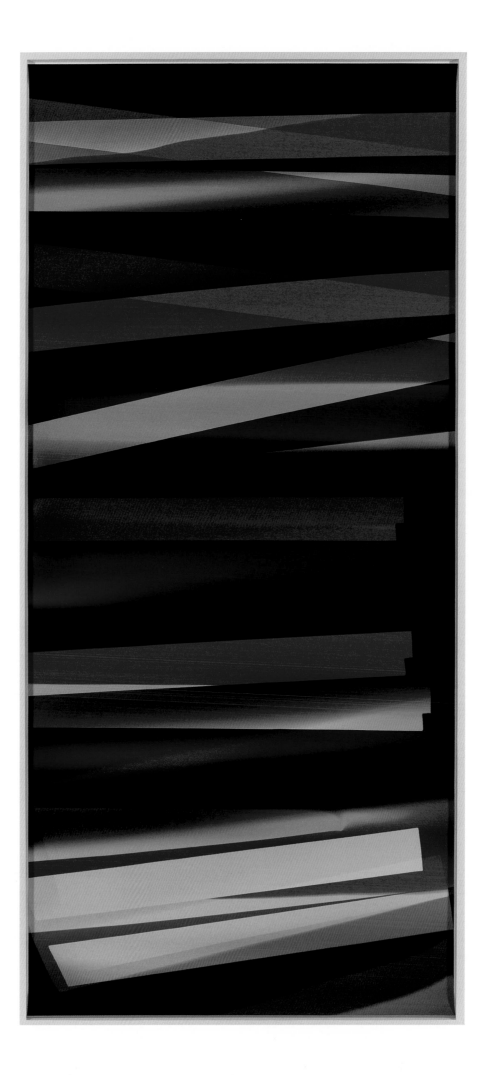

CHAPTER FOURTEEN

Into the Twenty-First Century

At midnight on December 31, 1999, people around the world stared at timepieces and wondered if they had stockpiled enough food and water to get them through the crisis that loomed as the clock struck twelve. They feared the so-called Millennium Bug, an elegantly simple glitch in the settings of the countless computers running factories, municipal water supplies, nuclear power plants, banking systems, hospital equipment, airplanes, air traffic control systems, and thousands of other crucial applications. When the clock struck twelve, there was scarcely a ripple in the world's computers, and lots of pundits had some explaining to do.

The defining catastrophe of the new century's first decade arrived on September 11, 2001, with the attacks on New York and Washington, D.C., followed by subsequent terrorist assaults and natural disasters across the globe. More years may pass before the lasting impact of so many violent events on visual practice can be definitively outlined. Nevertheless, the unprecedented rapid and copious global transmission of pictures taken of these catastrophes by professional and citizen photojournalists not only shaped public understanding of these events, but also became part of the public's expectation.

In photographic practice, many trends, subjects, and ideas made an easy transition to the twenty-first century. The convergence of photographic genres continued to strengthen. The relationship of photography to ephemeral art, performance art, and installation art expanded, as more artists turned to the medium to record and exhibit short-lived or fragile works. During the early years of the new millennium, photography, video, and installation art continued a late twentieth-century trend: they seemed increasingly in concert

through their use of large screens and immersive environments. In the late 1970s, Hiroshi Sugimoto (see p. 446) began to make long exposures of films projected in movie theaters. The resultant photographs showed only a cool, luminescent light on the screen. Similar effects of slowed time have proliferated in the past decades, in works ranging from the installation projects of Olafur Eliasson (b. 1967) to the video work of Douglas Gordon (b. 1966), and the grid of languid photographic portrait busts created by Hungarian Péter Forgács (b. 1950) in his 2009 *Col Tempo* project, which utilized Third Reich anthropological film and photography of Jewish subjects. More and more, war photography focused on the individual soldier, a trend noticed in the World War II era. At the same time, though, notions of globalization began to be more refined than in the late twentieth century. Of course, the greatest engine of change in the early twenty-first century was the tiny pixel, which made photography instantly available via computers and smart phones.

WAR AND PHOTOGRAPHY

The merger of art photography and photojournalism, evident in late twentieth-century practice, was further confirmed by images of and about the Iraq War. In her series *Bringing the War Home: House Beautiful* (2004), Martha Rosler re-employed the photomontage technique from her earlier series about the Vietnam War (see p. 438). She interrelated pictures of extravagant American domestic interiors, views of Saddam Hussein's palace, and war casualties. Gilles Peress, whose work equally encompasses art and photojournalism, took photographs in Iraq during 2005, when the war had clearly changed into a struggle with urban bombers and insurgents. In addition, painter-photographer Gerhard Richter created the book *War Cut* (2004), which contains reproductions of his abstract paintings juxtaposed with news accounts of the war.

14.1
WALEAD BESHTY, *Three Color Curl*, 2010. CMY/Five Magnet: Irvine, California, January 2nd 2010. Fujicolor Crystal Archive Super Type, color photographic paper.

The 2004 revelation of U.S. soldiers' amateur photographs showing prisoner abuse in Iraq's Abu Ghraib prison kindled what was to date perhaps the largest worldwide public interpretation of photographs. The Abu Ghraib debate centered on defining the significance of what the images represented. Views ranged from the notion that the photographs showed little more than a fraternity prank, to the idea that they recorded a repulsive spectacle of torture. The debate was sufficiently widespread that on May 6, 2004, President George W. Bush apologized publicly for the way in which the photographs humiliated the prisoners and their families, and added his take on the interpretation quandary. He remarked that he was "equally sorry that people seeing these pictures didn't understand the true nature and heart of America."[1]

The Abu Ghraib photographs were unknowingly made in the directorial mode that dominated late twentieth- and early twenty-first-century photographic practice. In many of these photographs, the prisoners were forced to act out scenes of humiliation for the camera. For example, the striking scene of a roughly hooded and cloaked figure, from whose outstretched hands dangle electrical wires associated with painful interrogation techniques, was scripted to trick both the subject and the viewer into thinking that torture was about to begin. Initially, the soldier-photographers only emailed the images to their friends, apparently in a spirit of amusement and camaraderie.

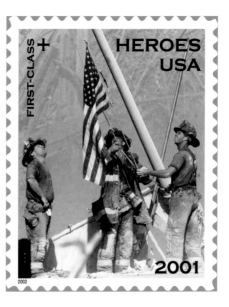

14.3
Heroes, 2001.
Postage stamp

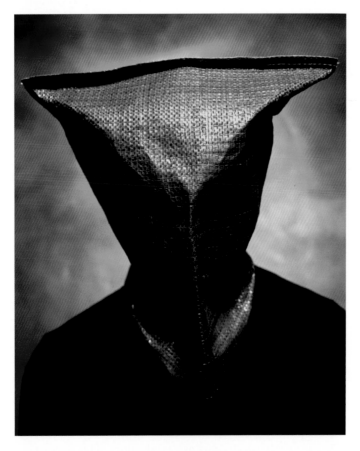

14.2
ANDREAS SERRANO, *Torture*, 2005. Cibachrome.

The images of hooded figures from Abu Ghraib instantly embarked on a new life in the arts. Andres Serrano created an interpretation that combines contradictory properties of sympathy and menace for the front cover of the *New York Times Magazine* (Fig. 14.2), and Richard Serra (b. 1939) created two lithographic interpretations. In Iraq, the artists' union quickly prepared paintings and sculptures that emphasized the prisoners as victims. Throughout the world, graphic designers converted the Abu Ghraib hooded figures into election campaign posters and magazine covers. The instantly recognizable silhouette transmogrified into a global symbol of threat, and it has remained hauntingly fresh.

While artists, writers, and photographers immediately reacted to the tumult in the century's first decade, history teaches that it often takes many years for a society to settle on the communally resonant symbolism with which to depict and memorialize catastrophes. It is rare for an artwork, such as Picasso's *Guernica*, made in 1937, months after the Basque village of the same name was used for bombing practice by the Nazis, to succeed in speaking to its own time and to subsequent generations.

Societies find it difficult and painful to reach consensus about visual symbols, as shown by the prolonged debate about the plans for new buildings and memorials on the New York City site of the September 11, 2001, attacks. Recognizing the difficulty of creating memorials that are meaningful to people living in the present and in the future, the United States Postal Service modestly restricted the scope of the postage stamp based on a famous photograph taken by Thomas E. Franklin (b. 1966) for *The Record*, a Bergen, New Jersey, newspaper. Called "Heroes," the stamp showed firefighters raising the U.S. flag over the smoldering ruins of the World Trade Center. Although it did not visually resemble Joe Rosenthal's *Marines Raising the Flag on Iwo Jima* (see Fig. 9.35), the public still recognized a similarity based on the expression of duty and sacrifice in both images. Moreover, the stamp functioned as a fundraiser for those who were bereaved on September 11 (Fig. 14.3).

SOLDIERS

Contemporary war photography stressed the experience of individual combatants, a tendency that became pronounced in photographic practice during World War II. The approach characterized the work of photographers such as W. Eugene Smith (see Fig. 9.34), and it hardened into custom during the Korean conflict, notably in David Douglas Duncan's portraits of soldiers for the "There was a Christmas" essay in *Life* magazine (see Fig. 11.2). During the Vietnam War, emphasis on the experience of individual soldiers was a dominant theme in the work of Larry Burrows (see Fig. 11.44), Philip Jones Griffiths (see Fig. 11.45), and Don McCullin (see Fig. 11.74).

In addition, both McCullin and American Civil War photographer Alexander Gardner (see Fig. 4.18) altered and enhanced the scenes they photographed with props. The ongoing discussion of the propriety of their actions involves several assumptions; chief among them is that topical photography should not be embellished in any way that would change how the average person would see the scene.

When French photojournalist Luc Delahaye (b. 1962) recorded the dead body of a Taliban soldier killed in a battle with Northern Alliance forces near the Afghan capital of Kabul (Fig. 14.4), he emphasized the posture of the dead soldier, so that it seemed lively and balletic, like James Nachtwey's street fighters (see Fig. 12.35). The dancelike stance was accentuated by the dead man's stocking feet; his shoes have been removed, perhaps by another soldier in need of them. More important, the figure has fallen in a pose that is visually reminiscent of a well-known scene in Christian art, the moment when the dead Christ is lifted down from the cross. The Christian symbolism seems to have given offense to Muslims and to Christians who, for different reasons, found it unsuitable for a Taliban combatant.

Like many contemporary photographers, Delahaye prefers large-format pictures, which give him a broad canvas on which to develop his distinctive palette of browns and grays, with

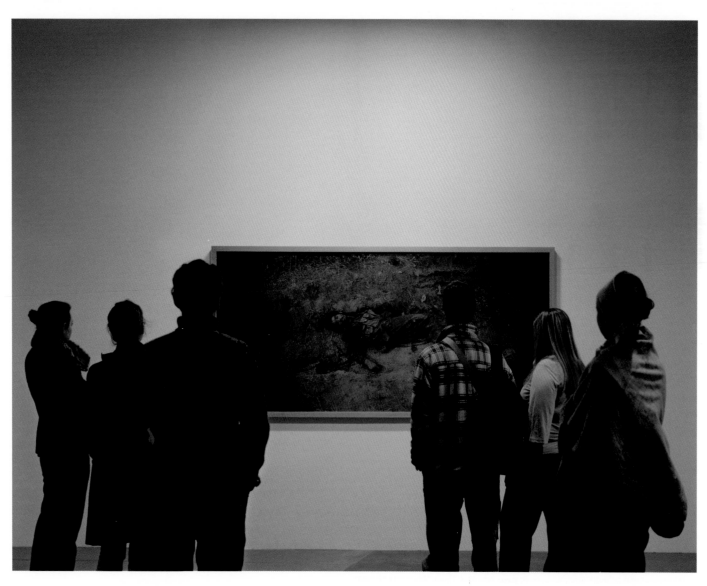

14.4
LUC DELAHAYE, *Exhibition View of Taliban*, 2001. Courtesy of the artist.

touches of warm color. Delahaye's work exists at that fertile confluence of painting, poetry, and photography that vitalizes contemporary photographic practice.

The portrayal of individual soldiers, rather than generals and battles, persisted throughout American representations of the Iraq and Afghanistan wars. From the beginning of the Iraq conflict, the *New York Times* printed and made available online small portraits of dead soldiers, following the convention set by *Life* magazine during the Vietnam War. Combat from the soldiers' point of view is presented by photographers embedded with the troops, such as Tyler Hicks (b. 1970), and these images often occupy the front page, above-the-fold, of the *Times* (Fig. 14.5). In addition, many photojournalists communicate text and pictures directly with audiences via Twitter accounts and websites.

Photographs by Suzanne Opton (b. 1948) of soldiers returning from active duty in Iraq to Fort Drum in New York State feature close-up portraits of the soldiers' heads (Fig. 14.6). The men and women in these pictures rest on the floor; no uniforms or other military paraphernalia identify them as soldiers. Through

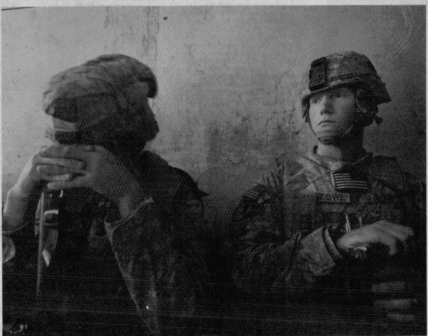

14.5
TYLER HICKS, from
An Outpost in Afghanistan's Borderland, front page, *New York Times*, November 10, 2008.

Front-page editors are willing to use photographs with subtle, suggestive colors that add to the topical information of images.

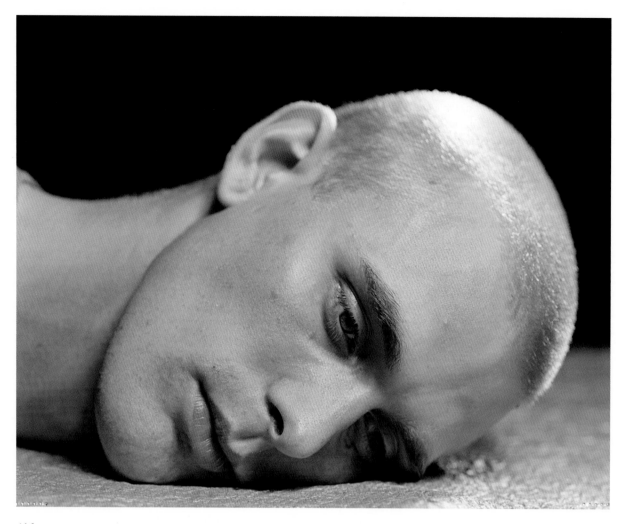

14.6
SUZANNE OPTON, *Soldier Birkholtz, 353 Days in Iraq; 205 Days in Afganistan* from *The Soldier + Citizen series,* **2004.**

In her portraits of soldiers returning from duty in Iraq, Opton concentrated on their heads and eliminated the identifying paraphernalia of uniforms and weapons.

these images, Opton surveys many interrelated ideas, including the notion of soldiers as both victors and victims, which is also found in David Douglas Duncan's work. In Opton's pictures, the soldier's pose hints at the possibility of physical or mental injury. Her headshots are reminiscent of the heads of statues toppled during warfare since ancient times in areas like Iraq. Opton's images have been displayed in a variety of spaces, including galleries and large outdoor commercial billboards. Like Delahaye's, her work connects art and photojournalism.

THE PAST IN THE PRESENT

During the first decade of the twenty-first century, the use of historical photographic materials and cameras continued to swell. Sally Mann depicted landscapes using the nineteenth-century glass-plate-based collodion process, and incorporated the medium's particular flaws as expressive effects in her work. Moreover, artists who were not trained in photography were attracted to the visual language of historical photographic processes. In addition, many photographers chose to use "found" or "orphaned" vernacular photographs in their work. Scrapbooks, albums, and online auction sites were mined for materials.

Black-and-white photography surged in high-school and college classes in the first years of the century, but the tide was short-lived, especially as film cameras began to vanish from shelves. In 2004, the Kodak Corporation announced that it would no longer make paper for black-and-white photography, prompting some commentators to suggest that black-and-white photography had become an outmoded or alternative process, along with daguerreotype, cyanotype, and photogravure.

SLIDE SHOWS

Prototypes of slides and slide projectors were used for education and entertainment before photography was invented. Drawings or paintings on glass were projected by means of lenses and oil lamps. Today, the humble slide, whether shown in a mechanical slide projector or via a graphics software program, commands surprising attention. New research has revealed that Thomas Eakins, the late nineteenth-century champion of American realist painting and draftsmanship, not only traced images projected by lantern slides on to several of his well-known canvases, but he also condensed figures from disparate photographs on to the picture plane, thus building up his images in a way that anticipated how digital artists use Photoshop today.

Artists and photographers whose work, public presentations, and personal records consist primarily of slides have a complex intellectual relationship with the projected still images, a connection explored in a wide-ranging exhibition, called "SlideShow," that began at the Baltimore Museum of Art in 2005, and which traveled the United States in 2006. The exhibition confirmed that, beginning in the 1960s, artists and photographers found much to love in the slide machine. Slides allowed photographers such as Nan Goldin continually to vary their presentations. Goldin's *The Ballad of Sexual Dependency* expanded to include her fashion photography, and was tailored to a specific subject, such as the AIDS crisis. In addition to Goldin, photographers such as Helen Levitt, Robert Smithson, Jan Dibbets, and, more recently, the team of Fischli and Weiss created works specifically for the slide projector, either dramatically engaging the pause between images, or, conversely, by using a dissolve mechanism to melt one image into another.

SCREENS

The intense light that pours through the slide as it is projected is similar not only to that of a film projector, but also to the concentrated, strong light of television, which became the dominant mass medium in the 1960s. Computer and smart phone screens also steep photographs in light, in a way that contrasts with viewing a photograph printed on paper. Light, the "photo" in "photography," emerged in the late twentieth century as an ephemeral medium that served the interests of Conceptual and Minimalist artists, as well as the growing number of twenty-first-century artists in all media who want to investigate perception.

One of the powerful linkages between the late twentieth century and the early twenty-first was the continuing swift convergence of various screen- and projected-image forms. As the world learned from the photographs taken in the Abu Ghraib prison, a digital camera image can be stored in a computer, which links to email, which links to the Internet, which links to other computers, to camera phones, and to the international news agencies and television networks. The speed with which digital images can be transmitted may have more social consequences than the transition from analog to digital camera. Also, surveillance camera images can be transmitted rapidly, and transmogrified by the recipients into forms ranging from simple posters to gallery art.

Digital technology also facilitates big photographs, such as those by Andreas Gursky, which emulate the edge-to-edge clarity of daguerreotypes, as well as the size and luminosity of the ubiquitous screens that cropped up in public and private spaces. Today, large screens are used not only for film and video, but also as flatscreen billboard advertisements in public places. The transition from analog devices, such as the slide projector, to digital devices was made easier because of the consumer's familiarity with lighted screens.

So ubiquitous is the radiant screen in contemporary life that the screen itself has become the subject of art. Chilean-born Alfredo Jaar (b. 1956) constructed his 2002 installation *Lament of the Images* by placing three illuminated wall texts on Plexiglas panels in a darkened room. The text explained three historical moments when, for widely varying reasons, crucial photographs were not available: the first, Nelson Mandela's February 11, 1990, release from prison, when he was unable to weep for joy, because after years of breaking rocks the powdery lime that covered his body and turned it white also impaired his ability to cry; secondly, the media blackout during the October 7, 2001, bombing of Kabul, Afghanistan, by U.S. forces, during which Western news agencies were prevented from obtaining live pictures; lastly, Corbis's reported withdrawal from public view of millions of news and historical photographs. After reading the texts, visitors to Jaar's installation pass into another room where they are momentarily blinded by a large, brightly lit screen that symbolizes the eradication of public information in the age of mass media (Fig. 14.7).

THE MEDIUM OF THE MOMENT

Reflecting on the prominence of photography in 2003, Peter Galassi, chief photography curator at New York's Museum of Modern Art, noted that "it is the medium of the moment."[2] Similarly, a 2002 *Art in America* article by critic Phyllis Tuchman announced that "photography rules right now." Just as those born after 1970 subliminally absorbed the Postmodern concern with ethnicity and gender long before they attended college, so they also never knew a time when photography was not broadly accepted in museums, galleries, and universities. For the young, the harsh financial sacrifices and intellectual ordeals for acceptance routinely faced by many photographers until the last two decades of the twentieth century are ancient history, as are the heated debates about media and photography that grew directly out of feminist and Postmodern criticism.

Through the use of computer-based photo-editing software at school, work, and home, the general public has become knowledgeable about photo manipulation. *Time* magazine's 1993 combination of various human faces into one image seemed bold and even upsetting (see Fig. 12.15), though the image itself did not appear complex to the eye. *Time*'s post-2008

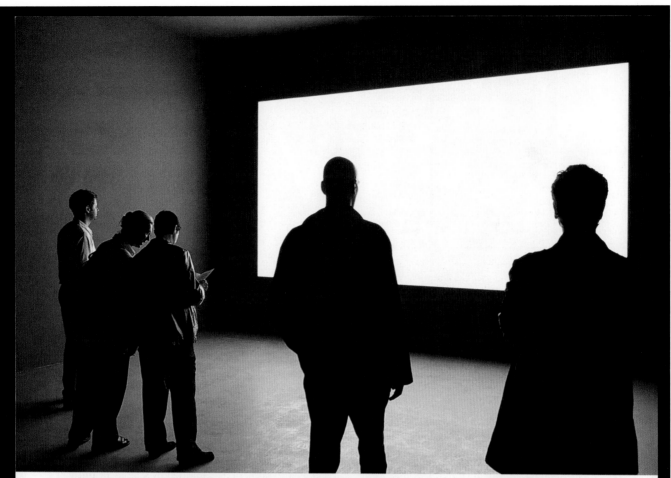

Alfredo Jaar: Lament of the Images, 2002, installation including (above) light wall in second room and (below) three texts on Plexiglas panels, each approx. 29½ by 23½ inches, in first room. All photos this article, unless otherwise noted, © Laurent Lecat.

Cape Town, South Africa, February 11, 1990.

Nelson Mandela is released from prison, after 28 years of brutal treatment by the apartheid regime. The images of his release, broadcast live around the world, show a man squinting into the light as if blinded.

More than half of Mandela's sentence was spent on Robben Island, a windswept rock surrounded by the treacherous seas of the Cape of Good Hope. Only seven miles off Cape Town, the island had been used as a maximum security prison for "non-white" men since 1959. Mandela's fellow inmates there included Walter Sisulu, Ahmed Kathrada, and Govan Mbeki, the father of current South African President Thabo Mbeki. Mandela later said that Robben Island was "intended to cripple us so that we should never again have the strength and courage to pursue our ideals."

In the summer of 1964, Mandela and his fellow inmates in the isolation block were chained together and taken to a limestone quarry in the center of the island, where they were put to work breaking rocks and digging lime. The lime was used to turn the island's roads white. At the end of each day, the black men had themselves turned white with limedust. As they worked, the lime reflected the glare of the sun, blinding the prisoners. Their repeated requests for sunglasses to protect their eyes were denied.

There are no photographs that show Nelson Mandela weeping on the day he was released from prison. It is said that the blinding light from the lime had taken away his ability to cry.

Kabul, Afghanistan, October 7, 2001.

As darkness falls over Kabul, the U.S. launches its first airstrikes against Afghanistan, including carpet bombing from B-52s flying at 40,000 feet, and more than 50 cruise missiles. President Bush describes the attacks as "carefully targeted" to avoid civilian casualties.

Just before launching the airstrikes, the U.S. Defense Department purchased exclusive rights to all available satellite images of Afghanistan and neighboring countries. The National Imagery and Mapping Agency, a top-secret Defense Department intelligence unit, entered into an exclusive contract with the private company Space Imaging Inc. to purchase images from their Ikonos satellite.

Although it has its own spy satellites that are ten times as powerful as any commercial ones, the Pentagon defended its purchase of the Ikonos images as a business decision that "provided it with excess capacity."

The agreement also produced an effective white-out of the operation, preventing western media from seeing the effects of the bombing, and eliminating the possibility of independent verification or refutation of government claims. News organizations in the U.S. and Europe were reduced to using archive images to accompany their reports.

The CEO of Space Imaging Inc. said, "They are buying all the imagery that is available." There is nothing left to see.

Pennsylvania, U.S.A., April 15, 2001.

It is reported that one of the largest collections of historical photographs in the world is about to be buried in an old limestone mine forever. The mine, located in a remote area of western Pennsylvania, was turned into a corporate bomb shelter in the 1950s and is now known as the Iron Mountain National Underground Storage site.

The Bettmann and United Press International archive, comprising an estimated 17 million images, was purchased in 1995 by Microsoft chairman Bill Gates. Now Gates' private company Corbis will move the images from New York City to the mine and bury them 220 feet below the surface in a subzero, low-humidity storage vault.

It is thought that the move will preserve the images, but also make them totally inaccessible. In their place, Gates plans to sell digital scans of the images. In the past six years, 225,000 images, or less than 2 percent of them, have been scanned. At that rate, it would take 453 years to digitize the entire archive.

The collection includes images of the Wright Brothers in flight, JFK Jr. saluting his father's coffin, important images from the Vietnam War, and Nelson Mandela in prison.

Gates also owns two other photo agencies and has secured the digital reproduction rights to works in many of the world's art museums. At present, Gates owns the rights to show (or bury) an estimated 65 million images.

14.7
ALFREDO JAAR, *Lament of the Images*, 2002. Installation including three texts on Plexiglas panels, each approximately 29.5 × 23.5 in. (75 × 60 cm), in the first room, and a light wall in the second room. Photograph by Laurent Lecat. Page from *Art in America*, September 2002, page 86.

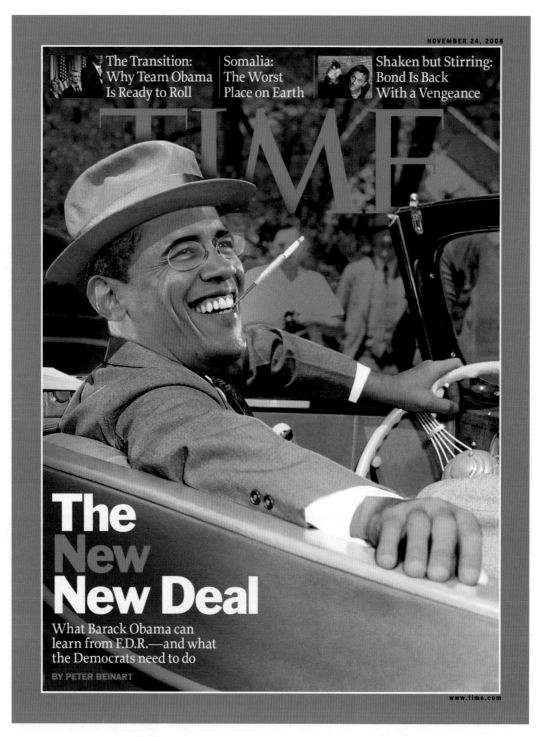

NOVEMBER 24, 2008

The Transition: Why Team Obama Is Ready to Roll

Somalia: The Worst Place on Earth

Shaken but Stirring: Bond Is Back With a Vengeance

TIME

The New New Deal

What Barack Obama can learn from F.D.R.—and what the Democrats need to do

BY PETER BEINART

www.time.com

14.8
ARTHUR HOCHSTEIN AND LON TWEETEN, Cover of *Time* magazine, November 24, 2008. Photo-illustration.

election depiction of President-elect Barack Obama (Fig. 14.8) generated a lot of excited discussion in newspapers and in blogs, but not discomfiture with the photographic process. The cover showed Obama's head and hands merged into a black-and-white photograph of Depression-era President Franklin Delano Roosevelt. Although many items in the original Roosevelt photograph were removed or reduced in importance, it was the

cover's jarring clash of scale and foreshortening that sparked public discussion. Since editing software such as Photoshop could have softened the discrepancies and adjusted the vanishing point, the disparities between the old and the new seem to have been intentional.

The nub of public reaction to the image was based on knowledge of how to use photo-editing software and belief about what resultant images should look like. In effect, the public's early 1990s fear about the deceptiveness of computer-generated photographs weakened during the first decade of the twenty-first century, and was replaced with pride in a skill widely admired by professional and amateur image-makers. During the last two decades, Photoshop has become a verb, and the wellspring of mostly affable competition to spot conspicuously poor or self-serving applications in news media. For their part, photo editors continue to worry that the ease with which photo-editing can be done in the field might spark an incidental or accidental bit of digital manipulation by a photographer while on assignment, thus damaging the credibility of a news organization.

The career of German photographer-sculptor Thomas Demand (b. 1964) also tracks the public understanding of the rise and current state of photography. Demand attended the Düsseldorf Art Academy (where, later, Andreas Gursky and Thomas Struth were enrolled) when the highly influential Bernd and Hilla Becher taught there. Demand, who studied sculpture, not photography, creates life-size models, mostly out of cut paper, based on photographs of notorious or tarnished settings—such as the passageway to serial killer Jeffrey Dahmer's apartment or the legendary staircase that survived the bombing of Dresden during World War II. He photographs these models and then destroys them. In sum, Demand often makes photographs of paper replications of news photographs. Thrice removed from the original, which itself was a reproduction, and devoid of people or little signs of wear and tear, Demand's scenes are chilly and restrained.

Occasionally, Demand painstakingly constructs a scene with no obvious paper trail in the media. *The Clearing* (2003) was purchased by New York's Museum of Modern Art, and shown in the museum's 2005 retrospective of Demand's work (Fig. 14.9). With the aid of thirty assistants, it took Demand three months to construct the scene. The photograph was given pride of place during the reopening of the refurbished museum, acknowledging the medium's elevated status in the art world. In the past, such a spot would have been awarded to a masterwork of modern painting, by an artist such as Picasso or Matisse. The image, which is about 16 feet wide and 6 feet tall, has a particular resonance in New York City, site of the attack on the World Trade Center. Its unstated subject, a startling daybreak moment Demand experienced in the Public Gardens of Venice, shows mist rising in response to the first rays of the sun, which strike the leaves in the upper left and the tree trunks on the right. The curators left it to viewers in New York to decide if the ambiguous title of *The Clearing* signaled a new beginning, or, as the photograph's flecks of brash orange might suggest, the dawn of an apocalyptic event.

Like Demand, artists in other media increasingly use photography and base their work on photographic icons. A critic for the *New Yorker* magazine suggested that today "painting owes as much to photography as the other way around."[3] Painters working in the early twenty-first century, such as Eric Fischl, Luc Tuymans (b. 1958), and Marlene Dumas (b. 1953) have enlarged their investigations of photography's formal language, particularly its light and its framing effects, in relation to the

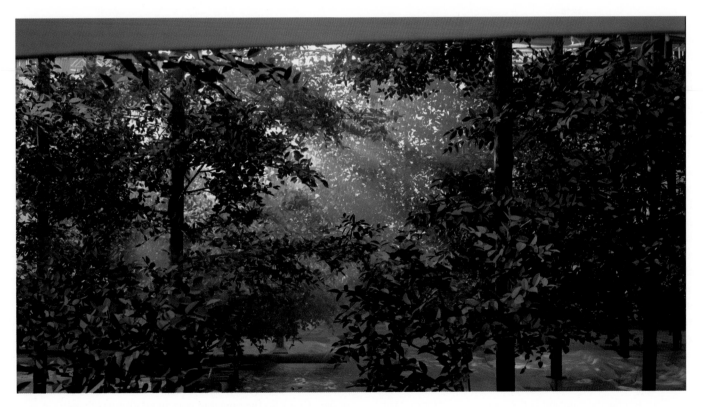

14.9
THOMAS DEMAND, *The Clearing,* **2003. Museum of Modern Art, New York. C-print.**

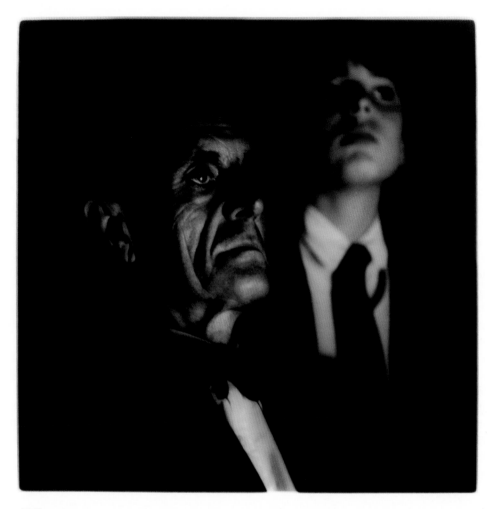

14.10
BILL HENSON, *Untitled, 28/77*, 1990–91, from the *Paris Opera Project* series. C-print.

conventions of painting. Of course, painting and photography have intersected before, in the paintings of Eakins and Degas, and more recently in the work of David Hockney and Gerhard Richter.

Today, the range of photographic sources turned to by artists from other media is much wider than in the past, ranging from adaptations of vernacular photographs, such as family snapshots, to news photographs and masterworks of the Western canon. At the same time, painters' tactics vary, including the reproduction of a photograph on canvas, application of paint directly on to a photograph, and digitally collaging materials. More and more, photographers create installations and videos, borrowing freely from photojournalism and art-historical images and styles. Just as artists frequently adapt photographs to their purposes, so too photographers increasingly make overt references to familiar paintings, mimicking an artist's typical style and subject matter. British-born Tom Hunter (b. 1965) created a series called *Persons Unknown*, in which he ennobled homeless people in poses and backgrounds closely based on the famous woman-at-the-window paintings by the Dutch painter Jan Vermeer (1632–1675). His other work focuses on youth in London, and enlists Pre-Raphaelite painting as the source for contemporary interpretations, such as the death of a young woman, whom

he posed as a jeans-wearing Ophelia, Hamlet's beloved, as envisioned in a painting by John Everett Millais (1829–1896).

The notion that photography can now successfully emulate masterworks of the Western tradition stems in part from the medium's recent increased status in the art world. Advertising photography, too, has been quick to take advantage of great works, sometimes to instigate publicity through shock and scandal. Just as Lejaren à Hiller produced a sensational interpretation of medical history (see p. 266), so too the Paris fashion house of Marithé and François Girbaud produced a 2005 billboard advertisement mimicking the poses in Leonardo da Vinci's *Last Supper*. It featured a female Jesus with other models, all wearing designer clothing. The public display brought on a lawsuit from the Roman Catholic Church for the abuse of a sacred image.

Undoubtedly, the strongest inheritance from the twentieth century is the directorial mode. A speculative article by Elizabeth Van Ness in the *New York Times* pointed out that film-directing has become a popular advanced degree among those who do not plan to take up movie-making. She suggested that consequently cinema studies might become the new M.B.A.[4] The association of directing with the power to command groups of people is sufficiently strong that students who want to go into business choose to learn film and video. Photographs in the directorial mode are plentiful worldwide, and have encouraged a second generation that has moved away from demands of big-budget productions. For example, Egyptian-born photographer Youssef Nabil (b. 1972) uses the camera to observe his life as if he were in a motion picture and uses the iconography of movie stills and old painted studio photographs to create portraits (Fig. 14.11). Indeed, work carried out by photographers not expressly involved in the technique has been pulled into its orbit. Notable among those caught up in the gravitational pull of directorial photography is Australian Bill Henson (b. 1955), among whose greatly varied work are large photographs overflowing with broody dark shadows that form the site of evocative narratives about youth and decay (Fig. 14.10). Although Henson obviously has made selections in these scenes, they are not directed in the manner of photographs like those of Gregory Crewdson, which require big budgets and a large crew. Nevertheless, images by Henson and others have been tugged into the force field of the directorial mode because they share some of its

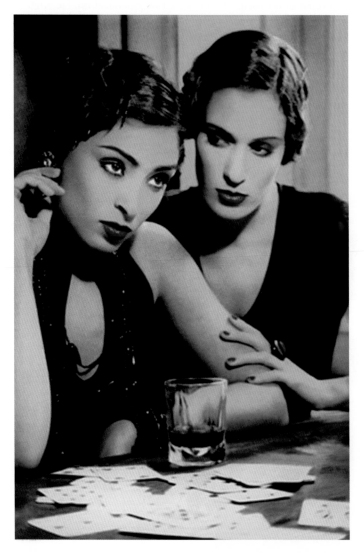

14.11
YOUSSEF NABIL, *Sweet Temptation, Cairo*, **1993. Hand-coloured gelatin silver print.**

dark, edgy anxiety. In 2008, some of Henson's photographs of nude teenagers, set in a Baroque swirl of light and shade, were taken from a gallery by police. The raid set off a countrywide discussion in Australia about censorship in relation to the imaging of children.

Not only has the directorial mode gained an international panoply of adherents and a firm market, but its look—intense detail and deeply saturated color—has been taken into consideration when editing prints that were not produced by photographer-directors. Glancing back at the photographs used on the front pages of leading world newspapers, from the late 1990s to about 2005, will demonstrate a shift toward vivid and portentous renderings where dark patches of shadow set the tone.

PHOTOGRAPHIC PRACTICE AND GLOBALIZATION

There is no doubt that early third-millennium calamities tarnished some of globalization's promise. Nevertheless, many of the questions that came to the fore were prefigured in the late twentieth century, and probably would have emerged regardless of events.

In the arts and in photographic practice today, globalization is being differentiated from globalism, defined as a mischievous return to utopian Modernism, with its yearning for universal cultural and social values. Looking back at the decade of the late 1980s to the late 1990s, curator Francesco Bonami observed that the West was confronted with new art from countries whose creative resources were largely hidden before the dissolution of the Soviet bloc. In response, the West "melted under the warmth of the multicultural electric heater." But after an initial fascination, the West reflexively looked inward at its own roots and, finding them insular, had to face the fact that life experience outside Western culture could nurture vital art.[5] For photography, as for the arts, many of the newly seeded questions about globalization have revolved around redefining identity issues, in an era when there is lessening consensus on what identity should mean for image-makers. For example, installation artist and photographer Yinka Shonibare believes that the time has come "to resist the temptation of defining artists by the narrow confines of nationality." He considers that the aesthetic and political concerns found in art should be understood to spring from an artist's judgment, not national origin.[6] Likely enough, globalization fostered questions about cultural territory, national identity, and social roots. But these queries do not have the same emphasis as those raised during the Postmodern period, when identity issues were frequently associated with an underclass, or with indigenous people who struggle to maintain their languages and custom.

In short, as some artists and photographers seek to move away from national and ethnic identification, others are making commitments to create art and photography that is directly and deliberately tied to the contemporary conditions of regions and nations. As Jean-Hubert Martin pointed out about the 2005–06 exhibition "Africa Remix," "being the same and different seems to be the paradoxical condition in which contemporary art evolves."[7]

While Shonibare rejects being tagged as a Nigerian-British photographer, several Mexican photographers and critics insist the image-making should be for and about regional Mexican issues. They take exception to what they understand to be the bland, international view of Gabriel Orozco (see p. 456), which ignores his origins and "de-localizes" his work from its roots in a region to the world.[8] In contemporary Mexican art and photography, the explicit Mexican combination of economic hardship, political corruption, migrant-worker exploitation, and drug trafficking has produced a milieu that Mexicans call the "aesthetics of corruption."[9]

In this climate, art and documentary photographers judge that the art most needed is that which identifies and interprets social conditions for a wide audience. Perhaps the most famous instance of this strategy is the photography of Mexican photographer Daniela Rossell (b. 1973), who documents the extravagant and conspicuous consumption of Mexico's rich in her series, *Ricas y Famosas* (*Rich and Famous*). The women who sit for Rossell's portraits are like rare hothouse plants, nurtured in an overheated environment that they can seldom leave because of the constant threat of kidnapping (Fig. 14.12). While Rossell's work has been shown internationally, its greatest meaning is found in Mexico. Her photographs are free from the interest in folklore and tradition that engaged Mexican art and photography in the past and fixed the country's international cultural identity. Moreover, they were not conceived as a visual example of an abstract theory, but formulated out of actual social conditions.

In Mexico, the dedication to making images about the present means focusing on the poverty and unemployment caused by the near-collapse of Mexican industry, which was brought on by the spread of global capitalism and by the North American Free Trade Agreement (NAFTA), which came into effect in 1994. What might be called critical nationalism is also abundantly apparent in the photographs that document the installations of Teresa Margolies (b. 1963). Like Gabriel Orozco, Margolies favors transient works of art that depend on photography to record them. For more than a decade, Margolies has given aesthetic expression to her country's high violent-death rate. Working in the morgue to which unidentified gunshot victims are often brought, she collected the soap and water used to wash corpses, and created a lyrical installation of floating bubbles to memorialize the dead. Both Rossell and Margolies reject the elitism of Postmodern theory and stress that their work should be accessible to and understandable by a wide swath of people. Their work indicates what may be the beginning of another shift, from social protest to social programs.

In India, Ravi Agarwal (b. 1958) makes photographs that give a glimpse of the inequities of economic globalization. He often configures his pictures of large cities, such as New Delhi, to show homeless workers living in the shadow of shiny new hotels and skyscrapers. Agarwal shares another pursuit that has become apparent in contemporary Mexico. Like the Mexican artists who set up organizations to help the poor find employment and food, he is an activist who founded Toxics Link, an environmental exchange service for grassroots organizations, and he is the head of Srishti, a citizens group that devises strategies to manage medical and municipal waste in India. In the United States,

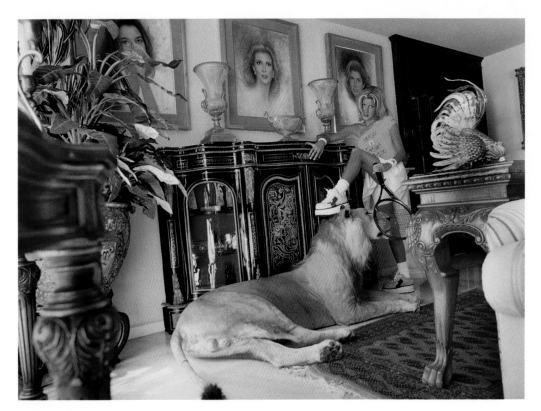

14.12
DANIELA ROSSELL, *Paulina with Lion* **from** *Ricas Y Famosas* **(Rich and Famous), 1999. Color photograph.**

A theme of conspicuous consumption runs through Rossell's often gold-toned photographs of Mexico's rich and famous residents. Here the subject, clothed in tennis garments, places a foot on the head of a stuffed lion, symbolizing her social clout.

photographer Lonnie Graham (b. 1953) not only makes images but also uses his financial resources to create human-betterment projects. For instance, he began the African-American Garden Project, which brought farmers from Africa to the United States to teach African agricultural techniques. He believes that "as artists we must not limit ourselves to our imaginations."[10]

In the past, photographers concerned with social change, such as Jacob Riis and Margaret Bourke-White, hoped to stimulate reform directly through their images; photographers in the newly independent India proposed that photography should be "of Indians, by Indians, for Indians" (see p. 326). By contrast, some contemporary photographers and artists consider it necessary to reach beyond their image-making into direct social action. The reaccentuation of the worth and distinctiveness of regions—coupled with the continuing interrogation of abstract, unifying systems, such as globalization and Modernism—has kindled further reflection on colonialism, not just as it was practiced in the past, but as it currently takes place. For example, Croatian visual artist Andreja Kulunčić (b. 1968) creates photo-based posters that confront contemporary social problems. In addition, she examines how Croatia's application to join the European Union encouraged the country's artists to seek more attention from international curators seeking new artworks. "We don't want to be colonized," Kulunčić declared, adding that outside curators have a fixed idea or stereotype about what Croatian art and photography are, an attitude that stifles both change and original thinking.[11]

Many issues that inflect contemporary discussion of globalization have been the subject of articles and exhibitions created by Okwui Enwezor. In shows such as "The Short Century" (2001) and "Documenta XI" (2002) Enwezor extensively displayed art and photography from developing countries. He is concerned that other curators tend to reject images and objects that refer to topical subject matter, or which are grounded in particular geographic locations and conditions.[12] To those who find documentary and even contemporary images without aesthetic appeal, Enwezor replies that today "boundaries between art, journalism, and sociology are essentially nonexistent."[13]

GLOBAL/LOCAL

In Dubrovnik, Croatia, during the spring of 2004, photographs from the war that gripped the former Yugoslavia for a decade were selected by ten photographers and exhibited at a new gallery called War Photo Limited, whose aim was to show people what happened in the nearby area during the war. Among the images were some by Ron Haviv (b. 1965), including a 1992 image from Bijeljina that shows a young Serb militiaman about to kick a prostrate woman in the head (Fig. 14.13). Haviv's photograph is untitled, but residents certainly would be able to deduce who was a Muslim and who a Serb. While the exhibition was free to locals, its aim was to educate international visitors from the cruise ships that dock in Dubrovnik. Conversely, in 2001, when Peru's Truth and Reconciliation Commission investigated the violence between 1980 and 2000, when about sixty thousand people were killed or disappeared, they issued their account in two forms. A five-thousand-page report on the history and social effects of the radical group called Shining Path was made available. Also, the commission believed that it could reach far more Peruvians if it created a photography

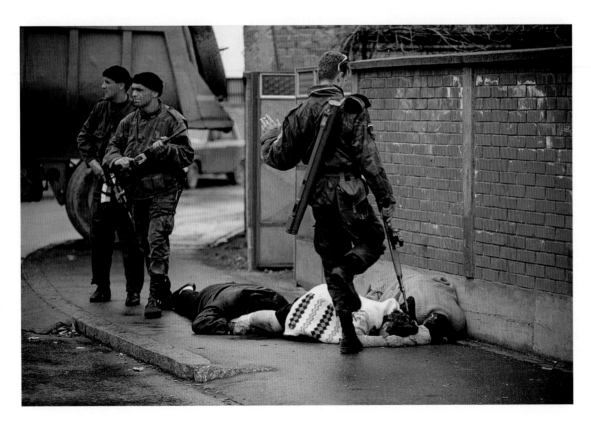

14.13
RON HAVIV, *Untitled* **from** *Blood and Honey: A Balkan War Journal,* **Bijeljina, Bosnia, March 31, 1992.**

The soldier's graceful balletic stance belies the cruelty of this scene as the viewer realizes that he is about to kick the prostrate and helpless woman at his feet.

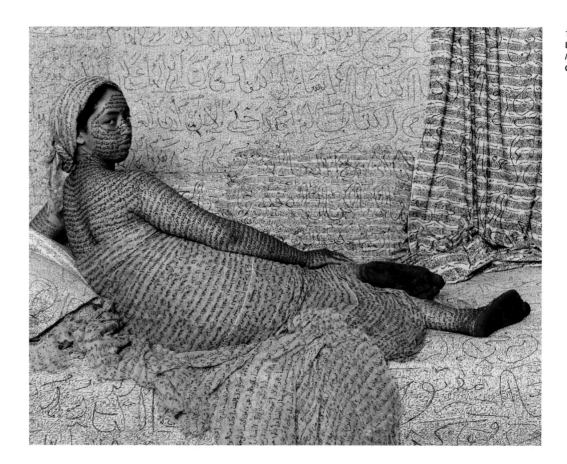

14.14
LALLA ESSAYDI, *Les Femmes du Maroc: Grande Odalisque*, 2008. Chromogenic print.

exhibition from the image bank of about 1,700 photographs. The high Andes city of Chorrillos, located in an area that saw much violence, was chosen as the site of a temporary museum called "Yuyanapaq," a Quechua word meaning "to remember." Peruvians by the thousands flocked to see photographs that were documentary as well as interpretive art. Since then, the exhibit has continued to be mounted in other areas of the country, in other parts of the world, and on the Internet. Although the photographs have worldwide interest, "Yuyanapaq" was mainly an exhibit by and for Peruvians. Similarly, "Why are We the Way We are?" a Guatemalan exhibition composed largely of photographs, started in Guatemala City during 2004 and continued circulating through 2005. Like the Peruvian show, the Guatemalan exposition was composed of images calculated to communicate the history of the country, including its recent armed conflicts. It used life-size photographs to create what was for some the first experience of looking directly into the eyes of an indigenous person. In one of the photo-installations, the viewer's face was reflected in a mirror placed in the center of multiple rows of headshots that emphasized the facial differences among Guatemalans. As Jim Volkert, then associate director of the Smithsonian's National Museum of the American Indian, observed, the show was not about art, but "its significance is that it has the ability to affect the culture of a country, and is rare in a museum context."[14]

During the early twenty-first century, the craving to break free from imposed ethnic and national identities has chafed against the desire to make photography for and about specific locales. The "Us and the Other" approach to art and photography continues to be challenged by the notion that non-Western art or photographic practice has been inflected by Western ideas and economics. The idea of the exotic, morally superior Other seems to be giving way to the observation that there is no outside intellectual space from which one can fashion a high-minded objective critique. That point of view was taken up at a controversial 2005 show organized at the International Center of Photography in New York City.

As its title implies, "White: Whiteness and Race in Contemporary Art" shifted the focus away from other identities and on to the one that is often assumed but seldom discussed. To grasp the cultural understanding of whiteness, Nancy Burson placed an advertisement for men who thought they looked like Jesus. She photographed them and then employed her composite technique to show how much skin color influences people's mental image of Christ.

THE ARAB WORLD

Not surprisingly, after September 11, 2001, studies and exhibitions of photography having to do with Islam or with Arab identity multiplied. At the 2003 Venice Bienniale, curator Catherine David organized a section called "Contemporary Arab Representations." She maintained that the word "representations" was far better than the word "art" to describe the various media presented in the show, including photography. Curators of photography and art exhibitions have had to confront the dilemma of defining the so-called Arab world, a term that is often used to imply cultural homogeneity where it does not exist. Wisely, Catherine David designated one country, Lebanon, as a laboratory in which to consider photographic practice. Other shows, such as "Nazar: Photographs from the Arab World," held during 2004 in the Netherlands, defined the Arab world as comprising places where Arabic is the predominant language. Many exhibitions also included images of what might be termed the Arab diaspora to Europe and North America. Palestine represents the most acute case of Arab dispersion, and, at the Venice Biennale of 2003, Sandi Hilal (b. 1973) and Alessandro Petti (b. 1973) created billboard-size enlargements of identity photographs and passports belonging to Palestinians but issued by the countries in which they were currently living in exile, such as Italy, Israel, and Jordan.

Many exhibitions of Arab photography, such as Fotofest 2014 in Houston, Texas, include numerous regional, national, or religious identities, which intentionally makes it difficult to generalize an Arab stereotype. For example, Morocco-born Lalla

Essaydi (1956) enlarges aspects of her experiences growing up with the traditions of Islam by creating a physical and intellectual space in which women are confined to silence, yet able to speak. Set in the very house where women in her family who disobeyed were isolated and not spoken to for a month, her subjects converse through the calligraphy that encompasses their figures. As Essaydi points out, the henna dye with which the words are written is a symbol of women's domain. Yet the predominance of calligraphy, traditionally an art reserved for men, works to subvert the women's silence and confinement. At the same time, the wealth of words creates a vivid contrast to the silent stereotypes of harems and concubines popular in nineteenth-century photography (see Fig. 2.58) (Fig. 14.14). The effort to differentiate Arabs was also taken up by Walid Raad (b. 1967), who combed the rich files of the Arab Image Foundation (A.I.F.) in Beirut, Lebanon, for ordinary photographs that would visually chronicle Arab diversity (Fig. 14.15). Ironically he found them among hundreds of commercial portraits made for ID cards and other public uses. Despite efforts to standardize the image, these conventional photographs show a great variety of physical

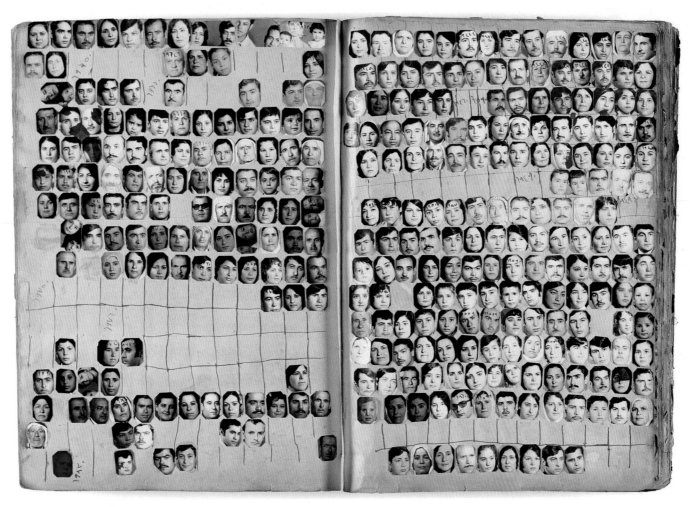

14.15
WALID RAAD AND AKRAM ZAATARI/ARAB IMAGE FOUNDATION, from *Mapping Sitting*, a project by Studio Soussi portrait index, Saida, Lebanon, 1934–86.
100 pages, approx. 150 portraits per page, Anis Soussi. Arab Image Foundation Collection.

focus

China

After the death of Mao Zedong in 1976 and the dissolution of the Cultural Revolution (1966–76), which forcibly attempted to bring the arts and photography into line with Chinese communist social objectives, Chinese photographers cautiously began to explore the limits of their freedom. While their exhibitions were sometimes shut down or denounced, the work that they were able to send abroad often received accolades, prompting the Chinese government to recognize that artistic freedom at home could help the country's image abroad.[16] Although impassioned debates about the social responsibilities of photography still affect them, photographers have increasing control over their own work.

As historian and photographer James Zeng Huang noted, in the years immediately after the Cultural Revolution, documentary photography was sometimes associated with the politically correct images that appeared in that era. But in the 1990s, documentary photography began to flourish anew. Yu Quanxing (b. 1962) spent a decade recording the lives of women in remote areas of western China, and Zhao Tielin (1948–2009) created sympathetic chronicles of the lives of prostitutes. James Zeng Huang's series on family planning depicted the clinics in which female sterilization (tubal ligation) was practiced in the late 1990s (Fig. 14.16).[17]

The efflorescence of Chinese photography accompanied the escalation of experimental art and access to visual technology that began in the 1990s.[18] Thus, many artists who work in other media became familiar with photographic practice and some even took it up exclusively. As happened in the West, the directorial mode attracted many Chinese photographers. Hong

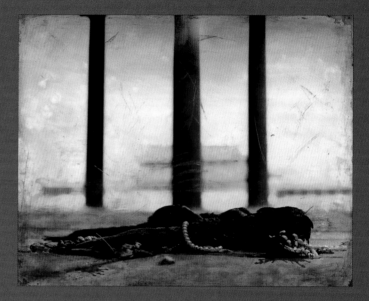

14.17
HONG LEI, *Autumn in the Forbidden City*, 1997. C-print.

Lei (b. 1960), a painter turned photographer, not only sets up the scenes he photographs, but also scratches and paints on the print's surface. One of his images uses the Forbidden City, China's ancient capital, as a backdrop. It features a bejeweled dead pheasant which was likely brought down to earth by the beads wound in its wings (Fig. 14.17). Hong's photographic work often derives its settings and motifs from traditional Chinese painting, where, for instance, pheasants and other birds adorn ideal landscapes. Hong fears the effects of globalization on Chinese tradition, and openly longs for the past glories of Chinese art. Nevertheless, his photographs are often glazed with blood-red color, an indication that he can also be critical of the past.

Chinese photographers sometimes associate photographic realism with Socialist Realism and the repressive period of the Cultural Revolution. Consequently, they temper the camera's ability to make imprints of the observable world. For example, Wang Jinsong (see pp. 463–64), whose work seems documentary, usually uses a grid to organize his many disparate pictures, and to break up the viewer's easy assumption of photographic realism. Similarly, the breadth of Zhuang Hui's images (see p. 425), and the great number of individuals packed into them, constitute works that are simulataneously documents and critiques of realist photography's shortcomings. Liu Zheng (b. 1969), sometimes referred to as China's August Sander, teasingly photographs realist sculpture as if the figures were alive. His seven-year project *The Chinese* is stylistically more adventuresome than

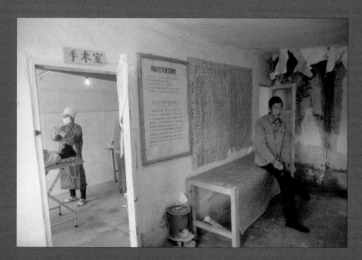

14.16
JAMES ZENG-HUANG, *Family Planning Project: Dr Jiang's Rural Clinic*, 1997.

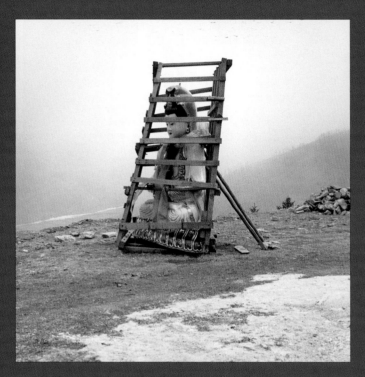

Sander was, yet it shares the encyclopedic urge to record the panoply of people and activities within a nation (Fig. 14.18).

As photographers in China continue to experiment with the limits of public expression, the human body has become increasingly central in their work. Performance art flourishes, and artists such as Chen Lingyang (b. 1975) have fused fantasy and feminism in a visual rumination on women in art. Chen's *25:00* shows a figure she calls the giantess, who is waiting for what Chen notes is the impossible twenty-fifth hour in the day when she will shake off her languor, realize her social worth, reflected in her physical size, and become "large" in the world. The sleeping giantess, digitally perched on the recently constructed buildings of modern urban China, seems equally decipherable as Chen and as the contemporary Chinese woman (Fig. 14.19).

While contemporary photographic practice flourishes, historic work created and preserved by official and unofficial photographers is slowly making its way into the public realm in China and elsewhere, hinting at the possibility that the most populous country on earth may eventually be able to construct its own photographic history.

14.18
LIU ZHENG, *Buddha in Cage, Wutai Mountain, Shanxi Province*, 1998.
Gelatin silver print.

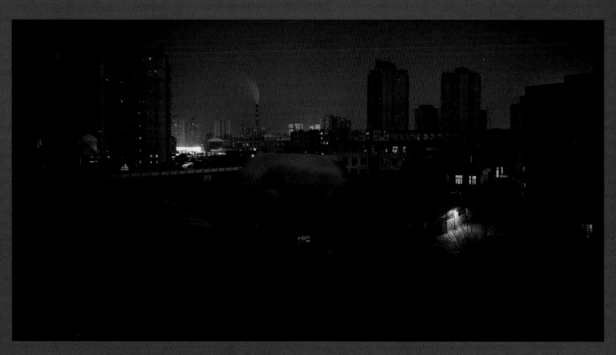

14.19
CHEN LINGYANG, *25:00*, 2002. Digitally combined photographs.

features, an aspect of identity photographs also emphasized in the Guatemalan exhibition "Why are We the Way We are?"

YOUTH AND BEAUTY

Throughout the last quarter of the twentieth century, beauty was held accountable for many of photography's lapses and misdeeds, especially in the area of social concern. In his enduringly influential essay, "On the Invention of Photographic Meaning" (1975), photographer-critic Allan Sekula savaged art for art's sake, writing that "the ills of photography are the ills of aestheticism," and that "aestheticism must be superseded, in its entirety, for a meaningful art, of any sort, to emerge."[19] Critic Hal Foster concurred in his popular anthology *The Anti-Aesthetic* (1983), whose title was drawn from a term in Walter Benjamin's authoritative essay "The Work of Art in the Age of Mechanical Reproduction."[20] Foster questioned whether the aesthetic was now a threadbare illusion.[21] Time and again, beauty has been sent packing to the cobwebbed attic of outmoded ideas. The anti-aesthetic persisted into the twenty-first century. For example, in 2003 Martha Rosler opined that, in the United States, "the debate over beauty has been deeply reactionary, a cry for 'art for art's sake' to return us to the grand old days when the critics were in control, patrons knew what to buy and artists didn't mess with politics."[22]

Mindful of the lessons from the recent past, a few photographers modestly began to explore what might constitute a fragile post-Postmodern beauty. For Dutch photographer Rineke Dijkstra (b. 1959), beauty is as tentative as the hesitant step being taken by the adolescent boy she photographed in Berlin's Tiergarten (Fig. 14.21). In her pictures of young men and women, some of whom she has photographed for years, Dijkstra secures both fact and symbol. Measured against the stark, blank faces of Thomas Ruff's photographs (see Fig. 12.43), Dijkstra's portraits are lush, informative, and loving. She is, in her own words, a believer in observing rather than in asking questions.

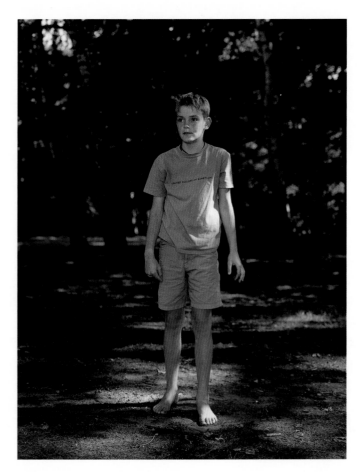

14.21
RINEKE DIJKSTRA, *Tiergarten, Berlin,* **August 13, 2000. C-print.**

Because she focuses on the vulnerable yet inevitable time of life when the innocence of childhood visibly and spiritually grows into experience, she has fashioned widely understood elegiac visual metaphors for lost innocence, coupled with a consolation that radiates from the calm surrender of her young subjects to the path of physical and mental maturity. More self-assured young adults inhabit the Arcadian color celebrations of American Ryan McGinley (b. 1977), whose self-published book, *The Kids are All Right* (2000), became a manifesto for post-AIDS, guilt-free sensuality – an influence still felt in youth-oriented depictions and advertising (Fig. 14.20). A more melancholic tone informs Bill Henson's photographs, especially his recent work, in which nude adolescent bodies populate a post-apocalyptic suburban night.

In 1999, Gregory Crewdson at Yale University in New Haven, Connecticut, helped organize a New York exhibition called "Another Girl, Another Planet" (the title a reference to the 1980s song by English punk band the Only Ones), which showcased the work of photographers who had studied with him, including Justine Kurland, Dana Hoey, Katy Grannan, Malerie Marder, and Jenny Gage. The show led to years of backhanded praise and reference to the women as "girl photographers," although they do not claim to be a group. Another Yale graduate from Crewdson's photography program, Anna Gaskell (b. 1969), was missing from that show, but seems closest to Crewdson in her

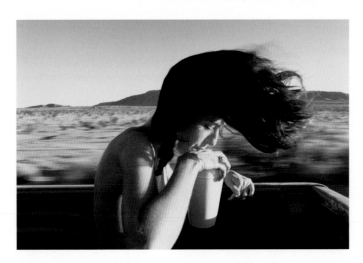

14.20
RYAN MCGINLEY, *Dakota (Hair),* **2004**

interest in the supernatural and the uncanny. Like the others, she constructs uneasy pictures, mostly of young women. In her series *Resemblance*, she presented a series of images in which young women (actually students at Phillips Academy in Andover, Massachusetts) seem to be creating an ideal human. Gaskell concocts dramatic moments filled with foreboding and hints of secret ritual (Fig. 14.22), based on her musings on works by Lewis Carroll, as well as by French author Villers de l'Isle Adam (1838–1889) and German author E. T. A. Hoffman (1776–1832). Gaskell's literary sources pinpoint a significant divergence within the late twentieth-century directorial mode; where television and the movies once acted as powerful visual sources, now myth, fairytales, and science fiction have also begun to play a part.

The American "girl photographers" were part of a larger and global refocusing on the experiences of young women. For example, the internationally successful film *Whale Rider* (2002) showed a New Zealand Maori girl coming of age by making a new place for herself in traditional culture; in *Bend It Like Beckham* (2002), an Asian-British teenager struggles not only with gender roles, but also with the tug of her family's heritage. Confident young women appear in *The Adventures of Guille and Belinda and the Enigmatic Meaning of their Dreams*, a series of photographs begun in 1999 by American-born Alessandra Sanguinetti (b. 1968), who divides her time between New York and Argentina. She palled around with two rural girls on and off for five years, and photographed them as they acted out their fantasies.

Since she was a teenager in the 1990s, Japanese photographer Hiromix (Toshikawa Hiromi, b. 1976) has recorded and circulated photographs of her everyday life. Known as the quintessential *onna no ko no shashinka*—usually translated as "girlie photographer"—she became an example to many young

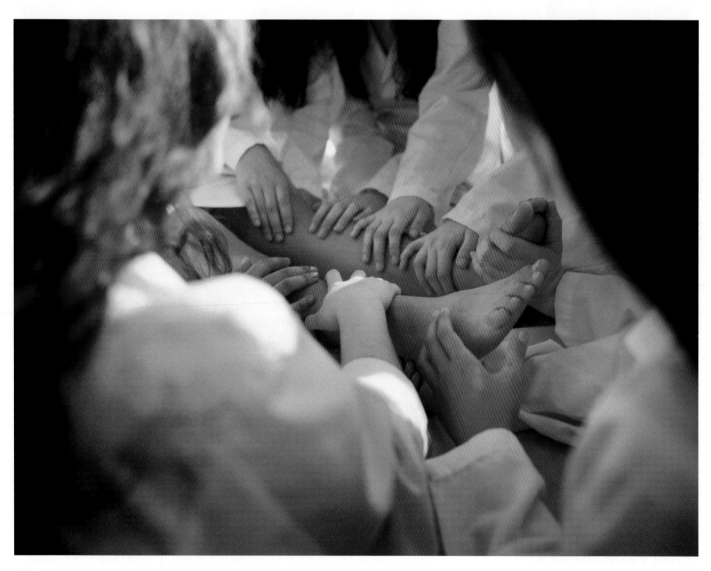

14.22
ANNA GASKELL, *Untitled No. 74* (from the *Resemblance* series), 2001. C-print.

An unsettling ambiguity often dominates Gaskell's work. Here, it is not clear whether the figures in white robes are performing laying on of hands to help or to thwart the person whose legs they are touching.

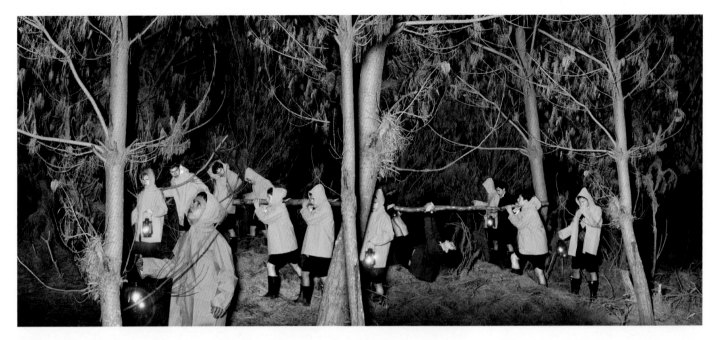

14.23
ANTHONY GOICOLEA, *Ash Wednesday*, 2001. Digital c-print. Courtesy the artist.

women. Today's girl photographer in Japan is more likely to direct eerie scenes involving teenagers and young women. For example, throughout the last decade, Japanese performance artist and photographer Miwa Yanagi (b. 1967) perfected menace-tinged digital fantasies about department store "elevator girls," who welcome and give directions in upscale Japanese department stores, and a series of chilling scenes based on fairytales. Another exhibition based on the notion of girlhood as an eccentric and absorbing phase of life was the internationally drawn exhibition "Girl's Night Out," which was shown across the United States in 2004–06. It featured photographers such as Daniela Rossell and Rineke Dijkstra. Perhaps the most interesting aspect of the show was its sponsor, the Neutrogena company, which makes skin-care products aimed at young consumers.

While images by women of womanhood were frequently created in the new century, images by men of manhood and boyhood also were produced. For example, Anthony Goicolea (b. 1971) is intrigued by the power of fairytales and science fiction to reveal psychic states. He has staged odd scenes that involve boys or male teenagers seemingly caught in the act of strange deeds, motivated by pubescent group-think and cultic initiation in an adult-free, alternative world (Fig. 14.23). Moreover, by using make-up, costumes, lighting, and photo-editing software, Goicolea plays all the parts in his elaborate scenarios himself.

SCIENCE AND SOCIETY

In the early twenty-first century, the public had unprecedented access to space photographs generated by cameras on board unmanned vessels, such as the Hubble Space Telescope, the

Mars Global Surveyor Orbiter, NASA's Mars rovers, the Cassini spacecraft and its lander, named Huygens, created by NASA and the European Space Agency, and Mars Express, which was launched by the European Space Agency. Pictures of vast cone nebulas, where stars are created, and gauzy remnants of supernovas, the remains of exploded stars, competed with images of Saturn's largest moon, Titan, cloaked in tangerine skies. The colors of outer space reminded some art critics and photographers of abstract paintings, and, at a conference held in 2003, they debated whether a photograph taken by a robot could be considered art.

Less debated was the way in which the photographs transmitted from distant spacecrafts obtain their color. The cameras on the Mars rovers take only black-and-white pictures. Filters and computer manipulation do the rest. Nevertheless, black-and-white images do not easily translate into color.[23] Just as colorized black-and-white films from the early twentieth century do not have the rich depth that color film produces, so the Mars rover pictures look more like they were dunked in orange Kool-Aid.

Raw black-and-white photographs of supernovas taken by the Hubble Space Telescope resemble blurry pictures of what look like pale mummified jellyfish floating in a dark sea. However, when colorized, they take on the appearance of bursting fireworks (Fig. 14.24). The color of space photographs is mostly created on this planet, both to intensify indications of color as they are rendered in black and white, and to please human eyes. So-called "raw images" are usually available on project websites, but they are generally not published in newspapers and magazines.

Ray Villard, long-time public relations director for the Hubble project, was candid in his assessment of colorization.

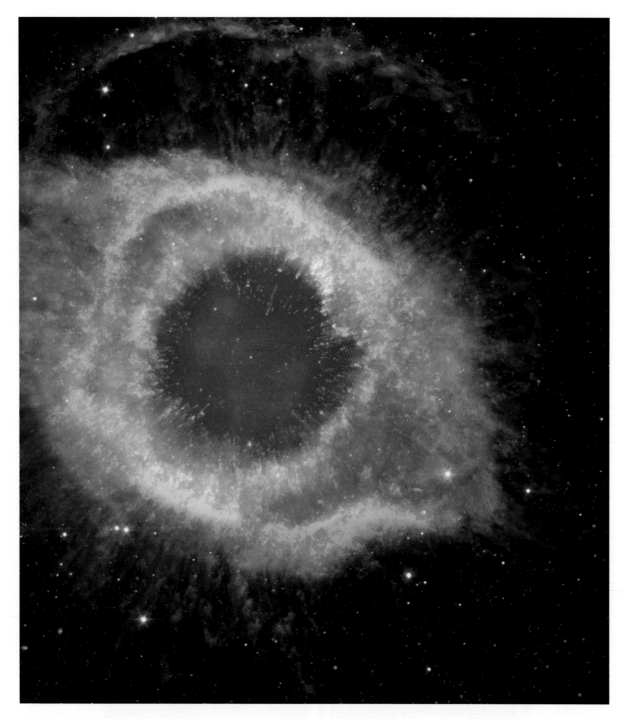

14.24
White Dwarf Star in Aquarius, 2006. Composite picture made up of visible data from Hubble and infrared data from Spitzer space telescopes.

"It's hard to tell the story if you don't have a stunning image to back it up," he said. In an attempt to convince the public that unmanned journeys to the cosmos are worth their huge cost, space photographs sport the digitally drenched color of art photographs and stills from action-adventure movies. Scientists in other disciplines routinely tint their work. For example, at the Oak Ridge National Laboratory in Tennessee, the sharpest picture ever made of atoms was tinted red, not because it appeared red, but to make it more attractive.

Geographic Information Systems (GIS), computer-driven applications that gather, store, and analyze images as well as text them, offer an innovative tool in fields ranging from the military to the humanities. GIS search for new and old photographs of sites, reconfigure and align the scale of the images, and then superimpose them in discrete layers, highlighting differences between and among the images. In the past, some of this time- and labor-intensive work could have been done in the darkroom. But the accumulation and "georectifying" of images is best accomplished when all the visual and textual information is digitized (Fig. 14.25).

GIS have created a new photo-based subfield in archeology. Old spy-plane and civilian aerial photographs are layered with pictures taken from U. S. space shuttles, Google Earth, and real-time data, to reveal previously unseen roads, canals, and buildings, as well as changes in herding and agricultural patterns. GIS also help to monitor looting, by showing, dating, and comparing looters' holes and damages. Because GIS are computer-based, an individual researcher can insert or remove images and data, tailoring the image strata to specific projects. GIS allow businesses and transportation centers to bring together real-time images and share observations. In the humanities, GIS have been applied to items too large or too delicate to be studied at first hand. For example, a digitized version of the Bayeux Tapestry, the lengthy eleventh-century cloth-based rendition of events surrounding the Norman Conquest of England, has been digitized with software that allows scholars to add historical sources, maps, art media, and comments that are shared among users.

The value of "then and now" or "repeat photography" has been increased by GIS. In 1889, German scientist Sebastian Finsterwalder began making pictures of Alpine glaciers to record and estimate their melting rates. His is one of oldest projects that the mostly self-assigned repeat photographers created worldwide, standing in the same place and making the same view over long periods of time. Vernacular versions of GIS,

such as Historypin and LookBackMaps, allow cell phone and computer users to obtain and layer historical photographs of locations, including their current spot. Users can then put themselves in the pictures, or add a new shot or a historical photograph not yet registered.[24]

While surveillance cameras have multiplied in urban areas, they have also entered the wilderness. The World Wildlife Fund placed thirty "camera traps" in the tropical forests of Indonesia, where they gather photographs of the rare Sumatran tiger. Camera traps also record tigers in Africa and jaguars in Central America. Because global warming has become apparent at the earth's fragile polar regions, these areas, and the animals that live there, have become the subject of scientific photographers, photojournalists, artists, and amateurs. For example, as part of his worldwide Genesis Project, through which he seeks to encourage a vast rediscovery of pristine nature, Sebastião Salgado accompanied an expedition to Antarctica sponsored by the United Nations Environment Programme (see p. 426). An ongoing project by Subhankar Banerjee (b. 1967) employs photography to support indigenous Arctic peoples while imaging how oil and coal exploration disrupt traditional ways of life.

Jean-Luc Mylayne (b. 1946) a serious amateur ornithologist, has led a nomadic life since 1976. His photographs deliberately erase his presence and the patient, philosophically based technique he uses to photograph birds. Because Mylayne spends many months studying particular species and individual birds before he makes a photograph, he has created only about 150

14.25
GIS. Portable devices like smart phones and tablets can be used to generate personal maps aligned with information taken from historic sites and traffic advisories.

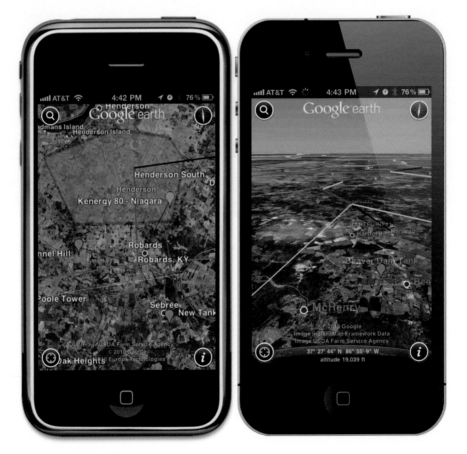

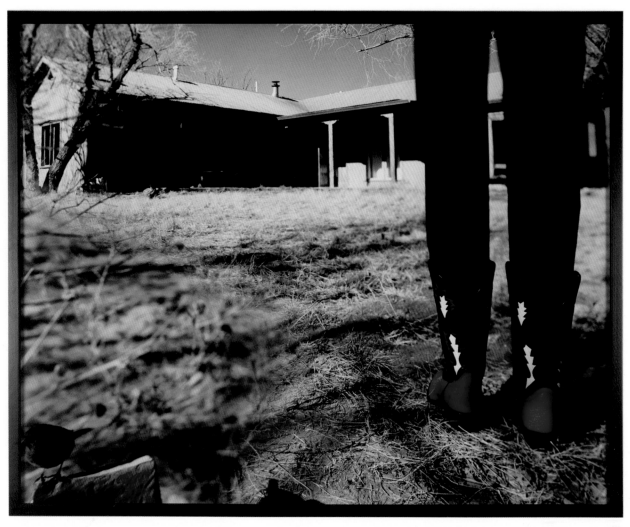

14.26
JEAN-LUC MYLAYNE, *N° 188, January February (Janvier Février) 2004,* 2007. C-print. Courtesy Gladstone Gallery.

images. Although he has described himself as a director, his work strongly diverges from the directorial mode typified by Gregory Crewdson. Mylayne does not work with large crews or create elaborate artificial sets. He accepts the bird's habitat as he finds it. Likewise, he does not concoct an implicit drama in terms of human emotion, nor does he compose solely for the ease of human perception. Instead, he waits patiently for the elements of the photograph, such as available light, time of the year, and the appearance of the bird, to come together (Fig. 14.26). Sometimes, viewers must search the photography to find the bird's presence. While Mylayne's art is based on confluences, it is primarily one of time.

PRE-PRODUCTION/POST-PRODUCTION

In the analog era of commercial and advertising photography, as well as in art-photographers' studios, time-consuming pre-production of a photograph, including such items as lighting and set design, was the norm. It was followed by extensive post-production editing and printing, achieved in darkrooms and print rooms. Pre- and post-production were standard practice in photojournalism, beginning with the photo editor's assignment choices. Photojournalists knew—and continue to know—that their images would be cropped and edited to suit a story's text and the paper's space.

Similar procedures are carried on in today's "light rooms", that is, with the software employed to edit digital images, which is used not only by professional photographers and artists but also by the general public. In late twentieth- and early twenty-first-century visual media, the software tools available to edit film, video, and photography received much attention. It seemed that most production problems could be fixed "in post." In tune with the times, the Lytro camera, an innovative light-gathering device introduced in 2011, adopted the advertising slogan, "Shoot now, focus later," because focusing is done with computer or smart-phone software after the picture is taken. The emphasis on post-production paralleled the extensive preparations made by contemporary art and commercial photographers.

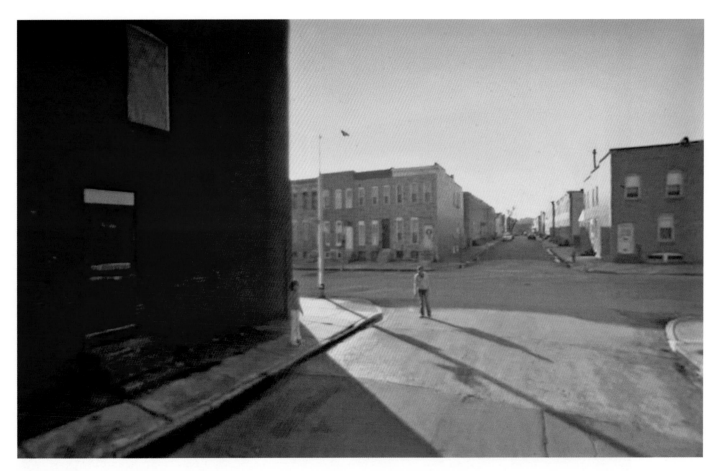

14.27
DOUG RICKARD, #39.177833, Baltimore, MD (2008), 2011.

Photographers who favor elaborate planning before a shoot, such as Thomas Demand and Walead Beshty (b. 1976) (Fig. 14.1), often seem to be carrying on Conceptual ideas. Indeed, Beshty conceived the elaborate preparations for his *Color Curl* series as physical and mental experiments with the medium. He folded and contoured light-sensitive photo-paper and then exposed it to colored light. Although his work has been called abstract, he denies that it is. Rather, the image is the result of a specific set of conditions, which Beshty hopes may produce some unanticipated results. By contrast, Doug Rickard's (b. 1968) images adapted from Google Earth's Street View pictures explore what might be called the post-production readymade. Rickard's earlier photographs concentrated on vernacular architecture as a symbol of human alienation and powerlessness. His *A New American Picture* series, exhibited in 2012, was created by photographing images on a computer screen. These images originated in the Google Earth protocol, in which a camera affixed to an automobile films from a fixed height, taking photographs every 65 feet. Software automatically blurs the faces of any humans in the Google Earth picture. Rickard uses that blur to symbolize the erasure of identity that goes on even as more visual information is gathered, as in a photograph taken in Baltimore, Maryland, labeled only with the longitude and latitude of the space given it by Google Earth (Fig. 14.25).

SCREENS AND PLATFORMS

The early twenty-first century witnessed an increase in journal and memoir photography, due more to the ease of digital recording and distribution than to artistic precedents in such popular work as Nan Goldin's *The Ballad of Sexual Dependency* and in the snapshot style introduced during the 1990s by influential contemporary photographers such as Corinne Day and Wolfgang Tillmans. The success of *Look-Look* magazine, which was founded in 2003, rests on its active solicitation of informal and art photographs and articles by young people, many of whom are in high school. *Look-Look* has given digital cameras to teenagers around the world and hired them to make pictures.

Digital cameras, camera-phones, photoblogs, and social media sites like Facebook, Twitter, and Pinterest encouraged people to create visual diaries. Often these efforts render an uncomplicated view of events great and small. At the same time, what has been called "diaristic" photography sets out clues to subjective feelings in pictures with indefinite and implied narratives. Diaristic photographers do not insist on a particular interpretation. As critic and diarist Craig Garrett observed, diarists avoid contemporary political issues by turning inward. They seem to say, "this is my life, my observation, my reality."[25] The diarists' procedures may seem akin to the literary or cinematic use of metaphor to suggest inner feelings, but the diaristic photograph is more open-ended. It does not stand for states of mind that elude description; rather, it invites the viewer to engage with the image and construct a narrative from his or her experience. Where photobloggers and camera-phone users often expect to communicate an idea or emotion through their pictures, diaristic photographers hope to spark a reaction or an independent narrative in the mind of the viewer. Noting a comparable mindset underlying Anna Gaskell's photographs, art historian Claire Daigle detected a diaristic mode that is "distinctly impersonal," signaling "a shift away from the subjective to the demonstrative."[26] So-called reality television, which features ordinary people doing or saying mundane and extraordinary things, may have faintly encouraged personal and diaristic photography, but the heat of reality television contrasts with the cool tone and "whatever" attitude of the diarists.

If the late twentieth century was the time of the computer revolution, then the last ten years have been the era of a quieter change, the development of "platforms," which allow operating systems in digital devices to communicate with each other, often wirelessly. In effect, digital cameras and camera-phones can upload their pictures on to Internet and social media sites, and people can link these devices to self-service printing machines that are available in malls and camera shops. Phones can send pictures to other camera-phones or to moblogs—that is, mobile phone blogs. Interestingly, while people sometimes want to print out their photographs, they increasingly do not want to do so at home, but choose to take advantage of the frequent technological upgrades at public photo kiosks and online services. Conse–quently, editing software manufacturers and photo kiosk firms try to appeal to those who want to edit and order photographs quickly, as well as customers who want to linger and use software more creatively. Photoblogs have multiplied rapidly since 2000. While the blogosphere presents Internet users with a huge number of choices, those choices are, as critic David Brittain pointed out, modeled on the global marketplace, where ideas coexist alongside commercial activities.[27] Bloggers do not consider the presence of commerce to be a drawback, and frequently point out that taste-makers should not narrow the photoblog's content.

The camera-phone is the slimmer, more democratic descendant of the simple Kodak camera that was first marketed in 1888. Because of its size, the camera-phone can be used stealthily in the public sphere, sometimes to the annoyance of people on the street whose actions have been fashioned into recorded dramas, edited by the camera-phone owner. Some public places, such as courtrooms, have banned camera-phones and use detectors to ferret them out. Nevertheless, so-called "cell-phone paparazzi" take full advantage of this device to capture the likeness of celebrities.

The escalating use of camera-phones has breathed new life into the simple snapshot and created many new photographers, especially among the young. It has encouraged self-portraiture and the practice of citizen photojournalism. With a digital camera or camera-phone ordinary people can join the hunt for candid celebrity photographs. For some, blogging text and photographs of personal life and current events has become a way of life. Chinese artist Ai Weiwei (b. 1957) has been streaming pictures and comments since 2005. Ai, who contributed to the design of China's Olympic National Stadium (popularly called "the Bird's Nest"), also created widely viewed reports from the 2008 earthquake in Sichuan province. Digital cameras and camera-phones have extended on-the-spot news reporting, like that created by Ai, to anyone with the means to own one. The current question for both digital camera and camera-phone pictures is how long they will last.

Yet this might be the wrong question to ask about images whose owners may never have made them material by printing them. The millions of digital images now on hard drives and memory chips may be changing the definition of the snapshot and family photography as a palpable, lasting record, the stuff of albums. In an era with so much fleeting imagery, the photograph may come to be understood like television broadcasts, which can be stored for future viewing but generally are not kept for the long term. One of the most profound effects of the waning of analog photography and the rise of digital is the way in which the new technology has dematerialized photographs. Among the long-term effects of this transformation is the mounting challenge to property rights, drafted in a prior age when mostly material things had value.

RETAKE

The first decade of the twenty-first century carried forward many of the themes that informed the preceding era. Concern for social, regional, and personal identity, the urgent aspects of global warming and globalization, and the jolts of history all found expression in twenty-first-century photography. Consequently photographers such as Rineke Dijkstra, Sebastião Salgado, and Anna Gaskell continue to work on themes that engaged them

in the 1990s. Digital means allowed professional and amateur photographers to make and edit their work more easily. But the major effect of the digital revolution for photography was the increased ease of transmitting, storing, and commenting on images. New digital archives appear every day; it has been estimated that people upload 4.5 million images a day to Flickr alone.

philosophy and practice

Re-Membering

In 2000, Adam Lamminan wrote in *Adbusters* about what he dubbed "the hidden potential of the post-postmodern crisis" of uncertainty. He summed up what he believed to be the popular effect of the movement on the young: "Everything is relative and nothing is sacred ... Many of us are either desperately clinging to a sinking ship of fixed ideals or floundering in a sea of ideas." But the "upside," as Lammiman called it, is that "it is no longer possible to ignore the existence of viewpoints different from your own. Seeing so many points of view, each with its weaknesses, makes it difficult to believe that your own ideas are flawless."[28] While less rigorously philosophical and more idealistic than the ideas of Postmodern photographers and theorists, this attitude infused early twentieth-century photographic practice.

The vast spread of digital communications, especially since the last decade of the twentieth century, created a scaffold that brought ideas together but did not necessarily seek to harmonize them. At first, especially in the early 1990s, digital technologies were thought by some to have the potential to muffle direct perception of the world. That fear was expressed in Aziz and Cucher's dystopian images of people whose senses have been obstructed (Fig. 12.14). About the same time, photographer and critic Joan Fontcuberta suggested that digital imaging means would multiply so rapidly that they would give the public a more sophisticated understanding of photographic objectivity. When Fontcuberta voiced that prediction, digital photo-editing software was employed primarily by professionals, not amateurs. A decade later, photo-management and -editing software is often included with digital camera and computer sales. Ironically, the best defense against dishonest photo manipulation has proved to be a public familiar with the means to alter and disseminate photographs. The 2007 and 2008 "Digital Forensics" articles in *Scientific American*, including Hany Farid's instruction on "5 Ways to Spot a Fake Photo," brought numerous responses, indicating the growing popularity of fake-spotting.[29] Several websites, addressed to audiences ranging from young children to professional photographers, have created forums to expose fakes and to discuss how they were produced.

Nevertheless, concern about the possible malevolent social effects of computer-manipulated photographs tended to overshadow other powerful ways in which photographs have been and will continue to be deceptive. Omitting images, such as the scenes of forced labor that Aleksandr Rodchenko excluded from his series on the building of Russia's White Sea Canal (see p. 240), can be as deceiving as reshaping pictures. Censorship of images is not just a historical practice. In 2004, the U.S. military ban on news agencies photographing the flag-draped coffins of soldiers killed in the Iraq conflict was tested when an employee of a military subcontractor took such a photograph. Spokespersons for the U.S. government stated that the ban was devised to protect the emotional sensitivity of families who have lost soldiers. In 2009, families of fallen soldiers were given the choice of whether to allow the coffin to be photographed.

With so many images digitally available, the screen has emerged as a primary setting for viewing images. In fact, image-makers in all of photography's genres routinely think about the digital appearance and transmission of their work. However valuable digital presentation may be, it dilutes the fact that in the past most photographs were not viewed on a brightly illuminated surface. Viewing photographs in a book, magazine, or gallery differs from seeing them on what seems to be a radiant window. Of course, there is no one proper setting in which to see photographs, even though some better approximate the images' original venues. The question of setting has haunted photography in a way not shared by other media. Although photography was disclosed to the world in 1839, there never developed specific civic sites where photographs can be seen, other than in art galleries and museums. While photographs will continue to be exhibited in physical settings, the diversity of the huge disembodied archive of Web-based photographs may play a large role in resituating photography in novel physical settings.

Yet the question remains: does the public have the stamina to see ghastly photographs? Is this a legal or an ethical issue? In her final book, *Regarding the Pain of Others* (2003), philosopher-critic Susan Sontag rethought the impact of horrific photographs, such as war photographs, which she had concluded in her earlier and influential work *On Photography* desensitized and, literally, de-moralized the public. But in her revised view, she proposed that the vast repository of war photographs that has accumulated since photography was invented does have a moral purpose. She pointed out that individual photographs, such as that by Ron Haviv (see Fig. 14.13), may tell us very little about the specific causes and motives of war. Nevertheless the collective social archive of war photographs serves as a constant reminder of human suffering and wickedness. "Let the atrocious images haunt us," Sontag declared. "Even if they are only tokens, and cannot possibly encompass most of the reality to which they refer, they still perform a vital function." She forcefully concluded that "remembering is an ethical act."[30]

EPILOGUE

Democratic access to images and to information developed as a permanent ideal in Western culture during the Enlightenment. It became attached to photography by the mid-nineteenth century, as in the enthusiasm expressed by an anonymous writer in an 1858 issue of the British journal the *Athenaeum*, who foresaw an educational revolution caused by stereographic photography, such that "perhaps in ten years or so the question will be seriously discussed … whether it will be of any use to travel now that you can send out your artist to bring home Egypt in his carpetbag to amuse the drawing room with" (see p. 79, note 9). Of course, international travel is a more common event these days, but it is still beyond the economic means of most of the world's people. While estimates project that sales of personal computers and related devices will continue to grow, most of this growth is in the West, although China, Latin America, Eastern Europe, and India are making important gains. Economic imbalances continue to produce inequities in knowledge.

At photography's inception, when thinkers such as François Arago and William Henry Fox Talbot speculated about the medium's future, they saw it integrated into art, science, and industry, without a peep of protest on the part of those affected by the changes it might bring. The way that photography faithfully indexed the world made the medium seem objective, like a faithful, aloof scribe, rather than an excitable, rabble-rousing partisan. Their scientific training disposed Arago and Talbot to predict that the medium's accepted neutral vision would become attached to the ideal of free and open information systems.

A positive, even lyrical perception of mass media's influential sway was constructed in the early twentieth century in reform movements as well as experimental art, and found adherents in the late twentieth century, such as Cuban-born artist-photographer Felix Gonzalez-Torres. Improvising on Alfred Stieglitz's renowned series of *Equivalents*, a set of cloud photographs made to demonstrate that symbols of transcendence were freely available to those who looked for them in nature (see Fig. 6.27), Gonzalez-Torres stacked in a gallery hundreds of inexpensively produced pictures of clouds to be taken away by visitors (see Fig. 12.2). Whereas Stieglitz's *Equivalents* eventually sold for hundreds of thousands of dollars, Gonzalez-Torres's mass-produced pictures were free.

Early twenty-first-century critics and the public picked up on the word "truthiness," invented by comedian Stephen Colbert in 2005. Colbert defined it as the "the truth we want to exist." A year later, it was discussed as the "summarizing concept of our age."[31] The idea's obvious correspondence to the extensive pre- and post-production practices made possible by digital media helped to propel it through art circles, and inspired the 2012–13 exhibition and book *More Real: Art in the Age of Truthiness*. Ironically, truthiness, with its aversion to fact, set off an international discussion on the nature of mediation, became a resource for art-making and criticism, and inspired several psychological studies on how people shape the truth.

There is no doubt that digital media, software, and networks have expanded the range and impact of photography, and introduced photographs, as well as data and image retrieval, into everyday life on an unprecedented scale. An eminent photographer remarked, "Après Photoshop, le déluge," mimicking the phrase attributed to Louis XV suggesting that chaos and ruin would follow after his reign. Yet photography's future is not a leaden certainty, driven by commerce and technology. Image-makers tend to respond to the inconsistencies and tensions of history, ideas, and practices as if they were chafing fault lines whose energy sparks new insight and expression. However much we must be on our guard for the negative social effects of new media, we have an equally important obligation to stay alert for and encourage new visions.

GLOSSARY

Abstract Expressionism A mid-twentieth-century art movement, principally in the United States, whose artists promoted the use of color and form to suggest mental states and emotions.

Albumen paper Light-sensitive paper used in conjunction with the collodion negative (see COLLODION PROCESS). Printing paper was coated with a mixture of egg white and salt, allowed to dry, and then sensitized with a silver nitrate solution. The sensitized paper was placed under a negative and exposed. Albumen paper offered a rich tonal range and a stability greater than the paper treated with salt and silver nitrate that was used to create the salt print. The print had a glossy surface, different from earlier processes, in which the image seemed to have sunk into the paper, like a watercolor. Albumen paper was perfected by Louis-Désiré Blanquart-Evrard, and quickly commercialized.

Ambrotype Also called collodion positive. By placing a dark backing behind a sheet of glass on which a negative image has been rendered, a positive image results. Housed in a case, like the daguerreotype. Popular in the mid-nineteenth century.

Angiogram An X-ray technique that highlights blood vessels.

Appropriation Literally, taking possession of. In art, appropriation refers to a strategy used in the late 1970s and 1980s in which an artist took advertising, historical, or popular imagery and incorporated it in a new work of art, so as to alter its meaning.

Aquatint An etching process added to engravings that produces light tones, resembling watercolor washes. Powdered resins are applied to the plate, which is then heated. As it melts, the resins create grains, which, when etched, produce tonal areas in the final print.

Autochrome Invented by Auguste and Louis Lumière in 1904 and marketed in 1907, the autochrome was the first practical method of making color photographs. Like the daguerreotype, the autochrome was a unique image, but developed on a glass plate, not metal or film. The process involved exposing a glass plate that had been covered with tiny granules of substances sensitive to colored light. In the darkroom, a positive was developed on the original glass plate, creating a transparency that could be seen by means of a hand-viewer, or through projection by a magic lantern device, precursor of the slide projector. The autochrome usually had a pebbly surface quality, which resulted from the little light-sensitive pellets used in the manufacturing process.

Beaux-Arts French for "fine arts." When applied to architecture, it denotes the academic Classical style that was taught at the École des Beaux-Arts in Paris. American architecture was particularly influenced by this style in the period 1885–1920.

Bromoil process A variety of the oil-pigment process introduced in 1907 that was easier than the oil-pigment process and could be used for enlargements. Bromo-gelatin paper was exposed to a negative, then bleached to eliminate the silver image. The remaining gelatin formed a relief print upon which color could be applied with a brush.

Calotype Also called the Talbotype, after its British inventor, William Henry Fox Talbot, who patented the process in 1841. As with Daguerre's generous donation of the daguerreotype to the world (which did not include England), there were legal restrictions on its use. Photographers had to apply for a

license, although Talbot gave the calotype process free to science and amateur photographers.

To create a calotype negative, from which a positive print is made, good-quality writing paper or drawing paper was saturated with a solution of silver nitrate. After the paper dried, it was dipped in a solution of potassium iodide. A light-sensitive layer of silver iodide resulted. This paper could be prepared ahead of time. Before use, it had to be coated with a mixture of silver nitrate and gallic acid to sensitize it. When the light-sensitive paper was exposed in the camera, it produced a latent image—that is, one that could not be seen by the eye. To bring out the latent image, the paper was washed in a mixture of silver nitrate and gallic acid, fixed with hypo, and flushed with water.

The negative was then placed over sensitized paper called salted paper, which had been brushed or dipped into a solution of sodium chloride or ammonium chloride or a mixture of the two. Both were sandwiched in a printing frame and exposed to sunlight until a positive print was registered. The print was then rinsed in water to decrease its light sensitivity.

Camera lucida From the Latin for "light room." The camera lucida was neither a light nor a room, but a prism, mounted on a slim rod attached to a drawing board. By adjusting the prism, an artist could create the illusion that a scene was projected on to the drawing board.

Camera obscura From the Latin for "dark room." The camera obscura was originally a darkened chamber with a hole or lens in one wall that allowed an image of the outside world to be projected on to the opposite wall. Small, portable versions were later constructed, which made it possible to copy images reflected on to a panel of translucent glass. The camera obscura ultimately became the box of the photographic camera.

Carte-de-visite Called a card photograph in the United States, the *carte-de-visite* was a small photographic portrait mounted on a cardboard backing that was about the size of a visiting card.

Chiaroscuro From the Italian for "light and dark," this refers to the contrasts between light and shade in a painting or a photograph. Chiaroscuro is often used to highlight an important subject and to create dramatic effects.

Cliché verre A coated glass photographic plate into which an artist scratches an image with a sharp stylus. Since light can move through the areas scratched away, the plate can be used as a photographic negative. It is placed on sensitized paper and exposed to light, which passes through the lines cut into the opaque coating. Many prints can be made from one plate.

Collage The combination of different materials, such as paper, paint, fabrics, photographs, newspaper clippings. Usually pasted on a board or artist's canvas.

Collodion process Also known as the wet-plate process. A technique developed by Frederick Scott Archer in 1851, in which glass plates were sensitized to light with a sticky substance called collodion mixed with light-sensitive silver salts. Unlike the calotype process developed by William Henry Fox Talbot, the collodion process was patent free, which increased its popularity with photographers. By the 1860s, the technique replaced both the daguerreotype and the calotype. Glass plates were covered with a solution of collodion, a sticky mixture of ether, guncotton, and alcohol, to which light-sensitive silver iodide and iodide of iron were added. The plate was then sensitized with a coating of distilled water and silver nitrate. While the plate was still damp, it was placed inside the camera and exposed. The method was dubbed the wet-plate process, because exposure time was diminished when the plate was damp. After exposure, the plate needed to be developed quickly. In the field, photographers set up traveling dark-tents, complete with chemicals.

The process required relatively strong light and long exposure times—sometimes minutes. Moreover, the process was especially sensitive to blue, yielding dull, blank white skies. Yet since the light-sensitive materials were caught up in the film of collodion, they did not leave the kind of paper fiber imprint that paper negatives did. The collodion process was used with albumen paper.

Collotype An adaptation of lithography used to make multiple prints derived from photographic negatives. Photosensitized gelatin was applied to a glass plate, and then exposed to a negative. After careful processing, the resulting plate could be inked and printed on paper.

Combination printing A technique that uses two or more negatives to make a final print. Parts of the sensitive paper are masked so that they will not develop, while a negative is printed where desired. The technique was used by early photographers, such as Gustave Le Gray, to compensate for overexposed skies, which did not register cloud formations.

Constructivism An early twentieth-century art and design movement originating in the young Soviet Union during the 1920s. Its emphasis on rejecting traditional materials and subjects, and its stress on the union of art and utilitarianism, soon became international.

C-print C-print (color print) is a term referring to any enlargement from a color negative. Loosely, a color print from any source.

Cubism An early twentieth-century art movement that began in Europe but which quickly generated an international following. In Cubist art, aspects of an object, such as inside and outside, as well as up and down, were presented simultaneously, yielding an array of geometric shapes.

Cyanotype A photographic technique invented by Sir John Herschel. It uses iron salts to produce a deep blue image, and is the source of the blueprint or dyeline process used today.

Dadaism An early twentieth-century art movement that began in Europe in the waning years of World War I, and which gained momentum and international influence directly after that conflict. Dadaists dwelled on the fragmentary and the incomplete, and instilled their work with postwar cynicism about human promise.

Daguerreotype A photographic technique taking its name from Louis-Jacques-Mandé Daguerre. It used a silver or silver-coated copper plate to register an image in a camera obscura. The daguerreotype was a unique image, not capable of making multiple copies. Daguerreotype plates were eventually standardized in terms of size (width first):

a whole plate: 6½ × 8½ inches
a half-plate: 4½ × 5½ inches
a quarter-plate: 3¼ × 4¼ inches
a sixth-plate: 2¾ × 3¼ inches
a ninth-plate: 2 × 2½ inches

Because early daguerreotypists sometimes had cameras made to their specifications, not all plates conformed to the standard. Also, large, so-called mammoth plates of no standard size were used in specially made cameras. Because the daguerrotype image was fragile and would fade when exposed to light, daguerrotypes were usually stored in closable cases.

Diana This inexpensive camera, which appeared in the 1960s, had several "flaws" that proved attractive to photographers by generating surprises in film development: it leaked light on to the film; the shutter could be opened repeatedly on the same frame, yielding multiple exposures; and the viewfinder did not see accurately through the lens.

Digital imaging Also termed computer-assisted imaging, this process is used to alter existing pictures, or to create images, called virtual images, that are not based on photographs taken of the real world. Digital cameras do not use film, but translate optical reality into visual bits called pixels (a new word derived from the term "picture elements") that can be stored in a computer. Electronic images may be shown on a computer screen or other visual monitors. Similarly, a scanner surveys an image and renders it into a mathematical language that can be stored and retrieved by the computer.

Direct positive (see NEGATIVE)

Dry plates Also called gelatin-silver bromide, or gelatin bromide photography. Perfected in the late 1870s from experiments begun in the 1850s, dry plates were mass-marketed in the 1880s. They were prepared by holding a light-sensitive mixture of silver nitrate, cadmium bromide, and gelatin at a constant temperature of 32° centigrade for several days. The resulting plate was commercially produced, freeing photographers from sensitizing and developing the wet collodion plate on the spot. The exposure time of the dry plate was so fast that it allowed photographers to record movement. Moreover, because of the quick exposure time, the camera could be held in the hands, rather than being placed on a tripod. By the early 1880s, dry plates were manufactured throughout Europe and North America.

Dye-transfer An involved process for making color prints, which allows the maker great control over the range of color at every stage of the process. It requires exposing a color transparency three times with different filters of blue, red, and green. The resulting black-and-white negatives are then used to make a matrix, a shallow-relief mold whose thickness is etched by the amount of light reaching it through the negatives. Thus the matrix is responsive to subtle color modulations. Each mold is immersed in blue, red, and green dye, respectively. After the molds have absorbed the colors, and the photographer or printer has made chemical adjustments to the tones and hues, the molds are sequentially printed on a sheet of photographic paper. The dye-transfer method produces one of the most stable—that is, permanent—color-printing processes.

Fauvism An early twentieth-century art movement that arose in France and emphasized the expressive rather than the naturalistic use of color. In French, *fauve* means "wild beast."

Focal length The distance from the center of the camera lens to the point behind the lens where light rays from an object passing through the lens come into focus.

Futurism An early twentieth-century art movement, primarily in Italy, whose blurred or abstract shapes were meant to celebrate the dynamism of the machine and the promise of industrialization.

Gravure Also called photogravure, this is an etching process modified to reproduce photographs. A copper plate is treated with resin or bitumen powder, then exposed to a piece of carbon tissue paper that has a negative image on it. When soaked in warm water, the image transfers to the surface of the plate. It is then chemically etched with ferric chloride solution, leaving a recessed image that will accept ink. The process could be used commercially to make many copies, or with a hand-press to make a few, as was done by the Pictorialists.

Gum-bichromate process Developed in the 1850s, the process became popular with Pictorial photographers during the late nineteenth century. The technique used the photograph as the basis of the image. A sheet of paper was brushed with gum arabic into which had been mixed potassium bichromate and a colored pigment. After it dried, the paper was exposed to a negative. The photochemically sensitive materials on the paper hardened in proportion to the amount of light received. The photographer then washed away the unhardened material, leaving a positive print. During the wash, the photographer could add color, or brush the print to create painterly effects.

Half-tone process The process whereby photographs may be printed with text in a book, newspaper, or magazine by relief or by lithography. It was called half-tone because it allowed the reproduction of tones between black and white. Applying a principle discovered by William Henry Fox Talbot, the half-tone uses a fine screen to break up the surface of a print into tiny dots whose size accords with the darkness and lightness of a picture. The screen is printed on a metal plate covered with gelatin mixed with bichromate. The gelatin hardens and the non-printing areas of the image are etched with acid. The half-tone process was used sporadically even before the late 1880s, when it was perfected, allowing newspapers routinely to include photographs.

Heliotype A method for reproducing photographs developed in the 1870s. It refined already existing lithographic processes for reproducing photographs in books. Like the woodburytype, it was not compatible with type.

Hypo Originally hyposulphite of soda, a substance that dissolved silver salts and stopped the further development of the silver. Today "hypo" is the related substance, sodium thiosulfate.

Installation art As the term suggests, installation art involves creating an art environment composed of many objects, rather than a single object or image. The technique was used by Constructivists and Dadaists, as well as artists in the late twentieth and early twenty-first centuries.

Latent image An image registered on a photographically sensitive surface, like paper or a metal plate, but which is not visible to the eye. The latent image must be developed through a chemical process.

Lithography A printing technique in which an image is reproduced on a flat surface, originally a stone, but later a copper or zinc plate, rather than by being cut or gouged into a surface, like metal or wood. To make a lithograph, the surface is treated in such a way that the areas intended to convey an image will hold ink, and the remaining or negative areas will repel ink.

Negative, positive, direct positive A negative is a photographically produced image in which the tones of the actual subject are reversed—that is, light areas are dark and darks are light. It is used to produce a positive print, in which the tones are re-reversed to create an image that reproduces optical reality. A direct positive is a unique, single image without a negative. In a direct positive print, like the daguerreotype, an image is produced on a surface and then treated chemically to imitate the tonal range of nature.

Oil-pigment process A process similar to the gum print. A piece of gelatin-coated paper was sensitized with potassium bichromate and exposed to a negative. Placed in a water bath, the print developed raised areas on the hardened gelatin. While wet, the print was brushed with pigments. The application of pigment could follow the subject of the negative, or be more expressive.

Outsider art Sometimes also called "self-taught art." The term was first used in the 1950s, but gained more prominence during the late twentieth century, as a way to recognize art produced by people who generally make their own guidelines and who work outside the conventional art world.

Pantograph An aid for copying prints and drawings. It consists of four bars, arranged in a parallelogram. A stylus is placed at the "V" joint of one set of bars and a drawing pencil is placed at the upper tip of the second set of bars. By tracing the stylus over a print, the drawing pencil makes an exact copy. The pantograph can also be used to enlarge or reduce an image.

Photogenic drawing A photographic technique developed by William Henry Fox Talbot that used light-sensitized paper to produce a negative from which multiple positive prints could be made.

Photogram Cameraless photographs made by casting light on photosensitive paper, or by placing objects directly on the light-sensitive surface. Some early photographers, such as William Henry Fox Talbot and Anna Atkins, made what would later be called photograms. The technique became popular with experimental photographers in Europe between World War I and World War II.

Photomontage A technique popular with experimental artists and photographers in the period after World War I. Images from such sources as advertising and newspapers were cut and reassembled to form composite images. Sometimes drawing or paint was applied. The final picture might be photographed or prepared for mechanical reproduction.

Physionotrace French engraver Gilles-Louis Chrétien adapted the pantograph to make engravings in 1786, calling his invention the physionotrace. An artist viewed the sitter through an eyepiece, moving it to trace the sitter's profile. A stylus in the lower area of the physionotrace tracked the eyepiece movements exactly, registering them in ink on paper. The portrait was then transferred to a copper plate, etched, and used to make multiple images. The central parts of the image were then engraved by hand.

Pictorialism An early twentieth-century movement in art photography, whose photographs were characterized by a soft focus, or in which the photographer's apparent hand-manipulation of the negative aimed to give the photograph the appearance of brushstrokes or other painterly effects.

Pinhole camera An extremely simple camera, sometimes constructed by children from cylindrical oatmeal containers. It is a light-tight container with a pinhole used as a lens at one end, and light-sensitive film or paper placed at the opposite end. Pinhole cameras produce wide-angle soft-toned pictures with a minimum of detail.

Platinum prints Known in the late nineteenth and early twentieth centuries as platinotypes after the Platinotype Company, which manufactured platinum paper, beginning in 1879. The paper was saturated with a light-sensitive mixture of potassium chloroplatinate and ferric oxalate. After exposure to a negative, the paper was washed with potassium oxalate, which precipitated out the platinum. An expensive, long-lasting, and stable process, the platinum print yields a wide range of soft-gray tones.

Positive (see NEGATIVE)

Precisionism An American art movement of the 1920s and 1930s in which objects were rendered as nearly abstract geometric shapes but were still recognizable.

Rayograph A term invented by the artist Man Ray, who used his own name to label the cameraless photographic images he produced by placing objects directly on to a sheet of photographically sensitive paper. The process is more widely known as a photogram.

Rotogravure An early twentieth-century printing process that allowed photographs to be printed with text. It was also the name for popular illustrated newspaper inserts, such as those found in Sunday papers. Fashion and high society were often subjects of the rotogravure.

Salt print One of the earliest photographic techniques to sensitize paper in order to make a photographic print. Paper was soaked in salt and then coated on one side with silver nitrate, yielding a light-sensitive silver chloride surface. The paper was then dried, placed under a negative, and exposed to light, producing a photographic print.

Silhouette portrait Drawing or cut-out profile of the human face derived from cast shadows.

Silkscreen A printmaking process in which a stencil is made on silk or a synthetic textile tightly stretched over a frame. The technique can be adapted to photography, in which case the photograph is imprinted on the textile, and the artist can adjust the colors.

Single-lens reflex camera (S.L.R.) A camera that uses a movable mirror placed between the lens and the film. This mirror projects the image as it is seen through the lens on to a focusing screen.

Social Realism An inexact phrase used to describe a tendency in art to dwell on societal ills and misfortunes. The term is also associated with the anti-experimental, highly descriptive propaganda art preferred by leaders of the Soviet Union, beginning in the 1930s.

Solarization A technique that involves briefly exposing a print or negative to light during the development process. Discovered by accident in the nineteenth century, the result is a reversal of tones along the edges of forms. Sometimes called edge reversal, solarization is somewhat unpredictable, making it a favorite of the Surrealists. It is also known as the Sabattier effect, for French photographer Antoine Sabattier (active 1850s), who is said to have discovered it.

Stereography A technique for producing photographs that gives the illusion of depth when a special viewer (stereoscope) is used. Two images taken from slightly different angles are printed on a card, which is put in the viewing device. Stereographs approximate the distance between the two human eyes that helps to produce depth perception.

The stereoscope was invented by Charles Wheatstone (1802–1875) in 1832, before photography was announced to the world. It was an awkward viewing apparatus that used mirrors to simulate what the right eye and the left eye see separately. In 1849, Sir David Brewster (1781–1868) perfected a smaller stereoscope, better adapted to viewing stereoscopic photographs in both the daguerreotype and calotype formats. The earliest stereoscopic daguerreotypes, such as Claudet's *The Geography Lesson* (Fig. 2.55), were taken with two cameras, each adjusted to mimic human sight. Twin-lens stereoscopic cameras were introduced in the mid-1850s.

Strobe Fast bursts of intermittent light used to illuminate moving subjects.

Tabloid More compact than nineteenth-century broadsheets, tabloid newspapers feature many illustrations, most of them photographs or derived from photographs. From the earliest post-World War I tabloids, the genre has featured sensational pictures, which carry as much meaning as the text.

Tintype An inexpensive photographic process that rendered images on thin sheets of iron, not tin. The tintype was lightweight, making it easy to send through the postal system.

Tomography A computer-assisted process that produces cross-sections of the human body (or other objects) and assembles them into a three-dimensional picture.

Toning During or after the development of a print, it might be treated with a chemical solution containing silver and another ingredient, such as gold, platinum, or selenium. Toning allows the photographer to create a soft overall coloration, usually ranging from light gold to sepia.

Transparency As the word implies, a transparency is a positive film that allows light to pass through it. Transparencies may be in color or in black and white. The most familiar kind of transparency is the 35mm color slide, but transparencies can be made in larger sizes.

Waxed-paper process An improvement to the calotype that allowed the light-sensitive paper to be prepared up to two weeks before exposure, and then developed a week after, though with variable results. As the name suggests, paper was coated with wax, then sensitized. It could be used wet, by being placed between two clean pieces of glass, or used dry. The prepared paper gave the photographer, especially when traveling, greater freedom and speed.

Wet plates (see COLLODION PROCESS)

Woodburytype A method of printing photographs for book illustrations. Woodburytype images could not be printed with text. Instead, they were tipped in—that is, pasted on separate sheets of paper in a book. Invented in 1866 by Walter Bentley Woodbury, the woodburytype used a gelatin film sensitized with potassium bichromate, which was exposed to a negative of the photograph to be copied. The resultant exposed film was then dipped in warm or hot water in a process that yielded a relief image, similar to low-relief sculpture, but much thinner. The various thicknesses of the gelatin corresponded to the different tones of the photograph. The negative was placed in a special press that transferred lead into the relief spaces. The lead mold was removed and used as the basis for printing a copy of the photograph.

PICTURE CREDITS

Laurence King Publishing has endeavored to contact all copyright owners. Any corrections or omissions will be noted for any future edition. Grateful thanks for their help go to: Janice Madhu of the George Eastman House, NY; Jacqueline Burns of the J. Paul Getty Museum, Los Angeles; Akiko Shiozawa in Tokyo. Collections are given in captions next to illustrations. The following abbreviation has been used: LOC/P&P (Library of Congress, Washington D.C./Prints & Photographs Division). Sources for illustrations not supplied by museums or collections, additional information, and copyright credits are given below.

page XI Rapho, Paris;
page XVI © 1989 Wm. B. Becker;
1.2 © Historical Picture Archive/Corbis; **1.7** The Bridgeman Art Library; **1.9, 1.20** Science & Society Picture Library, London; **1.10** Gilman Collection, Museum Purchase, 2005 (2005.100.800) Copy Photograph © The Metropolitan Museum of Art/Art Resource/Scala, Florence; **1.11** © Ville de Chalon-sur-Saône, France. Musée Nicéphore Niépce; **1.19** Gilman Collection, Purchase, Joseph M. Cohen Gift, 2005 (2005.100.725). ©2013. Image copyright The Metropolitan Museum of Art/Art Resource/Scala, Florence;
2.1 © Corbis/Hulton-Deutsch Collection; **2.7** Courtesy Hans P. Kraus, Jr., NY; **2.8, 2.10, 2.11** Science & Society Picture Library, London; **2.9** Glasgow University Library, Department of Special Collections; **2.15, 2.17** Gilman Collection/ Image copyright The Metropolitan Museum of Art/Art Resource/ Scala, Florence; **2.16** The National Media Museum/Science and Society Picture Library; **2.20** Illustration © 2009 Wm. B. Becker/photographymuseum.com; **2.30, 2.31** Courtesy John Wood, McNeese State University, Louisiana; **2.32** The Bridgeman Art Library; **2.35** Conaculta-INAH-SINAFAO-Fototeca Nacional, Mexico City; **2.36** Courtesy the Director, National Army Museum, London; **2.37** Research Library, Getty Research Institute, Los Angeles; **2.42** With thanks to Alison Doane; **2.43** Gilman Collection, Purchase, The Horace W. Goldsmith Foundation Gift, through Joyce and Robert Menschel, 2005 (2005.100.63).© 2013. Image copyright The Metropolitan Museum of Art/Art Resource/Scala, Florence; **2.48** Museum of Modern Art, New York/Scala, Florence; **2.50** Gift of John Goldsmith Phillips, 1976. Acc.n.: 1976.646. © 2013. Image copyright The Metropolitan Museum of Art/Art Resource/Scala, Florence; **2.51** © 1989 Wm. B. Becker; **2.52, 2.54** Private Collection, London; **2.53** With thanks to William Welling, NY; **2.57** © 1989 Wm. B. Becker; **2.60** Courtesy Strong Museum, Rochester, NY © 2005; **2.61** © National Portrait Gallery, Smithsonian Institution/Art Resource, NY; **2.62** Cincinnati Art Museum, Gift of James M. Marrs, M.D. Photo: Walsh 11/1999; **2.63** Courtesy Library of Congress, Washington D.C. Prints & Photographs Division LC-USA7-10881; **2.64** Museum of Fine Arts, Boston. Gift of Richard Parker in memory of Herman Parker 1994.124 © 2001 Museum of Fine Arts, Boston, All Rights Reserved; 2.65 Gift of I.N.P. Stokes and the Hawes family/Image copyright The Metropolitan Museum of Art/Art Resource/ Scala, Florence; **2.66, 2.71** Gilman Collection/Image copyright The Metropolitan Museum of Art/Art Resource/Scala, Florence;
page 74 LOC/P&P LC-USZ62-114481;
3.3 LOC/P&P. LC-USZ62; **3.4** Purchase, The Horace W. Goldsmith Foundation Gift, through Joyce and Robert Menschel, 1995 (1995.170.1).© 2013. Image copyright The Metropolitan Museum of Art/Art Resource/Scala, Florence; **3.5, 3.11, 3.18, 3.20** V&A Picture Library, London; **3.6** (64.677.4) © 2013. Image copyright The Metropolitan Museum of Art/Art Resource/Scala, Florence; **3.8** © Photothèque des Musées de la Ville de Paris/cliché Ladet; **3.9** Photo RMN, Paris; **3.10** Félix Nadar/Archives Photographiques © Centres des Monuments Nationaux, Paris; **3.14** Science & Society Picture Library, London; **3.15** Sotheby's Picture Library, London;
4.1 Gilman Collection/Image copyright The Metropolitan Museum of Art/Art Resource/Scala, Florence;
4.3, 4.27, 4.28, 4.29, 4.31, 4.32, 4.36, 4.42, 4.48 V&A Picture Library, London; **4.4** The Bridgeman Art Library; **4.6** © RMN-Grand Palais (Musée d'Orsay)/Hervé Lewandowski; **4.10** © National Portrait Gallery, Smithsonian Institution/Art Resource, NY; **4.11** LOC/P&P LC-USZ62-76355; **4.12** LOC/ P&P LC-USZ62-114481; **4.14** LOC/P&P # 18960u; **4.16** LOC/ P&P LC-B8171-557; **4.17** LOC/P&P LC-B8171-7798; **4.19** LOC/P&P LC-USZ62; **4.20** Digitally-enhanced version © 2008 Wm. B. Becker; **4.23** © BnF, Dist. - Grand Palais/image BnF/ RMN; **4.24** Illustrated London News; **4.30, 4.34** LOC/P&P; **4.43** © Christie's Images Ltd 2005; **4.44** Collection Centre Canadien d'Architecture/Canadian Centre for Architecture, Montréal PH1980:0048:04:010; **4.46** Gilman Collection, Purchase, Jennifer and Joseph Duke Gift, 2005 (2005.100.565). ©2013. Image copyright The Metropolitan Museum of Art/ Art Resource/Scala, Florence; **4.47** © RMN (Musée d'Orsay)/ Michèle Bellot; **4.50** National Museum of American Art, Smithsonian Institution, Washington, D.C.,bequest of Sara Carr Upton/Art Resource/Scala, Florence; **4.52** LOC/P&P C-USZ62-22284; **4.54** LOC/P&P LC-USZ62-50848; **4.58** LOC/P&P LC-USZ62; **4.59** © National Anthropological Archives, Smithsonian Institution #4042; **4.60** © National Anthropological Archives, Smithsonian Institution; **4.61** © Corbis; **5.1, 5.5, 5.12** V&A Picture Library, London; **5.9** © Hulton-Deutsch Collection/Corbis; **5.14** © Roger-Viollet/ Topfoto; **5.17** LOC/P&P LC-BH821-6803; **5.19** Bibliothèque de l'Institut de France, Paris/Photo RMN, Paris/Le Mage; **5.21, 5.22** © National Media Museum/Science & Society Picture Library; **5.24** © Bibliothèque Centrale M.N.H.N. Paris; **5.25** Rheinisches Bildarchiv, Cologne;
page 160 Courtesy George Eastman House, NY;
6.1 Wm. B. Becker Collection/PhotographyMuseum.com; **6.3** Private Collection; **6.4** Tonnesen Archive, Chicago; **6.5** LOC/P&P LC-USZ62-64301; **6.9, 6.41** V&A Picture Library, London;
6.10 Dayton Art Institute, Dayton, Ohio 1984.58. Gift of Mrs Lillian T. Snider; **6.12** Gift of Isaac Lagnado, in honor of Thomas P. Campbell, 2008 (TR.487.32008)/Image copyright The Metropolitan Museum of Art/Art Resource/ Scala, Florence; **6.13** Gilman Collection/Image copyright The Metropolitan Museum of Art/Art Resource/Scala, Florence; **6.16** ©2013. Digital image, The Museum of Modern Art, New York/Scala, Florence; **6.17** Gilman Collection, Purchase, Harriette and Noel Levine Gift, 2005/Image copyright The Metropolitan Museum of Art/Art Resource/Scala, Florence; **6.18** Art Seal Services; **6.21** LOC/P&P LC-USZ62-76355; **6.22** Purchase. Copy Print © 2001 Museum of Modern Art, NY/Art Resource/Scala, Florence; **6.24** Gift of Mrs Hermine M. Turner. Copy print © 2001 Museum of Modern Art, NY/Art Resource/Scala, Florence; **6.26** Alfred Stieglitz Collection, 1933. Acc. n.:33.43.39 © 2011. Image copyright The Metropolitan Museum of Art/Art Resource/Scala, Florence; **6.28** LOC/P&P LC-USZ62; **6.31** Collection Chris Mees, Design Documentation, Etchingham, East Sussex; **6.34** Gift of Mrs Hermine M. Turner. Photograph © 2001 Museum of Modern Art, NY/Art Resource/Scala, Florence; **6.35** © Musée d'Orsay, Dist. RMN-Grand Palais/Alexis Brandt; **6.36** Rare Book, Manuscript & Special Collections Library, Duke University, Durham, North Carolina; **6.38** Gift of Paul F. Walter. Museum of Modern Art, NY/Art Resource/Scala, Florence **6.40** Photographie J.H. Lartigue © Ministère de la Culture-France/A.A.J.H.L.; **6.43** LOC/P&P LC-USZ62-79449/© 1971 Aperture Foundation Inc., Paul Strand Archive; **6.44** Gift of Arthur Bullowa. Copy Print © 2001 Museum of Modern Art, NY/© 1971 Aperture Foundation Inc., Paul Strand Archive;
7.1 V&A Picture Library, London; **7.2** © Royal Geographical Society, London; **7.3** LOC/P&P USZ62/11036/301951; **7.4** Private Collection, London; **7.6** akg-images, London; **7.9** Purchase. © 2001 Museum of Modern Art, NY/Art Resource/ Scala, Florence; **7.13** © Collège de France; **7.15** © Succession Marcel Duchamp/ADAGP, Paris and DACS, London 2013; **7.16** Gift of Charles Bregler, 1977/The Bridgeman Art Library; **7.17** ©DACS 2013; **7.23** With thanks to Padre Fedele Merelli; **7.27** Préfecture de Police, Paris. All Rights Reserved; **7.28** Collection Arne Svenson © 1998; **7.31** Birmingham Central Library/John Whybrow Ltd; **7.33** Imperial War Museum # C02264; **7.35** American Museum of Natural History Library, image # 11604;
page 230 + 8.6 Research Library, Getty Research Institute, Los Angeles (930030)/© DACS 2013;
8.1 Merrill C. Berman Collection, NY, copy photo by Jim Frank; **8.4** Courtesy Daily News, NY; **8.5** American Stock/ Hulton Archive; **8.7** © ADAGP, Paris & DACS, London 2013; **8.8** © 1990 Photo Scala, Florence/© Rodchenko & Stepanova Archive, DACS 2013; **8.9** © Rodchenko & Stepanova Archive, DACS 2013; **8.10** © Christie's Images Ltd 2009/© Christian Schad Stiftung Aschaffenburg/VG Bild-Kunst, Bonn and DACS, London 2013; **8.11, 8.12** ©DACS 2013; **8.13** Stiftung Archiv der Akademie der Künste, Berlin/© The Heartfield Community of Heirs/VG Bild-Kunst, Bonn and DACS 2013; **8.14** Rheinisches Bildarchiv, Cologne/©Hattula Moholy-Nagy/DACS 2013; **8.15** © DACS 2013; **8.19** © Succession Marcel Duchamp/ADAGP, Paris and DACS, London 2013; **8.20** © ADAGP, Paris and DACS, London 2013; **8.22** Art Institute of Chicago, Julien Levy Collection, Gift of Jean and Julien Levy, 1975; **8.23** V&A Picture Library, London/© Man Ray Trust/ADAGP, Paris and DACS, London 2013; **8.24** Courtesy Edwynn Houk Gallery, NY/© Madame Brassai, Paris; **8.25** Courtesy Michael Senft, NY/© Man Ray Trust/ ADAGP, Paris and DACS, London 2013; **8.26, 8.27, 8.28** © ADAGP, Paris and DACS, London 2013; **8.29** Gilman Collection/Image copyright The Metropolitan Museum of Art/Art Resource/Scala, Florence; **8.30** Copy photo A. Guillard/Ville de Nantes, Musée des Beaux-Arts; **8.31** David H. McAlpin Fund. Copy print © 2001 Museum of Modern Art, NY/© Madame Brassai, Paris/Art Resource/Scala, Florence; **8.32** San Francisco Museum of Modern Art. Gift of Graham Nash/Estate of André Kertesz © 2013; **8.33** Gift of the Photographer. Copy print © 2001 Museum of Modern Art NY/Estate of André Kertesz © 2005/Art Resource/Scala, Florence; **8.34** © Henri-Cartier Bresson/Magnum Photos; **8.35** Courtesy & © Joseph Mulholland, Glasgow, candjm@ hotmail.com; **8.36** © G.Ray Hawkins, Gallery, Los Angeles/ Image copyright The Metropolitan Museum of Art/Art Resource/Scala, Florence; **8.37** © Man Ray Trust/Succession Marcel Duchamp/ADAGP, Paris and DACS, London 2013; **8.38** © Rodchenko & Stepanova Archive, DACS 2013; **8.39** © Hattula Moholy-Nagy/DACS 2013; **8.40** © Photo CNAC/ MNAM, Paris/RMN; **8.41** British Film Institute, London; **8.43** © Die Photographische Sammlung/SK Stiftung Kultur/ August Sander Archive, Köln/VG Bild-Kunst, Bonn and DACS, London 2013; **8.44** San Francisco Museum of Modern Art. Sale of Paintings Fund; **8.45** Photograph 1993 © The Metropolitan Museum of Art/© Albert Renger-Patz Archiv/ Ann und Jurgen Wilde, Köln/VG Bild-Kunst, Bonn/DACS, London 2013; **8.47** Retrograph Archive, London/© DACS 2013; **8.49** © Estate of George Hoyningen-Huene/Courtesy Staley-Wise Gallery, NY; **8.50** © Estate of Horst P. Horst/Art + Commerce; **8.52** © 2000 Willard Van Dyke Estate, courtesy James Enyeart; **8.53, 8.54** © Imogen Cunningham Trust; **8.55** Photograph by Ansel Adams. Used by permission of Trustees of the Ansel Adams Publishing Rights Trust. All Rights Reserved; **8.56** © Archie Miyatake, from the Toyo Miyatake Manzanar Relocation Center Collection; **8.58, 8.59** © 1981 Center for Creative Photography, Arizona Board of Regents; **9.1** LOC/P&P 211863 CC-USF34-134407C; **9.3** LOC/P&P LC-USZ62-117092; **9.5** LOC/P&P LC-USZ62-11491; **9.8** LOC/P&P LC-USW3-38330; **9.9** © Margaret Bourke-White /Time & Life Pictures/Getty Images; **9.13** Courtesy and © Berenice Abbott/Commerce Graphics Ltd, Inc.; **9.14** Used with special permission from Berea College Art Department, Berea, KY; **9.15** Microfilm Archives of Humbold-Universitat zu Berlin; **9.17** © Bill Brandt/Bill Brandt Archive Ltd; **9.18** © Aaron Siskind Foundation, NY; **9.19** Courtesy & © Donna Mussenden Van Der Zee; **9.20** Photograph © Morgan and Marvin Smith; **9.21** LOC/P&P LC-USZ62-42493; **9.24** Collection Miriam and Ira D. Wallach, Division of Art, Prints and Photographs, NY Public Library © Berenice Abbott/ Commerce Graphics Ltd, Inc.; **9.25** © Harold & Esther Edgerton Foundation, 2005, courtesy Palm Press, Inc.; **9.26**

TIMELINE The Cultural History of Photography

CULTURE AND POLITICS

PHOTOGRAPHY AND IMAGING

12TH TO 16TH CENTURIES
Several European churches used as camera obscura; first wood-block printing on paper in Germany
c. 1436: Gutenberg invents printing press
1446: First dated printed engraving from metal plate
Perspective machines devised to create 3D illusion

17TH CENTURY
Exploration and annexation of other lands undertaken by European nations; rise of European bourgeoisie and merchant classes leads to experiments and inventions and encourages realistic portraits for merchant families

17TH CENTURY
Pantograph invented
1609: Galileo invents first effective telescope
1668: Newton builds first reflecting telescope

18TH CENTURY
In England and France, mechanization encourages shift from agriculture to industry; Industrial Revolution begins; scientific method creates need for accurate visual record-keeping; silhouette portraits more common
1775: Lunar Society formed in Birmingham, England
1776: American Declaration of Independence
1789–99: French Revolution reduces dominance of upper class; continued exploration by Western European nations fosters theories of racial evolution and ethnology

18TH CENTURY
Camera obscura perfected, then made portable; Wedgwood and Davy experiment with fixing light-sensitive images using silver nitrate (published 1802)
1786 Chrétien creates physionotrace
1798: Senefelder perfects lithographic technique

EARLY 19TH CENTURY
c. 1816: Scattered movements of naturalism in art across Europe
1825: First passenger-carrying railroad in England

EARLY 19TH CENTURY
1806: Wollaston invents camera lucida
1816: Joseph Nicéphore Niépce experiments with lithography
1819: John Herschel experiments with hypo
1826: Niépce creates first positive image—*View from the Window at Le Gras*
c. 1828: Niépce meets Louis-Jacques-Mandé Daguerre

1830–40
1830s: Rise of urban middle classes, commerce, and industry
1830: Louis Philippe becomes "Citizen King" of France
1836: Mexicans defeat Texans at the Alamo
1837: Victoria becomes Queen of Great Britain
1839: First Opium War begins in China

1830–40
c. 1830: Florence invents poligraphie
Daguerre continues Niépce's work; develops latent image
1830s: William Henry Fox Talbot develops "photogenic drawing"
1832: Florence coins term *photographie*
1833–34: Talbot conceives fixing light-induced images; creates contact salt prints
1837: Daguerre discovers table salt as a stopping agent; creates daguerreotypes
1839: January 7—François Arago presents Daguerre's work to French Academy of Science; February 7—Herschel presents "photographic specimens" to Royal Society in London
1839: Hippolyte Bayard creates direct positives; *cliché verre* invented

1840–50
1840s: Philosophy of public works and education; rights for working classes; industrial capitalism creates middle-class professionals, scientists; rural subjects idealized in art; Western expansion into Asia, Africa, and Latin America
1840: Morse patents telegraph
1842: First Opium War ends; Europeans gain greater trade with China
1846: Potato famine in Ireland; California and New Mexico annexed by U.S.
1846–48: Mexican–American War; rise in American newspapers, war correspondents used for first time by U.S. newspapers; public appetite for up-to-date news; the *tableau vivant* becomes popular
1848: Revolution in Paris, Vienna, Venice, Rome, Warsaw, Berlin, Milan; *Communist Manifesto*; Livingstone crosses Africa; rise of interest in racial evolution leads to need for anthropological records
1849: California gold rush begins

1840–50
1840: Poe calls photography "a positively perfect mirror"
1840s: Ritter von Ettingshausen creates microscopic daguerreotype images; Herschel creates cyanotype; photographic portraits increase; photography arrives in China and India
1841: Talbot patents calotype
1844: Talbot shoots *The Open Door* and begins publication of *The Pencil of Nature*
1845: Foucault and Fizeau photograph sunspots; Hill and Adamson make some of earliest anthropological portraits
c. 1846: Martens invents rotating camera
1847: Southworth and Hawes photograph recreated historic events
1848–49: John McCosh earliest named war photographer; Southworth and Hawes create full-plate celebrity daguerreotypes

CULTURE AND POLITICS

1850–60

1850s: Increase in amateur photographers; advances in science and medicine; new interest in racial qualities/differences

1851: *New York Times* founded; Great Exhibition opens in London

1853: Crimean War begins

mid-1850s: Europeans undertake Grand Tour; growth and expansion of scientific subjects and colonial expansion bolster desire for stereographs; rise in periodicals using photographically derived engravings

1855: *Leslie's Illustrated Newspaper* founded

1856: Crimean War ends; Second Opium War begins

1857: Indian Mutiny; *Harper's Weekly* founded

late 1850s: debate about differences and similarities between photography and art

1859: Darwin's *On the Origin of Species*

1860–70

1860s: Advancement and growth of medicine, including antiseptics and anesthesia

1861: American Civil War begins

1864: War of the Triple Alliance begins

1865: Lincoln assassinated; American Civil War ends

1866: Alfred Nobel invents dynamite

1867: U.S. acquires Alaska; Marx's *Capital*; U.S. Congress sponsors survey of the Rockies

1869: First U.S. transcontinental railroad; Suez Canal opens

1870–80

1870s: Public and scientific interest in human expression; (1870s–80s) Impressionist movement in art

1870: Franco-Prussian War begins

1874: First exhibition of Impressionist paintings, Paris

1876: Centennial Exhibition, Philadelphia; battle of Little Big Horn: Sioux/ Cheyenne defeat U.S. Cavalry; Queen Victoria becomes Empress of India; Alexander Graham Bell invents telephone

1877: Reconstruction collapses in U.S.

1879: U.S. Bureau of Ethnology founded

1880–90

1880s: Symbolist movement in art; Zola proclaims that "metaphysical man is dead"; debate on photography as art form continues; Arts and Crafts movement gathers strength

1881: President Garfield assassinated

1885: European expansion into Africa

1886: Ives develops half-tone engraving process

1888: National Geographical Society founded in U.S.; *National Geographic* begins publication

1889: Johnstown floods in Pennsylvania; Eiffel Tower completed

late 1880s–1890s: Newspaper editors run camera columns; demand for more and faster information; illustrated newspapers and magazines increase worldwide; advertisers use photographs

PHOTOGRAPHY AND IMAGING

1850–60

1850s: Gum bichromate process developed; Sabattier thought to have discovered solarization

1850: Agassiz commissions slave portraits by J. T. Zealy; Historic Monuments Commission in France chooses calotypes for architectural inventory

1851: Mayall documents Crystal Palace; Frederick Scott Archer publishes collodion ("wet plate") process; Bond and Whipple's moon photograph at Great Exhibition, London; Société Héliographique formed

c. 1851 Le Gray invents dry waxed-paper process; Diamond experiments with collodion process, uses glass plates to record mental patients

1852–53 Atkins and Llewellyn create cyanotypes for scientific illustration; Durheim creates first "police photographs" in Switzerland

1853: Photographic Society of London formed

1854: Langenheims take daguerreotypes of solar eclipse in U.S.; Disdéri perfects and patents *carte-de-visite*

mid-1850s: Improved stereographic camera; "stereos" create photographic boom; war photographers take images of Crimean conflict; growth of commercial photography in Japan

1856–59: Le Gray merges negatives in "combination printing"

1856: Tintype developed

1858: William Lake Price's *A Manual of Photographic Manipulation*

late 1850s: Photomicrography perfected; some painters and more women take up photography

1860–70

1861: American war photographers create visual chronicle of conflict; tintypes flourish

1864–65: Nadar takes underground photos using carbon arc lamp

1866: Gardner's *Photographic Sketch Book of the Civil War*, 1865–66; Woodbury invents woodburytype; Barnard's *Photographic Views with Sherman's Campaigns*

1867: O'Sullivan official photographer for King survey

1868: O'Sullivan takes photos in Comstock mine by igniting magnesium wire

1869: Robinson's *Pictorial Effects in Photography*

1870–80

1870s: Dry plates perfected

1872: Celluloid production begins in U.S.

1872–77: Muybridge photographs horses in motion

1873: Platinotype invented in Britain

1874: International competition to record transit of Venus: Janssen develops "revolver camera"

1875: Dammann's *Ethnological Photographic Gallery of the Various Races of Man*

1877: Jackson's *Descriptive Catalogue of Photographs of American Indians*; (1877–80) Charcot's *L'Iconographie photographique*

1879: Klick develops photogravure process; Platinotype Co. manufactures platinum paper; birth of the platinum print

1880–90

1880s: Dry plates mass-marketed; photographs increasingly used in law and police work; Pictorialism gathers pace

1881: Photographic roll film invented in England and U.S.

mid-1880s: Pictorialist style flourishes

1886: Photographs reproduced in newspapers

1887: Muybridge's *Animal Locomotion*

1888: Eastman Dry Plate Co. introduces the No. 1 Kodak camera

1889: Emerson's *Naturalistic Photography*

late 1880s–early 1890s: More than 60 photographic journals and 161 photographic societies worldwide; press photographers and photographic agencies emerge; growth of paparazzi; black-and-white film perfected; hand cameras include shutters

1890–1900

1890s: Expressionist art in Germany; *Berliner Illustrirte* [sic] *Zeitung* founded
1890: Wounded Knee massacre
1892: Diesel engine patented; Ellis Island opens
1893: Chicago World's Fair promotes "ideal city"
1894: Sino-Japanese War begins
1896: Nobel's will establishes Peace Prize
1898: Spanish–American War; Curies discover radium
1899: Boer War begins

1890–1900

1890s: Photographic postcards popular; scenes of urban poor more commonplace; increased use of photography in criminology and anthropology; Riis's *How the Other Half Lives* with half-tone prints—social reform photography gains strength; Marey's *The Flight of Birds*
1891: Wiener Kamera Klub formed in Austria
1892: Linked Ring formed in Britain
1894: Edison introduces the kinetoscope; Photo-Club de Paris formed
1895: Lumières invent motion-picture projector; Röntgen discovers X-rays

1900–10

1900s: International Arts and Crafts movement continues; focus on Native Americans; artists and writers experiment with photography; social reform movements grows, especially in cities
1900: Boxer Rebellion in China
1901: Marconi makes first radio transmission; Queen Victoria dies; President McKinley assassinated
1903: Wright brothers make first powered flight; suffragettes campaign for vote in Britain; Ford organizes Ford Motor Co.
1904: St. Louis World's Fair; Russo-Japanese War begins; National Child Labor Committee founded in U.S.; *Daily Mirror* appears in Britain
1905: Einstein publishes theory of relativity
1906: San Francisco earthquake and fire; British Labour Party founded
1907: Cubist paintings exhibited in Paris
1908: Ford Motor Co. introduces the Model T
1909: Italian Futurism in art; Hine addresses N.C.L.C.

1900–10

1900s: Cameras miniaturized; photo-postcards increasingly common; Pictorialism flourishes
1900: Eastman Co. produces Brownie camera; snapshots increase
1901: Caffin's *Photography as a Fine Art*; Kodak Girl advertising image introduced
1902: Stieglitz, Steichen, and others found Photo-Secession
1903: *Camera Work* journal founded; Jack London's *The People of the Abyss*
1904: Lumières develop autochrome color process; Hine begins photographing Ellis Island immigrants
1905: Little Galleries of the Photo-Secession opens

1910–20

1910–25: Art Nouveau/Deco movement strengthens; tabloid newspapers more common; rotogravure printing process developed
1911: First Picasso exhibit in U.S.
1912: *Titanic* sinks
1913: Ezra Pound coins "Vorticism"; the Armory Show in New York
1914: World War I begins
1916: Dadaism begins in Zurich
1917: U.S. enters World War I; Bolshevik Revolution; Freud's *Introduction to Psychoanalysis*
1918: Tzara writes *Dada Manifesto*
1919: *New York Illustrated Daily News* founded; Treaty of Versailles ends World War I

1910–20

c. 1910: Coburn adopts Vorticism, and creates Vortescope to take abstract photographs (Vortographs)
1913: Bragaglia's *Fotodinamismo futurista*
1914–18: Aerial photography perfected during World War I
1915: D. W. Griffiths produces *The Birth of a Nation*
1917: *Camera Work*'s last issue; Pictorialism draws to end
c. 1919: Photomontage emerges in Europe

1920–30

1920s: Expansion of mass media and industrialization; postwar hardships in Central Europe and Germany; rapid expansion of automobiles, radios, electricity; Modernism gains ground in art
1920: League of Nations holds first meeting; U.S. women receive right to vote
1921: *AIZ* launched in Germany; Communist Party of China founded
1922: Mussolini forms fascist regime in Italy
1923: Hitler writes first volume of *Mein Kampf*
mid-1920s: Surrealism born in Paris
1927: Lindbergh makes first solo transatlantic flight; Stalin becomes ruler of Soviet Union; first "talking picture," *The Jazz Singer*, screened
1928: Television demonstrated publicly; *Vu* launched in France
1929: Wall Street Crash; Great Depression begins

1920–30

1920s: Group f.64 formed in California; documentary photography becomes popular; term "photojournalism" enters common usage; photomontage in art; photography used increasingly in advertising; Ansel Adams photographs Yosemite National Park; worker-photographers in Europe
1922: Teige writes "Foto-Kino-Film"; Man Ray's *Les Champs délicieux*
1923: Wirephoto transmissions begin
1924: Leica compact 35mm camera
1925: Flashbulb developed in Germany; Moholy-Nagy's *Malerei, Photographie, Film*
1928: Eastman Kodak makes 16mm color film; Howard's *Dead!* on cover of *Daily News*
1929: Motion picture film standardized; "Film und Foto" exhibition; August Sander's *Antlitz der Zeit*

CULTURE AND POLITICS

1930–40

1930s: Nazi Party gains power; unemployment rife in U.S. and Europe

1933: Hitler appointed German chancellor

1934: Hitler becomes Führer; U.S.S.R. enters League of Nations

1935: Franklin D. Roosevelt institutes Resettlement Administration (R.A.) and Works Project Administration (W.P.A.)

1936: *Life* magazine launched in U.S.; Edward VIII abdicates, George VI King of Great Britain and Northern Ireland; Spanish Civil War begins; Berlin Olympics; Walter Benjamin writes "The Work of Art in the Age of Mechanical Reproduction"

1937: *Hindenburg* explodes in New Jersey; Japan invades China; R.A. becomes the Farm Security Administration (F.S.A.); Chicago Institute of Design (New Bauhaus) founded

1938: *Picture Post* launched in Britain; House Un-American Activities Committee formed

1939: World War II begins; Spanish Civil War ends

1940–50

1941: Pearl Harbor bombed by Japanese; U.S. enters war; atomic bomb research begins in U.S.; "Indian Art of the United States" exhibition, New York

1942: F.S.A. subsumed into Office of War Information

1944: Normandy invasion (D-Day)

mid-1940s: First exhibitions of Abstract Expressionist art

1945: Yalta Conference; Germany surrenders; F.D.R. dies; atomic bomb dropped on Hiroshima, Nagasaki; Japan surrenders; United Nations founded

1946: Churchill's "Iron Curtain" speech

1947: Cold War established; India gains independence

1948: Mahatma Gandhi assassinated; Communists seize Czechoslovakia; Berlin airlift; nation of Israel proclaimed; U.N. Declaration of Human Rights; apartheid formalized in South Africa

1949: Soviets explode atomic bomb

1950–60

1950s: Pop art begins in Britain; McCarthyism expands; arms race continues

1950: Truman orders H-bomb development; Korean War begins; Vietnam "Police Action" begins

1951: Color television introduced in U.S.; *Drum* magazine founded in Johannesburg

1952: George VI dies; Elizabeth II becomes queen

1953: Eisenhower becomes president of U.S.; Stalin dies; Moscow announces explosion of H-bomb; Korean War ends; first commercial color television broadcast in U.S.

1954: Racial segregation banned in U.S. schools; polio vaccine used; U.S. tests H-bomb on Bikini Atoll

1955: Warsaw Pact signed

1957: Soviet Union launches *Sputnik I*, first space satellite

1959: Cuban Revolution; Xerox introduces the xerographic copier

1960–70

1960s: Anti-American demonstrations on U.S. campuses; Conceptual art movement grows

1961: Berlin Wall erected; Bay of Pigs invasion; Gagarin becomes first man to orbit earth

1962: Cuban missile crisis; James Meredith registers at University of Mississippi

1963: Pope John XXIII dies; civil rights rally in Washington, D.C.; President Kennedy assassinated

1965: Watts riots for six days in Los Angeles

1968: Robert F. Kennedy and Martin Luther King assassinated

1969: Nixon inaugurated as U.S. president; first live television space broadcast; Warhol founds *Interview* magazine

PHOTOGRAPHY AND IMAGING

1930–40

1930s: Documentary photography grows; Workers Film and Photo League founded in New York

1930: Technicolor introduces full-color film

1931: Exhibition of Foreign Advertising and Industrial Photography

1933: Brassaï's *Paris de nuit*; "Die Kamera" exhibition in Berlin; propaganda photography grows

1934: First Salon of Pure Photography

1935: Associated Press Wirephoto formed; newsreels featured at cinemas; Stryker supervises R.A.'s photographic activities

1936: Lange's *Migrant Mother*; Rothstein's *Fleeing a Dust Storm*; Bourke-White's cover of *Life*

1937: Museum of Modern Art "American Photographs" exhibition of photographic history

1938: Evans's *American Photographs*

1939: Lange's *An American Exodus*; Abbott's *Changing New York*; Edgerton develops lighting for aerial photography

1940–50

1940: Museum of Modern Art Department of Photography opens

1941: Evans and Agee's *Let Us Now Praise Famous Men*

1942: "Road to Victory" exhibition

1944: Kodak introduces Kodacolor film

1945: Miller's *Buchenwald*; "Power in the Pacific" exhibition; Rosenthal's *Iwo Jima*; Khaldei's *Reichstag*

1947: Edwin Land invents Polaroid camera; Capa and others found Magnum Photos

1950–60

1950: Ken Domon co-founds Shudan Photo Group; Duncan's "There Was a Christmas"

1952: Yamahata's *Atomized Nagasaki*

1954: Eastman Kodak introduces high-speed Tri-X film

1955: "Family of Man" exhibition, Museum of Modern Art; DeCarava's *The Sweet Flypaper of Life*

1958: Domon's *Hiroshima*; Robert Frank's *The Americans*

1960–70

1960: Polaroid develops high-speed film; Korda photographs Che Guevara; *Yves Klein Leaping into the Void*

1962: Kodak invents Instamatic camera; Ishimoto's *Chicago*; White's *Empty Head*; Porter's *In Wildness is the Preservation of the World*

1963: Society for Photographic Education formed; Hosoe's *Barakei*; Moore photographs Civil Rights movement

mid-1960s: "Social landscape" photography becomes popular

1966: "Twelve Photographers of the American Social Landscape" exhibition; Burrows's *At a First-aid Centre …*; Szarkowski's *The Photographer's Eye*

1967: Cole's "House of Bondage. New Documents" exhibition, New York; Rosler's *Bringing Home the War*

1968: Withers's *Workers Assembling for a Solidarity March*

1969: *Apollo 11*'s moon photograph

CULTURE AND POLITICS

1970–80

1970: Rhodesia declares itself a republic; Kent State antiwar protests and shootings

1971: Greenpeace founded

1972: *Life* magazine closes; Nixon visits Communist China; Watergate scandal; Bloody Sunday in Northern Ireland; Computed Tomography (C.T.) invented

1973: O.P.E.C. oil crisis; Pinochet overthrows Allende in Chile; Britain, Ireland, and Denmark enter European Common Market

1974: Nixon resigns; U.S. troops withdraw from Vietnam

1975: First U.S.–Soviet space link-up; Pol Pot assumes leadership in Cambodia—genocide begins

1976: Carter elected U.S. president; civil war in Nicaragua; Mao dies

1977: First manned flight of U.S. space shuttle; first M.R.I. test on human being

1978: Karol Wojtyla becomes Pope John Paul II

1979: Shah of Iran deposed; Thatcher becomes British prime minister; Soviet Union invades Afghanistan; Lyotard's *The Postmodern Condition*

1980–90

1980s: Rise of computer-related technology, digital imagery

1980: Iran–Iraq War begins; Polish Solidarity movement; Neo-Expressionism in art

1981: IBM creates first personal computer; Reagan inaugurated U.S. president

1983: Compact disks marketed; AIDS virus identified; U.S. invades Grenada

1984: Apple launches Macintosh computer; Indira Gandhi assassinated; miners' strike in Britain; Canon demonstrates digital electronic still camera

1985: Gorbachev becomes leader of Soviet Union; hole in ozone layer confirmed

1986: Space shuttle *Challenger* explodes; Chernobyl disaster; Irangate scandal in U.S.; Fuji introduces disposable camera

1987: First personal computers sold

1989: Berlin Wall demolished

1990–2000

1990s: Launch of Hubble Space Telescope; Gulf War begins

1990: Mandela freed

1991: Soviet Union collapses

1992: Earth Summit in Rio de Janeiro; single European market

1994: Russia invades Chechnya; North American Free Trade Agreement; massacres in Rwanda; Channel Tunnel connects England and France; Mandela president of South Africa;

1995: World Trade Organization formed; Oklahoma City bombings; evidence of global warming from Intergovernmental Panel on Climate Change

1996: Taliban forces seize power in Afghanistan; Rabin assassinated

1997: Deaths of Mother Teresa and Diana, Princess of Wales; China regains control of Hong Kong

1998: Kosovo conflict begins; India and Pakistan make nuclear tests

1999: Putin becomes Russian prime minister; camera-phone invented

2000–PRESENT

2000: Human DNA sequence established

2001: September 11—World Trade Center destroyed; October 7—U.S. bombs Kabul, Afghanistan

2003: Sharon elected Israeli prime minister; war and famine in Sudan; *Look-Look* magazine founded; U.S. and Britain launch war against Iraq; Saddam Hussein captured

2004: March 11—Madrid terrorist bombings; U.S. hands over power to Iraqi interim government; December 26—tsunami devastates South Asia

2005: July 7—London bombings; Hurricane Katrina devastates US Gulf Coast; October 1—Bali terrorist bombings

2008: Obama elected as 44th president of the United States; global financial crisis begins

PHOTOGRAPHY AND IMAGING

1970–80

1970: Duncan's *War without Heroes*; Filo's Kent State photograph; Haeberle and Brant's *Q. And Babies? A. And Babies*

1971: Jones Griffiths's *Vietnam, Inc.*

1972: Moriyama's *Stray Dog*; Owens's *Suburbia*; Ut's *Children Fleeing a Napalm Strike*

1973: Clark's *Tulsa*; Szarkowski's "From the Picture Press" exhibition; Dater's *The Feminine Eye in Photography*

1975: "New Topographics" exhibition, New York; Sekula's "On the Invention of Photographic Meaning"; digital camera created

1976: Facio and D'Amico's *Humanario*; Friedlander's *The American Monument*

1977: Sontag's *On Photography*; "Pictures" exhibition in New York

1978: First Colloquium of Latin American Photographers; Szarkowski's "Mirrors and Windows" exhibition; Sherman's *Untitled Film Stills*

1980–90

1980 Barthes's *Camera Lucida*

1981: Meiselas's *Nicaragua*

1982: Soviets take first color photographs of Venus; Burgin's *Thinking Photography*

1983: Kruger's *We won't play nature to your culture*; Goldin's *The Ballad of Sexual Dependency*

1986: Graham's *Beyond Caring*; Richards's *Exploding into Life*

1987: Clifford's *The Predicament of Culture*; Serrano's *Piss Christ*

1988: Killup's *In Flagrante*

1989: Gates establishes Corbis.com; *Adbusters* launched

1990–2000

1990s: Adobe Photoshop marketed; The Visible Human Project; Salgado's *An Uncertain Grace*

1991: Meyer's *The Temptation of the Angel*; (1991–92) Wall's *Dead Troops Talk*; "Pleasures and Terrors of Domestic Comfort" exhibition

1992: Sultan's *Pictures from Home*; Mann's *Immediate Family*

1993: MANUAL's *The Constructed Forest*; *Time* magazine's "The New Face of America"

1994: Aziz and Cucher's *Dystopia*

1997: Schneider's *Genetic Self-Portrait*; (1997–98) Mori's *Pure Land*; Mikhailov begins *Case Studies* series

1998: Gursky's *Bundestag, Bonn*

1999: "Another Girl, Another Planet" exhibition

2000–PRESENT

2000: Andujar awarded Lannan Foundation Cultural Freedom Prize; Willis's *Reflections in Black*

2002: Burtynsky's *Shipbreaking* series; Jarr's *Lament of the Images*

2003: Kodak announces end of slide projector manufacture; Sontag's *Regarding the Pain of Others*

2004: Photos of U.S. soldiers abusing Iraqi soldiers revealed; Kodak ends black-and-white photo paper manufacture

2005: (2005–06) "SlideShow" exhibition; "African Remix" exhibition

2008: "Impressed by Light: British Photographs from Paper Negatives, 1840–1860" exhibition

2008–2009 Eggleston: "The Democratic Camera [40 year retrospective]"

2009: Kodachrome discontinued by Kodak

2011: Large worker-photography exhibition, Madrid

2012: "The Rise and Fall of Apartheid," International Center of Photography, New York

2013: "Sebastião Salgado: Genesis" exhibition, Natural History Museum, London

NOTES

Introduction

1 J-D. Du Vernay, "Statistique de la photographie," *La Lumière* (September 1852), p. 155.
2 John Berger, *Ways of Seeing* (London and Middlesex, England: Penguin Books and British Broadcasting Corporation, 1972), p. 7.

Part One

Photography's Double Invention

1 Siegfried Kracauer, "Photography," in his *The Mass Ornament*, ed. and trans. by Thomas Y. Levin (Cambridge, MA: Harvard University Press, 1995), pp. 58–61. This essay and the others in *The Mass Ornament* were published in the newspaper *Die Frankfurter Zeitung*.

Chapter One

The Origins of Photography (to 1839)

1 For more information, see J. L. Heilbron, *The Sun in the Church: Cathedrals as Solar Observatories* (Cambridge, MA: Harvard University Press, 1999).
2 Oliver Wendell Holmes, "The Stereoscope and the Stereograph," *Atlantic Monthly*, vol. 3 (June 1859), pp. 738–39.
3 Eric Hobsbawm, T*he Age of Revolution, 1789–1848* (New York: Vintage Books, 1996), pp. 7–28.
4 For a review of perspective machines see Martin Kemp, *The Science of Art: Optical Themes in Western Art from Brunelleschi to Seurat* (New Haven, CT: Yale University Press, 1990), pp. 163–257. My discussion of perspective and drawing machines is indebted to this excellent text.
5 Gisèle Freund, *Photography and Society* (Boston, MA: David R. Godine, Publisher, 1980), p. 11.
6 Boris Kossoy, "Hercules Florence, Pioneer of Photography in Brazil," *Image*, vol. 20, no. 1 (March 1977), p. 17.
7 Kossoy 1977, pp. 16–19.
8 For the circumstances of Florence's invention, I am indebted to Boris Kossoy's essay "Photography in Nineteenth-Century Latin America: The European Experience and the Exotic Experience," in *Image and Memory: Photography from Latin America, 1866–1994*, ed. Wendy Watriss and Lois Parkinson Zamora (Austin, TX: University of Texas Press, 1998), pp. 21–25.
9 Quoted in Kossoy 1998, p. 25.
10 In 1842, Talbot wrote to Herschel that "Science is now cultivated by so many, that it is impossible that cases of simultaneous invention should not frequently arise." Quoted in Larry J. Schaaf, *Out of the Shadows: Herschel, Talbot and the Invention of Photography* (New Haven, CT: Yale University Press, 1992), p. 126.
11 Thomas Wedgwood and Sir Humphry Davy, "An Account of a Method of Copying Paintings upon Glass and of Making Profiles, by the Agency of Light upon Nitrate of Silver," reprinted in Beaumont Newhall, *Essays and Images* (New York: Museum of Modern Art, 1980), p. 16.
12 See a discussion of Niépce's processes in Helmut and Alison Gernsheim, *L. J. M. Daguerre: The History of the Diorama and the Daguerreotype*, 2nd, rev. ed. (New York: Dover Publications, Inc., 1968), pp. 51–64.

13 For a technical description of this process and many early photographic processes, see William Crawford, *The Keepers of Light: A History and Working Guide to Early Photographic Processes* (Dobbs Ferry, NY: Morgan & Morgan, 1979).
14 Quoted in Helmut and Alison Gernsheim, *L. J. M. Daguerre: The History of the Diorama and the Daguerreotype*, 2nd, rev. ed., pp. 80–81.
15 See Mary Warner Marien, *Photography and its Critics: A Cultural History, 1839–1900* (New York: Cambridge University Press, 1997), pp. 32–33.
16 Arago's statement and Gaucheraud's newspaper article are excerpted in English in Helmut and Alison Gernsheim, *L. J. M. Daguerre: The History of the Diorama and the Daguerreotype*, 2nd, rev. ed., pp. 82–85.
17 See the discussion in Larry J. Schaaf, *Out of the Shadows: Herschel, Talbot and the Invention of Photography*, pp. 23–25.
18 See Pierre G. Harmant, "Anno Lucis 1839," a three-part article in *Camera* (May 1977, no. 5, pp. 39–43; August, no. 8, pp. 37–41; October, no. 10, pp. 40–44). Also Robert Meyer, "Hans Thøger Winther: A Norwegian Pioneer in Photography," in *Shadow and Substance: Essays on the History of Photography*, ed. Kathleen Collins (Bloomfield Hills, MI: Amorphous Institute Press, 1990), pp. 39–48.
19 Bayard's note is reproduced in full in Michael Sapir, "The Impossible Photograph: Hippolyte Bayard's Self-Portrait as a Drowned Man," *Modern Fiction Studies*, vol. 40, no. 3 (Fall 1994), p. 623.
20 Quoted in Larry J. Schaaf, *Out of the Shadows: Herschel, Talbot and the Invention of Photography*, p. 49.
21 Letter from Charles Wheatstone to William Henry Fox Talbot, Document 3786, Fox Talbot Museum (Talbot's correspondence is available online through the Fox Talbot Museum at Lacock Abbey, Lacock, England).
22 Schaaf, p. 130.
23 Letter by William Henry Fox Talbot, dated January 30, 1839, published in the *Literary Gazette* (February 2, 1839). Quoted in Gail Buckland, *Fox Talbot and the Invention of Photography* (Boston, MA: David R. Godine, Publisher, 1980), p. 43. It is unknown if Talbot was actually preparing a report, or whether his claim to be doing so was an attempt to respond to the announcement of the daguerreotype.
24 Gail Buckland, p. 38.
25 William Henry Fox Talbot, *The Pencil of Nature* (London: Longman Brown, Green & Longmans, 1844–46), n.p. The book was reproduced in facsimile by Da Capo Press in 1969.
26 This experiment is described in Larry J. Schaaf, *Out of the Shadows: Herschel, Talbot and the Invention of Photography*, p. 40.
27 Quoted in Larry J. Schaaf, p. 42.
28 Quoted in Gail Buckland, *Fox Talbot and the Invention of Photography*, p. 39.
29 See Marien, *Photography and its Critics*, pp. 6, 35.
30 Quoted in Larry J. Schaaf, *Out of the Shadows: Herschel, Talbot and the Invention of Photography*, p. 57.
31 Schaaf, p. 71.
32 Schaaf, p. 75.
33 See Marien, *Photography and its Critics*, p. 17.
34 Quoted in Helmut and Alison Gernsheim, *L. J. M. Daguerre: The History of the Diorama and the Daguerreotype*, 2nd, rev. ed., pp. 101–2.

Chapter Two

The Second Invention of Photography (1839–1854)

1 "New Discovery in the Fine Arts," *New Yorker* (April 13, 1839), excerpted in Merry Foresta and John Wood, *Secrets of the Dark Chamber: The Art of American Daguerreotype* (Washington, D.C.: Smithsonian Institution Press, 1995), p. 224.
2 "New Discovery in the Fine Arts," p. 223.
3 "Self-Operating Processes of Fine Art: The Daguerotype [sic]," *Museum of Foreign Literature, Science and Art*, 35, n.s. 7 (January–April, 1839), p. 341.
4 For a discussion of the range of these meanings applied to photography see Jens Jäger, "Discourses on Photography in Mid-Victorian Britain," *History of Photography*, vol. 19, no. 4 (1995), pp. 316–21.
5 Fritz Kempe, *Daguerreotypie in Deutschland: Vom Charme der frühen Fotografie* (Seebruck am Chiemsee: Heering Verlag, 1979), p. 62.
6 *Athenaeum* (December 18, 1847), p. 1304, quoted in Jens Jäger, "Discourses on Photography in Mid-Victorian Britain," *History of Photography*, p. 317.
7 Francis Wey, "Exposé sommaire du but et des principaux éléments du journal," (1851), reprinted in Heinz Buddemeier, *Panorama, Diorama, Photographie* (Munich: Wilhelm Fink Verlag), pp. 253–54.
8 *Alexander's Weekly Messenger* (January 15, 1840), p. 38.
9 "Fine Arts," unsigned review of the Society of British Artists, *Athenaeum* (April 17, 1847), p. 416.
10 "Self-Operating Processes of Fine Art: The Daguerotype [sic]," p. 341.
11 Paul Greenhalgh, *Ephemeral Vistas: The Expositions universelles, Great Exhibitions and World's Fairs, 1851–1939* (Manchester: Manchester University Press, 1988), p. 145.
12 *The Golden Age of British Photography, 1839–1900*, ed. Mark Haworth-Booth (Millerton, NY: Aperture, 1984), p. 48.
13 William Henry Fox Talbot, *Some Account of the Art of Photogenic Drawing, or the Process by which Natural Objects May Be Made to Delineate Themselves without the Aid of the Artist's Pencil* (London: R. & J. S. Taylor, 1839), n.p.
14 Letter dated June 1839, quoted in Gail Buckland, *Fox Talbot and the Invention of Photography* (Boston, MA: David R. Godine, Publishers, 1980), p. 19.
15 William Henry Fox Talbot, *The Pencil of Nature* (1844–46; rpt. New York: Da Capo Press, 1969), n.p.
16 Larry J. Schaaf, *The Photographic Art of William Henry Fox Talbot* (Princeton, NJ: Princeton University Press, 2000), p. 166.
17 Francis Wey, "Album de la Société héliographique," *La Lumière* (May 18, 1851), p. 58. Quoted in Andre Jammes and Eugenia Parry Janis, *The Art of the French Calotype* (Princeton, NJ: Princeton University Press, 1983), p. 4.
18 Sander Gilman, *Seeing the Insane* (New York: J. Wiley, 1982), p. 189.
19 Hugh W. Diamond, "On the Application of Photography to the Physiognomic and Mental Phenomena of Insanity" (read before the Royal Society, May 22, 1856), reprinted in *The Face of Madness: Hugh W. Diamond and the Origin of Psychiatric Photography*, ed. Sander L. Gilman (New York: Brunner/Mazell, Publishers, 1976), p. 19.
20 Diamond, p. 20.
21 See Bates Lowry and Isabel Barrett Lowry, *The Silver Canvas: Daguerreotype Masterpieces from the J. Paul*

Getty Museum (Los Angeles, CA: The J. Paul Getty Museum, 1998), p. 112.

22 Diamond, p. 24.

23 Brian Wallis, "Black Bodies, White Science: Louis Agassiz's Slave Daguerreotypes," *Art in America*, vol. 9, no. 2 (Summer 1995), p. 40.

24 Daniel M. Fox and Christopher Lawrence, *Photographing Medicine: Images and Power in Britain and America since 1840* (New York: Greenwood Press, 1988), p. 24.

25 Fox and Lawrence, p. 25.

26 For further details, see the discussion in Bates Lowry and Isabel Barrett Lowry, *The Silver Canvas*, pp. 182–85.

27 See Olivier Debroise, *Mexican Suite: A History of Photography in Mexico*, trans. Stella de Sá Rego (Austin, TX: University of Texas Press, 2001), pp. 164–67.

28 Gina Rodriguez Hernández, "Cerro Gordo, abril 18 de 1847," in *Alquimia*, vol. 1, no. 2 (April 1998), pp. 44–45.

29 See Olivier Debroise, *Mexican Suite: A History of Photography in Mexico*, p. 166.

30 Beaumont Newhall, *The Daguerreotype in America* (New York: Dover Publications, Inc., 1976, 3rd rev. ed.), p. 88.

31 James R. Ryan, *Picturing Empire: Photography and Visualization of the British Empire* (Chicago, IL: University of Chicago Press, 1997), p. 28.

32 Alkis X. Xanthakis, *History of Greek Photography, 1839–1960* (Athens, GA: Hellenic Literary and Historical Archives Society, 1988) pp. 28–29.

33 Xanthakis, p. 30.

34 Yeshayahu Nir, *The Bible and the Image: The History of Photography in the Holy Land, 1839–1899* (Philadelphia, PA: University of Pennsylvania Press, 1985), p. 35. I am indebted to Nir's discussion and the work of Kathleen Stewart Howe in *Revealing the Holy Land: The Photographic Exploration of Palestine* (Santa Barbara, CA: Santa Barbara Museum of Art, 1997).

35 Quoted in Kathleen Stewart Howe, *Revealing the Holy Land*, p. 23. These daguerreotypes are now lost. Also see Robert Hershkowitz, *The British Photographer Abroad: The First Thirty Years* (London: Robert Hershkowitz Ltd., 1980), p. 80.

36 For a full discussion of the commission and its work, see André Jammes and Eugenia Parry Janis, *The Art of the French Calotype* (Princeton, NJ: Princeton University Press, 1983), especially pp. 52–66.

37 Malcolm Daniel, *The Photographs of Edouard Baldus* (New York: Metropolitan Museum of Art, 1994), pp. 21–24.

38 Eugenia Parry Janis and Josiane Sartre, *Henri Le Secq: Photographe de 1850–1860* (Paris: Flammarion, 1986), p. 116.

39 For Francis Wey's discussion, see "Du Naturalisme dans l'art de don principe et de ses conséquences" (*La Lumière*, vol. 1, 1851), reproduced in Heinz Buddemeier, *Panorama, Diorama, Photographie* (Munich: Wilhelm Fink Verlag, 1970), pp. 267–84.

40 See William Newton's address to the Photographic Society of London, printed in the *Journal of the Photographic Society*, vol. 1 (March 3, 1853), p. 6.

41 Gustave Le Gray, *Photographie: traité nouveau théorique et practique des procédés et manipulations sur papier ... et sur verre* (Paris: Lerebours et Secretan [1852]), p. 1. See also p. 3.

42 The Barbizon group was not only an art faction; it was also associated with democratic freedom because its subject, nature, was free to all and could be understood without having had a Classical education.

43 This image is discussed in William Welling, *Photography in America: The Formative Years* (Albuquerque, NM: University of New Mexico Press, 1978), p. 28.

44 *Daguerrean Journal*, vol. 1, no. 4 (January 1, 1851), p. 117. Quoted in Michael L. Carlebach, *The Origins of Photojournalism in America* (Washington, D.C.: Smithsonian Institution Press, 1992), p. 27.

45 See *Photography in Russia*, 1840–1940, ed. David Elliott (London: Thames and Hudson, 1992), p. 28.

46 *Photography in Russia*, p. 27.

47 Francis Wey, "Du Naturalisme dans l'art de don principe et de ses conséquences" (*La Lumière*, vol. 1, 1851), reproduced in Heinz Buddemeier, *Panorama, Diorama, Photographie*, p. 281. The quotation reads "et leurs portraits ne ressemblent point, comme certaines épreuves daguerriennes, des merlans frits séchés sur un plat d'argent."

48 Elizabeth Anne McCauley, *Industrial Madness: Commercial Photography in Paris, 1848–1871* (New Haven, CT: Yale University Press, 1994), p. 154.

49 T. S. Arthur, *Godey's Lady's Book*, 1849. Quoted in Floyd Rinhart and Marion Rinhart, *The American Daguerreotype* (Athens, GA: University of Georgia Press, 1981), pp. 113–14.

50 Quoted in Robert Taft, *Photography and the American Scene* (1938; rpt. New York: Dover Publications, 1964), p. 76.

51 Alan Trachtenberg, *Reading American Photographs: Images as History, Mathew Brady to Walker Evans* (New York: Hill and Wang, 1989), p. 26.

52 Deborah Willis, *Reflections in Black: A History of Black Photographers, 1840 to the Present* (New York: W. W. Norton & Co., 2000), p. 4.

53 Michael L. Carlebach, *The Origins of Photojournalism in America*, pp. 22–23.

54 Matthew R. Isenburg, "Southworth and Hawes: The Artists," in John Woods, *The Daguerreotype: A Sesquicentennial Celebration* (Iowa City, IA: University of Iowa Press, 1989), p. 75.

55 Albert Sands Southworth, "The Early History of Photography in the United States," in *Photography: Essays and Images*, ed. Beaumont Newhall (New York: Museum of Modern Art, 1980), p. 41.

56 The pivotal role of St. Andrews in photographic history is outlined in Robert Crawford, *The Beginning and the End of the World: St Andrews, Scandal, and the Birth of Photography* (Edinburgh: Birlinn Limited, 2011).

57 Sara Stevenson, "David Octavius Hill and Robert Adamson," in *British Photography in the Nineteenth Century: The Fine Art Tradition* (New York: Cambridge University Press, 1989), p. 53.

58 Talbot quoted in Larry J. Schaaf, *The Photographic Art of William Henry Fox Talbot* (Princeton, NJ: Princeton University Press, 2000), pp. 19, 59.

59 Letter from Hill to Mr. Bicknell, dated January 17, 1848, quoted in Colin Ford and Roy Strong, eds., *An Early Victorian Album: The Photographic Masterpieces (1843–1847) of David Octavius Hill and Robert Adamson* (New York: Alfred A. Knopf, 1976), p. 321.

60 Sara Stevenson, "David Octavius Hill and Robert Adamson," p. 43.

61 See discussion in Richard Rudisill, *Mirror Image: The Influence of the Daguerreotype on American Society* (Albuquerque, NM: University of New Mexico Press, 1971), pp. 218–19.

62 Michel Foucault, *Discipline and Punish: The Birth of the Prison*, trans. Alan Sheridan (New York: Vintage Books, 1979), p. 187.

63 See Marien, *Photography and its Critics: A Cultural History, 1839–1900* (New York: Cambridge University Press, 1997), p. 3, and the subsequent discussion.

64 Sir Francis Palgrave, "The Fine Arts of Florence," *Quarterly Review*, vol. 66 (1840), p. 326.

65 "Photogenic Drawing, or Drawing by Agency of Light," *Edinburgh Review*, vol. 154 (January 1843), pp. 160–61, 169.

66 John Ruskin, *The Works of John Ruskin*, ed. E. T. Cook and A. Wedderburn (London: G. Allen, 1903–12), vol. 33, p. 304.

67 "Otkrytie Dagera," in *Khudozhestvennaia gazeta*, no. 2 (January 15, 1840), pp. 11–12, quoted in *Photography in Russia*, p. 26.

68 Eugène Delacroix, "Le dessin sans maître, par Mme Elisabeth Cavé," *Revue des Deux Mondes*, vol. 3 (September 15, 1850), pp. 1144–45.

69 Gustave Flaubert, *Correspondance (1850–1854)* (Paris: Louis Conard, 1910), p. 427, and C.A. Sainte-Beuve, "De la littérature industrielle," *Portraits Contemporains*, vol. 2 (Paris: Michel Lévy Frère, 1889), p. 434. The comments appeared in September 1839.

70 E.-J. Delécluze, "Exposition de 1850," *Journal des Débats* (March 21, 1851), n.p.

71 For a fuller discussion of photography's critics, see Mary Warner Marien, *Photography and its Critics*, pp. 64–73.

Part Two
The Expanding Domain (1854–1880)

1 [Lady Elizabeth Eastlake], (Untitled Book Review) *Quarterly Review*, 101 (January–April 1857), pp. 442–43.

2 Keith F. Davis, "'A Terrible Distinctness': Photography and the Civil War Era," in *Photography in Nineteenth-Century America*, ed. Martha A. Sandweiss (New York: Harry N. Abrams, Inc., 1991), p. 137.

3 Roger Tayler, *Impressed by Light: British Photographs from Paper Negative, 1840–1860* (New York: Metropolitan Museum of Art, 2007) p. 134.

Chapter Three
Popular Photography and the Aims of Art

1 *Art Journal* (1860), p. 221, from frontispiece of Richard J. Huyda, *Camera in the Interior: 1858, H. L. Hime, Photographer: The Assiniboine and Saskatchewan Exploring Expedition* (Toronto: Coach House Press, 1975).

2 Francis Frith, "The Art of Photography," *Art Journal*, 5 (1859), pp. 71–72 (emphases Frith).

3 C. Jabez Hughes, "On Art Photography," *American Journal of Photography*, 3 (1861), p. 261.

4 For information on photographic journals in the United States, see William and Estelle Marder, "Nineteenth-century American Photographic Journals: A Chronological List," *History of Photography*, vol. 17, no. 1 (Spring 1993), pp. 95–100.

5 See the contemporary description from *New York Review*, reproduced in William Welling, *Photography in America: The Formative Years, 1839–1900* (Albuquerque, NM: University of New Mexico Press, 1978), p. 265.

6 Oliver Wendell Holmes, "The Stereoscope and the Stereograph," *Atlantic Monthly*, vol. 3 (June 1859), p. 744.

7 Oliver Wendell Holmes, "Sun-Painting and Sun-Sculpture," *Atlantic Monthly*, vol. 8 (July 1861), pp. 14–15.

8 Oliver Wendell Holmes, "The Stereoscope and the Stereograph," p. 747.

9 "Stereoscope: or Travel Made Easy," *Athenaeum*, no. 1586 (March 20, 1858), p. 371.

10 *Revue Photographique* (1862), p. 151, quoted in André Rouillé, "The Great Photography Debate," *Impact of Science on Society*, vol. 42, no. 4 (no. 168), p. 292.

11 John Mraz, *Looking for Mexico: Modern Visual Culture and National Identity* (Durham, NC: Duke University Press, 2009), pp. 21–22.

12 Elizabeth Anne McCauley, *A. A. E. Disdéri and the Carte de Visite Portrait Photograph* (New Haven, CT: Yale University Press, 1985), p. 220.

13 Christopher Date and Anthony Hamber, "The Origins of Photography at the British Museum," *History of Photography*, vol. 14, no. 4 (1990), p. 316.

14 Valerie Lloyd, *Roger Fenton: Photographer of the 1850s* (London: South Bank Board, 1988), p. 11.

15 Abigail Solomon-Godeau, *Photography at the Dock: Essays on Photographic History, Institutions, and Practices* (Minneapolis, MN: University of Minnesota Press, 1991), pp. 158–59.

16 See Howard B. Leighton, "The Lantern Slide and Art," *History of Photography*, vol. 8, no. 2 (1984), pp. 107–18.

17 Marcus Aurelius Root, *The Camera and the Pencil* (1864; rpt. Pawlet, VT: Helios, 1971), p. 28.

18 "Stereoscopes for Amateurs—Process of Producing Stereoscopic Photographs," *Scientific American*, 2 (June 2, 1860) p. 361. For a discussion of art reproduction and visual literacy, see Mary Warner Marien, *Photography and its Critics* (New York: Cambridge University Press, 1997).

19 "Fine Arts: New Publications" [review of the exhibition "Gems of Art Treasures"], *Athenaeum*, 1549 (July 4, 1857), p. 856.

20 Rembrandt Peale, "Portraiture," *Crayon*, 4, Part II (February 1857), p. 44 (emphasis Peale).

21 Charles Baudelaire, "Salon of 1859," in *Art in Paris*, p. 154.

22 Rembrandt Peale, "Portraiture," p. 44.

23 Eugène Delacroix, "Le dessin sans maître, par Mme. Elisabeth Cavé," *Revue des Deux Mondes*, 3 (September 15, 1850), pp. 1144–45.

24 For an international discussion of the painters who may have been influenced by photography see Nissan N. Perez, *Focus East: Early Photography in the Near East, 1839–1885* (New York: Harry N. Abrams, Inc., 1988), pp. 66–87.

25 Plate note, in Maria Morris Hambourg, Françoise Heilbrun, and Philippe Néagu, *Nadar* (New York: Metropolitan Museum of Art, 1995), p. 114.

26 Quoted in Maria Morris Hambourg, "A Portrait of Nadar," in Maria Morris Hambourg, Françoise Heilbrun and Philippe Néagu, *Nadar*, p. 25.

27 See Elizabeth Anne McCauley, I*ndustrial Madness: Commercial Photography in Paris, 1848–1871* (New Haven, CT: Yale University Press, 1994), p. 124.

28 Maria Morris Hambourg, plate note, in Hambourg, Heilbrun, and Néagu, *Nadar*, p. 113.

29 For a history of the *tableau vivant*, see Heinz K. Henisch and Bridget A. Henisch, *The Photographic Experience, 1839–1914* (University Park, PA: Pennsylvania State University Press, 1994), pp. 70–75.

30 For more information on Madame Warton's programs see Jack W. McCullough, *Living Pictures on the New York Stage* (Ann Arbor, MI: UMI Research Press, 1983), pp. 38–47.

31 William Crawford, *The Keepers of Light* (Dobbs Ferry, NY: Morgan & Morgan, 1979), p. 55. This book contains a useful key to the allegorical significance of the figures in *The Two Ways of Life*.

32 Maria Morris Hambourg, Pierre Apraxine, Malcolm Daniel, Jeff L. Rosenheim, and Virginia Heckert, *The Waking Dream: Photography's First Century, Selections from the Gilman Paper Company Collection* (New York: Metropolitan Museum of Art, 1993), p. 275.

33 Carol Mavor, *Pleasures Taken: Performances of Sexuality and Loss in Victorian Photographs* (Durham, NC: Duke University Press, 1995), and Susan H. Edwards, "Pretty Babies: Art Erotica or Kiddie Porn?" *History of Photography*, vol. 18, no. 1 (Spring 1994) pp. 38–46.

34 Anne Anninger and Julie Mellby, *Salts of Silver, Toned with Gold: The Harrison D. Horblit Collection of Early Photography* (Cambridge, MA: Houghton Library, Harvard University, 1999), p. 116.

35 Virginia Dodier, "Clementina, Viscountess Hawarden," in Mike Weaver, *British Photography in the Nineteenth Century: The Fine Art Tradition* (New York: Cambridge University Press, 1989), p. 145.

36 From a letter to John Herschel reproduced in Helmut Gernsheim, *Julia Margaret Cameron: Her Life and Photographic Work* (Millerton, NY: Aperture, 1975), p. 14.

37 Julia Margaret Cameron, "The Annals of My Glass House," in Beaumont Newhall, ed., *Photography: Essays and Images* (New York: Museum of Modern Art, 1980), p. 137.

38 See Mike Weaver, *Julia Margaret Cameron, 1815–1879* (Boston, MA: New York Graphic Society/Little

Brown Company, 1984), p. 138.

39 William Culp Darrah, "Nineteenth-Century Women Photographers," *Shadow and Substance: Essays on the History of Photography*, ed. Kathleen Collins (Bloomfield Hills, MI: Amorphous Institute Press, 1990), p. 89.

40 Jabez Hughes, "Photography as an Industrial Occupation for Women," *British Journal of Photography* (May 9, 1873), p. 223.

41 William Culp Darrah, "Nineteenth-Century Women Photographers," p. 89.

Chapter Four
Imaging of the Social World

1 Oliver Wendell Holmes, "The Stereoscope and the Stereograph," *Atlantic Monthly*, vol. 3 (June 1859), p. 748.

2 [John W. Draper], "Editorial Miscellany," *American Journal of Photography*, vol. 3 (1861), p. 320.

3 Callwell's *Small Wars: Their Principles and Purpose* was published in 1899. See the discussion in James R. Ryan, *Picturing Empire: Photography and the Visualization of the British Empire* (Chicago, IL: University of Chicago Press, 1997), p. 73. Also of related interest is André Rouillé, *L'Empire de la Photographie*, 1839–1870 (Paris: Le Sycomore, 1982).

4 James R. Ryan, p. 73.

5 [Eugéne Durieu], "Rapport," *Bulletin de la Société Française de Photographie* (February 1856), p. 50.

6 Donald E. English, *Political Uses of Photography in the Third French Republic, 1871–1914* (Ann Arbor, MI: University of Michigan Research Press, 1984), p. 8.

7 Helmut and Alison Gernsheim, *Roger Fenton: Photographer of the Crimean War* (London: Secker & Warburg, 1954), pp. 12–13.

8 See the discussion in Mike Weaver, "Le Gray—Fenton—Watkins," in *The Art of Photography, 1839–1989*, ed. Mike Weaver (New Haven, CT: Yale University Press, 1989), p. 96. Indeed, it may not have been the actual spot where the tragic military offensive took place. See Jennifer Green-Lewis, *Framing the Victorians: Photography and the Culture of Realism* (Ithaca, NY: Cornell University Press, 1996), p. 126.

9 *Photographic Journal*, vol. 2 (1855), p. 221.

10 Ulrich Keller, *The Ultimate Spectacle: A Visual History of the Crimean War* (London: Gordon and Breach, 2001), p. 136.

11 Fenton may not have been the first to offer photographic instruction to Queen Victoria and Prince Albert. They may have been taught by Dr. Ernst Becker, who was appointed librarian to Prince Albert and assistant tutor to the princes. See Francis Dimond and Roger Taylor, *Crown and Country: The Royal Family and Photography, 1842–1910* (New York: Viking, 1987), p. 14.

12 See *New York Times* (July 26, 1864), p. 4.

13 Cook's life and work are recounted in Jack C. Ramsay, Jr., *Photographer under Fire: The Story of George S. Cook, 1819–1902* (Green Bay, WI: Historical Resources Press, 1994).

14 Mary Panzer, *Mathew Brady and the Image of War* (Washington, D.C.: Smithsonian Institution Press, 1997), p. 103.

15 Vicki Goldberg, *The Power of Photography* (New York: Abbeville Publishing Group, 1991), p. 77.

16 Geo. Alfred Townsend ("Gath"), "The New York World Interview with Mathew Brady," in Vicki Goldberg, *Photography in Print* (New York: Simon and Schuster, 1981), p. 204.

17 Quoted in Josephine Cobb, "Photographers of the Civil War," *Military Affairs*, vol. 26, no. 2 (Fall 1962), p. 128.

18 *New York Times* (Monday, July 21, 1862), p. 5.

19 Described in Jack C. Ramsay, *Photographer under Fire*, p. 71.

20 *New York Times* (Monday, October 20, 1862), p. 5.

21 Oliver Wendell Holmes, "Doings of the Sunbeam," *Atlantic Monthly*, vol. 12 (July 1863), pp. 11–12.

22 At one point, the photograph was credited to Timothy O'Sullivan by Gardner.

23 Kathleen Collins, "Living Skeletons: Carte-de-visite Propaganda in the American Civil War," *History of Photography*, vol. 12, no. 2 (April–June 1988), p. 104.

24 Collins, pp. 103–20. A *carte-de-visite* in the William C. Darrah collection shows the Elmira prison as neat and orderly rows of white tents. See his *Cartes de Visite in Nineteenth Century Photography* (Gettysburg, PA: W. C. Darrah, Publisher, 1981), p. 83, pl. 189.

25 Wendy Watriss and Lois Parkinson Zamora, *Image and Memory: Photography from Latin America, 1866–1994* (Austin, TX: University of Texas Press, 1998), pp. 7, 411.

26 For this information, and a comprehensive discussion of photography during the French Commune, I am indebted to Donald E. English, in his book, *Political Uses of Photography in the Third French Republic, 1871–1914*.

27 Albert Boime, *Art and the French Commune* (Princeton, NJ: Princeton University Press, 1995), p. 5. Boime's book is a lucid account of the reaction of artists to the events of the Paris Commune.

28 Quoted in Boime, p. 194.

29 For more discussion of this print, see English, p. 24.

30 "Photographs from the Philippine Islands," *Photographic News*, no. 61 (November 4, 1859), p. 99.

31 S. Bourne, "Narratives of a Photographical Trip to Kashmir and Adjacent Districts," *British Journal of Photography* (November 23–28, 1866), pp. 559–60.

32 *The Golden Age of British Photography, 1839–1900*, ed. Mark Haworth-Booth (Millerton, NY: Aperture, 1984), p. 104.

33 B. A. and H. K. Henisch, "James Robertson of Constantinople: A Chronology," *History of Photography*, vol. 14, no. 1 (January–March 1990), pp. 30–31.

34 Mark Haworth-Booth, ed., *The Golden Age of British Photography*, p. 104, and "Photographieren auf Forschungsreisen: Robert Schlagintweit und seine Brüder erforschen die Alpen, Indien und Hochasien (1850–1857)," in *Silber und Salz: Zur Frühzeit der Photographie im deutschen Sprachenraum, 1839–1860*, ed. Bodo von Dewitz and Einhard Matz (Cologne and Heidelberg: Edition Braus, 1989), pp. 310–33.

35 Clark Worswich and Ainslie Embree, *The Last Empire: Photography in British India, 1855–1911* (Millerton, NY: Aperture, 1976), pp. 4–5. I am indebted to this book for information on the history of photography in India, as well as to Christopher Pinney's *Camera Indica: The Social Life of Indian Photography* (Chicago, IL: University of Chicago Press, 1997).

36 Vidya Dehejia, *India through the Lens, 1840–1911* (Washington, D.C.: Freer Gallery of Art and Arthur M. Sackler Gallery, Smithsonian Institution, 2000), p. 17.

37 See Roberta Wue, "Picturing Hong Kong: Photography through Practice and Function," in *Picturing Hong Kong* (New York: Asia Society Galleries and George Braziller, 1997), p. 28, n. 5. I am indebted to Wue for her insightful essay on early Hong Kong photography.

38 Jeffrey W. Cody and Frances Terpak, "Through a Foreign Glass: The Art and Science of Photography in Late Qing China," in *Brush and Shutter: Early Photography in China*, ed. Jeffrey W. Cody and Frances Terpak (Los Angeles: Getty Research Institute, 2011), pp. 34–35.

39 John Thomson, quoted in Roberta Wue, "Picturing Hong Kong," p. 38. For all his years in Asia, Thomson had two assistants, Akum and Ahong, the latter of whose names resembles A-Hung and Afong. For Ahong, see Stephen White, *John Thompson: A Window to the Orient* (New York: Thames and Hudson, 1985), p. 10.

40 John Thomson, quoted in Roberta Wue, "Picturing Hong Kong," p. 37. Afong was active from about 1859 to 1900.

41 Clark Worswick, *Japan: Photographs, 1854–1905* (New York: A Pennwick/Alfred A. Knopf, 1979), p. 30. Also see Terry Bennett, *Early Japanese Images* (Rutland, VT: Charles E. Tuttle Company, 1996), pp. 31–32. I am indebted to Worswick and Bennett for information on Japanese photography. Long considered lost, some of the Eliphalet Brown daguerreotypes may be held in Japanese museums. See Bennett, above, pp. 30–31; Hugh Cortazzi and Terry Bennett, *Japan: Caught in Time* (New York: Weatherhill, 1995), p. 31, and Eleanor M. Hight, "Japan as Artefact and Archive: Nineteenth-Century Photographic Collections in Boston," *History of Photography*, vol. 28 , no. 2 (Summer 2004), p. 112.
42 Julia Meech, "Woodblock Prints and Photographs: Two Views of Nineteenth-Century Japan," *Asian Arts* (Summer 1990), p. 56.
43 Clark Worswick, *Japan*, p. 136, and Terry Bennett, *Early Japanese Images*, p. 144.
44 Bill Jay, *Victorian Cameraman: Francis Frith's Views of Rural England, 1850–1898* (Newton Abbot, Devon: David & Charles, 1973).
45 Kathleen Stewart Howe maintains that De Clercq's religious photographs are unusual among French photographs of the Holy Land. She suggests that, unlike English religious education, which stressed Bible reading and a sense of historical place, French religious study emphasized Catholic creed. See *Revealing the Holy Land: The Photographic Exploration of Palestine*, essay by Kathleen Stewart Howe (Santa Barbara, CA: Santa Barbara Museum of Art, 1997), p. 28. The relationship between surveys and photography is also discussed in Nissan N. Perez, *Focus East: Early Photography in the Near East, (1839–1885)* (New York: Harry N. Abrams, Inc., 1988), pp. 77–80.
46 Richard Parkhurst and Denis Gérard, *Ethiopia Photographed* (London: Kegan Paul International, 1996), p. 20.
47 See Elizabeth Anne McCauley, *Industrial Madness*, p. 306, and Keith B. Davis, *Désiré Charnay, Expeditionary Photographer* (Albuquerque, NM: University of New Mexico Press, 1981), p. 19.
48 Quoted in Mark Haworth-Booth, ed., *The Golden Age of British Photography*, p. 114.
49 William Goetzmann, *Army Exploration in the American West, 1803–1863* (New Haven, CT: Yale University Press, 1959), pp. 427–29. The border survey was not the first time that a photographer accompanied a survey team in Canada. The Assiniboine and Saskatchewan topographical and geological survey of 1858 was photographed by an engineer-photographer, Humphrey Lloyd Hime. See Richard J. Huyda, *Camera in the Interior: 1858, H. L. Hime, Photographer: The Assiniboine and Saskatchewan Exploring Expedition* (Toronto: Coach House Press, 1975).
50 William H. Goetzmann, *Exploration and Empire: The Explorer and the Scientist in the Winning of the American West* (New York: Alfred A. Knopf, 1967), p. 231.
51 William H. Goetzmann, *Army Exploration in the American West*, p. 5.
52 William H. Goetzmann, *Exploration and Empire*, pp. 303–04.
53 Gardner was not alone in associating the Leutze mural with the railroad. The artist Fanny Palmer used the title in a 1868 lithograph showing the railroad crossing the west, and painter Andrew Melrose painted *Westward the Star of Empire*, a strange view in which the train glows in a way reminiscent of J. M. W. Turner's rendering of the train as sublime in *Rain, Steam, and Speed*. For more on Leutze and on art and the railroad, see *The West as America: Reinterpreting Images of the Frontier, 1820–1920*, ed. William Truettner (Washington, D.C.: Smithsonian Institution Press, 1991).
54 *New York Times* (May 8, 1867), p. 8.
55 James D. Horan, *Timothy O'Sullivan: America's Forgotten Photographer* (New York: Doubleday & Co., 1966), pp. 217–18.
56 Horan, p. 221.
57 Peter Bacon Hales, *William Henry Jackson and*

the Transformation of the American Landscape (Philadelphia, PA: Temple University Press, 1988), p. 95. I am indebted to Hales's work for my understanding of Jackson.
58 Hales, p. 96.
59 Robert Bartless Haas, *Muybridge, Man in Motion* (Berkeley, CA: University of California Press, 1976), p. 51.
60 For more information on Modoc war photography, see Peter Palmquist, "Imagemakers of the Modoc War: Louis Heller and Eadweard Muybridge," *Journal of California Anthropology* (Winter 1977), pp. 206–41.
61 Alan Axelrod, *Chronicle of the Indian Wars: From Colonial Times to Wounded Knee* (New York: Prentice Hall General Reference, 1993), pp. 208–09.
62 Axelrod, p. 203.
63 Robert M. Utley and Wilcomb E. Washburn, *The American Heritage: History of the Indian Wars* (New York: American Heritage Publishing Company, 1977), p. 266.

Chapter Five
Science and Social Science

1 Roslyn Poignant, "Surveying the Field of View: The Making of the R.A.I. Photographic collection," in *Anthropology and Photography*, 1860–1920, ed. Elizabeth Edwards (New Haven, CT: Yale University Press, 1992), p. 51.
2 Elena Barkhatova, "Realism and Document: Photography as Fact," in *Photography in Russia, 1840–1940*, ed. David Elliott (London: Thames and Hudson, 1992), p. 42. I am indebted to the essays in Elliott's book for an understanding of Russian photography.
3 Roslyn Poignant, "Surveying the Field of View," pp. 47–48. Edwards's book is a fine source for information on nineteenth- and early twentieth-century anthropological photography.
4 Edward Said, *Orientalism* (London: Routledge & Kegan Paul, 1978). The application of the term "Orientalism" to Asia has been much criticized in recent years. But in its loosest meanings, the word has come to signal illicit looking.
5 Clark Worswick, *The Last Empire: Photography in British India, 1855–1911* (Millerton, NY: Aperture, 1976), p. 9, and Robert A. Sobieszek and Carney E. S. Gavin, *Remembrance of the Near East: The Photographs of Bonfils, 1867–1907* (Rochester, NY: International Museum of Photography at George Eastman House, 1980), n.p.
6 Vidya Dehejia, *India through the Lens, 1840–1911*, p. 19.
7 Todd D. Smith, "Gay Male Pornography and the East: Re-orienting the Orient," *History of Photography*, 18 (Spring 1994), p. 17.
8 For a discussion of pornography, see Elizabeth Anne McCauley, *Industrial Madness*.
9 Roslyn Poignant, "Surveying the Field of View," p. 45.
10 The name was later changed to the Bureau of American Ethnology (B.A.E.).
11 For information on the American West and photography, see *Native Nations: Journeys in American Photography* (London: Barbican Art Gallery, 1998); Merry A. Foresta, *American Photographs: The First Century* (Washington, D.C.: Smithsonian Institution Press, 1996); and *The West as America: Reinterpreting Images of the Frontier, 1820–1920*, ed. William Truettner (Washington, D.C.: Smithsonian Institution Press, 1991).
12 Wendy Watriss and Lois Parkinson Zamora, *Image and Memory*, p. 43.
13 See Felicity Ashbee, "William Carrick: A Scots Photographer in St. Petersburg (1827–1878)," *History of Photography*, vol. 2, no. 3 (July 1978), p. 211.
14 Mary Bennett and Paul C. Juhl, *Iowa Stereographs: Three-Dimensional Visions of the Past* (Iowa City, IA: University of Iowa Press, 1997).

15 Oliver Wendell Holmes, "Doings of the Sunbeam," p. 15.
16 Quoted in Nancy Ann Roth, "Electrical Expressions: The Photographs of Duchenne de Boulogne," in *Multiple Views*, ed. Daniel P. Younger (Albuquerque, NM: University of New Mexico Press, 1991), p. 116.
17 Paul Ekman, "Introduction," *Charles Darwin, The Expression of the Emotions in Man and Animals* (New York: Oxford University Press, 1998), p. xiii. I am indebted to Ekman's research on Darwin and his use of photography, which appears throughout his edition of the 1872 book.
18 John O'Neill, "The Question of an Introduction: Understanding and the Passion of Ignorance," in *Freud and the Passions*, ed. John O'Neill (University Park, PA: Pennsylvania State University Press, 1996), p. 10.
19 Joan Copjec, "Flavit et Dissipati Sunt," in *October: The First Decade, 1976–1986*, ed. Annette Michelson, Rosalind Krauss, Douglas Crimp, and Jon Copjec (Cambridge, MA: MIT Press, 1987), p. 300.
20 Quoted in Sigrid Schade, "Charcot and the Spectacle of the Hysterical Body: The 'Pathos Formula' as an Aesthetic Staging of Psychiatric Discourse—A Blind Spot in the Reception of Warburg," *Art History*, vol. 18, no. 4 (December 1995), p. 510.
21 Oliver Wendell Holmes, *Atlantic Monthly*, vol. 10 (May 1863).
22 It exists today as the Armed Forces Institute of Pathology. For more information on medicine during the American Civil War, see Stanley B. Burns, *Early Medical Photography in America* (New York: Burns Archive, 1983), pp. 1444–69, which is a reprint of the August 1980 issue of *New York State Journal of Medicine*.
23 See *Confederate States Medical and Surgical Journal* (rpt. Metuchen, NJ: Scarecrow Press, 1976), p. 25.
24 Ann Thomas, "The Search for Pattern," in *Beauty of Another Order: Photography in Science*, ed. Ann Thomas (New Haven, CT: Yale University Press, 1997), p. 99.
25 Quoted in Ann Thomas, "The Search for Pattern," p. 100.
26 Frederic Luther, *Microfilm: A History, 1839–1900* (Annapolis, MD: National Microfilm Association, 1959), pp. 23–46.
27 For a discussion of this book, and nineteenth-century photographically illustrated books, see Carol Armstrong, *Scenes in a Library: Reading the Photograph in the Book, 1843–1875* (Cambridge, MA: MIT Press, 1998).
28 This event is extensively described in Ann Thomas, "Capturing Light: Photographing the Universe," in Ann Thomas, ed., *Beauty of Another Order: Photography in Science*, pp. 191–93.
29 For a full discussion, see Ann Thomas, "The Search for Pattern," pp. 86–88.
30 [Robert Cecil] Unsigned, untitled review, *Quarterly Review*, vol. 116, no. 232 (July and October 1864), p. 498.
31 Cecil, p. 499.
32 Thomas Thurston, "Hearsay of the Sun: Photography, Identity and the Law of Evidence in Nineteenth-Century American Courts," http://chmn. gmu.aq/photos/essay/intro.htm (February 1, 1999).
33 *The American Law Register* 1 (January, 1869) hypertext project http://chmn.gmu.aq/photos/text/ 17ALR1. htm
34 An exception is Captain W. W. Hooper's photographs of the Madras famine, 1876–77.
35 Quoted in John Falconer, "Willoughby Wallace Hooper: 'a craze about photography,'" *Photographic Collector*, vol. 4, no. 3 (Winter 1983), p. 259.
36 For photographs of the Suez Canal, see Nissan N. Perez, *Focus East: Early Photography in the Near East, 1839–1885* (New York: Harry N. Abrams, 1988).
37 See William Newton's address to the Photographic Society of London, printed in *Journal of the Photographic Society*, 1 (March 3, 1853), p. 6.
38 John Ruskin, *The Works of John Ruskin*, ed. E. T. Cook and A. Wedderburn (London: G. Allen, 1903–

1912), vol. 11, p. 212.
39 Ruskin, *Works*, vol. 20, pp. 96–97.
40 Henri de la Blanchère, *L'Art du photographe* (Paris: Amyot Editeur, 1859), p. 3.

Part Three
Photography and Modernity
(1880–1918)

1 Mark Twain letter, October 4, 1884, reproduced on http://www.twainquotes.com/Mental_telegraphy.html

Chapter Six
The Great Divide

1 Keith F. Davis, *An American Century of Photography: From Dry-Plate to Digital*, 2nd ed. (Kansas City, MO: Hallmark Cards, Inc., 1999), p. 16.
2 Margarett Loke, ed., *The World as it Was, 1865–1921: A Photographic Portrait from the Keystone-Mast Collection* (New York: Summit Books, 1980), p. 12.
3 Anon., "The Camera Epidemic," *New York Times* (August 20, 1884), p. 4.
4 Loke, ed., p. 16.
5 Ulrich Keller, "Photojournalism around 1900: The Institutionalization of a Mass Medium," in *Shadow and Substance: Essays on the History of Photography*, ed. Kathleen Collins (Bloomfield Hills, MI: Amorphous Institute Press, 1990), pp. 293–94.
6 James Lawrence Breese, "The Relations of Photography to Art," *Cosmopolitan*, vol. 18, no. 2 (December 1894), p. 140.
7 Jay Bochner, *An American Lens: Scenes from Alfred Stieglitz's New York Secession* (Cambridge, MA: MIT Press, 2005), p. 10.
8 See Malek Alloula, *The Colonial Harem* (Minneapolis, MN: University of Minnesota Press, 1986).
9 Michael Lesy, *Dreamland: America at the Dawn of the Twentieth Century* (New York: New Press, 1997), pp. xi–xii.
10 H. Roger Grant, *Railroad Postcards in the Age of Steam* (Iowa City, IA: University of Iowa Press, 1994), p. 4.
11 J. Wells Champney, "Fifty Years of Photography," *Harper's New Monthly Magazine*, vol. 79, no. 471 (August 1889), p. 366.
12 Emile Zola, *Le Roman expérimental* (Paris: Bernouard, 1982), p. 52.
13 Peter Henry Emerson, "Photography: A Pictorial Art," in *Amateur Photographer*, no. 3 (March 19, 1886), p. 138.
14 Peter Henry Emerson, *Naturalistic Photography for Students of the Art*, 1st ed. (1889; rpt. New York: Arno Press, 1972), p. 21, and Peter Henry Emerson, "Photography: A Pictorial Art," p. 138.
15 Peter Henry Emerson, "Photography: A Pictorial Art," p. 139.
16 J. C. Strauss, quoted in Christian A. Peterson, "The Photograph Beautiful, 1895–1915," *History of Photography*, vol. 16, no. 3 (Autumn 1992), p. 192.
17 Charles H. Caffin, *Photography as a Fine Art* (New York: Doubleday, Page & Co., 1901), pp. vii, 24.
18 For James Craig Annan, I am indebted to the essay "James Craig Annan: Brave Days in Glasgow," by William Buchanan, in *The Golden Age of British Photography*, 1839–1900, ed. Mark Haworth-Booth (Millerton, NY: Aperture, 1984), pp. 170–73.
19 Frederick H. Evans, "Opening Address," *Photographic Journal*, vol. 59 (April 30, 1900), p. 238.
20 Sadakichi Hartmann, "A Plea for Straight Photography," reproduced in Beaumont Newhall, *Photography: Essays and Images* (New York: Museum of Modern Art, 1980), pp. 185–88.
21 *Photo-Secession*, no. 1 (December, 1902), quoted in William Innes Homer, *Alfred Stieglitz and the Photo-*

Secession (Boston, MA: Little, Brown, and Co., 1983), p. 56.
22 For information on the Pictorialist photographic societies, see William Innes Homer, *Alfred Stieglitz and the Photo-Secession* and Margaret Harker, *The Linked Ring: The Secession Movement in Photography in Britain* (London: Heinemann, 1979).
23 Alfred Stieglitz, "The Photo-Secession," reproduced in Beaumont Newhall, *Photography*, p. 167.
24 Richard Whelan, *Alfred Stieglitz: A Biography* (Boston, MA: Little, Brown, and Co., 1995), p. 236.
25 Quoted in Whelan, p. 224.
26 See Elizabeth Anne McCauley, "The Making of a Modernist Myth," in Elizabeth Anne McCauley and Jason Francisco, *The Steerage and Alfred Stieglitz* (Berkeley: University of California Press, 2012).
27 Robert A. Sobieszek, *The Art of Persuasion: A History of Advertising Photography* (New York: Harry N. Abrams, Inc., 1988), p. 22, and Douglas Collins, *The Story of Kodak* (New York: Harry N. Abrams, Inc., 1990), p. 157.
28 For Käsebier, I have relied on Barbara L. Michael's monograph *Gertrude Käsebier: The Photographer and Her Photographs* (New York: Harry N. Abrams, Inc, 1992).
29 See the discussions throughout Patricia Johnston, *Real Fantasies: Edward Steichen's Advertising Photography* (Berkeley, CA: University of California Press, 1997).
30 Christian A. Peterson, "The Photograph Beautiful 1895–1915," *History of Photography*, vol. 16, no. 3 (Autumn 1992), p. 199.
31 Charles L. Mitchell, *American Amateur Photographer*, vol. 12 (December 1900), p. 567, quoted in Keith F. Davis, *An American Century of Photography: From Dry-Plate to Digital*, p. 51.
32 Quoted in Malcolm Daniel, *Edgar Degas, Photographer* (New York: Metropolitan Museum of Art, 1998), p. 24.
33 For a description of Strindberg's photography, see Linda Haverty Rugg, *Picturing Ourselves: Photography and Autobiography* (Chicago, IL: University of Chicago Press, 1997), pp. 81–131.
34 *Bernard Shaw on Photography*, ed. Bill Jay and Margaret Moore (Salt Lake City, UT: Peregrine Smith Books, 1989), p. 90.
35 Robert Doty, *Photo-Secession: Stieglitz and the Fine-Art Movement in Photography* (New York: Dover Publications, Inc., 1978), p. 51.
36 Doty, p. 34.
37 Ulrich F. Keller, "The Myth of Art Photography: An Iconographic Analysis," *History of Photography*, vol. 9, no. 1 (January–March 1985), p. 10.
38 Ulrich F. Keller, "The Myth of Art Photography: A Sociological Analysis," *History of Photography*, vol. 8, no. 4 (October–December 1984), p. 253.
39 Keller, p. 260.
40 Alfred Stieglitz, "Pictorial Photography," *Scribner's*, vol. 26, no. 5 (November 1899), p. 528.
41 Paul Strand, "Photography," *Seven Arts*, 2 (August 1917), p. 524.
42 Alfred Stieglitz, "Our Illustrations," *Camera Work*, no. 49/50 (June 1917), p. 36.
43 Paul Strand, "Photography," p. 524.
44 Strand, p. 524.

Chapter Seven
Modern Life

1 See the discussion in James R. Ryan, *Picturing Empire: Photography and the Visualization of the British Empire*, pp. 131–35.
2 Peter Bacon Hales, *Silver Cities: The Photography of American Urbanization, 1839–1915* (Philadelphia, PA: Temple University Press, 1983), pp. 243–60. I am indebted to Hales for his discussion of photography and urban reform.

3 Jacob Riis, "Flashes from the Slums: Pictures Taken in Dark Places by the Lightning Process," *Sun* [New York] (February 12, 1888), reprinted in Beaumont Newhall, ed., *Essays and Images*, p. 156.
4 For an insightful critique of Riis, see Sally Stein, "Making Connections with the Camera: Photography and Social Mobility in the Career of Jacob Riis," *Afterimage*, vol. 10, no. 10 (May 1983), pp. 9–16.
5 Quoted in *Photo Story: Selected Letters and Photographs of Lewis W. Hine*, ed. Daile Kaplan (Washington, D.C.: Smithsonian Institution Press, 1992), p. xxvii.
6 *Photo Story*, p. xxv.
7 Daile Kaplan, "'The Fetish of Having a Unified Thread': Lewis W. Hine's Reaction to the Use of the Photo Story in Life Magazine," *Exposure*, vol. 27, no. 2 (1989), p. 10.
8 Larry Peterson, "Producing Visual Traditions among Workers: The Uses of Photography at Pullman, 1880–1980," *Afterimage*, vol. 13, no. 2 (Spring 1992), p. 7.
9 Peterson, p. 5.
10 Wolfgang Ruppert, "Images of the Kaiserreich: the Social and Political Import of Photographs," in *German Photography, 1870–1970: Power of a Medium*, ed. Klaus Honnef, Rolf Sachsse, and Karin Thomas (Cologne: DuMont Buchverlad, 1997), p. 25.
11 Kevin Boyle and Victoria Getis, *Muddy Books and Ragged Aprons: Images of Working-Class Detroit, 1900–1930* (Detroit, MI: Wayne State University Press, 1997), p. 40.
12 David E. Nye, *Image Worlds: Corporate Identities at General Electric, 1890–1930* (Cambridge, MA: MIT Press, 1985), p. 81.
13 Peter Bacon Hales, *Silver Cities*, pp. 138–39.
14 Hales, p. 143.
15 Quoted in Melissa Banta and Curtis M. Hinsley, *From Site to Sight: Anthropology, Photography, and the Power of Imagery* (Cambridge, MA: Peabody Museum Press, 1986), p. 61.
16 Linda Dalrymple Henderson's article "X Rays and the Quest for Invisible Reality in the Art of Kupka, Duchamp, and the Cubists," *Art Journal*, 47 (Winter 1988), p. 331, and Marta Braun, *Picturing Time: The Work of Etienne-Jules Marey (1830–1904)* (Chicago, IL: University of Chicago Press, 1992), p. 291.
17 Quoted in Marta Braun, *Picturing Time*, p. 296.
18 Quoted in Elizabeth Johns, "An Avowal of Artistic Community: Nudity and Fantasy in Thomas Eakins's Photographs," in *Eakins and the Photograph* (Washington, D.C.: Smithsonian Institution Press, for the Pennsylvania Academy of Fine Art, 1994), p. 84.
19 Marta Braun, "The Expanding Present: Photographing Movement," in *Beauty of Another Order*, ed. Ann Thomas, p. 172.
20 Marta Braun, *Picturing Time*, pp. 237–38.
21 For a discussion of the Gilbreths' work in the context of scientific management, see Martha Banta, *Taylored Lives: Narrative Productions in the Age of Taylor, Veblen, and Ford* (Chicago, IL: University of Chicago Press, 1992), pp. 160–61.
22 Michael O'Malley, *Keeping Watch: A History of American Time* (Washington, D.C.: Smithsonian Institution Press, 1996), p. 233.
23 Peter E. Palmquist, *Elizabeth Fleischmann: Pioneer X-Ray Photographer* (Berkeley, CA: Judah L. Magnes Museum, 1990), and Bettyann Holtzmann Kevles, *Naked to the Bone: Medical Imaging in the Twentieth Century* (Reading, MA: Addison-Wesley, 1998), p. 125.
24 Joseph J. Corn, ed., *Imagining Tomorrow: History, Technology, and the American Future* (Cambridge, MA: MIT Press, 1986), p. 14.
25 The importance of the notion of a fourth dimension is exhaustively presented in Linda Dalrymple Henderson's *The Fourth Dimension and Non-Euclidean Geometry in Modern Art* (Princeton, NJ: Princeton University Press, 1983).
26 Giovanni Lista, "Futurist Photography," *Art Journal*, vol. 41, no. 4 (Winter 1981), p. 358.
27 Bettyann Holtzmann Kevles, *Naked to the Bone*, p. 53. My discussion of the X-ray owes to Kevles's

research and writing as well as to Linda Dalrymple Henderson's article "X Rays and the Quest for Invisible Reality in the Art of Kupka, Duchamp, and the Cubists," *Art Journal*, 47 (Winter 1988), pp. 323–40, and her "Francis Picabia, Radiometers, and X-Rays in 1913," *Art Bulletin*, vol. 71, no. 1 (March 1989), pp. 114–23.

28 Umberto Boccioni, "Futurist Painting: Technical Manifesto," quoted in Stephen Kern, *The Culture of Time and Space, 1880–1918* (Cambridge, MA: Harvard University Press, 1983), p. 185.

29 Cosmo Burton, "The Whole Duty of the Photographer," *British Journal of Photography*, vol. 36 (1889), p. 668 [emphases Burton].

30 E. F. im Thurn, "Anthropological Uses of the Camera," *Journal of the Anthropological Institute*, vol. 22 (1893), p. 184.

31 John Thomson, "Exploring with the Camera," *British Journal of Photography*, vol. 32 (1885), p. 373, quoted in James R. Ryan, *Picturing Empire: Photography and the Visualization of the British Empire* (Chicago, IL: University of Chicago Press, 1997), p. 43.

32 Quoted in James R. Ryan, *Picturing Empire*, p. 31.

33 For an extensive discussion of these photographs, see Ryan, *Picturing Empire*, pp. 30–44.

34 The saga of Stanley, Livingstone, and the images their encounter generated can be found in Joanna Skipworth and John M. MacKenzie, eds., *David Livingstone and the Victorian Encounter with Africa* (London: National Portrait Gallery, 1996). For Kalulu, see pp. 132–33.

35 Nicholas Monti, *Africa Then: Photographs, 1840–1918* (New York: Alfred A. Knopf, 1987), p. 9.

36 For a discussion of the importation of European ways in Africa, see Terence Ranger, "The Invention of Tradition in Colonial Africa," in *The Invention of Tradition*, ed. Eric Hobsbawm and Terence Ranger (New York: Cambridge University Press, 1983), pp. 211–62.

37 See Anne Baldassari, *Picasso and Photography* (Paris: Flammarion, 1997). Fortier is discussed throughout *Delivering Views: Distant Cultures in Early Postcards*, ed. Christraud M. Geary and Virginia-Lee Webb (Washington, D.C.: Smithsonian Institution Press, 1998).

38 Quoted in Nicholas Monti, *Africa Then: Photographs, 1840–1918*, p. 10.

39 Jorge Lewinski, *The Camera at War* (New York: Simon and Schuster, 1978), p. 56.

40 Quoted in Catherine A. Lutz and Jane L. Collins, *Reading the National Geographic* (Chicago, IL: University of Chicago Press, 1993), pp. 26–27. I have used this account to describe the Society's founding.

41 Quoted in Alison Devine Nordström, "Photography of Samoa: Production, Dissemination, and Use," in *Picturing Paradise: Colonial Photography of Samoa, 1875–1925* (Daytona Beach, FL: Southeast Museum of Photography, 1996), p. 14. I am indebted to this work for information on Samoan photography.

42 Alison Devine Nordström, "Photography of Samoa," p. 15. Eleanor M. Hight, "Japan as Artefact and Archive: Nineteenth-Century Photographic Collections in Boston," *History of Photography*, vol. 28, no. 2 (Summer 2004), p. 112.

43 For a discussion of tattoos and exotic Pacific island life, see Harriet Guest, "The Great Distinction: Figures of the Exotic in the Work of William Hodges," in *New Feminist Discourses*, ed. Isobel Armstrong (London: Routledge, 1992), pp. 296–341.

44 Allan Sekula, "The Body and the Archive," in *The Contest of Meaning*, ed. Richard Bolton (Cambridge, MA: MIT Press, 1989), p. 351. For more information on the use of photography in police work, see Sandra S. Phillips, Mark Haworth-Booth, and Carol Squiers, *Police Pictures: The Photograph as Evidence* (San Francisco, CA: San Francisco Museum of Modern Art and Chronicle Books, 1997).

45 Eugene S. Talbot, *Degeneracy: Its Causes, Signs, and Results* (London: Walter Scott, 1901), p. 18.

46 For a history of fingerprinting, see the inventor William J. Hershel's *The Origin of Finger-Printing by Sir William J. Hershel* (1916, rpt. New York: AMS Press, 1974).

47 My discussion of Clara Sheldon Smith owes to the research and writing of photographer Arne Svenson in his book *Prisoners* (New York: Blast Books, 1997).

48 Francis Galton, "Eugenics: Its Definition, Scope, and Aims," *American Journal of Sociology*, vol. 10, no. 1 (July 1904), p. 1.

49 Galton, p. 3.

50 Francis Galton, "Photographic Chronicles from Childhood to Age," *Fortnightly Review* (new series; vol. 31, January 1–June 1, 1882), p. 26.

51 Francis Galton, *Inquiries into Human Faculty and Its Development* (1883, 2nd ed. London and New York: Dent & Dutton, 1907), pp. 6, 222.

52 Susan D. Moeller, *Shooting War: Photography and the American Experience of Combat* (New York: Basic Books, 1989), p. 25. My discussion of the Spanish–American War owes to her analysis.

53 Margarett Loke, ed., *The World as it Was*, pp. 15–16.

54 Quoted in Lewis L. Gould and Richard Greffe, *Photojournalist: The Career of Jimmy Hare* (Austin, TX: University of Texas Press, 1977), p. 75. I have relied on this work for information on Jimmy Hare.

55 Gould and Greffe, p. 33.

56 For this dimension of the war, and for information on the British homefront, see John Taylor, *War Photography: Realism in the British Press* (London: Routledge, 1991), p. 20.

57 Peter Robertson, "Canadian Photojournalism during the First World War," *History of Photography*, pp. 39, 42–43.

58 Quoted in Bernd Weise, "Photojournalism from the First World War to the Weimar Republic," in *German Photography, 1870–1970: Power of a Medium*, ed. Klaus Honnef, Rolf Sachsse, and Karin Thomas (Cologne: DuMont Buchverlag, 1997), p. 54.

59 Nevertheless, photographs of World War I corpses were made, both by professional photographers and by amateurs with small cameras. Generally, they would not be shown until after the war.

60 Allyson Booth, *Postcards from the Trenches: Negotiating the Space Betweeen Modernism and the First World War* (New York: Oxford University Press, 1996), p. 21.

61 Quoted in Jane Carmichael, *First World War Photographers* (London: Routledge, 1989), pp. 34–35. I rely on Carmichael for her account of photography during the war.

62 The story of Canadian photographer Ivor Castle's fabricated "over the top" photographs is told in Michael L. Carlebach, *American Photojournalism Comes of Age* (Washington, D.C.: Smithsonian Institution Press, 1997), p. 91, and Peter Robertson, "Canadian Photojournalism during the First World War," *History of Photography*, vol. 2, no. 1 (January 1978), p. 44. Castle was not the only photographer to fake war photographs. Jean-Baptiste Tournassou, Chief of the Photography and Cinematography Organization for the French Army, also staged photographs of soldiers.

63 Bernd Weise, "Photojournalism from the First World War to the Weimar Republic," p. 53.

64 "The Real Thing," in *The Short Stories of Henry James*, ed. Clifton Fadiman (New York: Modern Library, n.d. c.1945.), p. 196.

65 Thomas Thurston, "Hearsay of the Sun: Photography, Identity and the Law of Evidence in Nineteenth-Century American Courts" [http://chnm. gmu.aq/photos/essay/intro.htm] (February 1, 1999).

66 Lewis Hine, "How the Camera May Help in Social Uplift," quoted in Maren Stange, *Symbols of Ideal Life: Social Documentary Photography in America, 1890–1950* (New York: Cambridge University Press, 1989), p. 86.

67 James Lawrence Breese, "The Relations of Photography to Art," *Cosmopolitan*, vol. 18, no. 2 (December 1894), p. 140.

68 Lewis Hine, "How the Camera May Help in Social Uplift," quoted in George Dimock, "Children of the Mills: Rereading Lewis Hine's Child-Labour Photographs," *Oxford Art Journal*, vol. 16, no. 2 (1993), p. 39.

Part Four
A New Vision (1918–1945)

1 Richard Guy Wilson, "America and the Machine Age," in *The Machine Age in America, 1918–1941*, ed. Richard Guy Wilson (Brooklyn, NY: Brooklyn Museum, 1986), p. 26.

2 Forrest McDonald, *The American Presidency: An Intellectual History* (Lawrence, KS: University of Kansas Press, 1994), pp. 441–42.

Chapter Eight
Art and the Age of Mass Media

1 Percy Wyndham Lewis, "The Children of the New Epoch," *The Tyro*, no. 1, 1921, p. 3.

2 Colin Osman and Sandra S. Phillips, "European Visions: Magazine Photography in Europe between the Wars," in Marianne Fulton, *Eyes of Time: Photojournalism in America* (Boston, MA: New York Graphic Society/Little, Brown and Company, 1988), p. 76. The word *Illustrirte* in *Berliner Illustrirte Zeitung* was idiosyncratically spelled. More correctly, it would have been *Illustrierte*.

3 Willi Münzenberg's life and career are discussed in Helmut Gruber's "Willi Münzenberg's German Communist Propaganda Empire, 1921–1933," *Journal of Modern History*, vol. 38, no. 3 (September 1966), pp. 278–97.

4 Colin Osman and Sandra S. Phillips, "European Visions," p. 76.

5 Osman and Phillips, p. 78.

6 Michael L. Carlebach, *American Photojournalism Comes of Age* (Washington, D.C.: Smithsonian Institution Press, 1997), p. 145.

7 Kurt Schwitters, translated and quoted in Maud Lavin, "Advertising Utopia: Schwitters as Commercial Designer," *Art in America* (October 1985), p. 137.

8 Edlef Köppen, "The Magazine as a Sign of the Times," in *The Weimar Republic Sourcebook*, ed. Anton Kaes, Martin Jay, and Edward Dimendberg, p. 644.

9 Vachel Lindsay, *The Art of the Moving Picture* (1916; 1922; New York: BiblioBazaar, 2006), p. 26.

10 Christopher Phillips, "Resurrecting Vision: European Photography between the World Wars," in *The New Vision: Photography between the World Wars* (New York: Metropolitan Museum of Art, 1989), p. 73. I am indebted to Phillips for my understanding of this period.

11 Hannes Meyer, "The New World," in *The Weimar Republic Sourcebook*, ed. Anton Kaes, Martin Jay, and Edward Dimendberg, pp. 445–46.

12 Quoted in Peter Galassi, "Rodchenko and Photography's Revolution," in Magdalena Dabrowski, Leah Dickerman, and Peter Galassi, *Alexsandr Rodchenko* (New York: Museum of Modern Art, 1998), p. 104.

13 See the extended discussion in Margarita Tupitsyn, *El Lissitzky: Beyond the Abstract Cabinet* (New Haven, CT: Yale University Press, 1999), pp. 20–21.

14 Quoted in Margarita Tupitsyn, *The Soviet Photograph, 1924–1937* (New Haven, CT: Yale University Press, 1966), p. 11.

15 Quoted in Christopher Phillips, "Resurrecting Vision," p. 84.

16 For a discussion of the history of the idea of "making strange," see Simon Watney, "Making Strange: The Shattered Mirror," in *Thinking Photography*, ed. Victor

Burgin (London: Macmillan, 1982), pp. 154–76.

17 Tristan Tzara, "Dada Manifesto 1918," in *Art in Theory, 1900–1990: An Anthology of Changing Ideas* (Oxford: Blackwell, 1992), p. 252.

18 Richard Hülsenbeck, "First German Dada Manifesto," in *Art in Theory, 1900–1990: An Anthology of Changing Ideas* (Oxford: Blackwell, 1992), p. 253.

19 The most comprehensive book on women photographers in Germany and their connection to the New Woman motif has yet to be translated into English. See *Fotografieren Hiess Teilnehman: Photografinnen der Weimarer Republik*, ed. Ute Eskilden (Düsseldorf: Richter Verlag, 1994).

20 See Maud Lavin, "Representing the New Woman," *Cut with a Kitchen Knife: The Weimar Photomontages of Hannah Höch* (New Haven, CT: Yale University Press, 1993), pp. 1–12.

21 Dawn Adès, *Photomontage* (London: Thames and Hudson, rev. ed., 1986), p. 28.

22 László Moholy-Nagy, "Unprecedented Photography," in *Photography in the Modern Era: European Documents and Critical Writings, 1913–1940*, ed. Christopher Phillips (New York: Metropolitan Museum of Art/Aperture, 1989), p. 84.

23 Quoted in Ades, *Photomontage*, p.12.

24 Moholy-Nagy, "Unprecedented Photography," p. 85.

25 László Moholy-Nagy, "Photography in Advertising," in *Photography in the Modern Era*, ed. Christopher Phillips, p. 90.

26 Johannes Molzahn, "Stop Reading! Look!" in *The Weimar Republic Sourcebook*, ed. Anton Kaes, Martin Jay, and Edward Dimendberg, p. 648.

27 Quoted in Kim Sichel, *Germaine Krull: Photographer of Modernity* (Cambridge, MA: MIT Press, 1999), p. 77. I am indebted to Sichel for my understanding of Krull.

28 "Les intellectuels allemands ne peuvent pas faire caca ni pipi sans des idéologies." Quoted in Dawn Adès, *Photomontage*, p. 114.

29 Adès, p. 115.

30 Francis Naumann, "The New York Dada Movement: Better Late than Never," *Arts* (February 1980), p. 143.

31 Maria Morris Hambourg, "From 291 to the Museum of Modern Art: Photography in New York, 1910–37," in Maria Morris Hambourg and Christopher Phillips, *The New Vision: Photography Between the World Wars*, pp. 15–16.

32 Quoted in Theodore E. Stebbins, Jr. and Norman Keyes, Jr., *Charles Sheeler: The Photographs* (Boston, MA: Museum of Fine Arts, 1987), p. 17.

33 Stebbins and Keyes, p. 25.

34 Stebbins and Keyes, p. 27.

35 See Sue Taylor, *Hans Bellmer: The Anatomy of Anxiety* (Cambridge, MA: MIT Press, 2000), and Therese Lichtenstein, *Behind Closed Doors: The Art of Hans Bellmer* (Berkeley, CA: University of California Press, 2001).

36 Kim Sichel, *Germaine Krull: Photographer of Modernity*, p. 106.

37 Quoted in Peter Galassi, *Henri Cartier-Bresson: The Early Work*, p. 39.

38 Henri Cartier-Bresson, *The Decisive Moment* (New York: Simon & Schuster, 1952), n.p.

39 Michael R. Taylor, "New York" in *Dada: Zurich, Berline, Hannover, Cologne*, Paris, ed. Leah Dickerman (Washington, D.C.: National Gallery of Art, 2006), p. 293.

40 Quoted in Victor Margolin, *The Struggle for Utopia: Rodchenko, Lissitzky, Moholy-Nagy, 1917–1946* (Chicago, IL: University of Chicago Press, 1997), p. 113.

41 Eleanor M. Hight, *Picturing Modernism: Moholy-Nagy and Photography in Weimar Germany*, p. 209.

42 Willi Warstat, "Photography in Advertising," in *The Weimar Republic Sourcebook*, ed. Anton Kaes, Martin Jay, and Edward Dimendberg, p. 651.

43 Dziga Vertov, "The Council of Three," in *Kino-Eye: the Writings of Dziga Vertov*, ed. Annette Michelson, trans. Kevin O'Brien (Berkeley, CA: University of California Press, 1984), p. 17.

44 James Curtis, *Mind's Eye, Mind's Truth: FSA Photography Reconsidered* (Philadelphia, PA: Temple University Press, 1989), pp. 77–78.

45 *August Sander: Citizens of the Twentieth Century*, ed. Gunther Sander, text Ulrich Keller, trans. Linda Keller (Cambridge, MA: MIT Press, 1986), pp. 8–9. I am indebted to this publication for my analysis of Sander.

46 *August Sander*, p. 19.

47 Eleanor M. Hight, *Picturing Modernism*, p. 203.

48 Karel Teige, "The Tasks of Modern Photography," in *Photography in the Modern Era*, p. 319.

49 Teige, pp. 318, 319. Teige's art and his theoretical writings are reviewed in Eric Dluhosch and Rostislav Suácha, *Karel Teige, 1900–1951: L'enfant terrible of the Czech Modernist Avant-Garde* (Cambridge, MA: MIT Press, 1999).

50 Walter Benjamin, "A Small History of Photography," in his *One-Way Street and Other Writings*, trans. Edmund Jephcott and Kingsley Shorter (London: NLB, 1979), p. 255.

51 Benjamin, p. 254.

52 Quoted in Melissa A. McEuen, *Seeing America: Women Photographers between the Wars* (Lexington, KY: University Press of Kentucky, 2000), p. 37.

53 Margarita Tupitsyn, *El Lissitzsky: Beyond the Abstract Cabinet*, p. 61.

54 See Christopher Phillips, "Resurrecting Vision," p. 95, and Benjamin H. D. Buchloh, "From Faktura to Factography," in *The Contest of Meaning: Critical Histories of Photography*, ed. Richard Bolton (Cambridge, MA: MIT Press, 1989), pp. 76–77.

55 Raoul Hausmann, "Photomontage," in *The Weimar Republic Sourcebook*, ed. Anton Kaes, Martin Jay, and Edward Dimendberg, p. 652.

56 Robert A. Sobieszek, *The Art of Persuasion: A History of Advertising Photography* (New York: Harry N. Abrams, Inc., 1988), p. 66.

57 Quoted in Therese Thau Heyman, "Modernist Photography and the Group f.64," in *On the Edge of America: California Modernist Art, 1900–1950*, ed. Paul J. Karlstrom (Berkeley, CA: University of California Press, 1996), p. 252.

58 Heyman, p. 256.

59 Quoted in Michel Oren, "On the 'Impurity' of Group f/64 Photography," *History of Photography*, vol. 15, no. 2 (Summer 1991), p. 122.

60 Weston's statement for the "Film und Foto" exhibition, quoted in David Travis, "Ephemeral Truths," in Sarah Greenough, Joel Snyder, David Travis, and Colin Westerbeck, *On the Art of Fixing a Shadow: One Hundred and Fifty Years of Photography* (Washington, D.C.: National Gallery of Art, 1989), p. 243.

61 Leah Ollman, "The Worker Photography Movement: Camera as Weapon," in *Multiple Views: Logan Grant Essays on Photography, 1983–89*, ed. Daniel P. Younger (Albuquerque, NM: University of New Mexico Press, 1991), p. 235.

Chapter Nine
Documentary Expression and Popular Photography

1 William Stott, *Documentary Expression and Thirties America* (New York: Oxford University Press, 1973), pp. 80–81.

2 See the extensive discussions of these media throughout William Stott, *Documentary Expression and Thirties America*.

3 John Grierson, "First Principles of Documentary" (1934–36), in *Imagining Reality: The Faber Book of Documentary*, ed. Kevin Macdonald and Mark Cousins (London: Faber and Faber, 1996), p. 101.

4 John Grierson, "The Documentary Idea: 1942," in *Grierson on Documentary*, ed. Forsyth Hardy (Berkeley, CA: University of California Press, 1966), p. 249.

5 Adams was addressing Roy Stryker, head of the Farm Security Section that produced photographs. See Roy E. Stryker and Nancy Wood, *In This Proud Land: America 1935–1943 as Seen in the FSA Photographs* (Greenwich, CT: New York Graphic Society, 1973), p. 8.

6 See Leah Bendavid-Val, *Propaganda and Dreams: Photographing the 1930s in the USSR and US* (New York: Edition Stemle, 1999).

7 William Stott, *Documentary Expression and Thirties America*, p. 26.

8 Maren Stange, "'The Record Itself': Farm Security Photography and the Transformation of Rural Life," in Pete Daniel, Merry A. Foresta, *Maren Stange, and Sally Stein, Official Images: New Deal Photography* (Washington, D.C.: Smithsonian Institution Press, 1987), p. 1.

9 Maren Stange, *Symbols of Ideal Life: Social Documentary Photography in America, 1890–1950* (New York: Cambridge University Press, 1989), p. 111.

10 Quoted in Lawrence W. Levine, "The Historian and the Icon: Photography and the History of the American People in the 1930s and 1940s," in *Documenting America, 1935–1943*, ed. Carl Fleishhauer and Beverly W. Brannan (Berkeley, CA: University of California Press, 1988), p. 39.

11 See Keith F. Davis's discussion in his *An American Century of Photography: From Dry-Plate to Digital*, 2nd, rev. ed. (Kansas City, MO, and New York: Hallmark Cards, Inc., in association with Harry N. Abrams, Inc., 1999), p. 165.

12 Quoted in Maria Morris Hambourg, "A Portrait of the Artist," in Maria Morris Hambourg, Jeff L. Rosenheim, Douglas Eklund, and Mia Fineman, *Walker Evans* (New York: Metropolitan Museum of Art, 2000), pp. 21–22.

13 Quoted in Belinda Rathbone, *Walker Evans: A Biography* (New York: Houghton Mifflin, 1995), p. 70. The original appeared in a book review by Evans titled "The Reappearance of Photography," in *Hound and Horn*, vol. 5, no. 1 (October–December 1931), p. 127.

14 Maria Morris Hambourg, "A Portrait of the Artist," in Maria Morris Hambourg et al., *Walker Evans*, p. 9.

15 James Agee and Walker Evans, *Let Us Now Praise Famous Men* (1941, rpt.; Boston, MA: Houghton Mifflin Co., 1988), p. xlvii.

16 Quoted in Sally Stein, "Peculiar Grace: Dorothea Lange and the Testimony of the Body," in *Dorothea Lange: A Visual Life*, ed. Elizabeth Partridge (Washington, D.C.: Smithsonian Institution Press, 1994), p. 59.

17 James Curtis, *Mind's Eye, Mind's Truth: FSA Photography Reconsidered*, pp. 75–76.

18 Jefferson Hunter, *Image and Word: The Interaction of Twentieth-Century Photographs and Texts* (Cambridge, MA: Harvard University Press, 1987), p. 97.

19 Keith F. Davis's discussion in his *An American Century of Photography*, p. 165.

20 Quoted in Vicki Goldberg, *Margaret Bourke-White: A Biography* (New York: Harper & Row, 1986), p. 115.

21 For new information on Bubley, see Bonnie Yochelson, *Esther Bubley on Assignment* (New York: Aperture, 2005).

22 *Documenting America*, 1935–1943, ed. Fleishhauer and Brannan; essays by Lawrence W. Levine and Alan Trachtenberg, p. 314.

23 Jefferson Hunter, *Image and Word*, pp. 14–15. In *Documentary Expression and Thirties America*, William Stott voices much the same opinion.

24 Deborah Frizzell, *Humphrey Spender's Humanist Landscapes: Photo-Documents, 1932–1942* (New Haven, CT: Yale Center for British Art, 1997), p. 24.

25 See Leah Ollman, "The Worker Photography Movement: Camera as Weapon," in *Multiple Views: Logan Grant Essays on Photography*, 1983–89, p. 226. Most articles on worker photography have not been translated from German.

26 Erika Wolf, "The Soviet Union: From Worker to Proletarian Photography," in *The Worker Photography Movement [1926–1939]: Essays and Documents* (Madrid: Museo Nacional Centro de Arte Reina Sofía,

2011), p. 36.

27 Erika Wolf, pp. 42–43

28 Leah Ollman, "The Worker Photography Movement," pp. 230–31.

29 See the discussion in Ute Eskilden, "The A-I-Z and the Arbeiter Fotograf: Working Class Photographers in Weimar," *Image*, vol. 23, no. 2 (December 1980), p. 7.

30 See Terry Dennett, "The British Film and Photo League," in *Creative Camera*, nos. 197–98 (May/June 1981), p. 91. The entire issue is devoted to worker photography. Also see Hanno Hardt and Karin B. Ohrn, "The Eyes of the Proletariat: The Worker-Photography Movement in Weimar Germany," *Studies in Visual Communications*, vol. 7, no. 3 (Summer 1981), pp. 46–57.

31 Leah Ollman, "The Worker Photography Movement," p. 233.

32 See the discussion throughout Maud Lavin, "Montage, Mass Culture, and Modernity: Utopianism in the Circle of New Advertising Designers," in Matthew Teitelbaum, ed., *Montage and Modern Life, 1919–1942* (Cambridge, MA: MIT Press, 1992), pp. 37–59.

33 Erik Barnouw, *Documentary: A History of the Non-Fiction Film* (New York: Oxford University Press, 2nd rev. ed., 1993), pp. 111–12.

34 For information on the Photo League, see Anne Tucker, "A History of the Photo League: The Members Speak," *History of Photography*, vol. 18, no. 2 (Summer 1994), pp. 174–84. Also see her "Aaron Siskind and the Photo League: A Partial History," *Afterimage*, vol. 9, no. 10 (May 1982), pp. 4–5.

35 See Mason Klein and Caroline Evans, *The Radical Camera: New York's Photo League, 1936–1951* (New Haven: Yale University Press, 2011). The Photo League was harassed by the F.B.I. for seven years, beginning in 1940; it finally disbanded in 1951, after its listing as a subversive communist front organization in 1947 made it difficult to continue.

36 Ute Eskilden, "Innovative Photography in Germany Between the Wars," in *Avant-Garde Photography in Germany, 1919–1939* (San Francisco, CA: San Francisco Museum of Modern Art, 1980), p. 35.

37 Ann Thomas, "The Search for Pattern," in *Beauty of Another Order: Photography in Science*, ed. Ann Thomas (New Haven, CT: Yale University Press, 1997), p. 110.

38 Peter Reichel, "Images of the National Socialist State," in Klaus Honnef, Rolf Sachsse, and Karen Thomas, eds., *German Photography, 1870–1970: Power of a Medium* (Cologne: DuMont Buchverlag, 1997), p. 72.

39 Quoted in Rolf Sachsse, "Photography as NS State Design Power's Abuse of a Medium," in *German Photography, 1870–1970*, p. 92.

40 Phillip Knightley, *The First Casualty: From the Crimea to Vietnam—The War Correspondent as Hero, Propagandist, and Myth Maker* (New York: Harcourt Brace Jovanovich, 1975), pp. 220–21.

41 Phillip Knightley, *The First Casualty*, pp. 210–12. For a recent continuation of the story, see Caroline Brothers, *War and Photography: A Cultural History* (London: Routledge, 1997), pp. 179–81.

42 Susan Moeller, *Shooting War: Photography and the American Experience of Combat* (New York: Basic Books, 1989), p. 192.

43 Mary Anne Staniszewski, *The Power of Display: A History of Exhibition Installations at the Museum of Modern Art* (Cambridge, MA: MIT Press, 1998), p. 223.

44 Staniszewski, p. 215.

45 Staniszewski, p. 224.

46 See the discussion of the photograph in Vicki Goldberg, *The Power of Photography* (New York: Abbeville Press, 1993), pp. 142–47.

47 Walter Benjamin, "The Work of Art in the Age of Mechanical Reproduction," in *Walter Benjamin, Illuminations*, ed. Hannah Arendt (New York: Schocken Books, 1969), p. 223.

48 Maud Lavin, "Montage, Mass Culture, and Modernity: Utopianism in the Circle of New Advertising Designers," in Matthew Teitelbaum, ed., *Montage and Modern Life, 1919–1942*, p. 59.

Part Five

Through the Lens of Culture
(1945–1975)

Chapter Ten
The Human Family

1 William Manchester, *In Our Time: The World as Seen by Magnum Photographers* (New York: American Federation of Arts and W. W. Norton & Co., 1989), pp. 423, 430.

2 John G. Morris, *Remembrance of Henri Cartier-Bresson*, the September 2004 issue of *News Photographer*, the journal of the National Press Photographers Association. Online at http://www.nppa.org/news_and_events/news/2004/08/jgm_hcb01.html

3 Edward Steichen, *The Family of Man* (New York: Simon and Schuster, 1955), pp. 4–5.

4 Christopher Phillips, "The Judgment Seat of Photography," in Richard Bolton, *The Contest of Meaning: Critical Histories of Photography* (Cambridge, MA: MIT Press, 1989), p. 28.

5 Quoted in Aline B. Saarinen, "The Camera Versus the Artist," compiled in "The Controversial Family of Man," *Aperture*, no. 3 (1955), p. 11.

6 Jacob Deschin, "Panoramic Show at the Museum of Modern Art," compiled in "The Controversial Family of Man," *Aperture*, no. 3 (1955), p. 8.

7 Barbara Morgan, "The Theme Show: A Contemporary Exhibition Technique," compiled in "The Controversial Family of Man," *Aperture*, no. 3 (1955), p. 24.

8 Eric J. Sandeen, *Picturing an Exhibition: The Family of Man and 1950s America* (Albuquerque, NM: University of New Mexico Press, 1995), pp. 43–49. I am indebted to Sandeen's writing for information on the exhibit.

9 Phoebe Lou Adams, "Through a Lens Darkly," *Atlantic Monthly*, no. 195 (April 1955), p. 72.

10 The Universal Declaration of Human Rights is available on the United Nations website. See http://www.un.org/Overview/rights.html

11 Eric J. Sandeen, *Picturing an Exhibition*, p. 27.

12 Melville J. Herskovits, *Cultural Relativism: Perspectives in Cultural Pluralism*, ed. Frances Herskovits (New York: Random House, 1972), p. 8.

13 For the history of the Che Guevera photograph, see Fernando Castro, "Crossover Dreams: Remarks on Contemporary Latin American Photography," in Wendy Watriss and Lois Parkinson Zamora, *Image and Memory: Photography from Latin America, 1866–1994* (Austin, TX: University of Texas Press, 1998), pp. 57–61, and Vicki Goldberg, *The Power of Photography* (New York: Abbeville, 1991), pp. 156–61.

14 The now-classic study is Eva Cockcroft, "Abstract Expressionism, Weapon of the Cold War," *Pollock and After: The Critical Debate*, ed. Francis Frascina (New York: Harper and Row, 1985), pp. 125–32.

15 Fernando Castro, "Crossover Dreams: Remarks on Contemporary Latin American Photography," in Wendy Watriss and Lois Parkinson Zamora, *Image and Memory*, p. 61. Castro's article is one of the few in English to recount the relationship of politics and photography in Latin America.

16 John Mraz, "Cuban Photography: Context and Meaning," *History of Photography*, vol. 18, no. 1 (Spring 1994), p. 88.

17 For the late survival of itinerant photography in Latin America see Ann Parker and Avon Neal, *Los Ambulantes: The Itinerant Photographers of Guatemala* (Cambridge, MA: MIT Press, 1982).

18 Raquel Tibol, [no title], in *Hecho en Latinoamérica* (Mexico City: Consejo Mexicano de Fotografía, 1978), p. 25.

19 Tibol, p. 28.

20 Maria Eugenia Haya (Marucha), "Photography in Latin America," *Aperture*, no. 109 (1987), pp. 68–69.

21 For a discussion of the work of Latin American

women making anthropological photographs, see Naomi Rosenblum, *A History of Women Photographers*, p. 196.

22 John Mraz, "Nacho Lopez, Photojournalist of the 1950s," *History of Photography*, vol. 20, no. 3 (Autumn 1996), p. 210.

23 Quoted in Olivier Debroise, *Mexican Suite: A History of Photography in Mexico*, trans. Stella de Sá Rego (Austin, TX: University of Texas, 2001), p. 197.

24 John Mraz, "Foto Hermanos Mayo: A Mexican Collective," *History of Photography*, vol. 17, no. 1 (Spring 1993), p. 88, n. 1.

25 The literature on Álvarez Bravo is replete with references to his Surrealism. An example is Charles Hagen's review of an exhibition: "A Mexican Master Surveys the Past," *New York Times* (Sunday, March 22, 1992), H37.

26 Paul Hill and Thomas Cooper, "Manuel Álvarez Bravo," in their *Dialogue with Photography* (New York: Farrar, Straus and Giroux: 1979), p. 231.

27 Hill and Cooper, p. 226.

28 Quoted in Jane Livingston, *Manuel Álvarez Bravo* (Boston, MA: David R. Godine, Publisher, 1978), p. ix.

29 Paul Hill and Thomas Cooper, "Manuel Álvarez Bravo," p. 233.

30 I am indebted to Nissan N. Perez for this interpretation, which appeared in "Visions of the Imaginary: Dreams of the Intangible," in *Revelaciones: The Art of Manuel Álvarez Bravo* (Albuquerque, NM: University of New Mexico Press, 1990), p. 18.

31 Heike Behrend, "A Short History of Photography in Kenya," in *Anthology of African and Indian Ocean Photography* (Paris: Review Noire, 1999), p. 161. I am indebted to this book and to *In/Sight: African Photographs, 1940 to the Present* (New York: Guggenheim Museum, 1996) for my understanding of African photography.

32 PMSL & JLP, [untitled section introduction] in *Anthology of African and Indian Ocean Photography* (Paris: Review Noire, 1999), p. 197.

33 Stephen F. Sprague, "Yoruba Photography: How the Yoruba See Themselves," *African Arts*, vol. 12, no. 1 (1978), pp. 52–59. I am indebted to this now classic article for my understanding of the subject.

34 G. Thomas, *History of Photography in India, 1840–1980* (N.P.: Anhandra Pradesh State Akademi of Photography, 1981), p. 45. A comprehensive history of photography in India, especially from the years immediately preceding Independence to the present, is sorely lacking.

35 Thomas, pp. 5, 49, 51.

36 For this discussion, I relied on the research and analyses by Christopher Pinney in his *Camera Indica: The Social Life of Indian Photographs* (Chicago, IL: University of Chicago Press, 1997).

37 Vinay Lal, "Reading between the Frames: Burden (and Freedom) of Photography," *Economic and Political Weekly*, vol. 35, no. 14 (April 1–7, 2000), p. 1170.

38 Yosuke Yamahata, *Nagasaki Journey: The Photographs of Yosuke Yamahata, August 10, 1945*, ed. Rupert Jenkins (San Francisco, CA: Pomegranate Artbooks, 1995), p. 19.

39 Quoted in Spencer R. Weart, *Nuclear Fear: A History of Images* (Cambridge, MA: Harvard University Press, 1988), p. 110.

40 I depended on the following sources for this discussion: Peter B. Hales, "The Atomic Sublime," *American Studies*, vol. 32 (Spring 1991), pp. 5–31; Vince Leo, "The Mushroom Cloud Photograph: From Fact to Symbol," *Afterimage*, vol. 13, nos. 1 and 2 (Summer 1985), pp. 6–12; and Spencer R. Weart's study, *Nuclear Fear*.

41 Mark Holborn, "Introduction," in *Eikoh Hosoe* (New York: Aperture, 1999), p. 5.

42 Shoji Yamagishi, "Introduction," in *New Japanese Photography*, ed. John Szarkowski and Shoju Yamagishi (New York: Museum of Modern Art, 1974), p. 11.

43 Mark Holborn, *Black Sun: The Eyes of Four—Roots and Innovation in Japanese Photography* (New York: Aperture, 1986), p. 10.

44 Holborn, p. 14.
45 Shomei Tomatsu, *Nagasaki, 11:02* (Tokyo: Shinchosa, 1995).
46 Edward Putzar, *Japanese Photography*, 1945–1985 (Tucson, AZ: Pacific West, Inc., 1987), p. 6.
47 For this and other aspects of the postwar Japanese experience, see John W. Dower, *Embracing Defeat: Japan in the Wake of World War II* (New York: W.W. Norton & Co./ New Press, 1999), p. 293.
48 Quoted in Fuminori Yokoe, "The Call of the Ocean of Memory," in Colin Westerbeck, *Yasuhiro Ishimoto: A Tale of Two Cities* (Chicago, IL: Art Institute of Chicago, 1999), p. 103.
49 Leo Rubinfien, "Investigations of a Dog," *Art in America* (October 1999), p. 134.
50 Rubinfien, p. 134.
51 Rubinfien, p. 135.
52 Rubinfien, p. 136.
53 Roland Barthes, "The Great Family of Man," in his *Mythologies*, trans. Annette Lavers (New York: Hill and Wang, 1972), pp. 100–01.

Chapter Eleven
The Cold War Era

1 Quoted in Helen Gee, *Photography of the Fifties: An American Perspective* (Tucson, AZ: Center for Creative Photography, 1983), p. 4.
2 Tom Engelhardt, *The End of Victory Culture: Cold War America and the Disillusioning of a Generation* (New York: Basic Books, 1995), p. 10.
3 David Riesman, with Nathan Glazer and Reuel Denny, *The Lonely Crowd: A Study of the Changing American Character* (abridged by the authors) (New York: Doubleday & Co., Inc., 1953).
4 Quoted in Lili Corbus Bezner, *Photography and Politics in America: From the New Deal into the Cold War* (Baltimore, MD: Johns Hopkins University Press, 1999), p. 14.
5 Aaron Siskind, "The Drama of Objects," in *Aaron Siskind, Pleasures and Terrors*, ed. Carl Chiarenza (Boston, MA: Little, Brown and Co., 1982), pp. 65–66.
6 See the discussion in Daniel Belgrad, *The Culture of Spontaneity: Improvisation and the Arts in Postwar America* (Chicago, IL: University of Chicago Press, 1998), pp. 49–56.
7 Sheryl Conkelton, "Seeing and Knowing the Order of Things," in *Frederick Sommer: Selected Texts and Bibliography*, ed. Sheryl Conkelton (New York: G. K. Hall & Co., 1995), p. 11.
8 Jerry Uelsmann, "Preface," *Photo Synthesis* (Gainesville, FL: University Press of Florida, 1992).
9 Quoted in Peter C. Bunnell, *Minor White: The Eye that Shapes* (Princeton, NJ: Art Museum, Princeton University, 1989), p. 17.
10 Quoted in Bunnell, *Minor White*, pp. 15–16.
11 Allan Sekula, "On the Invention of Photographic Meaning," in *Thinking Photography*, ed. Victor Burgin (London: Macmillan, 1982), p. 102.
12 Peter C. Mazio, "Introduction," *Robert Frank: New York to Nova Scotia* (Houston, TX: Museum of Fine Arts, 1986), p. 6.
13 Quoted in "History—His Story," in *The Pictures are a Necessity: Robert Frank in Rochester, NY, November 1988*. Occasional Papers no. 2, Rochester Film and Photo Consortium (Rochester, NY: University Educational Services at George Eastman House, 1989), p. 43.
14 Andy Grundberg, "Harry Callahan, Cool Master of the Commonplace, Dies at 86," *New York Times* (Thursday, March 18, 1999), B9.
15 Maren Stange, "'Illusion Complete within Itself': Roy DeCarava's Photography," *Yale Journal of Criticism*, vol. 9, no. 1 (1996), pp. 63–92.
16 Quoted in Keith F. Davis, *An American Century of Photography, From Dry-Plate to Digital* (Kansas City, MO, and New York: Hallmark Cards, Inc., in

association with Harry N. Abrams, Inc., 2nd, rev. ed., 1999), p. 288.
17 For a comparison of film noir and tabloid photography, see William Hannigan, *New York Noir: Crime Photos from the Daily News Archive* (New York: Rizzoli, 1999), especially pp. 20–22.
18 The textual source, if there is one, is not mentioned. See Jonathan Green, *American Photography: A Critical History 1945 to the Present*, p. 99.
19 Green, p. 106.
20 Bruce Davidson, *Bruce Davidson: Photographs* (New York: Agrinde/Summit Books, 1978), p. 10.
21 Jonathan Green, *American Photography*, p. 119.
22 Joseph Marshall, "The Moral Issue of a Pregnant Woman Shooting Up," *Photo Review*, vol. 16, no. 1 (Winter 1993), p. 5.
23 David Halberstam, [Introduction] in Bill Owens, *Suburbia*, ed. Robert Harshorn Shimshak (New York: Fotofolio, 1999), n.p. (p. 5).
24 Britt Salvesen, *New Topographics* (Göttingen: Steidl, 2010). Reprints the rare original text of the 1975 exhibition, and offers new insights in essays by Salvesen and Alison Nordström.
25 Jeffrey Kastner, "A Vision of Suburban Bliss Edged with Irony," *New York Times* (Sunday, March 19, 2000), AR36.
26 Quoted in Douglas Collins, *The Story of Kodak* (New York: Harry N. Abrams, Inc., 1990), p. 261.
27 Quoted in Maria Morris Hambourg, Jeff L. Rosenheim, Douglas Eklund, and Mia Fineman, *Walker Evans* (New York: Metropolitan Museum of Art, 2000), p. 137.
28 Quoted in Beaumont Newhall, *Supreme Instants: The Photography of Edward Weston* (Boston, MA: Little, Brown and Company, 1986), p. 43.
29 Douglas Collins, *The Story of Kodak*, p. 289.
30 For a full discussion of the impact of space photography, see Vicki Goldberg, *The Power of Photography*, pp. 52–57.
31 Marianne Fulton, "Changing Focus: The 1950s to the 1980s," in Marianne Fulton, *Eyes of Time: Photojournalism in America* (Boston, MA: Little, Brown and Company, 1988), p. 217.
32 David Robbins, *The Independent Group: Postwar Britain and the Aesthetics of Plenty* (Cambridge, MA: MIT Press, 1990), p. 55.
33 Robbins, p. 69.
34 Robert Smithson, "Art through the Camera's Eye," quoted in Robert Sobieszek, *Robert Smithson: Photo Works* (Albuquerque, NM: University of New Mexico Press, 1993), p. 32.
35 It is interesting to note that both Bill Brandt and Nigel Henderson photographed at Bethnal Green, a lower-class area of London, yet both also moved outside social documentary to more experimental forms of photography.
36 A. D. Coleman, "I'm Not Really a Photographer," *New York Times*, September 10, 1972, p. D35
37 Interview with Ed Ruscha, by John Coplans, *Artforum* (Feb 1965), reprinted in Ed Ruscha and Alexandra Schwartz, *Leave Any Information at the Signal* (Cambridge: MA: October Books, 2002), p. 24.
38 Quoted in Joshua Shannon, "Uninteresting Pictures: Photography and Fact at the End of the 1960s," in Matthew S. Witkovsky, ed., *Light Years: Conceptual Art and the Photograph, 1964–1977* (New Haven: Yale University Press, 2011), p. 91.
39 Quoted in Tony Godfrey, *Conceptual Art* (London: Phaidon Press Limited, 1998), p. 203.
40 Quoted in Michael Compton, *Marcel Broodthaers* (London: Tate Gallery, 1980), p. 13.
41 Quoted in Reiko Tomii, "Concerning the Institution of Art: Conceptualism in Japan," in *Global Conceptualism: Points of Origin* (New York: Queens Museum of Art, 1999), p. 26.
42 Robert Stearns, *Photography and Beyond in Japan* (Tokyo: Hara Museum of Contemporary Art, 1995), pp. 59–60.
43 John Szarkowski, *The Photographer's Eye* (New York: Museum of Modern Art, 1966), n.p.

44 See, for instance, John Szarkowski, *Looking at Photographs: 100 Pictures from the Collection of the Museum of Modern Art* (New York: Museum of Modern Art, 1973), p. 10.
45 John Szarkowski, *From the Picture Press* (New York: Museum of Modern Art, 1973), p. 6.
46 Kubler—and before him, the art historians Heinrich Wölfflin (1864–1945) and Alois Riegl (1858–1905)—insisted on a large time frame, not a decade.
47 Szarkowski, *Looking at Photographs*.
48 Szarkowski, *The Photographer's Eye*.
49 Quoted in Jonathan Green, *American Photography*, p. 187.
50 Szarkowski, *William Eggleston's Guide* (New York: Museum of Modern Art, 1976), pp. 6–8.
51 Szarkowski, *Mirrors and Windows: American Photography since 1960* (New York: Museum of Modern Art, 1978), p. 11.
52 John Szarkowski, p. 18.
53 John Szarkowski, p. 13.
54 John Szarkowski, p. 14.

Part Six
Convergences (1975 to the Present)

1 Cristina Vives Gutiérrez, "About the Idea, the Negative and Negation," in *Conceptual Art in Cuba* (Minneapolis: Parts, n.d. [2000]), n.p.

Chapter Twelve
Globalism, Technology, and Social Change

1 See Thomas McEvilley, "Toward a Creative Reversal," *Art in America* (January 2001), p. 41.
2 Young Kim, [untitled artist's statement] in Andy Grundberg, Rebecca Solnit, and Ronald Takaki, *Tracing Cultures* (San Francisco, CA: The Friends of Photography, 1995), p. 40.
3 For Hillman's ideas, see James Hillman, "The Practice of Beauty," in *Uncontrollable Beauty: Toward a New Aesthetics* (New York: Allworth Press, 1998), pp. 261–74.
4 Ann Thomas, "The Portrait in the Age of Genetic Mapping," in Gary Schneider, *Genetic Self-Portrait* (Syracuse, NY: Light Work, 1999).
5 Thomas, p. 32.
6 For a discussion of Delaroche's legendary comment, see Mary Warner Marien, *Photography and its Critics* (New York: Cambridge University Press, 1997), pp. 55–57.
7 Nicholas Mirzoeff, *An Introduction to Visual Culture* (London: Routledge, 1999), p. 88.
8 William J. Mitchell, *The Reconfigured Eye: Visual Truth in the Post-Photography Era* (Cambridge, MA: MIT Press, 1992), bookjacket. A similar, but less forceful, statement occurs in the text on p. 20.
9 Joan Fontcuberta, "Introduction," in Pedro Meyer, *Truths and Fictions: A Journey from Documentary to Digital Photography* (New York: Aperture Foundation, 1995), p. 9.
10 Fontcuberta, p. 10.
11 Fontcuberta, p. 12.
12 See David King, *The Commissar Vanishes: The Falsification of Photographs and Art in Stalin's Russia* (New York: Metropolitan Books, 1997).
13 For analyses of the Gulf War see Douglas Keller, *The Persian Gulf TV War* (Boulder, CO: Westview Press, 1992), and Michael Griffin and Jongsoo Lee, "Picturing the Gulf War: Constructing an Image of War in Time, Newsweek, and U.S. News and World Report," *Journalism and Mass Communication Quarterly*, vol. 72, no. 4 (Winter 1995), pp. 813–25.
14 Anthony Aziz and Sammy Cucher, "Notes from Dystopia," in *Photography after Photography: Memory*

and Representation in the Digital Age (Amsterdam and Munich: OPA and Siemens Kulturprogramm, 1996), pp. 126–28.

15 Aziz and Cucher, pp. 126–28.

16 See the discussion in Victor Burgin, "The Image in Pieces: Digital Photography and the Location of Cultural Experience," in *Photography after Photography*, p. 32.

17 Joan Fontcuberta, "Introduction," in Meyer, *Truths and Fictions*, p. 11.

18 Keith Cottingham, "Fictional Portraits," in *Photography after Photography*, p. 162.

19 Lynne Warren, "Miroslaw Rogala," in *Photography after Photography*, p. 52.

20 "Blood and Oil," *Economist* (March 4, 2000), p. 68.

21 Weston Naef and Sebastião Salgado quoted in Matthew L. Wald, "The Eye of the Photojournalist," *New York Times Magazine* (June 9, 1991), p. 58.

22 Vicki Goldberg, "Art, Facts, and Artifacts," *American Photographer* (March 1988), p. 26.

23 Stuart Hall, *Different* (London: Phaidon Press, 2001), p. 37.

24 Susan Kismaric, *British Photography from the Thatcher Years* (New York: Museum of Modern Art, 1990), p. 12.

25 Cornell Capa, quoted in Pooley, p. 40.

26 See, for example, John Worden, "Gimme Shelter," *Afterimage*, vol. 15, no. 10 (May 1988), p. 19.

27 Gilles Peress, *Telex Iran: In the Name of Revolution* (Zurich and New York: Scalo, 1997).

28 Donna Ferrato, *Living with the Enemy* (New York: Aperture, 1991), n.p.

29 Quoted in a 1987 interview with Marianne Fulton, in her "Changing Focus: The 1950s to the 1980s," in Marianne Fulton, *Eyes of Time: Photojournalism in America* (Boston, MA: Little, Brown and Company, 1988), p. 248.

30 Vicki Goldberg, "The Heroism of Anonymous Men and Women," *New York Times* (June 13, 1993), H35.

31 See, for example, *Anthropology and Photography, 1860–1920*, ed. Elizabeth Edwards (New Haven, CT: Yale University Press, 1992); and James Clifford, *The Predicament of Culture: Twentieth-Century Ethnography, Literature, and Art* (Cambridge, MA: Harvard University Press, 1988).

32 Allan Sekula, "Dismantling Modernism, Reinventing Documentary (Notes on the Politics of Representation)," in *Photography: Current Perspectives*, ed. Jerome Liebling (Rochester, NY: Light Impressions Corporation, 1978), p. 232.

33 Jolene Rickard, quoted in Theresa Harlan, "As in Her Vision: Native American Women Photographers," in *Reframing: New American Feminist Photographies*, ed. Diane Neumaier (Philadelphia, PA: Temple University Press, 1995), p. 115.

34 Harlan, p. 115.

35 Michael Kimmelman, "Can Suffering be too Beautiful?" *New York Times* (July 13, 2001), Section E, Part 2, 27.

36 Henry Hitchings, "What's Right in Front of You," *Times Literary Supplement* (July 18, 2003), p. 18.

37 David Byrne, "Foreword," in Lynne Cohen, *Occupied Territory* (New York: Aperture, 1987), p. 15.

38 J. M. Roberts, *Twentieth Century: The History of the World, 1901–2000* (New York: Viking, 1999), p. 613, n. 1. The Cambodian Genocide Program at Yale University can be accessed at www.yale.edu/cgp

39 Santu Mofokeng, "Trajectory of a Street-Photographer," in *Anthology of African and Indian Ocean Photography* (Paris: Review Noire, 1999), p. 269.

Chapter Thirteen
The Culture of Critique

1 Martha Rosler, *Positions in the Life World*, p. 33.

2 Abigail Solomon-Godeau, "Who is Speaking Thus? Some Questions about Documentary Photography," in *Photography at the Dock* (Minneapolis, MN: University of Minnesota Press, 1991), p. 183.

3 The poster/essay for *The Health and Safety Game* was written by Allan Sekula.

4 Fred Lonidier, "Working with Unions," in *Cultures in Contention*, ed. Douglas Kahn and Diane Neumaier (Seattle, WA: Real Comet Press, 1985), p. 103.

5 Martha Rosler, "In, Around, and Afterthoughts (On Documentary Photography)," in *The Contest of Meaning: Critical Histories of Photography*, ed. Richard Bolton (Cambridge, MA: MIT Press, 1989), p. 322.

6 Martha Rosler, *Positions in the Life World*, p. 44.

7 Andy Grundberg, "Two Camps Battle Over the Nature of the Medium," *New York Times* (Sunday, August 14, 1983), H 24.

8 Allan Sekula, "The Traffic in Photographs," *Art Journal*, vol. 41, no. 1 (Spring 1981), p. 20.

9 Allan Sekula, "The Body and the Archive," in *The Contest of Meaning: Critical Histories of Photography*, ed. Richard Bolton (Cambridge, MA: MIT Press, 1989), pp. 342–89.

10 Allan Sekula, "On the Invention of Photographic Meaning," in *Thinking Photography*, ed. Victor Burgin (London: Macmillan, 1982), p. 102.

11 Allan Sekula, "Dismantling Modernism, Reinventing Documentary (Notes on the Politics of Representation)," in *Photography: Current Perspectives*, ed. Jerome Liebling (Rochester, NY: Light Impressions Corporation, 1978), p. 231.

12 Sekula, p. 239.

13 Sekula, p. 251.

14 Allan Sekula, "The Body and the Archive," p. 379.

15 Roland Barthes, *Camera Lucida: Reflections on Photography* (New York: Hill and Wang, 1981), p. 73.

16 Douglas Crimp, *Pictures* (New York: Artists Space; Committee for the Visual Arts, 1977), p. 3. Another Crimp article, also titled "Pictures," was published in *October*, vol. 8 (Spring 1978), pp. 75–88. It expanded on the first article and brought the ideas to bear on artists not included in the original show, most notably Cindy Sherman.

17 Thomas Lawson, "Last Exit: Painting," *Artforum* (October, 1981), p. 45.

18 Sontag's book was compiled from essays she wrote in 1973, 1974, and 1977 for the *New York Review of Books*.

19 Abigail Solomon-Godeau, "Conventional Pictures," *The Print Collector's Newsletter*, vol. 12, no. 5 (November–December 1981), p. 138.

20 See, for example, the discussion in Abigail Solomon-Godeau, "Photography After Art Photography," in her *Photography at the Dock: Essays on Photographic History, Institutions, and Practices* (Minneapolis, MN: University of Minnesota Press, 1991), pp. 113–14.

21 David Rimanelli, [untitled review], *Artforum* (December 2000), p. 120.

22 Craig Owens, "The Discourse of Others: Feminists and Postmodernism," in Hal Foster, *The Anti-Aesthetic: Essays on Postmodern Culture* (Port Townsend, WA: Bay Press, 1983), p. 59.

23 See Griselda Pollock, "What's Wrong with Images of Women," *Screen Education*, no. 24 (October 1977), pp. 25–31, and Janet Wolff, *Feminine Sentences: Essays on Women & Culture* (Berkeley, CA: University of California Press, 1990).

24 Deborah Bright, "Of Mother Nature and Marlboro Men: An Inquiry into the Cultural Meanings of Landscape Photography," in *The Contest of Meaning: Critical Histories of Photography*, ed. Richard Bolton (Cambridge, MA: MIT Press, 1989), p. 139.

25 A. D. Coleman, "The Directorial Mode: Notes Toward a Definition," in his *Light Readings: A Photography Critic's Writings, 1968–1978* (Albuquerque, NM: University of New Mexico Press, 1998), pp. 250–54.

26 For a more complete discussion of the controversy see Steven C. Dubin, *Arresting Images: Impolitic Art and Uncivil Actions* (New York: Routledge, 1992).

27 Dubin, p. 100.

28 Quoted in Annette Grant, "Lights, Camera, Stand Really Still: On the Set with Gregory Crewdson," *New York Times* (Sunday, May 30, 2004), p. AR20.

29 Quoted in Gary Boas, "New Image Art," in *Artforum* (December 2000), p. 152.

30 Walker, Ursitti, and McGinniss, *Photo Manifesto: Contemporary Photography in the U.S.S.R.* (New York: Stewart, Tabori & Chang, 1991), p. 63.

31 Ulf Erdmann Ziegler, "Preface" to *Contemporary German Photography* (Cologne: Taschen Verlag, 1997), n.p.

32 Interview with Wang Jinsong by Stephanie Smith, in Wu Hung and Christopher Phillips, *Between Past and Future: New Photography and Video from China* (Chicago and New York: Smart Museum of Art and the International Center of Photography, 2004).

33 Göran Gnaudschun [artist's statement], in *Contemporary German Photography*, n.p.

34 Quoted in Jennifer Blessing, *Rose is a Rose is a Rose: Gender Performance in Photography* (New York: Guggenheim Museum, 1997), p. 208.

35 See Peter Weiermair, *Japanese Photography: Desire and Void* (Zurich: Edition Stemmle, 1997), p. 12.

36 Noriko Fuku, "I am a Photographer," in *An Incomplete History: Women Photographers from Japan, 1864–1997* (Rochester, NY: Visual Studies Workshop, 1998), p. 11.

37 Noriko Fuku, "I am a Photographer," p. 5.

38 I am grateful to Elizabeth Ferrer's interpretation in *A Shadow Born of Earth: New Photography in Mexico* (New York: American Federation of Arts, 1993), p. 85.

39 For an overview, see Laura U. Marks, "Minor Infractions: Child Pornography and the Legislation of Morality," *Afterimage*, vol. 18, no. 4 (November 1990), pp. 12–14.

40 See, for example, Carol Mavor, *Pleasures Taken: Performance of Sexuality and Loss in Victorian Photographs* (Durham, NC: Duke University Press, 1995), and Anne Higonnet, *Pictures of Innocence: The History and Crisis of Ideal Childhood* (London: Thames and Hudson, 1998).

41 For a comprehensive history of political debates involving images, see Steven C. Dubin, *Arresting Images: Impolitic Art and Uncivil Actions* (New York: Routledge, 1992).

42 See Robert Shlaer, *Sights Once Seen: Daguerreotyping Frémont's Last Expedition through the Rockies* (Albuquerque, NM: Museum of New Mexico, 2000).

43 See, for example, Bill McKibben, "The Problem with Wildlife Photography," *Doubletake* (Fall 1997), pp. 50–56.

44 Robert Adams, *Beauty in Photography: Essays in Defense of Traditional Values* (New York: Aperture, 1981), p. 13.

45 Marusia Bociurkiw, "The Transgressive Camera," *Afterimage*, vol. 16, no. 6 (January 1989), p. 18.

46 From the ACT UP flyer handed out at Nixon's 1988 show at the Museum of Modern Art, quoted in its entirety in Jan Zita Grover, "Visible Lesions: Images of the PWA," *Afterimage* (Summer 1989), p. 14.

47 Interview with David Hevey titled "A Radical Creature," [no author] *Creative Camera* (February–March 1992), pp. 28–30.

48 Bonnie Yochelson, *Esther Bubley on Assignment*, p. 72.

49 Joyce Kozloff [interview with Barbara Pollack] [www.jca-online.com/pollack.html].

50 See Abigail Solomon-Godeau, "Living with Contradictions: Critical Practices in the Age of Supply-Side Aesthetics," in her *Photography at the Dock*, pp. 134–48.

51 Jeff Rian, "On the Ground: Paris," *Artforum* (December 2004), p. 80.

Chapter Fourteen
Into the Twenty-First Century

1 Bradley Graham and David Von Drehle, "Bush Apologizes for Abuse of Prisoners," *Washington Post* (May 7, 2004), A01.

2 Deidre Stein Greben, "'The Medium of the Moment,'" *Art News Online* (February 2003), p. 1. www.artnewsonline.com

3 Unsigned review, "Art History," *New Yorker* (May 3, 2004), p. 19.

4 Elizabeth Van Ness, "Is a Cinema Studies Degree the New M.B.A.?" *New York Times* (March 6, 2005), pp. 1, 15.

5 Francesco Bonami, "The Road Around (or A Long Good-Bye)," in *Echoes: Contemporary Art at the Age of Endless Conclusions*, ed. Francesco Bonami (New York: Monocelli Press, Inc., 1996), p. 13.

6 Yinka Shonibare in dialogue with others in "Global Tendencies: Globalism and the Large-Scale Exhibition," ed. Tim Griffin, *Artforum* (November 2003), p. 154.

7 Jean-Hubert Martin, "The Reception of African Art," in *Africa Remix* (Ostfildern-Ruit, Germany: Hatje Cantz Publishers, 2005), p. 29.

8 See, for example, Klaus Biesenbach, "Mexico City: An Exhibition about the Exchange Rates of Bodies and Values," in *Mexico City: An Exhibition about the Exchange Rates of Bodies and Values*, ed. Klaus Biesenbach (New York: D. A. P., 2002), pp. 41–43.

9 Gilbert Vicario, "What Makes Art Mexican?" in *Made in Mexico*, ed. Gilbert Vicario (Boston, MA: Institute of Contemporary Art, 2004), p. 9.

10 Shannon Burke, "Lonnie Graham is the Spark," *The Grizzly* [Ursinus College], November 11, 2004, p. 3.

11 Andreja Kuluncic, quoted in Carol King, "To Be Noticed, Croatian Artists Set Their Sights on New York," *New York Times* (Thursday, June 23, 2005), p. E3.

12 Okwui Enwezor in dialogue with others, in "Global Tendencies: Globalism and the Large-Scale Exhibition," ed. Tim Griffin, *Artforum* (November 2003), p. 158.

13 Eleanor Heartney, "A 600-Hour Documenta," *Art in America*, vol. 19, issue 9 (September 2002), p. 95.

14 Quoted in Catherine Elton, "500 Tragic Years of Mayan Life, Shows in an Exhibition of Outreach and Hope," *New York Times* (August 23, 2004), p. E5.

15 Michael Hardt and Antonio Negri, *Empire* (Cambridge, MA: Harvard University Press, 2000), p. 393.

16 Richard Vine, "Sixty Ways of Looking at China" (interview with Wu Hong and Christopher Phillips), *Art in America* (June/July 2004), p. 126.

17 I am indebted to James Zeng Huang for his ongoing generous help in understanding the recent history of photography in China, and for his English translation of his 2005 article titled "Photojournalism in China: A Decade of Change."

18 This synopsis of Chinese photography is drawn from the catalog by Wu Hung and Christopher Phillips, *Between Past and Future: New Photography and Video from China* (Chicago and New York: Smart Museum of Art and the International Center of Photography, 2004).

19 Allan Sekula, "On the Invention of Photographic Meaning," in *Thinking Photography*, ed. Victor Burgin (London: Macmillan, 1982), p. 102.

20 Walter Benjamin, "The Work of Art in the Age of Mechanical Reproduction," in Walter Benjamin, *Illuminations*, ed. Hannah Arendt (New York: Schocken Books, 1969), p. 241.

21 Hal Foster, "Postmodernism: A Preface," in *The Anti-Aesthetic: Essays on Postmodern Culture*, ed. Hal Foster (Port Townsend, WA: Bay Press, 1983), p. xv.

22 Martha Rosler in dialogue with others, in "Global Tendencies: Globalism and the Large-Scale Exhibition," ed. Tim Griffin, *Artforum* (November 2003), p. 163.

23 Kenneth Chang, "How the Red Planet Came Down with Pink Blues," *New York Times* (February 10, 2004), p. F3.

24 Mary Warner Marien, *100 Ideas that Changed Photography* (London: Laurence King Publishing, 2012), pp. 206–207.

25 Craig Garrett, "Coerced Confessions: Snapshot Photography's Subjective Objectivity," *Flash Art International*, 36 (November–December 2003), p. 72.

26 Claire Daigle, "Pagan Stories: The Situations in Recent Art," *New Art Examiner*, vol. 25 (March 1998), p. 55.

27 David Brittain, "To Hell and Back: The Photoblog," *Source: The Photographic Review*, no. 43 (Summer 2005), p. 34.

28 Adam Lammiman, "Whose Reality is it Anyway?," *Adbusters*, no. 30 (June/July 2000), p. 18.

29 Hany Farid, "Digital Forensics: 5 Ways to Spot a Fake," *Scientific American* (June 8, 2008) http://www.sciam.com/article.cfm?id=5-ways-to-spot-a-fake

30 Susan Sontag, *Regarding the Pain of Others* (New York: Farrar, Straus and Giroux, 2003), p. 115.

31 Adam Sternberg, *New York* magazine (October 15, 2006), retrieved January 22, 2013.

BIBLIOGRAPHY

Many excellent books on individual photographers and movements have been published in recent years. This bibliography emphasizes English-language general histories, rather than monographs.

GENERAL HISTORIES OF PHOTOGRAPHY

Braive, Michel F. *The Photograph: A Social History*, trans. David Britt (New York: McGraw-Hill Book Company, 1966). Idiosyncratic, historically outdated, yet delightful array of European vernacular photography.

Campany, David, ed. *Art and Photography* (London: Phaidon, 2003). An overview of photography's place in recent art history, from the 1960s onward.

Daval, Jean-Luc. *Photography: History of an Art* (New York: Rizzoli, 1982). Oversize and beautifully printed review emphasizing European photography. Daval concentrates on the interaction of photography and other art media.

Eder, Josef Maria. *History of Photography*, trans. Edward Epstean (New York: Dover Publications, Inc., 1978). Eder's influence on the history of photography, through his chronological organization of the medium's technical developments in Europe (first translated in 1945), is still felt. No illustrations.

Freund, Gisèle. *Photography and Society* (Boston, MA: David R. Godine, 1980). Originally published in France. Freund's insistence on seeing European photography, especially French photography, in the context of political and social events, helped to shift scholarly focus from photography as art to the cultural history of photography.

Frizot, Michel, ed. *A New History of Photography* (Cologne: Könemann, 1998). Lavishly illustrated history, with articles primarily on photography in the United States and Europe. This book incorporates new directions in the field, such as research on the development of mass-media networks, fashion photography, and the use of photography in the development of ethnic stereotypes. Flawed by the excessive use of sepia in the reproductions.

Gernsheim, Helmut, with Alison Gernsheim. *The History of Photography from the Camera Obscura to the Beginning of the Modern Era*, 2nd ed. (New York: McGraw-Hill, 1969). With Beaumont Newhall (see below), the Gernsheims shaped the field of photographic history. The Gernsheim collection, now in the Harry Ransom Research Center at the University of Texas at Austin, is one of the few large private collections to remain intact.

Kevles, Bettyann Holtzmann. *Naked to the Bone: Medical Imaging in the Twentieth Century* (New Brunswick, NJ: Rutgers University Press, 1997). From X-rays to PET scans, Kevles provides an informative reflection on society's reaction to imaging the body, and frequently notes the uses to which artists put medical imaging.

Kosinski, Dorothy. *The Artist and the Camera: Degas to Picasso* (Dallas, TX: Dallas Museum of Art, 1999). Kosinski and others examine the sometimes hidden history of photography's impact on modern art.

Well researched and lavishly illustrated.

Lebeck, Robert, and Bodo von Dewitz. *Kiosk: A History of Photojournalism* (London: Steidl, 2002).

LeMagny, Jean-Claude, and André Rouillé, eds. *A History of Photography*, trans. Janet Lloyd (New York: Cambridge University Press, 1987). Individual articles mostly on European photographic history, written by leading historians and curators.

Newhall, Beaumont. *The History of Photography* (New York: Museum of Modern Art, 1982). Newhall's preference for so-called straight photography, whether in art, documentary, or photojournalism, was apparent from his first catalog, published in 1937, to this last edition. The influential historian and curator shaped the prominent collections at the Museum of Modern Art in New York City and George Eastman House in Rochester, New York.

Orvell, Miles. *American Photography* (New York: Oxford University Press, 2003). Ranging from portraiture and landscape photography to family albums, this book traces 150 years of the history of American photography.

Parr, Martin, and Gerry Badger. *The Photobook: A History*, vol. 1 (London: Phaidon, 2004). A comprehensive overview of the development of the photo-book from the very early days of photography to the present.

Rosenblum, Naomi. *A World History of Photography*, 3rd ed. (New York: Abbeville Press, 1997). Rosenblum led the way to the current rewriting of photographic history.

Her book includes long-overlooked women photographers, and reaches out to report on photography in the non-Western world.

Scharf, Aaron. *Art and Photography* (Harmondsworth, Middlesex: Penguin, 1974). One of the first books to investigate interactions between the fine arts and photography. Contains a useful bibliography.

Taylor, Brandon. *Collage: The Making of Modern Art* (New York: Thames and Hudson, 2004).

Thomas, Ann. *Beauty of Another Order: Photography in Science* (New Haven, CT: Yale University Press, 1997). Highly informative articles by Thomas and others in a catalog to the important exhibition of the same name at the National Gallery of Canada in Ottawa.

NINETEENTH-CENTURY PHOTOGRAPHY

Baldwin, Gordon, Malcolm Daniel, and Sarah Greenough. *All the Mighty World: The Photographs of Roger Fenton, 1852–1860* (New Haven, CT: Yale University Press, 2004). A comprehensive study of the influential British photographer.

Bann, Stephen. *Parallel Lines: Printmakers, Painters and Photographers in Nineteenth-Century France* (New Haven, CT: Yale University Press, 2001). An investigation of the interaction between painting, print-making, and photography in France at a time when technological advances precipitated enormous changes in the reproduction of images.

Bartram, Michael. *The Pre-Raphaelite Camera* (New York: New York Graphic Society, 1985). Painstaking and convincing look at the shared themes and visual techniques of painting and photography.

Batchen, Geoffrey. *Burning with Desire: The Conception of Photography* (Cambridge, MA: MIT Press, 1997). A critical, philosophically aware review of the formal, cultural, and political definitions of photography in its early decades.

Buerger, Janet E. *French Daguerreotypes* (Chicago, IL: University of Chicago Press, 1989). Largely based on the Cromer collection at George Eastman House in Rochester, New York, this book elucidates the multiple directions taken by the daguerreotype in mid-nineteenth-century France.

Carlebach, Michael L. *The Origins of Photojournalism in America* (Washington, D.C., Smithsonian Institution Press, 1992). An introduction to the integration of photographically based images into nineteenth-century newspapers.

Crawford, William. *The Keepers of Light* (Dobbs Ferry, New York: Morgan & Morgan, 1979). In his mixture of history and how-to-do-it, Crawford guides novice photographers through the chemistry and techniques of early photographic processes. This book is still sought after for its clear instructions.

Edwards, Elizabeth, ed. *Anthropology and Photography, 1860–1920* (New Haven, CT: Yale University Press, 1992). Seldom-seen images and insightful essays track the intertwined development of photographic practice and the science of anthropology.

Flukinger, Roy. *The Formative Decades: Photography in Great Britain, 1839–1920* (Austin, TX: University of Texas Press, 1985). Showcases the wealth of nineteenth-century photography housed in the libraries at the University of Texas at Austin. Accompanied by helpful notes on the works and photographers.

Foresta, Merry, and John Wood. *Secrets of the Dark Chamber: The Art of the American Daguerreotype* (Washington, D.C.: National Museum of American Art and Smithsonian Institution Press, 1995). Daguerreotypes from an exhibition at the National Museum of American Art in Washington, D.C., accompanied by writings on the medium produced by critics and photographers throughout the nineteenth century.

Galassi, Peter. *Before Photography: Painting and the Invention of Photography* (New York: Museum of Modern Art, 1981). Like Schwarz (below), Galassi speculated on the aesthetic forebears of photography. A still-controversial early essay by the director of the photography department at the Museum of Modern Art.

Gray, Michael, Arthur Ollman, and Carol McCusker. *First Photographs: William Henry Fox Talbot and the Birth of Photography* (New York: Powerhouse Cultural Entertainment, Inc., 2002). Accompanying an exhibition of the same name, this book contains several rarely seen images, together with short essays and a timeline.

Hambourg, Maria Morris, Pierre Apraxine, Malcolm Daniel, Jeff L. Rosenheim, and Virginia Heckert. *The Waking Dream: Photography's First Century: Selections from the Gilman Paper Company Collection* (New York: The Metropolitan Museum of Art, 1993). Richly illustrated review, augmented with extensive, succinct descriptions of individual works.

Hamilton, Peter, and Roger Hargreaves. *The Beautiful and the Damned: The Creation of Identity in Nineteenth Century Photography* (London: Lund Humphries in association with the National Portrait Gallery, 2001). An examination of the development of portrait photography in the nineteenth century, including how the *carte-de-visite* conferred social status and family albums were similarly used to establish a position within society.

Henisch, Heinz Z., and Bridget A. Henisch. *The Photographic Experience, 1839–1914: Images and Attitudes* (University Park, PA: Pennsylvania State University Press, 1994) and *The Painted Photograph, 1839–1914: Origins, Techniques, Aspirations* (University Park, PA: Pennsylvania State University Press, 1996). Drawn mostly from a collection of vernacular photography started by Henisch and Henisch before studies of the photography of everyday life became popular in the late twentieth century.

Jammes, Andre, and Eugenia Parry Janis. *The Art of the French Calotype* (Princeton, NJ: Princeton University Press, 1983). Photographic history's debt to collectors is evidenced in the images from the Jammes collection of French photography.

Jones, Kimberly, Simon Kelly, Sarah Kennel, and Helga Aurisch. *In the Forest of Fontainebleau: Painters and Photographers from Corot to Monet* (New Haven, CT: Yale University Press, 2008).

Keller, Ulrich. *The Ultimate Spectacle: A Visual History of the Crimean War* (London: Gordon and Breach, 2001). Using a range of pictorial materials including scientific diagrams, press illustrations, and academic paintings as well as photographs, this book gives an account of a war that was conducted under the eye of public scrutiny and whose aesthetic scripting was drafted on that basis.

Kemp, Martin. *The Science of Art: Optical Themes in Western Art from Brunelleschi to Seurat* (New Haven, CT: Yale University Press, 1989). Lavishly illustrated, Kemp's book incorporates detailed histories and technical data for optical instruments, such as the camera obscura, which preceded the invention of the photographic camera.

Marien, Mary Warner. *Photography and its Critics: A Cultural History, 1839–1900* (New York: Cambridge University Press, 1997). An analysis of U.S. and European critical writing on the medium.

McCauley, Elizabeth Anne. *Industrial Madness: Commercial Photography in Paris, 1848–1871* (New Haven, CT: Yale University Press, 1994). A comprehensive look at commercial photography and its consumers.

Rudisill, Richard. *Mirror Image: The Influence of the Daguerreotype on American Society* (Albuquerque, NM: University of New Mexico Press, 1971). Difficult-to-find social history of early photography that has survived the test of time.

Sandweiss, Martha A., ed. *Photography in Nineteenth-Century America* (Fort Worth, TX: Amon Carter Museum, and New York: Harry N. Abrams, 1991). Richly illustrated. Six scholarly essays trace the social interactions of photography. The first entry, Alan Trachtenberg's "Photography: the Emergence of a Keyword," is an invaluable introduction to the intricate interplay of photographic practice and cultural values.

Sandweiss, Martha A. *Print the Legend: Photography and the American West* (New Haven, CT: Yale University Press, 2002). Tells the intertwined stories of photography and the American West in the nineteenth century.

Schaaf, Larry J. *The Photographic Art of William Henry Fox Talbot* (Princeton, NJ: Princeton University Press, 2000). In this collection of Talbot's own writings, as well as those of his contemporaries, each of the 100 plates is reproduced at the actual size of the original. This is a record of Talbot's technological as well as his artistic achievements.

Schwarz, Heinrich. *Art and Photography: Forerunners and Influences: Selected Essays by Heinrich Schwarz*, ed. William E. Parker (Layton, UT: Peregrine Smith Books, 1985). Essays by the distinguished Czech museum curator, whose examination of the social and cultural forces that encouraged the invention of photography has been widely influential in photographic studies.

Seiberling, Grace. *Amateurs, Photography, and the Mid-Victorian Imagination* (Chicago, IL: University of Chicago Press, 1986). Intelligent analysis of the role that photography played in defining social class among British middle- and upper-class amateurs.

Taylor, Roger. *Impressed by Light: British Photography from Paper Negatives, 1840–1860* (New Haven, CT: Yale University Press, 2007).

Thomas, Alan. *Time in a Frame: Photography and the 19th-Century Mind* (New York: Schocken Books, 1977). An early attempt to conceive photography as the history of an idea.

PHOTOGRAPHY SINCE 1900

Birgus, Vladimir, ed. *Czech Photographic Avant-Garde, 1918–1948* (Cambridge: The MIT Press, 2002).

Blessing, Jennifer. *Rrose is a Rrose is a Rrose: Gender Performance in Photography* (New York: Guggenheim Museum, 1997). Reviews the philosophical unity linking early twentieth-century photographers such as Claude Cahun with contemporary artists such as Cindy Sherman.

Bright, Susan. *Art Photography Now* (New York: Aperture, 2005). A survey of the work of many important artist-photographers working today.

Campany, David, ed. *Art and Photography* (London: Phaidon, 2003). An overview of photography's place in recent art history.

Constructed Realities: The Art of Staged Photography (Zurich: Edition Stemmle, 1989/95). Attempts to define the staged photograph through a broad survey of work by American and European artists.

Cotton, Charlotte. *The Photograph as Contemporary Art* (London: Thames and Hudson, 2004). This book addresses the vocabulary and debates of photographic criticism.

Cox, Julian. *Road to Freedom: Photographs of the Civil Rights Movement, 1956–1968* (Atlanta, GA: High Museum of Art, 2008).

Dickerman, Leah. *Dada: Zurich, Berlin, Hannover, Cologne, New York, Paris* (Washington, D.C.: National Gallery of Art, 2008).

Doss, Erika, ed. *Looking at Life Magazine* (Washington, D.C.: Smithsonian Institution Press, 2001). A collection of articles that make full use of the magazine's archive.

Enwezor, Okwui, ed. *The Short Century: Independence and Liberation Movements in Africa, 1945–1994* (Munich: Prestel, 2001). Scholars examine popular imagery in post-World War II liberation movements.

Faber, Monika, and Janos Frecot. *Portraits of an Age: Photography in Germany and Austria, 1900–1938* (New York and Vienna: Neue Galerie and Albertina, 2005). A survey of portrait photographs that documents the changing image of middle-class society in Germany and Austria.

Francisco, Jason, and Elizabeth Anne McCauley. *The Steerage and Alfred Stieglitz* (Berkley: University of California Press, 2012).

Global Conceptualism: Points of Origin, 1950s–1980s (New York: Queens Museum of Art, 1999). Not primarily about photography, but demonstrates the extent to which photography became a major medium in North American, South American, European, African, and Asian art.

Goranin, Näkki. *American Photobooth* (New York: W. W. Norton & Co., 2008).

Graham-Brown, Sarah. *Images of Women: The Portrayal of Women in Photography of the Middle East, 1860–1950* (New York: Columbia University Press, 1988). Comprehensive, undervalued study of stereotypes, and also the role of women as photographers.

Griffith, Bronwyn A. E., ed. *Ambassadors of Progress: American Women Photographers in Paris, 1900–1901* (France: Musée d'Art Americain in association with the Library of Congress, Washington D.C., 2001). An exhibition in Paris revealed how American women

photographers influenced the international Pictorialist movement.
Grosenick, Uta, and Thomas Seelig, eds. *Photo Art: Photography in the 21st Century* (New York: Aperture, 2008).
Howarth, Sophie, ed. *Singular Images: Essays on Remarkable Photographs* (New York: Aperture, 2005). A series of commentaries by distinguished critics and photographic historians.
Janus, Elizabeth, ed. *Veronica's Revenge: Contemporary Perspectives on Photography* (Zurich: Scalo, 1998). Janus and others explore the scope of Marion Lambert's perceptive collection of American and European photographers and artists who use photography in their work.
Kemper, Sarah. *Virtual Anxiety: Photography, New Technologies, and Subjectivity* (Manchester: Manchester University Press, 1998). A reflection on the possible impacts of digitalization on photography.
Lahs-Gonzales, Olivia, and Lucy Lippard. *Women Photographers of the 20th Century* (St. Louis, MO: St. Louis Art Museum, 1997). International in scope and taking account of recent theoretical approaches.
McEuen, Melissa A. *Seeing America: Women Photographers between the Wars* (Lexington, KY: University Press of Kentucky, 2000). Engaging text on such photographers as Margaret Bourke-White.
Millstein, Barbara Head, ed. *Committed to the Image: Contemporary Black Photographers* (New York: Brooklyn Museum of Art in association with Merrell, 2001). Social commentary provided by ninety-five contemporary African-American photographers.
Mitchell, William J. *The Reconfigured Eye: Visual Truth in the Post-Photographic Era* (Cambridge, MA: MIT Press, 1992). Merges a technical account, now largely out of date, with the philosophical issues raised by digital imaging.
Oguibe, Olu, Okwui Enwezor, and Octavio Zaya, eds. *In/sight: African Photographers, 1940 to the Present* (New York: Guggenheim Museum, 1996). Scholars bring critical insights to the practice of postwar photography in Africa.
Phillips, Christopher, ed. *Photography in the Modern Era: European Documents and Critical Writings, 1913–1940* (New York: Metropolitan Museum of Art, 1989). Valuable resource for understanding photography between the world wars, with important articles by Gustav Klusis, Ossip Brik, and Karel Teige.
Pultz, John. *The Body and the Lens: Photography 1839 to the Present* (New York: Harry N. Abrams, 1995). A compact introduction to late twentieth-century concerns with the body as the primary site of human identity.
Reframings: New American Feminist Photographies (Philadelphia, PA: Temple University Press, 1995). Essays and images that underscore the diversity of women's photographic practice.
Salvesen, Britt, *New Topographics* (Göttingen, Germany, and Tucson, AZ: Steidl Publishers and the Center for Creative Photography, 2010).
Rosenblum, Naomi. *A History of Women Photographers* (New York: Abbeville Press, 1994). An encyclopedic account that has had a lasting impact on photographic studies. Especially strong on mid-twentieth-century figures.
Tupitsyn, Margarita. *The Soviet Photograph, 1924–1937* (New Haven, CT: Yale University Press, 1996). Compact look at interrelated political and aesthetic issues from the death of Lenin to the prewar period under Stalin.
Witkowsky, Matthew S., *Light Years: Conceptual Art and Photography, 1964–1977* (Chicago: Art Institute of Chicago, 2011).

HISTORIES OF ETHNIC, REGIONAL, AND NATIONAL PHOTOGRAPHY

Alibhai-Brown, Yasmin. *Imaging the New Britain* (London: Routledge, 2001). Although not a photography book, this is a perceptive and wide-ranging analysis of contemporary multicultural Britain in the shadow of the royal family. Provides useful background to contemporary British photographic practice.
Alison, Jane, ed. *Native Nations: Journeys in American Photography* (London: Barbican Art Gallery, 1998). Comprehensive look at photography of and by Native Americans, with text by many of the artists represented in the book.
Anthology of African and Indian Ocean Photography (Paris: Éditions Revue Noire, 1999). Beautifully printed images in a huge compilation devoted to recent historical scholarship, including that of the black diaspora from the point of view of Africans.
Badger, Gerry, and John Benton-Harris. *Through the Looking Glass: Photographic Art in Britain, 1945–1989* (London: Barbican Art Gallery, 1989).
Bezner, Lili Corbus. *Photography and Politics in America: From the New Deal to the Cold War* (Baltimore, MD: The Johns Hopkins Press, 1999). Bezner shows that American documentary photography cannot be separated from political reform movements and official reactions.
Billeter, Erika. *A Song to Reality: Latin-American Photography, 1860–1993* (Barcelona: Lunwerg Editores, 1998). Strong on documentary photography, and the continuing iconographic themes that inform Latin-American photography.
Carville, Justin. *Photography and Ireland* (London: Reaktion Books, 2011).
Cody, Jeffrey W., and Frances Terpak. *Brush and Shutter: Early Photography in China* (Los Angeles: Getty Research Institute, 2011).
Daniel, Pete, Merry A. Foresta, Maren Stange, and Sally Stein. *Official Images: New Deal Photography* (Washington, D.C.: Smithsonian Institution Press, 1987). A close examination of the politics behind the public idealism of photographic projects such as those carried out by the Farm Security Administration.
Davis, Keith F. *An American Century of Photography, From Dry-Plate to Digital: The Hallmark Photographic Collection*, 2nd ed., rev. (Kansas City, MO and New York: Hallmark Cards, Inc. in association with Harry N. Abrams, Inc., 1999). A clearly written, well-illustrated review of photography, with an emphasis on photography as art.
Debroise, Olivier. *Mexican Suite: A History of Photography in Mexico*, trans. and rev. by Stella de Sá Rego (Austin, TX: University of Texas Press, 2001). Covers twentieth-century photography by Mexicans and non-Mexicans. Canonical works, such as those of Manuel Álvarez Bravo, are accompanied by new research, especially into the vernacular uses of photography.
Dehejia, Vidya. *India: Through the Lens, Photography 1840–1911* (Washington, D.C.: Smithsonian Institution, 2000). Lavishly illustrated account of colonial photography with historical essays by scholars including John Falconer, curator of photographs for the outstanding Oriental and India Office Collections at the British Library in London.
Elliott, David, ed. *Photography in Russia, 1840–1940* (London: Thames and Hudson, 1992). Russian scholars and curators discuss major developments. Experimental movements in the 1920s are well known outside of Russia, but equal space is given to early efforts.
Ferrer, Elizabeth. *A Shadow Born of Earth: New Photography in Mexico* (New York: Universe Publishing, 1993). An eye-opening review of contemporary documentary as well as art photography.
Frasier, Karen M. *Photography and Japan* (London: Reaktion Books, 2011).
Gao Minglu, ed. *Inside Out: New Chinese Art* (Berkeley, CA: University of California Press, 1998). Gao brings together Western and Chinese scholars to review recent developments in contemporary Chinese art, which is frequently photo-based. (The history of photography in China has yet to be written.)
Golia, Maria. *Photography and Egypt* (London: Reaktion Books, 2010).
Green, Jonathan. *American Photography: A Critical History, 1945 to the Present* (New York: Harry N. Abrams, 1984). Still influential for its taxonomy of postwar photography, as well as the publications and the institutions that promoted the medium.
Hales, Peter Bacon. *Silver Cities: The Photography of American Urbanization, 1839–1915* (Philadelphia, PA: Temple University Press, 1983). Explores the use of photography in creating both visual histories of American cities and so-called "booster books" to promote commerce.
Haney, Erin. *Photography and Africa* (London: Reaktion Books, 2010).
Holborn, Mark. *Black Sun: The Eyes of Four: Roots and Innovation in Japanese Photography* (New York: Aperture, 1994). Concentrates on the influential postwar images of Hosoe, Tomatsu, Fukase, and Moriyama.
Honnef, Klaus, Rolf Sachsse, and Karin Thomas, eds. *German Photography 1870–1970: Power of a Medium* (Cologne: DuMont Buchverlag, 1997). Strongest in its account of photography and the rise of National Socialism, and the aftermath of World War II.
India: A Celebration of Independence, 1947 to 1997 (New York: Aperture, 1997). Reviews the work of Indian photographers such as Sunil Janah, and Western photographers such as Mary Ellen Mark, who have worked in India. (A comprehensive account of colonial and postcolonial photography in India is long overdue.)
Issa, Rose. *Iranian Photography Now* (Ostfildern, Germany: Hatje Cantz, 2008).
Kuehn, Karl Gernot. *Caught: The Art of Photography in the German Democratic Republic* (Berkeley, CA: University of California Press, 1997). Against the odds, some photographers countered photo-based propaganda with scenes of the harshness of everyday life and lyrical personal diaries that experimented with form.
Out of India: Contemporary Art of the South Asian Diaspora (New York: Queens Museum of Art, 1998). Many photo-based works by artists of Indian descent living around the world.
Pelizzari, Maria Antonella. *Trances of India: Photography, Architecture, and the Politics of Representation, 1850–1900* (Montreal and New Haven, CT: Canadian Centre for Architecture and Yale Center for British Art, 2003). A comprehensive and analytical review of late nineteenth-century photography about Indian identity.
Pinney, Christopher. *Camera Indica: The Social Life of Indian Photographs* (Chicago, IL: University of Chicago Press, 1997). Acknowledging his debt to French theorist Roland Barthes's influential book *Camera Lucida* (see below).
Rencontres de La Photographie Africaine: Bamako 2003: Rites sacrés/Rites profanes (Paris: Editions Eric Koehler, 2003) [Text in French and English]. An overview of historic and contemporary African photography.
Roberts, Claire, *Photography and China* (London: Reaktion Books, 2013).
Stange, Maren. *Symbols of Ideal Life: Social Documentary Photography in America, 1890–1950* (New York: Cambridge University Press, 1986). An in-depth examination of the documentary practice of Jacob Riis and Lewis Hine, as well as others who developed the notion of documentary photography.
Stathatos, John. *Image and Icon: The New Greek Photography, 1975–1995* (Athens: Hellenic Ministry of Culture, 1997). With Aris Georgiou, whose work is included in this survey, Stathatos has worked tirelessly to make Greek photographic practice better known, primarily through the yearly international festival of photography held in Thessaloniki. The most lavishly illustrated of his recent publications, this text uses a broad definition of landscape to encompass recent mixed-media work.
Stearns, Robert. *Photography and Beyond in Japan: Space, Time and Memory* (Tokyo: Hara Museum of Contemporary Art, 1995). A brief history of enduring themes in Japanese image-making. The last section concentrates on international figures such as Yasumasa Morimura and Nobuyoshi Araki.
Stott, William. *Documentary Expression and Thirties America* (New York: Oxford University Press, 1973). Reviews the definitions of documentary that influenced government-sponsored photographic projects, such the Farm Security Administration's work, as well as social science.
Taft, Robert. *Photography and the American Scene: A Social History, 1839–1889* (New York: Dover Publications, Inc., 1964). First published in 1938, Taft's extensive archival research and collection of anecdotes set the stage for the study of photography in the United States.
Trachtenberg, Alan. *Reading American Photographs: Images as History, Mathew Brady to Walker Evans* (New York: Hill and Wang, 1989). An insightful look at the impact of political and cultural developments on photography from the Civil War to the Depression years. Trachtenberg pioneered the inclusion of photographic

history in American Studies.

Ursitti, Christopher, and Joseph Walker. *Photo Manifesto: Contemporary Photography in the U.S.S.R.* (New York: Stewart, Tabori & Chang, 1991). Profusely illustrated, with solid analytic text describing the lively condition of photography during the dissolution of the Soviet Union.

Varma, Pavan K., and Alain Willaume, eds. *India Now: New Visions in Photography* (New York: Thames and Hudson, 2008).

Watriss, Wendy, and Lois Parkinson Zamora, eds. *Image and Memory: Photography from Latin America, 1866–1994* (Austin, TX: University of Texas Press, 1998). Large, well-illustrated catalog for an exhibition surveying historical and contemporary work.

Weiermair, Peter, and Gerald Matt, eds. *Japanese Photography: Desire and Void* (Zurich: Edition Stemmle, 1997). Well-illustrated account of contemporary Japanese photography, especially those figures who have acquired international reputations.

Welling, William. *Photography in America: The Formative Years, 1839–1900* (New York: Thomas Y. Crowell, 1978). What began as a compendium of nineteenth-century writings on photography was illustrated with carefully selected images.

Willis, Deborah. *Reflections in Black: A History of Black Photographers 1840 to the Present* (New York: W.W. Norton, 2000). An extensive look at African Americans who practice photography by a scholar who has spent her career researching the topic. Some reproductions, especially in the first third of the book, are inexplicably blurry, but the remainder are sharp and fresh.

Wride, Tim B. *Shifting Tides: Cuban Photography after the Revolution* (Los Angeles, CA: Los Angeles County Museum of Art, 2001). Cuban photographers did not shed their experimental tendencies, but participated in the international trend toward personal photography, with diary-like images that confound the better-known revolutionary propaganda photographs.

Xanthakis, Alkis X. *History of Greek Photography, 1839–1960*, trans. John Solman and Geoffrey Cox (Athens: Hellenic Literary and Historical Archives Society, 1988). Primarily Greek photographers, with many images of Classical architecture, as well as vernacular photography.

PHOTOGRAPHIC THEORY AND CRITICISM

Barthes, Roland. *Camera Lucida: Reflections on Photography*, trans. Richard Howard (New York: Hill and Wang, 1981). Barthes's meditation on a photograph of his mother as a child has become a standard reference in photographic studies, much as Proust's madeleine has come to signal the "remembrance of things past."

Berger, John. *Ways of Seeing* (London: British Broadcasting Corporation and Penguin Books, 1972). Influential essay, based on a B.B.C. television series, which discusses the impact of pictures, regardless of medium or context—for example, Ingres's *Odalisque* is paired with a bare-bosomed figure that illustrated a girlie magazine.

Bolton, Richard, ed. *The Contest of Meaning: Critical Histories of Photography* (Cambridge, MA: MIT Press, 1989). Thoughtful anthology of writings by such critics as Allan Sekula and Rosalind Krauss, selected to demonstrate the breadth of postmodern theory.

Bourdieu, Pierre. *Photography: A Middle Brow Art*, trans. Shaun Whiteside (Stanford, CA: Stanford University Press, 1990). First published in 1965, this book is a cross between anthropology and speculative criticism, in which the author stresses the relationship between taste, photographic practice, and social class.

Burgin, Victor, ed. *Thinking Photography* (London: Macmillan, 1982). With *The Contest of Meaning* (above), a compendium of influential critical writing, including essays by Walter Benjamin and Umberto Eco, as well as articles by Burgin.

Hight, Eleanor M., and Gary D. Sampson, eds. *Colonialist Photography: Imag(in)ing Race and Place* (London: Routledge, 2002). An analysis of photography's role in the social construct of the notion of race.

Pinney, Christopher, and Nicholas Peterson, eds. *Photography's Other Histories* (Durham, NC: Duke University Press, 2003). A collection of essays by leading critics on postcolonial photography.

Frederic J. Schwartz. *Blind Spots: Critical Theory and the History of Art in Twentieth-Century Germany* (New Haven, CT: Yale University Press, 2005). Reviews the work of influential German critics, such as Walter Benjamin and Siegfried Kracauer.

Solomon-Godeau, Abigail. *Photography at the Dock: Essays on Photographic History, Institutions, and Practices* (Minneapolis, MN: University of Minnesota Press, 1991). A collection of writings by one of the most incisive and persuasive contemporary critics of photographic practice.

Sontag, Susan. *On Photography* (New York: Farrar, Straus and Giroux, 1973). Contains six of Sontag's seven short essays on photography that first appeared in the *New York Review of Books*. Widely analyzed and discussed when they were published, the essays introduced ideas about mass media that are still prevalent.

Wells, Liz, ed. *Photography: A Critical Introduction*, 3rd ed. (London: Routledge, 2004). A largely successful attempt to integrate contemporary photographic theory with a history of twentieth-century photographic practice.

Wilder, Kelley, *Photography and Science* (London: Reaktion Books, 2009).

WEBSITES

Websites are making historical and contemporary photography widely available. Search engines can be used to pursue the names of individual photographers as well as ethnic and national collections. The few listed below only hint at the growing richness of the Web as a resource for photographic history.

Prominent among the general websites is the well-maintained site for George Eastman House, www.geh.org, which offers a timeline of photography, and is constantly enriched with new material. The United States Library of Congress, www.loc.gov, has a rich assortment of photographs displayed in its American Memory section, and frequently directs viewers to other themed sites where photographs can be found. Likewise, many museums have samples of their collection and exhibits on line, including the Smithsonian Institution, www.si.edu; the Metropolitan Museum of Art in New York, www.metmuseum.org; Getty Museum, www.getty.edu; the Museum of Contemporary Photography, www.mocp.org; and the Museum für Kunst und Gewerbe in Hamburg, Germany, www.mkg-hamburg. de. The collection of authors Helmut and Alison Gernsheim is held at the University of Texas at Austin, www.hrc.utexas. edu/collections/photography/holdings/gernsheim.

The Center for Creative Photography in Tucson has diligently digitized its holdings: www. creativephotography.org.

The American Museum of Photography is a museum without walls at www.photographymuseum.com. In addition, www.luminous-lint.com has emerged as a website with wide-ranging information on historical and contemporary photography. Its timelines are very useful.

In the United Kingdom, the National Media Museum offers film, photography, and television: www. nationalmediamuseum.org.uk. The New York Public Library's project to digitize much of its photography holdings has resulted in a fine online resource: www.nypl.org/locations/schwarzman/prints-and-photographs-study-room/photography-collection.

Major journals devoted to photography often have online exhibits and articles. See, for example, *Camera Austria*, www.camera-austria.at, and the *British Journal of Photography*, www.bjphoto.co.uk.

Some sites—such as www.lightwork.org and www.bjphoto. co.uk—collect and post links to a variety of websites devoted to historical and contemporary photography. Similarly, the International Center for Photography offers web samples of its exhibits at www.icp.org. The International Directory of Photography Historians lists the interests of more than a thousand specialists: http:// people.rit.edu/andpph/hpg.html; and the Women in Photography archive can be found at http://www.cla. purdue.edu/WAAW/palmquist/index.htm. Autograph: The Association of Black Photographers has changing exhibitions online at www.autograph-abp.co.uk/. Photography-now.com offers international samples of current exhibitions of contemporary photography.

Websites of special interest to photohistorians include the images and related materials about the French Commune to be found at www.ucc.ie/acad/appsoc/ tmp_store/mia/Library/history/france/paris-commune/ index.htm. Increasingly, specialized archives are being put online. For example, the United States Steel Gary [Indiana] Works are being digitized by Indiana University. See http://webapp1.dlib.indiana.edu/ussteel/

Various historical photographic techniques also have websites—for example, the Daguerrian Society at www.daguerre.org. Craig's Daguerrian Registry is primarily a source for collectors but also supports a list of daguerreotypists: see www.daguerreotype.com. The Harappa Web Site Project has a rich subsection on historical photography in India and Pakistan: www. harappa.com/photo3/index.html

Those interested in contemporary and former uses of the cyanotype can visit www.cyanotypes.com. The Stereoscopic Association can be found at www. stereoscopicsociety.org.uk. Sites for those interested in area studies or historical periods have also been founded. The Latin American photographic archive at Tulane University at www.tulane.edu/~latinlib contains fifty major collections. In general, entering the words "digital archive" plus a subject into a search engine will often produce less well-known collections of images about a specific topic.